D1323436

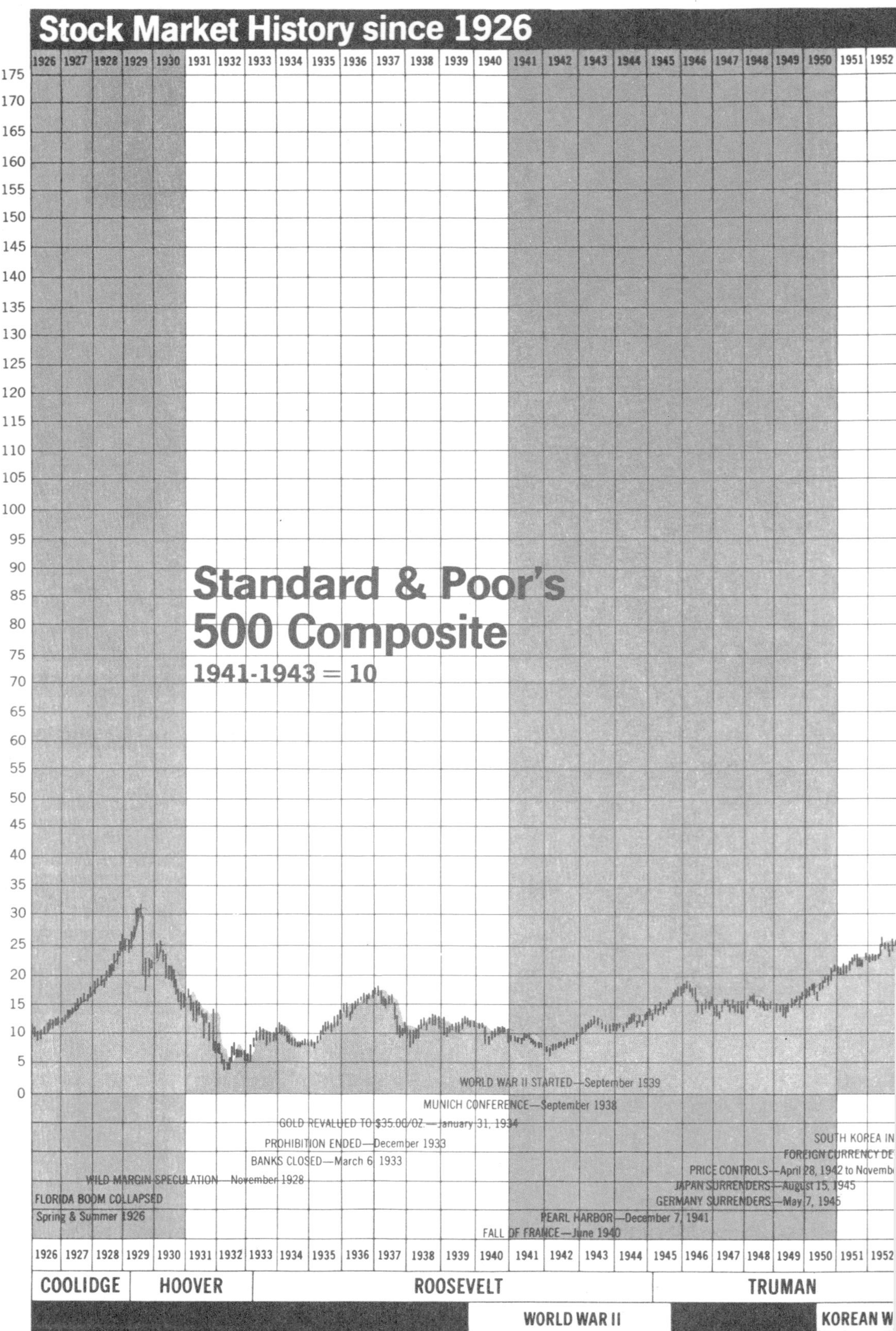

Stock Market History since 1926
Standard & Poor's 500 Composite
1941-1943 = 10
WORLD WAR II STARTED—September 1939
MUNICH CONFERENCE—September 1938
GOLD REVALUED TO $35.00/OZ.—January 31, 1934
PROHIBITION ENDED—December 1933
BANKS CLOSED—March 6, 1933
WILD MARGIN SPECULATION—November 1928
FLORIDA BOOM COLLAPSED
Spring & Summer 1926
PRICE CONTROLS—April 28, 1942 to Novemb
JAPAN SURRENDERS—August 15, 1945
GERMANY SURRENDERS—May 7, 1945
PEARL HARBOR—December 7, 1941
FALL OF FRANCE—June 1940
COOLIDGE
HOOVER
ROOSEVELT
TRUMAN
WORLD WAR II

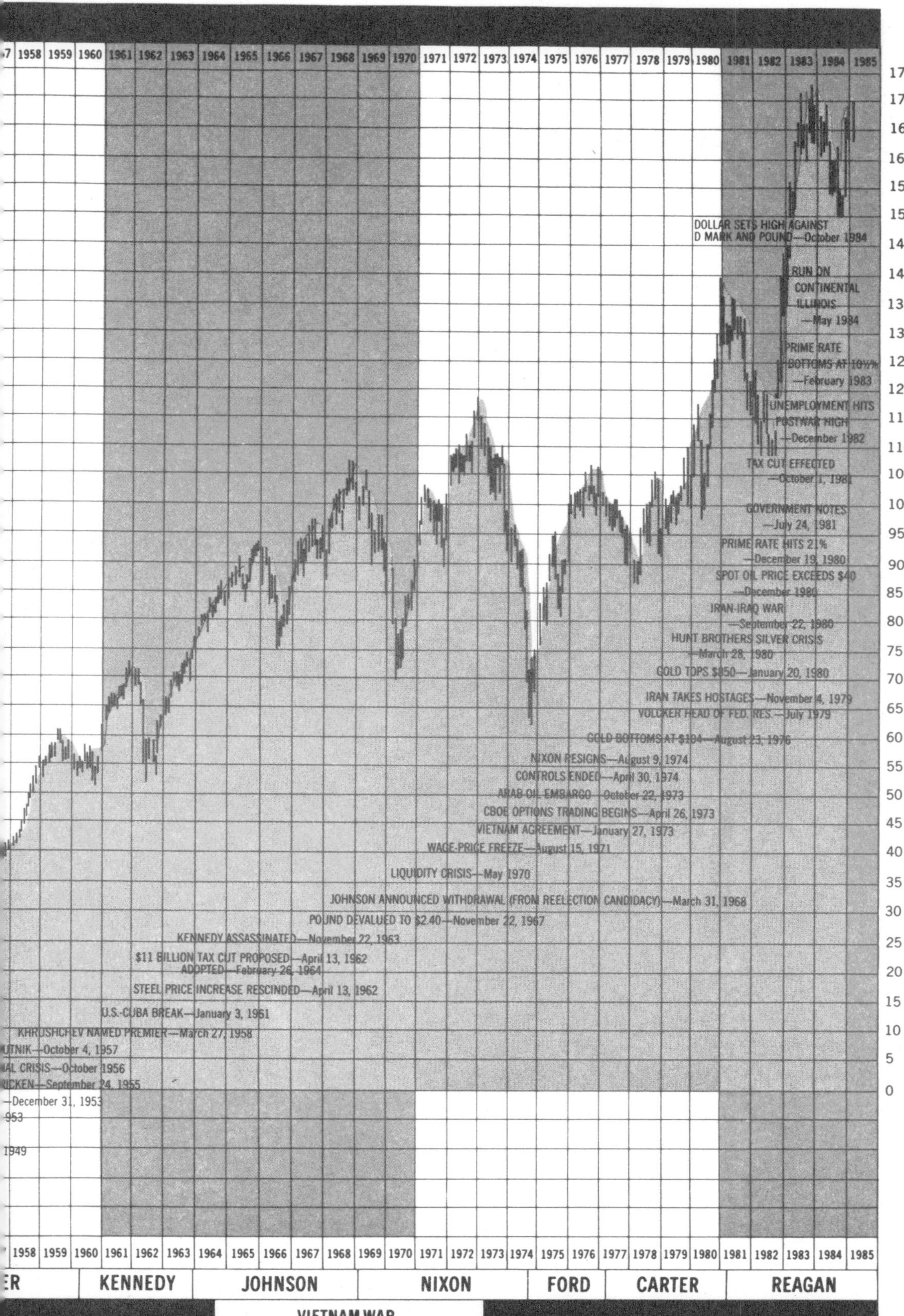

1958 1959 1960 1961 1962 1963 1964 1965 1966 1967 1968 1969 1970 1971 1972 1973 1974 1975 1976 1977 1978 1979 1980 1981 1982 1983 1984 1985
175
170
165
160
155
150
145
140
135
130
125
120
115
110
105
100
95
90
85
80
75
70
65
60
55
50
45
40
35
30
25
20
15
10
5
0
DOLLAR SETS HIGH AGAINST D MARK AND POUND—October 1984
RUN ON CONTINENTAL ILLINOIS —May 1984
PRIME RATE BOTTOMS AT 10½% —February 1983
UNEMPLOYMENT HITS POSTWAR HIGH —December 1982
TAX CUT EFFECTED —October 1, 1981
GOVERNMENT NOTES —July 24, 1981
PRIME RATE HITS 21% —December 19, 1980
SPOT OIL PRICE EXCEEDS $40 —December 1980
IRAN-IRAQ WAR —September 22, 1980
HUNT BROTHERS SILVER CRISIS —March 28, 1980
GOLD TOPS $850—January 20, 1980
IRAN TAKES HOSTAGES—November 4, 1979
VOLCKER HEAD OF FED. RES.—July 1979
GOLD BOTTOMS AT $104—August 23, 1976
NIXON RESIGNS—August 9, 1974
CONTROLS ENDED—April 30, 1974
ARAB OIL EMBARGO—October 22, 1973
CBOE OPTIONS TRADING BEGINS—April 26, 1973
VIETNAM AGREEMENT—January 27, 1973
WAGE-PRICE FREEZE—August 15, 1971
LIQUIDITY CRISIS—May 1970
JOHNSON ANNOUNCED WITHDRAWAL (FROM REELECTION CANDIDACY)—March 31, 1968
POUND DEVALUED TO $2.40—November 22, 1967
KENNEDY ASSASSINATED—November 22, 1963
$11 BILLION TAX CUT PROPOSED—April 13, 1962
ADOPTED—February 26, 1964
STEEL PRICE INCREASE RESCINDED—April 13, 1962
U.S.-CUBA BREAK—January 3, 1961
KHRUSHCHEV NAMED PREMIER—March 27, 1958
UTNIK—October 4, 1957
AL CRISIS—October 1956
ICKEN—September 24, 1955
—December 31, 1953
953
1949
1958 1959 1960 1961 1962 1963 1964 1965 1966 1967 1968 1969 1970 1971 1972 1973 1974 1975 1976 1977 1978 1979 1980 1981 1982 1983 1984 1985
ER
KENNEDY
JOHNSON
NIXON
FORD
CARTER
REAGAN
VIETNAM WAR

INVESTMENTS: ANALYSIS AND MANAGEMENT

McGRAW-HILL SERIES IN FINANCE

Consulting Editor
CHARLES A. D'AMBROSIO
University of Washington

Brealey and Myers Principles of Corporate Finance
Campbell Financial Institutions, Markets, and Economic Activity
Christy and Clendenin Introduction to Investments
Coates Investment Strategy
Doherty Corporate Risk Management: A Financial Exposition
Edmister Financial Institutions: Markets and Management
Francis Investments: Analysis and Management
Francis Management of Investments
Garbade Securities Markets
Haley and Schall The Theory of Financial Decisions
Hastings and Mietus Personal Finance
Henning, Pigott, and Scott International Financial Management
Jensen and Smith The Modern Theory of Corporate Finance
Lang and Gillespie Strategy for Personal Finance
Levi International Finance: Financial Management and the International Economy
Martin, Petty, and Klock Personal Financial Management
Robinson and Wrightsman Financial Markets: The Accumulation and Allocation of Wealth
Schall and Haley Introduction to Financial Management
Sharpe Portfolio Theory and Capital Markets
Stevenson Fundamentals of Finance
Troelstrup and Hall The Consumer in American Society: Personal and Family Finance

McGRAW-HILL FINANCE GUIDE SERIES

Consulting Editor
CHARLES A. D'AMBROSIO
University of Washington

Bowlin, Martin, and Scott Guide to Financial Analysis
Farrell Guide to Modern Portfolio Theory
Gup Guide to Strategic Planning
Riley and Montgomery Guide to Computer-Assisted Investment Analysis
Smith Guide to Working Capital Management
Weston and Sorge Guide to International Finance

Investments:

ANALYSIS AND MANAGEMENT

FOURTH EDITION

Jack Clark Francis

Bernard M. Baruch College
City University of New York

McGraw-Hill Book Company

New York St. Louis San Francisco Auckland
Bogotá Hamburg London Madrid
Mexico Montreal New Delhi Panama
Paris São Paulo Singapore
Sydney Tokyo Toronto

INVESTMENTS: ANALYSIS AND MANAGEMENT

INTERNATIONAL EDITION

2nd printing 1987

This book was set in Baskerville by Better Graphics.
The editors were Paul V. Short and Susan H. Ryf.
The designer was Ben Kann.
The production supervisor was Phil Galea.
New drawings were done by J & R Services. Inc.

Library of Congress Cataloging in Publication Data

Francis, Jack Clark.
Investments : analysis and management.

(McGraw-Hill series in finance)
Includes bibliographies and index.
1. Investments. 2. Securities. 3. Financial futures.
4. Arbitrage. I. Title. II. Series.
HG4521.F685 1986 332.6 85-23143

When ordering this title use ISBN 0-07-100417-3

Printed and Bound in Singapore by KIN KEONG PRINTING CO. PTE. LTD.

ABOUT THE AUTHOR

Jack Clark Francis is Professor of Economics and Finance at Bernard M. Baruch College, City University of New York. He was a Federal Reserve Economist; a Finance Professor at the Wharton School of Finance, University of Pennsylvania; a U.S. Army Officer; and a Finance and Quantitative Analysis Instructor at the University of Washington in Seattle. Professor Francis has had articles published in the *Journal of Finance, Journal of Financial and Quantitative Analysis, Financial Management, Journal of Futures Markets, Journal of Monetary Economics, Journal of Economics and Business, Quarterly Review of Economics and Business, Review of Business, Journal of Portfolio Management,* and other academic and Federal Reserve periodicals. He has also authored a book entitled *MANAGEMENT OF INVESTMENTS,* coauthored *PORTFOLIO ANALYSIS,* and coedited *Readings in Investments.* Professor Francis lives in Stamford, Connecticut.

to my father

Clark Francis

Born on October 2, 1907 in Cardwell, Missouri,

Passed away on January 29, 1981 in Indianapolis, Indiana,

A good family man,

A good Christian,

A successful entrepreneur,

I miss him.

contents

PART TWO
INTRODUCTION TO VALUATION AND RISK-RETURN THEORY

PART THREE
BOND VALUATION

THE CHARTERED FINANCIAL ANALYST (CFA) DESIGNATION

PART TEN

preface

The fourth edition of *Investments: Analysis and Management* is similar to the three preceding editions in most ways, but at the same time, different in some significant respects. Like the previous editions, this book was written to facilitate the learning of both the traditional institutional material and the newer, more abstract risk-return theories. These two different approaches to the study of investments management are integrated in a complementary fashion that places a comprehensive range of material between two covers. In addition, this fourth edition has been expanded.

EXPANDED COVERAGES

The market economics concepts on depth, breadth, and resilience have been discussed in an appendix to Chapter 3, entitled Security Markets, to give a better foundation in marketmaking. The appendix to Chapter 3 also reports other developments in security markets in the United States that interested readers may pursue. Chapter 4, about security law, has been extended slightly to introduce hotly debated topics like the new "shelf registrations" and the old Glass-Steagall Act. The end-of-chapter appendix on security market indices from the third edition has been expanded to stand alone as Chapter 7 in the fourth edition. The single force that has reshaped this edition more than anything else, however, is the new arbitrage pricing theory (APT).

Chapter 9, entitled Total Risk and Its Factors, contains no discussion of diversifiable risk and undiversifiable risk, as it did in the previous editions. The topics of diversifiable risk and undiversifiable risk have been postponed until the next chapter to make room for an expanded discussion of "risk factors" in Chapter 9. Risk factors called interest rate risk, purchasing power risk, market risk, default risk, management risk, and others are developed conceptually in Chapter 9 as the elements that combine to create an asset's total risk. This discussion of these risk factors was added to this edition to set the stage for the risk factors that are discussed more mathematically in the new arbitrage pricing theory (APT) chapter—Chapter 30.

The capital asset pricing model (CAPM), or security market line (SML) as it is also called, has been separated from the chapter that introduces risk; it has been expanded to stand alone as Chapter 10 in the fourth edition. A rigorous discussion of interest rate risk in Chapter 11 has been supplemented by new material about immunization and dedicated portfolios. The material on industry analysis that used to be part of the chapter on fundamental common stock analysis has been segregated and supplemented to stand alone as Chapter 17, entitled "Industry Analysis." Chapter 21, on short positions and options, has been expanded to include a better analysis of hedging and arbitrage. And, some new chapters have been added.

NEW CHAPTERS

Several entirely new chapters have been added to the fourth edition. The previous chapter about commodity futures contracts remains with little change as Chapter 22; it discusses the traditional commodity futures contract topics. But the traditional material about commodities has been augmented by a new chapter entitled Financial Futures, Chapter 23, that contains material about exciting new financial instruments. Chapter 24 is also an entirely new chapter—it is about international investing. Arbitrage pricing theory (APT), the newest investments theory, is the subject of Chapter 30. APT is discussed at the intuitive level and also graphically; a modest amount of simple algebra is also used to make precise statements. Then Chapter 30 goes on to discuss various aspects of the APT and review some empirical investigations of the new theory. The APT discussion in Chapter 30 was written to tie in with the discussions of the various risk factors that were found in the earlier chapters of the book. This edition was written to present the important new APT in an easy-to-understand manner.

As a result of the outpouring of new securities (particularly in the financial futures area) and new investments theory (primarily the arbitrage pricing theory), the fourth edition contains more new material than any previous edition. But the philosophy, direction, and tone of the book remain unchanged. The book was written to facilitate learning. The institutional background, the financial and economic theory, and the management practices are presented in an integrated fashion. The book abounds with references and cross-references. The material is explained on three different levels—verbally, graphically, and mathematically—where that is necessary to adequately explain the concept. And, as with the previous editions, the book benefited from criticisms and suggestions concerning previous editions and this manuscript, while it was being drafted.

ACKNOWLEDGMENTS

My colleagues at Baruch College helped me mold and shape this fourth edition. Harry Markowitz made helpful suggestions. But, more important, Harry provided the theoretical foundation for modern portfolio theory, and thus, for most of this book. Myself and the entire financial community are indebted to Harry Markowitz.

Harry Markowitz, Avner Wolf, Sam Dyckman, Steve Lillien, Gerry Pogue, Peter Gutmann, Kishore Tandon, Joel Rentzler, Wi Saeng Kim, and Giora Harpaz, are all Baruch College professors who helped me. Other professional colleagues have also lent a hand.

Professor Carl McGowan of Bentley College; Professor Joe Lavely of Berry College; Frank J. Fabozzi, the Walter E. Hanson Professor of Business and Finance at Lafayette College; Richard Bookstaber of Morgan-Stanley; Gary Gastineau from Kidder, Peabody and Company's Webster Management subsidiary, Ed Mader at E.F. Hutton; Professor H.K. Wu from the University of Alabama; Mr. Musa Essayyad from the University of Alabama; Mark Podems at Standard and Poors Corporation; Professor Mark Castelino from Rutgers University and Powers Research Company; Professor Stephen H. Archer at Willamette University; Edwin J. Stuart at the University of Texas; Professor Patric Casabona at St. John's University; Mr. Russell Cornelius of Rye, New York; Mr. Charles Cotterill of American Express; Professor Cheng Few Lee at the University of Illinois; James Morris at the University of Colorado; George Papaionnou at Hofstra University; Ms. Deborah Susan Francis of Seattle First National Bank; Phillip A. Horvath from Bradley University; Professor Gabriel Hawawini at INSEAD; Professor Kendall P. (Pat) Hill at the University of Alabama in Birmingham; Max G. Ansbacher at Bear Stearns and Company; Professor Owen K. Gregory of the University of Illinois; Bob Haugen of the University of Wisconsin at Madison; Professor Gunter Dufey of the University of Michigan; David Babbel of the Wharton School; Mr. Luke J. Sparvero at the University of Texas at Arlington; Joanne Hill; Brown Brothers; Harriman, Inc.; John Groth, Texas A&M; Richard Meyer, University of South Florida; and others whose names have inadvertently slipped my mind all made substantial improvements in the manuscript.

Graduate students working on their MBA and PhD degrees at Baruch College who helped me included Mr. John Brandt, Ms. Suzanne Michelle Goldburger, Mr. T.T. Wu, Ms. Nancy White, Mr. Jengren Chiou, Mr. Nikos Milanos, Ms. Nilufer Usmen, Mr. Celal Secilimis, Mr. Stuart Auslander, and Mr. Nusret Cakici. In addition, numerous other students helped their professor by passing on a casual comment, an anonymous note, or some helpful remark.

Research assistants, computer programmers, word processors, reviewers and typists who helped included Mrs. Maria Pia Seirup, Ms. Louise Jones, Ms. Polly Whittel, Ms. Tonia Berezecky, Ms. Alison Stooker, Ms. Mary Ann Verow, Ms. Emma Burling, Ms. Kimberely Comer, Ms. Judy Fazekas, Ms. Cynthia von Wnuck, Ms. Susan Wacker, Ms. Dea Mae Conrath, Ms. Cheryl Anton, Ms. Victoria Novoa, and Ms. Charlynn C. Maniatis.

REQUEST FOR ASSISTANCE

If you find things about this book that are wrong, that frustrate you, that are not clear, or that you think impede learning, please drop me a note and let me know. Compliments do not help me create a good book. Criticisms and suggestions make me think, reconsider, and rewrite. I appreciate and acknowledge suggestions and criticisms my readers share with me.

Jack Clark Francis

introduction

This is a book for investment managers or students of the investment management process. The book discusses marketable financial instruments such as common stocks, preferred stocks, bonds, puts, calls, and commodity futures contracts—to name a few. These assets, the markets in which they are traded, the laws governing the trading, valuation of the assets, construction of a diversified portfolio, and the important factors affecting investments management will be analyzed in the chapters which follow.

1-1 EVOLUTION OF INVESTMENTS TEACHING

The development of investments management can be traced chronologically through three different phases. First, investments management was a *skill* or an *art*. To make millions in the market, the traders of yesteryear needed to be steel-nerved gamblers who possessed a special cunning about the markets, were pathologically greedy, had the connections to raise large sums of capital, and had the deadpan poker faces to carry out all these activities without tipping their hands. The names of people who possessed some of these skills—names such as Vanderbilt, Morgan, Drew, Fisk, Gould—are still familiar today. However, the daring speculative ventures they and others undertook were made illegal in the United States by the passage of the Securities Act of 1934. This act outlawed price manipulation schemes.

The unscrupulous skills used to make large investment trading profit around the turn of the century require an attitude that is best learned by observation and experience. Studying textbooks is not the most effective way to learn such nonintellectual skills, so no textbooks were written. The spine-tingling stories of how millions were made and lost by manipulating the markets are to be found only in the records of congressional hearings and newspapers from the 1800s and early 1900s.

During the 1930s investments management entered its second phase, a phase of *professionalism*. After the first U.S. regulations governing investment trading were passed in 1933–34, the whole investments industry followed the lead previously taken by the New York Stock Exchange and seriously set about the task of upgrading its ethics, establishing standard practices, and cultivating a good public image. As a result, security and commodity exchanges tightened their entrance requirements; fair practice codes and self-policing bodies were set up to oversee investment activity; and investors busied themselves studying the fine print on their contracts, calculating financial ratios, and investigating the professional reputations of those with whom they dealt.

Since the professionalism of investments management began, investment textbook writers have been busy. As the body of investments law has expanded—and investment markets became safer places, so that ordinary people began investing—numerous books have been written describing the laws and procedures investors must follow.

More recently, investments management has begun to be more *scientific;* this is the third phase in its development. It is impossible to specify the date when one stage ended and the next began, but some people point to a paper published by Harry Markowitz[1] in 1952 as the beginning of a scientific approach—although scientific analysis of investments can be found as far back as 1900.[2] In fact, the last two phases, professionalism and scientific analysis, are currently advancing simultaneously.

One of the most recent developments in the professionalization of investments management is the designation of chartered financial analyst (CFA) for investment analysts who have passed a series of examinations to demonstrate their proficiency.[3] Interestingly, these exams have contained questions about economic theory and mathematical statistics—tools of the scientists. Thus, the professionalization of investments management is continuing, but assuming a more scientific bent. This book reflects that trend.

1-1.1 burgeoning literature dichotomized investments students

Since about 1960 the literature published about investments expanded at an accelerating rate. As had been true in the preceding decades, excellent books and articles appeared, explaining and rationalizing securities and other investments, the markets in which they were traded, and the relevant laws, procedures, and vocabulary. In addition, a whole new set of scientific research findings was published. Finance professors, security analysts, portfolio managers, economists, mathematicians, computer scientists, and others interested in investments management were partially dichotomized by the rapid publication of both traditional investments literature and the new esoteric scientific studies. Some people teaching investments seemed either to ignore the tradi-

[1] "Portfolio Selection," *Journal of Finance,* March 1952, vol. 7, no. 1, pp. 77–91.

[2] L. Bachelier, "Theory Speculation," *Ann. Sci. Ecole Norm. Sup.,* vol. 3, no. 1018 (Paris: Gauthier-Villars, 1900). Reprinted in Paul Cootner, *The Random Character of Stock Market Prices* (M.I.T., Cambridge, Mass., 1964), pp. 17–78.

[3] The chartered financial analyst (CFA) designation, the education and testing process required to attain the CFA designation, and the organization which administers the CFA program are explained in Part 10 of this book.

tional institutional material and concentrate on the new scientific literature, or vice versa. The two groups were almost mutually exclusive.

One of the aims of this book is to reverse the dichotomization by combining the most important elements from both the traditional camp and the new analytical group into one publication which suits the needs of both. The material is presented in such a fashion that those who want only the traditional material can find it—mostly in Chaps. 2 through 7, but elsewhere too. Those who want to confine their attention to analysis and exclude material about the investment institutions can do this by selecting relevant material from Chaps. 9 through 30.

1-1.2 organization

This text is written so that a beginning student can start at the front and move directly toward the back of the book. After Chap. 8, reference to the Mathematical Appendixes at the back of the book may be required to sustain progress. But the material does flow logically and increases in difficulty as the chapters pass, so that a front-to-back reading plan makes sense. However, too much material is included to be covered in most one-quarter or one-semester courses, so some chapters must be omitted. Which chapters are read is a matter of the professor's tastes. The book is laid out so that by picking and choosing among the chapters, the teacher can construct many different courses. Essentially, it is organized into ten main parts:

- Part 1, The Setting, explains the investment institutions found in the United States. Chaps. 2–7.
- Part 2, Introduction to Valuation and Risk-Return Theory, presents the theoretical foundation needed to make rational investment decisions. Chaps. 8–10.
- Part 3, Bond Valuation, shows how the time value of money affects security prices. Chaps. 11–13.
- Part 4, Common Stock Valuation, analyzes the procedures used by fundamental stock analysts. Chaps. 14–17.
- Part 5, The Movements of Stock Prices, reviews the debate between technical analysts and the random-walk theorists about the manner in which security prices fluctuate. Chaps. 18–19.
- Part 6, Other Investments, describes the characteristics of preferred stock, the long and short positions, options, futures contracts, and international investing. Chaps. 20–24.
- Part 7, Portfolio Theory, explains the techniques of modern, scientific portfolio analysis and management. Chaps. 25–29.
- Part 8, Arbitrage Pricing Theory (APT), reviews the latest asset valuation theory. Chap. 30.
- Part 9, Mathematical Appendixes, explains various mathematical and statistical tools used in some later chapters and chapter appendixes.
- Part 10, Chartered Financial Analyst (CFA), describes the CFA program.

These parts are fairly independent of one another. That is, they can be read without reference to the preceding parts; this is particularly true of Parts 1, 2, 3, and 5. Part 4 does assume a knowledge of Part 3, but those readers already familiar with the present value concept can read Part 4 independently. Part 3 presumes the reader has mastered Chap. 2. Part 6 utilizes tools that were developed in Part 2. Part 2 is not really essential to all parts of the book, but the material therein does touch on many important areas of financial investing.

All the parts are organized into related chapters that should usually be read in the order presented. But there is no reason why some of the later chapters in any part cannot be omitted. The end-of-chapter appendixes can certainly be skipped; most of them delve into a more detailed treatment of the material in the chapter. The majority of classes will read only those chapters which the professor feels might be particularly appropriate for the class within the time allotted.

The end-of-chapter appendixes are provided mainly for those students whose intellectual curiosity is not satiated by the chapter. The tiny bit of calculus which has crept into this book is confined to the appendixes; it is not essential for a basic grasp of the concepts under discussion. Instead, it is provided for those few readers who may want to see mathematical proof of some of the assertions made or to see how to use the tools under discussion to solve real problems. The Mathematical Appendixes (Part 9) are provided to help the student refresh his or her memory of mathematical procedures which are quickly forgotten if not used regularly.

1-2 THE OBJECTIVE OF INVESTMENT

This book is written to develop investment managers who are interested in investing their funds in assets which have the maximum expected rate of return at any selected level of risk or, conversely, the minimum risk with a given expected rate of return. An example involving the six hypothetical assets listed below should make this clearer. Figure 1-1 represents these six assets in risk-return space.

asset	expected rate of return	risk	dominated?
M	.1 = 10%	.1	No
B	.05 = 5%	.1	Yes, by *T* and *M*
C	.1 = 10%	.2	Yes, by *M* and *A*
A	.15 = 15%	.2	No
T	.05 = 5%	.05	No
E	.15 = 15%	.3	Yes, by *A*

That is, the six assets are plotted on the two-dimensional graph with their expected rate of return, denoted $E(r)$, on the vertical axis and their risk measured numerically on the horizontal axis.[4]

[4] The quantitative risk measure used in Fig. 1-1 is explained in detail in Chap. 9. The analysis of diversified portfolios of assets is introduced in Chap. 25. Chapter 25 explains why the individual assets graphed in Fig. 1-1 will be dominated by portfolios and that some of the dominated assets may be held as fractional parts of dominant portfolios.

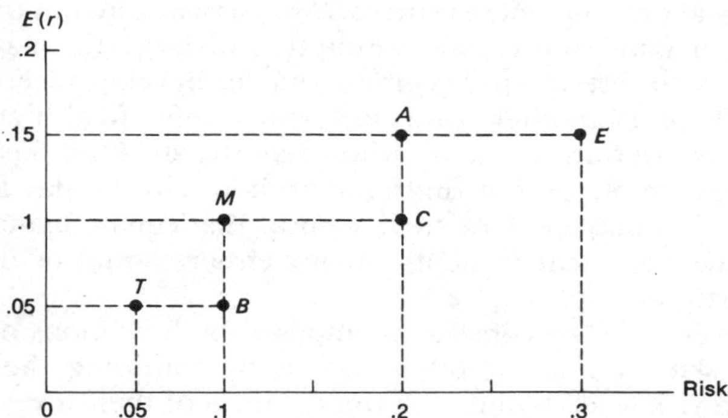

FIGURE 1-1 assets graphed in risk-return space.

According to the investment objective assumed, assets *T*, *M*, and *A* dominate assets *B*, *C*, and *E*, respectively, because they have less risk for their given levels of expected return. Similarly, assets *M* and *A* dominate assets *B* and *C*, respectively, because they have the largest expected rates of return in their risk classes. Thus, the type of investor addressed by this book will prefer investing in assets *T*, *M*, or *A* rather than in assets *B*, *C*, or *E*.

Which of the dominant assets the investor prefers depends on his or her own personal investment preferences. A timid investor will prefer dominant investment *T*, whereas an aggressive investor will prefer dominant investment *A*. A "medium investor," halfway between timidity and aggressiveness, will prefer asset *M*, but the investment objective assumes that no rational investor would prefer assets *B*, *C*, or *E*.

Stating that the investment objective is to select assets which have the maximum expected rate of return in their risk class is like saying the objective is to maximize the investor's expected wealth at some preferred level of risk, since the larger the rate of return, the larger the terminal wealth.[5] It should be noted that this objective assumes the investor is essentially greedy.[6] Stated less crassly, this book is written for investors who prefer to have more wealth rather than less wealth. Other objectives, such as accumulation of power, social reform, or attainment of prestigious position, may often be obtained through wealth if the manipulator has a sufficient amount of it. Therefore, we shall confine our attention to the wealth maximization objective within whatever risk class the investor prefers.

It is an oversimplification to assume that the objective of financial investing is pure and simple wealth maximization. There are constraints imposed by the law, and also by the investor's physical, financial, intellectual, and emotional resources. Limited personal resources frequently cause investors to select

[5] For a one-period time horizon the sentence is true. But for a multiperiod time horizon, the statement refers only to the geometric mean rate of return if the rates of return vary from period to period. The geometric mean return is explained in Mathematical App. F in Part 9 and/or Chap. 29.

[6] In particular, this book assumes that the investor is greedy in the long-run sense, which implies observance of the law. Short-run greed is myopic and can lead to such self-destructive activities as grand larceny and fraud (which, in turn, lead to jail, poor job prospects afterward, ad nauseam).

investments expected to yield only mediocre returns. *Risk aversion* is an important constraint on wealth maximization. The assumption of large financial risk can cause the investor to lose sleep, become irritable, develop ulcers, or even commit suicide. Time is another constraint which limits wealth accumulation. Many investors are only amateurs who "play the stock market" after work. These investors simply cannot find enough hours in the day to pursue every opportunity that may increase their wealth. Inadequate managerial skill can also limit people's achievements—many either cannot or do not want to manage a portfolio.

Most investors try to overcome the constraints imposed by limitations on their time, management skill, wealth, or other factors by confining their investments to a preferred risk level. By limiting the riskiness of their investments, these investors are usually able to limit the amount of time, managerial skill, and other factors which they must devote to investment management. For example, U.S. Treasury bonds are an investment which involves little risk or management effort if the investor is willing to earn uninspiring returns. The investment objective is covered in detail in Chap. 27 and its appendix—this material analyzes the rationale behind different investment objectives.

part one

THE SETTING

CHAPTER 2—Securities defines bonds, shares of stock, and other financial instruments and explains their owners' legal rights.

CHAPTER 3—Securities Markets explains how various securities markets operate.

CHAPTER 4—Securities Law describes some harmful securities transactions and the laws that have been enacted to curtail such harmful practices in the United States.

CHAPTER 5—Taxes outlines the most commonly encountered United States tax laws and tells how they affect investment decisions.

CHAPTER 6—Sources of Investment Information shows examples of investment information that is publicly available and tells how to acquire it.

CHAPTER 7—Security Market Indices lists many different market indicators and tells how to discriminate between the strong and the weak ones.

These initial chapters explain in some detail the places, people, transactions, laws, and institutions that constitute the market place for security transactions in the United States. This material is presented first so that the reader may be able to understand the more abstract material that follows in terms of this basic institutional background.

CHAPTER 2

securities

A *security* is a document that evidences specific claims on a stream of income and/or to particular assets. Debt securities include bonds and mortgages. Ownership securities include common stock certificates and the titles to marketable assets (such as the bill of sale for an art object, for example). In addition, preferred stock is a hybrid security which entitles its owner to a mixture of both ownership and creditorship privileges. This chapter defines and discusses various features of both debt and equity securities.

Table 2-1 suggests a method of classifying the main types of securities. The table furnishes a very compact summary of some of the salient points about the main categories of securities. This table should not be taken too literally, however. For example, the common stock issued by American Telephone and Telegraph is less risky than bonds of many risky, little corporations. Table 2-1 refers only to the main categories of securities; it is not a true description of each and every individual security issue.[1]

This chapter's discussion of securities begins with money market securities in Sec. 2-1 because they are the simplest kind of security. The U.S. government's debt securities are the topic of Sec. 2-2. Municipal bonds are examined in Sec. 2-3, and Sec. 2-4 delves into corporate bonds. Mortgage-backed securities are explained in Sec. 2-5. Equity instruments like common stocks are discussed in Sec. 2-6. Preferred stock is explained in Sec. 2-7. Convertible securities are the subject of Sec. 2-8. Then, some empirical market price data are presented in Sec. 2-9 in order to compare and contrast numerically the various securities.

[1] Tax laws that exempt intercorporate cash dividend payments from income taxes under certain circumstances, the tax-free coupons on municipal bonds, the existence of certain tax-exempt investors, the existence of different classes of common stock issued by the same corporation, and other real-world complications make Table 2-1 less than completely descriptive of reality. For these reasons Table 2-1 should be viewed as being a conceptual scheme rather than a specific case-by-case way to view the menu of investment securities.

TABLE 2-1 classification of security types by risk, return, and degree of owner control over management

security type	control	return	risk
Common stock	1, most	1, most	1, most
Preferred stock	2	2	2
Corporate bonds	3	3	3
Government bonds	4, least	4, least	4, least

Before turning our attention to specific debt securities, let's consider some general characteristics that apply to all debt securities. *Debt,* according to the dictionaries, is a condition that exists when one person owes something to another person. The dictionaries go on to explain that a *security* is a paper that is given as a pledge of repayment, or as evidence of debt or ownership. These definitions suggest that the phrase *debt securities* must refer to pieces of paper that evidence certain parties owe something to certain other parties. This chapter explores *marketable debt securities*—these are debt securities designed to be bought, sold, or traded in a securities market.

Investors buy debt securities in order to earn interest income from the security. That is, the investor lends money to the borrower who issued the debt security. But the investor expects to have the loan repaid with interest. The interest income is the inducement that causes the investor to give up the use of his or her funds and loan them at risk to some borrower who may be a total stranger.

There are many different kinds of marketable debt securities. They pay different rates of interest, they are available in different denominations, they have differing lengths of time until they come due for repayment, and some are more likely than others to be repaid. A wide variety of debt securities are discussed in this chapter. The discussion starts with the simplest kind of actively traded debt securities—the money market securities.

2-1 MONEY MARKET SECURITIES

Dictionaries explain that things which are *liquid* flow freely from one place to another without being significantly compressed or expanded. Following this general definition, money (that is, cash) is the most liquid of all securities because it is readily acceptable at its face value in markets everywhere. Essentially, money is a *perfectly liquid asset* that flows freely from hand to hand without losing any of its value in the process. Money is more liquid than, say, long-term bonds, which have uncertain market prices that can deviate significantly from their face values and thus can be difficult to convert back into the amount of money which was paid for the bond. Thus, bonds may be an illiquid investment, especially if they are not traded in active markets.

Highly marketable securities that have short terms until they mature and involve little or no risk of default are said to be "moneylike" and are called *money market securities.* Money market securities are the most liquid of all securities except cash. Large corporate investors typically use money market securities as a place to invest excess cash that may be available temporarily for a few weeks or months (for example, cash held in anticipation of paying quarterly federal income taxes). Money market securities pay varying rates of interest that are usually about equal to the rate of inflation.

All money market securities are short-term debts. In fact, all of them mature within 270 days or less because of a federal law (enforced by the Securities and Exchange Commission) that requires that all securities with longer maturities go through the costly registration process, which is described in detail in Chaps. 3 and 4.[2]

Another factor common to money market securities is that most of them pay interest to their investors by selling at a *discount* from their face (or maturity) values. Consider, for example, a U.S. Treasury bill. All *Treasury bills* are offered in denominations of $10,000, $15,000, $50,000, $100,000, $500,000, and $1 million. A 90-day T-bill with a $100,000 face value might sell for $98,000 when it is first issued by the U.S. Treasury Department. Then, the buyer can either hold this security for 90 days or sell it in the active secondary market anytime before it matures. Upon maturity, whoever owns this so-called T-bill can redeem it for its face value of $100,000. The $2,000 difference between the discounted purchase price of $98,000 and the maturity value of $100,000 is the interest paid to the T-bill's investor (or series of investors). Several other types of money market securities are discussed below.

Negotiable certificates of deposit are called "negotiable CDs" in the financial world. Negotiable CDs were originated by the First National City Bank in New York, in 1961. Citibank, as this huge bank is currently called, created them by announcing that it would issue large-denomination negotiable CDs and that a large, well known securities dealer, The First Boston Corporation, had agreed to create a secondary market (act as dealer) in these new securities. The idea worked and today it is well known that a negotiable CD is a receipt from a federally insured commercial bank for a deposit of $100,000 or more, with certain provisions attached. One of the provisions is that the deposit will not be withdrawn from the bank before some specific maturity date. Since the bank is insured by the Federal Deposit Insurance Corporation (FDIC), the CD is issued by a very safe financial institution. Thus, negotiable CDs are bought and sold in active secondary markets similar to the way Treasury bills are traded.

Banker's acceptances are no more than written promises to repay borrowed funds which borrowers give to banks. Then, if the potential borrower takes down the loan (that is, actually borrows the money), the lending bank is said to accept the banker's acceptance. Later, if the lending bank wants to withdraw the money it has invested in the loan before the loan expires, it sells the written promise to repay the loan (that is, the banker's acceptance) to another investor. Banker's acceptances may be resold to any number of new investors before the loan comes due and is repaid; there is an active secondary market in these moneylike pieces of debt.

Any investor who buys a banker's acceptance can collect the loan on the

[2] For more detail about the money markets and the securities traded there see Marcia Stigum, *The Money Market,* rev. ed. (Dow Jones-Irwin, Homewood, Ill., 1983).

date it is scheduled to be repaid. And if the borrower should default on the loan, the last investor also has legal recourse. This means that the last buyer of the banker's acceptance can collect from the bank that originated the banker's acceptance.

Commercial paper refers to the short-term promissory notes issued by "blue-chip" corporations. Blue-chip corporations are large, old, safe, well-known, national companies—Exxon and General Motors, for example. The maturities vary from 5 to 270 days, and the denominations are for $100,000 or more—usually more. These notes are not backed by any collateral; instead, commercial paper relies on the high credit rating of the issuing corporation.

It is customary for commercial paper issuers to maintain open lines of credit (that is, unused borrowing power at banks) sufficient to pay back all their commercial paper that is outstanding. The commercial paper issuers use the paper only because that type of credit can be quicker and easier to obtain than bank loans. The credit ratings of most commercial paper issuers are so high that the so-called prime (that is, highest-quality credit rating) commercial paper interest rate is essentially a riskless rate of interest that is approximately the same as the yields on negotiable CDs and banker's acceptances. One page from Standard & Poor's *Commercial Paper Rating Guide* is reproduced on page 157. It shows the names and ratings of a few corporations that regularly issue commercial paper.

Fed funds, the common name for *federal funds* loans, are overnight loans between commercial banks. Fed funds arise when a bank holds reserves in excess of those that the Federal Reserve System legally requires the bank to hold to meet its reserve requirement. Federal funds are thus simply bank reserves loaned from banks with excess reserves to banks with insufficient reserves. The interest rates on these 1-day bank loans is called the *federal funds rate*. The so-called fed funds rate is probably the interest rate studied most by money market economists in business, finance, and government policy-making agencies. It fluctuates quickly over a wide range and is generally acknowledged to be one of the best indicators of the U.S. monetary authority's (namely, the Federal Reserve System's) current regulatory attitude toward credit tightening or credit easing. Bankers obtain or sell federal funds simply by calling other bankers on the telephone to find the needed supply of funds or to sell fed funds, whichever is appropriate.

Eurodollar loans are also sometimes called petrodollar loans, Asian dollar loans, or "hot money flows." All these terms refer to large, short-term loans which are denominated in dollars. The loans are usually arranged by banks with large international operations such as the First National City Bank (or Citicorp or Citibank, as it is now called) in New York City or the Bank of America in San Francisco.[3] These loans tend to be made by businesses located in countries where current interest rate levels are low. Not surprisingly, the loans are typically made to borrowers in countries that have sound national

[3] Bank of America and Citibank are the two largest banks in the United States, and they also have the largest international operations. Other banks (particularly large New York City banks) arrange Eurodollar loans, however. Barclay's Bank, an English bank which is larger than any U.S. bank, for example, has branches in the United States and other countries as well. Barclay's thus arranges Eurodollar loans too. Large banks around the world arrange Eurodollar loans.

economies and higher levels of current interest rates. International bankers arrange Eurodollar loans for their banks' customers, or banks frequently borrow or lend Eurodollars for themselves. A broker's fee of one-tenth of 1.0 percent, or a yield spread of the same size, presents ample profit opportunity to interest a banker in arranging a multimillion Eurodollar loan for a client or for his or her own bank.

Repurchase agreements are commonly known as repos. Repos are devices that are usually used by securities dealers to help finance part of their multimillion dollar inventories of marketable securities for one or a few days. For instance, if a securities dealer ends a day of busy trading with an increase of $4 million in marketable securities in inventory but lacks the cash needed to pay for the additional securities, a repo may be sold to finance the $4 million of additional inventory overnight. The financially pinched securities dealer would pay a repo broker a finders fee (or broker's commission) to find an investor who had $4 million of unused cash that needed to be invested overnight. Then the securities dealer would sell $4 million worth of marketable securities to the overnight investor. And, at the same time that the cash-short securities dealer made the sale, that securities dealer would also make an agreement to repurchase the $4 million worth of securities back the next day at a slightly higher price than the sales price. That slightly higher price would be the interest income for the overnight investor who purchased the repo. Or, sometimes the securities dealers sell and repurchase their inventory at the same price and simply make an explicit interest payment to the investor. In repo transactions the investor is essentially making a short-term loan to the securities dealer that employs part or all of the securities dealer's inventory as collateral for the loan.

Repos that last longer than overnight are common too. These longer-term repos are called *term repos* and can span 30 days, or even longer sometimes. These repurchase agreements, especially the term repos, are marketable securities that are actively traded by telephone calls between the money market trading desks of different banks and brokerages across the United States.

The debt securities traded in money markets are all short-term securities that are largely free from the risk of default. If we expand our scope to include high-quality debt securities of all lengths of maturity, then U.S. government securities can be considered next.

2-2 U.S. GOVERNMENT SECURITIES

Since World War II, government securities have played an increasing role in the decisions of investors. In mid-1981 the total debt of the U.S. federal government grew to exceed $1 trillion—that is, one thousand billions of dollars. Almost every penny of this federal debt was interest-bearing debt. Most of it was in the form of U.S. Treasury bonds, notes, bills, certificates of indebtedness, and U.S. savings bonds. Demand for increased government services has also expanded the debt issues of government agencies and state and local governments. These debt issues have been increasing not only in absolute amounts but also on a per capita basis.

Government securities represent the amount of indebtedness of our governmental bodies. The owners of the securities are creditors; the governmental bodies are debtors. A clear distinction should be drawn between the debt of the federal government and the debt of state and local governments. In particular, the investor should be aware of different levels of risk involved and the different tax treatment for each. Therefore, they are discussed separately. United States government securities are discussed in this section. Municipal bonds are explained next—in Sec. 2-3.

United States government securities are of such high quality that their yield is often used as an example of a default-free interest rate. Indeed, they are very safe, since the U.S. government has unlimited power to tax or to print money whenever such action becomes necessary to obtain the money to pay its bills.

2-2.1 nonmarketable issues

Approximately 30 percent of the public debt consists of nonmarketable issues. These cannot be traded in the securities market; they are not transferable or negotiable; they cannot be used as collateral for a loan; they can be purchased only from the Treasury and they can be redeemed only by the Treasury. By far the major portion of nonmarketable securities are U.S. savings bonds, Series E and H and the new Series EE.

The EE savings bonds, which were introduced in 1980 to replace the old Series E bonds, pay much better interest rates than their predecessors. The EE government savings bonds yield interest rates which vary and are equal to 85 percent of whatever the market yield on 5-year Treasury securities is over the same holding period. Furthermore, the EE savings bonds guarantee a minimum yield of 7.5 percent, no matter how low the other market interest rates may fall. The redemption prices and yields of these bonds, if held to any point in time, are printed on the bond. However, if a savings bond is redeemed before its maturity date, the investor is penalized for the early redemption by being restricted to receive a low penalty rate of interest.

2-2.2 marketable issues

These issues make up about 70 percent of the federal debt. They are usually purchased from outstanding supplies through a dealer or broker. However, the purchaser may subscribe for new issues through any one of the twelve Federal Reserve Banks in the United States. The holder of marketable government securities stands to gain not only from the interest paid on these bonds, like the owner of nonmarketable bonds, but also from price appreciation (higher selling price than purchase price), unlike the owner of nonmarketable bonds. Bid-and-ask prices for these marketable issues are published daily in such newspapers as *The New York Times* and *The Wall Street Journal.* The prices are quoted in thirty-seconds of one percent of par; fractions are written as though they were decimals. For example, 70.16 means $70^{16}/_{32}$ percent of par. Chapter 11 explains in detail how the yield on these marketable issues is calculated. For now, however, potential investors should become aware of the types and maturities of the various issues that are available.

Treasury bills are extremely liquid short-term notes that mature in 13, 26, or 52 weeks from date of issue. The Treasury usually offers new bills every week, selling them on a discount from face value basis. Furthermore, T-bills are issued only on a "book entry" basis—the buyer never actually receives the security, only a receipt. The Treasury agent records the purchasers' transactions and issues receipts to the Treasury bill buyers instead of an actual T-bill security.

T-bills are never sold at a premium over their face values—only at a discount. The discount to investors is the difference between the price they have paid and the face amount they will receive at maturity. For example, a $10,000 Treasury bill maturing in 13 weeks (that is, "a 90-day T-bill" to bond traders) could be purchased for $9750 if it were to yield 10.6 percent at an annual rate (or 2.56 percent = .0256 = $250/9750 on a quarterly basis).[4] Then at the end of the 90 days the buyer would be repaid $10,000 by the U.S. Treasury. The $250 gain is the interest income for the 13 weeks; it equals the discount from the bond's face value when the bond was first sold.

Certificates of indebtedness are issued at par (or face) value. Later, after they are issued, certificates are traded in the market at prices which vary minute by minute. Certificates usually bear fixed interest rates. The fixed interest rate is printed on the certificate and never varies—it is called the coupon rate. The *coupon rate* tells what percent of the certificate's face value will be paid out in two semiannual coupon interest payments each year. Certificates usually mature about a year from the date of issue, but the Treasury can set the period of time to be any length of time up to 1 year. Certificates have not been issued by the U.S. Treasury in recent years.

Treasury notes are similar to certificates of indebtedness except with regard to their time until maturity. T-notes are bonds that typically have a maturity of from 1 to 7 years. They are marketable debt securities that pay coupon interest semiannually, just like the certificates. The Treasury issues T-notes periodically, and some issues are currently outstanding and are traded actively.

Treasury bonds comprise about 10 percent of the federal debt. Bonds differ from notes and certificates with respect to maturity; they generally run from 7 to 30 years from date of issue to maturity. Another significant difference is that some issues are *callable* at times prior to maturity.[5] If the bonds are selling in the market above par, their yield to maturity is calculated to the nearest call date. If they are selling at a discount, the yield to maturity is calculated on the basis of their maturity date. The yield to maturity is a compound average rate of return calculated over the bond's entire life—it is explained in more detail in Chap. 11. A bond's one-period rate of return is calculated over a shorter time period.

[4] The quarterly rate of 2.56 percent, or simply .0256, is annualized as follows:

$$\begin{aligned}(1.0 + qr)^4 &= (1.0 + ar)\\ &= (1.0256)^4 = 1.106399\end{aligned}$$

where qr denotes the quarterly rate and ar denotes the annual rate of interest. Subtracting 1 from both sides of the equation results in: .106399 = 10.6399 percent, or approximately 10.6 percent per year.

[5] There are several callable issues of Treasury bonds. They are listed in the newspaper quotations with the other Treasury bonds. For instance, the 12 percent coupon Treasury bonds that mature in August of 2013 are callable in 2008. The maturity year of this issue is therefore listed as: 2008–13.

BONDS' ONE-PERIOD RATES OF RETURN From the investor's point of view the most important outcome from an investment is the rate of income. The bond investor's one-period rate of return (or holding period return) is an important consideration to investors. Regardless of whether the period over which a bond's rate of return is calculated is a day, a week, a month, a quarter, a year, or 5 years, the definition of its one-period rate of return is given in Eq. (2-1a) below.

$$r_t = \frac{p_{t+1} - p_t + i_t}{p_t} \tag{2-1a}$$

The symbol r_t denotes the one-period rate of return in the tth period. The tth period can be whatever period you are interested in—this year, next week, or last quarter. The p_{t+1} and p_t terms are dollar quantities defined as the market price of the bond at the beginning of period $t + 1$ and period t, respectively. The i_t is the dollar amount of interest paid on the bond in period t. A numerical example should clarify all this.

If a bond sells at \$995 on January 1 of some year and it sold at \$950 on January 1 of the preceding year, then $p_{t+1} = \$995$. If this hypothetical bond paid \$50 interest per year, then its 1-year rate of return is 10 percent, as shown in Eq. (2-1b).

$$10.0\% = .1 = \frac{\$95}{\$950} = \frac{\$995 - \$950 + \$50}{\$950} \tag{2-1b}$$

If the bond's market price had fallen to \$852.50 instead of rising to \$995, the year's return would have been a negative 5 percent.

$$-5.0\% = -.05 = \frac{-47.50}{\$950} = \frac{\$852.50 - \$950 + \$50}{\$950} \tag{2-1c}$$

Equation (2-1a) is the one-period rate-of-return definition for a bond—this is also called the bond's holding period return.

Some people refer to a bond's one-period rate of return as its one-period yield. However, this language seems inadvisable because it could get confused with a bond's yield to maturity—a different concept that will be discussed later in Chap. 11.

2-2.3 special issues

Approximately 20 percent of the government debt consists of *special issues.* These federal obligations cannot be purchased by the public and are sold by the Treasury to those special government funds that have cash to invest. The Government Employees' Retirement Fund, the Federal Old-Age and Survivors Insurance Fund, and the National Service Life Insurance Fund are examples of such funds.

2-2.4 agency securities

The federal land banks, the Federal Home Loan Banks, the Central Bank for Cooperatives, the Federal National Mortgage Association (called Fannie Mae),[6] the Government National Mortgage Association (called Ginnie Mae),

[6] For a monetary economist's view of Fannie Mae, Ginnie Mae, Maggie Mae (or Magic), and Freddie Mac, see J. C. Francis, "Helping Americans Get Homes," *Business Review,* Philadelphia Federal Reserve Bank, January 1974. Free copies available from the bank on request.

the U.S. Postal Service, and the Federal Intermediate Credit Bank are all U.S. government agencies allowed to issue their own debt obligations. Such bonds are similar in substance to other government bonds. The federal government makes no guarantee that the interest and principal of these "independent" bonds will be paid; therefore, they must pay higher yields than federal bonds in order to induce investors to buy these riskier bonds. However, it would be poor political and economic policy for the government to allow any of its own agencies to default. There have been instances in which the Treasury has provided the funds needed to prevent any such financial embarrassment. The debt of two agencies is *officially* guaranteed by the Treasury: the outstanding debt of the District of Columbia Armory Board and some of the Federal Housing Administration (FHA) bonds. The income from federal agency bonds, as other federal government bonds, is taxable.

2-2.5 price quotations in newspapers

Figure 2-1 shows an example of how the market prices for U.S. government and agency bonds are listed in the newspapers. In the case of every government and agency bond listed in Figure 2-1, the left-hand column gives the maturity date of the issue. The lowercase letter n is printed after those issues which are Treasury notes. If the securities are coupon-paying bonds, then the second column gives the coupon rate. T-bills have no coupon rates since they are sold at discount so as to pay interest as price appreciation rather than by coupon payments. The bid and asked prices are in the next two columns of Fig. 2-1. For coupon-paying bonds the bid and asked prices are stated as percentages of the bonds' face value. For T-bills the bid and asked values are the market interest rates that the investor will earn if the T-bills are purchased at their respective bid or asked prices. The *bid price* is the highest price (stated as a percentage of face value) that any potential investor is willing to pay. The *asked price* is the lowest price that any potential seller is willing to take.[7] The

[7] For money market securities the bid and asked prices are stated as interest rates instead of percentages of face value in some newspapers. The bid and asked prices stated as interest rates are simply the yield to maturity an investor would earn if the T-bill were purchased at the current bid or asked market price, respectively.

FIGURE 2-1 newspaper excerpt showing United States government and agency bond prices for one day.

Government and Agency Bonds

(Prices in 32d of a point, composite bill yields in basis points)

BOND & NOTES

Date	Rate	Bid	Ask	Chg.	Yield
Aug, 79	n 6¼	99.30	100	.....	0.26
Aug, 79	n 6⅞	99.30	100	.....	0.26
Aug, 79	n 6⅝	99.26	99.28	.....	9.62
Sep, 79	n 6⅝	99.16	99.18	+ .1	10.05
Sep, 79	n 8½	99.22	99.24	.....	10.27
Oct, 79	n 7¼	99.11	99.13	.....	10.01
Nov, 79	n 6¼	99	99.2	.....	10.02
Nov, 79	n 6⅝	99.1	99.3	.....	10.25
Nov, 79	n 7	99.4	99.6	.....	10.22
Nov, 79	n 7⅛	99.2	99.4	– .1	10.11
Dec, 79	n 7⅛	98.27	98.29	.....	10.10
Dec, 79	n 7½	99	99.2	.....	10.03
Jan, 80	n 7½	98.25	98.27	– .1	10.13
Feb, 80	4	97.4	97.12	– .2	9.54
Feb, 80	n 6½	98.8	98.10	.....	10.06
Feb, 80	n 7⅝	98.22	98.26	.....	9.94
Mar, 80	n 7½	98.14	98.16	– .1	10.04
Apr, 80	n 7¾	98.16	98.20	– .1	9.81
May, 80	n 6⅞	97.26	97.30	.....	9.81
May, 80	n 8	98.22	98.26	.....	9.60
Jun, 80	n 7⅝	98.7	98.11	.....	9.65
Jun, 80	n 8¼	98.23	98.27	.....	9.67

TREASURY BILLS

Date		Bid	Ask	Chg.	Yield
-1979-					
Sep	20	9.32	9.08	–0.01	9.29
Sep	27	9.36	9.16	+0.01	9.39
Oct	4	9.40	9.22	–0.02	9.46
Oct	11	9.40	9.24	–0.02	9.50
Oct	16	9.35	9.17	–0.07	9.44
Oct	18	9.41	9.23	–0.01	9.51
Oct	25	9.43	9.25	+0.01	9.55
Nov	1	9.52	9.42	+0.07	9.75
Nov	8	9.51	9.41	+0.06	9.75
Nov	13	9.52	9.42	+0.03	9.78
Nov	15	9.55	9.53	+0.06	9.90
Nov	23	9.57	9.45	+0.07	9.83
Nov	29	9.55	9.45	+0.05	9.85
Dec	6	9.51	9.41	+0.05	9.83
Dec	11	9.50	9.40	+0.04	9.83
Dec	13	9.50	9.40	+0.04	9.83
Dec	20	9.50	9.38	+0.03	9.83
Dec	27	9.42	9.30	+0.02	9.76
-1980-					
Jan	3	9.43	9.35	.....	9.83
Jan	8	9.45	9.35	.....	9.85
Jan	10	9.45	9.37	–0.01	9.89

FEDERAL NATIONAL MTGS

Date	Rate	Bid	Ask	Chg.	Yield
Apr, 80	8.55	98.28	99.8	.....	9.74
Jun, 80	6.70	97.8	97.24	– .2	9.62
Jun, 80	8½	98.22	99.2	.....	9.69
Jul, 80	6⅞	97.8	97.24	– .2	9.54
Sep, 80	7½	97.16	98	.....	9.51
Sep, 80	8¾	98.22	99.6	– .2	9.56
Oct, 80	8.70	98.18	99.2	– .2	9.56
Dec, 80	6.60	96.4	96.28	.....	9.16
Dec, 80	8	98.4	98.20	.....	9.12
Mar, 81	7.05	96.12	96.28	.....	9.24
Mar, 81	7.35	96.24	97.8	.....	9.27
Apr, 81	6.85	95.28	96.12	.....	9.26
Apr, 81	10	100.28	101.4	.....	9.21
Jun, 81	7¼	95.24	96.24	.....	9.23
Jun, 81	7.95	97.12	97.28	.....	9.24
Jul, 81	8.85	98.28	99.8	– .2	9.28
Sep, 81	7¼	95.16	96.16	.....	9.14
Sep, 81	9⅜	99.28	100.4	– .2	9.29
Sep, 81	9.70	100.16	101.16	.....	8.88
Oct, 81	7⅞	96.24	97.8	– .4	9.30
Dec, 81	6.45	94.8	94.24	.....	9.01
Dec, 81	7.30	95.16	96.16	.....	9.00

column headed "Chg." contains the amount of price change from the previous day's closing price to the current day's closing price. The right-hand column headed "Yield" contains the yield to maturity the investor would earn if the security were purchased at the current market price and held to the maturity date.

2-2.6 zero coupon bonds called TIGRs and CATS

Some investors are not able to invest in U.S. government securities, even though they may prefer their default-free status, because the denominations are so large. The smallest denomination of Treasury bill that may be purchased, for example, is $10,000. Several large security brokerages have purchased multimillion dollar blocks of Treasury bonds and resold small shares in this pool of default-free Treasury securities at a slightly higher price than they paid. Thus, the brokers can profit by selling small investments in a pool of U.S. Treasury obligations. And, selling small shares in these large pools allows small investors to buy the Treasury bonds that they could not otherwise afford. Merrill Lynch, Pierce, Fenner & Smith has labeled these small shares in a big pool of Treasury obligations with the title of Treasury Investment Growth Receipts; they are called TIGRs, for short. Salomon Brothers, another large and innovative brokerage, has created a similar product and calls it Certificates of Accrual on Treasury Securities—or CATS, for short. Other brokerages have created similar products with different names. Some people refer to any of these securities as "zeros," since they pay coupons of zero.

In order to create its first TIGRs in 1982, Merrill Lynch bought $500 million face value of long-term Treasury bonds. Merrill then put these T-bonds into trust with a bank that was to act as custodian of the bonds for the TIGR investors. Merrill then created a series of certificates that mature at 6-month intervals as the semiannual coupon payments from the underlying Treasury bonds in the pool come due. The TIGR investor buys the certificate at a deep discount from its maturity value—the price gain is the investor's interest income. However, the TIGR investor receives nothing until the selected maturity date arrives—which might be months, years, or decades away. The further away the maturity date, the deeper the discount (and resulting price gain) to the investor.

The various brokerage firms that originated their own TIGRs or CATS (or whatever they may call them) usually promise their investors that they will create and maintain secondary markets where the certificates can be sold to another investor before they mature; this makes the certificates liquid investments. But under no circumstances can the Treasury securities that are held in the pool with a trustee be used as collateral by the investor or the custodian bank or anyone else. The pool of T-bonds is held in trust until the last TIGR matures and the pool is completely liquidated to repay it.

In order to buy a TIGR that will mature in the year 2004 with a face value of $14,000, an investor need only have spent $1000 in 1982 to buy the certificate, for example. This turns out to yield an average annual rate of return of 7.1 percent per year over the 22 years, if the TIGR is held to maturity. The disadvantage of investing in zero coupon bonds like the TIGRs and CATS is that taxable investors must pay income taxes on the implicit coupon interest each year—even though they do not receive it. So, zero coupon bonds cannot be used to delay income tax payments—only the income which is being taxed is postponed.

2-3 MUNICIPAL SECURITIES

The bonds of states, counties, parishes, cities, towns, townships, boroughs, villages, and any special municipal corporation tax districts (such as toll bridge authorities, college dormitory authorities, sewer districts, ad infinitum) are all referred to by security traders as *municipals.* They include the obligations of state and local commissions, agencies, and authorities as well as state and community colleges and universities. With such a wide assortment of issuing entities, there is naturally just as wide a variety of agreements with the bondholders.

Federal laws provide that the income derived from the obligation of a political subdivision be exempt from federal income taxes. This tax exemption applies to the coupon interest income, but not to any capital gains which may be earned, from municipal bonds. Thus, *munis*, as they are commonly called, are widely held by wealthy individuals and partnerships whose income may be taxed at the high personal tax rates.

The interest on municipal bonds can be paid in two ways—by giving a check to the bond's registered owner or by cashing in the coupons attached to a bearer bond as they come due. Tax evaders found the *bearer bonds* attractive because they didn't have to report to the federal government that they owned the bonds, since the interest income from municipals was tax-exempt. In addition, when the owner of the municipals sold or gifted them to another party, it was easy to avoid paying the capital gains or gift tax, respectively, because there was no registered list of owners that could be consulted to discern ownership changes. The federal government curtailed the issue of new bearer bonds by municipalities after 1981 by removing their tax-exempt status, unless the issue was registered. However, bearer bonds issued before 1981 will still be actively traded until they are all retired.

The disadvantage of owning bearer bonds is that thieves find them easy to steal and resell since the bond owner's name is not recorded on a registration list. In contrast, the owners of *registered bonds* are protected from bond theft because all registered owners must notify the trustee of the bond issue of any change in ownership. Furthermore, the new investor in the bond must have his or her name added to the list of registered owners. This registration procedure prevents stolen bonds from being easy to sell and makes tax evasion easier to discern.

Municipal bonds' tax-exemption advantage works to the benefit of the issuers. The bonds are generally regarded by investors as being lucrative because of their exemption from income taxes. This makes them easier for the municipality to issue. These popular bonds therefore typically command a premium in the form of lower market interest rates.

Not all municipal bonds are high-quality investments. Some local governments are already too burdened with debt or have a tax base so limited that experts refuse to consider the bonds as top rate. Other issues are supported only by limited revenue-producing property and are not considered able to guarantee payment. For example, New York City offered a bond issue in 1975 with a coupon rate of over 9 percent and was still unable to sell the issue.[8]

Municipal bonds, regardless of their exact contract provisions, fall into one of two categories, general or limited obligation bonds.

2-3.1 general obligation bonds

Often referred as to *full faith and credit bonds* because of the unlimited nature of their pledge, *general obligation* securities originate from government units that have unlimited power to tax property to meet their obligations and that promise to pay without any kind of limitation. About two-thirds of the bonds issued by actual governments such as those of states, counties, and cities are of this type because these entities have the revenue-generating (that is, taxing) power to go to the politically feasible limit to pay their debts.

2-3.2 limited obligation bonds

The term *limited obligation bonds* is applied when the issuer is in some way restricted in raising revenues used to pay its debts. *Revenue bonds* are the most significant form of limited obligation. The distinguishing aspect of such bonds is that they are entitled to the revenue generated only from the specific property that is providing service for which rates or fees are paid. These bonds are widely used to finance municipally owned utilities, such as water works, electricity, gas, sewage disposal systems, and even public swimming pools.

Municipal bonds pay income to their investors in two forms—interest payments and capital gains (or losses). They are just like the marketable U.S. Treasury bonds in this respect. Therefore, the one-period rate of return from a municipal bond investment is computed with Eq. (2-1*a*) on page 16, just like the returns from a Treasury bond.

2-3.3 insured municipal bonds

Even though the tax-exempt income from a municipal bond may be quite attractive to some investors, they may still shy away from these types of bonds if there is much chance that the issue might falter and not be able to repay its obligations. This understandable risk aversion makes it difficult for municipalities whose bonds do not receive the highest quality ratings to issue bonds. In the 1970s two firms set up business to insure bonds issued by municipalities that were not worthy of the highest quality credit ratings. The two firms are the American Municipal Bond Assurance Association (AMBAC) and the Municipal Bond Insurance Association (MBIA). Insuring municipal bond issues proved to be such a profitable business that several other firms were started up in the 1980s.

Standard & Poor's, a well-known bond rating agency, has agreed to give any municipal bond issue that AMBAC insures its highest quality credit rating. Thus, after its investigation, if AMBAC agrees to insure a municipality's bond issue, the issue will get a top credit rating it would never have been able to obtain otherwise. This makes it much easier for small and risky municipalities not only to sell their bond issues—but also to sell their issues at

[8] For more detail about practically any aspect of municipal bonds, see Frank J. Fabozzi, S. G. Feldstein, I. M. Pollack, and F. G. Zarb (eds.), *The Municipal Bond Handbook*, 2 vols. (Dow Jones-Irwin, Homewood, Ill., 1983).

lower interest rates. In fact, AMBAC's insurance will raise an issue's quality rating and lower its interest rate so much that the municipality's savings in interest expense might pay for AMBAC's insurance fee.

2-4 BONDS ISSUED BY CORPORATIONS

Essentially, a bond is what is commonly called an "I owe you" (or, more simply, an IOU). More particularly, a bond is a marketable, legal contract that promises to pay whoever owns it a stated rate of interest for a defined period and then to repay the principal at the specific date of maturity. Bonds differ according to their terms concerning provisions for repayment, security pledged, and other technical aspects. They represent the formal legal evidence of debt and are the senior securities of the firm.

2-4.1 the indenture contract

The *indenture,* or deed of trust, is the legal agreement between the corporation and the bondholders. Each bond is part of a group of bonds issued under one indenture. Thus, they all have the same rights and protection from the issuing company. Sometimes, however, bonds of the same issue may mature at different dates and have correspondingly different interest rates.

The indenture is a long, complicated legal instrument made up of carefully worded phrases containing the restrictions, pledges, and promises of the contract. The trustee, usually a bank, ensures that the issuing firm keeps its promises and obeys the restrictions of the contract; the trustee also takes any appropriate legal action to see that the terms of the contract are kept and that the rights of the bondholders are upheld. Because the individual bondholders are usually not in a position to make sure that the company does not violate its agreements and because the bondholders cannot take substantial legal action if the firm does violate them, the trustee assumes these responsibilities. The trustee does the "watchdog" job for all the bondholders.

2-4.2 general features of corporate bonds

TRUSTEE The *trustee* is a third party to the contract between the issuer and the investor. It is the trustee's job to make sure that the corporate issuer lives up to the provisions contained in the indenture contract.

BOND INTEREST Bond interest is usually paid semiannually, though annual payments are also popular. The method of payment depends upon whether the bond is a registered or coupon bond. The interest on *registered bonds* is paid to the holder by check. Therefore, the holders must be registered with the trustee of the bond issue to ensure proper payment. Registered bonds can be transferred only by registering the name of the new owner with the trustee and canceling the name of the previous owner. In contrast, *coupon bonds* have a series of attached coupons that are clipped off at the appropriate times and sent to a bank for collection of the interest.

If the coupon interest is paid to whoever may happen to be the bearer of the bond without checking to see who is its registered owner, the bonds are called *bearer bonds.* The ownership of bearer bonds may be transferred simply by physically handing them over to the new owner. The ease of transfer enjoyed by bearer bonds increases the danger of loss to their owner—anyone who picks up a bearer bond is its legal owner and no registration records exist to verify the true owner's identity.[9]

COUPON RATE The coupon rate is the interest paid on the face value of a corporate or a U.S. Treasury bond. It is one fixed dollar amount that is paid annually as long as the debtor is solvent. (Corporations' income bonds or adjustment bonds are the only exceptions.) The coupon rate is decided upon after the issuing corporation's investment banker has taken into account risk of default, the credit standing of the company, the convertible options, the investment position of the industry, the security backing of the bond, and the market rate of interest for the firm's industry, size, and risk class. After all these factors have been taken into account, a coupon rate is set with the objective that it will be just high enough to attract investors to pay the face value of the bond. Later, the market price of the bond may change from its face value as market interest rates change, while the contractual coupon rate remains fixed.

Generally, the higher the *yield* (or effective rate of return, as it is also called), the riskier the security.[10] Yield rather than coupon rate is more significant in buying bonds. If the bond is selling at a *discount,* its market price is below its face value. In this case, the yield is higher than the coupon rate. If it is selling at a *premium,* the market price of the bond is above its face value. In this case, the coupon rate is higher than the yield. In buying bonds, the investor should be aware of possible capital gains or losses due to changes in the market price of a bond, since this is as important as the interest income in calculating yield. Chapter 11 explains how to calculate bond yields.

MATURITIES Maturities vary widely. The actual term to maturity of a new bond issue changes after the bond is issued because as long-term bonds come closer and closer to their maturity dates, they become medium-term and then short-term bonds. Nevertheless, a bond is usually grouped by its maturity that existed on the date the bond was newly issued. *Short-term bonds* are any bonds maturing within 5 years. They are common in industrial financing and may be secured or unsecured. *Medium-term bonds* mature in 5 to about 10 years. If a bond is originally issued as a medium-term bond, it is usually secured by a real estate or equipment mortgage, or it may be backed by other security. *Long-term bonds* may run 20 years or more. Capital-heavy industries with long expectations of equipment life, such as railroads and utilities, are the greatest users of this form of bond financing.[11]

[9] The federal government curtailed the issue of new bearer bonds by municipalities after 1981 by removing the tax-exempt status. This was done primarily to reduce the frequency of tax evasion by municipal bond investors. However, previously issued bearer bonds are still traded.

[10] The term *yield* is used synonymously with *yield to maturity* or *average rate of return compounded annually to maturity*. These terms refer to the effective rate of return to the owner if the bond is held to maturity. Bonds' yields to maturity are discussed in detail in Chap. 11.

[11] For an analysis of the structure of corporate debt maturities see J. B. Silvers, "Liquidity, Risk and Duration Patterns in Corporate Financing," *Financial Management,* Autumn 1976, vol. 5, no. 3, pp. 54–64.

CALL PROVISION A call provision may be included in the indenture. This provision allows the debtor to call or redeem the bonds at a specified amount (above par) before maturity date. The difference between the par value of the bond and the higher call price is called the *call premium.* The call provision is advantageous to the issuing firm but potentially harmful to the investor. If interest rates should decline, it may be wise for the firm to call in its bonds and issue new ones at the lower market interest rate. This action, however, leaves investors with funds they can invest only at the lower interest rate. To compensate for the undesirable callable feature, a new issue of callable bonds will sell at a higher interest rate than a comparable issue of noncallable bonds.

SINKING FUND Sinking fund bonds are not special types of bonds but just a name given to describe the method of repayment. Thus, any bond can be a sinking fund bond if it is specified as such in the indenture. Sinking fund bonds arise when the company decides to retire its bond issue systematically by setting aside a certain amount each year for that purpose. The payment, usually a fixed annual dollar amount or a percentage installment, is made to the sinking fund agent, who is usually the trustee. This person then uses the money to call the bonds annually at some call premium or to purchase them on the open market if they are selling at a discount.

Sinking fund bonds have been common in industrial financing that involves some risk because risky debt issues are more attractive to investors with a promise of faster payment. Where risk is lower (for example, in utilities), sinking fund bonds are less frequently used. Approximately half the industrial issues and one-third of the utilities' issues have such a provision.[12]

SERIAL MATURITIES Serial bonds are appropriate for issuers that wish to divide their bond issues into a series, each part of the series maturing at a different time. Ordinarily the bonds are not callable, and the bond issuer pays each part of the series as it matures. Municipalities issue serial bonds more frequently than do corporate bond issuers.

2-4.3 secured bonds

The most important classifying criterion of corporate bonds is whether they are secured or unsecured. That is, what security, if any, has been pledged to help pay investors if the company should be unable to live up to its obligations, or should default?

If the indenture provides for a lien on a certain designated property, the bond is a secured bond. A lien is a legal right given to the bondholders, through the trustee, to sell the pledged property to obtain the amount of money necessary to satisfy the unpaid portion of interest or principal. Pledged security is naturally used to make the bonds more attractive to

[12] The potential investor in a sinking fund bond should investigate the provisions of the sinking fund's administration. Some bond issuers occasionally do not actually pass annual cash payments on to a third party who accumulates these monies safely in a sinking fund. Instead, only a bookkeeping entry may be made to indicate that some accounting category called "sinking fund" was credited—but no monies were actually set aside in a safe place to be cared for by a trustworthy third party. This latter type of sinking fund provides no protection for the investor.

investors by making them safer investments. The reasoning is that if investors see the bonds as safer than similar nonsecured bonds, they will pay a higher price or accept a lower interest rate for them. In reality, the security is seldom sold in the case of default. The company is usually reorganized, with new securities issued for the defaulted bonds. The presence of a lien on the property has a very favorable influence on the treatment of the bondholders' interests in the reorganization, however.

MORTGAGE BONDS A bond issue secured with a lien on real property or buildings is a mortgage bond. If all the assets of the firm are collateral under the terms of the indenture, it is called a *blanket mortgage*. The total assets need not be pledged, however; only some of the land or buildings of the company may be mortgaged for the issue. They can be first, second, or subsequent mortgages, each with its respective claim to the assets of the firm in case of default. A first mortgage is the most secure because it enjoys first claim to assets. A mortgage bond may be *open-end, limited open-end,* or *closed-end,* or it may contain an *after acquired property* clause.

An *open-end mortgage* means that more bonds can be issued on the same mortgage contract. The creditors are usually protected by restrictions limiting such additional borrowing. The open-end mortgage will normally also contain an *after acquired property* clause, which provides that all property acquired after the first mortgage was issued be added to the property already pledged as security by the contract. A *limited open-end mortgage* allows the firm to issue additional bonds up to a specified maximum (for example, up to 50 percent of the original cost of the pledged property). A *closed-end mortgage* means no additional borrowing can be done on that mortgage. This, with an after acquired property clause, guarantees an increasing security base for the creditors. Investors should know the kind of mortgage they have and the provisions that are behind their mortgage bonds, since they determine the risk and return of the investment.

COLLATERAL TRUST BONDS When the security deposited with the trustee of a bond issue consists of the stocks and bonds of other companies, these newly issued secured bonds are called *collateral trust bonds*. Since the assets of holding companies are usually largely in the form of stocks and bonds of their subsidiaries, holding companies are the main issuers of such bonds.

Collateral must, as a rule, be 25 to 33 percent greater than the value of the bonds in order to ensure adequate protection if liquidation is necessary. The borrower may remove this collateral and substitute other assets for it as long as the required margin of coverage is maintained. Such bonds are issued when the method is easier than issuing mortgage bonds or when the holding company wants to consolidate a number of smaller issues at a better market price.

2-4.4 unsecured bonds

Debenture bonds, or more simply, *debentures,* are unsecured bonds. They are issued with no lien against specific property provided in the indenture. They may be seen as a claim on earnings and not assets. This is not to say that the bondholders are not protected in case of default but, rather, that they are general creditors. All assets not specifically pledged or any balance remaining after payment of secured debts from assets previously pledged are available to pay the legal claims of general creditors. The debenture indentures usually take this added riskiness into account and contain specific protecting provisions. They may restrict any further issuing of debentures unless earnings over a certain number of years are two or three times what is needed to cover the original debenture interest. Another common clause says that if any secured debt is issued, the debentures will be secured by an equal amount. Sometimes working capital (that is, current assets minus current liabilities) must be maintained at a certain ratio to the principal amount of the debenture or the debtor is not allowed to pay dividends on its common stock.

SUBORDINATED DEBENTURES Subordinated debentures are simply debentures that are specifically made subordinate to all other general creditors holding claims on assets. These other creditors are usually suppliers or financial institutions that have granted credit and loans to the firm. Many debentures, because they are unsecured, have in recent years been issued as convertible debentures. They then have all the characteristics of bonds, but under certain conditions they may be converted into a specified number of shares of common stock. This conversion privilege is a "sweetener" to make the unsecured debt more attractive. Convertible bonds will be discussed more thoroughly later in this chapter (in terms of the common stock into which they are convertible) and also in the appendix to Chap. 21 (where their conversion option is analyzed).

2-4.5 bonds with special characteristics

Several types of bonds have general characteristics of bonds plus some special distinguishing characteristic. These types of bonds are given special names. For example, if a mortgage bond is secured so that it covers only part of the property of the firm or only a specific section of a railroad, it is called a *divisional bond.* It is the first mortgage on that operating division of the railroad or industrial firm. If the division is highly productive, the bonds will be strong; weak divisions will signify correspondingly weak bonds.

DIRECT LIEN BONDS These are special bonds secured by one piece of property such as a railroad terminal, dock, or bridge. Such a bond might then be referred to as a *terminal bond* or a *bridge bond.* If two or more companies own the property that is securing the bond, such as a railroad bridge, it is called a *joint bond.*

PRIOR LIEN BONDS These are bonds that have been placed ahead of the first mortgage, usually during the reorganization of a bankrupt firm. Only with the permission of the first mortgage bondholders can prior lien bonds be issued, taking priority over the first mortgage claim on assets.

JUNIOR MORTGAGE BONDS These bonds have a secondary claim to assets and earnings behind senior mortgage bonds. Because it is poor public relations for an issue to bear the title *second mortgage,* these issues typically have names such as *refunding mortgage* or *consolidated mortgage.*

ASSUMED OR GUARANTEED BONDS When a large firm (usually a railroad) takes over a small one in a merger or consolidation, the bonds of the small company must be recognized. If the small company is dissolved by the merger, the new entity assumes the liability represented by the bonds. These bonds are then covered not only by the specific property pledged in the indentures but also by the large firm's promise-to-pay clause.

If the merged company continues to operate as a unique division within the large company, its bonds will be guaranteed by the larger firm. Depending upon the willingness of the parent company to continue the guarantee through endorsement of the bonds, rental of its property, or some other legal agreement between the two companies, these bonds may be solid or very weak.

PARTICIPATING BONDS These bonds share in the earnings of the firm. They have a guaranteed rate of interest but may also participate in earnings up to an additional specified percentage. Because they have this characteristic of increased dividends with increased earnings, they are unpopular with the common stockholders of the company, who prefer to keep all earnings for themselves. For this reason, participating bonds are issued only by companies with poor credit positions. The most common users of such bonds have been bridge companies.

ZERO COUPON BONDS Zero coupon bonds pay no interest prior to maturity. Instead, they are sold at large discounts from their face (or maturity) value so that the investor's price gain is the interest income. Thus, the investor has no worry about reinvesting coupon interest receipts, perhaps at disadvantageous interest rates, because there are none. The main disadvantage of these bonds is that the U.S. Internal Revenue Service (IRS) taxes the price gains income as if it were received in annual cash payments. The income taxes must be paid each year even though the zero coupon bonds produce no cashflow until maturity. J. C. Penney was the first corporation to issue zero coupon bonds, in 1981; then, municipalities began to issue them in 1982.

PUT BONDS In 1974 Citicorp issued the first put bonds in the United States. In Canada these bonds have been issued for years; there they are called either extendables or retractables. These bonds all have an early redemption option that allows the bond's investor to put (or sell) the bond back to the issuer before the bond's maturity date at a price called the strike price. Investors benefit from this early redemption option because it essentially puts a floor under the bond's market price so that it cannot fall below the strike price.[13]

Mortgages are another category of special bonds. However, mortgages constitute such a large part of all outstanding debt in the United States that these securities are considered in the next section.

[13] Put options and the strike price of a put option are examined more deeply in chap. 21. For a detailed description of fixed income option valuation see Robert W. Kopprash, "Contingent Take-Down Options on Fixed Income Securities"; chap. 23 in Frank J. Fabozzi and I. M. Pollack (eds.), *The Handbook of Fixed Income Securities* (Dow Jones-Irwin, Homewood, Ill., 1982).

2-5 MORTGAGE SECURITIES

The dictionary says that a mortgage is a "pledge of property to secure payment of a debt." There are two general categories of mortgages: commercial mortgages and home mortgages. *Commercial mortgages* are usually bank loans that enable a growing business firm to buy more physical plant on credit. The new plant that is purchased becomes the collateral pledged against the commercial mortgage loan. In contrast, *home mortgages* are typically loans that a savings and loan association makes to a family to buy a home on credit. Mortgages are like collateral bonds that have real estate pledged as collateral.

Billions of dollars of mortgage loans are made every year in the United States. Savings and loan associations, commercial banks, mortgage bankers, life insurance companies, and mutual savings banks originate most mortgage loans. Then, federal government agencies such as the Federal National Mortgage Association (FNMA), Government National Mortgage Association (GNMA), and Federal Home Loan Banks (FHLB) buy many of the mortgages which the mortgage originator wants to liquidate.[14]

2-5.1 commercial mortgages and conventional home mortgages

Commercial mortgages are usually not bought and sold in active trading (or secondary) markets. The banks and other financial intermediaries that make these loans must hold them as long-term investments, because active secondary markets in which to trade commercial mortgages do not exist. Most commercial mortgages are illiquid because they are usually of such a large denomination (namely, millions of dollars) that few investors are large enough to trade such securities easily. Furthermore, it is impossible for mortgage buyers to obtain credit insurance for commercial mortgages in order to protect themselves if the commercial borrower defaults on the mortgage payments.

Home mortgages are of much smaller denomination than commercial mortgages. They range in size from small mortgages of only a few thousand dollars up to million-dollar mortgage pools that are made up of numerous smaller individual mortgages.[15] Although there are a sufficient number of mortgage investors to support active markets in securities of these denominations, few investors are willing to buy uninsured (that is, conventional) home mortgages. Insured home mortgages enjoy the kind of liquidity provided by an active trading (or secondary) market, which most conventional (or uninsured) mortgages cannot obtain because mortgage investors are usually afraid of the losses they may suffer if an uninsured mortgage defaults. In contrast to the less liquid conventional mortgages, securities backed by multimillion dollar pools of insured home mortgages are traded in active secondary markets.

[14] United States League of Savings Associations, *Savings Institutions Source Book,* 1984, Washington, D.C.

[15] For additional details about mortgages and mortgage-backed securities, see J. C. Francis, "Helping Americans Get Mortgages," *Business Review,* Philadelphia Federal Reserve Bank, January 1974, pp. 14–21. Also see W. Attebury, *Modern Real Estate Finance,* GRID Inc., Columbus, Ohio, 1972.

These mortgage security markets do a larger dollar volume of security trading than most stock exchanges in the United States.

2-5.2 insured home mortgages

The Veterans Administration (VA), the Federal Housing Authority (FHA), and GNMA are federal agencies that, for a small fee, will guarantee home mortgages against default. That is, if a home buyer cannot or does not pay off an insured mortgage, the federal agency that insured it will pay off the mortgage, so that the mortgage investor is protected against large losses. The insuring agency must then foreclose on the defaulted mortgage and sell the home which was used as collateral in order to regain its investment.

As a result of the federal agency guarantees, insured mortgages enjoy almost the same liquidity as high-quality securities (like U.S. Treasury bonds). The mortgages themselves are not traded. Instead, the mortgages are placed in multimillion dollar pools and bonds, called mortgage-backed securities, are sold to finance the purchase of the mortgages in the pool. Then the mortgage-backed securities are actively traded. This active trading does not take place in organized exchanges. Mortgage investors trade among themselves either directly (by telephone) or through mortgage brokers who work for securities brokerage firms and specialize in arranging mortgage trades for a fee.

Nearly all home and commercial mortgages are interest-bearing installment loan contracts that fully amortize themselves within three decades.[16] The business or family that obtained the mortgage loan typically repays it in equal-sized monthly payments that extend over the life of the mortgage contract. If the real estate that the mortgage financed is sold before all the mortgage is paid off, then the portion of the mortgage still outstanding on the sale date must be paid off with the proceeds from the sale—this is called *prepaying* a mortgage. However, until the date it is all paid off, the mortgage remains a marketable debt security that may be sold to a new investor (unless the mortgage contract explicitly forbids the mortgage lender to sell the mortgage—a rare clause in mortgage contracts).[17]

2-6 COMMON STOCK

Common stock is the first security of a corporation to be issued and the last to be retired. Common stock represents a share in the ownership of the firm. It has the last claim on earnings and assets of all other securities issued. But, it also has an unlimited potential for dividend payment through increasing earnings and for capital gains through rising prices. All other corporate

[16] Mathematical formulas to determine the installment payments necessary to amortize a loan with any given principal, interest rate, and term to maturity are shown and explained in various books. See chap. 18, app. B of *The Handbook of Fixed Income Securities.* The formulas for pass-through mortgage securities are explained there. Computer programs for home computers may also be purchased to calculate mortgage repayment schedules for any given interest rate and term to maturity.

[17] *The Handbook of Fixed Income Securities*, chaps. 17, 18, and 19 discuss mortgage investing in more detail.

securities (namely, corporate bonds and preferred stock) have a contract for interest or dividend payment that common stock does not have. If the firm should fail, common stockholders get what is left after everyone else has been repaid. The chance of a common stockholder recovering anything from a bankrupt firm is highly unlikely. As shown in Table 2-1, the investor's risk is higher with common stock than with any other category of security. As a result of this risk, investors refuse to invest in common stocks unless those stocks offer a rate of return sufficiently high to induce them to assume the possible losses that may result from the high risk.

When investors buy common stock, they typically receive certificates of ownership as proof of their part as owners of the firm. The certificate states the number of shares purchased, their par value, if any, and usually the transfer agent. When stock is purchased on the market (that is, when it is not a new issue purchased from the company), the new owner and the number of shares bought are noted in the stock record book of the transfer agent. The former shareholder's certificate is canceled and the new certificate sent to the registrar, which is usually another bank or trust company. The registrar checks to verify that no errors were made. When all checks are completed, the certificate is sent to the new shareholder.

2-6.1 common stockholders' voting rights

Common stock is voting stock. The power to vote for the board of directors and for or against major issues belongs to common stockholders because they are the owners of the corporation. Most stockholders are not very much interested in the voting power they possess and will sign and return the proxies that are mailed to them by the company. A *proxy* allows a named person, usually part of the management, to vote the shares of the proxy signer at the stockholders' meeting. The use of proxies usually allows management, which normally by itself does not control enough votes to run the company, to be able to vote its decisions into effect.

Many corporate charters allow for *cumulative voting,* which permits a stockholder to have as many votes as he or she has shares of stock times the number of directors being elected. The stock owner may cast all these cumulative votes for only one director or divide them among several. This provision allows for stockholders with a significant minority of shares to gain representation on the board of directors. As mentioned before, small and large institutional stockholders are usually not interested in voting or will vote with management. However, in some unusual instances stockholders have banded together to oppose management. In 1970, for example, several groups of General Motors stockholders, including some large institutions, chose to vote against management on its air pollution proposal in favor of stronger measures. This disenchanted minority of shareholders came to the annual stockholders' meeting, moved and seconded an environmental protection motion that cost GM millions of dollars, and the motion was discussed and voted on by all shareholders who were present at the meeting. If the minority had not been allowed to have their costly environmental proposal implemented as they desired, they could have used their cumulative voting power to fire a few people from the board of directors and elect environmentalists in their place. This threat enabled the minority interest to garner support for its motion by some shareholders who might not have supported it otherwise.

2-6.2 preemptive right

The *preemptive right* allows existing stockholders the right to subscribe to any new issue of stock so that they can maintain their previous fraction of total outstanding shares. Some states automatically make the preemptive right a part of every corporate charter; in others, its inclusion as part of the charter is optional. The reasoning behind the preemptive right is the recognition that stockholders are part owners of corporations and as such should have an interest in earnings and assets and a voice in management proportionate to the fraction of voting shares they own. The preemptive right, if exercised, prevents dilution of ownership control inherent in additional stock issues. For example, if Henry Ford owned 30 percent of the Ford Motor Company Inc., and the Ford Corporation floats a stock issue that doubles the number of shares outstanding, Mr. Ford's share of ownership and control diminishes to 15 percent unless he has the preemptive right (and either the cash or the borrowing power) that allows him to buy 30 percent of the new issue. The preemptive right, then, if exercised, guarantees the undiluted maintenance of voting control, share in earnings, and share in assets.[18]

2-6.3 par value

Par value is the face value of a share of stock. It was originally used to guarantee that the corporation receive a fair price for the value of the firm represented by a share of stock. The idea was to guarantee that the creditors' principal would be protected; however, in practice the concept did not work well. "Watered stock" was issued on many occasions; that is, stock was sold for less than its par value. For example, when United States Steel was formed in 1901, much of its stock was watered—sold at less than par. In 1912 New York became the first state to allow stock to be issued with no par value. Such stock can be issued at any price because it has no par to dictate a minimum value. However, since no-par stock's peak of popularity in the 1920s, corporations have largely given it up in favor of low-par shares. Today most companies set a low minimum par value on their stock at the level they feel sure is below the actual price the shares will command on the market. Railroad stocks still have high par values, with \$100, \$50, and \$25 being common. Utilities most frequently use \$5 or \$10 limits, while industrial firms most often choose a \$1 par value.

Investors must realize that the par value of the stock has very little to do with the value of their shares. They should be interested in the value of their stock as determined by earnings and capital gains and not by any value set as the par value of the stock.

The same misplaced concern is placed on *book value*. Book value per share can be calculated by adding the common stock and surplus accounts of the balance sheet and then dividing by the number of shares of common stock. Book value does give an indication of the assets of the corporation, but it has

[18] Occasionally a preemptive rights offering can be oversubscribed—that is, the existing shareholders submit preemptive bids for more shares than the underwriter had initially planned to offer. The so-called Green Shoe option can be invoked to cover this problem. The Green Shoe option comes from an underwriting in the 1950s for an issue of stock in the Green Shoe Manufacturing Company. This option provides the underwriter the opportunity to buy more shares than initially planned from the issuer in the event that an oversubscription occurs.

TABLE 2-2 comparison of 1981 par, book, and market values for shares of randomly selected corporations

corporation	par	common equity, (000), $	number of common shs., (000)	book value per share, $	range of mkt. price, $
Firestone Tire & Rubber	N.P.	1,443	52,104	25.00	9–14
General Motors Corp.	1.66	17,438	310,610	57.43	34–58
RCA Corporation	N.P.	1,438	75,460	19.06	17–32
Pan Am World Airways	.25	787	81,965	11.05	2–6
Shell Oil	1	9,245	308,954	29.92	38–59

Source: Standard & Poor's *Stock Market Encyclopedia,* Spring 1983.

no real effect on stock prices. During the Depression of the early 1930s and again during the depressed stock markets of the 1970s, many companies had high book values but found their stock was selling far below book value. Book and market values will probably be equal when the stock is issued, but after that, it appears that only coincidence will keep them equal at any given moment. Table 2-2 shows how book value and par value compare with the actual market price of the stock for a few randomly selected corporations. The variations in the three values for each corporation are wide.

2-6.4 classified common stock

Occasionally an investor will come across *classified common stock.* Traditionally the stock referred to as class A was nonvoting, dividend-paying stock issued to the public. Class B stock was voting stock and was held by management, which therefore had control of the firm. It paid no dividends, however, although the owners did enjoy the residual benefits of a growing company.

In the 1920s, classified common stock became very popular with managers and investment bankers because it allowed them to maintain complete control of a company with a minimal investment while still being able to sell stock to the public to finance expenditures. Investors, not much interested in voting rights, saw it as an attractive issue. It offered the speculative advantages of common stock and the protected stability and return of preferred stock. However, much criticism of classified stock arose, and in 1924 the New York Stock Exchange stopped listing any more issues of nonvoting, classified stock. More recently, however, small new companies have found the issuing of voting, classified stock advantageous. They sell class A stock, which pays regular dividends and carries full voting rights, to the public. Class B common is purchased by the organizers of the corporation, but it does not pay dividends until the firm's earnings have grown to respectable levels.

Classified common stock may become more popular in the future for several reasons. For instance, in 1984 the General Motors Corporation adopted Class E common stock as part of an executive incentive plan. The emergence of this classified common stock caused the New York Stock Exchange, where GM stock is listed, to reconsider its ban against listing corporations that issued classified common stock. The NYSE hated to delist GM because the exchange did much business in the issue. Some corporations are also considering the adoption of classified common stock as a means to discourage unwanted take-over offers from aggressive financiers (who are sometimes called "corporate raiders").

2-6.5 cash dividends

According to their investment goals, some stockholders may be very much concerned about dividends. There is no general rule regarding the size or regularity of dividends. Generally, however, rapidly growing corporations pay little or no dividends in order to retain as much capital as possible for internal financing. Established firms tend to pay out a larger portion of their earnings in dividends.

Some companies, for example, public utilities like American Telephone and Telegraph, take pride in their regular, substantial dividend policies. In contrast, other firms, such as Litton Industries, have no cash dividend payouts. At one time it was thought desirable to pay dividends and maintain some kind of stable policy toward them. Now most companies determine dividends according to the need of financing and investor expectation about growth. Dividends may or may not be important to the investor. If investors prefer regular income from large cash dividends, they will buy dividend-paying stock. If they are more concerned about making a capital gain (that is, a higher selling price than purchase price), they will look at the growth prospects of the company and prefer a firm which retains its earnings rather than pay cash dividends.

2-6.6 common stocks' one-period rate of return

Continuing the convention that p_t refers to the market price per security at the beginning of period t, the one-period rate of return from an equity share is defined in Eq. (2-2a).

$$r_t = \frac{p_{t+1} - p_t + d_t}{p_t} \tag{2-2a}$$

The d_t term in Eq. (2-2a) represents the cash dividends per share paid to shareholders of record during period t. Conceptually, p_t is the stock's purchase price if it had been bought at the beginning of the tth period and the quantity $p_{t+1} - p_t$ is called the capital gain or loss, depending on whether the stock appreciated or depreciated during the "period."[19] Calculating a stock's returns is more difficult if the corporation has split its shares or paid stock dividends.

2-6.7 stock dividends

Stock dividends are paid in shares of the issuing company's stock. When a stock dividend is paid, the stock account is increased and the capital surplus account is decreased. Except for these accounting entries, stock dividends and

[19] If p_t were used to denote *end*-of-period prices, Eq. (2-2a) must be modified as shown in Eq. (2-2b):

$$r_t = \frac{p_t - p_{t-1} + d_t}{p_{t-1}} \tag{2-2b}$$

Equations (2-2a) and (2-2b) produce identical results; they differ only by whether p_t denotes beginning- or end-of-period price.

stock splits are identical. For this reason, the New York Stock Exchange has adopted a rule calling all distributions of stock under 25 percent per share *dividends* and distributions over 25 percent *splits* even if the corporation involved calls its action something different.

2-6.8 stock splits

When a company divides its shares, it is said to have "split its stock." If a corporation had 2 million shares outstanding and split them 2 for 1, it would end up with 4 million shares outstanding. In a stock split, the firm must correspondingly reduce the par value of the common stock, but it does not change its capital stock and paid-in surplus accounts. If the firm's stock had a par of $1 before the split, then the 2 for 1 split would give it a par of 50 cents.

A corporation's major reason for splitting its stock is to reduce the stock's market value. The split divides the market price per share in proportion to the split. For example, a $100 per share stock will sell at $50 after a 2 for 1 split, just as $100 per share stock will sell for $50 after a 100 percent stock dividend. In both cases there will be twice as many shares outstanding so that the total market value of the firm is unchanged by such paper shuffling. In essence, stock splits and stock dividends do not affect the value of the firm or the share holder's returns (contrary to what many people think). In any event, most companies do not like the price of their stock to rise too high because the high cost may decrease its popularity. The $30 to $60 range seems to be most popular among investors. Thus, a stock split may be used to restore a popular market price.

2-6.9 calculating returns after splits

Equation (2-2*a*) can be rewritten as (2-2*c*). To calculate a common stock's single-period return after a stock split or stock dividend, Eq. (2-2*c*) may be useful.

$$r_t = \frac{\text{capital gain or loss} + \text{cash dividends}}{\text{purchase price}} \tag{2-2c}$$

Each share's price must be adjusted for stock splits and dividends before rates of return can be calculated. These price adjustments are needed to ensure that only actual changes in the investor's wealth will be measured, rather than the meaningless price changes which are associated with a stock dividend or split. For example, if a 2 for 1 split or a 100 percent stock dividend occurred, the share prices would be halved before the stock dividend or split (or doubled afterward) so that no changes in the investor's wealth would be attributed to it in calculating rates of return.

The following numerical example shows how a share of stock, originally selling for $100 per share, can fall to $50 per share owing to a 2 for 1 split or 100 percent stock dividend without changing the owner's 5 percent rate of return. The change in the unit of account (that is, the stock dividend or stock split) occurred between periods 2 and 3. Since the investor owns twice as many shares after the stock split but each share has half the previous market price, the investor's wealth is unchanged. And the investor's income in this simple example is $5 of cash dividends per period per $100 of investment both before and after the change in the unit of account, that is, a constant 5 percent

TABLE 2-3 a 2 for 1 stock split, or, equivalently, a 100 percent stock dividend

time period (t)	t = 1	t = 2	t = 3	t = 4
Market price per share	$100	$100	$50	$50
Cash dividend per share	$5	$5	$2.50	$2.50
Earnings per share	$10	$10	$5	$5
Number of shares held per $100 original investment	1	1	2	2
Rate of return per period	5%	5%	5%	5%
Shares outstanding	100,000	100,000	200,000	200,000

rate of return per period.[20] This numerical example is summarized in Table 2-3.

2-7 PREFERRED STOCK

Preferred stock is just that: preferred stockholders have preference over common stockholders (but not bondholders) as to after-tax earnings in the form of dividends and assets in the event of liquidation. Therefore, in terms of risk, the preferred stockholder is in a less risky position than the common stockholder but in a more risky position than the corporate bondholder. Preferred stockholders generally receive a higher rate of return on their investment than bondholders in compensation for the slightly greater risk they assume. However, they generally receive a lower rate of return than the common stockholder because they assume less risk. In fact, unlike common, preferred is limited (except with participating preferred) in the amount of dividends it can receive. If the firm is prosperous, the preferred receives only its stipulated dividend and all the residual earnings go to common stockholders. In terms of control, the preferred stockholder, as part owner, is in a better position than the bondholder, since the preferred stockholder is frequently given voting rights. Of course, common stockholders today are always given voting rights.[21]

2-7.1 voting

Prior to 1930, preferred stockholders had few, if any, voting rights. The theory was that as long as holders of this class of stock received their dividends, they should have no voice in the company. Currently, however, there is a pronounced trend to give preferred shares full voting rights. Moreover, nonvoting preferred may become voting stock if preferred dividend payments are missed for a stated length of time. This is consistent with the idea that as long as dividends are paid, preferred stock should have no voice in management. Also, nonvoting preferred may be given voting rights for spe-

[20] The true economic effect of stock dividends and splits is analyzed later in Chap. 19 along the lines of E. Fama, L. Fisher, M. Jensen, and R. Roll, "The Adjustment of Stock Prices to New Information," *International Economic Review,* February 1969, vol. 20, no. 2, pp. 1–21.

[21] See Chap. 20 for a risk-return–oriented economic analysis of the various features of preferred stock investing.

cial circumstances, such as authorization of a new bond or stock issue or the merger of the company.

2-7.2 preemptive right

Common-law statute gives share owners, common or preferred, the right to subscribe to additional issues to maintain their proportionate share of ownership. However, as was explained in the section on common stock, the existence of the preemptive right depends on the law in the state where the corporation was chartered and the provisions of the company's articles of incorporation. The right is a bit more likely to be waived (unless the state law forbids it) for preferred stock than for common, particularly if preferred is nonvoting.

2-7.3 par value

Most preferred stock has a par value. When it does, the dividend rights and call prices are usually stated in terms of par value. However, these rights would be specified even if there were no par value. It seems, therefore, as with common stock, that preferred that has a par value has no real advantage over preferred that has no par value.

2-7.4 dividends

Dividends are the most significant aspect of preferred stock, since preferred stockholders invest more for gain from dividends than for gain from capital appreciation. The dividend paid is usually a stipulated percentage of par value, or for a stock with no par, a stated dollar amount.

Most of the preferred issues outstanding today have a *cumulative dividend* clause. This means that the preferred stockholder is entitled to a dividend whether the firm earns it or not. If the corporation "misses" a preferred dividend, or any part of it, it is not lost but must be made up in a later year before any dividend can be paid to the common stock. For example, if a firm is unable to meet its $6 preferred dividend this year, but next year has $8 to disperse as dividends, all $8 will go to the preferred stock rather than $6 to preferred and $2 to common. After this payment, the firm will still owe $4 per share to its cumulative preferred stockholders.

Not all preferred stock is cumulative. *Noncumulative stock* is entitled to its dividends if they are earned. If they are not, the dividend is completely lost to the preferred stockholders. Of course, the corporation cannot legally pay dividends to its common stock if it has missed a preferred dividend during that dividend period (typically 1 year).

It should be noted that even with a cumulative provision, preferred stock carries no obligation to pay if the dividends are not earned. This provision may lead to difficulty if there is a question as to whether a dividend has been earned. If the directors decide to apply profits to a capital improvement (and who is to say what this is?) and not to pay a dividend, both the preferred stockholders and the common stockholders have no legal recourse; they are stuck with the directors' decision.

2-7.5 call feature

With many guarantees and "sweeteners" needed to make a preferred stock issue attractive, and with the preference and restrictions for dividend payments it demands, companies want to be in a position to call in these preferred shares if they become financially able. A redemption clause gives the company the right to redeem or call in the issues. As in a bond redemption, a preferred stock redemption is made at some time after the announcement of such action, and a call premium is paid above the par value of the stock and its regular dividend. Though railroads seldom have this privilege, almost all industrials and utilities carry it. The premium above par for utilities runs from 5 to 10 percent and from 10 to 20 percent for industrials. For both types of issuers, 10 percent is most common.

As with the bondholder, the call feature is seldom advantageous to a preferred stockholder. However, it is a desirable provision for the firm, since it allows a prospering corporation to bring an end to relatively high fixed charges, namely, preferred dividends. The call price has the effect of setting a ceiling price on preferred stock, since it is reasonable that an investor would be reluctant to pay a market price for a preferred share in excess of the amount for which the corporation could redeem it.

2-7.6 sinking funds

If a preferred stock issue is not convertible, it may include provisions for a *sinking fund.* This sinking fund may take the form of a simple accounting manipulation (debiting earned surplus and crediting a sinking fund for the preferred stock account), or it may entail an orderly annual retirement of the issue. If it is the latter, the shares will probably be redeemed at the call price unless the market price is significantly below the call price. In that case it might be less costly (even after brokerage commissions) for the firm to buy the preferred shares on the market.

A corporation's sinking fund for preferred stock has a much different legal status from that of a similar fund for bonds. A firm's inability to meet payments for a bond sinking fund may precipitate bankruptcy. Default on payments into a preferred stock sinking fund, though, has minor, if any, consequences. Occasionally, if the preferred stock is normally nonvoting, the preferred stockholders are given voting rights after a certain number of payments have been missed.

2-7.7 participating preferred stock

Participating preferred stock, like a participating bond, is uncommon. Both are entitled to a stated rate of dividends (interest) and then a share of the earnings available to be paid to the common stock. Since participating preferred stock is not very popular with the common shareholders, only weak firms will use such a provision as a "sweetener" to help sell this type of stock. Because preferred stock is basically a fixed-income investment like a bond but has few, if any, of the legal guarantees and recourses as to payment of interest that are inherent in a bond, the issuer may add protective clauses to the contract in order to make the stock safer and more salable.

2-7.8 adjustable rate preferred stock

Nine issues of preferred stock which had adjustable rather than fixed rates of cash dividend payments were marketed for the first time in the United States in 1982. These innovative new issues had dividend rates which were tied to the market interest rates on Treasury bonds and were adjustable quarterly. Most of the new issues allowed their rate of cash dividend payments to fall no lower than 7.5 percent and rise no higher than 15.5 percent. Corporate investors bought most of these preferred stocks because the tax law says that 85 percent of the intercorporate cash dividends are tax-exempt. Adjustable rate preferred stock may be viewed as a successful modification of an old security to fit into today's more dynamic market conditions.[22]

2-7.9 conclusions about preferred stock

In sum, preferred stock is a curious hybrid between debt and equity. Although it is technically a form of equity investment, it has many of the characteristics of debt, such as fixed-income return, sinking fund provisions, and call provisions. Its one-period rate of return is calculated with Eq. (2-2*a*) on page 32, like common stock returns.

2-8 CONVERTIBLE SECURITIES

A *convertible security* is a security that can be convertible into another security with different rights and privileges. More specifically, a convertible security is usually a preferred stock or a bond that can be converted into common stock. Once converted into stock, it cannot be changed back. If it is a bond, the convertible security provides the investor with a fixed interest payment; if preferred stock, with a stipulated dividend. The investor also receives the option to convert the instrument into common stock and thus has the speculative aspects of equity ownership.[23] The conversion option allows investors to participate in the residual earnings of the firm that are reflected in rises in the stock prices. They can earn their guaranteed fixed return until they are assured of a capital gain, convert, and make a profit. The convertible may also be an inflation hedge. If inflation significantly reduces the real value of the fixed interest payment, the common stock price may also be inflated, and convertible holders can benefit from converting their security.

Many convertibles have a specific period in which the issue may be converted. They may stipulate that conversion cannot take place until 2 or 3 years after the issue. This stipulation allows the money obtained through such financing to be utilized by the corporation for investment and growth that will show up in higher common stock prices only after a period of time. A limited issue will place a time limit as to when the conversion can take place, typically 10 to 15 years. Convertible preferred stocks are usually unlimited as to time horizon for conversion. An unlimited bond is eligible for conversion for the entire time the bond is outstanding.

As a rule, convertible securities are callable. The call privilege allows the company to call in the security for redemption just as it permits the company to call in preferred stock or a straight bond. The purpose of the call provision is not to redeem the bonds or preferred stock but to force conversion of the issue when the conversion value of the security is well above the call price. In practice, few convertibles are ever redeemed.

[22] "Variable Rate Preferred—The Tale of a Good Idea," *The New York Times*, Mar. 6, 1983, p. 10.

[23] Valuing the option portion of a convertible has been investigated. See M. H. Brennan and E. S. Schwartz, "Convertible Bonds: Valuation and Optimal Strategies for Call and Conversion," *Journal of Finance*, December 1977, pp. 1699–1715. J. E. Ingersol, Jr., "A Contingent Claims Valuation of Convertible Securities," *Journal of Finance*, May 1977, pp. 463–478.

2-8.1 conversion ratio

The *conversion ratio* is the ratio of exchange between the common stock and the convertible security. For example, a $1000 convertible bond may provide for a conversion to 10 shares of common stock. The *conversion price* is then simply the $1000 face value divided by the conversion ratio ($1000/10 = $100 per share conversion price). This ratio may be stated as 10 shares of stock for each bond.

There are instances when the conversion price is not constant over time. The conversion price might change simply with the length of time outstanding or with the proportion of the issue converted. A bond might have a conversion price of $100 per share the first 5 years, $105 per share for the next 5 years, $110 for the third 5 years, and so on. Under a provision stipulating increasing price with amount redeemed, a bond might have a conversion price of $100 per share for the first 25 percent of the shares converted, $105 for the second 25 percent, $110 for the third, and $115 per share for the final 25 percent converted. Such provisions for increasing conversion prices give the issuer some power to force investors to convert their issues as fast as possible when the market price has substantially exceeded the conversion price.

Conversion value is the market price per share of common stock times the conversion ratio. In the foregoing example, if the stock were selling at $105 per share, the conversion value of the bond would be 10 × $105 = $1050. If the price were $95 per share, the conversion value would be $950 for the $1000 face value bond.

The market price of a convertible security will usually be higher than its conversion value at time of issue. The difference between the two is the *conversion premium*. For example, suppose XYZ Corporation's convertible debentures are issued at par value of $1000 per bond. Further assume that the market price of the XYZ common stock was $88 per share on the date the convertible was issued and that the conversion ratio was $1000/$100 = 10. The conversion value was thus 10 × $88 = $880. Subtracting the $880 conversion value from the convertible bond price of $1000 gives a conversion premium of $120. Frequently the conversion premium is expressed as a percentage—for example, ($120/$880 equals) 13.6 percent conversion premium in this example.

2-8.2 dilution

Dilution of an investor's position is possible on both sides of a convertible issue. If the firm splits its stock or declares a stock dividend, the conversion value of the convertible instrument is lowered appropriately. For example, if the conversion price of a bond were $100 per share and the conversion ratio were 10 shares per bond, a 2 for 1 stock split would change the conversion ratio from 10 to 20 (just as the number of shares would be doubled) and the conversion price from $100 to $50 (just as the market price of the common stock would be halved).

The existing investors in a company's stock also run the risk of dilution of their position. They usually recognize this well before conversion takes place, and on the announcement of a convertible issue the market price of the stock often declines. To keep the current stockholders' position stable, the convertible security can be covered by the provision for preemptive rights in the corporate charter. Under this provision, the convertible must be offered to

TABLE 2-4 dilution effect of conversion

	debentures outstanding, $	converted, $
Earnings before interest and taxes	20,000,000	20,000,000
Interest on 7% debenture	3,500,000	0
Profit before taxes	16,500,000	20,000,000
Taxes at 50%	8,250,000	10,000,000
Profit after taxes	8,250,000	10,000,000
Shares outstanding	4,000,000	6,000,000
Earnings per share	$2.06	$1.67

the existing stockholders before it can be sold to the general public. However, over half the states allow corporations to deny preemptive rights in their corporate charters.

An example will illustrate the diluting effect of a convertible. We assume that a corporation issues $50 million of 7 percent convertible debentures at a conversion price of $25 per share. Upon conversion the total number of additional shares would be ($50 million/$25 =) 2 million new shares. Suppose that the company has 4 million shares outstanding originally and, for simplicity, no other debt. It expects earnings of $20 million in 3 years; the income tax rate is 50 percent. Table 2-4 shows what earnings per share would be before conversion and after conversion.

Table 2-4 shows that, with conversion, the earnings per share are diluted. The impact of such dilution upon the market share price must be carefully considered by the investors. However, when the debentures are converted, the corporation is relieved of the interest burden of debentures or the dividends to preferred stock. Conversion has the effect of issuing equity to pay debt.

2-8.3 reasons for convertible financing

This method of delayed equity financing gives several advantages to the corporation.[24] One is a delayed dilution of common stock and earnings per share as shown in Table 2-4. Another is that the firm is able to offer the bond at a lower coupon rate, or preferred stock at a lower dividend rate, than it would have to pay on a straight bond or preferred stock. The rule usually is that the more valuable the conversion feature, the lower the yield that must be offered to sell the issue—the convertible feature is a sweetener.

Companies with poor credit ratings may issue convertibles in order to lower the yield necessary to sell their debt securities. The investor should be aware that some financially weak companies will issue convertibles just to

[24] The following are some in-depth studies about various aspects of convertible security financing for the interested reader: G. J. Alexander, R. D. Stover, and D. B. Kuhnau, "Market Timing Strategies in Convertible Debt Financing," *Journal of Finance,* March 1979, pp. 143–155; M. H. Brennan and E. S. Schwartz, "Convertible Bonds: Valuation and Optimal Strategies for Call and Conversion," *Journal of Finance,* December 1977, pp. 1699–1715; E. F. Brigham, "An Analysis of Convertible Debentures: Theory and Some Empirical Evidence," *Journal of Finance,* March 1966, pp. 35–54; R. W. Melicher and J. R. Hoffmeister, "The Issue Is Convertible Bonds," *Financial Executive,* November 1977, pp. 46–50.

reduce their costs of financing, with no intention that the issue will ever be converted. There are also corporations whose credit rating is weak but who have great potential for growth. Such a firm will be able to sell a convertible debt issue at a near-normal cost, not because of the quality of the bond but because of the attractiveness of the conversion feature for this "growth" stock. Times of tight money and growing stock prices will find even very credit-worthy companies issuing convertible securities in an effort to reduce their cost of obtaining scarce capital.

A definite disadvantage to the firm that is financing with convertible securities is that it runs the risk of diluting not only the earnings per share of its common stock but also the control of the company. If a large part of the issue is purchased by one buyer, typically an investment banker or insurance company, conversion may shift the voting control of the firm away from its original owners and toward the converters. This is not a significant problem for large companies with millions of stockholders, but it is a very real consideration for the small firm or one just going public.

2-8.4 overhanging issue

When a company is unable to force the conversion of an issue because the market price of the common stock has not risen to a point that will induce investors to convert, the issue is said to be an *overhanging issue*. Ordinarily a company will plan for the issue to be converted within a certain period of time. A growth company may expect conversion within 18 months. The failure of the market price of the stock to rise sufficiently for conversion to occur might indicate a failure of the company to perform as expected. Such an overhanging issue can cause serious problems, since the company would find it difficult to gain market acceptance for another convertible issue or even for nonconvertible financing.

The possibility of an overhanging issue and the associated limitations on financial flexibility will definitely reduce the advantages of a convertible over an equity issue. A common stock issue brings in equity capital at the moment, whereas a convertible entails the uncertainty of whether it will ever be converted into common stock.

2-8.5 reasons for investing in convertible securities

The investor should be aware that the conversion option is not free. Convertible securities sell above the price of comparable nonconvertible securities. This additional cost may be worthwhile, however, for a convertible security has value in two forms rather than in just one. First, it has value as a bond or preferred stock. (Since convertible preferred stock and convertible bonds are so similar, the discussion will pertain equally to both.) Second, it allows the investor to hedge against the future. If the price of the stock rises, the convertible is valued at or near its conversion value. But if the market price should decline, the convertible value will fall only to its value as a straight bond.

To illustrate, assume a 20-year, 7 percent convertible debenture has been issued by the XYZ Corporation. A straight 20-year debenture for the same firm would require an 8 percent yield to maturity. The 7 percent bond must sell at a discount if it is to yield 8 percent to maturity. Consequently, a $1000 face value debenture must sell for about $902. Therefore, $902 is the value floor for XYZ's debenture. This means that if the market price of the stock should deteriorate to a point that makes the conversion value negligible, the bond price could not fall below $902. At that price, given that there is no significant change in the corporation's financial condition since the date of issue, the convertible will sell as if it were a straight bond. This bond "floor" is, of course, subject to the changes in interest rates and risk conditions of the firm, as are all bond prices. Bond valuation is covered in detail in Chaps. 11, 12, and 13.

It is interesting to note that the popularity of convertibles with institutional investors has to some extent meant higher premiums over bond value. Many institutions are legally restricted from speculating in common stock. The convertible bond helps them enjoy the benefits of rising prices in the stock market without violating the law. The institution can buy the convertible as a bond and either sell it as its value rises with the climbing stock prices or wait to convert the bond and immediately sell the stock without penalty. Indeed, convertible securities are attractive to all classes of investors, offering protection against falling stock prices and the speculative advantage of capital gains.[25]

2-9 EMPIRICAL EVIDENCE

Table 2-1, at the front of this chapter, suggested that the U.S. government Treasury bonds are the least risky investment and therefore have the lowest rate of income, on average, of the various types of securities. This chapter also suggested that, averaged over all of the different kinds of securities, common stock tends to have the highest risk and rate of return. Some explicit numerical analysis of empirical evidence is offered to substantiate these ideas.

A share of IBM common stock and a marketable U.S. Treasury bond are compared. These two securities were selected for comparison because they are so different. One is a residual-income security involving ownership risks; the other is a fixed-interest debt security involving no risk of bankruptcy.

2-9.1 time periods analyzed

For purposes of this inquiry, the stock and the bond are observed for over a decade. A decade is long enough for about two complete business cycles and numerous smaller temporary market disequilibriums to pass so that the long-run equilibrium tendencies of the securities can be seen.

Rather than observe the securities only at the beginning and the end of the sampled period, they will be observed every 6 months. This will produce 20 observations per decade instead of only two. Essentially, it is assumed that the securities are purchased, held 6 months, sold, and then repurchased and held for the next 6-month period, repetitively. This is a good framework in which to analyze a security's risk and return characteristics.

2-9.2 raw data for the bond

The raw data for the marketable Treasury bond are shown in Table 2-5. The bond pays a 3 percent coupon rate on its face value of $1000; that is, the owner of the bond receives $30 interest each year, or, actually, $15 every 6 months. When the bond matures on February 18, 1995, its owner will receive

[25] The conversion option of convertible securities is analyzed further in App. A of Chap. 21, where call options and warrants are also analyzed. For further information about convertible bonds see *The Handbook of Fixed Income Securities,* chap. 22.

TABLE 2-5 holding period returns for a U.S. Treasury bond

Name of issuer: U.S. Treasury
Type of security: marketable bond
Fixed income: 3% of face per annum
Maturity date: Feb. 15, 1995
Face value: $1000
Researcher: Nancy White
Source of data: *The Wall Street Journal*

half-year	beginning mkt price, $	semiannual coupon, $	RATE OF RETURN semiannual	RATE OF RETURN annual
1982-II	860.80	15	—	—
1982-I	840.50	15	4.2	8.4
1981-II	822.50	15	3.9	7.8
1981-I	820.40	15	2.1	4.2
1980-II	850.40	15	−1.8	−3.6
1980-I	690.90	15	25.2 high	50.4
1979-II	820.00	15	−13.9	−27.8
1979-I	750.40	15	11.3	22.6
1978-II	751.30	15	1.9	3.8
1978-I	750.40	15	2.1	4.2
1977-II	760.50	15	.6	1.3
1977-I	710.70	15	9.1	18.2
1976-II	840.30	15	−14.5 low	−29.0
1976-I	790.90	15	8.1	16.2
1975-II	810.50	15	−.6	−1.2
1975-I	760.40	15	8.6	17.2
1974-II	700.40	15	10.7	21.4
1974-I	740.70	15	−3.4	−6.8
1973-II	700.00	15	8.0	16.0
1973-I	740.70	15	−3.5	−7.0
1972-II	790.50	15	−4.4	−8.8
1972-I	760.60	15	5.9	11.8
1971-II	740.00	15	4.8	9.6
1971-I	720.60	15	4.8	9.6
1970-II	652.50	15	12.7	25.4
1970-I	680.90	15	−1.9	−3.8
1969-II	711.90	15	−2.2	−4.4
1969-I	730.00	15	−.4	−.8

Note: Second-half date is August 15 and the first-half date is February 15.

the $1000 face value. In the meantime, the market price fluctuates freely. The *income* to the owner of the bond is, first, $15 interest every 6 months plus, second, whatever capital gain or loss has occurred during the period. Thus, the owner's rate of income per period is calculated with Eq. (2-1*a*) on page 16.

2-9.3 raw data for the common stock

The raw data for the IBM common stock are shown in Table 2-6. The data sheet is more complicated for the common stock than for the bond because of stock splits and stock dividends, that is, changes in the unit of account. Column 1 of both Tables 2-5 and 2-6 shows the dates on which the market

TABLE 2-6 holding period returns for IBM stock

Name of firm: International Business Machines (IBM)
Type of security: common stock
Industry: electronic
Researcher: Nancy White
Source of data: Moody's Dividend Bulletin, NYSE daily stock price changes

	REPORTED DATA		ADJUSTED DATA			
half-year	closing market price	semiannual cash dividends	change in unit of account	closing market price	semiannual cash dividends	annual rate of return
1982-II	96.25	1.72		96.25	1.72	—
1982-I	60.63	1.72		60.63	1.72	High 131.3
1981-II	56.88	1.72		56.88	1.72	19.2
1981-I	57.88	1.72		57.88	1.72	2.5
1980-II	67.88	1.72		67.88	1.72	−24.40
1980-I	58.75	1.72		58.75	1.72	36.94
1979-II	64.37	1.72		64.37	1.72	−12.11
1979-I	73.37	1.72	4-1 (6/11/79)	73.37	1.72	−19.8
1978-II	298.50	5.74		74.63	1.43	.45
1978-I	257.25	5.00		64.31	1.25	36.0
1977-II	273.50	5.00		68.38	1.25	−8.3
1977-I	264.00	4.50		66.0	1.125	10.62
1976-II	279.12	3.50		69.75	.875	−8.2
1976-I	276.75	3.50		69.19	.875	4.1
1975-II	224.25	3.00		56.06	.75	49.5
1975-I	209.00	3.00		52.25	.75	17.33
1974-II	168.00	2.56		42.00	.64	51.86
1974-I	212.75	2.80		53.19	.70	−39.4
1973-II	246.75	2.80		61.69	.70	−25.3
1973-I	317.0	2.70	5-4 (5/10/73)	63.40	.675	−3.3
1972-II	402.0	2.70		80.4	.54	−40.9
1972-I	392.0	2.60		78.4	.52	6.4
1971-II	336.5	2.60		67.3	.52	34.53
1971-I	317.0	2.40		63.4	.48	13.8
1970-II	317.75	2.40		63.55	.48	1.0
1970-I	250.0	2.00		50.0	.40	55.8
1969-II	364.5	1.60		72.90	.32	Low −61.9
1969-I	337.75	1.30		67.55	.26	16.6
1968-II	315.0	1.30		63.0	.26	15.3
1968-I	353.75	2.60	2-1 (5/9/68)	70.75	.52	−20.4
1967-II	710.	2.60				

Note: First half ends June 30 and second half ends December 30.

price was observed. Columns 2 and 3 in both tables show the reported prices and cash flows (from either the stock's cash dividends or the bond's coupon interest). Column 4 in the two tables differs.

In Table 2-6 the fourth column indicates what changes occurred in the common stock's unit of account. For example, a 2 for 1 stock split or 100 percent stock dividend occurred in May 1968. Columns 5 and 6 show the

TABLE 2-7 comparison of IBM stock and U.S. Treasury bond data, 1969–1982

	Treasury bond, %	IBM stock, %
Arithmetic average rate of return	6.28	8.23
Range of returns	−29.0 to 50.6	−61.9 to 131.3
Standard deviation	15.96	37.0

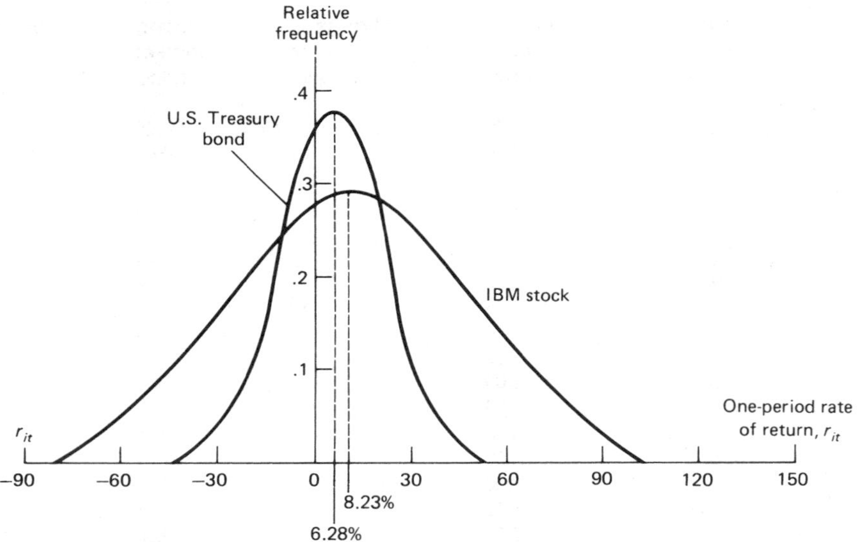

FIGURE 2-2 smoothed relative frequency distributions comparing the rates of return from a U.S. Treasury bond and IBM common stock, 1969–1982.

price and dividend data after they have been adjusted for the changes in the unit of account. For example, all reported prices and dividends prior to the 2 for 1 split in May 1968 are halved before being entered in the columns for adjusted data. If these adjustments for changes in the unit of account had not been made, it would appear as if a $710 investment in IBM in 1967 would have fallen to a market value of $353.75 by mid-1968. In fact, what happened is that the $710 share changed to two shares at $353.75 each during the 6 months, with a total value of 2 × $353.75 = $707.50. The owner's rate of income is calculated with the adjusted data using Eq. (2-2*c*) from page 32.

Table 2-7 compares the IBM stock and the Treasury bond with reference to several points. The IBM stock earned more income per dollar invested than the Treasury bond, and its rate of income was more erratic or variable than the income from the bond. Thus, the stock was a riskier investment. Figure 2-2 is a smoothed approximation of the relative-frequency distribution of the returns from the two assets. This graph shows that the stock has considerably more *variability in its rate of income*—that is, risk—than the bond because its probability distribution is wider. The purpose of this numerical example is to add realism to the assertion that common stock is typically riskier and has higher average returns than bonds.

2-10 CHAPTER SUMMARY

Debt securities come in many forms. The debt securities traded in the money markets all mature in less than 1 year and involve virtually no risk of default. The securities issued by the U.S. government and its agencies are also free from default risk, but their maturities vary from 1 to 30 years.[26] The tax-exempt municipal bonds, in contrast, involve elements of default risk if the issuing municipality falters. Corporate bonds are the most risky category of bonds. However, protective provisions in the indenture contract that governs the terms of a corporate bond issue can furnish some protection to the issue's investors if the issuer becomes bankrupt. Investors in residential mortgages can get relief from default risk by buying only insured mortgages. But no insurance is available to protect commercial mortgage investors.

The common stockholder has the right to receive a certificate to evidence share ownership, to receive dividends, to vote at the stockholders' meetings, and, in many states, the preemptive right to maintain a proportionate share in the corporation's assets, earnings, and voting control. But, in return for these advantages, the common shareholders are forced to accept (1) only a residual claim on the corporation's earnings after all other bills have been paid and (2) the last claim on the assets if the corporation goes bankrupt. If the corporation prospers, however, these last two claims can become very valuable investments.

Unlike common stockholders, preferred stockholders participate in the corporation's earnings to only a limited extent. Preferred stock offers (1) a secure cash dividend that has a prior claim on corporate earnings over the common stock dividend and (2) a fixed cash dividend return that is fairly secure. If the preferred issue is cumulative, then any missed cash dividend payments may be collected eventually, unless the issuer goes bankrupt. And, some issues of preferred stock allow their owners to vote at the common stockholders' meeting in the event that the preferred dividends are in arrears. Some issues of preferred are also backed by a sinking fund. High-grade preferred stock thus offers good security and a stable income if the issuing corporation flourishes.

Convertible preferred stocks combine all the features of ordinary preferred stock with the added benefit of being convertible into common stock in the event that the common appreciates nicely. Convertible preferred thus offers both safety features not found in common stock and the opportunity to participate in common stock's capital gains.

[26] Econometric analysis of the returns from Treasury obligations and other securities may be found in several studies published by V. Vance Roley. See the following partial list of his studies: co-authored by Benjamin M. Friedman and V. V. Roley, "Models of Long-Term Interest Rate Determination," *The Journal of Portfolio Management*, Spring 1980, pp. 35–45; "The Effect of Federal Debt-Management Policy on Corporate Bond and Equity Yields," *The Quarterly Journal of Economics*, November 1982, pp. 645–668. "The Role of Commercial Banks Portfolio Behavior in the Determination of Treasury Security Yields," *Journal of Money, Credit and Banking*, May 1980, vol. 7, pp. 353–369; "The Determinants of the Treasury Security Yield Curve," *Journal of Finance*, December 1981, vol. 26, pp. 1103–1126.

QUESTIONS

1. Differentiate between the coupon rate and a bond's one-period rate of return. Which should be more important to the potential investor? Why?
2. Why can an issuer's call provision in the indenture be potentially detrimental to a bondholder?
3. Why is an issue of participating bonds rather infrequent?
4. What characteristics do all money market securities have in common?
5. What are the differences between U.S. government marketable and non-marketable securities? Give examples of each.
6. What characteristics of municipal bonds are important to the potential investor?
7. Define the strike price of a put bond.
8. What do AMBAC and the MBIA do?
9. Compare and contrast commercial mortgages and residential mortgages.
10. What must the indenture contract have to say about an issue of mortgage bonds?
11. Differentiate between the coupon rate of a bond and a preferred stock's rate of cash dividends.
12. Would you expect the market price of a corporation's common stock to fluctuate the same way as the price of its preferred stock? Why or why not?
13. What are the advantages of investing in the common stock rather than the bonds of a corporation? What are the disadvantages?
14. "Stock dividends and stock splits have no effect on the value of a company." True, false, or uncertain? Discuss.
15. How much importance should be attached to book value and par value in evaluating the investment qualities of a corporation's common stock?
16. Why may a firm wish to raise capital through a convertible securities issue? Why may a firm prefer not to issue convertible securities?
17. From the point of view of the investor, what factors would be considered before investing in a convertible security rather than a straight bond or preferred stock?

SELECTED REFERENCES

Archer, Stephen H., G. Marc Choate, and George Racette, *Financial Management*, 2d ed. (Wiley, New York, 1983). Chapter 11 discusses common and preferred stock and bonds and how to find the value of these types of securities.

Fabozzi, Frank J., and Irving M. Pollack (eds.), *The Handbook of Fixed Income Securities* (Dow Jones-Irwin, Homewood, Ill., 1982). A collection of informative essays written by experts in the field of fixed-income (or debt) securities. Some algebra is used in describing the different securities.

Feldstein, Sylvan G., Frank J. Fabozzi, Irving M. Pollack, and Frank G. Zarb (eds.), *The Municipal Bond Handbook*, Vols. I and II (Dow Jones-Irwin, Homewood, Ill., 1983). These two thick volumes are comprehensive in their discussion of municipal bond topics. No mathematics in this collection of readings by experts in every phase of municipal bond analysis.

Schall, Lawrence D., and Charles W. Haley, *Financial Management,* 3d ed. (McGraw-Hill, New York, 1983). Chapters 20, 21, and 22 provide an easy-to-read and informative discussion of common stock, long-term debt, preferred stock, convertible securities, and warrants.

Scott, I. O., Jr., *Government Securities Markets* (New York: McGraw-Hill, 1965). A nonmathematical discussion of U.S. government bonds and their markets may be found in chaps. 1–3.

Weston, J. F., and E. Brigham, *Managerial Finance,* 7th ed. (Holt, New York, 1981). Chapters 19, 20, and 22 present a nonmathematical description of various types of securities.

CHAPTER 3 securities markets

After reading about the basic types of securities in Chap. 2, the next logical questions might be: Where do these securities come from? How are they subsequently bought and sold? Stated simply, the answers to these questions are that securities are originally issued by corporations, proprietorships, partnerships, and governments. Later, after the securities are initially issued, they are traded in various *securities markets*.

Securities markets are a multibillion dollar business today—a far cry from the auctioneers and merchants who bought and sold securities under a buttonwood tree on Wall Street in 1790. The markets have become so numerous and complex that they defy description in a few well-chosen words. It is the aim of this chapter to discuss the functions, operations, and trading arrangements available in securities markets in the United States and to evaluate briefly the efficiency of these markets. Indeed, the average college student has a vested interest in becoming knowledgeable on the subject: the New York Stock Exchange's 1984 census of share owners shows that almost three-fourths of the U.S. population owns—directly or indirectly—security investments.

3-1 INVESTMENT BANKING

Billions of dollars worth of new securities are issued in the U.S. securities markets each year. These new issues are called *primary issues*. The agent responsible for finding buyers for these brand new securities is called the *investment banker* or *underwriter*. The name "investment banker" is rather unfortunate, for these persons are not primarily investors or bankers. That is, they do not typically make permanent investments of their own funds, nor do they provide a place for safekeeping of funds as a savings banker would. What, then, do they do? Essentially, they purchase brand new issues from security issuers such as companies and governments, and then they arrange for their immediate resale to the investing public.

Who are investment bankers? Perhaps the names listed below sound familiar.

First Boston Corporation
Merrill Lynch, Pierce, Fenner & Smith
Goldman Sachs
Morgan Stanley
Salomon Brothers
Drexel Burnham Lambert

A few large firms such as those listed above do most of the underwriting for the entire investment banking industry. The investment banking industry is made up of several thousand different firms in the United States—but most of them are small and not widely known. In addition to being investment bankers, almost all these firms perform brokerage services and other financial functions. In fact, most of the largest investment banking firms have diversified themselves into department stores of finance. Merrill Lynch, Pierce, Fenner & Smith is a case in point. To name just a few of its activities, Merrill Lynch runs one of the largest brokerage operations in each of the following markets: government securities, securities issued by governmental agencies, commodities, options, financial futures, corporate bonds, preferred stocks, common stocks. Also, through its subsidiaries, Merrill Lynch provides real estate financing and investment advisory services. Thus, investment banking is only a small part of the huge Merrill Lynch operation. For instance, Merrill Lynch has far more stockbrokers who arrange trades between common stock investors in the secondary market than it has investment bankers who originate common stock issues in the *primary market*.

3-1.1 functions of the investment banker

ADVISORY In a corporation's first confrontation with an investment banker, the banker will serve in an advisory capacity. The underwriter will aid the firm considering whether or not to issue new securities in analyzing its financing needs and make suggestions about various means of financing. The underwriter may also function as an advisor in mergers, acquisitions, and refinancing operations. Occasionally, following a securities issue, the investment banker will be given a seat on the board of directors of the firm so that he or she may continue to give financial counsel to the firm and, in the process, help protect the underwriter's reputation as the sponsor of profitable, financially sound firms.[1]

ADMINISTRATIVE The investigations, paperwork, and "general red tape" are quite voluminous in a securities issue. The investment banker has the responsibility of seeing that they are all done in accordance with the relevant laws. Some of these specific administrative responsibilities will be discussed later.

UNDERWRITING The brief period elapsing between the time the investment banking houses purchase an issue from the issuer and the time they subse-

[1] The once common practice of a firm's placing "insiders," like its own investment banker, on its board of directors has come under harsh scrutiny from the SEC in recent years. It is believed that a group of "outsiders" could bring a more objective and less biased view to the management of the firm.

quently sell it to the public is *risky*. Because of unforeseen changes in market conditions, the underwriters face the possibility of either not being able to sell the entire issue or of selling it at less than the purchase price.

Underwriting refers to the guarantee by the investment banker that the issuer of the new securities will receive a certain minimum amount of cash for its new securities. Of course, inherent in this guarantee is some degree of risk for the investment bankers. It is the underwriter's intention to buy the securities from the issuer at less than the expected selling price. This intention is sometimes frustrated, however.

Not all new security issues are underwritten. If the investment banker finds one or more buyers for a new issue and arranges for a direct trade between issuer and investors, he or she is said to have made a *private placement.* Rather than perform the underwriting function, in a private placement the investment banker is compensated for acting as the middle link in bringing buyer and seller together and for his or her skills and speed in determination of a fair price and execution of the trade. Table 3-1 contains empirical statistics that indicate that bond issuers, especially small issuers, are able to get their bond issues sold cheaper by using direct placement rather than public offerings.

In a *public offering,* the investment banker may not assume the role of underwriter; instead the investment banker may agree to use certain facilities and services in distributing new shares on a *best efforts basis* while assuming no financial responsibility if all the securities cannot be sold. In these best efforts offerings the investment banker's charges are typically more than they would have charged for a direct placement but less than they would have charged for a fully underwritten public offering. Best efforts offerings are the exception rather than the rule, however. Usually the investment banker is the underwriter for public offerings.

DISTRIBUTION Distributing securities to investors is the central function of investment bankers. It is their primary concern to bring together buyer and seller, whether they actually buy and then sell the securities themselves, or

TABLE 3-1 a study of debt issues between 1947 and 1950 shows that issue costs as a percentage of the issue amount are less for private placements than for public issues

	PRIVATE PLACEMENTS			PUBLIC ISSUES		
issue size, millions of dollars	underwriting expenses, percent	other expenses, percent	total, percent	underwriting expenses, percent	other expenses, percent	total, percent
Under 0.50	1.7	1.1	2.8	7.3	2.9	10.2
0.50 to 0.99	1.4	0.9	2.3	5.5	3.2	8.7
1.00 to 2.99	0.9	0.5	1.4	3.5	2.1	5.6
3.00 to 4.99	0.6	0.4	1.0	1.4	1.3	2.7
5.00 to 9.99	0.6	0.3	0.9	0.9	1.0	1.9
10.00 to 24.99	0.3	0.3	0.6	1.0	0.7	1.7
25.00 and above	0.2	0.2	0.4	0.7	0.4	1.1

Source: A. B. Cohan, *Yields on Corporate Debt Directly Placed,* National Bureau of Economic Research, Washington, D.C., 1967, p. 127.

BOX 3-1
an investment banker's nightmare come true

In 1970 Duke Power Company issued $100 million in bonds. Several investment banking firms purchased the bonds and offered them for sale at 99.733 percent of their face value to yield 8.65 percent. After trying to sell them at this price for 2 weeks, the investment bankers still held $70 million worth of unsold bonds. Then they decided to disband and try selling the bonds on the open market. On the open market the bonds sold as low as 97, yielding 8.90 percent, and the investment banking syndicate stood to lose an estimated $800,000 on the financing.* Duke Power, though, had its needed cash and nothing to worry about. The investment bankers suffered the losses because they misjudged the market.

* "Interest Rates Climb on Bonds," *The New York Times*, Aug. 18, 1970, p. 47.

whether they simply act as intermediaries in bringing together issuer and investors in a private placement. To gain understanding of how a primary distribution of securities materializes, consider the issuance of a hypothetical $100 million debenture bond flotation by the XYZ Corporation.

3-1.2 an example of a public distribution

Mr. X and his associates of the XYZ Corporation have agreed that they need $100 million to build another large new factory. They need advice about how to raise this much capital; therefore, they go to a nearby investment banking house, say, ABC & Co., and seek counsel.

EARLY CONFERENCES The investment house that first reaches an agreement with the issuer is called the *originator;* the originator ultimately manages the flotation and coordinates the *underwriting syndicate* and *selling group*. At the outset, however, the originator and the issuer must determine how much capital should be raised, whether it should be raised by debt or equity, and whether XYZ Corp. is in a sound financial position. Investigations are conducted by accountants, engineers, and attorneys. The accountants assess the firm's financial condition. If the funds are to be used to acquire new assets, ABC's engineering consultants investigate the proposed acquisition. Attorneys will be asked to give interpretations and judgments about various documents involved in the flotation. And ABC & Co. will make an investigation of the firm's future prospects. Finally, the originator will draw up a tentative underwriting agreement between the issuer and investment banking house, specifying all terms of the issue except the specific price that will be set on the debenture.

THE UNDERWRITING SYNDICATE With most large issues, such as the one under discussion, the investment banker will form a purchase syndicate made up of a group of investment banking houses, usually 10 to 60. There are at least three advantages to forming an underwriting syndicate. First, since it spreads around the purchase cost, ABC & Co. is not faced with an enormous cash drain while the securities are being sold. Second, it lessens the risk of loss,

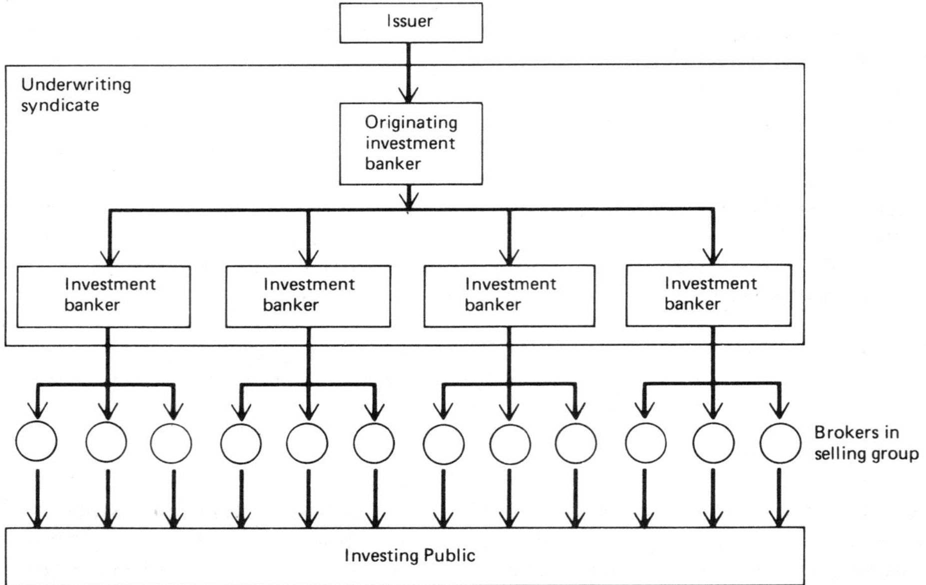

FIGURE 3-1 flowchart for a primary offering made through a syndicate of investment bankers.

since several firms would bear the loss in case of failure instead of only ABC & Co. Third, the utilization of several underwriters and their selling groups encourages a wider participation of final ownership of the new securities. Figure 3-1 illustrates the relationship between issuer, originator, underwriting syndicate, selling group, and the ultimate investors.

THE SELLING GROUP After the underwriters have purchased the issue from XYZ Corp., each uses its own selling group for distribution to the investing public. The selling group consists of other investment bankers, dealers, and brokers. Some firms, such as Merrill Lynch, Pierce, Fenner & Smith, perform all these functions—from managing underwriter in some issues to brokers in others.

DISCLOSURE REQUIREMENTS The federal law administered by the Securities and Exchange Commission (SEC) requires that a *registration statement* be filed with the commission. It must contain information for an investor to judge the investment quality of the new issue. After the filing of the statement, there is usually only a brief delay until the new issue may be offered for sale. During this period the SEC analyzes the registration statement to determine if the relevant information was provided. The SEC may act to delay approval or request amendments to the statement, in which case the waiting period may last days or weeks. In fact, most delays are caused by the large number of statements filed that must be processed by the SEC staff.

A portion of the registration statement is the *prospectus*. After approval and after the price has been set, it is reproduced in quantity and delivered to potential investors. Investors must have a prospectus before they can invest. It contains information about XYZ's history, about those individuals who hold large blocks of XYZ stock, and other facts pertinent to the evaluation of the debentures offered. At the risk of overstatement, it should be emphasized that SEC approval of the registration statement and the prospectus within is not an endorsement by the SEC of the investment value of the securities offered. Its approval implies only that adequate information has been revealed for investors to make their own judgment about the value of the security offer.

Not all issues must be registered with the SEC. Included in this exempt classification are government issues and companies regulated by governmental agencies. The latter must apply for exemption, however. Other issues that are likely to be exempt include (1) intrastate offerings, (2) issues that are offered to only a few investors, and (3) issues of less than $1.5 million, the most frequently exempted group. Exemption does not make the issuer and underwriters immune from legal action if fraud is involved in the flotation, however.

SETTING THE PRICE Perhaps the most difficult decision in a flotation is setting the "right" price. The right price is one that is not too low; this would be unnecessarily costly to the issuer. It also cannot be too high; this might cause losses for the underwriters. Therefore, a very delicate balance is necessary. Security valuation is too large a topic to delve into here—however, chapters in the latter part of the book are devoted to explaining how to estimate the value of securities.[2]

The price is generally set at the end of the registration period.[3] The syndicate prefers to wait to set the final price until the issue is ready for marketing so that it may have the latest, most up-to-date information on the market situation. As a rule, when the price is right, market conditions are good, and the issuer and underwriters are reputable, the flotation will "go out the window"; that is, it will be sold in a few days or even hours. When one or more of these conditions is lacking, it may become a "sticky issue," taking a week, month, or even more to sell, and it may result in multimillion dollar losses for the underwriting syndicate if it is a big deal.

MARKET STABILIZATION During the distribution period, the manager of an underwriting firm occasionally must *stabilize the price* of the issue to prevent its drifting downward. To achieve this objective, the underwriting syndicate's manager "pegs" the price by placing orders to buy the newly issued security at a specified price in the secondary market where the outstanding securities are trading. Although this procedure has been criticized as being a monopolistic price-fixing agreement, the SEC has nodded approval as long as full, prior disclosure of intent to stabilize is made. It is defended on the grounds that if

[2] Bond valuation is the topic of Chaps. 11, 12, and 13. Common stock valuation is the topic of Chaps. 14, 15, 16, and 17.

[3] "Shelf registration" is an expeditious new procedure for registering primary offerings. Shelf registration is discussed in the appendix to this chapter and, more briefly, in Chap. 4, entitled Securities Law.

price-pegging were not allowed, the risk of the underwriting syndicate would be greater; the underwriting cost to the issuer would increase correspondingly. The price-pegging activity usually continues for about 30 days after the issue begins.

If the issue has been badly priced, even the pegging operation does not help substantially. In the most extreme occurrence, the managing underwriter would start buying back everything that had been sold in an effort to keep the price up. In such a case, all the underwriters would experience severe losses.

3-1.3 flotation costs

Investment bankers earn their income as would any other merchants; that is, their selling price is greater than their purchase price. The difference is called the *spread.* In the case of XYZ Corp., let us assume there is a four-percentage-point spread. These percentage points are stated as a percent of the issue's face value. So, the investment banker, ABC & Co., bought the bonds for $960 each and they were ultimately sold to the investing public for their face value of $1000 each. That four points, then, is compensation for various costs such as investigations, the discount given to the underwriting syndicate, and the additional discount given to the selling group members. The spread may very likely be divided as follows: ABC & Co., the managing underwriter, would keep one-half of one point of the four-point spread for originating and managing the syndicate; the entire underwriting group would earn about one and one-half points; and the members of the selling group would earn the remaining two points. If the managing underwriters should sell to an ultimate buyer, they would receive the full four-point spread—one-half point as originator, one and one-half points as part of the underwriting syndicate, and two points as a retailer. Likewise, if the managing underwriter sold part of the issue to its own selling group, they would receive two points of the four-point spread—one-half as originator and one and one-half as part of the underwriting syndicate.

Of the various types of securities issued, the selling costs for bonds are much less than for either preferred stock or common stock. The selling costs for common stock range from 2 to 4 times more than for bonds and about 1.1 to 2 times more than for preferred stock, depending on the size of the issue. It seems reasonable that flotation costs of bonds would be less than for preferred or common stock because bonds are usually sold in large blocks to a small number of large institutional investors, whereas a stock issue may be sold to millions of stockholders. Thus, marketing costs and risk are significantly greater with stock issues.

Further, one need not look far to see why, as a percentage of gross proceeds, flotation costs for small issues are greater than for large issues. Fixed costs, such as registration fees and investigation expenses, account for about 85 percent of the cost of flotation. The greater the issue, then, the less the fixed cost per dollar of new issue. Moreover, as a general rule, small issues are made by less well known companies, and the less well known the company, the more obligated is the managing firm to make an extremely intensive investigation of the issuing firm. Also, marketing the issue of an unknown firm is much more difficult and thus more costly than launching the issue of a well-known firm. Therefore, flotation costs for small issues are higher than for large issues on a per-unit basis.

TABLE 3-2 issue costs as a percent of proceeds for registered issues of common stock during 1971–1975

	GENERAL UNDERWRITTEN CASH OFFERS			UNDERWRITTEN RIGHTS ISSUES			NONUNDERWRITTEN RIGHTS ISSUES
	underwriters'	other	total	underwriters'	other	total	total
Under 0.50	...	...	...	...	...	...	9.0
0.50 to 0.99	7.0	6.8	13.7	3.4	4.8	8.2	4.6
1.00 to 1.99	10.4	4.9	15.3	6.4	4.2	10.5	4.9
2.00 to 4.99	6.6	2.9	9.5	5.2	2.9	8.1	2.9
5.00 to 9.99	5.5	1.5	7.0	3.9	2.2	6.1	1.4
10.00 to 19.99	4.8	0.7	5.6	4.1	1.2	5.4	0.7
20.00 to 49.99	4.3	0.4	4.7	3.8	0.9	4.7	0.5
50.00 to 99.99	4.0	0.2	4.2	4.0	0.7	4.7	0.2
100.00 to 500.00	3.8	0.1	4.0	3.5	0.5	4.0	0.1
Average	5.0	1.2	6.2	4.3	1.7	6.1	2.5

Source: C. W. Smith, "Alternative Methods for Raising Capital: Rights versus Underwritten Offering," *Journal of Financial Economics*, December 1977, vol. 5, pp. 273–307, table 1, p. 277.

TABLE 3-3 average underwriting and administrative costs for underwritten public issues of bonds, 1960–1969, classified by size of issue

size of issue, millions of dollars	underwriters' compensation, percent	other expenses, percent
Under 0.50	13.6	6.2
0.50 to 0.99	7.7	5.2
1.00 to 1.99	6.4	3.0
2.00 to 4.99	4.6	1.7
5.00 to 9.99	1.6	0.9
10.00 to 19.99	1.2	0.6
20.00 to 49.99	1.1	0.4
50.00 and above	0.8	0.3

Source: R. Hillstrom and R. King (eds.), *1960–69: A Decade of Corporate and International Finance*, Investment Dealers Digest, Inc., New York, p. 18.

Tables 3-2 and 3-3 show the results from surveys of investment bankers about their charges. When compared, these tables indicate that it is considerably more expensive to issue common stock than to issue the same amount of debt securities. Second, a large part of the investment banking costs are fixed costs that do not vary with the size of the issue. As a result of these fixed costs, if the total costs of the issue are measured as a percent of the total capital raised, it is less expensive to have large issues than small issues.

In an effort to keep the underwriting costs of a new issue down, some potential issuers of new securities solicit bids on their issue from competing investment banking firms. The underwriter that offers to pay the highest net cash proceeds to the issuing corporation for the issue gets the deal. The law requires that public utility holding companies seek competitive bids for all their primary security issues rather than simply negotiate a fee structure with one selected underwriter. Research to determine the relative advantage of seeking competitive bids versus negotiating with only one investment banker suggests that the issuer gets about the same price for the issue either way.[4] However, potential issuers who do not solicit bids nevertheless probably "shop around" discreetly before settling on one underwriter. Thus, there is probably some indirect bidding competition on even those deals that appear to have a fee structure that was negotiated with only one investment banker.

3-2 ORGANIZED SECURITIES EXCHANGES

The individual who is interested in investing may either arrange for the purchase of stock through a bank or go directly to a broker. Most investors prefer to go directly to a local brokerage house and request the services of one of its brokers. Either way, after the initial paperwork has been completed, the investor's order will be relayed to one of the dealers handling the securities in which the investor is interested and the purchase will be consummated.

Individual investors most frequently utilize (through their brokers) the services of either the organized exchanges or the over-the-counter markets. These markets are called the *secondary markets.* Investors buy brand new securities from their issuer (or the issuer's investment banker) in the *primary market.* In the secondary market investors buy and sell securities among themselves so that the issuer never gets any direct cashflow from these trades. This discussion of the secondary markets begins with the organized exchanges, of which the largest and best known is the New York Stock Exchange (NYSE), also known as the "big board." Table 3-4 shows that the NYSE handled over 80 percent of all securities traded on organized exchanges registered with the Securities and Exchange Commission (SEC) dur-

[4] For similar research findings see D. E. Logue and R. A. Jarrow, "Negotiation versus Competitive Bidding in the Sale of Securities by Public Utilities," *Financial Management,* Autumn 1978, pp. 31–39.

TABLE 3-4 volume of 1981 trading by N.Y. Stock Exchange, American Exchange, and other exchanges in U.S.

	NUMBER OF SHARES		VOLUME BY VALUE, $	
	shares in millions	pct. of total	value in millions	pct. of total
N.Y.S.E.	12,843	80.7	415,913	84.8
American St. Exch.	1,472	9.3	26,385	5.4
Midwest St. Exchange* Pacific St. Exch.* Philadelphia St. Exch.* Boston Stock Exchange Cincinnati St. Exch.*	1,594	10.0	48,390	9.8

* For details about these exchanges, see R. J. Tewles and E. S. Bradley, *The Stock Market* (Wiley, New York, 1982), chap. 11.

Source: *New York Stock Exchange Fact Book,* 1983, p. 73.

ing 1981.[5] The American Stock Exchange (AMEX) followed far behind with only 10 percent of total volume. The other exchanges listed in Table 3-4 make up the balance (these are sometimes called regional exchanges). These smaller and less well known exchanges (and others that have since gone defunct) were particularly important historically when proximity to the trading market was vital because of the undeveloped communications media; and, they still provide a valuable service for small, local businesses whose securities are known only within a small area and for the issuers of municipal bonds. Today, however, approximately 90 percent of their trading volume is in stocks that are dually listed on the NYSE and the smaller exchanges. There are virtually no stocks listed on the NYSE that cannot also be bought and sold over the counter. Thus, one of the most important present functions of the small exchanges is to provide *competition* for the NYSE in dually listed securities.

3-2.1 functions

Probably the most essential function performed by any exchange is the creation of a *continuous market*—the opportunity to buy or sell securities immediately at a price that varies little from the previous selling price. Thus, a continuous market allows investments to be liquid and marketable. That is, the investors are not obligated to hold debt securities until maturity, or, if they have common stocks, infinitely long (since common stock never matures or expires unless the corporation is somehow dissolved).

An exchange also helps determine securities prices. Price is determined by buy and sell orders that flow from investors' demand and supply preferences. The exchanges bring together buyers and sellers from all over the nation and from foreign countries; anonymity between buyers and sellers is preserved as their agents transact whatever trades the investor orders.

The stock exchanges also provide a service to industry by indirectly aiding new financing. The ease with which investors can trade issues makes them more willing to invest in new issues.

3-2.2 organization

Since most of the other exchanges follow the organizational pattern of the New York Stock Exchange, this discussion will focus on the dominant features of the NYSE.

The New York Stock Exchange has been described as a *voluntary association*. More specifically, it is a corporation that endeavors to maintain a smoothly operating marketplace. The New York Stock Exchange, like other exchanges, is directed by a board of governors elected by its members. The NYSE board is composed of governors representing member firms and the public. The board is the chief policy-making body of the exchange. Among other duties, it approves or rejects applications of new members; it accepts or rejects budget proposals; it disciplines members through fines, suspension, or expulsion; it accepts or rejects proposals for new security listings; it submits requests to the SEC for changes; and it assigns securities to the various posts on the trading floor.

The main trading floor of the NYSE is about the size of a football field. There is an annex in which bonds and less actively traded stocks are bought

[5] The SEC is a federal agency that regulates securities markets in the United States. The SEC and securities markets regulation will be discussed in detail in Chap. 4.

and sold. Around the edge of both rooms are telephone booths, used primarily to transmit orders from the broker's office to the exchange floor and back again to the broker's office after execution of the order. On the floor are 18 U-shaped counters; each counter has many windows known as *trading posts*. A few of the 1550 or so (it changes constantly) domestic corporations listed on the NYSE are assigned to be traded at each of the posts on the trading floor.

3-2.3 NYSE membership

There are 1366 members of the NYSE. This number has remained constant since 1953. Memberships are frequently referred to as *seats,* although trading is conducted without the benefit of chairs. In 1969, seats sold at a record high of $515,000, but by 1977 they were down to only $35,000. In most years there are over 100 transfers of exchange memberships. The composition of the membership varies as to function, but most are partners or employees of brokerage houses.

COMMISSION BROKERS Approximately 400 to 450 of the 1366 seats on the NYSE are owned by commission brokers. These seats are owned in the individual's name, but a brokerage house may be financing the individual's purchase of the seat and therefore controlling the seat indirectly. Some large brokerage houses control more than one seat. For example, Merrill Lynch, Pierce, Fenner & Smith, the largest brokerage house, reputedly uses seven seats full-time (and also several other floor brokers during peak trading activity). If Merrill Lynch doesn't have a loan outstanding to the owners of these seats, which gives the firm control over the seat owner, then the firm is at least able to exert considerable control over the seats' owners because of the larger number of transactions (and the associated commission income) the firm directs to whatever floor broker it desires. These exchange members act as agents who buy and sell securities for clients of the brokerage house and as dealers for their own position. Members whose functions differ from those of commission brokers include floor brokers, floor traders, specialists, and odd-lot dealers.

FLOOR BROKERS Floor brokers may be described as broker's brokers. They are ordinarily free-lance members of the exchange, not brokers for a member firm. At peak activity periods, they will accept orders from other brokers, execute them, and receive part of their commission in return. Floor brokers are useful in that they help prevent backlogs of orders, and they allow many firms to operate with fewer exchange memberships than would be needed without their services.

FLOOR TRADERS Floor traders differ from floor brokers in that they trade only for themselves. They buy neither for the public nor for other brokers. They are speculators, free to search the exchange floor for profitable buying and selling opportunities. Sometimes floor traders buy and sell the same stock on the same day, an activity occasionally referred to as *day trading*. Floor traders trade free of commission, since they own their own seats and trade for themselves. However, over the years floor trading has declined—probably as a result of higher costs (transfer taxes and clearing fees), unfavorable federal and state income taxes, and stricter regulations.

SPECIALISTS Approximately 400 of the seats on the New York Stock Exchange are owned by members of the NYSE who have the title of "specialist." Specialists are assigned to posts on the trading floor where they specialize in the trading of one or more stocks. All specialists are monopoly market makers in one or more stocks on the NYSE. They may act as brokers or dealers in a transaction. As *brokers* the specialists execute orders for other brokers for a commission. As *dealers,* the specialists each buy and sell shares of the stock(s) in which they are specializing for their own accounts at their own risk. When there are more buy orders than sell orders, the specialists either raise the market price of the security over which they have control or sell shares out of their inventory to quell the demand. And, when there are more sell orders than buy orders, the specialists either lower the price or buy for their own accounts in order to equalize supply and demand.[6] That is, the specialists set the market prices for the securities in which they are assigned the market-making function as they carry out their assigned duty of making a smooth and continuous market. Members of the NYSE want to be specialists because the position provides substantial income if the security for which they are assigned the market-making function enjoys a high trading volume—specialists make the bid-and-ask spread off of every share that passes through their hands.

In order to keep from having their positions taken away from them the specialists are supposed to help achieve an orderly, continuous market, ensuring only small incremental changes in price from trade to trade. To become a specialist requires experience, ability as a dealer, a seat on the exchange, selection by the board of governors, and a minimum capital requirement. All specialists are required to have adequate capital to assume a position of at least 4000 shares of every stock in which they specialize. Each specialist on the floor of the exchange represents one of approximately 90 specialists firms that make the markets at the NYSE.

ODD-LOT DEALERS The purchase or sale of less than 100 shares of stock is referred to as an *odd-lot transaction.* Trades of 100 shares or multiples of 100 are referred to as *round-lot transactions.*[7] Formerly, odd-lot trades were executed through special odd-lot dealers who were members of the stock exchange in years past. In particular, the NYSE firm of Carlisle-DeCoppet and Company was well known for specializing in odd lots. Odd-lot dealers must buy in round lots, deliver a portion of the round lot to the odd-lot buyer (usually a small, amateur investor), and then be left holding in inventory the remainder of the round lot purchased. Odd-lot dealers used to be compensated for performing this service by charging a special fee on top of the usual brokerage fee. The fee made odd-lot trading very costly, in terms of the total commission cost, compared with trading in round lots. However, the situation has changed since May 1, 1975.

[6] For analysis of specialists' trading activities during periods of traumatic market change, see F. K. Reilly and E. F. Drzycimski, "Exchange Specialists and World Events," *Financial Analysts Journal,* July–August 1975, pp. 27–33.

[7] There are a few high-priced stocks for which a round lot is considered a 10-share trade.

Today some large brokerages (notably Merrill Lynch, Pierce, Fenner & Smith) handle odd-lot orders at negotiated rates that are lower than those the old odd-lot dealers used to charge. Furthermore, some stock exchange specialists have begun to deal in odd lots for the securities in which they make markets. Thus the odd-lot dealers have lost their profitable niche in the market system. Competition among the different dealers who are willing to deal in odd lots has driven odd-lot commissions down to more reasonable levels today. Round-lot commissions are discussed later in this chapter.

3-2.4 listing requirements

All firms whose stock is traded on an organized exchange must have at one time filed an application for listing. Some firms, such as American Telephone and Telegraph (AT&T), are listed on more than one exchange. The NYSE has the most stringent listing requirements of all the exchanges. For example, to be eligible the firm must have at least 2000 stockholders who are holders of round lots; there must be a minimum of 1 million shares outstanding that are publicly held by more than 2000 different stockholders; and the company must demonstrate earning power of at least $2.5 million before taxes at the time of listing. Among its other obligations, a firm applying for NYSE membership must be prepared to pay a listing fee and to make its financial statements continuously available to the investing public.

Once a company has met all the requirements for listing and is allowed to have its securities traded on the NYSE, it must meet certain requirements established by the exchange and the SEC in order to maintain that privilege. For example, the listed firm must publish quarterly earnings reports; it must fully disclose financial information annually; it must obtain SEC approval of proxy forms before they can be sent to stockholders; and insiders of the firm are prohibited from short selling.[8]

With the strict listing requirements and other requirements after membership, one wonders why firms seek listing on organized exchanges rather than settle for trading on the over-the-counter markets. Part of the answer lies in the fact that the listed firm benefits from a certain amount of "free" advertising and publicity, particularly if its stock is actively traded. This exposure probably has a favorable effect on the sale of its products to the extent that the company's name and its products are associated in the public's mind. Furthermore, some people claim that listing a stock on the NYSE enhances the prestige of the listing corporation. If true, that would aid the listed corporations in obtaining capital at a lower cost. But scientific research has cast grave doubts on the folklore of Wall Street, which claims that NYSE firms' securities sell at higher prices and thus the firms have lower costs of capital than corporations which are not listed on the NYSE.[9] However, the investor in a listed security may gain some small convenience from the large quantities of information published about the listed company (for example, the financial reports that the SEC requires the firms to distribute and news

[8] Short selling is discussed in Sec. 21-1 of Chap. 21.

[9] L. K. W. Ying, W. G. Lewellen, G. Schlarbaum, and R. C. Lease, "Stock Exchange Listings and Security Returns," *Journal of Financial and Quantitative Analysis,* September 1977, pp. 415–432. These researchers conclude that there are some immediate and temporary price increases associated with exchange listings. But later price declines appear to wipe out part or all of the earlier gains.

about dividends, new products, and new management) that are rapidly disseminated by the news media. Investors also can read in the financial pages the volume of trading that is being done in their companies and the daily high and low prices for shares traded.

In the final analysis, over half the total dollar volume of securities traded in the United States is accounted for by the over-the-counter (OTC) market rather than the organized exchanges, and most of the over-the-counter securities are not listed on any organized exchange. Thus, it would be erroneous to conclude that the OTC market is not also important as a security market in the United States.

3-3 OVER-THE-COUNTER MARKETS

The term "over the counter" is a bit anachronistic. It originated in the days when securities were traded over the counters of various dealers from their inventories. Now, however, the over-the-counter market is more a way to do business than it is a place. It is a way of trading securities other than on an organized stock exchange. The broker-dealers who engage in the trades of these securities are linked by a network of telephones, telegraphs, teletypewriters, and computer systems through which they deal directly with one another and with customers. Thus, prices are arrived at by a process that takes place over communication lines spanning thousands of miles and allows investors to select among competing market-makers (instead of one monopolistic market-maker in each security, such as the NYSE specialists).

3-3.1 securities traded

The securities traded over the counter range from the most risk-free (that is, U.S. government) bonds to the most speculative common stocks. Historically, the OTC markets have been more important as bond markets than as stock markets. Currently, virtually all U.S. government, state, and municipal obligations are traded over the counter, although U.S. government bonds are also traded at organized exchanges. More than 90 percent of corporate bonds are traded over the counter, although many of them are also listed on the NYSE.

The OTC stock market is not quite as large as the OTC bond market. About a third of stock trading in the United States is OTC—over 30,000 different common stock issues are traded this way. But, many of these issues generate virtually no trading activity because they are shares in small, local corporations that may be closely held by members of the family of the firm's founder. Also, many bank, insurance, and investment company stocks are traded over the counter because in the past the OTC markets required less financial disclosure. However, the 1964 amendments to the Securities Exchange Act of 1934 changed this so that OTC securities must disclose essentially the same information as the exchange-listed securities. Many preferred stock issues are traded over the counter. And practically all the securities listed on the NYSE are also being traded over the counter through the "third market," which is discussed in the appendix to this chapter.

3-3.2 broker-dealers

Of the registered broker-dealer houses (that is, those registered with the SEC), some are organized as sole proprietorships, some as partnerships, and many as corporations. Many of them have memberships in one or more stock exchanges. Some are wholesalers (that is, they buy from and sell to other dealers), some are retailers (selling mostly to the public), and some serve both functions. If the dealer buys and sells a particular security regularly, he or she is said to *make a market* in that security, serving much the same function as the specialist on the New York Stock Exchange. Broker-dealer firms can be categorized according to their specialties. For example, an OTC house specializes in OTC issues and rarely belongs to an exchange; an investment banking house that specializes in the underwriting of new security issues may diversify by acting as dealer in both listed and OTC securities; a commercial bank or a trust company may make a market in U.S. government, state, and local obligations; a stock exchange member house may have a separate department specifically formed to carry on trading in OTC markets; and there are houses that deal almost exclusively in municipal issues or federal government bond issues.

3-3.3 National Association of Security Dealers (NASD)

The National Association of Security Dealers (NASD) is a voluntary organization of security dealers that performs a self-regulating function for the OTC markets similar to that which the NYSE does for its members. To qualify as a registered representative (that is, as a partner, officer, or employee of a broker-dealer firm that does business directly with the public), the candidate must pass a written qualifying examination prepared by the NASD and file an application with the NASD. The applicant must be recommended by a partner, owner, or voting stockholder of a member organization. Once a member, any individual who violates the rules of fair practice outlined by the NASD is subject to censure, fine, suspension, or expulsion, just as a member firm would be. The NASD is designed to protect the interests of its members by creating a favorable public relations image for the OTC dealer.

The NASD also performs an advocacy function for its members. It lobbies in Congress, negotiates with the Securities and Exchange Commission, and prepares printed literature in an effort to represent favorably the interests of the OTC dealers and brokers who make up its membership.[10]

3-3.4 over-the-counter quotations

As mentioned previously, prices are determined by negotiated bid and asked prices on the OTC markets rather than by a monopolistic market-making specialist, as on the organized exchanges. But only the high, low, and closing prices of the OTC securities are published in most daily newspapers.

In 1971 a computerized communications network called NASDAQ (an acronym for the initials NASD and *automated quotations*) became operative in the OTC market. NASDAQ (pronounced Naz' dak) provides up-to-date bid-and-ask prices for thousands of securities in response to the simple pressing

[10] Unfortunately, the NASD's pleas for the continued development of a central market system with negotiated commissions that is equally open to all market-makers seem to have largely fallen on deaf ears since 1975 (namely, since the SEC instituted "May Day" on May 1, 1975). In particular, this has been reflected in a series of SEC rulings that are favorable to the NYSE and unfavorable to the development of the third and fourth markets and the people who started those markets. Most especially, Weeden & Co. (an old brokerage firm that bravely withdrew from the NYSE and went into direct competition with it to start the third market) suffered at the hands of several SEC rulings. See "A Stock Trading Test Could Presage Future of Securities Industry," *The Wall Street Journal*, Oct. 3, 1978, p. 1.

of appropriate keys on a computer terminal. When an inquiry is made the NASDAQ computer and telecommunications system instantly flashes prices on the screen of any computer terminal that is linked to NASDAQ's central computer. Thus, the OTC security sales representative can quickly obtain the bid-and-ask quotations of all dealers making a market in the stock he or she wishes to trade. After obtaining this information, the OTC broker then contacts the dealer offering the best price and negotiates a trade. The primary advantage to investors is the assurance that they are receiving the best price. Prior to the inception of NASDAQ, the investor was dependent on the stockbroker's diligence in acquiring bid-and-ask prices from several different market-makers; the broker would contact each individually. The investor could not be certain of receiving the best available price.

NASDAQ is designed to handle up to 20,000 stocks, but it currently lists only about 2500 (which is still considerably more than the approximately 1500 that are listed on the NYSE) because most of the other stocks are not active enough to be included within the system. Thus, NASDAQ has much unused capacity that may eventually be put to use by the inclusion of stocks listed on the exchanges. It is advantageous (for everyone except the NYSE specialists) to have all exchange-listed and OTC securities reported through NASDAQ; this makes it easier for investors to compare the prices from competing market-makers. Closer competition should minimize the costs and commission rates investors are charged to buy and sell securities.

Of the few thousand stocks quoted in NASDAQ, not all are published in *The Wall Street Journal* and other daily financial newspapers. In order to be included in the *national daily list* and be widely published, a stock must have at least three market-makers, a minimum of 1500 stockholders distributed throughout the country, and command what is called "investor interest."

In order to measure investor interest NASDAQ officials calculate the market value of trading in every issue at 6-month intervals. They multiply the average weekly volume of shares traded in each issue by the price per share to estimate the market value of a security's trading activity. The top 1400 stocks are placed on the "most active list" and the next 950 stocks are placed on the "supplementary list" of stocks for which trading data is to be published. Then the news media publish whatever they wish from these lists.

For those OTC stocks not included in the national daily list, a more comprehensive quotation service is provided by the National Quotation Bureau, an organization whose subscribers are primarily security dealers. It quotes prices of over 8000 securities on its daily "pink sheets." Its information is derived chiefly from wholesale OTC dealer firms.

3-4 TRADING ARRANGEMENTS

Before a buy or sell order can be executed, the stockbroker must have explicit orders about the trading arrangements desired by the customer. For example, the broker must know whether the customer wants to specify a market order, limit order, or stop order and also whether the customer prefers to buy on margin or pay cash. These trading arrangements are explained below.

3-4.1 types of orders

Investors have several options when placing a buy or sell order. They may request that the broker place a market order, stop order, limit order, or open order to buy or to sell.

MARKET ORDERS This type of order is the most common and most easily executed. With a market order, the customer is simply requesting that the securities be traded at the best possible price as soon as the order reaches the trading floor of the exchange. Market orders are usually traded very rapidly, sometimes in minutes after the order is given the broker, since no price is specified.

STOP ORDERS Sometimes called stop loss orders, these are usually designed either to protect a customer's existing profit or to reduce the amount of loss. For example, if Ms. Investor buys a stock for $50 and its current market price rises to $75, she has a *paper profit* of $25 per share. If Ms. Investor fears a drop in the current market price, she could request a stop order to sell at, say, $70. This stop order would in effect become a market order after the security fell to $70, and it would be executed as soon as possible after the stock's market price reached $70. The $70 liquidating price is not guaranteed, however. The stock might be down to $69 or $68 or even lower by the time it could be executed. However, the investor's profit position is protected to a large extent. Of course, the danger of using stop loss orders is that the investor runs the risk of selling a security with a future of long-run price appreciation in a temporary decline.

To protect herself from excessive losses, our Ms. Investor may issue a stop order at a price less than purchase price. For example, if she buys a stock for $50 but feels that it is a speculative investment, she may wish to request a stop order to sell at, say, $49 in order to minimize her loss.

Specialists on the NYSE must keep a record of stop orders. They are executed in order of priority (as are limit orders). That is, the first stop order received at a given price is the first order executed. An accumulation of stop orders at a certain price can cause a sharp break in the market of the issue involved. In such an event, it is quite likely that the exchange would suspend the stop orders, just at the time the traders really needed the protection. Thus, the value of a stop order can be considerably diminished under such a contingency.

STOP LIMIT ORDERS These orders specify both the stop price and the limit price at which the customer is willing to buy or sell. The customer must be willing to run the risk that the security will not reach the limit price, resulting in no trade. If the trade cannot be executed by the broker when the order reaches the trading floor, the broker will turn the order over to the specialist, who will execute the order if the limit price or better is reached. An example should clarify this complicated order.

Suppose that Mr. Morgan owned 2000 shares of a stock that was currently selling at $40, but Morgan feared that the price was poised for a decline. To allay his fears, Mr. Morgan places an order: "Sell 2000 at $38, stop and limit." As soon as the price of the stock falls to $38 the broker will attempt to execute the order at a price of $38 or better, but in no case at a price below $38. If the stock cannot be sold for $38 or better, there is no sale.

Mr. Morgan's stop limit order would have been more effective if it had been placed as follows: "Sell 2000 shares at $39 stop, $38 limit." If the price of the stock falls to $39, the broker will immediately endeavor to execute the stop portion of the stop limit order. If the stop order isn't executed at $39 for some reason, it may be executed at the $38 limit price or better. But, under no condition will the stock be sold at a price below $38. This second stop limit order is superior to the first stop limit order because there are more opportunities for it to be executed to Mr. Morgan's benefit.

A stop limit order to buy is executed in the reverse order of the stop limit order to sell. As soon as the stock's price reaches the stop level or higher, the stop order to buy is executed at the limit level or better—that is, at a price below the limit price, if possible. Unfortunately, the danger does exist that in a fast-moving market the prices may move so far so fast that even a well-placed stop limit order gets passed over without being exercised.

OPEN ORDER OR GOOD-TILL-CANCELED (GTC) ORDER These terms refer to the time in which the order is to remain in effect. An *open order* or a *GTC order* remains in effect indefinitely, whereas a *day order* remains in effect only for the day that it is brought to the exchange floor. The vast majority of orders are day orders, probably because the customer feels that conditions are right for trading on that specific day. Market conditions may change the next day. However, customers may prefer a GTC order, particularly for limit orders, when they are willing to wait until the price is right for trading. GTC orders must be confirmed at various intervals to remain in effect.[11]

3-4.2 margin buying

Technically, margin trading includes both margin buying and margin short selling. However, only a small portion of total trading on the margin is short selling. (Short selling is discussed in detail in Chap. 21; for now, the concern is with buying on margin.)

When investors buy stock on margin, they buy some shares with cash and borrow to pay for additional shares, using the paid shares as collateral. The shares paid for with the investor's money are analogous to the equity or down payment in an installment purchase agreement. The Federal Reserve Board of Governors controls the amount that may be borrowed. For example, if the Federal Reserve Board stipulates a 55 percent margin requirement, the investor must pay cash equal to at least 55 percent of the value of the securities purchased. The buyer may borrow funds to pay for no more than 45 percent of the cost of the securities. The Federal Reserve's margin requirements have varied from a low of 25 percent in the 1930s to a high of 100 percent in the 1940s.

The investor who wishes to buy on margin is required to open a *margin account* with a stockbroker. Then the investor is required by the NYSE to make a minimum down payment of $2000. Some brokerage firms require initial margin deposits in excess of the NYSE $2000 minimum.[12] To see how

[11] For more detail about the different kinds of orders and their meanings, read Richard Tewles and Edward Bradley, *The Stock Market*, chap. 7.

[12] Some of the most exclusive brokerage firms will not open even a cash account for a new client unless the client makes an initial deposit in excess of $250,000. The brokers at these brokerage firms are able to earn the largest commission incomes since they deal only with "substantial individuals" and institutional investors rather than small investors.

things work, let us assume the margin requirement is 55 percent and Mr. Investor wishes to purchase 100 shares of a $100 stock. In other words, he wishes to make a total investment of $10,000, but assume he has only $5500 cash of his own. Because of the Federal Reserve Board's 55 percent margin requirement, Mr. Investor can still buy 100 shares by paying cash for 55 shares and using them as collateral for a loan to pay for the other 45 shares. Assume Mr. Investor follows this procedure. Consider the position he will be in if his shares double in price, to $200 each, and, conversely, his position if the price of his shares drops by one-half, to $50 each.

THE GOOD NEWS FOR MR. INVESTOR If Mr. Investor's shares double in value from $100 to $200, his total profit will be $100 profit per share times 100 shares, or $10,000 before interest, commissions, and taxes. Compare this $10,000 gross gain with $100 profit per share times only 55 shares, or a $5500 gross profit, if he has not bought on margin (that is, if he has invested only his $5500 cash). Mr. Investor's gross profit increased because he bought on margin—as shown in the following T-accounts.

The Cash Purchase Summary follows:

Original Position without Margin

Market value	$5,500	Equity $5,500

Position without Margin After 100% Price Increase

Market value	$11,000	Equity $11,000

Total gain: ($100 per share) times (55 shares) equals $5500—that is, 100 percent return on the invested cash.

The Margin Purchase Summary follows:

Original Position with Margin

(assets)		(liabilities and net worth)
Market value	$10,000	$ 4,500 Debit balance (the loan)
		$ 5,500 Equity
		$10,000 Total

Position with Margin After 100% Price Rise

(assets)		(liabilities and net worth)
Market value	$20,000	$ 4,500 Debit balance (the loan)
		$15,500 Equity
		$20,000 Total

Total gain: ($100 per share) times (100 shares) equals $10,000—that is, 182 percent return on the invested cash, an example of favorable financial leverage.

THE BAD NEWS FOR MR. INVESTOR Next, let us suppose that Mr. Investor's shares decrease in price from $100 to $50 per share. The current market value of his investment has dropped from $10,000 to $5000. Compare again his position as a margin buyer with that of a nonmargin buyer. As a margin buyer, he has a $50 per share loss times 100 shares, or a $5000 loss. If he had not bought on margin and had purchased only 55 shares, his loss would have been $50 per share times 55 shares, or $2750. Thus we see that by buying stock on 55 percent margin, he can increase his loss as well as his profit. Mr. Investor's losses are summarized in the following T-accounts.

The Cash Purchase Summary follows:

Original Position without Margin

Market value	$5,500	Equity $5,500

Position without Margin After 50% Price Decline

Market value	$2,750	Equity $2,750

Total loss: ($50 per share) times (55 shares) equals $2750—that is, 50 percent of the invested cash is lost.

The Margin Purchase Summary follows:

Original Position with Margin

(assets)		(liabilities and net worth)
Market value	$10,000	$ 4,500 Debit balance (the loan)
		$ 5,500 Equity
		$10,000 Total

Position with Margin After 50% Price Decline

(assets)		(liabilities and net worth)
Market value	$5,000	$4,500 Debit balance (the loan)
		$ 500 Equity
		$5,000 Total

Total loss: ($50 per share) times (100 shares) equals $5000—that is, 91 percent of the invested cash is lost because of adverse financial leverage.

THE WORST NEWS FOR MR. INVESTOR—A MARGIN CALL The transactions summarized in the preceding T-accounts do not tell the entire story an investor needs to know. If the stock decreases in value sufficiently, Mr. Investor will receive a *margin call* from his broker—brokers also call it a *maintenance call*. That is, the broker calls and informs the client that it is necessary to put up more margin (that is, to produce additional cash "down payment"). If Mr. Investor cannot come up with the additional cash immediately, the broker must liquidate enough of the stocks Mr. Investor owns at their depressed price in order to bring the equity in the account up to the required level. Selling the margined shares of Mr. Investor is easily accomplished, since margin customers are required to deposit their stock as collateral for the loan from their broker. If anything is left over after the sale and subsequent loan payment, the investor receives the balance. By how much must the stock decrease in value before there is a margin call? The New York Stock Exchange has answered this question by stipulating a maintenance margin requirement.

According to the NYSE *maintenance margin* requirement, a margin call must occur when the equity in the account is less than 25 percent of the market value of the account. In the case of Mr. Investor, a margin call would have been required when his $10,000 margined purchase of common stock decreased in market value to below \$6000. Stated differently, if Mr. Investor's maintenance margin must be at least 25 percent of the market value of the account, this is equivalent to saying that the client's loan cannot be more than 75 percent of the account's market value. Mr. Investor's \$4500 loan is fixed and does not vary as the stock's price changes—this loan is 75 percent of a market value of \$6000. In practice, most brokers have higher margin maintenance requirements than the minimum set by the NYSE.

The Federal Reserve Board's Regulation T, called the "initial margin requirement," is effective only when the stock is sold short or on an initial margin purchase. After the initial purchase margin requirement has been met, the Federal Reserve Board's requirements are completely out of the picture. Even if the Fed's initial margin requirement is changed, this change affects only *new* margin purchases.

The primary benefit of buying on margin is that it allows investors to magnify their profits by the reciprocal of the margin requirement (that is, two times if the margin requirement is one-half, three times if it is one-third, and so forth). The major disadvantage is that it causes magnified losses of the same reciprocal if stock prices decline. There is the added disadvantage of fixed interest payments whether stock prices advance or decline. In sum, margin trading increases risk. Therefore it should be used only by those financially sophisticated individuals who can gracefully assume these added risks.

When an investor buys on margin, the one-period rate of return is defined in Eq. (3–1*a*).

$$r_t = \frac{p_{t+1} - p_t + d_t - i(1 - m)p_t}{mp_t} \qquad (3\text{–}1a)$$

Equation (3–1*a*) is different from Eq. (2–2*a*) for the nonmargin buyer's return. The percentage down payment, or margin, is denoted m in Eq. (3–1*a*). The denominator, mp_t, is the dollar amount of the margin buyer's equity investment, ignoring commissions. The margin buyer borrowed $(1 - m)p_t$ dollars at an interest rate of i, so the dollar amount of the interest expense, $i(1 - m)p_t$, is deducted from the numerator to obtain the net income return on equity.

For the sake of concreteness, Eq. (3–1*a*) is reproduced below as Eq. (3–1*b*) for the case from above in which Mr. Investor purchased a \$100 stock on 55 percent margin and then its price doubled to \$200. The interest rate Mr. Investor's brokerage firm charged him for the \$45 per share loan is presumed to be 10 percent (or $i = .1$). No cash dividends were received while Mr. Investor held the stock.

$$\frac{\$200 - \$100 + 0 - [(.1)(1.0 - .55)(\$100)]}{(.55)(\$100)} = \frac{\$95.50}{\$55} = 1.736 \qquad (3\text{–}1b)$$

Equation (3–1*b*) shows that Mr. Investor made 173.6 percent return when the price of the stock he bought doubled. Stated differently, margin transformed a 100 percent price rise into a 173.6 percent gain for the lucky investor. (The rate of return is 182 percent if the interest expense is ignored, as it was in the same example above.)

3-4.3 brokerage services

The investor services provided by brokerage houses include the following:

1. *Free safe-deposit vaults for securities.* If investors leave their securities with the broker for safekeeping, they are relieved of the responsibility of renting a safe-deposit vault or finding some other means of storage, and they do not have to physically transfer their securities to and from the broker's office every time they wish to buy or sell. If the investor owns bonds and leaves them with the broker, the broker will clip the coupons, collect the interest due, and credit the customer's account.
2. *Free literature compiled and published by the research department.* This literature ranges from a booklet of essential information for the beginning investor to computer printouts of the most up-to-date information on securities compiled by the financial analysts of the firm's research staff. Some brokerage houses also provide free newsletters and brochures on commodity prices, foreign exchange, and various industries.
3. *A market for all types of trading.* The firm can arrange trades from the most speculative of commodities to the most risk-free investments.
4. *A credit agency.* When a customer is buying on margin, the broker will loan the funds. The rate of interest charged is usually at least 1 percent over the prime rate; it varies with the amount of margin provided and the credit worthiness of the customer.
5. *Services competition.* A NYSE rule says that brokers are not allowed to give any client more than $25 worth of gifts per year—to make a more costly gift could be viewed as buying or bribing customers. However, some brokers "loan" cars to a favored customer for months at a time, wine and dine their best customers, and provide other "colorful" services in order to get lucrative customers. Such services were common before May 1, 1975, when fixed minimum commissions precluded price competition between exchange brokerages.

3-5 SUMMARY AND CONCLUSIONS

Primary securities markets are made by investment bankers who originate new issues of stocks and bonds. After the investment bankers' distribution is completed, the securities are traded in secondary markets. There are different types of secondary markets in the United States—organized exchanges like the NYSE and the over-the-counter market. The types of brokers that work the secondary markets range from austere discount brokerages like Charles Schwab & Company (which are discussed in the appendix to this chapter), which supply only the bare-bones services, to the most costly full-service brokerages, like Merrill Lynch.

When an investor gives trading orders to his or her broker, instructions should be given about whether the transaction is to be a cash deal or on margin. Then the client must decide whether to issue a market order, a stop limit order, a stop order, a good-till-canceled order, or a day order.

One of the most important modifications in the securities industry in recent decades went into effect on May 1, 1975. On that date the SEC abolished the fixed minimum commissions that, for more than a century, had given organized exchanges like the NYSE market-making powers that subsidized their profits at the expense of investors. This beneficial development was caused by economic pressures from the third and fourth market, block positioners and institutional investors that almost destroyed the NYSE during the 1970s. These more recent developments and others are discussed in the appendix to this chapter for those who wish to study more detail about the structure of the stock markets in the United States.

QUESTIONS

1. What benefits do security exchanges provide for the country in which they reside?
2. What types of securities are most frequently traded over the counter?
3. How are selling prices determined over the counter and on the organized exchanges?
4. What are the advantages and disadvantages of trading on margin?
5. If the margin requirement is 65 percent and Mr. Investor intends to purchase 100 shares of $50 per share stock, what is the minimum down payment he will be required to make? Explain.
6. "Price-pegging assures the investment banking syndicate that no losses will be incurred." Is the preceding statement true, false, or uncertain. Explain.
7. Do you see any conflict of interest between a stockbroker's roles as (a) a sales representative working to maximize commission income and (b) an investment advisor who is trying to give her or his clients advice to maximize their wealth? Explain.
8. What functions are performed by the investment banker?
9. What is a "market order"?
10. Who are the people called "floor brokers" within an organized exchange and what do they do?

NOTE: Questions number 11 and thereafter presume a knowledge of the appendix to Chap. 3.

11. Define the terms "breadth," "depth," and "resiliency" as they relate to securities markets.
12. What is a "block positioner"? Do block positioners help or hinder the specialists on the organized exchanges?
13. What are some of the benefits associated with efficient security markets?
14. In years past, the managers of large portfolios which spend thousands of dollars on brokerage commissions each year have been offered bribes (for example, free vacations, free research assistance, free prostitutes, gifts of various kinds, and other forms of illegal "payola," "under-the-table money," or "kickbacks") by unethical brokers in order to lure them into directing their portfolio transactions to the unethical brokers. What effect do you think negotiated brokerage commissions will have on such practices? Explain.
15. List the pros and cons of having America's stock market policed by, first, the SEC or some other government agency, and second, competition in one big national securities market that is all reported through one computer system like NASDAQ and that has negotiated commission rates. Issues involved include: Would the SEC or competition be the least costly way for a nation to

regulate its security markets? Are both needed? Are there certain types of problems that the SEC or competition is not suited to regulate?

16. Do the specialists on the organized exchanges make those markets more or less efficient in your opinion? Why?
17. What are the ITS and the NSTS? What is their purpose? Which one is better?
18. What was accomplished by the SEC's rule 19c-3? Explain.
19. Compare and contrast the NYSE's DOT, the Philadelphia Stock Exchange's PACE, and American Exchange's PER.

SELECTED REFERENCES

Garbade, Kenneth, *Securities Markets,* McGraw-Hill, 1982. The book provides an excellent economic analysis of the determinants of an efficient securities market system in chaps. 20 through 26. Mathematical statistics are used.

Loll, Leo M., and Julian G. Buckley, *The Over-the-Counter Securities Market,* (Prentice-Hall Inc., Englewood Cliffs, N.J., 1981). Chapters 8 through 11 describe various securities markets in significant detail. This book is studied by most people who are preparing to take the exam to be a registered representative.

Mulhern, John J., "The National Stock Market: Taking Shape," *Business Review,* Federal Reserve Bank of Philadelphia, September–October 1980, pp. 3–11. An easy-to-read and informative explanation of recent developments in the U.S. stock markets. Copies of this booklet are available free on request.

Scott, Ira O., *Government Securities Market,* McGraw-Hill, New York, 1965. The market for U.S. Treasury securities is explained in chaps. 2 and 3.

Stigum, Marcia, *The Money Market: Myth, Reality and Practice,* Dow Jones-Irwin, 1983, revised edition, Homewood, Illinois. A book that explains how money markets work, in easy-to-read detail.

Tewles, Richard J., and Edward S. Bradley, *The Stock Market,* (New York: Wiley, 1982). This book describes in detail the institutions and practices that make up securities markets in the United States. No mathematics used.

APPENDIX 3A

securities markets developments

Chapter 3 discussed the most important aspects of the securities markets in the United States. This appendix delves into more subtle and abstract market developments. These more sophisticated elements of the market's evolution are an extension of the basic concepts introduced in Chap. 3.

APP. 3A-1 THE THIRD AND FOURTH MARKETS

Security markets in the United States are sometimes classified under the following four categories.

FIGURE APP. 3A-1 subsets of the secondary markets.

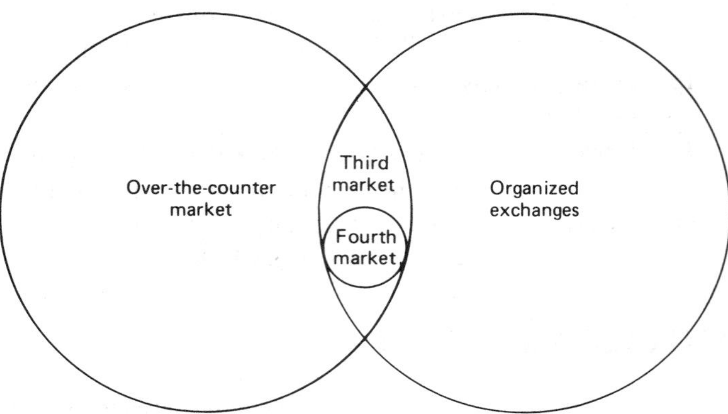

1. *Primary markets*—where new issues are underwritten and distributed by investment bankers. See Sec. 3-1 of this chapter.
2. *Secondary markets*—where previously issued securities are traded in the organized exchanges and over the counter. See Secs. 3-2 and 3-3, respectively.
3. *The "third market"*—an over-the-counter market in exchange-listed securities (which is a subset of the secondary market).
4. *The "fourth market"*—a communications network between investment institutions (which is another subset of the secondary market).

The third market is less well known than the larger secondary market. The third market seems to have reached its peak of importance in about 1975, but it is still a competitive force in the securities markets. The fourth market operates in such a discreet manner that it is difficult to obtain details about it. Figure App. 3A-1 illustrates the relationship between the organized exchanges, the third market, and the fourth market.

the third market

The third market is a subset of the secondary market that does something unique. In the third market listed securities—primarily those listed on the New York Stock Exchange (NYSE)—are traded over the counter. The third market is part of the over-the-counter market. It consists of securities broker-dealers, each making markets in anywhere from a few to a few hundred securities. These third-market dealers stand ready to buy or sell for their own accounts in sizes ranging from an odd lot to large blocks.[13] In those listed

[13] Some Wall Street veterans may be familiar with the name of Weeden. Weeden & Co. was the largest and oldest third-market firm in the United States during the 1970s. Weeden & Co. was started after the Weeden family had owned a seat on the NYSE for a long time. Then, Donald Weeden and his brothers sold their NYSE seat and bravely set themselves up to compete with the NYSE—a job they performed successfully for several years. In its heyday Weeden & Co. made markets in approximately 300 NYSE listed stocks plus numerous bonds. Weeden & Co. traded in quantities as small as odd lots up through large blocks of tens of thousands of shares. Because of adverse rulings by the SEC, Weeden & Co. was forced to merge, after years of third-market pioneering and leadership that benefited the investing public. After its merger Weeden & Co. became a division of the NYSE member firm of Moseley, Hallgarten, Estabrook, and Weeden, Inc.

securities in which it chooses to deal, each dealer owns an inventory (including short positions). Thus, the third-market broker-dealers are market-makers who are in direct competition with the specialists of the NYSE, AMEX, and other exchanges.

The third market developed as a response to the absence of commission-rate discounts for those who trade in large blocks of stock on the NYSE. Prior to 1968 the NYSE's commission charge for, say, 20,000 shares was 200 times its round-lot charge for 100 shares. This system made trading in large blocks very expensive. One way to achieve lower commission charges, then, was to seek an OTC market-maker who "made markets" in NYSE-listed securities. The OTC dealers were not bound to the minimum commission rates that members of the NYSE set for themselves prior to May 1, 1975.[14]

THIRD-MARKET PARTICIPANTS The main participants in the third market are institutional investors such as bank trust accounts, mutual funds, and pension funds. These institutional investors seek to trade in the third market because they believe that they can reduce their commission cost, obtain a better price, effect a more rapid transaction, or accomplish some combination of the above by trading in the third market. Some small broker-dealers who are not members of an organized exchange are also active customers in the third market; that is where they are able to obtain the exchange-listed securities that they sell at negotiated commissions. Private individuals and small odd-lot customers also do their business through the third market, but not to a large extent. Most small investors are unaware of the third market's existence.

Since the third-market-makers deal almost exclusively with broker-dealers and institutions, the services offered (such as securities research, safe-deposit vaults, and sales representatives) are minimal. Third-market dealers also do not own seats on the NYSE, which are expensive to maintain. Therefore their overhead costs tend to be lower. These costs savings are usually reflected in lower net transactions costs to the investors who trade in the third market. The gross profits taken out of a transaction by a third-market dealer are sometimes only a fraction as much as the gross profits taken out of a similar transaction conducted by one of the full-service brokerage firms.[15]

[14] In 1971 the SEC required that the portion of each order in excess of $500,000 be subject to a negotiated fee rather than the minimum commission rate that the organized exchanges required. This ruling made the organized exchanges more competitive with the third market in large-block trades. Then, the NYSE's fixed minimum commission rate schedule was completely outlawed by the SEC on "May Day" (May 1, 1975).

[15] *New York Stock Exchange Fact Book,* 1982. For additional details about the determinants of brokerage commissions, see the following studies: H. Demsetz, "The Cost of Transacting," *The Quarterly Journal of Economics,* vol. 87, February 1968, pp. 33–53; Peter Gutmann, "The Unreported Side of Martin's Report," *Magazine of Wall Street,* Sept. 13, 1971, pp. 22–23; T. W. Epps, "The Demand for Brokers' Services: The Relation between Security Trading Volume and Transaction Cost," *The Bell Journal of Economics,* vol. 7, no. 1, Spring 1976, pp. 163–194; R. O. Edmister, "Commission Cost Structure: Shifts and Scale Economies," *Journal of Finance,* vol. 33, no. 2, May 1978, pp. 477–486. See the references in appendix footnotes 19, 20, 21, 22, and 23, too, for other published commission cost studies.

the fourth market

The fourth market refers to those institutional investors and wealthy individuals who *directly* buy and sell securities from each other. Most fourth-market trades are put together by an intermediary who collects a fee, but the fourth-market participants completely bypass the normal brokerage services. Little is known about these direct trades, since only the two parties to the trade and perhaps a person who helped arrange the transaction are involved—and registration is not required.

A DEFINITION OF THE FOURTH MARKET The *fourth markets* are essentially communication networks among institutional investors that trade large blocks. The functions of inventory carrying, risk-bearing, investment research, credit provision, and dealing in other markets are lacking in the fourth market. The fourth-market-maker is usually one individual or a few persons who communicate the buy and sell desires of their clientele to block traders and thus facilitate directly negotiated sales. The fourth-market organizer may collect a small commission or a flat annual retainer for helping to arrange these large transactions. Generally, the costs of trading large blocks are smaller in the fourth market than in other markets. Other reasons for operating in the fourth market include the expectation of obtaining a better price through direct negotiation, savings on commissions, rapid execution, and/or a desire to retain anonymity. These advantages suggest that use of the fourth market may become more widespread in the future, particularly as large institutional investors continue to grow in importance.

Fourth-market trading represents a threat to the organized exchanges. Its mere existence represents a competitive force in the marketplace and encourages the exchanges and the OTC to handle large blocks efficiently at a lower cost—this, essentially, tends to reduce the profits earned by the specialists on the organized exchanges, the OTC market-makers, and all brokers.

MARKET-MAKERS IN THE FOURTH MARKET There are several privately owned fourth-market organizations. Each one operates slightly differently. Some use telephones to communicate with their institutional customers, whereas others keep their customers directly in touch with one another by using a computer telecommunications network.[16] For example, consider a fourth-market firm named Instinet, which operates out of New York City by computer network and geographically dispersed terminals.

If Mr. Instinet Subscriber wants to buy or sell, he might begin by querying the memory of the Instinet computer to learn what currently existing market prices exist. When Mr. Subscriber decides that he wants to trade he enters the name of the stock, its bid or asked price, and the number of shares into Instinet's computer network, plus a code number through which he can be contacted. This entry, which is essentially an offer to buy or sell, prints out on

[16] The original fourth-market-making firm, Tomasso & Co., has been forced to withdraw from this market by fierce competition from the so-called block positioners at the large brokerage firms such as Merrill Lynch, Pierce, Fenner & Smith; Salomon Brothers; Goldman Sachs; Morgan Stanley; and First Boston Corporation. However, a computer network like the one described in the text, named Instinet, has survived for over a decade against the large brokerages.

the computer terminals of other Instinet subscribers around the world. If another subscriber is interested, they may contact Mr. Subscriber and actually dicker over the price using the computer terminals in their offices. If they agree on the price and size of a trade, the market-maker's computer automatically closes the trade and prints out confirmation slips for both subscribers. The deal is completed without a middle party (such as a specialist) who charges a standard commission, carries inventories, or provides other services. And the buying and selling subscribers never even need learn each other's identity. This anonymity is valued by some fourth-market clients.[17]

APP. 3A-2 DISCOUNT BROKERS, BLOCK POSITIONERS, AND THIRD-PARTY RESEARCH FIRMS

Other groups, in addition to the third market and fourth market, compete to get clients' trades by offering reduced commission rates. "Discount brokers" and "block traders" are two important categories of brokers in the secondary market that maintain downward pressure on the commission rates by offering their special types of brokerage services at a low rate. In addition, security research companies called "third-party researchers" work through brokerage firms to lure commission dollars into their pockets by selling research for "soft dollars." Each of these phenomena is discussed below.

discount brokers

Discount brokerages seek to attract clients by offering lower brokerage commissions than the so-called full-service brokerages. Merrill Lynch, Pierce, Fenner & Smith and E. F. Hutton are examples of large full-service brokerages. The *full-service brokerages* typically have well-paid brokers (also known as account executives, registered representatives, or customers men and women) who are college graduates to deal with the clients. In addition, full-service brokers provide free investment research advice for their clients, free safekeeping of the clients' securities, pretty air-conditioned offices that the clients may visit, and other customer services that are paid for by the high commission rates they charge. The discount brokers do not provide these amenities for their clients—they just do the clerical paperwork that every brokerage must do and charge minimal commission rates for this minimal service. Charles Schwab & Co. is the largest discount brokerage firm in the United States.[18] The second largest firm is Quick & Reilly Inc. Source Securities is another large firm in the field of over 100 discount brokerages in the United States. Table App. 3A-1 lists the main discount brokerage firms.

[17] Instinet is a registered trademark of the Institutional Networks Corporation, 122 East 42 Street, Suite 1001, New York, NY 10168.

[18] Charles Schwab & Co. was acquired by the largest bank holding company in the United States, BankAmerica, in 1983. When the Federal Reserve Board allowed this merger, it was widely interpreted as a significant limitation on the provisions of the Glass-Steagall Act (which requires the separation of commercial banking and investment banking). Later in 1983 Chase Manhattan Bank acquired a discount brokerage firm named Rose & Co. And, also in 1983, dozens of banks either acquired a discount broker subsidiary or started one of their own. It appears that the discount brokerage business will have a bright future in the 1980s.

TABLE APP. 3A-1 the largest discount brokerages*

Andrew Peck Associates (800-221-5873), New York City
Chemical Investor Services (800-223-5566), New York City
Fidelity/Source (800-225-2097), Los Angeles, New York City, San Francisco, Atlanta, et al.
Icahn & Co. (800-221-5735), Chicago, New York City, Miami
Marquette de Bary & Co. (800-221-3305), New York City
Muriel Siebert & Co. (800-221-4206), New York City
Olde & Co. (800-942-5959), Chicago
Ovest (800-221-5713), New York City
Parr Securities (800-221-3720), New York City
Rose and Co. (212-619-3333), New York City
C. Schwab and Company (800-442-2525), San Francisco, New York City, et al.
Quick & Reilly (800-221-8252), New York City, Chicago, Philadelphia, St. Louis, Milwaukee, Miami, et al.

* Numerous commercial banks acquired or started their own discount brokerage subsidiaries in 1983. Thus, the banks are also offering these services.

Because of the emergence of the third market, the fourth market, and the discount brokers, the investors in the United States now enjoy the additional choices provided by competitive multiple market-makers in some listed securities. Even though the organized exchanges, the secondary market, the third market, and the discount brokers operate separately from each other, they do not operate independently of one another. The third-market-makers and the specialists continuously watch the security market prices posted by their competing market-maker—they cannot afford to differ very far or they would lose their clientele.

The National Association of Security Dealers Automated Quotations (NASDAQ) system should contribute to the growth of the third market and the discount brokers. As NASDAQ expands to include more listed stocks of the various organized exchanges, it promises to foster further competition between the organized exchanges and the third market and to benefit investors by promoting more efficient securities pricing and lower commissions. As competition drives brokerage commissions down, securities research and other services provided free by full-service brokers may be discontinued unless paid for separately from the commissions—that is sometimes called "unbundling" of the brokerages' services. *Unbundling* means that the various brokerage services would be sold separately for a fee rather than be given away by the full-service brokerages as part of their standard service.

block positioners

Whenever 10,000 or more shares of one stock are traded in one transaction, it is called a *block trade.* The largest single block ever traded on the NYSE occurred on March 14, 1972, when 5,245,000 shares of American Motors common stock changed hands. Block trading on the NYSE, for example, has increased to comprise approximately 30 percent of the exchange's total volume of shares traded in recent years.

Because multiple buyers must usually be lined up to purchase a block, a special type of broker called a *block positioner* has developed. Published research indicates that the block positioners can routinely handle large blocks and rarely cause the market price of the issue to change significantly.[19] Most block positioners are employees of brokerage firms that own seats on the NYSE—these large firms have both the capital to carry a block in inventory and the connections to distribute it. Block positioners also operate in the third market.

The commission rates charged by block positioners are small. One-fourth of 1 percent is not an unusual commission rate for a block trade. In contrast, odd lots typically garner commissions of from 1 to 6 percent—because there are no economies of scale in these small transactions. The low commission rates offered by the block positioners are another source of economic competitive pressure that helps maintain *negotiated brokerage commissions* on the organized exchanges. In their competition to obtain clients, the different brokers will dicker or negotiate the commission rate they will charge for the transaction.

third-party research firms

The SEC has decreed that under "appropriate circumstances" a securities broker may provide a money manager with securities research that is provided by a "third party." This ruling opened the door for brokerage firms to handle security trades for clients who also want specific kinds of research, and then to spend the brokerage commissions to pay for two things: (1) the administrative costs of handling the clients' security transactions, and (2) hiring outside third-party researchers who provide the specific research that the client desires.

The payment arrangements behind third-party research deals are usually kept confidential, even though they are legal. Typically, the third-party research firms agree to sell their research findings for *"hard dollars"*—or cash, as it is more commonly called. The broker-dealer receives *"soft dollars,"* otherwise known as brokerage commission dollars, for executing trades for the client who receives the research service. The broker-dealer then gives part of the so-called soft dollar commission income from the client to the third-party researcher to pay the hard dollar fees for the research work that was supplied. Third-party researchers typically receive annual retainers of about $15,000 for each client who buys their research through a broker-dealer. The broker-dealer typically expects at least $25,000 per year in soft dollar commission income from each client who uses the third-party research. The $10,000 per-year difference stays with the broker-dealer as a contribution toward over-

[19] A. Kraus and H. Stoll, "Price Impacts of Block Trading on the NYSE," *Journal of Finance*, June 1972, pp. 569–588; Robert Radcliffe, "Liquidity Costs and Block Trading," *Financial Analysts Journal*, July–August 1973, pp. 73–80; Paul Grier and Peter Albin, "Nonrandom Price Changes in Association with Trading in Large Blocks," *Journal of Business*, July 1973, pp. 425–433; Nicholas Close, "Price Reaction to Large Transactions in the Canadian Equity Market," *Financial Analysts Journal*, November–December 1975; Larry Dann, David Mayers, and Robert Raab, "Trading Rules, Large Blocks, and the Speed of Price Adjustment," *Journal of Financial Economics*, January 1977, pp. 3–22; Kenneth Carey, "Nonrandom Price Changes in Association with Trading in Large Blocks: Evidence of Market Efficiency in Behavior of Investor Returns," *Journal of Business*, October 1977; Robert Reback, "Nonrandom Price Changes in Association with Trading in Large Blocks: A Comment," *Journal of Business*, October 1974; Heidi Fiske, "Can the Specialist System Cope with the Age of Block Trading?" *Institutional Investor*, August 1969; Richard West, "Institutional Trading and the Changing Stock Market," *Financial Analysts Journal*, May–June 1971, pp. 17–24, 71–72, and 78.

head expenses and profit. Commission expense dollars that are directed by the investor to pay for third-party research are called soft dollars because the investor is typically an investment institution (such as a bank, for instance) that normally spends tens of thousands of dollars per year on commissions in the normal conduct of their business. Thus, the third-party research is obtained for money that would have to be spent on commissions anyway, rather than paid for with "hard dollars."

Legal third-party research agreements have allowed entrepreneurial security analysts, economists, and other types of consultants to open up their own shops and build up a list of clients who want their research without all the bother and expense of starting up a broker-dealer firm themselves. Institutional investors like this arrangement because it allows them to purchase the unique variety of research services they want by paying for them with soft dollars.

Some of the services provided by third-party researchers for soft dollars are among the most exotic offerings available. Sophisticated econometric forecasts by Wharton Econometric Forecasting (WEFA), Chase Econometrics, and Data Resources Incorporated (DRI) can be obtained through some third-party research suppliers. Barr Rosenberg Associates (BARRA) provides what is sometimes lightly referred to as "Barr Rosenberg's bionic betas," and other services as well, through third-party arrangements. And firms like Analytic Systems, AMTECH, International Risk Management, Quantec, and MIT System Dynamics National Model provide other sophisticated delicacies for the discerning research buyer. However, most third-party research firms provide traditional security buy and sell recommendations. [20]

APP. 3A-3 THE MARKET QUALITIES OF DEPTH, BREADTH, AND RESILIENCY

Perfectly *liquid* assets are *perfectly marketable* and suffer no shrinkage in value as a result of being liquidated hurriedly. Or, stated from a negative viewpoint, *illiquid* assets are not readily marketable—either price discounts must be given or sales commissions must be paid, or both of these costs must be incurred by the seller in order to find a new investor for an illiquid asset. The less marketable an asset is, the larger are the price discounts and/or the commissions that must be given up by the seller in order to effect a quick sale. The amount of such price concessions demanded from the sellers in a security market is one indicator of how much marketability risk investors are exposed to in that market.

definition of the bid-asked price spread

Most securities markets have two prices posted for every security traded there—both a bid price and an asked (or offered) price. The NYSE, for example, has bid and asked prices for every stock it lists. But only one price is printed for each security in the newspapers around the world each day. This single price is called the *execution price;* it is the price at which the last trade of the day was executed. Publishing only the execution price rather than both

[20] For more details about third-party research, see Julie Rohrer, "Soft Dollars: The Boom in Third-Party Research," *Institutional Investor,* April 1984, pp. 73–80.

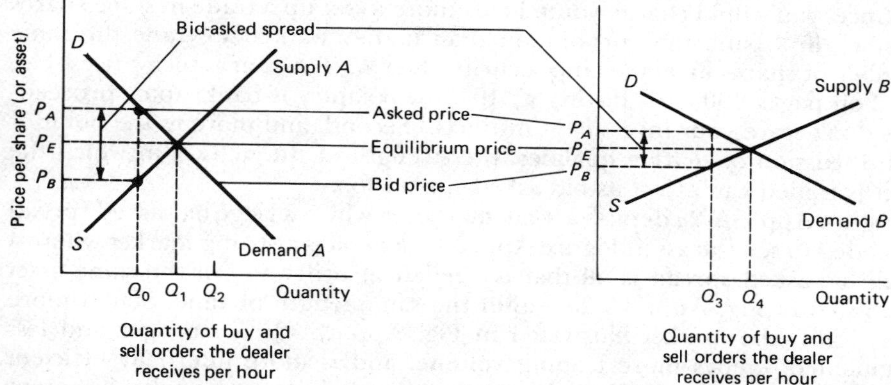

FIGURE APP. 3A-2(*a*) and (*b*) supply and demand schedules for the same asset in a weak market and a strong market.

the bid and asked prices may be a public relations gimmick designed (1) to make things look simple, and (2) to conceal from casual observers the cut the brokers take out of every transaction.

You can sell an asset to the highest bidder at a price called its bid price. And you can buy an asset at the lowest price at which it is offered—called its asked (or offered) price. The bid price is always below the asked price. The bid-asked price spread is the cost of selling an asset quickly. Seen differently, the bid-asked spread is the dealer's reward for making a market in the asset.[21]

The bid-asked spread can be thought of as being (1) the price discount the seller had to give up to sell the asset quickly, or alternatively, (2) the broker's commission for handling the transaction. Or if the intermediary was a dealer instead of a broker, the bid-asked spread is the dealer's compensation for buying the asset and carrying it in inventory until another buyer can be found.

Figure App. 3A-2*a* and App. 3A-2*b* illustrates three different prices. The equilibrium price, P_E, is the price that would equate supply and demand in a perfect market. For example, in a perfect market taxes, brokers' commissions, and other transactions costs would not exist. Thus, the equilibrium price is a theoretical price that will never emerge in a real-world market. The bid price, P_B, is the highest purchase price known available in the market; the asked (or offered) price, P_A, is the lowest price at which the asset is offered for sale.

strong and weak markets contrasted

An asset may not be easily marketable for either or both of two basic reasons. First, the asset itself may be intrinsically undesirable. For an example of an undesirable asset, consider a corporation that issued a common stock while it was being sued in bankruptcy court—this stock would be risky to carry in inventory and hard to sell. As a result, if you were a securities dealer, for

[21] George J. Benston and Robert L. Hagerman, "The Determinants of Bid-Asked Spreads in the Over-the-Counter Market," *Journal of Financial Economics*, vol. 1, December 1974, pp. 353–364; Harold Demsetz, "The Cost of Transacting," *Quarterly Journal of Economics*, vol. 82, February 1968.

instance, you would charge your clients more to set up a trade in some shares of stock in a bankrupt corporation than if they wanted to trade the same number of shares in a blue-chip security. (See W. T. Grant's stock prices, Fig. 11-2 on pages 290–291, during its 1975 bankruptcy if bankruptcy proceedings don't scare your investment instincts.) Second, and more to the point of this discussion of market qualities, the strength of the market in which the asset is traded can affect its bid-asked spread too.

Figure App. 3A-2*a* depicts a weak market in which a large bid-asked spread is needed to sell the asset. Figure App. 3A-2*b* depicts a strong market where a small bid-asked spread is all that is needed in order to sell the same asset illustrated in Fig. App. 3A-2*a* within the same length of time. Stated more analytically, the market illustrated in Fig. App. 3A-2*b* is stronger and less fragmented, enjoys more trading volume, and is more internally efficient than the weak market in Fig. App. 3A-2*a* because the strong market has more *depth, breadth,* and *resiliency.*

The terms "depth," "breadth," and "resiliency" are defined in the remainder of this section. A securities market should have considerable depth, breadth, and resiliency or else investors who trade securities there will be exposed to marketability risk.

market depth defined

A market that is *deep* has buy and sell orders for the asset traded in that market that continuously exist both above and below the market price. As a result, when there is an imbalance in the quantity of buy and sell orders in a deep market, the resulting price changes are small. Markets that lack depth are called *shallow markets.* The market prices of assets traded in shallow markets typically jump about in an erratic and disconcerting fashion because there are few orders to buy and sell and the price range between these sparse orders is wide. The New York Stock Exchange provides a deeper market for most of the securities it lists than do most foreign security markets, for example.

Figure App. 3A-2*b* illustrates how the price changes necessary to find a buyer or seller for a given quantity of a specific security are smaller than are needed in the weaker market shown in Fig. App. 3A-2*a*. The strong market in Fig. App. 3A-2*b* enjoys more depth than the market in Fig. App. 3A-2*a*. That is, orders to buy or sell that are *quickly and easily found* extend far above and below the bid and asked prices in the strong market of Fig. App. 3A-2*b*, but they extend over only a limited range in the shallow market.

By definition, the transaction-to-transaction price changes are smaller in a deep market than in a shallow market. Therefore, a market-maker for an asset who enjoys a *depth of orders* instead of a shallow order flow is less likely to suffer losses on assets carried in inventory. As a result of this reduced risk of doing business, the bid-asked spreads that dealers charge are less in deep markets than they are in shallow markets.

In order for a market to have depth, it does not matter whether the market participants are all assembled at a single geographic location or widely dispersed around the world. But the market participants must have a good, fast, inexpensive communication system with each other so that they can locate and quickly act upon all bid and asked prices. *Fragmented markets* lack depth because, by definition, some bid and asked prices may go undiscovered for significant intervals of time—the buyers and sellers have trouble communicating their trading desires to each other in a fragmented market. In contrast, a geographically dispersed market that enjoys centrally reported offers to trade through computerized telecommunications (such as NASDAQ) is not a fragmented market—it can be a deep and unfragmented market if the requisite array of bid and asked prices are continuously present through computer hookups.

breadth and resiliency defined

A market is said to be *broad* or have *breadth* if the bid and asked orders exist in substantial volume. Markets that operate with few buyers and sellers at any given moment and generate only a moderate volume of orders are called *thin markets.*[22] Comparing parts *a* and *b* of Fig. App. 3A-2 reveals that the market in Fig. App. 3A-2*b* has more breadth than its weak counterpart because the quantity of orders generated by the same equilibrium price is larger in the strong market, as indicated by the fact that $Q_4 > Q_1$ in the two figures. Dealers operating in a broad market should be willing to charge smaller bid-asked spreads than dealers in thin markets, because the broad markets provide more transactions on which the dealers can collect their bid-asked spread.[23]

When an imbalance between the buy and sell orders arriving at the market arises, an appropriate price change is all that is needed to restore the proper order balance. When new orders pour in immediately after the price changes in a market, that market is said to be *resilient.* Fast and inexpensive market communications are necessary for a market to be resilient. And dealers in a resilient market should be willing to charge smaller bid-asked spreads because there is less risk that they will be stuck holding an inventory of assets they cannot sell if the price falls. Thus, resilience is a valuable quality for a market to possess.

marketability from the viewpoint of a NYSE specialist

As explained above in Sec. 3-2 of this chapter, NYSE specialists are monopoly market-makers in whatever stock the exchange assigns them. In their role as market-makers, one of the specialists' duties is to collect limit orders and stop orders from customers all over the world, record these orders in their *order book,* and execute these orders expeditiously ahead of their own orders at the time indicated on the customers' orders.[24] Figure App. 3A-3 is a hypothetical bid page from the order book of a NYSE specialist who is making a market in

[22] For more detail see Kenneth Garbade, *Security Markets* (McGraw-Hill, New York, 1982), chap. 26.

[23] Kalman Cohen, Steven Maier, Robert Schwartz, and David Whitcomb, "The Returns Generating Process, Returns Variance, and the Effect of Thinness in Securities Markets," *Journal of Finance,* vol. 33, March 1978; Thomas Epps, "Security Price Changes and Transaction Volume: Some Additional Evidence," *Journal of Financial and Quantitative Analysis,* March 1977, vol. 14.; Richard Rogalski, "The Dependence of Prices and Volumes," *The Review of Economics and Statistics,* May 1978; George Tauchen and Mark Pitts, "The Price Variability-Volume Relationship of Speculative Markets," *Econometrica,* vol. 51, March 1983.

[24] A moment's consideration suggests to those familiar with computers that the specialist job could probably be performed faster, cheaper, and more surely by using a computer. However, the exchange members are reluctant to computerize themselves out of a lucrative job. N. H. Hakansson, A. Beja, and J. Kale, "On the Feasibility of Automated Market Making by a Programmed Specialist," *Journal of Finance,* vol. 40, no. 1, March 1985, pp. 1–20.

FIGURE APP. 3A-3 four numerical examples of different degrees of breadth and depth in a specialist's order book for a stock

bid price	thin and shallow	thin but deep	broad but shallow	broad and deep
$68	100	100	500	500
$67	100	100	500	500
$66	0	300	0	700
$65	0	300	0	900
$64	0	300	0	1500

a stock with a current market price of $68.50 per share. The figure shows four numerical examples of how breadth and depth might differ for the stock.

Summarizing, a market has *depth* when orders exist both above and below the price at which the security is currently trading. A market has *breadth* when the orders referred to in the preceding sentence exist in substantial volume. A market is *resilient* when price changes that are caused by order imbalances are immediately followed by an outpouring of new orders. Any given market will be more deep, broad, and resilient when information dissemination about prices and transactions costs is wide, fast, and accurate.

APP. 3A-4 EFFICIENT SECURITIES MARKETS

An *efficient capital market* can be defined as a market that will channel liquid capital quickly and accurately to where it will do the nation the most good. For example, if a competent woman discovers and patents a "better mousetrap," forms a mousetrap corporation, and sells shares of stock in it to the investing public, an efficient market will channel funds out of the stock of inferior firms and reallocate these funds so that they are invested in the securities of the manufacturer of the better mousetrap. This reallocation of capital funds will materialize only if two conditions are met. First, the woman who holds the patent on the better mousetrap must be able to obtain a fair appraisal of her product's value in the securities markets. This appraisal is essential in order for her to be able to sell common stock and thus raise the capital funds she requires to start producing the better mousetrap. However, in order for this first condition to occur a second condition must also be met. Second, the market-makers must charge brokerage commissions that are not too high, or the profit incentives that motivate the inventive woman and her potential investors to start to work will diminish.

Essentially, the Better Mousetrap Corporation, or any business, requires two kinds of market efficiencies in order to grow and prosper: (1) *external market efficiency*, that is, the existence of outsiders who can quickly and accurately appraise the true economic value of an enterprise so that they know what price to pay for a share in it, and (2) *internal market efficiency*, that is, the ability of a market to equate the supply of and the demand for its securities at a reasonable brokerage commission cost (or, equivalently, bid-asked spread).

We will now discuss the two types of market efficiencies and their impact on the allocation of resources.

external or pricing efficiency[25]

External efficiency "means that new information is widely, quickly, and cheaply available to investors, that this information includes what is knowable and relevant for judging securities and is rapidly reflected in their prices."[26] As a result of external efficiency, the price of a security should fully reflect available information.[27]

Sometimes a securities market deemed to be externally efficient (the New York Stock Exchange, for example) is said to be a fair game for its participants. Essentially, the "fair game" label refers to the fact that no significant number of investors consistently uses inside information in order to earn profits by trading with other investors who do not have access to the same information. Of course, some investors in a market that is externally efficient may be "ripped off" because they were too lazy to investigate before they invested, but this represents an example of investor laziness rather than an external inefficiency. As long as all investors can get the same set of information if they work at it, the investors are participating in a fair-game market, which can also be called an externally efficient market.

Efficient security markets are very desirable. They allocate capital when and to where able business executives need it and reward the investors who provide this needed capital with adequate returns. On the other hand, incompetent business managers and investors will be disciplined by failure in an efficient market—the price of securities in a badly managed firm will fall because of lack of demand. As a result, attention will be drawn to the firm's incompetent management and the incompetents will be forced to seek other tasks for which they are better suited.

IMPEDIMENTS TO EXTERNAL OR PRICING EFFICIENCY The securities markets in the United States today are considered by some to be the most efficient in the world. However, imperfections that allow capital to be misallocated do exist. Some of the major imperfections in the capital market mechanism are as follows:

1. *Uninterested shareholders.* Shareholders frequently assign their voice in management to the corporation's executives by signing proxy statements. Ineffective management may thus be perpetuated until such time as a majority of shareholders becomes dissatisfied with their returns, refuses to sign proxy statements, and votes in new management.[28]

[25] R. R. West, "On the Difference between Internal and External Market Efficiency," *Financial Analysts Journal,* November–December 1975, pp. 30–34.

[26] J. Lorie and R. Brealey, *Modern Developments in Investment Management* (Praeger, New York, 1972), p. 101.

[27] E. F. Fama, "Efficient Capital Markets: A Review of Theory and Empirical Work," *Journal of Finance,* May 1970, p. 383.

[28] One of the early classic studies documenting the phenomenon of stockholder apathy was A. A. Berle and G. C. Means, *The Modern Corporation and Private Property* (Macmillan, New York, 1934). Also see Michael C. Jensen and W. H. Meckling, "Theory of the Firm: Managerial Behavior, Agency Costs and Ownership Structure," *Journal of Financial Economics,* October 1976, vol. 3, no. 4, pp. 305–360. A collection of studies dealing with this topic may be found in *Journal of Financial Economics,* vol. 11, April 1983.

2. *Earnings retention used for financing.* Most corporations prefer to finance their expansion by retaining earnings rather than by using new securities. Such internal financing is cheaper than the issuance of new securities, but it allows management to ignore the price of the firm's securities in the financial markets and thereby avoid the discipline of the market.
3. *Investor ignorance.* Some investors buy securities on the basis of rumors or "hot tips" without investigating to determine whether the investment has true value.
4. *Mob speculation.* Hysteria temporarily determines security prices when mob speculation (such as that which followed President Kennedy's assassination) occurs. This condition results in incorrectly priced securities, which, in turn, leads to misallocation of capital to unproductive uses.[29]

In the final analysis, the more diligently that investors investigate before they invest, the more externally efficient their capital markets will be. However, even after a market is externally efficient, it still cannot allocate resources efficiently unless it is also internally efficient.

internal or operational efficiency

If a security market were perfectly efficient externally, then the market price of every security would equal the security's true economic value. However, it would still not be possible for the externally efficient market to allocate resources efficiently unless the cost and speed required to trade securities were reasonable; this is where internal efficiency becomes relevant. All the securities must be *immediately marketable* in order for a market to be internally efficient. Furthermore, the brokerage commission charges for trading securities (or what is often the same thing, the spread between the bid and the asked price) must not be so high that they will discourage the frequent transactions necessary to keep the market's trades reflecting current conditions.

In order for a securities market to continuously provide its investing customers with the opportunity to transact their buy and sell orders quickly at a low cost per transaction and thus be *internally efficient,* the market must have competing market-makers. The market-makers should stand ready to accommodate transactions by purchasing for their own inventories from investors who wish to sell and by being ready to sell to investors from their own inventories of securities. That is, the market-makers should continuously maintain bid (that is, their offering price to buy) and asked (their offer to sell) prices for all securities in which they choose to deal. And the brokerage commission, or the bid-asked spread, charged by these dealers should not be high—it should be only enough to provide a fair rate of return for competent market-makers.

The New York Stock Exchange provides an interesting case of improved internal efficiency. The NYSE's transactions efficiency was improved by a law

[29] On November 22, 1963, when President Kennedy was assassinated, the Dow Jones Industrial Average (DJIA) fell 24.5 points in 27 minutes. On the next trading day most shares reopened trading at the prices they had 5 minutes before the assassination. For an analysis of NYSE specialists' effectiveness in protecting the market from mob hysteria and other destabilizing factors, see A. Barnea, "Performance Evaluation of NYSE Specialists," *Journal of Financial and Quantitative Analysis,* September 1974, pp. 511–536.

that took effect on May 1, 1975—called "May Day" on Wall Street. Before May Day, the NYSE had refused to let its chosen securities be listed on any other exchanges. Furthermore, all the NYSE member firms agreed never to charge less than some fixed, minimum level of brokerage commission on every transaction they handled. Thus, although the securities prices on the NYSE fluctuated, the fee for the NYSE's brokerage service was not negotiable (that is, it had a fixed minimum level that was profitable for NYSE member firms to support). As a result, the NYSE was a monopoly market-maker and a noncompeting, price-fixing cartel.

However, the Securities and Exchange Commission decreed that the NYSE must cease its price-fixing cartel on May 1, 1975, and as a result, the NYSE's internal efficiency improved rapidly. The commission rate that NYSE brokerages charged for their service dropped approximately 25 percent immediately, and continued reductions of lesser importance followed.[30] Also, competition from other market-makers, who went into competition with the NYSE by making over-the-counter markets in the NYSE-listed stocks, probably also improved the depth, breadth, and resiliency of the market for securities that benefited from having more than one market-maker. Almost everyone except the NYSE member firms benefited from the improvement in the NYSE's internal efficiency. Even noninvestors who have never owned a security benefit from increased market efficiency because resources are allocated more effectively.

resource allocation

The labor and capital resources in an economy should be mobile so that they can go to the highest bidder. The highest bidder is presumably willing to pay more than lower bidders because of more urgent and/or more profitable uses for the resources. Thus, if labor and capital are mobile, they will be used at the time and the place that will tend to increase everyone's health, welfare, or happiness (as measured by gross national product per capita, for example) the most. This is also true of investment funds, since they are one particular kind of capital.

Efficient security markets—in both the internal and the external senses—will make investment capital more mobile and thus help allocate resources so that they can be put to the best use. All this means simply that if someone does invent a truly better mousetrap, efficient markets will provide the capital financing needed to manufacture the product on a large scale and we will all be able to enjoy better mousetraps as a result. This benefit will not be obtained without some work, however. The next section explains how an investor can help develop internally efficient markets (and also save on commission costs) by negotiating with security brokers over the fees for their services.

[30] R. O. Edmister, "Commission Cost Structure: Shifts and Scale Economies," *Journal of Finance*, vol. 33, no. 2, May 1978, pp. 477–486; J. L. Hamilton, "Competition, Scale Economies, and Transaction Costs in the Stock Market," *Journal of Financial and Quantitative Analysis*, vol. 11, pp. 779–802; J. L. Hamilton, "Marketplace Fragmentation, Competition, and the Efficiency of the Stock Exchange," *Journal of Finance*, March 1979, vol. 34, no. 1, pp. 171–187; Hans Stoll, "The Pricing of Security Dealer Services: An Empirical Study of NASDAQ Stocks," *Journal of Finance*, vol. 33, pp. 1153–1172; "Wall Street Is Finding after Ten Years, That It Enjoys Unfixed Rates," *Wall Street Journal*, April 22, 1985, pp. 1 and 18.

APP. 3A-5 NEGOTIATING BROKERS' COMMISSIONS

Although the commissions paid to stockbrokers are usually lower when they are determined by competition rather than by the NYSE's fixed minimum commission schedule, these commissions are still an important cost in securities trading, and they should be evaluated. To furnish a guideline against which investors can gauge their commission negotiations, the old NYSE fixed minimum commission schedule may be useful.

pre-1975 NYSE commission schedules

Tables App. 3A-2 and App. 3A-3 contain the fixed minimum commission schedules used by all NYSE member brokerages until they were declared illegal by the SEC in 1975.

Round lots represent 100-share groups or multiples of 100 shares. To illustrate the use of Table App. 3A-2, assume 100 shares of a $10 stock are purchased for a total transaction value of $1000. The pre-1975 commission would be:

$$\begin{array}{lr} 1.3\% \times \$1{,}000 = & \$13 \\ & +\ 12 \\ \hline \text{Commission:} & \$25 \end{array}$$

To illustrate the use of Table App. 3A-3, assume the investor purchased 2000 shares of a security for $30 per share for a total transaction value of $60,000. The commission for this purchase would then be:

$$\begin{array}{rcr} .4\% \times \$60{,}000 & = & \$240.00 \\ + & & 142.00 \\ +\ \$6 \text{ for each 100 shares up to 1000} & = & 60.00 \\ +\ \$4 \text{ for each 100 shares beginning at 1100 shares} & = & 40.00 \\ \text{Total commission} & = & \$482.00 \end{array}$$

TABLE APP. 3A-2 pre-1975 NYSE rates for single 100-share orders

amount involved	minimum commission
under $100	negotiated
$100–799	2% plus $6.40
$800–2,499	1.3% plus $12
$2,500–4,780	.9% plus $22
$4,780 and over	$.65 per share

TABLE APP. 3A-3 pre-1975 NYSE rates for multiple round lots

amount involved	minimum commission
$100–2,499	1.3% plus $12
$2,500–19,999	.9% plus $22
$20,000–29,999	.6% plus $82
$30,000–300,000	.4% plus $142
Over $300,000	Negotiated

Other noncommission transactions costs that cannot be negotiated are explained below.

TRANSFER TAXES The SEC assesses the stock exchanges 1 cent per $500 of securities sold. The exchanges shift this fee onto the selling customers. In the example of 100 shares of stock sold at $35 per share for a total value of $3500, the SEC fee would be

$$\$3500/\$500 = 7$$
$$7 \times 1¢ = 7¢$$

To summarize, assume the investor both buys and sells 100 shares of stock *X* at $35 per share. The total transaction costs under the now-discontinued rate schedule would be

$$\begin{aligned} \text{Commission on purchase } (.9\% \times \$3{,}500) + \$22 &= \$\ 53.50\} \\ \text{Commission on sale } (.9\% \times \$3{,}500) + \$22 &= \ \ 53.50\} \\ \text{SEC fee} &= \ \ \ \ .07 \\ \text{Total transaction costs} &= \$107.07 \end{aligned}$$

Investors with large portfolios should be able to negotiate commission rates below the old rates simply by threatening to take their business to another broker. Small investors have less bargaining power because brokers will not lose much commission if a small transaction is taken elsewhere. However, the transactions costs just outlined set forth some rough guidelines for inexperienced investors to guard their own interests in their dealings with stockbrokers. Of course, the best advice is simply: shop before you buy brokerage services. A phone call or two to discount brokerage houses might provide even the most inexperienced investor with a commission savings that will more than offset the cost of the phone call.

The commission rates from a large United States discount brokerage are published in Table App. 3A-4 to provide a comparison with the pre-1975 fixed minimum commissions from the NYSE shown in the preceding paragraphs.

discount broker's commission rates are lower

TABLE APP. 3A-4 discount broker's commission rate schedule*

amount involved	commission rates
0–$3,000	$18 plus 1.2% of the transaction
$3,001–7,000	$36 plus .6% of the transaction
$7,001–56,000	$57 plus .3% of the transaction
Over $56,000	The commission is 72% below the pre-1975 fixed NYSE rates shown in the tables above, but not less than $225

* The discount broker's commission rates shown here are subject to minimums and maximums. The minimum charge is 8 cents per share for the first 600 shares and 4 cents per share thereafter; maximum commission is 45 cents per share for orders of 100 or more shares.

TABLE APP. 3A-5 investor's savings from a large discount brokerage's commissions relative to pre-1975 NYSE rates†

shares in the trade	price per share	old NYSE minimum commission*	discounter commission	dollar savings	percent savings
100	$55	$ 80.73	$ 45.00	$ 35.73	44%
300	$ 8	$ 67.32	$ 46.80	$ 20.52	30%
500	$25	$204.30	$ 94.50	$109.80	54%
800	$45	$414.82	$165.00	$249.82	60%
4,000	$20	$797.36	$225.00	$572.36	72%

* Since May 1975 several of the nation's largest brokerage firms have increased their standard retail commissions.

† These discount broker's commissions may be revised upward or downward at any time.

Table App. 3A-5 illustrates the general nature of the determinants of the commission rates.[31] An investor who shops conscientiously for brokerage services should be able to find good service at prices similar to those suggested in Table App. 3A-5. Table App. 3A-1 on page 76 lists the names of discount brokers.

APP. 3A-6 THE NATIONAL MARKET SYSTEM (NMS)

President Gerald Ford signed into law the Securities Acts amendments of 1975—it was the most significant piece of securities legislation in over 40 years. The major provision of this law was the requirement that the Securities and Exchange Commission (SEC) oversee actions by the securities industry to develop a new national market system (NMS hereafter). The new law did not specify the exact form of the NMS. The law merely says that the United States public would benefit from having one big competitive national securities system that is centrally administered. This big unified, central stock market should be made up of the NYSE, the AMEX, the organized regional exchanges, and the OTC market.

In the new market, fully negotiated commission rates would be the rule. Competing dealers should vie among themselves to make markets in any given stock. And the commission rates should be negotiated between the investor and the broker because stockbrokers would compete with one another in the new market by price competition—that is, by reduced commissions. But all dealers in a given stock would tend to sell it at about the same price because their offering prices would be forced to compete in one nationwide computer hookup. Consequently, investors could buy the stock wher-

[31] Chris Welles, "Discounting: Wall Street's Game of Nerves," *Institutional Investor*, 1976, pp. 27–33; Linda Snyder, "Wall Street's Discount Houses Are Selling Hard," *Fortune*, March 1977, pp. 117–118; Arthur M. Louis, "The Stock Market of the Future—Now," *Fortune*, Oct. 29, 1984, pp. 105–108.

ever it is offered at the lowest price or wherever they found the lowest brokerage commissions. For example, a Philadelphia investor could easily trade through a market-maker in Denver or in New York City.

Proponents of a new centralized stock market believe that several improvements would result. Specifically, they contend that the national market system (or a good market of any kind) would (1) be conveniently located, and (2) have minimum sales commissions and minimize transactions costs. The present stock markets perform these services, but a reorganized national market system could provide them more effectively.

1. *Convenient location.* To assure its success, the new market should be convenient for all investors—ideally, it should blanket the nation. If the NYSE and AMEX in New York, the other organized regional exchanges located around the United States, and the thousands of OTC market-makers across the country were connected by one centralized computer and public reporting system, they could all operate as one market. In fact, a communication system that meets most of these specifications is already in operation. It is NASDAQ. As mentioned earlier in this chapter, the National Association of Security Dealers' Automated Quotation (NASDAQ) system is a big computer connecting thousands of leased computer terminals located in the offices of most OTC brokers and dealers across the nation.

   After NASDAQ was in operation, a nationwide quotation system named the Composite Quotation System (CQS) was started. The CQS reports the prices and volume of shares traded for all securities listed on exchanges in the United States. The CQS was expanded to include both listed and unlisted securities in 1978 and was brought under the control of the Consolidated Quotation Association. This expansion is an important step in the development of a national clearance and settlement system and centrally reported national securities market—it helps ensure that all investors have access to the same information.[32]

2. *Lower commissions and transactions costs.* Discount brokers have long been stealing customers from the full-service brokerages merely by selling the same securities at a lower cost (stock price plus commission fee). If all dealers competed directly in one big market, all would have to adjust their prices in order to stay in the running. Thus the public would have a better chance of obtaining the best commission rate available—a *competitively* determined commission.

   Not only could a central computer bring many geographically separated brokers and dealers under one market reporting system, but, once established, it should be relatively inexpensive to operate. After a computer system like NASDAQ is purchased and operating, running a few thousand more transactions through it would cost relatively little. The costs of keeping the computer running must be paid whether or not it is busy. And the computerized market, once it is functioning, should minimize back-office paperwork delays and jam-ups and reduce costly administrative expenses. These cost savings would be passed on to the participating stockbrokers in the form of lower charges for trading their customers' securities. Consequently, brokers who buy and sell securities through a computerized central market should incur lower transac-

[32] Telerate, Reuters, and Quotron are companies that compete in the United States to bring up-to-the-minute security price quotations to brokers, banks, and money managers. Reuters Inc. also provides this service in Europe. These firms charge fees for their services rather than operate through a trade association like the NASD.

tions costs per trade. Competition between the different market-makers subscribing to the central computer system should force them to pass on most of these savings. Thus, reduced brokerage fees or improved services would await buyers and sellers of securities in the national market system legislated by the Securities Acts amendment of 1975.

A geographically fragmented stock market that was connected by one central computer system (like NASDAQ, for instance) can provide a better securities market. But how well the benefits of a new market are realized will depend upon sound planning and skillful implementation.[33]

APP. 3A-7 RECENT DEVELOPMENTS

Since the Securities Acts amendments of 1975 legislated the development of a new National Market System (NMS), various changes have occurred. The SEC's decree that all brokerage commissions be determined by competitive negotiations after May 1, 1975 ("May Day") was the first major change. Brokerage commissions have dropped substantially since May Day, resulting in greater operational efficiency in U.S. securities markets. And the composite tape that has been operational on the NYSE since 1975 has increased competition between brokers and market-makers. By reporting the prices at which any given security is offered for sale on the NYSE, the third market, and the fourth market on one reporting system to which all parties have access, the composite tape has forced the competing market-makers to compete more directly. A number of other new changes that have been made to help implement the NMS are described below.

more operational efficiency for small orders on the exchanges

Thousands of small transactions for odd lots and small round-lot transactions come to the floors of the New York Stock Exchange (NYSE), the American Exchange (AMEX), and the other organized exchanges each day. There is no need for these small routine orders to be routed through costly and cumbersome floor brokers for delivery to and execution by the specialist, who makes a market for the stock on the floor of the exchange. Therefore, the operational efficiency of several exchanges has been increased by cutting these unnecessary intermediaries (that is, the floor brokers) out of the routine flow of small orders.

In 1976 the NYSE inaugurated the designated order turnaround (DOT) system to allow brokerages to transmit a client's small buy and sell orders directly to the specialist who handled the stock, without going through a floor broker. Since then the AMEX started a similar program it calls the post execution reporting (PER) system. The Philadelphia Stock Exchange (PSE) started up the Philadelphia automated communications and execution (PACE) system. The PSE's PACE is similar to another new system started at the Pacific Stock Exchange—both of these new systems not only route brokers' orders directly to the specialists, they also allow for automated reporting

[33] Shelby White, "The New Central Marketplace: The Debate Goes On," *Institutional Investor,* vol. 10, 1976, pp. 30–31; Julius W. Peake, "The National Market System," *Financial Analysts Journal,* vol. 34, 1978, pp. 25–28.

of the transaction. Thus, they are even more operationally efficient than the DOT and PER systems.

The routing of orders to competing exchanges where better prices may be available has also been made possible by the SEC's rule 19c-3 and various automated market linkage systems.[34]

SEC rule 19c-3 supports the development of ITS and NSTS

The Securities and Exchange Commission (SEC) passed its rule 19c-3—this new rule strikes down any securities exchange rules that prohibit members of an exchange from trading securities listed on that exchange off-board in a competing market. The NYSE fought the SEC's rule 19c-3 by claiming that such a rule would fragment and weaken securities markets. But this was apparently just an assertion made by the NYSE in an effort to maintain its profitable monopolistic market-making position over the stocks it listed.

Supporters of the SEC's rule 19c-3 saw no reason why the NYSE should be allowed to monopolize all orders flowing there if better prices were available to clients in other markets. After all, the over-the-counter dealers had been competing successfully with each other for years through NASDAQ—in a way that benefited the public interest. Why shouldn't the NYSE specialists compete in the same manner? NYSE rules that forbid its member firms to take any of their trades to another market in order to find a better deal for their client clearly obstructed the development of the NMS legislated by the Securities Acts amendments of 1975.

After trying to avoid competing with other market-makers, the NYSE knuckled under and started allowing its members to trade all NYSE-listed issues that were newly listed after the SEC's rule 19c-3 with competing market-makers if they desired. And, soon thereafter, the NYSE started its intermarket trading system (ITS). The Cincinnati Stock Exchange (CSE) had already eagerly developed a similar system which it ambitiously named the national securities trading system (NSTS).[35]

The ITS and NSTS are both centralized quotation systems that link competing markets together electronically through a computer. Essentially, these systems allow brokers in one market to see competing prices offered by competing market-makers in other markets. Brokers can then seek out better prices for their clients in other markets if another market is currently offering a better deal on a security. This is the kind of healthy competition that supporters of the Securities Acts amendments of 1975 were seeking when they legislated the NMS.

the SEC's rule 415 allowed shelf registrations

In 1982 the Securities and Exchange Commission (SEC) handed down its rule 415. This new rule streamlines the process of registering stock and bond issues with the SEC before they can be sold to investors. Section 3-1 of this chapter explained how investment bankers have traditionally counseled potential issuers of new security offerings and then registered the issue with the

[34] John J. Mulhern, "The National Stock Market: Taking Shape," *Business Review,* September–October 1980, pp. 3–11.

[35] Chris Welles, "The Showdown Over Rule 390," *Institutional Investor,* December 1977, pp. 33–38, 125–130; "A Little Exchange That's Thinking Big," *Business Week,* Jan. 17, 1983, p. 100.

SEC before they sold it to the investing public. Today, the same information must be filed with the SEC before an issue is legally registered and approved by the SEC. But, the SEC's new rule 415 has given companies that have in excess of $150 million of stock outstanding in the hands of investors who are unaffiliated with the corporation an expeditious new procedure to register and issue their new securities.

In the form that was permanently adopted in December 1983, rule 415 makes it possible for an issuer to register once and for all the securities it plans to come out with during the next 2 years. Since the issuer can handle the registration paperwork with the SEC itself in advance of the future issues under rule 415, the issuer need not commit itself to an investment banker until the issue is ready to be sold. Later, when the market conditions are good and the issuer is ready for the new infusion of cash, the previously registered issue can be taken off of the "shelf" at the SEC and issued to the public without any further disclosures. The investment bankers dislike this new procedure because it means that they must (1) accept lower fees since the issuers can handle the registration paperwork for themselves, (2) bid for the issue in competition with other investment bankers at the time it is ready to be issued, and (3) hastily set up an underwriting syndicate to distribute whatever issues the investment bankers may have bid for successfully. But most chief financial officers (CFOs) prefer the procedure under the new SEC rule 415 because they need not be so dependent on an investment banker. In any event, the new rule moves the U.S. securities markets one step closer to a new NMS because it beneficially increases competition in securities markets.[36]

[36] Beth McGoldrick, "Life with Rule 415," *Institutional Investor,* February 1983, pp. 129–133; "Investment Banking: Coping with the New Risks," *Institutional Investor,* February 1983, p. 130; Neil Osborn, "The Furor Over Shelf Registration," *Institutional Investor,* June 1982, pp. 61–71; David S. Kidwell, M. Wayne Marr, and G. Rodney Thompson, "SEC Rule 415: The Ultimate Competitive Bid," *Journal of Financial and Quantitative Analysis,* June 1984, vol. 19, no. 2, pp. 183–196.

The SEC's rule 415 and many other important new securities market developments are analyzed in Y. Amihud, T. S. Y. Ho, and R. A. Schwartz (eds.), *Market Making and the Changing Structure of the Securities Industry* (Lexington Books, D. C. Heath and Company, Lexington, Mass., 1985).

securities law

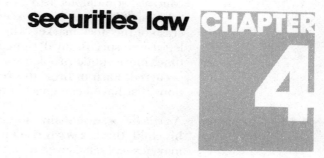

The United States has one of the strongest economies in the world because it has efficient capital markets. Businesspeople in the United States can raise the funds they need to start new businesses or expand existing businesses by selling common stock, preferred stock, or bonds in a ready-and-waiting capital market. The capital markets in the United States channel billions of dollars from savers to investors every year. If these investment funds were not available to the business community, the American economy would stagnate, unemployment would rise, and gross national product (that is, national income) per capita would fall. Good capital markets are essential to maintain everyone's welfare.

To maintain and augment its capital markets, the U.S. government has taken various legal steps to ensure that the markets are fair and honest places where small savers and big investors alike can place their funds. In particular, laws forbidding fraud and price manipulation have been passed and federal agencies have been established specifically to enforce these securities laws. This chapter explains the various laws, legal agencies, and codes that govern capital markets and the investment industry in the United States. However, before examining these various programs, it will be helpful to consider the market disorders, fraudulent activities, and price manipulation schemes that led to federal regulation of securities markets.

4-1 THE ABUSES THAT MOTIVATED PASSAGE OF SECURITIES LAWS

Most of the worst abuses in the securities markets occurred before any federal security regulations existed. A number of states had passed so-called blue-sky laws, but they were deficient in many respects. Often by the time the state officials got around to prosecuting for the sales of worthless or fraudulent securities, the promoters had long since left the state and were not, therefore, subject to its jurisdiction. Mainly because of a lack of effective federal legal controls, scandalous activities using "wash sales," "corners on the market," "churning," "pools," and excessive "pyramiding of debt" preceded the great crash of the stock market, which lasted from 1929 to 1933. In 1933 and 1934, legislation specifically designed to curb those activities was enacted. Since that time, more subtle problems involving "insider information" and fraud have occurred. Each of these disorders will be discussed briefly before the regulations that have been enacted to stop them are examined.

4-1.1 wash sales

A *wash sale* is, essentially, no sale at all. For example, if a man sells securities to his child, this is a wash sale (assuming he can control his child). Or, someone may buy *and* sell a given quantity of some security in the same day; this, too, is a wash sale. The purpose of a wash sale is to establish a record of a sale. This may be done to establish a tax loss or to deceive someone into believing that the market price has changed.

For example, suppose a dishonest investor were trying to purchase shares in the Ajax Corporation at less than the current market price of $40 per share. If Ajax shares were inactively traded, wash sales could be used to create the illusion of a falling price. The dishonest investor could buy and sell his or her own shares of Ajax at prices below $40, using fictitious names and several different securities brokers. The prices of these sales would be a public record. This would create the illusion that Ajax shares had fallen in price. Then the dishonest investor might be able to purchase shares in Ajax at less than $40 from an innocent party who owned shares but was unaware that the low prices from the wash sales were fraudulently generated.

The Securities Exchange Act of 1934 made wash sales illegal. Swindlers who use wash sale schemes can be fined and/or sent to jail.

4-1.2 corners

An investor who "corners the market" in some security or commodity buys all of that item that is for sale. This person then owns the only source of supply. This monopolistic seller who has the corner can then arbitrarily raise the price simply by withholding the supply of the item offered for sale. Eager buyers will bid up the price in hopes of coaxing some supply of the item out on the market so that they may purchase it. Price manipulators who obtain a corner on the market of some asset may then liquidate it at a high price for a capital gain. Or, a price manipulating speculator might corner a market in hopes of trapping or "squeezing" short sellers by withholding the supply that is offered for sale, and then waiting while eager short sellers bid up the price as they try unsuccessfully to buy the item that they need to deliver. After the price is bid up to higher levels, the party that has the market cornered can sell the item to the short sellers at high prices that will throw them for substantial losses.

Short sellers are speculators who sell an asset they do not own.[1] They expect the price of that asset to fall, enabling them to purchase the asset at the new lower price and then deliver at the higher price at which they had *previously* arranged to sell it. Thus, short sellers profit from price declines. To see how a manipulating speculator who obtains a corner on the market can squeeze short sellers and profit from this action, consider the example in Box 4-1.

[1] Short selling is defined and discussed in detail in Sec. 21-1 of Chap. 21.

BOX 4-1
cornering the market in the "good old days"

One of the more spectacular market corners was obtained by Commodore Cornelius Vanderbilt in 1862. Vanderbilt started buying stock in the Harlem Railroad in New York City for $8 per share. He continued until the price was driven up to $100 per share and he had control of the railroad. Then Vanderbilt extended the railroad into Manhattan. Daniel Drew, a ruthless price manipulator, had also purchased shares in the railroad as the price rose. However, Drew wanted more profit, so he conspired to sell his shares to drive the price down and simultaneously to take a short position in the stock in order to profit from its decline in price. Drew influenced Boss Tweed and other dishonest New York City politicians to repeal the railroad's legal franchise to operate. Then Drew sold all his holdings and also sold 137,000 shares short with the expectation that the price would fall rapidly from $100. The price fell to $72 but Vanderbilt used his great wealth to purchase every share that appeared for sale—he cornered the market. Vanderbilt then raised the price of his shares to $179, and Drew was thrown for a loss on his short sales of 137,000 shares. There were only 27,000 shares of stock in Harlem Railroad outstanding! So, Drew was forced to settle with the buyers of the 137,000 shares he had contracted to deliver at prices below $100 while Vanderbilt held the price at $179. Since Vanderbilt had cornered the market, Drew's losses became Vanderbilt's gains.

In this colorful case, a large price manipulator became the victim of an even larger and more well-heeled price manipulator. Although there is a little justice in this case, many unnamed but innocent investors were also unjustly hurt in the process.

The Securities Exchange Act of 1934 made price manipulation in securities markets illegal.

4-1.3 churning

Law books define *churning* as the abuse of a customer's confidence for the personal gain of a securities broker by frequent and/or large transactions that are disproportionate to the size and nature of the customer's account. Churning is a very common and also a very safe way for securities brokers to steal funds from their clients' accounts while escaping detection by all but the most watchful of clients. Brokers are able to profit from churning a client's account because the broker earns a commission on every purchase and every sale regardless of whether the customer gains or loses on the trade. Churning occurs when a broker feeds clients "hot tips" that motivate them to buy and/or sell. Sales commissions are thus generated for the broker whether or not the client gains from the transactions. The practice is called "churning" because it involves *turning over* a client's account.

It is very difficult for a client who has been robbed by a broker to prove that churning occurred, provided the broker used some discretion. For example, if the broker merely plants the seed that blooms into a fruitless trade by giving the client worthless hot tips, it is difficult for the hapless client to even recognize that he or she was victimized. And furthermore, if the broker, who typically handles numerous accounts, does not churn any single account too frequently, it is difficult to prove that any churning occurred. There is, after all, no law that makes a broker liable for unprofitable trades a client may voluntarily undertake.

Successful civil lawsuits based on churning are rare; only the most obviously unscrupulous brokers and/or the brokerage houses end up paying damages to their clients. An example of an easy-to-win case of churning, for instance, is where a broker executes trades for a client's account without obtaining the client's permission to execute the trade.[2]

The federal government made churning a crime under Section 10(b) of the Securities Exchange Act of 1934 and rule 10b-5 of the Securities and Exchange Commission (SEC).

4-1.4 pools

A *pool* is a formal or informal association of two or more persons with the objective of manipulating prices and profiting therefrom. When this objective is completed, the pool is dissolved. A few manipulators may verbally agree to operate as a pool, or a contract involving many members can be drawn up. Some of the pool members may provide capital; some may provide inside information; some may manage the pool's operations; or all may participate in all those functions. Some pools have hired managers for a fee or a percentage of the profits. Some pools even have had specialists from securities exchanges in collusion as hired managers or members of the pool. In general, pools do not tend to conform to any particular organizational format.

During the early 1900s there were basically two kinds of pools—trading pools and option pools. A *trading pool* purchased the shares in which it was interested in the open market. The trading pools usually tried to acquire the securities quietly and discreetly in order to keep from driving up the security's price while they were buying by disseminating unfavorable publicity about the firm.

After a trading pool or an option pool had accumulated large quantities of the security at favorable prices, it would work to manipulate the price upward. Favorable information about the firm would often be disseminated in the form of rumors or hot tips. Pool members who were brokers would recommend the security to their customers. Pool members within the firm whose securities were being manipulated would issue favorable publicity about the firm. Radio commentators and news reporters were paid by some pools to recommend securities. Pools also churned the market in their security by transacting numerous wash sales to call attention to the security and make it appear to have an active market at rising prices. The pool's tactics were often successful in manipulating naive investors into bidding up the price of the pool's security.

When the market price of the pool's securities reached a high figure and was supported there by strong demand, the pool would liquidate its holdings as quietly as possible. In liquidating, it was essential to be discreet so as not to break the wave of optimism supporting the price—a colluding specialist on an

[2] See the appendix to this chapter for an intriguing churning case, *Hecht v. Harris, Upham & Co.*

BOX 4-2
the Sinclair option pool of 1929

One of the most profitable pools was the Sinclair Consolidated Oil option pool of 1929. While Sinclair stock was selling in the $28 to $32 range, a contract was obtained from the Sinclair Company granting the pool an option to buy 1,130,000 shares at $30 per share. The pool then purchased 634,000 shares in the open market to bid up prices. The pool exercised its option, then liquidated all its holding while the stock was selling in the $40 range. The pool also sold 200,000 shares short as the price fell. The pool's total profit was approximately $12.5 million from the following sources: $10 million profit from optioned shares purchased at $30 per share; $500,000 profit from shares purchased in the market; $2 million profit from the short sales.

Source: Stock Exchange Practices, 73d Cong., 2d Sess., Senate Report 1455, p. 63.

profit, pool members then went on to sell short in anticipation of the fall in price which was likely to ensue. Any profits earned by pools were losses for investors who were not in the pool.

An *option pool,* on the other hand, would arrange to acquire all or most of its securities at advantageous prices under option contracts. Many option pools had members who were on the board of directors of the firm whose securities were being manipulated. This board would vote to grant the pool options to buy blocks of new shares at a set price. When the market price rose above this option price, the pool would exercise its option to purchase the shares from the manipulated corporation and then turn around and sell these shares at the higher market price to the public. This maneuver diluted the profits accruing to the shareholders of the corporation who were not in the pool. The directors in the pool sometimes rationalized the income they derived from the pool by saying it was compensation for their services as directors. See Box 4-2 for a case about a pool's operations.

The Securities Exchange Act of 1934 outlawed pool activities. The act made price manipulation illegal; required that all pools be reported; forbade members of exchanges to participate in pools; forbade the churning and wash sales often used by pools; and required corporation executives, directors, and other insiders to report their transactions in the securities of their firm to the Securities and Exchange Commission.

4-1.5 the Great Crash

On September 3, 1929, the Dow Jones Industrial Average (DJIA) closed at 381. On October 2, 1929, the DJIA fell 49 points, only to be followed by a drop of 43 points the next day. On October 23, 1929, the DJIA had dropped to 306—a decline of nearly 20 percent in less than 2 months—and it continued to drop. The worst bear market in the history of the United States had begun. The ensuing market decline continued for over 3 years. On July 8, 1932, the DJIA closed at 41—less than 11 percent of its peak level in 1929! This was the era of the Great Crash and the Depression. Demand for goods

TABLE 4-1 unemployment in the U.S. during the Depression

year	unemployed	percent	year	unemployed	percent
1929	1,550,000	3.2	1935	10,610,000	20.1
1930	4,340,000	8.7	1936	9,030,000	16.9
1931	8,020,000	15.9	1937	7,700,000	14.3
1932	12,060,000	23.6	1938	10,390,000	19.0
1933	12,830,000	24.9	1939	9,480,000	17.2
1934	11,340,000	21.7	1940	8,120,000	14.6

Source: U.S. Dept. of Commerce, Bureau of the Census, *Historical Statistics of the U.S., Colonial Times to 1957* (Washington, D.C., 1960), p. 73.

and services decreased as pessimism set in and credit began to tighten. The Depression was a period of agonizing economic adjustment. Unemployment spread, reaching a peak of 24.9 percent in 1933 (see Table 4-1).

As unemployment rose, demand for goods continued to drop and prices fell. From 1929 to 1931 the price of a dozen eggs fell from 30 to 18 cents and corn sank from 80 to 32 cents per bushel in spot commodity markets.[3] Millions of unemployed consumers' purchases dropped to mere subsistence levels. As retail sales declined, inventories swelled and production at many factories ceased. Numerous businesses shut down and eventually went bankrupt because of lack of sales.[4]

Loan foreclosures occurred, and most creditors fell behind on their contractual repayments. As a result, commercial banks lacked liquid assets, and some defaulted when depositors demanded their money. When bank depositors could not obtain their funds, the news spread like wildfire. A banking panic began that caused even some of the most soundly managed banks to become temporarily insolvent; there were "runs" on the banks by panic-stricken depositors who withdrew their deposits and then hoarded the money in their homes. From 1930 through 1932 over 5,000 banks failed because they did not have the cash on hand to pay out to panic-stricken depositors who hurriedly withdrew their demand deposits as part of a run on the bank. These thousands of failed banks caused a loss of $3 billion in deposit currency. President Roosevelt closed all banks on March 6, 1933—it was euphemistically called a "national banking holiday." A week later some of the banks were allowed to reopen on a restricted basis if they were solvent.

Due to the massive unemployment, widespread losses, deprivation, and anguish associated with the Depression, there was a great public demand for reform. Securities markets, which were only partly to blame for creation of the economic bubble that burst in 1929, were dealt with swiftly. The Securities Act of 1933 and Securities Exchange Act of 1934 formed the basis for the regulations that still govern securities markets in the United States. These and other regulations passed at about the same time forbid wash sales, corners on the market, pools, dissemination of fraudulent information, and use of in-

[3] U.S. Dept. of Commerce, Bureau of the Census, *Historical Statistics of the U.S., Colonial Times to 1957* (Washington, D.C., 1960), pp. 294–304.

[4] J. K. Galbraith, *The Great Crash* (Houghton Mifflin, Boston, 1961).

sider information for speculative profits. Full disclosure of the financial conditions of firms issuing securities publicly was required, and the Federal Reserve Board was given control over margin requirements so it could limit speculative excesses resulting from borrowing too heavily and/or pyramiding debt. These changes and others have diminished the frequency of price manipulation schemes and other destabilizing forms of speculation and have increased the robustness and stability of the security markets in the United States.

4-2 SECURITIES REGULATIONS PASSED FROM 1930 to 1934

In order to curb fraudulent practices, excessive debt pyramiding, dissemination of misleading or fraudulent information, and market breaks such as the Great Crash of 1929, and generally to increase the stability of securities markets in the United States, the Congress enacted securities regulations. The most important of these regulations governing the activity in securities markets are outlined below. The laws are explained in chronological order to show how legislative thinking evolved and to familiarize the reader with the individual acts.

4-2.1 laws existing prior to the Great Crash

The U.S. government did little to regulate securities markets prior to 1933. Postal laws forbade using the mails to defraud; however, no noteworthy prosecutions were made for securities fraud under these statutes. Because two major stock exchanges, the New York Stock Exchange (NYSE) and the Curb Exchange (as the American Stock Exchange was called until 1953) were both located in the state of New York, New York State had statutes and legal precedents relating to securities markets. But these state laws were too localized to be very effective.

In 1912 the Sixty-second Congress instituted the Pujo investigation of the "money trust." The investigation was aimed at breaking up the concentration of interlocking directors of large banks and corporations. The investigation resulted in some drastic recommendations for strengthening securities markets, but not in any legislation. It took the Great Crash of 1929 and the resulting public outcry to obtain the needed legislative programs. Thus, the securities laws that followed the Great Crash unfortunately resulted from the crisis rather than from foresight and planning.

4-2.2 Glass-Steagall Act of 1933

In 1933 Representative Henry Bascom Steagall and Senator Carter Glass pushed a law through Congress that was officially named *the Banking Act of 1933*. The Glass-Steagall Act, as it is more popularly called, forbade commercial banks from conducting two important activities: (1) paying interest on demand deposits, and (2) conducting any investment banking activities.[5]

Most countries around the world allow their banks to pay interest on checking account deposits. But the Glass-Steagall Act made it illegal for banks

[5] The one aspect of the Glass-Steagall Act that has been received favorably is the establishment of the Federal Deposit Insurance Corporation (FDIC) to insure the deposits of banks that elect to pay for the insurance, and to open their books to the FDIC's bank examiners.

in the United States to pay interest on checking account deposits until *the Depository Institutions Deregulation and Monetary Control Act of 1980* (sometimes called DIDC) was enacted to implement such interest payments. Money market mutual funds probably would never have come into existence if the commercial banks had always been allowed to pay competitive rates of interest on their demand deposits. The second activity denied to United States banks by the Glass-Steagall Act is still not allowed: banks and their subsidiaries were prohibited from underwriting primary issues of corporations' stocks and bonds. Essentially, commercial banks are denied the opportunity to perform investment banking activities.

As a result of the Glass-Steagall Act, the mighty House of Morgan, for instance, was split. The House of Morgan was one of most profitable and most powerful financial houses on Wall Street—it was founded by the famous financier J. P. Morgan. The House of Morgan was split into two firms in order to separate its commercial banking activities from its investment banking activities. Both firms are still famous and powerful around the world in financial circles. Today, Morgan Guaranty Trust is America's fifth largest bank—a status this aristocratic bank enjoys without benefit of branches. In most years, Morgan Guaranty has the highest rate of profit of all large banks in the United States, and it is widely agreed to be the most prestigious bank in the United States. In the same vein, Morgan Stanley is the most prestigious investment banking firm in the United States.[6] In the early 1930s it was politically popular to split up a financial powerhouse like the House of Morgan, perhaps because politicians wanted to "pin the blame" for the Great Crash and the Depression on a handy scapegoat.

The Glass-Steagall Act was enacted largely on the basis of Depression-era ignorance and fears rather than concrete evidence that financial centralization is harmful. Today, the Glass-Steagall Act is frequently viewed differently. American banks are falling behind in competing with merchant banks abroad because many of these foreign banks are allowed to perform both commercial banking and investment banking and other services too.[7] Most foreign countries don't usually tie their banks down with as many legal restrictions as the United States banks have. Some of the banking restrictions in this country (such as the laws governing interest payments, branching, diversified activities, and international finance) are becoming increasingly recognized as archaic and as a hindrance to the financial strength of the country's banks. In fact, there is serious talk in high governmental chambers about repealing major portions of the Glass-Steagall Act.

4-2.3 the Securities Act of 1933

The Securities Act of 1933 (the Securities Act, hereafter) deals largely with primary issues of securities. This act, also known as the "truth in securities law," was supplemented by the Securities Exchange Act of 1934 (SEA). The

[6] One can gain some idea of the financial community's high regard for Morgan Guaranty Trust and Morgan Stanley by reading "Why the Blue-Chips Bank on Morgan," *Fortune*, July 13, 1981, pp. 36–42. The two Morgan firms are typically described in the financial press with glowing superlatives.

[7] For a discussion about the competitive disadvantage of U. S. banks, see Charles N. Henning, William Piggott, and Robert Haney Scott, *International Financial Management* (McGraw-Hill, New York, 1978), pp. 202–203.

SEA extends some of the disclosure requirements for primary issues to many secondary issues.[8]

The primary purpose of these two laws is to require security issuers to fully disclose all information about themselves that affects the value of their securities. The Securities Act also prohibits certain types of fraud; let us consider it in some detail before discussing the SEA.

REGISTRATION OF NEW ISSUES The main objective of the Securities Act is to provide the potential investor in *primary* issues with a *full disclosure of the information needed* to make a wise investment decision about new securities. To achieve this objective, the Securities Act specifies that the issuing firm and the investment banker must register the issue. Registration involves filing with the SEC audited financial statements, other information about the firm, and information about the underwriting agreement. Information required in the registration is listed below.

1. A statement as to the nature of the issuer's business, its organization, and its financial structure
2. A list of directors and officers of the issuer, their addresses, and their salaries
3. Details about the issuer's arrangements for bonuses, stock options, and profit sharing
4. Contracts the issuer may have with subcontractors, consultants, and others
5. Audited balance sheets and income statements of the issuing firm for several preceding years
6. Copies of the issuer's articles of incorporation, bylaws, trust indentures, and agreement with the investment banker
7. A statement about other securities the issuer has outstanding and the rights of these other issues
8. A statement about the terms on which the issuer offers its shares to the public
9. Any other statements the SEC may require and any other information that may materially affect the value of the securities

Registration statements may be obtained at the SEC by the general public.

PROSPECTUS The first part of the registration statement is prepared in the form of a booklet for public dissemination and is called a *prospectus*. It contains most of the information in the registration statement. According to the Securities Act, a prospectus *must be given to every investor* to whom the investment banker's syndicate sells the new securities. Thus, whether or not investors can comprehend the data in the prospectus, they are provided with one to ensure that they have information to make a decision.

Surprisingly, the Securities Act does not require that a prospectus be delivered before orders for the registered security may be solicited, received, or even accepted, but only that its delivery precede or accompany delivery of the security itself to the customer. Several commentators have criticized this

[8] A *primary* issue is a new issue of securities from the issuer to the investing public in which the issuing firm receives the cash proceeds. A *secondary* issue involves sales of previously outstanding shares among members of the investing public—the issuer receives no cash.

aspect of the act; they urge that the law require delivery of a prospectus before an order is taken for the issue.

After a firm registers the required information with the SEC, it must wait at least 20 days before issuing the securities. During this waiting period the SEC investigates the proposed prospectus to ensure that all the required information has been *disclosed*. The proposed prospectus may be circulated during this waiting period, but it must have a note in red ink on its front cover stating that it has not yet received SEC approval for issuance as a final prospectus. A prospectus so marked is sometimes called a *red herring*.

If the issuer and the investment banker are not notified otherwise, they may issue their securities after the 20-day wait. By permitting securities to be issued, the SEC in no way implies its approval of them as a good investment. SEC disapproval of a proposed prospectus merely indicates that in the opinion of the SEC insufficient information has been disclosed for investors to analyze if they wish. An actual prospectus may be obtained from any stockbroker for the price of a phone call to request it.

SHELF REGISTRATION In 1982 the SEC modified the registration process slightly in order to reduce red tape for issuers. In that year the SEC adopted Rule 415 to allow large corporations to file registration statements with details about the firm's long-run financing plans. This rule makes it possible for a corporation that files a so-called shelf registration statement to issue at a later date the stocks and/or bonds detailed in its long-run plan on file at the SEC without filing another separate registration statement for each individual issue.

The two main advantages that result from corporations being able to use shelf registration statements on file at the SEC are (1) that the financial managers of corporations that are considering issuing securities are not so burdened with bureaucratic red tape at the SEC, and (2) that aggressive investment bankers can see issuers' advance plans merely by investigating the SEC's public files. Public availability of this information about plans for possibly forthcoming securities issues allows small investment bankers who are not well known a chance to bid for upcoming primary issues.

Shelf registration shortcuts some red tape at the SEC for issuing companies, but it is not intended to reduce the availability of the information investors need to make rational investments decisions. Potential investors in every securities issue must still be given a prospectus.[9]

THE "SMALL ISSUES" EXEMPTION According to Regulation A of the SEC, a firm issuing less than $1,500,000 per year of new securities need not comply with the full registration requirement. Such issuers are required only to furnish potential investors with an offering circular containing a limited amount of unaudited financial information.

[9] See Neil Osborn, "The Furor over Shelf Registration," *Institutional Investor*, June 1982, pp. 61–71. See also *Fortune*, March 22, 1982, for an informative article about rule 415. For an up-to-date law school textbook discussion of rule 415 that laymen can appreciate, see Martin L. Budd and Nicholas Wolfson, *Securities Regulations: Cases and Materials* (Michie Company, Charlottesville, Va., 1984), pp. 215–225.

SECONDARY SALES Secondary sales are also exempt from registration under the Securities Act. Under this act, if more than 90 days have passed and the primary issue is completely distributed, the securities traded in the secondary market need not be accompanied by a prospectus, although it may have been required in the primary issue. However, the SEA requires issuers of securities traded in secondary markets to register and file information with the SEC. Thus, the SEA extends the full disclosure provisions of the Securities Act to cover secondary markets. This regulation will be discussed in more detail later in this chapter.

PRIVATE OFFERING EXEMPTION The Securities Act also exempts from the registration requirements stock issues offered to a small group of private subscribers who are sufficiently experienced or informed that the disclosure requirements are not necessary for their protection and who are purchasing the shares as an investment and not for resale to the public. Therefore, each purchaser is required to sign a letter stating that she or he is purchasing the shares for investment purposes. Hence, the shares issued under this exemption are often referred to as *letter stock*. The SEC has required that letter stock investors not sell their shares for at least 2 years after purchase as proof of their investment motives.

"NO SALE" EXEMPTION The Securities Act does not require the registration of securities issued in exchange for outstanding stock of the issuer as in a merger or consolidation. The original rationale for this rule was that a merger or acquisition is not ordinarily regarded as a sale because individual shareholders have little or no choice in the matter—they typically just go along with whatever the directors or controlling officers have decided. However, in 1972 rule 145 reversed the "no sale" view and required SEC registrations for business combinations such as mergers and acquisitions. Essentially, mergers and acquisitions are now viewed as security sales that are subject to the full disclosure of information requirements of the 1933 Securities Act.

ANTIFRAUD PROVISIONS In addition to the requirements pertaining to full disclosure of information, the Securities Act contains some antifraud provisions. It provides court remedies against security salespersons or others who are disseminating untrue or misleading information about securities. Courts finding that fraudulent statements have been made about specific securities can issue injunctions to stop such action and require other civil law remedies, such as reimbursement for damages.

The Securities Act limits the techniques that can be used to sell securities. It provides the basis for a later SEC ruling that all public securities dealers must deal fairly, because they offer their services to the public. This ruling provides a basis for prosecuting security salespersons who issue misleading advice or act to perpetrate other frauds.

When the Securities Act was first passed, there was widespread concern that industry's legitimate needs for funds would be hampered by the imposition of risks of legal liability or by the risk of harassment by shareholder suits. Nevertheless, the Securities Act provides for both civil and criminal liability when fraud occurs in connection with the issuance of securities or in the registration filed with the SEC; the test of time has shown that the concern was ungrounded.

A significant case under the Securities Act is *Escott v. Bar Chris Construction Co.* In 1961 Bar Chris, which was in the business of constructing bowling alleys, filed a registration statement with the SEC for new debentures containing inaccuracies and misstatements. After the facts became known, a lawsuit was brought on behalf of individuals who had purchased the debentures. The court held the corporation and its underwriters liable for damages for the inaccuracies. All persons who signed the registration statement or who were officers, directors, or partners of the issuer at the time the registration statement was filed were held liable if it was shown that they failed to exercise *due diligence* in investigating the situation or in making the true facts known. The court also held that any accountant who certifies portions of a registration statement that later turns out to be false can be held liable. The court stated that even if a firm's accountants, underwriters, and lawyers do not know the true facts, they are under a duty to investigate the situation with "due diligence," and if they do not, they can be held liable.

The Bar Chris decision has produced consternation in the investment community. What has most distressed business executives is (1) the possibility of being held liable when they had no intent to deceive; and (2) the lack of clear standards by which they can know if they have investigated with "due diligence." But this legal precedent did help the investing public obtain fuller disclosure of the information they needed to invest wisely.

4-2.4 the Securities Exchange Act of 1934 (SEA)

After the Securities Act of 1933 was passed, its limitations were quickly recognized, so the Congress immediately set about extending its provisions by enacting the Securities Exchange Act of 1934 (SEA). The primary objectives of the SEA are to (1) provide adequate information about securities traded in secondary markets in order to facilitate their evaluation and discourage price manipulation and (2) establish the Securities and Exchange Commission (SEC). The SEA also provides for the regulation of credit for security purchases and contains antifraud provisions.

SEC ESTABLISHED The SEA charged the SEC with the responsibility for regulating securities markets. The SEC is located in Washington, D.C., and is headed by five commissioners who are appointed by the President with the consent of the Congress. In recent years the SEC has had a staff well in excess of a thousand people and a multimillion dollar annual budget.

DISCLOSURE FOR SECONDARY SECURITIES In order to ensure full disclosure of information for securities traded in secondary markets, the SEA requires that an annual registration statement and other periodic reports be filed for public inspection with the SEC as a prerequisite for the listing of a security for trading. The Securities Acts amendments of 1964 extended these registration requirements to securities traded in over-the-counter markets if the issuing firm has total consolidated assets in excess of $3 million and meets other requirements.

Since the SEA originated the SEC, the SEC has developed the 8-K, 10-K, and 10-Q forms on which corporations are required to report their activities.

Corporations must file their periodic financial statements on the 10-K forms. Significant current developments must be reported on the 8-K forms as they occur. Unaudited financial reports must be filed quarterly on the 10-Q forms.

REGISTRATION OF ORGANIZED EXCHANGES The SEA grants the SEC considerable authority over organized exchanges such as the New York Stock Exchange (NYSE). It requires that all exchanges register with the SEC and agree to (1) comply with the letter and spirit of the law, (2) adopt bylaws or rules for expelling and disciplining members of the exchange who do not conduct their activities in a legal and ethical manner, and (3) furnish the SEC with copies of its rules and bylaws and any amendments that are adopted. Within these guidelines the exchanges are free to regulate themselves. If an exchange fails to follow the guidelines, the SEC can intervene in the affairs of the exchange and alter penalties, expel members of the exchange, or even close the exchange. As a matter of practice, the SEC rarely has intervened.[10]

CREDIT REGULATION Before the Great Crash in 1929, some speculators purchased securities by making small down payments in the neighborhood of 10 percent of the purchase price from their own funds and then borrowing the other 90 percent. As these securities rose in price, some lenders would count the capital gains as new equity. This interpretation entitled the borrower to borrow even more money. This pyramiding of debt on top of unrealized paper profits was disastrous when the market crashed in 1929.

When securities prices began to fall in 1929, security price declines equal to speculators' 10 percent down payments were common. Thus, the first market decline bankrupted imprudent speculators who had overextended themselves by pyramiding debt. When lenders, many of them banks, tried to sell the securities they held as collateral, they often found the value was not sufficient to cover the debt. In order to avoid further capital losses, lenders who held securities as collateral hurriedly dumped the shares on the market for liquidation. This dumping probably accelerated the market's decline and further aggravated the financial crisis. The instability in the banking system and the money supply caused by pyramids of debt that came crashing down deepened the economic depression of the early 1930s.

The members of Congress who wrote the SEA wanted to prohibit dangerous debt pyramids. Since the Federal Reserve Board is charged with controlling the money supply and credit conditions, it was given the authority to set margin requirements for credit purchases of securities.[11]

[10] The SEC did intervene by forcing the organized security exchanges to abandon their fixed minimum commission schedules no later than May 1, 1975—this date is well known on Wall Street as "May Day." Another example of the SEC imposing its rules on the organized exchanges occurred in 1979 when the SEC's rule 19c-3 took effect. Rule 19c-3 requires the organized exchanges to allow their member firms to trade any new stock listed after April 26, 1979, either on the floor or off the floor of the exchange. The purpose of these two rules was to force the organized exchanges to comply with Securities Acts amendments of 1975 and establish a competitive National Market System (NMS), as discussed in the appendix of Chap. 3.

[11] The Board of Governors of the Federal Reserve System also controls banks' reserve requirements and Federal Reserve open-market operations, and it sets the discount rate at which commercial banks may borrow from one of the 12 Federal Reserve Banks.

The Federal Reserve then wrote Federal Reserve Regulations T and U to cover initial margin requirements. The initial margin is the percentage of the purchase price that investors must be able to pay with their own funds. Regulations T and U allow the Board of Governors of the Federal Reserve to set the margin requirements for loans made by banks, security brokers, and dealers. In recent years the margin requirement has varied between 50 and 80 percent.[12] Thus, if the margin is 65 percent, an investor cannot initially borrow more than 35 percent of the market value of any security he or she purchases on credit. Maintenance margins (that is, margins that must be maintained as the prices of the securities vary after their purchase) may be set by the securities exchanges.

The SEA also limited security dealers' total indebtedness to 20 times their net capital. This provision is intended to keep securities firms from using excessive debt to carry inventories of securities that could bankrupt the firm in a market decline. Brokers and dealers hold the securities for many of their customers in the firm's name. As a result, the customers would suffer if the firm holding their assets went bankrupt. The SEA's limit on dealers' debt is therefore primarily intended to protect the investor rather than, as it may seem, the dealers and brokers.

PROXY SOLICITATION The SEA requires that the SEC establish rules to govern solicitations by registered issuers to obtain their shareholders' votes (that is, proxies) on matters to come before the shareholders meeting (such as election of directors). In response to this statute, the SEC requires that all proxy solicitations contain (1) a reasonable amount of information about the issues to be voted upon, (2) an explanation of whether management or the stockholders proposed the issue, (3) a place for the shareholder to express approval or disapproval of each issue with the exception of election of directors, and (4) a complete list of candidates if the proxy solicitation is for election of directors. All proxy solicitations and consent forms must be submitted to the SEC for approval before they are sent to shareholders.

In this day of widespread share ownership and massive corporations, the SEC has sought to effect "shareholders' democracy" by making proxy solicitation possible by insurgent groups without the incursion of huge costs. This objective is achieved by requiring that corporate management include a statement or proposal of up to 100 words by an insurgent group when management solicits proxies. This provision makes it less likely that an incompetent corporate management can perpetuate itself through proxy control.

[12] For a critical analysis of the effectiveness of margin requirements, see T. G. Moore, "Stock Market Margin Requirements," *Journal of Political Economy,* April 1966, pp. 158–167. For an analysis of the special margins imposed by the NYSE and AMEX, see James A. Largay, "100% Margins: Combating Speculation in Individual Security Issues," *Journal of Finance,* September 1973, pp. 973–986.

In 1985 the U.S. Treasury and the Federal Reserve Board both proposed that control of margin requirements be taken away from the Federal Reserve Board and given to the security exchanges. This modest deregulation proposal was debated publicly and remained unresolved at the date of this printing.

Margin trading is discussed in detail in Section 3-4.2 of Chap. 3.

EXEMPTIONS FROM THE REGULATIONS Securities of the federal, state, and local governments, securities that are not traded across state lines, and any other securities the SEC wishes to specify are exempt from registering with the SEC. Certain organized exchanges may also be exempted from registering if the SEC chooses. As a matter of practice, certain small, local exchanges have been exempted from SEC registration (namely, the exchanges in Honolulu and in Wheeling, West Virginia). As a result, many of the provisions of the SEA do not apply to these exempted securities and exchanges. The SEC's Regulation A under the Securities Act of 1933 deals with these exemptions; and so, they are often called "Reg A issues."

INSIDER ACTIVITIES Corporation directors, officers, and other executives and technicians who have access to inside information about the firm that employs them are forbidden by the SEA from earning speculative profits from trading in the firm's securities. To enforce this prohibition, the SEA requires that every officer, director, and owner of more than 10 percent of a listed firm must file a statement, called an *insider report,* of his or her holdings of that firm's securities for each month in which a change in those holdings occurs. These insider reports are made public. For example, *The Wall Street Journal* prints insider reports occasionally.

Section 16 of the SEA of 1934 forbids insiders from making short sales in their firm's shares. The act also entitles stockholders to recover any speculative profits (that is, gains on holdings of less than 6 months' duration), or losses avoided, that were obtained with the aid of insider information. And a 1984 amendment to the SEA provides for treble damages—that is, the corporation that employs the inside trader can recover $3 for every $1 the insider

BOX 4-3
Texas Gulf Sulphur Corporation's insiders

One of the most famous and significant cases dealing with the use of insider information is the *Texas Gulf Sulphur* case. In late 1963 Texas Gulf began drilling what turned out to be one of the richest mineral deposits discovered in the twentieth century. Although the initial drilling results of November 1963 were remarkable, announcement of the discovery was not made to the public until April 16, 1964. The firm indicated that this delay was necessary to complete a land acquisition program and to permit further tests to be made to determine with certainty the magnitude of the discovery.

During the period from November until the announcement, various officers and employees of the corporation purchased shares and options on the corporation's stock, at prices ranging from $18 to $30 per share, as did various private parties who were tipped off. On the date of the announcement, the stock was selling at about $36, and subsequently the increase was even more dramatic, rising to as high as $160 per share 3 years later. In the suit that followed, a federal court of appeals found the officers and employees of Texas Gulf guilty of trading in the corporation's shares without disclosing all "material facts" to the public; an activity that, in effect, was fraudulent and deceitful.

gained. These provisions have greatly diminished the occurrence of option pools and other price manipulation schemes involving the complicity of insiders. However, insider information violations of a different variety do still occur. In fact, the SEC is still pressing new cases against insiders in an effort to prevent corporate officials and others from benefiting from the information available to them at the public's expense.[13] See Boxes 4-3 and 4-4 for relevant cases.

[13] For recent details about legal thinking and legal precedents dealing with insider trading, see *Business Week*, April 29, 1985, cover story "Insider Trading" on pages 78–92, and also the article entitled "Switzerland's Stone Wall" on page 92 of the same issue. Furthermore, see *The New York Times*, May 6, 1985, for the stories about insider trading entitled "Thayer, Ex-Defense Deputy, Gets 4-Year Prison Term in Stock Case" (page 1) and "Sentences Getting Stiffer" on page D4.

Box 4-4
the case of Merrill Lynch's tippees

Another landmark case pertaining to insider information was decided in 1966. Merrill Lynch, Pierce, Fenner & Smith was the underwriter for a proposed issue of Douglas Aircraft Corporation's debentures. This relationship resulted in a case involving more subtle insider information problems. In preparing the financial reports and registration statements to precede the issue of debentures, Merrill Lynch learned that Douglas's profits would be lower than generally anticipated. Before Douglas announced these earnings, Merrill Lynch's salespeople provided 12 institutional investors who were Merrill Lynch customers with this information. The 12 recipients of this insider information sold their Douglas stock on the basis of this tip.

The SEC charged Merrill Lynch *and* the 12 recipients of insider information with unlawful use of insider information. Merrill Lynch accepted the penalties without admitting guilt. The 12 "tippees" were censured. In a public statement an SEC examiner said of the 12 institutions, "Blindness toward their obligations to the investing public must be attributed to undue self-interest."* Such actions seem to indicate that the SEC tends to give a strict interpretation to the law forbidding the use of insider information.** However, only time will reveal the list of legal precedents that will govern insiders' conduct in the future.†

* *The Wall Street Journal*, Aug. 16, 1968, p. 1, col. 6, and July 1, 1970, p. 12.

** Section 10(b) of the SEA involves more subtle legal issues than the application of Section 16. Section 16 permits the stockholders to recover short-term profits earned by an insider regardless of whether or not the insider information was misused. On the other hand, Section 10(b) deals with fraudulent activities perpetrated by insiders or outsiders. The misuse of insider information is only one area Sec. 10(b) covers.

In general, the SEC deals harshly with the users of insider information. In one case, the printer that printed a prospectus was prosecuted for using information gained from that prospectus while working on it—before it was released to the public.

† The insider information cases of (1) *Ray Dirks v. SEC* and (2) *U.S. v. Chiarella* will be landmark cases when they exhaust their appeals. Rule 10(b)-5 and Section 16(b) of the SEA are key laws governing the use of insider information. For details, see M. L. Budd and N. Wolfson, *Securities Regulation* (The Michie Company, Charlottesville, Va., 1984), chaps. 8 and 9.

Down through the years, SEC rulings and court decisions have broadened the definition of an "insider." SEC actions seem to be endeavoring to shift profit seekers' interest away from seeking hot tips and insider information and toward security analysis instead. As this will tend to decrease the possibility of price manipulation and increase the economic efficiency of securities markets, it is a desirable trend in public policy.

PRICE MANIPULATION The SEA, as noted earlier, specifically forbids certain price manipulation schemes such as wash sales, pools, circulation of manipulative information, and making false and misleading statements about securities. However, it does allow investment bankers to manipulate prices to the extent that they temporarily stabilize a security's price during a primary offering.

The SEA also authorizes the SEC to supervise trading in the options (that is, puts and calls) markets.[14]

4-3 SECURITIES REGULATIONS ENACTED FROM 1935 TO THE PRESENT

4-3.1 Public Utility Holding Company Act of 1935

In 1928 the Federal Trade Commission (FTC) began a review of the public utility industry. The FTC uncovered a system of huge utility empires that were organized to profit their owners rather than serve the public needs. Therefore, the Congress enacted the Public Utility Holding Company Act of 1935 (the 1935 Act, hereafter).

Section 11(a) of the Public Utility Holding Company Act of 1935 gave the SEC the responsibility and the authority "to determine the extent to which the corporate structure . . . may be simplified, unnecessary complexities thereby eliminated, voting power fairly and equitably distributed . . . and the properties and business thereof confined to those necessary and appropriate to the operations of an integrated public utility system."

The 1935 Act also gave the SEC the power to regulate the terms and form of securities issued by utility companies, regulate the accounting systems they use, approve all acquisitions and dispositions of assets and securities, and regulate intercompany transactions such as the payment of cash dividends and the making of loans. Thus, the 1935 Act puts the SEC in a position of importance with respect to the activities listed above in regulating public utilities in the United States. The SEC doesn't use these powers much today, however, because the abuses in the public utility area are no longer a problem.

4-3.2 Maloney Act of 1936

Essentially an amendment of the SEA, the Maloney Act was adopted at the request of the over-the-counter (OTC) security dealers and provides for their self-regulation. The act stipulates that one or more associations of "qualified" OTC brokers and dealers may apply for registration with the SEC. The group

[14] In 1981 the SEC and the Commodity Futures Trading Commission (CFTC) announced an administrative pact between the two governmental agencies that clarified their jurisdiction over recently developed financial futures and option products. Essentially, the SEC oversees almost all options trading, while the CFTC regulates almost all futures contracts and options on futures. See "Pact Opens New Kinds of Futures," *The Wall Street Journal*, Dec. 8, 1981, pp. D1 and D16.

may regulate itself within the guidelines laid down by the SEC, and it may grant discounts on securities traded among its members. OTC dealers who are not members of an association deal with members of an association by paying full retail prices for any securities they purchase. This provides a strong incentive for all OTC dealers to belong to an association.

NATIONAL ASSOCIATION OF SECURITIES DEALERS (NASD) To date, only one association of OTC dealers has registered with the SEC under the provisions of the Maloney Act; it is the National Association of Securities Dealers (NASD). The NASD has about 2800 member firms representing about 200,000 people selling securities in the nearly 7000 branch offices that comprise the OTC market. The NASD is headed by a board of governors that is assisted by 13 district business conduct committees. The association has established a testing procedure that must be passed by any individual wishing to join it; a set of rules forbidding fraud, manipulation, and excessive profit taking; a uniform practices code that standardizes and expedites routine transactions such as payments and deliveries; and a program to discipline its members for illegal or unethical conduct.

NASD DISCIPLINE PROCEDURES In addition to conducting themselves in an ethical manner, member firms of the NASD must submit their financial statements for inspection at any time the association wishes. If any violation is discovered in these audits or if a violation is reported from any source, the NASD disciplines its own members. After hearing the charge against the member and the member's defense, one of the NASD's business conduct committees passes judgment. The charge may be dismissed, or penalties involving suspension and/or fines in the tens of thousands of dollars may be levied. Expulsion from the NASD is the severest penalty, since nonmembers cannot obtain the purchase discounts needed to survive as dealers. All decisions may be appealed to the NASD's board of governors, the SEC, or the courts.

The SEC possesses direct power over the NASD. In particular, it must be given copies of all rules adopted by the NASD (or any other association of OTC dealers that may be formed). It may suspend or revoke the association's registration for failure to follow its guidelines. And the SEC may review and alter the verdict in any judicial proceedings convened by the association. However, the SEC does lack the power to write rules for an OTC association, a power it has for the organized exchanges.

4-3.3 Trust Indenture Act of 1939

An indenture is a contract, written by a firm that issues bonds, stipulating certain promises the firm makes to its bondholders. A common provision of an indenture is that the issuing corporation can pay no dividends on common stock if the bond's interest payments are in arrears. A trustee (for example, a bank) is appointed to monitor the issuing corporation on behalf of the bondholders and to make certain that the provisions of the indenture are not violated. If a provision is violated, the trustee should bring a suit against the issuing corporation on behalf of the owners of the indentured securities. If this relationship is to function properly, the trustee must be independent of the issuing corporation so that it is not reluctant to bring suit.

Prior to 1939, corporations were sometimes able to violate the provisions of their indentures. These corporations might appoint their own banks as trustees, for example. Such a bank was dependent upon the indentured corporation for income and was therefore reluctant to sue it if it violated its indenture. To overcome such weakness, the Trust Indenture Act of 1939 requires that the indenture clearly specify the rights of the owners of the indentured securities, that the issuing corporation provide the trustee periodic financial reports, and that the trustee not impede its willingness or legal right to sue the issuing corporation.

4-3.4 Investment Company Act of 1940 (ICA)

The Investment Company Act of 1940 (ICA) is the main piece of legislation governing mutual funds and closed-end investment companies. The ICA extends the provisions of the Securities Act and the SEA. These earlier acts require that the investment companies (like other issuers of securities) avoid fraudulent practices, fully disclose their financial statements, and give their prospectuses to potential investors. The ICA also requires investment companies to publish statements outlining their investment goals (for example, growth, income, or safety), not to change their published goals without the consent of the shareholders, to obtain the stockholders' approval of contracts for management advice for the fund, to include outsiders on their boards of directors, to follow uniform accounting procedures, and to operate the fund for the benefit of its shareholders rather than for the benefit of its managers.

The ICA of 1940 was modified slightly by the Investment Company Amendments Act of 1970. These 1970 amendments (1) asked for a standard of "reasonableness" with respect to the management fees charged to manage the assets of a mutual fund; (2) restricted the adoption of new management contracts;[15] and (3) placed a ceiling of 5 percent of asset value on the sales charges that could be deducted from a fund.

4-3.5 Investment Advisors Act of 1940 (IAA)

The Investment Advisors Act of 1940 (IAA) requires individuals or firms that *sell advice* about securities or investments to register with the SEC. These investment advisors are required to observe the legal guidelines pertaining to fraud, price manipulation, and other factors outlined earlier. A set fee or a percentage of the assets managed is a permissible compensation plan for advisors under this law.

Although it has some good provisions, the IAA is not a totally effective means of protecting investors. One of the deficiencies of the law is that practically anyone can qualify as an investment advisor. Although advisors must register with the SEC and disclose their age, experience, education, and other background information, the SEC cannot deny anyone the right to sell investment advice unless it can show that the customers would be cheated or defrauded if they paid for the advice. Since it is difficult to prove that an investment advisor who has never studied accounting, finance, or economics,

[15] Under the 1970 amendments to the Investment Company Act, performance-based fee agreements are permitted between investment advisors and registered investment companies. For an economic analysis of the issues, see Franco Modigliani and Gerald A. Pogue, "Alternative Investment Performance Fee Agreements and Implications for SEC Regulatory Policy," *The Bell Journal of Economics*, vol. 6, no. 1, Spring 1975, pp. 127–159.

for instance, will necessarily hurt investors with whatever advice he or she may purvey, it is essentially impossible to deny charlatans the right to sell their advice. As a result, some advisors with dubious backgrounds operate by advertising themselves as being "investment advisors registered with the SEC."

The SEC has developed some policies that tend to limit the advertising practices of investment advisors. It forbids their using selected testimonials from customers; offering free advice unless it actually is free and without obligation; making "false and misleading" statements; and indicating that some graph, chart, or formula can be used by itself to make investment decisions.

The IAA also provides a basis on which investors can ask the courts to cancel investment management contracts and return fees paid to the advisor. But the IAA still allows ample opportunities for a naive and trusting investor to be "ripped off" by unqualified or unethical investment advisors. Therefore, investors seeking to procure investment advice should be independently critical consumers of such services.

4-3.6 Securities Investor Protection Corporation (SIPC)

The Securities Investor Protection Corporation (SIPC, or "sip-ic") was established in 1970 by an act of Congress to assist the clients of bankrupt brokerage firms. The act requires that all registered securities brokers and dealers and all members of national securities exchanges join SIPC and pay dues (which are like insurance premiums) of one-fourth of 1 percent of the firm's gross revenues, or less.[16] Mutual fund salespeople, insurance agents, and investment advisors need not join SIPC.

SIPC dues are accumulated in a fund that is used to repay clients of a bankrupt brokerage firm if the firm loses the client's money or securities and does not have the capital to repay the loss. SIPC was formed to free investors from worry about selecting a brokerage by providing insurance to protect investors in case their brokerage firm fails. It is believed that this insurance will make more people willing to invest their funds (rather than hoard them, for example) and thus help U.S. industrial development grow.

4-3.7 Commodity Futures Trading Commission (CFTC) Act of 1974

Commodity futures contracts are a marketable security that has a legislative history dating back before the laws governing the financial securities. Starting in 1884 there was a new bill about trading futures contracts introduced in Congress almost every year—most of these bills proposed a ban on trading in futures contracts. In those early days of finance most people did not understand futures contracts. As a result of this ignorance they naively imagined that trading in futures contracts destabilized market prices or was some form of evil gambling—some people still cling to these naive notions.

The Grain Futures Act of 1922 was the first bill to impose federal government authority over futures trading. This first bill raised standards at the commodity futures exchanges and improved trading practices. However, a

[16] For details about SIPC, see "SIPC to Raise Broker Fees May 1, Weights Giving Its Insurance Fund Bigger Cushion," *The Wall Street Journal*, Apr. 12, 1983, p. 2. The dues were only $25 per member per year until SIPC paid off enough losses to deplete its capital. Then, the dues are temporarily raised to replenish SIPC's coffers.

major commodity price debacle in 1933 led to the amendment and renaming of the Grain Futures Act; the new law was named the Commodity Exchange Authority Act of 1936.

The Commodity Exchange Act (CEA) of 1936 established the Commodity Exchange Authority (CEA) as a regulatory body. The CEA was a regulatory branch of the U.S. Department of Agriculture (USDA) that regulated trading in domestic agriculture commodities from 1936 until 1974. The CEA had the authority to grant approval for new futures contracts to be publicly traded, police the registration of the commodity futures commission merchants, investigate charges of cheating and fraud in commodity trading, and prevent price manipulation in domestic U.S. commodity trading. Commodity futures trading started growing rapidly in the 1960s and the tiny CEA proved inadequate to handle the larger work responsibilities. Therefore, the Commodity Futures Trading Commission Act of 1974 passed all the CEA's regulatory authority onto a new, larger independent regulatory agency it established called the Commodity Futures Trading Commission (CFTC).

The CFTC is an independent federal regulatory agency overseen by five commissioners who are appointed by the President of the United States. The CFTC also has a staff of economists and other regulatory officials who research the commodity markets in an effort to discern what rules and regulations about commodity futures trading will best promote the public welfare.

In addition to establishing the CFTC and giving it the powers that had previously been assigned to the CEA, the 1974 act also gave the CFTC authority to go into court and sue any person or organization that violated the CFTC Act; take charge of a commodity market in an "emergency" situation and direct whatever actions it deemed necessary to restore an orderly market; and issue "cease and desist" orders, violation of which subjects the offending party to criminal or civil sanctions and a stiff fine. Moreover, one of the most sweeping changes brought about by the CFTC Act was to grant the CFTC authority over the *entire* futures trading industry—that is, all commodities in the world that are traded in the United States, rather than merely the domestically produced commodities.[17]

4-3.8 Employee Retirement Income Security Act of 1974

Coincident with the extraordinary growth of pension funds since 1940 have been a number of abuses by fund managers that resulted in the loss of pension benefits to hapless and unsuspecting employees. Not infrequently, these abuses stemmed from the imprudent risks taken by fund managers in deploying the funds entrusted to them. In an attempt to eliminate such disasters, Congress passed the Employee Retirement Income Security Act of 1974 (called ERISA) to protect workers' pensions. Among ERISA's provisions is the so-called prudent man rule. ERISA stipulates that the fiduciary caretakers (that is, the portfolio managers) of pension funds covered by the act are liable not only for the preservation of the fund's principal but also for

[17] For more detail read Warren W. Lebeck, "The Origins of Futures Markets," in Nancy H. Rothstein (ed.), *The Handbook of Financial Futures* (McGraw-Hill, New York, 1983). In the same book see also John H. Stassen, "Trading Rules and Regulations," and "Regulatory Considerations."

sufficient growth through "prudent investments" to be able to pay retirement benefits when due in the future.

The *prudent man rule* that appears throughout securities laws was first articulated by Mr. Justice Samuel Putman in 1830, in the famous case of *Harvard College v. Amory.*[18] Justice Putman said:

> All that can be required of a trustee . . . is that he shall conduct himself faithfully and exercise a sound discretion. He is to observe how men of prudence, discretion and intelligence manage their own affairs, not in regard to speculation, but in regard to the permanent disposition of their funds, considering the probable income as well as the probable safety of the capital to be invested. . . .

While the word "prudent" has been left somewhat vaguely defined by the U.S. Congress and the state legislatures that refer to the prudent man rule, the term apparently refers to some "average" rate of return with an "average" assumption of risk. The returns from Standard & Poor's 500 market index, for example, might be such an average yardstick. If the courts enforce this line of thinking (which they have not done, as yet), pension fund managers need to be able to defend their investment track records in a court of law or else they may find themselves liable for damages resulting from the inadequate investment returns they were able to earn for their clients. Such damages could easily run into the millions of dollars for a case involving one of the multibillion dollar pension funds.

4-3.9 Securities Acts amendments of 1975 (SAA)

President Gerald Ford signed the SAA into effect in 1975 and thereby mandated a change in U.S. securities markets. The most comprehensive securities legislation in over 40 years, the SAA mandated the development of the National Market System (NMS). The amendments did not specify the details of the NMS, leaving that to be determined by the competitive economic forces in the security markets themselves—subject, of course, to the approval of the SEC. The new act merely indicated that the NMS should comprise a competitive environment which would result in maximum efficiency and liquidity. As a result of this law, the organized exchanges discontinued their fixed minimum commission rate schedules, began to allow exchange-listed stocks to be traded off the floor of the exchanges by their member firms, developed the consolidated tape, developed the intermarket trading system (ITS), and implemented other changes that are discussed in the appendix to Chap. 3.

4-3.10 the bankruptcy laws

In addition to the securities laws outlined above, there is some business law that is relevant for investors. The Bankruptcy Act of 1938, which was revised and updated by the Bankruptcy Act of 1978, is one example of a business law that sometimes concerns investors.[19] Essentially, the Bankruptcy Act requires

[18] William H. Cooper, "Problems with the Prudent Man Rule," Trusts and Estates, vol. 121, no. 3, March 1982, pp. 68–76. The article reviews different aspects of the prudent man legal standard as it has been applied and interpreted.

[19] A book that is devoted to describing the various aspects of bankruptcy is Edward I. Altman, *Financial Distress: A Complete Guide to Predicting, Avoiding and Dealing with Bankruptcy*, Wiley, New York, 1983. Chapter 1 discusses bankruptcy law and the Bankruptcy Reform Act of 1978. An economic theory of bankruptcy is presented in J. C. Francis, Harold Hastings, and Frank Fabozzi, "Bankruptcy as a Mathematical Catastrophe," in Haim Levy (ed.), *Readings in Finance*, vol. 4 (J. A. I. Press, Greenwich, Conn., 1983).

that courts or court-appointed trustees oversee the affairs of firms against which bankruptcy charges have been filed. Furthermore, the law requires that in bankruptcies involving listed securities the bankruptcy courts should ask the SEC for an advisory opinion concerning whatever financial reorganization may result from the bankruptcy proceeding. Let us briefly consider the different types of bankruptcy proceedings.

A company that files for protection from its creditors under Chapter XI of the federal bankruptcy laws receives instant relief from its financial problems, regardless of whether or not the firm is insolvent. The very act of filing freezes all claims and lawsuits against the troubled firm and may allow it to get out from underneath unprofitable leases, labor agreements, or other contracts. Furthermore, the company continues to operate under the bankruptcy court's protection while its case is being resolved.

Under the Bankruptcy Reform Act of 1978, a Chapter XI filing can be voluntary (that is, by the firm's own executives) or involuntary (by the firm's creditors). The only criterion for filing is that the firm is not paying its debts. After filing, the firm continues to operate under the court's protection while completing a repayment or *reorganization* plan. A committee of the troubled firm's unsecured creditors is usually appointed by the court to oversee a reorganization that will provide both financial and operating rehabilitation for the firm. The reorganization plan must contain means of execution and must be approved by the court. In addition, a plan is approved only if two-thirds in amount and one-half in number of the allowed claims consent to it. Typically, reorganization plans call for reduced creditor claims and/or extension of the payments over a longer time period.

A more drastic legal procedure may be initiated under Chapter X of the federal bankruptcy laws. This bankruptcy filing may be initiated either voluntarily by the troubled debtor firm or by three or more of the firm's creditors with total claims in excess of $5000. Since Chapter X proceedings are designed for the more hopeless and complex bankruptcy cases, a statement explaining why relief cannot be obtained under Chapter XI is required.

Under Chapter X bankruptcy proceedings an independent, disinterested trustee is appointed by the court to assume control of the firm during the bankruptcy proceedings and to prepare a reorganization plan, if possible. If the firm cannot be saved by reorganization, then the trustee oversees the auction of any remaining assets the troubled firm may have. Then the trustee distributes the cash proceeds of the auction to the creditors. But if a reorganization of the firm is possible, a new management team is usually appointed by the trustee. Such reorganizations almost always provide for cancellation of all junior claims against the firm—essentially, the old common stock is all declared null and void, and thus becomes irrevocably worthless. The more senior securities (such as preferred stock or bonds) are then usually downgraded to become the new common stock. Such drastic reorganizations must be approved by two-thirds or more of all creditors. If the firm's total assets exceed its total liabilities so that its old common stock has some positive value, then the majority of the common stockholders' votes must approve the reorganization too.

Bankruptcy law becomes of interest to investors for various reasons. First, news about bankruptcy proceedings can cause those who are speculating on the firm's future to buy and sell its securities in a fashion that generates significant speculative profits and losses. For example, when the Chrysler Corporation narrowly averted bankruptcy because of a situation that was regularly reported by the newspapers in 1980 through 1982, some of the price changes in its securities were breathtaking. Another reason that investors should not be heedless of the bankruptcy laws is that at some time, through some unfortunate investment, their own interests may be drawn into the bankruptcy courts. That is, people who were initially hopeful investors may eventually become frustrated creditors participating in a bankruptcy case.

4-3.11 other laws

In addition to the laws outlined above, there are a few laws that partly govern activity in securities markets. The Bank Holding Company Act of 1970, for instance, forbids banks or their holding companies from owning certain nonbanking assets. These laws and a few others that have not been mentioned typically have a minor effect on securities markets and the SEC.

4-3.12 enforcement powers

Under the laws reviewed above and several other statutes, private citizens are granted powers with which to enforce securities regulations. For example, one individual may charge another individual with fraud or other criminal offenses related to dishonest securities dealings which carry fines of up to $10,000 and imprisonment of up to 2 years. Or an individual may bring a civil suit against a securities firm or a securities exchange and be reimbursed for damages, cause the courts to discipline the offender, or both.

The SEC may also take action to require conformance with the securities laws. And the CFTC can take legal actions to force commodity traders to observe the laws relevant to commodity trading. Both agencies are granted the right to suspend trading in particular securities or commodities within their jurisdiction, to suspend the registration of an entire exchange, to expel officers or members of an exchange who operate illegally, to suggest changes in an exchange's rules and bylaws and require their implementation, to collect financial statements and records, to conduct investigations and hearings as needed to enforce the law, to obtain injunctions requiring the cessation of activities violating the securities and/or commodity trading laws, and to obtain writs requiring violators to comply with the law.

4-4 CONCLUSIONS ABOUT FEDERAL REGULATORY PROGRAMS

The regulatory system just outlined has greatly reduced the incidence of fraud and price manipulation, increased market stability, and fostered thoughtful investment analysis. For example, the Pecora hearings, conducted in 1933 and 1934, revealed that during 1927 and 1928 a group of highly respected investment houses had underwritten $90 million of Peruvian government bonds that, by the investment brokers' admission, would never have sold at all had adequate disclosure requirements been in effect at the time. Fortunately, in recent years the market seems to have been largely free of such flagrant abuses. Nevertheless, the regulatory program has been far from perfect and bears constant evaluation and improvement.

Enforcement of security laws and development of new regulatory programs for the United States are largely the responsibility of the SEC. Background information on this governmental agency will provide insight into this commission's powers.

The SEC's daily operations are governed by directors, associate directors, and assistant directors of its various divisions. These directors are in turn overseen by the five SEC commissioners. The vast majority of the commissioners and directors who have managed the SEC since its inception have been attorneys. Unfortunately, the homogeneity of their educational backgrounds has imparted a myopic outlook to the SEC's management. Strange as it may sound, the SEC's professional staff contains very few economists, financial analysts, and accountants. Indeed, some of the SEC's management staff know precious little about economics and finance.

The SEC seems to have at least recognized the problem in recent years, as evidenced by its encouragement of its staff to take night courses in economics and finance at local universities. Also, the SEC created a position for a certified public accountant who is supposed to work with the accounting profession and the SEC's attorneys in developing better accounting statements. Although these changes represent improvement, the federal agency charged with overseeing the nation's securities markets, investment advisors, mutual funds, and other investment activities still appears to some observers to be undersupplied with professional financial economists.[20]

QUESTIONS

1. Briefly outline the background leading to the development of a system in the United States for regulating the securities markets after 1933.
2. What harm can come to a nation's financial markets and economy from corners on the market and pools?
3. Compare and contrast the Securities Act of 1933 and the Securities Exchange Act of 1934 with respect to registration of securities.
4. What is a prospectus? What is its purpose? When should prospectuses be provided? When the SEC releases a prospectus, does it imply that it recommends the issue for investment?
5. What is the SEC? How did it develop? What functions does it perform? How could it be strengthened?
6. How is credit that is used to purchase securities regulated?
7. Is it illegal to trade securities on the basis of a hot tip from an employee of the firm that issues the securities? Explain.
8. What is the NASD? How did it develop? What are its functions? What powers can it use to enforce the law?
9. What is an indenture? What precautions discourage violation of an indenture?
10. What legislation governs the activities of mutual funds? What are the restrictions on the funds?

[20] For a scholarly investigation and criticism of the way the SEC is run, see Susan M. Phillips and J. Richard Zecher, *The SEC and the Public Interest* (M.I.T., Cambridge, Mass., 1981). The authors of this book are financial economists whose research efforts appear to have been noticed in Washington, D.C. Ms. Phillips left academia to be director of the CFTC.

11. "The SEC's actions tend to ensure that investors will not lose their savings by investing them in securities." True, false, or uncertain? Explain.
12. What is the CFTC? What does it govern?

SELECTED REFERENCES

Budd, Martin L., and Nicholas Wolfson, *Securities Regulation: Cases and Materials* (The Michie Company, Charlottesville, Va., 1984). An easy-to-read law school textbook, large sections of which laypeople can read and understand.

Hammer, Richard M., Gilbert Simonetti, Jr., and Charles T. Crawford (eds.), *Investment Regulation Around the World* (Ronald Press, Somerset, N.J., 1983). A collection of readings about the investment regulations in countries foreign to the United States.

Jennings, Richard W., and Harold Marsh, Jr., *Securities Regulation: Cases and Materials*, 4th ed. (Foundation Press, Mineola, N.Y., 1977). A popular law school textbook that is easy for laypeople to read. No mathematics.

Loss, Louis, *Securities Regulation*, 3 vols. (Little, Brown, Boston, 1961). This set of legal volumes is written for persons specializing in securities law. No mathematics is used, but the volumes use technical legal terms.

Phillips, Susan M., and J. Richard Zecher, *The SEC and the Public Interest* (M.I.T., Cambridge, Mass., 1981). This scholarly economic analysis and criticism of the SEC was written by two professors of finance who worked at the SEC. No mathematics is used.

Securities and Exchange Commission, Securities Act of 1933, release no. 4725; Securities Exchange Act of 1934, release no. 7425. The SEC provides these and numerous other releases to document and explain its legal activity in the securities industry.

Tewles, Richard J., and Edward S. Bradley, *The Stock Market*, 4th ed. (Wiley, New York, 1982). Chapters 17 and 18 present a discussion of the history and administration of securities law in the United States. No mathematics.

APPENDIX 4A

Hecht v. Harris, Upham & Co.—a true case of churning

Bertha came to the United States from England as a poor immigrant when she was a young woman. She worked most of her life as a $125 per month housekeeper for a Mr. Hecht. Late in life her fortunes improved; she married her employer, who was an affluent man. Prior to her marriage, in 1939 Bertha had opened a brokerage account for herself with $2000 of her own money. She opened this account near her home in San Francisco with a securities broker named Asa Wilder.

From 1939 to 1955 Bertha's account grew in value from $2000 to $65,000 as a result of additional deposits, dividend income, and capital gains. During those 16 years Bertha's account showed a total of 32 sales and 41 purchases. She never had more than five sales in 1 year, and none in some years. Essentially, that is, Bertha's account was traded infrequently. Over those years Mr. Wilder and Bertha became friendly even though Mr. Wilder became employed at a different brokerage firm than the one where Bertha's account was maintained.

In 1955 Mr. Hecht died and left his 62-year-old widow an estate with a net value of $502,532. After Hecht's death, Bertha and Asa Wilder started a close business and social relationship. Mrs. Hecht transferred $42,000 of her personal account from Walston and Company to Hooker and Fay Co., where Mr. Wilder was then employed. When Bertha received the proceeds from Mr. Hecht's estate, they also were placed in her account at Hooker and Fay. In May 1957 Mr. Wilder left Hooker and Fay to become a registered representative (that is, a securities broker) and commodities manager at Harris, Upham and Company's San Francisco office. At that time the Hecht account of $533,161 was transferred to Harris, Upham and Co. under Mr. Wilder's guidance.

Bertha Hecht dealt with Asa Wilder through Harris, Upham and Co., and socially as well, for over 6 years after Mr. Hecht passed away. However, in March of 1964 Mrs. Hecht's tax consultants advised the perky 71-year-old widow that her account at Harris, Upham and Co. was seriously depleted. At that time its value was down to $251,161.

Suit was brought jointly against Asa Wilder and Harris, Upham and Co. in a California District Court by Bertha Hecht for recovery of $1,109,000. This suit claimed damages for three reasons: (1) The Hecht account had been converted from a blue-chip investment account to a low-grade speculative securities and commodity account; (2) Asa Wilder traded excessively in the account for the purpose of generating commissions; and (3) Asa Wilder had defrauded Bertha Hecht by self-dealing in two different securities transactions.

The court found that, if it were still intact, Mrs. Hecht's original Harris, Upham & Co. account would have had a value of approximately $1,026,775. Dividend and bond interest would have amounted to $194,135 instead of only the $124,237 earned under Asa Wilder's handling. The court also learned that during the 6 years and 10 months that Asa Wilder handled widow Hecht's account at Harris, Upham and Co. he entertained his client. During this time Mrs. Hecht had paid for:

1. $91,000 in commissions and markups on securities
2. $98,000 in commissions on commodity trades
3. $13,000 in interest on loans advanced to Mrs. Hecht's margin account

During this period of 6 years and 10 months there had been about 1300 transactions in 200 different corporate stocks and 9000 commodity transactions. Essentially, the account was traded very actively.

In assessing the role of Mr. Wilder's employer in allowing widow Hecht's account to be depleted, the court pointed out that, although it was only one-tenth of 1 percent of the total of accounts in the San Francisco office, the Hecht account had supplied, in commissions and interest, at least 4.7 percent of the office's total income. Furthermore, the charges against the Hecht account, stated as a percent of the value of the account, were about 50 times the average. If the brokerage firm had monitored its accounts better, these unusual statistics would have pinpointed what Asa Wilder was doing with the Hecht account so that the problem could have been overcome.

In defending his own actions, Mr. Wilder pointed out that he was paid on salary rather than on straight commission; therefore, he had no incentive to churn widow Hecht's account. The court pointed out, however, that Mr. Wilder had received bonuses and pay increases that corresponded chronologically with the points in time when he was depleting the Hecht account most actively. Three months after Mr. Wilder lost the Hecht account, his so-called salary was reduced from $1250 per month to $850 per month. Thus it appeared that his income was related to the brokerage's income from the Hecht account.

The court concluded that Mrs. Hecht was guilty of laziness and therefore could not rightfully assert that her account was wrongfully or unwillingly converted to a speculative account. On the issue of excessive trading (or churning) the court ruled that Mrs. Hecht should receive $143,000 in damages, that is, the full amount of commissions she had paid to Harris, Upham and Co. during the 6 years and 10 months her account resided there. On the issue of the two fraudulent self-dealing security transactions perpetrated by Asa Wilder on widow Hecht, the court granted Bertha Hecht $232,000 in damages.

CHAPTER 5 taxes

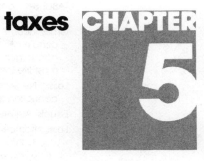

There is an old saying in the United States that sooner or later two things will get us all—death and taxes. Fortunately, not only can taxes be postponed, they can sometimes be avoided completely!

The structure of taxes in the United States encourages certain activities (for example, long-term investing) and discourages other types of activities (such as short-term price speculation). This chapter explains the tax structure so that judicious investors can postpone, reduce, or eliminate their tax payments. After all, if you can legally postpone paying your taxes for 1 year, that is like getting an interest-free loan. This chapter explains the essence of the tax structure in the United States and suggests completely legal and ethical ways to postpone and avoid taxes.

5-1 FEDERAL PERSONAL INCOME TAXES

Federal income taxes are the largest tax most people pay. Most working people pay more than 20 cents out of every dollar they earn to the Internal Revenue Service (IRS), the tax collecting arm of the U.S. government. If someone refuses to pay or cheats on taxes, the IRS can have the federal courts review the case. The federal courts can hand down penalties that involve years in the federal penitentiary if a large-scale case of dishonest tax evasion is uncovered. Since such heavy legal penalties can be invoked, it behooves each of us to familiarize ourselves with the tax law. Remember, ignorance of the law is not a legally acceptable defense.

5-1.1 federal taxes on personal income

Individuals who earn wages, salaries, and other types of income are legally allowed to deduct certain of their costs from their total income (called *gross income)* in order to determine what part of their income is *taxable income*. Table 5-1 summarizes the process used to derive a taxpayer's taxable income.

TABLE 5-1 deriving taxable income

Gross income: (Includes wages, salaries, rent received, unemployment compensation under certain circumstances, alimony received, etc., but excludes such things as interest on municipal bonds, gifts, inheritances, some social security benefits, child support payments received, and most life insurance proceeds)

Less: Necessary business expenses, certain moving expenses, payments to an IRA or Keogh plan, deduction for a married couple when both work, alimony paid, etc.

Equals: Adjusted gross income

Less: Itemized personal deductions such as:

1. Interest expense on loans being paid off
2. Charitable contributions (with certain maximum limitations)
3. Various state and local taxes
4. Medical and prescription drug expenses in excess of 5% of adjusted gross income
5. Casualty losses in excess of $100 per loss that exceed 10% of adjusted gross income
6. Various miscellaneous deductions

Less: The zero bracket amount (an alternative explained below*)

Less: Exemption of $1000 for each allowable exemption**

Equals: Taxable income

* Instead of itemizing deductions, the taxpayer may take the zero bracket amount, which is, in effect, a fixed standard deduction that has been built into the tax tables. The zero bracket amount in 1984 is $3400 for married individuals filing a joint return or for certain surviving spouses, $2300 for single taxpayers and heads of household, and $1700 for married individuals filing separately. Nonresident aliens, dependent children with unearned income, and certain married taxpayers who file separately are denied the right to claim the zero bracket amount.

** In 1984 taxpayers were allowed a $1000 exemption for themselves and for each dependent person who met specific criteria. Additional exemptions were allowed for taxpayers age 65 and over and for blind taxpayers. As of 1985 both the zero bracket amount and the exemptions have been indexed to the inflation rate. For an analysis of indexing the federal income tax schedule, see John A. Tatom, "Federal Income Tax Reform In 1985: Indexation," *REVIEW* (Federal Reserve Bank of St. Louis), vol. 67, no. 2, February 1985, pp. 5–12.

For example, a single person who lives with no financial dependents and earns a salary of $15,000 per year is allowed a *standard* (nonitemized) deduction of $2300 per year.[1] This taxpayer is also allowed one exemption of $1000 for himself or herself.

If the taxpayer in Table 5-2 were the sole supporter of a spouse and one child, then he or she would be entitled to larger deductions than a single person. The family supporter would be entitled to a nonitemized standard

[1] This "standard deduction" is built into the tax tables. Therefore, it is not deducted by the taxpayer in deriving taxable income.

TABLE 5-2 calculating taxable income from gross income for two hypothetical taxpayers

single taxpayer		married taxpayer filing jointly with 1 child
$15,000	Gross income	$15,000
−1,000	Exemptions	−3,000
$14,000	Taxable income	$12,000

deduction of $3400 built into the tax tables and three exemptions (worth $3000) rather than a $2300 deduction built into the tax tables and a $1000 exemption.

After a taxpayer has determined the amount of taxable income, the tax schedule can be consulted to find out the amount of taxes to be paid on it.

5-1.2 the progressive federal income tax rates

There are two important characteristics about the U.S. federal income tax schedule. First, the taxes are stated as a percentage of the taxable income. Second, this percentage increases as the taxpayer's taxable income increases—this is called a *graduated* or *progressive tax schedule.* Tables 5-3 and 5-4 show the tax rates for a single taxpayer and a married taxpayer, respectively.

TABLE 5-3 federal income tax schedule for single taxpayers, 1984

If taxable income is:	The tax is:
Not over $2,300	No tax.
Over $2,300 but not over $3,400	11% of the excess over $2,300
Over $3,400 but not over $4,400	$121, plus 12% of the excess over $3,400
Over $4,400 but not over $6,500	$241, plus 14% of the excess over $4,400
Over $6,500 but not over $8,500	$535, plus 15% of the excess over $6,500
Over $8,500 but not over $10,800	$835, plus 16% of the excess over $8,500
Over $10,800 but not over $12,900	$1,203, plus 18% of the excess over $10,800
Over $12,900 but not over $15,000	$1,581, plus 20% of the excess over $12,900
Over $15,000 but not over $18,200	$2,001, plus 23% of the excess over $15,000
Over $18,200 but not over $23,500	$2,737, plus 26% of the excess over $18,200
Over $23,500 but not over $28,800	$4,115, plus 30% of the excess over $23,500
Over $28,800 but not over $34,100	$5,705, plus 34% of the excess over $28,800
Over $34,100 but not over $41,500	$7,507, plus 38% of the excess over $34,100
Over $41,500 but not over $55,300	$10,319, plus 42% of the excess over $41,500
Over $53,300 but not over $81,800	$16,115, plus 48% of the excess over $55,300
Over $81,800	$28,835, plus 50% of the excess over $81,800

TABLE 5-4 federal income tax schedule for married taxpayers filing joint returns and certain widows and widowers, 1984

If taxable income is:	The tax is:
Not over $3,400	No tax.
Over $3,400 but not over $5,500	11% of the excess over $3,400
Over $5,500 but not over $7,600	$231, plus 12% of the excess over $5,500
Over $7,600 but not over $11,900	$483, plus 14% of the excess over $7,600
Over $11,900 but not over $16,000	$1,085, plus 16% of the excess over $11,900
Over $16,000 but not over $20,200	$1,741, plus 18% of the excess over $16,000
Over $20,200 but not over $24,600	$2,497, plus 22% of the excess over $20,200
Over $24,600 but not over $29,900	$3,465, plus 25% of the excess over $24,600
Over $29,900 but not over $35,200	$4,790, plus 28% of the excess over $29,900
Over $35,200 but not over $45,800	$6,274, plus 33% of the excess over $35,200
Over $45,800 but not over $60,000	$9,772, plus 38% of the excess over $45,800
Over $60,000 but not over $85,600	$15,168, plus 42% of the excess over $60,000
Over $85,600 but not over $109,400	$25,920, plus 45% of the excess over $85,600
Over $109,400 but not over $162,400	$36,630, plus 49% of the excess over $109,400
Over $162,400	$62,600, plus 50% of the excess over $162,400

As of 1985 the tax rates, the zero bracket amount, and the allowances for personal exemptions have been adjusted annually for inflation. These annual inflation adjustments are designed to avoid the effect of "bracket creep," which occurs as most people's salaries are pushed up by inflation into higher income tax brackets each year. Of course, Congress may change these tax plans at any time.

Reconsider the two taxpayers shown in Table 5-2 in order to see examples of how to determine the amount of taxes due. The single person's taxable income of $14,000 incurs a federal income tax bill of $1801, calculated as follows with Table 5-3.

	$1,581	from Table 5-3
Plus:	$ 220	equals 20% of the $1100 excess over $12,900
	$1,801	total federal income tax

In contrast, the married person, who was the sole supporter of a spouse and one child, has taxable income of $12,000, from Table 5-2. Using Table 5-4, the married person's taxes are found to be only $1101.

	$1,085	from Table 5-4
Plus:	$ 16	equals 16% of the $100 excess over $11,900
	$1,101	total federal income tax

The married couple claiming three exemptions pays $700 less in tax than the single taxpayer claiming one exemption who has the identical gross income.

The tax benefit of marriage holds true only if one of the two spouses earns a large majority of the family's income. If both spouses earn roughly equal incomes, there is a "marriage penalty"; that is, the total tax calculated by filing jointly is greater than if each spouse were allowed to file as a single taxpayer. The Economic Recovery Tax Act (ERTA) of 1981 reduced this "marriage penalty" by providing for an additional deduction of up to $3000 for both itemizing and nonitemizing taxpayers.

5-1.3 income averaging

Other methods exist for calculating an individual's federal income tax. One of these methods is known as *income averaging* and should be used by those individuals enjoying a substantial increase in income over prior years. Most kinds of income are averageable—including capital gains, gambling income, and income from gifts and inheritances. For those taxpayers having unusual fluctuations in income this method of arriving at tax due represents a device to ease somewhat the tax bite in peak income years.

5-1.4 alternative minimum tax

Congress has also devised a method of taxing individuals at a rate greater than those shown in Tables 5-3 and 5-4. The method is known as the *alternative minimum tax* (AMT), which is based on alternative minimum taxable income (AMTI). The alternative minimum tax typically applies only to those individuals with large capital gains or those claiming large tax preferences. The computation method adds back the capital gains deduction (discussed in the next section), certain tax preferences from tax-sheltered investments, the $100/$200 dividend exclusion, and certain itemized deductions, to name just a few. Then, the taxpayer gets a flat deduction of $40,000 if filing a joint return, $30,000 if single, and $20,000 if married and filing separately. The AMT rate is a flat 20 percent of the balance. If the AMT is greater than the tax computed using the rates in Tables 5-3 and 5-4, then the taxpayer is liable for the AMT. The intent of Congress in developing the AMT is to help close the various loopholes in the tax laws—to see that everyone pays a "fair share."

5-1.5 investment interest expense limitation

An additional provision in the tax law, to close a loophole of the active investor, was added to the Internal Revenue Code in 1976. This provision limits the deduction for investment interest paid to $10,000 per year *plus* net investment income. This provision discourages investors from borrowing large sums for investment purposes by denying them the ability to offset the resulting interest expense paid from their ordinary (noninvestment) income. Any unused interest deductions may be carried over to future years when the interest expense limitation does not apply. Note, however, that interest expense paid on home mortgages is not subject to this investment interest expense limitation. However, if the proceeds of a home mortgage are used for investment purposes (such as stocks, bonds, options, etc.), the home mortgage interest then becomes subject to the investment interest expense limitation. The reader may at this point be correctly concluding that the U.S. system of taxation has become extraordinarily convoluted in an effort to achieve equity.

5-1.6 wash sales

The active investor should also be aware of the *wash sale provisions* of the Internal Revenue Code. These provisions prohibit deduction of loss on sale or exchange of stock if substantially similar stock or securities are acquired within 30 days prior to or 30 days subsequent to the sale or exchange. The provisions also apply where the taxpayer enters into a contract or option to acquire substantially similar stock or securities. This limitation applies regardless of whether the taxpayer voluntarily and intentionally sells the stock in order to register a loss for income tax purposes, is forced to sell, or sells in order to prevent a greater loss. The loss of the deduction is only temporary, however, since the basis of the substantially similar stock includes the loss on the stock that was sold and disallowed. Thus, any recognition of loss is postponed until the sale of the new stock.

5-1.7 long-term capital gains taxes at preferential rate

Capital gains and losses arise out of the exchange of capital assets, which include such things as securities and real estate. The sale or exchange of these capital assets may result in *long-term gain or loss* or *short-term gain or loss*, depending upon the length of the holding period. If the capital asset is held for more than 6 months, gain is defined as long-term and is afforded preferential tax treatment.[2] If the capital asset is held 6 months or less, the gain is short-term and receives ordinary income tax treatment.

To compute the amount of tax on capital gains, first combine the amount of long-term capital gains and losses to arrive at a single net long-term capital gain or loss figure. Then combine the amount of short-term capital gains and losses to arrive at a single net short-term capital gain or loss figure. If both long-term and short-term net figures are gains, find the tax on the net short-

[2] Prior to the enactment of the 1984 Tax Reform Act, the long-term capital gain holding period was over 1 year.

term gain at the ordinary income tax rate and the tax on the net long-term gain at the preferred tax rate. If one net figure is a gain and the other is a loss, combine the two and figure the tax using the preferred rate if the net overall capital gain is long-term or the ordinary tax rate if the net overall capital gain is short-term.

Short-term and long-term capital gains are taxed at the same ordinary tax rate. However, 60 percent of a taxpayer's net long-term capital gains are allowed as a deduction (which essentially makes 60 percent of them tax-exempt); this lowers the effective tax rate on long-term gains. The reason for this tax break is to encourage U.S. taxpayers to make long-term investments (rather than be short-term speculators) and thus stimulate the development of the U.S. economy. To see how the capital gains tax works, consider an example.

Suppose Ms. L. T. Investor buys one share of GM stock at $50 a share on February 1 and sells it at $70 a share on March 1 of the next year. This $20 per share capital gain is a long-term gain since she owned the stock for 13 months—that is, more than 6 months. Also, suppose that the stock paid cash dividends of $5 per year while Ms. Investor owned it. Cash dividends are taxed as ordinary income (like salary income). So, the cash dividends are not counted as capital gains. Finally, assume that Ms. Investor is single and earns $15,000 per year of taxable salary income. Table 5-3 shows that she is in the 24 percent tax bracket. Of her $20 per share long-term capital gain, 60 percent of it is excluded from taxable income. If she pays tax at the 24 percent rate, she is taxed on $8 (equals 40 percent of the $20), the taxable portion of the gain, or $1.92 capital gains taxes. This is summarized below.

	$ 70	selling price
Less:	$ 50	buying price
	$ 20	long-term capital gain
Times:	.4	since 60% (or 6⁄10) is tax-exempt
	$ 8	taxable long-term capital gain
Times:	.24	since her tax bracket is 24%
	$1.92	long-term capital gains tax payable

Note that the $1.92 capital gains tax is actually only 9.6 percent (=.096 = $1.92/$20) of Ms. L. T. Investor's $20 gain. In contrast, her ordinary salary income and her $5 dividend incur a 24 percent tax rate—this is why the capital gains tax is called preferential.

As a result of the preferential tax rate, some taxpayers prefer to assume the price change risks associated with securities investments rather than put their money in a riskless, federally insured savings account that pays a guaranteed rate of interest. Interest income is taxed at the higher ordinary income tax rates. Wealthy people who are in high income tax brackets often seek long-term capital gains income instead of ordinary income, for example.

In addition to the capital gains tax, the federal income tax code gives another preferential tax break to the recipients of cash dividends.

5-1.8 cash dividend exclusion

Individual investors may receive up to $100 per year in cash dividends free from federal income tax (or $200 on a joint tax return). However, all cash dividends over this $100 exclusion are taxed as ordinary income. The purpose of this law is to encourage the millions of small individual savers in the United States to buy ownership shares in the U.S. economy.

In addition to the cash dividend exclusion, certain bond interest is also tax-exempt.

5-1.9 tax-exempt municipal bonds

Municipal bonds are bonds issued by municipalities (such as cities and school districts) to raise funds to finance local projects, as previously explained in Chap. 2. The Internal Revenue Code specifies that the interest income from municipal bonds is completely exempt from federal income taxes. The purpose of this tax exemption is to make it easier for municipalities to sell their bonds and thus finance the advancement of their locality. After all, if people were asked to select between a General Motors Corporation bond and a bond issued by the Slippery Rock Sewer System, both paying the same rate of interest, who would buy the municipal bond? Most municipal bonds need the tax-exempt interest as an added incentive to attract investors away from the other competing bond issues. The reason that municipal bond interest is tax-exempt, however, is different. The Constitution of the United States prohibits federal taxation of the states.

For example, consider an investor who is in the 30 percent income tax bracket and is trying to select between a municipal bond and a corporate bond of equivalent riskiness, both of which pay a 10 percent rate of interest. The calculations in the right-hand side of Table 5-5 show that the municipal bond offers (10 percent less 7 percent equals) 3 percentage points more after-tax rate of return than the corporate bond.

Wealthy individuals typically prefer the tax-exempt municipal bonds more than investors with more modest incomes because the wealthy are usually in

TABLE 5-5 comparative after-tax interest rate computations for a municipal and a corporate bond

	before-tax interest rate	after-tax interest rate
Tax-exempt municipal bond	10.0%	10.0%
Taxable corporate bond	10.0%	(1.0 − .3) × 10.0% = 7.0%

TABLE 5-6 after-tax returns to investors in various tax brackets

Tax bracket	32%	36%	39%	42%	45%	48%	50%
after-tax return, %	before-tax return, %						
4.50	6.62	7.03	7.38	7.76	8.18	8.65	9.00
5.00	7.35	7.81	8.20	8.62	9.09	9.62	10.00
5.50	8.09	8.59	9.02	9.48	10.00	10.58	11.00
6.00	8.82	9.37	9.84	10.34	10.91	11.54	<12.00>
6.50	9.56	10.16	10.66	11.21	11.82	12.50	13.00
7.00	10.29	10.94	11.48	12.07	12.73	13.46	14.00
7.50	11.03	11.72	12.30	12.93	13.64	14.42	15.00
8.00	11.76	12.50	13.11	13.79	14.55	15.38	16.00

the higher income tax brackets. In fact, the higher the investor's income tax bracket, the more incentive there is for the investor to seek tax-exempt bond interest. This fact is illustrated in Table 5-6.

The values in Table 5-6 show the after-tax rates of return for investors in different income tax brackets. The table shows, for instance, that an affluent investor in the 50 percent tax bracket must earn a before-tax return of 12 percent in order to get an after-tax return of 6 percent. This 6 percent after-tax return is found by multiplying the 12 percent before-tax return by (1.0 minus the 50 percent tax rate)—these numbers are marked in Table 5-6.

Stated differently, the affluent investor would be just as well off with a municipal bond paying 6 percent interest as with a corporate bond paying 12 percent. Tax shelters for individuals' contributions to their own retirement funds are another example of tax incentive programs to encourage specific personal behavior.

5-2 TAX-SHELTERED RETIREMENT PLANS

Practically all adults save in order to be able to enjoy a few luxuries in their retirement years. Furthermore, the federal government does not want a large pool of elderly people to be suffering because of inadequate retirement funds. For these reasons, several tax-sheltered retirement plans have been passed into law. Although these plans are essentially savings plans, they offer two additional tax incentives. First, the money saved from current income and put in these retirement plans may be deducted from gross income to determine taxable income. That is, appropriately administered retirement savings qualify as a legal tax deduction. Second, the interest income, cash dividends, and any capital gains from retirement funds are not taxable until the taxpayer retires (and typically falls into a lower tax bracket) and actually consumes the retirement funds.

To see how tax-sheltered retirement savings plans work, consider an individual who has $10,700 taxable income. Let's now assume this individual saves $1500 in a tax-sheltered retirement plan. Table 5-7 shows calculations indicating that this retirement saver enjoys an income tax savings of $300 by saving $1500 for his or her own retirement.

TABLE 5-7 tax savings from an individual's $1500 retirement savings

without retirement plan		with retirement plan
$10,700	Taxable income	$10,700
0	Contribution to retirement plan	−1,500
$10,700	Taxable income	$ 9,200
× .20	Assumed average tax rate of 20%	× .20
$ 2,140	Income taxes	$ 1,840
− 1,840	Subtract lesser tax ←	
$ 300	Income tax savings from plan	

There are many different types of tax-sheltered retirement plans. Four of the most popular plans are as follows:

1. Appropriately administered company pension and profit-sharing plans
2. An individual retirement account (IRA hereafter)
3. Keogh plan
4. Tax-sheltered annuity

Each of the four different tax-sheltered retirement plans is discussed briefly below.

5-2.1 retirement plans paid by employers

Most large companies provide some kind of employee pension plan to supplement the employees' wage and salary payments. The employees who receive these pension plan benefits need not pay income taxes on these delayed and indirect forms of compensation until they are retired and receiving their pension payments. Thus, the plans are: (1) tax-sheltered, and (2) paid for by employers.

One of the main reasons firms choose to provide costly pension plans for their employees is to increase the stability of their workforce. Typically, the employee must work for the firm for 10 to 15 years before pension benefits become fully *vested.* Vesting occurs when an employee obtains a legally enforceable claim on pension benefits, which cannot be taken away even if that person resigns or is fired. A federal law called the Pension Reform Act of 1974 governs the vesting procedure. But employees are encouraged to remain on their jobs for at least 10 years in order for their pension benefits to become guaranteed (or vested) even if they change jobs later. Thus, the pension plan presumably helps employers retain more experienced and loyal workers and, in turn, reduces the costs of continually training new employees.

The size of an employee's retirement benefit varies in direct proportion to the income the employee receives as a worker. So, retired presidents receive larger pensions than retired janitors, for instance.

5-2.2 individual retirement accounts (IRA's)

Any individual may establish his or her own personal individual retirement account (IRA). This tax-sheltered retirement plan was established by the Pension Reform Act of 1974, which is also named the Employee Retirement Income Security Act (ERISA). All that an employee need do to set up an IRA is go to a convenient bank, savings and loan association, mutual fund, brokerage firm, or life insurance company, fill out the appropriate forms, and make cash deposits. An individual's IRA contribution is limited to the lesser of $2000 or 100 percent of their compensation each year. IRAs are available to all gainfully employed individuals regardless of how large their annual earnings are or whether or not they are included in their employer's retirement plan.

An IRA participant can make contributions every year, or only occasionally—whenever desired. In order to discourage people from using the IRA as a way to save taxes by using it as a savings account, a penalty of 10 percent is levied on any withdrawals made before the age of 59½ years. In addition to the 10 percent penalty for early withdrawal, the entire amount of the early IRA withdrawal becomes immediately subject to ordinary income taxes. As a result of these fines, IRAs cannot be used as tax shelters for short-run savings; using them for this purpose is considered tax evasion.

When an IRA is established, the participant must select an investment vehicle for his or her tax-sheltered retirement contributions. Some common investments follow:

1. *Common stocks.* Most mutual funds accept IRA contributions.
2. *Bonds.* Most bond mutual funds accept IRA deposits.
3. *Savings Accounts.* Most commercial banks and savings and loan associations offer interest-paying IRA deposit plans.

A variation of the IRA is known as the simplified employee pension (SEP). It is an employer-sponsored type of IRA, covering all eligible employees, whose dollar contribution and withdrawal limits are based on the Keogh plan rules (discussed below).

5-2.3 Keogh plan

A Keogh plan is a tax-sheltered retirement plan similar to an IRA. The main differences involve (1) the size of the allowed contributions, and (2) the source of the worker's income. The Keogh plan is available to *self-employed* people so that they may establish their own pension plans. Keogh plan participants can contribute up to 25 percent of compensation or $30,000 per year, whichever is less. However, Keogh contributions are subject to a 10 percent early withdrawal fine, as with IRA accounts.

Another retirement plan available to certain types of employees is called the 401(k) plan.

5-2.4 401(k) plans

The so-called 401(k) plans were named for the section of the Internal Revenue Code in which they are described. They are becoming widely used. The unique feature of a 401(k) plan is that it allows employees to choose between (1) having their employer contribute a portion of their salary directly to the 401(k) plan, in which case the employees' tax is deferred on that portion of their salary, or (2) electing to have the employer pay the amount directly to them, in which case employees are taxed currently for the total amount. If employees choose to defer receipt of income, they avoid current taxation until they choose to withdraw the funds, presumably at a time when they are in a lower tax bracket. The employer, however, can take a current tax deduction for the payments. This deduction reduces the employer's current taxable income in the usual fashion.

Most employers offer a 401(k) plan under which the employer will match all or a portion of an employee's contributions. For example, for every dollar an employee contributes to a 401(k) plan, the employer may agree to match 50 cents up to some stated limit. Therefore, if Mr. Sam Saver's monthly earnings are $5000 and he chooses to contribute 6 percent per month to his employer's 401(k) plan, he is taxed on $4700 [= $5000 − (.06 × $5000)]. In addition, Sam's employer would contribute $150 per month (= 50% × 6% × $5000). Thus, $450 of untaxed earnings would be contributed monthly to the 401(k) plan in Sam's name. But the principal and income would be taxed in the year of withdrawal. However, the 401(k) plan must be a part of a profit-sharing or stock bonus plan that has been approved by the IRS in order to obtain the tax deferral privilege.

An individual may participate in *both* a 401(k) plan and an IRA. However, if an individual's funds are limited such that only one plan is practically feasible, the 401(k) plan is generally the more favorable option for three reasons: (1) the employee may borrow from the 401(k) plan, (2) the employee may make withdrawals without penalty (for reasons specified in the plan document), and (3) the 401(k) plan allows favorable income tax treatment.

Tax-sheltered annuities provide another retirement plan that certain types of employees should consider.

5-2.5 tax-sheltered annuities

Employees of tax-exempt charitable, educational, and religious organizations and public school teachers can establish their own personal tax-exempt annuities or custodial accounts. An *annuity* is an investment that yields fixed periodic payments during its lifetime. A custodial account is a person's investment portfolio that has been placed under the custody of some money manager such as a bank's trust department or a mutual fund. Employees of nonprofit organizations can contribute up to $30,000 a year to the tax-sheltered annuities or custodial accounts of their choice. All the employees need to do is to fill out the forms so that the money is withheld from their pay and sent to the selected investment by the employer. Early withdrawals are discouraged under this plan, as with the IRAs and Keogh plans.

After a taxpayer reaches retirement age, tax planning should not be discontinued just because the taxpayer may have established a tax-sheltered retirement plan. Estate taxes that must be paid on the value of a deceased person's assets should also be considered. And gift taxes should be considered as well. Both of these taxes are discussed in Sec. 5-3.

5-3 ESTATE AND GIFT TAXES

Estate planning is something that affluent people should do in order to keep their wealth from being taken away by estate taxes and/or gift taxes. The estate tax is discussed first. Next, tax-exempt gifts are suggested as a legal way to reduce estate taxes.

5-3.1 estate (or death) taxes

Although dead people do not have to pay taxes, their estates are taxable. The federal estate tax is progressive so that those who die with substantial riches fall in a higher estate tax bracket than do the moderately wealthy. The estate tax schedule is shown in Table 5-8.

A deceased taxpayer's taxable estate is less than the gross estate because of deductions allowed by the tax law. For married people, the most significant deduction is the marital deduction, which is unlimited. This marital deduction can eliminate estate taxes when the first spouse dies. However, the problem of estate tax minimization remains with the spouse who dies last.

In order to maximize the portion of their estate that heirs may inherit, some people make gifts to eliminate the appreciation in value of the donated assets from their taxable estates. But all gifts are not tax-free—gift taxes are explained in the following section.

5-3.2 gift taxes

Anytime one person gives money to another person without receiving goods or services of equal value in return, the IRS considers this amount to be

TABLE 5-8 unified federal estate and gift tax rates*

(1) over	but not over	tax on (1)	tax rate on excess over (1)
0	10,000	0	18
10,000	20,000	1,800	20
20,000	40,000	3,800	22
40,000	60,000	8,200	24
60,000	80,000	13,000	26
80,000	100,000	18,200	28
100,000	150,000	23,800	30
150,000	250,000	38,800	32
250,000	500,000	70,800	34
500,000	750,000	155,800	37
750,000	1,000,000	248,300	39
1,000,000	1,250,000	345,800	41
1,250,000	1,500,000	448,300	43
1,500,000	2,000,000	555,800	45
2,000,000	2,500,000	780,800	49
2,500,000	3,000,000	1,025,800	53
			**
Over 3,000,000		1,290,800	55

* Lifetime transfers (gifts) and transfers at death are cumulated for the purpose of determining the applicable rate for transfers at death.

** In the case of decedents dying and gifts made in 1988 and thereafter, the maximum transfer rate is scheduled to be 50% on transfers in excess of $2,500,000.

subject to the gift tax laws. The gift tax schedule is shown in Table 5-8; it has been the same as the estate tax schedule since 1976. However, certain moderate-sized gifts are exempt from the gift tax.

Up to $10,000 per individual per year may be given to as many people as the taxpayer desires, without incurring any gift tax. Unlimited amounts may be given to one's spouse tax-free. When the gift giver dies, the deceased person's total taxable gifts are added to the estate and the unified gift tax schedule shown in Table 5-8 is applicable.

The death taxes shown in Table 5-8 apply to the total amount of (1) cumulative taxable gifts given before the donor died, plus (2) the portion of the donor's estate remaining after death. The deceased person's gifts are added to the deceased's estate and taxed in unison in order to stop people from "gifting away" their assets in order to avoid estate taxes. These death taxes are being reduced, however, through what is known as a unified credit. The credit is unified since it applies to the combined amount of an individual's gift taxes and death (estate) taxes.

Table 5-9 shows that in 1984 the first $96,300 of cumulative gift and estate taxes (of more than $10,000 annual exclusion per person) were subject to the unified credit and therefore not payable. The table also shows that this 1984 unified *tax credit* of $96,300 was equivalent to the first $325,000 of the assets in the estate being tax-exempt. These tax credits (and their equivalent estate tax exemptions), according to Table 5-9, increase annually through 1987. This is essentially an annual reduction in gift and estate taxes.

TABLE 5-9 annual changes in unified estate and gift tax credits and equivalent exemptions that apply to amounts in Table 5-8

year	unified tax credit	equivalent asset exemption
1984	$ 96,300	$325,000
1985	$121,800	$400,000
1986	$155,800	$500,000
1987 and after	$192,800	$600,000

Unlike people, corporations may live forever. And even if a corporation dies (that is, goes bankrupt) it incurs no gift or estate taxes. However, corporations must pay taxes on their incomes. Corporations that invest funds are able to enjoy some of the same tax breaks as do individual investors. The federal corporate tax structure is explained in Sec. 5-4.

5-4 FEDERAL CORPORATE INCOME TAXES

Corporations are legal entities that exist to allow the ownership of a firm to be subdivided into shares that are readily transferable. Unlike a proprietorship or a partnership, which are both considered to be extensions of the people who own them, corporations are treated by the law as separate entities. This has unfortunate tax implications because the income earned by corporations is taxed twice. First, the corporation pays corporate income taxes on about half of every dollar of earnings—this is explained in more detail below. Second, the people who own the corporation's shares must also pay federal income taxes on whatever dividends and/or capital gains their shares yield—as explained earlier in this chapter. This *double taxation* not only seems unfair, it also dampens incentive to make corporate investments, which would strengthen the U.S. economy. Looking at the brighter side, however, the corporate income tax rate structure is simple and easy to compute.

5-4.1 the corporate tax structure

A corporation must pay a federal income tax that involves five different tax rates, as listed in Table 5-10. For example, consider a corporation that earns $70,000 of taxable income. This corporation will pay a total federal income tax of $14,250 on this income, as illustrated in Table 5-11.

Corporations' *marginal tax rates* on additional increments of income vary from 15 percent up to 46 percent on each additional dollar of income. The example in Table 5-11 shows that the *average tax rate* on $70,000 of income is

TABLE 5-10 the Federal Corporate Income Tax Law of 1983

1. Corporations must pay 15% of their first $25,000 of income in federal income taxes.
2. Corporations must pay 18% of any income between $25,000 and $50,000 in federal income taxes.
3. Corporations must pay federal income taxes of 30% on income between $50,000 and $75,000.
4. Corporations are taxed at 40% of their income between $75,000 and $100,000.
5. Corporations must pay 46% on all income over $100,000 per year in taxes.

TABLE 5-11 computation of federal corporate income taxes on $70,000 of income

incremental or marginal tax rate	times	portion of total income	equals	portion of total tax
15% = .15	×	$25,000	=	3,750
18% = .18	×	25,000*	=	4,500
30% = .30	×	20,000**	=	6,000
Totals		$70,000		$14,250

Average tax rate $= 20.4 = .204 = \frac{\$14,250}{\$70,000}$

* The amount between the first $25,000 and $50,000.

** The amount over the first $50,000.

20.4 percent. That is, the total taxes of $14,250 are 20.4 percent of the total income of $70,000 when averaged over all three relevant corporate tax brackets. As a result of this averaging over the progressive marginal (or graduated) income tax brackets, the average corporate tax rate starts at the minimum *marginal tax rate* of 15 percent for incomes of $25,000 or less. The *average tax rate* then rises progressively toward the maximum marginal tax rate of 46 percent as the corporation's income increases.

As with the individual income tax, the corporate income tax is subject to various rules that effectively modify the corporate tax rate structure. There are add-on taxes, such as the accumulated earnings tax, personal holding company tax, and minimum tax. There is also a special corporate capital gains tax rate.

5-4.2 accumulated earnings tax

The accumulated earnings tax is a special tax on those corporations choosing to accumulate earnings beyond the "reasonable needs" of the business. The alternative to accumulating income is payment of dividends. Closely held businesses are understandably reluctant to pay dividends when their shareholders are not in need of income from dividend distributions (since the corporate income is then taxed a second time, to the individuals receiving the dividends).

The accumulated earnings tax rate follows:

27½%—on first $100,000

38½%—on balance over $100,000

Congress deems it reasonable for a corporation to accumulate $250,000 per year to provide for future contingencies. Thus, the first $250,000 retained each year in most corporations is above suspicion (the first $150,000 per year for personal service corporations). Amounts accumulated (not paid out in dividends) in excess of these exempt amounts are subject to the accumulated earnings tax at the rates shown above if the corporation cannot demonstrate reasonable needs for such accumulation.

5-4.3 personal holding company tax

Another weapon used by the government to ensure corporate distribution to shareholders is the 50 percent personal holding company tax. To oversimplify, a personal holding company's principal function is the collection of interest, dividends, and other passive income as well as so-called incorporated talents, incorporated country estates, and incorporated yachts. There is no exemption nor reasonable needs test as with the accumulated earnings tax. One hundred percent of undistributed earnings is taxed at 50 percent.

The incentive to accumulate earnings was greater prior to 1982 than it is today. Prior to 1982 the top marginal tax rate for individuals was 70 percent and for corporations 46 percent, resulting in a 24 percent spread. Today the top bracket for individuals is 50 percent and for corporations 46 percent, for a 4 percent spread. The tax penalty for distributing corporate income has thus been substantially reduced.

5-4.4 minimum tax on items of tax preference

A corporation is assessed a minimum tax in addition to its regular tax if its items of tax preference exceed the greater of $10,000 *or* its regular corporate income tax for the year. The rationale behind this add-on tax is the same as for individuals who are subject to the alternative minimum tax—to help ensure that corporations as well as individuals pay their fair share of taxes. Items of tax preference for corporations are similar to those for individuals. They include, but are not limited to, the excess of accelerated depreciation on real property over straight-line depreciation, excess depreciation for pollution control facilities, excess of percentage depletion deductions over adjusted basis, and similar items.

5-4.5 corporate capital gains

Corporate capital gains are taxed at a flat 28 percent rate. Because corporations are not entitled to the 60 percent deduction of the individual taxpayer, corporations realize an advantage from capital gain treatment only if the capital gain is subject to a marginal rate in excess of 28 percent under the regular corporate rate. Thus, as in Table 5-11, a corporation realizing only $50,000 of taxable income in 1984 paid the same tax (namely, $8250 equals 15 percent of $25,000 plus 18 percent of $25,000), whether it was ordinary income, net capital gain, or a combination of the two.

The maximum disparity between the corporate rate on net capital gains and ordinary income is 18 percentage points (28 percent as compared to 46 percent), while for the individual the spread can reach 30 percentage points (20 percent effective maximum capital gain rate versus 50 percent ordinary rate). Nevertheless, corporations probably pursue capital gains as intently as do individuals.

Although the corporate tax rate structure varies significantly from the individual taxpayer's rate structure, there are many similarities in deductions allowed. An explanation of a few key deductions follows in the next sections.

5-4.6 interest expense deduction

As with the individual taxpayer, the corporate taxpayer is also entitled to deduct interest expense. The corporation has the added advantage of not being subject to the individual's interest expense limitation. The ability to deduct interest expense is a critical factor in a corporation's financing decisions. In general, a business may finance expansion either through earnings retention, debt, or equity. If earnings are insufficient, a debt or equity financing decision is required.

Strictly in terms of taxes, financing with debt is superior to equity because of the deductibility of interest and nondeductibility of dividends. Financing with debt gives rise to additional deductions since the costs of issuing debt can be deducted over the term of the indebtedness while the costs of equity financing are nondeductible capital items.

The nondeductibility of dividends not only makes debt financing relatively attractive, it has many other ramifications as well, especially for the closely held corporation. Since salaries and wages are deductible expenses for the corporation, this encourages shareholder-employees to withdraw corporate earnings in the form of salaries rather than nondeductible dividends. Of course, such arrangements are feasible only to the extent compensation paid to shareholder-employees can be justified, according to the IRS, as "a reasonable allowance . . . for personal services actually rendered." Compensation deemed excessive by the IRS will be disallowed and treated as a dividend. Although the possibility of disallowance is omnipresent, especially when earnings fluctuate widely and shareholder earnings are adjusted annually to exhaust the earnings, many closely held businesses still pay out in salaries their entire earnings year-in and year-out. There are other methods by which shareholders may withdraw funds from a corporation that will give rise to a tax deduction at the corporate level. They include interest on shareholder loans to the corporation, rent on property leased by the shareholders to the corporation, and royalties on patents owned by the shareholders and used by the corporation. These transactions, however, must be bona fide business arrangements rather than disguised dividends.

Corporations are also permitted some tax savings on income received from investments in other corporations (called intercorporate cash dividends).

5-4.7 the corporate dividend received deduction

To avoid the possibility of having cash dividend income taxed repeatedly when one corporation owns shares in other corporations, the IRS tax code allows a tax break for *intercorporate dividend payments*. Eighty-five percent of most cash dividends that one corporation receives from other corporations are not taxable.[3] Stated differently, only 15 percent of intercorporate dividends are taxable. Thus, if a corporation in the 46 percent income tax bracket receives cash dividends from another corporation in which it owns shares, the effective tax rate on these intercorporate dividends is only 6.9 percent, as shown below:

(100% − 85% =)	15% = .15	taxable portion
Times:	46% = .46	income tax bracket
	6.9% = .069	effective income tax rate

There is no tax on intercorporate dividends when one corporation owns 80 percent or more of another.

5-4.8 accelerated cost recovery system (ACRS) depreciation deductions

A tax deduction significant to all businesses, particularly capital intensive ones, is depreciation expense. Calculation of depreciation for accounting purposes and for tax purposes is not necessarily the same. This text discusses straight-line and accelerated calculation methods in Chap. 16. Section 16-2 (on page 462) compares the unrealistically rapid *accelerated cost recovery system* (ACRS) depreciation guidelines with the more realistic traditional depreciation schedules. For tax purposes the Economic Recovery Tax Act (ERTA) of

[3] The dividend-received deduction is reduced when the stock is debt-financed.

1981 made depreciation calculation for tax purposes very simple—it provides tables for 3-year, 5-year, 10-year, 15-year, and 18-year life assets.

The taxpayer does have other write-off options, but ACRS provides the fastest ones. The Internal Revenue Code defines such assets as autos, light-duty trucks, machinery and equipment used for research and experimentation, and special tools as 3-year property. Five-year property includes such items as heavy-duty trucks, lathes, most production line equipment, most office furniture, machines and equipment, ships, and aircraft. Ten-year property includes mobile homes, railroad tank cars, and some public utility property. Included in the 15-year category is low-income housing, and the 18-year category includes most other real estate.

Depreciation deductions are valuable to a business not only because they provide tax savings, but also because they create cash inflow from tax savings without a proportional periodic cash outflow. Roughly speaking, depreciation deductions represent a mythical reserve that accumulates to replace the asset that is wearing out. Although businesses rarely establish specific reserves for asset replacement, the Internal Revenue Code recognizes and provides for this need. The deduction is also a congressional tool to adjust for the needs of the economy: more liberal deductions to stimulate the economy (through capital infusion) and more restrictive deductions to rein in an "overactive economy." Another tool that congress uses to achieve economic goals through capital expansion/contraction is the use of the investment tax credit.

5-4.9 investment tax credit (ITC)

Congressional intent in devising the investment tax credit was clearly to achieve economic goals. Elementary macroeconomic courses emphasize the force of capital spending by business as a method of stimulating the economy. The investment tax credit is an ingenious device to help achieve such goals. Very simply, businesses are allowed a credit (that is, a deduction from their tax liability) of up to 10 percent of the cost of qualifying capital expenditures. The rules are somewhat complicated, but the general rule is that up to 10 percent credit is allowed for a taxpayer's investment in tangible personal property and certain other tangible property but not for buildings and structural components of buildings. Both new and used property can qualify. The estimated useful life of the property at the time it is placed in service determines the percentage of the basis of the new property (up to $125,000 of the cost of used property) considered to be a qualified investment. The useful life for investment credit purposes must be the same as the useful life used in computing the depreciation allowance. Percentages applied to the qualified investment for ACRS property are: 100 percent for 5-year, 10-year, and 15-year property, and 60 percent for 3-year recovery property. In addition, there are some restrictions built into the Internal Revenue Code to prevent abuse of the significant tax advantages the investment tax credit offers.

5-5 INVESTMENT AND TAXATION

The obvious question is "How should I manage my investments so as to minimize tax payments?" In view of the numerous tax laws described earlier

Box 5-1
a good tax strategy for many investors

> Don't liquidate assets that are accumulating capital gains as long as they continue to gain. However, when an investment turns bad and starts losing, realize the loss as quickly as possible by selling the loser.

in this chapter, you might expect that it would be impossible to give one simple answer to this question. While it is true that one simple tax strategy that will minimize each investor's tax payments cannot be articulated, one simple rule of considerable applicability and value is shown in Box 5-1.

The tax strategy recommended above is a buy-and-hold strategy that was extended to include a provision for the speedy recognition of losses. The buy-and-hold policy for investments that are gaining in value is predicated on the long-term capital gains preferential tax rate, combined with an obvious reluctance to liquidate a good investment. There is no reason to sell an investment if (1) you expect continued capital gains, (2) holding the asset a little longer will qualify it to be taxed at the lower tax rate on long-term capital gains, or (3) both 1 and 2 are true. Furthermore, the buy-and-hold strategy will minimize the brokerage commissions that accompany every buy or sell transaction. And whatever capital gains taxes must be paid can be put off until the sale actually occurs.

In contrast to the buy-and-hold-the-gainers strategy, it is usually wise to sell investments that register disappointing losses as quickly as possible. Losers should be liquidated hastily for two reasons: to stop the losses from increasing, and to recognize the losses in the short term (that is, 1 year or less) so that they may be written off against ordinary income and thus reduce the tax bill. This latter portion of the recommended strategy is called *taking advantage of tax losses.*

5-6 SUMMARY AND CONCLUSIONS

Both private individuals and corporate entities are required by law to pay progressive income taxes in the United States. However, the capital gains from long-term investments are taxed at a lower rate in order to encourage investing behavior. Gift and estate taxes, which are also progressive, encourage estate planning in order to avoid making Uncle Sam a partner in the distribution of accumulated wealth. Also, various tax-deferred pension plans are available to encourage private individuals to plan for their own retirement.

The preceding outline of federal taxes may elicit three different reactions. First, the laws seem unfair; that is, they distribute the tax burden over different classes of taxpayers in such a way as to hurt certain groups and benefit other groups. Some possible solutions to this problem are usually examined in a full-semester course in welfare economics.

A second common response to the tax laws is that the tax system seems overpowering. The complex array of tax regulations requires specialized training in order to operate under them without overpaying. This problem can be overcome by hiring a tax accountant.[4]

A third common reaction to the tax laws is the belief that taxes are simply too high. One result is a large and growing "subterranean economy" of tax evaders who work for income they do not report to the federal government.[5] This is a problem for the United States that can be overcome by lowering the income tax rates. In any event, analysis of these problems is beyond the scope of this text.

QUESTIONS

1. Name three allowable deductions from adjusted gross income in arriving at a person's taxable income; a corporation's taxable income.
2. Assume the taxable income (not including capital gains and losses) of Mr. and Mrs. Taylor, filing a joint return, is $20,000. The Taylors, during the taxable year, also incurred $5000 in long-term capital gains, $3000 in short-term capital gains, $2000 in long-term capital losses, and $1000 in short-term capital losses. Figure the Taylors' tax due, assuming no other deductions or unusual circumstances.
3. How is the corporate federal income tax rate structured?
4. Jack Lind has a marginal tax rate of 48 percent and must choose between a tax-free municipal bond paying 9 percent and a taxable security paying 15 percent. Assuming all other factors are equal, which security should he choose? Why?
5. What are the major benefits from investing in an IRA or a Keogh plan?
6. What are the disadvantages of investing in an IRA plan? A Keogh plan?
7. What is the difference between marginal and average tax rates?
8. Compare and contrast the effects on investor behavior that result from the difference between long-term capital gains and short-term capital gains.
9. Do you believe that the tax schedule should be graduated (or progressive), as it is in the United States? Explain.
10. What is meant by a "wash sale"? What is its effect on an individual's taxable income?
11. What are the tax rates imposed by the accumulated earnings tax and the personal holding company tax? What is the reason for levying these additional taxes on corporations?

[4] This chapter presents only a thumbnail sketch of the federal tax laws in the United States. Many details were omitted to make for easier reading. The state taxes were ignored completely because they are much smaller than the federal taxes. As a result, this chapter cannot be used to train tax experts. There are many college-level tax accounting courses that must be mastered in order to become a tax expert.

[5] Peter M. Gutmann, "The Subterranean Economy," *Financial Analysts Journal*, November–December 1977; P. M. Gutmann, "Are the Unemployed, Unemployed?" *Financial Analysts Journal*, September–October 1978; P. M. Gutmann, "The Subterranean Economy Five Years Later," *Across the Board* (the Conference Board Magazine), vol. 20, no. 2, February 1983.

12. Assume that Countessa Corporation had ordinary taxable income of $100,000 and capital gains income of $20,000. Also assume Countessa Corporation purchased a $16,000 automobile to be used in its business, subject to the full investment tax credit (depreciation expense was deducted in arriving at ordinary taxable income). What is Countessa's final tax liability?

SELECTED REFERENCES

Bittker, Boris, and James A. Eustice, *Federal Income Taxation of Corporations and Shareholders* (Warren, Gorham & Lamont, Boston, 1979).

Kess, Sidney, and Bertil Westin, *Estate Planning Guide* (Commerce Clearing House, 1977). A comprehensive analysis of estate planning for most types of situations; includes the changes in planning techniques resulting from the 1976 Tax Reform Act.

Prentice-Hall, *Federal Tax Course* (Prentice-Hall, Englewood Cliffs, N.J., 1983). A comprehensive text, revised annually, that explains with numerous examples the tax law.

U.S. Treasury Department, Internal Revenue Service, *A Guide to Federal Estate and Gift Taxation,* Publication 44B (Government Printing Office, Washington, D.C.). A concise summary of federal estate and gift taxes. Examples are sparse; legal terms are plentiful.

U.S. Treasury Department, Internal Revenue Service, *Tax Guide for Small Business,* Publication 334 (Government Printing Office, Washington, D.C., annual). Explains the tax laws that apply to businesses, including sole proprietorships, partnerships, and corporations.

U.S. Treasury Department, Internal Revenue Service, *Your Federal Income Tax,* Publication 17 (Government Printing Office, Washington, D.C., annual). Explains many specific problems and gives examples.

APPENDIX 5A

the taxation of hedges, futures contracts, short sales, and options

This appendix sketches the way hedges (see Chaps. 21, 22, and 23), futures contracts (Chaps. 22 and 23), and short sales (Chaps. 21, 22, and 23) are taxed.

APP. 5A-1 TAXATION OF HEDGES AND COMMODITY FUTURES CONTRACTS

The general rule governing regulated futures contracts states that contracts that have not been closed by year's end *must* be treated as if sold on the last day of the tax year, and the amount of any gain or loss is to be determined by the contract's fair market value on that last day. (Any gain or loss from a prior year is reflected to avoid double taxation.) Capital gain or loss is treated as if:

(1) 40 percent of the gain or loss is short-term capital gain or loss, and (2) 60 percent of the gain or loss is long-term gain or loss. This tax treatment represents a 32 percent maximum effective tax rate.

Hedging transactions, typically entered into by a taxpayer to reduce the risk of price changes, interest rate changes, or currency fluctuations, are treated as ordinary gains or losses.

Commodity futures contracts on financial instruments such as Treasury bills are determined to be capital assets or noncapital assets according to the rules on hedges and commodity futures transactions as outlined above. The commodities futures tax rules extend to index contracts as well—that is, futures on financial indices such as the Standard and Poor's 500 index. These futures contracts on stock indices, as well as options on index futures, receive the same treatment enjoyed by commodities futures contracts—a 32 percent maximum effective tax rate.[6]

APP. 5A-2 TAXATION OF SHORT SALES AND OPTIONS

Those individuals entering into transactions in which they sell securities short normally incur a short-term capital gain or loss. Although it is theoretically possible to incur a long-term capital gain or loss, it happens rarely and the circumstances are sufficiently complex to be beyond the scope of this text. However, the gain or loss is capital (not ordinary) if the asset used to close the short sale is capital, which is typically the case.

The writer (issuer) of put and/or call options incurs a capital gain when the buyer fails to exercise his or her option. Since options are normally written for short terms, the gain is short-term. When a put or call is exercised, the writer (issuer) applies the premium he or she received to adjust the cost basis of the securities purchased.

The holder (purchaser) of the put or call realizes a capital loss when the option is not exercised. If the option is exercised, however, the cost of the call option is included in determining the total cost basis of the underlying security. When a put is exercised and the holder sells the shares named in it, the cost of the "put" is offset against the amount received for the stock.

[6] For specific information about income taxes on financial futures contracts, see Jude P. Zwick, "Federal Income Tax Considerations," in Nancy H. Rothstein (ed.), *The Handbook of Financial Futures* (New York: McGraw-Hill, 1983). Also see F. A. Ernst and J. P. Tyrrell, "Taxation of Commodity Transactions," chap. 6 in Perry J. Kaufman (ed.), *Handbook of Futures Markets* (New York: Wiley-Interscience, 1984).

CHAPTER 6 sources of financial information

This chapter describes various sources of financial news and information. These sources are useful to professional financial analysts and amateurs alike. Studying the information sources described in this chapter can give investors insights and broaden their exposure to valuable information.

Usually, an investment inquiry should begin with an inquiry into *world affairs*. Wars, epidemics, international tensions—all affect nations' economies and securities markets. A financial analyst should develop a picture of world conditions and then an estimate of the impact of these conditions on the *national economy*. At that point, the analyst can focus on *specific industries*. Labor negotiations, changes in legislation, sales, and the competition within the industry must be considered. Only after all this background investigation has been completed is the financial analyst ready to examine a particular *firm*. Obviously, a good financial analyst must consult many sources of news and other information.

The remainder of this chapter discusses information sources about world affairs, national economies, industries, and industrial firms—in that order. Computer facilities that may be used to assist economists and financial analysts are discussed at the end of the chapter.

6-1 WORLD AFFAIRS

Two extremely useful financial newspapers are *The New York Times* and *The Wall Street Journal.* These papers carry complete and current reports on political and economic conditions around the world.[1]

[1] *The Economist* and the *Financial Times* are international newspapers published in London that are useful to international investors. They are both very expensive, however, costing about $300 per year for delivery in the United States.

6-1.1 The New York Times

The New York Times (NYT) is a daily newspaper noted for its objective coverage—"All the news that's fit to print" is the *NYT*'s slogan. The *NYT* has a large business and financial section toward the back of every edition that some people judge to be superior to those of some purely business newspapers. This section reports financial news, market data from various markets, and stories about individual firms and industries. With the exception of certain regular features, the *NYT* carries much of the same financial news as *The Wall Street Journal.* The *NYT*'s coverage of world affairs is probably better than that of any other paper in the United States.

6-1.2 The Wall Street Journal

The Wall Street Journal (WSJ) is published 5 days a week. It is written for a national audience interested in finance and, in particular, investments.[2] The *WSJ* reports world, national, and financial news and news about industries and firms. It also reports the opinions of economists and various financial experts about the course of future events.

Regular *WSJ* items useful to investors include feature-length articles and columns such as "Outlook," "Labor Letter," "Tax Report," "Insider Information," "Dividend News," "Earnings Digest," "Heard on the Street," "Abreast of the Market," and "Bond Markets." The paper also reports price and volume data daily for assets traded on the NYSE, AMEX, the OTC markets, the bond markets, foreign exchange markets, the options exchanges, and other financial markets.[3]

The *NYT* tends to do a better job than the *WSJ* when it comes to reporting world affairs and money market facts. The *WSJ* tends to top the *NYT* in its reporting of individual companies. However, both these newspapers report facts that affect the decisions of American businesspeople. Additional facts about world affairs and how they affect American business interests are reported in newsletters published by large U.S. commercial banks and federal government departments.

6-1.3 Barron's

Barron's is a weekly financial newspaper that makes no attempt to report world, national, or local news. *Barron's* "Statistical Section" typically fills about half this 50-page newspaper; it includes security price and volume quotations, mutual fund statistics, commodity market data, the "Market Laboratory," the "Pulse of Industry and Trade," and other compilations of market data. The title "Statistical Section" can be misleading, however, because only raw data are published.

[2] Subscriptions to the *WSJ* cost $63 per year for second-class postage delivery to your door. Instructors interested in using the *WSJ* in class may contact Educational Service Bureau, Dow Jones & Company, P.O. Box 300, Princeton, N.J. 08540, for information about student subscription programs and various free teaching materials.

[3] Dow Jones & Company publishes the *WSJ* and *Barron's* financial newspapers and prepares the Dow Jones Industrial Average, the Dow Jones Transportation Average, and the Dow Jones Utility Average. These three averages are very popular and receive wide coverage through the Dow Jones & Company newspapers.

6-2 NATIONAL AFFAIRS

Price movements of most securities are highly attributable to movement in the price level of the entire securities market. Thus, if the level of market indices can be forecast, much information about the future prices of most securities will be provided. Changes in market indices tend to precede changes in the national economy by 2 to 6 months and sometimes more. Thus, forecasting the level and direction of the national economy accurately a year in advance is extremely useful in predicting the direction of security price movements.[4] Some large banks publish economic forecasts that can be useful.

6-2.1 bank newsletters

Certain large banks publish newsletters on economic conditions. Reports in these newsletters usually focus on the general economic outlook, and they also often refer to the expected effects of economic changes on the securities market. Chase Manhattan Bank's *Business in Brief*, the Bank of New York's *General Business Indicators*, Citibank's *Monthly Economic Letter*, and Morgan Guaranty Trust Company of New York's *Morgan Guaranty Survey* are available free upon request. A short letter to these banks' Economic Research Department is all that is needed.

The *Federal Reserve Bulletin* is a monthly summary of economic data published by the Federal Reserve Board.[5] The bulletin is one of the handiest sources of raw economic data on many topics. The St. Louis Federal Reserve Bank also publishes weekly and monthly economic newsletters that it sends to subscribers and that contain some of the best monetary economic analyses available to the public, and they are free of charge.[6]

These bank newsletters are easy to read. Graphs and tables of numbers may be included, but mathematics and technical terms are used sparingly. The Federal Reserve Board also sells the *Historical Chart Book* and the *Monthly Chart Book* for $1.25 per copy. Each of these publications contains over 100 pages of readable charts of economic and financial data.

6-2.2 U.S. government publications

Several summaries of macroeconomic data may be obtained from U.S. government sources. These sources contain information that can be used in forecasting.

The U.S. Department of Commerce publishes monthly the *Survey of Current Business (SCB)*. The first part of the *SCB* consists of an evaluation of business conditions and developments. The second part contains a statistical summary covering prices, wages, production, business activity, and many other factors. There are also weekly statistical updates.

The Department of Commerce also publishes a summary of the *SCB* data in *Long-Term Economic Growth (LTEG)*. *LTEG* is published by the department's

[4] Geoffrey H. Moore, *Business Cycles, Inflation, and Forecasting,* National Bureau of Economic Research Study Number 24 (Ballinger Publishing Company, Cambridge, Mass., 1980), pp. 187–202.

[5] Annual subscriptions cost $20 and may be obtained by writing to the Division of Administrative Services, Board of Governors of the Federal Reserve System, Washington, D.C. 20551.

[6] For subscriptions, write to the Federal Reserve Bank of St. Louis, P.O. Box 442, St. Louis, MO 63166.

HOW TO READ CHARTS

Basic Data

(Dec.) (Nov.) (Nov.) (Mar.)
P T P T

Peak (P) of cycle indicates end of expansion and beginning of recession (shaded area) as designated by NBER.

Solid line indicates monthly data. (Data may be actual monthly figures or moving averages.)

Broken line indicates actual monthly data for series where a moving average is plotted.

Solid line with plotting points indicates quarterly data.

Parallel lines indicates a break in continuity (data not available, extreme value, etc.).

Trough (T) of cycle indicates end of recession and beginning of expansion as designated by NBER.

Arabic number indicates latest month for which data are plotted. ("9" = September)

Dotted line indicates anticipated data.

Roman number indicates latest quarter for which data are plotted. ("IV" = fourth quarter)

Various scales are used to highlight the patterns of the individual series. "Scale A" is an arithmetic scale, "scale L-1" is a logarithmic scale with 1 cycle in a given distance, "scale L-2" is a logarithmic scale with two cycles in that distance, etc.

9
Scale L-2
90
80
70
60
50
40
IV
Scale L-1½
140
120
100
80

Diffusion Indexes

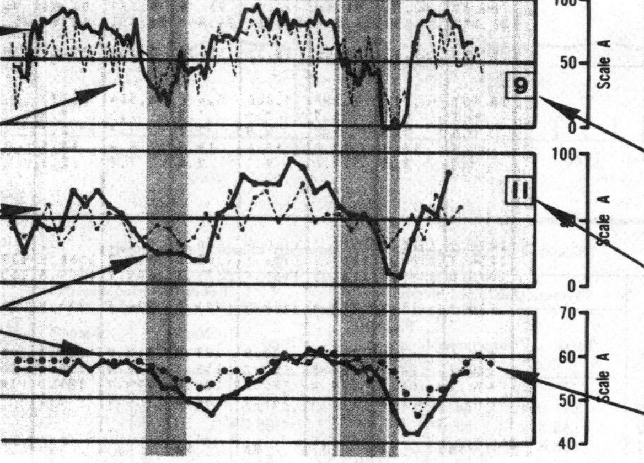

Solid line indicates monthly data over 6- or 9-month spans.

Broken line indicates monthly data over 1-month spans.

Broken line with plotting points indicates quarterly data over 1-quarter spans.

Solid line with plotting points indicates quarterly data over various spans.

Diffusion indexes and rates of change are centered within the spans they cover.

Arabic number indicates latest month for which data are used in computing the indexes.

Roman number indicates latest quarter for which data are used in computing the indexes.

Dotted line indicates anticipated quarterly data over various spans.

Rates of Change

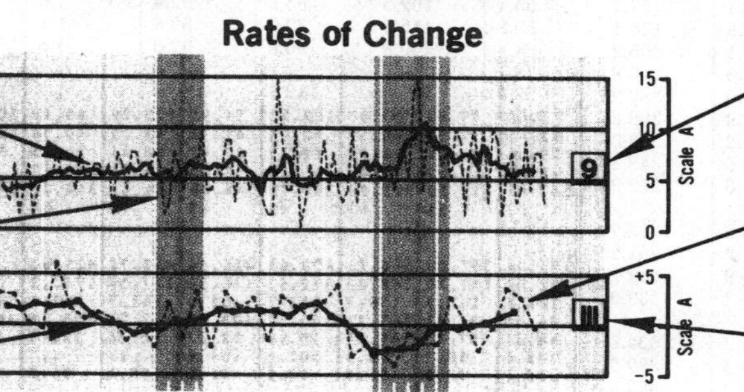

Solid line indicates percent changes over 3- or 6-month spans.

Broken line indicates percent changes over 1-month spans.

Solid line with plotting points indicates percent changes over 3- or 4-quarter spans.

Arabic number indicates latest month used in computing the changes.

Broken line with plotting points indicates percent changes over 1-quarter spans.

Roman number indicates latest quarter used in computing the changes.

FIGURE 6-1 explanation of charts in *Business Conditions Digest* (*BCD*).

GROSS PRIVATE DOMESTIC INVESTMENT

According to revised estimates for the second quarter, business fixed investment rose $23.3 billion (annual rate) and residential investment outlays rose $4.5 billion. There was a $48.5 billion increase in inventories following an increase of $73.8 billion in the first quarter.

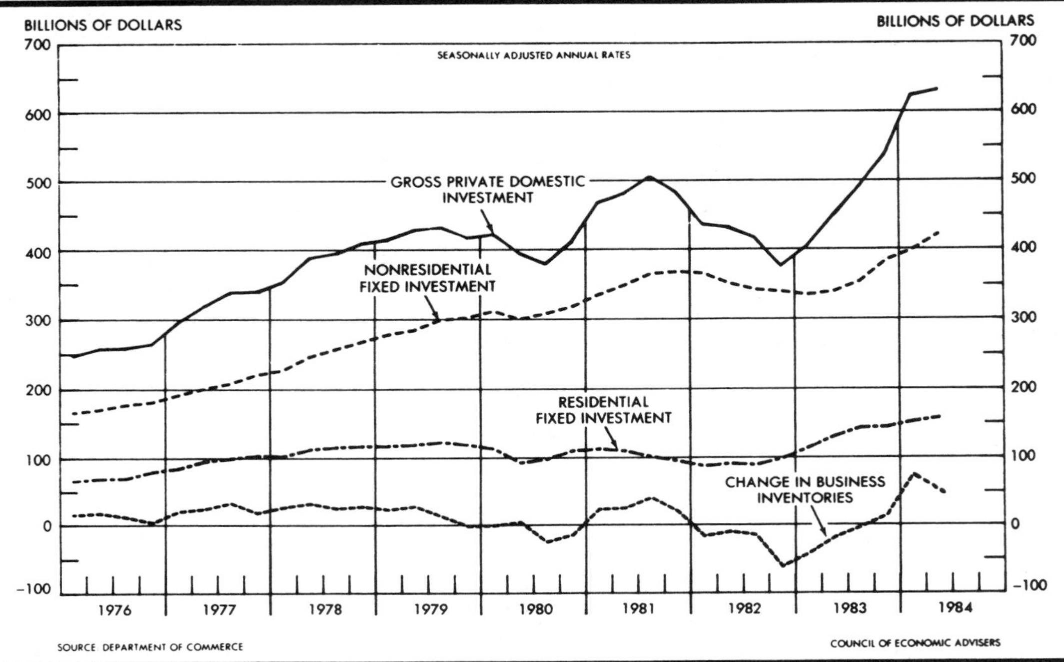

[Billions of dollars; quarterly data at seasonally adjusted annual rates]

Period	Gross private domestic investment	Nonresidential fixed investment			Residential fixed investment				Change in business inventories	
		Total	Structures	Producers' durable equipment	Total	Nonfarm structures	Farm structures	Producers' durable equipment	Total	Nonfarm
1972	195.0	121.0	44.1	76.9	63.8	61.5	0.7	1.5	10.2	9.6
1973	229.8	143.3	51.0	92.3	68.0	65.6	.7	1.7	18.5	15.2
1974	228.7	156.6	55.9	100.7	57.9	54.8	1.3	1.8	14.1	16.0
1975	206.1	157.7	55.4	102.3	55.3	52.4	1.0	1.9	−6.9	−10.5
1976	257.9	174.1	58.8	115.3	72.0	68.8	1.1	2.1	11.8	13.9
1977	324.1	205.2	64.4	140.8	95.8	92.0	1.5	2.3	23.0	21.9
1978	386.6	248.9	78.7	170.2	111.2	107.0	1.7	2.5	26.5	25.4
1979	423.0	290.2	98.3	191.9	118.6	114.0	1.7	2.9	14.3	8.6
1980	401.9	308.8	110.9	197.9	102.9	98.1	1.8	3.0	−9.8	−4.5
1981	484.2	353.9	135.3	218.6	104.3	99.8	1.3	3.2	26.0	18.2
1982	414.9	349.6	142.1	207.5	91.4	86.6	1.5	3.3	−26.1	−24.0
1983	471.6	352.9	129.7	223.2	132.2	127.6	1.0	3.6	−13.5	−3.1
1982: I	436.2	365.7	148.8	216.9	87.5	83.4	1.0	3.2	−17.0	−20.9
II	431.2	351.2	142.7	208.5	90.9	85.9	1.7	3.3	−10.9	−9.5
III	415.9	342.2	138.4	203.8	89.0	84.5	1.3	3.3	−15.3	−11.1
IV	376.2	339.3	138.4	201.0	97.9	92.5	2.1	3.3	−61.1	−54.3
1983: I	405.0	334.6	130.4	204.2	113.3	108.9	1.0	3.4	−42.9	−32.6
II	449.6	339.3	125.6	213.6	129.8	125.3	.9	3.5	−19.4	−5.4
III	491.9	353.9	126.2	227.8	142.3	137.7	.9	3.7	4.3	11.6
IV	540.0	383.9	136.6	247.3	143.4	138.7	.9	3.8	12.7	14.1
1984: I	623.8	398.8	142.2	256.7	151.2	146.4	.9	3.9	73.8	60.6
II [r]	626.4	422.1	151.2	271.0	155.7	150.6	1.1	4.0	48.5	44.7

NOTE.—Series beginning 1981 are as revised in July issue of *Economic Indicators*.

Source: Department of Commerce, Bureau of Economic Analysis.

FIGURE 6-2 sample page from *Economic Indicators*.

Census Bureau and contains over 250 pages of numerous time series relating to economic conditions.[7]

The National Bureau of Economic Research (NBER) studies business cycles by using its widely publicized indicators. Its findings are published by the Census Bureau. Each month *Business Conditions Digest (BCD)* publishes the NBER's table of economic indicators and charts their values, along with other business data.[8] The 30 leading indicators, 15 coincidental indicators, 7 lagging indicators, and 7 international comparisons are given in the first part of the issue, along with other economic information and primary data. The final section of *BCD* examines trends, cyclical indicators, and other data. Figure 6-1 shows how to read the charts in *BCD*, and Figures 13-3 and 15-2, on pages 378 and 430, respectively, contain excerpts from the type of graphs published in *BCD*.[9]

The President's Council of Economic Advisors publishes the monthly *Economic Indicators*,[10] which is a compendium of time series and graphs, and the *Annual Economic Review*. Figure 6-2 shows a page from *Economic Indicators*.

The Federal Trade Commission and the SEC publish the *Quarterly Financial Report for Manufacturing Corporations*,[11] which contains aggregate balance sheet and income statement information for all manufacturing corporations. The categories "profits per dollar sales" and "annual rate of profit on stockholder's equity at end of period" are shown by industry and by asset size. If you are comparing different industries, this information can be quite helpful.

Most government publications are oriented toward the national economy and the effects of its cycles and other fluctuations on various industries. Such information is useful to the investor in predicting the impact of future movements of the economy on security prices.

6-3 INVESTMENT INFORMATION SERVICES

Syntheses of fundamental financial information about industries and individual firms are published by investment information services. Such firms offer subscriptions to their daily, weekly, and monthly publications. The cost of a subscription is deductible from an investor's income, according to federal personal income-tax regulations. Large public libraries usually carry the publications of one or more of these services, which may be consulted free of charge. The leading services are as follows:

[7] *SCB* and *LTEG* may be obtained from the Superintendent of Documents, U.S. Government Printing Office, Washington, D.C. 20402. Subscriptions to the *SCB* are $35 per year. *LTEG* costs $3.75 per copy.

[8] A 1-year subscription to *BCD* costs $44 in the United States and $55 in foreign countries. Write to Superintendent of Documents. See footnote 7 for the address.

[9] In viewing the various exhibits in this chapter, it is important to remember that these examples are invalid (and, in some cases, might even make counterproductive investment recommendations) when they become outdated. When making investment decisions, it is always wise to have the most recent and complete information available upon which to base the decisions.

[10] Subscriptions to *Economic Indicators* are $19.50 per year. Write to Superintendent of Documents. See footnote 7 for the address.

[11] Subscriptions are $14; write to Superintendent of Documents. See footnote 7 for address.

Standard & Poor's Corporation (owned by McGraw-Hill)
25 Broadway
New York, N.Y. 10004

Moody's Investors Services, Inc. (owned by Dun & Bradstreet)
99 Church Street
New York, N.Y. 10007

The Value Line Investment Survey (owned by Arnold Bernhard & Co.)
711 Third Avenue
New York, N.Y. 10017

Most of Standard & Poor's and Moody's information is based on the reference volumes *S&P Corporation Records* and *Moody's Industrial Manuals*. *Moody's Industrial Manuals* are thick, bound volumes that give complete investment data for a period of years and the financial history of hundreds of companies. They are specialized: there are different books for industrial, transportation, utility, bank and financial, and government securities. Unlike Moody's manuals, *S&P Corporation Records* are arranged alphabetically by the names of the companies rather than by industry. Frequent bulletins keep the six-volume set of *S&P Corporation Records* up to date. Twice weekly, Moody publishes a report to keep its manuals current.

6-3.1 Standard & Poor's

Standard & Poor's (S&P) massive *S&P Corporation Records* discusses the affairs of each company listed, using the following topic headings: Capitalization and Long-term Debt; Corporate Background, with such subheadings as sales backlogs, subsidiaries, affiliates, principal properties, capital expenditures, employees, officers, directors, and executive offices; Bond Descriptions, with such subheadings as trustee, purpose of issue, sinking fund, redemptions, security, dividend restrictions, and price range; Stock Data, with such subheadings as voting power, capital changes, capital stock offered through rights, stock issued under convertibles, capital stock sold, stockholders, transfer agent, listings, and dividends; and Earnings and Finances, with such subheadings as auditors, consolidated earnings statements, adjusted earnings, quarterly sales, property account analysis, maintenance and repairs, consolidated income statement, and consolidated balance sheet.

The Outlook is a weekly publication of S&P. It surveys market conditions and recommends common stocks to investors. It also contains special articles, reports on individual firms, discussions of stocks currently in favor, a report on overall business conditions, a market forecast and recommendations, and sometimes a "stock for action." A special annual issue of *The Outlook* is published with a forecast for the coming year. This forecast is divided into such categories as best low-priced stocks, candidates for dividend increases, rapid growth stocks for long-term profits, and stocks for action in the year ahead. Figure 6-3 shows a sample page of investment recommendations from *The Outlook*. In addition to investment recommendations, market index data are published in both tabular and graphical form. Figure 7-1 on page 177 shows some market indices from *The Outlook*. The major Standard & Poor's stock price indices are illustrated graphically in Figure 10-1 on page 253. Standard & Poor's also publishes an annual paperback book, *Security Price Index Record*, that contains data back to 1928 for all 90 of the Standard &

Group 1: Foundation stocks for long-term gain

These issues are basic building blocks for a portfolio. They offer the prospect of long-term appreciation, along with moderate but growing income. The investor seeking to build an estate should start with stocks from this list, augmenting them with issues from other groups according to one's objectives and temperament.

Earnings Per Share ($) 1983	E1984	E1985	Indicated Div. $	1982-84 Price Range	Recent Price	P/E Ratio	Yield %		Annual Growth Rates —for Latest 5 Years— Sales	Earn.	Div.	▼Price Action vs. Mkt. 11-28-80 to 8-12-82	Since 8-12-82	Listed Options Traded	Last Page Ref.
4.31	A5.95	7.00	2.60	71 1/2-23 5/8	60	8.6	4.3	Assoc. Dry Gds. (Jan.)	20%	16%	7%	1.86	1.21	..	645
3.95	4.40	4.70	2.20	44 7/8-27 3/4	39	8.3	5.6	CPC Int'l	4	6	11	1.35	0.76	..	599
1.50	↓3.40	4.00	1.80	39 -19 5/8	28	7.0	6.4	Dow Chemical	8	−18	10	0.81	0.90	C	645
3.01	A3.40	↓3.80	1.40	42 1/2-15 1/4	42	11.1	3.3	Heinz (H.J.) (Apr.)	11	16	15	1.58	1.52	..	711
9.04	10.75	12.50	3.80	134 1/4-48 3/4	125	10.0	3.0	•Int'l Business Machines	14	11	4	1.29	1.22	C	711
5.22	A5.35	↓5.50	2.60	63 1/4-38 7/8	57	10.4	4.6	•Procter & Gamble (Jun.)	13	11	12	1.68	0.82	A	711
3.73	4.25	5.00	1.20	78 1/2-30	45	9.0	2.7	Schlumberger Ltd.	17	19	22	0.55	0.80	C	599
7.23	7.85	8.50	2.44	55 3/8-20 1/2	49	5.8	5.0	•Security Pacific	12	9	10	1.32	1.31	..	545
5.20	[1]5.20	5.40	1.85	39 5/8-19 7/8	38	7.0	4.9	Sonat Inc.	22	17	20	0.97	0.94	..	599

Group 2: Stocks with promising growth prospects

These stocks promise to enjoy well above average growth rates in earnings per share for the foreseeable future. Although most of the issues command relatively high P/E ratios, the premiums are, in our view, justified. Income is not a consideration here.

Earnings Per Share ($) 1983	E1984	E1985	Indicated Div. $	1982-84 Price Range	Recent Price	P/E Ratio	Yield %		Latest 5-Year Growth Rates Sales	Earn.	No. of Earn. Gains '78-'83	Interim ■Earn. Trend	▼Price Action vs. Mkt. 11-28-80 to 8-12-82	Since Aug. 12, '82	Listed Options Traded	Last Page Ref.
2.86	3.35	3.70	1.20	53 3/8-25 3/8	43	11.6	2.8	Abbott Laboratories	15%	18%	5	+18%	1.51	0.91	Ph	699
3.00	3.45	3.95	1.60	50 3/8-25 3/8	46	11.6	3.5	•Bristol-Myers	10	14	5	+17	1.70	1.01	C	583
4.37	5.20	6.25	2.30	70 1/2-39 7/8	68	10.9	3.4	•Emerson El. (Sept.)	10	9	5	+16	1.96	0.76	A	635
1.47	A1.74	2.10	0.44	32 3/8- 9 7/8	22	10.5	2.0	Nat'l Med. Ent. (May)	51	29	5	+16	1.08	1.18	A	635
†2.05	†2.70	†3.15	†0.40	49 1/8-10 7/8	38	15.9	0.8	•Northern Telecom	1.	..	4	+17	1.62	2.09	T	595
3.85	A4.08	4.40	1.60	62 1/2-28 5/8	46	10.5	3.5	Syntex (July)	19	25	5	− 2	1.62	0.75	C	583
1.74	2.60	3.25	1.24	38 1/4-19 1/8	32	9.8	3.9	•Thomas & Betts	7	−2	4	+52	1.03	1.01	...	583
1.09	A1.25	1.70	0.20	36 7/8-10 11/16	29	17.1	0.7	•Unitrode Corp. (Jan.)	29	26	5	+27	0.87	1.37	...	635

A bullet (•) before the name of a stock in the group indicates that the issue is currently considered to be among the best situated in the group.

*↑Upward change in earnings estimate or dividend rate since last publication of the Master List; ↓downward change. E-Estimated. A-Actual. *Of following year.*

Listed options traded: C-Chicago Board Options Exchange; A-American Stock Exchange; Pac-Pacific Stock Exchange; Ph-Philadelphia Stock Exchange; T-Toronto Stock Exchange.

Price/Earnings Ratios are based on latest shown estimated or actual earnings.

▼A figure above 1.0 indicates that the stock outperformed the S&P industrial stock price index in this period. It is computed by taking the ratio of the stock's price at the end of the period vs. the beginning of the period and dividing it by the corresponding ratio of the index. The time periods covered are updated periodically to conform to the latest major market cycle.

■This column compares share earnings of the latest six months with those of the corresponding year-earlier period.

††This figure shows the degree to which the stock's dividend and price change offset the sharp increase in the consumer price index in the five years through 1983. A figure of 1.0 would indicate that the impact of inflation was completely offset.

[1]Including a $0.39 reversal of reserves for refunds, but excluding the $1-$1.25 potentially favorable effect of the Boise Cascade joint venture cancellation. [2]Not calculable; company was formed in May 1981. [3]Before nonrecurring gain. [4]Excl. $1.30 a share write-off. [5]Not available; company spun off from AT&T effective January 1, 1984. [6]Company went public in October 1983. [7]Includes certain non-operating items relating to recent California public utility commission decisions. †Canadian funds.

546 **October 3, 1984** **The Outlook**

FIGURE 6-3 sample page from S&P's *The Outlook.*

¶S&P 500 •Options Index	Ticker Symbol	Name of Issue (Call Price of Pfd. Stocks)	Market	Com. Rank. & Pfd. Rating	Par Val.	Inst.Hold Cos	Inst.Hold Shs. (000)	Principal Business	Price Range 1971-82 High	1971-82 Low	1983 High	1983 Low	1984 High	1984 Low	Sep. Sales in 100s	September, 1984 Last Sale Or Bid High	Low	Last	%Div. Yield	P-E Ratio
1	INMA	**Intermagnetics Gen'l**	OTC	NR	10¢	11	678	Mfr superconductive mtls	20¾	4¼	23⅜	5¾	7⅜	3½	3221	6½	4⅝	4⅞B	...	d
2	IMI	**Intermark, Inc**	AS	B	1	8	51	Operating-holding co	15¼	¼	16⅝	6⅛	17¼	11	464	15⅛	14¼	14⅜	0.8	16
3	SQDWS	**Wrrt(Pur ½shr Square D $44⅜)**	AS	...	...	2	79		...	...	...	...	4	2⅝	154	3⅜	2⅞	2⅞	...	...
4	INTR	**Intermec Corp**	OTC	B	60¢	17	790	Mfr printing/reading prdts	14 3/16	1/16	20¼	12 11/16	18¾	13	1551	17⅝	16¼	16¾B	...	25
5	ITM	**Intermedics Inc**	NY,M,Ph	B	10¢	30	2867	Cardiac pacemakers,med prod	37¾	8⅜	30¼	13¾	19¾	10¼	1823	13⅞	11⅝	11⅝	...	d
6	IMET	**Intermetrics Inc**	OTC	NR	1¢	10	546	Computer software prod & svc	17⅝	7	20¾	8⅜	9¼	5⅞	864	7¼	6⅝	7B	...	
7	INMT	**Intermountain Gas [55]Ind[56]**	OTC	B+	1	5	75	Sells nat gas: southern Idaho	22½	8⅞	18¼	12⅛	33⅝	16	4580	33⅝	31½	33½B	4.8	9
8	IMLB	**Intermountain Labs**	OTC	B—	No	...	...	Veterinary diagnostic lab sv	3⅜	⅜	5⅛	2⅜	5	2	343	2⅜	2⅛	2⅜B	...	22
9	IAL	**Int'l Aluminum**	NY,M,P	B+	1	18	1432	Mfr & sale aluminum prod	19½	1	24¾	16⅞	21⅞	14¾	313	17⅝	17⅛	17⅛	4.2	9
10	IBKWA	**Int'l Bank,Wash DC'A'**	OTC	↑B	1	9	149	Hldg insur,fin'l,mfg,invest	14⅝	2⅝	12⅜	8⅛	9⅞	5⅝	1306	6⅞	6½	6⅞B	...	d
11	IBK	**Int'l Banknote**	AS,Ph	↓C	1	21	2730	Prints securities,currencies	7⅞	¼	7⅜	4⅛	6	2⅞	7308	4⅝	3¾	4¼	...	d
12	WS	**Wrrt(Purch 1 com at $7)**	AS,Ph	...	...	11	3039		...	...	2½	1¾	3	1⅛	2795	1¾	1¼	1½	...	...
¶13•[1]	IBM	**Int'l Bus. Machines**	[2]NY,B,C,M,P,Ph	A+	1¼	1611	304304	Lgst mfr business machines	98	37⅝	134¼	92¼	128½	99	197993	128½	120⅞	124¼	3.5	12
14	ICEYF	**Int'l Capital Eq Ltd**	OTC	NR	5¢	4	223	Fin'l svs:Eq lsg/purch	13	3¾	9	4¾	9½	4¾	167	5½	5	5B	...	d
15	ICLB	**Int'l Clinical Labs**	OTC	B	33⅓¢	39	2822	Regional lab systems	21¾	¾	33	18¾	27	15	4142	22	16¼	17B	...	18
16	INC	**Int'l Controls**	AS,P	B+	10¢	23	1032	Electronics/aerospace	24⅜	⅛	18⅞	13½	18¼	13½	2277	18¼	16½	18⅛	1.4	11
17	INDQ	**Int'l Dairy Queen**	OTC	B+	1	11	366	Lmtd menu stores: franch'g	24½	1	40	21¼	40	32½	485	40	39	39B	...	12
¶18•[3]	IFF	**Int'l Flavors/Fragr**	NY,C,M,Ph	A	12½¢	155	16831	Creator & mfr, used by others	49⅜	16⅝	35¾	23¾	29¼	22⅞	14372	27¼	24	24½	4.4	12
19	IGAM	**Int'l Game Tech**	OTC	NR	1¢	11	451	Mfr coin oper video games	17⅝	7⅜	17⅞	8¾	20	11½	4915	17⅜	15½	16¼B	...	11
¶20	HR	**Int'l Harvester**	NY,B,C,M,P,Ph	C	20	85	12837	Truck mfr: farm mchy: constr	45½	2¾	14¾	4	13⅝	5⅛	33032	8⅝	7⅛	7⅜	...	d
21	WS A	**Wrrt A(Purch 1 com at $5)**	NY	...	...	10	340	& ind'l eq:turbo mchy	...	...	10⅞	1	9⅜	2⅞	5336	5⅞	4⅛	4⅝	...	...
22	Pr C	**$5.76 cm Cv C Pfd([69]54.03)**	NY,M	C	No	12	2468		49¼	6¼	39⅝	8¼	39	23½	317	34¼	31	31½	...	...
23	Pr A	**$3[70]cm Cv A Pref(25)**	NY	NR	No	...	...		...	...	55	20½	50⅝	20¾	182	32	26¾	26½B	...	...
24	Pr D	**Cv Jr D[71]Pref(25)**	NY	NR	No	...	...		...	...	...	...	28	17¾	1049	27	22	23	...	...
25	HYD	**Int'l Hydron[72]**	AS	NR	1¢	8	356	Mfrs soft contact lenses	...	...	14	11	17¼	8⅝	3987	17¼	11⅞	16⅞	...	39
26	IIP	**Int'l Income Ppty**	AS	NR	1¢	9	626	Real estate investment trust	10¾	7	9¾	8	10	8¼	58	10	9⅝	9¾B	9.0	20
27	IKNG	**Int'l Kings Table**	OTC	B—	No	14	725	Smorgasbord restaurants	5⅝	⅝	21⅞	5⅜	19⅛	11⅜	1396	17	15¾	16½B	...	13
28	ILFC	**Int'l Lease Finance**	OTC	NR	10¢	4	220	Leas'g/sale of jet aircraft	...	...	15⅜	7⅝	16¼	10½	1367	14½	13	14¼B	...	11
¶29•[1]	IGL	**Int'l Minerals/Chem**	NY,B,C,M,P,Ph	B	5	162	15859	Phospate rock:chemicals	66½	6¾	49	31⅜	49	32⅞	28598	42⅝	39⅞	40¾	6.4	10
30	Pr	**4% cm Pfd (110) vtg**	NY,M	A	100	...	...	potash,hydro-carbons	54½	28½	38½	33½	35¾	30¼	14	32	30¾	31½B	12.7	...
31	IMMC	**Int'l Mobile Machs**	OTC	NR	1¢	2	29	Develop ultraphone system	13⅝	2⅜	14⅝	5½	10⅝	6¾	6578	8⅝	7⅛	8½B	...	d
32	IMC	**Int'l Multifoods**	NY,M	A	1	43	3458	Flours, durum prods, feeds	34¼	8⅜	36⅝	29	33	23	2467	27¼	23⅝	25¾	6.8	8
¶33•[1]	IP	**Int'l Paper**	NY,B,C,M,P,Ph,Mo	B+	1	382	27526	World's largest paper maker	79¾	28½	60	46	59⅞	46	52774	56	50⅛	50⅜	4.8	9
34	PWR	**Int'l Pwr Machines**	AS	NR	10¢	4	147	Uninterruptible power sys	22½	6	12⅜	6⅞	8⅜	5⅜	164	6⅜	5⅝	5⅝	2.8	d
35	PRO	**Int'l Proteins**	AS	C	16⅔¢	1	37	Mfr & dstr fishmeal: shrimp	26⅞	1⅝	6⅛	2⅞	4¾	2¾	239	3⅝	3¼	3⅜	...	d
36	IRF	**Int'l Rectifier**	NY,M,P	↓C	1	21	1315	Semiconductors,antibiotics	15⅜	1½	23⅞	5 3/16	26½	13⅝	3914	25⅛	21⅞	22⅝	...	26
37	IRIS	**Int'l Remote Im Sys**	OTC	NR	No	9	382	Image analy medic sys-dev	5	½	10	2⅞	4	1¼	4513	1⅝	1¼	1⅜B	...	d
38	IRDV	**Int'l Research & Dev**	OTC	B+	1	10	490	Safety evaluation,drugs,chem	20	½	14	6¼	10½	8	466	8¾	8¼	8½B	3.8	10
39	IROC	**Int'l Royalty & Oil**	OTC	NR	1⅔	...	...	Oil royalty int:No Am/int'l	2¾	⅛	⅞	¼	½	⅛	303	¼	⅛	¼B	...	d
40	INS	**Int'l Seaway Trading**	AS	B—	1	1	7	Brand name import'd footw'r	15½	⅞	10⅛	6½	11	8⅛	15	8½	8⅛	8⅛	...	...
41	INSH	**Int'l Shipholding**	OTC	B—	1	5	19	Ocean shipping	20¾	7	18	9½	15	11¾	122	12¾	12¾	12¾B	...	4
42	ITCP	**Int'l Technology**	OTC	NR	1	8	389	Hazardous waste disposal svc	...	...	15¾	14½	18½	12	1632	18½	16¾	17¼B	...	18
43	ITHB	**Int'l Thoroughbred**	OTC	NR	10¢	2	117	Breed, lease race horses	3⅜	1	6	3	5¾	4¼	12410	5¾	4⅞	5⅝B	...	94
44	ITSI	**Int'l Totalizator Sys**	OTC	NR	No	...	...	Comput'zed pari-mut wager'g	2⅝	1¾	7⅜	2¼	6⅝	2⅜	2144	3⅞	2⅞	3⅝B	...	d
45	ITCO	**Int'l Transtech**	OTC,B	NR	5¢	...	...	Dev vehicle propane cv sys	23½	5	16½	2¾	4¾	1½	298	2⅜	1½	2B	...	d

Uniform Footnote Explanations—See Page 1. Other: [1]CBOE:Cycle 1. [2]Mo,To. [3]CBOE:Cycle 2. [51]△$3.67,'83. [52]△$0.74,'84. [54]Co may extend wrrts. [55]Plateau Resources offer for com,$26 to Oct 31 [56]IMG Holdings offer for com,$33.50 to Sep 28. [57]△$0.46,'80. [58]△$0.03,'80. [59]If com price equals 200% of exercise price. [60]Incl $1146M comp. [61]△$0.38,'80. [62]Fiscal Jun'82 & prior. [63]△$0.13,⊙$1.48,'83. [64]Accum on Pfd. [65]Incl pension. [66]□$3.09,'80. [67]△$8.57,□$1.20,'81. [68]□$3.04,△$1.57,'83. [69]To 10-14-84,scale to $50 in'90. [70]Divds cm fr 11-15-85. [71]Divds cm at 120% of cash declared on com stk. [72]SmithKline Beckman plans acquis,$18. [73]⊙$0.34,'83. [74]•$1.07,'83. [75]□$0.75,△$0.16,'80. [76]□$0.34,'81. [77]△$0.17,'82. [78]□$0.97,'84. [79]Incl $0.412 return of capital. [80]△$0.10,'81. [81]△$4.34,'81. [82]□$0.87,'82. [83]Deferred comp. [84]8 Mo Jun,'81.

Common and Preferred Stocks — Int-Int 119

Index	Cash Divs. Ea. Yr. Since	Dividends: Latest Payment Per$	Date	Ex. Div.	Total $ So Far 1984	Ind. Rate	Paid 1983	Financial Position Mil-$: Cash& Equiv.	Curr. Assets	Curr. Liab.	Balance Sheet Date	Capitalization: LgTrm Debt Mil-$	Shs. 000 Pfd.	Com.	Earnings $ Per Shr. Years: End	1980	1981	1982	1983	1984	Last 12 Mos.	Interim Earnings: Period	$ Per Shr. 1983	1984	Index
1		None Since Public				Nil		5.95	16.5	3.94	5-27-84	1.74		5082	My	0.06	•0.12	d0.82	d1.58	d0.78	d0.78				1
2◆	1978	Q0.03	9-14-84	8-27	0.09	0.12	0.14	1.41	75.4	38.1	6-30-84	84.5		4123	Mr	0.80	0.35	[51]0.11	[52]1.03		0.92	12 Mo Jun	0.36	0.92	2
3		Terms&trad. basis should be checked in detail						Redeemable at $22						1122	Co may accelerate expir'n to 10-1-86[53]							Wrrts expire 10-1-88[54]			3
4◆		None Since Public				Nil		0.15	17.5	5.19	6-30-84			4544	Mr	0.41	0.16	0.48	0.66		0.68	3 Mo Jun	0.10	0.12	4
5◆		None Since Public				Nil		n/a	106.	43.8	4-29-84	54.9		10245	Oc	1.26	1.72	0.78	d0.93		d0.53	9 Mo Jul	d0.15	0.25	5
6		None Since Public				Nil		0.83	14.1	8.03	5-31-84	1.05		2892	Fb	0.30	0.40	0.47	0.02		0.05	3 Mo May	0.01	0.04	6
7	1964	Q0.40	10-26-84	10-1	1.56	1.60	1.40	5.78	20.0	18.6	6-30-84	22.9	54	1508	Sp	1.23	1.15	2.16	3.17		3.84	12 Mo Jun	3.31	3.84	7
8◆		None Since Public				Nil		0.13	2.60	1.33	4-30-84	0.56		2503	Ja	d0.01	0.05	0.20	0.17		0.11	6 Mo Jul	0.11	0.05	8
9	1966	Q0.18	10-10-84	9-14	0.72	0.72	0.60	5.49	57.0	15.8	6-30-84	6.29		4511	Je	[57]2.06	1.63	1.29	1.40	1.98	1.98				9
10	1955	0.06¼	6-29-84	6-15	0.12½	Nil	0.40	Equity per shr $12.94			6-30-84	45.4	360	12939	Dc	1.06	1.00	0.56	0.40		d0.77	6 Mo Jun	0.57	d0.60	10
11	1982	0.02	6-15-84	6-4	0.04	Nil	0.08	7.36	66.9	48.8	6-30-84	63.4	248	16739	Dc	[58]0.07	0.60	■d0.28	■d1.08		d1.39	6 Mo Jun	d0.38	d0.69	11
12		Terms&trad. basis should be checked in detail						Cash or 10% Sub Deb'98						5720	Co may accelerate to 7-31-85*							Wrrts expire 8-1-88			12
13	1916	Q1.10	9-10-84	8-8	3.00	4.40	3.71	4260	18178	9178	6-30-84	[60]3646		610834	Dc	[61]5.72	▲5.63	7.39	9.04	E10.75	9.82	6 Mo Jun	3.84	4.62	13
14		None Since Public				Nil		Equity per shr $3.74			4-30-84	2.01		2161	Jl	d0.82	0.30	[62]0.19	0.05		d0.10	9 Mo Apr	d0.02	d0.17	14
15◆		None Paid				Nil		8.13	31.6	19.8	5-31-84	20.0		6842	Au	0.46	0.51	0.60	▲0.85		0.93	9 Mo May	▲0.59	0.67	15
16◆	1982	S0.12½	7-24-84	6-25	0.22½	0.25	0.20	14.8	60.2	17.2	3-31-84	14.9		p3572	Dc	1.47	2.08	2.21	[63]1.50		1.58	6 Mo Jun	0.90	0.98	16
17		None Since Public				Nil		2.77	23.8	24.8	6-1-84	28.0		2101	Nv	1.34	1.72	2.17	2.94		3.23	6 Mo May	1.13	1.42	17
18	1956	Q0.27	10-10-84	9-20	1.08	1.08	1.04	74.2	315.	81.1	6-30-84			36703	Dc	1.73	1.81	1.73	1.87	E2.10	1.88	6 Mo Jun	1.08	1.09	18
19		None Since Public				Nil		1.31	46.4	18.5	6-30-84	2.76		7927	Dc	1.05	1.90	0.96	1.08	E1.50	1.34	6 Mo Jun	0.47	0.73	19
20		0.30	1-15-81	12-22		[64]Nil		273.	1306	1236	7-31-84	[65]1413	4917	56590	Oc[66]	d9.82[67]	d20.27	■d51.39	[68]d14.23	Ed1.75	d4.02	9 Mo Jul	d11.71	d1.50	20
21		Terms&trad. basis should be checked in detail						Wrrts expire 12-15-93						10908	Co may extend to 12-15-99										21
22		1.44	10-15-81	9-9		Nil		Conv into 1⅓ com,$37.50					3000		Oc	bd0.06	bd0.67	bd2.67	bd0.93			Accum $15.88 to 7-15-84			22
23		None Paid				Nil		Conv into 3.75 shrs com					1316		Oc										23
24		None Paid				Nil		Cv after 7-15-84 into 3.125 com					3000		Oc										24
25		None Since Public				Nil		10.3	35.7	10.2	6-30-84	1.83		11208	Dc			•pNil	•[73]0.36		0.43	6 Mo Jun	•0.18	0.25	25
26	1979	0.22	8-24-84	8-6	0.65	0.88	0.80	Equity per shr $7.83			6-30-84	3.86		9098	Dc	d0.09	•0.27	0.49	0.37		0.48	6 Mo Jun	0.17	0.28	26
27◆		0.016	11-15-79	10-9		Nil		1.46	2.56	7.86	4-7-84	11.0		2847	Je	d0.32	d0.35	0.18	0.84	P1.27	1.27				27
28◆		None Since Public				Nil		Equity per shr $5.04			5-31-84	229		11611	Nv	0.40	0.43	▲0.89	[74]1.08		1.24	6 Mo May	0.38	0.54	28
29◆	1971	Q0.65	9-28-84	9-10	2.60	2.60	2.60	149.	614.	326	6-30-84	p348	98	p27295	Je[75]	5.97	[76]5.97	[77]▲4.96	3.02	[78]4.01	4.01				29
30	1942	Q1.00	9-28-84	9-10	3.00	4.00	4.00						98		Je	b6.22	b5.62	b3.55	b2.92	b4.61					30
31		None Since Public				Nil		1.76	2.66	1.98	6-30-84	1.04	395	7353	Dc	d0.14	d0.12	d0.39	d0.81		d0.94	6 Mo Jun	d0.35	d0.48	31
32	1923	Q0.44	10-15-84	9-24	1.76	1.76	[79]1.70½	19.4	244.	105.	5-31-84	93.2	45	8100	Fb	[80]3.35	4.07	4.32	4.03	E3.30	2.94	6 Mo Aug	1.36	0.27	32
33	1946	Q0.60	9-15-84	8-20	1.80	2.40	2.40	256.	1291	563.	3-31-84	999	3026	49851	Dc	5.97	[81]5.74	▲2.72	▲4.61	E5.50	4.65	6 Mo Jun	▲2.15	▲2.19	33
34	1981	Q0.04	9-17-84	8-29	0.12	0.16	0.16	1.14	16.3	5.20	6-30-84		400	3820	Dc	0.72	0.69	0.25	d0.07		d0.10	6 Mo Jun	d0.06	d0.09	34
35		0.05	12-15-80	11-21		Nil		3.67	26.0	27.9	6-30-84	6.29		2115	Dc	▲1.50	d1.10[82]	d1.38	d0.31		d0.58	6 Mo Jun	d0.09	d0.36	35
36◆		0.16	10-1-81	9-4		Nil		2.26	60.3	24.4	7-1-84	14.9		7135	Je	1.62	0.62	d0.42	■d2.77	•0.88	0.88				36
37		None Since Public				Nil		3.99	5.83	0.44	6-30-84			13231	Dc	d0.17	d0.16	d0.28	d0.28		d0.27	6 Mo Jun	d0.12	d0.11	37
38	1973	Q0.08	8-24-84	8-6	0.24	0.32	0.15	3.13	5.73	6.10	6-30-84	0.70		2913	Dc	0.38	0.20	0.24	0.75		0.85	6 Mo Jun	0.32	0.42	38
39◆		0.007	5-5-81	4-20		Nil		0.05	0.15	0.03	6-30-84			6543	Sp	0.02	0.01	d0.01	Nil		d0.01	9 Mo Jun	0.01	Nil	39
40	1983	0.05	6-21-83	5-27		Nil	0.05	1.35	16.6	7.38	5-31-84	[83]0.48		656	Fb	0.70	d0.94	0.31	0.03		0.07	6 Mo Aug	0.16	0.20	40
41◆		None Paid				Nil		12.9	38.4	35.8	6-30-84	84.0		1123	Dc	d3.66	•2.52	▲1.66	5.73		3.54	6 Mo Jun	2.69	0.50	41
42		None Since Public				Nil		2.31	35.1	21.0	6-30-84	19.2	180	5283	Mr	0.84	■0.60	0.48	1.00		0.97	3 Mo Jun	0.26	0.23	42
43		None Since Public				Nil		73.8	80.3	6.48	3-31-84	43.5	16834*	39499	Je		[84]0.01	0.05	0.02		0.06	9 Mo Mar	0.04	0.08	43
44		None Since Public				Nil		0.35	5.16	4.56	6-30-84			2865	Dc	d1.07	•0.15	•0.28	•0.22		d0.73	6 Mo Jun	•0.20	d0.75	44
45◆		None Since Public				Nil		0.35	1.74	1.51	6-30-84	1.55		798	Dc		d1.26	d2.64	d1.06		d0.90	6 Mo Jun	d0.13	•0.03	45

◆ **Stock Splits & Divs By Line Reference Index** [2]4-for-3,'80:10%,'80,'81:3-for-2,'83. [4]2-for-1,'83. [5]3-for-2,'80. [8]2-for-1,'81:3-for-2,'83. [15]3-for-2,'81,'83. [16]5-for-4,'81. [27]5-for-3,'83:10%,'84. [28]2-for-1,'83. [29]3-for-2,'80. [36]2-for-1,'83:Prop 3-for-2 stk split. [39]3-for-1,'81. [41]1-for-2 REVERSE,'83. [45]1-for-2 REVERSE,'84.

FIGURE 6-4 data on 45 preferred and common stocks from Standard and Poor's *Stock Guide*. *Note*: The data were current at the time they were published. However, the most recent data should be consulted before reaching any conclusions. (*Source*: Standard & Poor's Corporation, 25 Broadway, New York, N.Y.)

Poor's different industry stock price indices. The *Stock Price Index Record* also contains other financial market data from past years. Moody's publishes the *Stock Survey,* which is a weekly publication that is similar to Standard & Poor's *The Outlook.*

S&P publishes the monthly pocket-sized *Stock Guide* and the similar *Bond Guide.* These two booklets contain many of the salient financial statistics from the voluminous *S&P Corporation Records.* Each of these booklets is a concise summary of investment information about various issues. Figure 6-4 shows two adjacent pages of the *Stock Guide.* Figure 6-5 is an explanation of S&P's stock ratings. The *Stock Guide* also contains lists under the categories "stock for potential appreciation," "recommended stocks primarily for appreciation," "candidates for dividend increases," "candidates for stock splits," and "25 of the best low-priced stocks." The back pages of the *Stock Guide* contain data about the hundreds of publicly available mutual funds. Figure 6-6 shows a page from S&P's *Bond Guide.* Figure 6-7 explains the bond ratings used by S&P.

Standard & Poor's *Commercial Paper Rating Guide* is a monthly booklet. The booklet briefly discusses every major issuer of commercial paper and indicates a quality rating for the issuer's money market security. Figure 6-8 shows a page from the Standard & Poor's *Commercial Paper Rating Guide* that explains the corporation's commercial paper rating practices. Figure 6-9 shows a sample page of corporate ratings from the *Commercial Paper Rating Guide.*

6-3.2 Moody's

The voluminous *Moody's Industrial Manuals* contain fundamental financial information about hundreds of firms. For each firm information is presented under the following headings and subheadings: Capital Structure, with subheadings on long-term debt and capital stock history, subsidiaries, business and products, and principal plants and properties; Management, with subheadings on officers, directors, general counsel, auditors, stockholders, employees, general office address, and unfilled orders; Income Accounts, with subheadings on comparative income account, supplementary P & L (profit and loss) data, comparative balance sheets, property account, and a description of reserves; Financial and Operating Data, with subheadings on statistical records, data adjusted for stock splits and stock dividends, financial and operating ratios and analysis of operations; Long-term Debt, with subheadings on authorized debt, call dates, sinking fund, security, sales and leasebacks, dividend restrictions, rights on default indenture modification, term loans, notes payable, revolving credit agreement, and other notes; and Capital Stock, with subheadings on authorized stock, dividend restrictions, voting rights, preemptive rights, transfer agent, registrar, stock subscription rights, and debenture subscription rights.

Moody's Handbook of Widely Held Common Stocks is issued four times a year and gives a brief summary of about 1000 firms. Figure 6-10 shows a sample page. For each firm the price is charted and compared with the industry's price trend. Financial background, current developments, and future prospects are reported, along with the financial statistics for several years. S&P's counterpart to *Moody's Handbook* is the *Stock Market Encyclopedia,* which also covers about 1000 stocks. Figure 6-11 shows a report from S&P's *Stock Market Encyclopedia.*

EARNINGS AND DIVIDEND RANKINGS FOR COMMON STOCKS

The investment process involves assessment of various factors—such as product and industry position, corporate resources and financial policy—with results that make some common stocks more highly esteemed than others. In this assessment, Standard & Poor's believes that earnings and dividend performance is the end result of the interplay of these factors and that, over the long run, the record of this performance has a considerable bearing on relative quality. The rankings, however, do not pretend to reflect all of the factors, tangible or intangible, that bear on stock quality.

Relative quality of bonds or other debt, that is, degrees of protection for principal and interest, called creditworthiness, cannot be applied to common stocks, and therefore rankings are not to be confused with bond quality ratings which are arrived at by a necessarily different approach.

Growth and stability of earnings and dividends are deemed key elements in establishing Standard & Poor's earnings and dividend rankings for common stocks, which are designed to capsulize the nature of this record in a single symbol. It should be noted, however, that the process also takes into consideration certain adjustments and modifications deemed desirable in establishing such rankings.

The point of departure in arriving at these rankings is a computerized scoring system based on per-share earnings and dividend records of the most recent ten years—a period deemed long enough to measure significant time segments of secular growth, to capture indications of basic change in trend as they develop, and to encompass the full peak-to-peak range of the business cycle. Basic scores are computed for earnings and dividends, then adjusted as indicated by a set of predetermined modifiers for growth, stability within long-term trend, and cyclicality. Adjusted scores for earnings and dividends are then combined to yield a final score.

Further, the ranking system makes allowance for the fact that, in general, corporate size imparts certain recognized advantages from an investment standpoint. Conversely, minimum size limits (in terms of corporate sales volume) are set for the various rankings, but the system provides for making exceptions where the score reflects an outstanding earnings-dividend record.

The final score for each stock is measured against a scoring matrix determined by analysis of the scores of a large and representative sample of stocks. The range of scores in the array of this sample has been aligned with the following ladder of rankings:

A+	Highest	B+	Average	C	Lowest
A	High	B	Below Average	D	In Reorganization
A−	Above Average	B−	Lower		

NR signifies no ranking because of insufficient data or because the stock is not amenable to the ranking process.

The positions as determined above may be modified in some instances by special considerations, such as natural disasters, massive strikes, and non-recurring accounting adjustments.

A ranking is not a forecast of future market price performance, but is basically an appraisal of past performance of earnings and dividends, and relative current standing. These rankings must not be used as market recommendations; a high-score stock may at times be so overpriced as to justify its sale, while a low-score stock may be attractively priced for purchase. Rankings based upon earnings and dividend records are no substitute for complete analysis. They cannot take into account potential effects of management changes, internal company policies not yet fully reflected in the earnings and dividend record, public relations standing, recent competitive shifts, and a host of other factors that may be relevant to investment status and decision.

FIGURE 6-5 Standard & Poor's explanation of its common stock quality rating categories. (*Source*: Standard & Poor's *Stock Guide*, 1984.)

CORPORATE BONDS — **Ind-Int 81**

Title-Industry Code & Co. Finances (In Italics) / Individual Issue Statistics — Exchange	Ind / Interest Dates	Chgs. 1981 / S&P Quality Rating	Eligible	Times Earn. 1982 / Bond Form	Times Earn. 1983 / Legality (M a, N H, N Y)	Yr. End	Cash & Eqv / Redemption Provisions: Refund Earliest/Other	Current Assets / Call Price: For S.F.	Liabs	Date / Call Price: Regular	L. Term Debt (Mil $) / Out-st'd'g (Mil $)	Debt % Prop / Underwriter Firm	Year	Interim Times Earn. Period / Price Range 1972-82 High	1972-82 Low	Interim 1983 / 1983 High	Interim 1984 / 1983 Low	1984 High	1984 Low	Mo. End Price Sale(s) or Bid	Curr Yield	Yield to Mat.
Indianapolis Water	*74*	*2.73*		*2.55*	*2.89*	*Dc*	*0.25*	*5.93*	*9.83*	*6-84*	*48.9*	*34.4*		*12 Mo Jun*		*2.68*	*2.99*					
1st 8½s '86	Jj15	AA	X	R	- √ -	....	100		100	18.0	G2	'76	105	75¼	95¼	88⅛	96¼	94	96⅛	8.84	11.64
Ingersoll-Rand Co.	*41c*	*2.83*		*1.56*	*0.69*	*Dc*	*165*	*1482*	*596*	*3-84*	*554*	*95.0*		*3 Mo Mar*		*0.40*	*1.37*					
• SF Deb 8.05s 2004	Ms	A-	X	R	- √ -	....	[1]100		±104.83	74.6	M8	'74	100	50	73½	63¼	65¾	56½	62¾	12.83	13.50
• SF Deb 12⅞s 2010	mS	A-	X	R	- √ -	[2]107.725	[3]100		±110.815	150	M8	'80	103	76	107½	98½	90	90	93⅛	13.83	13.85
• Nts 8¾s '85	Mn	A-	X	R	- √ -	....	....		100	100	M8	'75	107⅝	77	98¼	94½	98	95.81	97⅝	8.96	12.61
• Nts 12⅜s '90	mS	A-	X	R	- √ -	....	....		[4]100	150	M8	'80	103	82	104½	99	100¾	92½	98	12.63	12.86
Inland Steel Co.	*66a*	*1.91*		*d1.06*	*0.20*	*Dc*	*38.2*	*842*	*541*	*3-84*	*773*	*45.3*		*3 Mo Mar*		*d0.23*	*1.14*					
• 1st K 4⅜s '87	jJ	BBB	X	CR	- - √	....	100		±100⅛	12.3	K2	'57	81½	56¾	78½	68½	80½	78¾	79⅛	5.53	13.49
• 1st L 4½s '89	Fa	BBB	X	CR	- - √	....	100		±100⅛	14.0	K2	'59	80⅝	53	70	61¼	71½	70	71½	6.29	13.23
• 1st M 6½s '92	jD	BBB	X	R	√ - √	....	100		±101	24.0	K2	'67	93	47	71⅛	56⅛	66¾	60⅝	61½	10.57	14.70
• 1st O 8¾s '95	jJ15	BBB	X	R	√ - -	....	100		±101½	55.0	K2	'70	110½	53½	82⅛	68½	76	62	67½	12.96	14.86
• 1st P 8⅛s '99	Ao15	BBB	X	R	√ - -	....	100		±103½	52.6	K2	'74	105¾	53⅛	81	65	72	62	68	13.05	14.09
• 1st Q 9½s 2000	mS	BBB	X	R	√ - -	[5]104	100		±104½	84.4	K2	'75	110	59⅛	81	70⅛	75⅜	67	s67⅜	14.05	14.84
• 1st R 7.90s 2007	Jj15	BBB	X	R	√ - -	[6]103.90	[7]100		±105.10	125	K2	'77	100	47	71	56¼	64	51	58½	13.50	14.00
• 1st S 11¼s '90	Jd	BBB	X	R	- - -	....	....		[8]100	150	F2	'80	101½	74	98½	87	93	86	87½	12.86	14.53
Integrated Resources, Inc.	*26*	*2.16*		*1.98*	*3.24*	*Dc*	*137*	*449*	*269*	*3-84*	*99.9*	*327*		*3 Mo Mar*		*1.63*	*2.19*					
• SrSubSFDeb 8⅜s '97	Ao15	BBB-	X	R	- - -	....	[9]100		100	[10]85.6	D7	'82	70	50⅛	77⅛	67½	72	58⅜	71¼	12.11	13.41
• SrSubSFDeb 12⅛s '99	Mn15	BBB-	X	R	- - -	....	[11]100		±104½	15.5	B1	'79	110½	67	101	90	93½	80¼	86⅜	14.86	15.17
INTERCO, Inc.	*68c*	*4.19*		*3.45*	*4.67*	*Fb*	*95.1*	*1125*	*283*	*5-84*	*208*	*50.5*		*3 Mo May*		*3.12*	*3.96*					
• Nts 14¼s '91	Fa15	A+	X	R	- √ -	....	....		[12]100	75.0	G2	'81	102	92⅛	No Sale		103¼	101	102	13.97	13.77
InterFirst[13] Corp[14]	*10a*	*1.12*		*1.13*	*0.88*	*Dc*					*560*			*6 Mo Jun*		*1.10*	*1.03*					
• SF Deb 9¾s '99	mN15	BBB+	X	R	- - -	....	[15]100		[15]104⅛	27.0	G2	'74	110	57¼	85	74	80	68	72	13.54	14.31
Nts 12¾s '89	aO	BBB+	X	R	- - -	....	....		[16]100	100	G2	'82	103⅛	99⅞	104⅛	99	103½	95⅞	98¾	12.91	13.09
• Cv[17] Flt'g Rt Nts[18] 11.60s '87	fA	BBB+	X	R	√ - -	....	....		[19]100	100	B9	'79	100	87	99¼	95½	98½	87	87⅛	13.31	....
Interlake, Inc.	*66b*	*4.59*		*1.69*	*3.03*	*Dc*	*99.6*	*377*	*166*	*6-84*	*114*	*47.9*		*6 Mo Jun*		*1.89*	*4.40*					
• SF Deb 8.80s '96	fA	BBB+	X	R	- - -	....	100		±102.30	30.8	K2	'71	107½	53⅞	77¾	71½	77⅛	67	s77⅛	11.41	12.55
Intermark, Inc	*17a*	*1.31*		*0.97*	*1.32*	*Mr*	*1.41*	*75.4*	*38.1*	*6-84*	*84.5*	*330*		*12 Mo Jun*		*0.89*	*1.33*					
• Sr Sub SF Deb 11⅞s '99	mS15	B-	Y	R	- - -	....	[20]100		104.35	20.0	D7	'79	93⅛	68½	93	81	82¼	73⅛	77⅛	15.40	15.92
• Sub SF Deb 13.20s '98	aO	B-	Y	R	- - -	[21]100	[22]100		100	[10]33.0	D7	'83	....	....	94	89	94	93⅞	80⅝	16.37	16.83
Int'l Bank, Wash D.C.	*26*	*3.21*		*2.61*	*1.75*	*Dc*					*47.5*			*3 Mo Mar*		*3.62*	*d2.11*					
Sub SF Deb 15¾s 2000	fA	B	Y	R	- - -	....	[23]100		[24]±109½	20.0	D3	'80	99½	80	105	92	105	94¼	100⅛	15.73	15.72
Int'l Banknote	*30a*	*2.18*		*0.37*	*d1.26*	*Dc*	*7.36*	*66.9*	*48.8*	*6-84*	*63.4*	*111*		*6 Mo Jun*		*d0.72*	*d1.26*					
• Sub Deb[25] 10s '98	fA	NR		R	- - -	....	[26]100		[19]110	[10]40.0	O3	'83	....	....	68½	68	73	59½	59½	16.81	18.02
Int'l Business Machines	*48a*	*9.13*		*10.71*	*15.06*	*Dc*	*5368*	*17667*	*9421*	*3-84*	*[27]3846*	*23.8*		*3 Mo Mar*		*11.38*	*14.07*					
• Nts 9½s '86	aO	AAA	X	R	√ √ -	....	....		100	500	S1	'79	103½	78	100½	94½	97½	93	s94⅝	10.04	12.51
• Deb 9⅜s 2004	aO	AAA	X	R	√ √ -	[28]102½	[29]100		105¼	500	S1	'79	99⅝	64½	92⅝	79⅞	84½	73	s80⅜	11.66	11.97
Int'l Harvester Co	*9a*	*d0.67*		*d2.67*	*d0.93*	*Oc*	*280*	*1361*	*1335*	*4-84*	*[30]1403*	*192*		*6 Mo Apr*		*d0.91*	*0.38*					
• SF Deb 8⅝s '95	mS	CCC	Y	R	- - -	....	100		±102¼	43.8	M8	'70	112½	21	68	35⅛	64⅞	50	58⅞	14.65	17.01
• SF Deb 6¼s '98	Ms	CCC	Y	R	- - √	....	....		±102¼	14.0	M8	'68	88	21	55	29	50	41	44⅞	13.93	16.60
• SF Deb 18s 2002	jD15	CCC	Y	R	- - -	....	[31]100		±117	65.1	Exch	'82	55⅛	46⅛	109¾	53½	110⅞	94¼	s104⅛	17.29	17.25
• SF Deb 9s 2004	Jd15	CCC	Y	R	- - -	....	[32]100		±104.92	84.1	M8	'74	105½	21	69⅛	34⅛	65⅛	50	s56⅛	16.04	16.61
• SF Sub Deb 4⅝s '88	Ms	CC	Y	CR	- - -	....	*[33]100		100	13.0	Exch	'63	90	30	78	30	76⅛	68½	70⅛	6.60	16.12
• SF Sub Deb 4.80s '91	Ms	CC	Y	R	- - -	....	*[33]100		±101	24.0	Exch	'66	83	20	64⅞	27¾	80	64⅞	75	6.40	10.14
Int'l Harvester Credit	*26e*	*1.14*		*1.20*	*1.13*	*Oc*	*149*			*4-84*	*[34]2853*			*6 Mo Apr*		*1.13*	*1.14*					
• Deb 8⅝s '91	fA	CCC	Y	R	- - -	Z±101 1/16	....		±102⅛	50.0	M8	'71	108½	31	74	44	75	64	s68⅞	12.52	16.29
• Deb 7⅜s '93	Fa	CCC	Y	R	- - -	Z±101¼	....		±102½	59.9	M8	'72	101¾	30	66	41¼	67½	55⅞	63⅞	11.94	15.43
• Deb 7½s '94	Jj15	CCC	Y	R	- - -	Z±101 5/16	....		±102.62	74.8	M8	'73	100⅛	29	64	42½	64½	53⅝	56⅛	13.36	17.03

Uniform Footnote Explanations—See Page 1. Other: [1]Fr 3-1-85. [2]Red rest'n(12.875%)to 9-1-90. [3]Fr 9-1-91. [4]Fr 9-1-86. [5]Red rest'n(9.55%)to 9-1-85. [6]Red rest'n(7.9%)to 1-15-87. [7]Fr 1-15-88. [8]Fr 6-1-87. [9]Fr 4-15-90. [10]Incl disc. [11]Fr 5-15-89. [12]Fr 2-15-88. [13]Was First Int'l Bancshares. [14]See First United Bancorp. [15]Fr 11-15-84. [16]Fr 10-1-87. [17]Conv into 8 1/2% Deb'09 thru 7-31-86. [18]To 1-31-85,then 1/2% above T-Bill rate,etc. [19]Fr 8-1-86. [20]Fr 9-15-89. [21]Red rest'n(14 3/4%)to 10-1-88. [22]Fr 10-1-89. [23]Fr 8-1-90. [24]Fr 8-1-85. [25]Usable at par with 1988 wrrts. [26]Fr 8-1-88. [27]Incl $1195M comp. [28]Red rest'n(9.415%)to 10-1-89. [29]Fr 10-1-85. [30]Incl pension. [31]Fr 12-15-93. [32]Fr 6-15-85. [33]PF100. [34]Incl current debt.

FIGURE 6-6 data on 45 corporate bonds from Standard and Poor's *Bond Guide*. *Note*: These data were current at the time they were published. However, the most recent data shouid be consulted before reaching any conclusions. (*Source*: Standard & Poor's Corporation, 25 Broadway, New York.)

STANDARD & POOR'S Corporate and Municipal Debt Rating Definitions

A Standard & Poor's corporate or municipal debt rating is a current assessment of the creditworthiness of an obligor with respect to a specific obligation. This assessment may take into consideration obligors such as guarantors, insurers, or lessees.

The debt rating is not a recommendation to purchase, sell or hold a security, inasmuch as it does not comment as to market price or suitability for a particular investor.

The ratings are based on current information furnished by the issuer or obtained by Standard & Poor's from other sources it considers reliable. Standard & Poor's does not perform any audit in connection with any rating and may, on occasion, rely on unaudited financial information. The ratings may be changed, suspended or withdrawn as a result of changes in, or unavailability of, such information, or for other circumstances.

The ratings are based, in varying degrees, on the following considerations:

I. Likelihood of default-capacity and willingness of the obligor as to the timely payment of interest and repayment of principal in accordance with the terms of the obligation;
II. Nature of and provisions of the obligation;
III. Protection afforded by, and relative position of, the obligation in the event of bankruptcy, reorganization or other arrangement under the laws of bankruptcy and other laws affecting creditors' rights.

AAA Debt rated AAA has the highest rating assigned by Standard & Poor's. Capacity to pay interest and repay principal is extremely strong.

AA Debt rated AA has a very strong capacity to pay interest and repay principal and differs from the higher rated issues only in small degree.

A Debt rated A has a strong capacity to pay interest and repay principal although it is somewhat more susceptible to the adverse effects of changes in circumstances and economic conditions than debt in higher rated categories.

BBB Debt rated BBB is regarded as having an adequate capacity to pay interest and repay principal. Whereas it normally exhibits adequate protection parameters, adverse economic conditions or changing circumstances are more likely to lead to a weakened capacity to pay interest and repay principal for debt in this category than in higher rated categories.

BB, B, CCC, CC Debt rated BB, B, CCC and CC is regarded, on balance, as predominantly speculative with respect to capacity to pay interest and repay principal in accordance with the terms of the obligation. BB indicates the lowest degree of speculation and CC the highest degree of speculation. While such debt will likely have some quality and protective characteristics, these are outweighed by large uncertainties or major risk exposures to adverse conditions.

C The rating C is reserved for income bonds on which no interest is being paid.

D Debt rated D is in default, and payment of interest and/or repayment of principal is in arrears.

Plus (+) or Minus (−): The ratings from "AA" to "B" may be modified by the addition of a plus or minus sign to show relative standing within the major rating categories.

Provisional Ratings: The letter "p" indicates that the rating is provisional. A provisional rating assumes the successful completion of the project being financed by the debt being rated and indicates that payment of debt service requirements is largely or entirely dependent upon the successful and timely completion of the project. This rating, however, while addresssing credit quality subsequent to completion of the project, makes no comment on the likelihood of, or the risk of default upon failure of such completion. The investor should exercise his own judgment with respect to such likelihood and risk.

NR Indicates that no rating has been requested, that there is insufficient information on which to base a rating, or that S&P does not rate a particular type of obligation as a matter of policy.

Debt Obligations of issuers outside the United States and its territories are rated on the same basis as domestic corporate and municipal issues. The ratings measure the creditworthiness of the obligor but do not take into account currency exchange and related uncertainties.

Bond Investment Quality Standards: Under present commercial bank regulations issued by the Comptroller of the Currency, bonds rated in the top four categories (AAA, AA, A, BBB, commonly known as "Investment Grade" ratings) are generally regarded as eligible for bank investment. In addition, the Legal Investment Laws of various states impose certain rating or other standards for obligations eligible for investment by savings banks, trust companies, insurance companies and fiduciaries generally.

Standard & Poor's publication "CreditWeek" contains a section entitled "CreditWatch" indicating whether certain events have positive or negative implications with respect to the ratings of the debt of certain issuers.

Standard & Poor's does not act as a financial advisor to any issuer in connection with any corporate or municipal debt financing. Standard & Poor's receives compensation for rating debt obligations. Such compensation is based on the time and effort to determine the rating and is normally paid either by the issuers of such securities or by the underwriters participating in the distribution thereof. The fees generally vary from $1,000 to $10,000 for municipal securities, and from $1,500 to $20,000 for corporate securities. While Standard & Poor's reserves the right to disseminate the rating, it receives no payment for doing so, except for subscriptions to its publications.

FIGURE 6-7 Standard & Poor's explanation of its bond quality rating categories. (*Source*: Standard & Poor's *Bond Guide*, 1984.)

EXPLANATION OF HEADINGS

Rating: This is S&P's commercial paper rating. (For definitions of ratings see page ii.) For those issuers selling commercial paper secured by mortgages, the rating will be followed by "CTN" (collateral trust notes) or "MBN" (mortgage-backed notes). For those issuers selling commercial paper backed by irrevocable revolving credit agreements or by letters of credit, the rating will be followed by "IRC" or "LOC," respectively.

Dealer: This section contains either:

1) the dealer's name if the issuer issues through a dealer; see page xvi for Directory of Dealers;
2) "Privately Placed" if the commercial paper is offered to a restricted list of investors and accordingly, the identity of the dealer has been omitted; see page xvi; or
3) "Direct Issue" and a phone number. These issuers issue commercial paper themselves and their phone numbers are provided.

Long-Term Debt Rating: The highest public rating on the issuer's long-term debt is provided. The ratings are assigned numbers corresponding to the list below to indicate the level of long-term debt that is rated.

[1]First mortgage bonds	[5]Senior-ranking ind. rev. bonds
[2]Other secured debt	[6]Subordinate-ranking ind. rev. bonds
[3]Senior unsecured debt	[7]General obligation bonds
[4]Subordinated debt	[8]Revenue bonds

[9]Preliminary rating

Bank Line Policy: A statement about the issuer's bank line policy appears here.

Rating Rationale: This is a concise paragraph outlining the business of the issuer and the key factors that determined the commercial paper rating. When a rating has changed from the previous month the rationale will highlight the reasons for the change. Following the rationale will be the initials of the S&P contact assigned to the issuer. See page v for the list of S&P contacts.

STANDARD & POOR'S COMMERCIAL PAPER RATING DEFINITIONS

A Standard & Poor's Commercial Paper Rating is a current assessment of the likelihood of timely payment of debt having an original maturity of no more than 365 days.

Ratings are graded into four categories, ranging from 'A' for the highest quality obligations to 'D' for the lowest. The four categories are as follows:

'A': Issues assigned this highest rating are regarded as having the greatest capacity for timely payment. Issues in this category are delineated with the numbers 1, 2 and 3 to indicate the relative degree of safety.

'A-1': This designation indicates that the degree of safety regarding timely payment is either overwhelming or very strong. Those issues determined to possess overwhelming safety characteristics will be denoted with a plus (+) sign designation.

'A-2': Capacity for timely payment on issues with this designation is strong. However, the relative degree of safety is not as high as for issues designated "A-1".

'A-3': Issues carrying this designation have a satisfactory capacity for timely payment. They are, however, somewhat more vulnerable to the adverse effects of changes in circumstances than obligations carrying the higher designations.

'B': Issues rated 'B' are regarded as having only an adequate capacity for timely payment. However, such capacity may be damaged by changing conditions or short-term adversities.

'C': This rating is assigned to short-term debt obligations with a doubtful capacity for payment.

'D': This rating indicates that the issue is either in default or is expected to be in default upon maturity.

The commercial paper rating is not a recommendation to purchase or sell a security. The ratings are based on current information furnished to Standard & Poor's by the issuer or obtained from other sources it considers reliable. The ratings may be changed, suspended or withdrawn as a result of changes in or unavailability of such information.

FIGURE 6-8 Standard & Poor's explanation of its commercial paper ratings. (*Source*: *Commercial Paper Rating Guide*, 1984.)

Interlake Inc. **Rating:** A-2

Dealer: Goldman, Sachs & Co. **Long-Term Debt Rating:** BBB+[3]

Bank Line Policy: 100% backup for commercial paper outstanding.

Rating Rationale: Interlake is an integrated iron and steel maker; it also produces packaging materials, material handling and storage equipment, and ferroalloys; and has growing businesses in powdered metals and investment castings. It sells commercial paper mainly for working capital needs. The company has emerged from the recent recession with supportive financial measures and is currently in an earnings recovery./DVD

Intermountain Power Agency, Utah **Rating:** A-1

Dealer: Salomon Brothers **Long-Term Debt Rating:** A+

Bank Line Policy: 100% backup for commercial paper outstanding.

Rating Rationale: IPA is issuing $300 million in commercial paper to finance the construction of a two-unit coal plant in Utah. Commercial operation dates are July 1986 and July 1987. Construction is 45% complete on unit one and 11% complete on unit two. Three-quarters of the project's energy has been sold under take or pay contracts to Los Angeles and five other municipalities in southern California to offset more expensive oil and gas purchases. The rating reflects the strong financial position and economic base of the participants, sound management, and strong legal arrangements. The construction risk associated with the project offsets these strengths./PE

International Business Machines Corp. **Rating:** A-1+

Dealer: Salomon Bros. **Long-Term Debt Rating:** AAA[3]

Bank Line Policy: Bank lines of $3.1 billion are available.

Rating Rationale: IBM, the world's largest computer manufacturer, issues commercial paper for working capital needs. IBM's dominant industry position and high levels of investment in R&D and capital spending has produced an excellent operating record. Profit margins and return on capital are extremely healthy and debt leverage is conservatively maintained. Strong cash flow and exceptional liquidity are additional positives./HSG

FIGURE 6-9 sample page from Standard & Poor's *Commercial Paper Rating Guide*, September 1984. *Note*: The information was current when published, but since conditions can change rapidly, later reports may give different opinions about the same security. (*Source*: Standard & Poor's Corporation, 25 Broadway, New York.)

MC DONALD'S CORPORATION

LISTED	SYM.	LTPS♦	STPS♦	IND. DIV.	REC. PRICE	RANGE (52-WKS.)	YLD.
NYSE	MCD	114.8	104.9	$0.77	47 (adj.)	49 - 37	1.6%

INVESTMENT GRADE. RAPID GROWTH HAS BEEN ACHIEVED IN BOTH REVENUES AND EARNINGS.

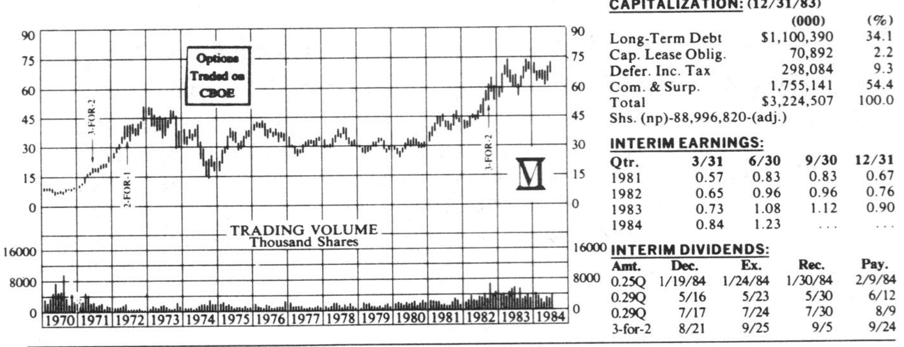

CAPITALIZATION: (12/31/83)

	(000)	(%)
Long-Term Debt	$1,100,390	34.1
Cap. Lease Oblig.	70,892	2.2
Defer. Inc. Tax	298,084	9.3
Com. & Surp.	1,755,141	54.4
Total	$3,224,507	100.0

Shs. (np)-88,996,820-(adj.)

INTERIM EARNINGS:

Qtr.	3/31	6/30	9/30	12/31
1981	0.57	0.83	0.83	0.67
1982	0.65	0.96	0.96	0.76
1983	0.73	1.08	1.12	0.90
1984	0.84	1.23	...	...

INTERIM DIVIDENDS:

Amt.	Dec.	Ex.	Rec.	Pay.
0.25Q	1/19/84	1/24/84	1/30/84	2/9/84
0.29Q	5/16	5/23	5/30	6/12
0.29Q	7/17	7/24	7/30	8/9
3-for-2	8/21	9/25	9/5	9/24

BACKGROUND:

McDonald's develops, licenses, leases and services a nationwide system of drive-in self-service restaurants. All units are similar in design and serve a standardized 9menu of moderately priced food. As of 12/31/83, there were 5,371 units operated by franchisees, 1,949 units operated by the Company and 458 units operated by affiliates. Outside of the U.S. there are 1,527 units in operation in 31 countries and the Virgin Islands. Revenues in 1983 were derived from: Company owned units sales, 75%; licensed restaurants, 23%; other 2%. Independent operators normally lease on a 20-year basis with rental derived as a percentage of sales, with a minimum fixed rent.

RECENT DEVELOPMENTS:

Net income for the quarter ended 6/30/84 increased 13% to $108.6 million. Sales were up 12%. For the six months, net income advanced 13%. Sales were also up 13%. Sales by all Company operated, franchised and affiliated restaurants gained 18%. International sales were helped by CHICKEN MCNUGGETS which were introduced in Canada and Japan in early 1984. During the second quarter 116 new restaurants were opened. An additional 162 restaurants were under construction at 6/30 including 36 in international markets.

PROSPECTS:

Sales and earnings are expected to continue upward. Results will continue to benefit from drive-thru and playland additions. The expansion of international operations will continue. The number of international restaurants has increased substantially at a compounded annual growth rate of 16%, over the past five years. Between 175 and 200 new restaurants will be added in 1984. International restaurants represent 20% of the worldwide number of restaurants, compared with 14% five years ago.

STATISTICS:

YEAR	GROSS REVS. ($mill.)	OPER. PROFIT MARGIN %	RET. ON EQUITY %	NET INCOME ($mill.)	WORK CAP. ($mill.)	SENIOR CAPITAL ($mill.)	SHARES (000)	EARN. PER SH.$	DIV. PER SH.$	DIV. PAY. %	PRICE RANGE	P/E RATIO	AVG. YIELD %
74	729.0	22.2	20.4	67.4	11.5	348.5	89,303	0.75	Nil	–	28⅛ - 9⅜	24.9	–
75	941.5	21.9	21.0	86.9	18.0	428.4	90,035	0.97	Nil	–	26⅞ - 11⅞	20.1	–
76	1,175.9	21.8	20.9	110.1	5.1	490.0	91,159	1.21	0.03	3	29⅜ - 21⅝	21.1	N.M.
77	1,406.1	21.7	21.3	136.7	d6.7	687.9	90,957	1.50	0.08	5	23⅝ - 16¾	13.5	0.4
78	1,671.9	22.9	20.4	162.7	d8.5	782.8	91,137	1.78	0.14	8	26⅞ - 19½	13.0	0.6
79	1,937.9	21.5	19.8	188.6	d27.6	966.1	90,448	2.07	0.23	11	23 - 17⅜	9.7	1.1
80	2,215.5	22.3	19.4	220.9	d98.7	969.8	90,314	2.45	0.33	14	23⅛ - 16⅛	8.0	1.7
81	2,515.8	22.8	19.3	264.8	d176.7	925.5	90,508	2.90	0.42	15	32⅜ - 21½	9.3	1.6
82	2,769.5	23.1	19.7	300.6	d178.2	1,055.9	89,879	3.33	0.53	16	43¾ - 25¾	10.1	1.6
83	**3,062.9**	**24.1**	**19.6**	**342.6**	**d198.5**	**1,171.3**	**88,997**	**3.83**	**0.65**	**17**	**49⅝ - 36½**	**11.3**	**1.5**

♦Long-Term Price Score — Short-Term Price Score; see page 4a. Adjusted for 3-for-2 stock splits, 10/82 and 9/84.

INCORPORATED:
March 1, 1965 – Delaware

PRINCIPAL OFFICE:
McDonald's Plaza
2111 Enco Drive
Oak Brook, Ill. 60521
Tel: (312) 887-3200

ANNUAL MEETING:
First Monday in May

NUMBER OF STOCKHOLDERS:
25,798

TRANSFER AGENT(S):
American National Bank & Trust Co., Chicago, Ill.
Royal Trust Co., Toronto, Can.

REGISTRAR(S):
American National Bank & Trust Co., Chicago, Ill.
Montreal Trust Co., Toronto, Can.

INSTITUTIONAL HOLDINGS:
No. of Institutions: 452
Shares Held: 56,763,202-(adj.)

OFFICERS:
Chmn. & Ch. Exec. Off.
F.L. Turner
Pres. & Ch. Oper. Off.
M.R. Quinlan
Exec. V.P., Secy. & Gen. Counsel
D.P. Horwitz
Vice Pres. & Treas.
R.B. Ryan

FIGURE 6-10 sample page from *Moody's Handbook of Widely Held Common Stocks*. *Note*: The information was current when published, but since conditions can change rapidly, later reports may give different opinions about the same security. (*Source*: Moody's Investors Services Inc., 99 Church Street, New York.)

In addition to its monthly *Bond Guide*, S&P publishes the weekly *Bond Outlook*, and Moody's publishes the *Bond Survey*. Both cover similar data about the corporate and municipal bond markets, attractive convertibles and new issues, changes in bond ratings, bonds called for payment, and similar terms.

6-3.3 Value Line

The *Value Line Investment Survey* differs somewhat from the Moody's and S&P publications. Value Line Inc. reports on 1400 stocks in 60 industries, covering each stock in detail once every quarter. Figure 6-12 shows one of Value Line's quarterly reports for a firm. Supplements are issued to Value Line subscribers each week to keep the financial reports up to date. About 85 stocks are usually included in the three- or four-page supplements. Once per quarter Value Line issues industry reports like the one shown in Figure 6-13.

A unique feature of Value Line's service is its investment scoring system. Value Line rates every stock from 1 to 5 with respect to four factors: quality, performance in the next 12 months, appreciation potential in 3 to 5 years, and income from dividends. Value Line suggests that investors select securities with the highest weighted average rating. Investors select the weights to be assigned to each rated item to reflect their investment preferences.

A second distinctive feature of Value Line is the quality of its investment advice. In studies to determine the profitability of the investment advice given by various brokerages and investment advisors, Value Line ranks as one of the better sources. On the average, Value Line's recommendations yield a portfolio that earns a few percentage points more return per year than could be earned by picking a large portfolio randomly.[12] These studies suggest that Value Line's recommendations are better than picking stocks randomly. Such favorable studies have never been published for other investment advisory services by unbiased outside researchers.

6-3.4 information about put and call options

Standard & Poor's publishes a paperback book entitled *Options Handbook* that primarily provides information about the corporation that issued the securities to which the option applies. In this respect, the *Options Handbook* is similar to Standard & Poor's *Stock Market Encyclopedia*. In addition to information about the corporation on which the options are traded, the *Options Handbook* contains pieces of essential information about the options themselves.

Value Line Inc. publishes a weekly magazine named *Value Line Options and Convertibles* that contains much valuable information about the corporation that issued the securities on which the options are written, along with valuable information of particular interest to option buyers and writers. In the opinion of some observers, the *Value Line Options and Convertibles* periodical provides option traders with the best available information that can be obtained at a modest price.

[12] Fisher Black, "Yes, Virginia, There Is Hope: Tests of the Value Line Ranking System," *Financial Analysts Journal*, September–October 1973. L. D. Brown and M. S. Rozoff, "The Superiority of Analyst Forecasts as a Measure of Expectations: Evidence from Earnings," *Journal of Finance*, March 1978, vol. 33, no. 1, pp. 1–16. S. Basu, "The Investment Performance of Common Stocks in Relation to Their Price-Earning Ratios," *Journal of Finance*, vol. 32, no. 3, June 1977, pp. 663–682.

McGraw-Hill, Inc.

1452

NYSE Symbol MHP

Price	Range	P-E Ratio	Dividend	Yield	S&P Ranking
Jun. 19'84 44	1984 $45\frac{1}{4}$-34	17	1.24	2.8%	NR

Summary

McGraw-Hill is a major supplier of informational products and services for businesses, education and industry through a broad range of media, such as magazines (including Business Week), textbooks, information systems, technical and scientific books, financial services, and economic information services. It also owns and operates four television stations. McGraw-Hill is the parent company of Standard & Poor's.

Current Outlook

Earnings for 1984 are expected to advance from the $2.52 a share reported for 1983.

The quarterly dividend was raised 15%, to $0.31 from $0.27, with the March, 1984 payment.

Revenues and earnings in 1984 should benefit from strong advances in educational services, information services, and Standard & Poor's. Favorable advances are also expected from books, publications, and broadcasting. A strong recovery is anticipated from Data Resources, Inc.

Operating Revenues (Million $)

Quarter:	1984	1983	1982	1981
Mar.	300	276	261	235
Jun.		308	282	255
Sep.		345	315	298
Dec.		365	335	323
		1,295	1,194	1,110

Revenues for the March, 1984 quarter rose 8.8%, year to year. Margins widened, and led by gains from publications, Standard & Poor's and broadcasting, pretax earnings advanced 17%. After taxes at 48.8% in both periods, net income also gained 17%.

Common Share Earnings ($)

Quarter:	1984	1983	1982	1981
Mar.	0.53	0.45	0.40	0.35
Jun.		0.55	0.48	0.41
Sep.		0.79	0.67	0.65
Dec.		0.73	0.65	0.58
		2.52	2.20	1.97

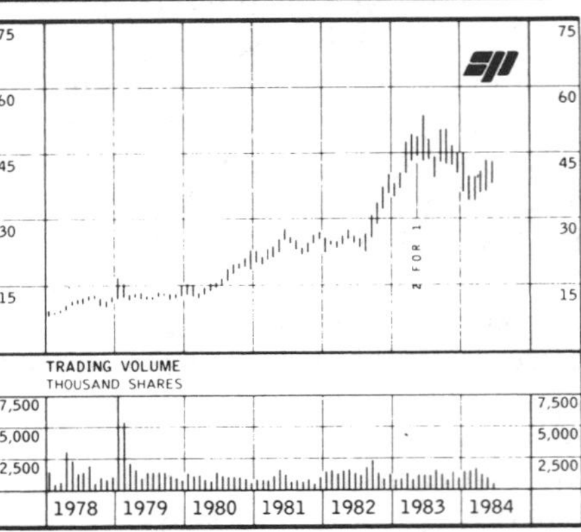

Important Developments

Jun. '84—MHP acquired Center for Communications Management, Inc., the nation's leading supplier of rate data and other information on telecommunications services.

May '84—The company agreed in principle to acquire Educational Management Services, Inc. (EMS) for $1,225,000 in cash. EMS designs, develops, and markets microcomputer software and custom courseware used primarily for educational and training purposes.

Apr. '84—MHP acquired the publishing assets of Sapphire Books, Pty., Ltd, based in Sydney, Australia. Sapphire is a leading publisher of educational texts.

Next earnings report due in late July.

Per Share Data ($)

Yr. End Dec. 31	[1]1983	[1]1982	1981	[1]1980	[1]1979	[1]1978	[1]1977	[1]1976	1975	1974
Book Value	**8.54**	6.99	6.15	4.88	3.77	4.92	4.25	3.80	3.34	2.90
Earnings[2]	**2.52**	2.20	1.97	1.74	1.55	1.29	1.04	0.82	0.67	0.61
Dividends	**1.08**	0.94	0.84	0.76	0.64	0.50	0.40	0.32	0.28	0.25
Payout Ratio	**43%**	43%	43%	44%	41%	39%	38%	38%	40%	40%
Prices—High	**$53\frac{7}{8}$**	$40\frac{1}{2}$	28	$23\frac{1}{8}$	17	$13\frac{1}{8}$	10	$8\frac{5}{8}$	$6\frac{7}{8}$	$4\frac{1}{2}$
Low	**35**	$22\frac{1}{2}$	$19\frac{3}{4}$	$12\frac{1}{8}$	$11\frac{7}{8}$	$8\frac{1}{4}$	$7\frac{7}{8}$	$6\frac{1}{2}$	3	$2\frac{3}{4}$
P/E Ratio—	**21-14**	18-10	14-10	13-7	11-8	10-6	10-8	10-8	10-4	7-4

Data as orig. reptd. Adj. for stk. div(s). of 100% Jun. 1983. **1.** Reflects merger or acquisition. **2.** Bef. spec. item(s) of −0.01 in 1974.

June 26, 1984

Standard & Poor's Corp.
25 Broadway, NY, NY 10004

1452

McGraw-Hill, Inc.

Income Data (Million $)

Year Ended Dec. 31	Revs.	Oper. Inc.	% Oper. Inc. of Revs.	Cap. Exp.	Depr.	Int. Exp.	Net Bef. Taxes	Eff. Tax Rate	[3]Net Inc.	% Net Inc. of Revs.
[1]1983	1,295	255	19.7%	49.2	27.7	2.00	[2]247	48.8%	126	9.8%
[1]1982	1,194	222	18.6	42.0	24.8	1.87	[2]215	48.8%	110	9.2%
1981	1,110	202	18.2%	37.9	22.5	4.63	[2]191	48.8%	98	8.8%
[1]1980	1,000	189	18.9%	20.9	20.8	8.47	[2]171	49.2%	86	8.6%
[1]1979	880	159	18.0%	25.2	15.0	5.76	[2]153	49.2%	77	8.7%
[1]1978	761	136	17.9%	18.0	11.8	2.96	[2]132	51.2%	64	8.4%
[1]1977	659	112	16.9%	13.5	9.8	3.08	[2]107	51.5%	51	7.8%
[1]1976	590	91	15.4%	7.5	8.7	3.35	[2] 85	51.5%	40	6.9%
1975	536	75	14.0%	9.9	8.8	5.19	[2] 67	49.9%	33	6.2%
1974	510	68	13.4%	5.7	8.5	7.51	[2] 59	48.2%	30	5.9%

Balance Sheet Data (Million $)

Dec. 31	Cash	——Current—— Assets	Liab.	Ratio	Total Assets	Ret. on Assets	Long Term Debt	Common Equity	Total Cap.	% LT Debt of Cap.	Ret. on Equity
1983	127	592	362	1.6	1,053	12.6%	3.5	616	662	0.5%	21.8%
1982	77	506	331	1.5	945	12.0%	11.3	541	589	1.9%	21.2%
1981	65	470	318	1.5	879	11.8%	14.5	496	543	2.7%	21.0%
1980	29	395	286	1.4	786	11.3%	17.5	437	482	3.6%	20.9%
1979	26	361	293	1.2	743	11.3%	20.1	388	432	4.7%	21.0%
1978	93	363	205	1.8	616	10.8%	29.8	341	390	7.6%	19.6%
1977	83	317	179	1.8	550	9.8%	33.5	300	350	9.6%	17.8%
1976	46	267	149	1.8	482	8.6%	41.2	263	325	12.7%	15.7%
1975	20	237	140	1.7	454	7.4%	49.8	237	308	16.2%	14.1%
1974	15	227	148	1.5	445	6.9%	58.0	218	295	19.7%	14.0%

Data as orig. reptd. **1.** Reflects merger or acquisition. **2.** Incl. equity in earns. of nonconsol. subs. **3.** Bef. spec. item(s) in 1974.

Business Summary

McGraw-Hill is a major provider of informational products and services through publications, information systems, service businesses, and TV broadcasting. Segment contributions in 1983:

	Revs.	Profits
Books	32%	25%
Publications	29%	25%
Information Systems	17%	23%
Standard & Poor's	10%	14%
Data Resources, Inc.	6%	3%
Broadcasting	6%	10%

The Books and Education Services division publishes books and other materials for educational, industrial, professional, and general markets.

The Publications division publishes magazines and newsletters devoted to industrial, commercial, and professional fields, including "Business Week" magazine.

The Information Systems division issues construction statistics, catalogs on building suppliers, real estate information, and computer product information.

Standard & Poor's supplies a broadly based line of financial information and advisory services.

Economic information services are provided by Data Resources, Inc.

TV stations include KMGH-TV, Denver; WRTV, Indianapolis; KGTV, San Diego; and KERO-TV (UHF), Bakersfield (Calif.).

Dividend Data

Dividends have been paid since 1937. A dividend reinvestment plan is available.

Amt. of Divd. $	Date Decl.	Ex-divd. Date	Stock of Record	Payment Date
0.27	Jul. 27	Aug. 22	Aug. 26	Sep. 13'83
0.27	Oct. 26	Nov. 21	Nov. 28	Dec. 13'83
0.31	Jan. 25	Feb. 21	Feb. 27	Mar. 12'84
0.31	Apr. 25	May 22	May 29	Jun. 12'84

Capitalization

Long Term Debt: $3,465,000.

$1.20 Conv. Preference Stock: 20,010 shs. ($10 par); red. at $40; conv. into 3.3 com.

Common Stock: 50,188,584 shs. ($1 par). The McGraw family controls about 20%. Institutions hold about 57%. Shareholders of record: 8,430.

Office—1221 Avenue of the Americas, NYC 10020. **Tel**—(212) 512-2000. **Chrmn**—H. W. McGraw, Jr. **Pres & CEO**—J. L. Dionne. **Sr VP-Secy**—R. N. Landes. **VP-Treas**—R. J. Webb. **Investor Contact**—M. A. Cooper. **Dirs**—V. R. Alden, J. B. Cave, K. K. Clarke, J. L. Dionne, P. O. Lawson-Johnston, W. J. McGill, H. W. McGraw, Jr., J. L. McGraw, A. J. Pifer, L. Putze, W. T. Seawell, H. S. Tuthill, A. O. Way, T. S. Weber, Jr., G. R. Webster. **Transfer Agents**—Manufacturers Hanover Trust Co., NYC; Manufacturers Hanover Trust Co. of California, San Francisco. **Incorporated** in New York in 1925.

Information has been obtained from sources believed to be reliable, but its accuracy and completeness are not guaranteed. William H. Donald

FIGURE 6-11 sample page from Standard & Poor's *Stock Market Encyclopedia. Note*: The information was current when published, but since conditions can change rapidly, later reports may give different opinions about the same security. (*Source*: Standard & Poor's Corporation, 25 Broadway, New York.)

McDONALD'S CORP. NYSE-MCD

RECENT PRICE **50** | P/E RATIO **11.1** (Trailing: 12.2 Median: 12.0) | RELATIVE P/E RATIO **1.12** | DIV'D YLD **1.7%** | **320**

High	6.6	6.9	17.3	34.4	34.2	28.1	26.9	30.5	23.7	26.9	23.1	23.1	32.4	43.7	49.7	53.9
Low	3.6	4.1	6.6	16.5	19.6	9.5	11.9	21.7	16.8	19.5	17.5	16.1	21.5	25.8	36.6	40.9

Institutional Decisions

	2Q'83	3Q'83	4Q'83	1Q'84	2Q'84
to Buy	111	101	86	112	113
to Sell	106	98	108	92	84
Hldg's(000)	52540	50734	52184	53289	54802

Insider Decisions 1983

	M	J	J	A	S	O	N	D	J	F	M	A	M	J	J
to Buy	2	1	0	3	6	9	4	5	3	2	3	2	1	0	0
to Sell	1	3	2	0	1	2	0	5	0	0	8	6	0	7	2

1986 | 1987 | 1988 | 1989

October 5, 1984 Value Line

TIMELINESS (Relative Price Performance Next 12 Mos.) **2** Above Average

SAFETY (Scale: 1 Highest to 5 Lowest) **1** Highest

BETA 1.00 (1.00 = Market)

1987-89 PROJECTIONS

	Price	Gain	Ann'l Total Return
High	110	(+120%)	23%
Low	90	(+ 80%)	17%

© Value Line, Inc.

1968	1969	1970	1971	1972	1973	1974	1975	1976	1977	1978	1979	1980	1981	1982	1983	1984	1985		87-89E
1.25	1.78	2.32	3.29	4.43	6.66	8.16	10.46	12.90	15.46	18.34	21.43	24.53	27.80	30.81	34.42	**38.90**	**44.60**	Revenues per sh	**64.40**
.16	.23	.29	.41	.55	.79	1.04	1.38	1.73	2.22	2.66	3.16	3.77	4.48	5.06	5.93	**6.75**	**7.75**	"Cash Flow" per sh	**11.70**
.12	.17	.22	.30	42	.58	.76	.96	1.21	1.50	1.78	2.08	2.44	2.91	3.33	3.83	**4.40**	**5.05**	Earnings per sh (A)	**7.75**
--	--	--	--	--	--	--	--	.04	.07	.14	.23	.33	.42	.52	.65	**.76**	**.90**	Div'd Decl'd per sh (B)	**1.50**
.20	.55	.62	.65	1.32	2.06	2.64	2.49	2.52	3.32	3.89	4.84	4.54	4.63	5.54	5.87	**6.50**	**7.00**	Cap'l Spending per sh	**9.50**
.49	.65	1.26	1.58	2.28	2.94	3.70	4.60	5.76	7.07	8.74	10.53	12.63	15.14	17.01	19.72	**23.00**	**27.15**	Book Value per sh (C)	**42.50**
71.26	72.62	83.22	84.43	86.97	88.94	89.30	90.03	91.16	90.96	91.14	90.45	90.31	90.51	89.88	89.00	**88.50**	**88.50**	Common Shs Outst'g (D)	**90.00**
31.8	29.0	26.1	40.1	59.8	48.9	25.5	22.4	21.3	13.8	12.6	9.6	8.3	9.5	9.9	11.4	Bold figures are		Avg Ann'l P/E Ratio	**13.0**
1.91	1.76	1.87	2.56	4.10	4.82	3.57	2.99	2.73	1.81	1.72	1.39	1.10	1.15	1.09	.96	Value Line		Relative P/E Ratio	**1.10**
--	--	--	--	--	--	--	--	.2%	.3%	.6%	1.1%	1.6%	1.5%	1.6%	1.5%	estimates		Avg Ann'l Div'd Yield	**1.5%**

CAPITAL STRUCTURE as of 6/30/84
Total Debt $1290.3 mill. **Due in 5 Yrs** $600 mill.
LT Debt $1162.0 mill. **LT Interest** $120 mill.
Incl. $75.5 mill. capitalized leases.
(LT interest earned: 7.0x; total interest coverage: 6.5x) (37% of Cap'l)
Leases, Uncapitalized Annual rentals $72.8 mill.
Pension Liability None in '83 vs. None in '82
Pfd Stock $66.5 mill. **Pfd Div'd** $5.9 mill.
1,330,828 shs. adjustable rate cum. (no par; $50 liq. value), ea. conv. into $50 worth of common (or cash, at company's option) (2% of Cap'l)
Common Stock 88,228,496 shs. (adjusted for 3-for-2 split 9/84) (61% of Cap'l)

1974	1975	1976	1977	1978	1979	1980	1981	1982	1983	1984	1985		87-89E
729.0	941.5	1175.9	1406.2	1671.9	1937.9	2215.5	2515.8	2769.5	3062.9	**3440**	**3950**	Revenues ($mill)	**5800**
25.0%	25.9%	25.9%	27.6%	27.3%	26.5%	27.7%	28.4%	28.7%	30.1%	**30.0%**	**30.0%**	Operating Margin	**31.0%**
25.4	37.3	48.1	65.4	79.8	97.0	119.8	140.6	154.3	185.5	**210**	**240**	Depreciation ($mill)	**360**
67.4	86.9	110.1	136.7	162.7	188.6	220.9	264.8	300.6	342.6	**390**	**450**	Net Profit ($mill)	**700**
50.2%	49.5%	49.3%	48.8%	48.0%	45.3%	45.1%	45.0%	44.9%	45.4%	**45.0%**	**45.0%**	Income Tax Rate	**45.0%**
9.3%	9.2%	9.4%	9.7%	9.7%	9.7%	10.0%	10.5%	10.9%	11.2%	**11.3%**	**11.4%**	Net Profit Margin	**12.1%**
11.5	17.9	5.1	d6.7	d8.5	d27.6	d98.7	d176.7	d178.2	d198.5	**d200**	**d225**	Working Cap'l ($mill)	**d300**
353.5	444.0	496.6	687.9	782.8	966.1	969.8	925.5	1055.9	1171.3	**1200**	**1250**	Long-Term Debt ($mill) (E)	**1300**
330.5	414.3	525.4	643.1	796.3	952.2	1140.9	1370.7	1528.6	1755.1	**2100**	**2450**	Net Worth ($mill)	**3900**
11.7%	12.2%	12.8%	12.5%	12.4%	11.9%	12.7%	13.7%	13.5%	13.5%	**13.5%**	**14.0%**	% Earned Total Cap'l	**14.5%**
20.4%	21.0%	21.0%	21.3%	20.4%	19.8%	19.4%	19.3%	19.7%	19.5%	**18.5%**	**18.5%**	% Earned Net Worth	**18.0%**
20.4%	21.0%	20.2%	20.3%	18.8%	17.7%	16.8%	16.5%	16.6%	16.2%	**15.5%**	**15.5%**	% Retained to Comm Eq	**14.5%**
--	--	4%	4%	8%	11%	13%	14%	16%	17%	**18%**	**19%**	% All Div'ds to Net Prof	**20%**

CURRENT POSITION ($MILL.)	1982	1983	6/30/84
Cash Assets	44.1	66.5	65.0
Receivables	88.0	89.0	100.7
Inventory(FIFO)	23.5	26.6	25.9
Other	44.5	49.3	46.7
Current Assets	200.1	231.4	238.3
Accts Payable	153.8	179.4	164.6
Debt Due	100.2	101.0	128.3
Other	124.3	149.5	145.9
Current Liab.	378.3	429.9	438.8

ANNUAL RATES of change (per sh)	Past 10 Yrs	Past 5 Yrs	Est '81-'83 to '87-'89
Revenues	20.5%	15.0%	*13.0%*
"Cash Flow"	24.5%	18.5%	*14.5%*
Earnings	22.5%	17.5%	*15.0%*
Dividends	—	44.5%	*19.0%*
Book Value	22.5%	19.0%	*16.0%*

Cal-endar	QUARTERLY REVENUES ($ mill.) Mar. 31	June 30	Sept. 30	Dec. 31	Full Year
1981	562.1	650.0	668.1	635.6	2515.8
1982	616.7	724.9	737.6	690.3	2769.5
1983	663.1	786.6	830.1	783.1	3062.9
1984	758.4	882.0	**920**	**879.6**	**3440**
1985	**870**	**1000**	**1060**	**1020**	**3950**

Cal-endar	EARNINGS PER SHARE (A) Mar. 31	June 30	Sept. 30	Dec. 31	Full Year
1981	.57	.84	.83	.67	2.91
1982	.65	.96	.97	.75	3.33
1983	.73	1.07	1.12	.91	3.83
1984	.85	1.23	**1.29**	**1.03**	**4.40**
1985	**.97**	**1.40**	**1.48**	**1.20**	**5.05**

Cal-endar	QUARTERLY DIVIDENDS PAID (B) Mar. 31	June 30	Sept. 30	Dec. 31	Full Year
1980	.062	.088	.088	.088	.33
1981	.088	.111	.111	.111	.42
1982	.111	.133	.133	.146	.52
1983	.146	.166	.166	.166	.65
1984	.166	.193	.193	.205	

BUSINESS: McDonald's Corporation licenses and operates a chain of 7,935 self-service restaurants throughout the U.S., Canada and overseas under the name of "McDonald's". Outlets serve standardized menu of a few low-priced foods. About 70% of units are operated by independent licensees; 5% by overseas affiliates. Foreign ops. provide 22% of revs., 17% of profits. Company does not sell equipment, food, or supplies to franchisees. Labor costs, 22% of sales; advertising and promotion, 4.5%. '83 deprec. rate: 4.6%. Has 136,000 empls.; 25,800 shrhldrs. Insiders own 13% of common stock. Chairman: Fred L. Turner. Pres.: Michael Quinlan. Inc.: Del. Address: 1 McDonald's Plaza, Oak Brook, IL 60621.

Rarely has Big Mac's position in the fast food industry seemed so strong. Its recent sponsorship of the Olympic Games underscored the fact that McDonald's can overwhelm competitors with the sheer volume of its advertising. For example, McDonald's has more than twice as many restaurants as archrival Burger King, and it's probably spending three times as much on *network* TV. Under these conditions—despite ad themes that aren't particularly memorable and a menu that's still relatively limited—it's not hard to stay number one.
Earnings continue to grow at a 15% annual rate. In fact, profits would be growing at a faster pace this year if "other income" (including capital gains on the sale of restaurants) weren't running below year-earlier levels, and if margins at company-operated restaurants weren't off. We think management is deferring price increases in company stores in order to build customer traffic, but also because the biggest contributor to McDonald's bottom line—franchising income—is growing at a rate of over 20% this year (probably due to more aggressive menu pricing in franchised stores). We expect earnings growth to remain in the 15% range even if the economy slows a bit in 1985. We still consider this stock timely.
Continued expansion, inflation, and margin improvement overseas are the keys to our 3- to 5-year projections. The company's expansion strategy has long been to add at least 500 new restaurants to its system each year, which would translate into annual growth rates of 5%-6% in the second half of this decade. Inflation, which we peg at 5%-6% annually over the next few years, tends to "automatically" boost McDonald's franchising income, since it's calculated as a percentage of franchisees' sales. Finally, the company is gradually building up economies of scale in a number of important foreign markets. In our opinion, this stock has superb 3- to 5-year appreciation potential for an issue of such quality (Safety: 1). **Note:** *All data on this page have been adjusted for the recent 3-for-2 split.* T.W.P.

Restated Revenues (and Operating* Margins) by Business Line

	1981	1982	1983	1984
Company Stores	1915.9(17.0%)	2094.8(16.9%)	2297.4(18.0%)	2570(17.5%)
Licensed Stores	561.3(84.8%)	620.4(85.0%)	703.7(84.7%)	820(85.0%)
Other	38.6(100.0%)	54.3(100.0%)	61.8(100.0%)	50.0(100.0%)
Company Total	2515.8(33.4%)	2769.5(33.8%)	3062.9(35.0%)	3440(35.0%)

*Before unallocated corporate expenses.

(A) Based on average shares outstanding. Next earnings report due late Oct. Estimated current cost egs./sh.: '83, $3.00. (B) Next dividend meeting about Oct. 17. Goes ex about Oct. 23. Approximate dividend payment dates: Feb. 9, June 12, Aug. 9, Nov. 4. (C) Incl. intangibles. In '83: $144.1 mill., $1.62/sh. (D) In millions, adjusted for stock splits and dividends. (E) Incl. capitalized leases as of 1977.

Company's Financial Strength	A+
Stock's Price Stability	85
Price Growth Persistence	35
Earnings Predictability	100

Factual material is obtained from sources believed to be reliable but cannot be guaranteed.

FIGURE 6-12 sample company report from *Value Line Investment Survey. Note*: The information was current when published, but since conditions can change rapidly, later reports may give different opinions about the same security. (*Source*: Value Line Inc., 711 Third Avenue, New York.)

Growth prospects remain good for most of the fast food companies under Value Line review. Year-to-year same-store sales gains inevitably are starting to ease; comparisons became much more "difficult" in the third quarter than they were in the first half. But we don't expect customer traffic to actually start slipping unless the economic slowdown we project for 1985 develops into a full-blown recession. Moreover, accelerating expansion programs will tend to keep top-line growth relatively strong next year. (Over the long run, however, more aggressive construction plans are likely to mean more intense competition—especially if the economy doesn't continue to cooperate.)

Costs remain in good shape, for the most part. We see no major problems on the horizon in either the commodity or the labor markets. The current political environment is not one in which the minimum wage is likely to be boosted. And the upward pressure on meat prices that we expect over the next few quarters can be easily offset by modest adjustments in menu prices.

This industry's overall Timeliness rank is well above average. Four stocks carry our top rank (1) for expected relative performance over the next 12 months: *Collins Foods, Piccadilly, Shoney's,* and *Wendy's. McDonald's* also is a timely commitment (rank: 2).

COMPOSITE STATISTICS: FAST FOOD SERVICE INDUSTRY							
1980	1981	1982	1983	1984	1985	© Value Line, Inc.	87-89E
5821.9	6756.5	8063.7	9183.5	***10500***	***12000***	Sales ($mill)	***18500***
18.9%	19.3%	19.4%	19.5%	***19.5%***	***19.5%***	Operating Margin	***19.0%***
254.0	298.8	366.5	437.3	***520***	***600***	Depreciation ($mill)	***900***
376.3	473.3	563.5	632.9	***735***	***840***	Net Profit ($mill)	***1250***
43.5%	43.6%	43.9%	44.2%	***44.0%***	***44.0%***	Income Tax Rate	***43.0%***
6.5%	7.0%	7.0%	6.9%	***7.0%***	***7.0%***	Net Profit Margin	***6.8%***
d57.4	d52.0	d23.8	d3.5	***d25.0***	***d35.0***	Working Cap'l ($mill)	***d100***
1777.6	1805.3	2143.6	2294.4	***2450***	***2600***	Long-Term Debt ($mill)	***3400***
2096.2	2603.7	3182.8	3723.6	***4425***	***5150***	Net Worth ($mill)	***7800***
12.0%	12.9%	12.6%	12.4%	***12.5%***	***12.5%***	% Earned Total Cap'l	***12.5%***
18.0%	18.2%	17.7%	17.0%	***16.5%***	***16.5%***	% Earned Net Worth	***16.0%***
14.9%	15.2%	14.8%	14.0%	***13.5%***	***13.5%***	% Retained to Comm Eq	***13.0%***
17%	16%	17%	18%	***18%***	***18%***	% All Div'ds to Net Prof	***20%***
8.4	9.7	9.7	11.6	Bold figures are Value Line estimates		Avg Ann'l P/E Ratio	***13.0***
1.12	1.18	1.07	.98			Relative P/E Ratio	***1.10***
2.0%	1.7%	1.7%	1.5%			Avg Ann'l Div'd Yield	***1.5%***

Unit Sales: Slimmer Gains On Tap

The fast food industry didn't really begin feeling the effects of the nation's economic recovery until the middle of 1983. For the first couple of quarters of the upturn, consumers seemed intent upon satisfying their pent-up demand for big-ticket durables. Perhaps some demand for restaurant meals got "pent up" during this period; in any case, sales of many fast food chains accelerated dramatically during the summer and fall of 1983. A number of them have posted double-digit "real" unit sales increases over most of the subsequent year. Sales growth should remain relatively healthy for the balance of 1984 and 1985. (Consumer spending on food away from home has taken a remarkably stable percentage of disposable income—roughly 4%—for many years.) Nevertheless, smaller year-to-year volume gains might dampen investor enthusiasm.

What's behind Wall Street's preoccupation with same-store customer traffic? Logically enough, it's the substantial leverage that even small changes in sales can exert on store-level earnings (and thus the all-important marginal return on investment), due to the high level of fixed and semi-fixed costs in the restaurant industry. It's important to note, however, that real sales increases do not automatically boost the bottom line. *Ponderosa,* for example, achieved an eye-popping 25% customer count gain in its latest fiscal quarter, yet its share earnings actually fell. Reason: Part of the growth came from the rollout of a breakfast buffet, which entailed high initial food and labor costs. Several other chains, including Pillsbury's Burger King and *Wendy's,* also are adding breakfast menus or other new products that are generating large customer traffic gains—whose "normal" impact on earnings is being muted temporarily by startup-type costs and/or lower built-in profit margins. Management's eventual goal, of course, is to extract profits at least proportional to the added revenues.

INDUSTRY TIMELINESS: 15 (of 91)

In any event, the upbeat tone of industry sales trends seems to have more than offset upward pressure on interest rates in the planning of construction programs for 1985 and beyond. *Wendy's* recently announced that it would accelerate expansion of its company-operated restaurant base from an 11% pace in 1984 to 16% in 1985. Very few other fast feeders are likely to step up their capital spending *that* much, but many companies plan to boost their new-unit growth rates moderately, and virtually all will at least maintain them.

Is There Room For Everyone As The Industry Matures?

Just about everyone, in our opinion. Those who keep their finances in order and stay in tune with changing consumer tastes should have little trouble maintaining their current expansion paces into the 1990s. But there will always be companies putting themselves at risk by expanding too rapidly, marketing their concepts poorly, embracing the wrong new product, etc. And it's entirely possible that the margin for error will shrink as the restaurant industry increasingly is dominated by large, efficient companies. (Much of the growth of the well-known national chains has come at the expense of "mom and pop" operators—not each other.)

Assuming the U.S. economic boom gives way to a more sustainable growth rate, the fast food industry's current expansion plans, in aggregate, will be a step or two ahead of growth in consumer demand. This implies some downward pressure on marginal returns on investment in this industry. In that kind of environment, mediocre operators are likely to struggle, and some could fail if an increasingly competitive situation is compounded by a severe recession. Investors, should note, however, that most of the large, well-capitalized companies we follow are more likely to take advantage of such circumstances than to be victimized by them. *T.W.P./M.L.C.*

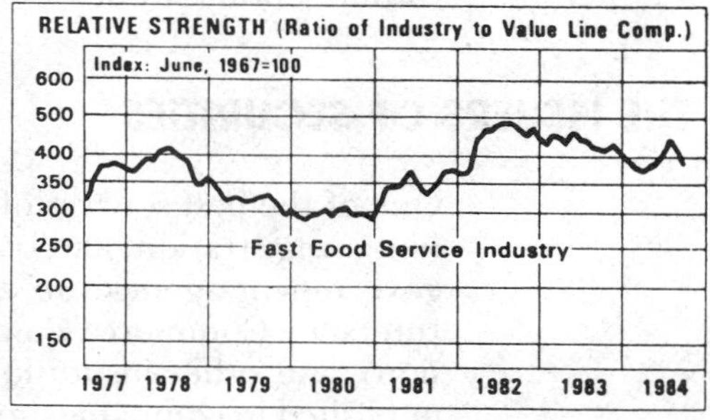

FIGURE 6-13 sample industry report from *Value Line Investment Survey. Note*: The information was current when published, but since conditions can change rapidly, later reports may give different opinions about the same security. (*Source*: Value Line Inc., 711 Third Avenue, New York.)

6-4 BROKERAGE HOUSES

Brokerage houses are the offices of securities brokers and dealers. In order to expedite their sales efforts these brokerage offices usually carry one or more of the leading investment surveys for their customers' use. However, large brokerages maintain their own research departments that generate information for their customers. A broker's research department disseminates publications, usually in the form of market newsletters or reviews, upon request. The department makes analyses of industries and individual companies. Upon request some research departments will also analyze portfolios and make specific recommendations tailored to a customer's investment goals. A brokerage that is too small to maintain a research staff may use a research company, such as Argus Research or Data Digests; sometimes small brokerages even use newsletters from the larger brokerage houses.

Most of the major brokerage firms in the United States have research departments. The largest securities brokerages are listed in Table 6-1.

Nearly every large city in the United States has a branch sales office of several of the firms listed in Table 6-1. Each brokerage firm's research department produces reports in the form of booklets that are mailed to anyone requesting them. The reports are sent at no cost in order to attract customers.

Some brokerages have the reputation of being "retailers," as opposed to being primarily institutional brokerages or investment bankers. These retail brokerages sell primarily to individual investors—the "little people." In order to attract the small investor, they provide numerous services either free or at a minimum charge. Merrill Lynch, Pierce, Fenner & Smith is the most prominent retail brokerage. Among the free services such firms frequently provide for their customers are up-to-the-minute financial news, information about commodities and bonds as well as common stock, and safekeeping of securities.

Although the large retail brokerages strive to maintain a good reputation for fair dealing, their salespeople's advice should not be followed blindly. The brokerages' publications enable investors to get a quick look at the market and the particular brokerage's feelings about it. Wise investors, however, will never rely on the report of just one firm or investment service, but will examine other views before investing.

6-5 THE ISSUERS OF SECURITIES

One of the best sources of financial information is the issuing firm itself. The filing, registration, and other statements required by the NYSE, the SEC, the government agencies in charge of regulating various industries (such as the Interstate Commerce Commission and the Federal Communications Commission), and other institutions provide detailed information that usually is not published in companies' annual and quarterly reports. Such detailed information is of little value to the casual investor, but it can be very useful to the serious analyst. Details about expenses, maintenance, interest, receivables, inventories, depreciation, sources and application of the funds, employment

TABLE 6-1 the 25 largest brokerage houses in the United States

1982 rank	1983 rank	name of firm	total capital	equity capital	subordinated debt	excess net capital	number of employees	number of offices	number of registered representatives
1	1	Merrill Lynch & Co.	$1,685,277,000	$1,432,882,000	$252,395,000	$119,561,000	37,882	910	10,200
2	2	Salomon Brothers Holding Co.	1,091,600,000	888,500,000	203,100,000	222,700,000	2,478	9	727
4	3	Shearson/American Express	836,615,000	552,553,000	284,062,000	261,025,000	10,342	352	3,967
3	4	The E.F. Hutton Group	608,061,000	414,703,000	193,358,000	115,910,000	13,400	364	5,300
5	5	Goldman, Sachs & Co.	478,000,000[1]	363,000,000	115,000,000	443,600,000	3,145	15	834
6	6	Prudential-Bache Securities	443,474,000	437,974,000	5,500,000	31,740,000	9,600	250	3,900
9	7	The First Boston Corp.	341,161,000	271,109,000	70,052,000	212,689,000	1,889	17	608
8	8	Paine Webber	313,738,000	232,344,000	81,394,000	93,791,392	9,642	234	3,557
7	9	Dean Witter Reynolds	300,875,000	298,980,000	1,895,000	93,754,000	12,000	345	4,800
15	10	Bear, Stearns & Co.	275,825,000	204,000,000	71,825,000	193,141,800	3,100	12	800
12	11	Donaldson, Lufkin & Jenrette	249,036,000	157,323,000	91,713,000	70,000,000	3,588	44	650
11	12	Stephens	248,268,788	248,268,788	—	66,051,352	146	1	82
10	13	Morgan Stanley & Co.	247,000,000	170,700,000	76,300,000	116,477,552	2,336	6	643
13	14	Drexel Burnham Lambert	241,307,000	162,600,000	78,707,000	53,385,000	4,561	52	1,400
16	15	Warburg Paribas Becker-A.G. Becker	225,840,000	175,230,000	50,610,000	67,705,027	2,732	20	320[2]
14	16	Lehman Brothers Kuhn Loeb	201,599,000	176,599,000	25,000,000	29,840,000	2,534	10	510
21	17	Smith Barney	167,800,000	134,600,000	33,200,000	38,300,000	4,750	90	1,600
17	18	Kidder, Peabody & Co.	151,436,000[2]	135,230,000	16,206,000	16,763,000	4,716	72	1,702
19	19	A.G. Edwards & Sons	143,015,000[2]	143,015,000	—	85,415,000	3,484	206	1,738
22	20	Shelby Cullem Davis & Co.	140,263,644	140,263,644	—	—	12	2	5
18	21	Allen & Co.	130,663,000	130,663,000	—	—	NA	1	4
20	22	Thomson McKinnon Securities	126,079,211	58,942,711	67,136,500	57,168,295	3,620	107	1,600
23	23	Spear, Leeds & Kellogg	114,000,000	103,000,000	11,000,000	6,842,000	834	12	90
24	24	L.F. Rothschild, Unterberg, Towbin	102,633,000	76,693,000	25,940,000	21,120,000	1,424	9	528
—	25	The Securities Groups	90,025,000	90,025,000	—	—	115	9	NA

Source: Institutional Investor, April 1983, p. 273.

costs, wasting of assets, and treatment of nonrecurring special items are only a few of the items that must be reported to the SEC in publicly available reports.

6-5.1 forms 8-K, 9-K, and 10-Q and registration statements

In accordance with Regulation S-X, dealing with "complete disclosure," the SEC requires four kinds of reports from firms whose securities are traded publicly. These reports deal with registration, periodic reporting, insider trading, and proxy solicitations. The 8-K form is a report that firms registered with the SEC are required to file for each month in which any action occurs affecting the debt, equity, amount of capital assets, voting rights, or other aspects of the firm. The 9-K form is an unaudited report required every 6 months, containing revenues, expenses, gross sales, and special items. The 10-Q form is an unaudited quarterly report.

The information in the 8-K, 9-K, and 10-Q forms is only a portion of the information a firm is required to register with the SEC when it plans to issue new securities. When preparing a primary issue of securities, a firm is required by the Securities Act of 1933 to make a full disclosure of additional information about the issuance of the new securities, the purpose for which the new capital is to be used, information about the management, and professional opinions about various aspects of the new undertaking. The firm is required to file a registration statement with the SEC at least 20 days before it may sell its new securities. The first part of this registration statement is the *prospectus*. Prospectuses are available free to the public. The law requires that every investor who buys shares in a new issue be given a prospectus.

6-5.2 annual reports and interviews with executives

Investors may also obtain information about a firm by reading its annual report or interviewing its executives. However, both these sources may be biased. Only events that have a favorable impact on the firm's prospects are discussed in most cases, for management is reluctant to publicize its errors.

6-6 PROFESSIONAL JOURNALS

Various professional organizations and publishing companies publish periodicals containing articles relevant to financial investing. Some of the more prominent journals are briefly discussed here.

6-6.1 *Financial Analysts Journal*

The *Financial Analysts Journal (FAJ)* is a bimonthly publication of the Financial Analysts Federation, which is an association of financial analysts and others devoted to the professional advancement of investment management and security analysis.[13]

The *FAJ* addresses itself to the field of financial investments. It typically contains articles on economic viewpoint, investment management, and investment analysis. It also publishes articles on industry reviews, corporation finance, bond analysis, accounting, and similar investment topics. The articles are written primarily by finance professors, finance executives, and financial technicians.

[13] Subscriptions are $36 per year and may be obtained from *Financial Analysts Journal*, 1633 Broadway, New York, NY 10019.

6-6.2 Financial Management

Financial Management is published quarterly by the Financial Management Association. It is intended for executives interested in the financial management of business firms, but it also contains investment-related articles on such topics as stock splits, dividend policy, mergers, and stock listings.[14]

6-6.3 Institutional Investor

Institutional Investor is published monthly and is aimed at professional investors and portfolio managers, with emphasis on what is happening in the investment industry.[15] The magazine is full of promotional literature and is written by a paid professional staff. No intellectual material or mathematical formulas are used in the articles in *Institutional Investor*. This magazine and the one discussed next specialize in publishing articles for busy investment executives.

6-6.4 Journal of Portfolio Management

The *Journal of Portfolio Management* is published quarterly.[16] The intent of the journal is to function as a forum for the publication of academic research of use to the practicing portfolio manager. Over half the articles are written by academicians, designed to be read by investment executives.

6-6.5 Journal of Finance

The *Journal of Finance* is published five times a year by the American Finance Association, a professional organization primarily for finance professors, finance executives, and business economists. An annual membership fee of $25 entitles members of the association to receive a subscription to the *Journal of Finance (JF)* at no additional fee.[17] The *JF* typically contains about a dozen studies done by finance professors, a few comments on previously published articles, and reviews of recently published finance books. The papers published range from sophisticated mathematical analysis to descriptions of finance institutions. All phases of finance are covered—investments, corporation finance, public finance, real estate finance, international finance, and money and banking.

6-6.6 Journal of Financial and Quantitative Analysis

The *Journal of Financial and Quantitative Analysis (JFQA)* is a quarterly academic finance journal that also publishes a few applied mathematics papers. The *JFQA* is published jointly by the Western Finance Association and the graduate school of business of the University of Washington. Subscriptions cost $20 per year in the United States and $25 per year for foreign mailings.[18] Each issue of the journal contains about 10 articles submitted by professors of finance, business economics, statistics, and econometrics. Analytical articles

[14] Subscriptions are $25 per year and may be obtained from: Financial Management Assoc., Executive Director, College of Business Administration, University of South Florida, 4202 Fowler Avenue, Tampa, FL 33620.

[15] Subscriptions are $95 per year and may be obtained from *Institutional Investor*, Inc., 488 Madison Avenue, New York, NY 10022.

[16] Subscriptions are $90 per year and may be obtained from *Journal of Portfolio Management*, Subscription Department, 488 Madison Avenue, 14th floor, New York, NY 10022.

[17] Subscribers should write to Professor Robert G. Hawkins, Graduate School of Business Administration, New York University, 100 Trinity Place, New York, NY 10006.

[18] Subscriptions may be obtained from the *Journal of Financial and Quantitative Analysis*, Graduate School of Business Administration, Mackenzie Hall, University of Washington, Seattle, WA 98195.

employing mathematical and statistical studies of financial problems are found in the *JFQA*.

6-6.7 *Journal of Financial Economics (JFE)*

The *Journal of Financial Economics (JFE)* is a quarterly academic journal that is essentially managed by the finance faculty of the University of Rochester and published by Elsevier Science Publishers.[19] Each issue contains about seven articles that usually employ mathematics and/or statistics to investigate investments problems. Practically all the articles are written by professors of finance.

6-6.8 *Journal of Business (JOB)*

The *Journal of Business (JOB)* is a quarterly academic journal published by the University of Chicago.[20] The journal typically contains about six analytical articles dealing with a wide range of business topics; investments studies seem to be the most popular topic. Professors of business and economics author the articles in most cases.

6-7 PROFESSIONALLY MANAGED PORTFOLIOS

Information about mutual funds (that is, open-end investment companies) and closed-end investment companies is published by several sources. The investment companies themselves, especially the mutual funds, are always eager to mail out copies of their prospectuses and other promotional literature. And there are firms that provide information about investment companies. Three of the more prominent firms in this field are Arthur Wiesenberger Services, Inc.; Vickers Associates, Inc.; and Donoghue's Moneyletter, Inc.

6-7.1 Arthur Wiesenberger Services, Inc.

Arthur Wiesenberger Services, Inc. (a subsidiary of Warren, Gorham, and Lamont Publishers, Inc.) primarily sells information about open-end and closed-end investment companies. The firm annually publishes a large book entitled *Investment Companies*. Several early chapters of *Investment Companies* are devoted to explaining the differences between open-end and closed-end investment companies, regulations pertaining to investment companies, pertinent tax laws, and other facts. The greater part of the book is a description of the management, holdings, and history of large investment companies. It describes individual investment companies and compares the performance of some mutual funds. Figure 28-1 on page 834 is an excerpt from *Investment Companies*.

Wiesenberger Services also publishes *Charts and Statistics*, a companion volume to *Investment Companies*; *A Guide to Mutual Fund Withdrawal Plans*, a review of the income withdrawal plans of various investment companies; *Dividend Calendar*; *Reinvestment Prices*; *Range of Offering Prices*; *Mutual Affairs*;

[19] Subscriptions cost $20 per year and are available from Elsevier Science Publications, P.O. Box 851, CH-1001, Lausanne 1, Switzerland.

[20] Subscriptions cost $22 per year and may be obtained from *Journal of Business*, The University of Chicago Press, Journals Division, P.O. Box 37005, Chicago, IL 60637.

Investor Aids; and other books and pamphlets sold primarily to sales representatives for investment companies. Wiesenberger also sells two expensive ($1,000 per month) security-selection services, *Findings and Forecasts* and *Wiesenberger 333 Stock Service*. Full information may be obtained by writing to the company.[21]

6-7.2 Vickers Associates

Vickers Associates, Inc., publishes *Vickers Guide to Investment Company Portfolios*, which contains information about each of the large investment companies. Vickers Associates also publishes monthly pamphlets showing in detail the purchases and sales of the large investment companies.[22]

Portfolio Transactions by 75 Leading Investment Companies, *Vickers Favorite Fifty*, *Over-the-Counter Favorites*, and *Industry Group Summary* are summaries of current investment activity that are sold to investors seeking hot tips. *Vickers Favorite Fifty* lists stocks that are or were popular with investment companies at various dates. In addition to information about the holdings of investment companies, Vickers sells information about the portfolios of college endowment funds and insurance companies.

6-7.3 Donoghue's Moneyletter

Mutual funds that invest only in debt securities maturing in less than 1 year (that is, money market securities) are called "money market funds." William E. Donoghue has a firm in Holliston, Massachusetts, that compiles and tabulates investment data on the dozens of money market mutual funds operating in the United States. Donoghue's *Moneyletter* is published 24 times per year and gives current information about money market fund investing; Fig. 28-2 on page 835 is an excerpt from this periodical. Donoghue's *Money Fund Report* is a similar periodical for larger investors. Donoghue also publishes the *Money Fund Directory* semiannually, which gives detailed information about each money market mutual fund.[23]

6-8 DATA FILES FOR COMPUTERS

As computers have developed, the cost per computation has dropped. At the same time, equipment and programs have advanced and become easier to use. As a result, financial analysis in various forms is now being done by computer. Some firms market financial information in a form that may be read directly into a computer as raw input data.

6-8.1 the CRSP file

The Center for Research in Security Prices (CRSP) file is a magnetic tape that may be used as raw input data. There are two different versions of the CRSP tape for sale—the monthly and the daily versions. The CRSP monthly tape contains monthly prices, quarterly cash dividends, and stock dividend and

[21] Arthur Wiesenberger Services, Inc., a Division of Warren, Gorham, and Lamont, Inc., 870 Seventh Avenue, New York, NY 10017.

[22] Vickers Associates, Inc., 226 New York Avenue, Huntington, NY 11743.

[23] Donoghue's *Money Fund Reports*, P.O. Box 411, Holliston, MA 01746.

split information for every firm listed on the NYSE since 1926.[24] A daily prices version of the CRSP tape may also be purchased, but the daily tape goes back only to the 1960s. The CRSP tape costs tens of thousands of dollars per year to rent, so usually only large, well-funded institutions that are dedicated to ongoing research can afford them. However, educational institutions can rent the CRSP tape at much lower prices.

6-8.2 the ISL data

Interactive Data Corporation (IDC) sells a quarterly magnetic computer tape with daily stock trading volumes and prices and quarterly dividends and earnings for all NYSE and AMEX securities and some OTC securities; it is called the ISL tape. ISL tapes may be purchased and updated periodically.[25] The same data are also available in book form. Standard & Poor's publishes them in volumes entitled *Daily Stock Price Records*; each volume contains one quarter of data for hundreds of companies. Data management can be a problem with ISL tapes because, for example, 20 different quarterly tapes must be used to obtain 5 years of observations on one stock.

6-8.3 Compustat tapes

Standard & Poor's Compustat Services, Inc., sells a financial data base called Compustat.[26] Compustat is a magnetic tape to be read by a computer's tape-drive input device or through an authorized time-sharing vendor. The Compustat tape contains 20 years of annual data for more than 6000 stocks. Quarterly data on 2700 stocks from 1972 are also available.[27] There are 173 annual data items and 65 quarterly data items for each company on the tapes. The tapes are updated 12 times a year at no charge over the basic subscription price of $60,000 per year for corporate customers.

6-8.4 the PDE file

Standard & Poor's Compustat Services, Inc., also has the prices, dividends, and earnings (PDE) file, which contains monthly stock prices, quarterly dividends per share, quarterly earnings per share, monthly trading volume, stock dividend or split information, book value per share, the stock exchange where the stock is traded, the Compustat file code number, the CUSIP number, the industry number, and the stock exchange ticker symbol for about 5500 stocks. The tape also contains price, dividend, and earnings data on the various Standard & Poor's and other stock market indices. Purchasers of the Compustat annual and quarterly tapes and other interested parties may obtain the PDE tape at a modest price; the PDE are nearly all taken from the Compustat tapes.

6-8.5 the Value Line data base

Value Line maintains machine-readable data files on the 1650 corporations it analyzes and publishes in its *Value Line Investment Survey*. The complete data files containing stock prices and financial statement data, some of it going

[24] The tape may be purchased from the Center for Research on Security Prices, University of Chicago, 1101 East 58 Street, Chicago, IL 60607.

[25] IDC is a subsidiary of Chase Manhattan Bank. The ISL tape may be purchased from the Interactive Data Corporation, 1114 Avenue of the Americas, 6th floor, New York, NY 10036.

[26] Compustat may be purchased by writing to Compustat Services, 7400 S. Alton Court, Englewood, CO 80110.

[27] All the Compustat data and more can be obtained from a different financial data base firm named Disclosure, 5161 River Road, Bethesda, MD 20816, phone 301-951-1300. Annual subscriptions to the Disclosure Tape are available to colleges for $4500. The corporate rate is $20,000 per year.

back as far as 1954, may be purchased from Value Line in the form of magnetic tapes for several hundred dollars. Value Line also sells an abbreviated version of these data on floppy disks called Value/Screen for $495 per year. These floppy disks are available for personal computers like the IBM-PC, Compaq, other IBM-PC compatibles, Apple, Franklin Ace, and others. Contact Value Line at the address given above on page 148 to obtain their data.

6-8.6 the Berkeley options data base

The University of California at Berkeley obtains market data from the Chicago Board of Trade about the options traded there and compiles them to be sold. Daily bid and asked prices are available from 1976 to the present. These data may be purchased by contacting the business school at the Berkeley campus.

6-8.7 the Chicago Board of Trade commodity data

The Chicago Board of Trade (CBT) has been compiling commodity price information in machine-readable form since 1981. These data are available on a transaction-to-transaction basis or on a daily basis and may be purchased in the form of magnetic tapes. The data are also available in booklets that have been printed and sold by the CBT for many years. These sources of data may be acquired through the CBT itself.

The computer-accessible financial data files discussed above are far too expensive for most individual investors to purchase. However, some large universities and corporations provide these useful facilities for their students and employees at no cost to the individual user in order to expedite financial research. In addition to access to these data files, the financial researcher must either be able to program the computer to use the data or be able to employ the services of an able computer programmer.

6-9 SOFTWARE SERVICES FOR COMPUTERS

Computer programs (sometimes called software packages) are available to do some clerical-type analysis and statistical work. Most of these programs can use one of the data files discussed above as raw input data. The program reads the data file, performs the requested work, and prints out the results.

These software packages can usually be adapted to different computer systems. They calculate financial ratios, make interfirm and interindustry comparisons, do various kinds of statistical analyses, and perform other repetitive tasks.

6-9.1 the Statistical Package for the Social Sciences (SPSS)

The Statistical Package for the Social Sciences (SPSS) is a large package of computer programs for statistical analysis that is well documented, with an easy-to-read users' manual. The package contains routines to compile descriptive statistics and perform many different kinds of sophisticated statistical analyses. These programs are written in various forms and are ready for use with IBM, CDC, Univac, or Xerox Sigma computers of various sizes.[28]

[28] See N. Nie, C. H. Hull, J. G. Jenkins, and D. H. Bent, *SPSS*, 2d ed. (McGraw-Hill, New York, 1975). This is a large, easy-to-read paperback book dealing with practically every phase of the SPSS package.

6-9.2 the Bio-Med package

The Bio-Med package, originally prepared for medical research at the University of California, Los Angeles (UCLA), is now a widely used software package containing programs to do several different kinds of sophisticated statistical analysis. The excellent book of documentation that accompanies the Bio-Med programs rounds out a useful package employed in many business schools. It may be obtained at a low cost from UCLA.

6-9.3 INVESPAK

INVESPAK is a package of 25 different computer programs, written in the BASIC language, that perform various kinds of financial analysis computations. These include such tasks as calculating risk and return statistics for investment assets as well as brokerage commissions and margin requirements; estimating the value of stocks, bonds, convertible securities, warrants, and put and call options; and performing Markowitz portfolio analysis to create an efficiently diversified portfolio.[29]

6-9.4 the TK!Solver program

Software Arts Inc., the computer software company that is most famous for creating the VisiCalc spreadsheet program, has also written other programs that it sells. TK!Solver is an equation processing program that sells for $500 and will solve complex equations (for example, the *N*th degree polynomials used in present value work) for the value of any one variable in the program.[30]

6-9.5 the Time-Series Program (TSP)

One of the most sophisticated econometric packages that has been available in recent years is called the Time-Series Package (TSP). The program was originally written for large computers, but more recently a version for personal computers has been published for sale by McGraw-Hill Book Company. Written in collaboration with the original authors of the TSP program, the new scaled-down program is called Micro-TSP. The Micro-TSP package will run on an IBM-PC; it transforms variables, links up with other unrelated programs (like VisiCalc), calculates statistics (like the Durbin-Watson) that are unique to time-series analysis, prepares plots for a line printer, and performs sophisticated econometric algorithms (like the Cochrane-Orcutt autoregressive first-order scheme to overcome serial correlation problems and two-stage least-squares analysis). The program may be obtained on a floppy disk with a booklet of documentation telling how to use it, from McGraw-Hill.[31]

[29] See William B. Riley, Jr., and Austin H. Montgomery, Jr., *Guide to Computer Assisted Investment Analysis* (McGraw-Hill, New York, 1982). If you don't want to go through the labor of typing the programs into your personal computer yourself, you can obtain floppy disks with all 25 programs from McGraw-Hill for a fee.

[30] The TK!Solver program is available from Software Arts Inc., 27 Mica Lane, Wellesley, MA 02181.

[31] Quantitative analysis is, in addition to being respected, becoming increasingly popular among professional investment analysts. See Barbara Donnelly, "Wall Street's Quants Come into Their Own," *Institutional Investor*, November 1984, pp. 181–187. To get Micro-TSP write: MICRO-TSP Editor, College Division, McGraw-Hill Book Co., 1221 Avenue of the Americas, New York, NY 10020.

6-9.6 Bookstaber's *Complete Investment* Book

Richard M. Bookstaber is the author of the book entitled *The Complete Investment Book*, published by Scott-Foresman in 1985. The book includes listings of many computer programs that perform investment analysis. The computer programs are written in the Microsoft BASIC language (which is commonly used with IBM-PCs). The book has four main sections, entitled "Bonds," "Stocks," "Technical Systems," and "Options." Each chapter within the sections addresses a different trading strategy. The computer programs may be copied out of the book itself, or Dr. Bookstaber will sell the programs on floppy disks at a low price for those who do not desire to spend hours entering the code.[32]

6-10 SUMMARY

The New York Times and *The Wall Street Journal* are the most accessible sources of news that affects business in the United States. Also, investors can read about the U.S. economy in periodic newsletters sent out free by major banks and in U.S. government publications, such as the *Survey of Current Business.*

Information on selected industries and individual firms is available by subscription to an information service, such as Value Line, Standard & Poor's, or Moody's. The major brokerage houses disseminate free publications giving their investment opinions. And investors can obtain audited financial statements from the SEC.

Investors who wish to have their funds managed for them can obtain detailed information about the various mutual funds by buying reports published by Arthur Wiesenberger Services and by reading Donoghue's *Money Fund Report.*

Professional financial analysts who seek to fully analyze massive economic and financial data may buy the raw data in machine-readable form from various vendors. To complete the analysis, computer hardware and software can be obtained from a number of suppliers.

QUESTIONS

1. The financial newspapers contain analytical studies aimed at determining the cause-and-effect relationships between various economic variables. Is this true, false, or uncertain? Explain.

[32] There is approximately one program for each chapter in Bookstaber's book. For $70 Dr. Bookstaber will mail a disk containing every one of these programs entered separately on a disk and a manual explaining how to use the software. Or, for $90 Bookstaber will send a larger program that is menu-driven and links all the separate programs together with a graphics capability to form a sophisticated investments analysis package that entails every aspect discussed in his book. Those who wish to acquire Bookstaber's programs on a disk and the accompanying documentation can send their check to: The Complete Investment Software, P.O. Box 205, Short Hills, NJ 07078. These programs would cost hundreds of dollars to have keypunched commercially and many thousands of dollars to have created commercially.

2. Write an essay that describes how the NYSE index and the S & P composite index are constructed and that compares and contrasts these two indices. *Hint*: This task may require the use of Chap. 7.
3. Select a publicly traded security and compare the reports on it found in Standard & Poor's *Stock Market Encyclopedia*, in *Moody's Handbook of Widely Held Common Stocks*, and in the *Value Line Survey*. Write a page about the significant differences among these three sources. (This assignment will require outside research, since only Standard & Poor's common stock ratings are explained in this book. See Figs. 6-6 and 6-10 to start.)
4. Write a short essay contrasting Moody's Aa bond rating with Standard & Poor's AA bond rating. (This may require outside research, since bond ratings are explained only briefly in this book. See Fig. 6-7.)
5. Where could an investor interested in buying shares in a mutual fund find information that would help in choosing a fund?
6. If you had to prepare a graph of AAA-grade corporate bond yields showing the path of the interest rate time series monthly for the last 10 years, where could you find the raw data quickly, easily, and inexpensively?

security market indicators

Investors who follow the market want to know, "How's the market doing?" Security market indicators have been constructed to answer this question quickly and easily. The Dow Jones Industrial Average (DJIA) is an example of a well-known, widely quoted stock market indicator. The DJIA is widely quoted, if for no other reason, because *The Wall Street Journal* and *Barron's* are two widely read financial newspapers that are published by Dow Jones & Company—the same firm that compiles the DJIA.

Technically speaking, the DJIA is an average, not an index. A stock market *average* is merely a weighted or unweighted average stock price for a specified group of stocks. In contrast, an index is a series of pure index numbers. Stock market indices usually employ more refined methods to measure the general level and changes in stock prices than do stock market averages.

Index numbers are void of dollar values or other units of measure. Stock market indices are usually calculated as ratios of dollar values. They are "pure numbers" that are used for making comparisons between different index numbers in the same series or other index numbers. An index is usually a weighted average ratio that is calculated from an average of a large number of different stocks. The index numbers in a particular time series of index numbers are all constructed from the same base date and base value (which is usually set to be 100, 10, or 1) to make them directly comparable. Some year in the past is selected as the base year from which the index's base value is calculated in order to impart a sense of time perspective to the index.

7-1 DIFFERENT AVERAGES AND INDICES EXIST FOR DIFFERENT USES

Many different security market indices and averages exist and are published. Some stock market averages and indices are listed below.

- The Dow Jones Industrial Average

- The Dow Jones Transportation Average
- The Dow Jones Utility Average
- Moody's Industrial Average
- Moody's Railroad Stock Average
- Moody's Utility Stock Average
- Standard & Poor's Stock Averages from 90 different industrial categories
- Standard & Poor's 400 Industrial Stocks Average
- Standard & Poor's 20 Transportation Stocks Average
- Standard & Poor's 40 Utility Stocks Average
- Standard & Poor's Financial Stocks Average
- Standard & Poor's Composite 500 Stocks Average
- *The New York Times* Index
- Value Line Average
- Wilshire 5000 Equity Index
- New York Stock Exchange Average
- Center for Research on Security Prices (CRSP) Index
- National Quotation Board Index of Over-the-Counter Stocks
- American Stock Exchange (ASE) Index
- *Barron's* 50 Stock Average

Bond indices follow:

- Dow Jones 40 Bonds Index
- Salomon Brothers Corporate Bond Index
- Standard & Poor's Municipal Bond Index
- Standard & Poor's U.S. Government Bond Index

The following commodity indices are available.

- Dow Jones Indices of Spot Commodity Prices
- Dow Jones Futures Commodity Index

The security market indicators listed above are published in financial newspapers (like *Barron's*) and business periodicals (such as the various Standard & Poor's and Moody's publications).

The averages and indices above are indicators of different things and are useful for different purposes.[1] For example, someone who is searching for a growth industry would be more interested in Standard & Poor's indices of stocks from 90 different industrial categories than in the Standard & Poor's Composite 500 Stocks Average from all industries. Figure 7-1 illustrates

[1] Stock market indices have been used as a basis for constructing the so-called index funds. This interesting application is discussed in A. F. Ehrbar, "Index Funds—An Idea Whose Time Is Coming," *Fortune*, June 1976, pp. 145–154; Harvey Shapiro, "How Do You Really Run One of These Index Funds?" *Institutional Investor*, February 1976; K. P. Ambachtsheer and J. L. Farrell, "Can Active Management Add Value?" *Financial Analysts Journal*, November–December 1975, pp. 39–48.

S&P Indexes of the Securities Markets

Monthly stock price indexes—1941-43 = 10

	Sept. Month End	% Change from Prev. Month	Sept. †Avg.	Oct. 3	—†1984 Range— High	Low
500 Composite	166.10	− 0.3	166.11	162.44	169.28	147.82
400 Industrials	187.41	− 1.1	188.10	183.24	191.24	167.75
20 Transportation	140.20	0.3	138.71	136.05	161.46	117.21
40 Utilities	71.27	+ 3.6	69.71	70.53	71.30	62.90
40 Financial	17.56	+ 3.5	17.43	16.90	18.85	14.09
Capital Goods	177.38	+ 2.1	178.04	172.60	181.96	156.87
Consumer Goods	157.39	− 0.4	157.28	153.64	158.30	138.93
High Grade	125.62	+ 0.1	125.15	123.08	127.37	114.06
Low Priced	482.72	− 0.2	477.91	469.36	576.21	399.23
INDUSTRIALS						
Aerospace/Defense	244.32	− 3.4	251.10	239.47	59.11	194.44
Aluminum	131.53	− 6.3	134.46	128.69	195.39	122.58
Automobile	104.66	+ 5.4	101.98	102.37	107.52	83.04
Excl. General Motors	43.49	+ 5.9	42.65	41.40	44.48	33.20
Auto Parts—After Mkt.	23.81	+ 0.4	23.36	23.02	24.98	20.34
Auto Parts—Orig. Equip.	28.27	− 0.5	27.81	27.13	31.47	23.79
Auto Trucks & Parts	63.25	− 5.8	65.26	62.28	78.33	56.05
Beverages: Brewers	79.05	− 0.5	79.19	76.39	86.34	71.74
Distillers	298.16	0	296.71	293.64	319.95	257.88
Soft Drinks	180.36	+ 0.4	178.48	177.88	180.66	144.48
Building Materials	90.45	− 1.5	89.92	87.09	98.20	76.73
Chemicals	66.93	− 5.3	67.70	65.02	75.82	61.85
Chemicals (Miscellaneous)	19.50	− 2.5	19.88	19.09	20.36	16.92
Coal	299.42	+ 2.0	290.02	292.78	339.39	272.25
Communication—Equip./Mfrs.	37.43	− 3,2	37.37	36.09	40.31	29.24
Computer & Bus. Equip.	174.78	− 1.1	175.40	170.66	182.67	152.53
Excl. I.B.M.	258.29	− 4.8	264.30	251.12	316.27	232.05
Computer Services	38.27	+ 1.2	38.06	37.52	38.63	25.35
Conglomerates	30.94	− 2.6	31.00	30.66	34.16	28.64
Containers: Metal & Glass	73.75	+ 1.1	73.11	73.10	74.16	54.12
Paper	426.83	− 7.2	447.50	404.97	463.60	337.07
Copper	39.14	− 8.7	39.59	39.92	60.10	35.02
Cosmetics	50.63	+ 1.2	50.81	49.31	51.11	45.28
Drugs	259.10	− 2.3	259.90	258.02	270.08	244.97
Electrical Equipment	499.39	− 1.9	498.62	485.93	525.36	438.77
Electronic Major Cos	180.33	− 1.5	182.19	174.53	187.63	158.09
Electronics—Instrumentation	67.84	− 6.6	69.11	64.73	83.48	61.95
Semiconductors/Components	48.72	−14.6	51.53	47.48	60.15	43.07
Entertainment	270.91	+ 1.7	270.72	265.70	299.86	250.37
Fertilizers	18.50	− 0.5	18.80	18.24	20.96	14.84
Foods	147.04	+ 2.6	146.29	145.26	148.58	127.19
Forest Products	19.33	− 4.9	19.79	18.93	24.57	18.22
Gaming Cos.	12.34	− 5.6	12.92	12.20	14.08	10.87
Gold Mining	143.93	+ 4.6	135.95	144.65	191.33	120.61
Hardware & Tools	12.95	− 0.8	12.95	12.70	14.63	10.78
Homebuilding	40.48	+ 5.2	38.99	38.50	50.82	32.20
Hospital Management	59.39	−11.9	61.87	57.28	68.21	52.65
Hospital Supplies	56.27	− 9.8	59.24	53.94	72.50	53.53
Hotel-Motel	104.26	+ 0.9	103.11	101.22	117.84	94.66
Household Furnish. & Appliances	276.21	+ 1.8	274.13	266.55	355.26	244.32
Leisure Time	123.66	− 2.1	125.33	123.20	126.73	101.01
Machine Tools	156.19	+ 0.4	158.77	148.59	210.98	132.78
Machinery: Agricultural	42.59	+ 1.9	41.81	40.03	60.69	34.82
Construction & Mat. Handling	261.42	− 8.5	272.18	257.77	376.53	249.52
Industry/Specialty	137.10	− 3.8	139.02	134.50	165.00	123.96
Metals—Miscellaneous	102.93	− 5.3	102.06	99.95	131.90	86.47
Mobile Homes	120.84	+ 2.5	118.59	113.92	169.89	92.31
Offshore Drilling	121.47	+14.5	113.45	118.48	131.98	87.01
Oil Composite	339.69	+ 2.4	334.60	336.61	339.45	284.48
Crude Producers	799.62	− 0.7	794.70	794.43	851.47	735.37
Integrated: Domestic	401.43	+ 2.1	404.40	408.79	412.54	339.76
Int'l. Integrated	141.74	+ 3.1	139.40	139.41	141.68	118.16
Oil Well Equip. & Service	1354.79	− 2.4	1337.03	1317.27	1609.62	1209.26
*Canadian Oil & Gas Exploration	21.46	+ 3.2	20.90	21.43	21.56	16.59
Paper	332.28	− 7.4	345.06	326.61	363.14	293.12
Pollution Control	62.20	+ 3.6	60.53	59.05	65.91	41.17
Publishing	797.16	− 2.7	822.46	784.29	839.88	677.26
Publishing (Newspapers)	66.19	− 5.2	67.14	63.45	70.35	53.28
Radio-TV Broadcasters	1155.57	− 1.2	1169.03	1117.58	1187.39	920.10
Restaurants	82.91	− 0.7	82.91	80.61	86.01	68.41
Retail Stores Composite	159.57	+ 0.1	158.82	152.21	160.39	134.21
Department Stores	347.51	− 0.3	347.16	338.51	359.08	289.75
Retail Stores (Drug)	63.51	+ 2.5	62.33	60.79	62.80	50.35
Food Chains	105.78	+ 2.8	103.53	103.22	105.14	83.48
Gen. Merchandise Chains	13.30	− 1.0	13.30	12.51	13.68	11.19
Retail (Miscellaneous)	226.70	+ 1.1	222.95	213.35	227.42	179.41
Shoes	110.80	− 5.7	112.35	109.14	119.17	101.59
Soaps	225.04	0	224.06	226.06	227.86	198.56
Steel	37.61	− 0.6	37.03	36.21	52.07	34.99
Excl. U.S. Steel	34.88	− 1.5	34.46	33.75	50.56	32.67
Textiles: Apparel Mfrs.	63.53	− 0.3	62.88	62.97	77.63	58.87
Textile Products	91.84	− 4.7	94.32	93.18	118.95	89.86
Tires and Rubber Goods	187.42	+ 0.3	185.23	178.40	215.75	163.42
Tobacco	180.25	+ 3.8	177.15	175.49	180.25	148.22
Toys	18.66	+ 1.3	18.60	18.48	18.80	12.14
UTILITIES						
Electric Companies	38.96	+ 4.9	37.58	38.67	38.70	34.02
Natural Gas Distributors	117.20	+ 5.1	112.06	116.16	117.88	101.38
Pipelines	256.02	+ 4.2	245.97	252.03	261.34	219.83
Telephone (New)	110.06	+ 2.2	108.91	108.66	110.83	95.66
TRANSPORTATION						
Air Freight	38.35	− 0.8	38.81	37.06	43.79	28.42
Airlines	138.56	+ 0.1	135.92	135.55	184.30	119.71
Railroads	105.58	+ 0.9	103.03	102.16	114.73	87.59
Truckers	156.66	− 3.1	160.45	153.54	197.41	130.01
FINANCIAL						
Banks—New York City	66.26	+ 6.8	64.64	62.92	71.89	52.50
Outside N.Y.C.	95.92	+ 7.0	92.49	91.41	116.07	77.95
Life Insurance	466.94	+ 2.7	455.71	460.44	463.85	396.50
Multi-Line Insurance	26.59	− 0.2	26.75	26.22	27.96	22.07
Property-Casualty Insurance	186.89	+ 3.5	184.11	181.01	200.96	145.05
Savings & Loan Holding Cos.	24.86	+21.9	23.53	23.83	39.54	20.25
Personal Loans	127.85	− 2.3	128.02	128.23	133.36	98.80
*Brokerage Firms	46.98	− 7.7	49.89	42.91	54.53	37.09
*Real Estate Investment Trusts	3.81	+ 4.7	3.76	3.81	3.82	3.50
*Investment Cos.	63.38	+ 0.1	62.57	62.02	78.21	57.32
*Investment Cos. (Bond Funds)	8.01	+ 2.6	7.91	7.90	8.81	7.68

*Not included in composite indexes.

†Figures for 500 Composite, Industrials, Transportation, Utilities, and Financial based on daily indexes. All others based on weekly indexes.

The market last week

Daily Stock Price Indexes

	Oct. 5	Oct. 4	Oct. 3	Oct. 2	Oct. 1	Sept. 28
500 Composite						
H.	163.32	163.22	163.59	165.24	166.10	166.96
L.	162.51	162.44	162.20	163.55	164.48	165.77
C.	162.68	162.92	162.44	163.59	164.62	166.10
400 Industrials						
H.	184.27	184.21	184.62	186.53	187.41	188.44
L.	183.27	183.24	182.94	184.56	185.62	187.02
C.	183.39	183.83	183.24	184.62	185.75	187.41
20 Transportation						
H.	137.38	136.38	136.94	139.76	140.29	140.78
L.	135.80	135.63	135.62	136.67	138.57	139.68
C.	136.90	135.80	136.05	136.93	138.89	140.20
40 Utilities						
H.	70.88	70.76	70.86	70.88	71.27	71.48
L.	70.64	70.51	70.41	70.49	70.57	71.15
C.	70.79	70.67	70.53	70.52	70.70	71.27
40 Financial						
H.	17.06	17.00	17.16	17.37	17.56	17.72
L.	16.93	16.90	16.87	17.16	17.34	17.50
C.	16.99	16.96	16.90	17.16	17.36	17.56

Weekly Bond Yields %

Composite	Oct. 3	Sept. Avg.	1984 Range High	Low
AAA	—Discontinued—			
AA	12.87	12.97	14.23	12.19
A	13.21	13.31	14.54	12.49
BBB	14.03	14.03	15.32	13.06

Industrials	Oct. 3	Sept. Avg.	1984 Range High	Low
AAA	12.25	12.37	13.66	11.79
AA	12.66	12.84	14.13	12.02
A	13.06	13.21	14.42	12.33
BBB	14.15	14.14	15.12	12.83

Utilities	Oct. 3	Sept. Avg.	1984 High	Low
AAA	—Discontinued—			
AA	13.08	13.09	14.45	12.33
A	13.35	13.40	14.78	12.64
BBB	13.91	13.93	15.60	13.18

Government	Oct. 3	Sept. Avg.	1984 High	Low
Long Term	12.35	12.33	13.89	11.51
Intermediate	12.53	12.56	13.79	11.33
Short Term	11.97	12.12	13.22	10.70
Municipal	10.47	10.17	11.14	9.48

Other key interest rates

	Last Week	Two Weeks Ago	1984 Range High	Low
Three-Month Treasury Bills	10.19%	10.20%	10.65%	8.89%
Money-Market Funds	10.49	10.51	10.72	8.70
Prime Lending Rate	12.75	12.75	13.00	11.00
S&P 500 Stocks	4.66	4.53	4.97	4.21

S&P 500 Annual Average Total Return

1 Year Ending Sept. 28, 1984	5 Years Ending Sept. 28, 1984	10 Years Ending Sept. 28, 1984
+ 4.60%	+ 14.24%	+ 15.42%

FIGURE 7-1 Standard & Poor's stock price index data. (*Source*: *The Outlook*, p. 536, Standard & Poor's Corporation, 25 Broadway, New York.)

values for the Standard & Poor's indices, which are published with other information weekly in its publication *The Outlook*.

Market indices furnish a handy summary of historical price levels in the markets from which they were derived. This type of information has several uses. First, a person who owns several securities in some given market or industry can quickly get an indication of how market movements have affected the market value of his or her portfolio. Curious investors need only check the value of an index of similar securities and determine the percentage change in it in order to get an indication of how their own portfolios fared. This is much faster than checking the prices of each security separately. Second, indices are useful for historical analysis. By analyzing market indices and other economic indicators, an analyst can detect some consistent relationships between different indices and sectors of the economy. These types of relationships can be useful. If an index is a dependable leading index, it may be useful for forecasting.

Some people suggest that indices have other important uses. Some believe, for example, that by charting an index over time it is possible to detect patterns that are repeated at various phases of the market's rise and fall. Then the patterns from this one index can be used to forecast that market's future direction. These charting activities, called *technical analysis*, are discussed in more detail in Chaps. 18 and 19.

7-2 CONSTRUCTION OF INDICES

Every market index is constructed differently. A well-constructed market index will give an indication of the prices of the entire population under consideration. A poorly constructed index will indicate only what an unrepresentative sample of the population is doing.

In the selection of a market index with which to work, or the design of a new index, analysts should consider such factors as sample size, representativeness, weighting, convenient units.

SAMPLE SIZE The sample should be a significant fraction of the population studied because larger samples generally give clearer indications about what the underlying population is doing. On the other hand, if the sample is too large, it will be too costly to compile.

REPRESENTATIVENESS The sample should contain heterogeneous elements representing all sections of the population. For example, a sample of securities should not be limited to large firms or firms that are all in the same industry.

WEIGHTING The various elements in the sample should be assigned weights that correspond to the actual investment opportunities in the population under study. For example, a security's weight in some index might be proportional to the fraction of total market value represented by all the firms' shares outstanding. Or equal weights could be used to represent the probability of selecting any given security with random sampling—this would be like selecting stocks by throwing an unaimed dart. The equal weights could represent the results of a "no skill" investment strategy, for instance.

CONVENIENT UNITS An index should be stated in units that are easy to understand and that can be easily used to answer relevant questions.[2]

7-3 COMPARISON OF TWO STOCK MARKET INDICES

So many security market indices exist that it isn't practical to describe each different one. However, it is instructive to compare and contrast one of the best indices with one of the worst. Therefore, let us compare the popular and highly publicized Dow Jones Industrial Average (DJIA) with the more sophisticated but relatively unheard of Center for Research on Security Prices (CRSP) Index in light of the criteria listed above in Sec. 7-2.

The CRSP index is sold commercially to businesses. College researchers get substantial discounts, but the CRSP data are still costly. The data are updated only every 3 months; thus they are never sufficiently current to be useful for current events analysis. The CRSP tape is used primarily by academic researchers who are performing statistical analysis on decades of data. In contrast, the DJIA is published daily by Dow Jones & Company, owner of *The Wall Street Journal* and *Barron's* newspapers—both newspapers discuss the DJIA liberally.

SAMPLE SIZE The CRSP index contains every NYSE stock (approximately 1300) so that the sample equals the entire NYSE population. The DJIA is an average of 30 securities listed on the NYSE. Thus, the DJIA samples 2.3 percent of the population.

REPRESENTATIVENESS The DJIA contains only securities of the large, old, blue-chip firms. No small firms and no new firms are in the DJIA. In contrast, the CRSP includes every security listed on the NYSE. The disadvantage of using large samples, such as the CRSP index employs, is the cost. Since computers are now being used to do the clerical work, however, such costs are not as big a problem today as they used to be.

[2] Other factors should be considered in the design of a sample or an index, but they are beyond the scope of this discussion. The interested reader may find entire courses and books on the subject of experimental design and sampling: H. A. Latane, D. L. Tuttle, and Wm. E. Young, "Market Indices," *Financial Analysts Journal*, September–October 1971, pp. 75–85; J. H. Lorie and M. T. Hamilton, "Stock Market Indices," in *Modern Developments in Investment Management*, 2d ed., James Lorie and Richard Brealey (eds.) (The Dryden Press, Hinsdale, Ill., 1978), pp. 78–93; P. H. Cootner, "Stock Market Indexes: Fallacies and Illusions," *Commercial and Financial Chronicle*, Sept. 29, 1966 [reprinted in *Modern Developments in Investment Management*, James Lorie and Richard Brealey (eds.), pp. 94–100]; H. Working, "Note on the Correlation of First Differences of Averages in a Random Chain," *Econometrica*, vol. 28, no. 4, October 1960, pp. 916–918; L. Fisher, "Some New Stock Market Indexes," *Journal of Business*, supplementary issue of January 1966, pp. 191–225; P. L. Cheng and M. K. Deets, "Statistical Biases and Security Rates of Return," *Journal of Financial and Quantitative Analysis*, January 1971, pp. 977–994; Barr Rosenberg, "Statistical Analysis of Price Series Obscured by Averaging Measures," *Journal of Financial and Quantitative Analysis*, September 1971, pp. 1083–1094.

WEIGHTING The CRSP weights each security equally.[3] Thus, if 1300 securities are listed on the NYSE at a given date, the CRSP assigns each a weight of 1/1300. The equal weights used in the CRSP represent the proportions that would result if a portfolio were selected in a random manner, for example, with an unaimed dart. That is, every security has an equal chance of being selected by an unskilled person.

The DJIA presently uses an arbitrary weighting system. In 1928, when the DJIA was expanded to 30 stocks, the 30 market prices were simply summed up and divided by 30 to obtain the DJIA. Thus, equal weights (of 1/30) were assigned to the 30 securities used in 1928. Over the years, however, as some of the 30 securities underwent stock splits and stock dividends, the weights of 1/30 for each asset became inappropriate. To adjust for these changes, the weights of all 30 shares were increased.

Let us assume, for example, that the first of the 30 securities to be split was split 2 for 1. This split would leave two shares, each worth half as much, so the prices of the 29 original shares plus one of the new smaller shares would be summed up and the total would be divided by 29½ instead of 30.[4] This weighting system is equivalent to selling the split share and investing the proceeds evenly in all 30 remaining shares.

The adjustment process described in the preceding paragraph was not particularly rational in 1928, but it became more irrational and meaningless as some securities in the sample grew more than others. In the 1980s the 30 securities in the average were divided by 1.314 and the DJIA was in the 800 to 1300 range; the average price of the 30 shares was about $65. As a result, the weights used in the DJIA do not relate to any relevant values or market opportunities.

CONVENIENT UNITS The DJIA has ranged between 800 and 1300 points in recent years. Dow Jones & Company has explained that each of these points equals about a 7-cent change in the market value of an "average share of stock." The points themselves are void of any intrinsically meaningful economic interpretation.

Unlike the DJIA, the CRSP index contains market prices, percentage changes in the prices, and two different rates of return—one that includes cash dividends and one that omits cash dividends.[5] Since the rate of return is the most important outcome for most investments and since it is the best

[3] The CRSP also has an index in which each security is weighted by its importance (that is, market value–weighted) in the total NYSE market.

[4] Split shares usually increase in value, but this is due to retained earnings or growth in earnings and is unrelated to the split. The effects of stock splits and stock dividends, analyzed in Chap. 19, are seen to be nil, on average. The Dow Jones Industrial Average is explained in "Revised Dow Jones Industrials to Add IBM and Merck, Delete Chrysler and Esmark," *The Wall Street Journal*, June 28, 1979, p. 5.

[5] The file is actually a magnetic computer tape that contains price relatives *(PR)* rather than rates of return (denoted r). The relationship between price relatives and rates of return is shown below, where p_t denotes the dollar price at time period t.

$$PR = (p_{t+1}/p_t) = (1 + r_t)$$

standard for investment comparisons, the percentages and rates of return are quite convenient.

7-4 MAINTENANCE PROBLEMS WITH SECURITY MARKET INDICES

After a security market index is constructed, situations periodically arise that require its revision. The three main problems that make index revision necessary are (1) stock splits, (2) a change in the number of stocks in the sampled list, and (3) substitutions to replace unsatisfactory securities. The way these three problems affect the DJIA and the CRSP index are considered below.

STOCK SPLITS The strange way that stock splits are reflected in the divisor of the DJIA was explained above in the section entitled "Weighting." As a result of the Dow Jones procedure, the relative importance of stocks that split decreases and the importance of nonsplit stocks increases in the computation of the DJIA. There is no logic behind these shifts in the relative weights of the stocks in the DJIA.[6]

The CRSP index, on the other hand, handles stock splits more logically. This index is constructed from prices and returns that are adjusted to nullify any changes in the unit of account (namely, stock dividends or splits). Then, each different security in the index is assigned either an equal weight or a market value weight that is unaffected by stock splits.

CHANGE IN SAMPLE SIZE When the DJIA was first constructed in 1884 it contained 12 stocks. The sample size was increased to 20 stocks in 1916. The present sample size of 30 stocks was adopted in 1928. As for the CRSP index, selection of a sample size has never been a problem because the entire population has been used to compute the index since its inception.

SUBSTITUTIONS Substitutions can be a recurrent and troublesome problem for an index computed from a small sample—like the DJIA. There have been many substitutions in the DJIA over the decades. One of the more interesting substitutions involved IBM stock. IBM was added to the DJIA in 1932 and then deleted in 1939 in order to make room for American Telephone and Telegraph (AT&T). The logic behind this substitution was too tortured to understand in hindsight.[7] In 1979 IBM was added back into the DJIA. More specifically, Chrysler and Esmark were deleted and replaced by IBM and

[6] H. L. Butler and J. D. Allen, "Dow Jones Industrial Average Re-Examined," *Financial Analysts Journal*, November–December 1979, pp. 23–32. Butler and Allen discuss the effect of stock splits and substitutions on the DJIA. Andrew T. Rudd examines the DJIA statistically in "The Revised Dow Jones Industrial Average," *Financial Analysts Journal*, November–December 1979, pp. 57–63.

[7] The sample used in the DJIA is not only small, it doesn't even contain all industrial stocks, as the DJIA title implies it should. More specifically, the public utility stock of AT&T in the DJIA is obviously not an industrial stock. It appears that a substitution for AT&T is in order.

Merck & Co. It was felt that the two new stocks were more "blue-chip" than the two that were eliminated.

Substitutions in the CRSP are more logical and of only minor importance because of the small weight given to each individual stock. Stocks are added to or deleted from the CRSP index only when they are listed or delisted from the NYSE.[8]

7-5 CONTRASTING DIFFERENT MARKET INDICATORS

The preceding comparison of the DJIA and the CRSP stock market indicators makes the DJIA seem weak and inadequate. Surprisingly, however, the two indicators are highly positively correlated with each other.[9] In fact, almost all the stock market indicators for stock markets in the United States are highly positively correlated with each other. Consider the following nine stock market indicators; their correlation coefficients are shown in Table 7-1.

1. Dow Jones Industrial Average (DJIA)
2. Standard & Poor's 400 Industrial Stocks Average (S&P400)
3. Standard & Poor's 500 Composite Stocks Average (S&P500)
4. New York Stock Exchange (NYSE) Average
5. American Stock Exchange (ASE) Average
6. Over-the-Counter (OTC) Industrial Stocks Average (OTCIND)
7. OTC Composite Stocks Average (OTCCOMP)
8. CRSP Equally Weighted Stocks Index (CRSPEQ)
9. CRSP Value Weighted Stocks Index (CRSPVW)

[8] L. Fisher and J. Lorie, "Rates of Return on Investments in Common Stock," *Journal of Business*, January 1964, pp. 1–21. This article explains the CRSP file and presents some of the data. Professor Fisher has also prepared some additional indices, which are published in "Some New Stock Market Indexes," *Journal of Business*, January 1966, pp. 191–225.

[9] Correlation coefficients are defined in Mathematical App. D at the end of the book.

TABLE 7-1 correlation coefficients between different stock market indicators*

	DJIA	S&P400	S&P500	NYSE	ASE	OTCIND	OTCCOMP	CRSPEQ	CRSPVW
DJIA	1.0								
S&P400	.958	1.0							
S&P500	.963	.987	1.0						
NYSE	.949	.989	.981	1.0					
ASE	.675	.798	.796	.836	1.0				
OTCIND	.773	.801	.819	.837	.702	1.0			
OTCCOMP	.798	.827	.856	.846	.762	.821	1.0		
CRSPEQ	.934	.946	.955	.949	.854	.743	.806	1.0	
CRSPVW	.945	.948	.957	.953	.858	.760	.815	.920	1.0

* Monthly returns from 1973 to 1983.

TABLE 7-2 common stocks total rates of return for all yearly holding periods from 1926 to 1981 (percent per annum compounded annually)

to the end of	from the beginning of 1926	1927	1928	1929	1930	1931	1932	1933	1934	1935	1936	1937	1938	1939	1940	1941	1942	1943	1944	1945
1926	11.6																			
1927	23.9	37.5																		
1928	30.1	40.5	43.6																	
1929	19.2	21.8	14.7	−8.4																
1930	8.7	8.0	−0.4	−17.1	−24.9															
1931	−2.5	−5.1	−13.5	−27.0	−34.8	−43.3														
1932	−3.3	−5.6	−12.5	−22.7	−26.9	−27.9	−8.2													
1933	2.5	1.2	−3.8	−11.2	−11.9	−7.1	18.9	54.0												
1934	2.0	0.9	−3.5	−9.7	−9.9	−5.7	11.7	23.2	−1.4											
1935	5.9	5.2	1.8	−3.1	−2.2	3.1	19.8	30.9	20.6	47.7										
1936	8.1	7.8	4.9	0.9	2.3	7.7	22.5	31.6	24.9	40.6	33.9									
1937	3.7	3.0	0.0	−3.9	−3.3	0.2	10.2	14.3	6.1	8.7	−6.7	−35.0								
1938	5.5	5.1	2.5	−0.9	−0.0	3.6	13.0	16.9	10.7	13.9	4.5	−7.7	31.1							
1939	5.1	4.6	2.3	−0.8	−0.1	3.2	11.2	14.3	8.7	10.9	3.2	−5.3	14.3	−0.4						
1940	4.0	3.5	1.3	−1.6	−1.0	1.8	8.6	11.0	5.9	7.2	0.5	−6.5	5.6	−5.2	−9.8					
1941	3.0	2.4	0.3	−2.4	−1.9	0.5	6.4	8.2	3.5	4.3	−1.6	−7.5	1.0	−7.4	−10.7	−11.6				
1942	3.9	3.5	1.5	−1.0	−0.4	2.0	7.6	9.3	5.3	6.1	1.2	−3.4	4.6	−1.1	−1.4	3.1	20.3			
1943	5.0	4.7	2.9	0.6	1.3	3.7	9.0	10.8	7.2	8.2	4.0	0.4	7.9	3.8	4.8	10.2	23.1	25.9		
1944	5.8	5.5	3.8	1.7	2.5	4.8	9.8	11.5	8.3	9.3	5.7	2.6	9.5	6.3	7.7	12.5	22.0	22.8	19.8	
1945	7.1	6.9	5.4	3.5	4.3	6.6	11.5	13.2	10.4	11.5	8.4	5.9	12.6	10.1	12.0	17.0	25.4	27.2	27.8	36.4
1946	6.4	6.1	4.7	2.8	3.5	5.6	10.1	11.6	8.8	9.7	6.8	4.4	10.1	7.7	8.9	12.4	17.9	17.3	14.5	12.0
1947	6.3	6.1	4.7	3.0	3.7	5.6	9.8	11.2	8.6	9.4	6.7	4.5	9.6	7.5	8.5	11.4	15.8	14.9	12.3	9.9
1948	6.3	6.1	4.7	3.1	3.8	5.6	9.6	10.8	8.4	9.1	6.6	4.6	9.2	7.3	8.2	10.6	14.2	13.2	10.9	8.8
1949	6.8	6.6	5.3	3.8	4.5	6.3	10.1	11.2	9.0	9.7	7.4	5.6	10.0	8.3	9.2	11.5	14.8	14.0	12.2	10.7
1950	7.7	7.5	6.4	4.9	5.6	7.4	11.1	12.3	10.2	11.0	8.9	7.3	11.5	10.0	11.0	13.4	16.6	16.1	14.8	13.9
1951	8.3	8.1	7.1	5.7	6.4	8.2	11.7	12.9	11.0	11.7	9.8	8.4	12.4	11.1	12.1	14.3	17.3	16.9	15.9	15.3
1952	8.6	8.5	7.5	6.2	6.9	8.6	12.0	13.2	11.3	12.1	10.3	9.0	12.8	11.6	12.5	14.6	17.4	17.1	16.1	15.7
1953	8.3	8.1	7.2	5.9	6.5	8.2	11.4	12.4	10.7	11.4	9.6	8.3	11.9	10.7	11.5	13.4	15.7	15.3	14.3	13.7
1954	9.6	9.5	8.6	7.4	8.1	9.7	12.9	14.0	12.4	13.1	11.6	10.4	13.9	12.9	13.9	15.8	18.2	18.0	17.4	17.1
1955	10.2	10.2	9.3	8.2	8.9	10.5	13.7	14.7	13.2	13.9	12.5	11.4	14.8	13.9	14.9	16.8	19.1	19.0	18.5	18.4
1956	10.1	10.1	9.2	8.2	8.8	10.4	13.4	14.4	12.9	13.6	12.2	11.2	14.4	13.5	14.4	16.1	18.2	18.1	17.5	17.3
1957	9.4	9.3	8.5	7.4	8.1	9.5	12.3	13.2	11.8	12.4	11.0	10.0	13.0	12.1	12.8	14.3	16.2	15.9	15.2	14.9
1958	10.3	10.2	9.5	8.5	9.1	10.6	13.3	14.3	12.9	13.6	12.3	11.4	14.3	13.5	14.3	15.8	17.6	17.5	16.9	16.7
1959	10.3	10.3	9.5	8.6	9.2	10.6	13.3	14.2	12.9	13.5	12.3	11.4	14.2	13.4	14.1	15.6	17.3	17.1	16.6	16.4
1960	10.0	10.0	9.3	8.3	8.9	10.3	12.8	13.7	12.4	13.0	11.8	10.9	13.5	12.8	13.5	14.8	16.4	16.1	15.6	15.3
1961	10.5	10.4	9.7	8.8	9.4	10.8	13.3	14.1	12.9	13.4	12.3	11.5	14.1	13.4	14.0	15.3	16.9	16.7	16.2	16.0
1962	9.9	9.9	9.2	8.3	8.8	10.1	12.5	13.2	12.1	12.6	11.4	10.7	13.0	12.3	12.9	14.1	15.5	15.3	14.7	14.4
1963	10.2	10.2	9.5	8.7	9.2	10.5	12.8	13.5	12.4	12.9	11.8	11.1	13.4	12.7	13.3	14.5	15.8	15.6	15.1	14.9
1964	10.4	10.4	9.7	8.9	9.4	10.6	12.9	13.6	12.5	13.0	12.0	11.3	13.5	12.9	13.5	14.5	15.8	15.6	15.2	14.9
1965	10.4	10.4	9.8	9.0	9.5	10.7	12.9	13.6	12.5	13.0	12.0	11.3	13.5	12.9	13.4	14.5	15.7	15.5	15.0	14.8

TABLE 7-2 common stocks total rates of return for all yearly holding periods from 1926 to 1981 (percent per annum compounded annually)

to the end of	from the beginning of 1926	1927	1928	1929	1930	1931	1932	1933	1934	1935	1936	1937	1938	1939	1940	1941	1942	1943	1944	1945
1966	9.9	9.8	9.2	8.4	8.9	10.1	12.2	12.8	11.8	12.2	11.2	10.5	12.6	12.0	12.4	13.4	14.5	14.3	13.8	13.6
1967	10.2	10.2	9.6	8.8	9.3	10.4	12.5	13.1	12.1	12.5	11.6	10.9	12.9	12.4	12.8	13.8	14.9	14.7	14.2	14.0
1968	10.2	10.2	9.6	8.9	9.3	10.4	12.4	13.1	12.1	12.5	11.6	10.9	12.9	12.3	12.8	13.7	14.7	14.5	14.1	13.9
1969	9.8	9.7	9.1	8.4	8.9	9.9	11.8	12.4	11.4	11.8	10.9	10.3	12.1	11.6	12.0	12.8	13.8	13.6	13.1	12.9
1970	9.6	9.6	9.0	8.3	8.7	9.7	11.6	12.2	11.2	11.6	10.7	10.1	11.9	11.3	11.7	12.5	13.5	13.2	12.8	12.5
1971	9.7	9.7	9.1	8.4	8.9	9.9	11.7	12.2	11.3	11.7	10.8	10.2	11.9	11.4	11.8	12.6	13.5	13.3	12.8	12.6
1972	9.9	9.9	9.3	8.7	9.1	10.1	11.9	12.4	11.5	11.9	11.0	10.5	12.1	11.6	12.0	12.8	13.7	13.5	13.0	12.8
1973	9.3	9.3	8.7	8.1	8.5	9.4	11.1	11.7	10.8	11.1	10.3	9.7	11.3	10.8	11.1	11.8	12.7	12.4	12.0	11.7
1974	8.5	8.4	7.8	7.2	7.5	8.4	10.1	10.6	9.7	10.0	9.1	8.5	10.1	9.5	9.8	10.5	11.2	10.9	10.5	10.2
1975	9.0	8.9	8.4	7.7	8.1	9.0	10.6	11.1	10.2	10.6	9.8	9.2	10.7	10.2	10.5	11.1	11.9	11.6	11.2	11.0
1976	9.2	9.2	8.7	8.0	8.4	9.3	10.9	11.4	10.5	10.9	10.1	9.5	11.0	10.5	10.8	11.5	12.2	12.0	11.6	11.3
1977	8.9	8.8	8.3	7.7	8.1	8.9	10.5	10.9	10.1	10.4	9.6	9.1	10.5	10.0	10.3	10.9	11.6	11.4	11.0	10.7
1978	8.9	8.8	8.3	7.7	8.0	8.9	10.4	10.8	10.0	10.3	9.6	9.0	10.4	9.9	10.2	10.8	11.5	11.3	10.9	10.6
1979	9.0	9.0	8.5	7.9	8.2	9.1	10.6	11.0	10.2	10.5	9.8	9.2	10.6	10.1	10.4	11.0	11.7	11.4	11.1	10.8
1980	9.4	9.4	8.9	8.3	8.7	9.5	11.0	11.4	10.6	10.9	10.2	9.7	11.1	10.6	10.9	11.5	12.2	11.9	11.6	11.4
1981	9.1	9.1	8.6	8.1	8.4	9.2	10.6	11.0	10.3	10.6	9.9	9.4	10.7	10.2	10.5	11.1	11.7	11.5	11.1	10.9

to the end of	from the beginning of 1946	1947	1948	1949	1950	1951	1952	1953	1954	1955	1956	1957	1958	1959	1960	1961	1962	1963	1964	1965
1946	−8.1																			
1947	−1.4	5.7																		
1948	0.8	5.6	5.5																	
1949	5.1	9.8	11.9	18.8																
1950	9.9	14.9	18.2	25.1	31.7															
1951	12.1	16.7	19.6	24.7	27.8	24.0														
1952	13.0	17.0	19.4	23.1	24.6	21.2	18.4													
1953	11.2	14.2	15.7	17.9	17.6	13.3	8.3	−1.0												
1954	15.1	18.4	20.4	23.0	23.9	22.0	21.4	22.9	52.6											
1955	16.7	19.8	21.7	24.2	25.2	23.9	23.9	25.7	41.7	31.6										
1956	15.7	18.4	19.9	21.9	22.3	20.8	20.2	20.6	28.9	18.4	6.6									
1957	13.2	15.4	16.4	17.7	17.6	15.7	14.4	13.6	17.5	7.7	−2.5	−10.8								
1958	15.3	17.5	18.7	20.1	20.2	18.8	18.1	18.1	22.3	15.7	10.9	13.1	43.4							
1959	15.1	17.1	18.1	19.3	19.4	18.1	17.3	17.2	20.5	15.0	11.1	12.7	26.7	12.0						
1960	14.0	15.8	16.6	17.6	17.5	16.2	15.3	14.9	17.4	12.4	8.9	9.5	17.3	6.1	0.5					
1961	14.8	16.5	17.3	18.3	18.3	17.1	16.4	16.2	18.6	14.4	11.7	12.8	19.6	12.6	12.9	26.9				
1962	13.3	14.8	15.4	16.1	15.9	14.7	13.9	13.4	15.2	11.2	8.5	8.9	13.3	6.8	5.2	7.6	−8.7			
1963	13.8	15.2	15.8	16.6	16.4	15.3	14.6	14.3	15.9	12.4	10.2	10.8	14.8	9.9	9.3	12.5	5.9	22.8		
1964	13.9	15.3	15.9	16.6	16.4	15.4	14.7	14.4	16.0	12.8	10.9	11.5	15.1	10.9	10.7	13.5	9.3	19.6	16.5	
1965	13.8	15.1	15.7	16.3	16.2	15.2	14.6	14.3	15.7	12.8	11.1	11.6	14.7	11.1	11.0	13.2	10.1	17.2	14.4	12.5
1966	12.6	13.7	14.2	14.7	14.4	13.4	12.7	12.4	13.4	10.7	9.0	9.2	11.7	8.2	7.7	9.0	5.7	9.7	5.6	0.6
1967	13.1	14.2	14.6	15.1	14.9	14.0	13.4	13.1	14.2	11.6	10.1	10.5	12.8	9.9	9.6	11.0	8.6	12.4	9.9	7.8
1968	13.0	14.0	14.5	14.9	14.7	13.8	13.3	13.0	14.0	11.6	10.2	10.5	12.7	10.0	9.8	11.0	8.9	12.2	10.2	8.6
1969	12.0	13.0	13.3	13.7	13.4	12.5	11.9	11.6	12.4	10.1	8.7	8.9	10.7	8.2	7.8	8.7	6.6	9.0	6.8	5.0
1970	11.7	12.6	12.9	13.2	13.0	12.1	11.5	11.1	11.9	9.7	8.4	8.6	10.2	7.8	7.5	8.2	6.3	8.3	6.4	4.8

1971	11.8	12.6	12.9	13.3	13.0	12.2	11.6	11.3	12.0	10.0	8.8	8.9	10.5	8.3	8.0	8.7	7.1	9.0	7.4	6.1
1972	12.0	12.9	13.2	13.5	13.3	12.5	12.0	11.7	12.4	10.5	9.4	9.5	11.0	9.0	8.8	9.5	8.1	9.9	8.6	7.6
1973	10.9	11.7	11.9	12.2	11.9	11.2	10.6	10.3	10.8	9.0	7.9	7.9	9.2	7.3	6.9	7.5	6.0	7.4	6.0	4.9
1974	9.4	10.1	10.2	10.4	10.1	9.3	8.7	8.2	8.7	6.9	5.7	5.7	6.7	4.8	4.3	4.6	3.0	4.1	2.5	1.2
1975	10.2	10.9	11.1	11.3	11.0	10.3	9.7	9.4	9.9	8.2	7.1	7.1	8.2	6.4	6.1	6.5	5.2	6.3	5.1	4.1
1976	10.6	11.3	11.5	11.7	11.5	10.8	10.3	9.9	10.4	8.8	7.8	7.9	9.0	7.3	7.1	7.5	6.3	7.5	6.4	5.6
1977	10.0	10.7	10.8	11.0	10.7	10.0	9.5	9.2	9.6	8.1	7.1	7.1	8.1	6.5	6.2	6.6	5.4	6.4	5.4	4.6
1978	9.9	10.5	10.7	10.9	10.6	9.9	9.4	9.1	9.5	8.0	7.1	7.1	8.0	6.5	6.2	6.6	5.5	6.5	5.4	4.7
1979	10.2	10.8	10.9	11.1	10.8	10.2	9.7	9.4	9.8	8.4	7.5	7.6	8.5	7.1	6.8	7.2	6.2	7.1	6.2	5.6
1980	10.7	11.3	11.5	11.7	11.5	10.9	10.4	10.2	10.6	9.2	8.4	8.5	9.4	8.1	7.9	8.3	7.4	8.4	7.6	7.1
1981	10.3	10.8	11.0	11.2	10.9	10.3	9.9	9.6	10.0	8.7	7.9	7.9	8.8	7.5	7.3	7.6	6.8	7.6	6.9	6.3

to the end of	from the beginning of 1966	1967	1968	1969	1970	1971	1972	1973	1974	1975	1976	1977	1978	1979	1980	1981
1966	−10.1															
1967	5.6	24.0														
1968	7.4	17.3	11.1													
1969	3.2	8.0	0.8	−8.5												
1970	3.3	7.0	1.9	−2.4	4.0											
1971	5.1	8.4	4.8	2.8	9.0	14.3										
1972	7.0	10.1	7.5	6.7	12.3	16.6	19.0									
1973	4.0	6.2	3.5	2.0	4.8	5.1	0.8	−14.7								
1974	0.1	1.4	−1.5	−3.4	−2.4	−3.9	−9.3	−20.8	−26.5							
1975	3.3	4.9	2.7	1.6	3.3	3.2	0.6	−4.9	0.4	37.2						
1976	5.0	6.6	4.9	4.1	6.0	6.4	4.9	1.6	7.7	30.4	23.8					
1977	3.9	5.3	3.6	2.8	4.3	4.3	2.8	−0.2	3.8	16.4	7.2	−7.2				
1978	4.1	5.4	3.9	3.2	4.5	4.6	3.3	0.9	4.3	13.9	7.0	−0.5	6.6			
1979	5.1	6.3	5.0	4.5	5.9	6.1	5.1	3.2	6.6	14.8	9.7	5.4	12.3	18.4		
1980	6.7	8.0	6.9	6.5	8.0	8.4	7.8	6.5	9.9	17.5	13.9	11.6	18.7	25.2	32.4	
1981	5.9	7.1	6.0	5.6	6.9	7.2	6.5	5.2	7.9	14.0	10.6	8.1	12.3	14.3	12.2	−4.9

Source: R. G. Ibbotson and R. A. Sinquefield, *Stocks, Bonds, Bills and Inflation* (Financial Analysts Research Foundation, Charlottesville, Va., 1982), pp. 88–89.

TABLE 7-3 correlation matrix for HPRs from various market indexes*

	NYSE	AMEX	OTC	total common stock	preferred stock	LT corp. bond	int. corp. bond	commercial paper
NYSE	1.000							
AMEX	0.884	1.000						
OTC	0.876	0.897	1.000					
Total common stock	0.998	0.911	0.902	1.000				
Preferred stock	0.371	0.439	0.178	0.356	1.000			
LT corp. bond	0.282	0.313	0.124	0.266	0.863	1.000		
Int. corp. bond	0.422	0.322	0.254	0.405	0.827	0.897	1.000	
Commercial paper	−0.454	−0.576	−0.343	−0.450	−0.067	0.029	0.027	1.000
Total corp. fixed	0.279	0.309	0.120	0.263	0.894	0.986	0.925	0.089
Total corporations	0.982	0.906	0.910	0.987	0.424	0.354	0.473	−0.395
Farms	−0.101	−0.281	−0.144	−0.109	−0.144	0.055	0.146	0.327
Housing	−0.271	−0.206	−0.241	−0.270	−0.068	−0.004	0.121	0.635
Total real estate	−0.227	−0.312	−0.232	−0.231	−0.122	0.017	0.153	0.576
U.S. Treasury bills	−0.459	−0.574	−0.317	−0.450	−0.084	0.019	−0.010	0.980
U.S. Treasury notes	−0.174	−0.037	−0.264	−0.187	0.574	0.669	0.606	0.517
U.S. Treasury bonds	−0.041	−0.005	−0.176	−0.059	0.737	0.754	0.695	0.184
U.S. govt. agencies	−0.073	−0.025	−0.171	−0.088	0.657	0.739	0.682	0.412
Total govt. bonds	−0.229	−0.194	−0.314	−0.244	0.648	0.688	0.611	0.470
Short munic.	−0.439	−0.573	−0.314	−0.435	−0.057	0.048	0.049	0.981
LT munic.	0.201	0.268	0.089	0.191	0.782	0.877	0.789	−0.043
Total munic.	0.192	0.261	0.080	0.182	0.783	0.878	0.789	−0.031

	total corp. fixed	total corporations	farms	housing	total real estate	U.S. Treasury bills	U.S. Treasury notes	U.S. Treasury bonds
Total corp. fixed	1.000							
Total corporations	0.352	1.000						
Farms	0.063	−0.126	1.000					
Housing	0.056	−0.258	0.427	1.000				
Total real estate	0.062	−0.233	0.767	0.906	1.000			
U.S. Treasury bills	0.072	−0.393	0.380	0.641	0.604	1.000		
U.S. Treasury notes	0.678	−0.106	0.059	0.254	0.194	0.439	1.000	
U.S. Treasury bonds	0.770	0.004	−0.053	0.029	−0.013	0.131	0.832	1.000
U.S. govt. agencies	0.757	−0.009	0.018	0.157	0.108	0.328	0.962	0.855
Total govt. bonds	0.724	−0.170	0.032	0.203	0.141	0.417	0.911	0.934
Short munic.	0.104	0.376	0.298	0.600	0.537	0.956	0.524	0.180
LT munic.	0.847	0.257	0.048	−0.107	−0.056	−0.048	0.688	0.762
Total munic.	0.850	0.248	0.053	−0.100	−0.049	−0.036	0.695	0.767

	U.S. govt. agencies	total govt. bonds	short munic.	LT munic.	total munic.
U.S. govt. agencies	1.000				
Total govt. bonds	0.910	1.000			
Short munic.	0.431	0.467	1.000		
LT munic.	0.748	0.688	−0.032	1.000	
Total munic.	0.755	0.698	−0.020	1.000	1.000

* Appendix D at the end of Chap. 15 explains the meaning of correlation coefficients.

Source: R. C. Ibbotson and C. L. Fall, "The United States Market Wealth Portfolio," *Journal of Portfolio Management*, Fall 1979, Table 6.

As shown in Table 7-1, the American Stock Exchange (ASE), which has the lowest correlations with the other U.S. stock markets, nevertheless has a robust .67 as its lowest correlation coefficient. This is a highly significant positive correlation—the other U.S. stock market indicators are even more highly correlated.[10]

7-5.1 the naive buy-and-hold strategy

Market indices are used to answer many different investment questions. One of the most common questions in the minds of potential investors is "What kind of return can I earn if I invest in common stocks?" The answer to this question is shown in Table 7-2.

Table 7-2 shows the annual rates of return from the Standard & Poor's 500 Stocks Composite Average over every year and every combination of consecutive years from 1926 to 1981. These rates of return show what an investor who reinvested all cash dividends and paid no income taxes or brokerage commissions would have earned if he or she neither suffered unusually bad luck nor enjoyed unusually good luck. The returns in Table 7-2 are sometimes referred to as the returns from a *naive buy-and-hold strategy*. That is, the returns in Table 7-2 are what might have been earned by a naive investor who selected a diversified portfolio of NYSE stocks randomly and then simply held onto them while reinvesting all the cash dividends in the portfolio.

Table 7-2 is useful in answering the question often asked by new investors, "What can I expect if I invest in a portfolio of diversified common stocks?" But no index can answer every question an investor might ask. For instance, Table 7-2 gives only vague clues about what to expect from an investment in only one particular stock instead of a diversified portfolio. (Such an undiversified investment would probably yield more variability than the returns from the diversified "portfolio" shown in Table 7-2.) Various different market indices exist with which a wide variety of investor questions can be answered.

7-5.2 comparing indices from different markets

Table 7-3 shows the correlation coefficients between investment returns from several different markets in the United States. This table shows that the stock markets are all highly positively correlated, just as Table 7-1 showed. In addition, Table 7-3 illustrates that the stock market returns are not so highly correlated with the returns from other assets. In fact, the stock market returns are slightly negatively correlated, on average, with the returns from several types of bonds and real estate investments listed in Table 7-3. Investment managers need to know how the price of each assets category reacts to the same basic economic forces if they are going to manage their investments well.

Table 7-4 contains summary statistics calculated from the different indices for which correlation coefficients were shown in Table 7-3. The geometric mean rate of return, the arithmetic average rate of return, and the standard deviations of the year-to-year rates of return for each different index are in

[10] Levels of significance are highly dependent on the size of the underlying sample. When using the normal distribution (that is, for sample sizes in excess of 30), a simple correlation coefficient in excess of .35 is significantly different from zero. For large samples .20 is a significant correlation coefficient.

TABLE 7-4 U.S. capital market total annual returns 1947–1978

	compound return	arithmetic mean	standard deviation
Common stocks			
NYSE	10.16%	11.56%	17.73%
OTC	12.63	14.79	21.79
Total	10.34	11.79	18.02
Fixed-income corporate securities			
Preferred stocks	2.92	3.31	9.20
Long-term corporate bonds	2.21	2.42	6.72
Intermediate corporate bonds	3.87	4.00	5.48
Commercial paper	4.27	4.29	2.37
Total	2.89	3.03	5.53
Corporate securities total	8.19	9.07	13.84
Real estate			
Farms	11.69	11.88	6.79
Residential housing	6.88	6.93	3.28
Total	8.14	8.19	3.53
U.S. government securities			
U.S. Treasury bills	3.51	3.53	2.11
U.S. Treasury notes	3.65	3.73	3.71
U.S. Treasury bonds	2.39	2.56	6.17
Agencies	4.01	4.08	3.92
Total	3.17	3.23	3.78
Municipal (state & local) bonds			
Short-term	2.44	2.45	1.37
Long-term	1.69	2.01	8.20
Total	1.75	2.02	7.62
Market total	6.88	6.97	4.65

Source: R. G. Ibbotson and Carol L. Fall, "The U.S. Wealth Portfolio: Components of Capital Market Values and Returns," *Journal of Portfolio Management*, Fall 1979,

Table 7-4.[11] The geometric mean and the arithmetic mean are two similar, but slightly different, ways of calculating the average rate of return. The standard deviation is a statistic that measures the variability of returns (or the range of returns) over which the investment experienced fluctuations—riskier investments have larger standard deviations of returns.

By comparing the summary statistics in Table 7-4 with the correlation coefficients between the different indices shown in Table 7-3, an inexperienced investor can gain insights into different investment possibilities that would take a lifetime of practical experience to accumulate. However, care must be taken in interpreting such statistics.

Figure 7-2 illustrates how $1 invested in some of the different indices shown in Tables 7-3 and 7-4 in 1946 would grow over several decades. Money invested in municipal bonds appears at a glance to have earned the worst

[11] The geometric mean rate of return is defined and discussed in Mathematical App. F at the back of this book.

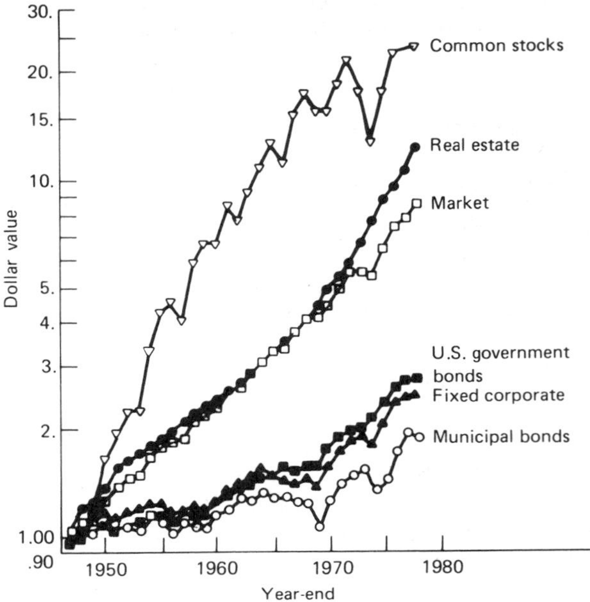

FIGURE 7-2 cumulative wealth indices of capital market security groups (year-end 1946 = $1). (*Source*: R. G. Ibbotson and Carol L. Fall, "The U.S. Wealth Portfolio: Components of Capital Market Values and Returns," *Journal of Portfolio Management*, Fall 1979).

returns, on average, of any of the investment indices in the figure. This is a hasty and erroneous conclusion, however. Recall that the coupon interest from municipal bonds is exempt from federal income taxes. Thus, on an after-tax basis the returns from the municipal bonds were higher than the returns from some of the other investments in Fig. 7-2 which yield higher before-tax returns.

7-6 CHAPTER SUMMARY AND CONCLUSIONS

There are two major categories of security market indicators—the average, and the more scientific index. Market indices (like the CRSP index) are more sophisticated than market averages (like the DJIA) for three main reasons: (1) indices have base years to facilitate comparisons, (2) indices can employ some meaningful weighting system if it is appropriate, and (3) indices are usually measured in more useful units of measurement than are averages.

Dozens of different security market averages and indices are tabulated and published in the United States every day. Stock market indicators for each different market and for various categories of stocks within each market, bond market indicators for different categories of bonds, commodity indices for different categories of commodities (such as grains, metals, and meats) and for each commodity exchange, and foreign exchange indices are all prepared daily. Numerous economic indices such as the consumer price index, which is used to measure inflation, are also used by businesspeople. Each different index is supposed to give a valid indication of the level of the prices of some important group of market assets. Each index should be scrutinized before using it for exacting purposes, however, because some are biased and unrepresentative.

A well-constructed index uses a statistically significant sample of the population being surveyed; this sample is selected so that it provides a representative indication of the entire population being studied. A good index also employs a weighting system founded on economic logic—such as an equally weighted securities index, to show how the average random investor should do without any good or bad luck. Also, it is always better to use an index that is reported in convenient units rather than in numbers that don't lend themselves to making meaningful comparisons.

After a good index is selected, it must still be watched to ensure that it is properly maintained. Securities markets indices must adjust properly for stock dividends and splits. Changes and substitutions in the list of assets being sampled should be made judiciously, too.

In the final analysis, it is fairly easy to construct a satisfactory stock market index for the United States. To a large extent the prices of all common stocks are simultaneously and systematically affected by the basic economic forces so that they all move through the alternating bull (that is, appreciating price trend) and bear (namely, price decline) market periods together. Thus, a poorly constructed average like the DJIA is highly positively correlated with the more scientific CRSP index. Different markets, such as the commodity and bond markets, however, require the selection of separate market indices because these markets "march to a different drummer."

QUESTIONS

1. What is the difference between a stock market average and a stock market index?
2. Compare and contrast the two following weighting systems frequently used in the construction of stock market indices. (1) Equal weights—every stock in the index is assigned an equal weight or proportion. (2) Value-weighted—every stock is assigned a weight that corresponds to its total market value stated as a proportion relative to the aggregate market value of all securities in the market in which it is traded.
3. What tasks are stock market indicators used for?
4. What considerations are relevant when either constructing a new market indicator or selecting an existing one to use? Explain.
5. What are the major criticisms made against the popular DJIA?
6. How are the so-called value-weighted weights calculated when constructing a stock market index? What is the value weighting system of weights supposed to represent?
7. Consider the three following NYSE stock market indicators:
   a) CRSP Value Weighted Index
   b) CRSP Equally Weighted Index
   c) DJIA

   Which of these three NYSE market indicators is best? Explain why.

8. Table 7-3 shows that the correlation coefficients between the various common stock market indicators, real estate indicators, bond market indicators, and the other major categories of market indicators differ substantially. Why are these different major categories of market indicators so uncorrelated, while the indicators shown in Table 7-1 are all so highly positively correlated?
9. Make a list of the 30 stocks that are used in the construction of the DJIA. Of what segment of stocks traded on the NYSE do you think this index is representative? Explain.

SELECTED REFERENCES

Fabozzi, Frank J., and Gregory M. Kipnis (eds.), *Stock Index Futures* (Dow Jones-Irwin, Homewood, Ill., 1984). Chapter 5, entitled "Stock Market Indicators," explains details about stock market index construction.

Ibbotson Associates, *Stocks, Bonds, Bills and Inflation: 1985 Yearbook*, (Chicago, 1985). This 151-page book updates the similar book by Ibbotson and Sinquefield that is also in this reference section.

Ibbotson, Roger G., and Rex A. Sinquefield, *Stocks, Bonds, Bills and Inflation: The Past and the Future* (Financial Analysts Research Foundation, Charlottesville, Va., 1982). This small book presents an easy-to-read explanation of how different security market and economic indicators are constructed, with the aid of a little first-year college algebra. Graphs and tables of the summary statistics yield themselves to comparisons that will be insightful to astute investors.

Teweles, Richard J., and Edward S. Bradley, *The Stock Market*, 4th ed. (Wiley, New York, 1982). Chapter 19 is an easy-to-read, nonmathematical discussion of stock market averages and indices. The chapter ends by explaining how the Dow theory (about charting stock prices in hopes of finding revealing patterns) uses stock market averages.

part two

INTRODUCTION TO VALUATION AND RISK-RETURN THEORY

Part two introduces the basic valuation model and relates it to the various investment risks. The intrinsic economic value of a market asset is the present value of the future income.

$$\text{Present value} = \sum_{t=1}^{T} \frac{\text{income}_t}{(1 + k)^t}$$

where k is the appropriate risk-adjusted discount rate for the asset.

CHAPTER 8—*price =?= value* explains the basic principles of valuation that are used to discern underpriced and overpriced securities.

CHAPTER 9—*total risk and its factors* defines total risk quantitatively and discusses the various risk factors that contribute to an asset's total risk.

CHAPTER 10—*the characteristic line and the capital asset pricing model* shows how to statistically partition an asset's total risk from all factors into two mutually exclusive portions called diversifiable (or unsystematic) risk and undiversifiable (or systematic) risk and traces the asset pricing implications of this analysis.

The three chapters that make up part two introduce fundamentally important valuation and risk concepts that are used throughout the later chapters.

price =?= value

Stock prices fluctuate endlessly. Figure 10-1 on page 253 illustrates the fluctuations in stock prices. All the chapters that follow this one are addressed either directly or indirectly to answering the question, "What determines security prices?" To answer this question it will be necessary to study abstract concepts about price, value, return, and risk. Before discussing the meanings and implications of these words, it may be best to consider the essence of the economic process that determines security prices.

8-1 COMPARING PRICE WITH VALUE

A security's *value* determines its price. But not all the 30 million people in the United States who own securities know that fact; the ones who don't are the unfortunate investors who are most likely to be "ripped off." Professional and semiprofessional investors follow the more scientific procedure of forming estimates of a security's value (which are sometimes called intrinsic-value estimates, present value estimates, or economic value estimates) before they make a decision to buy or sell a security. To see how these value estimates determine security prices, consider the buy-sell decision rules summarized in Box 8-1.

The buy-sell decision rules in Box 8-1 are simple to understand, but they are difficult to implement because it is hard to obtain good estimates of an asset's true economic value. Some security analysts earn annual salaries in excess of $100,000 per year for merely providing and explaining their value estimates for a few securities. For example, an expert automotive analyst might be responsible for only the following four stocks—Ford, Chrysler, General Motors, and American Motors. But if this analyst can correctly predict the direction in which the prices of these four stocks move over an extended period of time, he or she will develop a "track record" for making good predictions and will develop a "following of investors." As a result, some

BOX 8-1
the buy-sell decision rules for investors

THE BUY RULE If a security's price is below its value, it is underpriced and should be bought and held in order to reap capital gains in the future. More succinctly, if the actual market price of security i at the tth instant in time is p_{it} and its intrinsic economic value is v_{it}, then the buy rule is stated as follows:

If ($p_{it} < v_{it}$), buy

THE SELL RULE If the ith security's actual market price at time t is above the security's true value estimated at the same time, then sell the security to avoid losses when its price falls down to the level of its value.

If ($p_{it} > v_{it}$), sell

THE DON'T TRADE RULE If the ith asset's market price equals its economic value, then the price is in equilibrium and is not expected to change. That is, the asset is correctly priced and there is no profit to be made from buying or selling it.

If ($p_{it} = v_{it}$), don't trade

stock brokerage can profit from paying this analyst a six-figure annual salary because the expert's following will generate trading commissions for the brokerage firm in excess of the high salary. In addition, the analyst can earn some nice trading profits for his or her own account. This example suggests the economic worth of being able to prepare good value estimates for a security.

8-2 THE BASIC VALUATION MODEL

The chapters that follow this one explain how to estimate security values in order to detect overpriced and underpriced securities. The specific valuation process used to find the value of the different kinds of securities varies with the type of security. But, the valuation process outlined in Box 8-2 is the basic economic mechanism employed to value all securities.

BOX 8-2
the present value model

The present value of a market asset is the discounted present value of the income the investor may expect to receive from the asset.

$$\text{Present value} = \frac{\text{Income}_1}{(1+i)^1} + \frac{\text{Income}_2}{(1+i)^2} + \frac{\text{Income}_3}{(1+i)^3} + \cdots \qquad (8\text{-}1)$$

The equation gives the present value of a stream of income returns expected to start at time $t = 1$. These future dollar returns are discounted at discount rate i (the discount rate is like a risk-adjusted interest rate).

The static present value model shown in Box 8-2 illustrates how a security's value (or present value or economic value or intrinsic value) is calculated. After the security's present value is determined, a buy-sell investment decision can be made by comparing the security's market price to its intrinsic value, as suggested in Box 8-1.

8-3 THE DYNAMICS OF VALUATION AND INVESTMENT

In practice, the valuation process is more complex than suggested in Boxes 8-1 and 8-2. One problem encountered in practice involves the amount of confidence to give the security analyst's value estimate. A security analyst's value estimate is rarely in the form of a single specific price estimate. More often, the estimate is given with a *margin for error*. For example, an expert analyst might estimate that XYZ stock is worth $30 per share plus or minus a $5 per share margin for error. This means the analyst estimates the equity share's value to be within the $25 to $35 range. Thus, the buy-sell rules shown in Box 8-1 are a bit oversimplified.

Another practical problem results from the fact that a security's risk and return, and thus also its value, will probably change with the passage of time. For example, selling a security puts downward pressure on its market price (if market supply exceeds market demand at the moment of the sale), and buying a security may bid up its price (if the market's supply-for-sale of the security does not increase simultaneously). As a result of any change in its price level, the security's expected future capital gains or losses must be revised, and this affects its estimated future income.

Also, the security's risk may change. The risk of a stock or bond would increase, for example, if the issuing corporation borrowed funds (and thereby increased the ratio of the firm's debt to its total assets) in order to undertake a new venture that involved possible losses. Any increase in risk raises the risk-adjusted discount rate in the present value formula and thus lowers the security's value (as illustrated in Box 8-2). The step-by-step reaction of a vigilant investor to the increased riskiness of the investment described above is summarized below.

1. Estimate both the estimated dollar income from the security if you should buy it and the appropriate risk-adjusted discount rate to be used in the present value formula shown in Box 8-2. (The risk-return relationship is illustrated in Fig. 9-3 on page 217.)
2. Estimate the security's present value using the discount rate and income forecast obtained from step 1.
3. Use the three buy-sell decision rules in Box 8-1 to decide whether to buy, sell, or do neither.
4. See if the market price changes as a result of buy and sell orders from you and other investors. If changes occur, return to step 1 and repeat the process to determine if further action is advisable.

Security analysts must continually reevaluate the securities they are assigned to follow. Thus, the valuation process is more realistically represented

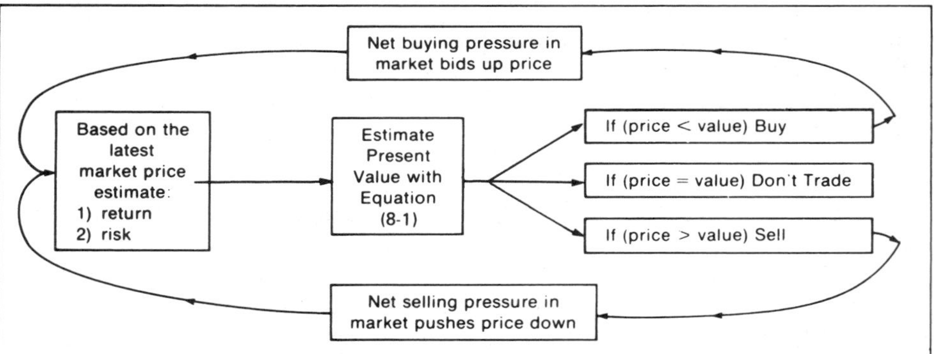

FIGURE 8-1 flow chart of the continuous valuation process.

by the dynamic valuation process illustrated in Fig. 8-1. The flow chart in Fig. 8-1 is a never-ending loop of reconsidering the value, comparing the price and the value, and then reconsidering the buy-sell decision based on the latest estimates. Every time a new piece of information about a security is obtained, that security's value may change. Thus, values fluctuate continuously. And the buying and selling pressures in the marketplace keep market prices in continuous motion as they pursue the *continuously changing values*. This is what makes being a security analyst a fast, exciting, and dangerous job.

8-4 COOTNER'S PRICE-VALUE INTERACTION MODEL

In order to explain how stock prices would fluctuate in a market where price-value comparisons were continuously being made, Paul Cootner suggested that security prices can be viewed as a series of constrained random fluctuations around their true intrinsic value.[1] Cootner hypothesizes the existence of two groups of investors. The first group can be referred to as the "naive investors," those who have access only to the public news media for their information. They might be amateur analysts, or people who select stocks by throwing unaimed darts at a list of stocks. They might be speculators, or people who base their investment decisions upon their interpretations of the public news and their financial circumstances. Naive investors will recognize few, if any, divergences from intrinsic values. They are more likely to invest on the basis of hot tips when they have excess liquidity and at other times when the investment may or may not be wise.

The second group of investors are the "professional investors," those who have the resources to discover news and develop estimates of intrinsic value before the naive investors even get the news. As a result, the professionals will recognize significant deviations from intrinsic value and initiate trading that tends to align the market price with the intrinsic value.

[1] P. H. Cootner, "Stock Prices: Random versus Systematic Changes," *Industrial Management Review*, Spring 1962, vol. 3, no. 2, pp. 24–45.

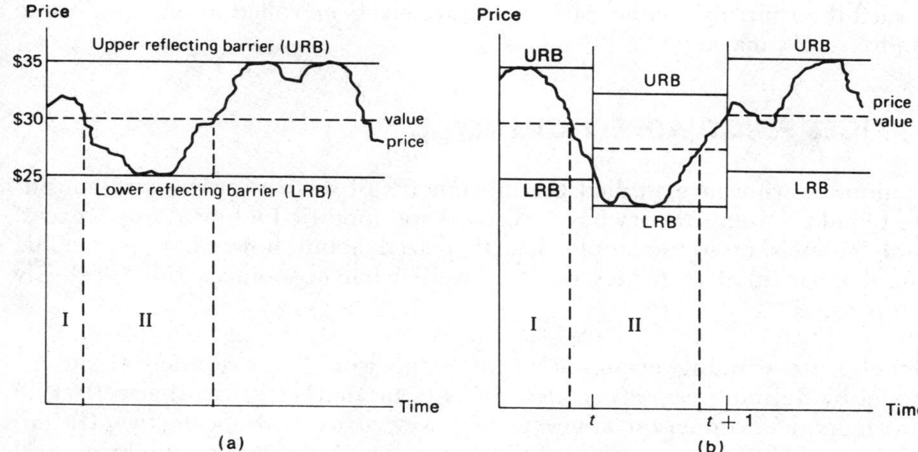

FIGURE 8-2 hypothetical charts of random stock price fluctuations within fixed limits: (*a*) no change in intrinsic value; (*b*) intrinsic value changes at periods *t* and *t* + 1.

Figure 8-2 illustrates how security prices might fluctuate over time in the hypothetical market Cootner describes. The dashed lines represent the professional investors' *consensus value estimate*. Note that the intrinsic value of the security illustrated in Fig. 8-2*b* changes at times t and $t + 1$, while the value remains unchanged at $30 in Fig. 8-2a. Since trading by naive investors is not necessarily based on correct interpretation of the latest news, these investors may ineptly buy securities whose market prices are above their intrinsic values. Such naive buying is illustrated in Fig. 8-2*a* and 8-2*b* by the price fluctuating above the value in phase I. After this initial overoptimistic buying, naive investors may ineptly sell the stock when its price is below its value, as shown in phase II of Fig. 8-2*a* and 8-2*b*. Unprofitable speculative trades by naive investors and trades made to obtain needed liquidity (for example, to pay for an emergency medical operation) are responsible for the aimless price fluctuations that can cause prices to diverge from values.

When a security's price does differ significantly from its true intrinsic value, the professional investors find it profitable to correct this disequilibrium. Small deviations are not profitable to correct because the profits are not sufficient to pay for the brokerage commissions. But when prices are significantly out of line the professionals bid up low prices or liquidate overpriced securities. In effect, the professionals erect "reflecting barriers" around the true intrinsic value.[2] These reflecting barriers are represented by the solid lines above and below the intrinsic value lines in Fig. 8-2. The upper reflecting barrier is denoted URB and the lower reflecting barrier is labeled LRB. Prices will fluctuate freely within the reflecting barriers. But when prices reach these barriers, the professionals' action will cause prices to move

[2] William Feller, *An Introduction to Probability Theory and Its Applications*, 3d ed., vol. 1 (Wiley, New York, 1968), pp. 436–438. These pages provide a discussion of a random walk with reflecting barriers.

toward their intrinsic value. Such a market has been called an intrinsic-value random-walk market.[3]

8-5 EQUILIBRIUM PRICES FLUCTUATE EFFICIENTLY

Economists who have studied the movements of security prices and considered Paul Cootner's theory have accepted and modified it in varying degrees. Paul Samuelson, for example, has theorized about how Cootner's model would perform if securities markets were what economists call "perfectly competitive."

8-5.1 Samuelson's continuous equilibrium

Nobel Prize–winning economist Paul Samuelson has extended Cootner's model by defining *perfectly efficient prices* to be market prices that reflect all information.[4] Samuelson suggests that a security with perfectly efficient prices would be in "continuous equilibrium." This continuous equilibrium will not be static through time, however. Every time a new piece of news is released, the security's intrinsic value will change and the security's market price will adjust toward the new value. It is the speed of this price adjustment process that gauges the efficiency of a price. A perfectly efficient security's price is in a "continuous equilibrium" such that the intrinsic value of the security vibrates randomly and the market *price equals the fluctuating intrinsic value* at every instant in time. If any disequilibrium (of even a temporary nature) exists, then the security's price is less than perfectly efficient.[5] Of course, actual market prices are not perfectly efficient because different security analysts typically assign different value estimates to any given security.

Actual market prices can pursue only a *consensus estimate* of any given security's intrinsic value, since security analysts' value estimates differ. If most security analysts' value estimates happen to be similar at a point in time, then the consensus value estimate may vary only within a small range. In this case, the security's price will be almost perfectly efficient as it fluctuates in a narrow range around its changing equilibrium economic value, as shown in Fig. 8-3*a*. In Fig. 8-3 a security's intrinsic value falls at time period $t + n$ when some bad news about the security emerges.

In contrast to the situation illustrated in Fig. 8-3*a*, consider Fig. 8-3*b*, which represents another security with an identical intrinsic value at every point in time. However, this second security of equal value "fell in disfavor" (a Wall Street phrase which means that few investors were interested in buying it), and large divergences between the security's price and its value occurred. As shown in Fig. 8-3*b*, the second security's price fluctuated far below its value

[3] Eugene Fama, "The Behavior of Stock Market Prices," *Journal of Business*, January 1955, p. 36.

[4] Paul Samuelson, "Proof That Properly Discounted Present Values of Assets Vibrate Randomly," *The Bell Journal of Economics and Management Science*, Autumn 1973, pp. 369–374.

[5] Eugene Fama, "Efficient Capital Markets: A Review of Theory and Empirical Work," *Journal of Finance*, May 1970, pp. 383–417; Eugene Fama, "The Behavior of Stock Market Prices," *Journal of Business*, January 1965.

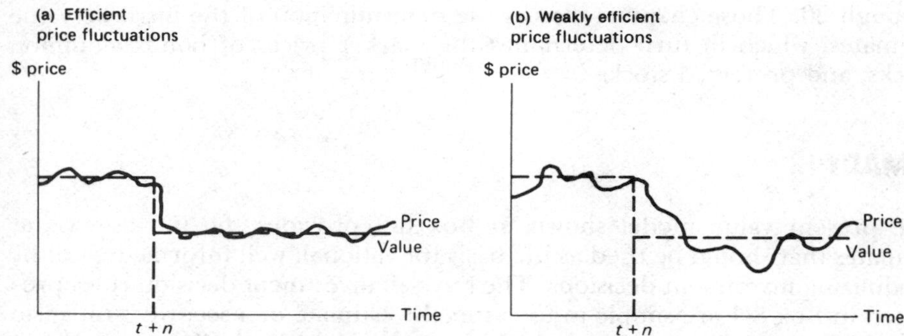

FIGURE 8-3 more and less efficient security prices: (*a*) efficient price fluctuations: (*b*) weakly efficient price fluctuations.

(that is, inefficient price movements occurred) as a result of insufficient interest from investors who would continuously estimate the security's value, compare value and price, and make buy-sell decisions rapidly.

8-5.2 the random-walk theory

For years, security analysts and financial economists have studied and discussed what is sometimes called the *random-walk theory* of security prices. According to the random-walk theory, a security's market price should fluctuate randomly around its intrinsic value because (1) the new information arrives at random intervals throughout every day, (2) this new information causes security analysts to reestimate the values of the securities affected by the new information, and (3) market trading based on the buy-sell rules shown in Box 8-1 causes security prices to fluctuate randomly as they pursue constantly changing intrinsic values.

The random-walk theory of stock prices is like Paul Cootner's model, illustrated in Fig. 8-2, without the reflecting barriers.[6] Or, in a more idealistic model, the prices of securities in a random-walk market might fluctuate in continuous equilibrium if investors were continuously informed and were in uniform agreement (an admittedly heroic assumption) about the securities' intrinsic values. In any event, the valuation process underlying both Cootner's model and the random-walk model is summarized by the continuous flow chart shown in Fig. 8-1.

Detailed statistical studies of security prices discussed in later chapters (see, for example, Chap. 19) reveal that security price changes do tend to fluctuate randomly, as described in the models above.[7] These statistical findings attest to the realism of the market mechanism illustrated above in Figs. 8-2 ad 8-3. Readers who are interested in learning more about how security analysts prepare their estimates of a security's intrinsic value can read Chaps. 9

[6] Paul Cootner (ed.), *The Random Character of Stock Market Prices* (M.I.T., Cambridge, Mass., 1964).

[7] Eugene Fama and others have given the name *efficient markets* to security markets in which the prices fluctuate randomly around their intrinsic values in a narrow range. Eugene Fama, op. cit.

through 20. Those chapters discuss the determination of the intrinsic value estimates, which in turn determines the market prices of bonds, common stocks, and preferred stocks.

8-6 CHAPTER SUMMARY

The present value model shown in Box 8-2 provides the intrinsic value estimates that should be used as the basis for rational, well-informed, wealth-maximizing investment decisions. The buy-sell investment decision rules presented in Box 8-1 are simple to use after the estimate of a security's intrinsic value is obtained. The intrinsic value estimates and the buy-sell decisions must be used more than once for each security, however. Securities' intrinsic values change continuously because every time a piece of new information becomes available it may cause security analysts to change their assessment of the intrinsic value of one or more securities. It is these changes in the intrinsic value estimates which motivate investors to buy and bid up or sell and push down the ever-changing securities prices. The continuous flow chart shown in Fig. 8-1 illustrates the never-ending series of investment decisions that keep security analysts busy.

QUESTIONS

1. Look up the dictionary definitions of the words "value" and "price." Compare and contrast these two words in a short essay.
2. Why must a security analyst have estimates of a security's risk and return before preparing estimates of the security's value? *Hint*: What determines the value of the appropriate discount rate in the present value model?
3. Should the value of a security be stable or should it fluctuate? What should change the value of a security?
4. Define the term "efficient price." Explain it.
5. Suppose the chairperson of the board of General Motors (GM) appeared on the late night news of every television station in the United States tonight and announced that GM had discovered an oil well on every parking lot it owned around the world. Assuming the executive would not distort the truth, how would the announcement affect the market price of GM stock? Would the price of GM move upward in a trend as more and more investors learned of the GM discovery each day and then bid the stock's price up day after day as they reached their decisions to buy the stock after a learning lag? Explain.
6. Investor naivete is a source of inefficient price movements (as explained in Paul Cootner's model of market price determination). Briefly discuss five other factors that probably cause prices to differ from values.
7. There are millions of part-time amateur investors in the United States. However, there are only 15,000 members of the Financial Analysts Federation (FAF); these constitute most of the full-time professional investment managers. Given that there are millions of amateur investors and, in contrast, only thousands of professional investors, which group do you think dominates the

market? That is, do you think that security prices fluctuate randomly because there are mostly part-time amateur investors in the market? How can a small number of professional investors have a significant impact on security prices?

SELECTED REFERENCES

Brealey, Richard A., *An Introduction to Risk and Return from Common Stocks*, 2d ed. (M.I.T., Cambridge, Mass., 1983). Chapter 1 of this easy-to-read book is entitled "Technical Analysis and Random Walks"—it is particularly relevant to the discussion in this chapter. No mathematics.

Working, Holbrook, "A Theory of Anticipatory Prices," *American Economic Review*, May 1958, pp. 188–199. The late Professor Working was one of the most important theoreticians and econometric researchers in the area of security prices. (He usually discussed commodity futures rather than stocks or bonds, but the logic is the same.) The paper provides an articulate review of this scholar's thoughts about the determination of market prices. No mathematics.

CHAPTER 9 total risk and its factors

"Risk" is an important word as it applies to financial investments. In fact, "risk" is more than just a word—it is a concept. There are different factors that cause different types of risk. This chapter defines investors' *total risk* and analyzes the factors that contribute to total risk.

This chapter defines total risk *quantitatively* so that it may be treated in an analytical manner. Chapter 10 goes on to show how to statistically divide the total risk of an asset into two parts—diversifiable risk and undiversifiable risk. Chapter 30 presents a new theory, called the arbitrage pricing theory, that can be used to isolate and measure the various *risk factors* that may be present in any particular asset's total risk.[1]

The risk analysis techniques of this chapter and Chap. 10 provide an important foundation for understanding many topics throughout the rest of this book.

9-1 DEFINING TOTAL RISK ANALYTICALLY

Webster's dictionary defines *risk* as "the chance of injury, damage, or loss." This is an intuitively pleasing definition, and few people would disagree with it. However, this verbal definition is not very analytical. Verbal definitions are interpreted in different ways by different people. They can be made clearer only by means of other verbal definitions or by examples that are not always entirely appropriate and are rarely concise. Such definitions do not yield to measurement. Frequently, they are not even exact enough to allow objects possessing the defined characteristic (here, "risk") to be ranked in terms of

[1] This chapter suggests that an asset's total risk is the sum of various "risk factors" defined in the chapter. This discussion is informative and insightful, and it introduces the concept of linear additive risk factors that is the basis for the new arbitrage pricing theory explained in Chap. 30.

that characteristic. Thus, it seems desirable to develop a surrogate for the dictionary definition of risk that is amenable to quantification.

9-1.1 quantitative surrogates

If risk analysis is to proceed, a quantitative financial risk surrogate is needed.[2] However, if this surrogate is to be intuitively pleasing, it must measure, either directly or indirectly, "the chance of injury, damage, or loss" so that it may be used synonymously with the word "risk." The quantitative financial risk surrogate used in this text is measured from the investment's probability distribution of rates of return.

9-1.2 probability distribution of rates of return

The rate of return is the single most important outcome from an investment. Therefore, the quantitative risk surrogate focuses on rates of return. Considerations of whether a stock is a growth stock, whether the company's "image is pleasing," or whether the firm's product is "glamorous" are relevant only to the extent they affect its rate of return and riskiness.

In an uncertain world, investors cannot tell in advance exactly what rate of return an investment will yield. However, they can formulate a probability distribution of the possible rates of return. Figure 9-1 shows three probability distributions of returns for AT&T, Borden, and Firestone common stock.

A probability distribution may be either subjective or objective. An *objective probability distribution* is formed by measuring objective historical data. A *subjective probability distribution* is formed by simply writing down someone's hunches and assigning probabilities to them. Of course, what occurred historically may influence hunches about the future. But if the probability distribution is not stationary over time, historical probability distributions of rates of return are not much help in forecasting the future probability distributions upon which investment decisions are based. Luckily, most firms' probability distributions of rates of return and the statistics describing them do not seem to change very much as time passes.[3] Thus, objective distributions almost always influ-

[2] Quantification is occurring in many fields. For example, a biology student may now major in biometrics at most universities. Biometrics involves measuring biological phenomena. By testing new drugs and detecting subtle cause-and-effect relationships (for example, lung cancer and smoking), biometricians are extending the ability of the medical profession. Within the social sciences, quantification progress is accelerating, too. Most psychology departments today offer programs in psychometry—that is, the measuring of mental traits. The IQ test is probably the best-known psychometric instrument. However, psychometric tools measure many subtle traits besides intelligence. Economics departments are offering majors in econometrics. Econometricians develop mathematical economic models which they test statistically. Econometricians are expanding the study of economics from rationalization of observable phenomena to a science of measuring, testing, and predicting, and they are winning Nobel prizes.

[3] Marshall Blume, "On the Assessment of Risk," *Journal of Finance*, March 1971, pp. 1–10; O. A. Vasicek, "A Note of Using Cross-Sectional Information in Bayesian Estimation of Security Betas," *Journal of Finance*, December 1973, pp. 1233–1239; R. C. Klemkosky and J. D. Martin, "The Adjustment of Beta Factors," *Journal of Finance*, September 1975, pp. 1123–1128; B. Rosenberg and J. Guy, "Beta and Investment Fundamentals," *Financial Analysts Journal*, May–June 1976; F. J. Fabozzi and J. C. Francis, "Beta as a Random Coefficient," *Journal of Financial and Quantitative Analysis*, March 1978, pp. 101–115; J. C. Francis, "Statistical Analysis of Risk Surrogates for NYSE Stocks," *Journal of Financial and Quantitative Analysis*, December 1979, pp. 981–997. Several of these articles are reproduced in *Readings in Investments*, edited by J. C. Francis, Cheng-Few Lee, and Donald Farrar (McGraw-Hill, New York, 1980).

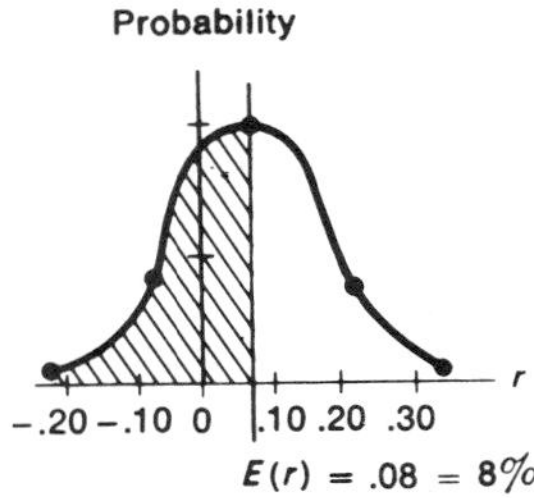

i	p_i	r_i
1	.05	.38 = 38%
2	.2	.23 = 23%
3	.5	.08 = 8%
4	.2	−.07 = −7%
5	.05	−.22 = −22%
	1.0	

$E(r) = .08 = 8\%$

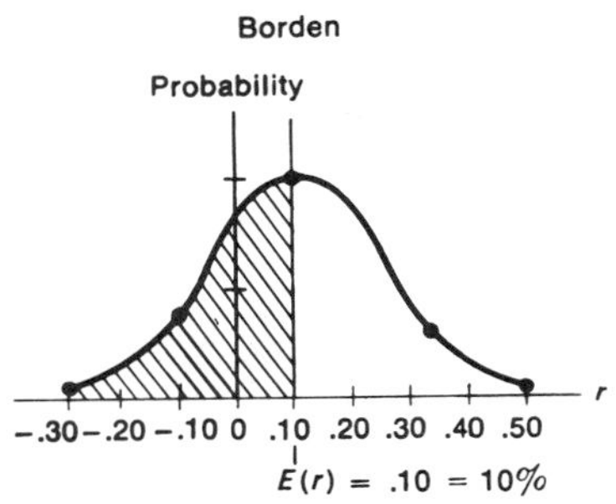

i	p_i	r_i
1	.1	.5 = 50%
2	.2	.3 = 30%
3	.4	.1 = 10%
4	.2	−.1 = −10%
5	.1	−.3 = −30%
	1.0	

$E(r) = .10 = 10\%$

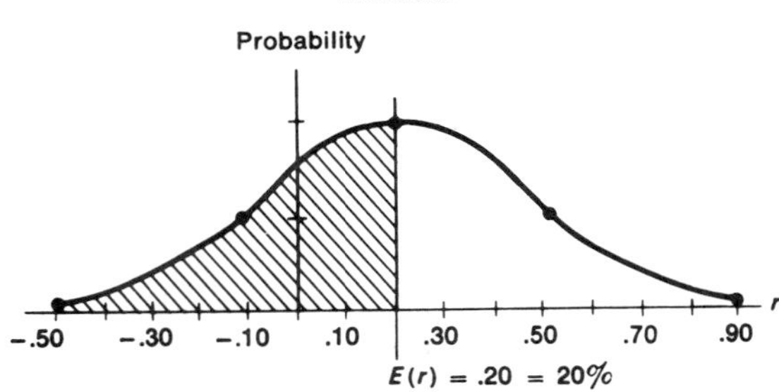

i	p_i	r_i
1	.1	.9 = 90%
2	.25	.5 = 50%
3	.3	.2 = 20%
4	.25	−.1 = −10%
5	.1	−.5 = −50%
	1.0	

$E(r) = .20 = 20\%$

FIGURE 9-1 subjectively derived finite probability distributions of rates of return.

ence the development of subjective distributions and in many cases are good estimates of what the future holds.

Probability distributions of returns are essential in deriving a quantitative financial risk surrogate. Investors tend (consciously or subconsciously) to focus on the probability distribution of rates of return. In particular, investors want to know the average rate of return they can expect from each potential investment and the risk associated with that investment.

9-1.3 expected return

The expected return is a weighted *average return* using the probabilities for weights; it measures the average or central tendency of the probability distribution of returns (see Box 9-1).

BOX 9-1
definition of the expected rate of return $E(r)$

The *expected return* is the sum of the products of the various one-period rates of return times their probabilities. Equation (9-1) defines the expected return symbolically.

$$E(r) = \sum_{t=1}^{T} p_t r_t \tag{9-1}$$

$$= p_1 r_1 + p_2 r_2 + p_3 r_3 + p_4 r_4 + p_5 r_5$$

where r_t denotes the tth rate of return from the probability distribution, p_t is the probability that the tth rate of return occurs, and there are T possible rates of return.

The calculations below are for the expected value of the Borden probability distribution in Fig. 9-1.

$$E(r) = p_1 r_1 + p_2 r_2 + p_3 r_3 + p_4 r_4 + p_5 r_5$$

$$= (.1)(.5) + (.2)(.3) + (.4)(.1) + (.2)(-.1) + (.1)(-.3)$$

$$= .05 + .06 + .04 - .02 - .03$$

$$= .1 = 10\%$$

The expected return is the mathematical expectation or the mathematical expected value of the different rates of return that are possible. Mathematical statisticians call the expected value the *first moment* of the probability distribution. The second moment (about the mean) of a probability distribution is called the variance.[4]

9-1.4 variance and standard deviation of returns

The wideness of a probability distribution of rates of return is a measure of uncertainty or risk. That is, the more an investment's return varies around its expected return, the larger is the investor's uncertainty. The risk or wideness of the probability distribution can be measured with the variance of returns defined in Eq. (9-2). The calculations are for the Borden Company data from Fig. 9-1.

$$\sigma^2 = \sum_{t-1}^{5} p_t [r_t - E(r)]^2 \tag{9-2}$$

$$= p_1 [r_1 - E(r)]^2 + p_2[r_2 - E(r)]^2 + p_3[(r)_3 - E(r)]^2 + p_4 [r_4 - E(r)]^2 + p_5 [r_5 - E(r)]^2$$

$$= (.1)(.5 - .1)^2 + (.2)(.3 - .1)^2 + (.4)(.1 - .1)^2 + (.2)(-.1 - .1)^2 + (.1)(-.3-.1)^2$$

[4] The first four statistical moments are the mean, variance, skewness, and kurtosis. These four moments are discussed in Mathematical App. C at the end of the book. Expectation operators are explained in Mathematical App. B.

BOX 9-2
definition of total risk

An asset's *total risk* equals its total variability of returns. Total variability of returns is measured using either the variance or the standard deviation of the one-period rates of return. The standard deviation is defined in Eq. (9-3); it is the square root of the variance.

$$\text{Standard deviation of returns} = \sqrt{\text{variance } (r)} = \sigma \tag{9-3}$$

The standard deviation and the variance both equate dispersion around the expected value—the wideness of the probability distribution—with total risk.

$$= .016 + .008 + 0 + .008 + .016$$

$$= .048 \qquad \text{rate of return squared}$$

The standard deviation is defined in Box 9-2. Borden's standard deviation is calculated below.

$$\sigma = \sqrt{\sigma^2}$$

$$= \sqrt{.048}$$

$$= .22 = 22\% = 22 \text{ percentage points}$$

The standard deviation is stated in rates of return, but the variance is stated in terms of the "rate of return squared." Since it is more natural to discuss rates of return rather than rates of return *squared,* risk is sometimes measured with the standard deviation of returns. However, for statistical purposes it is sometimes more convenient to use the variance rather than the standard deviation when discussing risk. Conceptually, either risk definition is appropriate since they are simply positive mathematical transformations of each other.[5]

9-1.5 symmetric probability distribution of returns

If risk is defined as the chance of loss or injury, it seems more logical to measure risk by the area in a probability distribution that is *below* its expected return. This procedure can be difficult, and it is unnecessary if the probability distribution is *symmetric.*

Figure 9-2 shows three probability distributions of returns—one skewed left, one symmetric, and one skewed right. The symmetric distribution has no skewness. The area on one side of the expected return of a symmetric distribution is the mirror image of the area on the other side of the expected return.

[5] The standard deviation and the variance are what mathematicians call positive monotone transformations of each other. Other risk measures exist that differ more markedly. For a discussion of different quantitative risk surrogates and why the "variability of return" definition that is inherent in the standard deviation of returns was selected see J. C. Francis and S. H. Archer, *Portfolio Analysis,* 1st ed. (Prentice-Hall, Englewood Cliffs, N.J., 1971), chap. 11. See also Harry Markowitz, *Portfolio Selection* (Wiley, New York, 1959), chap. 9.

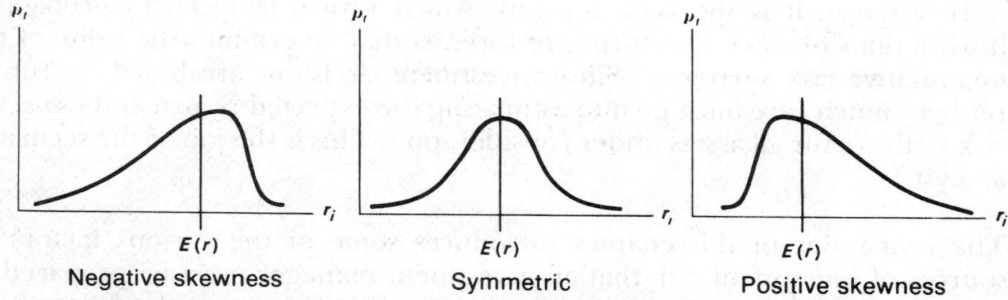

FIGURE 9-2 three probability distributions with different types of skewness.

Empirical studies of historical probability distributions of returns indicate they are not significantly skewed if short differencing intervals (for example, if 1 month elapses between p_t and p_{t+1}) are used.[6] Consequently, it is not important whether variability of returns is measured on one or both sides of the expected return.

Measuring total variability of return (that is, risk) on both sides of the expected return with the standard deviation and variance includes surprisingly good returns (that is, returns above the expected return) in the risk measure. But as long as the probability distributions of returns are fairly symmetric, the way the risk of a group of assets is measured does not change in any meaningful way. Measurements of each asset's *total* variability of return will be twice as large as measurements of that asset's variability below the expected return if its probability distribution is symmetric. As long as total variability of return on both sides of the expected return is used consistently as a risk surrogate, the risk measurements of all assets will still result in the same risk rankings for a group of assets. Since the standard deviation and variance are such common statistics and will rank assets' risk in the same order as a more complicated measure (for example, of variability below the expected return), they will be used as quantitative financial risk surrogates.[7] This approach will also be simpler than trying to measure only the lower half of the distribution. Measuring risk by the standard deviation and variance is equivalent to *defining risk as total variability of returns* about the expected return or, simply, as variability of returns.

[6] J. C. Francis, "Skewness and Investors' Decisions," *Journal of Financial and Quantitative Analysis*, March 1975, pp. 163–172. Also, see the first part of the appendix to Chap. 19 for an intuitive explanation with graphs. L. Fisher and J. H. Lorie, "Some Studies of Variability of Returns on Investments in Common Stocks," *Journal of Business*, April 1970, pp. 99–134. J. C. Francis and S. H. Archer, *Portfolio Analysis*, 2d ed. (Prentice-Hall, Englewood Cliffs, N.J., 1979); see tables 14-2 and 14-3 and chaps. 14 to 16 about nonsymmetric distributions of returns. Alan Kraus and Robert H. Litzenberger, "Skewness Preference and the Valuation of Risk Assets," *Journal of Finance*, September 1976, pp. 1084–1100.

[7] Harry Markowitz, *Portfolio Selection* (Wiley, New York, 1959), chap. 9. Markowitz explains the use of the variance instead of his semivariance (svr), which measures variability below the expected return. By his definition:

$$\text{svr} = \sum_{t-1}^{n} P_t \,[\text{bar}_t - E(r)]^2$$

where bar_t is the tth *below average rate of return*. The bars are shaded in Figure 9-1.

In essence, it is the accuracy with which future (subjective) probability distributions of rates of returns are forecast that determines the value of the quantitative risk surrogate. Since investment decisions are based on future returns, much care must go into estimating the expected return and expected risk statistics for all assets under consideration. This is the job of the securities analyst.[8]

9-1.6 the factors that make up an asset's total risk

The remainder of this chapter introduces some of the various factors or sources of investment risk that an investment manager must be prepared to analyze.[9] Each of the remaining sections in this chapter is devoted to one investment risk factor. These different investment risk factors are referred to throughout the rest of this book.

Default risk arises because firms may eventually go bankrupt. Some default risk is systemically related to the business cycle, which affects almost all investments. However, some default risk is caused by changes that are unique to the afflicted company.

Interest rate risk arises from changes in the level of market interest rates. Interest rate risk is predominantly an undiversifiable risk because the levels of all interest rates tend to rise and fall together and to affect the values of all assets similarly.

Market risk arises because bull and bear market conditions tend to affect all securities systemically.

Management risk arises when the people who manage an investment asset make errors that decrease the asset's value. Thus, management risk is that part of total risk caused by bad business decisions.

Purchasing power risk is caused by inflation, which erodes the purchasing power of invested dollars.

Marketability risk is that portion of an asset's total risk caused by discounts and selling commissions that must be given up to sell an illiquid asset.

Political risk is that portion of an asset's total variability of return caused by changes in the political environment (for instance, a new tax law) that affect the asset's market value.

Callability risk is variability of return caused by the fact that a security may legally be called for a forced sale.

Convertability risk is variability of return caused by the fact that a market security (such as a bond) may be converted to another security (such as a common stock).

The above types of risk are independent but can occur simultaneously, nevertheless. For example, a management error that occurs when interest rates are low may be overcome; the same error could bankrupt the firm if it were to occur when interest rates (and thus interest expenses) were high. In

[8] Gordon Alexander and J. C. Francis, *Portfolio Analysis*, 3d ed. (Prentice-Hall, Englewood Cliffs, N.J., 1985), deals explicitly with procedures the security analyst can use to estimate risk and return statistics. See chaps. 5 and 6 of the Alexander/Francis book.

[9] Stephen A. Ross, "The Arbitrage Theory of Capital Asset Pricing," *Journal of Economic Theory*, December 1976, vol. 13, pp. 341–360.

this example management risk interacts with interest rate risk. The above list of risk factors is not exhaustive. Empirical research is under way to identify the factors that make up an asset's total risk.[10] The remainder of this chapter and its appendix introduce those risk factors which are likely to contribute to the total risk of an asset.

9-2 THE DEFAULT RISK FACTOR

Default risk is that portion of an investment's total risk that results from changes in the financial integrity of the investment. For example, when a company that issues securities moves either further away from or closer to bankruptcy, these changes in the firm's financial integrity are reflected in the market prices of its securities. The variability of return that investors experience as a result of changes in the credit-worthiness of a firm that issues investment securities is their default risk.[11]

An investor who purchases common stocks, preferred stocks, bonds, or other corporate securities must face the possibility of default and bankruptcy by the issuer. Financial analysts usually can foresee bankruptcy because deteriorating financial ratios and default on debt (when the firm is unable to pay its bills) almost always precede it. Occasionally an act of God, such as a flood or earthquake, may destroy, for instance, all a manufacturing company's assets. And if this firm were to have no insurance to cover the losses, a sudden bankruptcy could result.

Almost all the losses suffered by investors as a result of default risk are *not* the result of actual defaults and/or bankruptcies. Investor losses from default risk usually result from security prices falling as the financial integrity of a healthy firm that issued the securities *weakens*. By the time an actual bankruptcy occurs, the market prices of the troubled firm's securities will have already declined to near zero. So, the bankruptcy losses would be only a small part of total losses resulting from the process leading up to the default. Nevertheless, since losses due to default risk occur as a firm's financial integrity deteriorates in a way that increases the likelihood the firm may someday go bankrupt, it is useful to begin by reviewing the legal bankruptcy proceedings.

[10] Richard Roll and Stephen A. Ross, "An Empirical Investigation of the Arbitrage Pricing Theory," *Journal of Finance*, December 1980, vol. 35, no. 5, pp. 1073–1104. Arbitrage pricing theory, the subject of Chap. 30 of this book, explains how to evaluate the individual elements that combine to form an asset's total risk.

[11] Default risk may be further divided into two subcomponents. The two parts of a security's default risk might be called business risk (from the assets on the issuing firm's balance sheet) and financial risk (from the liabilities on the issuing firm's balance sheet).

It is tempting to say that default risk is proportional to the probability of not getting back the principal of the investment. But, this is not a satisfactory concept, because this probabilistic definition differs from the variability of return definition that underlies modern risk analysis. We can say, however, that an asset's variability of return and its probability of not returning the investor's principal both increase monotonically as the asset's default risk increases.

9-2.1 bankruptcy law

When a corporation fails to make a scheduled payment of interest or principal on a debt, the firm is said to be in *default* on that obligation.[12] If payment is not made within a relatively short period, a lawsuit almost inevitably follows.

A question that arises in most bankruptcy hearings is whether the firm's assets should be liquidated and the proceeds divided among the creditors. A *liquidation* occurs if the bankruptcy court feels the resulting value would exceed that likely to be obtained if the firm were to continue in operation.

If the firm's assets are liquidated in a bankruptcy, the proceeds of the liquidation are paid out to creditors according to the following list of legally established priorities:

First priority: The attorney's fees and court costs associated with the bankruptcy proceeding are paid off first.

Second priority: Any remaining proceeds from the bankruptcy go to pay back wages due to workers, up to a maximum of $2000 per worker.

Third priority: Any remaining proceeds are used to pay back taxes to any federal, state, and local governments.

Fourth priority: If any auction proceeds are left (and sometimes none are left at this stage), creditors holding *secured* loans are paid. For example, mortgage lenders and the holders of collateralized loans made to the company would be paid. This class of creditors typically receives only about half the money owed them by the bankrupt firm.

Fifth priority: If any funds remain, the company's *general* (or unsecured) *creditors* are paid. Debenture bondholders and suppliers that sold to the firm on credit are in this class. It is commonplace for general creditors to receive about 10 cents on every dollar the bankrupt company owes them, but even this paltry sum will not be paid unless all higher-priority claims have been paid in full.

Sixth priority: Preferred stockholders are paid if any auction proceeds are still left. Two cents on each dollar paid for preferred stock might be considered a good liquidation receipt at this step on the ladder of priorities.

Seventh priority: Common stockholders are paid last; they usually receive nothing from their investment.[13]

REORGANIZATION If the value of the firm's assets when employed as part of a "going concern" appears to exceed the value in liquidation, a "reorganization" of the firm and its liabilities may be ordered by the bankruptcy court. Such proceedings are usually conducted under the provisions of Chapter X of the Federal Bankruptcy Act. At least two-thirds of the firm's creditors must concur with the proposed reorganization. If substantial amounts of bonds are held by the public, the SEC must also approve.

[12] A corporation unable to meet its obligatory debt payments is said to be *technically insolvent.* If the value of a firm's assets falls below its liabilities, it is said to be insolvent in the *bankruptcy* sense. While details differ from case to case, the typical bankruptcy situation begins with a default of one or more required payments. If agreements with creditors cannot be obtained, the corporation itself usually files for bankruptcy. Subsequent developments involve the bankruptcy courts, court-appointed officials, representatives of the firm's creditors, the management of the firm, and others. See Sec. 4-3.10 of Chap. 4, about the bankruptcy laws.

[13] From the administrative office of the U.S. courts, table of bankruptcy statistics, 1969.

Typically, creditors are given new claims in the reorganized firm, intended to be at least equal in value to the amounts that would have been received in liquidation. For example, holders of debentures might receive preferred stock in the reorganization, while holders of subordinated debentures might become common stockholders. Stockholders might be left without any interest in the firm; that is, they might lose their entire investment if the bankruptcy judge decrees it.

Among the goals of reorganization are a fair treatment of various classes of securities and the elimination of impossible debt obligations. Presumably, a plan that the troubled firm's debt and equity investors might agree upon among themselves could be considered equitable.

ARRANGEMENTS. Another procedure is available to distressed corporations. Chapter XI of the Federal Bankruptcy Act authorizes certain corporations to voluntarily seek an "arrangement" in which debts may be extended to longer maturities and/or reduced. While Chapter XI proceedings are going on, the corporation is protected by the court from creditor lawsuits. Eventually, a plan for handling debts will be proposed. If a majority of creditors approves, the changes can be made and the firm returned to a solvent status to see if it can survive.[14]

9-2.2 default risk and bankruptcy

Small- and medium-sized firms are much more likely to default and move toward bankruptcy than are large corporations. And defaults increase during hard times—namely, economic recessions and depressions. However, any firm can go bankrupt at any stage in the business cycle. W. T. Grant, for example, a large nationwide retail chain, went bankrupt in 1975, after a recession.

W. T. GRANT In order to show how a firm deteriorates financially over time and how this affects the firm's investors, Table 9-1 was compiled for the highly publicized bankruptcy in 1975 of W. T. Grant. This table lists W. T. Grant's monthly bond and stock prices, earnings, and dividend data for the 3 years before bankruptcy was declared. The data show clearly that the firm's earnings and bond quality ratings deteriorated precipitously for the 2 years before October 1975, when the bankruptcy was declared. Moreover, the corporation discontinued its cash dividend over a year before the bankruptcy. Thus, there were some easily observable warnings of the firm's failure.

The way that Grant's stock and bond prices collapsed month by month to near-zero levels *before* the bankruptcy was declared suggests that investors were aware of the firm's weakening condition. The existence of a larger number of sellers than buyers caused such steadily declining security prices. Only the firm's most naive investors can have been surprised by W. T. Grant's bankruptcy announcement in October 1975. Furthermore, the 2 years of steadily falling stock and bond prices that preceded W. T. Grant's bankruptcy

[14] For more details about bankruptcy see Edward I. Altman, *Corporate Financial Distress* (Wiley, New York, 1983). See also C. W. Smith and J. B. Warner, "On Financial Accounting: An Analysis of Bond Covenants," *Journal of Financial Economics*, June 1979, vol. 7, no. 2, pp. 117–161.

TABLE 9-1 the W. T. Grant bankruptcy

date	Standard & Poor's bond rating	bonds' price per $100 of face value	bonds' yield to maturity	common stock price	quarterly earnings per share	quarterly cash dividend
Jan. 1973	BBB	$80.125	6.88%	$39.00		
Feb. 1973	BBB	79.00	7.15%	31.50	$ 2.70	$.375
Mar. 1973	BBB	78.15	7.27%	27.375		
Apr. 1973	BBB	76.875	7.44%	22.375		
May 1973	BBB	77.75	7.37%	17.25	2.40	.375
June 1973	BBB	78.00	7.34%	17.375		
July 1973	BBB	69.875	8.57%	19.00		
Aug. 1973	BBB	65.125	9.39%	18.75	2.41	.375
Sept. 1973	BBB	70.00	8.58%	21.25		
Oct. 1973	BBB	74.125	7.95%	18.75		
Nov. 1973	BBB	75.375	7.78%	12.50	1.90	.375
Dec. 1973	BB	65.00	9.49%	10.875		
Jan. 1974	BB	65.00	9.51%	11.375		
Feb. 1974	BB	64.00	9.70%	9.00	.59	.15
Mar. 1974	BB	61.00	10.31%	7.625		
Apr. 1974	BB	61.125	10.32%	7.25		
May 1974	BB	51.00	12.62%	6.625	.50	.15
June 1974	BB	51.00	12.65%	5.25		
July 1974	B	50.875	12.72%	4.625		
Aug. 1974	B	30.00	20.57%	3.25	.08	0
Sept. 1974	B	28.125	21.48%	3.00		
Oct. 1974	B	31.125	20.07%	2.625		
Nov. 1974	B	28.25	21.77%	2.50	(.47)*	0
Dec. 1974	CCC	23.00	25.67%	1.875		
Jan. 1975	CCC	28.00	22.07%	2.375		
Feb. 1975	CCC	27.125	22.71%	3.375	(.47)*	0
Mar. 1975	CCC	32.50	19.67%	5.00		
Apr. 1975	CCC	31.50	20.26%	4.875		
May 1975	CCC	35.00	18.61%	4.125	(15.71)*	0
June 1975	CCC	41.00	16.23%	4.125		
July 1975	CCC	39.00	17.05%	4.00		
Aug. 1975	CCC	36.00	18.36%	3.50	(19.06)*	0
Sept. 1975	CC	25.00	24.50%	2.89		
Oct. 1975	C	15.00	bankruptcy declared			

* Parentheses signify losses.

Source: Standard & Poor's *Bond Guide*, published monthly 1973–1975; *ISL Daily Stock Price Manuals.*

are an example of how most losses from default risk occur *before* bankruptcy proceedings start. It behooves investors to investigate before they invest.

9-2.3 quality ratings for bonds and stocks

Financial services such as Standard and Poor's, Moody's, and Dun & Bradstreet continuously study thousands of different corporations and analyze their financial situations. Figures 6-5 and 6-7 on pages 153 and 155, respectively, explain the quality ratings of AAA, AA, and A; BBB, BB, and B;

TABLE 9-2 defaults and bond ratings

period	AAA	AA	A	BBB
1920–1929	.12%	.17%	.20%	.80%
1930–1939	.42%	.44%	1.94%	3.78%
1920–1939	.30%	.30%	1.1%	2.3%

Source: W. B. Hickman, *Corporate Bond Quality and Investor Experience* (National Bureau of Economic Research, Washington, D.C., 1958).

CCC, CC, and C; and DDD, DD, and D that Standard and Poor's assigns to the stocks and bonds it rates. The other financial services assign similar quality ratings.[15]

The second column of Table 9-1 reveals how the quality ratings for W. T. Grant's bonds yield valuable information. Grant's bond ratings dropped to a very low level before the firm failed. Table 9-2 provides further evidence that bond quality ratings are valuable in assessing the likelihood of a firm's going bankrupt.

W. B. Hickman, a financial economist, studied hundreds of different bonds and their quality ratings over the two decades 1920 to 1940.[16] He computed the percentage of firms in each bond quality rating category that went bankrupt. Table 9-2 shows that a smaller percentage of firms went bankrupt at all quality levels in the 1920s than in the 1930s—because the Great Depression hit the country in the 1930s. More important, in each period sampled a larger percentage of firms with low quality ratings went bankrupt than firms rated high. This strongly suggests that the quality ratings the financial services sell to their subscribers can be helpful in assessing the financial risks that can lead ultimately to default, reorganization, or bankruptcy.

DETERMINANTS OF QUALITY RATINGS The financial services assign quality ratings that measure the default (or bankruptcy) risk of bond and stock issues and then sell these ratings to the rated companies and the financial services' subscribers. A firm's default risk is essentially determined by (1) the amount of funds available to the issuer relative to the amount of funds required by contract to be paid to bondholders (or expected to be paid to the stockholders) modified by (2) the strength of the security owner's claim for payment. To differentiate among securities in terms of default risk and quality ratings, the investor can analyze the firm's financial statements and financial ratios. But the following section sketches how the financial services assign quality ratings to an issue of securities.

[15] The different rating agencies seldom give different ratings for the same security. If two financial services do give the same security different ratings, it is referred to as a *split rating*. The few differences that do occur are rarely more than one rating grade level apart. This attests to the similarity of the different bond and stock rating services' ratings.

[16] For similar results see H. G. Fraine and R. H. Mills, "Effects of Defaults and Credit Deterioration on Yields of Corporate Bonds," *Journal of Finance*, September 1961.

Ratios. To analyze corporate bonds, the single most important factor is probably some "times fixed charges earned ratio."

$$\text{Times fixed charges earned ratio} = \frac{\text{income earned by firm}}{\text{firm's fixed charges}} \tag{9-4}$$

For this ratio, some measure of earnings for a period of time is taken as the amount of income available with which to pay fixed charges. And the amount of interest on bonds and/or cash dividends on common stock for that period is the amount required. The greater the amount of earnings relative to the amount of interest and/or cash dividends, the greater the ratio and the greater the ability to pay during that period. Different financial analysts calculate the times fixed charges earned ratio using quantities that are defined differently.[17]

The requirement to pay. The other main element considered in determining a security's quality rating is the strength of the requirement to pay. The relative strength of the requirement to pay is largely determined by the terms of the indenture contract between the company and its bondholders. A company that has issued bonds has a contract with its bondholders to pay specified amounts on particular dates. If it fails to make payments, it violates its contract, and the bondholders have the legal remedies of creditors, such as instituting receivership or trusteeship for a company. In contrast, stockholders enjoy no such legal promise to pay dividends, and accordingly the consequences to the company of nonpayment of dividends are much less severe. In particular situations there are many different circumstances that affect the strength of the requirement to make payments to security holders. But the contrast between the legal positions of bondholders and stockholders is sufficient to illustrate that financial risk is related to the strength of the requirement to pay.

MEANING OF QUALITY RATINGS The bond ratings published by such investment information services as Moody's and Standard & Poor's (S&P) indicate the default risk associated with the purchase of securities by assigning individual issues of securities to risk classifications. The term "high grade" is applied to issues with low financial risk. The highest-grade bonds are designated "Aaa" by Moody's and "AAA" by S&P. The next-highest grade (that is, the next-lowest level of financial risk) is designated "Aa" by Moody's and "AA" by S&P, and the third level is designated "A" in both systems. There are three "B" classifications and three "C" classifications for bonds, differentiated in the same manner as the A classifications and representing higher levels of risk. S&P has a "D" classification for bonds in default, which Moody's does not use.

There are several rating or ranking systems for preferred and common stocks. S&P ranks stocks in seven groups, with A+ the highest grade (lowest risk) and C the lowest grade (highest risk). These rankings relate to measures

[17] For common stocks, for instance, the usual measure of how much funds are available is earnings per share; the amount of funds "required" is the amount of cash dividends generally expected by investors. When a company has paid a certain amount of cash dividends per share in the past, the amount may be considered the expected amount. If the trend has been upward, the usual expectation is that it will continue upward.

Common stock analysis is the topic of Chaps. 14, 15, 16, and 17. Bond default risk analysis is studied in Chap. 12.

of historical stability and growth of earnings and dividends.[18] No assessment of the future financial abilities of issuers is involved.

9-2.4 risk and return

It would seem that investors should require issuers of high-risk securities to pay higher rates of return than issuers of low-risk securities; otherwise, why should investors assume the greater risk of loss or even bankruptcy?

Figure 9-3 shows the relationship between risk and corporate bond yields at different times. Corporate bonds yield progressively higher interest rates as

[18] Standard & Poor's, *Stock Guide* (New York, 1979).

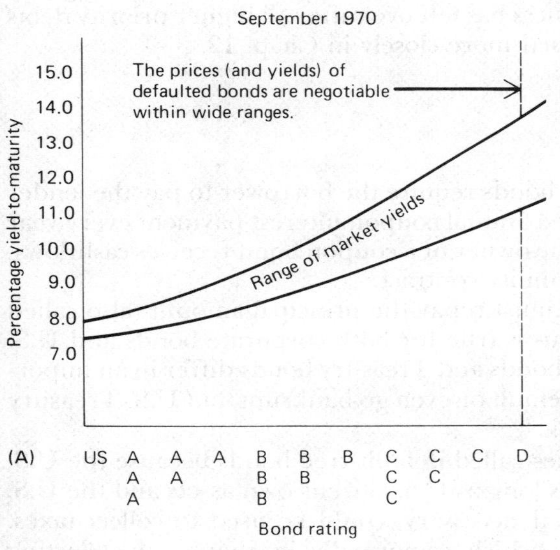

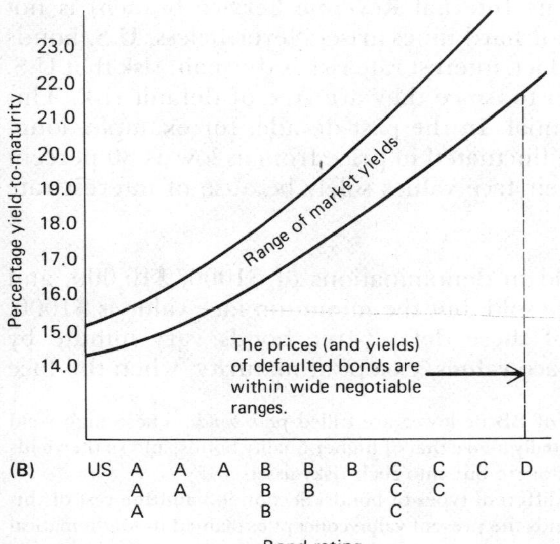

FIGURE 9-3 the default risk structure of market interest rates on (*a*) September 1970 and (*b*) July 1981. Note that (*i*) the level of all interest rates rose, (*ii*) the positive risk-return trade-off does not disappear as the level of interest rates changes, and (*iii*) the yields (and thus, the prices) of defaulted bonds are negotiable within a wide range.

their financial integrity and quality ratings deteriorate. Bond prices vary inversely with interest rates; therefore, the quality ratings directly affect bond prices because the ratings affect the bond's risk-adjusted interest rates. Federal Reserve Board policy, fiscal policy, the supply of and demand for loanable funds, and other factors that constantly change cause the relationship between discount rate and bond ratings to shift every day. But high-risk bonds must always pay the highest returns in order to attract investors.[19]

The trade-off between the risk that investors undertake and the rate of return they are paid is not limited to bonds. Stock investors also try to avoid risk. As a result, common stocks must, on average, pay higher rates of return than bonds because common stockholders have only a residual claim against whatever assets (if any) the business has left over after all higher priority debts are paid. Default risk is examined more closely in Chap. 12.

9-3 THE INTEREST RATE RISK FACTOR

A bond is a legal contract. Most bonds require the borrower to pay the lender (that is, the bond investor) a fixed annual coupon interest payment every year until the bond matures. Thus, the owner of a coupon bond receives cashflows, as does the beneficiary of an annuity contract.

At maturity, the bond issuer must repay the principal amount (also called the face value) of the bond. This is true for both corporate bonds and U.S. Treasury bonds. But corporate bonds and Treasury bonds differ in an important respect: corporations can default or even go bankrupt, but U.S. Treasury bonds are free from default risk.[20]

Treasury bonds are sometimes called default-free bonds because the U.S. Treasury cannot go bankrupt as long as U.S. citizens own assets and the U.S. government has an army that, if necessary, could be used to collect taxes. Therefore, the U.S. Treasury (which is normally in charge of collecting federal income taxes through its Internal Revenue Service branch) is not likely to become bankrupt even if hard times arise. Nevertheless, U.S. bonds experience interest rate risk. In fact, interest rate risk is the main risk that U.S. Treasury obligations are subject to, since they are free of default risk. This interest rate risk can be substantial. In the past decade, for example, long-term U.S. Treasury bonds have fluctuated in price from as low as 80 percent to as high as 120 percent of their face values solely because of interest rate risk.

9-3.1 changes in the market prices of bonds

Treasury bonds are usually sold in denominations of \$1000, \$10,000, and \$100,000. Larger face values are sold, but the minimum face value is \$1000. However, the market prices of these default-free bonds vary minute by minute and rarely equal their face values, except at maturity, when the face

[19] Bond issues with quality ratings of BB or lower are called *junk bonds*. These high-yield bonds have a default rate that is substantially above that of higher quality bonds, and so the yields offered must be higher to induce investors to buy into such risky assets.

[20] See Chap. 2 for a description of different types of bonds. Section 9-3 and the rest of this book presume that the reader understands the present value concept explained in Mathematical App. A at the end of the book.

value must be repaid to the lender. The factor that makes a \$1000 Treasury bond with decades to maturity vary in price from \$800 to \$1200 is the changing market interest rates.

The market price of a bond can be calculated to the penny by observing the current market interest rate—or yield to maturity, as it is more properly called—and using it to find the present value of the bond's cashflows. The cashflows are all known in advance—they are the annual coupon interest payments plus the face value at maturity. For example, a \$1000 Treasury bond with a 10 percent coupon rate will pay \$100 per year up to and including the year of its maturity, and then it will also repay the \$1000 principal. The various present values this default-free bond may assume as its time to maturity varies from zero years to infinity are illustrated in Fig. 9-4 for market interest rates of 9 percent, 10 percent, and 11 percent. The market price of a bond will always exactly equal its present value, so these calculated values are informative.

9-3.2 determinants of interest rate risk from price fluctuations

The present values illustrated in Fig. 9-4 (and the prices of all coupon-paying bonds for that matter) are calculated with Eq. (9-5) below.

$$\text{Present value} = \sum_{t=1}^{T} \frac{\text{coupon}_t}{(1.0 + \text{yield})^t} + \frac{\text{face value}}{(1.0 + \text{yield})^T} \tag{9-5}$$

The word "yield" in Eq. (9-5) is short for the bond's yield to maturity, a rate of return measure that is compounded over the expected life of the bond.[21]

[21] Strictly speaking, a bond's yield to maturity can be defined as the discount rate that equates the present value of all the bond's future cashflows to the bond's current market price. A bond's yield to maturity is discussed in more detail in Chap. 11. The yield to maturity is called the internal rate of return from the asset in most capital budgeting discussions. Sometimes the yield to maturity is called the dollar-weighted rate of return.

FIGURE 9-4 how a change in interest rates affects market prices for bonds of varying lengths of maturity.

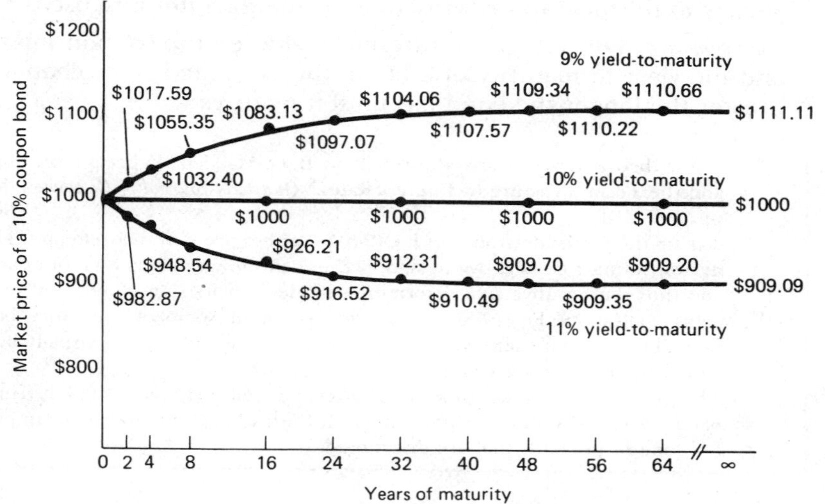

CHANGES IN MARKET INTEREST RATES The two present value theorems shown in Box 9-3, below, can be discerned from Fig. 9-4, or by mathematically analyzing Eq. (9-5).

Present value theorem one is illustrated in Fig. 9-4. The present value of the bond is higher along the curve calculated with the 9 percent interest rate than it is along the lower curve, which represents the same bond's present values calculated with an 11 percent rate. That is, the bond's present value at any given time to maturity moves inversely with the interest rate used to discount the cashflows.[22]

Present value theorem two is also relevant to Fig. 9-4. The 10 percent Treasury bond's present values fluctuate over a much wider range at the longer maturities than at the shorter maturities. That is, the bond has more interest rate risk as the *futurity* of its cashflows increases. Figure 9-5 shows how the various market interest rates that induce these bond value changes have varied during recent years.

[22] Chen, Roll, and Ross have found a statistically significant relationship between asset returns and the (orthogonalized) market interest rates from long-term bonds (and several other economic variables, too). See Nai-Fu Chen, Richard Roll, and Stephen A. Ross, "Economic Forces and the Stock Market: Testing the APT and Alternative Asset Pricing Theories, "CRSP Working Paper Number 119, December 1983. Their results are also referred to in Richard Roll and Stephen A. Ross, "The Arbitrage Pricing Theory Approach to Strategic Portfolio Planning," *Financial Analysts Journal*, May–June 1984, pp. 14–29. The relationship between the individual risk factors and the total risk of an asset are discussed more fully in this book's Chap. 10 and most particularly in the chapter about arbitrage pricing theory (APT), Chap. 30.

BOX 9-3

two basic bond price theorems

The following two theorems about the relationship of bond prices and yield to maturity may be discerned from graphs like Fig. 9-4.*

Theorem one: Bond prices (or the present value of anything) move inversely to the yield to maturity (that is, the discount rate used).**

Theorem two: For any given difference between the coupon interest rate and the yield to maturity of a bond, the associated price change will be greater the longer the bond has until it matures.†

* These theorems were derived formally by B. G. Malkiel, "Expectations, Bond Prices, and the Term Structure of Interest Rates," *Quarterly Journal of Economics*, May 1962, pp. 197–218.

** Taking the partial derivative of Eq. (9-5) furnishes proof of theorem one. This partial derivative must be negative in sign, because all the numerical quantities are positive and thus the negative sign determines the derivative's sign. Similar differential calculus analysis of Eq. (9-5) can provide proof of some of the other bond price theorems. Or, more simply, most of these theorems can be seen visually by studying and comparing Figs. 9-4 and 9-5.

† Theorem two is not true for some long-term discounted bonds, but it is true for most bonds. And theorem two is never horribly misleading—it merely oversimplifies for a few long-term bonds that are discounted.

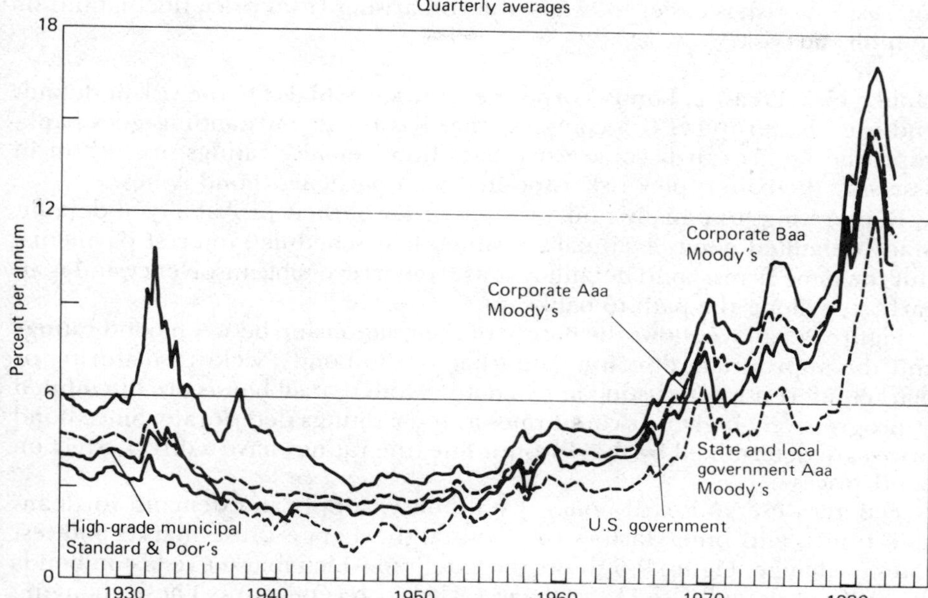

FIGURE 9-5 market yields to maturities over time. (*Source*: *Historical Chart Book*, Federal Reserve Board of Governors, Washington, 1983, p. 97.)

COUPON RATE CHANGES A bond investor seeking to avoid the interest rate risk arising from price fluctuations (described by present value theorems one and two) may do so by investing in short-term bonds (say, bonds with 1 year to maturity) rather than in bonds with more futurity (that is, longer maturities). Then, however, another kind of interest rate risk is encountered, coupon rate risk.

If an investor keeps funds invested over a number of years by buying a new 1-year bond every time an old 1-year bond matures, each of these successive 1-year bonds will bear a different coupon interest rate. Bonds' coupon interest rates can vary over just as wide a range as their market interest rates. Figure 9-5 illustrates how these market interest rates have varied in recent years. Thus, an investor who buys only short-term bonds must buy a succession of bonds with varying coupon interest rates.

Coupon interest rates that fluctuate year to year (which are the source of the only cashflows from a bond before it matures) create *coupon rate risk*. This risk that arises from changing coupon interest income can take its toll, for example, on retired people who depend on coupon income to buy their food each month. However, the coupon rate risk will at least reduce the other kind of interest rate risk (that is, the risk of price fluctuations) associated with bonds with long periods to maturity. Each investor must decide which type of interest rate risk is easier to bear—the risk arising from price fluctuations or coupon rate risk.[23]

9-3.3 corporate bonds

Unlike U.S. Treasury bonds, corporate bonds are subject to the risk of default and even bankruptcy. If a company that has bonds outstanding goes bankrupt, the bonds can become worthless. Bond quality ratings are useful in assessing the bankruptcy risk associated with particular bond issues.

Bond ratings essentially rank issues in order of their probability of default. Many defaulted bonds eventually resume their scheduled interest payments. But for some firms, bond default results from irreversible insolvency and is an early step along the path to bankruptcy.

Figure 9-3 above shows the nature of the relationship between bond ratings and the appropriate discount rate (that is, the bond's yield to maturity, or market interest rate) existing at two dates. Note that all bonds are discounted at progressively higher discount rates as their ratings deteriorate. Since bond prices are determined by the discount rate, the ratings have a direct effect on bond prices.

Federal Reserve Board policy, fiscal policy, supply and demand for loanable funds, and other factors that constantly change cause market interest rates to change. Figure 9-5 shows the extent to which market yields on bonds in different default-risk classes have varied in recent years. These changing credit conditions can turn bond markets into speculative markets, because present value theorems one and two apply to corporate bonds in exactly the same way they apply to government bonds. Thus, corporate bonds are also subject to the two kinds of interest rate risk—coupon rate risk and price change risk. The only difference between the default-free Treasury bonds and the more risky corporate bonds is that the corporate bonds must pay higher rates of interest in order to induce investors to assume their risk of default. However, since all interest rates tend to rise and fall together (as shown in Fig. 9-5), the corporate bonds' interest rates merely fluctuate at a level higher than the level at which Treasury bonds' interest rates fluctuate.

9-3.4 common stocks

Even preferred and common stocks experience interest rate risk. Preferred and common stocks usually pay cash dividends. The dividend yield from a share of preferred or common stock is defined below.

$$\text{Dividend yield} = \frac{\text{cash dividend per share}}{\text{market price per share}}$$

The coupon yield (or current yield) from a bond is defined below.

$$\text{Coupon yield} = \frac{\text{coupon interest per year}}{\text{market price per bond}}$$

[23] If bond investments can be held for years until they mature (this is how pension funds and life insurance companies invest most of their funds), then price fluctuations are easy to bear. But if bond investments might need to be liquidated in an emergency when bond market prices are low, then the risk from price fluctuations is unbearable, and short-term bonds would be the less risky investment alternative.

The dividend yield from a share of stock and the coupon yield from a bond are both rates of periodic cashflow that make up part of the investors' total rate of return. Yet these two cash yield measures are different, because of bankruptcy considerations.

A bond's coupon interest payment is a contractual payment that cannot vary in amount or timing, or else the issuing company will be sued in bankruptcy court. Cumulative cash dividends on preferred stocks must likewise be paid if the issuing firm does not want to be sued by shareholders. But most preferred stock issues have noncumulative cash dividends, which may be skipped if the issuing corporation experiences hard times. Cash dividends are paid to common stockholders only if the issuing firm's board of directors sees fit. Common stockholders' cash dividends can be canceled completely if the firm's profitability is dubious and if paying dividends might increase the chance of bankruptcy. This bankruptcy risk makes the cash dividend yield paid to common stockholders considerably more risky than bondholders' coupon yield. Nevertheless, the present value model is still relevant in deter-

FIGURE 9-6 cash dividend yields on common stock averages and bond average yield moving together.

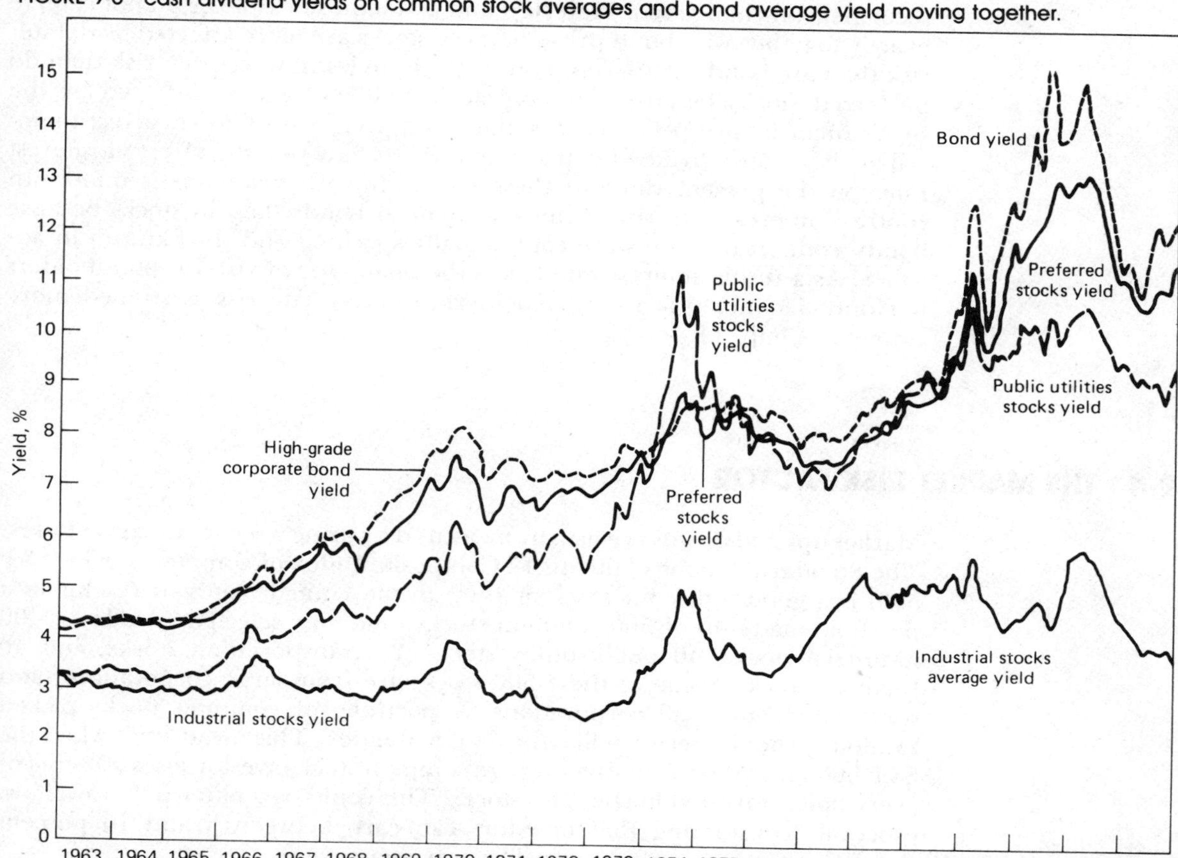

mining the prices of stocks. It is through the present value mechanism that interest rate risk affects the prices of preferred and common stocks. Considering how cash dividend yields tend to move with interest rates as time passes can help in understanding why stocks experience some interest rate risk.

Figure 9-6 illustrates how the average dividend yields of preferred and common stock fluctuate together with the average market interest rate of bonds over a period of years. Common stock has the lowest average dividend yield because some industrial common stocks pay little or no cash dividends—their stockholders receive most of their return in capital gains. The preferred stock has the highest average dividend yield because preferred stockholders receive only cash dividend income; furthermore, the preferred stock must pay a higher yield than bonds pay because preferred stock involves more default risk than do bonds. In spite of these differences, the various yields shown in Fig. 9-6 tend to fluctuate together; this similarity is the result of interest rate risk.

Common stocks and preferred stocks have interest rate risk because their estimated values are the present values of all future cash dividends. Thus, when the prevailing level of interest rates changes, the present values of these securities can change too. Preferred and common stock prices do not change exactly together with bond prices because stocks are more affected by default risk than are bonds. Also, common stocks have less interest rate risk than do preferred stocks because common stock dividends are so affected by the firm's financial prospects. That is, the profit prospects of a firm affect financial analysts' cash dividend expectations so strongly that the effect of interest rates on the present value of these uncertain cash dividends is minor. In contrast, interest rate risk is more evident in bonds than in stocks because bonds' coupon payments are contractually specified and thus known in advance. As a result, interest rate risk is the main type of risk for bondholders but only a minor risk for stockholders. Interest rate risk is studied more closely in Chap. 11.

9-4 THE MARKET RISK FACTOR

Market ups and downs are usually measured by using a security market index. The Standard & Poor's 500 Stocks Composite Index of common stocks (S&P 500) is a good index for stock markets in the United States. It resembles a portfolio made up of 500 common stocks randomly selected as follows: 400 industrial stocks, 40 public-utility stocks, 20 transportation stocks, and 40 financial stocks. Some of these 500 stocks are from large corporations, and some are from small corporations. A portfolio of common stocks picked randomly should perform like the S&P 500 index. This means that when the S&P 500 falls 20 percent, the average common stock investor loses 20 cents of every dollar invested in common stocks. This could be a bitter pill to swallow, especially considering that investors can earn between 5 and 10 percent simply by putting money in a riskless savings account.

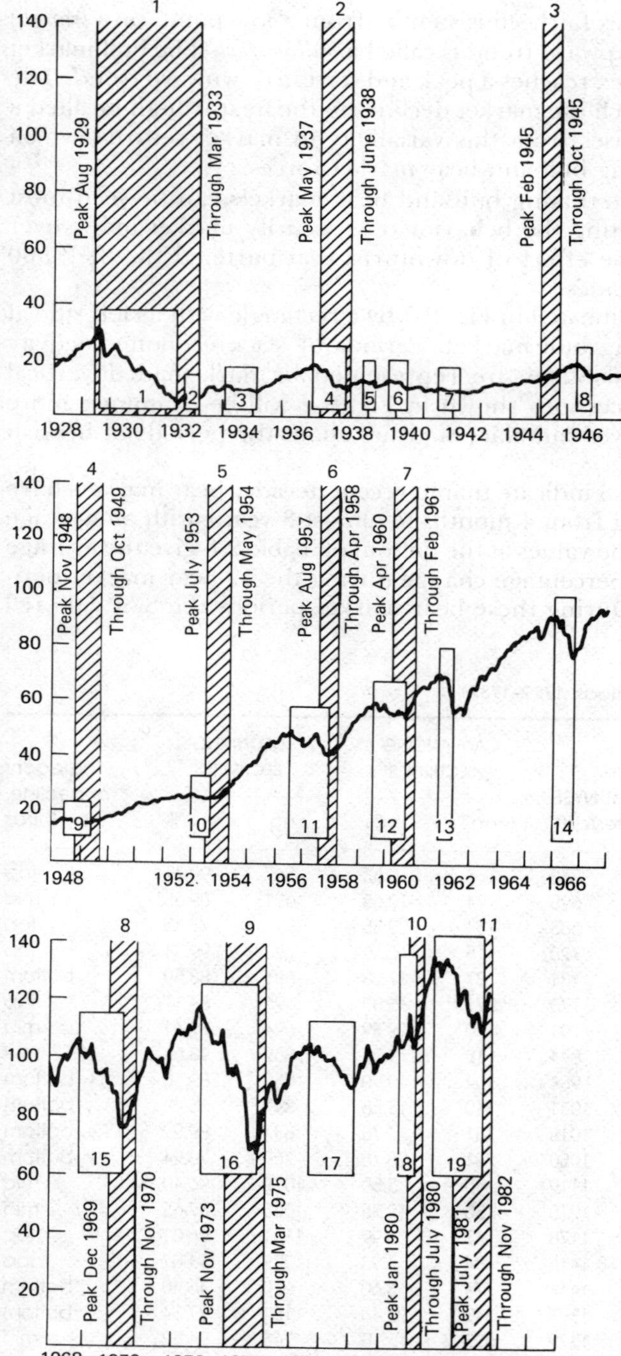

FIGURE 9-7 S&P 500 index fluctuates through bull and bear markets.

9-4.1 bull markets are punctuated by bear markets

When a security index rises fairly consistently (from a low point, or a *trough*) for a period of time, this upward trend is called a *bull market*. The bull market ends when the market index reaches a peak and starts a downward trend. The period of time during which the market declines to the next trough is called a *bear market*. *Market risk* arises from this variability in market returns, which results from the alternating bull and bear market forces.

The effects of these alternating bull and bear markets can be seen most clearly in a graph illustrating the behavior of a security market index over time. Figure 9-7 shows the effect of downturns that buffeted the S&P 500 significantly in recent decades.

Each bear market is delineated in Fig. 9-7 by a rectangle with its left side at the peak of the preceding bull market. Periods of slack economic activity (recessions) in the United States are represented by dark-shaded vertical stripes. The economic recessions shown in Fig. 9-7 will be examined more closely later. Table 9-3 gives summary statistics about the periods of bearish market activity.

Figure 9-7 and Table 9-3 indicate that in recent decades bear markets have lasted for periods ranging from 4 months to almost 3 years, with an average duration of 14 months. The values at the bottom of Table 9-3 give the average duration of and average percentage change during the 19 bear market periods shown in the table. During these bear market periods the S&P 500 fell

TABLE 9-3 advance-decline data for 19 bear market periods, 1929–1982

bear market dates	duration in months	change in S&P 500, %	no. of NYSE stocks tested*	ADVANCING SECURITIES no.	ADVANCING SECURITIES %	DECLINING SECURITIES no.	DECLINING SECURITIES %	category of decline, by thirds
7/29–6/32	36	−84.76	570	3	0.53	567	99.47	top
9/32–3/33	7	−24.58	695	74	10.65	621	89.35	mid
2/34–3/35	14	−25.71	683	154	22.55	529	77.45	top
2/37–4/38	15	−45.39	728	5	0.69	723	99.31	top
11/38–4/39	6	−17.14	771	87	11.28	683	88.59	bottom
10/39–6/40	9	−25.04	773	277	35.83	496	64.17	top
7/41–4/42	8	−23.59	794	100	12.59	694	87.41	mid
5/46–11/46	7	−21.44	874	12	1.37	862	98.63	mid
6/48–6/49	13	−16.94	954	104	10.90	850	89.10	bottom
1/53–9/53	9	−11.12	1031	140	13.58	891	86.42	bottom
7/56–12/57	18	−17.32	1018	181	17.78	837	82.22	bottom
7/59–10/60	16	−10.06	1050	281	26.76	769	73.24	bottom
12/61–6/62	7	−22.46	1112	40	3.50	1072	96.40	mid
1/66–10/66	10	−17.35	1215	150	12.35	1065	87.65	mid
12/68–6/70	19	−29.02	1178	47	3.99	1131	96.01	top
1/73–12/74	24	−43.35	1416	84	5.93	1332	94.07	top
9/76–3/78	19	−15.81	1444	774	53.60	670	46.40	bottom
1/80–4/80	4	−10.67	1523	342	22.46	1181	77.54	bottom
11/80–7/82	21	−19.38	1379	623	45.18	766	54.82	mid
Averages	14	−25.42			16.40		83.59	

* Some of the NYSE-listed stocks (it varies from bear market to bear market) were not considered because they went bankrupt, disappeared because they were merged into a larger firm, or were eliminated by some other filter.

between 10 percent and 85 percent, with an average decline of over 25 percent. Of course, to a certain extent, these statistics about bear markets are influenced by the arbitrary parameters employed in delineating the bearish periods.[24]

9-4.2 counting the stocks that fall and that gain in price

A glance at Fig. 9-7 shows that the market average sometimes has rising months during bear market periods (for example, look at September and October 1973). In fact, every bear market period delineated in Fig. 9-7 includes brief upturns in the market index. Furthermore, if we were to study graphs of the prices of individual stocks, we would see that the price of an individual stock can rise even when the market indices are falling. That is, a given stock can move in the opposite direction from the market averages, at least temporarily. These observations allow us to define a *bear market* as a period of time during which securities prices show a general tendency to decline.

A natural question for the potential investor to ask is, "Do some pathological stocks have higher prices at the end of a bear market than they had at the start?" This is an important question because the profitability of investing during a bear market depends on how many stocks (if any) are experiencing rising prices. To answer this question, a computer analyzed the market prices of every NYSE stock for each bear market.

First, the computer program examined only those stocks that were listed on the NYSE throughout each bear market. So, for instance, those corporations that went bankrupt or were merged and thus lost their independent identity were not considered at all. Second, the program checked the month-end market prices of every continuously listed NYSE stock at the start and end of each bear market to see whether the price had advanced (risen) or declined (fallen) overall. Finally, the program calculated the number of stocks that had advanced and the number that had declined in each bear market examined. Table 9-3 gives the results of this analysis.

The average figures at the bottom of Table 9-3 indicate that about 84 percent of NYSE stocks ended the typical bear market at a price lower than the price at the start of the market downturn. The analysis also revealed that almost every stock rose in price for at least 1 month during every bear market period. Nevertheless, the vast majority of stocks were pulled downward by the bearish conditions.

9-4.3 bull market parameters

Figure 9-7 shows that bull markets predominate over bear markets. Table 9-4 presents some bull market summary statistics. A comparison of these bull market statistics with the bear market statistics in Table 9-3 indicates than 63 percent (or 375) of the 593 months from June 1932 to November 1980 inclusive were bullish. Table 9-4 also contains other statistics that measure just how profitable common stock investing tends to be in bull markets.

[24] Any market decline in excess of 10 percent that lasted several months was arbitrarily defined as a bear market in compiling the statistics reported in this section. This definition is not sacrosanct. In particular, some of the one-third smallest bear markets may be easily contested. See the right-hand column of Table 9-3 for delineation of which third (that is, top, middle, or bottom third) a bear market occupies.

TABLE 9-4 data on 18 bull markets

bull market number	trough month /year	peak month /year	duration in months	S&P 500 average's values	% increase in S&P
1	6/32	9/32	3	4.77– 8.26	73.16
2	6/33	2/34	8	6.23– 11.32	81.70
3	3/35	2/37	23	8.41– 18.11	115.33
4	4/38	11/38	7	9.89– 13.07	32.15
5	4/39	10/39	6	10.83– 12.90	19.11
6	6/40	7/41	13	9.67– 10.26	6.10
7	4/42	5/46	49	7.84– 18.70	138.52
8	11/46	6/48	19	14.69– 16.82	14.49
9	6/49	1/53	38	13.97– 26.18	87.40
10	9/53	7/56	34	23.27– 48.78	109.62
11	12/57	7/59	19	40.33– 59.74	48.12
12	10/60	12/61	14	53.73– 71.74	33.51
13	6/62	1/66	43	55.63– 93.32	67.75
14	10/66	12/68	26	77.13–106.50	38.07
15	6/70	1/73	31	75.59–118.40	56.63
16	12/74	9/76	21	67.07–105.50	57.29
17	3/78	1/80	21	88.82–115.30	29.81
		total	375	total	1,008.76
		average	19.73	average	53.09

The S&P 500 appreciated an average of 53.09 percent in the 17 bull markets delineated in Table 9-4. The smallest gain was 6 percent in the short bull market of 1940 to 1941; the largest was 138 percent during the 1942 to 1946 period. This 138 percent gain means that an investor who picked stocks at random should have more than doubled the value of his or her portfolio of common stocks in that 4-year period. Results like these yield what is lightly referred to as the thrill of investing—namely, easy profits. But don't forget, even during the 4 bullish years from April 1942 to May 1946 a few bad stock selections could have bankrupted an unlucky investor. There is no guarantee that every investor will do as well as the averages during a bull market. Some investors will make worse than average selections; some will do better than average.

Table 9-4 shows that the bull markets varied in length from 3 months to 49 months, with an average life of 19.73 months. Note that the average life of 14 months for a bear market (see Table 9-3) is much less than the average bull market's duration. Thus, bear markets are typically briefer than bull markets. The fact that there were about twice as many bullish months as bearish months helps explain the long-run upward trend in stock market prices that is clearly shown in Fig. 9-7.

It is a pleasure for stock market investors to fantasize about the stock market's long-term upward trend and about those bullish times during which the market value of a portfolio could be more than doubled quickly with virtually no effort (as was the case in the 1935 to 1937, 1942 to 1946, or 1953 to 1956 bull markets). However, the thought of losing more than 84 cents out of every dollar invested in common stocks in less than 3 years (as was the case in the 1929 to 1932 bear market) brings a person's feet back down to the ground with a discomforting thud. The obvious question is, "What causes the stock market indices to rise and fall like a breathtaking roller coaster?"

9-4.4 buying low and selling high—good investment timing

According to a definition formulated by two experts on economics, a *business cycle* is

> . . . a type of fluctuation found in the aggregate economic activity of nations that organize their work mainly in business enterprises; a cycle consists of expansions occurring at about the same time in many economic activities, followed by similarly general recessions, contractions, and revivals which merge into the expansion phase of the next cycle; this sequence of changes is recurrent but not periodic; in duration business cycles may last from more than one year to ten or twelve years; they are not divisible into shorter cycles of similar character with amplitudes approximating their own.[25]

The main element that causes the stock market to rise bullishly and then fall bearishly again and again is the fact that the nation's economy follows a cycle of recessions and expansions.[26] This can be seen by studying the 11 dark-shaded periods of recession shown in Fig. 9-7.[27]

By studying Fig. 9-7 one can see that the stock market appears to fall into a bear market *before* almost every recession. The bear market that started in January 1973, for instance, preceded the recession that started in November 1973. Occasionally, the stock market falls into bearish periods when no recession is at hand. For example, the bear markets in 1962 and 1966 did not precede recessions. However, 10 of the 19 bear markets shown in Fig. 9-7 anticipated actual recessions that were evidently correctly predicted by security analysts.

Since the *anticipation of recessions* appears to be the cause of most bear markets, it behooves investors to study past recessions so that they can attempt to forecast recessions. Investors can protect their portfolios by withdrawing invested funds before the onset of the bear market. Buying just before security market prices rise in a bull market and selling just before the start of a

[25] W. C. Mitchell and A. F. Burns, *Measuring Business Cycles* (National Bureau of Economic Research, New York, 1946).

[26] For a detailed and expert discussion, see Geoffrey H. Moore, *Business Cycles, Inflation and Forecasting* (Ballinger, Cambridge, Mass., 1980), chap. 9. National Bureau of Economic Research Studies in Business Cycle Number 24.

[27] Empirical research by Ross and Roll indicates that unanticipated changes in industrial production is a significant risk factor. Other significant risk factors exist. Richard Roll and Stephen A. Ross, "The Arbitrage Pricing Theory Approach to Strategic Planning Portfolio Planning," *Financial Analysts Journal*, May–June 1984, pp. 14–26. Arbitrage pricing theory, the topic of Chap. 30 of this book, shows how the different risk factors that make up total risk can be evaluated independently.

bear market—that is, buying low and selling high—is called good *investment timing*.[28]

9-4.5 Piccini's study of market peaks

Economist Raymond Piccini studied 13 recessions in an effort to determine the length of time that normally elapses between a stock market peak (that is, the start of a bear market) and the onset of a recession.[29]

[28] Valuable information about business cycle indicators can be gained from the following references: *Handbook of Cyclical Indicators: A Supplement to the Business Conditions Digest*, U.S. Department of Commerce, Bureau of Economic Analysis, Washington, D.C., May 1977; *Business Conditions Digest*, U.S. Department of Commerce, Bureau of Economic Analysis, U.S. Government Printing Office, Washington, D.C.; *Survey of Current Business: National Income and Product Accounts of the U.S., 1929–1965 Statistical Tables: A Supplement to the Survey of Current Business*, U.S. Department of Commerce, U.S. Government Printing Office, Washington, D.C., 1966. Studies of security price movements that each explain different viewpoints include the following: Michael W. Keran, "Expectations, Money and the Stock Market," *Review*, Federal Reserve Bank of St. Louis, January 1971, pp. 16–31; Stephen F. LeRoy and R. D. Porter, "The Present-Value Relation: Tests Based on Implied Variance Bounds," *Econometrica*, 1981, vol. 49, pp. 555–574; B. G. Malkiel and John Cragg, "Expectation and the Structure of Share Prices," *American Economic Review*, September 1970; Raymond Piccini, "Stock Market Behavior around Business Cycle Peaks," *Financial Analysts Journal*, July–August 1980, pp. 55–57; William Poole, "The Relationship of Monetary Decelerations to Business Cycle Peaks; Another Look at the Evidence," *Journal of Finance*, June 30, 1975, pp. 697–711.

[29] R. Piccini, "Stock Market Behavior around Business Cycle Peaks," *Financial Analysts Journal*, July–August 1980, pp. 55–57.

FIGURE 9-8 S&P 500 average percentage differences from levels at business cycle peaks. (*Source*: *Financial Analysts Journal*, exhibit one, p. 56, July–August 1980.)

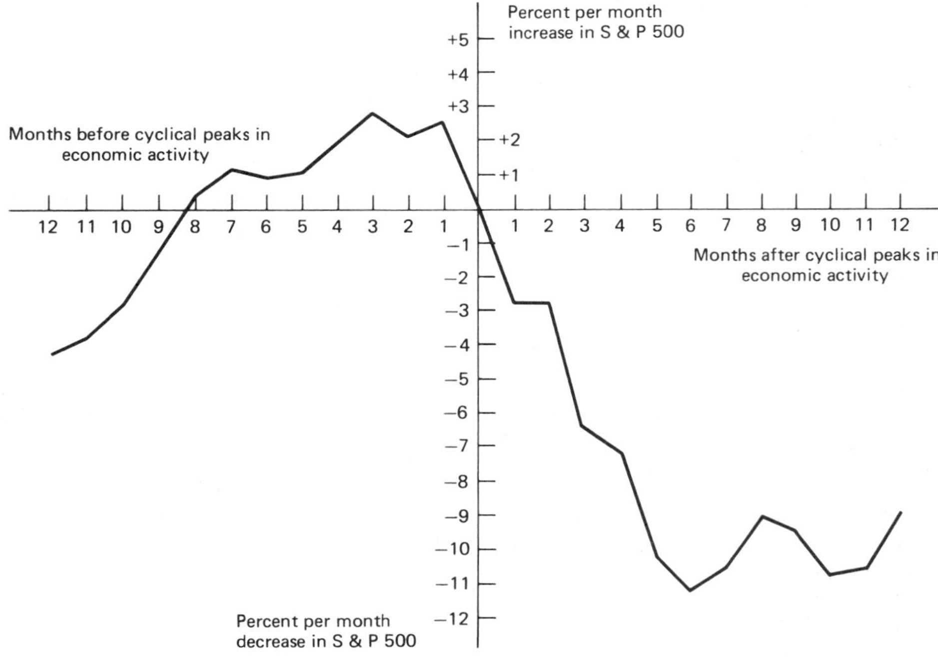

Although the durations of bear markets and recessions differ, Piccini was able to point out some market tendencies worth remembering. First, 1 to 3 months before a recession starts is typically a good time for an investor to sell common stocks. Piccini reached this conclusion because the market peaks 1 to 3 months before the month of the peak in economic activity, on average. Second, if an investor waits until 6 months after a recession starts (that is, after the economic peak), the market index will be down 11 percent from where it was when the recession started, on average. This is a good time to start thinking about buying common stocks in order to enjoy the new bull market.

Figure 9-8 illustrates the relationship between the average percentage changes in the Standard & Poor's 500 Stocks Composite Average and the peaks and troughs in business activity that Piccini studied. The figure shows the average number of months by which the stock market's ups and downs lead and lag the National Bureau of Economic Research's official peak month in business activity, averaged over 13 recessions. Although every bear market deviated from this average pattern, Fig. 9-8 shows market tendencies that are worthwhile for investors to consider.

9-5 THE MANAGEMENT RISK FACTOR

Most people know that high-level executives earn princely salaries, occupy luxurious offices, and wield enormous power within their organizations. None of this should make us forget, however, that even the very highest executive is merely mortal and capable of making a mistake or a poor decision. This section assesses how the errors business managers sometimes make can affect investors who buy shares in their firms. Investors must be wary of these managers; they are in a position to make both gross and subtle errors. There are so many different kinds of management errors that it is not feasible to enumerate all the management risks to which investors expose themselves.

Only a few management errors will be discussed below. These difficulties are reviewed to broaden your appreciation of some of the problem areas a security analyst must consider. Watching for management errors requires an attitude of vigilance and sensitivity rather than an uncanny ability to forecast specific incidents.

9-5.1 acts of God

An *act of God* is an extraordinary interruption of events by a natural cause. Floods, earthquakes, hordes of destructive insects, and bolts of lightning are examples. These events can be neither prevented nor foreseen, and they usually entail great costs to those involved. Conscientious business managers can, however, reduce the risk of great financial loss by insuring their plant and equipment and taking other steps to prepare for such catastrophes.

When an act of God wreaks disaster upon a business firm, the costs of the misfortune typically fall on the firm's insurance company (if the firm has insurance), on any employees who may be harmed, and, ultimately, on the firm's investors. Consider, for example, the terrible winter that buried the northeastern portions of the United States under a record snowfall during January and February 1977. This heavy snowfall was accompanied by extremely cold temperatures and soaring demand for natural gas, electricity, and oil for heating purposes. In some states, there were power failures caused by snow and ice. Thousands of businesses and schools were closed for weeks, millions of workers were furloughed, and millions of dollars worth of fruit and vegetables were destroyed by cold that reached as far south as Florida. The nation's gross national product was reduced by billions of dollars. Since most businesses were not insured against or otherwise prepared for this catastrophe, their investors suffered stock price declines totaling millions of dollars.

Many of the losses from the cold weather of 1977 would have been averted if business managers and governmental planners had ordered better insulation for their buildings, stockpiled extra heating supplies and other raw materials, made contingency plans to allow for foul weather, and purchased insurance against such losses. Shortsightedness caused many companies to suffer financial losses that reduced the value of their securities in the market. Thus, investors in those firms also suffered losses which could have been transferred to insurance companies that were better equipped to handle them. Many investors attempted to have inept business managers fired—but this is like closing the door to the chicken coop after the fox has eaten the hens. In any event, this is one sort of management risk to which investors expose themselves.

9-5.2 product obsolescence

Losses can occur if management allows a firm's product to become obsolete. Theoretically, a business corporation will live forever if it is well managed. When shareowners sell out or employees change jobs, die, or retire, new people take their places. This transfer of roles enables businesses to survive for generations. Products, too, must sometimes be replaced if they grow old, go out of style, suffer decreasing usefulness, or otherwise become obsolete.

It is up to management to overcome the problem of obsolescence by developing and maintaining active research and development (R&D) programs. Annual expenditure for R&D to generate new products for the firm to produce and sell is a sign of a farsighted top management. For example, if the buggy manufacturers of 1900 had reinvested some of their profits in R&D, they might have survived in the 1930s as horseless carriage manufacturers. The steam-engine manufacturers of the 1940s had to learn how to manufacture diesel locomotives to survive in the 1960s. The American Locomotive Corporation and Baldwin Locomotive Corporation, for example, used to be huge steam-engine manufacturing companies; then General Motors pulled away their customers with diesel engines and drove them out of business. Television manufacturers in the 1950s had to develop color sets in order to compete in the markets of the 1960s. The Detroit automotive giants must produce smaller, more fuel-efficient cars if they are to stand up to foreign car competition in the 1980s.[30] Clearly, management must make changes to avoid *product obsolescence*.

The road to corporate success is littered with bankrupt corporations that did not develop new products to replace obsolete ones. In many cases, blame can be directly attributed to management error. Not enough of the firms'

[30] See "Despite Losses, GM Could Emerge Even Bigger and Stronger than Ever," *The Wall Street Journal*, Aug. 7, 1980, p. 19.

profits were spent on R&D to develop new products. Instead, nearsighted top management tried to make bigger short-run profits by cutting R&D budgets. The resulting permanent losses to these firms' investors were management's fault.

9-5.3 loss of important customers

A product usually becomes obsolete over a period of years. However, it is commonplace for a business firm to lose a customer with no prior warning. Competitors constantly win customers from each other. A firm that suddenly loses a *large* customer can go bankrupt rapidly.

It is a management error to let a company become dependent on one customer or a few customers whose loss could financially embarrass the firm. Every firm's top management should strive to develop a broad and diversified group of customers. Ideally, no single customer will be capable of ruining a supplying firm merely by changing suppliers.

It is easy to obtain a diversified customer group in some industries. Retail department stores, supermarkets, dry cleaning stores, filling stations, airlines, and theaters, for example, usually do not depend on any one customer to maintain a profitable level of sales. However, some businesses are dependent upon one customer or a few.

Any small firm that supplies parts (say, rearview mirrors, floor carpets, or radio antennas) to an automobile firm is likely to be entirely dependent on the auto giant for its existence. Small firms often lack the diversified sales force and manufacturing technology needed to obtain new customers and may exist solely to supply one customer. This precarious position indicates that the firm is poorly managed.

Of course, some industries are composed of oligopolistic competitors who dominate the buying of raw materials for that industry. If a firm finds itself selling to only a few monopsonistic or oligopolistic customers, the firm should diversify into another industry to help prolong its existence.

9-5.4 agency theory

Reading about management errors can leave one with a cynical outlook. It is possible, for example, to hastily conclude that conscientious business executives are merely mortal people who make mortal errors because they become tired, are too busy, or may not be sufficiently well-educated to make better decisions. However, a theory is developing to replace this cynicism with informed insight. Doctors Jensen and Meckling have hypothesized an economic theory about *principal-agent relationships* that can explain some of the management errors discussed above.[31] Knowledge of this theory is worthwhile because the insights it yields may enable security analysts to make better forecasts and predictions. Let us consider this theory.

An agent-principal relationship exists whenever decision-making authority must be delegated. Corporations are an example of a common principal-agent relationship—a corporation's shareholder/owners delegate the day-to-day decision-making authority to managers who are hired employees rather than substantial owners. Jensen and Meckling argue that corporate managers who have little or no ownership interest in the corporation that employs them

[31] The roots of agency theory can be traced back many years. See, for example, A. A. Berle and G. C. Means, *The Modern Corporation and Private Property* (Macmillan, New York, 1934).

have more incentive to consume certain nonpecuniary benefits than they would if they were substantial owners of the firm.[32] The nonpecuniary benefits to which Jensen and Meckling refer might include nonsalary benefits like company-supplied luxury cars for executives, liberal expense accounts, corporate jets, some personally gratifying corporate acquisition, and other comforts and ego-bolsterers for managers. Jensen and Meckling suggest that owners work harder to maximize the value of the firm than employees, if all other factors are equal. That is, to the extent that ex post rewards and punishments are not perfect and just, employed managers may not expend as much ex ante effort to generate profitable investment opportunities as they would if they owned the firm where they worked.

The Jensen-Meckling agency theory reasons that many stock market investors are rational, intelligent people who can discern the conflict of interest that exists between the economic welfare of the corporate owners and the corporation-employed managers. Jensen and Meckling maintain that this conflict of interest is more or less built into the corporate decision-making process because corporate managers who are merely employees can, and sometimes do, abuse the powers vested in them to act as agents for the owners. As a result of this conflict of interest, investors will discriminate by paying more for shares in an owner-managed firm than they would pay for shares in an identical corporation managed by employees who own little or no ownership interest in the firm. This difference in the value between the owner-managed and the employee-managed corporations is defined as the *agency cost*.

Eugene Fama argues against the Jensen-Meckling agency theory.[33] Fama contends that in a well-functioning market for productive resources (such as managers and capital), significant agency costs should not exist. Fama reasons that corporation managers must seek employment in competitive markets, compete against their peers within the corporate environment, and thus face the discipline of the competitive marketplace. Furthermore, Fama points out, managers face the harsh discipline and also enjoy the opportunities provided by competitive markets for managerial talent. More specifically, to the extent that good managers see a market for their services that provides alternative employment opportunities, good managers should be motivated by any other more lucrative opportunities to work up to their full potential in an effort to gain positions that will pay them more.

Barnea, Haugen, and Senbet,[34] and also Haugen and Senbet,[35] have presented a third view that rationalizes the existence of the Jensen-Meckling

[32] Michael C. Jensen and William H. Meckling, "Theory of the Firm: Managerial Behavior, Agency Costs and Ownership Structure," *Journal of Financial Economics*, 1976, vol. 3, pp. 305–360. See also Michael C. Jensen and William H. Meckling, "Rights and Production Functions: An Application to Labor-Managed Firms and Codetermination," *Journal of Business*, 1979, vol. 52, pp. 469–506.

[33] Eugene F. Fama, "Agency Problems and the Theory of the Firm," *Journal of Political Economy*, 1980, vol. 88, pp. 288–307.

[34] Amir Barnea, Robert A. Haugen, and Lemma W. Senbet, "A Rationale for Debt Maturity and Call Provisions in the Agency Theoretic Framework," *Journal of Finance*, vol. 35, December 1980, pp. 1223–1224.

[35] R. A. Haugen and L. W. Senbet, "Resolving the Agency Problems of External Capital through Options," *Journal of Finance*, June 1981, pp. 569–581.

agency theory and, at the same time, acknowledges the insights provided by Fama's critique of the agency theory. Barnea, Haugen, and Senbet argue that the issuing of complex securities (namely, executive stock options and puts) can resolve the inherent conflicts between the shareholders and the managers of a corporation.

In analyzing the normative issues of agency theory, researchers have recognized different motivating factors (that is, different arguments in the utility function) between the owner/principals and the agent/employees. Recognizing these differences has enabled researchers to develop optimal incentive contracts that minimize agency costs.[36] More recently, Fama and Jensen—who had previously opposed each other concerning the agency theory—have co-authored studies that note the survival of the "open corporation" even in the face of agency costs. They suggest that corporate survival may be attributable to benefits that professional managers bring to the corporation.[37]

Agency theory is still evolving. Economic researchers are currently investigating various aspects of the theory in an effort to validate, refine, or reject it. Some of these studies delve into events (for example, a large sample of corporation mergers) to see if the event raises or lowers the value of the owners' equity shares. If this research determines that a significant agency cost does exist, that would explain how management errors like those reviewed above continue to occur in a competitive business world. And it would suggest that owner-managed corporations are better investments than employee-managed firms.[38]

9-6 THE PURCHASING POWER RISK FACTOR

Webster's dictionary states that *inflation* is "an increase in the amount of currency in circulation, resulting in a relatively sharp and sudden fall in its value and rise in prices." Economics textbooks often characterize inflation simply as an increase in the general level of prices. This section focuses on the effect that inflation has on investment decisions. It behooves investors to try to deal rationally with purchasing-power risk because inflation will erode their wealth if they don't.

9-6.1 money illusion

Purchasing-power risk denotes the fact than an investor's money assets (such as cash, savings, and bond investments) may lose their purchasing power

[36] D. W. Diamond and R. Verrecchia, "Optimal Managerial Contracts and Equilibrium Security Prices," *Journal of Finance*, May 1982, vol. 37, pp. 225–288; S. Grossman and O. Hart, "Takeover Bids, the Free-Rider Problem, and the Theory of the Corporation," *The Bell Journal of Economics and Management Science*, Spring 1980, pp. 42–64; Bengt Holstrom, "Moral Hazard and Observability," *The Bell Journal of Economics and Management Science*, Spring 1979, vol. 10, pp. 74–91; Bengt Holstrom, "Moral Hazard in Teams," *The Bell Journal of Economics and Management Science*, Autumn 1982, vol. 12, pp. 324–340; Steven Shavell, "Risk Sharing and Incentives in the Principal and Agent Relationship," *The Bell Journal of Economics and Management Science*, Spring 1979, vol. 10, pp. 55–73.

[37] Eugene Fama and Michael C. Jensen, "Separation of Ownership and Control," *Journal of Law and Economics*, June 1983a, vol. 26; Eugene Fama and Michael C. Jensen, "Agency Problems and Residual Claims," *Journal of Law and Economics*, June 1983b, vol. 26.

[38] The April 1983 issue of the *Journal of Financial Economics* is devoted to articles about different aspects of agency theory. Interested readers may see vol. 11, nos. 1–4.

because of inflation. An investment may lose its purchasing power even though its price is continually rising. Many investors do not understand how an investment may suffer purchasing-power losses when its market price moves upward—these investors have *money illusion*, a phrase economists use to describe a certain type of naive behavior. People who have money illusion mistakenly believe that if they have more money, they must be richer. This belief does not take into account the way money can lose its buying power because of inflation. For example, if the amount of wealth you have doubles during a period when the price level quadruples, you are poorer even though you have more money.

Investor losses to inflation can be measured. However, one should understand how inflation is measured before studying purchasing-power losses.

9-6.2 measuring the rate of inflation

Economists measure the rate of inflation by using a price index that they construct. The consumer price index (CPI) is a popular price index in the United States. It is tabulated by the U.S. government's Bureau of Labor Statistics and measures the cost of a representative basket of consumer goods. This basket contains specified quantities and qualities of various items of food, clothing, housing, and health care bought by the average urban household. Bureau of Labor Statistics employees go to stores around the United States every month and note the prices of consumer goods to obtain realistic CPI data.

Of course, the price of this hypothetical basket of goods changes from month to month. The amount of that change is stated as a percentage of the CPI for the previous month, and this figure is the rate of inflation.

In other words, the rate of inflation between month 1 and month 2 is the difference between the CPI for those months, divided by the CPI for month 1, as shown below in Eq. (9-6*a*). The inflation rate is denoted q.

$$q = \frac{\text{CPI for month 2} - \text{CPI for month 1}}{\text{CPI for month 1}} \tag{9-6a}$$

If the cost of the market basket goes from \$200 to \$202 in 1 month, the rate of inflation would be 1 percent, as shown below.

$$q = \frac{\$202 - \$200}{\$200} \tag{9-6b}$$

$$= \frac{\$2}{\$200} = .01 = 1.0\%$$

An inflation rate of 1 percent per month is equivalent to about 12 percent per year. More precisely, if the CPI increases by 1 percent in some month, this monthly rate of 1 percent is converted to an annual rate by adding 1 to the rate of price increase and then raising that quantity to the power 12 to get the annual rate of inflation of 12.68 percent, as shown below.

$$(1.0 + 1.0\% \text{ per month})^{12} = 1.01^{12} = 1.1268 = 1.0 + 12.68\%$$

It is the common practice to annualize inflation rates (as well as interest rates) so that they can be compared easily.

There is more than one rate of inflation relevant to each period of time. Goods that enjoy strong demand, such as homes, will usually experience

TABLE 9-5 consumer price index (CPI) data

	CONSUMER PRICES, ALL ITEMS		
year and month	index (1967 = 100)	change over 1-month span, %	change over 6-month spans (annual rate, %)
1982			
January	282.5	0.4	3.5
February	283.4	0.2	4.4
March	283.1	−0.1	6.0
April	284.3	0.4	6.2
May	287.1	0.9	6.2
June	290.6	1.1	6.6
July	292.2	0.5	6.6
August	292.8	0.3	4.7
September	293.3	0.0	1.8
October	294.1	0.4	1.4
November	293.6	0.0	0.7
December	292.4	−0.3	0.8
1983			
January	293.1	0.3	1.4
February	293.2	−0.1	2.3
March	293.4	0.1	3.3
April	295.5	0.7	3.4
May	297.1	0.4	4.3
June	298.1	0.2	5.0
July	299.3	0.4	4.4
August	300.3	0.4	4.2
September	301.8	0.4	4.3
October	302.6	0.4	4.8
November	303.1	0.4	
December	303.5	0.2	

Source: *Business Conditions Digest*, U.S. Department of Commerce, February 1984, p. 84.

faster rates of inflation than goods that aren't in strong demand. Also, the rate of inflation for each good varies from month to month.

Table 9-5 contains month-by-month data for the CPI and the rate of inflation. A 6-month time span is used to obtain inflation estimates because it is felt this would yield a better picture of the trends than would a 12-month span. The 6-month figures are increased appropriately to obtain annualized rates of change.

9-6.3 real returns versus nominal returns

After inflation has been measured, it should be compared to investment returns. To avoid money illusion, an important question is, "Are your investments' rates of return higher than the rate of inflation?"

When you read in a newspaper that a savings account pays an annualized rate of return of 6 percent, for example, that is the investment's *nominal rate of return*. Nominal rates of return are *money rates of return*; that is, they are not adjusted for the effects of inflation. A numerical example should clarify this.

For purposes of illustration, assume that a savings deposit earns a nominal interest rate (or nominal rate of return) of 6 percent, $r = .06 = 6\%$, during some 1-year period. Thus, if \$100 were deposited, it would grow to \$100(1.0

$+ r) = \$100(1.06) = \$106$ in that year. However, if we also assume that the rate of inflation during that year is $q = .06 = 6$ percent, then the real value (in terms of current purchasing power) of the \$100 savings at the end of the year is still only \$100 after we divide the nominal rate by the inflation rate to get the real rate, as shown below.

$$\frac{(\$100)\ (1.0 + r)}{1.0 + q} = \frac{(\$100)(1.06)}{1.06} = \$100$$

In this example the nominal rate of return was eroded by an equal inflation rate so that the savings account's purchasing power didn't increase even though there were 6 percent more dollars in it.

Generally speaking, an asset's nominal future value after earning a nominal rate of r for one period is related to its present value as shown below:

$$\text{Nominal future value} = (\text{present value})\ (1.0 + r)$$
$$(\$106) = (\$100)\ (1.06)$$

And an asset's *real (or inflation-adjusted) future value* is calculated as shown in the following equation:

$$\text{Real future value} = \frac{\text{nominal future value}}{1.0 + \text{inflation rate}}$$

An investment's "real rate of return" during some time period is calculated by dividing 1 plus the asset's nominal rate of return, $(1.0 + r)$, by 1 plus the rate of inflation, $(1.0 + q)$, during the same time period. Equation (9-7*a*) defines this *real rate of return*, denoted rr. Equation (9-7*a*) is similar to the preceding dollar value equation.

$$1.0 + rr = \frac{1.0 + r}{1.0 + q} \tag{9-7a}$$

Equation (9-7*a*) can be equivalently restated as Eq. (9-7*b*).

$$rr = \frac{1.0 + r}{1.0 + q} - 1.0 \tag{9-7b}$$

For example, if a common stock earns a 10 percent nominal rate of return, $r = .1 = 10\%$, for a year when the inflation rate is 8 percent, $q = .08 = 8\%$, the stock's real rate of return is less than 2 percent in that year.

$$1.0 + rr = \frac{1.10}{1.08} = 1.0185, \text{ or } rr = 1.85\% \tag{9-7c}$$

This investment in common stock results in a 1.85 percent increase in *real* purchasing power. The only portion of an investment's nominal rate of return that results in increased consumption opportunities for an investor is the real rate of return. The rest of the investment's nominal rate of return is wasted on compensating for purchasing power lost to inflation. Investors who suffer from money illusion fail to realize this and erroneously believe that the investment in this example yields more than a 1.85 percent gain.

You can now see how it is possible for an investment that earns a positive nominal rate of return to earn a *negative* real return. Consider a savings account that pays 6 percent interest in a year when inflation is 8 percent. This savings account has a *negative* real rate of return, as shown in Eq. (9-7*d*) below.

$$rr = \frac{1.0 + r}{1.0 + q} - 1 = \frac{1.06}{1.08} - 1 = .9815 - 1 = -.0185 \qquad \text{(9-7}d\text{)}$$

Investors with money illusion would think that the savings account has increased their wealth by 6 percent when, in fact, their purchasing power has decreased by 1.85 percent.

If an investment has a negative real rate of return, that does not necessarily mean that the investor would have been better off without the investment. After all, if money is held in cash (earning no interest, so that $r = 0$) instead of being invested in, say, a 6 percent savings account, as in the previous example, the investor will suffer an 7.4 percent loss in purchasing power.

$$rr = \frac{1.0 + r}{1.0 + q} - 1 = \frac{1.0}{1.08} - 1 = .926 - 1 = -.0740$$

Thus, it is better to earn 6 percent than to hold cash, even though both alternatives earn a negative real return. Of course, the objective of wise investors is to earn a positive real return.[39] Box 9-4 shows a shortcut method for calculating real or nominal rates of return to expedite attainment of the objective.

[39] Some detailed studies on the effect of inflation on stock prices are as follows: (1) A. A. Alchian and R. A. Kessel, "Redistribution of Wealth through Inflation," *Science*, September 1959, pp. 535–539. (2) M. Arak, "Inflation and Stock Values: Is Our Tax Structure the Villain?" *Quarterly Review Federal Reserve Bank of New York*, Winter 1980–1981, vol. 5, pp. 3–13. (3) Z. Bodie, "Common Stocks as a Hedge against Inflation," *Journal of Finance*, May 1976, vol. 31, pp. 459–470. Z. Bodie and V. I. Rosansky, "Risk and Return in Commodity Futures," *Financial Analysts Journal*, May–June 1980, pp. 27–39. (4) R. A. Brealey, "Inflation and the Real Value of Government Assets," *Financial Analysts Journal*, January–February 1979, vol. 35, pp. 18–21. (5) P. Cagan, *Common Stock Values and Inflation—The Historical Record of Many Countries*, National Bureau of Economic Research, Report No. 13, March 1974. (6) E. F. Fama and G. W. Schwert, "Asset Returns and Inflation," *Journal of Financial Economics*, 1977, vol. 5, pp. 115–146. (7) J. Jaffee and G. Mandelker, "'The Fisher Effect' for Risky Assets: An Empirical Investigation," *Journal of Finance*, May 1976, vol. 31, pp. 447–470. (8) H. Hong, "Inflation and the Market Value of the Firm: Theory and Empirical Tests," *Journal of Finance*, September 1977, vol. 32, pp. 1031–1048. (9) J. Lintner, "Inflation and Security Returns," *Journal of Finance*, May 1975, vol. 30, pp. 259–280. (10) F. Modigliani and R. A. Cohn, "Inflation, Rational Valuation and the Market," *Financial Analysts Journal*, March–April 1979, vol. 35, pp. 24–44. (11) B. Moore, "Equity Values and Inflation: The Importance of Dividends," *Lloyds Bank Review*, July 1980, pp. 1–15. (12) S. A. Moosa, "Inflation and Common Stock Prices," *Journal of Financial Research*, Fall 1980, vol. 3, pp. 115–128. (13) C. R. Nelson, "Inflation and Rates of Return on Common Stocks," *Journal of Finance*, May 1976, vol. 31, pp. 471–483. (14X) B. A. Oudet, "The Variation of the Return on Stocks in Periods of Inflation," *Journal of Financial and Quantitative Analysis*, March 1973, vol. 8, pp. 247–258. (15) F. K. Reilly, G. L. Johnson, and R. E. Smith, "Inflation, Inflation Hedges and Common Stocks," *Financial Analysts Journal*, January–February 1970, vol. 26, pp. 104–110. (16) G. W. Schwert, "The Adjustment of Stock Prices to Information about Inflation," *Journal of Finance*, March 1981, vol. 36, pp. 15–29. (17) J. C. Van Horne and W. F. Glassmire, Jr., "The Impact of Changes in Inflation on the Value of Common Stocks," *Journal of Finance*, September 1972, vol. 27, pp. 1081–1092.

BOX 9-4

an easy approximation for calculating nominal returns

Although they understand the economic logic of calculating real rates of return, some people dislike using Eq. (9-7*a*) because it requires a division that must be calculated with tedious decimal point accuracy.

$$1.0 + rr = \frac{1.0 + r}{1.0 + q} \tag{9-7a}$$

These folks have simplified Eq. (9-7*a*) by multiplying both sides of the equation by the quantity $(1.0 + q)$ and rearranging to obtain the mathematically equivalent Eqs. (9-8*a*), (9-8*b*), and (9-8*c*) below.

$$1.0 + r = (1.0 + rr)\,(1.0 + q) \tag{9-8a}$$

$$1.0 + r = 1.0 + rr + q + (q)\,(rr) \tag{9-8b}$$

$$r = rr + q + (q)\,(rr) \tag{9-8c}$$

Equations (9-8*a*), (9-8*b*), and (9-8*c*) show that the nominal rate of return, r, can be defined in three different but mathematically equivalent ways. Furthermore, a close look at Eq. (9-8*c*) reveals an easy shortcut calculation that yields fair approximations of the nominal rate of return.

The people who are looking for a shortcut for calculating the nominal rate of return reason that the product of q times rr in Eq. (9-8*c*) will often be a tiny value that can probably be ignored with little loss of accuracy. Therefore, they restate Eq. (9-8*c*) in the simplified form shown in Eq. (9-9) to expedite their calculations.

$$r = rr + q \tag{9-9}$$

Equation (9-9) is a good approximation of Eq. (9-8*c*) if the values of q and rr are so small that their product is not significantly different from zero. More specifically, when the inflation rate is not up into the double digits Eq. (9-9) is an easy way to calculate the nominal rate of return without creating an approximation that is terribly misleading.

Next, let us investigate the nominal rates of return that the typical investor earns from different types of investments with the concurrent rate of inflation. The purpose of making this comparison is to discern those types of investments that yield the best *real* returns.

9-6.4 comparing investment returns with inflation rates

After learning how to see through the "illusory veil of money" and discern the real dollars, the next question that investors typically ask is, "What should I invest in to earn the best real rate of return?" To determine the average inflation-adjusted investment experience with different types of assets, financial analysts have prepared various hypothetical portfolios. A common stock portfolio, a portfolio of U.S. Treasury bonds, a portfolio of long-term corporate bonds, and a portfolio of U.S. Treasury bills were prepared by randomly selecting a representative sample of each of these types of securities. These portfolios were formed without any attempt to pick either the best or the worst securities in each category. The portfolios thus represent indices of average investment performance. These investment indices are useful by themselves, for comparison with each other, and for comparison with the rate of inflation.

Figure 9-9 shows how $1 invested at the end of 1925 would probably have grown if it had been invested in each of the four different types of investment portfolios and then continually reinvested for the next 55 years. The different investments' annual rates of return and the concurrent inflation rate were calculated as explained below.

COMMON STOCKS The Standard & Poor's 500 Stocks Composite Index of diversified common stocks with all cash dividends reinvested was used as an

FIGURE 9-9 wealth indices of investments in the U.S. capital markets 1926–1981. (*Source*: R. G. Ibbotson and R. A. Sinquefield, *Stocks, Bonds, Bills and Inflation: The Past and the Future*, 1982 edition, Financial Analysts Research Foundation, Charlottesville, Va., p. 4, exhibit 1.)

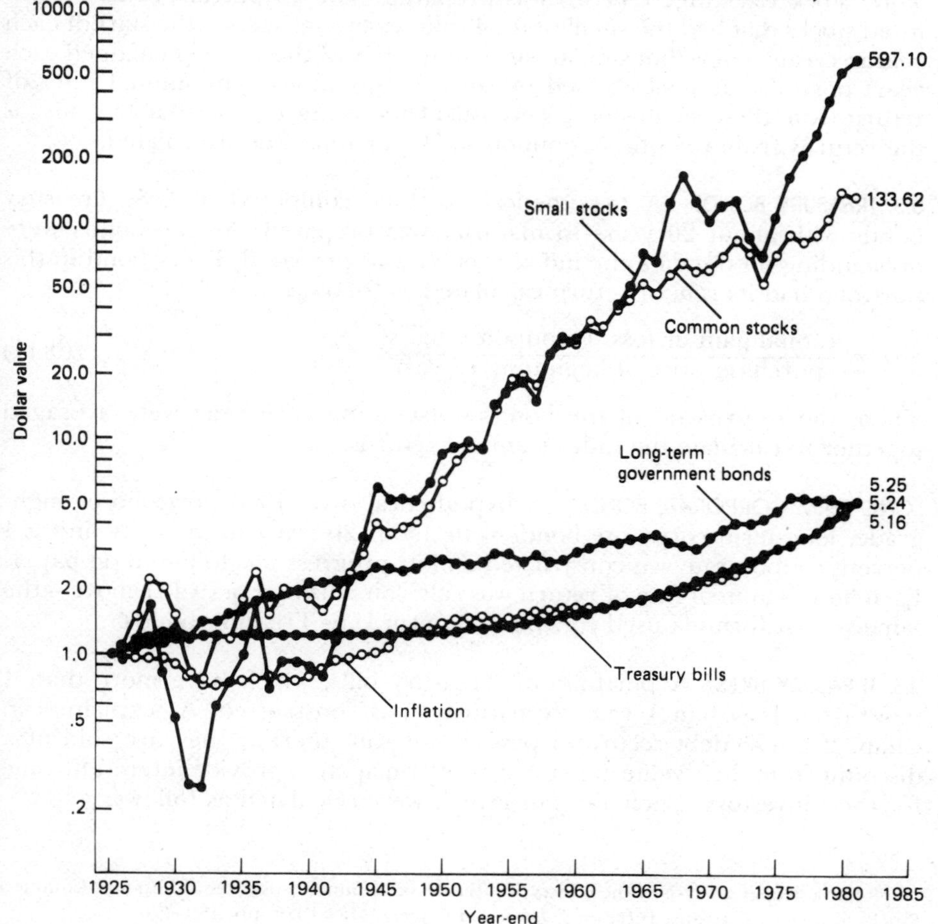

index of normal stock market returns. Each common stock's rate of return was calculated as follows:

$$r = \frac{\text{capital gain or loss + cash dividend}}{\text{purchase price at beginning of year}} \tag{9-10}$$

Adjustments were made to compensate for any stock that had a stock split or stock dividend, so that these changes would not distort the returns. Then, all 500 stocks' annual rates of return were averaged together each year using their relative market values as weights. Thus, stocks in the larger companies were given larger weights to represent the fact that there are more investment opportunities (namely, more shares of stock outstanding) in a large firm than in a small firm. Figure 9-9 shows that this hypothetical common stock portfolio had a greater value after 55 years than most of the other hypothetical portfolios.[40]

COMMON STOCKS IN SMALL CORPORATIONS A hypothetical portfolio of the common stocks with the smallest total value of all issues listed on the New York Stock Exchange (NYSE) was prepared. The 20 percent of all NYSE-listed stocks that had the smallest total values were selected at the start of each year to create a new (but similar, since only a few of these stocks changed each year) portfolio of stocks issued by small corporations. The annual rates of return from these small stocks were calculated using Eq. (9-10) above, just as the returns from the other common stock portfolio were calculated.

U.S. TREASURY BONDS A hypothetical portfolio composed of U.S. Treasury bonds with about 20 years to maturity was prepared. All the bonds were outstanding on the date the index's return was prepared. Every bond in this portfolio had its rate of return calculated as follows:

$$r = \frac{\text{capital gain or loss + coupon interest}}{\text{purchase price at beginning of year}} \tag{9-11}$$

Then, the returns of all the bonds outstanding each year were averaged together to calculate the index's annual returns.

LONG-TERM CORPORATE BONDS A hypothetical diversified portfolio of high-grade, long-term corporate bonds with about 20 years to maturity and a 4 percent coupon rate was constructed and its progress was followed on paper. Each bond's annual rate of return was calculated using Eq. (9-11) above—the same return formula used for the long-term U.S. Treasury bonds.

U.S. TREASURY BILLS A portfolio of Treasury bills, which have more than 1 month but less than 1 year to maturity, was constructed. As explained in Chap. 2, these debt securities pay no coupon interest; they are sold at a discount from their value at maturity (or principal) to provide interest income for their investors. Their rates of return were calculated as follows:

[40] For a deeper analysis of the effects of inflation on common stocks see Zvi Bodie, "Common Stocks as a Hedge Against Inflation," *Journal of Finance*, May 1976, pp. 459–470.

$$r = \frac{\text{capital gain or loss}}{\text{purchase price}} \qquad (9\text{-}12)$$

Then, the average of all outstanding Treasury bills was calculated to obtain the yearly returns for the index.

INFLATION RATES The rate of inflation was calculated using Eq. (9-6) for each of the 55 years illustrated in Fig. 9-9. Figure 9-9 was prepared by starting with $1 in each investment category as of December 1925. Then, each investment's annual return was used to increase or decrease the value of the investment at the end of the preceding year, and this was done for 55 years.[41]

9-6.5 concluding remarks about purchasing power risk

A wise investor should compare the inflation rate with the nominal rates of return from different investments to see if the investments' real rates of return are positive or negative. Investors should focus on these real returns (1) to avoid being fooled by the money illusion fallacy and (2) to detect those investments that will maximize their purchasing power.[42]

The common stocks issued by the small corporations had the highest long-run gains of any of the securities considered. Figure 9-9 indicates that a $1 investment in common stock grew to $597.10 in 55 years. The Treasury bills had the weakest performance. The T-bills' original dollar grew to $5.25 in 55 years, a return that was almost exactly equal to the cumulative inflation rate over the same 55 years. The CPI (which reflects the rate of inflation) grew from a level of $1 in December 1925 to $5.24 at the end of 1981. This means that the cost of a representative basket of consumer goods cost 5.24 times as much in 1981 as it did at the end of 1925. Since the hypothetical portfolio of Treasury bills increased about this same amount, it may be concluded that the T-bills had a positive nominal rate of return, but a zero real rate of return. Figure 9-10 contains summary statistics to help clarify this picture.

The summary statistics in Fig. 9-10 are averages measured over 55 years. These averages should be useful in planning investments. But if basic economic conditions change, these historical averages may become irrelevant or even misleading. For example, the inflation rate and market interest rates in the United States doubled between the early 1960s and the early 1980s. Furthermore, these changes did not occur smoothly—there were erratic year-to-year fluctuations. Dealing profitably with changes such as these requires constant vigilance. In the final analysis it is *unanticipated inflation* rather than

[41] Armen A. Alchian and Reuben A. Kessel, "Redistribution of Wealth through Inflation," *Science*, Sept. 4, 1959, vol. 130, no. 3375, pp. 535–539.

[42] For an empirical analysis of agricultural commodities as an inflation hedge and a comparison with investments in common stocks and bonds see Zvi Bodie and Victor I. Rosansky, "Risk and Return in Commodity Futures," *Financial Analysts Journal*, May–June 1980, pp. 27–39. Essentially, this study reports that the nominal returns from a portfolio of futures contracts on agricultural commodities and the portfolio's risk were about the same as the return and risk from Standard & Poor's 500 Stocks Index. But, the agricultural commodity futures were a better inflation hedge than the stocks. Furthermore, the returns from the commodities were negatively correlated with common stock returns.

Series	Geometric mean*	Arithmetic mean	Standard deviation	Distribution
Common stocks	9.1%	11.4%	21.9%	
Small stocks	12.1	18.1	37.3	
Long-term corporate bonds	3.6	3.7	5.6	
Long-term government bonds	3.0	3.1	5.7	
U.S. Treasury bills	3.0	3.1	3.1	
Inflation	3.0	3.1	5.1	

*The geometric mean rate of return is explained in Mathematical App. F at the end of this book.

FIGURE 9-10 basic series: total annual returns (1926–1981). (*Source*: R. G. Ibbotson and R. A. Sinquefield, *Stocks, Bonds, Bills and Inflation: The Past and the Future*, 1982 edition, Financial Analysts Research Foundation, Charlottesville, Va., p. 15, exhibit 3.)

the well-known historical rates of inflation that is the essence of purchasing power risk.[43]

9-7 CONCLUSIONS ABOUT RISK AND RISK FACTORS

The *total risk* of an asset may be defined as the total variability in the asset's one-period rates of return. The total risk of an asset may be perceived as being the sum of several different contributing risk factors that each increase the asset's total variability of return in some way, as shown on page 245.[44]

[43] Ross and Roll's empirical research indicates that unanticipated inflation is a significant risk factor. Other significant risk factors also exist. Richard Roll and Stephen A. Ross, "The Arbitrage Pricing Theory Approach to Strategic Planning Portfolio Planning," *Financial Analysts Journal*, May–June 1984, pp. 14–26. Arbitrage pricing theory, the topic of Chap. 30 of this book, shows how the different risk factors that make up total risk can be statistically evaluated.

[44] The various risk factors are additive only under certain conditions that are discussed with reference to the arbitrage pricing theory, in Chap. 30. The appendix to Chap. 9 discusses the callability, convertibility, and political risk factors for those who are interested.

Default risk factor (if present)
Plus: interest rate risk factor (if present)
Plus: market risk factor (if present)
Plus: management risk factor (if present)
Plus: purchasing power risk factor (if present)
Plus: marketability risk factor (if present)
Plus: political risk factor (if present)
Plus: callability risk factor (if present)
Plus: convertibility risk factor (if present)
Plus: other risk factors (if present)

Equals: total risk

The risk factors present in any individual asset are different from the risk factors in most other assets—every combination of risk factors is unique. Bonds, for instance, usually derive the largest portion of their total risk from the interest rate risk factor. In contrast, many common stocks are affected only slightly by the interest rate risk factor and, instead, are affected primarily by the default and management risk factors.

It is assumed throughout this text that rational investors are risk-averse—they dislike risk from whatever factor or combination of factors it may be derived.[45] As a result, financial analysts, security analysts, and portfolio managers labor to perceive the risk factors present in whatever asset they are analyzing and to delineate the significance of each risk factor that is present in that asset's make-up.[46] The following chapters will explain how these risk factors interact and how they affect asset values.

QUESTIONS

1. What are the advantages and the disadvantages of research and development expenditures in the corporate budget?
2. Define the terms below:
   a. Bull market
   b. Bear market
   c. Market risk
   d. Business cycle
3. Archibald Scott observed that some common stocks experienced good price rises during the last bear market. Therefore, he plans to continue to be a consistently active investor in the future regardless of whether the stock market is experiencing a bullish trend or a bearish trend. Scott says that he has

[45] Rational people may undertake small risks, such as gambling for the sake of entertainment. The appendix to Chap. 27 shows that people who have positive but diminishing marginal utility of wealth (that is, are economically rational) tend to avoid significant risks, however.

[46] Richard Roll and Stephen A. Ross, "An Empirical Investigation of the Arbitrage Pricing Theory," *Journal of Finance*, December 1980, vol. 35, no. 5, pp. 1073–1104. This is a pioneering study that attempted to isolate and identify the risk factors using empirical data. See Chap. 30 of this book for a discussion of this study.

studied past bear market stock prices and "found several good price-gaining stocks during every month of the last two bear markets." Comment on Scott's investment plans for the future.

4. After studying Raymond Piccini's findings in Fig. 9-8, Sally Overton heard two economists predict that the current economic boom would peak and turn downward into the beginning of a recession. This recession was expected to start 5 months ahead. On the basis of Piccini's results and the two forecasts, Overton has decided to invest her life savings in a widely diversified portfolio of common stocks and then to liquidate 4 months from now, 1 month before the forecasted recession starts. Overton reasons that this strategy will allow her to take advantage of the last few months of bullish price rises before the bear market starts. How do you evaluate Overton's strategy?

5. On Friday, November 22, 1963, President John F. Kennedy was assassinated as he rode in a car in a parade in Dallas, Texas. News of the killing flashed around the world. When the news reached the NYSE, hysterical selling began that caused officials to close the exchange early. In the 27 minutes between the arrival of the news of the assassination and the closing, many stock prices dropped by as much as $5 or $10 per share. The DJIA fell 24.5 points in those 27 minutes. However, when the exchange reopened on the following trading day (that is, on Monday, November 25) the shares were at the prices they had been *before* the tragic news. On the first trading day following the funeral, the DJIA leaped 32 points. In your opinion, did the market temporarily collapse because of default risk, management risk, interest rate risk, market risk, or what? Explain.

6. Write a short essay defining total risk verbally and explain how this definition is consistent with using the variance of returns as a quantitative risk surrogate.

7. Write one-sentence definitions of each of the following:
   a. Purchasing power risk
   b. Interest rate risk
   c. Market risk
   d. Management risk
   e. Default risk
   f. Total risk

   For additional credit define political risk, callability risk, convertibility risk, and marketability risk, which are discussed in the appendix to Chap. 9.

8. How do bankruptcy proceedings relate to the default risk of investment securities?

9. Compare and contrast the following terms:
   a. Expected value
   b. Weighted average
   c. Arithmetic mean
   d. Median

   Write a short essay that compares these statistics phrases with each other, giving special reference to the random variable in a probability distribution of possible returns from an investment. *Hint*: Consult a textbook about mathematical statistics and/or mathematical probabilities.

10. If such bond rating agencies as Moody's and S&P raise the rating of a bond issue from Baa or BBB to A, what effect is this likely to have on the stock and bond prices of the firm? Explain.

11. Does purchasing power risk pose more of a threat to people who are working and saving for their retirement or to retired people? Explain.
12. Which of the following two categories of investment assets is the best hedge against inflation—real assets (such as real estate, homes, diamonds, gold, silver, and rental property) or monetary assets (such as savings account deposits, cash in a lockbox, and bond investments)? Why? What factors unrelated to purchasing power risk should also be considered in selecting between these two categories of investment assets?
13. Suppose that a representative basket of consumer goods cost $200 on January 1, 1980, and that the same basket cost $242 on January 1, 1982. What was the rate of inflation per year for 1980 and 1981? Show your calculations.
14. Why do the market prices for U.S. Treasury bonds decline as interest rates rise? Why do they rise as interest rates decline?

Note: The following questions apply to the material in the appendix to Chap. 9.

15. What are the disadvantages of investing in a market asset that is not easily marketable?
16. Compare and contrast the marketability risk of two different NYSE stocks. Select a blue-chip stock that has thousands of shares traded each day for one of your stocks. Select another NYSE stock traded only infrequently with which to compare the high-volume stock. In your comparison, consider the following factors: the daily high and low prices, and the bid-asked spreads. *Hint*: You may have to ask a stockbroker to obtain this information for you—or you could write to the NYSE and request it.
17. Why do convertible bonds from a given firm sell at a different yield to maturity than nonconvertible bonds issued by the same firm that are identical in every respect except the convertibility?

SELECTED REFERENCES

Agmon, Tamir, and M. Chapman Findlay, "Domestic Political Risk and Stock Valuation," *Financial Analysts Journal*, November–December 1982, pp. 3–6. This article defines *political risk* and shows how it can affect security values.

Bodie, Zvi, "Common Stocks as a Hedge Against Inflation," *Journal of Finance*, May 1976, pp. 459–470. Mathematical statistics are used to analyze the effects of *inflation* on equity shares. Empirical data are also used to test the models derived.

Brennan, M. J., and E. S. Schwartz, "Convertible Bonds: Valuation and Optimal Strategies for Call and Conversion," *Journal of Finance*, December 1977, pp. 1699–1716. The paper mathematically derives guidelines for finding the value of convertible bonds and highlights some *convertibility risk* considerations.

Garbade, Kenneth, *Securities Markets* (McGraw-Hill, New York, 1982). This textbook focuses on the economic analysis of security markets. In particular, chaps. 20, 24, and 26 discuss the concepts of a market's breadth, depth, resiliency, thinness, the bid-asked spread, and other characteristics useful in analyzing *marketability risk*. The book also devotes a few pages in chap. 17 to explaining callable bonds that are relevant to *callability risk*.

Ibbotson, R. G., and R. A. Sinquefield, *Stocks, Bonds, Bills and Inflation: The Past and the Future*, Monograph 15 (Financial Analysts Research Foundation, Charlottesville, Va., 1982). This empirical study compares the returns from common stocks, corporate bonds, Treasury bills, and T-bonds with the consumer price index. The easy-to-read booklet contains many tables of informative data from the 1925–1981 sample period and various risk factors.

Markowitz, H., *Portfolio Section* (Wiley, New York, 1959). This classic book explains portfolio analysis. Chapters 2 and 4 delve into probability distributions, standard deviations, expected returns, and the characteristic line. Chapter 9 discusses the semivariance. Algebra and finite probability are used in these chapters to rationalize quantitative surrogates for total risk.

Sauvain, H., *Investment Management*, 3d ed. (Prentice-Hall, Englewood Cliffs, N.J., 1967). Chapters 5 through 7 discuss financial, purchasing power, and interest rate risk. No mathematics used.

Teweles, Richard J., and Edward S. Bradley, *The Stock Market*, 4th ed. (Wiley, New York, 1982). Chapter 26 provides a good description of convertible bonds that sheds light on *convertibility risk*.

APPENDIX 9A

other risk factors

The major risk factors are interest rate risk, purchasing power risk, market risk, default risk, and management risk. These risk factors were discussed in Chap. 9. In addition to these major risk factors there are some other significant risk factors that are usually of lesser importance. This appendix discusses some of these other risk factors.

APP. 9A-1 THE MARKETABILITY RISK FACTOR

Marketability risk, as differentiated from the market risk of bull and bear markets, is that portion of an asset's total variability of return resulting from price discounts given or sales commissions that must be paid in order to sell the asset in a hurry.

Perfectly liquid assets are perfectly marketable and suffer no marketability risk. Or, stated from a negative viewpoint, illiquid assets are not readily marketable—either price discounts must be given or sales commissions must be paid, or both these costs must be incurred by the seller, in order to find a new investor for an illiquid asset. The more illiquid an asset is, the larger are the price discounts and/or the commissions that a seller must give up in order to effect a quick sale.

You can buy an asset at its bid price and sell it at its asked (or offered) price. The bid price is always below the asked price, as shown in Fig. App. 3A-2 on page 79. The bid-asked spread is the cost of selling an asset quickly. Seen differently, the bid-asked spread is the dealer's reward for making a market in the asset.

The bid-asked spread can be thought of as the sum of (1) the price discount the seller has to give up to sell the asset quickly and (2) the broker's commission for handling the transaction. Or, if the intermediary is a dealer instead of a broker, the bid-asked spread is the dealer's compensation for buying the asset and (it is hoped, only temporarily) carrying it in inventory until another buyer can be found.

APP. 9A-2 THE POLITICAL RISK FACTOR

Political risk may be thought of as the exploitation of a politically weak group to benefit a politically strong group, with the efforts of various groups to improve their relative positions increasing the variability of return from the affected assets. Whether the changes that cause political risk are sought by political or by economic interests, the resulting variability of return is called political risk if it is accomplished through legislative, judicial, or administrative branches of the government that can be manipulated politically.

International investors face political risk in the form of expropriation of nonresidents' assets, foreign exchange controls that prohibit foreign investors from withdrawing their funds, disadvantageous tax and tariff treatments, a requirement that nonresident investors give partial ownership to local residents, and unreimbursed destruction of foreign-owned assets by hostile residents of the foreign country. Foreign investors are forced to deal with *international political risk* by requiring higher expected rates of return from foreign investments than from domestic investments, by obtaining guarantees from high-level government officials in writing, and by using nonrecourse financing provided by the foreign country before undertaking any foreign investing. Although most political risk discussions focus only on international political risk, domestic political risk should not be overlooked.

Domestic political risk takes the form of environmental regulations, zoning requirements, fees, licenses, and, most frequently, taxes of one form or another. The taxes may be property taxes, sales taxes, income taxes, or employment taxes. Taxes are levied on a readily identifiable, politically weak group such as owners of real estate, buyers of luxury goods or "sinful goods" (such as the consumers of liquor), high-income earners, or employers. The passage of new tax laws or the modification of previously existing taxes can be foretold only probabilistically, if at all. The tax proceeds are transferred from the readily identifiable, politically weak group to a more politically powerful group. The tax and the transfer of the wealth are accomplished through the jurisdiction of some governmental unit that can be manipulated politically.

The effects of political risk on investment values can be traced explicitly through the discounted present value of cash dividends model. Equation (App. 9A-1) indicates that the present value of a share of stock equals the discounted present value of all cash dividends the equity share is expected to pay to its owners from now (that is, time period $t = 0$) to infinity.

$$p_0 = \frac{d_1}{(1 + k)^1} + \frac{d_2}{(1 + k)^2} + \frac{d_3}{(1 + k)^3} + \cdots \quad \text{(App. 9A-1)}$$

where

d = cash dividend per share paid in time period t
k = risk-adjusted discount rate
p = stock's present value

Political risk can change the value of the share of common stock in Eq. (App. 9A-1) in two different ways. First, if a new corporate income tax were imposed on the corporation or an old income tax were raised, for example, the firm would not be able to pay its investors cash dividends as large as expected before the income tax increase. This politically legislated tax would reduce the investment's value—an example of political risk at work.

The second way that political risk can cause variability in the common stock's value is through risk changes. Care must be taken to avoid "double-counting" when risk adjustments are made, however. If cash dividends were correctly adjusted in the numerator of Eq. (App. 9A-1), only pure risk changes justify a further adjustment to the discount rate in the denominator of the equation. When political change does cause a pure change in risk, however, this change will pass through the discount rate and cause political variability of return for investors who bought the stock.[47]

APP. 9A-3 THE CALLABILITY RISK FACTOR

As explained in Chap. 2, some issues of bonds and preferred stock are issued with a provision that allows the issuer to call them in for repurchase if the issuer desires. Issuers like these call provisions because it allows them to refund outstanding fixed-payment securities with a newer issue if market interest rates drop to a level below the level being paid on the outstanding securities. But whatever the issuing company gains by calling in an issue is gained at the expense of the investors who had the misfortune to have their securities called. Investors should view the call provision as a threat that may deprive them of a good investment at a time when their funds can be refunded only at a lower rate of yield.

That portion of a security's total variability of return derived from the possibility that the issue may be called commands a risk premium that comes in the form of a slightly higher expected rate of return. This additional return should increase in proportion to the risk that the issue is called. The following array of categories shows how callability risk varies with the terms attached to the call provision.

[47] This section draws from an article by Tamir Agmon and M. Chapman Findlay, "Domestic Political Risk and Stock Valuation," *Financial Analysts Journal*, November–December 1982, pp. 3–6.

1. Securities that are noncallable at any time during their life have no callability risk.
2. An issue that is noncallable for refunding, but that can be recalled for redemption with funds from sources other than a refunding (such as retained earnings), is the second safest category.
3. The third category is the largest and most difficult to define because it involves one or both of two different kinds of call protection. One kind of call protection is a stipulation that the issue may not be called for a certain number of years (such as 5, 10, 15, or 20) after the issue is new; the issue is then callable on short notice after the protected period is past. The other kind of call protection is a call premium that allows the issuer to call the securities at any time, but only at a premium (of 10 percent, for example) over their face value. The risk protection from these provisions increases with the number of years before the call may be allowed to occur and/or with the size of the call premium.
4. Callability risk is the greatest with those issues that are callable at any time on short notice. These securities may yield as much as 70 or 80 basis points more than an equivalent issue not callable under any conditions.[48]

APP. 9A-4 THE CONVERTIBILITY RISK FACTOR

Callability risk and convertibility risk are similar in two respects. First, both these provisions are contractual stipulations included in the terms of the original issue. Second, both these provisions alter the variability of return (that is, the risk) from the affected security. *Convertibility risk* is that portion of the total variability of return that an investor in a convertible bond or a convertible preferred stock experiences because of the contractual possibility that the investment may be converted into the issuer's common stock.

Sometimes bonds and preferred stocks are issued with the stipulation that they may be converted into the issuing corporation's common stock if the investor wishes to do so, as explained in Chap. 2. Essentially, the convertibility right attached to some bonds and/or preferred stocks gives their investors the option to buy shares of the corporation's common stock at some future date and fixed price by using the bond or preferred stock valued at its face value to pay for the purchase. The value of the conversion right of a security can be assessed by comparing the price of a nonconvertible security with the price of a similar convertible security.[49]

[48] F. Jen and J. Wert, "The Effect of Call Risk on Corporate Bond Yield," *Journal of Finance*, December 1967; Zvi Bodie and Benjamin Freidman, "Interest Rate Uncertainty and the Value of Bond Call Protection," *Journal of Political Economy*, February 1978; Edwin Elton and Martin Gruber, "The Economic Value of the Call Option," *Journal of Finance*, September 1972; Gordon Pye, "The Value of a Call Option on a Bond," *Journal of Political Economy*, April 1966; Gordon Pye, "The Value of Call Deferment on a Bond: Some Empirical Results," *Journal of Finance*, December 1967.

[49] Convertible securities are discussed in E. O. Thorp and S. T. Kassouf, *Beat the Market: A Scientific Stock Market System* (Random House, New York, 1967), chap. 10. See also M. J. Brennan and E. S. Schwartz, "Convertible Bonds: Valuation and Optimal Strategies for Call and Conversion," *Journal of Finance*, December 1977, pp. 1699–1716.

the characteristic line and capital asset pricing model (CAPM)*

Chapter 9 defined the *total risk* of an asset as the asset's total variability of return and went on to show how to measure total risk statistically with the "variance," or the "standard deviation of returns." This chapter expands on the material presented in Chap. 9 by showing that the total risk of an asset can be statistically divided into two parts: diversifiable risk and undiversifiable risk.

Undiversifiable risk
Diversifiable risk
Total risk

Partitioning total risk into these two mutually exclusive segments yields an important insight called the capital asset pricing model (CAPM hereafter), or, synonymously, the security market line (SML). Let us begin this chapter's exploration of new facets of risk by defining diversifiable risk and undiversifiable risk.

UNDIVERSIFIABLE RISK STEMS FROM SYSTEMATIC VARIABILITY *Undiversifiable risk* is that portion of total variability in return caused by factors which *simultaneously* affect the prices of all marketable securities.[1] The systematic nature of these

* Chapter 10 presumes a knowledge of Chap. 9.

[1] The simultaneity of systematic stock price movements was first documented using monthly data by J. C. Francis, "Intertemporal Differenes in Systematic Stock Price Movements," *Journal of Financial and Quantitative Analysis*, June 1975, pp. 205–219. A later study refines Francis' measurements by using daily data; see G. A. Hawawini and A. Vora, "Evidence of Intertemporal Systematic Risks in the Daily Price Movement of NYSE and AMEX Common Stocks," *Journal of Financial and Quantitative Analysis*, 1979. The Hawawini-Vora study suggests that sometimes there is a one- or two-day lead or lag in the speed with which some stock prices react to systematic changes.

price changes bestows on them immunity from much of the risk reduction effects of diversification. Thus, *systematic risk* is synonymously called undiversifiable risk.

Changes in the economic, political, and sociological environment which affect securities markets are sources of systematic risk. Systematic variability of return is found in nearly all securities in varying degrees because most securities move together loosely in a systematic manner. Figure 10-1 shows how averages of 20 railroad stocks, 55 utility stocks, and 425 industrial stocks all tend to vary in price together: this is systematic variability. The prices of nearly all individual common stocks tend to move together in the same manner; that is why nearly all stocks listed on the New York Stock Exchange (NYSE) are significantly positively correlated with one another. In fact, the NYSE index (or any other stock index for the NYSE, for that matter) explains about 30 percent of the variation in the price movements of the approximately 1700 stocks listed there.[2]

Firms that have high proportions of systematic risk within their total risk include American Zinc, Lead and Smelting Company; Chicago Pneumatic Tool Company; Lafayette Radio Electronics; Lin Broadcasting Corporation; Liberty Homes Inc.; Memorex Corporation; Microdata Corporation; Northwest Airlines; Erie-Kansas-Texas Railroad; Peoria and Eastern Railroad; U.S. Rubber; Hoffman Machinery Corporation; and PanAm Airlines.

[2] Marshall Blume, "On the Assessment of Risk," *Journal of Finance*, March 1971, pp. 1–10. J. C. Francis, "Statistical Analysis of Risk Surrogates for NYSE Stocks," *Journal of Financial and Quantitative Analysis*, December 1979.

FIGURE 10-1 Standard & Poor's stock market price index quarterly averages fluctuate together. (*Source*: *1983 Historical Chart Book*, Board of Governors of the Federal Reserve System, p. 92.)

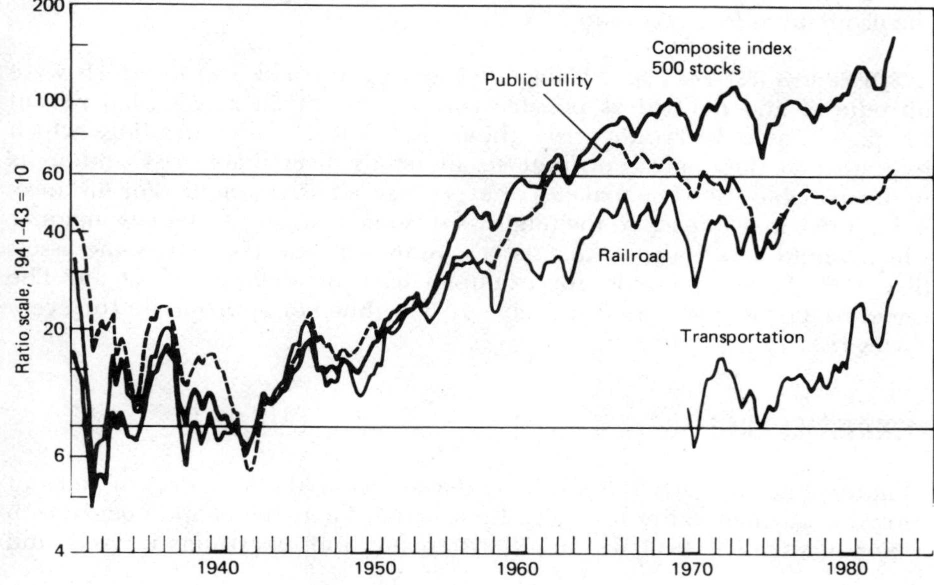

It will be noted that the firms with high systematic risk tend to be those providing basic industrial goods (such as railroads, tool companies, and rubber companies) and highly levered firms which have cyclical sales (like the airlines and home builders), and small firms with high-technology products which might become rapidly obsolete (like the computer companies). The sales, profits, and stock prices of these firms follow the level of economic activity and the level of the securities markets to a high degree. As a result, these firms tend to have high degrees of undiversifiable risk.

DIVERSIFIABLE RISK COMES FROM UNSYSTEMATIC CHANGES *Diversifiable risk* is that portion of total risk which is unique to a firm or industry. Changes such as labor strikes, management errors, inventions, advertising campaigns, shifts in consumer taste, and lawsuits cause unsystematic variability of returns in a firm. Since unsystematic changes affect one firm, or at most a few firms, they must be forecast separately for each firm and for each individual incident by any security analyst who is attempting to predict the price movements of an asset. And, more importantly, since unsystematic security price movements are statistically independent from one another, they may be reduced via diversification. Thus, unsystematic risk is synonymously called *diversifiable risk*.

The proportion of total variability which is unsystematic varies widely from firm to firm. The total risk of a few firms is all unsystematic risk. Coca-Cola, U.S. Tobacco, Wrigley Company, American Snuff Company, AT&T, and Homestake Mining Company are firms which have large proportions of unsystematic risk and small proportions of systematic risk.

Many of the firms with low proportions of systematic risk and high proportions of unsystematic risk produce nondurable consumer goods. Sales, profits, and stock prices of these firms do not depend on the level of industrial activity or the stock market. As a result, these firms might have their best years when the economy is in a recession.

CONTRIBUTING RISK FACTORS Table 10-1 lists various risk factors which were introduced and defined as possible components of an asset's total risk in Chap. 9. Table 10-1 categorizes these risk factors under headings which indicate that they may contribute to an asset's diversifiable risk and/or its undiversifiable risk. The makeup of every asset's risk is unique. For instance, default risk may impact on the total risk of some asset in a systematic manner which would contribute to that asset's undiversifiable risk. Or, some assets (like U.S. Treasury bonds, for example) have no default risk at all. The categorization hypothesized in Table 10-1 is thus not appropriate for every asset's risk.

10-1 THE CHARACTERISTIC LINE

Chapter 9 argued that the standard deviation (or the variance) of rates of return was a quantitative surrogate for *total risk*. Then, this chapter began with a nonquantitative explanation of systematic and unsystematic risks and

BOX 10-1
the categories of risk factors that make up total risk

Table 10-1 shows how the risk factors discussed in Chap. 9 are related to the risk partition explained in Chap. 10.

TABLE 10-1 sources of risk

1. Sources of Undiversifiable Risk:
   Systematic interest rate risk (if present)
   Plus: Systematic purchasing power risk (if present)
   Plus: Systematic market risk (if present)
   Plus: Systematic management risk (if present)
   Plus: Systematic default risk (if present)
   Plus: Systematic marketability risk (if present)
   Plus: Systematic callability risk (if present)
   Plus: Systematic convertibility risk (if present)
   Plus: Other systematic risk factors (if present)
2. Sources of Diversifiable Risk:
   Plus: Unsystematic interest rate risk (if present)
   Plus: Unsystematic purchasing power risk (if present)
   Plus: Unsystematic market risk (if present)
   Plus: Unsystematic management risk (if present)
   Plus: Unsystematic default risk (if present)
   Plus: Unsystematic marketability risk (if present)
   Plus: Unsystematic callability risk (if present)
   Plus: Unsystematic convertibility risk (if present)
   Plus: Other Unsystematic risk factors (if present)

Aggregate: Total risk

their sources. Do not be misled by the nonquantitative discussion at the beginning of this chapter, however. It is possible to measure the systematic and unsystematic risks of an asset by using quantitative risk surrogates. A statistical tool which we shall refer to as the *characteristic line* is employed to measure systematic, or undiversifiable, risk and unsystematic, or diversifiable, risk.

Figure 10-2 illustrates the characteristic line for the common stock issued by the Kaiser Aluminum and Chemical Corporation.[3] Statistically speaking, characteristic lines are ordinary least-squares regression lines of the form shown in Eq. (10-1). Statistics books sometimes call our characteristic line the simple linear regression model.[4]

[3] The term *characteristic line* is from Jack L. Treynor, "How to Rate Management of Investment Funds," *Harvard Business Review*, January–February 1965, pp. 63–75. Mr. Treynor appears to be the first person to perceive the concept of undiversifiable risk: Jack L. Treynor, "Toward a Theory of Market Value of Risky Assets," unpublished manuscript, 1961.

[4] Mathematical App. D, in Part 9, provides a brief review of the definitions of terms such as regression line, correlation coefficient, and standard error.

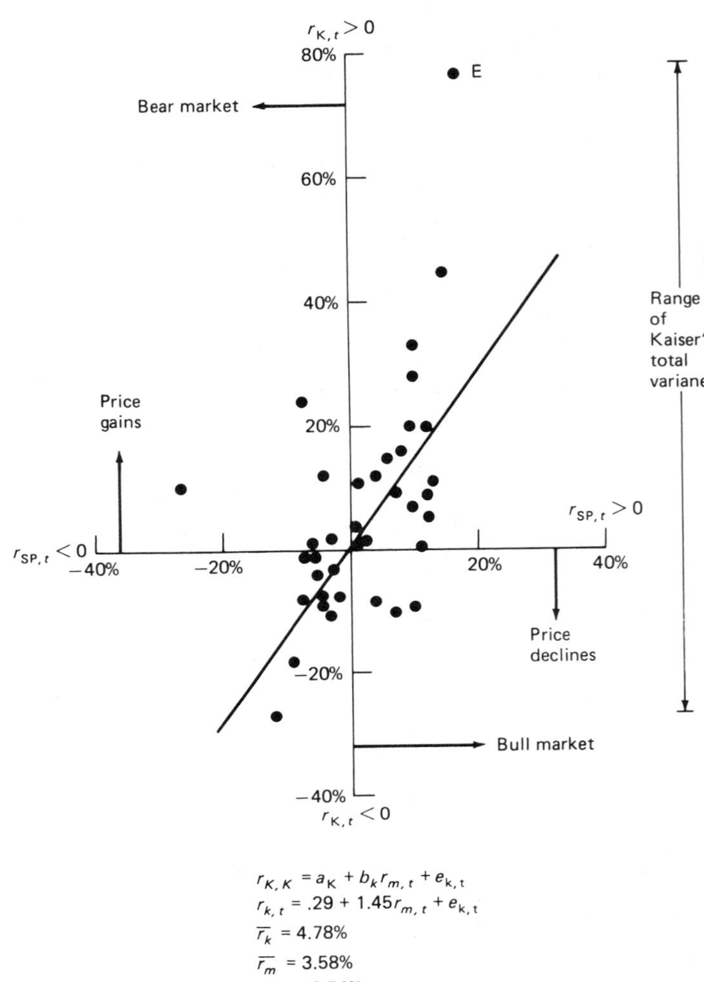

FIGURE 10-2 characteristic line for Kaiser Aluminum and Chemical common stock

$$r_{it} = a_i + b_i r_{mt} + e_{it} \tag{10-1}$$

where

a_i and b_i = the regression intercept and slope statistics, respectively
e_t = the random error around the regression line which occurs in period t

A characteristic line graphically represents the nature of systematic and unsystematic risks; it shows the relationships of some asset with the market. Each characteristic line is thus a *market model* for one security.

10-1.1 market returns: the characteristic line's independent variable

The action of the stock market is measured along the horizontal axis of Fig. 10-2 in terms of rates of change or rates of return from the market at different time periods, denoted r_{mt}. Equation (10-2) shows how rates of change in the market are calculated, using Standard & Poor's (SP) market index.[5] A number of other market indices could also have been used.

$$r_{mt} = \frac{SP_{t+1} - SP_t}{SP_t} \tag{10-2}$$

where

SP_{t+1} = the dollar amount of the S&P index at the beginning of period $t + 1$

SP_t = the value of the index at the beginning of period t

These period-by-period rates of change in the market index are downward-biased estimates of average returns available in the market because cash dividends are excluded. There is no reason why dividends should not be included in r_{mt} or why other market indices should not be used in determining characteristic lines. However, once a market index is adopted, it should be used *consistently* in determining all characteristic lines if all are to be comparable.

10-1.2 asset returns—the characteristic line's dependent variable

Rates of return for which the characteristic line is being prepared are calculated by using Eq. (2-2) for stocks.

$$r_{it} = \frac{p_{t+1} - p_t + d_t}{p_t} \tag{2-2}$$

where

d_t = cash dividend in period t from stock i

p_t = market price at beginning of period for ith stock

p_{t+1} = end-of-period price for period t or, equivalently, the beginning price for period $t + 1$

Returns on the ith asset are the dependent variable on the vertical axis of Fig. 10-2. If the ith asset has any systematic risk, part of its variation in rates of return is dependent upon the independent variable—returns on the market. Monthly, quarterly, semiannual, or annual returns may be used to prepare a characteristic line.[6]

[5] Appendix 10B provides some empirical market returns which were calculated with Standard & Poor's 500. See *Standard & Poor's Trade and Securities Statistics*, an annual book of statistics which is updated with monthly supplements.

[6] It is desirable to have at least 30 observations over a sample period of no longer than a decade when estimating the characteristic line. Thirty observations are suggested because that is where small sample theory typically ends and the large sample theory begins. For example, the T distribution may be dropped and the normal distribution used in its place. The reason a decade is suggested as an upper limit for the sample period is because sample periods that are too long encompass time periods during which the firm may change.

10-1.3 estimating a characteristic line

The characteristic line is a line of best fit. It may be estimated intuitively; it may be fit to historical data by hand; or ordinary least-squares (OLS) regression may be used. If historical data are to be used, the first step in estimating the characteristic line for some asset is to calculate the periodic returns on the asset as defined in Eq. (2-2) and the returns on the market as defined in Eq. (10-2). The time periods used for calculating returns on the asset and the

TABLE 10-2 Kaiser Aluminum & Chemical Corporation return data

	RAW DATA, $		ADJUSTED DATA, $		quarterly dividend yield, %	quarterly price change, %	quarterly rate of return, %
year/quarter	begin price	cash dividend	begin price	cash dividend			
1974.1	20.000	0.188	10.000	0.094	0.094	11.88	12.82
1974.2	22.375	0.188	11.188	0.094	0.840	−25.14	−24.30
1974.3	16.750	0.250	8.375	.125	1.49	−13.43	−11.94
1974.4	14.500	0.250	7.250	.125	1.72	−11.20	−9.47
1975.1	12.875	0.300	6.438	.150	2.32	74.74	77.07
1975.2	22.500	0.300	11.250	.150	1.33	43.89	45.22
1975.3	32.375	0.300	16.188	.150	.926	−28.18	−27.26
1975.4	23.250	0.300	11.625	.150	1.29	19.35	20.64
1976.1	27.750	0.300	13.875	.150	1.08	19.81	20.90
1976.2	33.250	0.300	16.625	.150	.902	10.52	11.42
1976.3	36.750	0.300	18.375	.150	.816	−.68	.1360
1976.4	36.500	0.300	18.250	.150	.821	.0	.8219
1977.1	36.500	0.300	18.250	.150	.821	−2.39	−1.572
1977.2	35.625	0.350	17.813	.175	.982	3.856	4.839
1977.3	35.000	0.350	18.500	.175	.945	−12.83	−11.89
1977.4	32.250	0.350	16.125	.175	1.08	−4.260	−3.175
1978.1	30.875	0.400	15.438	.200	1.29	−5.667	−4.372
1978.2	28.125	0.400	14.563	.200	1.37	9.441	10.81
1978.3	31.875	0.400	15.938	.200	1.25	15.29	16.54
1978.4	36.750	0.400	18.375	.200	1.36	−2.721	−1.360
February 1, 1979: a 2 for 1 split was effective							
1979.1	17.875	0.250	17.875	.250	1.39	11.18	12.587
1979.2	19.875	0.250	19.875	.250	1.25	−7.547	−6.289
1979.3	18.375	0.300	18.375	.300	1.63	13.60	15.23
1979.4	20.875	0.300	20.875	.300	1.43	−9.580	−8.143
1980.1	18.875	0.300	18.875	.300	1.58	.662	2.251
1980.2	19.000	0.300	19.000	.300	1.57	4.605	6.184
1980.3	19.875	0.350	19.875	.350	1.76	32.07	33.83
1980.4	26.250	0.350	26.250	.350	1.33	−11.90	−10.57
1981.1	23.125	0.350	23.125	.350	1.51	9.729	11.24
1981.2	25.375	0.350	25.375	.350	1.37	−10.83	−9.458
1981.3	22.625	0.350	22.625	.350	1.54	−19.88	−18.34
1981.4	18.125	0.350	18.125	.350	1.93	−11.72	−9.793
1982.1	16.000	0.350	16.00	.350	2.18	−10.93	−8.750
1982.2	14.250	0.150	14.250	.150	1.05	−11.40	−10.35
1982.3	12.625	0.150	12.625	.150	1.18	7.920	9.108
1982.4	13.625	0.150	13.625	.150	1.10	10.09	11.19
1983.1	15.000	0.150	15.000	.150	1.00	6.666	7.666
1983.2	16.000	0.150	16.000	.150	.937	27.34	28.28

TABLE 10-3 returns to calculate characteristic line

time period, t	independent variable, returns on market	dependent variable, returns on asset i
$t = 1$	r_{m1}	r_{i1}
$= 2$	r_{m2}	r_{i2}
$= 3$	r_{m3}	r_{i3}
$= 4$	r_{m4}	r_{i4}
.	.	.
.	.	.
.	.	.
.	.	.
.	.	.
$t = T$	r_{mT}	r_{iT}

Regression model: $r_{it} = a_i + b_i r_{mt} + e_{it}$ Eq. (10-1)
Characteristic line: $r_i = a_i + b_i r_m$ Eq. (10-3a)

market must be *simultaneous* because the characteristic line model measures an investment asset's simultaneous reactions to market pressures.

Table 10-2 shows the quarterly data used to fit the characteristic line for Kaiser Aluminum and Chemical Corporation's common stock. These data can be obtained from the sources of financial information discussed in Chap. 6. After the rates of return on the ith asset and some market index data have been gathered, they can be arranged as shown in Table 10-3.

The rates of return from the market and the asset may be plotted as shown in Fig. 10-2. Point E in this figure, for example, is a point where the market return was 17 percent and Kaiser's return was 77 percent during the same time period. Each dot represents the rate of return on the asset and the market during a given time period. A line of best fit can be "eyeballed" through these points, or a regression line can be calculated. The dependent variable r_i is regressed onto the independent variable r_m. It is best to fit the regression line because additional statistics, such as the correlation coefficient, can be obtained once the regression line is determined.

10-1.4 interpreting the characteristic line

Equation (10-3) represents the characteristic line for the ith asset. Equation (10-3a) is like Eq. (10-1) except that the residual return left unexplained by the regression, e, has been averaged out to zero when summed up over all the observations, and thus it does not appear in the equation. The time subscripts in Eq. (10-1) have also been deleted because Eq. (10-3a) was fit through the multiple time periods over which the returns were observed.

$$r_i = a_i + b_i r_m \tag{10-3a}$$

The term a_i is called the *alpha coefficient* for security i; it is the intercept point where the characteristic line intercepts the vertical axis.[7] Alpha is an estimate of the ith asset's rate of return when the market is stationary, $r_{mt} = 0$. The term b_i is called the *beta coefficient*; it measures the slope of the characteristic line.

[7] Statistically speaking, the alpha intercept statistic is defined as follows: $a_i = \bar{r}_i - b_i\bar{r}_m = E(r_i) - b_i E(r_m)$

The beta coefficient in the characteristic line is defined mathematically in Eq. (10-4*a*) and (10-4*b*).

$$b_i = \frac{\text{cov}(r_i, r_m)}{\text{var}(r_m)} \tag{10-4a}$$

$$= \frac{\text{units of rise}}{\text{units of run}} = \text{slope of characteristic regression line} \tag{10-4b}$$

where

$\text{cov}(r_i, r_m)$ = the covariance[8] of returns of the *i*th asset with the market

$\text{var}(r_m)$ = the variance of returns for the market index

The beta coefficient is an *index of systematic risk*. Beta coefficients may be used for (ordinal) rankings of the systematic risk of different assets. However, the beta coefficient is not a (cardinal) measure which may be compared directly with total or unsystematic risk. If the beta is larger than one, that is, if $b > 1.0$, then the asset is more volatile than the market and is called an *aggressive asset*. If the beta is smaller than one, $b < 1.0$, the asset is a *defensive asset*: it is less volatile than the market. Most assets' beta coefficients are in the range from .5 to 1.5. But, Kaiser is an aggressive stock with a high degree of systematic risk. Kaiser's beta of 1.50 indicates that its return tends to increase 50 percent more than the return on the market average when the market is rising. When the market falls, Kaiser's return tends to fall 150 percent of the decrease in the market. The characteristic line for Kaiser has an above-average correlation coefficient of $\rho = .68$ indicating that the returns on this security follow its particular characteristic line slightly more closely than the average stock. This tendency may be determined by visually noting that the points tend to fit around the characteristic line in Fig. 10-2.

10-1.5 partitioning risk

Statistically, total risk is measured by the variance of returns, denoted var(r). This measure of total risk may be partitioned[9] into the systematic and unsystematic components as follows:

$$\begin{aligned} \text{var}(r_i) &= \text{total risk of } i\text{th asset} \\ &= \text{var}(a_i + b_i r_m + e) \qquad \text{substituting } (a_i + b_i r_m + e) \text{ for } r_i \\ &= \text{var}(b_i r_m) + \text{var}(e) \qquad \text{since var}(a_i) = 0 \qquad (10\text{-}5) \\ &= b_i^2\,\text{var}(r_m) + \text{var}(e) \qquad \text{since var}(b_i r_m) = b_i^2\,\text{var}(r_m) \\ &= \text{systematic} + \text{unsystematic risk} \qquad (10\text{-}5) \end{aligned}$$

The unsystematic risk measure, var(e), is called the *residual variance* (or *standard error squared*) in regression language.

[8] The covariance is defined as follows:

$$\text{cov}(r_{ij}r_m) = \left(\frac{1}{T}\right) \sum_{t=1}^{T} [(r_i - \bar{r}_i)(r_m - \bar{r}_m)] = \rho_{im}\sigma_i\sigma_m$$

[9] Used in this context *partition* is a technical statistical word which means to divide the total variance into *mutually exclusive* and *exhaustive* pieces. This partition is only possible if the returns from the market are statistically independent from the residual error terms that occur simultaneously, $\text{cov}(r_{mt}, e_{it}) = 0$. The mathematics of regression analysis will orthogonalize the residuals and thus ensure that this condition exists.

The percentage of systematic risk is measured by the coefficient of determination (ρ^2) for the characteristic line. The percentage of unsystematic risk equals ($1.0 - \rho^2$). More specifically,

$$\frac{\text{Unsystematic risk}}{\text{Total risk}} = \frac{\text{var}(e)}{\text{var}(r_i)} = (1.0 - \rho^2) \tag{10-6a}$$

$$\frac{\text{Systematic risk}}{\text{Total risk}} = \frac{b_i^2\ \text{var}(r_m)}{\text{var}(r_i)} = \rho^2 \tag{10-6b}$$

Studies of the characteristic lines of hundreds of stocks listed on the NYSE indicate that the average correlation coefficient is $\rho = .5$, approximately.[10] This means that about $\rho^2 = 25$ percent of the total variability of return in most NYSE securities is explained by movements in the whole market; that is, systematic risk averages about one-fourth of total risk for most NYSE stocks.

Average systematic risk	25% $= \rho^2$
Average unsystematic risk	75% $= 1 - \rho^2$
Total risk	100% $= 1.0$

The systematic changes are common to all stocks and are impossible to diversify away; they are *undiversifiable*.

[10] Mathematical App. D discusses correlation, regression, and the characteristic line and defines the residual variance, coefficient of determination, and other regression terms. See also B. F. King, "Market and Industry Factors in Stock Price Behavior," *Journal of Business*, January 1966, p. 151. King says, in effect, that the average market effect is 50 percent of total risk; this implies $\rho = .7$. Marshall Blume, however, found an average ρ of about .5 in "On the Assessment of Risk," *Journal of Finance*, March 1971, p. 4. See also O. A. Vasicek, "A Note on Using Cross-Sectional Information in Bayesian Estimation of Security Betas," *Journal of Finance*, December 1973, pp. 1233–1239. J. C. Francis, "Statistical Analysis of Risk Surrogates for NYSE Stocks," *Journal of Financial and Quantitative Analysis*, December 1979.

TABLE 10-4 risk and return statistics from characteristic line regression

	Kaiser	market portfolio
Total risk variance of returns $= \text{var}(r)$	.038	.008
Unsystematic risk = residual variance $= \text{var}(r_e)$	.020	0*
Systematic risk measure $= b_i^2\,[\text{var}(r_m)] = \rho^2[\text{var}(r_i)]$	.018	.008
Beta coefficient = index of systematic risk	1.45	1.0
Systematic risk percentage $= \rho^2 =$	.47 = 47%	1.0 = 100%

* Chapter 24 shows that by diversifying internationally, risk that was considered undiversifiable within the domestic context can become, in whole or in part, diversifiable within the context of multinational investments.

Kaiser Aluminum's common stock is a riskier-than-average common stock in terms of total risk and systematic risk, as indicated by the statistics in Table 10-4.[11]

10-2 THE CHARACTERISTIC LINE: A CLOSER EXAMINATION

The characteristic line describing the period-by-period interaction between the rates of return of asset i and the rates of change in some market index was defined in Eq. (10-1); it is a model of market forces as they affect the ith asset. The characteristic line is also called the *market model* or the *single-index model* by some financial economists.[12]

10-2.1 graphing characteristic lines

For prediction purposes, the *conditional expectation* of Eq. (10-1), which was previously shown above as Eq. (10-3*a*), is useful. The conditional expectation is restated equivalently as Eq. (10-3*b*) below.

$$E(r_i|r_m) = a_i + b_i r_m \tag{10-3b}$$

Equations (10-3*a*) and (10-3*b*) are like Eq. (10-1) except that the residual return left unexplained by the regression, e, has been averaged out to zero when summed up over all the observations, and thus does not appear in conditional expectation. Stated differently, the mathematical expectation of the residual term is zero, $E(e) = 0$. The time subscripts in Eq. (10-1) have also been deleted because Eq. (10-3*a*) is an *ex ante* (or future expectation) model. In contrast, Eq. (10-1) is an *ex post* (or historical data–oriented) model that employs time subscripts to refer to the time series of single period rates of return represented by the model.

The characteristic line's alpha intercept term may have a positive, zero, or negative value for any given asset. But the statistic is usually very near zero in value for most assets. This alpha has no asset-pricing implications and cannot be used for investment performance evaluation.[13]

[11] Statements about the relative degree of total risk are made in the context of a long-run horizon—that is, over at least one complete business cycle. Obviously, an accurate short-run forecast which says that some particular company will go bankrupt next quarter makes it more risky than Kaiser, although the latter may have had more historical variability of return.

[12] The first printed discussion of the characteristic line was by Harry Markowitz, *Portfolio Selection*, Wiley, New York, 1959), pp. 97–101: Markowitz called it an *index model*. The next printed record of the model was in the doctoral dissertation of William F. Sharpe at University of California at Los Angeles. Markowitz was on Sharpe's dissertation committee and apparently passed his ideas on to Sharpe. Sharpe referred to the model as the *single-index model* in an article which summarized his dissertation entitled "A Simplified Model for Portfolio Analysis," *Management Science*, vol. 9, no. 2, pp. 277–293, January 1963. Working independently of Markowitz and Sharpe, Jack L. Treynor published an article entitled "How to Rate Management of Investment Funds," *Harvard Business Review*, vol. 43, no. 1, pp. 63–75, January-February 1965. Treynor referred to the model as the *characteristic line*, and this book has adopted Treynor's name for the model because it seems the most descriptive. Professor Eugene Fama appears to be the first to have referred to the model as the *market model*, and his students at the University of Chicago have followed his choice of term in many instances.

[13] The alpha intercept term of the characteristic line in terms of risk-premiums does have investment performance implications which are explained by M. C. Jensen, "The Performance of Mutual Funds in the Period 1945 through 1964," *Journal of Finance*, May 1968, pp. 389–416.

The beta regression slope coefficient has an average value of unity. Most betas lie in the range between .5 and 1.5, and the betas which lie the farthest away from unity have a tendency to regress back toward unity with the passage of time.[14]

Two possible forms that Eq. (10-1) may assume are shown in Fig. 10-3. Equation (10-1), or equivalently Eq. (10-3*b*), has been fitted to (1) a firm which has returns that are positively correlated with the returns on the market and (2) a firm whose returns are negatively correlated with the market. For these two firms, the characteristic lines indicate that when the rate of return for the market portfolio is r_{m1}, the security is expected to earn a return of r_{i1}. In statistical language, $E(r_{i1})$ is called the conditional expectation that is conditional on the value of r_{m1}.

In terms of capital market theory language, the asset in Fig. 10-3*a* has more systematic risk than the asset in Fig. 10-3*b*. It has a positive slope coefficient b_i, positive covariance of returns with the returns from the market portfolio *m*, and positive correlation of returns with returns on *m*. The firm in Fig. 10-3*b* has a negative regression slope coefficient b_i, negative covariance, and negative correlation coefficient. Thus the asset in Fig. 10-3*b* will decrease the risk of a portfolio which is correlated with *m* (as most portfolios are) more than the asset in Fig. 10-3*a*. Most simply, the asset in Fig. 10-3*b* is the better candidate for risk-reducing diversification purposes.

10-2.2 unsystematic risk is residual variance

Any time Eq. (10-1) results in a correlation coefficient below positive unity, the observations will not all lie on the regression line; of course, this is the typical case graphed in Figs. 10-2 and 10-3. The vertical deviations of the observations from the regression line are called *residual errors* and are denoted *e* in Eq. (10-1). Although the least-squares regression technique used to derive Eq. (10-1) or (10-3*b*) minimizes the sum of the squared errors (that is, minimum Σe_{it}^2) over all the observations, the sum is still a positive value. The term

[14] M. Blume, "Betas and Their Regression Tendencies," *Journal of Finance*, June 1975, pp. 785–795. W. F. Sharpe and G. Cooper, "Risk-Return Classes of NYSE Stocks, 1931–67," *Financial Analysts Journal*, March–April 1972. J. C. Francis, "Statistical Analysis of Risk Coefficients for NYSE Stocks," *Journal of Financial and Quantitative Analysis*, vol. XIV, no. 5, December 1979, pp. 981–997.

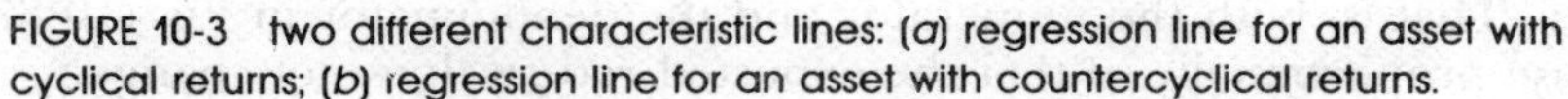
FIGURE 10-3 two different characteristic lines: (*a*) regression line for an asset with cyclical returns; (*b*) regression line for an asset with countercyclical returns.

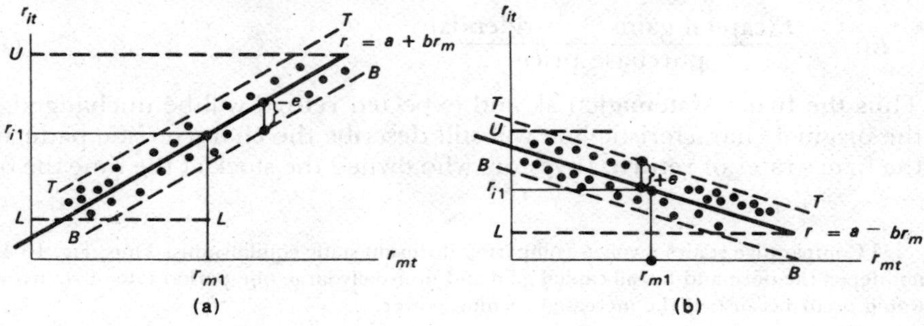

$\sigma^2(r_i|r_m)$ is called the *residual variance around the regression line* in statistical terms, or *unsystematic risk* in financial market theory language.

$$\sigma^2(r_i|r_m) = \frac{\sum_{t=1}^{T} e_{it}^2}{T} \tag{10-7a}$$

$$= \frac{\sum_{t=1}^{T} (r_{it} - a_i - b_i r_{mt})^2}{T} = \text{var}(e) \tag{10-7b}$$

In Fig. 10-3 the *total* range over which the returns varied is represented graphically by the vertical distance between the upper (U) and lower (L) horizontal dashed lines. The *residual* or *unsystematic* range of variability is represented graphically by the vertical distance between the top (T) and bottom (B) dashed lines, which are parallel to the characteristic line. These dashed lines (U, L, T, and B) are not any kind of boundary lines; they are merely added to depict graphically the total risk (between U and L) and unsystematic risk (between T and B).

10-2.3 comparative statics for a change in profitability[15]

If a firm were to experience a change in earning power, its characteristic line might or might not move. Suppose a technological breakthrough occurred which increased a firm's income at every level of sales. If the increased earnings raised the firm's expected rate of return at any given sales volume by one percentage point, the characteristic line might shift upward by one percentage point on the vertical axis. Figure 10-4 represents one possible shift.

In Fig. 10-4 the rise in the characteristic line is measured by the change in the intercept coefficients, $a_2 - a_1$. If the firm is to *continue* to yield a higher rate of return to its shareholders, it must experience an increase in systematic risk in order to maintain an equilibrium tradeoff relationship between expected return and systematic risk. Thus, the slope of the firm's characteristic line must increase from b_1 to b_2, as shown in Fig. 10-4.

If an increase in systematic risk does not accompany the rise in earnings, a once-and-for-all capital gain will result from the increase in earnings. This capital gain will raise the firm's purchase price enough so that its expected return will not change, although future dividends may be expected to remain higher. That is, both the numerator and the denominator in Eq. (10-8) will increase proportionally so that the expected return does not change.

$$E(r) = \frac{E(\text{capital gains} + \text{dividends})}{\text{purchase price}} \tag{10-8}$$

Thus the firm's systematic risk and expected return will be unchanged, and the original characteristic line will still describe the characteristic pattern for the firm's rates of return. Investors who owned the stock at the time the once-

[15] Comparative statics involves comparing different static equilibriums. Thus, Fig. 10-4 does not depict the once-and-for-all capital gain and unusually large one-period rate of return which would occur because of the increased earning power.

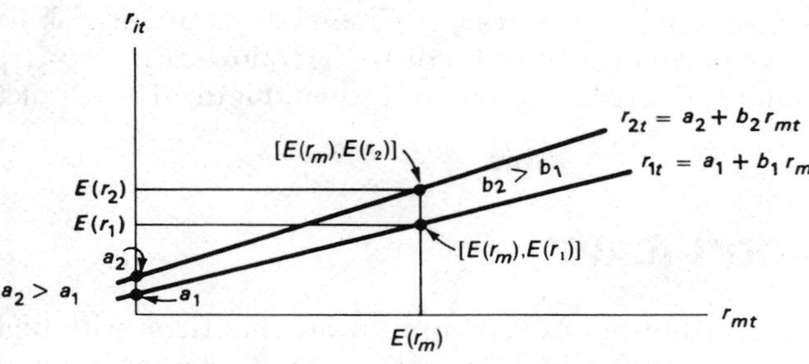

FIGURE 10-4 comparative statics of a change in earning power with a change in systematic risk.

and-for-all capital gain occurred will have captured the capitalized value of the earnings increase (that is, the big one-time capital gain).

10-2.4 firms with different beta coefficients

All simple linear regression lines pass through the *centroid* where the expected value (or mean) of both variables occurs. Since the characteristic line is a regression line, it must pass through this point $[E(r_m), E(r_i)]$. The centroids and three different characteristic lines are shown graphically in Fig. 10-5.

Suppose one firm depicted in Fig. 10-5 is a steel manufacturer, denoted S. Such a firm's sales and profits will likely follow the level of activity in the national economy. As a result, the steel firm has a beta regression slope (systematic risk) coefficient of unity. The second firm is the noncyclical firm denoted F, which might be a food manufacturer; its beta coefficient is zero, and so its returns are not expected to vary owing to systematic risk factors. The third hypothetical firm shown in Fig. 10-5 is a red ink manufacturer, denoted I. This firm is unique in that its returns characteristically covary inversely with the rate of return from the market. Supposedly, red ink sells better in recessions and depressions when accountants make more entries in red ink; so the red ink manufacturer has a beta coefficient of $-\frac{1}{2}$.

As a result of the basic difference in the characteristic of each business, the three firms in Fig. 10-5 all have drastically different beta coefficients,

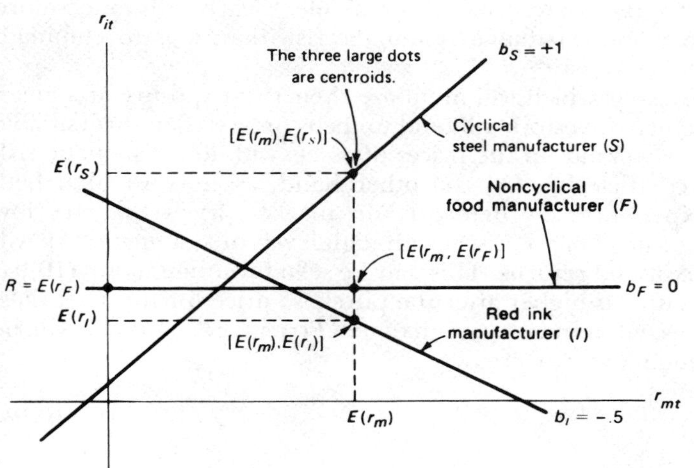

FIGURE 10-5 comparison of three firms with different systematic risks.

$b_S > b_F = 0 > b_I$. Since expected returns are a function of systematic risk for all assets, the three firms' expected returns also differ as follows: $E(r_S) > E(r_F) = R > E(r_I)$, where R denotes the risk-free rate of return. Figure 10-5 depicts these facts graphically.

10-3 THE CAPITAL ASSET PRICING MODEL (CAPM)

Studies of the probability distributions of returns indicate that firms with high total risk and high systematic risk tend also to have high average rates of return. This is what financial economists would intuitively expect. Investors demand high rates of return to induce them to invest in risky assets, reminding one of the widely quoted axiom that "there is no such thing as a free lunch." This "free lunch" principle asserts that you cannot expect to get something for nothing. This is also true of investment returns. Investors who want to earn high average rates of return must take high risks and endure the associated loss of sleep, the possibility of ulcers, and the chance of bankruptcy.

In Chap. 1 it was suggested that wealth-maximizing, risk-averting investors will seek investments which have the maximum expected return in their risk-class. Their expected happiness (or utility) from investing is derived as indicated from the unspecified function below.

$$E(U) = f[\mathrm{E}(r), \sigma]$$

The investment preferences of wealth-seeking, risk-averse investors represented by the function above cause them to maximize their expected utility (that is, happiness), which is a function of an investment's expected return $E(r)$ and total risk σ. Such investors will seek to (1) maximize their expected return in any given risk-class, or conversely, (2) minimize their risk at any given rate of expected return. However, in selecting individual assets, investors will not be particularly concerned with the asset's total risk, σ. The unsystematic portion of total risk can be easily diversified away by holding a portfolio of several different securities. However, systematic risk affects all stocks in the market and is therefore undiversifiable. Clearly, it is much more difficult to eliminate undiversifiable systematic risk than it is to eliminate diversifiable unsystematic risk.

In the search for assets which will minimize their risk exposure at a given level of expected return, investors will tend to focus on assets' undiversifiable systematic risk. They will bid up the prices of assets with low systematic risk (that is, low beta coefficients). On the other hand, assets with high beta coefficients will experience low demand and market prices that are low relative to assets' income. That is, assets with high levels of systematic risk will tend to have high expected returns. This may be seen by noting in Eq. (10-9*a*) that the expected return is higher after the purchase price for the asset falls. Obviously, the expected return ratio, denoted $E(r)$ in Eq. (10-9*a*), will be larger after the denominator decreases.

$$E(r) = \frac{E(p_{t+1}) - p_t + d_t}{p_t} \tag{10-9a}$$

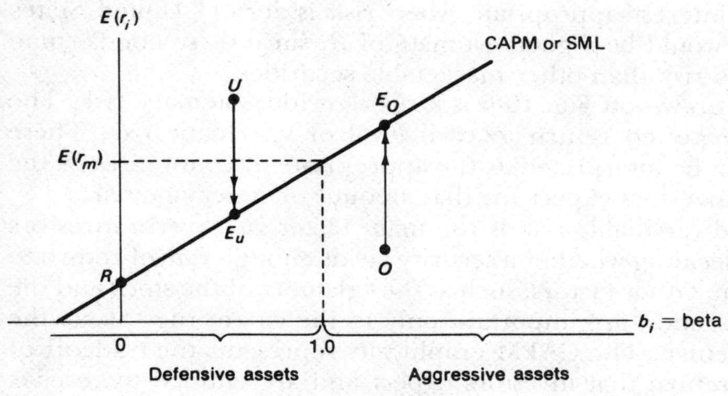

FIGURE 10-6 the security market line (SML), or capital asset pricing model (CAPM).

$$E(r) = \frac{\text{expected income}}{\text{market purchase price}} \tag{10-9b}$$

An asset with high systematic risk (that is, a high beta) will experience price declines until the expected return it offers is high enough to induce investors to assume this undiversifiable risk. This price level is the *equilibrium price,* and the expected return is the *equilibrium rate of return* for that risk-class.

Figure 10-6 shows the capital asset pricing model (CAPM), or security market line (SML), as it is also called, which graphically depicts the results of the price adjustments (that is, the equilibrium prices and expected returns) from this risk-averse trading.

The CAPM, or SML, is a linear relationship in which the expected average rate of return of the *i*th asset is a linear function of that asset's systematic risk as represented by b_i. Symbolically, Eq. (10-10) represents the CAPM.

$$E(r_t) = R + cb_i \tag{10-10}$$

where

b_i = the independent variable representing the systematic risk of the *i*th asset; it determines the dependent variable $E(r_i)$, the average expected rate of return for asset i

R = the vertical axis intercept

c = the slope of the CAPM[16]

[16] The slope of the CAPM is defined as follows:

$$c = \frac{\text{rise}}{\text{run}} = \text{slope of CAPM}$$

$$= \frac{E(r_m) - R}{b_m} = E(r_m) - R \qquad \text{since } b_m = 1.0$$

This slope is the risk-return tradeoff in the security market and is called the "market price of risk."

R is the rate of interest appropriate when risk is zero.[17] United States Treasury bill yields would be a good estimate of R, since these bonds come closer to having zero risk than other marketable securities.

Any vertical line drawn on Fig. 10-6 is a *risk-class* for systematic risk. The CAPM relates an expected return to each level of systematic risk. These expected returns can be interpreted as the appropriate discount rates or the cost of capital that investors expect for that amount of systematic risk.

Systematic or undiversifiable risk is the main factor risk-averse investors should consider in deciding whether a security yields enough rate of return to induce them to buy it. Other factors, such as the "glamor" of the stock and the company's financial ratios, are important only to the extent they affect the security's risk and return. The CAPM graphically represents the tradeoff of systematic risk for return that investors expect and are entitled to receive. This implies that the CAPM has asset-pricing implications.

10-3.1 asset's price movements

After an asset's average return and systematic risk have been estimated, they may be plotted in reference to the CAPM. In equilibrium every asset's $E(r)$ and beta systematic risk coefficient should plot as one point on the CAPM. To see why this is true, consider Fig. 10-6, which shows two assets denoted O and U. Asset U is underpriced because its average rate of return is too high for the level of systematic risk it bears. Asset O is overpriced because its expected rate of return is too low to induce investors to accept its undiversifiable risk. These two assets should move to the CAPM, as shown by the arrows to their equilibrium positions at the points marked E.

To see why assets O and U are incorrectly priced, reconsider Eq. (10-9c), which defines the expected rate of return for a common stock.

$$E(r) = \frac{\text{expected capital gains or loss} + \text{expected cash dividends}}{\text{purchase price}} \tag{10-9c}$$

To reach their equilibrium positions on the CAPM, assets O and U must go through a temporary price readjustment. Assuming the assets' systematic risk remains unchanged, the expected return of U must fall to E_U and the expected return of O must rise to E_O. To accomplish this move to an equilibrium rate of return, the denominator of Eq. (10-9c) must rise for asset U and must fall for asset O. Assets O and U or any marketable capital asset (such as a portfolio, stock, bond, or real estate) will be in disequilibrium unless its risk

[17] Black has suggested a model in which it is not necessary to assume the existence of a riskless rate; see Fischer Black, "Capital Market Equilibrium with Restricted Borrowing," *Journal of Business*, July 1972, pp. 444–454. In Black's model the riskless interest rate is replaced by a portfolio which has a beta equal to zero but still has positive variance of returns. The zero-beta portfolio is uncorrelated with the market portfolio, so that its total risk and its unsystematic risk are identical and both are positive quantities. This portfolio is created by holding risky securities and leveraging and selling short. Some preliminary empirical estimates of the rates of return on the zero-beta portfolio have been published; see F. Black, M. C. Jensen, and M. Scholes, "The Capital Asset Pricing Model: Some Empirical Tests," published in *Studies in the Theory of Capital Markets*, a book of unpublished studies edited by M. C. Jensen and published by Praeger, New York, 1972. Professor G. Alexander has shown an algorithm which could be used to obtain estimates of the returns from a zero-beta portfolio: "An Algorithmic Approach to Deriving the Minimum Variance Zero-Beta Portfolio," *Journal of Financial Economics*, March 1977.

and return lie on the CAPM. Supply and demand will set to work as outlined above to correct any disequilibrium from the CAPM.

10-3.2 market imperfections

The operation of the rational forces of supply and demand can be expected to move assets lying off the CAPM toward the CAPM, but because of market imperfections, all assets' risk-return characteristics never lie exactly on the CAPM. Some market imperfections which preclude attainment of a complete equilibrium are:

1. *Transaction costs.* The stockbroker's commissions and transfer taxes associated with each security transaction drain away investors' incentive to correct minor deviations from the CAPM.
2. *Differential tax rates on capital gains.* Since capital gains are taxed differently from dividends and interest, the after-tax rate of return (atr) defined in Eq. (10-11) differs with the investor's tax bracket. Thus, each investor envisions a slightly different CAPM in terms of after-tax returns:

$$\text{atr}_t = \frac{d_t(1 - t_0) + (p_{t+1} - p_t)(1 - t_g)}{p_t} \tag{10-11}$$

where

t_0 = the ordinary income tax rate
t_g = the capital gains rate

3. *Heterogeneous expectations.* Different investors assess the systematic risk of any given asset differently and therefore perceive different equilibrium rates of return as being appropriate for any given asset.
4. *Imperfect information.* Some investors are irrational; some are uninformed; and some receive financial news later than others.

Because of market imperfections, all assets are not expected to lie exactly on the CAPM. Therefore, in practice, the CAPM is actually a band rather than a thin line. The width of this band varies directly with the imperfections in the market. As a result, the CAPM cannot be used to pinpoint an asset's equilibrium price. Instead, it can suggest only a range of prices for an asset.

10-4 EMPIRICAL RISK-RETURN ESTIMATES

Section 9-1 explained how to measure an asset's expected rate of return and its total risk, and Sec. 10-1 showed how to measure an asset's systematic risk and unsystematic risk. Economic logic, suggesting that investors should demand higher returns to induce them to buy investments with high systematic risk, was explained too. The next logical question is: If stocks' betas and average returns are actually measured over a period of time, will the high beta stocks really have higher rates of return? Or, put more crassly: Is this CAPM theory really any good? Empirical tests of the CAPM theory were published by William F. Sharpe and Guy Cooper; their work is described in the following paragraphs. Similar studies by other researchers have both extended the

CAPM to embrace other variables and, also, reached conclusions which align with the basic CAPM reviewed here.[18]

10-4.1 the sample and the statistics

In the Sharpe-Cooper study, monthly stock prices for hundreds of NYSE stocks from 1926 to 1967 provided the raw data. Monthly rates of return were first calculated by using Eq. (2-2) for every stock and every month. Second, betas were calculated with Eq. (10-4*a*), using 5 years (or 60 monthly observations) of rates of return. Third, an annual rate of return was calculated for each stock. Fourth, the stocks were all grouped into risk deciles based on their beta coefficients. The risk-classes were based on the 5 years *preceding* the year in which the annual return was calculated to simulate picking stocks for future investment based on 5 years of past data—a procedure that assumes betas are stable over time.

The procedure was replicated for hundreds of stocks every year from 1931 to 1967. Betas were calculated from 5 years of data, risk deciles formed from the betas, annual returns measured during the sixth year, and then the procedure was repeated for the next year. When the procedure had been repeated once for each (5 + 1 equals) 6-year period from 1931 to 1967, the 10 risk deciles from each of the 37 years were averaged to obtain average risk deciles and average annual returns. Figure 10-7 shows the beta coefficients averaged over all stocks in all years for the 10 risk-classes. The annual returns averaged over all stocks and all years in each risk decile are shown in Fig. 10-8.

10-4.2 CAPM estimates

A simple linear regression of the form shown in Eq. (10-12) was fitted through the 10 average betas, denoted b_i from Fig. 10-7, and their associated average annual returns, denoted $\bar{r}_i$ from Fig. 10-8, for $i = 1, 2, \ldots, 10$ deciles.

$$\bar{r}_i = a + b(b_i) \tag{10-12}$$

Figure 10-9 shows a graph of the risk-return relationship delineated by the study.

The Sharpe-Cooper study is a scientific investigation which was painstakingly constructed so as to avoid introducing bias. Some sampling error exists

[18] Empirical tests of the CAPM include: M. Blume and I. Friend, "A New Look at the Capital Asset Pricing Model," *Journal of Finance*, March 1973, pp. 19–34; F. Black, M. C. Jensen, and M. Scholes, "The Capital Asset Pricing Model: Some Empirical Tests," in M. C. Jensen (ed.), *Studies in the Theory of Capital Markets*, Praeger, New York, 1972; M. Blume and F. Husic, "Price, Beta and Exchange Listing," *Journal of Finance*, May 1973, pp. 283–299; M. Miller and M. Scholes, "Rates of Return in Relation to Risk: A Re-Examination of Some Recent Findings," in M. C. Jensen (ed.), *Studies in the Theory of Capital Markets*, Praeger, New York, 1972, pp. 47–78; E. F. Fama and J. MacBeth, "Risk, Return and Equilibrium: Empirical Tests," *Journal of Political Economy*, May/June 1973, pp. 607–636; M. R. Reinganum, "Misspecification of Capital Asset Pricing: Empirical Anomalies Based on Earnings Yields and Market Values," *Journal of Financial Economics*, March 1981, pp. 19-46; R. Litzenberger and K. Ramaswamy, "The Effect of Personal Taxes and Dividends and Capital Asset Prices: Theory and Empirical Evidence," *Journal of Financial Economics*, June 1979, pp. 163–195; R. W. Banz, "The Relationship between Return and Market Value of Common Stocks," *Journal of Financial Economics*, March 1981, pp. 3–18; deficiencies in the preceding empirical tests are pinpointed by Richard Roll, "A Critique of the Asset Pricing Theory's Tests," *Journal of Financial Economics*, March 1977, pp. 129–176.

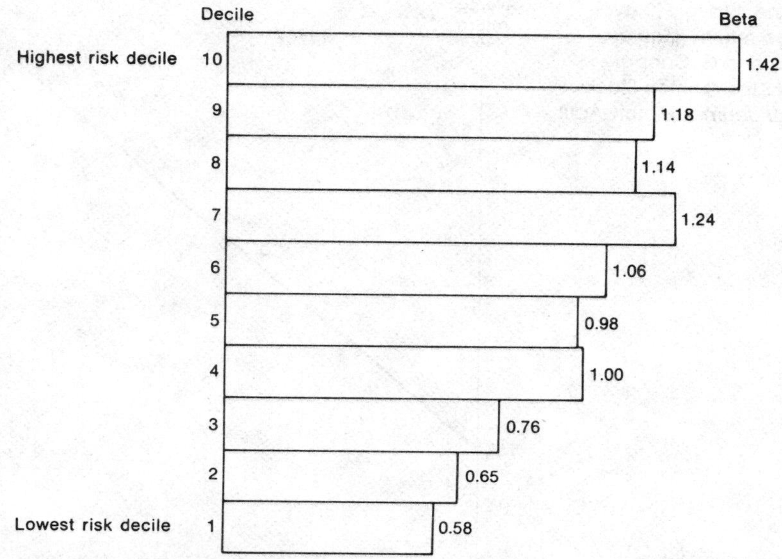

FIGURE 10-7 average betas for risk deciles, 1931–1967. (*Source*: redrawn from W. F. Sharpe and G. Cooper, "Risk-Return Classes of N.Y.S.E. Common Stocks, 1931–67," *Financial Analysts Journal*, March–April 1972.)

FIGURE 10-8 average annual rates of return by risk deciles, 1931–1967. (*Source*: redrawn from W. F. Sharpe and G. Cooper, "Risk-Return Classes of N.Y.S.E. Common Stocks, 1931–67," *Financial Analysts Journal*, March–April 1972.)

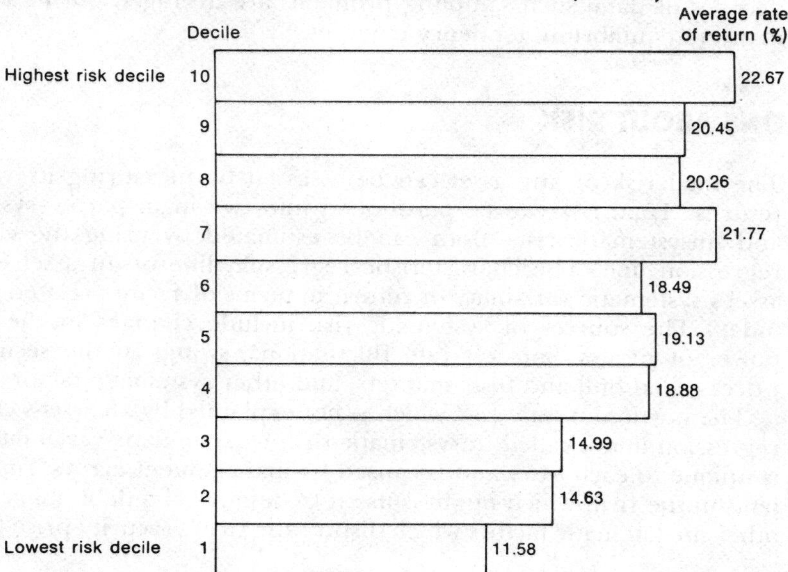

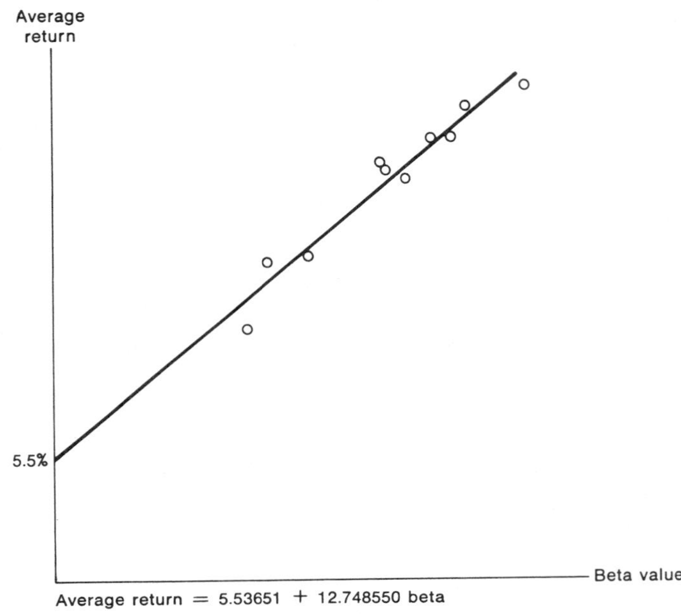

FIGURE 10-9 regression line through 10 average betas and 10 average returns. (*Source*: redrawn from W. F. Sharpe and G. Cooper, "Risk-Return Classes of N.Y.S.E. Common Stocks, 1931–67," *Financial Analysts Journal*, March–April 1972.)

in the study as it does in every statistical study, but the statistics do support the theory. In the long run, buying stocks with high (or medium or low) degrees of systematic risk was shown to yield portfolios with high (or medium or low) average future rates of return. On a single-stock basis, this may not occur because the single stock selected may go bankrupt, experience a change in its systematic risk, or undergo some other change which was not representative of the behavior of most stocks. However, by using hundreds of stocks and decades of data, such sampling problems are averaged out to zero and the market's equilibrium tendency emerges.

10-5 CONCLUSIONS ABOUT RISK

The total risk of any asset can be assessed by measuring its variability of returns. Total risk can be partitioned into two main parts—systematic risk and unsystematic risk. Both can be estimated by using the characteristic regression line. The characteristic regression line of an asset explains the asset's systematic variability of return in terms of factors related to a market index. The sources of systematic risk include changes in the purchasing power of money, interest rate fluctuations, swings in the security market prices called bull and bear markets, and other systematic factors.

The portion of total risk which is not explained by an asset's characteristic regression line is called unsystematic risk. Unsystematic variability of returns is unique to each asset and is caused by management errors, financial problems in the firm which might cause it to default on a debt obligation, and/or other unsystematic factors which disturb the firm's security price fluctuations.

Since unsystematic variations are unique to each firm, they can be easily diversified away to zero by spreading the funds to be invested across the securities of several unrelated firms. Systematic risk, on the other hand, is more difficult to diversify because it is common to all assets in the market to some extent. Within a given market (for example, the stock market), assets with high degrees of systematic risk must be priced to yield high rates of return in order to induce investors to accept high degrees of risk which are essentially undiversifiable within that market. The CAPM illustrates the positive relation between assets' systematic risks and their expected or average rates of return. Empirical tests support the validity of the CAPM.

QUESTIONS

10-1. Write a short essay defining total risk verbally, and explain how this definition is consistent with using the variance of returns as a quantitative risk surrogate.

10-2. Make a probability distribution of your starting salary per month when you graduate. What quantitative risk surrogate would you use to measure the risk of these dollar quantities? What problems are presented by simply using the standard deviation of your dollar salary as a quantitative risk surrogate?

10-3. Write one-sentence definitions of each of the following: (*a*) total risk, (*b*) systematic risk, (*c*) unsystematic risk, (*d*) diversifiable risk, and (*e*) undiversifiable risk.

10-4. Gather 10 years of quarterly data from 1974-IQ to 1983-IVQ inclusive for IBM common stock and prepare a regression like the one shown in Fig. 10-2. The needed stock market index data are in Appendix 10B. Calculate rates of return for the asset and estimate the characteristic line for the asset. Is it a defensive or an aggressive asset? Does the characteristic line for the asset have much predictive power? Is the asset good for diversification purposes? Has the beta coefficient for IBM shifted during the latest four quarters?

10-5. How do you expect the total risk of a mutual fund to be divided between systematic and unsystematic risk?

10-6. Assume that a firm added a new product to its line that decreased the overall riskiness of the firm. For example, a highly cyclical rubber company began producing red ink. How would this affect the value of a share of the firm's stock? Use a diagram of the CAPM to show the asset-pricing implications of this change in the firm.

10-7. Could you as a security analyst expect to find any worthwhile information by studying the residual error from the characteristic line regression? Explain.

10-8. Are the beta coefficients in the characteristic line stable through time? Explain. Is it worthwhile to study betas if they are intertemporally unstable?

10-9. Do you believe that an asset's unsystematic risk should have no effect on its market price, as the capital asset pricing model (CAPM) suggests? Explain.

SELECTED REFERENCES

Breeden, D. T.: "An Intertemporal Asset Pricing Model with Stochastic Consumption and Investment Opportunities," *Journal of Financial Economics*, September 1979, pp. 265–296. Advanced calculus is employed to develop an extension of the capital asset pricing model (CAPM) which maximizes the investor's expected utility from consumption. Breeden's model maximizes the investor's lifetime utility from consumption over multiple time periods and explains consumption-investment decisions. As a result, asset prices depend on their covariances with aggregate *consumption* rather than with any market index.

Sharpe, W. F.: "Capital Asset Prices: A Theory of Market Equilibrium under Conditions of Risk," *Journal of Finance*, September 1964, pp. 425–552, reprinted in *Readings in Investments*, J. C. Francis, Cheng-Few Lee, and Donald Farrar (eds.), McGraw-Hill, New York, 1983. This classic article suggests the asset pricing implications of systematic risk. Sharpe develops the risk-return relationship for portfolios (that is, the capital market line, or the CML) and for individual assets (namely, the CAPM). Calculus is used only in the footnotes. A knowledge of elementary statistics is assumed.

APPENDIX 10A

beta stability

The statistics from a security's characteristic line contain much information about various aspects of the stock's price movements and can be useful in predicting how the security will react to changes in the condition of the market from bullish rises to bearish declines. However, when the data points (that is, the dots in Fig. 10-2) do not fit closely around it, the characteristic line's predictive power diminishes accordingly. Since the correlation coefficient, ρ, is a goodness-of-fit statistic which measures how well the data points fit around the characteristic line (or any regression line), this statistic gives some indication of how much faith should be placed in its associated beta coefficient.

The characteristic line statistics shown at the bottom of Table App. 10A-1 for Homestake Mining, for example, have a correlation coefficient of .01 for the sample period from January 1927 through June 1935. Table App. 10A-1 shows that the squared coefficient of correlation is called the *coefficient of determination*. The coefficient of determination tells what percent of the total variance in the stock's price is explained by the regression. The coefficient of determination for Homestake for the 1927–1935 sample of only 1 percent (that is, .01) documents the fact that the data points did not fit Homestake's characteristic line closely.

Securities which have very low goodness-of-fit statistics for their characteristic lines (like the early Homestake data, for example) frequently have beta coefficients that are *random coefficients*. These random coefficients are essentially wild beta coefficients which move up and down over a wide range in

TABLE APP. 10A-1 beta coefficients change over time

firm	time period, month/year	beta	ρ^2*
Union Oil of California	1/27–6/35	.55	.58
	7/35–12/43	.57	.49
	1/44–6/51	.97	.45
	7/51–12/60	.98	.32
IBM	1/27–6/35	.49	.49
	7/35–12/43	.25	.26
	1/44–6/51	.56	.29
	7/51–12/60	.86	.23
May Department Stores	1/27–6/35	.83	.74
	7/35–12/43	.64	.49
	1/44–6/51	.72	.35
	7/51–12/60	.82	.32
Atlantic Coast Line Railroad	1/27–6/35	1.2	.73
	7/35–12/43	1.26	.7
	1/44–6/51	1.7	.43
	7/51–12/60	1.63	.57
Homestake Mining Corporation	1/27–6/35	.042	.01
	7/35-12/43	.235	.07
	1/44-6/51	.333	.09
	7/51–12/60	.465	.11

*ρ^2 = coefficient of determination for characteristic regression line
= correlation coefficient squared
= percent of variation explained

Source: Marshall E. Blume, "The Assessment of Portfolio Performance: An Application of Portfolio Theory," unpublished doctoral dissertation, University of Chicago, March 1968.

a spurious fashion as the characteristic line is fit over and over during different sample periods. Furthermore, a firm's beta may change drastically if, for instance, it undertakes production of new products with a complete new management team. But year after year most firms' probability distributions of returns and betas are similar (that is, they are relatively stable through time). Table 10A-1 shows how the betas for a few firms have behaved with the passage of time. Considering that the data for these calculations span 33 years, the stability of the statistics over time for May Department Stores, for instance, is impressive.[19]

[19] Explicit studies of beta stationarity include W. F. Sharpe and G. Cooper, "Risk-Return Classes of New York Stock Exchange Common Stock, 1931–67," *Financial Analysts Journal*, March–April 1972; M. E. Blume, "On the Assessment of Risk," *Journal of Finance*, March 1974, pp. 1–10; Nancy Jacob, "The Measurement of Systematic Risk for Securities and Portfolios: Some Empirical Results," *Journal of Financial and Quantitative Analysis*, March 1971, pp. 815–834; R. C. Klemkosky and J. D. Martin, "The Adjustment of Beta Factors," *Journal of Finance*, September 1975, pp. 1123–1128; J. C. Francis, "Statistical Analysis of Risk Surrogates for NYSE Stocks," *Journal of Financial and Quantitative Analysis*, December 1979.

APP. 10A-1 FRANCIS'S STUDY OF INTERTEMPORAL STABILITY OF RISK STATISTICS

It is important to ask whether the beta coefficient and the standard deviation statistics for different securities are stable through time or whether they jump around randomly (like the Homestake Mining statistics shown at the bottom of Table App. 10A-1, for instance). If the statistics gyrate wildly, they have little value to financial analysts because today's historical statistics are a poor predictor of the future riskiness of an investment.

Dr. J. C. Francis analyzed 750 NYSE stocks over a decade in order to assess the stability of three statistics which measure the riskiness of financial assets. The three statistics Francis analyzed are (1) the beta coefficient from the characteristic line, (2) the correlation coefficient, which measures how closely the data points fit around the characteristic line, and (3) the standard deviation, which measures the asset's total risk.

Francis divided the decade he studied up into two 60-month subsamples and measured the three statistics he analyzed for 750 different stocks. After calculating all these statistics over the first 5 years (or 60 months) and also over the second 5 years, he arranged them into *arrays* with the largest values at the top of the list and the smallest statistics at the bottom of the list. Six arrays were thus constructed, as listed below.

1. An array of 750 betas over the first 60 months.
2. An array of 750 betas over the second 60 months.
3. An array of 750 standard deviations over the first 60 months.
4. An array of 750 standard deviations over the second 60 months.
5. An array of 750 correlation coefficients over the first 60 months.
6. An array of 750 correlation coefficients over the second 60 months.

Then Francis divided each of the six arrays of 750 statistics up into ten equal-sized deciles with 75 stocks' statistics in each *decile*. He then arranged these six arrays of deciles of statistics into the transition matrix shown in Table App. 10A-2 in order to see how stable the statistics were from one 5-year subsample until the next 5-year subsample. Table App. 10A-2 is actually three different transition probability matrices—one for betas, one for standard deviations, and one for correlation coefficients—all assembled in one matrix.

The transition probability matrix for betas in Table App. 10A-2 shows, for example, that .4267 (or 42.67 percent) of the betas in the top decile in the first 5 years turned up in the top decile in the next 5-year period. Slightly over a quarter (.2533 or 25.33 percent, to be exact) of the betas in the top decile declined in value enough to be in the second decile in the second 5-year period. Note that betas in the top decile in the first 60-month subsample dropped into every one of the deciles except the eighth decile in the following 60-month subsample. But only .0133 (or 1.33 percent) fell clear down into the tenth decile in the next 5-year subsample. After studying the entire transition matrix, it appears that very few betas rose or fell more than two or three

TABLE APP. 10A-2 transition matrix, percentile in year t versus percentile in year $t + 5$

deciles	1	2	3	4	5	6	7	8	9	10
Beta1	0.4267	0.2533	0.0800	0.0400	0.0533	0.0400	0.0533	0.0000	0.0400	0.0133
StdD1	0.5067	0.1867	0.0800	0.0667	0.0667	0.0400	0.0267	0.0133	0.0133	0.0000
Corr1	0.1867	0.200	0.1067	0.1600	0.0667	0.0400	0.1067	0.0667	0.0533	0.0133
Beta2	0.1867	0.2933	0.1600	0.0933	0.0800	0.0267	0.0533	0.0533	0.0267	0.0267
StdD2	0.2267	0.2400	0.2133	0.1467	0.0800	0.0267	0.0267	0.0267	0.0000	0.0133
Corr2	0.2000	0.1600	0.1600	0.1600	0.0800	0.0133	0.0400	0.0400	0.1067	0.0400
Beta3	0.1733	0.1200	0.2000	0.1333	0.1067	0.1333	0.0667	0.0267	0.0133	0.0267
StdD3	0.1200	0.1867	0.2000	0.1867	0.0800	0.0800	0.0400	0.0667	0.0267	0.0133
Corr3	0.1200	0.1067	0.1200	0.0800	0.0400	0.1867	0.0933	0.1200	0.0800	0.0533
Beta4	0.0933	0.0667	0.1867	0.1733	0.1733	0.1067	0.0267	0.0667	0.0800	0.0267
StdD4	0.0800	0.1467	0.2267	0.0667	0.1200	0.1600	0.0933	0.0533	0.0533	0.0000
Corr4	0.0933	0.1467	0.1333	0.0267	0.1067	0.1467	0.0800	0.0933	0.0933	0.0800
Beta5	0.0667	0.1067	0.1067	0.1467	0.1200	0.1200	0.1067	0.0933	0.1067	0.0267
StdD5	0.0533	0.1333	0.0667	0.1467	0.2267	0.0800	0.1467	0.1067	0.0400	0.0000
Corr5	0.1200	0.1067	0.0933	0.0800	0.0933	0.0400	0.1333	0.1467	0.0667	0.1200
Beta6	0.0400	0.0667	0.0933	0.1067	0.0933	0.2000	0.1600	0.1467	0.0667	0.0267
StdD6	0.0000	0.0533	0.0800	0.2400	0.1600	0.1200	0.1600	0.0800	0.0667	0.0400
Corr6	0.0667	0.0800	0.1067	0.1333	0.0667	0.1867	0.0533	0.0933	0.1200	0.0933
Beta7	0.0000	0.0533	0.0533	0.1200	0.0933	0.0800	0.1600	0.2000	0.1600	0.0800
StdD7	0.1033	0.0267	0.0933	0.0933	0.1200	0.2000	0.1867	0.1333	0.0933	0.0400
Corr7	0.0667	0.0667	0.0667	0.0933	0.1200	0.0667	0.1600	0.0933	0.1333	0.1333
Beta8	0.0000	0.0267	0.0667	0.1067	0.1600	0.1733	0.1333	0.0800	0.0667	0.1867
StdD8	0.0000	0.0267	0.0400	0.0267	0.1067	0.1467	0.1733	0.1867	0.1333	0.1600
Corr8	0.0667	0.0533	0.0667	0.1200	0.1733	0.1467	0.1333	0.1333	0.0000	0.1067
Beta9	0.0133	0.0133	0.0400	0.0533	0.0667	0.0933	0.1467	0.2267	0.1600	0.1867
StdD9	0.0000	0.0000	0.0000	0.0267	0.0400	0.1067	0.0667	0.2133	0.2400	0.3067
Corr9	0.0400	0.0400	0.0933	0.0667	0.0933	0.1067	0.1067	0.1333	0.1867	0.1333
Beta10	0.0000	0.0000	0.0133	0.0267	0.0533	0.0267	0.0933	0.1067	0.2800	0.4000
StdD10	0.0000	0.0000	0.0000	0.0000	0.0000	0.0400	0.0800	0.1200	0.3333	0.4267
Corr10	0.0400	0.0400	0.0533	0.0800	0.1600	0.0667	0.0933	0.0800	0.1600	0.2267

Source: J. C. Francis, "Statistical Analysis of Risk Statistics for NYSE Stocks," *Journal of Financial and Quantitative Analysis*, December 1979, vol. XIV, no. 5, p. 992, table 4.

deciles during a 5-year period. The betas in the deciles around the median (that is, the fiftieth percentile) moved into the farthest deciles.[20]

Further study of Table App. 10A-2 reveals that the standard deviations are the most stable of the three statistics analyzed by Francis. For example, .2267 (or 22.67 percent) of the standard deviations that started out in the fifth decile in the first 60-month subsample ended up in the same decile in the next 5-year subsample. This finding means that most common stocks' total risk, and also the width of the probability distributions of returns shown in Fig. 9-1, are fairly stable through time.

The correlation coefficients were the least stable statistics analyzed by Francis. Only .0933 (or 9.33 percent) of the correlations that started in the fifth decile in the first subsample were still in the fifth decile 5 years later, for example. Findings like this mean that simply because an asset's data points fit closely around that asset's characteristic line in one 5-year period does not mean that that asset will experience the same goodness-of-fit in the following 5-year period.

The three transition matrices in Table App. 10A-2 suggest that betas, standard deviations, and correlations may not be as stable as financial analysts might desire. Nevertheless, these risk statistics do appear to exhibit sufficient intertemporal stability to make it worthwhile for serious financial analysts to study them.[21]

APP. 10A-2 THE RANDOM COEFFICIENT MODEL

The classic characteristic line model of Eq. (10-1) must be modified slightly to embrace the securities which experience changing betas. Equation (App. 10A-1) is identical with Eq. (10-1) in every respect except one—the beta in Eq. (App. 10A-1) has a time subscript.[22]

$$r_{it} = a_i + b_{it} r_{mt} + e_{it} \qquad \text{(App. 10A-1)}$$

The time subscript on the beta indicates that the beta may assume a different value in each time period—that is, $\text{var}(b_{it}) > 0$ as t changes—if appropriate. Empirical research indicates[23] that the unstable characteristic line model of

[20] The median betas probably changed deciles more than the extreme betas because the values of the statistics in the fourth, fifth, and sixth deciles were compressed into a narrow numerical range. In contrast, the highest and lowest deciles included a wider range of values so that larger numerical changes were needed to move out of these extreme deciles.

[21] The Francis study also presents models that are useful in predicting the future values of betas, standard deviations, and correlations which yield better predictions than merely extrapolating historical values into the future. See J. C. Francis, "Statistical Analysis of Risk Statistics for NYSE Stocks," *Journal of Financial and Quantitative Analysis*, December 1979, vol. XIV, no. 5, Eqs. 5 and 6.

[22] P. A. V. B. Swamy, *Statistical Inference in Random Coefficient Regression Models*, Springer-Verlag, Berlin, 1971. H. Theil, *Principles of Econometrics*, Wiley, New York, 1971, sec. 12-4.

[23] F. J. Fabozzi and J. C. Francis, "Beta as a Random Coefficient," *Journal of Financial and Quantitative Analysis*, March 1978. F. J. Fabozzi and J. C. Francis, "Stability Tests for Alphas and Betas over Bull and Bear Market Conditions," *Journal of Finance*, September 1977. F. Fabozzi and J. C. Francis, "The Effects of Changing Macroeconomic Conditions on Alphas, Betas, and the

Eq. (App. 10A-1) is appropriate for some of the stocks listed on the NYSE, for example. Making continual adjustments for these changing betas creates much additional work for the security analysts.[24]

Francis and Fabozzi published the first study suggesting that beta was a random coefficient in a significant minority of the common stocks listed on the NYSE.[25] Some financial analysts argued that practically all betas were stable.[26] Professors Lee and Chen joined the debate by publishing arguments which tend to support the Francis-Fabozzi position that beta coefficients do move about erratically.[27] No definitive consensus has been reached about the stability of the beta coefficient. However, a scholarly debate on the topic is proceeding.[28]

Single Index Model," *Journal of Financial and Quantitative Analysis*, June 1979. S. J. Kon and G. C. Jen, "Estimation of Time Varying Systematic Risk and Performance for Mutual Fund Portfolios: An Application of Switching Regression," *Journal of Finance*, May 1978. B. Rosenberg, "A Survey of Stochastic Regression Parameters," *Annals of Economic and Social Measurement*, vol. 2, no. 4, pp. 381–397, 1973. B. Rosenberg and J. Guy, "Beta and Investment Fundamentals," *Financial Analysts Journal*, May–June 1976.

[24] Practically all preceding empirical research with the characteristic line has been limited to a partial-equilibrium analysis in which individual securities interactions with some stock market index are measured. Professor Roll has suggested that a general equilibrium analysis would be a more appropriate context in which to test the risk-return capital market theory. Richard Roll, "A Critique of the Asset Pricing Theory's Tests; Part 1: On Past and Potential Testability of the Theory," *Journal of Financial Economics*, vol. 4, no. 2, pp. 129–176, March 1977. Roll would include commodities, bonds, art objects, real estate, and investments in human capital in the market index. The validity of Roll's general equilibrium suggestion is acknowledged. However, at the present time no general market index of the scope Roll visualizes is generally accepted. Furthermore, the validity and importance of the *partial-equilibrium analysis* with the characteristic line is in no way diminished by Roll's suggestion.

Published estimates of a broad-based portfolio have been prepared by R. G. Ibbotson and Carol L. Fall, "The U.S. Wealth Portfolio: Components of Capital Market Values and Returns," *Journal of Portfolio Management*, Fall 1979; and, more recently, R. G. Ibbotson and L. B. Siegel, "The World Market Wealth Portfolio," *Journal of Portfolio Management*, Winter 1983, pp. 5–17.

[25] F. J. Fabozzi and J. C. Francis, "Beta as a Random Coefficient," *Journal of Financial and Quantitative Analysis*, March 1978.

[26] Rodney L. Roenfeldt, Gary L. Griepentrog, and Christopher C. Pflaum, "Further Evidence of the Stationarity of Beta Coefficients," *Journal of Financial and Quantitative Analysis*, March 1978, pp. 117–121. See also Gordon J. Alexander and P. George Benson, "More on Beta as a Random Coefficient," *Journal of Financial and Quantitative Analysis*, vol. 17, March 1982, pp. 27–36.

[27] Cheng Few Lee and Son N. Chen, "A Random Coefficient Model for Re-Examining Risk-Decomposition Method and Risk-Return Relationship Tests," *Quarterly Review of Economics and Business*, vol. 20, Winter 1980, pp. 58–69.

[28] G. J. Alexander, P. G. Benson, and C. E. Swann, "Random Coefficient Models of Security Returns: A Comment," *Quarterly Review of Economics and Business*, vol. 23, no. 1, Spring 1983, pp. 99–106. Cheng Few Lee and Son-Nan Chen, "Random Coefficient Models of Security Returns: A Comment," *Quarterly Review of Economics and Business*, vol. 23, no. 1, Spring 1983, pp. 106–109. Shyam Sunder, "Stationarity of Market Risk: Random Coefficient Tests for Individual Common Stocks," *Journal of Finance*, vol. 35, September 1980, pp. 883–896. Kenneth Garbade and Joel Rentzler, "Testing the Hypothesis of Beta Stationarity," *International Economic Review*, vol. 22, no. 3, 1981, pp. 577–587. Gabriel Hawawini, "Why Beta Shifts As the Return Interval Changes," *Financial Analysts Journal*, May–June 1983. Diana R. Harrington, "Whose Beta Is Best?" *Financial Analysts Journal*, July–August 1983, pp. 67–74. Meir I. Schnellr, "Are Better Betas Worth the Trouble?" *Financial Analysts Journal*, May–June 1983, pp. 74–77.

Firms which undergo drastic changes in their product mix, financial structure, and management team will probably experience changes in average return, standard deviation, and systematic risk. For the majority of firms, however, the probability distributions of returns are stationary enough that a rational investor should be willing to pay money to find out what they are. This does not imply perfect stability—just sufficient stability to make the information valuable for investment decisions.[29]

APPENDIX 10B

data for Standard & Poor's 500 Stocks Composite Index

In order to calculate characteristic lines, it is necessary to have rates of change in some market index. Table App. 10B-1 lists quarterly observations on Standard & Poor's (S&P) 500 Stocks Composite Index for several years. These data can be used to calculate the rates of price change or rates of return for the market.

The S&P 500 index is made up of 425 industrial, 20 railroad, and 55 utility stocks. It is like a portfolio of 500 different common stocks. The weight of each of these stocks is proportional to the total market value of the firm's outstanding securities.

The S&P 500 price index may be thought of as the price of a share of stock in a hypothetical portfolio. This price index is so constructed that from 1941 to 1943 it had a base value of 10. The percentage changes in the price index are good estimates of the average rate of price change for marketable common stocks listed on the New York Stock Exchange.

The quarterly dividend series is like a cash dividend paid on one of the hypothetical shares in the S&P 500 portfolio. It represents the weighted average cash dividend for all 500 shares in the portfolio. This dividend is divided by the S&P 500 price index to obtain the weighted average dividend yield for the 500 firms in the sample. This dividend yield is at an annual rate, that is, four times the quarterly rate.

[29] Evidence about the stability of the beta coefficient has been published; see R. L. Roenfeldt, G. L. Griepentrog, and C. C. Pflaum, "Further Evidence of the Stationarity of the Beta Coefficient," *Journal of Financial and Quantitative Analysis*, March 1978. In addition, suggestions have been offered about how to adjust beta coefficients in order to obtain more useful statistics. Kalman Cohen, Gabriel Hawawini, Steven Maier, Robert Schwartz, and David Whitcomb, "Estimating and Adjusting for the Intervaling-Effect Bias in Beta," *Management Science*, 1984. Elroy Dimson, "Risk Measurement When Shares Are Subject to Infrequent Trading," *Journal of Financial Economics*, 1979, pp. 197–226. Myron Scholes and Joseph Williams, "Estimating Beta from Non-Synchronous Data," *Journal of Financial Economics*, 1977, pp. 309–327. J. C. Francis, "Statistical Analysis of Risk Statistics for NYSE Stocks," *Journal of Financial and Quantitative Analysis*, December 1979, vol. 14, no. 5, pp. 981–997.

TABLE APP. 10B-1 Standard & Poor's 500 Stocks Composite Index rate of return data

year/ quarter	S&P begin of quarter	S&P end of quarter	S&P latest 12-month dividend	S&P quarterly dividend	S&P quarterly dividend yield, %	S&P quarterly price change rate, %	S&P total return, %	Risk-free rate, %
1974.1	97.68	93.25	3.44	.8600	.880	−4.53	−3.654	7.462
1974.2	93.25	86.02	3.50	.8750	.938	−7.75	−6.815	7.600
1974.3	86.02	63.39	3.59	.8975	1.04	−26.30	−25.26	8.268
1974.4	63.39	70.23	3.60	.9000	1.41	10.79	12.21	8.286
1975.1	70.23	82.64	3.67	.9175	1.30	17.67	18.97	7.336
1975.2	82.64	94.85	3.71	.9275	1.12	14.77	15.89	5.873
1975.3	94.85	82.93	3.71	.9275	.977	−12.56	−11.58	5.401
1975.4	82.93	90.90	3.68	.9200	1.10	9.61	10.71	6.337
1976.1	90.90	102.24	3.69	.9225	1.01	12.47	13.49	5.684
1976.2	102.24	103.59	3.76	.9400	.919	1.32	2.239	4.953
1976.3	103.59	104.17	3.85	.9625	.929	.559	1.489	5.169
1976.4	104.17	107.00	4.05	1.012	.971	2.716	3.688	5.169
1977.1	107.00	99.21	4.19	1.047	.978	−7.280	−6.301	4.698
1977.2	99.21	100.10	4.36	1.090	1.09	.897	1.995	4.624
1977.3	100.10	96.74	4.50	1.125	1.12	−3.356	−2.232	4.829
1977.4	96.74	93.82	4.67	1.167	1.20	−3.018	−1.811	5.472
1978.1	93.82	88.46	4.80	1.200	1.27	−5.713	−4.434	6.137
1978.2	88.46	95.09	4.91	1.227	1.38	7.494	8.882	6.408
1978.3	95.09	102.96	5.02	1.255	1.31	8.276	9.596	6.481
1978.4	102.96	96.73	5.07	1.267	1.23	−6.050	−4.819	7.315
1979.1	96.73	100.90	5.20	1.300	1.34	4.310	5.654	8.680
1979.2	100.90	101.99	5.34	1.335	1.32	1.080	2.403	9.358
1979.3	101.99	108.56	5.51	1.377	1.35	6.441	7.792	9.377
1979.4	108.56	105.76	5.65	1.412	1.30	−2.579	−1.278	9.631
1980.1	105.76	102.18	5.80	1.450	1.37	−3.385	−2.014	11.80
1980.2	102.18	114.93	5.94	1.485	1.45	12.47	13.93	13.45
1980.3	114.93	127.13	6.07	1.517	1.32	10.61	11.93	10.04
1980.4	127.13	136.34	6.16	1.540	1.21	7.244	8.455	9.235
1981.1	136.34	136.57	6.28	1.570	1.15	.168	1.320	13.71
1981.2	136.57	129.77	6.39	1.597	1.16	−4.979	−3.809	14.36
1981.3	129.77	117.08	6.52	1.630	1.25	−9.778	−8.522	19.61
1981.4	117.08	122.74	6.63	1.657	1.41	4.834	6.250	15.08
1982.1	122.74	113.79	6.72	1.680	1.36	−7.291	−5.923	12.02
1982.2	113.79	108.71	6.81	1.702	1.49	−4.464	−2.968	12.89
1982.2	108.71	121.97	6.85	1.712	1.57	12.19	13.77	12.35
1982.4	121.97	138.34	6.87	1.717	1.40	13.42	14.82	9.705
1983.1	138.34	153.02	6.91	1.727	1.24	10.61	11.86	7.935
1983.2	153.02	168.91	6.94	1.735	1.13	10.38	11.51	8.081

Quarterly observations of an empirical surrogate for the riskless rate are also shown in Table App. 10B-1. U.S. Treasury bills with 3 months to maturity were observed monthly, and then 3-months' yields were averaged to obtain the yield reported for the quarters.

part three

BOND VALUATION

Bonds are the simplest type of security on which to make a value assessment. And, most of the major risk factors affect bond investors. Chapters 11, 12, and 13 discuss the interaction between investment risk factors and bond valuation.

CHAPTER 11—*interest rate risk and bond valuation* shows how to determine a bond's economic value and how to measure its interest rate risk with mathematics. The basic valuation model furnishes the fundamental engine for the analysis:

> **Basic Valuation Model** The intrinsic economic value of a market asset is the present value of the future income.
>
> $$\text{Present value} = \sum_{t=1}^{T} \frac{\text{income}_t}{(1 + k)^t}$$
>
> where k is the appropriate risk-adjusted discount rate for the asset.

CHAPTER 12—*default and purchasing power risk in bonds* analyzes the effects of these two risk factors on bond values.

CHAPTER 13—*market interest rates* interprets empirical interest rate data within the economic theory of interest.

Chapters 11, 12 and 13 explain how to value bonds and also set the stage for the common stock valuation discussion of Chaps. 14, 15, 16 and 17.

bond valuation

In order to decide whether to buy or to sell a security, an investor must compare the security's market price with its value to determine if the security is over- or underpriced. The *value* of a bond is simply the present value of all the security's future cashflows.[1] The buy or sell decision can be made as soon as the value of the bond is known.

The buy or sell decision rules were introduced in Box 8-1, on page 196. In terms appropriate for both stocks and bonds, Chap. 8 explained how to use the present-value model (see Box 8-2, on page 196) to find the value of a security. The purpose of the present chapter is to show how to use the present value model to calculate the value of a bond, which is the simplest type of security to analyze.

Of all the different kinds of bonds in existence, the U.S. Treasury bond is the easiest to value, because there is presumably no chance that the U.S. Treasury will go bankrupt. Corporate bonds, which can go bankrupt, are a little more complicated to analyze. They are analyzed after the default-free Treasury bonds are examined.

Let us begin by considering the numbers that are used in the present value model.

11-1 THE PRESENT VALUE MODEL AND BOND VALUATION

Chapters 8 and 9 discussed the time value of money and interest rate risk and introduced the present value model. The present value formula is given again in Eq. (11-1*a*).

[1] This chapter presumes a knowledge of the present-value model which was explained in Chap. 9 under the heading Interest Rate Risk. See Mathematical App. A at the end of this book for present value tables.

$$\text{Present value} = \frac{\text{coupon}_1}{(1 + \text{interest rate})^1} + \frac{\text{coupon}_2}{(1 + \text{interest rate})^2} + \ldots + \frac{\text{coupon}_T + \text{face value}}{(1 + \text{interest rate})^T} \quad (11\text{-}1a)$$

The three terms that appear on the right-hand side of Eq. (11-1*a*) are discussed below.

Market interest rate: The interest rate, or discount rate, or yield to maturity, is an interest rate which changes constantly; thus, it must be obtained from current market reports.[2] Assume an interest rate of 10 percent (which is also stated as .10). The yield to maturity is represented by the symbol ytm.

Face value: The bond's face value (or principal value) and the time when it is due to be repaid (its maturity date) are printed on the bond and are fixed throughout the bond's life. Assume that a $1000 face value bond is to be repaid in 3 years (that is, $T = 3$).

Coupon: The coupon is the product of the coupon rate and the face value. The timing of coupon interest payments is also important. Assume a coupon rate of 6 percent; thus the bond pays $60 (equals $1000 times 6.0 percent or .06) on the last day of each year of its 3-year life.

Substituting the values assumed in the preceding paragraphs into Eq. (11-1*a*) yields the following formula:

$$\begin{aligned}\text{Present value} &= \frac{\$60}{(1 + .10)^1} + \frac{\$60}{(1 + .10)^2} + \frac{\$60 + \$1000}{(1 + .10)^3} \\ &= \$54.545 + \$49.586 + \$796.393 \\ &= \$900.52\end{aligned}$$

The present value calculation above suggests that the bond is worth $900.52. One of the convenient aspects of bond valuation is that everyone uses this formula; thus, everyone would agree that this bond is worth $900.52.

The information needed to use the present value formula to value a bond is easy to obtain. The bond's principal amount, its coupon interest payments, and the dates of these cashflows are all printed on the bond: They never change. The only difference of opinion likely to arise in valuing a bond is in selecting the appropriate interest rate to use for discounting the cashflows. At any given time, different discount interest rates are appropriate for different bond issues. These differences exist because different bonds have different risks of default, but default risk is an issue we will postpone until we discuss corporation bonds later in this chapter.

11-2 VALUING A RISKLESS BOND

There is a large, active market in U.S. Treasury bonds (which are different from the nonmarketable U.S. savings bonds). The prices of these marketable

[2] The effective interest rate for a bond is the same as the bond's yield to maturity. The yield to maturity is the discount rate that equates the present value of all the bond's future cashflows with the current market price of the bond.

pieces of the national debt vary from day to day; they are published daily in many newspapers. Figure 11-1 is an excerpt from a financial newspaper which shows the prices of marketable Treasury bonds.

The first column of the newspaper excerpt in Fig. 11-1 gives each bond issue's coupon interest rate. The coupon interest rate, denoted i, applies to the bond's face value. Many U.S. Treasury bonds are sold in \$1000 denominations; that is, their face value, denoted F hereafter, is \$1000. Thus, a \$1000 face value bond (that is, $F = \$1000$) which has a 3½ percent coupon rate (namely, $i = .035 = 3.5$ percent) pays \$35 interest [$iF = (3.5 \text{ percent}) \times (\$1000)$] per year every year until it matures and repays its principal of $F =$ \$1000 to its owner. The bonds' maturity dates are the year and month shown in the second and third columns of the newspaper excerpt.

The fourth and fifth columns in Fig. 11-1 give the bid (that is, the highest price a potential buyer has bid) and asked (that is, the lowest offering) prices stated as percentages of each bond's face value. The numbers to the right of the decimal places in the bid and asked prices are the number of thirty-seconds of one percentage point. For example, suppose the bid price of some bond is shown as 72.8 in Fig. 11-1. This refers to 72⁸⁄₃₂, or 72.25 percent of its face value; thus a \$1000 face value bond is bid at \$722.50. Similarly, a \$10,000 face value denomination is bid at \$7225. The sixth column is the change in the bid price since the close of the previous trading day. A change of +.4, for example, means the bid price is up four thirty-seconds of a percentage point over the previous day. The seventh column gives the bond's yield to maturity based on its current market price.

A bond's yield to maturity (ytm) can be interpreted as the bond's average compounded rate of return if the bond is bought at the current asked price and held until it matures and the face value is repaid. That is, the *yield to maturity* is the discount rate that equates the present value of all cashflows to the purchase price of the bond. (The ytm is called the internal rate of return in capital budgeting discussions.)

To show how to determine the value of a bond, a hypothetical U.S. Treasury bond like the 3½'s of 1998 will be analyzed.[3] This bond's present

[3] If the bond were purchased between the dates when the semiannual interest payments occurred, the seller would receive accrued interest from the party purchasing the bond. For example, if the bond were sold 3 months after a semiannual interest payment, the purchaser would pay the market price of the bond on that date plus half the \$17.50 interest earned but not yet received by the party selling the bond. For the sake of simplicity, accrued interest will not be discussed in this chapter. Ignoring the accrued interest introduces an approximation into the calculations.

The following formula is used in determination of accrued interest.

$$\text{Accrued interest} = \frac{\text{days since last interest payment}}{\text{days between last and next coupon payments}} \times \text{semiannual interest payment}$$

Note that the "days" are counted from the delivery date instead of the transaction date. For a more detailed discussion see Robert W. Kolb, *Interest Rate Futures,* Robert F. Dame Publishing, Richmond, 1982, pp. 76–79. Or, Sidney Homer and Martin L. Leibowitz, *Inside the Yield Book,* Prentice-Hall, Englewood Cliffs, N.J., 1972, Chap. 13. Or, see Marcia Stigum, *Money Market Calculations,* Dow Jones-Irwin, Homewood, Ill., 1981, pp. 87–105; the 1983 revised edition discusses this on pages 56–57.

Treasury Issues/*Bonds, Notes & Bills*

Representative mid-afternoon Over-the-Counter quotations supplied by the Federal Reserve Bank of New York City, based on transactions of $1 million or more.

Decimals in bid-and-asked and bid changes represent 32nds; 101.1 means 101 1/32. a-Plus 1/64. b-Yield to call date. d-Minus 1/64. n-Treasury notes.

Treasury Bonds and Notes

Rate	Mat.	Date	Bid	Asked	Bid Chg.	Yld.
9⅞s,	1986	Feb n	97.17	97.21	+ .2	11.75
14s,	1986	Mar n	102.28	103	+ .1	11.78
11½s,	1986	Mar n	99.18	99.22	+ .3	11.73
11¾s,	1986	Apr n	99.26	99.30	+ .2	11.79
7⅞s,	1986	May n	94.8	94.12	+ .2	11.74
9⅜s,	1986	May n	96.8	96.12	+ .2	11.87
12⅝s,	1986	May n	100.31	101.3	+ .2	11.89
13¾s,	1986	May n	102.18	102.22	+ .2	11.90
13s,	1986	Jun n	101.19	101.23	+ .1	11.89
14⅞s,	1986	Jun n	104.14	104.18	+ .1	11.94
12⅝s,	1986	Jul n	101	101.4	.....	11.93
8s,	1986	Aug n	93.17	93.21	+ .2	11.84
11⅜s,	1986	Aug n	99.4	99.8	+ .1	11.83
12⅜s,	1986	Aug n	100.20	100.22	+ .1	11.97
12¼s,	1986	Sep n	100.15	100.19	− .1	11.91
6⅛s,	1986	Nov	90.12	91.12	+ .7	10.74
11s,	1986	Nov n	98.7	98.11	.....	11.90
13⅞s,	1986	Nov n	103.11	103.15	.....	11.99
16⅛s,	1986	Nov n	107.16	107.20	+ .1	11.99
10s,	1986	Dec n	96.6	96.10	+ .4	11.90
9s,	1987	Feb n	93.27	93.31	.....	11.97
10⅞s,	1987	Feb n	97.21	97.25	.....	11.97
12¾s,	1987	Feb n	101.14	101.18	+ .1	11.98
10¼s,	1987	Mar n	96.3	96.7	.....	12.04
12s,	1987	May n	100.1	100.5	.....	11.93
12½s,	1987	May n	100.24	100.26	− .1	12.13
14s,	1987	May n	104.5	104.9	− .1	12.06
10½s,	1987	Jun n	96.8	96.12	.....	12.08
12⅜s,	1987	Aug n	100.20	100.22	.....	12.09
13¾s,	1987	Aug n	103.26	103.30	.....	12.10
11⅛s,	1987	Sep n	97.18	97.22	+ .1	12.06
7⅝s,	1987	Nov n	89.7	89.23	− .1	11.62
12⅝s,	1987	Nov n	101.6	101.10	+ .1	12.11
11¼s,	1987	Dec n	97.19	97.23	.....	12.12
12⅜s,	1988	Jan n	100.22	100.26	+ .2	12.07
10⅛s,	1988	Feb n	94.15	94.19	+ .2	12.11
12s,	1988	Mar n	99.20	99.24	+ .2	12.09
13¼s,	1988	Apr n	103.1	103.9	− .1	12.09
8¼s,	1988	May n	89	89.8	− .2	11.98
9⅞s,	1988	May n	93.9	93.17	− .1	12.12
13⅝s,	1988	Jun n	104.3	104.5	− .1	12.22
14s,	1988	Jul n	105.6	105.14	.....	12.17
10½s,	1988	Aug n	94.23	94.31	+ .1	12.16
15⅜s,	1988	Oct n	109.20	109.28	+ .3	12.22
8¾s,	1988	Nov n	89.13	89.21	+ .1	11.99
11¾s,	1988	Nov n	98.16	98.20	.....	12.18
14⅝s,	1989	Jan n	107.22	107.30	.....	12.20
11⅜s,	1989	Feb n	97.6	97.14	.....	12.14
14⅜s,	1989	Apr n	107.2	107.10	− .2	12.23
9¼s,	1989	May n	90.8	90.16	− .2	11.98
11¾s,	1989	May n	98.7	98.15	.....	12.19
14½s,	1989	Jul n	107.23	107.31	.....	12.26
13⅞s,	1989	Aug n	105.16	105.20	− .2	12.31
11⅞s,	1989	Oct n	98.19	98.27	.....	12.19
10¾s,	1989	Nov n	94.12	94.20	.....	12.19
12¾s,	1989	Nov n	101.22	101.24	− .1	12.25
10½s,	1990	Jan n	93.7	93.15	− .2	12.21
3½s,	1990	Feb	88.28	89.28	− .2	5.71
10½s,	1990	Apr n	93	93.8	− .2	12.21
8¼s,	1990	May	85	85.16	− .3	11.85
10¾s,	1990	Jul n	93.24	94	.....	12.22
10¾s,	1990	Aug n	93.25	94.1	.....	12.20
11½s,	1990	Oct n	96.24	97	+ .1	12.22
13s,	1990	Nov n	102.31	103.7	+ .3	12.24
11¾s,	1991	Jan n	97.21	97.29	+ .3	12.24
12⅜s,	1991	Apr	100.13	100.17	+ .4	12.25
14½s,	1991	May n	109.21	109.29	+ .2	12.28
13¾s,	1991	Jul n	106.10	106.14	− .4	12.33
14⅞s,	1991	Aug n	111.16	111.24	+ .4	12.30
14¼s,	1991	Nov n	108.27	109.3	+ .1	12.30
14⅝s,	1992	Feb n	110.25	111.1	+ .2	12.31
13¾s,	1992	May n	106.24	107	.....	12.31
4¼s,	1987-92	Aug	88.28	89.28	− .1	5.87
7¼s,	1992	Aug	76.30	77.14	.....	11.71
10½s,	1992	Nov n	91.2	91.10	.....	12.21
4s,	1988-93	Feb	89.4	90.4	+ .5	5.48
6¾s,	1993	Feb	73.17	74.1	+ .1	11.69
7⅞s,	1993	Feb	77.25	78.9	+ .1	12.06
10⅞s,	1993	Feb n	92.21	92.29	− .2	12.25
10⅛s,	1993	May n	88.22	88.30	+ .3	12.23
7½s,	1988-93	Aug	75.6	75.22	− .3	12.03
8⅝s,	1993	Aug	80.28	81.4	− .3	12.16
11⅞s,	1993	Aug n	97.22	97.30	− .2	12.26
8¾s,	1994	Aug	80.18	80.26	− .3	12.13
12⅝s,	1994	Aug n	101.31	102.3	− .5	12.25
10⅛s,	1994	Nov	88.2	88.10	− .3	12.16
3s,	1995	Feb	88.30	89.30	− .3	4.21
10½s,	1995	Feb	89.25	90.1	− .3	12.22
10⅜s,	1995	May	89.3	89.11	− .3	12.19
12⅝s,	1995	May	102.8	102.16	− .2	12.20
11½s,	1995	Nov	95.20	95.28	− .2	12.19
7s,	1993-98	May	66.26	67.10	+ .3	11.90
3½s,	1998	Nov	88.28	89.28	.....	4.47
8½s,	1994-99	May	75.15	75.31	− .3	12.03
7⅞s,	1995-00	Feb	70.27	71.3	+ .4	12.05
8⅜s,	1995-00	Aug	73.30	74.6	− .1	12.06
11¾s,	2001	Feb	97.3	97.11	+ .3	12.13
13⅛s,	2001	May	106.24	107	− .2	12.14
8s,	1996-01	Aug	71.2	71.18	+ .1	11.96
13⅜s,	2001	Aug	108.22	108.30	− .1	12.12
15¾s,	2001	Nov	125.8	125.16	+ .6	12.17
14¼s,	2002	Feb	115.10	115.18	+ .1	12.09
11⅝s,	2002	Nov	95.24	96	+ .4	12.18
10¾s,	2003	Feb	89.12	89.20	+ .2	12.18
10¾s,	2003	May	89.13	89.21	+ .5	12.16
11⅛s,	2003	Aug	92.3	92.11	+ .3	12.17
11⅞s,	2003	Nov	97.24	98	+ .2	12.15
12⅜s,	2004	May	101.17	101.25	.....	12.14
13¾s,	2004	Aug	111.27	112.3	− .1	12.13
8¼s,	2000-05	May	71.9	71.17	+ .2	12.01
7⅝s,	2002-07	Feb	66.20	66.28	.....	11.88
7⅞s,	2002-07	Nov	68.6	68.14	− .1	11.91
8⅜s,	2003-08	Aug	71.20	71.28	+ .2	11.96
8¾s,	2003-08	Nov	74	74.8	.....	12.05
9⅛s,	2004-09	May	76.22	76.30	+ .1	12.07
10⅜s,	2004-09	Nov	86.6	86.14	+ .2	12.11
11¾s,	2005-10	Feb	96.29	97.5	+ .2	12.11
10s,	2005-10	May	83.15	83.23	+ .1	12.07
12¾s,	2005-10	Nov	104.15	104.23	+ .3	12.13
13⅞s,	2006-11	May	113.8	113.16	− .1	12.10
14s,	2006-11	Nov	114.1	114.19	− .11	12.09
10⅜s,	2007-12	Nov	86.7	86.15	+ .1	12.07
12s,	2008-13	Aug	98.28	99.4	− .2	12.11
13¼s,	2009-14	May	108.31	109.3	+ .2	12.09
12½s,	2009-14	Aug	103.11	103.15	− .4	12.06

U.S. Treas. Bills

Mat. date	Bid (Discount)	Asked (Discount)	Yield
-1984-			
9-27	4.85	4.51	4.57
10- 4	9.81	9.75	9.91
10-11	9.88	9.80	9.98
10-18	9.84	9.78	9.98
10-25	9.69	9.63	9.85
11- 1	10.15	10.11	10.36
11- 8	10.16	10.10	10.37
11-15	10.14	10.08	10.37
11-24	10.25	10.19	10.51
11-29	10.26	10.22	10.56
12- 6	10.26	10.22	10.58
12-13	10.26	10.22	10.60
12-20	10.24	10.20	10.60
12-27	10.19	10,13	10.55
-1985-			
1- 3	10.18	10.10	10.54
1-10	10.19	10.13	10.59
1-17	10.25	10.17	10.66
1-24	10.27	10.21	10.72
1-31	10.28	10.20	10.73
2- 7	10.30	10.24	10.80
2-14	10.31	10.25	10.83
2-21	10.33	10.27	10.88
2-28	10.31	10.27	10.90
3- 7	10.30	10.24	10.89
3-14	10.31	10.27	10.95
3-21	10.28	10.24	10.94
4-18	10.26	10.20	10.91
5-16	10.28	10.22	10.97
6-13	10.28	10.22	11.01
7-11	10.33	10.27	11.12
8- 8	10.33	10.27	11.18
9-85	10.28	10.24	11.22

Source – Federal Reserve Bank.

FIGURE 11-1 price quotations from hypothetical newspaper for Treasury obligations.

value will be found, assuming that 6 percent is the yield to maturity; that is, the market yield of 6 percent will be used as the discount rate. The dollars of interest per year paid on the bond is i times F (that is, 3.5 percent × $1000), or $35 per year. This bond pays its 3½ percent coupon rate in semiannual payments of $17.50 when the face value F is $1000. Thus the bond's compounding interval, or "period," is 6 months. Assume that there are exactly twenty 6-month periods until the bond matures and the face value of $1000 is received. The appropriate market rate of return or discount rate is the bond's yield to maturity, ytm = 6 percent per annum, or 3.0 percent per 6-month period.[4]

The *discount factor* for cashflows received t periods in the future and discounted at the interest rate ytm is the quantity $1/(1 + \text{ytm})^t$. Present value tables (for example, Table A-1 in the Mathematical App. A at the rear of the book) contain the discount factors for a wide range of time spans and different rates of discount (or interest). The cashflows in the tth period, denoted c_t, are $c_t = \$17.50$ for periods $t = 1, 2, \ldots, 19$ half-years plus $c_{20} = \$1017.50$ when the bond matures at the end of 10 years. The present value of these cashflows is calculated in Eq. (11-1*a*). Mathematically, the problem is to find the present value, denoted p_0.

$$p_0 = \sum_{t=1}^{10 \text{ years}} c_t/(1 + \text{ytm})^t \qquad (11\text{-}1a)$$

Equation (11-1*a*) is restated to allow for semiannual payments.

$$p_0 = \sum_{t=1}^{20 \text{ half-years}} \$17.50/(1 + .03)^t + \$1000/(1 + .03)^{20} \qquad (11\text{-}1b)$$

$$= \$814.3475$$

The present value of $814.35 will be the asked price for the 3½ percent coupon U.S. Treasury bonds maturing in November 1998, assuming that there are twenty 6-month periods (or 10 years before maturity) if the market-determined yield to maturity is 6 percent. The market price of the bond should not deviate one single penny from its present value if the market interest rate equals the ytm of 6 percent and no other factors change.

In practice, a bond may actually be traded at any price between the bid and asked prices. The reason is that the actual yield may vary a few hundredths of 1 percent from day to day as the market rates fluctuate randomly from minute to minute. These hundredths of a percentage point are called *basis points*. Sometimes a basis point is lightly referred to as an "01." However, the teaching point has been made and is restated succinctly: Since all the cashflows from a U.S. Treasury bond investment are known in advance, the bond's value (and thus its market price) is determined by the market interest rates (that is, the yields to maturity). The bond's market price will not remain above its value because investors will sell and drive its price down until the

[4] The ytm's of 6 and 3 percent were assumed so that easy-to-find present value tables could be used to check the calculations.

	YEARS TO MATURITY															
yield	1	2	3	4	5	6	7	8	9	10	11	12	13	14	15	16
0.0	110.00	120.00	130.00	140.00	150.00	160.00	170.00	180.00	190.00	200.00	210.00	220.00	230.00	240.00	250.00	260.00
1.00	108.93	117.78	126.53	135.20	143.79	152.29	160.70	169.03	177.28	185.44	193.53	201.53	209.46	217.30	225.07	232.76
2.00	107.88	115.61	123.18	130.61	137.89	145.02	152.01	158.87	165.59	172.18	178.64	184.97	191.18	197.27	203.23	209.08
3.00	106.85	113.49	119.94	126.20	132.28	138.18	143.90	149.46	154.85	160.09	165.17	170.11	174.90	179.54	184.06	188.43
4.00	105.82	111.42	116.80	121.98	126.95	131.73	136.32	140.73	144.98	149.05	152.97	156.74	160.36	163.84	167.19	170.41
4.25	105.57	110.91	116.04	120.95	125.66	130.17	134.50	138.65	142.63	146.45	150.11	153.62	156.98	160.20	163.30	166.26
4.50	105.32	110.41	115.27	119.93	124.38	128.64	132.71	136.61	140.34	143.90	147.31	150.57	153.69	156.67	159.52	162.25
4.75	105.07	109.90	114.52	118.92	123.12	127.13	130.96	134.61	138.09	141.41	144.58	147.60	150.49	153.24	155.87	158.38
5.00	104.82	109.40	113.77	117.93	121.88	125.64	129.23	132.64	135.88	138.97	141.91	144.71	147.38	149.91	152.33	154.62
5.25	104.57	108.91	113.03	116.94	120.65	124.18	127.53	130.71	133.72	136.59	139.31	141.90	144.35	146.68	148.89	150.99
5.50	104.32	108.41	112.29	115.96	119.44	122.73	125.85	128.81	131.61	134.26	136.77	139.15	141.41	143.54	145.56	147.48
5.75	104.07	107.92	111.56	115.00	118.24	121.31	124.21	126.95	129.54	131.98	134.29	136.48	138.54	140.49	142.33	144.07
6.00	103.83	107.43	110.83	114.04	117.06	119.91	122.59	125.12	127.51	129.75	131.87	133.87	135.75	137.53	139.20	140.78
6.25	103.58	106.95	110.12	113.09	115.89	118.53	121.00	123.33	125.52	127.58	129.51	131.33	133.04	134.65	136.16	137.59
6.50	103.34	106.47	109.40	112.16	114.74	117.16	119.44	121.57	123.57	125.44	127.20	128.85	130.40	131.86	133.22	134.50
6.75	103.09	105.99	108.69	111.23	113.60	115.82	117.90	119.84	121.66	123.36	124.95	126.44	127.84	129.14	130.36	131.50
7.00	102.85	105.51	107.99	110.31	112.47	114.50	116.38	118.14	119.78	121.32	122.75	124.09	125.34	126.50	127.59	128.60
7.25	102.61	105.04	107.30	109.40	111.36	113.19	114.89	116.47	117.95	119.32	120.60	121.79	122.90	123.94	124.90	125.79
7.50	102.37	104.56	106.61	108.50	110.27	111.90	113.42	114.84	116.15	117.37	118.50	119.56	120.53	121.44	122.29	123.07
7.75	102.13	104.10	105.92	107.61	109.18	110.64	111.98	113.23	114.39	115.46	116.45	117.37	118.23	119.02	119.75	120.43
8.00	101.89	103.63	105.24	106.73	108.11	109.39	110.56	111.65	112.66	113.59	114.45	115.25	115.98	116.66	117.29	117.87
8.25	101.65	103.17	104.57	105.86	107.05	108.15	109.17	110.10	110.97	111.76	112.49	113.17	113.80	114.37	114.90	115.39
8.50	101.41	102.71	103.90	105.00	106.01	106.94	107.79	108.58	109.30	109.97	110.58	111.15	111.67	112.14	112.58	112.99
8.75	101.17	102.25	103.24	104.14	104.98	105.74	106.44	107.09	107.68	108.22	108.72	109.17	109.59	109.98	110.33	110.66
9.00	100.94	101.79	102.58	103.30	103.96	104.56	105.11	105.62	106.08	106.50	106.89	107.25	107.57	107.87	108.14	108.39
9.25	100.70	101.34	101.93	102.46	102.95	103.40	103.80	104.17	104.51	104.83	105.11	105.37	105.61	105.82	106.02	106.20
9.50	100.47	100.89	101.28	101.63	101.95	102.25	102.51	102.76	102.98	103.18	103.37	103.54	103.69	103.83	103.96	104.07
9.75	100.23	100.44	100.64	100.81	100.97	101.12	101.25	101.37	101.48	101.57	101.66	101.75	101.82	101.89	101.95	102.01
10.00	100.00	100.00	100.00	100.00	100.00	100.00	100.00	100.00	100.00	100.00	100.00	100.00	100.00	100.00	100.00	100.00
10.25	99.77	99.56	99.37	99.20	99.04	98.90	98.77	98.66	98.55	98.46	98.37	98.30	98.23	98.16	98.11	98.05
10.50	99.54	99.12	98.74	98.40	98.09	97.82	97.56	97.34	97.13	96.95	96.78	96.63	96.50	96.37	96.26	96.16
10.75	99.31	98.68	98.12	97.61	97.16	96.75	96.38	96.04	95.74	95.47	95.23	95.01	94.81	94.63	94.47	94.33

11.00	99.08	98.25	97.50	96.83	96.23	95.69	95.21	94.77	94.38	94.02	93.71	93.42	93.17	92.94	92.73	92.55
11.25	98.85	97.82	96.89	96.06	95.32	94.65	94.05	93.52	93.04	92.61	92.22	91.88	91.57	91.29	91.04	90.82
11.50	98.62	97.39	96.28	95.30	94.41	93.63	92.92	92.29	91.72	91.22	90.77	90.37	90.01	89.68	89.39	89.14
11.75	98.39	96.96	95.68	94.54	93.52	92.61	91.80	91.08	90.44	89.86	89.35	88.89	88.48	88.12	87.79	87.50
12.00	98.17	96.53	95.08	93.79	92.64	91.62	90.71	89.89	89.17	88.53	87.96	87.45	87.00	86.59	86.24	85.92
12.25	97.94	96.11	94.49	93.05	91.77	90.63	89.62	88.73	87.93	87.23	86.60	86.04	85.55	85.11	84.72	84.37
12.50	97.72	95.69	93.90	92.31	90.91	89.66	88.56	87.58	86.72	85.95	85.27	84.67	84.14	83.66	83.24	82.87
12.75	97.49	95.28	93.32	91.59	90.06	88.71	87.51	86.46	85.52	84.70	83.97	83.33	82.76	82.25	81.81	81.42
13.00	97.27	94.86	92.74	90.87	89.22	87.76	86.48	85.35	84.35	83.47	82.70	82.01	81.41	80.88	80.41	80.00
13.25	97.05	94.45	92.16	90.15	88.39	86.83	85.46	84.26	83.20	82.27	81.45	80.73	80.10	79.54	79.05	78.62
13.50	96.82	94.04	91.59	89.45	87.57	85.91	84.46	83.19	82.07	81.09	80.23	79.48	78.82	78.24	77.73	77.28
13.75	96.60	93.63	91.03	88.75	86.75	85.01	83.48	82.14	80.97	79.94	79.04	78.26	77.57	76.97	76.44	75.98
14.00	96.38	93.23	90.47	88.06	85.95	84.11	82.51	81.11	79.88	78.81	77.88	77.06	76.35	75.73	75.18	74.71
14.25	96.16	92.82	89.91	87.37	85.16	83.23	81.55	80.09	78.82	77.70	76.74	75.89	75.16	74.52	73.96	73.47
14.50	95.95	92.42	89.36	86.69	84.38	82.36	80.61	79.09	77.77	76.62	75.62	74.75	73.99	73.34	72.77	72.27
14.75	95.73	92.02	88.81	86.02	83.60	81.51	79.69	78.11	76.74	75.56	74.53	73.63	72.86	72.19	71.61	71.10
15.00	95.51	91.63	88.27	85.36	82.84	80.66	78.78	77.15	75.73	74.51	73.46	72.54	71.75	71.07	70.47	69.96
15.25	95.29	91.23	87.73	84.70	82.08	79.83	77.88	76.20	74.75	73.49	72.41	71.48	70.67	69.97	69.37	68.85
15.50	95.08	90.84	87.19	84.05	81.34	79.00	77.00	75.26	73.77	72.49	71.38	70.43	69.61	68.90	68.30	67.77
15.75	94.86	90.45	86.66	83.40	80.60	78.19	76.12	74.35	72.82	71.51	70.38	69.41	68.58	67.86	67.25	66.72
16.00	94.65	90.06	86.13	82.76	79.87	77.39	75.27	73.45	71.88	70.55	69.40	68.41	67.57	66.85	66.23	65.70
16.25	94.44	89.68	85.61	82.13	79.15	76.60	74.42	72.56	70.97	69.60	68.44	67.44	66.58	65.85	65.23	64.70
16.50	94.22	89.30	85.09	81.50	78.44	75.82	73.59	71.69	70.06	68.68	67.49	66.48	65.62	64.89	64.26	63.72
16.75	94.01	88.91	84.57	80.88	77.73	75.05	72.77	70.83	69.18	67.77	66.57	65.55	64.68	63.94	63.31	62.77
17.00	93.80	88.54	84.06	80.26	77.04	74.29	71.96	69.99	68.31	66.88	65.67	64.64	63.76	63.02	62.39	61.85
17.25	93.59	88.16	83.56	79.65	76.35	73.54	71.17	69.16	67.45	66.01	64.78	63.74	62.86	62.12	61.48	60.95
17.50	93.38	87.78	83.05	79.05	75.67	72.81	70.39	68.34	66.61	65.15	63.91	62.87	61.98	61.24	60.60	60.07
17.75	93.17	87.41	82.55	78.45	74.99	72.08	69.62	67.54	65.79	64.31	63.06	62.01	61.12	60.38	59.74	59.21
18.00	92.96	87.04	82.06	77.86	74.33	71.36	68.86	66.75	64.98	63.49	62.23	61.17	60.28	59.54	58.91	58.38
18.25	92.76	86.67	81.56	77.27	73.67	70.65	68.11	65.97	64.18	62.68	61.41	60.35	59.46	58.71	58.09	57.56
18.50	92.55	86.31	81.08	76.69	73.02	69.95	67.37	65.21	63.40	61.89	60.62	59.55	58.66	57.91	57.29	56.76
1875	92.34	85.94	80.59	76.12	72.38	69.26	66.64	64.46	62.63	61.11	59.83	58.77	57.87	57.13	56.51	55.99
19.00	92.14	85.58	80.11	75.55	71.75	68.57	65.93	63.72	61.88	60.34	59.06	58.00	57.11	56.36	55.74	55.23
20.00	91.32	84.15	78.22	73.33	69.28	65.93	63.17	60.88	58.99	57.43	56.14	55.08	54.20	53.47	52.87	52.37
25.00	87.41	77.46	69.60	63.38	58.48	54.60	51.53	49.11	47.20	45.69	44.50	43.55	42.81	42.22	41.75	41.38
30.00	83.74	71.45	62.16	55.13	49.81	45.79	42.76	40.46	38.72	37.41	36.41	35.66	35.09	34.66	34.34	34.09

FIGURE 11-2 sample page from book of bond tables for 10 percent coupon bonds.

price equals its present value. Similarly, the price will not be below the bond's present value because the price would be bid up until it equaled the present value by investors who know how to calculate bond values. These buying and selling pressures were illustrated in Box 8-1, on page 196.

11-3 A BOND'S YIELD TO MATURITY

U.S. Treasury bonds contain no default risk and offer no opportunity for growth in their contractual income; therefore, the default and growth factors do not affect their prices. However, the discount rate (or, equivalently, the yield to maturity, ytm) and the term to maturity T do vary and do affect the prices of Treasury bonds and other bonds. The following discussion shows how bond prices are affected by the discount rate and the term to maturity and how to calculate a bond's yield to maturity.

11-3.1 bond tables

Tables have been prepared to show the correct price for a bond of any given term to maturity and any appropriate market interest rate. Figure 11-2 shows the page from a book of bond tables for bonds with 10.0 percent coupon rates.[5] The values in this table show the percentage of face value for which bonds with a 10.0 percent coupon rate should sell if they are to yield the rate shown in the left column. Books of bond tables have a separate page for various rates of coupon interest. These books of bond tables have been the most popular way to find a bond's yield to maturity for decades. However, inexpensive hand-held calculators are available today that can quickly calculate an exact yield to maturity.

The values in Fig. 11-2 were calculated using Eq. (11-1*a*), as shown in the preceding example. By the use of bond tables, however, the tedious present value calculations may be avoided. The bond tables may be used for two problems. If the term to maturity is known, the bond tables can be used to look up (1) the bond price if the yield to maturity is known or (2) the yield to maturity if the market price is known.

11-3.2 solving the formula for a bond's yield to maturity (ytm)

When it is necessary to determine the yield to maturity of a bond, three methods may be used. First, if a bond table is available, the yield may be quickly and easily found for a given price and maturity. The second way to determine yields is more cumbersome. The *yield to maturity* for a bond is the discount rate which equates the present value of all net cashflows to the cost of the investment. Since the coupon interest iF, the face value F, the purchase price p_0, and the cashflows c_t are known quantities (that is, they are printed on the bond and written in the issue's indenture contract), Eq. (11-2*a*) may be solved for the only unknown value in the equation. The only unknown value in Eq. (11-2*a*) is the exact yield to maturity (ytm).

[5] Technically, bond tables are appropriate for corporate and municipal bonds but not for U.S. Treasury bonds; the number of days in the semiannual periods are counted slightly differently. However, the differences are worth considering only for transactions involving millions of dollars of bonds. This difference is the reason that calculated present values may differ slightly from the values found in the appropriate bond table.

$$p_0 = \sum_{t=1}^{T} \frac{\text{cashflow}_t}{(1 + \text{ytm})^t} \tag{11-2a}$$

$$= \sum_{t=1}^{T} \frac{iF}{(1 + \text{ytm})^t} + \frac{F}{(1 + \text{ytm})^T} \tag{11-2b}$$

It is difficult to evaluate a Tth root polynomial like those given in Eq. (11-1a) and (11-2a). Such Tth root equations are usually solved by a laborious trial-and-error procedure using different values of the discount rate until the one is found which yields the desired mathematical equality. Such computations may be expedited by using a calculator. Appendix 11A also gives two computationally efficient formulas to estimate the ytm.

Someone who invests in a coupon-paying bond will earn the yield to maturity promised on the purchase date if and only if all of the following three conditions are fulfilled.

1. The bond is held until it matures rather than being sold at a price which differs from its face value before its maturity.
2. The bond does not default on any of its cashflows. That is, the bond issuer pays all coupons and the principal in full at the scheduled times.
3. All cashflows (namely, the coupon payments) are immediately reinvested at an interest rate equal to the promised yield to maturity.

11-3.3 about the reinvestment rate

As mentioned above, a bond's yield to maturity is based on the assumption that all cashflows throughout the bond's life (namely, the coupon interest) are immediately reinvested at the yield to maturity. Of course, this assumption is not always true; the interest income might be consumed, for example, rather than reinvested. This is equivalent to reinvesting the funds at a zero rate of return, and the realized yield to maturity will be reduced accordingly by such disinvestments.

Table 11-1 illustrates the effects of different reinvestment rates on a bond's realized yield to maturity. The table shows the total realized compounded

TABLE 11-1 an 8 percent noncallable 20-year bond bought at 100 to yield 8 percent

	INTEREST ON INTEREST					
reinvestment rate, %	% of total return	amount, $	coupon income, $	capital gain or discount	total return, $	total realized compound yield, %
0	0	0	1600	0	1600	4.84
5	41	1096	1600	0	2696	6.64
6	47	1416	1600	0	3016	7.07
7	53	1782	1600	0	3382	7.53
8†	58†	2201†	1600†	0	3801†	8.00†
9	63	2681	1600	0	4281	8.50
10	67	3232	1600	0	4832	9.01

† Yield from yield book.

rate (that is, the effective yield to maturity) for an 8 percent coupon (i = 8 percent = .08) bond bought at face value 20 years before it matured. Table 11-1 shows that only 4.84 percent total yield to maturity is realized if the coupon interest is consumed instead of being reinvested. Essentially, the bond's yield to maturity is reduced by consuming the coupons rather than reinvesting them because the investor will not get to earn the *interest on the interest.* But the same bond has a realized total yield of 9.01 percent if the coupons are reinvested at 10 percent. This shows the importance of the reinvestment opportunities and highlights an often-ignored source of a bond risk: the *reinvestment rate risk* can cause a bond's realized yield to vary.

11-3.4 different bond yield and return measures

Discussions about bonds are complicated by the fact that every bond has different ways to measure its yield. More specifically, every bond has two ways to measure its yield and also two ways to measure its rate of return. These four different bond yield concepts are briefly compared and contrasted below.

1. *Coupon rate.* The coupon rate or nominal rate, denoted i, is that fixed rate of interest which is printed on the bond certificate. Coupon rates are contractual rates that cannot be changed after the bond is issued. (Coupon rates cannot be calculated for Treasury bills and other zero coupon bonds.)
2. *One-period rate of return.* The single period (for example, the 1-month or 1-year period) rate-of-return formula for a coupon bond is shown below. [Equation (11-3) can also be used to calculate the one-period rate of return for zero-coupon bonds like Treasury bills simply by putting a zero in for the coupon interest.]

$$r_t = \frac{\text{capital gain or loss} + \text{coupon interest}}{\text{purchase price}} \tag{11-3}$$

FIGURE 11-3 the relation between different yield measures for a 6% coupon bond.

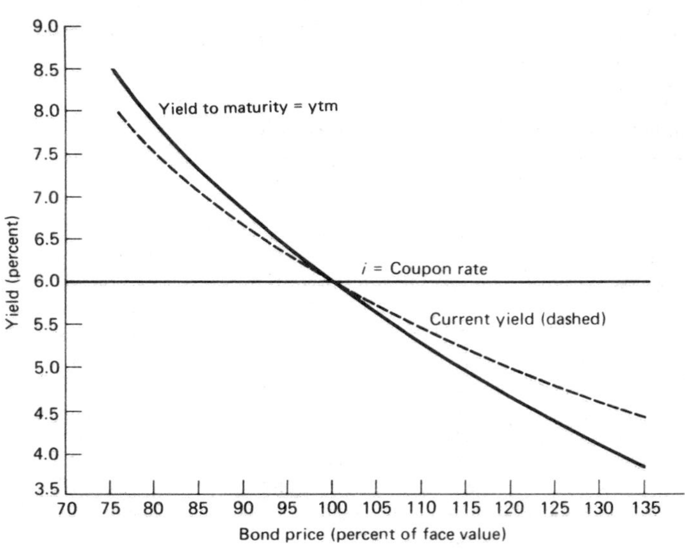

The one-period rate of return r varies from positive to negative in each period as the bond experiences capital gains and losses, respectively.

3. *Current yield.* Every bond that pays coupon interest has the current yield or coupon yield, defined below.

$$\text{Current yield} = \frac{\text{dollars of coupon interest per year}}{\text{current market price}} \tag{11-4}$$

For example, a 6.0 percent coupon bond with $1000 face value which is selling at the discounted price of $900 has a current yield of ($60/$900 = .0666 =) 6.66 percent. The current yield is an annual cashflow measure based on current market prices.

4. *Yield to maturity.* The internal rate of return or yield to maturity, designated ytm, of a bond is the discount rate that equates the present value of a bond's cashflows to the bond's current market price. The ytm is a compounded multiperiod effective rate of return that is earned if the bond is held to its maturity date and does not default.

Figure 11-3 illustrates how three of these four different interest rate measures interact with the market price of their related bond.[6] Figure 11-3 illustrates three price-interest rate relationships for a default-free bond with $1000 face value, 6.0 percent coupon rate, and 25 years until maturity. The one-period rate of return is not shown in this figure because it depends on both the beginning- and the end-of-period prices of the bond, which are not conveyed in the figure. Figure 11-3 depicts graphically the fact that the market price of a bond varies inversely with both its yield to maturity and its current yield.

Thus far we have only discussed one measure of a bond's *time dimension*—a bond's term (or time or years) to maturity. There is another, less obvious, time dimension to a bond—it is called the bond's *duration*.

11-4 MACAULAY'S DURATION (MD)

In 1938 F. R. Macaulay suggested studying the *time structure* of a bond by measuring its *average term to maturity,* or *duration,* as it is more commonly called.[7] A bond's *duration* may be defined as the weighted average number of years until the cashflows occur, where the relative present values of each cash payment are used as the weights. The formula for Macaulay's duration (MD hereafter) is given in Eq. (11-5).

[6] The mathematical relationship between the true yield to maturity and the approximate yield to maturity as well as the relationship between the current yield are examined by G. A. Hawawini and A. Vora, "On the Theoretic and Numeric Problems of Approximating the Bond Yield to Maturity," *Engineering Economist,* vol. 25, no. 4, 1980, pp. 301–325.

[7] F. R. Macaulay, *Some Theoretical Problems Suggested by the Movement of Interest Rates, Bond Yields and Stock Prices in the United States Since 1856,* National Bureau of Economic Research, Columbia, New York; 1938.

$$\text{MD} = \frac{\sum_{t=1}^{T} [c_t t/(1 + \text{ytm})^t] + FT/(1 + \text{ytm})^T}{v_0} \tag{11-5a}$$

$$\text{MD} = \frac{\sum_{t=1}^{T} t\left[\frac{c_t}{(1 + \text{ytm})^t}\right] + T\left[\frac{F}{(1 + \text{ytm})^T}\right]}{v_0} \tag{11-5b}$$

Weighted average maturity MD	=	Maturities (or time periods) of payments, t and T	×	Proportion of bond's value accounted for by the payment (in square brackets)

11-4.1 a numerical example

A small numerical example should clarify the duration calculations. Consider a hypothetical bond with the characteristics listed below:

Face value = F = \$1000

Yield to maturity = ytm = 6.0 percent = .06

Coupon rate = i = 7.0 percent = .07

Annual coupon payments = iF = .07 (\$1000) = \$70 = c_t

Number of years to maturity = T = 3 years

Market price = p_0 = \$1026.73

Premium over face = $p_0 - F$ = \$1026.73 − \$1000 = \$26.73

The present value of this bond is calculated with Eq. (11-1*a*) to obtain the value of \$1026.73 shown below. This bond's duration is calculated by using the numerical values from the present value calculations above inserted into Eq. (11-5). The 3-year bond's duration is 2.8107 years, as shown below.

As Eq. (11-5) and the computations above show, a bond's duration is simply the weighted average time which elapses until the bond's various cashflows are received, using the relative present values of each payment as a weight.

(1) year, t	(2) cashflow	(3) $1/(1 + \text{ytm})^t$	(4) = (2) × (3)
1	\$ 70	.9434 = $1/(1.06)^1$	\$ 66.04
2	70	.8900 = $1/(1.06)^2$	62.30
3	1070	.8396 = $1/(1.06)^3$	898.39
			\$1026.73 = v_0

(1) year, t	(2) present value of cashflow from column 4 above	(3) present value as proportion of v_0	(4) column 3 × column 1
1	\$ 66.04	.0643	.0643
2	62.30	.0607	.1214
3	898.39	.8750	2.6250
		1.0	2.8107 = MD

11-4.2 contrasting duration with years to maturity

In all cases, a coupon-paying bond's duration is less than or equal to its term to maturity (that is, MD $\leq T$). If a bond's only cashflow is made to repay the principal and interest on the bond's date of maturity, then the bond's term to maturity is identical with its duration. More succinctly, if $iF = 0$, then MD $= T$. However, as stated above, for bonds with periodic coupon interest pay-

BOX 11-1

the relationship between a bond's term to maturity and Macaulay's duration

The following theorems describe the relationship between Macaulay's duration (MD) and the number of years until a bond matures (denoted T):

MD THEOREM 1 A bond's duration equals its term to maturity if and only if it is a zero-coupon bond (that is, a pure discount bond) or a one-period coupon-bearing bond.

MD THEOREM 2 A coupon-bearing bond with a finite maturity of more than one period ($1 < T < \infty$) has a duration which is less than its term to maturity.

MD THEOREM 3 The duration of a perpetual bond (for example, British Consuls have $T = \infty$) is equal to [1.0 + (1.0/ytm)] irrespective of its coupon rate.

MD THEOREM 4 The duration of a coupon-bearing bond selling at or above its face (or par) value increases monotonically with its term to maturity and approaches the quantity [1.0 + (1.0/ytm)] as its term to maturity approaches infinity.

MD THEOREM 5 The duration of a coupon-bearing bond selling at a market price below its face value reaches a maximum before its maturity date reaches infinity and then recedes toward the limit [1.0 + (1.0/ytm)].

MD THEOREM 6 The duration of a coupon-bearing bond selling below its par (or face) value reaches its maximum value when T reaches the value indicated in Eq. (11-6) below.

$$T = \frac{1.0}{\log(1.0 + \text{ytm})} + \frac{1.0 - \text{ytm}}{\text{ytm} - i} + \frac{\text{ytm} - i}{i(1.0 + \text{ytm})^T \log(1.0 + \text{ytm})} \tag{11-6}$$

MD THEOREM 7 The duration of a coupon-bearing bond selling below par reaches its maximum at a maturity which is directly related to the bond's coupon rate and inversely related to the bond's yield to maturity.

MD THEOREM 8 The longer a coupon-paying bond's term to maturity, the greater the difference between its term to maturity and its duration.

The theorems above are illustrated in Fig. 11-4. These theorems were derived mathematically; see Gabriel Hawawini, "On the Relationship between Macaulay's Bond Duration and the Term to Maturity," *Economic Letters*, vol. 12, 1984.

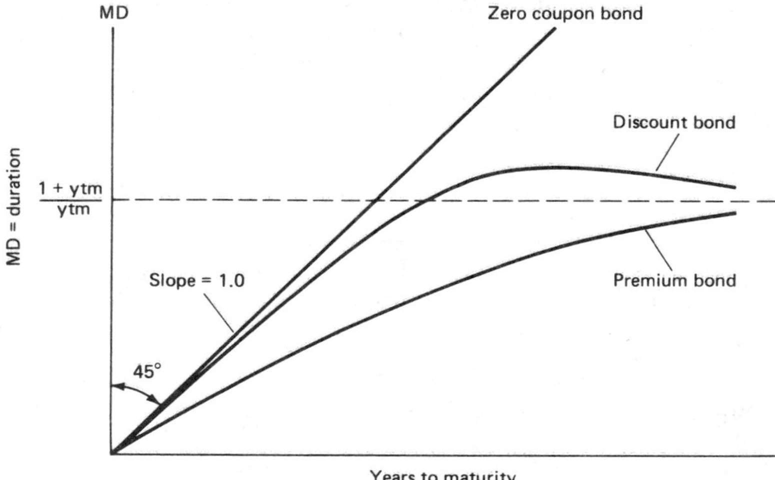

FIGURE 11-4 duration and term to maturity for premium, par, and discount bonds.

ments (which most bonds have) the duration of the bond will be less than the bond's term to maturity. In the numerical example above, for instance, the annual coupons of $70 caused the 3-year bond to have an average term to maturity or duration of 2.8107 years. Earlier and/or larger cashflows always shorten the duration (or average life) of a bond investment. Figure 11-4 illustrates the relationship between the term to maturity and the duration of a bond, and Table 11-2 shows the number of years' duration for several different bonds which are priced to yield 6.0 percent if held to maturity.

A bond's years of duration are considered to be a better measure of the *time structure* of an investment's cashflows than its years to maturity T, because the duration reflects the amount and timing of every cashflow rather than merely the length of time until the final payment occurs. Furthermore, Macaulay's

TABLE 11-2 bond duration in years for bond yielding 6 percent under different terms

years to maturity	VARIOUS COUPON RATES			
	.02	.04	.06	.08
1	0.995	0.990	0.985	0.981
5	4.756	4.558	4.393	4.254
10	8.891	8.169	7.662	7.286
20	14.981	12.980	11.904	11.232
50	19.452	17.129	16.273	15.829
100	17.567	17.232	17.120	17.064
	17.667	17.667	17.667	17.667

Source: L. Fisher and R. L. Weil, "Coping with the Risk of Interest Rate Fluctuations: Returns to Bondholders from Naive and Optimal Strategies," *Journal of Business,* October 1971, p. 418.

duration is a measure of the bond's *interest rate risk.*[8] An interest rate risk measure for bonds, called interest rate elasticity, and the relationship between a bond's elasticity and its duration are explained in the following paragraphs.

11-5 INTEREST RATE ELASTICITY (IE) AND INTEREST RATE RISK

Economists call a bond's price elasticity with respect to a change in the bond's yield to maturity its *interest rate elasticity.* Interest rate elasticity is denoted IE_{it} for the ith bond; it is defined in Eq. (11-7a).[9]

$$IE_{it} = \frac{\text{percent change in price for bond } i \text{ in period } t}{\text{percent change in yield to maturity for bond } i} \tag{11-7a}$$

$$IE_{it} = \frac{\Delta p_0/p_0}{\Delta \text{ytm}/\text{ytm}} < 0 \tag{11-7b}$$

A bond's interest elasticity will always be a negative number since a bond's price and its yield to maturity always move inversely. If the ith bond's yield to maturity, say, doubles during any time period, this percent change is a positive 100.0 percent (= +1.0), as shown below:

$$\text{Percent change in yield} = \frac{\Delta \text{ ytm}}{\text{ytm}} = 100.0\% = +1.0$$

If the bond's price simultaneously drops by 70 percent (that is, −.7 = −70.0 percent), then this bond's elasticity is a negative seven-tenths:

$$IE_{it} = \frac{\Delta\, p_0/p_0}{\Delta \text{ ytm}/\text{ytm}} = \frac{-70.0\%}{+100.0\%} = \frac{-.7}{+1.0} = -.7$$

A bond's elasticity of negative seven-tenths means that *any* percentage change in the bond's ytm will cause a simultaneous inverse percentage change in the bond's price which is seven-tenths as large.

11-5.1 how duration determines interest rate elasticity

A bond's price elasticity can be calculated directly with Eq. (11-7a). Alternatively, one can use the mathematical relationship between a bond's elasticity and its duration shown in Eq. (11-8) to find IE_{it} if MD_{it} is already known.[10]

[8] It has been shown that:

$$MD_{it} = \frac{dp_{it}}{p_{it}} \frac{-d(\text{ytm}_{it})}{1 + \text{ytm}_{it}}$$

M. H. Hopewell and G. G. Kaufman, "Bond Price Volatility and Term to Maturity: A Generalized Respecification," *American Economic Review,* September 1973, pp. 749–753; and R. A. Haugen and D. W. Wichern, "The Elasticity of Financial Assets," *Journal of Finance,* September 1974, pp. 1229–1240.

[9] The Greek letter delta Δ in Eq. (11-7a) denotes change.

[10] Equations (11-7), (11-8) and other insights were provided by Robert A. Haugen and Dean W. Wichern, "The Elasticity of Financial Assets," *Journal of Finance,* September 1974, pp. 1229–1240. See also J. R. Hicks, *Value and Capital,* 2d ed., Oxford, New York, 1965, p. 186.

$$(-1.0)\ \mathrm{IE}_{it} = \mathrm{MD}_{it}\ \frac{\mathrm{ytm}}{1 + \mathrm{ytm}} \tag{11-8}$$

Equation (11-8) indicates that anything which causes the ith bond's duration to increase (such as more years to maturity and/or a lower coupon rate) also increases the bond's elasticity. For example, increasing a bond's term to maturity tends to increase its duration as shown in Fig. 11-4, and therefore its elasticity is increased as shown in Eq. (11-8).

11-5.2 measuring a bond's interest rate risk

Interest rate risk may be defined as price fluctuations in a security caused by simultaneous changes in its discount rate (which is the yield to maturity for a bond). Thus, bonds with high levels of interest rate risk will experience larger price changes than bonds with less interest rate risk from any given change in the bond's yield to maturity.[11] A bond's elasticity measures its interest rate risk.

To show how a bond's percentage price fluctuations from any change in its yield are inexorably determined by the bond's elasticity, Eq. (11-7b) is rewritten as Eq. (11-9) below.

$$\left(\frac{\Delta p_0}{p_0}\right)_{it} = \mathrm{IE}_{it}\left(\frac{\Delta \mathrm{ytm}}{\mathrm{ytm}}\right)_{it} \tag{11-9}$$

Equation (11-9) is derived simply by solving Eq. (11-7b) for the instantaneous

[11] Bonds with high levels of interest rate risk will experience larger price changes than bonds with low levels of interest rate risk in all cases when the yield curve experiences parallel shifts. However, if the yield curve changes slope, then sometimes bonds with low levels of interest rate risk could experience the larger price changes.

FIGURE 11-5 market prices for a 3% coupon, $1000 face value bond at various maturities at 2%, 3%, and 4% discount rates (compounded annually).

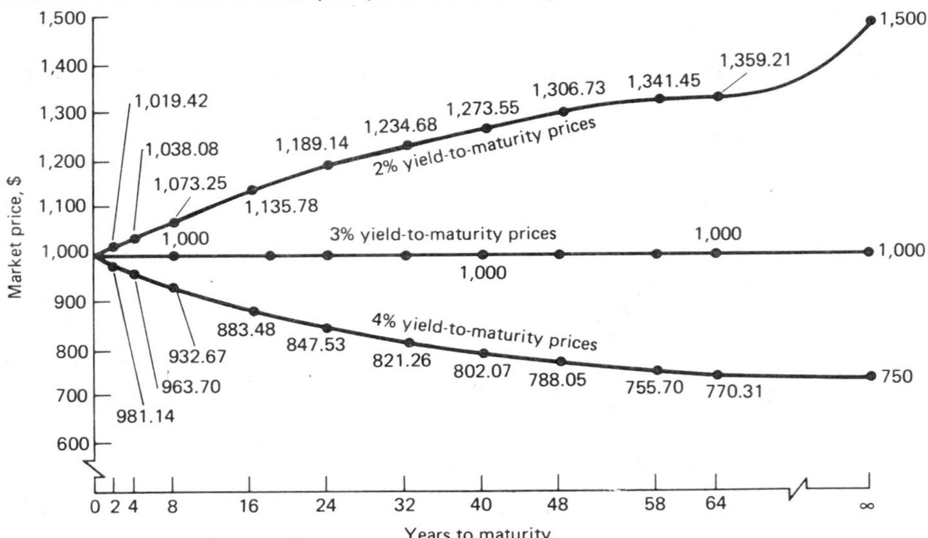

BOX 11-2
five bond price theorems

BP THEOREM 1 Bond prices move inversely against bond yields.[12]

BP THEOREM 2 For any given difference between the coupon rate i and the yield to maturity, the accompanying price change will be greater the longer the term to maturity T.[13]

BP THEOREM 3 The percentage price changes described in theorem 2 increase at a diminishing rate as T increases.

BP THEOREM 4 For any given maturity, a decrease in yields causes a capital gain which is larger than the capital loss resulting from an equal increase in yields.[14]

BP THEOREM 5 The higher the coupon rate i on a bond, the smaller will be the percentage price change for any given change in yields (except for 1-year and perpetual bonds).

percentage price change, denoted $(\Delta p_0/p_0)_{it}$. Equation (11-9) shows mathematically that, at the tth instant in time, the ith bond's elasticity will determine the size of its percentage price change when its yield to maturity changes.

11-5.3 bond price theorems

After learning about the interrelationship between a bond's term to maturity, its duration, and its elasticity, five bond price theorems can be introduced to summarize these interrelationships.[15] The five bond price theorems are shown in Box 11-2; these theorems can also be discerned from the definition of interest rate elasticity and also from Fig. 11-5.

Figure 11-5 illustrates the price analysis applied to a bond with a 3 percent coupon rate. The infinite number of different prices that a 3 percent coupon, default-free bond could assume when market interest rates (that is, the bond's yield to maturity) were 2, 3, or 4 percent are graphed over all possible terms to maturity. Figure 9-4, on page 219, shows the same analysis of a bond which has a 10 percent coupon rate at market interest rates of 9, 10, and 11 percent, for purposes of comparison.

[12] Taking the following partial derivative of Eq. (11-2a) furnishes proof of theorem 1.

$$\frac{d(p_0)}{d(\text{ytm})} = \sum_{t=1}^{T} \frac{-tc_t}{(1+\text{ytm})^{t+1}} < 0$$

This partial derivative must be negative in sign, because all the numerical quantities are positive, and thus the negative sign determines the derivative's sign. Similar differential calculus analysis of Eq. (11-2a) can provide proof of some of the other bond price theorems.

[13] BP theorem 2 is not true for very long-term bonds that are selling at a discount. However, theorem 2 is true for all other bonds, and it is not far from being true for the long-term discounted bonds. Considering the simplicity of the theorem, it contains enough valuable information to be worthy of study with the caveat about long-term discounted bonds in mind.

[14] This assumes yields change from the same starting value whether they move up or down.

[15] These theorems were derived formally by B. G. Malkiel, "Expectations, Bond Prices, and the Term Structure of Interest Rates," *Quarterly Journal of Economics*, May 1962, pp. 197–218.

Theorems 1 and 2 were explained in Chap. 9 at page 220 when interest rate risk was introduced. Theorem 3 is true because a bond's duration (and thus, its elasticity) increases at a diminishing rate as its term to maturity increases, as illustrated in Fig. 11-4. Theorem 3 (and several other theorems as well) can be discerned more directly from Figs. 9-4 and 11-5. Theorem 4 is true because the quantity ytm/(1.0 + ytm) in Eq. (11-8) changes more when the bond's yield to maturity decreases than it does when the bond's yield increases by any given amount (assuming both the increase and the decrease started from the same yield to maturity). As a result, the bond's elasticity (that is, interest rate risk) changes more when the bond's yield falls than when it rises by the same amount. And finally, theorem 5 is true because a bond with a high coupon rate (that is, larger cashflows early in the bond's life) will have a shorter duration, smaller price elasticity, and less interest rate risk than a bond which is similar in every respect except for a lower coupon rate.

11-5.4 price speculation with riskless Treasury bonds

The market prices published in Fig. 11-1 show that the market prices of U.S. Treasury bonds, which are the most risk-free assets in the world, vary significantly from their face values. For example, the U.S. Treasury's 8's of 1996 to 2001 were selling at the asked price of $715.625 per $1000 face value. This $715.625 price was deeply discounted below the bond's face value because market interest rates were high above the bond's coupon rate. If purchased for $715.625 and held to maturity, the bond offers a capital gain of ($1000 − $715.625) = $284.375. The bond can also be sold to another investor before it matures at whatever the market price is at that time. In any event, there is an opportunity for price speculators to profit by trading in U.S. government bonds. Consider the implications of the five bond price theorems for a bond price speculator.

As theorem 1 stated, the market prices of government bonds move inversely with interest rates. Equation (11-2*a*) shows mathematically and Fig. 11-5 illustrates graphically how this price fluctuation comes about. If a price speculator foresees a drop in market interest rates, he or she anticipates a rise in the market prices of Treasury bonds (and other bonds too). In this case, the speculator would buy (that is, take a long position in) marketable U.S. Treasury bonds. On the other hand, the speculator who expected a rise in interest rates would expect bond prices to fall. In this latter case, the speculator would sell marketable Treasury bonds short to profit from the expected price fall.

Theorem 2 states that the price fluctuations are larger in bonds which have longer terms to maturity. This is true for all bonds except a few long-term bonds selling at discounted prices. Figure 11-5 illustrates this graphically. However, it is difficult to discern the slight divergence from theorem 2 for the long-term discounted bonds (that is, the bonds that have ytms above their coupon rate). Speculators in bond prices should prefer long-term to short-term bonds for this reason, but theorem 3 implies that speculators need not go to the very longest term bonds to obtain large price fluctuations.

Theorem 4 implies that speculators can profit more by buying bonds (that is, taking a long position) during a decline in interest rates than by selling short during a period when an equal rise in interest rates (starting from the same level) is expected. Theorem 5 explains that bonds with small coupon rates will undergo larger capital gains (or losses) to attain a high (or low) yield to maturity than similar bonds with higher coupon rates because their prices are more volatile.[16]

11-6 IMMUNIZING AGAINST INTEREST RATE RISK

Duration is useful to financial managers, analysts, and economists; it measures both the time structure of a bond and the interest rate risk. Duration is a key concept in structuring a bond portfolio. One of the most popular applications of the duration measure occurs when a bond investor wants to use "immunization" in order to "lock in" an interest rate. Immunization will provide a compound rate of return over the period immunized that equals the portfolio's yield to maturity regardless of fluctuations in the market interest rates. An example is instructive.

11-6.1 immunization—the single bond case

Suppose that current interest rates are at an all time peak. Bond investors who expect market interest rates to fall in the future will want to buy bonds at the peak in interest rates for two reasons. First, as bond price theorem 1 explained, bonds will enjoy capital gains if their market interest rates do decline. Second, yields are most enticing and rewarding to bond investors at a time when market rates are high. So, bond investors who expect interest rates to decline attempt to buy bonds at the peak in interest rates, when their market prices are the cheapest.

Suppose that Ms. Carol Reed, controller of the Palmer Corporation, wanted to invest $1000 of Palmer's cash in a U.S. Treasury bond with a 9 percent coupon rate and face value of $1000 and suppose that this T-bond would mature in 10 years. Let us also assume that Ms. Reed needs exactly $1000 to pay a bill the Palmer Corporation has coming due in exactly 10 years. From our study of duration we learned that an investor like Ms. Reed cannot protect the Palmer Corporation from changes in interest rates with the purchase of a 10-year bond. Synchronizing the date when the $1000 bill must be paid with the date the $1000 bond matures will not assure the Palmer Corporation of having the correct amount of cash on hand to pay the bill. This surprising conclusion arises partly as a result of the reinvestment problem.

A reinvestment problem arises when the reinvestment of future coupon interest occurs at future market interest rates that are expected to be further and further below the original target yield if market rates decline as expected. Note from Table 11-3 that as interest rates shift and remain at their new levels for the rest of the 10-year period, the total "holding period return" on a 9 percent par bond due in 10 years varies significantly. The initial effect of a change in market interest rates appears in the value of the asset, a capital gain (or loss) occurs immediately.

After an initial change in interest rates that is presumed to occur right after

[16] Table 2-5 on page 42 shows the market prices of a Treasury bond as market interest rates varied.

TABLE 11-3 total return on a 9 percent, $1000 bond due in 10 years and held through various reinvestment rates

income source	reinvestment interest rate, %	HOLDING PERIOD IN YEARS 1	3	5	6.79*	9	10
Coupon income	5	$ 90	$270	$450	$611	$ 810	$ 900
Capital gain or loss		287	234	175	100	39	0
Interest on interest		1	17	54	105	191	241
Total return		$378	$521	$679	$816	$1,040	$1,141
(and yield)		(37.0%)	(15.0%)	(11.0%)	(9.0%)	(8.5%)	(8.2%)
Coupon income	7	$ 90	$270	$450	$611	$ 810	$ 900
Capital gain or loss		132	109	83	56	19	0
Interest on interest		2	25	78	149	279	355
Total return		$224	$404	$611	$816	$1,108	$1,255
(and yield)		(22.0%)	(12.0%)	(10.0%)	(9.0%)	(8.6%)	(8.5%)
Coupon income	9	$ 90	$270	$ 450	$611	$810	$900
Capital gain or loss		0	0	0	0	0	0
Interest on interest		2	32	103	205	387	495
Total return		$ 92	$302	$554	$816	$1,197	$1,395
(and yield)		(9.0%)	(9.0%)	(9.0%)	(9.0%)	(9.0%)	(9.0%)
Coupon income	11	$ 90	$270	$450	$611	$810	$900
Capital gain or loss		−112	−95	−75	−56	−18	0
Interest on interest		2	40	129	261	502	647
Total return		$ 20	$215	$504	$816	$1,294	$1,547
(and yield)		(2.0%)	(6.7%)	(8.5%)	(9.0%)	(9.7%)	(9.8%)

* Duration of a 9 percent bond bought at par and due in 10 years.

Source: Peter E. Christensen, Sylvan G. Feldstein, and Frank J. Fabozzi "Bond Portfolio Immunization," in Frank J. Fabozzi and Irving M. Pollack (eds.), *The Handbook of Fixed Income Securities,* Dow Jones-Irwin, Homewood, Ill., 1983, chap. 36, p. 808, exhibit 1.

the Palmer Corporation buys the $1000 T-bond, the remainder of the decade proceeds without further changes in market interest rates. However, as the decade progresses, the *interest-on-interest* component of a bond's total return exerts a stronger influence.[17] By the end of the decade, Table 11-3 shows that the interest on interest dominates the capital gain (or loss) in determining the bond's total return over the decade. This outcome makes sense. Capital gains occur quickly, whereas changes in reinvestment rates take time to exert their effect on the bond's total return gradually over the decade.

[17] To be more precise the interest on interest equals the interest on reinvested coupons plus interest on interest from interest on reinvested coupons.

Two opposing forces operate on the total return of a bond—first, interest on interest, and, second, the bond's market price fluctuations. After considering these opposing forces, the natural question to ask is: At some point in the future do the opposing forces of capital gain and reinvestment returns exactly equal or offset one another? More specifically, if market interest rates jump from, say, 9 to 11 percent and a capital loss occurs right after the $1000 T-bond is purchased, at what point in the future will that capital loss be made up by reinvesting the coupon income payments at the higher future interest rate of 11 percent? The two offsetting forces of capital value and reinvestment return exactly offset each other when the bond investment has been continuously maintained for the *duration* of the bond. In this case the 10-year T-bond's duration is 6.79 years. Stated differently, in order to earn the 9 percent target return, the original yield to maturity at the time of purchase, it is necessary to hold the bond investment for the period of its duration—6.79 years. In contrast, to lock in a market rate of 9 percent for a 10-year period, Ms. Reed must invest the Palmer money in a bond with a *duration* of 10 years. The time to maturity for a par bond with a duration of 10 years is approximately 23 years.

From Table 11-3 we note that the calculations are worked out for interest rate fluctuations as high as 11 percent and as low as 5 percent. The interesting point, however, is that as the interest rate fluctuates from 5 to 11 percent, the Palmer Corporation is still able to earn the 9 percent total return if the investment position is maintained for 6.79 years—the duration of the bond.

11-6.2 immunizing a bond portfolio

The objective of a portfolio manager who immunizes a portfolio is to totally eliminate the portfolio's interest rate risk. Immunization does not attempt to reduce any risk other than interest rate risk.

Immunization is said to exist if the total value of a portfolio of bonds at the end of some specified planning horizon is equal to the ending value the portfolio was expected to have when it was purchased. If the portfolio is fully immunized, the returns from it will be no less than the returns promised over the planned holding period at the time the investment was made. A simple example of a company that owns a two-bond portfolio should help clarify the meaning of this definition.

Consider again the hypothetical Palmer Corporation which is presumed to have a loan that is scheduled to be repaid in one lump sum 10 years in the future. However, let us increase the assumption about the size of the portfolio. Assume in the paragraphs below that the Palmer Corporation has a $200,000 debt coming due in 10 years that Ms. Carol Reed wishes to immunize by using $200,000 of the corporation's cash to purchase 200 T-bonds that have 10-year maturities and face values of $1000 each. Call the $200,000 liability the first item in the Palmer portfolio. Assume that the Palmer Corporation also has $200,000 in cash. Call this starting cash asset the second item in the company's portfolio of only two items. To invest the cash in the Palmer portfolio for 10 years without taking any chance of suffering losses because of interest rate risk, the firm might purchase a $200,000 zero-coupon default-free bond that matures in 10 years. If this default-free bond could be selected so that its maturity date occurred simultaneously with the due date of the outstanding $200,000 debt, it would be convenient for the Palmer Corporation. By matching the maturity date of an asset and a liability of the same size, Ms. Reed could eliminate all interest rate risk in Palmer's two-item portfolio. This is the simplest kind of portfolio protection or immunization against interest rate risk. The portfolio would be fully protected from interest rate risk for the 10 years until the $200,000 lump sum loan is repaid.

The example of the Palmer Corporation's two-item $200,000 portfolio is so simple that it is unrealistic. The example is unrealistic in the following three respects: (1) The needed zero-coupon bonds (or simply "zeros" as they are sometimes called) may not be available. This makes simply matching the maturity dates of assets and liabilities impractical. (And, if the asset is a coupon bond, its duration will be less than its term to maturity.) (2) It is typically impossible to find fixed-income assets of any kind that have maturity dates that synchronize exactly with the due dates of the existing liabilities. (3) Assets do not typically come in the exact denomination (such as $200,000) that equals the liability that is to be paid with the proceeds. As a practical matter it is usually necessary to construct a portfolio of coupon bonds which have differing maturity dates and different denominations. Solving the problems created by these three realities leads to the *duration-matching immunization strategy*.

THE DURATION-MATCHING IMMUNIZATION STRATEGY A portfolio of bonds can be immunized, essentially, by selecting the bonds in the portfolio so that the *weighted average* value for their Macaulay's duration (MD) exactly equals the duration of an equal-sized offsetting liability. For instance, if the Palmer Corporation had a $200,000 liability that was coming due in 10 years and had to be repaid in one lump sum, this liability would have Macaulay's duration of 10 years (that is, MD = 10 years) since no payments occur before the lump sum repayment date. The corporation's controller might immunize this $200,000 liability by purchasing two bonds which had a weighted average duration of 10 years and a combined value of $200,000 at their duration (as differentiated from their maturity). This transaction would fully immunize the $200,000 Palmer portfolio. The duration of a portfolio equals the dollar-weighted average of the durations of the bonds that make up the portfolio, as shown in Eq. (11-10).[18]

$$\text{MD}_p = \frac{V_1\,(\text{MD}_1) + V_2\,(\text{MD}_2)}{V_1 + V_2} \tag{11-10}$$

where

V_1 and V_2 = the dollar values of the two bonds in the portfolio

MD_1 and MD_2 = the two bonds' respective durations

MD_p = the weighted average duration of the two bonds in the Palmer portfolio

[18] Equation (11-10) is not exact, it is an approximation. Since the yield to maturity is an input to the duration calculation, every asset that has a different ytm will have its duration affected differently by a change in the level of the market interest rates. To be accurate in calculating the duration for a portfolio, the aggregate cashflows for the entire portfolio must be used to calculate the portfolio's duration.

It has been shown in Table 11-3 and elsewhere[19] that even if the market interest rates fluctuate up and down during the life of a portfolio, the portfolio can nevertheless be fully immunized against interest rate risk losses. This immunization operates as explained by Bierwag and Kaufman below.[20]

> If interest rates change after the bond is purchased, the investor is subject to two risks: (1) a price risk arising from the possibility of selling the bond at a price different from the amortized bond book basis and (2) a coupon reinvestment risk arising from reinvesting the coupons at interest rates different from the yield to maturity of the bond at the time of purchase. The impact of these risks on realized returns varies in opposite directions with changes in interest rates. Increases in interest rates will reduce the market value of a bond below its amortized basis but increase the return from reinvestment of the coupons. Conversely, decreases in interest rates will increase the market value of a bond above its amortized basis but decrease the return on the reinvestment of the coupons. In order for a bond to be immunized from changes in interest rates after purchase, the price risk and the coupon reinvestment risk must offset each other. It follows that duration must be the time period at which the price risk and the coupon reinvestment risk of a bond or bond portfolio are of equal magnitude but opposite in direction.

The duration-matching immunization strategy described in the preceding quotation converts a portfolio of assorted coupon-paying bonds into what is essentially a single zero-coupon bond with a maturity equal to the desired investment period. By thus keeping the weighted average duration of the assets equal to the duration of the liability, the bond portfolio manager is able to immunize the portfolio against interest rate risk.

"DURATION WANDERING" AND REBALANCING The duration of a bond will not move in one-to-one correspondence with the passage of time, as shown above in Fig. 11-4. Therefore, Ms. Reed, or any investment manager, must monitor and "rebalance" the bonds in a portfolio on an annual or as-needed basis in order to maintain the portfolio's duration at the value that will eliminate its interest rate risk. To illustrate, suppose the remaining life in the planning period for the Palmer portfolio has declined by a year—from a decade to 9 years. The duration of the original 10-year bond in the Palmer portfolio will have declined by less than a year—to approximately 9.2 years. To neutralize the risky effects of this "duration-wandering" tendency, Ms. Reed should rebalance the portfolio in order to match the duration of the bond with the remaining time in the planning period. *Rebalancing* the portfolio, in this case, would consist of selling off the original 10-year bond and buying a different

[19] Redington first showed how Macaulay's duration worked for the assets and liabilities of a firm in F. M. Redington, "Review of the Principle of Life Office Valuations," *Journal of the Institute of Actuaries,* vol. 78, 1952, pp. 286–340, which is reprinted in Gabriel A. Hawawini (ed.), *Bond Duration and Immunization: Early Developments and Recent Contributions,* Garland, New York, 1982. Fisher and Weil went on to show that a duration-matching strategy would almost perfectly immunize the value of a portfolio even though market interest rates fluctuated, see Lawrence Fisher and Roman L. Weil, "Coping With the Risk of Market Interest Rate Fluctuations: Returns to Bondholders from Naive and Optimal Strategies," *Journal of Business,* October 1971, pp. 408–431.

[20] Quotation from G. O. Bierwag and George G. Kaufman, "Coping With Interest Rate Fluctuations: A Note," *Journal of Business,* vol. 50, no. 3, July 1977, p. 365.

bond that had a shorter duration to keep the duration of the portfolio in line with the debt's maturity date. Left unchecked, unavoidable duration-wandering will cause the market value of the Palmer portfolio to fluctuate significantly in a fashion that may be costly. However, by monitoring and adjusting the portfolio's duration, Ms. Reed can immunize it in the face of multiple shifts in interest rates.

PROBLEMS WITH IMMUNIZATION Immunizing a portfolio of debts is not as simple as it may seem initially.[21] First of all, it is important not to forget that the duration of a bond portfolio and the remaining length of the investment period will decrease at slightly different rates with the passage of time. Figure 11-4 illustrates how a bond's duration does not decrease in a one-to-one correspondence with the passage of chronological time. As a result of the difference between decreasing time until a debt matures and the duration measure, the bond portfolio will need to be rebalanced periodically to keep its duration equal to the remaining term of the investment horizon. If the portfolio is not rebalanced periodically, an initially perfect immunization will become increasingly imperfect as time passes.[22]

Market interest rates fluctuate continually during every hour of every day. These fluctuations cause a second problem for portfolio managers who are endeavoring to immunize their portfolios. Since the yield to maturity is one of the determinants in every formula for duration, the changing yields to maturity which go on constantly in the financial markets cause fluctuations in bonds' durations. Dealing with these random and unexpected changes in the durations of the assets and liabilities in their portfolio causes a source of constant concern that portfolio immunizers refer to as "stochastic process risk." Essentially, *stochastic process risk* refers to uncertainty arising from the shape of and shifts in the yield curve. This stochastic process risk is a second problem which can render a fully immunized portfolio imperfect and in need of rebalancing.[23]

[21] "Pension Funds Switch to Bonds Helps Securities Firms but Isn't without Risks," *Wall Street Journal,* August 21, 1984.

[22] The experiences of different portfolio managers who are attempting to immunize their portfolios is discussed superficially by Diane Hal Cooper, "To Immunize, or Not To?" *Institutional Investor,* February 1982, pp. 89–94. A more scientific discussion of how to immunize by using interest rate futures is found in Robert W. Kolb, *Interest Rate Futures,* Robert F. Dame Inc, Richmond, 1982, pp. 164–180.

[23] Immunization, rebalancing immunized portfolios, and dealing with the "stochastic process risk" that results from changes in the yield curve that affect bonds' durations is all discussed in the following easy-to-read survey article. G. O. Bierwag, George G. Kaufman, and Alden Toevs, "Duration: Its Development and Use in Bond Portfolio Management," *Financial Analysts Journal,* July–August 1983, pp. 15–35.

The article discusses the implications of the definition of duration which explicitly recognizes the term structure of interest rates. The duration definition below, for example, which differs from the duration definition in Eq. (11-5), recognizes the term structure by appending a time subscript to each period's interest rate.

$$MD = \frac{\sum_{t=1}^{T} [c_t t/(1 + \text{ytm}_t)^t] + FT/(1 + \text{ytm}_t)^T}{v_0}$$

A third possible problem arises from future inflation rates, which could accelerate and create the need to increase certain liabilities (such as future pension fund payments) accordingly. However, if an immunization strategy has the investment assets that were purchased to meet the future liabilities shackled down to a specific rate of return, the future value of the offsetting assets may prove to be inadequate to fund the inflating future liabilities.

A fourth disadvantage of establishing an immunized portfolio is that the funds invested in bonds (or bondlike) assets cannot be invested in common stocks or other investments that may be more lucrative. If future common stock returns continue to exceed bond returns by as much as they have over past decades, the opportunity cost of high stock market returns that are lost by investing in an immunized portfolio could be significant.[24]

Finally, a fifth problem that some people cite as a reason not to immunize a portfolio is the default risk that occurs when bonds other than U.S. Treasury obligations are put into the portfolio. The introduction of default risk into a portfolio that is immunized against interest rate and funding risks is seen as being counterproductive. Municipal and corporate bonds can default and even become bankrupt and, in so doing, disrupt an otherwise effective immunization strategy.

Immunization is a new scientific tool that portfolio managers added to their box of work tools during the 1980s. Numerous researchers are laboring over further developments in the procedure.[25] Strategies already exist to overcome most of the objections listed above.

11-7 CHAPTER SUMMARY

The introduction to interest rate risk in Chap. 9 explained the present value model initially. The present chapter started by showing how to calculate the value of a default-free bond with that present value model. Then the yield to maturity was defined as the discount rate that equates the present value of a bond's future cashflows with its current market price. Different methods for obtaining yield-to-maturity estimates were discussed. The yield to maturity was then contrasted with other bond return and bond yield concepts.

In discussing how to deal with changes in the term structure of interest rates that cause "stochastic process risk" in measuring duration, the authors state (on their p. 15) that "the evidence suggests that the Macaulay measure of duration performs reasonably well in comparison to its more sophisticated counterparts and, because of its simplicity, appears to be cost-effective." However, readers who wish to learn more about this problem should read the survey article and the references it cites. In particular, see pp. 19–24.

[24] Table 7-4 on page 189 shows statistics comparing the long-run rates of returns from different categories of investment assets. In the long run common stock returns exceed bond returns so much that some investors may be well advised to avoid an immunized portfolio that yields a specified rate of return in favor of riskier but higher common stock returns. Adopting an immunization strategy is more desirable when high market interest rates can be locked in.

[25] H. Gifford Fong and Frank J. Fabozzi, *Fixed Income Portfolio Management*, Dow Jones-Irwin, Homewood, Ill., 1985, Chap. 6.

Macaulay's duration (MD) was introduced and defined as the average length of time that the funds remain tied up in an investment. The MD formula revealed that a bond's duration is simply the weighted average length of time until each cashflow is received, using each cashflow's relative present value as the weights. MD was shown to be a different measure of the time structure of a bond's cashflows than was the bond's term to maturity. Then a bond's interest rate elasticity (IE) was defined and shown to be a measure of a bond investment's interest rate risk. The exact mathematical relationship between MD and IE was reviewed to show that MD was also a measure of a bond's interest rate risk. MD was then used to create immunized portfolios to reduce the portfolio owner's interest rate risk.

QUESTIONS

11-1. What is the duration of a bond that has a yield to maturity of 6 percent and a perpetual maturity? British consols are an example of such bonds; these bonds are issued by the United Kingdom. They pay coupon interest forever, but the principal is never supposed to be repaid.

11-2. What is the relationship between a bond's coupon rate and its duration?

11-3. "It is possible for a bond portfolio manager to immunize the portfolio against any interest rate risk." True, false, or uncertain? Explain.

11-4. What happens to a bond's duration if the bond's yield to maturity rises?

11-5. "Duration does not correspond with the exact date of any particular cashflow that a default-free bond may experience. Therefore duration is a worthless measure of the time structure of a bond's cashflows." True, false, or uncertain?

11-6. Calculate the present value and duration of a bond paying an 8.0 percent coupon rate annually on its $1000 face value if it has 8 years until its maturity and has a yield to maturity of 9.0 percent. Show your computations. What is this bond's interest rate elasticity? (*Hint:* Read App. 11B for a simple formula to ease your computation.)

11-7. Reconsider the bond described in Question 6 above. If the bond's yield to maturity was 8.0 percent, what would be its present value? Duration? Elasticity? What can you conclude from this problem about the relationship between (*a*) the level of market interest rates and (*b*) interest rate risk?

11-8. Why do some of the Treasury bonds shown in Fig. 11-1 have more than one year listed under the Maturity heading?

11-9. Under what conditions would a bond's coupon rate be larger than its current yield? Explain.

11-10. What is the bid-asked spread for the 3½'s of 1998 listed in Fig. 11-1? Does anyone profit from this spread? Explain.

11-11. Would you prefer to invest in (*a*) a 10-year bond with a 4.5 percent coupon rate which is selling at 89.89 percent of its face value or (*b*) a similar 10-year bond which is selling at par and has a 5.85 percent coupon rate? Assume that both bonds are issued by the same firm and have the same provisions in every respect, except that their coupon rates differ. Explain why you

on behalf of its Pension Fund has sold

$450,000,000

of Equities as part of an Asset Restructuring Program and has purchased a Dedicated Portfolio of Fixed Income Securities totaling

$1,100,000,000

The undersigned assisted Chrysler Corporation in the execution of this program. The sale of Equities and the Purchase of Fixed Income Securities took place on July 19, 1984.

Salomon Brothers Inc

One New York Plaza, New York, New York 10004
Atlanta, Boston, Chicago, Dallas, London (affiliate)
Los Angeles, San Francisco, Tokyo (affiliate)
Member of Major Securities and Commodities Exchanges

FIGURE 11-6 tombstone from *New York Times* announcing that Salomon dedicated the Chrysler pension portfolio.

prefer one bond over the other. (*Hint:* Read App. 11A for computational shortcuts.)

11-12. Consider the tombstone from Salomon Brothers (Fig. 11-6). It appeared on p. D19 of the August 19, 1984, issue of the *New York Times*. Assume that Salomon's average commission rate on the common stock was ¼ of 1 percent to sell the stock and the previously owned bonds, plus another ¼ of 1 percent for all new securities purchased. How much in commissions did the Chrysler Corporation pay to dedicate its pension fund? (*Hint:* Read App. 11C to learn about dedicated-pension strategies.)

SELECTED REFERENCES

Bierwag, G. O., George G. Kaufman, and Alden Toevs, "Duration: Its Development and Use in Bond Portfolio Management," *Financial Analysts Journal*, July–August 1983, pp. 15–35. An easy-to-read survey of the research that led to duration as a useful tool for bond portfolio managers. Only a little elementary algebra is used.

Bookstaber, R., *The Complete Investment Book* (Scott, Foresman, and Company, Glenview, Ill., 1985). Chapter 8 explains immunization graphically, formulates the linear program problem to do immunization, and publishes a computer program written in BASIC language to perform the algorithm. See page 173 for further details about the computer program.

Fisher, Lawrence, and Roman L. Wiel, "Coping With the Risk of Market-Rate Fluctuations: Returns to Bondholders from Naive and Optimal Strategies," *Journal of Business,* October 1977, pp. 408–431. This study investigates the effectiveness of immunization in reducing interest-rate risk. Portfolio management with a shifting term structure of interest rates is simulated. Only elementary algebra is used.

Haugen, R. A., and D. W. Wichern, "The Elasticity of Financial Assets," *Journal of Finance,* September 1974, pp. 1229–1240. Algebra and differential calculus are used to derive both the duration and elasticity measure of interest rate risk from the present value model of security valuation. Bankruptcy risk is also considered in the analysis so that it is relevant for both stock and bond valuation.

Hopewell, M. H., and G. G. Kaufman, "Bond Price Volatility and Term to Maturity: A Generalized Respecification," *American Economic Review,* September 1973, pp. 749–753. Differential calculus is used to show that Macaulay's duration is a measure of interest risk for bonds.

APPENDIX 11A

bond valuation: calculating the yield to maturity expeditiously

This appendix explains how to calculate a bond's yield to maturity (YTM) quickly and with considerable accuracy.

If the bond analyst does not have the time to find the precise discount rate to fit into Eq. (11-2) (from page 293), an approximate yield to maturity can be obtained with fewer computations. Two easy-to-calculate approximation techniques are explained below.

APP. 11A-1 AN EASY-TO-UNDERSTAND FORMULA FOR YIELD APPROXIMATIONS

An intuitively logical method may be used to find a bond's approximate yield to maturity, denoted aytm. Equation (App. 11A-1*a*) defines this approximate yield-to-maturity formula.

$$\text{aytm} = \frac{\text{average capital gain or loss per year} + \text{annual coupon interest}}{\text{average investment}}$$

$$= \frac{[(F - p_0)/T] + iF}{(p_0 + F)/2} \qquad \text{(App. 11A-1}a\text{)}$$

T = number of years until the bond's maturity
p_0 = purchase price (or present value)
i = coupon interest rate per annum

For example, for a 3½ percent coupon bond maturing in 25 years, the approximate yield to maturity is calculated as shown below. Assume the market price is \$770 for a F = \$1000 face value bond.

$$\text{aytm} = \frac{(\$1000 - \$770)/25 + (.035)(\$1000)}{(\$770 + \$1000)/2} \qquad \text{(App. 11A-1}b\text{)}$$

$$= \frac{(\$230/25) + \$35}{(\$770 + \$1000)/2}$$

$$= \frac{\$9.20 + \$35}{\$885} = \frac{\$44.20}{\$885} = .0499 = 4.99\% \text{ approximate yield to maturity}$$

As pointed out previously, bond analysts and monetary economists who work with bonds regularly refer to 1/100 of one percentage point as a *basis point.* The error of 16 basis points calculated below is why Eq. (App. 11A-1*a*) is said to yield only approximations.

.0515	The bond's exact yield to maturity
−.0499	Approximation calculated in the example above
.0016	Error from example with Eq. (App. 11A-1*b*)

Equation (App. 11A-1*a*) may also be solved for P_0 and used to estimate the market price for a given yield to maturity.

Equation (App. 11A-1*a*) is easy to understand because it aligns with one's economic concept of the yield-to-maturity measure. The numerator is a measure of the average income per year, and the denominator is the amount of funds invested each year averaged over the bond's life. It seems intuitively correct to measure the yield to maturity by taking the ratio of these two quantities. Unfortunately, the intuitively pleasing Eq. (App. 11A-1*a*) produces answers that are only approximately correct.

APP. 11A-2 A BETTER YIELD-TO-MATURITY APPROXIMATION

Doctors Hawawini and Vora surveyed decades of work by various analysts and reported several formulas which yield better approximations to a bond's exact yield to maturity than does Eq. (App. 11A-1*a*) above.[26] Equation (App. 11A-2*a*) produces easy-to-calculate approximations which are quite close to the exact yield to maturity.

[26] Gabriel A. Hawawini and Ashok Vora, "Yield Approximations: A Historical Perspective," *Journal of Finance*, vol. 37, no. 1, March 1982, pp. 145–156 (see Eq. II.5) in table II).

$$\text{aytm} = \frac{[(F - p_0)/T] + iF}{.6p_0 + .4F} \qquad \text{(App. 11A-2}a\text{)}$$

where

i = coupon rate of the bond

T = number of years left until the bond matures

p_0 and F = purchase price and face value of the bond, respectively

Note that the numerators of Eq. (App. 11A-1a) and (App. 11A-2a) are identical—they both define the average income per year. The denominator of Eq. (App. 11A-2a), however, differs from that of Eq. (App. 11A-1a). The present value is given more weight in the denominator of Eq. (App. 11A-2a) than in Eq. (App. 11A-1a). Thus Eq. (App. 11A-2a) gives better estimates of the true ytm.

Using the same values employed above with Eq. (App. 11A-1a), an analogous numerical example calculated with Eq. (App. 11A-2a) is shown below.

$$\text{aytm} = \frac{(\$230/25) + \$35}{.6(\$770) + .4(\$1000)} = \frac{\$44.20}{\$862} = .0513 = 5.13\% \qquad \text{(App. 11A-2}b\text{)}$$

The error of 2 basis points from Eq. (App. 11A-2b) is smaller than the error of 16 basis points obtained using the same hypothetical values in Eq. (App. 11A-1a) above.

.0515	The bond's exact yield to maturity
−.0513	Approximate yield to maturity with Eq. (App. 11A-2b)
.0002	Error from Eq. (App. 11A-2b)

APP. 11A-3 COMPUTER PROGRAMS

Computer software to calculate the yield to maturity (ytm) can either be written, or it can be purchased commercially. One of the best software packages to calculate the ytm that is available commercially is sold for several hundred dollars by Software Arts Inc. It is called TK!Solver. Some colleges and corporations have the TK!Solver program available to be used cost-free.

Software Arts Inc. is a computer software company that is best known for its famous spreadsheet program named Visi-Calc that sold thousands of copies during the eary 1980s. However, Software Arts has other, completely different programs for sale too. TK!Solver is a computer program that does equation processing in a personal computer—on an IBM PC or on an Apple, for instance. TK!Solver solves Nth degree polynomials, trigonometric functions, and other complex equations for any single variable in the equation. Then the program will either save and/or print out the solution in various formats such as lists or graphs.

Dr. Richard Bookstaber has also written computer programs in BASIC language that calculate a bond's yield to maturity, present values at different selected discount rates, and the realized yield over a multiyear holding period if the bond is sold before it matures. These programs are listed in a book by Dr. Bookstaber entitled *The Complete Investment Book*, published and sold by Scott, Foresman, and Company of Glenview, Illinois.[27]

APPENDIX 11B

bond valuation: a more tractable expression for Macaulay's duration

Macaulay's duration can be restated in a mathematically equivalent formula that is easier to use. Thus, the intuitively clear, but computationally burdensome, Eq. (11-5) from page 296 is restated below as Eq. (App. 11B-1) to expedite calculations.

$$\text{MD} = \frac{i(1.0 + \text{ytm})\,(\text{ADF}) + T(\text{ytm} - i)\,(\text{DF})}{i + (\text{ytm} - i)\,(\text{DF})} \qquad \text{(App. 11B-1)}$$

where

DF = discount factor for ytm: $1.0/(1.0 + \text{ytm})^T$

ADF = annuity discount factor: $(1.0 + \text{ytm})^T/i$ = present value of a T period one-dollar annuity at the rate ytm

Substituting the numerical values from the example, on page 296, into Eq. (App. 11B-1) results in the following computation:

$$\text{MD} = \frac{.07(1.0 + .06)\,(2.673) - 3(.01)\,(.8396)}{.07 - .01\,(.8396)} = \frac{.173148}{.061604} = 2.8107$$

Comparing the value obtained above with the value obtained on page 296 reveals that identical solutions are obtained with Eqs. (11-5) and (App. 11B-1). But, using Eq. (App. 11B-1) is much easier than computing T different discounted cashflows and summing them as required by Eq. (11-5).[28]

[27] See chap. 2 of *The Complete Investment Book* by Richard Bookstaber, Scott, Foresman, and Company, 1985, Glenview, Ill. See page 173 of this book for more information about Bookstaber's computer programs.

[28] Equation (App. 11B-1) was derived by Professor Gabriel Hawawini in chap. 2: "On the Mathematics of Macaulay's Duration," of a book he edited: *Bond Duration and Immunization Early Developments and Recent Contributions,* Garland, New York, 1982. See also Jess H. Chua, "A Closed Form Formula for Calculating Bond Duration," *Financial Analysts Journal,* May–June 1984, pp. 76–78.

APPENDIX 11C

bond valuation: a dedicated-pension strategy

This appendix introduces the *dedicated-pension strategy*, a formal plan for bond investing that minimizes the funding risk for a portion of a defined benefit pension plan. Pension fund management is a big, sophisticated financial undertaking because pension funds are now and will continue to be the largest investors in the United States.

Dedication deals with duration and immunization considerations and goes on to address a broader range of portfolio objectives that concern pension fund managers. Dedicating part of a pension fund also involves synchronizing a pension fund's cash inflows and outflows, analysis of the pension fund's actuarially determined future liabilities, and attempts to reduce the corporation's cost of funding its pension obligations. A 1982 case involving the pension fund of a hypothetical company named the Palmer Corporation will be explained as a vehicle for the discussion.

There are two techniques for dedicating a portfolio: (1) multiple period immunization and (2) cashflow matching. The second method is more popular because it is the simpler of the two techniques.[29] The Palmer case discussed below is a case of cashflow matching.

APP. 11C-1 DETERMINING THE CORPORATION'S KNOWN PENSION LIABILITIES

The *first step* taken to establish a dedicated strategy for the Palmer Corporation's pension fund was to forecast the corporation's benefit payout obligations to the portion of its work force that is already retired in 1982. Table App. 11C-1 shows the year-by-year schedule of annual nominal dollar payments that the Palmer Corporation is legally obligated to make to its retirees over a 30-year period. Schedules of expected benefit payouts like Table App. 11C-1 are prepared by actuaries who consider the retirees' mortality projections, spousal benefits, and cost-of-living adjustments that may reasonably be expected in the future. Such schedules of actuarially expected pension obligations should be reviewed by external actuarial consultants to determine whether the assumptions on which the projections are based remain accurate and to extend the projections as a basis for new plans.

The Palmer Corporation's not-yet-retired workers comprise a larger potential pension fund liability than do its already retired workers. However, the Corporation's uncertain obligation to its not-yet-retired workers is not being funded by a dedicated bond portfolio. Uncertainty about the current workers' turnover rate, mortality rate, retirement age, future layoffs and hirings, and other factors make it difficult to estimate the Palmer Corporation's retirement obligation to its not-yet-retired workers. Therefore, only that $328,586,813

[29] For a more in-depth discussion of immunization see H. Gifford Fong and Frank J. Fabozzi, *Fixed Income Portfolio Management,* Dow Jones-Irwin, Homewood, Ill., 1985.

TABLE APP. 11C-1 Palmer Corporation's schedule of expected benefit payouts, 1982

year	payout amounts
1982	$ 8,067,461
1983	23,225,960
1984	22,444,547
1985	21,626,503
1986	20,776,913
1987	19,897,961
1988	18,994,617
1989	18,062,762
1990	17,117,618
1991	16,147,201
1992	15,163,588
1993	14,177,133
1994	13,188,631
1995	12,192,553
1996	11,224,388
1997	10,266,058
1998	9,338,069
1999	8,433,031
2000	7,575,599
2001	6,767,880
2002	5,996,468
2003	5,278,810
2004	4,604,799
2005	3,939,332
2006	3,439,599
2007	2,934,052
2008	2,497,460
2009	2,093,629
2010	1,748,721
2011	1,447,570
Total Liability	$328,568,813

Source: This example is adapted from Peter E. Christensen, Sylvan G. Feldstein, and Frank J. Fabozzi, "Dealing With High Corporate, State, and Municipal Pension Costs by 'Dedicating' a Bond Portfolio," in Frank J. Fabozzi and Irving M. Pollack (eds.), *The Handbook of Fixed Income Securities*, 1983, chap. 37, p. 283, exhibit 4, Dow Jones-Irwin, Homewood, Ill. 60430.

portion of the Corporation's total pension funding obligation that is easy to assess actuarially because it is comprised of known retirees is being committed to a dedicated pension strategy. A different corporation's management might have decided to dedicate more or less of its total pension obligation.

APP. 11C-2 SELECTING THE OPTIMUM PORTFOLIO OF ASSETS

After the actuaries have provided the Palmer Corporation with an estimate of its expected benefit payout obligations, as shown in Table App. 11C-1, the *second step* in the dedication procedure is to delineate whatever constraints the pension fund manager at the Palmer Corporation wants to place on the dedicated bond portfolio. That is, the pension fund manager must specify what quality of bonds from what sector of the bond market are to be purchased and dedicated to meeting the schedule of expected annual liabilities. The financial managers of the Palmer Corporation stipulated that they wanted only U.S. Treasury obligations in their dedicated bond portfolio; this is a simple investment constraint.[30]

The third and final step in establishing a dedicated-pension portfolio plan is to specify the reinvestment rate assumption to be used in planning for the cash inflows and outflows. This *third step* is much more important than it may seem, because the timing of cash receipts and disbursements frequently cannot be synchronized. In particular, if the selected reinvestment rate that the actuary approves is high enough, it may be advantageous for the pension fund manager to purchase bonds with high yields that mature before the date of the liability they were purchased to fund and then reinvest the maturing principal at the reinvestment rate for the short time until the liability comes due. Thus, we see that the reinvestment rate explicitly affects the optimum pension fund investment decisions.

High market interest rates of over 13 percent were available from U.S. Treasury bonds in 1982 when the Palmer pension portfolio was dedicated. After considering those investment opportunities Palmer's actuaries and auditors selected 13.08 percent as the appropriate reinvestment rate.

After the schedule of expected benefit payouts has been actuarially estimated in step one, the portfolio constraints have been laid down by the financial managers of the sponsoring corporation in step two, and the reinvestment rate has been selected and approved by the actuaries and the auditors in step three, the pension fund manager can set about structuring the least-cost dedicated-pension fund portfolio. Structuring a least-cost pension portfolio that will fully fund or defease the expected benefit payouts is a complicated task for which the pension fund manager will usually retain a financial consultant.

The financial consultant that structures the dedicated-pension portfolio will formulate the portfolio selection problem as a linear programming (LP) problem that is solved by computer. A linear program (LP) is a mathematical programming problem that employs linear equations and inequalities as constraints while it either maximizes or minimizes some objective that is also a linear equation, such as finding the least-cost way of funding a pension obligation over 30 years. This LP program must select for each year from among the numerous bond issues available the appropriate quantities of each issue that have maturity dates that precede the dates when the estimated pension payments must be made and also have the least cost when the income

[30] If the pension fund's managers were seeking higher rates of return, they might have stipulated a more complicated constraint. For example, more aggressive pension fund managers might stipulate that corporate bonds of AA grade or better quality ratings be selected, with a maximum of 20 percent of the portfolio to be invested in the bonds of foreign corporations.

Pragmatically speaking, the optimum portfolio is selected using a mathematical programming algorithm called *linear programming* (LP). The investment constraints thus determine what bonds the LP computer program is given from which to make its selection and what inequality or equality constraints are placed on the LP selection algorithm.

TABLE APP. 11C-2 the Palmer Corporation's dedicated-pension portfolio of U.S. Treasury bonds selected in 1982

par amount, in thousands of dollars	coupon rate	maturity date
673	11.125	8/31/82
3,000	12.125	10/31/82
3,000	14.125	4/30/83
3,000	15.500	10/31/83
2,600	13.875	4/30/84
3,200	12.125	9/30/84
3,000	13.375	3/31/85
3,100	15.875	9/30/85
2,600	14.000	3/31/86
3,200	14.875	6/30/86
3,900	16.125	11/15/86
2,900	13.750	8/15/87
3,100	12.375	1/15/88
3,200	14.000	7/15/88
3,000	14.625	1/15/89
7,800	14.500	7/15/89
2,000	10.750	8/15/90
3,000	13.000	11/15/90
4,600	14.500	5/15/91
9,400	14.625	2/15/92
3,100	8.625	8/15/93
2,900	9.000	2/15/94
2,000	8.750	8/15/94
2,700	10.125	11/15/94
5,300	10.375	5/15/95
2,400	12.625	5/15/95
12,000	11.500	11/15/95
2,900	8.500	5/15/99
3,300	7.875	2/15/00
3,800	11.750	2/15/01
12,000	15.750	11/15/01
8,700	14.250	2/15/02
2,500	11.750	2/15/10

Source: Peter E. Christensen, Sylvan G. Feldstein, and Frank J. Fabozzi, "Dealing With High Corporate, State, and Municipal Pension Costs by 'Dedicating' a Bond Portfolio," in Frank J. Fabozzi and Irving M. Pollack (eds.), *The Handbook of Fixed Income Securities*, 1983, chap. 37, p. 825, exhibit 5, Dow Jones-Irwin, Homewood, Ill. 60430.

from the reinvestments is considered.[31] Table App. 11C-2 shows the dedicated-pension portfolio selected to meet the needs of the Palmer Corporation by purchasing only round lots of bonds.

Structuring a dedicated-pension portfolio that has a high probability of meeting all the pensions' funding needs in every year usually requires that low-quality bonds that might default in the years ahead not be considered as

[31] Most colleges offer operations research, management science, or applied mathematics courses that explain how to formulate and solve linear programming (LP) problems.

potential investments. Callable bond issues and issues that are backed by large sinking funds should also not be included in the portfolio because they may be redeemed before their maturity dates. In addition, after a dedicated-pension portfolio is established, the quality of its assets should be reviewed and the portfolio rebalanced at least once per year.

APP. 11C-3 COMPARING CASH INFLOWS AND CASH OUTFLOWS

Table App. 11C-3 lists and compares the annual cash receipts and disbursements for the Palmer Corporation's dedicated-pension portfolio over the 30-

TABLE APP. 11C-3 summary of the Palmer portfolio's cashflow match

years	maturing principal	coupon income	reinvestment income	liability payments	surplus deficits	cumulative surplus
1982	673,000	2,503,309	8,049	−1,991,886	1,192,471	1,192,471
1983	6,000,001	17,225,743	136,890	−23,395,126	−32,493	1,159,979
1984	5,600,001	16,376,368	115,092	−22,639,894	−548,433	611,546
1985	6,200,001	15,589,118	125,441	−21,831,010	83,551	695,097
1986	8,900,001	14,747,806	139,292	−20,989,299	2,797,800	3,492,897
1987	6,800,001	13,347,306	223,511	−20,117,685	253,133	3,746,030
1988	6,300,001	12,442,307	181,143	−19,220,445	−296,995	3,449,036
1989	10,800,002	11,583,120	203,721	−18,295,716	4,291,127	7,740,162
1990	2,000,000	10,232,745	303,141	−17,353,893	−4,818,006	2,922,156
1991	7,600,001	9,822,745	240,129	−16,389,795	1,273,081	4,195,237
1992	9,400,002	8,273,371	419,266	−15,409,479	2,683,160	6,878,397
1993	3,100,001	7,585,997	266,296	−14,423,738	−3,471,445	3,406,952
1994	4,900,001	7,188,122	151,788	−13,435,751	−1,195,841	2,211,111
1995	10,400,002	6,745,935	282,143	−12,441,571	4,986,508	7,197,619
1996	12,000,002	5,066,373	980,330	−11,466,433	6,580,272	13,777,891
1997		4,376,373	763,687	−10,505,644	−5,365,585	8,412,306
1998		4,376,373	411,971	−9,570,064	−4,781,721	3,630,586
1999	2,900,000	4,376,373	161,191	−8,659,294	−1,221,730	2,408,856
2000	3,300,001	3,999,935	158,856	−7,789,960	−331,167	2,077,688
2001	3,800,001	3,646,748	174,601	−6,969,810	651,539	2,729,227
2002	20,700,003	1,858,624	1,076,967	−6,189,324	17,446,270	20,175,497
2003		293,750	1,261,810	−5,458,227	−3,902,667	16,272,830
2004		293,750	1,009,177	−4,773,300	−3,470,373	12,802,457
2005		293,750	780,738	−4,105,701	−3,031,213	9,771,244
2006		293,750	583,442	−3,564,531	−2,687,339	7,083,904
2007		293,750	408,293	−3,060,435	−2,358,391	4,725,513
2008		293,750	256,204	−2,606,610	−2,056,656	2,668,857
2009		293,750	122,502	−2,194,587	−1,778,335	890,522
2010	2,500,000	146,875	102,462	−1,834,878	914,459	1,804,981
2011			77,319	−1,522,835	−1,445,517	359,465
2012			4,150	−361,893	−357,743	1,721
Totals:	133,873,022	183,567,913	11,129,600	−328,568,813	1,721	

Source: Peter E. Christensen, Sylvan G. Feldstein, and Frank J. Fabozzi, "Dealing With High Corporate, State, and Municipal Pension Costs by 'Dedicating' a Bond Portfolio," in Frank J. Fabozzi and Irving M. Pollack (eds.), *The Handbook of Fixed Income Securities,* 1983, chap. 37, p. 826, exhibit 6, Dow Jones-Irwin, Homewood, Ill.

year planning horizon. In every year the cash receipts from maturing principal and coupon interest income almost exactly equals the cash outflow requirements specified by the actuary that were previously enumerated in Table App. 11C-1.[32] Since most of the portfolio's coupon income is being paid out shortly after it is received to fund the pension's liabilities, the portfolio is assuming very little reinvestment risk.[33] This also allowed the portfolio to lock in the high interest rates of over 13 percent that existed in 1982 when the portfolio was dedicated and thus benefit from these high-yield investment opportunities.

Table App. 11C-3 contains no bond price information because bond prices have nothing to do with the Palmer portfolio's annual cash inflows and outflows. The portfolio's default-free Treasury bonds are held until their maturity so that all coupon income and principal payments can be assumed to occur as expected in formulating the portfolio's LP problem. However, even if corporate bonds that suffered deteriorating quality ratings and the associated declines in their market prices were included in the portfolio, these price declines would not affect the cashflows in Table App. 11C-3 as long as the bonds' issuers punctually met all their scheduled coupon and principal payments.

APP. 11C-4 SAVINGS TO THE PALMER CORPORATION

Table App. 11C-4 lists the market prices that existed on August 2, 1982, for all the bonds listed in Table App. 11C-2. Note that the aggregate market value of all the bonds in the Palmer portfolio was $135,271,091 on that date. This amount was adequate to fully fund the total benefit payouts of $328,586,813 that are listed in Table App. 11C-1 if none of the bonds defaults. The average yield to maturity for the Palmer portfolio was 13.21 percent on August 2, 1982, reflecting the high yields available in the market on that date.

Table App. 11C-5 summarizes the potential benefits to the Palmer Corporation from dedicating part of its pension portfolio. These savings are predicated upon the willingness of Palmer's actuaries to raise their reinvestment rate assumption from the old 7.0 percent rate to the new rate of 13.08 that was current and appropriate on August 2, 1982. The portfolio's internal rate of return of 13.08 percent on August 2, 1982, was the appropriate reinvestment rate assumption based on the current market investment opportunities that could be locked in on that date. The actuaries had previously adopted the 7.0 percent reinvestment rate assumption in the years before the Palmer pension's funding risk was reduced by dedication of a portion of the pension portfolio.

At the old reinvestment rate of 7.0 percent the present discounted value of the Palmer Corporation's expected benefit payouts is shown in Table App.

[32] A large surplus of $17,446,270 was selected by the linear program (LP) for the year 2002 because there were no desirable Treasury bond issues available in the subsequent years.

[33] The linear program (LP) was formulated with a reinvestment rate assumption of 13.08 percent while the market yields on U.S. Treasury bonds were over 13 percent in 1982 when the Palmer portfolio was dedicated. As a result, the LP determined that the least-cost way to fund Palmer's pension liabilities was to lock in the high current rates rather than earn the lower reinvestment rate of 13.08 percent.

TABLE APP. 11C-4 pricing of the bonds in the Palmer dedicated bond portfolio*

bond name	face value, in thousands of dollars	coupon rate	maturity date	yield mat/call	price	market value
Treasury	673	11.125	8/31/82	9.86	100.065	704842
Treasury	3,000	12.125	10/31/82	10.49	100.317	3101458
Treasury	3,000	14.500	4/30/83	12.07	101.626	3159946
Treasury	3,000	15.500	10/31/83	12.65	103.129	3211411
Treasury	2,600	13.875	4/30/84	12.97	101.313	2726329
Treasury	3,200	12.125	9/30/84	12.85	98.623	3287422
Treasury	3,000	13.375	3/31/85	13.07	100.624	3153582
Treasury	3,100	15.875	9/30/85	13.41	106.126	3456679
Treasury	2,600	14.000	3/31/86	13.36	101.748	2767790
Treasury	3,200	14.875	6/30/86	13.39	104.374	3382276
Treasury	3,900	16.125	11/15/86	13.69	107.624	4331851
Treasury	2,900	13.750	8/15/87	13.40	101.250	3121229
Treasury	3,100	12.375	1/15/88	13.29	96.501	3009648
Treasury	3,200	14.000	7/15/88	13.40	102.378	3297253
Treasury	3,000	14.625	1/15/89	13.55	104.501	3155750
Treasury	7,800	14.500	7/15/89	13.50	104.379	8194975
Treasury	2,000	10.750	8/15/90	13.22	88.002	1859778
Treasury	3,000	13.000	11/15/90	13.29	98.498	3038360
Treasury	4,600	14.500	5/15/91	13.55	104.747	4961032
Treasury	9,400	14.625	2/15/92	13.55	105.624	10566399
Treasury	3,100	8.625	8/15/93	13.15	74.001	2418066
Treasury	2,900	9.000	2/15/94	13.09	76.002	2325135
Treasury	2,000	8.750	8/15/94	13.05	74.251	1566202
Treasury	2,700	10.125	11/15/94	13.15	81.747	2265643
Treasury	5,300	10.375	5/15/95	13.23	82.563	4493456
Treasury	2,400	12.625	5/15/95	13.21	96.373	2377763
Treasury	12,000	11.500	11/15/95	13.19	89.501	11035299
Treasury	2,900	8.500	5/15/99	12.91	70.001	2082755
Treasury	3,300	7.875	2/15/01	13.15	64.187	2238726
Treasury	3,800	11.750	2/15/01	13.28	89.499	3608092
Treasury	12,000	15.750	11/15/01	13.58	115.000	14204267
Treasury	8,700	14.250	2/15/02	13.38	105.999	9797030
Treasury	2,500	11.750	2/15/10	13.19	89.375	2370645
					Total Market value:	$135,271,091

* Prices as of August 2, 1982.

Average maturity: 1/15/93. Average coupon: 13.059 percent. Average yield: 13.21 percent. Internal rate of return: 13.08 percent.

Source: Peter E. Christensen, Sylvan G. Feldstein, and Frank J. Fabozzi, "Dealing With High Corporate, State, and Municipal Pension Costs by 'Dedicating' a Bond Portfolio," in Frank J. Fabozzi and Irving M. Pollack (eds.), *The Handbook of Fixed Income Securities,* 1983, chap. 37, p. 827, exhibit 7, Dow Jones-Irwin, Homewood, Ill. 60430.

11C-5 to be $190,184,656. Stated differently, Palmer's pension fund could have been fully funded in 1982 by putting $190,184,656 into the fund and reinvesting all cash inflows at 7.0 percent until they were disbursed. If the reinvestment rate were increased from 7.0 to 13.08 percent in 1982, however, only $135,271,091 would have been needed to fully fund the same expected

TABLE APP. 11C-5 report of the Palmer portfolio's reduced funding requirements

Total expected benefit payments	$328,568,813
Present value of total benefit payments (7% assumed)	$190,184,656
Portfolio cost (market value) (13.08% assumed)	$135,271,091
Potential savings	$54,913,565
Percent savings	29%

Source: Peter E. Christensen, Sylvan G. Feldstein, and Frank J. Fabozzi, "Dealing With High Corporate, State, and Municipal Pension Costs by 'Dedicating' a Bond Portfolio," in Frank J. Fabozzi and Irving M. Pollack (eds.), *The Handbook of Fixed Income Securities,* 1983, chap. 37, p. 828, exhibit 8, Dow Jones-Irwin, Homewood, Ill. 60430.

benefit payments. This 29.0 percent reduction from $190,184,656 to $135,271,565 is directly reflected in how much the Palmer Corporation is required to pay in cash to fund its legal pension fund obligation. The decrease of $54,913,565 is additional income for the Palmer Corporation that was attained by dedicating a portion of its pension fund in order to convince its actuaries to raise their reinvestment rate assumption.

why should the actuaries change their minds?

It may appear that the only reason the Palmer Corporation was able to save $54 million was merely that its actuaries arbitrarily changed their minds about what reinvestment rate assumption to use. This is an oversimplified interpretation of the facts that should be clarified. In truth, the higher reinvestment rate resulted from the Palmer Corporation's switch to a dedicated-pension strategy that reduced its funding risk by locking in high market rates that were available in 1982. The actuaries were willing to raise their reinvestment rate assumption to 13.08 percent because it was clear that the dedicated-pension fund had obtained 30-year default-free investments that safely yielded 13.08 percent.

Prior to adopting the dedicated-pension strategy in 1982 the Palmer Corporation had invested its pension funds in actively managed common stock investments. While the Palmer actuaries acknowledged that common stock investments average significantly higher rates of return than bond investments, they also knew that the common stock investments typically suffer much more variability of return from year to year than do the bond investments (as shown in Table 7-4, on page 189, for instance). As a result of the high risks associated with common stock investing, the actuaries decided that 7.0 percent was the average rate of return they should select in their conservative judgment to use as a reinvestment rate assumption for whatever portion of the Palmer pension portfolio was invested in common stocks. However, in 1982 when a $328,568,813 portion of the Palmer pension was committed to a dedicated-pension strategy that locked in the high 13.08 percent market yields for the next 30 years, the actuaries saw fit to adopt the higher 13.08 percent reinvestment rate assumption for this portion of the pension funds. The only investment risk that might deter the dedicated-pension funds from earning 13.08 percent return over the next 30 years was that the small portion of total portfolio income from reinvestment income might decrease if future market interest rates fell. But, even if this unfortunate outcome did occur, the reinvestment income was such a small portion of the dedicated-pension portfolio's total income that the portfolio's long-run goals would not be greatly reduced.

the benefits for the Palmer Corporation

Because the adoption of a dedicated-pension strategy allows the Palmer Corporation to fund its legal obligations to its retired workers with greater precision, the Corporation is able to enjoy the following five benefits.

1. Conservative low reinvestment rate assumptions (of 7.0 percent) can be replaced with conservative reinvestment rate assumptions that are much higher (13.08 percent, in this case).
2. Increasing the reinvestment rate assumption greatly reduces the present value of scheduled benefit payouts listed in Table App. 11C-1.
3. The Palmer Corporation can enjoy new options, such as reducing its annual payments into the pension fund or increasing employee retirement benefits.
4. Reduced pension funding requirements can relieve pressure on management to raise the income of the Palmer Corporation.
5. Dedication of the portion of its pension obligation owed to retired employees almost entirely eliminates the funding risk from that large part of Palmer's overall pension obligation. As a result, Palmer's future income and expense statements will not report such large and disconcerting fluctuations in its unfunded liabilities.

The benefits listed above are available to any company or governmental agency that has pension funding obligations to be funded, if the sponsor of the pension plan is willing to adopt a well-conceived dedicated-pension strategy. Furthermore, all dedicated-pension strategies need not be exactly like the Palmer Corporation's plan. Provision for more active portfolio management can be provided. Cost-of-living benefits can be included in the pension plans. Either fewer or more than the currently retired workers can be brought into a dedicated-pension fund. Moreover, financial futures contracts can be employed to immunize the dedicated-pension portfolio against interest rate risk.[34]

[34] Richard Bookstaber, *The Complete Investment Book,* published by Scott, Foresman and Company, Glenview, Ill., 1985. See chap. 8 about duration, immunization, and the linear programming formulation to immunize a bond portfolio. Bookstaber lists a BASIC language computer program to immunize a portfolio of bonds (pp. 91–94). The program may also be purchased from Dr. Bookstaber on a floppy disk, as explained on page 173 of this book.

default risk and purchasing power risk in bonds

Bond investors face several different kinds of risks. First, there is the *interest rate risk* which affects all bondholders every day as the market prices of all outstanding bonds move inversely to their market yields. Interest rate risk was introduced in Chap. 9 and discussed in more detail in Chap. 11. *Market risk* is a second risk factor to consider; it is caused by the fluctuations in market interest rates. Market risk was introduced in Chap. 9 and will be considered again, as it applies to bonds, in Chap. 13.[1] Unlike common stocks, the fluctuations in market interest rates are the most powerful driving force behind fluctuations in the market prices of bonds. Third, there is the *risk of default* and perhaps even bankruptcy. Default risk was introduced in Chap. 9. Fourth is *purchasing power risk,* which was also introduced in Chap. 9. Some additional aspects of default risk and purchasing power risk which are of special interest to bond investors are the subject of this chapter. Bond default risk is examined first.

[1] Market risk and interest rate risk are sometimes difficult to distinguish between when analyzing bonds. This separation is most easily seen with bonds by considering what happens when a bond's quality rating is raised and, simultaneously, market interest rates are pushed up by rising inflationary expectations. As a result of the increased quality rating, a bond's price tends to rise because bond prices move inversely with the lower bond yield that typically results from higher quality ratings. At the same time, however, the same bond's price may actually fall because inflationary expectations rose and drove up the general level of market interest rates enough to offset the tendency for the bond's price to rise because its quality rating was raised. In order to statistically measure interest rate risk separately from market risk, the arbitrage pricing theory (APT) is used. The APT, presented in Chap. 30, explains how different risk factors can be "extracted" by using factor analysis to "orthogonalize" them. The more subjective distinctions made between the default risk and the purchasing power risk factors in this chapter are established to set the stage for those who are endeavoring to conceptualize the nature of APT risk factors.

In 1975 investors who owned bonds issued by the W. T. Grant Corporation watched their investment fall into default.[2] Table 9-1, on page 214, shows the effect this default had on W. T. Grant investors month by month for the 3 years leading up to the actual declaration of bankruptcy. The general procedure used to develop bond quality ratings and the effect of bond ratings on the market prices of corprate bonds will be discussed in the following section.

12-1 DETERMINING CORPORATE BOND QUALITY RATINGS

Moody's Investor Services, Standard & Poor's (S&P), and Fitch's are the major firms that evaluate the default risk of bond issues and publish their quality ratings. As a matter of company policy, S&P rates practically all nonbank corporate bond issues of $5 million and over, whether or not the issuer requests it. For a fee ranging from $500 to over $1500, S&P will periodically reevaluate its rating and continually publish it year after year. Such continuing ratings make the bond issue easier to trade in the bond markets than if it were not continuously rated, so the issuer usually is glad to pay for this service that helps provide an active market for its own securities.

Figure 12-1 depicts the 12-step process followed at S&P in the development and maintenance of a bond issue's quality rating. It usually takes weeks to complete the process, although the process can be hurried if necessary to get a new issue ready for the market. After the background research is completed in steps 4 through 7, the quality rating to be assigned to a given issue is finalized in steps 8 through 11. The bond issue's quality rating is then released to the public in the last step.

Figure 6-7, on page 155, lists and defines S&P's various quality ratings. The bond rating procedures used at Moody's are similar to those used at S&P. The methods and results of different bond rating agencies are similar—that is, the ratings of any given bond issue by the different rating firms are usually identical. The next section explores the factors that determine corporate bond ratings.[3] There are two main considerations: the issuer's financial condition and the indenture contract that governs the issuing firm.

12-1.1 the issuer's financial condition

In Fig. 12-1, step 8 is where the rating agency decides what quality rating to assign. The most important pieces of financial information about the issuer that are considered are:

- The level and trend of the issuer's financial ratios
- The issuer's significance and size

[2] It can be shown that default risk is independent of interest rate risk (and related factors such as premiums, discounts, and years to maturity). H. Bierman and J. E. Hass, "An Analytic Model of Bond Risk Differentials," *Journal of Financial and Quantitative Analysis* (JFQA), December 1975, pp. 757–773. See also J. B. Yawitz, "An Analytical Model of Interest Rate Differentials and Different Default Recoveries," *JFQA*, September 1977, pp. 481–490.

[3] The Appendix to this chapter discusses the special financial ratios used to determine the quality ratings of municipal bonds.

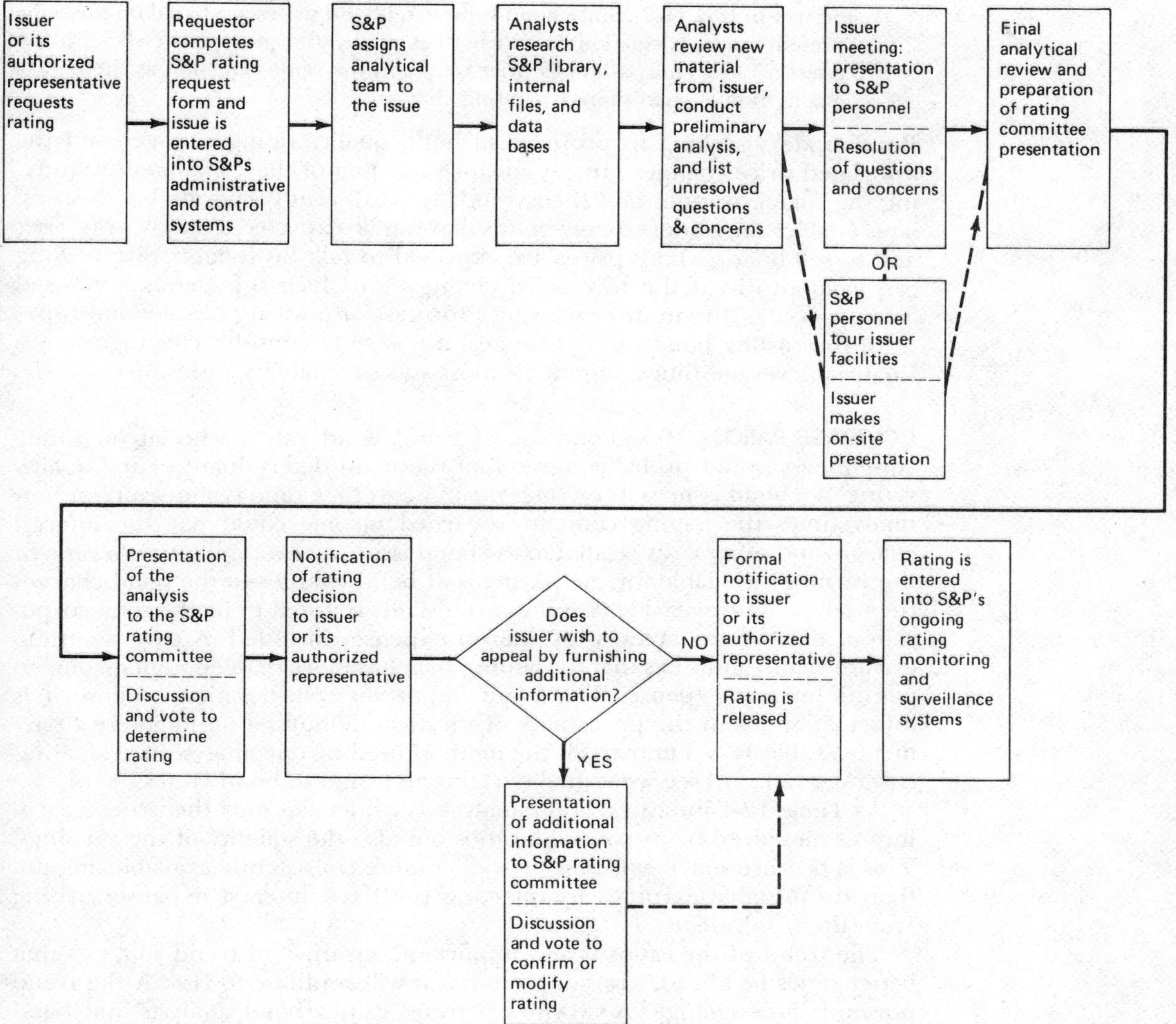

FIGURE 12-1 S&P corporate bond rating process flow diagram.

FINANCIAL RATIOS Here is an example of how a firm's financial ratios can affect the market prices of the firm's bonds:

1. The firm's coverage ratios fall (or rise), indicating an increased chance that the firm will (or will not) default on its bonds. As a result, the bond quality rating agencies lower (or raise) the rating they publish.
2. When a firm's quality rating falls (or rises), the appropriate interest rate to use in Eq. (11-1), on page 289, rises (or falls), as shown in Fig. 9-3, on page 217.
3. When the interest rate changes in the present value calculations, the bond's value moves inversely with the interest rate (as explained by bond price the-

orem 1 in Box 11-2). Since bond values and bond prices are based on the same present value calculations, bond market prices also move inversely with the interest rate. Thus, a bond's price moves in the same direction as the bond's quality rating when there is a rating change.

Bond traders seeking to profit from bond quality rating changes and the associated price changes can get advance warning of these changes by studying the financial ratios and their trends for different corporate bond issues. This enables the traders to buy bonds that can be expected to enjoy price rises and to sell bonds whose prices are expected to fall. Such aggressive trading can yield profits if the forecasted changes on which the trends are based actually occur. But an investor whose forecasts are wrong can go bankrupt.

In forecasting bond rating changes, it is wise to consider coverage ratios, financial leverage ratios, liquidity ratios, and profitability ratios.

COVERAGE RATIOS Most bond analysts and bond raters who sit on rating committees would probably agree that the main determinant of the quality rating of a bond issue is its *coverage ratio*. A coverage ratio is a measure of how many times the issuing company's earned income could pay the interest charges and other costs related to the bond issue. A coverage ratio is a ratio of the earnings available for the payment of bond charges to the bond charges themselves. The available earnings are usually defined to be the total corporate income before taxes, with interest expenses included. A coverage ratio greater than 1 indicates that the issuing firm has more than enough income to pay its interest expense. This is an important consideration because it is information about the probability of the firm defaulting on its interest payments. Table 12-1 summarizes the method used by one analyst in evaluating coverage ratios to see what quality rating to assign to bond issues.

As Table 12-1 indicates, bond analysts consider not only the issuer's earnings as measured by its coverage ratios but also the stability of the earnings. This is because stable earnings provide a more consistently available amount than do unstable earnings for meeting the fixed interest expenses arising from the firm's debts.

The trend of the ratios is also important. An upward trend suggests that better times lie ahead, assuming the ratios will continue to rise. A flat trend portends little change. A downward trend causes bond analysts and bond

TABLE 12-1 coverage ratios and quality ratings

coverage ratio	stability of earnings	relative quality
6 and over	Cyclical	Very high
4 and over	Stable	Very high
3 to 6	Cyclical	Medium to high
2 to 4	Stable	Medium to high
Under 3	Cyclical	Low
Under 2	Stable	Low

Source: Jerome B. Cohen, Edward D. Zinbarg, and Arthur Zeikel, *Investment Analysis and Portfolio Management*, 4th ed., R. D. Irwin, Homewood, Ill., 1982, p. 481.

raters who project the decline into future years to warn potential investors that troubled times may lie ahead and to suggest lower quality ratings for the bond issuer.

Different bond analysts may compute coverage ratios differently. For instance, the coverage ratios may be calculated on income on a before-tax or an after-tax basis. Or, some bond analysts may prefer to include lease payments and sinking fund payments with interest payments and calculate a ratio called the *times fixed charges earned ratio*. Such changes would lower the ratios in Table 12-1, since including taxes and lease and/or sinking fund payments lowers a firm's ratios if everything else remains unchanged.

A low times interest earned ratio may be the result of two causes. First, earnings may be too low. If so, the firm's poor profitability would also show up as low rates of return on assets and as rates of return on equity that are below those of most other firms. Second, the firm may be too deeply in debt and thus incur too much interest expense. If so, this will also show up as high financial leverage ratios. The section below explains financial leverage ratios.

FINANCIAL LEVERAGE RATIOS Companies that use borrowed funds (rather than the owner's equity) to expand are said to be using *financial leverage*. Ideally, money will be borrowed at a low interest rate and reinvested within the firm at a rate of return that exceeds the interest rate on the debt: the difference is profit. It is possible, however, for a firm to get too deeply into debt. If a firm uses too much financial leverage (that is, borrows too much), its fixed interest expense will grow to such a high level that if profits fall even slightly, the firm will not be earning enough to pay its contractual interest expense. This can lead quickly to bankruptcy; that is why bond investors are interested in evaluating the indebtedness of issuing firms.

Three of the most popular ratios used to measure financial leverage are the total debt to equity ratio, the long-term debt to capitalization ratio, and the long-term debt to equity ratio. The terms used in these three ratios are standard items from a firm's balance sheet, except for capitalization, a financial term that accountants no longer employ in their statements. A firm's *capitalization* is the total short-term debt (except current liabilities), long-term debt, and equity (or net worth)—that is, the capital funds committed to the firm.[4]

Each bond analyst usually has a favorite leverage ratio, though most bond analysts use more than one leverage ratio in order to assess the firm's level of indebtedness from different perspectives. The above ratios tend to increase or decrease together as a firm uses more or less, respectively, borrowed money.

Certain problems arise with the use of financial leverage ratios. Some of these problems relate to what is called off-balance-sheet debt. The items used

[4] There is no one sacrosanct definition of a firm's capitalization. The definition varies substantially from industry to industry, but also, to a lesser degree, from one financial executive to the next. These disagreements are not all taken lightly. In enforcing capital adequacy requirements on banks, bank examiners get into heated discussions with bankers—because the stakes are high.

to calculate the ratios above may ignore guarantees made by the firm and other types of long-term liabilities that do not normally appear on balance sheets. This results in understated leverage ratios. Some financial analysts simply ignore this problem. However, most analysts handle the problem by adding an amount to the firm's liabilities equal to the present value of its future lease payments and other off-balance-sheet debt. A difficulty is that different bond analysts may make different types of adjustments and thus come up with different leverage ratios for the same firm. This complicates interfirm comparisons of the ratios.

Another problem with the calculation of financial leverage ratios is how to decide whether to use book values or market values because, for example, the market prices of bonds fluctuate from day to day and thus differ from the book value shown in the liability section of the issuing firm's balance sheet. When the two methods produce quite different ratios, the financial analyst usually calculates the leverage ratios using both book and market values. Either way, it is possible to get an idea about whether or not the firm is too deeply in debt and to discern the trend of its indebtedness over time.

LIQUIDITY RATIOS If a firm is too deeply in debt, the associated high interest expenses may consume all the firm's earnings and keep it teetering on the edge of insolvency. Financial analysts can use any of several *liquidity ratios* to evaluate the solvency of a firm and thus to determine whether the firm will be able to pay its bills on time.

SOLVENCY RATIOS The two most common liquidity ratios are the current ratio and the quick ratio:

$$\text{Current ratio} = \frac{\text{current assets}}{\text{current liabilities}} \tag{12-1}$$

$$\text{Quick ratio} = \frac{\text{current assets} - \text{inventories}}{\text{current liabilities}} \tag{12-2}$$

These solvency ratios evaluate the ability of a firm to pay bills currently coming due.

Current liabilities are bills due to be paid within 1 year. Current assets include cash, marketable securities, accounts receivable, inventory, and any other asset that should in the normal course of business turn into cash within 1 year.

Some analysts say that a normal, healthy firm should have a current ratio of 2. Thus, the firm has $2 of current assets for every $1 of current liabilities. However, other values are commonly considered safe; the norm varies from industry to industry.

Critics of the use of the current ratio point out that the portion of current assets held in inventory is not liquid unless customers are eagerly waiting to buy it and pay cash for it. These analysts prefer to use the quick ratio. A quick ratio of 1 is sometimes suggested as a minimum standard because it means there is one dollar of cash, marketable securities, and accounts receivable (all of which are more liquid than inventory) for each dollar of bills due to be paid in the current year. Other liquidity ratios measure liquidity indirectly; these are called *turnover ratios.*

TURNOVER RATIOS Turnover ratios are used to measure the *activity* within a firm. Use of these ratios is based on the premise that assets not being actively employed must not be very useful and are therefore probably not very liquid or profitable. Below are four ratios that measure asset turnover and thus give an indirect indication of how liquid and profitable are the assets.

$$\text{Accounts receivable turnover} = \frac{\text{annual sales}}{\text{average accounts receivable}} \tag{12-3}$$

$$\text{Collection period in days} = \frac{\text{accounts receivable}}{\text{average day's sales}} \tag{12-4}$$

$$\text{Inventory turnover ratio} = \frac{\text{annual sales}}{\text{average inventory}} \tag{12-5}$$

$$\text{Total asset turnover} = \frac{\text{annual sales}}{\text{total assets}} \tag{12-6}$$

The accounts receivable turnover ratio and the collection period in days ratio give some indication of the liquidity of the current asset called accounts receivable. The inventory turnover ratio measures how rapidly a firm sells out and replaces its inventory. The total asset turnover ratio is designed to gauge whether all the assets owned by a firm are being used or whether some are lying dormant. Bond rating agencies, bond investors, and others who have loaned the firm money can get different perspectives on the firm's liquidity and how well managed the firm is by studying the turnover ratios.

The use of the turnover ratios can be illustrated by example. Suppose that the *ABC Corporation* has an accounts receivable turnover ratio of 6 and an inventory turnover ratio of 12. Since there are 12 months in 1 year, the turnover ratio of 6 means that ABC's accounts receivable turn over once every 2 months, averaged over the entire year. ABC's inventory turnover of 12 means that the inventory turned over once each month, on average. Stated differently, we can conclude that ABC allows its customers an average of 2 months to pay their bills and has an inventory that averages 1 month old. Assume that ABC's total asset turnover ratio is 3; this is no easy interpretation. The asset turnover ratio must be compared with its own historical values to determine the trend and also compared with the asset turnover ratios of ABC's competitors to get a relevant perspective. The next question is: Are these turnover ratios high or low? A standard of comparison is needed to answer this question.

Accounts receivable collected within 2 months might be normal for a neighborhood grocery store that sells on credit or for a public utility that issues monthly bills to its customers. But a 1-month collection time would be absurdly fast for a savings and loan association's home mortgage department, because home mortgage loans have their payments spread out over an average length of 25 years in the United States. As far as the inventory is concerned, a 1-month-old inventory would simply be impossible for the products produced by quality whisky distilleries, construction companies that build skyscrapers, or shipyards that assemble ocean liners. However, a fresh-fish market or a vegetable dealer had better never be caught with an inventory as old as a month; health inspectors would probably close the business for selling unfit food. Thus, each industry has its own normal turnover ratios, and so a firm's turnover ratios may usually be compared only with those of competing firms and the firm's own historical ratios.

CASHFLOW RATIOS The cashflows generated by a firm are divided by the firm's total long-term debt to measure *cashflows as a percentage of debt*. If such cashflow ratios indicate that a firm's interest expense cashflow stated as a percent of its debt is less than the firm's interest rate paid on total long-term debt, the firm may default on its interest payments. Unless the firm has liquid assets to sell off or is willing to incur new debts to pay interest on its old debts, the troubled firm faces imminent financial disaster. The determinants of a firm's cashflows are listed below.

Adjusted income: Adjusted income is the firm's normal operating income before taxes.

Interest expense on long-term debt: Interest expense is added back into the firm's income after interest expense because the resulting income-before-interest expense is a cashflow that may be used to pay interest expense.

Depreciation: Depreciation is an expense item deducted from the firm's revenue to allow for the replacement of plant and equipment that declines in value because of fair wear and tear. But the replacements and/or repairs need not actually be made simply because the bookkeeping entry deducting depreciation expense is made. Thus, depreciation is a noncash expense that financial analysts view as a cashflow that can be used for interest expense or to repair the firm's physical assets, whichever is most needed.

Another cashflow ratio is found by calculating the total of the three cashflow items listed above and then dividing this total cashflow by the total interest expense on the firm's long-term debt. Solvency cannot be maintained in the long run unless this latter cashflow ratio exceeds 1.

PROFITABILITY RATIOS It may not be apparent why bond quality rating agencies and bond investors should be particularly concerned with a firm's profitability. After all, even if a company's profits were to double, only the firm's common stock would appreciate in value. Since bonds earn only their fixed interest rate, an increase in profitability does not directly imply capital gains for bonds. Nevertheless, bond ratios and bond investment analysts are interested in the profitability of firms issuing bonds because profitability is probably the single best indicator of a firm's financial health. One of the more useful profitability ratios is the rate of return on total assets ratio.

$$\text{Rate of return on total assets} = \frac{\text{net profit before taxes}}{\text{total assets}} \tag{12-7}$$

The rate of return on assets will be lowest for firms in any given industry that have too many assets, high debt levels, low earnings, or some combination of these problems.

A profitability ratio that can reveal more about an earnings' weakness is the operating margin ratio:

$$\text{Operating margin} = \frac{\text{operating income}}{\text{sales}} \tag{12-8}$$

Operating income is a firm's pretax earnings before depreciation and interest expense (that is, before nonoperating expenses) are deducted to obtain the firm's taxable income. Dividing operating income by sales gives the percentage of every sales dollar available to pay overhead expenses and contribute toward profits. If this ratio is too low, it means the firm should either raise its sales price per unit or cut its direct manufacturing (or operating) costs, or do both.

Another popular profitability ratio is the pretax rate of return on permanent capital ratio:

$$\begin{matrix}\text{Pretax rate of return}\\ \text{on permanent capital}\end{matrix} = \frac{\text{pretax income + interest}}{\text{permanent capital}} \tag{12-9}$$

The sum of pretax income and interest is the total amount a firm has available to pay its interest expenses. *Permanent capital* is a firm's permanently committed capital funds and is the sum of short-term debt not currently coming due, long-term debt, and net worth (or total equity).

The pretax rate of return on permanent capital ratio states the firm's income as a percent of its permanent capitalization. It is useful for comparison with current interest rates. If the ratio does not exceed current interest rates, the company is probably not earning enough to pay its interest expense; this condition will result in low bond quality ratings.

Profitability ratios are useful both for historical comparisons with the firm's own ratios in order to discern trends within the firm and for comparisons with the firm's competitors in order to find strengths or weaknesses.[5] These ratios are also used by bond raters in assigning quality ratings to the firm's bond issues.

FINANCIAL RATIOS AND BOND QUALITY RATINGS In explaining how it rates industrial bonds, Standard & Poor's (S&P) made the statement shown in Box 12-1.[6] When examining Box 12-1, remember that different ratios are favored by each bond analyst and each bond rating agency and that for any given set of ratios, different values are appropriate for each industry. Also, do not forget that through the ups and downs of the normal business cycle the values of every firm's ratios vary in a cyclical fashion. Thus, bond rating is not as simple as Box 12-1 may appear to suggest.

[5] Financial service firms like Standard & Poor's, Moody's, and Value Line calculate numerous financial ratios every year for at least 10 years back. These ratios are then published in tabular form and sold. Such ratios are calculated every year for thousands of large and medium-sized firms. (See Chap. 6, pages 147–163.)

[6] Readers who desire detailed numerical examples of financial ratio calculations should consult a book written about that topic. For a modern treatment of the topic see George Foster, *Financial Statement Analysis,* Prentice-Hall, Englewood Cliffs, N.J., 1978. For a more traditional discussion of the topic see *Standard & Poor's Rating Guide,* McGraw-Hill, New York, 1979.

BOX 12-1

average relationships between ratios and bond ratings

Of all the financial ratios and measures that have been discussed, the ones that usually carry the most weight in rating determinations are pretax fixed-charge coverage, cashflow to long-term debt, pretax return on total capital invested, and long-term debt to capitalization. The following table provides 5-year average values of those financial measures for a representative sample of industrial companies with long-term debt ratings in each of the rating categories considered to be investment grade.

rating category	pretax fixed-charge coverage	cashflow to long-term debt	pretax return on long-term capital	long-term debt to capitalization
AAA	17.5 times	185%	28.5%	16.0%
AA	9.5 times	70%	22.0%	26.0%
A	5.5 times	45%	17.0%	33.0%
BBB	4.2 times	35%	15.5%	37.5%

Source: Standard & Poor's Rating Guide, McGraw-Hill, New York, 1979, p. 42.

THE DEMISE OF W. T. GRANT—AN ACTUAL CASE This chapter's discussion of financial ratios and bond quality ratings can be exemplified by a review of W. T. Grant's bond prices and bond ratings, which were presented in Table 9-1, on page 214. That corporation's deteriorating financial ratios demonstrate the relationships discussed in the preceding paragraphs.

In the early 1970s, the W. T. Grant Corporation was a large chain with over 1000 retail stores coast to coast in the United States. The firm went bankrupt in October 1975. Figure 12-2 depicts how this company's financial ratios deteriorated as it neared bankruptcy. Table 9-1 also lists the quality ratings of Grant's bonds, its earnings per share, and its cash dividends per share for the last 3 years of the firm's life.

Panel A of Fig. 12-2 illustrates how W. T. Grant's common stock price declined in comparison with the S&P stock market indices. In the lower panels, many financial ratios are graphed for W. T. Grant. Panel B of Fig. 12-2 shows how Grant's profitability declined in 1973 and 1974, leading to bankruptcy in 1975. Panel C of Fig. 12-2 shows how the turnover ratios declined together during 1970 and remained at depressed levels until the bankruptcy. Liquidity ratios are graphed in Panel D of Fig. 12-2; the firm's liquidity trickled away steadily until the end. Panel E of Fig. 12-2 shows how Grant endeavored to survive on borrowed money as its profitability declined. Note that Grant's total debt to equity ratio increased more than its long-term debt to equity ratio. This difference existed because most of the troubled firm's borrowing was done with short-term debt and accounts payable that were past due. Essentially, the troubled company delayed paying its current bills as its solvency diminished. Table 9-1 shows how Grant's financial deterioration was reflected in its declining bond quality ratings.

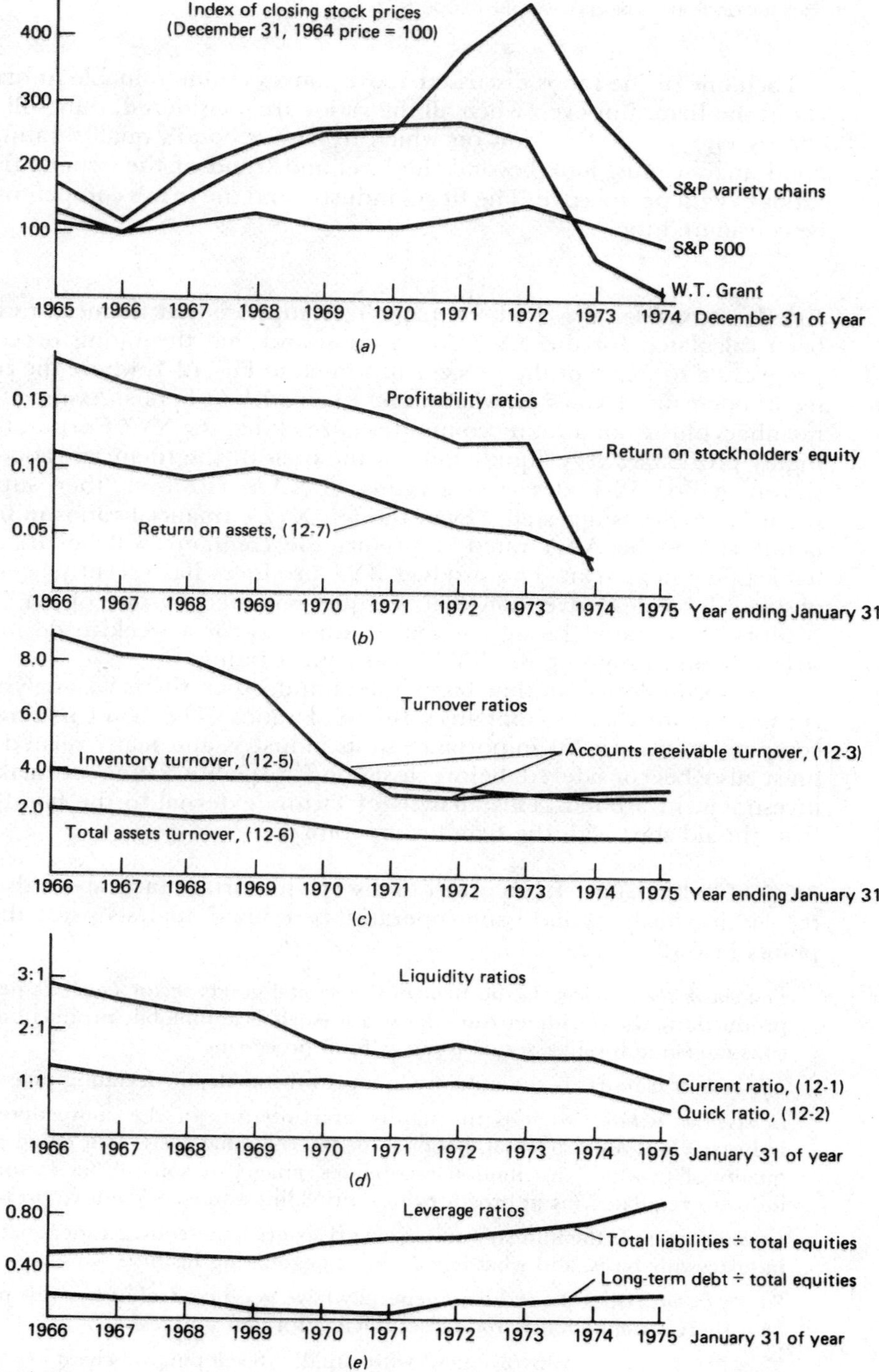

FIGURE 12-2 W. T. Grant Company stock prices and selected ratios for the fiscal years ending January 31, 1966 to 1975. (*Source*: "Cashflows, Ratio Analysis and the W. T. Grant Company Bankruptcy," *Financial Analysts Journal*, July–August 1980, p. 52, exhibit 1.)

Each one of the ratios discussed above conveys some valuable information about the firm. But even when all the ratios are considered, they still do not convey enough information on which to base a bond's quality rating. The bond analyst must look beyond the level and trend of the issuer's financial ratios to gain perspective. The firm's industry and the firm's competitors must be considered too.

12-1.2 the economic significance and size of the issuer

Briefly reconsider Fig. 12-1, on page 327. Suppose that financial ratios had been calculated for the XYZ Corporation and that the rating process had progressed to step 8 of the process illustrated in Fig. 12-1, where the committee of bond raters votes on what rating to give XYZ's bonds. Assume that the members of the bond rating committee agreed that the XYZ Corporation was highly profitable, very liquid, and, on the basis of the financial ratio criteria shown in Box 12-1, deserved a rating of AAA. However, then suppose a financial analyst suggested, "Even though XYZ's financial ratios indicate its bonds should be AAA rated, I predict the company will be driven into bankruptcy next year. The product XYZ produces has recently been made obsolete by a new invention that was just patented by one of XYZ's competitors." The bond rating committee adjourns for a week to do more research before assigning the XYZ bond issue a rating.

This example shows that bond raters and other financial analysts must consider more than a company's financial ratios. The bond issuing firm's competition, its size, its importance in its industry, and many related factors must also be considered before assigning a quality rating or making an investment in a bond. This analysis of factors external to the bond-issuing firm should start with the firm's competitors.

THE ISSUER'S INDUSTRY In an effort to discern important facts about the industry within which a bond issuer operates, S&P bond analysts study the seven points below.[7]

Position in the economy: Is the firm in the capital-goods sector (such as machinery production), the consumer-durables sector (such as automobile production), or the consumer-nondurables sector (such as food processing)?

Life cycle of industry: Is the industry in a growth, stable, or declining phase?

Competitive nature: What is the nature and intensity of the competition in the industry? Is it on a regional, national, or international basis? Is it based on price, quality of product, distribution capabilities, image, or some other factor? Is the industry regulated (as in broadcasting), providing some competitive protection?

Labor situation: Is the industry unionized? If so, are labor contracts negotiated on an industrywide basis, and what is the recent negotiating history?

Supply factors: Does the industry generally have good control of key raw materials, or is there a dependence upon questionable foreign sources?

Volatility: Is there an involvement with rapidly developing or changing technolo-

[7] *Standard & Poor's Rating Guide,* McGraw-Hill, New York, 1979, p. 28.

gies? Is there a dependence upon a relatively small number of major contracts (as is sometimes the case in the aerospace industry)?

Major vulnerabilities: Is the industry likely to be a prime target for some form of political pressure (such as the jawboning over prices to which the steel industry has often been subjected)? Are substantial environmental expenditures likely to be mandated (as has been the case in the metals industry)? Are near-term energy shortages possible? What is the ease of entry into the industry?

Answers to the questions above inform the bond analyst about the industry's growth potential, problems that may plague the industry, and the stability of the industry's sales. After these questions are answered, the analysis of the bond issuer can move on to a consideration of the issuer's competitive situation within its industry. These points must be investigated in this order before a bond issue can be meaningfully evaluated.

THE ISSUER'S COMPETITORS The key questions that S&P raters consider when evaluating an issuer's competition are listed below.[8] The questions are primarily about the firm whose bonds are being rated in order to keep the research into competition from becoming an aimless and costly inquiry into each of the bond issuer's competitors. The cost of the research on competition can be limited by inquiring only into how the competition affects the bond issuer.

Market share: Does a company have a large enough portion of the market share (be it regional, national, or international) to significantly influence industry dynamics? This may be especially important in a market dominated by only a few producers. Does the company have the opportunity to exercise price leadership? Does the company offer a full range of products or have proprietary products or a special niche in the market?

Technological leadership: Is the company usually among the first with new developments, or is it typically a follower? How do research and development expenditures compare with the industry average?

Production efficiency: Is the company a relatively low-cost producer? Are its facilities newer or more advanced than the average? Is it more or less vertically integrated than the average? If mandated expenditures (such as for pollution control) are required, has the company already complied to a greater or lesser extent than its competitors? Does the company face a more onerous labor situation than its competitors?

Financial structure: How does a company's use of leverage and various types of financing vehicles compare with that of others in the industry?

After the bond raters have answered the questions above to their satisfaction, they are ready to turn their attention to the last phase of bond rating, studying the new issue's indenture contract. Essentially, the bond rating committee endeavors to gauge the impact of the various protective provisions provided to enhance the safety of the bond buyer's investment.

[8] *Standard & Poor's Rating Guide,* McGraw-Hill, New York, 1979, pp. 29–30.

12-2 THE PROVISIONS IN THE ISSUE'S INDENTURE

The bond owners' rights are spelled out in the legal instrument called the *indenture*. The various protective provisions spelled out in the indenture can raise the quality rating for an issue by as much as one or two grades if a strong issuer grants liberal provisions. For example, if the bond issue's indenture pledges as collateral a large, modern office building that could be easily rented or sold, this protects the bond investors if the issuer should go bankrupt. The bond investors could get ownership of the collateral in a bankruptcy proceeding and sell it to recover the funds they invested in the issuing firm. In spite of the importance of these provisions, however, they are less important than the issuer's earning power. All the liberal protective provisions in the world will not get a high quality rating for a firm that faces a future of continuing losses.

The bond issuer commonly provides the following types of protective provisions to ensure the safety of the bondholder's investment.

- The issuer pledges specific assets as collateral.
- The issuer subordinates other legal claims on its assets or income.
- The issuer provides for a sinking fund with which to pay off the bonds even if the issuer defaults on its other debts.
- The issuing firm's management promises to operate the firm in certain ways to protect the bondholders.

These various provisions are considered in more detail below.

COLLATERAL A paragraph in a bond indenture which specifies that certain assets of the issuing company become the property of the bond investors to do with as they wish if the issuer defaults on the interest or principal payments of the bond issue is called a *collateral provision*. Many bond issues have no collateral provision, but those that do are rated somewhat higher (other factors being equal).

Debentures are bonds that have no assets pledged as collateral to help guarantee the bondholders that they will be repaid in case of a bankruptcy (see Chap. 2). If the issuer does go bankrupt, the debenture owners will find themselves placed in the undesirable category of "general creditors" by the bankruptcy court. General creditors include the public utilities, suppliers of raw materials who sold on credit, and other junior-level creditors. It is common for general creditors to be repaid only 10 cents of every dollar they are owed when a bankruptcy suit is settled. To avoid this disheartening prospect, bond investors can buy mortgage bonds, for example, in order to obtain a collateral provision. Mortgage bonds have a prior claim in bankruptcy on the specific asset (for example, a new factory that the proceeds of the bond issue financed) pledged as collateral.

Bondholders do not get a collateral provision for nothing. Such a provision increases the bond issue's price per bond slightly, and it lowers the interest income yield. So by buying collateralized bonds, the investor gives up some money in order to get a safer investment; this is a risk-return tradeoff.

SUBORDINATION In order to make safety-conscious investors more willing to buy bonds, clauses can be included in the indenture that subordinate certain claims or assets. A *subordination clause* places the bond issue or other bond issues or specified creditors in an inferior or secondary legal position with respect to the issuer's assets if the issuer defaults on the interest or principal payments.

The so-called *after-acquired property clause* is an example of a subordination clause. Such a clause states that if an issuer acquires additional assets after a first mortgage bond (or other type of collateralized bond, as specified) is outstanding, these new assets will automatically become part of this first mortgage bond's collateral. Such a clause protects the first mortgage bondholders from having the firm acquire newer assets with later mortgage bond issues against which the first mortgage bond owners would hold no claim. In effect, this clause subordinates the claim of any later mortgage bond buyers to the first mortgage bondholders' claim: first mortgage bondholders can claim their old assets and all the newer assets as collateral, too.

Another fairly common subordination is the *dividend test clause*. Such a clause limits the claim of the common stockholders (who essentially run the corporation through their voting power at annual stockholders' meetings) on corporate profits. Profits might be used to pay either cash dividends to stockholders or interest to bondholders. The dividend test clause specifies that the issuer cannot pay annual cash dividends in excess of annual earnings. Such a clause helps ensure that if the firm suffers losses, its borrowing power and liquid assets will be retained to pay bondholders rather than used to pay cash dividends to the common stockholders. Several other similar clauses also subordinate maximization of common stockholders' profit to bondholders' safety.

SINKING FUNDS A sinking fund provision also subordinates the common stockholders' interest in maximizing corporate profits to the bondholders' desire for safety. A *sinking fund* is a fund into which the bond issuer is required to pay every year. The sinking fund provision in some indentures requires that the sinking fund deposits be held by a third party (for example, a bank that holds them in escrow) to be used solely to repurchase the bonds at some future date. This type of sinking fund guarantees the bondholders that the money needed to repay their loan is being safely accumulated. But, this accumulation of funds does not maximize the issuer's profit. Thus, aggressive common stockholders who want their profits maximized may object to sinking fund provisions.

A sinking fund clearly provides increased safety of repayment for bondholders. After a number of years' annual payments have been safely accumulated in the sinking fund, the rating agencies may acknowledge the protection provided to investors by raising the issue's quality rating. An improved quality rating will increase the bond's market price and thus enrich the bondholders. Furthermore, sinking funds that are well funded may provide price supports for their bonds. That is, if the sinking fund has a policy of repurchasing bonds in the market when their market prices fall sufficiently low, this policy constitutes a price support that keeps the bonds' prices from falling below a specific price. This way of holding up bond prices benefits the bondholders, but sinking funds can also work to the detriment of bondholders, in two significant respects.

First, some sinking fund provisions provide that bonds may be redeemed at stipulated dates before the issue matures. Thus, an investor may have gone to the trouble of evaluating a bond issue and purchasing a bond at what is considered to be an attractive yield to maturity only to have the investment snatched away by a sinking fund prematurity-date purchase. Such sinking fund purchases are most likely to occur when interest rates are low and the investor has no good reinvestment alternative. Second, issues with sinking funds pay lower yields because they offer their bondholders greater safety. This is an example of the risk-return tradeoff: The lower-risk investments can attract buyers at lower rates of return.

OTHER PROTECTIVE PROVISIONS Some indenture contracts forbid the issuer to sell off its own assets in order to lease the same assets back again later. The purpose of such a sale-and-leaseback arrangement is to free capital invested in plant and equipment so that it may be spent for other purposes. Meanwhile, the use of the asset is ensured because the seller of the asset contracts to lease it back as part of the sales agreement. Bondholders want provisions against sale-and-leaseback transactions because they deplete the issuer's collateral assets; a leased asset is no collateral.

Debt test clauses are common in issues of speculative grade bonds. Such provisions limit the issuer's ability to create additional debt and thereby protect bondholders in two ways. First, they limit the issuer's ability to undertake rapid expansion, which is usually risky. Second, if the issuer should go bankrupt, such clauses limit the number of creditors that must quarrel over the remaining assets.

Negative pledge clauses limit the issuer's ability to pledge assets as collateral for any future borrowings. This protects existing bondholders from having to face senior bankruptcy claims that might have arisen with later issues of other collateralized bonds.

Prohibitions against the sale of subsidiary corporations are common. Such provisions allow the issuer to sell major subsidiaries only if they immediately repay the previously outstanding debt. This protects bondholders from losing important sources of income or collateral assets that the issuer owns through its subsidiaries.

It should now be apparent that there is an almost unlimited variety of provisions that can be inserted in an indenture. The ingenuity with which safety-seeking bondholders encumber issuers' management is refreshing. Remember, however, that nothing is granted for free. Every protective provision bondholders obtain reduces the rate of return they can expect to earn from their bonds. There are rare exceptions to this rule, but generally the natural economic order of things requires a tradeoff of risk for return.

12-3 BOND PRICES AND BOND QUALITY RATING CHANGES

When profits turn into consistent losses, a company is forced to deplete its liquid assets to pay its bills as they come due. When both profitability and liquid assets are gone and the firm cannot borrow any more money, it defaults on its debt payments. However, the bond quality ratings of a company which is moving from good health to bankruptcy will decline as the firm's financial ratios deteriorate. For example, Table 9-1, on page 214, shows how the bond quality ratings and bond prices of the W. T. Grant Corporation declined and the yields to maturity rose as that firm moved into bankruptcy over a 3-year period.

12-3.1 publicly available information forewarned of the bankruptcy

W. T. Grant was a large, old, well-known retailing chain with stores across the United States. The company filed a bankruptcy plea on itself in October 1975. At that time it had $1.02 billion in assets and $1.03 billion in liabilities. The corporation owed debts to 3500 merchandise suppliers who had sold to it on credit, to 27 bank lenders, and to its bondholders. Figure 12-2 above illustrates how the Grant Corporation's financial condition deteriorated as it approached bankruptcy.

Perusal of the financial data in Fig. 12-2 and Table 9-1 suggests that investors who purchase bonds in a deteriorating corporation like W. T. Grant should be able to sell their bonds before the firm goes completely bankrupt and thus avoid extensive losses. By simply observing the predictions of disaster which seem implicit in the declining bond quality ratings, constantly deteriorating financial ratios, and falling security prices, it should be possible to avert such catastrophic bond investments.

Scrutiny of the data in Fig. 12-2 and Table 9-1 raises an important question in this regard, however. Did the bond's price fall (and inversely, the yield to maturity rise) in *delayed reaction* to the falling quality ratings, or was the reverse situation true? That is, did astute investors foresee the oncoming bankruptcy before the bond rating agencies? If so, such astute investors could have sold their bonds *before* the quality ratings were lowered. Thus, this question arises: When a company like W. T. Grant deteriorates (or, just the opposite, grows in profitability and liquidity and has its rating raised), do the bond rating changes contain any valuable information? After all, if the bond rating changes lag behind changes in bond market prices, then the ratings are a worthless source of information to bond investors.

12-3.2 empirical analysis of bond rating changes and bond prices

Dr. Mark Weinstein analyzed the monthly market price changes of 132 different bonds which were associated with 100 different bond rating changes occurring between July 1962 and July 1974.[9] He studied 32 (that is, 132 − 100) more bonds than rating changes because some bond issuers had more than one bond issue outstanding at the time of their rating change, and the prices of all outstanding bonds were analyzed for each rating change. Dr. Weinstein investigated to find if bond prices reacted to quality rating changes with a lead or a lag, or simultaneously; or if they did not react at all.

Of the 132 bonds Weinstein analyzed, 60 had rating increases and 72 had decreases. He found small price reactions which occurred *before* the rating changes. These bond price changes were symmetrical and were in opposite directions for the quality rating increases and the decreases—just as you might expect. The negative monthly percentage price changes associated with

[9] Mark I. Weinstein, "The Effect of a Rating Change Announcement on Bond Prices," *Journal of Financial Economics*, December 1977, vol. 5, no. 3, pp. 329–350.

the rating decreases were reversed in sign and added to the positive monthly percentage price changes associated with the rating increases. Weinstein did this in order to determine the average bond price response pattern month by month before and after a rating change without regard to the direction of the change.

As explained in Chaps. 9 and 11, all bond prices fluctuate inversely with market interest rates. Therefore, the systematic bond price movements which are caused when the level of all market interest rates is rising or falling must be filtered out of the bond price changes in order to discern the price reactions which may be attributed purely to a rating change. Weinstein used three bond price change measures defined in Eqs. (12-10), (12-11), and (12-12) to accomplish this task.

$$u_{it} = r_{it} - r_{pt} \tag{12-10}$$

where

u_{it} = unsystematic or abnormal percentage price change which may be attributed to the rating change of bond i in month t

$$r_{it} = \frac{p_{it} - p_{i,t-1}}{p_{i,t-1}} \tag{12-11}$$

where

r_{it} = percent price change per month for the ith rating-changed bond in the tth month

p_{it} = market price of bond at the end of the tth month

$p_{i,t-1}$ = market price at the beginning of the tth month

$$r_{pt} = \frac{p_{pt} - p_{p,t-1}}{p_{p,t-1}} \tag{12-12}$$

= percent price change per month in month t from a diversified portfolio of bonds (denoted by the subscript p) all of which have the same quality rating as the ith bond

The abnormal percentage price change for the ith bond in the tth month measured by Eq. (12-10) may also be affected by unsystematic factors other than rating change. For example, the ith bond might experience unsystematic price gains (that is, $u_{it} > 0$) or losses (namely, $u_{it} < 0$) from an abnormally large purchase or sale, respectively, of the bonds by some substantial investor that was totally oblivious of the ith bond's rating change. In order to average over these irrelevant causes of abnormal bond price changes and focus only on rating change reactions, Dr. Weinstein averaged the unsystematic percentage price changes over all 132 bonds studied, as shown in Eq. (12-13).

$$U_t = \frac{1}{N}\sum_{i=1}^{N} u_{it} \tag{12-13}$$

where

$N = 132$ = the number of bonds studied

U_t = average unsystematic or abnormal percentage bond price change t months from the rating change month

Note: t was set to zero for the rating change month for all 132 bonds.

In addition to summing over all 132 bonds in order to average out to zero all unsystematic changes not caused by rating changes, Weinstein adjusted the time subscripts, denoted t. He set $t = 0$ for the rating change month for all the 132 bonds studied regardless of the month in which their rating change occurred. Thus the statistic U_0 measures the average unsystematic risk-adjusted price change reaction from dozens of different months—all of which have been averaged over 132 different bonds. As a result, the value of U_t is void of any date in time; it is stated relative to the sampled bonds' rating change month.

To further average out any unsystematic reactions which were unrelated to the rating changes, Dr. Weinstein cumulated the monthly U_t from B months before the rating change month to A months afterward. The formula for these cumulative abnormal returns is shown in Eq. (12-14).

$$\text{Cumulative abnormal returns} = \sum_{t=B}^{A} U_t = \sum_{t=B}^{A} \left(\frac{1}{N} \sum_{i=1}^{132} u_{it} \right) \tag{12-14}$$

Table 12-2 shows the results Dr. Weinstein obtained from various applications of his procedure. Next, Weinstein divided the sum of the averages defined in Eq. (12-14) by the quantity $(B - A)$ months to obtain a mean monthly abnormal return over the period near the rating change month, as shown in Eq. (12-15).

$$\text{Mean monthly abnormal return} = \frac{1}{A - B} \sum_{t=B}^{A} U_t \tag{12-15}$$

The eight portfolios shown in Table 12-2 represent eight different summations of the average monthly unsystematic percentage price changes U_t. They are called portfolios because each one represents the results of holding a different portfolio of diversified bonds all of which experienced rating changes at different calendar dates from July 1962 to July 1974. The second

TABLE 12-2 unsystematic price change statistics for bonds which experienced rating changes

	value of B	value of A	from *B* to *A* cumulation of U_t returns	mean monthly abnormal returns	standard error	*t* statistic of mean monthly abnormal return
1	−7	−1	0.009	0.002	0.133	0.01
2	−1	0	0.623	0.623	0.396	1.59
3	0	+6	0.162	0.027	0.137	0.20
4	−7	+6	0.442	0.034	0.096	0.36
5	−19	−13	0.385	0.064	0.113	0.69
6	−13	−7	0.358	0.060	0.123	0.48
7	−19	−7	1.204	0.100	0.071	1.41
8	−19	−1	1.278	0.278	0.061	1.16

Source: Mark I. Weinstein, "The Effect of a Rating Change Announcement on Bond Price," *Journal of Financial Economics,* December 1977, vol. 5, no. 3, pp. 329–350, table 4.

and seventh portfolios are the most interesting because they experienced the most statistically significant abnormal price reactions.

Portfolio 2 summarizes the results from buying bonds 1 month before their rating was changed (that is, at time $B = -1$) and then selling the bonds 1 month later (that is, A months after the change, so $A = 0$). This strategy yielded an average abnormal return which was positive on average; its value was 623/1000 of 1 percent. Using the standard deviation of the abnormal returns around their mean (called the standard error of the estimate by statisticians) as a measure of sampling errors allows the t statistic defined in Eq. (12-16) to be computed:

$$t \text{ statistic} = \frac{\text{mean monthly abnormal return} - \text{zero}}{\text{standard error}} \tag{12-16}$$

The second portfolio's t statistic of 1.59 indicates that the portfolio's mean monthly abnormal return was 1.59 standard errors above a mean value of zero. The mean value of zero was assumed in order to test the hypothesis that the abnormal price response differed significantly from zero. This outcome would happen infrequently (that is, with only a probability of .0559) as a result of mere sampling distribution. Essentially, there is a slightly abnormal price reaction in the month of the rating change. But this rating change response is so small, on average, that it would not even pay the brokerage commissions associated with buying and selling the bonds to obtain the abnormal return.

Portfolio 7 is the only other portfolio which appears to have experienced a rating change price reaction which differs from zero sufficiently to be of interest. The data in Table 12-2 show that bond portfolio strategy 7 earned a cumulative abnormal return of 1.204 percent over the 1-year period from 19 months before to 7 months before the rating change. This is equal to 1/10 of 1 percent per month abnormal return over the year from 1½ years to ½ year prior to the rating change.[10]

IMPLICATIONS OF THE WEINSTEIN STUDY In summary, the statistics in Table 12-2 are consistent with the hypothesis that (1) bond prices do not react after their ratings have been changed, (2) bond prices experience a tiny abnormal reaction in the rating change month, and (3) bond prices accomplish most of their price change reactions about 1 year in advance of having their ratings changed. The implication of (1) and (2) is that, after you allow for the brokerage commissions to buy and sell, it would not be worthwhile to trade bonds because their quality rating was changed if you did not trade until after the change was announced to the public.

Overall, Dr. Weinstein's findings imply that bond investors should not waste their time and money on Moody's, Standard & Poor's, or any other bond ratings. Changes in the quality rating of the issuing corporation (such as the W. T. Grant changes shown in Table 9-1) largely lag, and thus they appear

[10] Dr. Weinstein's results refine the conclusions presented in an earlier empirical analysis of bond price reactions to bond rating changes. Paul Grier and Steven Katz, "The Differential Effects of Bond Rating Changes among Industrial and Public Utility Bonds by Maturity," *Journal of Business,* April 1976, vol. 49, no. 2, pp. 226–239.

to be a delayed reaction to changes in a bond issuer's actual quality as reflected in the bonds' market prices.[11]

The Weinstein study suggests that bond market prices are unbiased and efficient estimators of bonds' true economic values. Apparently, when the quality of a bond issuing company changes, both the price and value of its bonds change together in advance of any changes in published bond ratings. This evidence suggests that bond market prices fully reflect all publicly disseminated information. In fact, Weinstein's results suggest that as a result of the buying and selling done by astute bond analysts the prices *anticipate* the publicly announced rating changes. Only detailed financial analysis and planning should yield any bond trading profits as a result of bond rating changes.

Trading bonds that have already had their quality ratings changed does not seem to offer any chance of earning easy trading profits. However, the common stock of the bond issuing corporation may react significantly to the change in the bond issuer's quality rating. That is a subject worthy of further research.

12-4 STOCK PRICE REACTIONS TO BOND RATING CHANGES

Professors Paul A. Griffin and Antonio Z. Sanvicente (GS hereafter) analyzed 63 downgradings and 65 upgradings of bond ratings during the sample period from 1960 to 1975 in order to estimate the effect of these changes on the market prices of the issuing corporations' common stock.[12] GS analyzed the stocks' one-period rates of return in order to detect any unusual or abnormal common stock returns which might result from the rating change in the corporation's bond. The painstaking scientific methodology used by GS and their financial findings are reviewed below.

12-4.1 analysis of stock returns

The basic random variable studied by GS was the one period rate of return defined below.

$$r_t = \frac{\text{capital gains or loss} + \text{cash dividends}}{\text{purchase price}} \tag{12-17}$$

All the shares were adjusted for the stock splits and stock dividends before the rates of return were calculated. This adjustment ensured that only actual

[11] Professor Holbrook Working suggested that a price change may anticipate the event which causes the price change if market analysts foresee the future with any success; see "A Theory of Anticipatory Prices," *American Economic Review*, May 1958, pp. 188–199.

[12] P. A. Griffin and A. Z. Sanvicente, "Common Stock Returns and Rating Changes: A Methodological Comparison," *Journal of Finance*, vol. XXXVII, no. 1, March 1982, pp. 103–119. The study actually employed three different methods to gauge the effects of a bond rating change on the issuer's stock. However, only the results of one method are reported here for the sake of expedition. Interested readers may consult the original study to see all the results. See also G. Pinches and C. Singleton, "The Adjustment of Stock Prices to Bond Rating Changes," *Journal of Finance*, March 1978, pp. 29–44.

An informative study which investigates statistical methodologies related to bond ratings was done by Robert S. Kaplan and Gabriel Urwitz, "Statistical Models of Bond Ratings: A Methodological Inquiry," *Journal of Business*, vol. 52, no. 2, April 1979, pp. 231–261.

changes in the investor's wealth would be measured rather than the meaningless price changes which are associated with a stock dividend or split. For example, if a 2 for 1 split or 100 percent stock dividend occurred, the share prices would be halved before the stock dividend or split (or doubled afterward) so that no changes in the investor's wealth would be attributed to it in calculating rates of return.

CHARACTERISTIC LINE USED In order to have a standard of comparison with which a corporation's rates of return may be compared, it is necessary to make adjustments for the differences in returns resulting from bull- or bear-market swings in price. The characteristic regression line, which was introduced in Chap. 10 as a way to quantify undiversifiable systematic risk and diversifiable unsystematic risk, was employed.[13] The characteristic line is a simple linear regression; it is defined in Eq. (12-18). A characteristic line regression was calculated for each common stock studied in order to adjust for changes in the stock market's condition.

$$r_{it} = a_i + b_i r_{mt} + z_{it} \tag{12-18}$$

where

r_{it} = monthly rate of return from the *i*th stock in the *t*th month

r_{mt} = one month return from the Lorie-Fisher stock market index during the *t*th month

a_i = alpha intercept for the *i*th stock, a regression statistic

b_i = beta systematic risk coefficient = regression slope coefficient for the *i*th stock

z_{it} = residual return for the *i*th stock in the *t*th month = an unsystematic price change caused by an abnormal nonmarket event

RESIDUAL ERRORS The residual errors z_t around the time of the corporation's bond rating change were the focus of the GS study. Figure 10-3, on page 263, shows the hypothetical characteristic line for some firm to illustrate its usefulness in filtering out the bull- and bear-market effects. The residual or unexplained portion of the *i*th stock's rate of return in the *t*th time period is calculated by subtracting known quantities. The *i*th stock's actual rate of return in period *t*, denoted r_{it}, has its same period's expected (or forecasted) rate of return, the quantity $(a_i + b_i r_{mt})$, subtracted to obtain the positive or negative residual, denoted z_{it}, as shown below.

$$z_{it} = r_{it} - (a_i + b_i r_{mt}) \tag{12-19}$$

If the residual error at the time of the bond rating change was zero ($z_t = 0$), this means that the security's rate of return was right on the characteristic line and that the change had no positive or negative effects on an investor's normal pattern of returns. If the residual error was positive (that is, a positive z_t), graphically speaking it was above the characteristic line because the bond

[13] In order to obtain the full benefit from this discussion, the reader may wish to review the characteristic line in Chap. 10.

rating change was apparently boosting returns above their normal pattern. A negative residual error (that is, a negative z_t) occurs when the actual rate of return is below the characteristic line and some negative influence is affecting that period's rate of return. If the bond rating changes create anything of value, then the residual errors could be positive when bonds are upgraded and negative when bonds are downgraded.

MONTHLY RESIDUAL ERRORS AVERAGED The residual errors about the characteristic line are the results of many influences other than bond rating changes. Therefore, it is not realistic to examine the residuals of an *individual* firm's common stock which are associated with its bond's rating change and draw general conclusions about how all stocks react to having their bonds' rating changed. To overcome the problem with individual influences, the regression residuals were averaged in each month over 63 bonds which were downgraded and, separately, 65 which were upgraded. Essentially, two portfolios of average residuals were created, one for upgraded bonds and another for downgraded bonds. These average residuals for portfolios of upgraded bonds, and separately, portfolios of only downgraded bonds, were calculated for each of the 11 months before the rating change (namely, $t = -11, -10, \ldots, -1$), and also, the month in which the bond rating change occurred (that is, time period $t = 0$). This approach should average out to zero any influences which are not due to the bond rating change. If the average residuals are significantly different from zero in the months around the time of the change, this disparity indicates that the change affected the value of the corporation's common stock. Equation (12-20) defines the average residual, denoted $\bar{z}_t$, for the tth month before or after the month in which the rating change occurred.

$$\bar{z}_t = \frac{1}{N} \sum_{i=1}^{N} z_{it} \qquad \text{for } N = 63, 65 \tag{12-20}$$

The time subscripts in Eq. (12-20) do not correspond to calendar months. Instead, the month in which any given bond's rating change occurs is defined to be month $t = 0$, and all other months are numbered in accordance with the month $t = 0$. For instance, the average residuals, say, 6 months before and after the bond rating change month would be denoted $\bar{z}_t = -6$ and $\bar{z}_t = 6$, respectively.

CONTROL GROUP STOCKS As a final step to filter out any statistical biases, GS searched out 128 common stocks which did not have their bond ratings changed but were like the 128 (the 65 upgradings plus 63 downgradings) corporations which did have their bond ratings changed in other ways. GS did this by having their computer screen through financial data on thousands of corporations. GS had the computer select 128 corporations which were in the same industry, of the same approximate size, and with similar liquidity and debt ratios, but which did not have their bond ratings changed. These 128 similar corporations which had no bond rating change are called the *control group* corporations.

GS performed the statistical analysis procedures described above on the 128 control group corporations in order to have something against which they could compare the results from the 128 corporations whose bond ratings were changed. Essentially, GS were good financial analysts who created a standard of comparison for their statistics; they used good scientific methodology in order to avoid drawing erroneous conclusions. GS began by calculating the characteristic line of Eq. (12-21) for all 128 corporations in the control group.

$$r_{cit} = a_{ci} + b_{ci} r_{mt} + z_{cit} \tag{12-21}$$

where

r_{cit} = monthly rate of return from the ith control group stock in the tth month

r_{mt} = 1-month return from the Lorie-Fisher stock market index during the tth month

a_{ci} = alpha intercept for the ith control group stock

b_{ci} = beta systematic risk coefficient = regression coefficient for the ith control group stock

z_{cit} = residual return for the ith control group stock in the tth month = an unsystematic price change caused by an abnormal event

Equation (12-21) is exactly like Eq. (12-18) except that the subscript c has been added to indicate that the characteristic line represents a corporation from the control group.

The residual error for each control group corporation was calculated with Eq. (12-22), which is exactly like its counterpart Eq. (12-19) above except for the additional subscript of c.

$$z_{cit} = r_{cit} - (a_{ci} + b_{ci} r_{mt}) \tag{12-22}$$

After obtaining residuals for every control group common stock, GS aligned or synchronized them to correspond in time with the residuals from the similar stocks whose bond ratings were changed. GS then subtracted the control group's monthly average residuals to obtain the residual difference u_t, as shown in Eq. (12-23).

$$u_t = \bar{z}_t - \bar{z}_{ct} \tag{12-23}$$

The residual difference u_t is a portfolio-like return measure which has had bull- and bear-market price movements eliminated via the characteristic line, has had other unsystematic sources of return averaged out to zero in Eq. (12-20), and has had any possible other-than-rating-change effects which might affect similar firms eliminated in Eq. (12-23). The residual difference defined in Eq. (12-23) is the best unbiased measure of monthly rating change effects that GS could devise.

CUMULATIVE RESIDUAL ERRORS In order to measure the cumulative month-by-month effect that the rating change may have, the average monthly residual differences from Eq. (12-23) were summed chronologically over the 11 months which preceded the rating change month. Equation (12-24) defines these cumulative abnormal residual, designated CAR, differences.

$$\text{CAR} = \sum_{t=-11}^{-1} \bar{u}_t = \sum_{t=-11}^{-1} (\bar{z}_t - \bar{z}_{ct}) \tag{12-24}$$

TABLE 12-3 GS residual difference statistics calculated with Eq. (12-24)

	averaged over 63 downgradings	averaged over 65 upgradings
CAR from 11 months before the event month $t = 0$	−.1129	+.0322
From the event month only	−.0182	−.0131

Source: P. A. Griffin and A. Z. Sanvicente, "Common Stock Returns and Rating Changes: A Methodological Comparison," *Journal of Finance*, vol. XXXVII, no. 1, March 1982, tables V and VI, results from 1960–1975.

The lower limit of the monthly summation, $t = -11$, indicates that the residual differences were summed from 11 months before the rating change month up through 1 month before the rating change. So, the upper limit of the months' summation is $t = -1$. Table 12-3 contains residual difference summary statistics from the GS study.

12-4.2 implications of the GS findings

The values in the top line of Table 12-3 indicate that over the 11 months before the month in which the bond ratings were changed the common stock prices fell 11.29 percent and rose 3.22 percent in an unsystematic manner which could well be associated with the downgradings and upgradings, respectively. These are the net effects after all other influences have been statistically purged. The signs of these values are what intuition suggests would occur. These results suggest that astute bond analysis of events expected to occur 1 year ahead could yield returns which were modestly above average, before the brokerage commissions to buy and sell the bonds are deducted. These returns would be further diminished by the commission costs. However, a different and more discouraging interpretation of these same values is also possible.

Classic statistical significance tests indicate that none of the four values in Table 12-3 are significantly different from zero at the .05 level of significance. Stated differently, all of the statistics in Table 12-3 should be "taken with a grain of salt" because they may be the result of factors not allowed for in the conscientious statistical procedures used by GS. In fact, GS suggest the possibility that the bond rating agencies may change bond ratings in response to movements in market prices, rather than the market prices moving in response to rating changes. After all, the rating changes do *lag the market price changes* by months.

The bottom line in Table 12-3 indicates that in the month of the event (that is, month $t = 0$) the stocks associated with downgraded or upgraded bonds earn returns which are 1.82 percent and 1.31 percent below average, respectively. These two values are small, the upgrading's stock price reaction is not even of the sign we might expect, and both numbers are not statistically significantly different from zero. These results suggest that by the time the rating agencies have gotten around to publicly announcing changes in a bond's quality rating, enough of the investing public has already revised the issuer's stock price so that the announcement of the rating change is worthless news. Stated differently, trading stocks based on recently announced bond rating changes is no way to capture speculative profits.

12-5 BOND RETURNS AND PURCHASING POWER RISK

Bonds are called dollar-denominated assets because they promise to make their payments in dollars rather than in real goods such as food or clothing. This means that any coupon interest payments and the principal repayment which are contractually promised to the bonds' owners are fixed dollar quantities which do not increase with the inflation that will almost surely occur during the bonds' life. As a result of any inflation, bondholders are repaid in dollars which have less purchasing power over real (that is, physical) goods than the dollars which were originally invested in the bonds. This loss in purchasing power over real goods which all bond investors will most likely experience is the *purchasing power risk* from bond investing. Purchasing power risk is often larger than investors realize because they are unaware of the rate of inflation and its implications.

It is surprising that most investors are not better informed about inflation, because various U.S. government agencies prepare and freely disseminate inflation estimates to the public media. Although it is not perfect, the most popular price index in the United States is the *Consumer Price Index (CPI)* prepared by the U.S. Bureau of Labor Statistics. The CPI measures the cost of a representative market basket of about 400 different goods and services which are regularly consumed by an urban, middle class American family. Current prices for these goods are gathered from 56 different urban areas around the United States and then assigned weights based on the areas' relative proportions of the total population. The prices of most of the 400 items which make up the CPI are observed regularly. Table 9-5, on page 237, shows CPI statistics published by the U.S. government.

The main conceptual problems with the CPI involve how the commodities which make up a representative consumer's market basket are selected, how changes in people's buying preferences are reflected, and how services and capital goods for use in the index are priced. Even though it is imperfect, the CPI is probably the best inflation index in the world. It will be used in this chapter to measure inflation in the United States.

As explained above in Sec. 9-5, inflation measurements are fundamental to dealing with purchasing power risk. The relation between the value of the CPI in the tth time period (denoted CPI_t) and the rate of price inflation (denoted q) is shown in Eqs. (12-25*a*) and (12-25*b*).

$$q_t = \frac{\text{CPI}_t - \text{CPI}_{t-1}}{\text{CPI}_{t-1}} \quad \text{for one period} \tag{12-25a}$$

$$(1 + q_t)^n = \frac{\text{CPI}_{t+n}}{\text{CPI}_t} \quad \text{for } n \text{ periods} \tag{12-25b}$$

Equation (12-25*a*) measures the one-period rate of inflation. The quantity in Eq. (12-25*b*) is called a *value relative* for measuring inflation over multiple periods. Column 7 of Table 12-4 shows the annual rates of inflation in the CPI over the years from 1926 to 1981.

12-5.1 long-term bond yields exceed inflation

Table 12-4 also shows the market rates of return for both long-term corporate and U.S. Treasury bond indices which were calculated with Eq. (12-26).

$$r_t = \frac{(p_t - p_{t-1}) + c_t}{p_{t-1}} \quad \text{for 1 year} \qquad (12\text{-}26)$$

where

c_t = coupon interest payment in the tth year

p_t = price level of the portfolio of bonds that make up the index

r_t = money rate of return per period = nominal return

The annual rates of return for long-term corporate bonds and U.S. Treasury bonds calculated with Eq. (12-26) are shown in columns 4 and 5, respectively, of Table 12-4.

Figure 9-10, on page 244, contains summary statistics calculated from the 57 annual returns in Table 12-4 to aid in comparing the risk and return from the various investments. Bear in mind that these returns are all stated on a before-commissions and before-tax basis. The returns after the transactions costs are deducted would be less.

12-5.2 Treasury bill yields

Column 6 of Table 12-4 indicates the results of a series of reinvestments in 1-month Treasury bills. Equation (12-27) defines how these Treasury bill returns were computed.

$$r_t = \frac{p_t - p_{t-1}}{p_{t-1}} \qquad (12\text{-}27)$$

Comparing the annual yields from the Treasury bills with the annual rates of inflation in the CPI reveals that the Treasury bill investment's yield approximately equaled the rate of inflation, on average, as shown in Fig. 9–10.

12-5.3 common stock comparison

To provide more perspective on the bond returns, the returns from a common stock index also are shown in Table 12-4 and Fig. 9-10. Standard & Poor's composite index made up from 500 different NYSE stocks was used. The annual rates of return for a diversified portfolio of common stocks that were selected randomly were calculated from this stock price index. The cash dividend index was included to obtain total returns. Equation (12-28) shows how the rates of return for the stock market index were calculated.

$$r_t = \frac{(\text{SP500}_t - \text{SP500}_{t-1}) + (\text{SP500 cash dividends}_t)}{\text{SP500}_{t-1}} \qquad (12\text{-}28)$$

The data in Table 12-4 and the summary statistics in Fig. 9-10 show that, on average, the common stocks earned much greater returns than any of the bond investments. One should not hastily conclude from this difference, however, that common stock investments are better than bond investments. The common stocks must pay higher returns to compensate their investors for assuming the greater risks associated with common stock investing.

Comparing the risk statistics in Fig. 9-10 for common stocks with the bonds' risk statistics is informative. An investment's risk or variability of return can be measured by its standard deviation of returns or the range over which its returns fluctuate. Comparing the fluctuations of the common stock index's returns (from a high of 54.0 percent to a low of −43 percent is a range of 97 percent) with the bonds' risk statistics indicates that the stock index is a far

TABLE 12-4 year-by-year total returns, 1926–1981

							INFLATION ADJUSTED				
year	common stocks	small stocks	long-term corporate bonds	long-term government bonds	U.S. Treasury bills	percent change in CPI, q	common stocks	small stocks	long-term corporate bonds	long-term government bonds	U.S. Treasury bills
1926	0.1162	0.0028	0.0737	0.0777	0.0327	−0.0149	0.1325	0.0181	0.0896	0.0937	0.0478
1927	0.3749	0.2210	0.0744	0.0893	0.0312	−0.0208	0.4008	0.2441	0.0963	0.1112	0.0523
1928	0.4361	0.3969	0.0284	0.0010	0.0324	−0.0097	0.4507	0.4129	0.0380	0.0103	0.0422
1929	−0.0842	−0.5136	0.0327	0.0342	0.0475	0.0019	−0.0852	−0.5146	0.0304	0.0318	0.0452
1930	−0.2490	−0.3815	0.0798	0.0466	0.0241	−0.0603	−0.2009	−0.3412	0.1480	0.1127	0.0889
1931	−0.4334	−0.4975	−0.0185	−0.0531	0.0107	−0.0952	−0.3725	−0.4438	0.0837	0.0458	0.1159
1932	−0.0819	−0.0539	0.1082	0.1684	0.0096	−0.1030	0.0260	0.0542	0.2330	0.2999	0.1239
1933	0.5399	1.4287	0.1038	−0.0008	0.0030	0.0051	0.5325	1.4198	0.0973	−0.0071	−0.0037
1934	−0.0144	0.2422	0.1384	0.1002	0.0016	0.0203	−0.0342	0.2181	0.1154	0.0777	−0.0187
1935	0.4767	0.4019	0.0961	0.0498	0.0017	0.0299	0.4328	0.3614	0.0644	0.0193	−0.0278
1936	0.3392	0.6480	0.0674	0.0751	0.0018	0.0121	0.3234	0.6279	0.0545	0.0621	−0.0104
1937	−0.3503	−0.5801	0.0275	0.0023	0.0031	0.0310	−0.3702	−0.5933	−0.0039	−0.0285	−0.0274
1938	0.3112	0.3280	0.0613	0.0553	−0.0002	−0.0278	0.3482	0.3661	0.0912	0.0850	0.0280
1939	−0.0041	0.0035	0.0397	0.0594	0.0002	−0.0048	0.0035	0.0157	0.0442	0.0623	0.0045
1940	−0.0978	−0.0516	0.0339	0.0609	0.0000	0.0096	−0.1070	−0.0616	0.0240	0.0307	−0.0095
1941	−0.1159	−0.0900	0.0273	0.0093	0.0006	0.0972	−0.1955	−0.1723	−0.0644	−0.0807	−0.0890
1942	0.2034	0.4451	0.0260	0.0322	0.0027	0.0929	0.1014	0.3245	−0.0618	−0.0560	−0.0833
1943	0.2590	0.8837	0.0283	0.0208	0.0035	0.0316	0.2222	0.8355	−0.0036	−0.0109	−0.0278
1944	0.1975	0.5372	0.0473	0.0281	0.0033	0.0211	0.1730	0.5057	0.0257	0.0069	−0.0175
1945	0.3644	0.7361	0.0408	0.1073	0.0033	0.0225	0.3343	0.6996	0.0177	0.0831	−0.0190
1946	−0.0807	−0.1163	0.0172	0.0010	0.0035	0.1817	−0.2291	−0.2617	−0.1439	−0.1595	−0.1552
1947	0.0571	0.0092	−0.0234	−0.0263	0.0050	0.0901	−0.0316	−0.0747	−0.1056	−0.1083	−0.0793
1948	0.0550	−0.0211	0.0414	0.0340	0.0081	0.0271	0.0267	−0.0465	0.0129	0.0059	−0.0192
1949	0.1879	0.1975	0.0331	0.0645	0.0110	−0.0180	0.2091	0.2191	0.0317	0.0837	0.0293

1950	0.3171	0.3875	0.0212	0.0006	0.0120	0.0579	0.2462	0.3135	−0.0351	−0.0547	−0.0439
1951	0.2402	0.0780	−0.0269	−0.0394	0.0149	0.0587	0.1723	0.0188	−0.0816	−0.0933	−0.0418
1952	0.1837	0.0303	0.0352	0.0116	0.0166	0.0088	0.1735	0.0213	0.0261	0.0027	0.0076
1953	−0.0099	−0.0649	0.0341	0.0363	0.0182	0.0062	−0.0162	−0.0713	0.0277	0.0299	0.0118
1954	0.5262	0.6058	0.0539	0.0719	0.0086	−0.0050	0.5337	0.6138	0.0590	0.0771	0.0136
1955	0.3156	0.2044	0.0048	−0.0130	0.0157	0.0037	0.3111	0.2000	0.0010	−0.0167	0.0119
1956	0.0656	0.0428	−0.0681	−0.0559	0.0246	0.0286	0.0363	0.0138	−0.0944	−0.0824	−0.0040
1957	−0.1078	−0.1457	0.0871	0.0745	0.0314	0.0302	−0.1340	−0.1708	0.0550	0.0429	0.0011
1958	0.4336	0.6489	−0.0222	−0.0610	0.0154	0.0176	0.4095	0.6219	−0.0391	−0.0772	−0.0022
1959	0.1195	0.1640	−0.0097	−0.0226	0.0295	0.0150	0.1030	0.1468	−0.0243	−0.0371	0.0143
1960	0.0047	−0.0329	0.0907	0.1378	0.0266	0.0148	−0.0100	−0.0473	0.0747	0.1211	0.0116
1961	0.2689	0.3209	0.0482	0.0097	0.0213	0.0067	0.2604	0.3118	0.0412	0.0030	0.0144
1962	−0.0873	−0.1190	0.0795	0.0689	0.0273	0.0122	−0.0986	−0.1300	0.0665	0.0560	0.0149
1963	0.2280	0.2357	0.0219	0.0121	0.0312	0.0165	0.2081	0.2156	0.0054	−0.0043	0.0144
1964	0.1648	0.2352	0.0477	0.0351	0.0354	0.0119	0.1514	0.2210	0.0354	0.0229	0.0232
1965	0.1245	0.4175	−0.0046	0.0071	0.0393	0.0192	0.1031	0.3906	−0.0235	−0.0120	0.0197
1966	−0.1006	−0.0701	0.0020	0.0365	0.0476	0.0335	−0.1303	−0.1009	−0.0308	0.0027	0.0136
1967	0.2398	0.8357	−0.0495	−0.0919	0.0421	0.0304	0.2035	0.7835	−0.0779	−0.1190	0.0113
1968	0.1106	0.3597	0.0257	−0.0026	0.0521	0.0472	0.0607	0.2992	−0.0206	−0.0478	0.0046
1969	−0.0850	−0.2505	−0.0809	−0.0508	0.0658	0.0611	−0.1384	−0.2951	−0.1345	−0.1058	0.0045
1970	0.0401	−0.1743	0.1837	0.1210	0.0653	0.0549	−0.0145	−0.2188	0.1225	0.0628	0.0098
1971	0.1431	0.1650	0.1101	0.1323	0.0439	0.0336	0.1063	0.1272	0.0742	0.0955	0.0099
1972	0.1898	0.0443	0.0726	0.0568	0.0384	0.0341	0.1509	0.0096	0.0373	0.0221	0.0041
1973	−0.1466	−0.3090	0.0114	−0.0111	0.0693	0.0880	−0.2177	−0.3681	−0.0706	−0.0913	−0.0175
1974	−0.2647	−0.1995	−0.0306	0.0435	0.0800	0.1220	−0.3478	−0.2893	−0.1373	−0.0708	−0.0378
1975	0.3720	0.5282	0.1464	0.0919	0.0580	0.0701	0.2833	0.4303	0.0717	0.0205	−0.0114
1976	0.2384	0.5738	0.1865	0.1675	0.0508	0.0481	0.1820	0.5026	0.1324	0.1143	0.0026
1977	−0.0718	0.2538	0.0171	−0.0067	0.0512	0.0677	−0.1313	0.1754	−0.0477	−0.0701	−0.0156
1978	0.0656	0.2346	−0.0007	−0.0116	0.0718	0.0903	−0.0229	0.1325	−0.0841	−0.0942	−0.0171
1979	0.1844	0.4346	−0.0418	−0.0122	0.1038	0.1331	0.0455	0.2686	−0.1558	−0.1295	−0.0262
1980	0.3242	0.3988	−0.0262	−0.0395	0.1124	0.1240	0.1787	0.2440	−0.1349	−0.1470	−0.0105
1981	−0.0491	0.1395	−0.0096	0.0185	0.1471	0.0894	−0.1385	0.0453	−0.0924	−0.0666	0.0533

Source: R. G. Ibbotson and R. A. Sinquefield, *Stocks, Bonds, Bills, and Inflation: The Past and the Future*, exhibits 4 and 11 on pages 17 and 30, respectively.

more risky investment than any of the bond indices. Thus common stock investors do get higher returns than bond investors, on average. However, they must suffer lost sleep and the greater possibilities of a nervous breakdown or of bankruptcy because their investment is riskier. Thus, the common stock investors earn the higher return they typically obtain.

12-5.4 real versus nominal returns

As explained above in Sec. 9-6, "money illusion" is a phrase economists attribute to individuals who are so naive as to think they are wealthy merely because they have *more money* than other people. This belief is naive because it ignores the effects of inflation on the money's purchasing power. People who have a money illusion have not learned to distinguish between real wealth and nominal wealth. Real wealth is what truly matters; nominal wealth can be illusory during inflationary times.

Equations (12-26) through (12-28) define the one-period nominal rates of return on long-term bonds, Treasury bills, and common stocks, respectively. None of the equations measures real returns, however. Table 12-4 and Fig. 9-10 were prepared to suggest comparing nominal investment returns to the inflation rate in order to form estimates of the real returns. But to calculate each security's real (that is, inflation-adjusted) rate of return, Eq. (12-29) is used.

$$rr_t = r_t - q_t \tag{12-29}$$

The term r_t in Eq. (12-29) is the one-period nominal rate of return for the tth time period calculated with Eq. (12-26), (12-27), or (12-28). The inflation rate for the tth period, q_t, was defined in Eq. (12-25*a*). After the inflation rate is subtracted from the nominal rate of return as shown in Eq. (12-29), a good approximation of the *real rate of return* for time period t, denoted rr_t, is obtained. (See Box 9-4 on page 240 about the approximation.)

The real rate of return measures the percentage increase in real purchasing power an investment yielded in a given period rather than its nominal (or dollar) return. Columns 8 through 12 of Table 12-4 show the annual real rates of return from various investment averages. An investment asset will have a positive nominal return, $r_t > 0$, and a negative real return, $rr_t < 0$, during any period in which its nominal return was less than the inflation rate, $r_t < q_t$.

12-6 CHAPTER SUMMARY

The present-value model of Eq. (11-1) is used in bond valuation. Sometimes the most difficult part of the bond rating process is determining the appropriate market interest rate to use as the discount rate; this is where the bond quality rating is useful. Standard & Poor's bond rating committees use the 12-step process depicted in Fig. 12-1 to assign quality ratings to bonds. Figure 12-1 illustrates how the bond rating committee weighs many factors and arrives at a final assessment (at step 8 of the figure).

Bond rating committees and bond investors use financial ratios and guidelines such as the ones given in Box 12-1 to place a bond issue tentatively into a quality category. This tentative rating is reexamined in light of the issue's economic significance and competitive position, and the tentative rating may be shaded upward or downward as deemed appropriate. Finally, the protective provisions are evaluated to determine the final quality rating, with guidelines gained from years of experience helping analysts assess the impact of the various clauses. (For example, if a profitable issuer has outstanding at the same time a debenture bond and a mortgage bond, the collateralized bond will typically be rated one notch above the unsecured debenture if the two issues are about equal in all other respects.)

The relationship between the appropriate discount rate and a bond's quality rating changes continuously through time, as shown in Fig. 9-3, on page 217. Federal Reserve Board policy, fiscal policy, the supply and demand for loanable funds, and many other factors cause this relationship to change from day to day. Figure 9-5 shows the extent to which market yields on bonds with different risks of default have varied in recent years. The only difference between default-free Treasury bonds and corporate bonds is that corporate bonds must pay higher rates of interest in order to induce investors to assume the default risk. Since interest rates tend to rise and fall together, as shown in Fig. 9-5, corporate bonds' interest rates merely fluctuate at a slightly higher level than do Treasury bonds' interest rates.

Bond rating agencies like Standard & Poor's, Moody's, and Fitch's spend considerable resources assessing the quality of individual bond issues. These bond ratings seem to have some validity because (1) they vary directly with the market interest rates available in the bond markets on any given date, (2) the bond quality ratings are written into the investment guidelines handed down by most state governments, and (3) bond issuers pay thousands of dollars annually merely to have their bond issues rated currently. Empirical evidence compiled by Weinstein and by Griffin and Sanvicente, however, raised serious questions about whether the bond ratings determined the market yields, or whether the reverse was true. The quality ratings for outstanding bond issues lag the changes in the stock and bond prices by so many months that it seems as if the market prices may be guiding the rating agencies in their rating assignments.

Purchasing power risk is like a hidden tax. Inflation takes away from (or, if you prefer, taxes) the creditors and tends to give what it takes to debtors. If the debtors pay a nominal interest rate which is below the rate of inflation, inflation definitely benefits debtors at the expense of their lender. Therefore, bond investors, who are essentially lenders, cannot afford to overlook the purchasing power risk, which rises with the inflation rate.

The default risk is greatest on low-grade corporate bonds, and the purchasing power risk is worst in the high-inflation economies of the world. In the final analysis, however, one of the wonderful things about bond investment (as opposed to bond price speculation) is that investors can be relatively free from worry about interest income fluctuations if they so desire. By simply buying a high-grade bond with little risk of default which offers contractual interest payments and repayment of the principal at specified times, the investor can have peace of mind and earn a yield to maturity which is known in advance. However, for the brave-hearted security analysts who do default risk analysis and monetary economists who forecast inflation and interest rates, the bond markets offer opportunities for profitable speculating too.

QUESTIONS

12-1. Assume that in July 1979 the Exxon 6's of 1997 bonds have a 10 percent yield to maturity. That is, the Exxon Corporation's issue of bonds that paid 6 percent and will mature in 1997 were yielding 10 percent. Assuming that the bond matured in exactly 18 years, how could you calculate its present value?

12-2. Compare and contrast the Exxon 6's of 1997 selling at 75 with Zapata Corporation's 10¼'s of 1997 quoted at 87¾ on July 20, 1979. Express your ideas in terms of risk and return of these two bonds. Explain the reasons for the differences between them.

12-3. Compare home mortgages to collateralized bonds with a sinking fund.

12-4. Why would an investor prefer to buy bonds with a sinking fund provision? Why might investors tend not to want a sinking fund provision for bonds they owned?

12-5. Explain why the yields on short-term bonds fluctuate more than the yields on long-term bonds, and yet the prices of long-term bonds nevertheless fluctuate more than the prices of short-term bonds.

12-6. Dr. Weinstein's study of bond price movements showed that substantial gains could be earned by buying corporate bonds a day or two after their quality rating was upgraded. True, false, or uncertain? Explain.

12-7. What did Dr. Weinstein use as a standard for comparison or yardstick against which to gauge the price movements of the corporate bonds that had their ratings changed?

12-8. Why might you (or Professors Griffin and Sanvicente) suspect that when a corporation has its bond rating changed this event might affect the market price of its common stock?

12-9. How did researchers Griffin and Sanvicente filter the effects of bull- and bear-market fluctuations out of the stock price movements they studied?

12-10. Do you think that bond rating agencies like Standard & Poor's and Moody's give any heed to the market prices of the issuer's bonds and/or common stock when they change the quality ratings to outstanding issues? (*Hint*: Consider the research results of Dr. Weinstein and Professors Griffin and Sanvicente.)

SELECTED REFERENCES

Ibbotson, Roger G., and Rex A. Sinquefield, *Stocks, Bonds, Bills and Inflation: The Past and the Future,* 1982 ed. The Financial Analysts Federation, Charlottesville, Va. An easy-to-read empirical analysis of market premiums for default risk and purchasing power risk in stock and bond indices. The empirical work is well grounded in the received theory of financial economics.

APPENDIX 12A

default risk analysis for municipal bonds

This chapter, especially the section on financial ratios, was oriented toward corporate bonds. Some of the ratios suggested would be inappropriate for analyzing bonds issued by municipalities. Municipalities, such as towns, cities, school districts, sewer districts, and toll bridge authorities, issue a special type of bond to raise funds for their construction projects. These municipal bonds are different from the corporate bonds issued by businesses in the respects listed below:

- Municipalities do not earn profits; rather, they endeavor to provide optimum service at minimum cost.
- The interest income from municipal bonds is exempt from federal income taxes.
- Municipal projects are usually narrow rather than broad in scope. For example, with sewer-district bonds, proceeds go only for the construction of one sewer. The cash from the sale of the bonds cannot be spent for any other purpose.

Because of their unique characteristics, municipal bonds are analyzed differently from corporate bonds. The purpose of this appendix is to briefly sketch a few ideas about how to estimate the default risk in municipal bonds.

APP. 12A-1 REVENUE BONDS AND GENERAL OBLIGATION (GO) BONDS

With respect to the probability of default, municipal bonds can be divided into two main categories: revenue bonds (also called *assessment bonds*) and general obligation bonds (or GO bonds, also called *full-faith-and-credit bonds*).

Revenue bonds are bonds the interest and principal of which must be repaid from the revenues generated by the project built with the bond issue's proceeds. For example, toll bridge collections are the only source of revenue from which a toll bridge authority's bonds can be repaid. The city in which the toll bridge is located cannot tax the local residents to pay off the toll bridge bonds. If people do not use the toll bridge, the toll bridge authority will default on its bonds.

General obligation bonds are so called because it is a general legal obligation of the entire municipality to see that the bonds do not go into default. Suppose that a toll bridge were built by a city (rather than by a toll bridge authority), and because of a lack of use the toll bridge revenues were insufficient to pay off the GO bonds used to finance the bridge. The city could then collect sales taxes, property taxes, dog taxes, or any other kind of taxes from its residents to pay off the toll bridge bonds. The full faith and credit of the bond's issuer, which in this case was assumed to be a city, stands behind GO bonds, not merely the revenues from the project financed.

revenue bonds

When an issue of revenue bonds defaults, the courts are reluctant to auction off the bankrupt project in order to see that the bond's investors are repaid. The assets are usually viewed as vital public facilities that should be used only for public welfare. So municipal bonds' collateral should be viewed as essentially untouchable (this is also true of GO bonds). Thus the project's income is the only source of funds from which to pay revenue bond investors their interest and principal.

In analyzing the potential income behind an issue of revenue bonds, the analyst focuses on the asset that is supposed to generate the revenue. For example, if the revenue bond's proceeds are to be used to pay for a toll bridge, the important questions are: How frequently will the toll bridge be used? How much will the toll be? What chance is there that a competing toll bridge or ferryboat will make the toll bridge suffer losses?

The financial analysis of revenue bonds usually centers on the so-called coverage ratio. The numerator of the *coverage ratio* is the total revenues of the asset—for example, the total annual tolls from a toll bridge. The denominator is the bond issue's debt service charges—that is, the total annual interest and debt repayment requirements. A ratio of 1.5 to 2.0 is considered respectable.

The ratios used to analyze GO bonds are entirely different.

GO bonds

Municipal bond analysts have devised special ratios with which to evaluate the full faith and credit of the municipality issuing GO bonds. Four of the more popular ratios are discussed below.

the debt to asset ratio

The *debt to asset ratio* is the ratio of the municipality's debts that are dependent on the municipality's tax income over the city's so-called assets (that is, the assessed value of the municipality's taxable real estate). The tax statistics are usually readily available because cities use them every year to levy property taxes on their residents.

Municipal bond analysts feel it is dangerous for large cities to have debt in excess of 10 percent of their taxable assets. For small cities, 8 percent is considered maximum. Experience suggests that beyond these values municipalities cannot reasonably be expected to repay without defaulting.

A serious problem sometimes encountered in measuring the debt to asset ratio is due to overlapping taxes. For example, if a city and the state in which it is located both charge property taxes on the same assets, it is practically impossible to calculate meaningful debt to asset ratios. In that case, other ratios become more important.

the debt per capita ratio

The *debt per capita ratio* measures the amount of debt per person that a municipality has incurred. It is the ratio of the municipality's total debt to the city's total population. Small cities can have debt of up to about $300 per resident and still enjoy investment-grade quality ratings, if other ratios are also sound. Larger cities can go up to $500 before their ratings are hurt.

debt service as a percent of the total budget

This ratio measures the percentage of a municipality's annual spending budget that goes to interest payments and debt repayments due that year. The municipality's total annual interest expense and current debt retirement obligations are the numerator, called the *total debt service charges*. The denominator is the total budgeted operating expense. As a rule, debt service charges should not exceed 12 percent of the municipality's budget.

the proportion of total debt maturing in 5 years

This ratio is simply the fraction of a municipality's total debt that will be maturing and thus will require either repayment or refunding (or "rolling over," as it is also called) within the next 5 years. Too much debt coming due too soon could strain the municipality's ability to stay solvent. If this proportion exceeds one-fourth, caution is advisable.

other considerations

In addition to the four ratios above, municipal bond analysts consider the municipality's *sociological trends* and its *demonstrated financial responsibility*.

If the general populace of a city is moving away so that the city has a shrinking tax base, this is an undesirable *sociological trend*. If the middle class, in particular, is moving into the surburban towns and leaving poorer people to populate the city, this is another sociological trend that can undermine municipal bond ratings. It is believed that middle-class people's homes and neighborhoods and the kinds of retail stores they support are a big part of what makes a city a pleasant place to live. Furthermore, the middle class people are the doctors, lawyers, schoolteachers, skilled blue-collar workers, and business people. If the middle class flees a city, the inner city becomes an unappealing mixture of business buildings, hotels, and poor neighborhoods that cannot generate sufficient tax revenues.

The best measure of any organization's *financial responsibility* is its ability to avoid deficit financing. Persistent deficit financing by a municipality casts doubt on the future ability of the community to either sell new bonds or roll over the outstanding debt with replacement debt. No one wants to loan money to an organization that spends more than it takes in year after year.

APP. 12A-2 MUNICIPAL BOND RATINGS

Standard & Poor's publishes quality ratings on approximately 6,000 municipal bond issues. These ratings are important to investors who do not have time to do their own financial analysis. For example, a West Coast investor interested in bonds issued by an East Coast municipality would have to go to great expense to get past financial statements, current budgets, expenditure plans, and a sociological analysis of the eastern municipality (unfortunately, municipalities do not publish annual reports, as do corporations). Standard & Poor's itself, for example, requests audited financial statements from the issuing municipality in order to obtain facts on which to base its published ratings.[14]

As might be imagined, municipal bonds are traded inactively in small OTC bond markets located in or near the issuing municipality. Local banks, wealthy local individuals, and large local businesses that have some interest in the municipality frequently buy entire issues through direct placements. Directly

[14] Standard & Poor's publishes some of the raw financial data for the municipalities it rates. These financial data and the municipalities' ratings are in *Standard & Poor's Municipal Bond Selector*, a periodic paperback booklet.

placed investments are usually held to maturity. Such issues never even receive quality ratings. As a result, the markets for many municipal bonds are weak, localized, and sometimes nonexistent. Thus, it is important to see if a given municipal bond is actively traded before undertaking any further investigation.[15]

APPENDIX 12B

rating corporate bonds statistically

Professors Pinches and Mingo (P&M)[16] have shown how to use a statistical procedure called multiple discriminant analysis (MDA) to estimate bond ratings based on six statistics for a firm. Essentially P&M fit four linear equations like Eq. (App. 12B-1) to classify bonds into one of five categories.

$$z_{iJ} = f_{i1}x_{1J} + f_{i2}x_{2J} + f_{i3}x_{3J} + f_{i4}x_{4J} + f_{i5}x_{5J} + f_{i6}x_{6J} \qquad \text{(App. 12B-1)}$$

where

i = 1, 2, 3, 4, 5 ratings

J = 1, 2, . . . , n bonds issues

The six explanatory variables are defined below for firm J's bonds:

x_{1J} = subordination of the issue is measured by setting x_1 to zero or unity to indicate whether or not it is subordinated

x_{2J} = years of consecutive cash dividends, a measure of stability

x_{3J} = size of the bond issue, a measure of the issue's marketability

x_{4J} = 5-year average of net income divided by interest expense, a coverage ratio

x_{5J} = 5-year average of long-term debt over net worth, a leverage measure

x_{6J} = net income over total assets, a measure of profitability for the J company

The f_i coefficients in Eq. (App. 12B-1) are numbers estimated statistically so that the discriminant score, denoted z_J for the jth bond, would give the best indication of whether that bond issue is in the ith quality rating. For example, for the first category (i = 1), which is the AAA-grade rating, if a bond issue's

[15] Those interested in a more detailed treatment of municipal bond analysis should consult Hugh C. Sherwood, *How Municipal and Corporate Debt Is Rated,* Wiley, New York, 1976, chap. 13); see also *Standard & Poor's Rating Guide*, McGraw-Hill, New York, 1979, chaps. 18–24 and appendixes); also see Robert Lamb and Stephen P. Rappaport, *Municipal Bonds,* McGraw-Hill, New York, 1980. More recently, see *The Municipal Bond Handbook*, vols. I and II, Dow Jones-Irwin, Homewood, Ill., 1983. Volume I is edited by F. J. Fabozzi, S. G. Feldstein, I. M. Pollack, and F. G. Zarb. Volume II is edited by S. G. Feldstein, F. J. Fabozzi, and I. M. Pollack.

[16] G. E. Pinches and K. A. Mingo, "A Multivariate Analysis of Industrial Bond Ratings," *Journal of Finance,* March 1973, pp. 1–32.

discriminant score is not high enough, that bond is not classified in the first category. Instead, the bond's discriminant score is next calculated for the second function ($i = 2$) to see whether z_j is high enough to qualify the bond to be in category 2 (that is, a AA-grade bond). This process goes on through the third and fourth discriminant scores, respectively. If a bond's discriminant score is not high enough to qualify for any of the first four categories (that is, $i = 1, 2, 3,$ or 4), the bond is assigned to category 5, which is grade B and below.[17]

In testing their model, P&M correctly classified 92 out of a sample of 132 bonds; that is, 70 percent were correctly classified. Multiple discriminant analysis appears to be a useful statistical tool for rating bonds. Multiple regression models can also be employed fruitfully in rating bond issues statistically.[18]

[17] R. A. Eisenbeis and R. B. Avery, *Discriminant Analysis and Classification Procedures,* Lexington Books, Lexington, Mass., 1972).

[18] Robert S. Kaplan and Gabriel Urwitz, "Statistical Models of Bond Rating: A Methodological Inquiry," *Journal of Business,* vol. 52, no. 2, April 1979, pp. 231–262. Kaplan and Urwitz developed a model to estimate bond ratings which works very well. However, when testing their model against a common multiple regression model, they report that the multiple regression model is nearly as accurate at classifying bond issues' ratings as their more sophisticated model.

the level and structure of market interest rates

The price of a bond moves inversely to its yield to maturity with decimal-point mathematical precision. Therefore, the best approach to predicting bonds' prices is to first explain their yields to maturity. The yields to maturity of all bonds are market interest rates which fluctuate minute by minute. These fluctuations in bond market interest rates may be viewed as arising from two sources—those which are internal and those which are external to the issuing firm:[1]

1. Changes *inside* the issuing firms alter the probability that the bond investors might suffer losses from default or bankruptcy. This risk factor is peculiar to corporation and municipal bonds; it is called *default risk.* Default risk was introduced in Chap. 9 and analyzed further in Chap. 12.
2. Changes *outside* the issuing firm affect similar bonds simultaneously. Changes in the supply and demand for credit, changes in the inflation rate (which was introduced in Chap. 9 under the heading of Purchasing Power Risk), and changes in the macroeconomic environment (which was also introduced in Chap. 9 under the heading of Market Risk) are factors external to the individual corporations which affect their bond yields and prices. Those factors which are external to the firm determine the level and structure of market interest rates and, thus, bond prices.

The market interest rates, or yields to maturity, which are the focus of this entire chapter were called the appropriate discount rate for finding a bond's present value in Chaps. 11 and 12. These rates are sometimes also called the risk-adjusted cost of debt capital or the investor's required rate of return.[2]

[1] In order to reap the full benefit from Chap. 13, the reader should fully understand Chap. 11, Bond Valuation, and Chap. 12, Default Risk and Purchasing Power Risk in Bonds.

[2] Care should be taken not to become confused about bonds' *one-period rates of return* as defined in Eq. (2-1). Chapter 11 discusses only bonds' *yields to maturity,* and these multiperiod rates of return are different from the one-period rates of return.

However, regardless of what you call the yield to maturity, explaining bond values is easy once the appropriate yield to maturity is known; just use Eq. (11-2) to find any bond's exact value.[3]

13-1 THE LEVEL OF INTEREST RATES

The term structure of interest rates (that is, the shape of what is called the *yield curve*) refers to the relationship between yields for bonds which are identical in every respect except their term to maturity. Studying the term structure of interest rates addresses questions like: "Why are the yields of some issuers' bonds which have 20 years to maturity usually higher than the same issuers' bonds with fewer years to maturity, if all other factors are equal?" Such questions are addressed later in this chapter. This section deals with the *level,* but not the structure, of interest rates. It answers questions about why all interest rates are high or low, rising or falling.

Market yields to maturity are determined by many things. The most basic determinant of interest rates is what economists call the *real rate of interest,* or the rate at which capital grows in the physical sense. For example, consider a stock of capital that consists of 10 coconut trees on an island. If the 10 coconut trees produce enough nuts and leaves to maintain the fertility of their soil, sustain the people who tend them, and increase to 11 coconut trees in a year, the trees may be viewed as a stock of capital that grew at 10 percent per year. Economists call this basic rate of interest the real rate of interest. The real rate of interest is not published in newspapers, as are the nominal interest rates.

In addition to the real rate of interest, market interest rates are also affected by various risk-premiums which investors may demand. In order to undertake risky investments, lenders (such as bond investors) may require one or more *risk-premiums* to be paid over and above the real rate of interest to induce them to lend their funds when the risk of loss exists. The determination of default risk-premiums for bonds and the relationship between bond yields and bond quality ratings was explained in Chap. 9. Other kinds of risk-premiums which bond investors may demand will be explained below.

Since interest rates and loans are typically in nominal money quantities rather than real physical quantities, the nominal interest rate must contain an allowance for the rate of price change so that lenders' wealth will not be eroded away by inflation. For example, if a lender loans $100 for a year at 5 percent interest, the lender will be repaid $105. But, if inflation at a rate of 10

[3] Some bond analysts stress the similar and simultaneous way in which the market price and market yield to maturity of a bond are determined. This approach is technically valid because, as a glance at the present value model of Eq. (11-1) will show, the present value of a bond and its yield to maturity are merely different sides of the same coin. The approach used in this book does not deny the simultaneity of the present value and *yield;* however, it does not emphasize this simultaneity either. Instead, it explains the present value of a bond as being determined by *yield to maturity.* That is, the *yield* is treated as an explanatory or causal variable which determines the bond's price. This latter approach is followed because it avoids the cumbersome discussion of bonds with different face values and focuses more expeditiously on the common denominator which can be used to compare and contrast all debt securities—namely, the investment's market-determined interest rate.

percent exists, $E(\Delta P/P) = 10$ percent, this \$105 will have the purchasing power a year later of $1/1.1 = 90.9$ percent of \$105, or \$95.44 because of the inflation.[4] Thus, the lender must charge 5 percent interest plus 10 percent inflation allowance, or 15 percent per year to allow for the inflation. In this case, the lender will be repaid \$115 [= \$100 times (100 percent + 5 percent + 10 percent)]. After 10 percent inflation, the \$115 has a real purchasing power of $1/1.1 = 90.9$ percent of \$115, or \$104.54. The lender thus gained only a \$4.54 increase, or 4.54 percent, in purchasing power by loaning money at 15 percent interest during a year in which inflation was 10 percent. This shows that lenders need to raise interest rates by at least the rate of inflation in order to maintain the real purchasing power of their wealth. This inflation adjustment is called the *Fisher effect,* after an economist named Irving Fisher, who first explained it decades ago.[5]

The manner in which the three determinants of interest rates (that is, the real rate of interest, risk-premiums, and the rate of expected price change) are combined is summarized symbolically in Eq. (13-1).

$$\begin{pmatrix}\text{Nominal,}\\ \text{or market}\\ \text{interest,}\\ \text{rate}\end{pmatrix} = \begin{pmatrix}\text{real}\\ \text{rate of}\\ \text{interest}\end{pmatrix} + \begin{pmatrix}\text{various}\\ \text{possible}\\ \text{risk-}\\ \text{premiums}\end{pmatrix} + \begin{pmatrix}\text{expected}\\ \text{rate of}\\ \text{inflation}\end{pmatrix} \qquad (13\text{-}1)$$

Equation (13-1) is a model of how the *level* of interest rates is determined.

The level of interest rates refers to how high all interest rates tend to be. For example, suppose that the real rate of interest is 3 percent per year (3 percent = .03), that lenders require a 2 percent risk-premium for loans of some given risk-class (2 percent = .02), and that expected inflation is 2 percent per year [$E(\Delta P/P) = 2$ percent = .02]. According to Eq. (13-1), this implies that the nominal interest rate for loans of this given risk-class is (3 percent + 2 percent + 2 percent =) 7 percent per year. If inflationary expectations rise from 2 to 4 percent per year, Eq. (13-1) implies that nominal interest rates will rise to (3 percent + 2 percent + 4 percent =) 9 percent per year. This increase from 7 to 9 percent is a change in the *level* of interest rates which would increase all interest rates.

13-1.1 measuring the effects of inflationary expectations

An economist named Dr. William Gibson, among others, published scientific evidence showing how the public's inflationary expectations, $E(\Delta P/P)$, determine market interest rates.[6] Gibson estimated a series of regressions of the form shown in Eq. (13-2).

[4] The symbol E denotes the mathematical expectation; it is defined in Mathematical App. B. The Greek letter delta, Δ, means *change* when it is used in economics. The symbol P might represent the consumer price index (CPI), for example. Therefore, ΔP means price change, and $E(\Delta P/P)$ represents an expected percentage price change, that is, the expected inflation rate.

[5] Irving Fisher discussed the effects of inflation on market interest rates in *Appreciation and Interest,* Macmillan, New York, 1896, pp. 75–76. The ideas were expanded later in Fisher's book *The Theory of Interest,* Macmillan, New York, 1930. For a different view which is critical of Fisher's well-received theory see Steven C. Leuthold, "Interest Rates, Inflation and Deflation," *Financial Analysts Journal,* January–February 1981, pp. 28–41.

[6] W. E. Gibson, "Interest Rates and Inflationary Expectations: New Evidence," *American Economic Review,* December 1972, pp. 854–865. A more sophisticated study was done by W. P. Yohe and D. S. Karnosky, "Interest Rates and Price Level Changes, 1952–69," *Review,* St.

$$\text{ytm}_{it} = A_i + B_i E(\Delta P/P)_t + z_{it} \qquad E(z_{it}) = 0 \tag{13-2}$$

In Eq. (13-2) ytm_{it} designates the market interest rate or yield to maturity of the ith bond issue in time period t, and $E(\Delta P/P)_t$ denotes inflationary expectations in period t. The A_i and B_i terms are the regression intercept and slope coefficients (see Mathematical App. D about regression) for the ith bond issue. Regression Eq. (13-2) tries to explain the market yield of the ith bond in the tth period in terms of the rate of inflation which was expected in that period.

Gibson used surveys taken at different times from dozens of economists' inflation forecasts for 1 year in the future to find the consensus of inflationary expectations. Surveys of U.S. economists from coast to coast were taken every 6 months for 18 years; $E(\Delta P/P)_t$ denotes their average forecast for the tth time period's inflation. Table 13-1 shows the regression results.

Regression Eq. 13-2 was fitted for five different bond issues. The coefficients of determination, denoted $\bar{R}^2$ in Table 13-1, measure the percentage of variation in the bond yields to maturity explained by the concurrent inflationary expectations variable, $E(\Delta P/P)$. Since the lowest $\bar{R}^2$ is .76 (= 76 percent for 3-month Treasury bills), this means that over three-quarters of the changes in interest rates can be explained with inflationary expectations. All five slope coefficients, B_i, approximate unity, indicating that if the rate of inflation changes by a certain amount, interest rates change by about the same amount. The smaller regression slope coefficients for the bonds with longer terms to maturity may be interpreted to mean that 1 year's inflation expectations have a smaller effect on long-term bond yields than on the yields of short-term bonds. The intercept terms A_i in Eq. (13-2) are estimates of the real rate of interest plus the risk-premium (which should be zero for U.S. Treasury bonds) in Eq. (13-1). For example, for Treasury bonds with 10 years and over to maturity, the intercept is A = 3.23 percent during the sampled period.

These regression statistics attest to the importance of inflationary expectations in the determination of market interest rates during the period sampled. The annual inflation rate and interest rate data shown in Table 12-4 on pages

Louis Federal Reserve Bank, December 1969. This readable survey and empirical test is available free in pamphlet form as reprint no. 49 from the St. Louis Fed. A more esoteric study is by M. Feldstein and O. Eckstein, "The Fundamental Determinants of the Interest Rate," *Review of Economics and Statistics,* November 1970, pp. 303–374. Most recently, see E. Fama, "Short-Term Interest Rates as Predictors of Inflation," *American Economic Review,* June 1975, pp. 269–282.

TABLE 13-1 Gibson's regression statistics for Eq. (13-2)

i	yields (r's) from:	intercept A_i	slope B_i	$\bar{R}^2$
1	3-month Treasury bills	2.20	.93	.76
2	6-month Treasury bills	2.04	1.09	.78
3	9- to 12-month Treasury bills	2.19	1.06	.79
4	3- to 5-year Treasury notes	2.92	.89	.83
5	10-year Treasury bonds	3.23	.67	.85

352–353 and Fig. 13-3 on page 378 furnish further evidence of the way interest rates move up and down with inflation.

13-1.2 supply and demand for credit

Although both the regression statistics in Table 13-1 and the data in Table 13-2 present strong evidence that rising rates of inflation pushed up interest rates during the 1960s and 1970s, there are changes in interest rates that were not related to inflationary factors. These as-yet-unexplained changes are the result of various risk-premiums (which will be explained in the next section) and changes in the supply of and demand for loanable funds caused by disintermediation, "crowding out," the ebb and flow of the business cycle, and other factors.[7]

13-1.3 market interest varies with the stage of the business cycle

The business cycle affects credit conditions by affecting the supply and demand for funds. Business economists at banks, bond portfolio managers, and others who must forecast day-to-day changes in interest rates study flow-of-funds tables which show where credit inflows (namely, savings) and credit outflows (that is, borrowings) originate in an effort to ascertain the effects of short-run changes in the supply and demand for loanable funds. During a period of economic expansion, the unemployment rate falls, business activity quickens, and businesses borrow money to build bigger plants and to finance more inventory, accounts receivable, and equipment purchases. The resulting credit demands bid up interest rates. In contrast, during slowdowns and recessions, unemployment increases, manufacturing activity slows, and demand for credit shrinks; thus interest rates fall, if all other factors are constant.

13-1.4 crowding out bids up market interest rates

President Ronald Reagan pushed income tax cuts through the Congress during his first term in the White House (1980–1984). However, Congress did not reduce the level of federal spending to reflect these reduced tax revenues. As a result, federal budget deficits of approximately $200 billion per year occurred. The U.S. Treasury had to sell $200 billion of bonds per year to raise the money to pay for the government's deficit spending. These huge deficits caused problems.

[7] *Intermediation* refers to the activity of financial intermediaries like banks and savings and loan associations (S&Ls) as they intermediate between savers and investors. Financial intermediaries accept many small savings deposits, pool them, and then make large loans to finance business expansion and home building. *Disintermediation* is the reverse; savers withdraw their savings from financial intermediaries and thus cause a reduction in loanable funds. Rising interest rates cause disintermediation because banks and savings and loan associations are reluctant to accept deposits which obligate the institution to pay high interest rates on their savings accounts. Credit crunches are a result of interest rates pushed up by tight credit conditions and inflation rather than the cause of the high interest rates themselves.

In 1969–1970, for example, nonprice rationing of loanable funds resulting from disintermediation occurred when market interest rates were pushed by inflation to levels in excess of the legal ceilings (imposed by the Federal Reserve's Regulation Q, for example) that savings institutions could pay. As a result, savers withdrew their savings and invested them in market securities with higher market-determined yields. The credit crunch of 1969–1970 resulted. Similar credit crunches occurred in 1966 and 1959 and almost occurred at other recent times. Hopefully, credit crunches will not occur in the 1980s because the bank regulatory authorities are relaxing the interest rate ceilings (like Regulation Q) that cause disintermediation.

TABLE 13-2 average yields and related statistics over recent sample periods

	1955–1967		1968–1979		1955–1979	
yields to maturity*:	average	variance	average	variance	average	variance
AAA	4.25%	.42	7.88	.853	5.99	3.93
AA	4.36	.426	8.12	.86	6.17	4.16
A	4.52	.42	8.34	.89	6.35	4.29
BBB	4.97	.48	8.90	1.04	6.86	4.61
Long-term Treasury bonds	3.88	.38	7.01	1.50	5.38	3.35
Intermediate-term Treasury bonds	3.89	.53	7.01	1.25	5.39	3.31
Short-term Treasury bonds	3.66	.60	6.92	1.87	5.22	3.84
Monetary sector statistics:						
Intermediate-term–long-term yield difference*	.01	.03	.01	.49	.01	.25
Price-earnings ratio†	16.59	7.08	13.46	16.82	15.08	14.00
N.B. reserves†	16,442	2,244	27,317	24,830	22,656	144,169
Inflation‡	1.69%	1.18	7.06	10.20	4.26	12.70
Real sector:						
Unemployment	5.04	1.23	5.75	2.16	5.38	1.80
Capacity utilization§	83.76	23.54	82.516	19.59	83.16	21.96
Financial ratios (national averages)¶:						
Rate of return on equity	10.96	3.30	12.68	5.96	11.79	5.30
Current ratio	2.43	.01	1.99	.01	2.22	.06
Quick ratio	.47	.01	.25	.00	.37	.02
Equity/debt ratio	3.93	.20	2.39	.02	3.19	.70

* Standard & Poor's Corporation, *Standard & Poor's Trade and Securities Statistics,* 1976.

† Board of Governors of the Federal Reserve System, *Federal Reserve Bulletin,* Washington, D.C., published monthly.

‡ U.S. Department of Commerce, Bureau of Economic Analysis, *Business Conditions Digest,* Washington, D.C., published monthly (GNP implicit deflator).

§ Trustees of the University of Pennsylvania, *Wharton Quarterly,* Philadelphia, Pennsylvania, Summer 1976 (manufacturing, mining, and utilities statistic).

¶ Federal Trade Commission, *Quarterly Financial Report,* U.S. Government Printing Office, Washington, D.C.

Source: J. C. Francis, "Bond Risk Premia," *Journal of Financial and Quantitative Analysis,* November 1976, and an unpublished updated study.

In 1983 the U.S. economy was emerging from a recession and businesses were starting to demand bank loans and other forms of credit to expand their factory operations and to finance larger inventories. Thus, businesses and the U.S. Treasury were both trying to borrow whatever loanable funds were available. The resulting demand for credit exceeded the available supply of loanable funds, and some hopeful businesses were *crowded out* of the credit markets by the massive borrowing demands of the U.S. Treasury. This crowding out—that is, the borrowing competition between businesses and the federal government—bid up market interest rates to levels above what they would have been if the government had balanced its budget. More concisely, crowding out caused high interest rates during 1983 and 1984.

Essentially, market interest rates may be viewed as being the *"price" of credit.* When the demand for credit exceeds the supply of loanable funds, market interest rates are bid up by those who are seeking to borrow.

The level of inflationary expectations and the phase of the business cycle are two of the main factors usually affecting interest rates. But, various kinds of risk-premiums which rise and fall can also have an important effect on market interest rates.

13-2 YIELD SPREADS

Yield spreads are the differences between the yields of any pair of bonds—usually a default-free U.S. Treasury bond and another, more risky, bond. Yield spreads are defined in Eq. (13-3) for the tth time period.

$$\begin{pmatrix}\text{Yield on}\\ \text{risky bond}\end{pmatrix}_t - \begin{pmatrix}\text{U.S. Treasury}\\ \text{bond yield}\end{pmatrix}_t = (\text{yield spread})_t \qquad (13\text{-}3)$$

Yield spreads like the one in Eq. (13-3) may also be called *risk-premiums* because they measure the additional yield that risky bonds pay to induce investors to buy more-risky bonds rather than less-risky bonds.

13-2.1 the cyclical portion of the yield spreads

Table 13-2 shows some yield spread statistics which were measured from Standard & Poor's average yields for different classes of bonds. The table shows that over the period 1955–1979, for example, AA-grade corporate bonds paid an average risk-premium of .78 of 1 percent, or 78 basis points (that is, 6.17 percent less 5.39 percent), over similar term (namely, intermediate-term) U.S. Treasury bonds.

The data in Table 13-2 show that yield spreads averaged larger in the 1968 to 1979 sample period than they did from 1955 through 1967. However, Table 13-3 shows that yield spreads vary with the business cycle.[8] The right-

[8] Chen, Roll, and Ross have found a statistically significant relationship between common stock returns and the (orthogonalized) market interest rate yield spreads (and several other economic variables too). See Nai-Fu Chen, Richard Roll, and Stephen Ross, "Economic Forces and the Stock Market: Testing the APT and Alternative Asset Pricing Theories," CRSP Working Paper no. 119, December 1983. Their results are also referred to in "The Arbitrage Pricing Theory Approach to Strategic Portfolio Planning" by Richard Roll and Stephen Ross in the May–June 1984 issue of *Financial Analysts Journal,* pp. 14–29. The relationship between the individual risk factors and the total risk of an asset are discussed more fully in this book's Chap. 30, about the arbitrage pricing theory (APT).

TABLE 13-3 market rates and yield spreads at economic peaks and troughs

date	RATES AND YIELD SPREADS, IN PERCENT, FOR SECURITIES AS FOLLOWS					
	AAA	AA	A	BBB	I-T*	(BBB–I-T*)
August 1957 (peak)	4.13	4.27	4.39	5.11	3.84	1.27
April 1958 (trough)	3.63	3.82	4.03	4.82	2.58	2.24
April 1960 (peak)	4.44	4.56	4.75	5.34	4.13	1.21
February 1961 (trough)	4.28	4.40	4.66	5.22	3.74	1.48
December 1969 (peak)	7.65	7.83	8.10	8.67	7.47	1.20
November 1970 (trough)	7.79	8.31	8.69	9.38	6.52	2.86
November 1973 (peak)	7.76	7.95	8.17	8.67	6.83	1.84
March 1975 (trough)	8.63	8.86	9.08	9.66	6.92	2.74
January 1980 (peak)	10.98	11.36	11.59	12.12	10.70	1.42
July 1980 (trough)	10.63	10.96	11.25	12.10	9.72	2.38
July 1981 (peak)	14.11	14.54	14.79	15.74	14.11	1.63

* I-T stands for an average of intermediate-term U.S. Treasury bonds.
Source: National Bureau of Economics Research Peaks and Troughs.

hand column of Table 13-3 shows, for example, how the average risk-premiums on BBB-grade bonds varied over the business cycle. Other yield spreads may be calculated from the data, which show that all risk-premiums tend to be larger at economic troughs than at the peaks in economic activity. This cyclical fluctuation can be forecast and used to establish profitable hedges between bonds in different classes which are expected to have opening or closing yield spreads.

Risk-premiums are higher at economic troughs for two main reasons. First, unemployment, fear of job loss, and risk-aversion are higher during recessions. Therefore, most investors demand larger risk-premiums to induce them to buy risky bonds. Second, the corporations which issue bonds typically experience reduced sales and profits during recessions. Since the issuers are more subject to bankruptcy during recessions, investors require larger risk-premiums.[9] These cyclical changes in the risk-premiums in Eq. (13-1) are one more reason why market interest rates fluctuate. However, there are other noncyclical causes for risk-premiums to change.

13-2.2 the noncyclical risk-premiums

The yield spreads between different debt securities open and close from year to year for some reasons which are not cyclical and easy to predict. Investors may demand risk-premiums of varying amounts for any of the following reasons.

[9] Lawrence Fisher, "Determinants of Risk Premiums on Corporate Bonds," *Journal of Political Economy,* June 1959, pp. 217–237; W. Braddock Hickman, *Corporate Bond Quality and Investor Experience,* Princeton University Press for the National Bureau of Economic Research, 1958; *Statistical Measures of Corporate Bond Financing Since 1900,* Princeton, 1960; George E. Pinches and Kent A. Mingo, "A Multivariate Analysis of Industrial Bond Ratings," *Journal of Finance,* March 1973, pp. 1–18. In addition to the risk-premiums which investors demand that *vary over the business cycle,* the current supply of and demand for loanable funds also affects yield spreads; see Ray C. Fair and Burton G. Malkiel, "The Determination of Yield Differentials between Debt Instruments of the Same Maturity," *Journal of Money, Credit and Banking,* November 1971, pp. 733–749.

1. *Fears of future inflation.* Table 13-1 shows regression statistics from Gibson's regression Eq. (13-2). These statistics indicate that Gibson's inflation model explained the variations in market interest rates very well during the 1960s and 1970s in terms of the concurrent rates of inflationary expectations. This was a period of steadily accelerating rates of inflation to higher and higher levels to which the public was unaccustomed; thus each new higher rate of inflation was unanticipated. But, Gibson's inflation model did not explain why market interest rates remained at double-digit levels during the period 1980–1984, for example, while the inflation rate crashed down from 12 percent to only 4 percent. Gibson's inflation model could not explain this phenomenon because it did not allow for investors' *fears* that double-digit rates of inflation might not be easy to extinguish. As a result of widely held fears during the early 1980s that double-digit inflation would resume, investors largely ignored the fall in the actual rate of inflation. Instead, investors demanded new high "fear of inflation" risk-premiums during the early 1980s to induce them to buy bonds at a time when they were afraid of renewed double-digit inflation.

2. *Domestic political fears.* The daily purchases and sales of bonds by hundreds of bankers and investment managers has a continuous and substantial impact on yield spreads. Most of these professional financial people scrutinize the current events news for political developments that have economic and financial implications. The political expectations and fears of these money managers are thus reflected in yield spreads. For instance, if the financial community thinks that a liberal President and Congress might get elected in the United States and raise taxes to finance liberal spending programs in the years ahead, political fears that the higher taxes might stifle people's incentive to work would tend to increase yield spreads. Financial newspapers like the *Wall Street Journal* frequently report that the financial community appears to have reached some consensus forecast of the future based on its current assessment of political eventualities, and even explain how the financial community's political expectations influence yield spreads and other aspects of the economic environment.

3. *Foreign political fears.* International investors face the risk that the governments of foreign countries in which they wish to invest may be suddenly overthrown, the risk that the existing government may swing far to the right or left in its political policies, the risk that the foreign currency may be devalued, the risk of civil uprising, ad nauseam. As a result of these perplexing uncertainties some investors demand risk-premiums from foreign investments over and above the risk-premiums they expect from domestic investments to induce them to assume the risks of foreign investing.

4. *Fears of military upheaval.* When a country becomes involved in a war, it usually causes the country to spend more on the war effort than can be collected in tax revenues, and federal deficits result. Most governments do not finance their war deficits by selling federal debt obligations. Instead, governments usually finance war deficits by printing new money at an inflationary rate which is sufficient to cover the deficit spending. The resulting rates of inflation undermine and destroy the country's security values and eventually the country's general economy, if the war lasts very long. Experienced financial economists have observed this wartime phenomenon over and over again in modern history. Futhermore, when a country is engaged in a war, the chance always exists that the country may suffer domestic damage if the enemy invades it.

Fears of this financially bleak and physically scary environment cause investors to require high risk-premiums to invest in either corporate or government bonds from countries that are about to enter a war or are already engaged in a war.

In addition to changes in the level of interest rates which result from changing rates of inflation, changing credit conditions, cyclical changes in yield spreads, and unusual risk-premiums, there are also changes in what economists call the "term structure of interest rates." These changes in the term structure of interest rates result from a different set of influences which are examined in the next section.

13-3 THE TERM STRUCTURE OF INTEREST RATES

The combined effects of changes in inflationary expectations and changing credit market conditions cause the *level* of market yields to vary over a wide range from year to year. However, these facts reveal nothing about the term structure of interest rates. Different bonds have different terms to maturity. For example, the U.S. Treasury, corporations such as American Telephone and Telegraph (AT&T) and General Motors (GM), and other organizations which borrow in the bond markets have different bond issues outstanding with maturities ranging from 3 months to over 30 years. Moreover, any given bond issuer usually has, on any given day, *different yields to maturity* on its various bond issues which differ only with respect to their *term to maturity.* For a given bond issuer, the structure of yields for bonds with different terms to maturity (but no other differences) is called the *term structure of interest rates. Ceteris paribus,* the term to maturity of a bond will affect its yield. Thus, Eq. (13-1) must be extended as shown below in Eq. (13-4) to reflect how the market interest rate of the *i*th bond at the *t*th time period is affected by varying the bond issue's term to maturity.

$$\begin{pmatrix}\text{Nominal, or}\\ \text{market interest,}\\ \text{rate for } i \text{ at } t\end{pmatrix} = \begin{pmatrix}\text{real}\\ \text{rate of}\\ \text{return}\end{pmatrix} + \begin{pmatrix}\text{risk-}\\ \text{premiums}\\ \text{for } i \text{ at } t\end{pmatrix} + \begin{pmatrix}\text{expected}\\ \text{rate of}\\ \text{inflation}\\ \text{at time } t\end{pmatrix} + \begin{pmatrix}\text{term}\\ \text{structure of}\\ \text{interest rates}\\ \text{for } i \text{ at } t\end{pmatrix} \tag{13-4}$$

The purpose of this section is to examine the manner in which a bond's term to maturity affects its yield to maturity. Figure 13-1 shows graphs of several hypothetical yield curves; these yield curves illustrate the term structure of interest rates graphically.

This section of the chapter focuses on the term structure of interest rates, or, if you prefer, the *yield curve.* By eliminating all variables which do not affect this term structure, the analysis is simplified and expedited. This can be done by limiting the discussion to the various maturities of U.S. government bonds. All U.S. Treasury bonds have identical *default risk*-premiums of zero. By restricting discussion to marketable U.S. government bonds we have, in financial parlance, limited our discussion to the *Treasury yield curve.*

The *term structure of interest rates* for U.S. government bonds, or the *yield curve* as it is also called, may be defined as the relationship between yields and

FIGURE 13-1 yield curve patterns of U.S. government securities for years characterized by sudden changes in inflation and for periods with steady inflation. [*Source*: Zvi Lerman, "The Structure of Interest Rates and Inflation," in Haim Levy (ed.), *Research in Finance*, 1983, vol. 4, p. 207.]

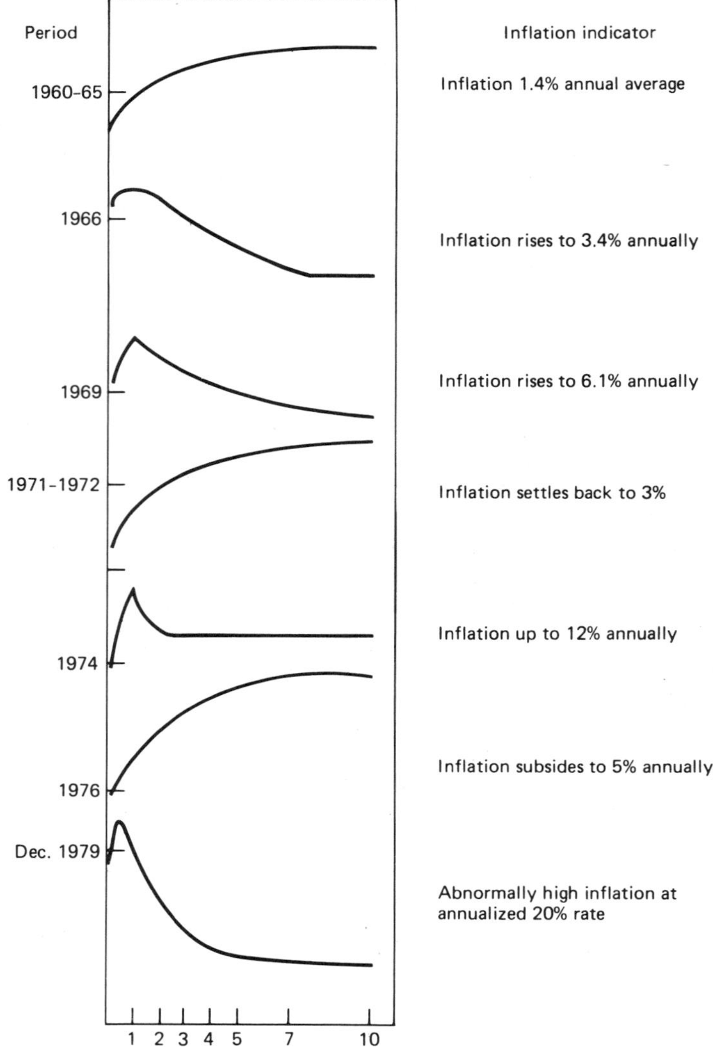

maturities for bonds in given default risk-classes. The yield curve changes a little every day, and there are different yield curves for each risk-class of bonds. The yield curve for AAA corporate bonds, for example, is different from the yield curve for U.S. Treasury bonds on any given day. Figure 13-2 illustrates the risk differentials between several hypothetical yield curves for bonds from different risk-classes. The yield curves for the riskier classes of bonds are at a higher level than the yield curve for less risky bonds—the difference in levels is due to the difference in risk-premiums. Further, the yield curves for riskier bonds are not so stable as the yield curve for U.S. Treasury bonds. Therefore, we shall confine our attention to the yield curve

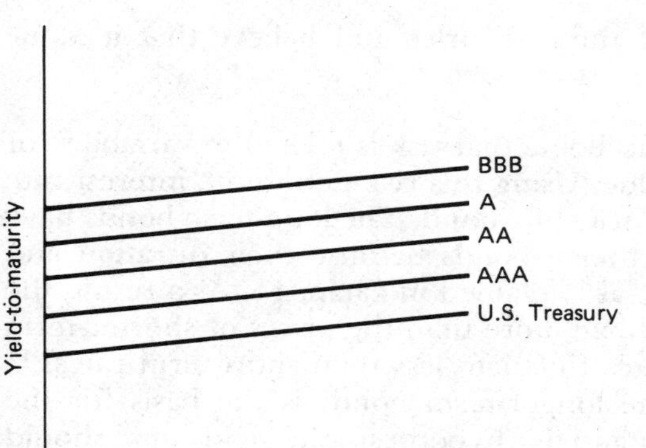

FIGURE 13-2 yield curve shapes.

for U.S. Treasury bonds throughout the remainder of this chapter to expedite the discussion.

13-4 THREE MAIN THEORIES ABOUT DETERMINATION OF YIELD CURVES

Traditionally, there have been three main theories about how the shape of the yield curve is determined:

1. The *liquidity premium theory* assets that long-term yields should average higher than short-term yields. This theory maintains that investors pay a price premium (resulting in lower yields) on short maturities to avoid the interest rate risk which is more prevalent in the long maturities. Thus, an upward sloping curve is considered "normal."
2. The *expectations theory* asserts that long-term yields are the average of the short-term yields prevailing during the intervening period. This implies that if all investors expected rates to (*a*) rise, the yield curve would slope upward, (*b*) remain unchanged, the yield curve would be horizontal, or (*c*) fall, the yield curve would slope downward.
3. The *segmentation (or hedging) theory* asserts that the yield curve is composed of a series of somewhat independent maturity segments. For example, the commercial banks predominantly demand short maturities, savings and loans mainly demand intermediate maturities, long-term bonds are purchased mostly by life insurance companies. Thus, yields on each segment of the yield curve are determined independently by the supply-and-demand conditions existing in that maturity segment.

Five bond price theorems were listed in Box 11-2 and discussed in Chap. 11. With these bond pricing theorems as a background, consider each of the three theories about the term structure of interest rates in some depth. After these theories have been explained, a discussion will integrate them into one unified theory. It should be pointed out, however, that some people adhere rigorously to only one of these theories and believe that it alone explains the term structure of interest rates.[10]

13-4.1 liquidity premium hypothesis

Assume, as we shall throughout this book, that risk is related to variability of return or dispersion of market value. Using this risk definition, interest rate risk increases with the term to maturity of a bond. The long-term bonds have more interest rate risk than short-term bonds because their duration and interest elasticity are larger values, as explained in Chap. 11. As a result, the prices of long-term bonds do fluctuate more than the prices of shorter-term bonds (even though long-term rates fluctuate less than short-term rates).[11] The large price fluctuation in the longer-term bonds is the basis for the *liquidity premium hypothesis*. According to this hypothesis, the yield curve should be typically sloping upward at longer maturities because investors demand higher returns to hold the risky long-term bonds.

> Liquidity preference produces asymmetry in the relationship between short-term and long-term rates at cycle peaks and troughs. It accounts for the failure of short-term rates to exceed long-term rates at peaks by as much as they fall below long-term rates at troughs.[12]

Advocates of the liquidity premium theory support their opinion by taking yield curves from each phase of several business cycles and showing that the average of short-term Treasury bond rates is less than the average of long-term Treasury bond rates. Graphically speaking, this means that, on average, the yield curve is upward sloping at the longer maturities. Although this is usually true, it is not conclusive proof of the validity of the liquidity premium theory; reasons do exist to suggest that one might doubt the liquidity premium theory.

Four reasons why the liquidity premium theory might be reversed (that is, why higher rates should be observed for short-term bonds) have been suggested by those who doubt the theory.[13] First, with the passage of time, short-term rates fluctuate in an uncertain manner. Investors in short-term maturities must, therefore, face a series of reinvestments at risky and uncertain returns. Second, increased transaction and information costs required to refinance frequently in the short-term maturities (instead of in fewer longer-

[10] Chen, Roll, and Ross have found a statistically significant relationship between common stock returns and the (orthogonalized) slope of the yield curve (and several other economic variables too). See Nai-Fu Chen, Richard Roll, and Stephen Ross, "Economic Forces and the Stock Market: Testing the APT and Alternative Asset Pricing Theories," CRSP Working Paper no. 119, December 1983. Their results are also referred to in "The Arbitrage Pricing Theory Approach to Strategic Portfolio Planning," by Richard Roll and Stephen Ross, in the May–June 1984 issue of *Financial Analysts Journal*, pp. 14–29. The relationship between the individual risk factors, such as the slope of the yield curve, and the total risk of an asset are discussed in this book's Chap. 30, about the arbitrage pricing theory (APT).

[11] J. B. Yawitz, G. H. Hempel, and W. J. Marshall, "The Use of Average Maturity as a Risk Proxy in Investment Portfolios," *Journal of Finance*, vol. XXX, no. 2, May 1975, tables 1 and 2.

[12] R. Kessel, *The Cyclical Behavior of the Term Structure of Interest Rates*, National Bureau of Economic Research, occasional paper no. 91, 1965.

[13] F. Modigliani, Richard Sutch, et al., *Supplement to Journal of Political Economy*, August 1967. B. P. Malkiel's book *The Term Structure of Interest Rates*, Princeton, 1966, also discusses the liquidity premium hypothesis.

term bond issues) reduce net returns from such investments. Third, investors in long-term bonds can reduce their risk by hedging (that is, by synchronizing their assets and liabilities to mature simultaneously). For example, there is no uncertainty about the maturity value or maturity date of long-term high-quality bonds. Thus, long-run fund requirements can be hedged by buying long-term bonds which mature when the investor expects the funds will be needed. Fourth, the yield curve could slope downward because investors expect lower inflation premiums, and consequently lower interest rates, in the future than at present. Here, then, are four possible reasons why the long-term bonds might sell at higher prices and lower yields.

Although the case for the existence of liquidity premiums is weakly made, it still contains some truth, and most economists give it some weight in their thinking.

13-4.2 the expectations hypothesis

The expectations hypothesis asserts the long-term rates are the average (or, more precisely, the geometric mean) of the short-term rates expected to prevail between the current period and the maturity date of the bonds.[14] For example, using the simple arithmetic average, if 1-year rates are now 10 percent and are expected to be 11 percent next year, then rates on 2-year bonds today will be approximately 10.5 percent.

$$10.5\% = \frac{10\% + 11\%}{2 \text{ years}} = \text{2-year average}$$

If we assume that the forward interest rate that we expect to exist 3 years ahead is 15 percent, then we can calculate the current (or spot) rate on a 3-year loan to be the average of the next three consecutive 1-year future rates, as shown below.

$$12\% = \frac{10\% + 11\% + 15\%}{3 \text{ years}} = \text{3-year average}$$

In developing the expectations hypothesis, two general types of interest rates will be discussed. These interest rates are sometimes referred to as the spot and the future rates; or, some people use the phrase "forward rate" in place of "future rate," the words future and forward being synonymous. The terms *spot* and *future,* or, if you prefer *spot* and *forward,* are used in the same way they are used in discussing commodities to distinguish between items for current delivery and items for future delivery, respectively. Think of money as being simply another commodity, think of the price of money for future delivery as being the principal plus interest—denoted [(principal) $(1 + r)$].

Future (or forward) rates, denoted ${}_tF_{t+1}$, refer to the yield to maturity for bonds which are expected to *exist in the future.* More specifically, ${}_tF_{t+1}$ denotes the yield to maturity (or market interest rate or future rate) which is currently expected to apply to some future 1-year bond which will exist during time period t. Spot rates, denoted ${}_0S_t$, refer to the interest rates for bonds which *currently exist* and are being currently bought and sold at time $t = 0$. More

[14] Mathematical Appendix F explains the geometric mean rate of return, or time-weighted rate of return, as it is also called. The geometric mean return is contrasted with the yield to maturity, or dollar-weighted rate of return, as it is also called. See also Appendix 13B.

BOX 13-1
mathematical statement of the expectations hypothesis

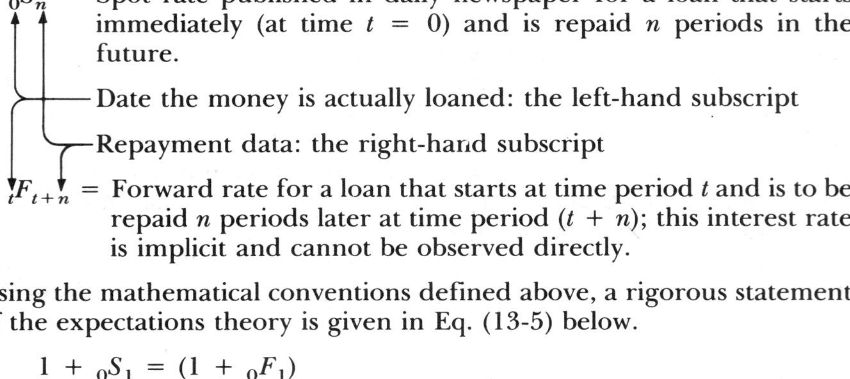

$_0S_n$ = Spot rate published in daily newspaper for a loan that starts immediately (at time $t = 0$) and is repaid n periods in the future.
Date the money is actually loaned: the left-hand subscript
Repayment data: the right-hand subscript
$_tF_{t+n}$ = Forward rate for a loan that starts at time period t and is to be repaid n periods later at time period $(t + n)$; this interest rate is implicit and cannot be observed directly.

Using the mathematical conventions defined above, a rigorous statement of the expectations theory is given in Eq. (13-5) below.

$$
\begin{aligned}
1 + {}_0S_1 &= (1 + {}_0F_1) \\
(1 + {}_0S_2)^2 &= (1 + {}_0F_1)\,(1 + {}_1F_2) \\
(1 + {}_0S_3)^3 &= (1 + {}_0F_1)\,(1 + {}_1F_2)\,(1 + {}_2F_3) \\
&\dots\dots\dots \\
(1 + {}_0S_n)^n &= (1 + {}_0F_1)\,(1 + {}_1F_2)\dots(1 + {}_{n-1}F_n)
\end{aligned}
\tag{13-5}
$$

specifically, $_0S_n$ denotes the market interest rate (or yield to maturity) for a currently existing bond which matures n periods in the future. These conventions are used in making the rigorous statement of the expectations hypothesis shown as Eq. (13-5) in Box 13-1.

The forward rates $_1F_2$, $_2F_3$, . . . , $_{n-1}F_n$ are implicit; that is, these future rates cannot be observed. In contrast, the spot rates $_0S_n$'s can be observed; they are printed in the newspapers daily. This means that the implicit future rates can be determined for any future period or series of future years by solving Eq. (13-5) for the appropriate value of $_nF_{n+1}$. This is not a statement of economic behavior; it is simply a mathematics problem. The implicit market interest rate for a one-period loan which is expected to exist t periods in the future can be found by solving Eq. (13-6*a*) for $_tF_{t+1}$ as shown below.

$$(1 + {}_tF_{t+1}) = \frac{(1 + {}_0S_{t+1})^{t+1}}{(1 + {}_0S_t)^t} \tag{13-6a}$$

$$= \frac{(1 + {}_0S_1)\,(1 + {}_1F_2)\,(1 + {}_2F_3)\dots(1 + {}_tF_{t+1})}{(1 + {}_0S_1)\,(1 + {}_1F_2)\,(1 + {}_2F_3)\dots(1 + {}_{t-1}F_t)} \tag{13-6b}$$

It is similarly possible to determine the implicit future rates for multiperiod bonds. For a bond with a life of n periods which starts in period t and ends in period $t + n$, the yield over the life (that is, over the n periods) of this bond can be derived from Eq. (13-7*a*).

$$\left(\frac{(1 + {}_0S_{t+n})^{t+n}}{(1 + {}_0S_t)^t}\right)^{(1/n)} = \tag{13-7a}$$

$$= \sqrt[n]{(1 + {}_tF_{t+1})(1 + {}_{t+1}F_{t+2})\dots(1 + {}_{t+n-1}F_{t+n})} \tag{13-7b}$$

$$= (1 + {}_tF_{t+n}) \qquad (13\text{-}7c)$$

where

${}_tF_{t+n}$ = market yield for an n-period bond that starts in future period t and matures in the farther future period $t + n$

The relations suggested by the expectations hypothesis will not hold exactly in the "real world" because transactions costs (such as sales commissions and taxes) will inhibit trading. However, ignoring transactions costs, arbitrage ensures that Eq. (13-5) will tend to hold if many bond traders are profit seekers. Recall that arbitrage is a series of transactions which yield a certain return; arbitrage is not uncertain or risky. Arbitrage between maturities will tend to maintain the expectations theory as it is represented in Eq. (13-5). This is an economic theory based on a mathematical identity.

13-4.3 Arbitrage

Some investors will rearrange their bond portfolios and cause bond prices and yields to be revised according to Eq. (13-5) because they expect to profit from such a move. For example, suppose inequality (13-8) occurs; this violates Eq. (13-5).

$$(1 + {}_0S_T)^T > (1 + {}_0F_1)(1 + {}_1F_2) \ldots (1 + {}_{T-1}F_T) \qquad (13\text{-}8)$$

Some profit-seeking investors who have money to invest for T periods will buy the existing long-term bond yielding ${}_0S_T$. This will drive up its price and drive down its yield until Eq. (13-8) becomes an equality that aligns with Eq. (13-5).

After profit-maximizing investors purchase the long-term bond yielding ${}_0S_T$, its price may later drop because of changing credit conditions and/or changing expectations. In this case, the investor must hold the long-term bond until it matures to attain the yield ${}_0S_T$. Since it is not always possible for profit-seeking investors to hold long-term bonds until they mature, they may sell them after their price has fallen and inequality (13-8) exists again. In this case, the sale will lower the bond's price and increase inequality (13-8). As a result of such disadvantageous sales (which even a profit-seeking speculator may sometimes be forced to make), the arbitrage process cannot be expected to maintain Eq. (13-5) as an exact equality. However, the actions of these profit seekers will *tend* to make current yields (that is ${}_0S_t$) a function of expected future yields (that is, the ${}_tF_{t+1}$'s) as suggested by the expectations theory of Eq. (13-5).[15]

One empirical test which supports the expectations theory as designated by Eq. (13-5) is simply to compare the interest rate forecasts inherent in the yield

[15] Rigorous monetary economics makes a distinction between spot rates and the yield to maturity of a bond that explains why arbitrage will not maintain inequality (13-8) as an equation continuously and why some bonds will never lie exactly on the yield curve. The difference is that a bond's spot rate is a time-weighted (or geometric mean) rate of return, while the yield to maturity is a dollar-weighted rate of return that differs from the time-weighted rate of return whenever the yield curve is not horizontal at the bond's yield to maturity. The implicit reinvestment rate is the key to this difference. Mathematical Appendix F at the end of this book explains the difference between the dollar-weighted and the time-weighted rates of return. Appendix 13B discusses the economics of the difference. Or, see the following article, Willard T. Carleton and Ian A. Cooper, "Estimation and Uses of the Term Structure of Interest Rates," *Journal of Finance*, September 1976, vol. XXXI, no. 4, especially pp. 1067–1068.

curve of some past date with the record of business activity after that date. Assuming that the professional investors have worthwhile ideas at any moment about the future level of business activity, and also assuming that they believe the level of interest rates follows the level of business activity, it then follows directly from the definition of the expectations hypothesis that the yield curve should usually slope up preceding economic expansions and down preceding contractions. Without recognizing the implicit reasoning, a business executive's version of the expectations theory would be: "Declining

FIGURE 13-3 market interest rates for various instruments. (*Source*: *Business Conditions Digest*, August 1984, p. 34, chart B7, U.S. Dept. of Commerce, U.S. Government Printing Office.)

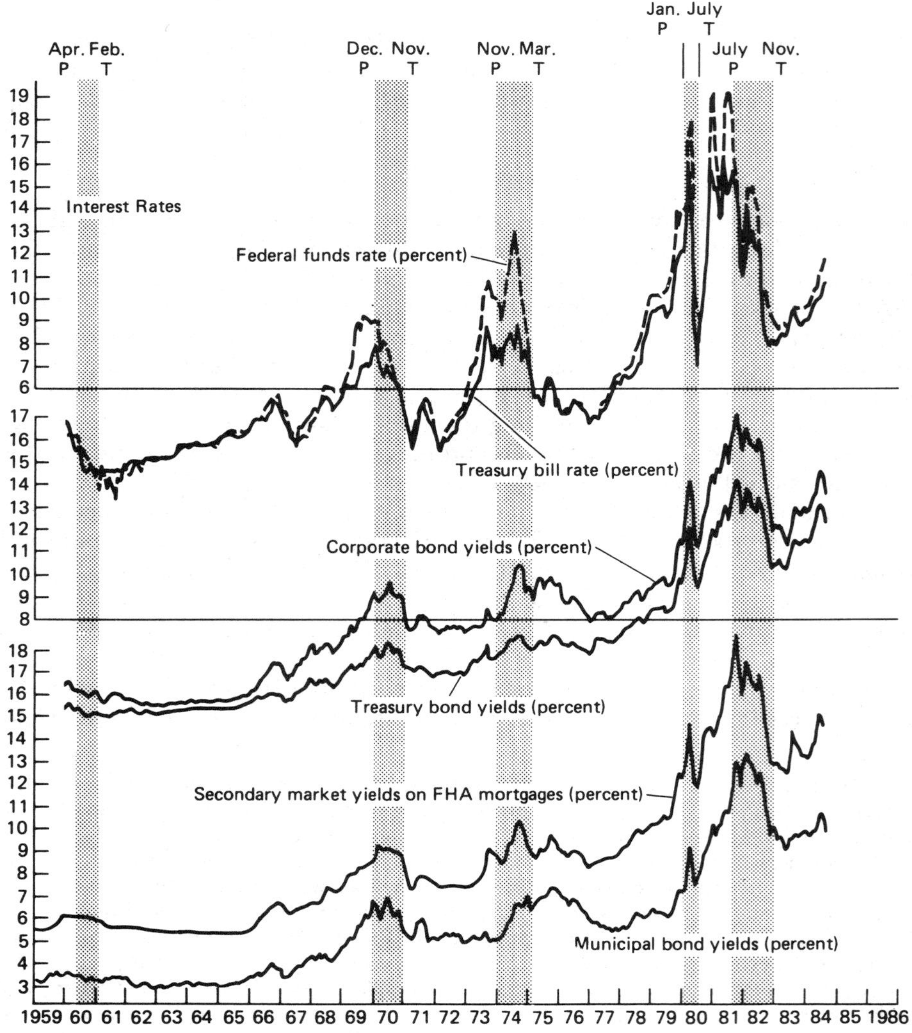

business activity during the period of time presented by the yield pattern will result in a negatively sloped yield pattern," or vice versa for rising rates.

The data in Fig. 13-3 tend to bear out this version of the expectations hypothesis. A yield curve constructed at nearly any of the cyclical peaks would slope downward, or a yield curve drawn at nearly any of the troughs would slope upward.[16] The yield curves existing at the economic troughs are the classic upward-sloping yield curves which forecast expectations of rising interest rates. It is seen more frequently than other shapes. This is usually attributed to the predominance of optimism over pessimism.[17] However, it also supports the liquidity premium theory and is the "proof" frequently used to support that theory.

13-4.4 the segmentation theory

The pure segmentation theory asserts that lenders and borrowers confine themselves to certain segments of the yield curve for the following reasons:

1. Legal regulations, such as "legal lists," which limit the investments that banks, savings and loan associations, insurance companies, and other institutions are allowed to make.
2. The high cost of information, which causes investors to specialize in one market segment.
3. The fixed maturity structure of the liabilities which various bond investors tend to have (for example, life insurance companies and pension funds tend to have long-term liabilities which may be forecast by an actuary) that lead them to hedge their liabilities with assets of equivalent maturity.
4. Simply, irrational preferences.

As a result, the rates on different maturities tend to be determined independently by the supply-and-demand conditions in the various market segments.

The segmentation theory is also referred to as the *hedging theory*. The implication of this name is that investors are typically obligated by some particular maturity pattern of liabilities. Given the maturity of an investor's liabilities, he or she can hedge against capital losses in the bond market by synchronizing asset and liability maturities. Thus, each investor is confined to some maturity segment which corresponds to his or her liability maturities. Figure 13-4 shows a grossly simplified conception of how the yield curve might be segmented.

Those individuals who do interpret the yield curve as being completely determined by independent markets dealing in different maturities are usually persons who deal solely in one of those market segments. Such individuals may be overimpressed by the sheer dollar volume of the transactions and the immediate price reactions they witness. It is possible that to some extent these persons are victims of their own myopic activities; they may be unaware of the

[16] Peaks and troughs are official National Bureau of Economic Research estimates.

[17] B. P. Malkiel, "Expectations, Bond Prices and the Term Structure of Interest Rates," *Quarterly Journal of Economics,* May 1962, pp. 206–213. See also J. W. Conard, *An Introduction to the Theory of Interest Rates,* University of California Press, Berkeley, 1959, part III. These readings show that what might be erroneously interpreted as complicated behavioral assumptions about investors are actually simple wealth maximizing behavioral assumptions. The discussions support the expectations theory.

FIGURE 13-4 segmented yield curve.

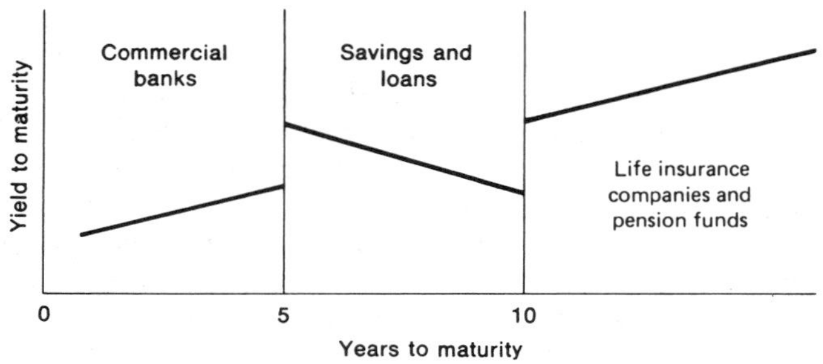

constant activities of professional profit-seeking arbitrageurs who are risk-indifferent and view all securities as substitutes.

Some profit-seeking arbitrageurs earn their living by smoothing out irregularities in the yield curve. Although these professional arbitrageurs may be few in number, their presence and effectiveness are attested to by the relative smoothness of the yield curve of any date. That is, sharp kinks such as those shown in Fig. 13-4 are nonexistent: The actual turns in the yield curve are smoother and less exaggerated.[18]

13-4.5 riding the yield curve

Some bond portfolio managers attempt to increase their portfolio's yields by undertaking a bond investment strategy called "riding the yield curve." This strategy may be undertaken whenever the yield curve is upward-sloping (that is, the long-term rates are higher than the short-term rates) regardless of whether the yield curve is smooth or kinky.

Riding the yield curve is a buy-and-hold strategy in which the bond investor purchases an intermediate- or long-term bond when the yield curve is sloped upward and is expected to maintain that slope and level. The purchased bond is then simply held in order to obtain the capital gains that occur as the bond moves closer to its maturity date and thus rides down the yield curve. That is, in addition to the bond's coupon interest, the bond investor earns capital gains resulting from the lower market yields which are encountered as the bond matures. Of course, the danger inherent in this strategy is that the level of interest rates may rise or that the short-term end of the yield curve may swing upward. Either development would cause the bond investor to suffer a capital loss. Profit opportunities such as these prompt professional bond investors to

[18] Traditionally, yield curves have been estimated by hand simply by "eyeballing" a line of best fit through data points representing bonds in a homogeneous default risk-class. More recently, however, more scientific models have been developed. Some of the algorithms tend to generate smooth yield curves; see S. W. Dobson, "Estimating Term Structure Equations with Individual Bond Data," *Journal of Finance,* March 1978, pp. 75–92. However, some other algorithms generate more kinky estimates of the yield curve; see J. H. McCulloch, "Measuring the Term Structure of Interest Rates," *Journal of Business,* January 1971, pp. 19–31. Michel Houglet, "Estimating the Term Structure of Interest Rates for Non-Homogeneous Bonds," Ph.D. dissertation, University of California, Berkeley, 1980. Gary S. Shea, "Pitfalls in Smoothing Interest Rate Term Structure Data: Equilibrium Models and Spline Approximations," *Journal of Financial and Quantitative Analysis,* vol. 19, no. 3, September 1984, pp. 253–270.

study monetary economics on a regular basis and work at forecasting the yield curve.

13-5 CONCLUSIONS ON TERM STRUCTURE

There is no consensus among businesspeople and economists about which of the preceding theories concerning the term structure is descriptive of reality. There is an undeniable element of logic in each of the three theories, and each is supported to a certain extent by empirical data. In fact, a combination of all three theories probably furnishes the best description of the elements determining the term structure of interest rates.

In essence, expectations of future rates determine a yield curve. However, the yield curve based on pure expectations (denoted *EE* in Fig. 13-5) is unobservable. Liquidity premiums which increase with the term to maturity are superimposed on top of the yields that are purely a function of expectations. Thus, a yield curve such as *YY* in Fig. 13-5, which is observable, represents a combination of the rates determined by expectations plus liquidity premiums (the liquidity premiums are equal to the vertical distance between *YY* and *EE*). This means that the liquidity premium theory is not invalidated by the occasional existence of a downward-sloping yield curve.

The long-term end of the yield curve is determined by the expectations and liquidity premiums that investors demand to induce them to hold these bonds. The stationary nature of the long-term end of the yield curve over the years reflects the constancy of long-run expectations and liquidity premiums.

The segmentation theory explains the frequent movements in the short-term end of the yield curve. The Federal Reserve's Open Market Committee endeavors to control the money supply and exert pressures on market interest rates by buying and selling millions of dollars of Treasury bills on a day-to-day basis. Thus, the Fed interacting with the liquidity needs of commercial banks are the primary supply and demand forces at work on the short-term end of the yield curve. The wide and frequent swings in that portion of the yield curve which has less than 1 year to maturity may be largely attributed to changes in these supply and demand factors. The effects of these forces on the yield curve are segmented and therefore diminish rapidly in the intermediate- and long-term maturities.

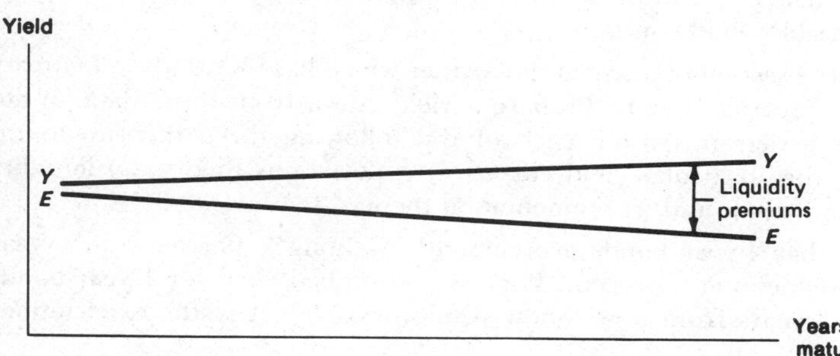

FIGURE 13-5 a yield curve determined by expectations and liquidity premiums.

13-6 CONCLUSIONS ABOUT THE LEVEL OF RATES

The determinants of the level of interest rates are easier to discern than the determinants of the term structure of interest rates. Inflationary expectations, crowding out, and risk-premiums associated with fears of possible inflation upturns in the future have been the important factors in the determination of the level of market yields since the mid-1960s. However, at certain times shifts in the credit supply and demand can result in faster interest rate changes than shifting inflationary expectations alone would dictate. Changes in the risk-premiums which occur as the phases of the business cycle change can contribute significantly to movements in the level of market rates of interest too.

Since bond prices are strongly affected by market interest rates, forecasting interest rates is an important task of a bond portfolio manager. Therefore, bond portfolio managers should be monetary economists as well as bond analysts if they hope to maximize profits.

QUESTIONS

13-1. Compare and contrast (*a*) changes in bond prices caused by changes in the level of interest rates with (*b*) those caused by changes in the term structure of interest rates.

13-2. How should the inflationary expectations of investors in 1-year bonds and investors in 20-year bonds differ?

13-3. If you managed a bank's multimillion-dollar portfolio of bonds, what would you do if you were convinced a credit crunch which would send market interest rates skyrocketing was beginning? How might other bond portfolio managers behave if they also expected a credit crunch, and how would their actions affect your job?

13-4. When actual U.S. Treasury bond yields for a given day are plotted against the terms to maturity to draw a yield curve, why do all the data points not lie exactly on the yield curve if it is drawn to be smooth? Does the fact that not all of the data points lie on the yield curve refute the expectations theory of interest rates in any way? Explain. *Hints:* (1) Think about income taxes. (2) See App. 13B.

13-5. Define the term yield curve. What financial variables which affect interest rates are held constant throughout the length of the yield curve? Why are these variables held constant?

13-6. Cut out the section of a recent newspaper which has the yields to maturity for U.S. Treasury bonds. Prepare a yield curve from these data. Write separate paragraphs using each of the following three theories to rationalize this particular yield curve: (*a*) expectations theory, (*b*) liquidity premium theory, and (*c*) segmentation theory.

13-7. Assume that 4-year bonds are currently yielding 7 percent and 3-year bonds are yielding 6 percent. What is the implied yield for 1-year bonds starting 3 years from now? Show your work. *Hint:* Use the expectations theory.

13-8. Give two reasons why the yield curve might be expected to slope upward most of the time, and also give two reasons why it might slope downward.

13-9. Why should government economic policymakers care about the yield curve? A portfolio manager? An investment banker?

13-10. Bond dealers define a bear hedge as a transaction in which "a short sale of longs is hedged by going long shorts"; that is, a short position of long-term bonds is hedged by taking a long position in short-term bonds. Why would a bond dealer enter such a bear hedge? (Refer to Chap. 21 for an explanation of long and short positions.)

SELECTED REFERENCES

Culbertson, J. A., "The Term Structure of Interest Rates," *Quarterly Journal of Economics,* November 1957, pp. 485–517; also, Michaelson, "Comment," ibid., February 1963, pp. 166–174; and J. A. Culbertson, "Reply," ibid., November 1963, pp. 691–696. This series of nonmathematical articles articulates the viewpoint of advocates of the segmentation theory.

Federal Reserve System, Board of Governors, Historical Chart Book Washington. This monthly pamphlet may be purchased for 60 cents by writing to the Federal Reserve. It provides a valuable summary of financial and economic data in chart form.

Malkiel, B. G., "Expectations, Bond Prices, and the Term Structure of Interest Rates," *Quarterly Journal of Economics,* May 1962, pp. 197–218. A discussion and analysis of the relation between yield changes and bond prices. This article uses differential calculus and utility theory. It develops bond pricing theorems and explains the simple behavioral assumptions behind the expectations hypothesis.

Meiselman, D., *The Term Structure of Interest Rates,* Prentice-Hall, Englewood Cliffs, N.J., 1962. The book explains the expectations hypothesis and supporting data using regression analysis and elementary difference equations.

Yohe, W. P., and D. S. Karnosky, "Interest Rates and Price Level Changes, 1951–69, *Review,* St. Louis Federal Reserve Bank, December 1969." A readable survey of relevant literature and explanation of Almon distributed-lag regression analysis which shows the positive relation between inflation and market interest rates.

APPENDIX 13A

bond swaps

As a result of the ever-changing yield spreads which exist in the bond markets, the managers of bond portfolios sometimes attempt to profit from a bond trading tactic called bond swaps. In general, a *bond swap* may be defined as the purchase and sale of equal amounts of similar bonds which are undertaken in an effort to increase a bond portfolio's rate of return. The four most common types of bond swaps are explained below; they are called:

1. Substitution swaps
2. Intermarket spread swaps
3. Rate anticipation swaps

4. Pure yield pickup swaps

The substitution swap is explained first because it is the simplest of all four types of bond swaps.[19] In the following discussion of bond swaps the bond which is to be sold (TBS) if the swap is consummated is called the *TBS bond* and the bond which is to be purchased (TBP) to complete the swap is called the *TBP bond.*

APP. 13A-1 THE SUBSTITUTION SWAP

The substitution swap involves bonds which are perfect substitutes (in theory, at least) in every respect except their prices (or equivalently, their yields to maturity). In order for two bonds to be perfect substitutes, both the TBS bond and the TBP bond must have identical quality ratings, identical numbers of years to maturity, identical coupon interest payments, the same sinking fund provisions, the same marketability, and equivalent call features and must be identical in every other aspect described in their respective indenture contracts. The TBS bond and the TBP bond can differ only with respect to their yields (and prices), and that key difference is the basis for the substitution bond swap.

All bond swaps are based on faith in one of the basic economic axioms. The particular axiom which forms the basis for bond swaps states that the same good cannot sell at different prices in the same marketplace. Such a price disparity between homogeneous goods would not endure if it temporarily emerged, because the economic *law of one price* suggests that profit-seeking price speculators would buy the homogeneous good (for example, shares of some particular security) from the cheapest supplier and sell it to the highest bidder as long as it was profitable to continue to do so; this is called simple *arbitrage.* The price speculators would continue this arbitrage until they bid up the cheapest supplier's selling price with their purchases and/or drove down the highest bidder's offering price through repeated selling. When the cheapest seller's price was bid up and/or the highest buyer's price was driven down to the point where the buy and the sell prices were equal throughout the marketplace (except for the shipper's charges for transportation allowance to get the goods from the seller to the buyer, the salesperson's commissions, etc.), then and only then would the arbitrage become unprofitable and therefore cease. Thus, when potential arbitrage profits are detected in the bond markets, substitution bond swaps go on until bonds which are perfect substitutes have equal market prices.

To further clarify the nature of a substitute bond swap, consider a hypothetical example. Suppose that a bond swapper has a TBS bond which has 30 years to maturity, yields 7 percent if held to maturity, and is currently priced at its par value (so that its coupon rate equals its yield to maturity). Then the bond swapper finds another bond issued by an almost identical corporation

[19] Richard Bookstaber, *The Complete Investment Book,* Scott, Foresman, and Company, Glenview, Ill. 1985. See chap. 7 about bond swaps. Bookstaber lists a BASIC language computer program to analyze bond swaps; see Bookstaber's pages 77–79. The program may also be purchased from Dr. Bookstaber on a floppy disk as explained on page 173 of this book.

which has identical provisions. That is, this TBP bond has 30 years to maturity, a 7 percent coupon rate, and the same quality rating as the TBS bond and is identical in every other respect except the market price (or, equivalently, the yield). Because of what economists call a temporary market imperfection or because the bond swapper is unable to see that the TBS bond is not really a perfect substitute for the TBP bond, the TBP bond is priced to yield 7.10 percent. The 10-basis-point yield pickup opportunity between the two presumably identical bonds will motivate profit-seeking arbitrageurs to swap the TBP bonds for their TBS bonds. Furthermore, this arbitrage should continue profitably for the bond swapper until the yields and prices of the two bonds are equal or until the bond swapper bankrupts himself by continuously undertaking poorly conceived swaps which cause him to suffer repeated losses. The latter would occur if the TBS and TBP were not perfect substitutes, as the swapper has erroneously thought.

APP. 13A-2 MEASURING GAINS FROM THE SUBSTITUTION SWAP

Bond swaps are undertaken because some bond portfolio manager or bond speculator expects to profit in the future as the price of the TBS bond is realigned with the price of the TBP bond. The time which elapses while the prices of the two swapped bonds become realigned is called the *workout time*. The workout time can be as short as a few weeks if the bond swapper is rewarded by the market for detecting a true market imperfection which is corrected quickly by a rush of profitable arbitrages, or the workout time can be as long as the period before the bonds mature. Assuming that the two swapped bonds do not default, they will mature with prices equal to their face values and yields equal to their yields to maturity as of the day they were purchased. Thus, in the hypothetical example of a substitute swap above, the workout time might drag on for as long as 30 years.

It is impossible to know the length of the workout time for a swap before the swap is undertaken. Therefore, some workout time assumption must be made in order to calculate the additional rate of return which is expected to be gained from any potential bond swap. For purposes of illustration a 1-year workout time will be assumed and used to analyze the substitution swap example explained above.

The substitution swap of two bonds each of which had 7 percent coupon rates and 30 years to maturity was undertaken because the TBP bond yielded a modest 10 basis points more than the presumably identical TBS bond which was priced at par to yield 7 percent. The present value of the TBP bond was thus $987.70, calculated with Eq. (11-1) or by using a book of bond yields. In order to construct a concrete example for further analysis, it is assumed that the two bonds are in fact identical and that their yields converge on 7 percent within a 1-year workout time. Thus, both the TBS bond and the TBP bond will be selling for their face values of $1000 at the end of the workout time. Of course, the TBS bond will yield 7 percent over the workout year because its price always equals its face value of $1000, and its yield to maturity never varies from 7 percent. However, the TBP bond will experience capital gains as its yield falls from 7.1 to 7.0 percent and causes it to earn a compound yield of

TABLE APP. 13A-1 profitability calculations for a hypothetical substitution swap

Assumptions:

1. The TBS bond was a 30-year bond which continuously sold at its par value to yield its coupon rate of 7%.
2. The TBP bond was purchased at $987.70 to yield 7.1% over its 30-year life, but its price rose to $1000 as its yield fell to 7.0% during the year after it was purchased.
3. The workout time was 1 year.
4. All cashflows were reinvested at 7%.

	TBS bond	TBP bond
Original bond investment	$1000.00	$987.70
Two $35 semiannual coupons	$70.00	$70.00
Interest at 7% for 6 months on first coupon	$1.23	1.23
Bond's price at end of workout year	$1000.00	$1000.00
Total dollars at end of workout	$1071.23	$1071.23
Total dollar gain during workout	$71.23	$83.53
Gain per dollar of investment	.07123	.08458
Year's realized compound yield	7.0%	8.29%

Conclusion: The swap earned 129 basis points for one year.

Source: S. Homer and M. L. Leibowitz, *Inside the Yield Book*, Prentice-Hall, Englewood Cliffs, N.J., 1972, table 29.

8.29 percent during the 1-year workout time. In other words, this hypothetical swap yielded 1.29 percent, or 129 basis points, yield improvement on a one-time basis during the workout year. The profitability calculations for this bond swap are shown in Table App. 13A-1.

APP. 13A-3 THE RISKS INHERENT IN BOND SWAPS

The calculations in Table App. 13A-1 assume a 1-year workout time. If the workout takes longer, then the capital gains must be spread over more years and the realized gain per year of workout time diminishes. Speaking approximately, the realized compound yield during the workout period varies inversely to the length of the workout time. Table App. 13A-2 shows several different realized compound yield gains if the substitute swap of two 30-year bonds is consummated and the yield is calculated as outlined in Table App. 13A-1. The results are shown in Table App. 13A-2 under different assumptions about the workout time. At the very worst, the swap would take the entire 30-year lives of the bonds to work out. In this case, only an additional 4.3 basis points per year from the 30 workout years would be obtained. This small increase in the additional yield does not seem sufficient to induce a risk-averse bond swapper to undertake the risks associated with the swap.

The risks associated with a bond swap are too substantial to ignore. The swap should promise a sufficiently large gain in realized yield to (1) pay for the bond brokerage commissions generated by the swap and also (2) compensate the bond swapper for the risks incurred. There are four types of risks involved in a bond swap; they are listed below.

1. The workout time is longer than anticipated. This lowers the realized additional yield per year of workout (as shown in Table App. 13A-2).
2. The yield spreads may move adversely (that is, in a direction opposite to that anticipated). For example, in the substitution swap example above, if the yield spread opened up to more than 10 basis points rather than closing toward zero as anticipated, the bond swappers could suffer losses from the swap. Such losses might result if, for example, the quality rating of the TBP bond were downgraded during the workout time, which would cause the yield to maturity to rise above 7.1 percent.
3. The overall level of all interest rates may change in an adverse movement. For example, if accelerating inflation caused the interest rates of the TBP bond, the TBS bond, and all other bonds to rise appreciably, then the substitution swapper could suffer losses. Even if the yield spread narrowed to zero as hoped, a rise in interest rate levels would cause all 30-year bonds to plunge in price (because they have long durations and high interest rate elasticities, as explained in Chap. 11). If interest rates are expected to rise, the portfolio manager should switch to cash holdings or bonds with shorter maturities and, thus, less interest rate risk in order to minimize losses.
4. The TBP bond may not be the type of substitute for the TBS bond which was wanted. To use the substitution swap for another example, if the TBP bond was intrinsically a more risky bond than the TBS bond, then the yields could never be expected to converge and produce additional yield. Thus, the bond swapper should analyze the bonds carefully before entering into a swap if the desired gains are ever going to materialize. The intermarket spread swap explained below is particularly vulnerable to this type of risk.

APP. 13A-4 THE INTERMARKET SPREAD SWAP

A second major category of bond swaps is the intermarket spread swaps. These swaps involve a TBS bond and a TBP bond which are different in some respect. The swapped bonds may have different coupon rates but may be issued by the same corporation or governmental organization and may be similar in every other respect, for example. Tables 13-2 and 13-3 above present some summary statistics which can be helpful in planning intermarket spread swaps.

TABLE APP. 13A-2 the relation between the workout time and the realized yield gain for the hypothetical substitution swap

workout time, years	realized compound yield gain, basis points per year
30	4.3
20	6.4
10	12.9
5	25.7
1	129.0
½	258.8
¼	527.2

Source: A. Homer and M. L. Leibowitz, *Inside the Yield Book,* Prentice-Hall, Englewood Cliffs, N.J., 1972, table 30.

For an example of an intermarket spread swap consider swapping a 25-year TBS U.S. Treasury bond with a 7 percent coupon rate which is selling at par to yield 7 percent. The TBS bond is to be swapped for another 25-year U.S. Treasury TBP bond. The TBP bond has a 5 percent coupon rate and is selling at a discount from par to yield 6.60 percent if held to maturity. The 40-basis-point spread is adverse for the holder of the TBP bond; but if the yield spread opens further to 50 basis points, the swap is nevertheless advisable. If the 7 percent TBS bond is sold and replaced by the TBP bond (that is, the two are swapped), there are three ways the yield spread could increase from 40 to 50 basis points:

1. The 7 percent TBS bond's yield could rise from 7.0 to 7.10 percent.
2. The 5 percent TBS bond's yield could drop from 6.60 to 6.50 percent.
3. Some combination of both (1) and (2) could occur.

If the expected yield spread increase materializes from any of these three possibilities, the lower-coupon TBP bond will outperform the higher-coupon TBS bond because the TBP bond has more interest rate risk (as measured by its duration or elasticity) than the TBS bond.

To see the advisability of the hypothetical intermarket spread swap, consider the three possible outcomes listed in the preceding paragraph.

1. If the high-coupon 7 percent TBS bond experiences a 10-basis-point increase in its yield as the yield spread widens, the resulting capital loss would be avoided because the TBS bond would have been liquidated in the swap.
2. If the low-coupon 5 percent TBP bond experienced a 10-basis-point decrease in its yield as the yield spread widens, then a significant capital gain would occur for the benefit of the swapper who acquired the bond.
3. If some combination of both (1) (that is, some increase in the TBS bond's yield) and (2) (namely, some capital gain on the TBP bond) occurs, then the swap yields some of each of the associated benefits.

The bond swapper suffers by earning the lower yield of only 6.60 percent on the TBP bond rather than the higher 7.0 percent yield on the TBS bond. However, if the workout time for this swap is short, then the bond swapper only suffers this reduced yield a short time. After the workout time, the swap can be reversed (that is, the TBS bond can be repurchased and the TBP bond sold), and two benefits will thereby occur: (1) the swap will have realized a "pickup" of about 1.0 percent of the value of the bonds because of the realized capital gain on the TBP bond and/or the capital loss which was avoided on the TBS bond and also (2) the higher yield to maturity offered by the TBS bond will be regained when the swap is reversed and the TBS bond is repurchased. Of course, these benefits are obtained only if the bond swapper's expectations for the yield spread's widening 10 basis points do in fact materialize. If the yield spread narrows unexpectedly or all interest rates rise significantly, then the bond swapper would have been better off holding cash which paid no interest income at all.[20]

[20] Most bond swap suggestions are offered, as might be expected, by bond brokers who hope to earn trading commissions if the swaps occur. Since a bond broker gains commission income regardless of whether the swap is profitable for the bond investor, the advice of a broker may be biased and self-serving. Furthermore, the broker probably will not explain the risk of the significant losses which are possible. Thus, the advice of all security brokers should be scrutinized.

APP. 13A-5 THE RATE ANTICIPATION SWAP

If a bond investor foresees a probable change in the level of all interest rates, then a rate anticipation swap should be considered. For example, if the national economy is advancing toward a boom (or falling into the trough of a recession) so that the rate of inflation and thus all interest rates may be expected to rise (fall), then long-term bonds should be sold (bought) and swapped for holdings of cash or short-term bonds in order to avoid capital losses (earn capital gains) from the anticipated changing level of interest rates. Other types of rate anticipation swaps also exist. But risks associated with these as well as almost all other bond swaps are inversely proportional to the ability of the bond swapper to forecast market interest rates.

APP. 13A-6 THE PURE YIELD PICKUP SWAP

The fourth category of bond swaps is the pure yield spread pickup swap; it is a simple transaction based on no expectation of market changes, so that the risks associated with erroneous forecasts are absent. This swap is accomplished by selling a bond which has a given yield to maturity and simultaneously buying a similar bond which offers a higher yield to maturity.

APPENDIX 13B

forward and spot rates and yield to maturity

The present value (p_0) of a bond may be represented in terms of the bond's yield to maturity (ytm), spot (S) rates of interest, or forward rates (F), respectively, as shown in Eq. (App. 13B-1).

$$p_0 = \sum_{t=1}^{n} \frac{C_t}{(1 + \text{ytm})^t} = \sum_{t=1}^{n} \frac{C_t}{(1 + S_t)^t} = \sum_{t=1}^{n} \frac{C_t}{\prod_{i=1}^{t} (1 + F_i)} \qquad \text{(App. 13B-1)}$$

Equation (App. 13B-1) makes the same statement in three different ways. Expanding each of the three bond price formulas above in Eq. (App. 13B-1) to the first two time periods' terms results in the three formulas shown below as Eqs. (App. 13B-2), (App. 13B-3), and (App. 13B-4).

$$p_0 = \frac{C_1}{1 + \text{ytm}} + \frac{C_2}{(1 + \text{ytm})^2} + \cdots \qquad \text{(App. 13B-2)}$$

$$= \frac{C_1}{1 + S_1} + \frac{C_2}{(1 + S_2)^2} + \cdots \qquad \text{(App. 13B-3)}$$

$$= \frac{C_1}{1 + F_1} + \frac{C_2}{(1 + F_1)(1 + F_2)} + \cdots \qquad \text{(App. 13B-4)}$$

where

p_0 = present value

C_t = cashflow occurring at time t

ytm = yield to maturity (or, internal rate of return, or, dollar-weighted rate of return)

S_t = discount rate applied to a payment received t periods from now, that is, the spot or current interest rate on a bond that matures t periods in the future

F_t = discount rate implicitly applied at $t - 1$ to a payment receivable at time t, that is, the forward or future interest rate on a one-period bond.

APP. 13B-1 SPOT AND FORWARD RATES

To begin with, let us ignore dollar quantities and instead focus on the relationships between the three interest (or discount) rates denoted F_t, S_t, and ytm. The *spot rate* is the geometric mean (which is defined in Mathematical App. F) or time-weighted rate of return of the forward rates (F). Equation (App. 13B-5), and the equivalent formulas numbered (App. 13B-6) and (App. 13B-7), show relationships between the spot and forward rates.[21]

$$(1 + S_t)^t = (1 + F_1)(1 + F_2) \ldots (1 + F_t) \qquad \text{(App. 13B-5)}$$

$$S_t = \sqrt[t]{(1 + F_1)(1 + F_2) \ldots (1 + F_t)} - 1 \qquad \text{(App. 13B-6)}$$

$$1 + F_t = (1 + S_t)^t / (1 + S_{t-1})^{t-1} \qquad \text{(App. 13B-7)}$$

Compare and contrast the spot and forward rates with the yield to maturity. A bond's *yield to maturity* is the weighted average of forward rates where weights are determined in accordance with the size of the cashflows occurring at each point in time. Consider an arithmetic example.

Assume the existence of a bond with 3 years remaining to maturity, with an annual coupon of \$100. The bond's cashflows are C_1 = \$100, C_2 = \$100, and C_3 = \$1100. Suppose that the forward rate term structure is: $F_1 = .10$, $F_2 = .11$, and $F_3 = .15$ for the three periods. Given these assumed numerical values allows us to calculate the spot rates of interest as shown in Table App. 13B-1. After computing the price of the bond, the yield to maturity can be determined to be the discount rate that equates the present values of all the cashflows to the bond's price. That value in this case is ytm = .11817851 = 11.817851 percent. The present value of the same bond is calculated below using the various discount rates discussed above.

[21] In a different vein, Eqs. (App. 13B-5), (App. 13B-6), and (App. 13B-7) can be viewed as being a formal statement of the expectations theory about the term structure of interest rates. The yield to maturity is typically substituted in place of the spot rate in these equations, however, when stating the expectations theory.

TABLE APP. 13B-1 calculations for the spot rates

In the first time period the spot rate and future rates are the same.

$$(1.0 + F_1) = (1.0 + S_1) = 1.10$$

or, after subtracting 1,

$$F_1 = S_1 = .10 = 10.0\%$$

For the second period's spot rate,

$$\sqrt[2]{(1 + F1)\,(1 + F2)} - 1.0 = S_2$$

or, substituting in values,

$$\sqrt[2]{(1.10)(1.11)} - 1.0 = S_2 = .104988688 = 10.4988688\%$$

For the third period,

$$\sqrt[3]{(1 + F_1)\,(1 + F_2)\,(1 + F_3)} - 1.0 = S_3$$

or,

$$\sqrt[3]{(1.10)(1.11)(1.15)} - 1.0 = S_3 = .119793223 = 11.9793223\%$$

APP. 13B-2 CALCULATING PRESENT VALUES

Using the spot or forward rates of interest from the numerical example in Table App. 13B-1, the present value of the bond paying a coupon of $100 per year for 3 years is computed in Table App. 13B-2. The ytm associated with that price is also calculated in Table App. 13B-2.

Tables App. 13B-3 and App. 13B-4 show how the present value and the associated ytm was calculated for 2-year and 1-year bonds, respectively. Next, let us examine the different yield curves that are imbedded in the numerical examples above.

TABLE APP. 13B-2 calculations for the present value and the associated ytm for $100 coupon 3-year bond

$$p_0 = \frac{\$100}{1.1} + \frac{\$100}{(1.1)(1.11)} + \frac{\$1100}{(1.1)(1.11)(1.15)}$$

$$= \frac{\$100}{1.1} + \frac{\$100}{(1.104988688)^2} + \frac{\$1100}{(1.119793223)^3}$$

$$= \$90.9091 + \$81.9001 + 783.32921 = \$956.2031$$

The yield to maturity (ytm) that is derived from the price of $956.2031 is calculated and found to be ytm = .1182 = 11.82 percent after rounding off, as shown below.

$$p_0 = \frac{\$100}{1.11817851} + \frac{\$100}{(1.11817851)^2} + \frac{\$1100}{(1.11817851)^3}$$

$$= 89.4312 + 78.9793 + 786.7908 = \$956.2031$$

TABLE APP. 13B-3 calculations for the present value and the associated ytm for $100 coupon 2-year bond

$$p_0 = \frac{\$100}{1.1} + \frac{\$1100}{(1.1)(1.11)}$$

$$= \frac{\$100}{1.1} + \frac{\$1100}{(1.104988688)^2}$$

$$= \$90.9091 + \$900.90090 = \$991.801$$

The yield to maturity (ytm) that is derived from the price of $991.801 is calculated and found to be ytm = .104754 percent, as shown below.

$$p_0 = \frac{100}{1.104754} + \frac{\$1100}{(1.104754)^2}$$

$$= \$90.51788 + \$901.2837 = \$991.801$$

APP. 13B-3 THE TERM STRUCTURE OF INTEREST RATES

Using completely general terms, the "term structure of interest rates" is a relationship between time and interest rates. The interest rates used in portraying the term structure of interest may be yields to maturity, spot rates, and/or forward rates.

Term structures of interest *should* be formulated in terms of spot rates or forward rates of interest, since the yield to maturity changes if the size of the coupon changes. As Carleton and Cooper[22] pointed out:

> As many people have shown, the concept of yield to maturity . . . is an ambiguous concept. For a conventional bond (if not for some hybrid financial contracts or real asset purchase), the expected cash flow pattern implies a unique yield to maturity as a solving—or internal—rate of return. Its economic meaning is moot, however, inasmuch as reinvestment of intermediate cash flows at the solving rate is implied. To borrow a concept from capital budgeting literature, the price of an asset equals its present value only in the sense that its cash flows have been discounted at the market's return requirements. It is true that associated with each bond is a derived yield to maturity, but that does not give us license to say that yield to maturity is a market-required rate, exogenous to the individual bond in question.

[22] W. T. Carleton and Ian A. Cooper, "Estimation and Uses of the Term Structure of Interest Rates," *Journal of Finance,* September 1976, vol. XXXI, no. 4, pp. 1067–1083.

TABLE APP. 13B-4 calculations for the present value and the associated ytm for $100 coupon 1-year bond

$$p_0 = \frac{\$1100}{1.1} = \$1000$$

The yield to maturity (ytm) that is derived from the price of $1000 is easily seen to be ytm = .10 = 10.0 percent.

TABLE APP. 13B-5 different yields to maturity for differing maturities with two different bonds

	TIME PERIODS UNTIL MATURITY		
	1	2	3
Present value of $100 coupon bond given future rates	$1000.00	$991.80	$956.19
ytm of $100 coupon bond	.10	.1047	.1182
Present value of $500 coupon bond given future rates	$1363.64	$1683.05	$1932.31
ytm of $500 coupon bond	.10	.1042	.1151

The term structures of interest under three different formulations are graphed below in Figs. App. 13B-1, App. 13B-2, and App. 13B-3. The most commonly graphed term structure is the third, but this is the least informative of the three term structures, and it is ambiguous as well. In Fig. App. 13B-1 the term structure is independent of the timing cashflows.

In Fig. App. 13B-2 the term structure is independent of the timing of cashflows. But, in Fig. App. 13B-3 the term structure depends upon the cashflow stream. For different bonds that have coupons of $100 and $500, the calculations are shown in Table App. 13B-5.

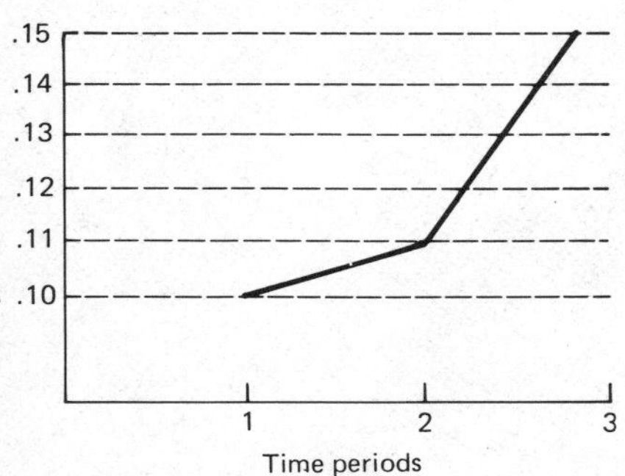

FIGURE APP. 13B-1 forward interest rate term structure

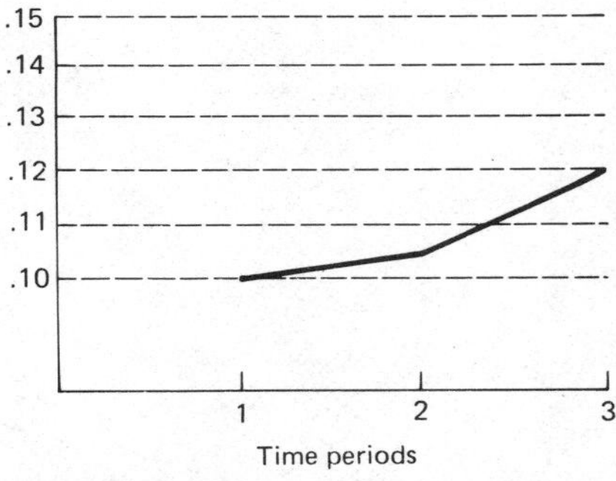

FIGURE APP. 13B-2 spot interest rate term structure

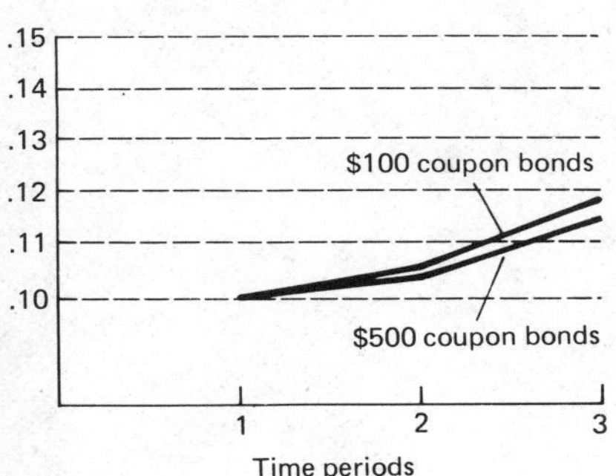

FIGURE APP. 13B-3 yield to maturity term structure

Consider a bond selling for $1932.3078 and having an annual coupon of $500. The yield to maturity on this $500 coupon bond will be 11.51 percent if it matures in 3 years. However, the bond maturing in 3 years with $100 per year coupons that was analyzed above with spot and forward rates has a yield to maturity of 11.82 percent. Table App. 13B-5 shows other yields to maturity for these two hypothetical bonds with varying terms to maturity. This contrast between 3-year bonds with different coupons illustrates why we cannot determine the correct "market yield to maturity" independent of a particular bond, and why the yield to maturity is not unique over dates. On the other hand, the term structure of interest using either the spot or forward rates of interest applies to any financial instrument, regardlesss of the size or timing of the cashflows.

The key to the differences highlighted in this discussion is the differences in the implicit reinvestment rate assumptions that underlie each different formulation of the problem. The yield-to-maturity calculations implicitly assume that all cashflows are immediately reinvested at the yield to maturity until the bond's maturity—a highly dubious assumption during periods of volatile market interest rates. It is more realistic to assume that any cashflows are reinvested at the future rates.

part four

COMMON STOCK VALUATION

The value of a share of common stock, like the value of a bond, is the present value of all the income flowing to the owner of the stock. Common stockholders, however, are owners of the corporation who receive an uncertain stream of *residual* income. That is, stockholders are not at all like debtors, who receive contractual streams of income. Therefore, common stock valuation must deal with measuring the riskiness of the investment. The riskiness of a common stock is important because that is what determines the discount rate to be used in finding the stock's present value. This risk is involved in common stock investing because there is uncertainty about the stream of residual income a stockholder can expect. Chapters 14 through 17 explain the concepts of risk and income as they interact to determine the value of a share of stock. Each of the four chapters in Part 4, except Chap. 16, relies on material explained in the preceding chapter; therefore they should be read in the order presented. These chapters show how to estimate the value of an individual asset so that the investor will be able to tell whether the asset is overpriced or underpriced.

common stock valuation theory*

Chapters 11, 12, and 13 explained how to find the value of bonds. Bond valuation is simple because a bond's cashflows are unambiguously known in advance, and the discount rate can be determined within a narrow range. In contrast, several ambiguities and uncertainties frustrate the exact determination of common stock values. This chapter examines the most important of these problems. Several common stock valuation models will be the focus of this chapter.

14-1 DEFINITION OF A MODEL

Models have been described as simplified versions of reality. The models with which this chapter deals are mathematical models. Like airplane models, they represent reality. They relate certain independent variables, such as dividends and earnings, to a dependent variable, the value of the common stock. Symbolically, the models studied will be of the form $V = f(X_1, X_2, \ldots, X_n)$, where V denotes the value of the asset and $X_1, X_2, \ldots, X_n$ represent those independent variables which determine value. These models will explicitly depict each variable's interaction with the other variables. They are simplified versions of the financial processes that actually determine asset prices.

In an effort to keep things simple, models abstract from many variables and instead focus only on the main determinants. For example, none of the models contains variables representing presidential assassinations, changes in Federal Reserve monetary and credit policy, the timing and impact of changes in the level of economic activity, and numerous other variables which do not directly affect the value of common stock. All the models do, however, contain

* Readers who wish to omit the abstract theory and go to more directly applicable techniques of common stock analysis may skip Chap. 14 and go on to Chap. 15. However, Chap. 11 is needed as background for Chaps. 14 and 15.

a variable representing the asset's income, since income is the most important determinant of value. In this chapter, the important conceptual issues related to the valuation of equity shares in a nonlevered firm are explained. Chapters 15 through 19 deal with common stock valuation on a more pragmatic level.

14-1.1 the basic valuation model

The value of a common stock is simply the present value of all the future income which the owner of the share will receive. This valuation model is the same for all stocks and all bonds. It is summarized symbolically in Eq. (14-1).

$$\text{Value} = \sum_{t=1}^{T} \frac{\text{income for period } t}{(1.0 + \text{appropriate discount rate})^t} \tag{14-1}$$

Using this valuation model on stocks is more difficult than using it on bonds because of two main problems. First, it is not known in advance what a stock's income will be in each future period, and, second, it is not clear what the appropriate discount rate should be for a particular stock. This chapter examines suggested solutions to these problems which have been offered by various financial analysts and economists. Before getting into these different valuation models, however, a brief review of the symbols used is provided.

14-1.2 symbols

The mathematical models in this chapter use the following symbols, which are defined here for easy reference.

v_t = present value of one share of common stock at period t

e_t = earnings per share at time period t

d_t = dividends per share at time period t paid to stockholders of record at the start of period t

r_t = *average* internal rate of return of all investments within the firm during time period t

k_t = appropriate discount rate at time t = firm's cost of capital as determined by its risk

f = retention ratio (which is assumed constant) = fraction of e which is retained inside the firm

$1 - f$ = payout ratio = (dividends/earnings) = fraction of e paid out to investors as a cash dividend

$g = fr$ = rate of growth in earnings, which is assumed to remain constant

t = a counting index indicating time period, for example, a quarter or a year

n_t = number of shares of stock outstanding at time period t

$\Delta n_t = n_{t+1} - n_t$ = number of new shares (if any) sold during period t at the ex-dividend price per share.

Capital letters are used to denote total amounts for the firm as a whole.

V_t = total value of firm at tth time period $= \sum^{n} v_t = n_t v_t$

D_t = total dividends paid to all stockholders of record at start of tth period $= \sum^{n} d_t = n_t d_t$

E_t = total earnings of firm in period $t = \sum^{n} e_t = n_t e_t$
T = the last time period, or the terminal period
I_t = total investment in tth period $= E_t - D_t + \Delta n_t v_t$
$D_{t+1,t}$ = total dividends payable at period $t + 1$ to stockholders of record at period t (but not to new stockholders) $= n_t d_t$

14-2 CAPITALIZING DIVIDENDS

J. B. Williams and M. J. Gordon have developed a model relating an equity share's value to its dividend income.[1] They hypothesized that the value v of a share of stock equals the present value of the infinite ($t = \infty$) stream of dividends d to be received by that stock's owner.

$$v_0 = \sum_{t=1}^{\infty} \frac{d_t}{(1+k)^t} = \frac{d_1}{1+k} + \frac{d_2}{(1+k)^2} + \cdots + \frac{d_\infty}{(1+k)^\infty} \tag{14-2}$$

In Eq. (14-2), k is the capitalization rate which is appropriate for the firm's risk-class. Retained earnings are assumed to increase future dividends in this model. Thus, it does not ignore retained earnings: it treats them indirectly.

The logic of the dividend model is undeniable. Cash dividends are the only income from a share of stock which is held to infinity. So, the value of a share of stock which is held to perpetuity could only be the present value of its stream of cash dividends from now until perpetuity. But, you may ask, what if the share is sold in a few years? The model includes this possibility.

14-2.1 selling shares

If an investor sells a share after, say, three periods, the present value of that share is as shown in Eq. (14-3*a*), according to the logic of the dividend model.

$$v_0 = \sum_{t=1}^{3} \frac{d_t}{(1+k)^t} + \frac{v_3}{(1+k)^3} \tag{14-3a}$$

$$= \frac{d_1}{1+k} + \frac{d_2}{(1+k)^2} + \frac{d_3 + v_3}{(1+k)^3} \tag{14-3b}$$

The v_3 term represents the value of the share in period $t = 3$ when it is sold. Further, according to the logic of Eq. (14-2), v_3 is the present value of all dividends from period $t = 4$ to infinity; this is represented symbolically as Eq. (14-4).

$$v_3 = \sum_{t=1}^{\infty} \frac{d_{t+3}}{(1+k)^t} \tag{14-4a}$$

$$= \frac{d_4}{(1+k)^1} + \frac{d_5}{(1+k)^2} + \frac{d_6}{(1+k)^3} + \cdots + \frac{d_\infty}{(1+k)^\infty} \tag{14-4b}$$

To show how the dividend model encompasses situations in which a share is sold before infinity, Eq. (14-4*b*) is substituted into Eq. (14-3*b*) to obtain Eq. (14-3*c*):

[1] M. J. Gordon, *The Investment, Financing and Valuation of the Corporation*, Irwin, Homewood, Ill., 1962. J. B. Williams, *The Theory of Investment Value*, Harvard, Cambridge, Mass., 1938.

$$v_0 = \frac{d_1}{1+k} + \frac{d_2}{(1+k)^2} + \frac{d_3}{(1+k)^3} + \frac{d_4/(1+k)^1 + \cdots + d_\infty/(1+k)^\infty}{(1+k)^3} \tag{14-3c}$$

Since

$$\frac{d_{n+3}/(1+k)^n}{(1+k)^3} = \frac{d_{n+3}}{(1+k)^n(1+k)^3} = \frac{d_{n+3}}{(1+k)^{n+3}}$$

Eq. (14-3*c*) can be equivalently rewritten as Eq. (14-3*d*):

$$v_0 = \frac{d_1}{1+k} + \frac{d_2}{(1+k)^2} + \frac{d_3}{(1+k)^3} + \frac{d_4}{(1+k)^{3+1}} + \frac{d_5}{(1+k)^{3+2}} + \cdots + \frac{d_\infty}{(1+k)^\infty} \tag{14-3d}$$

Comparison of Eqs. (14-3*d*) and (14-2) will reveal that they are equal. This shows the indirect manner in which the dividend model considers retained earnings and capital gains. That is, v_0 includes v_3, the value of the share in the future. And v_3 includes capital gains which result from retained earnings. Thus, the dividend model does not ignore the effects of capital gains or retained earnings.

14-2.2 definitions and relationships in dividend model

In order to show the interaction of earnings, dividends, retained earnings, and the growth rate of the firm, the model treats these variables explicitly as shown below. Dividends are related to earnings by defining dividends to be equal to the payout ratio $(1 - f)$ times earnings, as shown in Eqs. (14-5*a*) and (14-5*b*).

$$D_t = (1 - f)E_t = \text{total cash dividends} \tag{14-5a}$$

$$d_t = (1 - f)e_t = \text{cash dividends per share} \tag{14-5b}$$

Total corporate retained earnings of fE dollars are assumed to be reinvested within the all-equity firm at a rate of return of r. Since the firm we are discussing here has borrowed no money, it can only grow from retained earnings. This allows earnings to grow at the rate of $g = fr$ per period as shown in Eq. (14-6*a*), assuming no new outside capital is invested.

$$\left.\begin{aligned} E_t &= (1+g)^t(E_0) \\ &= (1+fr)^t(E_0) \end{aligned}\right\} \quad \text{total earnings growth} \tag{14-6a}$$

$$\left.\begin{aligned} e_t &= (1+g)^t(e_0) \\ &= (1+fr)^t(e_0) \end{aligned}\right\} \quad \text{per share earnings growth} \tag{14-6b}$$

As long as the retention ratio is a positive number ($f > 0$), dividends per share will grow as shown in Eq. (14-7*a*) if no new shares are issued.

$$d_t = (1 - f)(1 + fr)^t(e_0) \tag{14-7a}$$

$$= (1 - f)(1 + g)^t(e_0) \tag{14-7b}$$

$$= (1 - f)(e_t) \qquad \text{since } e_t = e_0(1+g)^t \tag{14-7c}$$

In the case where some fraction f of earnings is retained and earns a return of r within the firm, the present value of a share of stock is determined by substituting Eq. (14-7a) into Eq. (14-2) to obtain Eq. (14-8). In Eq. (14-8) the beginning cash dividend per share is restated in terms of the beginning earnings per share by substituting $e_0(1 - f)$ in place of d_0 to produce:

$$v_0 = \sum_{t=1}^{\infty} \frac{e_0(1 - f)(1 + fr)^t}{(1 + k)^t} \tag{14-8}$$

Equation (14-2) may be rewritten equivalently as Eq. (14-9a) by using Eq. (14-7a).[2]

$$\sum_{t=1}^{\infty} \frac{d_0(1 + fr)^t}{(1 + k)^t} = \sum_{t=1}^{\infty} \frac{d_0(1 + g)^t}{(1 + k)^t} = \frac{d_1}{k - g} \tag{14-9a}$$

Equation (14-8) may be rewritten equivalently as Eq. (14-9b) by substituting $e_0(1 - f)$ for d_0 in Eq. (14-9a), as shown below.

$$v_0 = \sum_{t=1}^{\infty} \frac{e_0(1 - f)(1 + g)^t}{(1 + k)^t} \tag{14-8}$$

$$= \frac{d_1}{k - g} \tag{14-9a}$$

$$= \frac{e_1(1 - f)}{k - g} \tag{14-9b}$$

One of the advantages of the dividend model is that it may be rewritten equivalently in different forms. For example, Eqs. (14-2), (14-8), (14-9a), and (14-9b) are all useful representations of the same model. Equation (14-8) explicitly shows the relationship of earnings e_0, dividend policy f, internal profitability r, and the firm's cost of capital k in the determination of the value of the stock. This model may be used to determine the value per share by defining all the variables on a per-share basis as shown, or the model may be used to value the entire firm by using the total quantities represented by the variables in capital letters.

14-2.3 the effects of dividend policy

Equation (14-9c) is particularly useful for studying the effects of dividend policy (as represented by the variable f) on value. First, consider the normal firm where the internal rate of return on new investment equals the discount rate (that is, $r = k$).

$$v_0 = \frac{e_1(1 - f)}{k - fr} = \frac{e_1(1 - f)}{k - g} \quad \text{since } g = fr \tag{14-9c}$$

$$= \frac{e_1(1 - f)}{k(1 - f)} \quad \text{if } r = k$$

$$= \frac{e_1}{k} \tag{14-10}$$

Equation (14-10) shows that regardless of the firm's initial earnings, e_1, or

[2] See footnote 1 in Chap. 15 for the details of the mathematical proof that Eq. (14-9a) is an equality and not merely approximately true.

riskiness (which determines k), the firm's value is not affected by dividend policy. That is, when $r = k$, dividend policy is irrelevant since f, which represents the firm's dividend policy, cancels completely out of Eq. (14-10).

Equation (14-10) is also proof that capitalizing earnings is equivalent to capitalizing dividends when $r = k$, regardless of the payout ratio. Equation (14-10), which capitalizes only earnings, was derived from Eq. (14-8). Equation (14-9*a*) which capitalizes dividends, was also derived from Eq. (14-8). This shows mathematical proof of the equivalence of capitalizing dividends and capitalizing earnings when $r = k$. When $r = k$, the quantity $1/k$ is the same as the price-earnings ratio (or earnings multipliers shown in Table 15-3).

Table 14-1 uses the dividend model Eq. (14-9*c*) to show the effects of various dividend policies, as represented by the value assigned to f, on the value of a hypothetical share. The values in Table 14-1 are computed on the assumption that earnings per share are $e_1 = \$5$, the firm's cost of capital is constant at $k = 10$ percent, and the internal profitability of the firm varies, that is, $r = 5$, 10, and 15 percent.

Table 14-1 shows the effect of various values of r, k, d, and e in determining v. Inspection of Eq. (14-9*c*) and Table 14-1 reveals that the optimal dividend policy depends on the relationship between the firm's internal rate of profit r and its discount rate k.

TABLE 14-1 numerical solutions for dividend model

$$V = \frac{e_1(1 - f)}{k - fr} \qquad (14\text{-}9c)$$

growth firm, $r > k$	declining firm, $r < k$	normal firm, $r = k$
$r = 15\%$ $k = 10\%$ $e_1 = \$5$	$r = 5\%$ $k = 10\%$ $e_1 = \$5$	$r = 10\%$ $k = 10\%$ $e_1 = \$5$
If $f = 60\%$, $v = \$200$. $v = \frac{5(.4)}{.1 - (.6)(.15)}$ $= \frac{2}{.01} = \$200$	If $f = 60\%$, $v = \$28.57$. $v = \frac{5(.4)}{.1 - (.6)(.05)}$ $= \frac{2}{.07} = \$28.57$	If $f = 60\%$, $v = \$50$. $v = \frac{5(.4)}{.1 - (.6)(.1)}$ $= \frac{2}{.04} = \$50$
If $f = 20\%$, $v = \$57.14$. $v = \frac{5(.8)}{.1 - (.2)(.15)}$ $= \frac{4}{.07} = \$57.14$	If $f = 20\%$, $v = \$44.44$. $v = \frac{5(.8)}{.1 - (.2)(.05)}$ $= \frac{4}{.09} = \$44.44$	If $f = 20\%$, $v = \$50$. $v = \frac{5(.8)}{.1 - (.2)(.1)}$ $= \frac{4}{.08} = \$50$
Conclusion: v increases with the retention rate f for firms with growth opportunities, $r > k$.	Conclusion: v increases with the payout ratio $(1 - f)$ for declining firms, $r < k$.	Conclusion: v is not affected by dividend policy when $r = k$.

14-2.4 growth firms

Firms which earn a return on invested funds r that is higher than their cost of capital or discount rate k are *growth firms*. Growth firms have $r > k$, and maximize their value by retaining all earnings for internal investment. For example, IBM has been a growth stock because of technological breakthroughs combined with a marketing and service strategy that gave the company profitable market penetrating powers. As a result of the strong marketing position it attained, IBM was able to operate very profitably. This enviable position allowed IBM to raise capital at a cost of k percent per year and reinvest it internally at a higher rate of r percent per year. Firms with such profitable investments available would be foolish not to reinvest all their earnings if they could not raise capital externally. The model accurately depicts this situation and shows that paying dividends would decrease such a firm's value (unless the firm could borrow).

14-2.5 declining firms

Firms which do not have profitable opportunities to invest may be called *declining firms*. A firm typically declines because its product becomes obsolete, its sales continue to decline, and no further investment within the firm is profitable. Examples of declining firms can be found in the buggy-whip industry from 1930 to 1960. Declining firms have so few, if any, profitable investment opportunities that their return on investment r remains below their cost of capital or discount rate k. In this case, the firm maximizes its value (that is, the value of its owners' shares) by paying out everything it earns to its shareholders as cash dividends. In fact, the optimal financial decision would be for the firm to liquidate itself and pay one big final cash dividend as soon as possible. In a capitalistic system, the recipients of these dividends will either spend them or search out better investments. Either way, the capital will be used more productively.

14-2.6 normal firms

The vast majority of firms have precious few growth opportunities (that is, investments with $r > k$). These firms operate in a tedious (but nevertheless worthwhile) static equilibrium where the internal rate of return from their investments just equals their cost of capital or discount rate, $r = k$. For these firms, dividend policy has no effect on value in the dividend model. That is, the value of the firm is unchanged whether it pays out 10 percent of its earnings as dividends, or 90 percent, or any other percentage. The numerical example in Table 14-1 portrays this case too.

14-2.7 growth in size not equivalent to growth in value

It is easy to be deceived into thinking that a firm which is getting bigger is a growth firm. For example, consider a hypothetical railroad which experiences an increase in its total sales, enlarges its labor force, increases profits, and sees its stock price rise. Does this make the railroad's stock a growth stock? No, not necessarily. This hypothetical railroad may be getting physically larger by retaining earnings and selling new issues of common stock to the public. These funds are raised at a weighted average cost of capital of k. Then they are reinvested and earn a rate of return of r. However, if $r = k$, the *present* value of dollars invested does not grow. The value of funds invested in the railroad tends to increase only enough to compensate investors for bearing the risk and inconvenience of postponing consumption in order to make the investment.

Increases in the railroad's share prices are due to earnings retention. The retained earnings earn a rate r, causing earnings and dividends per share to grow. However, future dividends and capital gains must be discounted at the appropriate discount rate k to find their present value. As long as $r = k$, the *present value* of future dividends and capital gains just equals the present value of the earnings which were retained to finance this expansion. Thus, the railroad gets physically bigger in size and the price of its shares rises, but the *present value* of an investment in it does not increase. If it paid out 100 percent of its earnings in dividends, the firm could still continue to get bigger by issuing new securities instead of retaining earnings. Either way, the present value of the benefits received from a dollar invested would be unchanged because $r = k$. Therefore, simply getting bigger does not make a corporation a growth firm.

14-2.8 simplifications in dividend model

The present value of cash dividends model is a valuable teaching device to show the effects of dividend policy on an all-equity firm under different assumptions about profitability. However, the *simplified* nature of the model can lead to conclusions which are true for the model but not true *in general.* Consider the simplifying assumptions which underlie the dividend model.

1. There is *no external financing*. The dividend model contains no debt and interest expense variables or allowance for new shares to be issued. As a result, every penny of dividends comes directly out of retained earnings in the model, and since retained earnings are the only source of funds with which the firm may expand, dividend policy and investment must compete for the firm's earnings.
2. The internal rate of return r of the firm is *constant*. This ignores the diminishing marginal efficiency of investment which would normally reduce r as a firm's investment was increased.
3. The appropriate discount rate k remains *constant*. Thus, the model ignores the possibility of a change in the firm's risk-class and the resulting change in k.
4. Since the firm and its stream of earnings are *perpetual*, T goes to infinity.
5. *No taxes* exist. This simplification will be relaxed later.
6. The growth rate $g = fr$ is *constant forever*.
7. The following relationship must not be violated: $k > fr = g$. If $g > k$, the value of a share would be infinite. However, it is *realistic to assume* that $k > g$.
8. The firm's dividend policy, as represented by the symbol f, is presumed to remain *fixed to infinity*.

Let us consider the problems which are introduced by these eight assumptions. The analysis will provide a review of capital budgeting and financing (that is, corporation finance) and of how such matters affect dividend policy and the value of the firm.

NO OUTSIDE FINANCING The dividend model *confounds* dividend policy with the investment program of the firm. Since the model does not include sources of funds from external financing, every dollar of dividends takes away a dollar from earnings retained for investment. When such a situation exists, either the firm's investment program, its dividend policy, or both will be

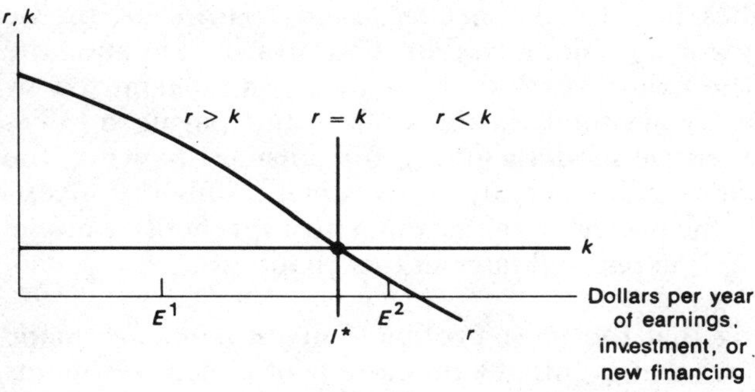

FIGURE 14-1 a firm's investment opportunities.

suboptimal. This problem is represented graphically in Fig. 14-1. A review of the optimum investment program shows the result of ignoring external financing.

Figure 14-1 shows dollars per year on the horizontal axis and the values of r and k on the vertical axis. The exhibit depicts some hypothetical firm's investment opportunities as it makes its financial plans for the next year. Both the corporation's total profit and its total investment are measured on the horizontal axis in dollars per year. The firm's marginal cost of capital equals its average cost of capital k, as represented by the horizontal line at k percent per year.[3] The rates of return r on each investment open to the firm are shown as decreasing as more investment occurs; this reflects the assumption that the most profitable investments will be made first and the poorer investments made last. The total dollar value of the annual investments is also measured along the horizontal axis. In Fig. 14-1 I^* dollars of investment occurs where $r = k$. I^* is the optimal investment regardless of whether the capital to finance this investment is raised by selling stocks, bonds, or preferred stock, by retaining earnings, or by obtaining a loan (assuming k does not change).

To the left of I^* dollars of investment, the internal rate of return is larger than the firm's cost of capital, $r > k$, and the firm could increase its value by expanding investment to I^*. If earnings are only E^1, I^* still is the amount of investment which will maximize the firm's value. The firm should invest I^* if

[3] Capital budgeting students will notice that investments up to I^* have positive net present values, but investments over I^* (for example, E^2) have negative net present values. Figure 14-1 is oversimplified for the sake of brevity. Actually, because of corporate income taxes, the real firm's cost of capital decreases if debt capital is used, *ceteris paribus*, and the average rate of return on investment is not shown. The discussion omits the difference between the marginal return and the average return, but some writers have shown the importance of this distinction in terms of such models. See Douglas Vickers, "Profitability and Reinvestment Rates: A Note on the Gordon Paradox," *Journal of Business*, July 1966, pp. 366–370. The assertions made in this chapter that firms which have $r = k$ are not growth firms is true only if r is the average rate of return. If $r' = k$, where r' is the marginal rate of return, then $r > r' = k$, and the firm is a growth firm. Strictly speaking, $r' = k$ is the optimum condition. If $r = k$, this implies $r' < k$, which is suboptimal because some investments have been undertaken which have marginal returns less than the marginal cost of capital. See E. Lerner and W. Carleton, "The Integration of Capital Budgeting and Stock Valuation," *American Economic Review*, September 1964, pp. 683–702. Lerner and Carleton examine the effects of a diminishing marginal efficiency of investment on the dividend model.

it has to sell new securities to raise the needed funds. However, in the dividend model, outside financing is not included. Thus, for this situation the model would show that the owner's wealth (that is, v) was maximized by retaining and investing the firm's total earnings of E^1 and paying no dividends. In a more comprehensive model allowing for outside financing, the firm should sell new securities to finance the I^* investment; only this investment would truly maximize the owner's wealth. A more comprehensive model which allows new financing is explicated later in this chapter.

CONSTANCY OF *r* Assuming that the most profitable investments are made first, common sense indicates that eventually no more profitable investments will be left. This is correctly represented graphically in Fig. 14-1 by a declining investment r curve. However, the dividend model assumes that r is constant (an assumption which is true, if it is ever true, only over a tiny range of investments).

If total earnings in Fig. 14-1 were E^2 dollars, for example, the dividend model indicates that they should all be paid out in dividends because $r < k$ at E^2. In a more comprehensive model which recognizes that r declines, the optimal policy would be to retain earnings of I^* for investment and pay dividends of $E^2 - I^*$ dollars. Since the model always indicates that the optimal dividend payout is either one of three policies (namely, zero, 100 percent, or irrelevant), the dividend policy which actually maximizes the owner's wealth will rarely be indicated by this oversimplified model.

CONSTANCY OF *k* A firm's cost of capital or appropriate discount rate k varies directly with the risk of the firm. Figure 14-2 is a graph of the capital asset pricing model (CAPM), or security market line (SML), as it is also called, which shows that as the risk of a firm (or any asset) increases, the appropriate discount rate rises too. The present value of the firm's income moves inversely with the discount rate. By assuming that the discount rate k is constant, the model abstracts from these effects of risk on the value of the firm. Risk measurement and the appropriate discount rate were discussed in Chaps. 9, 10, and 12.

INFINITE LIFE It is usually realistic to assume that a modern corporation endures perpetually. It will have new managements, and probably new products, too, as time passes, but the legal corporate shell can live forever.

NO TAXES This unrealistic simplifying assumption is relaxed in a more comprehensive model developed later in this chapter. The differential tax rates on dividends and capital gains are considered.

FIGURE 14-2 the discount rate k is determined by risk.

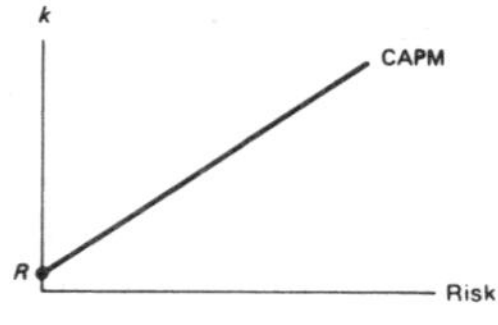

CONSTANT GROWTH RATE This assumption is merely a simplification of reality. It can be easily changed without changing the conclusions. The assumption that g does not change is made merely to simplify the mathematics of the model.

COST OF CAPITAL EXCEEDING GROWTH RATE, $k > g$ This assumption is realistic. Although a firm could sustain very high growth rates over the period of a few years, no firm could double or triple its earnings every year indefinitely. If a firm's earnings doubled annually for very many decades, its total profit would grow to exceed the gross national product (GNP) of the United States.

CONSTANT DIVIDEND PAYOUT RATIO, $(1 - f)$ The assumption that the firm has a constant retention rate f is merely another effort to simplify the mathematical form of the model. If f did change far in the future, the conclusions of the model would not be changed because the present value of future dollars is smaller. Furthermore, this assumption is fairly realistic. Many firms do tend to maintain a fixed retention rate when it is *averaged* over several years.

Beginning social scientists should not become discouraged about the dividend model because it is built on eight more or less (mostly less) realistic assumptions. Remember, a model is supposed to be a simplified version of reality. The simplifications were made for good reasons: to keep the mathematics as simple as possible and to focus only on the main issues in the valuation theory of equity shares. The model yielded some fascinating insights; for example, would you have believed that dividend policy does not affect the value of most normal firms? This issue is analyzed further below.

14-2.9 Gordon's bird-in-the-hand model

Dr. Gordon has studied the effects of relaxing the simplifying assumptions of the dividend model, and he has performed econometric tests using empirical data.[4] He concludes that dividend policy is irrelevant when $r = k$ and all the simplifying assumptions are maintained. However, when these assumptions are realigned to conform more closely with reality, Dr. Gordon concludes that dividend policy *does* affect the value of a share even though $r = k$. The introduction of risk into the model is Gordon's way of reaching the conclusion that dividend policy does matter in the "real world."

With the introduction of risk and uncertainty, the appropriate discount rate k *varies* as risk and uncertainty vary.[5] Gordon suggests that risk and uncertainty increase with futurity; that is, the further one looks into the future, the more uncertain things (namely, dividends) become. Therefore, Gordon suggests that k should not be held constant. Rather, k increases further in the future. Future dividends should be discounted at a higher discount rate than current dividends. Symbolically, Gordon says $k_t > k_{t-1}$ for

[4] M. J. Gordon, op. cit., chaps. 6–14.

[5] "Risk" and "uncertainty" are used synonymously in this book to refer to probabilistic outcomes where the probability distribution is known. Uncertainty is not used here in the Knightian sense that the probability distribution is not known, as suggested by Frank H. Knight, *Risk, Uncertainty, and Profit*, Houghton Mifflin, Boston, 1921.

$t = 1, 2, \ldots,$ because of increasing risk and uncertainty in the future.[6] He rewrites his basic model Eq. (14-2) as Eq. (14-11) with a subscript on the discount rates to represent uncertainty by specifying that $k_t > k_{t-1}$. The subscripts on k change to represent Gordon's assumptions that k changes in the future.

$$v_0 = \sum_{t=1}^{\infty} \frac{d_t}{(1 + k_t)^t}$$

$$= \frac{d_1}{(1 + k_1)} + \frac{d_2}{(1 + k_2)^2} + \frac{d_3}{(1 + k_3)^3} + \cdots + \frac{d_t}{(1 + k_t)^t} + \cdots \tag{14-11}$$

Equation (14-11) is sometimes lightly referred to as the "bird-in-the-hand" model, since near dividends are valued above distant dividends.[7] If the average of the discount rates in Eq. (14-11) equals the constant discount rate in Eq. (14-2), then Eq. (14-2) and the bird-in-the-hand model, Eq. (14-11), are equal. However, it is unlikely the k_t's average out to equal k in Eq. (14-2).

To show the impact of uncertainty on dividend policy, Dr. Gordon suggests that the first cash dividend, namely, d_1 in Eq. (14-11), be *retained and reinvested* to earn a constant internal rate of return r into perpetuity. The earnings from this reinvestment are rd_1 dollars per period per share into perpetuity. If these additional earnings are paid out as increases to the other regular dividends (that is, $d_2, d_3, \ldots$), the value of the stock is represented by Eq. (14-12).

$$v'_0 = \frac{0}{1 + k_1} + \frac{d_2 + rd_1}{(1 + k_2)^2} + \frac{d_3 + rd_1}{(1 + k_3)^3} + \cdots + \frac{d_t + rd_1}{(1 + k_t)^t} + \cdots \tag{14-12}$$

Even though r equals the average of all the k_t's, the value of the stock in Eq. (14-12) is less than the value of the stock in Eqs. (14-2) and (14-11). Symbolically, $v_0 > v'_0$ because the average of the k_t's for $t = 1, 2, \ldots,$ is a smaller average discount rate than the average of the k_t's for $t = 2, 3, \ldots,$.

If the cash dividends were the same dollar amount and the discount rate had remained constant as in Eq. (14-2), the value of the firm would be unchanged by shifting dividends with regard to time. Equation (14-13) shows the present value of the income from the reinvested d_1 if $r = k$.

$$\sum_{t=1}^{\infty} \frac{rd_1}{(1 + k)_t} = \frac{rd_1}{k} = d_1 \qquad \text{if } r = k \tag{14-13}$$

Thus, if $r = k_t$ for all time periods, shifting d_1 to a later period does not affect v_0 because the present value of the perpetual income rd_1 is d_1. However in $k_t > k_{t-1}$, as in Eq. (14-12), the income from the reinvested dividend (that is, rd_1) is discounted at a higher average discount rate, since the average of k_t for $t = 2, 3, \ldots,$ is larger than the average of k_t for $t = 1, 2, 3, \ldots,$. Thus $v'_0 < v_0$, which shows how dividend policy can affect value in a world of uncertainty.

[6] The first article to correctly analyze the implicit behavior of the risk-adjusted discount rate over time was A. A. Robichek and S. C. Myers, "Conceptual Problems in the Use of Risk-Adjusted Discount Rates," *Journal of Finance*, vol. 21, December 1966, pp. 727–730.

[7] The phrase comes from an old saying: "A bird in the hand is worth two birds in the bush."

By merely introducing uncertainty into the model, Gordon has shown how dividend policy can affect the value of a common stock.[8] Uncertainty explains why some investors value a dollar of dividend income more than a dollar of capital gains income. These investors value dividends above capital gains because dividends are easier to predict, less uncertain, and less risky, and are therefore discounted with a lower discount rate. When uncertainty of the type shown in Eq. (14-11) exists, the present value of a dollar of dividends is larger, the sooner the dividend is received.

14-3 MM'S DIVIDEND IRRELEVANCE ARGUMENT

Two financial economists, Dr. Franco Modigliani and Dr. Merton Miller (called MM hereafter, for brevity), disagreed with Dr. Gordon's bird-in-the-hand model, which shows that a firm's dividend policy affects its value.[9] MM constructed the simpler one-period dividend valuation model developed below from Eq. (14-2) as a basis for their dividend irrelevance argument.

14-3.1 one-period dividend valuation model

The multiperiod dividend valuation model, Eq. (14-2) or (14-3*b*), can be simplified to a one-period dividend valuation model by assuming that the share of stock is sold after one period, as shown below in Eq. (14-14):

$$v_0 = \frac{d_1}{1+k} + \frac{d_2}{(1+k)^2} + \cdots + \frac{d_\infty}{(1+k)^\infty} \tag{14-3d}$$

$$= \frac{d_1 + v_1}{1+k} \tag{14-14a}$$

because, if a share is sold after one period (at $t = 1$), the term v_1 can be substituted in place of the share's future dividends.

$$\sum_{t=1}^{\infty} \frac{d_{1+t}}{(1+k)^t}$$

To find the value of the entire firm in period t, MM merely multiply both sides of Eq. (14-14*a*) by the number of shares outstanding in period t, denoted n_t, to obtain Eq. (14-14*b*), as shown below.

$$v_t = \frac{d_t + v_{t+1}}{1+k_t} \tag{14-14a}$$

$$n_t v_t = V_t = \frac{n_t(d_t + v_{t+1})}{1+k_t} = \frac{D_t + V_{t+1}}{1+k_t} \tag{14-14b}$$

To expedite mathematical manipulation, MM base their model on the following simplifying assumptions:

1. *Perfect capital markets.* In a perfect capital market no buyer or seller is large enough for his or her individual transactions to affect prices, financial informa-

[8] M. J. Gordon, "Optimal Investment and Financing Policy," *Journal of Finance*, May 1963, pp. 264–272.

[9] M. H. Miller and F. Modigliani, "Dividend Policy, Growth and the Valuation of Shares," *Journal of Business*, October 1961, pp. 411–433.

tion is freely available to everyone so that uninformed investors may be ignored, and no taxes, brokers' commissions, or other transfer costs exist to deter investors from seeking a profit-maximizing equilibrium.

2. *Investors value dollars of dividends and dollars of capital gains equally.* This assumption is partially the result of assuming that no tax differential exists between dividends and capital gains.
3. *No risk or uncertainty.* Investors can forecast future prices and dividends with certainty, and therefore one discount rate is appropriate for all securities and all time periods. In this case $r = k = k_t$ for all t.

14-3.2 MM fundamental principle of valuation

Under the assumptions just listed, the price of each share must adjust so that the rate of income (that is, the rate of dividends plus capital gains) on every share will be equal to the appropriate discount rate and be identical for all assets over any given interval of time. This *fundamental theorem of valuation* means that the rate of return from a share of common stock, as defined in Eq. (14-15), is equal for all firms over any given period of time.

$$r_t = \frac{d_t + v_{t+1} - v_t}{v_t}$$

$$= \frac{\text{cash dividends + capital gains or loss}}{\text{purchase price}} \tag{14-15}$$

The fundamental theorem says that the rate of economic income defined in Eq. (14-15) will be equal for all shares in perfect markets which are at equilibrium when no differences in risk exist. This fundamental valuation model is true because MM assumed away everything which might interfere with its validity.[10]

The important implication of MM's fundamental principle of valuation is that all firms in all periods will have the same cost of capital k. This is true because a firm's cost of capital k equals the investor's rate of return r. So, if all firms' r_t's must be equal by the fundamental principle of valuation, their k_t's must all be equal too ($r = k$). The quantities r and k are just two different sides of the same coin.

14-3.3 MM's proof of dividend irrelevance

If a firm has a change in the number of shares outstanding, this change is denoted $\Delta n_t = n_{t+1} - n_t$. In the case that new shares are issued (or old ones repurchased as treasury stock), Eq. (14-14*b*) should be rewritten as Eq. (14-16) to reflect possible changes in the value of the firm.

$$V_t = \frac{D_t + V_{t+1} - \Delta n_t v_{t+1}}{1 + k_t} \tag{14-16}$$

[10] Some people object to the models which social scientists like MM build because the models are based on simplifying assumptions. However, the objection is not valid. Social scientists seek basic economic truth by assuming away realistic details like taxes and uncertainty and by employing the powerful logic of mathematics to their simplified models. This approach has just as much credibility as do the experiments conducted by the physical scientists who conduct their gravity experiments, for instance, in sealed vacuum chambers where winds do not blow and birds do not fly.

The quantity $\Delta n_t v_{t+1}$ is subtracted from V_{t+1} in the numerator of Eq. (14-16) to reflect the change in the number of shares outstanding. The total value of all these *new* shares is defined in Eq. (14-17).

$$\begin{aligned}\Delta n_t v_{t+1} &= n_{t+1}v_{t+1} - n_t v_{t+1} \\ &= v_{t+1}(n_{t+1} - n_t) \end{aligned} \tag{14-17}$$

Since MM's model allows for the issuance (or retirement) of shares, the firm can raise (or repay) capital to pay dividends and *also* undertake the optimal investment program (as explained in Fig. 14-1). Thus, dividend and investment policies are not perversely intertwined in MM's model as they were in Eq. (14-2), the multiperiod dividend model. As a result, MM's model yields more valid conclusions about the effects of cash dividends than does the dividend model.

Changes in the firm's investment in total assets, denoted I_t, may be financed through either earnings retention $(E_t - D_t)$ or the issuance of new shares $(\Delta n_t v_{t+1})$. It follows that the proceeds of any new common stock issue must therefore equal the new investment less any retained earnings, as shown by Eq. (14-18).

$$\begin{aligned}\Delta n_t v_{t+1} &= I_t - (E_t - D_t) \\ &= I_t - E_t + D_t \end{aligned} \tag{14-18}$$

If Δn_t is negative, this represents the case where assets are sold or earnings are retained to purchase outstanding shares (that is, treasury stock).

Using these symbols, MM show that the value of the firm is unaffected by its dividend policy by substituting Eq. (14-18) into Eq. (14-16) to obtain Eq. (14-19*a*), as shown below.

$$V_t = \frac{D_t + V_{t+1} - \Delta n_t v_{t+1}}{1 + k_t} \tag{14-16}$$

$$= \frac{D_t + V_{t+1} - (I_t - E_t + D_t)}{1 + k_t}$$

$$= \frac{V_{t+1} - I_t + E_t}{1 + k_t} \tag{14-19a}$$

The restatement of the total value of the firm with external financing in Eq. (14-19*a*) is consistent with the previous statement of the firm's value in Eqs. (14-16) and (14-14*b*). However, since it is possible to restate the value of the firm Eq. (14-19*a*) without dividends, D_t, this proves that dividends have *no effect* on the value of the firm when external financing is used. As shown in Fig. 14-1, dividends affect the firm's value only when the firm finances all investment *internally*. When external financing is utilized, dividend policy has no effect on the value of the firm under MM's simplifying assumptions.

14-3.4 subjective arguments for dividend relevance

Some students of finance are not impressed by Modigliani and Miller's dividend irrelevance model. Therefore, to supplement Dr. Gordon's bird-in-the-hand model, these people have dissented with MM by offering the following subjective arguments for the relevance of dividend policy in valuing equity shares.

RESOLUTION OF UNCERTAINTY Some advocates of dividend relevance have supported the bird-in-the-hand model by pointing out that investors prefer to receive cash dividends because the payout resolves their uncertainty. If a firm retains its earnings, there is uncertainty about when and if those retained earnings will cause capital gains.

CLIENTELE THEORY The popular clientele theory is a second subjective theory which suggests that dividend policy affects stock prices. It asserts that certain stocks attract certain kinds of investors because the investors prefer the firm's dividend payout policies. For example, widows who are counting on their investment income to keep them out of the poorhouse are supposed to buy public utility stocks which tend to pay good cash dividends. In contrast, high-income investors are assumed to want growth stocks which pay no cash dividends and instead have large capital gains which enjoy a preferential income tax.

The differential tax treatment of capital gains and dividends requires that the before-tax rate of return as defined in Eq. (14-15) be rewritten thus:

$$\text{atr}_t = \frac{d_t(1 - T_0) + (v_{t+1} - v_t)(1 - T_g)}{v_t} \qquad T_0 > T_g \tag{14-20}$$

where

atr_t = after-tax rate of return at period t
T_0 = tax rate on ordinary income
T_g = capital gains rate

Since MM's fundamental principle of valuation and all their models are based on the definition of the rate of return, dropping the assumption of no taxes will change all their models. MM freely state that "the tax differential in favor of capital gains is undoubtedly the major systematic imperfection in the market."[11] Nevertheless, MM still conclude that dividend policy has no effect on share values.

MM reason that the lower capital gains tax is not important for several reasons. First, many investors' capital gains and dividends are taxed equally (namely, charitable and educational institutions, foundations, pension trusts, and low-income retired people). Second, MM begin their own clientele theory by pointing out that all stocks have a long-run average payout ratio between

[11] M. H. Miller and F. Modigliani, op. cit., p. 432.

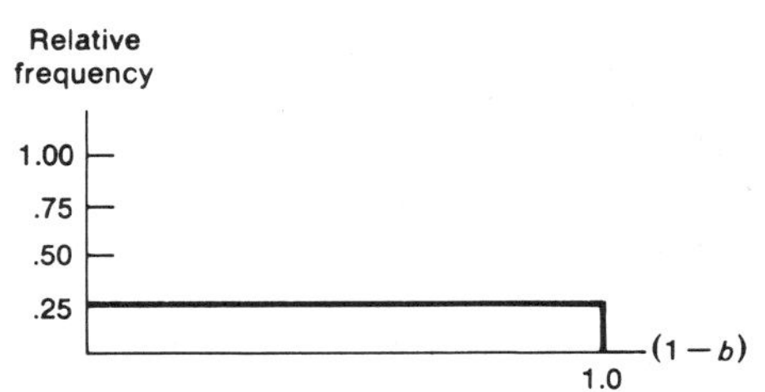

FIGURE 14-3 hypothetical relative-frequency distribution of payout ratios supplied by firms.

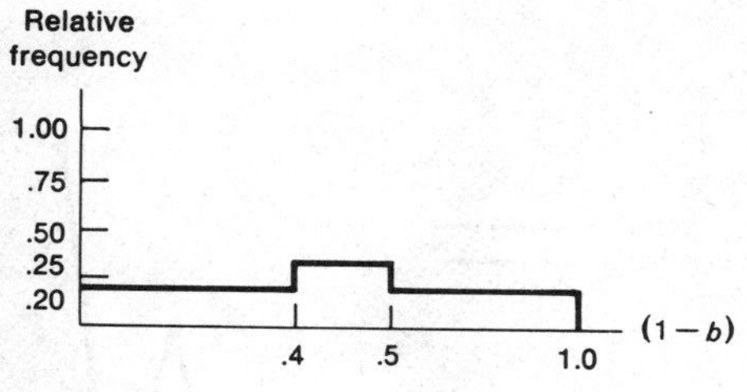

FIGURE 14-4 hypothetical relative-frequency distribution of payout ratios desired by investors.

zero and 100 percent (or, equivalently, 1.0). Figure 14-3 shows a hypothetical relative-frequency distribution of the payout ratios *supplied* by all the firms issuing stock. If investors have preferences for given payout ratios, they could be surveyed and the clientele for each payout ratio could be ascertained. Figure 14-4 shows a hypothetical relative-frequency distribution of payout ratios *desired* by investors. A comparison of the supply and demand for various payout ratios represented by Figs. 14-3 and 14-4 reveals a shortage of payout ratios in the 40 to 50 percent range and an oversupply of all other payout ratios.

MM reason that the market prices of stocks with payout ratios in the scarce 40 to 50 percent range will be bid up. The other firms' prices will be relatively lower because of lack of demand. If the managements of these firms are perceptive, they will note how much more demand exists for firms whose payout ratios are in the 40 to 50 percent range, and they will change their payout ratios until supply equals demand at each payout ratio. Thus, each firm will attract a *clientele* of investors who prefer its payout policies. For example, a consistent dividend-paying firm like American Telephone and Telegraph (AT&T) would not have as many high-income investors who prefer capital gains as growth stocks like IBM. MM[12] go on to point out that:

> Even if there were a shortage of some particular payout ratio, investors would still normally have the option of achieving their particular savings objectives without paying a premium for the stocks in short supply by buying appropriately weighted combinations of the more plentiful payout ratios.

INFORMATIONAL CONTENT Some people have argued that information is conveyed from a corporation's top management to its stockholders through the firm's dividend policy. Stockholders are viewed as outsiders who are not fully aware of what is going on in their firm.[13] Therefore, they look for signals about their firm, and a corporation's cash dividend policy is one of the easiest places to find information from top management.

For example, if a corporation announces a cash dividend reduction, some investors may interpret this change as evidence that the firm's earning power has been permanently reduced. Some of these bearish shareholders may sell the stock and drive its price down because they think earnings may never

[12] Ibid.

[13] Frank H. Easterbrook, "Two Agency-Cost Explanations of Dividends," *American Economic Review,* vol. 74, no. 4, September 1984, pp. 650–659.

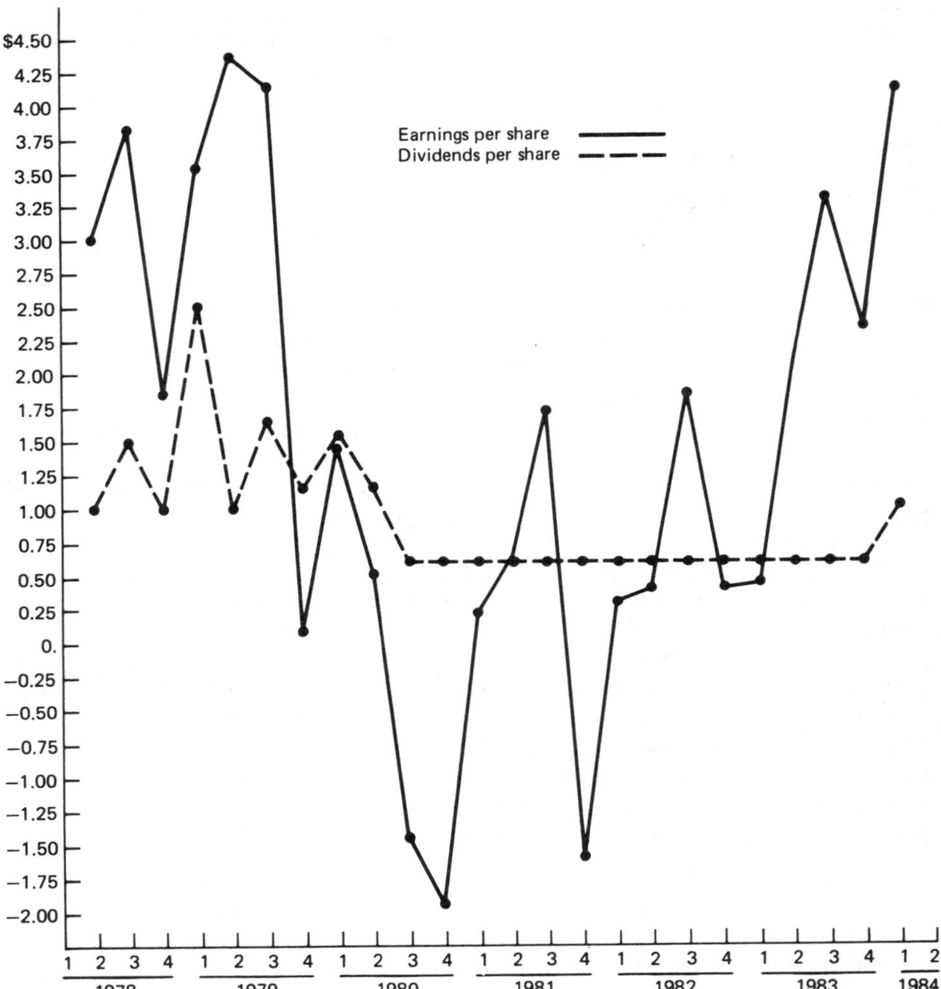

FIGURE 14-5 dividends and earnings per share for General Motors Corporation.

recover their upward trend. This appears to be what happened to General Motors in 1980, as shown in Fig. 14-5, when the company did not earn enough to pay its cash dividends out of current earnings. In fact, GM's stock price declined until early 1982. Many other illustrations like Fig. 14-5 could be drawn to support the notion that cash dividends convey valuable investment information to both past and potential investors.

INVESTORS' LIQUIDATION COSTS A final argument in support of cash dividends as a means of increasing owners' wealth is based on stockbrokers' commissions. If a shareholder must liquidate some shares to obtain needed cash, a brokerage commission must be paid to sell the shares. Many of the commission costs could be avoided if corporations would all pay cash dividends regularly.

14-3.5 arguments favoring dividend retention

Among those who believe that a firm's dividend policy does affect the value of its shares, there is a group that argues *for* and another group which argues *against* cash dividends. The latter group disagrees with the subjective arguments that cash dividends are desirable because they resolve uncertainty, convey information, and provide cashflows for needy clientele. This group offers the following points in support of earnings retention (which tends to cause capital gains).

TAX DIFFERENTIAL The most powerful and undeniable argument against cash dividends is the fact that they are taxed at a higher rate than capital gains [see Eq. (14-20) above]. This tax differential is a good rationale for earnings retention.

THE FLOTATION COSTS OF ISSUES Those who favor earnings retention point out that the firm can expand on retained earnings instead of on new security issues. This allows the firm to avoid paying a fee to an investment banker to float new security issues to raise capital with which to finance expansion.

SALE OF STOCK AT LOWER PRICE A subjective argument favoring dividend relevance is that new shares of stock which are sold to replace money paid out in cash dividends will drive down the market price of the outstanding shares.[14] The point of this position is that investors should prefer the stock of firms which retain earnings. The value of the shares will not be depressed by diluting sales of new shares to obtain cash with which to pay cash dividends.

14-3.6 conclusion about dividend policy

The preceding discussion embraced many aspects of the intellectual discussion about dividend policy. Valuation models were introduced. Models showing the relevance and the irrelevance of dividend policy were analyzed. The arguments for and against cash dividend payment were reviewed. What is the final answer? Are dividends really irrelevant?

MM's dividend irrelevance model is more general than Gordon's bird-in-the-hand model because the MM model allows external financing. Further, MM's clientele theory (see Figs. 14-3 and 14-4) is more logical than stories about widows' cash needs and other subjective arguments. However, the burden of heavier taxation on cash dividends is difficult to dismiss. Overall, it seems that dividend policy is probably irrelevant, but investors in high tax brackets logically dislike cash dividends. The problem with reaching this conclusion is that most business persons and amateur investcrs believe the opposite: They think cash dividends are desirable. So, alas, the dividend debate continues unresolved.

[14] John Lintner, "Dividends, Earnings, Leverage, Stock Prices, and the Supply of Capital to Corporations," *Review of Economics and Statistics*, August 1962. This article is a classic piece of research about cash dividends.

TABLE 14-2 some empirical data on a dozen stocks that paid no cash dividends for a decade or more, 1970–1980

stock	INVESTORS' RATE OF RETURN: annual average[(1)]	INVESTORS' RATE OF RETURN: return's rank in *Fortune* 500
NVF	41.7%	2
National Semiconductor[(2)]	33.3%	7
Teledyne[(2)]	32.2%	9
Tosco[(2)]	28.9%	17
Data General[(2)]	25.3%	34
Penn Central	19.9%	78
Digital Equipment[(2)]	17.4%	96
Lockheed	13.9%	143
Median for *Fortune* 500	9.4%	250
LTV	6.9%	284
Crown Cork & Seal	4.6%	342
DPF[(2)]	(5.7%)	451
Memorex[(2)]	(13.9%)	463

(1) The one-period rate of return calculated with Eq. (14-15) compounded annually from 1970 to 1980.

(2) The corporation has never paid cash dividends.

Source: *Fortune*, May 4, 1981, p. 351.

Several statistical studies with empirical data have endeavored to discern whether or not a corporation's cash dividend policy affects the market value of its common stock shares.[15] The results of these studies suggest that dividends may have a positive effect on stock prices, but the results are generally of marginal significance. Table 14-2 contains some simple and easy-to-understand empirical data that are also not conclusive. However, the data in Table 14-2 strongly suggest that a corporation's cash dividend *policy* does not affect the market price of its shares. The data in the table are thought-provoking.

In a different vein, an important common stock valuation question which ignores the long-run effects of dividend policy is: Do cash dividend payments cause any short-term stock price fluctuations?

[15] The following empirical studies more or less reach the conclusion that cash dividends have a positive but marginally significant effect on the market value of equity shares: F. Black and M. Scholes, "The Effects of Dividend Yield and Dividend Policy on Common Stock Prices and Returns," *Journal of Financial Economics*, May 1974, vol. 1, pp. 1–22. M. J. Brennan, "Taxes, Market Valuation and Corporate Financial Policy," *National Tax Journal*, 1970, vol. 23, pp. 417–427. E. J. Elton and M. J. Gruber, "Marginal Stockholder Tax Rates and the Clientele Effect," *Review of Economics and Statistics*, February 1970, vol. 52, pp. 68–74. R. H. Litzenberger and K. Ramaswamy, "Dividends, Short Selling Restrictions, Tax-Induced Investor Clienteles and Market Equilibrium," *Journal of Finance*, May 1980, vol. 35, pp. 469–481. R. H. Litzenberger and K. Ramaswamy, "The Effect of Personal Taxes and Dividends on Capital Asset Prices," *Journal of Financial Economics*, June 1979, vol. 7, pp. 163–195. M. H. Miller and M. Scholes, "Dividends and Taxes," *Journal of Financial Economics*, December 1978, vol. 6, pp. 333–364. W. F. Sharpe and H. B. Sosin, "Risk, Return and Yield, New York Stock Exchange Common Stocks, 1928–1969," *Financial Analysts Journal*, March–April 1976, vol. 32, pp. 33–42.

14-4 EFFECTS OF CASH DIVIDENDS

It was explained above that the value of a common stock equals the present value of its future income. If this is true, the market price of a share of common stock should drop when cash dividends are paid by an amount equal to the present value of that dividend, since a cash dividend payment decreases the present value of the share. Let us denote this dropoff in market price associated with payment of cash dividends as DO, which is defined in Eq. (14-21).

$$\text{DO} = (\text{closing price before dividend}) - (\text{closing price ex-dividend}) \quad (14\text{-}21)$$

Dr. D. Durand and A. May of Massachusetts Institute of Technology published a study of the behavior of American Telephone and Telegraph (AT&T) stock after cash dividends were paid.[16] AT&T was chosen for the study because (1) its stock had a broad, orderly, active market and (2) its $2.25 quarterly cash dividend was large in relation to the 12.5 cents stock price changes (that is, only ⅛ point changes are posted), which facilitated measuring the DO. A total of 43 quarterly dividend dates from 1948 to 1959 were examined. The average of the 43 DOs was $2.16, which was 96 percent of the $2.25 cash dividend paid. The data for all 43 quarterly dividends are shown in Table 14-3.

The data in Table 14-3 strongly support the theory that the value of a stock is the present value of its future income. Tax effects account for the small

[16] D. Durand and A. May, "The Ex-Dividend Behavior of American Telephone and Telegraph Stock," *Journal of Finance*, March 1960, pp. 19–31.

TABLE 14-3 dropoffs in AT&T stock at 43 quarterly dividends of $2.25

DO, $	DO/$2.25, %	Mar. '48– Sept. '52	Dec. '52– Mar. '57	June '57– Mar. '59	row totals
1¼	50		1		1
1⅜, 1½	55, 60				
1⅝	72		2		2
1¾	78	2	1	1	4
1⅞	83	3	2		5
2	89	5	2	1	8
2⅛	94	3	3	1	7
2¼	100	2	1	2	5
2⅜	106		3	1	4
2½	111				
2⅝	117	1	1	1	3
2¾	122	1			1
2⅞	127		1		1
3, 3⅛, 3¼	133, 138, 144				
3⅜	150	1		1	2
Totals		18	17	8	43
Average		$2.15	$2.07	$2.34	$2.16
DO/$2.25		96%	92%	104%	96%

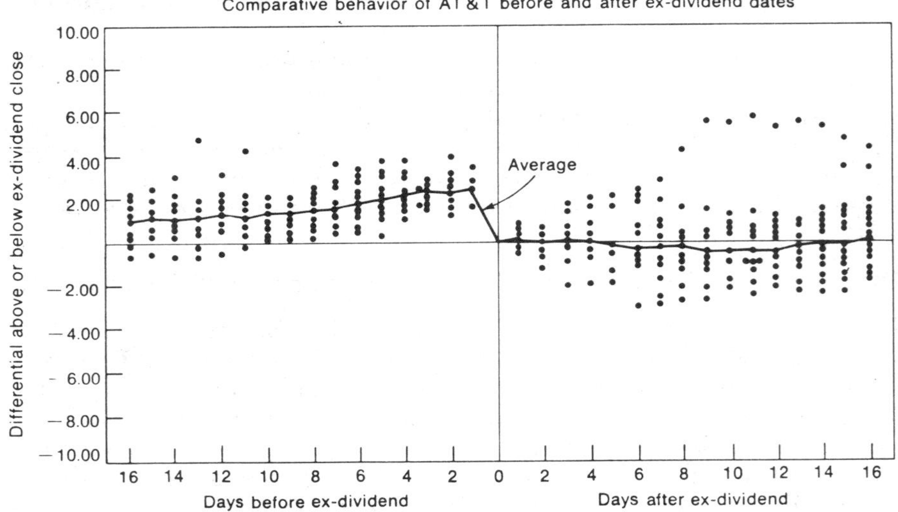

FIGURE 14-6 graph of price drop-off on AT&T stock. (*Source*: from D. Durand and A. May, "The Ex-Dividend Behavior of American Telephone and Telegraph Stock," *Journal of Finance*, March 1960, pp. 19–31.)

difference between the dropoff and the dividend; that is, shrewd investors who intend to sell the stock prefer to sell it shortly before the dividend is paid so that they may recognize their income as capital gains (rather than dividends, which are taxed at the higher ordinary income tax rate). This tendency drives the price down slightly before cash dividends are paid and keeps the DO from being as large as the cash dividend.

Figure 14-6 shows the price action of AT&T around the time of its quarterly dividends from 1948 to 1952. The line through the points traces the average dollar amount the market price fluctuated around the ex-dividend market price.

This line rises gradually as the dividend date approaches and the present value of the dividend increases. Then the dropoff occurs simultaneously with the dividend. It is clearly not advisable to purchase a stock a few days prior to its dividend date (unless the purchaser is tax-exempt). The price would drop after the dividend, and the new investor, having received the dividend, must pay ordinary income tax on it. Thus, the after-tax dividend income is less than the capital loss. Trading shares to capture cash dividends is no way to beat the market.

14-4.1 conclusions about cash dividend effects

Cash dividends are a source of real income to the investor. The market recognizes the present value of cash dividends and adjusts the price of the stock accordingly. The data compiled by Durand and May indicate that the market has a slight preference for capital gains over dividends, but in view of the income tax structure, this is rational.

It seems that on the average the market views dividends in a rational manner and cannot be beaten or fooled into erroneous values by dividend gimmicks. The data seem to support the Modigliani-Miller thesis (explained in Sec. 14-3) that dividend policy is irrelevant, except for possible tax effects.

The tax advantage gained by purchasing stocks just after cash dividends are paid and selling them shortly before the next cash dividend is useful only to investors in very high income tax brackets. When the risks associated with holding the security between dividend dates and the sales commissions incurred in buying and selling are considered, this strategy is not likely to beat the market.[17]

14-5 DIFFERENT APPROACHES TO VALUATION

Finance professors, fundamental security analysts, economists, and others have suggested several approaches to determining the values of common stocks. Three of the more popular approaches involve capitalizing (that is, finding the present value of) three different streams of money.

1. *The cashflow approach.* The advocates of this approach—mostly finance professors and economists—suggest that the value of a security is the present value of the cashflows it produces. Chapter 11 stressed this approach in valuing bonds, since their cashflows are known in advance.
2. *The dividend approach.* This approach suggests that the value of a common stock is the present value of all its expected cash dividends.
3. *The stream-of-earnings approach.* This approach suggests that the value of a security is the present value of all its future earnings. This approach is supported by many fundamental security analysts.

At this point, the obvious question is: What do investors capitalize—net cashflows, dividends, or earnings? MM have shown that, properly formulated, all three approaches are identical.

MM start to equate these three seemingly divergent valuation approaches by extending Eq. (14-19*a*) to cover longer time spans. Thus, Eq. (14-19*a*) may be rewritten as Eqs. (14-19*b*) and (14-19*c*).

$$V_t = \frac{E_t - I_t + V_{t+1}}{1 + k} \tag{14-19b}$$

$$= \frac{E_t - I_t}{1 + k} + \frac{V_{t+1}}{1 + k} \tag{14-19c}$$

Looking beyond one period to T periods in the future causes Eq. (14-19*c*) to expand to Eq. (14-22):

$$V_0 = \sum_{t=1}^{T-1} \frac{E_t - I_t}{(1 + k)^t} + \frac{V_T}{(1 + k)^T} \tag{14-22}$$

[17] For a review of other investigations of cash dividend dropoffs and a more detailed analysis of this phenomenon, see Kenneth M. Eades, Patrick J. Hess, and E. Han Kim, "On Interpreting Security Returns during the Ex-Dividend Period," *Journal of Financial Economics*, March 1984, vol. 13, no. 1, p. 34.

When T is infinitely large, $V_T/(1 + K)^T$ becomes zero and Eq. (14-22) can be rewritten as Eq. (14-23):

$$V_0 = \sum_{t=1}^{\infty} \frac{E_t - I_t}{(1 + k)^t} + 0 \tag{14-23}$$

14-5.1 the cashflow approach

Consider for a moment the cashflow in period t, denoted C_t. The cashflow is the difference between cash inflows and cash outflows. More specifically, the cashflow from a firm is its earnings less the investments necessary to maintain the firm, as shown in Eq. (14-24).

$$C_t = E_t - I_t \tag{14-24}$$

According to the advocates of the discounted cashflow approach, the value of the firm is given by Eq. (14-25).

$$V_0 = \sum_{t=1}^{\infty} \frac{C_t}{(1 + k)^t} \tag{14-25}$$

Substituting Eq. (14-24) in Eq. (14-25) yields Eq. (14-23). This shows the equivalence of the cashflow valuation model to Eq. (14-23) and its predecessors, Eqs. (14-19*a*), (14-14*a*), and (14-16).

14-5.2 the stream-of-earnings approach

Those who do not approve of the discounted stream-of-earnings approach typically attack it on two points. First, these detractors charge that stockholders cannot withdraw earnings from the corporation as they are earned; they must wait for cash dividends to be paid, and the retained earnings may never be received. When $r = k$ and markets are perfect, this argument is empty. In this case the market value of a share increases by an amount equal to retained earnings. Thus, stockholders who want their earnings can have them by liquidating some of their holdings.

Second, the earnings approach is sometimes attacked for "double counting." The double-counting advocates charge that all earnings are counted as income when they are earned. Then *earnings on retained earnings* are counted as income again later. The problem with some double-counting advocates is that they define income inappropriately.[18] The earnings E_t less new investments I_t required to maintain future earnings, as defined in Eq. (14-26), correspond with economists' definition of truly *consumable* income.

$$\text{True economic earnings} = E_t - I_t \tag{14-26}$$

Economists and many others correctly assert that the retention of accounting profits in the firm to maintain its future income (but not increase it) is not the retention of true income, although the accounting profession calls it "retained earnings." Thus, the stream-of-earnings approach, properly formulated, says the value of the firm is the present value of all *true economic earnings* as defined in Eq. (14-23).

[18] Section 16-5 explains in more detail how accountants' definition of income is distorted and misleading and can actually lead to "double counting."

$$V_t = \sum_{t=1}^{\infty} \frac{E_t - I_t}{(1 + k)^t} \tag{14-23}$$

Thus, MM show that if it is properly formulated (that is, if earnings are defined properly), the stream-of-earnings approach is equivalent to the other valuation approaches. In practical applications, it is the responsibility of the financial analyst to adjust accounting profit to conform to the true economic income if the stream-of-earnings approach is to be used.

To see the necessity of adjusting accounting earnings to conform to the concept of economic income, consider, say, the color television industry. The RCA Corporation dominated the industry in the 1960s because it developed the technology to mass-produce the only good color TV tubes in the world. Thus, when RCA went into mass production of color television sets, RCA's competitors who wanted to avert bankruptcy and possibly even maintain their future income undiminished had to invest much or all their *accounting profit* internally to develop the technology to produce color TV sets. The depreciation flows provided by the firms' old assets were not sufficient to finance these new assets for color television production. This investment of accounting profit most certainly was not the retention of true income—true income is something which its recipients should be free to consume if they please. The so-called retained earnings could not be withdrawn from the firm and consumed without decreasing the firm's ability to compete and earn in the future. Any television manufacturer that did not move into the production of color sets in the 1960s would more than likely be unable to compete in the television industry of the 1970s. This RCA case shows (1) the need for the financial analyst to adjust reported accounting income, (2) the rationale behind valuation Eq. (14-23), and (3) the weakness of the accounting definition of income as it compares with the economic concept of income.

14-5.3 the dividend approach

The dividend approach, properly formulated, says that the discounted value of the dividends coming to a *given share* of stock equals the value of that share. This is equivalent to taking the present value of *all* future dividends of the firm only if *no* new shares were issued or old ones retired. Let $D_{t,1}$ denote total dividends of the firm *paid in period t to stockholders of record at period t = 1*. Dividends paid on new shares issued after $t = 1$ should not be included in present value of $D_{t,1}, D_{t+1,1}, D_{t+2,1}, D_{t+3,1}, \ldots, D_{\infty,1}$. The present value of the firm to stockholders of record at $t = 1$ is given by Eq. (14-27*a*).

$$V_1 = \sum_{t=1}^{\infty} \frac{D_{t,1}}{(1 + k)^t} \tag{14-27a}$$

$$= \frac{D_{1,1}}{1 + k} + \sum_{t=2}^{\infty} \frac{D_{t,1}}{(1 + k)^t}$$

$$= \frac{1}{1 + k}\left[D_{(t,1)} + \sum_{t=2}^{\infty} \frac{D_{t+1,1}}{(1 + k)^t}\right] \tag{14-27b}$$

The present value at $t = 2$ of the future dividend stream $D_{t,1}$ equals the present value at $t = 2$ of the dividend stream $D_{t,2}$ times a fraction

$[1 - \Delta n_1/n_2]$ representing the ratio of the number of shares outstanding at $t = 1$ to the number of shares outstanding at $t = 2$. Equation (14-28) represents this symbolically.

$$\sum_{t=1}^{\infty} \frac{D_{t+1,1}}{(1 + k)^t} = \left[\sum_{t=1}^{\infty} \frac{D_{t+1,2}}{(1 + k)^t}\right]\left(1 - \frac{\Delta n_1}{n_2}\right) \tag{14-28}$$

Substituting Eq. (14-28) into Eq. (14-27*b*) yields Eq. (14-29):

$$V_1 = \frac{1}{1 + k}\left\{D_{1,1} + \left[\sum_{t=1}^{\infty} \frac{D_{t+1,2}}{(1 + k)^t}\right]\left(1 - \frac{\Delta n_1}{n_2}\right)\right\} \tag{14-29}$$

Multiplying the quantity inside the brackets by the quantity inside the large parentheses in Eq. (14-29) yields

$$n_2 v_2\left(1 - \frac{\Delta n_1 V_2}{n_2 v_n}\right) = V_2 - \Delta n_1 v_2$$

by using the definitions below in Eq. (14-30).

$$\begin{aligned} V_2 &= n_2 v_2 \\ &= \sum_{t=1}^{\infty} \frac{D_{t+1,2}}{(1 + k)^t} \end{aligned} \tag{14-30}$$

Substituting the quantity $V_2 - \Delta n_1 v_2$ in place of the product of the quantity in brackets and the quantity in parentheses in Eq. (14-29) yields Eq. (14-31).

$$V_1 = \frac{1}{1 + k}(D_{1,1} + V_2 - \Delta n_1 v_2) \tag{14-31}$$

$$V_t = \frac{D_t + V_{t+1} - \Delta n_t v_{t+1}}{1 + k} \tag{14-16}$$

Since $D_{1,1} = D_t$ at $t = 1$, Eq. (14-31) is equivalent to the basic valuation Eq. (14-16), from which Eq. (14-23) and others were derived. Thus, MM show that, properly formulated, the dividends approach is equivalent to the earnings and net cashflow approaches.

14-6 SUMMARY AND CONCLUSIONS

The theory of finance is not definitive about the effect of dividend policy on the value of an equity share. Dr. Gordon's so-called "bird-in-the-hand" model demonstrated how uncertainty about the future can make a share which pays cash dividends more valuable than a share which is identical in every way, except that its cash dividend policy is more restrictive. Doctors Modigliani and Miller, in turn, developed a more general dividend valuation model which permits external financing. MM, using their model, prove that dividend policy has no effect on the value of a share. The fact that MM's model is more general (that is, it allows outside financing) makes it more acceptable than more restrictive models. However, when differential income taxes on dividends and capital gains are considered, a good case can be made for retaining all earnings to maximize the value of normal and growth firms. Thus, the theory is at odds with the popular notion among many business executives that cash dividends have the ability to affect the value of common stock.

Theoretical analysis of several commonly used valuation models was highly informative. Valuation models based on cashflows, earnings, and dividends were all shown to be equivalent when properly formulated. Moreover, the analysis of these models was helpful in clarifying exactly how they should be formulated to yield consistent results. In the next chapter, the dividend valuation model embraced by Gordon, MM, and other analysts as well—that is, Eq. (14-2)—is reformulated in a more pragmatic manner, and fundamental security analysis methods which have been popular on Wall Street for decades are analyzed within the context of this model.

QUESTIONS

14-1. Define the phrase *financial model.*

14-2. For a firm with earnings per share of $10, dividends per share of $6, a cost of equity capital of 10 percent, and an internal rate of return of 15 percent, calculate its value by using the dividend model.

14-3. Discuss the simplifying assumptions which MM's and Gordon's models have in common. Can any problems arise from using such simplifications?

14-4. Do investors capitalize dividends or earnings in estimating the value of a stock?

14-5. "Dividend policy is irrelevant." True, false, or uncertain? Explain.

14-6. Compare and contrast the importance of dividend policy with and without the preferential tax rates on capital gains by using any model you prefer. Assume that the internal rate of return r equals the firm's cost of capital k and that capital gains are taxed at half the rate for ordinary income.

14-7. How can the present value of a share's cash dividends be equal to the present value of the share's earnings when dividends are almost always less than earnings?

14-8. Critically analyze the proposition on which Gordon's bird-in-the-hand model is based, that is, that uncertainty increases with futurity.

14-9. Why do Modigliani and Miller use the same discount rate k to find the value of three different income streams: dividends, earnings, and cashflows?

14-10. "A common stock that never pays any cash dividends is worthless." True, false, or uncertain? Explain.

SELECTED REFERENCES

Friend, Irwin, and Marshall Puckett, "Dividends and Stock Prices," *American Economic Review*, September 1954, pp. 656–682. An empirical test to determine whether investors capitalize dividends or earnings. Regression analysis is used.

Gordon, M. J., *The Investment, Financing, and Valuation of the Corporation*, Irwin, Homewood, Ill., 1962. A full discussion of Gordon's model for capitalizing dividends and a review of some of the literature. Some calculus used, mostly algebra.

Miller, M. H., and F. Modigliani, "Dividend Policy, Growth and the Valuation of Shares," *Journal of Business*, October 1961, pp. 411–433. The theory of valuation for shares in an all-equity corporation is analyzed with some analysis and review of relevant theories. Freshman college algebra used.

Modigliani, F., and M. H. Miller, "The Cost of Capital, Corporation Finance and the Theory of Investment; Corporate Income Taxes, and the Cost of Capital: A Correction," *American Economic Review*, June 1958, pp. 433–443. More recently, see Miller's "Debt and Taxes," *Journal of Finance*, May 1977, vol. XXXIII, no. 2, pp. 261–276. The valuation of a corporation which uses debt is explained. Freshman college algebra is used.

fundamental common stock analysis

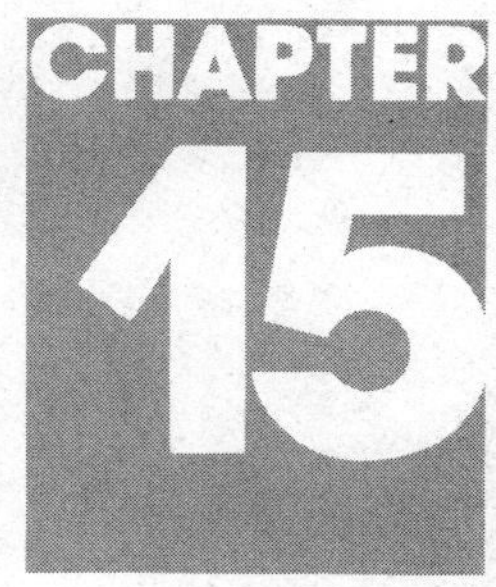

Security analysis is the basis for rational investment decisions. If a security's estimated value is *above* its market price, the security analyst will recommend buying the stock. If the estimated value is *below* the market price, the security should be sold before its price drops. This buying and selling process is what determines the market price of a security. Underpriced stocks are purchased until their price is bid up to equal their value. Overpriced stocks are sold, which drives their price down. Astute analysts continue to give "sell" instructions until the price is driven down to their estimate of its value—that is, until it is down to what they think it is "worth." In a perfectly efficient securities market, prices always equal values as a result of the buying and selling pressures just described. However, the values of securities are continuously changing as news about the securities becomes known, and this flux is what makes life exciting for security analysts. They must keep up-to-date value estimates for the securities with which they are working, or they will make bad (that is, unprofitable) buy and sell recommendations and lose their invested funds and/or their job.

This chapter explains how fundamental common stock analysts—that is, analysts who study the fundamental facts affecting a stock's value rather than follow fads or charts—do their investment research. Fundamental analysts delve into companies' earnings, their managements, the economic outlook, the firm's competition, market conditions, and many other factors. However, all their research is based on the valuation model explained below.

15-1 THE PRESENT VALUE OF CASH DIVIDENDS

The true economic value or *intrinsic value* of a share of common stock, like the value of a bond or other asset, equals the present value of all cashflows from the asset. Letting d_{it} denote the ith shares' (for example, General Motors) cash dividends per share paid in the tth period (say, the third quarter of 1985 might be used as one of the time periods), and letting k_i represent the ith stock's risk-adjusted discount rate (or cost of equity capitalization rate) means that the ith share's value, denoted p_i, is given by the present value formula in Eq. (15-1a), or equivalently by Eqs. (15-1b) and (15-1c).

$$p_{i0} = \sum_{t=1}^{\infty} \frac{d_{it}}{(1 + k_i)^t} \tag{15-1a}$$

$$= \sum_{t=1}^{\infty} \frac{d_{i0}(1 + g_i)^t}{(1 + k_i)^t} \qquad \text{since } d_{it} = d_{i0}(1 + g_i)^t \tag{15-1b}$$

$$= \frac{d_{i1}}{k_i - g_i} \tag{15-1c}$$

The growth rate for dividends, the g symbol, is presumed constant in writing Eqs. (15-1b) and (15-1c); therefore $d_{it} = d_{i0}(1 + g_i)^t$. This simplification allows the algebraic manipulation necessary to derive Eqs. (15-1c) and (15-1b).[1]

[1] If dividends grow at some constant rate, denoted g, then future dividends are related to current dividends as shown below. First note that Eq. (15-1a) can be rewritten as Eq. (a).

$$p_0 = \sum_{t=1}^{\infty} \frac{d_0(1 + g)^t}{(1 + k)^t} \tag{a}$$

$\sum d_0 x = d_0 \sum x$ because d_0 is a constant. This relation means that Eqs. (15-1b) or (a) may be rewritten as shown below.

$$p_0 = d_0 \sum_{t=1}^{\infty} \frac{(1 + g)^t}{(1 + k)^t} \tag{b}$$

$$= d_0 \left(\frac{1 + g}{1 + k} + \frac{(1 + g)^2}{(1 + k)^2} + \frac{(1 + g)^3}{(1 + k)^3} + \cdots \right) \tag{c}$$

Multiplying Eq. (c) by $[(1 + k)/(1 + g)]$ yields Eq. (d).

$$p_0 \frac{1 + k}{1 + g} = d_0 \left[1.0 + \frac{1 + g}{1 + k} + \frac{(1 + g)^2}{(1 + k)^2} + \cdots \right] \tag{d}$$

Subtracting Eq. (c) from the preceding equation yields Eq. (e).

$$\left(\frac{1 + k}{1 + g} - 1 \right) p_0 = d_0 \tag{e}$$

By assuming that $k > g$, the preceding equation can be rearranged as

$$\left[\frac{(1 + k) - (1 + g)}{1 + g} \right] p_0 = \left[\frac{k - g}{1 + g} \right] p_0 = d_0 \tag{f}$$

Multiplying Eq. (f) by the quantity $(1 + g)$ and rearranging yields Eq. (g).

$$p_0(k - g) = d_0(1 + g) = d_1 \tag{g}$$

where $d_0(1 + g)^1 = d_1$ denotes "next period's" dividends per share. Equation (15-1c) can be obtained by rearranging the preceding equation as follows.

$$p_0 = \frac{d_1}{k - g} \tag{15-1c}$$

15-2 FUNDAMENTAL ANALYSTS' MODEL

Most common stock analysts prepare their estimates of intrinsic value per share by multiplying the *i*th stock's normalized earnings per share, denoted e_{it} for the *t*th period, times the share's earnings multiplier, m_{it}, as shown in Eq. (15-2).

$$p_{it} = e_{it}m_{it} \tag{15-2}$$

The security analyst gets the earnings per share from the corporation's accountants and then normalizes it, as explained in Chap. 16, to obtain e_{it}.

15-2.1 the earnings multiplier

The economic theory to explain the earnings multiplier is obtained simply by dividing both sides of Eq. (15-2) or (15-1*b*) by normalized earnings per share, e_{it}, as shown in Eq. (15-3*a*):

$$m_{i0} = \frac{p_{i0}}{e_{i0}} = \sum_{t=1}^{\infty} \frac{(d_{i0}/e_{i0})(1+g_i)^t}{(1+k_i)^t} \quad \text{at time } t = 0 \tag{15-3a}$$

$$= \frac{p_{i0}}{e_{i0}} = \frac{d_{i0}}{e_{i0}} \sum_{t=1} \frac{(1+g_i)^t}{(1+k_i)^t} \tag{15-3b}$$

$$= \frac{d_{i1}/e_{it}}{k_i - g_i} \tag{15-3c}$$

The earnings multiplier is frequently called the *price-earnings ratio*.[2] The ratio d_{it}/e_{it} in Eqs. (15-3*a*) and (15-3*b*) is called the *dividend payout ratio*; it is about 50 percent for most corporations.

The remainder of this chapter focuses on the pragmatic approaches security analysts use to estimate a stock's appropriate earnings multiplier as defined in Eqs. (15-3*a*) and (15-3*c*) and the intrinsic value of the share. The factors which determine a security's dividend growth rate g are explained first. However, the primary topics for the remainder of the chapter are the factors which cause securities markets to value a stock like, say, American Telephone and Telegraph at 10 times its earnings per share in 1973 after valuing the same share at 22 times its earnings in 1961. However, before discussing earnings multipliers, a more direct approach to the valuation of a corporation is considered, that is, simply appraising its assets to find their sales value. This approach is not recommended because a corporation should not be considered to be merely a collection of physical assets. A viable corporation is one that produces some product of value and earns income. If the corporation's assets cannot produce income, they have no economic value.

[2] The equity share valuation model represented by Eqs. (15-1), (15-2), and (15-3*a*) has been developed by B. G. Malkiel, "Equity Yields, Growth, and Structure of Share Prices," *American Economic Review*, December 1963, pp. 1004–1031, and "The Valuation of Public Utility Equities," *Bell Journal of Economics and Management Science*, 1970, pp. 143–160, and by B. G. Malkiel and J. G. Cragg in "Expectations and the Structure of Share Prices," *American Economic Review*, September 1970, pp. 601–617.

15-2.2 asset values

The asset value of a security is determined by estimating the liquidating value of the firm, deducting the claims of the firm's creditors, and allocating the remaining net asset value of the firm over the outstanding junior securities (namely, shares of stock). The asset value of a firm is usually estimated by (1) consulting a specialist in appraising asset values and/or (2) consulting an accountant about the book value of the firm.

Asset values are important in determining the market value of a company when it may go bankrupt, but that is about the only time asset values are important. In the case of probable bankruptcy, the firm's income and dividends will probably not be continued and will therefore have negligible value: The firm's value is dependent upon the prices its assets will bring at sale. But for prosperous firms asset values need not be considered. The intrinsic value of a prosperous firm or "going concern" typically far exceeds the value of the firm's physical assets.

Table 15-1 shows some of the data for American Telephone and Telegraph (AT&T) which would be used in estimating the intrinsic value of a share of the firm's common stock. The lack of relationship between book asset values and market values is apparent in these data; this is typical. In most cases, asset values may be ignored when valuing common stock (except for a nonoperating asset which may be sold without affecting the firm).

15-3 EARNINGS MULTIPLIERS: A PRAGMATIC APPROACH

Much of the fundamental security analyst's work centers on determining the appropriate capitalization rate or, equivalently, the appropriate multiplier to use in valuing a particular security's income. The main factors which must be considered in determining the correct multiplier are (1) the risk of the security, (2) the growth rate of the dividend stream, (3) the duration of any expected growth, and (4) the dividend payout ratio. Also, as the national economy and credit conditions change, interest rates, capitalization rates, and multipliers change. Table 15-2 suggests the general nature of the relationship

TABLE 15-1 selected financial data for American Telephone & Telegraph (AT&T) common stock on a per-share basis

year	book value, $	range of market price, $	per-share earnings, $	average price-earnings ratio, times	per-share cash dividend, $	dividend payout ratio, %
1982	$69.07	64-50	8.38	7	5.40	64%
1981	67.52	61-47	8.55	6	5.40	63%
1980	65.51	56-45	8.19	6	5.00	61%
1979	63.43	64-51	8.04	7	5.00	62%
1978	60.67	64-56	7.74	8	4.60	59%
1977	57.78	65-58	6.97	9	4.20	60%
1976	55.08	64-50	6.05	9	3.80	63%
1975	52.86	52-44	5.13	10	3.40	66%
1974	51.40	53-39	5.27	9	3.24	61%
1973	49.40	55-45	4.98	10	2.87	58%

TABLE 15-2 capitalization rates and their equivalent multipliers when income is constant

capitalization rate (*k*), %	riskiness	equivalent multiplier (1/*k*)
1	Negligible risk	100 times
2		50
4		25
6		16.7
8		12.5
10	Medium risk	10
15		6.7
20		5
25		4
33		3
50	High risk	2

between capitalization rates, multipliers, and risk when growth in income is zero. With this general background in mind, the determinants of intrinsic values are examined below. First, earnings multipliers are analyzed.

15-3.1 earnings multipliers

In determining the price-earnings ratio to use in valuing a firm's securities, three factors must be estimated: the capitalization rate, the dividend growth rate, and the dividend payout ratio. As shown in Fig. 15-1, capitalization rates vary with the firm's risk-class and the prevailing market conditions. This inquiry into earnings multipliers begins with the multipliers for a normal market; later, the effects of bull or bear markets will be examined.

A *normal market* is a market in which most security prices are experiencing slow, steady growth and the average price-earnings ratio is in the low to mid-teens. Figures 15-2, 15-4, and 15-5 show the cyclical fluctuations in the stock market and some market-related economic statistics during recent years. When average earnings multipliers drop below 13 times, many market prices are deflated. When average earnings multipliers rise above approximately 18, it is the result of a bull market, and many stocks are overpriced. The defini-

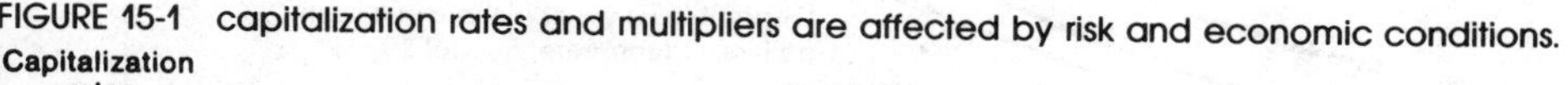
FIGURE 15-1 capitalization rates and multipliers are affected by risk and economic conditions.

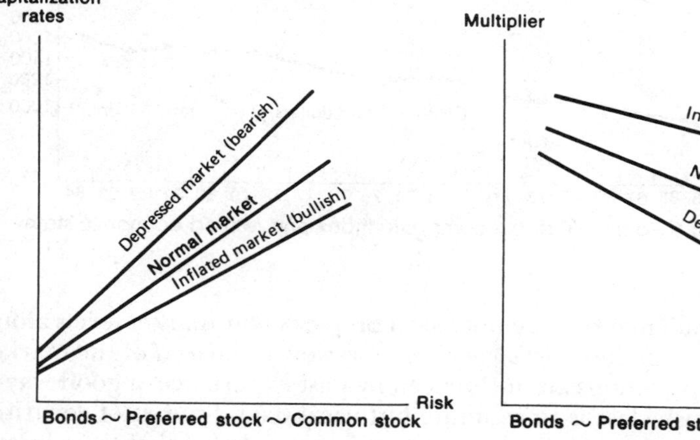

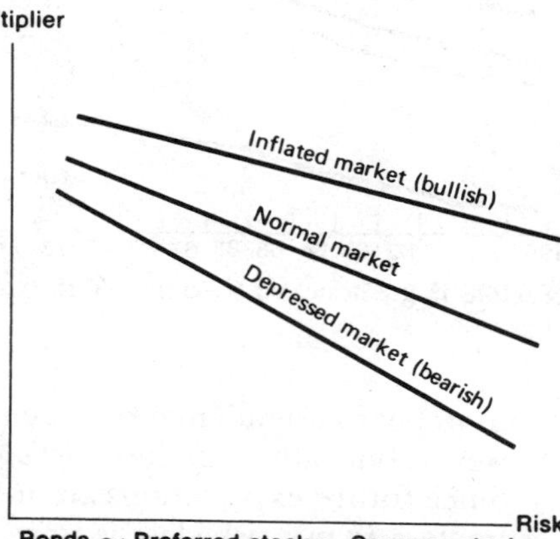

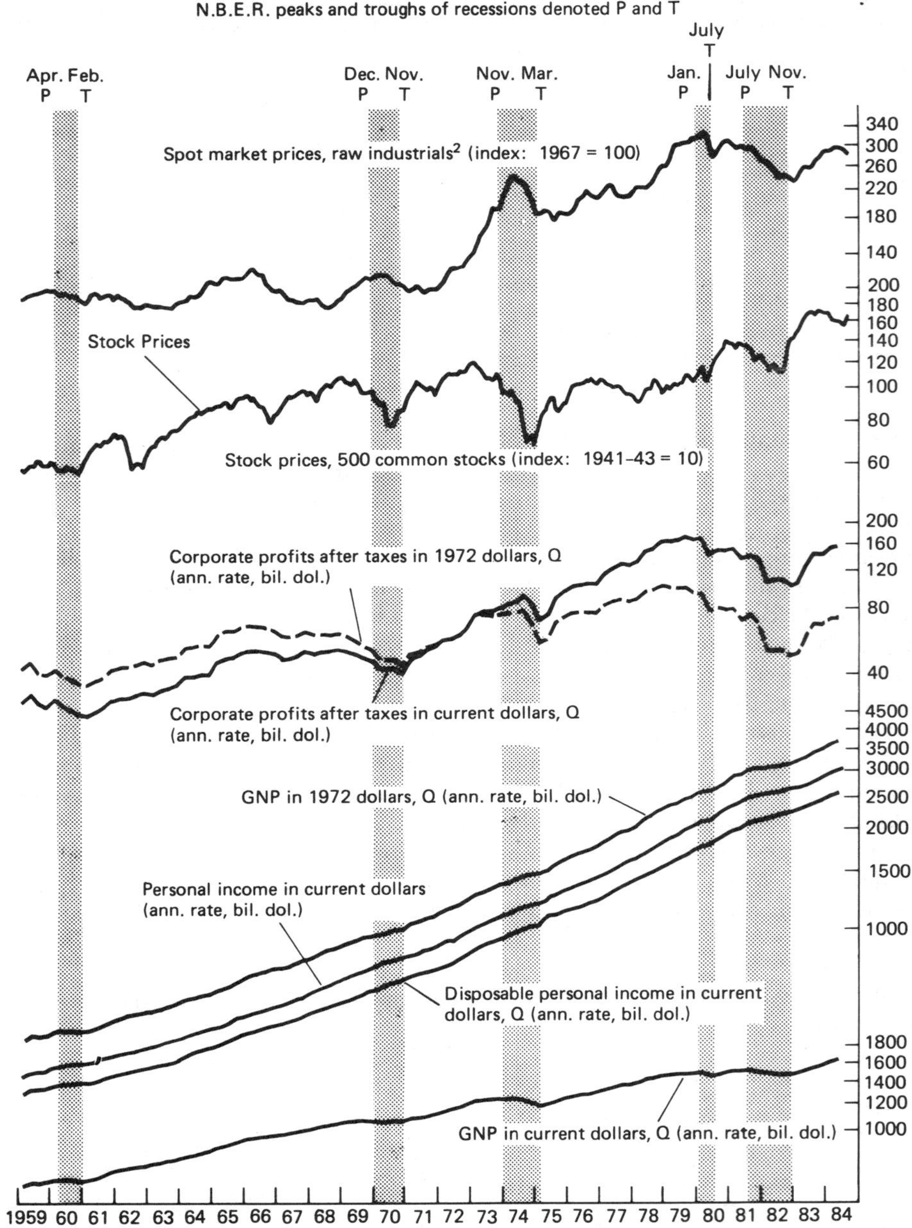

FIGURE 15-2 Standard & Poor's 500 stocks composite index and related economic statistics.

tions of bear and bull markets are not based on particular market levels alone, however, but rather on the *direction of changes* as well as the *level* of the market.

Since future expectations are influenced by past experience, a good way to estimate a firm's risk-class is to examine historical data. Studies of securities listed on the New York Stock Exchange (NYSE) have shown that their histor-

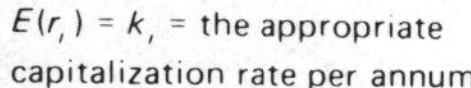

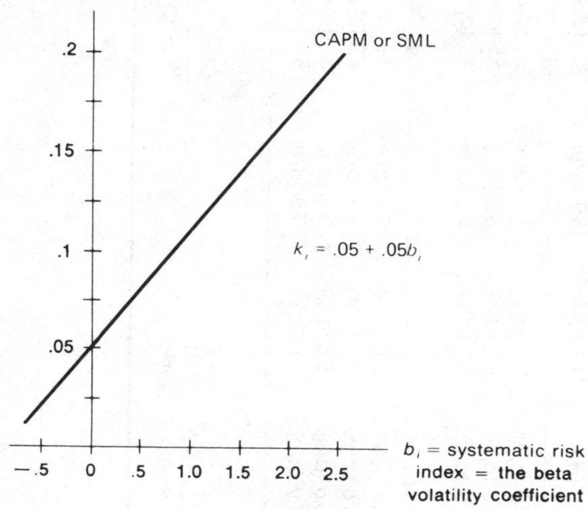

FIGURE 15-3 the capital asset pricing model (CAPM) or security market line (SML) for normal market conditions.

ical average earnings capitalization rate varies directly with the security's volatility coefficient (measuring systematic or undiversifiable risk). Figure 15-3 depicts the risk-return relationship called the capital asset pricing model (CAPM).[3] The CAPM illustrates the positive relationship between an asset's undiversifiable risk (as measured by its beta coefficient, from Chap. 10) and the appropriate discount rate (or expected rate of return) for the asset. The fundamental analysts can measure the risk of the company in recent periods, adjust these historical risk statistics for any expected changes, and then use these forecasted risk statistics to obtain capitalization rates from Fig. 15-3.[4]

The capitalization rates in Fig. 15-3 are for normal markets. If the analysis is being performed during an inflated market, for example, the capitalization rates in Fig. 15-3 should be adjusted downward to increase the earnings multiplier in line with prevailing conditions. The reverse is true if pessimism prevails and the market is depressed. After the capitalization rate has been determined, the growth rate in dividends per share must be estimated.

15-3.2 estimated growth rates affect multipliers

If a security is expected to become more valuable in the future, this anticipated rise in value will tend to make it more valuable now. In order to place a current value on future growth in value, that growth must be estimated before it occurs. The growth rate in dividends or earnings per share is a good measure of growth in a firm's earning power in most cases. It is usually fairly simple to estimate the growth rate in cash dividends or earnings per share. Measuring these growth rates is discussed in Chaps. 16 and 17.

[3] The capital asset pricing model (CAPM) or, as it is also called, the security market line (SML) in Fig. 15-3 is the author's subjectively adjusted estimate based on empirical regressions. Empirical estimates of the SML may be found in F. Black, M. C. Jensen, and M. Scholes, "The Capital Asset Pricing Model: Some Empirical Tests," in M. C. Jensen (ed.), *Studies in the Theory of Capital Markets*.

[4] Chapters 10, 16, and 30 explain how to measure a stock's risk in more detail. The following footnote cites research studies about how to measure systematic risk with the beta coefficient in order to impute a capitalization rate.

TABLE 15-3 price-earnings ratios for various risk-classes and various rates of dividend or earnings growth in normal markets

type of risk	capitalization rate (*k*), %	growth rate in div. (*g*), %	APPROPRIATE P/E RATIO IF EARNINGS GROWTH CONTINUES FOR: 5 years	10 years	15 years	20 years	25 years	forever
Outcome fairly certain, low risk: example: high-quality preferred stock	2	0	50 (*d/e*)	50 (*d/e*)	50 (*d/e*)	50 (*d/e*)	50 (*d/e*)	50 (*d/e*)
		1	52.4 (*d/e*)	54.8 (*d/e*)	57 (*d/e*)	59.0 (*d/e*)	61.1 (*d/e*)	101 (*d/e*)
	4	0	25 (*d/e*)	25 (*d/e*)	25 (*d/e*)	25 (*d/e*)	25 (*d/e*)	25 (*d/e*)
		1	26.2 (*d/e*)	27.2 (*d/e*)	28 (*d/e*)	28.8 (*d/e*)	29.5 (*d/e*)	33.7 (*d/e*)
		2	27.4 (*d/e*)	29.6 (*d/e*)	31.6 (*d/e*)	33.3 (*d/e*)	35 (*d/e*)	51 (*d/e*)
Some uncertainty, medium risk: example: an established business	6	0	16.7 (*d/e*)	16.7 (*d/e*)	16.7 (*d/e*)	16.7 (*d/e*)	16.7 (*d/e*)	16.7 (*d/e*)
		2	18.2 (*d/e*)	19.5 (*d/e*)	20.5 (*d/e*)	21.4 (*d/e*)	22.1 (*d/e*)	25.5 (*d/e*)
		4	19.9 (*d/e*)	22.8 (*d/e*)	25.5 (*d/e*)	27.9 (*d/e*)	30 (*d/e*)	52 (*d/e*)
	10	0	10 (*d/e*)	10 (*d/e*)	10 (*d/e*)	10 (*d/e*)	10 (*d/e*)	10 (*d/e*)
		3	11.3 (*d/e*)	12.3 (*d/e*)	13 (*d/e*)	13.5 (*d/e*)	13.8 (*d/e*)	14.7 (*d/e*)
		6	12.8 (*d/e*)	15.1 (*d/e*)	17 (*d/e*)	18.6 (*d/e*)	20 (*d/e*)	26.5 (*d/e*)
	14	0	7.1 (*d/e*)	7.1 (*d/e*)	7.1 (*d/e*)	7.1 (*d/e*)	7.1 (*d/e*)	7.1 (*d/e*)
		4	8.3 (*d/e*)	9 (*d/e*)	9.6 (*d/e*)	9.8 (*d/e*)	9.9 (*d/e*)	10.4 (*d/e*)
		8	9.7 (*d/e*)	11.7 (*d/e*)	13.2 (*d/e*)	14.3 (*d/e*)	15.2 (*d/e*)	18 (*d/e*)
High degree of uncertainty, high risk: example: new business	20	0	5 (*d/e*)	5 (*d/e*)	5 (*d/e*)	5 (*d/e*)	5 (*d/e*)	5 (*d/e*)
		4	5.8 (*d/e*)	6.1 (*d/e*)	6.3 (*d/e*)	6.3 (*d/e*)	6.3 (*d/e*)	6.5 (*d/e*)
		8	6.6 (*d/e*)	7.6 (*d/e*)	8.2 (*d/e*)	8.3 (*d/e*)	8.3 (*d/e*)	9 (*d/e*)
		12						
	26	0	3.8 (*d/e*)	3.8 (*d/e*)	3.8 (*d/e*)	3.8 (*d/e*)	3.8 (*d/e*)	3.8 (*d/e*)
		4	4.4 (*d/e*)	4.6 (*d/e*)	4.6 (*d/e*)	4.6 (*d/e*)	4.6 (*d/e*)	4.7 (*d/e*)
		8	5 (*d/e*)	5.5 (*d/e*)	5.6 (*d/e*)	5.6 (*d/e*)	5.6 (*d/e*)	6 (*d/e*)
		12	5.7 (*d/e*)	6.7 (*d/e*)	7.2 (*d/e*)	7.2 (*d/e*)	7.2 (*d/e*)	8 (*d/e*)

Formulas to derive multipliers:

(d/e) = payout ratio

$$M = \left[\sum_{t=1}^{p} \frac{(1 + g_1)^t}{(1 + k)^t} + \sum_{t=p+1}^{\infty} \frac{(1 + g_1)(1 + g_2)^{t-p}}{(1 + k)^t}\right]\left(\frac{d}{e}\right)$$

$$M = \frac{(d/e)(1 + g)}{(k - g)}$$

It is important to develop accurate estimates of the firm's dividend (or earnings) growth rate and the period of time this growth may be expected to continue. Table 15-3 contains numerical values that need to be multiplied by the common stock's dividend payout ratio, *d/e*, to obtain the appropriate earnings multiplier. Table 15-3 shows that the growth rate and the expected duration of growth in dividends have an important influence on the earnings multipliers. In fact, the growth rate is as important as the capitalization rate in preparing estimates of the appropriate earnings multipliers.

ESTIMATING INTRINSIC VALUE WITH ZERO EARNINGS GROWTH To see how the multipliers in Table 15-3 are used to estimate intrinsic values, consider a hypothetical example. Suppose that security markets were normal and that a security analyst had estimated the risk and growth statistics for the ABC Company. Assuming ABC's beta systematic risk coefficient, which measures its undiversifiable risk, was estimated to be $b = 1.0$, Fig. 15-3 indicates that the appropriate capitalization rate for the firm is $k = 10$ percent.

Two different security analysts' estimates of a security's beta systematic risk coefficient should not differ appreciably since the betas tend to be fairly stationary over time.[5] However, when a difference does occur, the security

[5] See the following research about beta coefficients—an index of systematic risk. Papers by Frank J. Fabozzi and J. C. Francis include: (1) "Beta as a Random Coefficient," *Journal of Financial and Quantitative Analysis*, March 1978, pp. 101–116. (2) "Stability Tests for Alphas and Betas over Bull and Bear Market Conditions," *Journal of Finance*, September 1977. (3) "The Effects of Changing Macroeconomic Conditions on Alphas, Betas, and the Single-Index Model," *Journal of Financial and Quantitative Analysis*, June 1979. (4) "The Stability of Mutual Fund Systematic Risk Coefficients," *Journal of Business Research*, 1980, pp. 263–275. (5) "Heteroscedasticity in the Single-Index Model," *Journal of Economics and Business*, Spring 1980, vol. 32, no. 3, pp. 243–248. (6) "Industry Effects and the Determinants of Beta," *Quarterly Review of Economics and Business*, vol. 19, no. 3, Autumn 1979, pp. 61–74. See also the following articles by J. C. Francis: (1) "Analysis of Equity Returns: A Survey with Extensions," *Journal of Economics and Business*, Spring/Summer 1977, vol. 29, no. 3, pp. 181–192. (2) "Statistical Analysis of Risk Coefficients for NYSE Stocks," *Journal of Financial and Quantitative Analysis*, vol. XIV, no. 5, December 1979, pp. 981–997. See also the following research. (1) G. J. Alexander and N. L. Chervany, "On the Estimation and Stability of Beta," *Journal of Financial and Quantitative Analysis*, March 1980, vol. 15, pp. 123–137. (2) E. K. Altman, B. Jacquillat, and M. Levasseur, "Comparative Analysis of Risk Measures: France and the United States," *Journal of Finance*, December 1974, vol. 29, pp. 1495–1511. (3) M. E. Blume, "Betas and Their Regression Tendencies," *Journal of Finance*, June 1975, vol. 30, pp. 785–796. (4) M. E. Blume, "On the Assessment of Risk," *Journal of Finance*, March 1971, vol. 26, pp. 1–10. (5) E. Dimson, "Risk Measurement When Shares Are Subject to Infrequent Trading," *Journal of Financial Economics*, June 1979, vol. 7, pp. 197–226. (6) E. Dimson and P. R. Marsh, "The Stability of UK Risk Measures and the Problem of Thin Trading," *Journal of Finance*, forthcoming. (7) A. A. Eubank, Jr., and J. K. Zumwalt, "An Analysis of the Forecast Error Impact of Alternative Beta Adjustment Techniques and Risk Classes," *Journal of Finance*, June 1979, vol. 34, pp. 761–776. (8) L. Fisher and J. Kamin, "Good Betas and Bad Betas," unpublished paper, Center for Research into Security Prices, University of Chicago, November 1971. (9) N. Jacob, "The Measurement of Systematic Risk for Securities and Portfolios: Some Empirical Results," *Journal of Financial and Quantitative Analysis*, March 1971, vol. 6, pp. 815–834. (10) R. C. Klemkosky and J. D. Martin, "The Adjustment of Beta Forecasts," *Journal of Finance*, September 1975, vol. 30, pp. 1123–1128. (11) S. J. Kon and W. P. Lau, "Specification Tests for Portfolio Regression Parameter Stationarity and the Implications for Empirical Research," *Journal of Finance*, May 1979, vol. 34, pp. 451–465. (12) M. Scholes and J. Williams, "Estimating Betas from Nonsynchronous Data," *Journal of Financial Economics*, December 1977, vol. 5, pp. 309–328.

(Footnote 5 continues)

analyst must rely on experience and judgment in selecting a capitalization rate if the discrepancies cannot be attributed to errors in the risk forecasts. Usually two estimates of the appropriate capitalization rate will not diverge very much, and the analyst can simply use their average as a capitalization rate. However, if a significant divergence is present which cannot be rationalized, the analyst may have found a security whose price is significantly out of equilibrium. Such disequilibrium situations can result in considerable profits for an investor who is willing to assume the risks associated with such uncertainties.

For ABC Company (the same hypothetical firm), the capital asset pricing model (CAPM) in Fig. 15-3 indicated a capitalization rate of 10 percent.[6] If no dividend growth is expected for ABC, the appropriate earnings multiplier from Table 15-3 is 10 times the payout ratio *d/e*. The price-earnings ratio was derived by finding the present value of unity each year to infinity and multiplying this value by the payout ratio, as shown in Eq. (15-4*a*).

$$\text{Zero-growth earnings multiplier} = \sum_{t=1}^{\infty} \frac{1}{(1 + \text{capitalization rate})^t} \frac{d_1}{e} \tag{15-4a}$$

$$= \frac{d_1/e}{\text{capitalization rate}} \tag{15-4b}$$

Equation (15-4*b*) is a simplified but equivalent version of Eq. (15-4*a*).

Assume that ABC's normalized earnings per share are currently $4 per

(13) W. F. Sharpe, "The Capital Asset Pricing Model: A 'Multi-Beta' Interpretation," in H. Levy and M. Sarnat (eds.), *Financial Decision Making under Uncertainty*, Academic Press, New York, 1977. (14) W. F. Sharpe and G. M. Cooper, "Risk-Return Classes of New York Stock Exchange Stocks, 1931–1967," *Financial Analysts Journal*, March–April 1972, vol. 28, pp. 46–54. (15) O. A. Vasicek, "A Note on Using Cross-Sectional Information in Bayesian Estimation of Security Betas," *Journal of Finance*, December 1973, vol. 28, pp. 1233–1239. The following studies discuss the use of accounting data to estimate risk: (16) W. Beaver, P. Kettler, and M. Scholes, "The Association between Market-Determined and Accounting-Determined Risk Measures," *Accounting Review*, October 1970, vol. 45, pp. 654–682. (17) W. Beaver and J. Manegold, "The Association between Market-Determined and Accounting-Determined Measures of Systematic Risk: Some Further Evidence," *Journal of Financial and Quantitative Analysis*, June 1975, vol. 10, pp. 231–284. (18) G. Foster, *Financial Statement Analysis*, Prentice-Hall, Englewood Cliffs, N. J., 1978. (19) N. J. Gonedes, "Evidence on the Information Content of Accounting Numbers: Accounting-Based and Market-Based Estimates of Systematic Risk," *Journal of Financial and Quantitative Analysis*, June 1973, vol. 8, pp. 407–444. (20) B. Rosenberg, "Extra Market Components of Covariance among Security Prices," *Journal of Financial and Quantitative Analysis*, March 1974, vol. 9, pp. 263–294. (21) B. Rosenberg and J. Guy, "Beta and Investment Fundamentals," *Financial Analysts Journal*, May–June 1976, vol. 32, pp. 60–72, and July–August 1976, vol. 32, pp. 62–70. (22) B. Rosenberg and W. McKibben, "The Prediction of Systematic and Specific Risk in Common Stocks," *Journal of Financial and Quantitative Analysis*, March 1973, vol. 8, pp. 312–334. Roll's paper contains a theoretical discussion of the importance of choosing the appropriate market measure: (23) R. Roll, "A Critique of the Asset Pricing Theory's Tests; Part 1: On Past and Potential Testability of the Theory," *Journal of Financial Economics*, March 1977, vol. 4, pp. 129–176.

[6] The theoretical capital asset pricing model (CAPM) is defined as follows: $E(r_i) = R + [E(r_m) - R]b_i$. It is assumed in Fig. 15-3 that $R = .05 = 5.0$ percent and $E(r_m) = .1 = 10.0$ percent and thus the CAPM assumes the specific form $E(r_i) = .05 + (.1 - .05)b_i$. See Chap. 10 for details about the CAPM.

year and that its average payout rate is 50 percent of earnings. Applying the earnings multiplier of (1/.1 =) 10 times to these earnings implies that the intrinsic value of ABC is about (10 × $4 × .5 =) $20 per share.

Of course, there are numerous places where errors may creep into estimates of normalized earnings, the dividend payout ratio, the capitalization rate, and the dividend growth rate. Therefore, it is not certain that the intrinsic value is exactly $20 per share. It is possible that an error of plus or minus 10 percent, which is the range from $18 to $22, could occur in a carefully prepared analysis of a mature company. Therefore, if the stock were selling at $15, it would seem to be underpriced and therefore a good buy. However, if it were selling at $18.50 or $21.75, it might be correctly priced and thus not as interesting.

ESTIMATING INTRINSIC VALUE WITH PERPETUAL EARNINGS GROWTH If it is assumed that ABC's earnings are currently $4 per share but will grow with cash dividends forever at, say, 3 percent per year, the intrinsic value estimate will be quite different from what it was with zero growth. Table 15-3 shows that for a capitalization rate of 10 percent and a growth rate of 3 percent, the correct multiplier is 14.7 times *d*/*e*. This multiplier is derived by finding the present value (using a capitalization rate of $k = .1 =$ 10 percent) of a stream of numbers starting at unity and growing at a rate of $g =$ 3 percent per year into infinity. Equation (15-5*a*) shows the mathematical model representing these computations.

$$\text{Earnings multiplier for perpetual growth} = \sum_{t=1}^{\infty} \frac{(1 + \text{earnings growth rate})^t}{(1 + \text{capitalization rate})^t} \frac{d_1}{e} \tag{15-5a}$$

$$= \frac{d_1/e}{(\text{capitalization rate} - \text{growth rate})} = \frac{d_1/e}{k - g} \tag{15-5b}$$

Equation (15-5*b*) is equivalent to Eq. (15-5*a*). Note that Eq. (15-5*b*) is also equal to Eq. (15-4*b*) when the earnings growth rate is zero.

For beginning earnings of $4 per share, a perpetual growth rate of 3 percent, and a cash dividend payout rate of one-half (that is, $d/e = .5$), the intrinsic value estimate is (14.7 × $4 × .5) for the intrinsic value to be in the range from ($29.40 ± 10 percent =) $32.34 to $26.46.

ESTIMATING INTRINSIC VALUE WITH TEMPORARY GROWTH It is not likely that a well-managed firm's growth will remain zero, nor is it likely that a firm can maintain its dividend growth at a high level forever. Therefore, suppose ABC's dividends are expected to grow at 3 percent for 5 years and then level off. In this case, Table 15-3 indicates that the appropriate price-earnings multiplier is 11.3 times *d*/*e*. This implies that a most likely estimate of the intrinsic value is (.5 × 11.3 × $4 =) $22.60. But the intrinsic value could range from ($22.60 ± 10 percent =) $20.34 to $24.86, allowing the 10 percent margin for error.

As seen above, the intrinsic value of ABC is highly dependent on its dividend growth. Zero growth implies ABC is worth $20 per share, while perpetual growth at 3 percent implies a value of $29.40. Between these two extremes a value of $22.60 is implied if dividends grow at 3 percent for 5 years and then level off and have zero growth thereafter.[7]

15-3.3 the payout ratio and the multiplier

The preceding examples demonstrated the effect that the size and duration of the growth rate in dividends can have on the earnings multiplier.[8] The effects of the dividend payout ratio are more direct than the effect of growth rate and thus easier to see. The theoretical analysis that led up to the values shown in Table 15-3 indicates that, if other things remain constant, reducing a corporation's dividend payout cuts its multiplier and thus its intrinsic value proportionately. The important question related to the payout ratio is how to evaluate it. That is, since corporations' dividends per share are a different percentage of their earnings per share practically every quarter, what is the best estimate of a firm's payout ratio? A glance at the right-hand column of Table 15-1, for example, shows how AT&T's payout ratio fluctuated from 66 to 59 percent within the 4 years from 1975 through 1978. Most corporations' payout ratios fluctuate more than this because the firms endeavor to maintain undiminished cash dividends while their earnings fluctuate violently at times. And when a corporation incurs a loss (that is, negative earnings per share), its payout ratio is simply undefined for that period. Stated differently, negative payout ratios have no rational economic interpretation.

Estimating the payout ratio which a stable public utility like AT&T seeks to maintain is simple. Table 15-1 shows that no losses were incurred and the payout ratio fluctuates symmetrically around 60 percent from year to year. For a more risky company, it is necessary to estimate the corporation's *normalized earnings* per share averaged over the complete business cycle. Earnings analysis is investigated in Chap. 16, and the procedure for finding normalized earnings is explained there. After a share's normal earnings are estimated, all that need be done is divide normalized earnings per share into the corporation's regular cash dividend per share to find the payout for use in the determination of an earnings multiplier. Unfortunately, in a few cases this straightforward procedure is inappropriate.

About a dozen large corporations have adopted the policy of reinvesting all corporate earnings in order to maximize their internally financed growth—that is, their dividend policy is to have a zero payout ratio. (Table 14-2, on page 416, lists those corporations which have elected to pay no cash dividends and shows how their market prices performed.) Although this payout ratio is logical if the corporations have profitable investment opportunities, it means Eq. (15-3*a*) cannot be used for those multipliers without some adjustments. Other pathological cases exist for which the model in Eq. (15-3*a*) also will not work. For example, what if a corporation keeps borrowing funds with which to pay cash dividends that bear no relation to its earnings? The once mighty Penn Central Railroad did so when it continued to pay cash dividends year

[7] Tables of price-earnings ratios computed under numerous growth rates and discount rates are available in Joe Lavely and Paul E. Ruckman, *Simultaneous Compounding and Discounting*, Lexington Books, Lexington, Mass., 1979.

[8] Robert A. Haugen and Dean W. Wichern, "The Elasticity of Financial Assets," *Journal of Finance*, September 1974, pp. 1229–1240. C. C. Holt, "The Influence of Growth Duration on Share Prices," *Journal of Finance*, September 1962, pp. 465–475.

after year until its $5 billion bankruptcy in 1970. For these unusual cases, the fundamental security analyst must use the corporation's past earnings multipliers as a starting point. Then past multipliers can be adjusted to derive earnings multipliers with which to estimate a share's intrinsic value. Past earnings multipliers are useful in estimating future earnings multipliers for those corporations which have unusual payout ratios, because the past multipliers implicitly contain the market's estimate of the payout. Even normal corporations with positive dividend payout policies and dividend payments that are highly positively correlated with earnings, as shown in Fig. 15-4, may be analyzed more effectively sometimes by making reference to historical earnings multipliers.

15-3.4 subjective factors affect multipliers

In the estimation of a stock's intrinsic economic value, there are many subjective considerations. Care must be taken in weighting the different impacts of these subjective factors on d_t, e_t, g, and k so as not to double-count the effect of one change in d_t, e_t, g, or k unless it truly affects more than one of these variables. Unfortunately, many changes (for example, the addition or deletion of a product line, mergers, or a new competitor) can affect the expected values of d_t, e_t, g, and k simultaneously; this is the time when special care must be used to incorporate the change into all the affected variables properly without double counting or overcompensating. The firm's management and financial position are two of the more important factors which involve subjective evaluations that can affect d_t, e_t, g, and k.

MANAGEMENT EVALUATION In forecasting the risk and earnings of a given corporation, fundamental analysts also consider management. The depth and

FIGURE 15-4 aggregate corporate profits, taxes, dividends, and retained earnings.

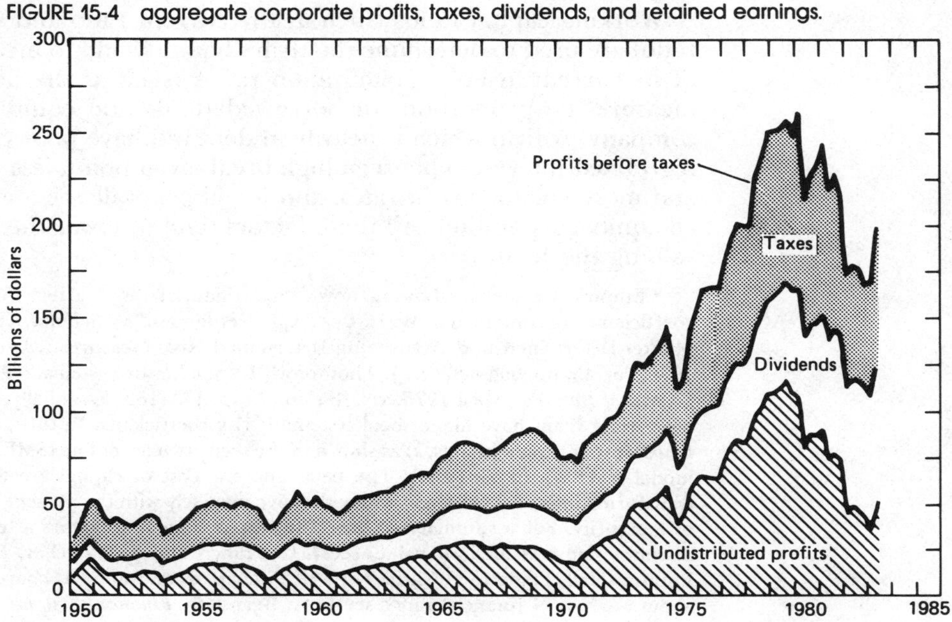

experience of management; its age, education, and health; the existence of personalities that are bottlenecks in an organization; and management's ability to react effectively to changes—all affect the firm's risk and its future income. The research and development (R&D) program should also be considered. For example, if a company has new discoveries or advanced technology which will give it a competitive advantage in the future, the potential benefit tends to have a favorable effect on the forecasted intrinsic value of its securities by decreasing risk and/or increasing earnings growth. Section 9-5 (pages 231–235) discussed these and other problems involved in assessing the qualifications of a corporation's management under the heading Management Risk.

Assessing the ability of management and the value of ongoing research is difficult. Capable managers do not fit an easily recognizable stereotype, and the most trivial technological development can be extremely profitable. Making such evaluations is more of a personal skill than a science. The more widely educated, experienced, and sensitive the analyst is, the better he or she will be able to recognize significant factors and assess their value.

ANALYSIS OF FINANCIAL RATIOS In an effort to forecast earnings, dividends, and their multipliers, financial statements must be considered. Financial analysis can also shed light on how well-managed the firm is, what its growth areas are, and how risky its operations are. These factors affect the multipliers used to derive the intrinsic value estimates.[9] Financial analysis starts by adjusting the financial statements to overcome inconsistencies and "window-dressing" gimmicks. In Chap. 16 some cases are analyzed in which corporations misrepresent their annual income. These misleading accounting practices must be detected and corrected so that meaningful financial ratios can be calculated and evaluated.

Working capital ratios (such as the current ratio and inventory turnover ratio) are used to determine the firm's liquidity and to measure the efficiency of its current assets. Capitalization ratios (such as the debt to equity ratio) measure the proportions of borrowed funds and equity used to finance a company. A firm which is heavily in debt will have poor capitalization ratios, high fixed-interest expense, a high break-even point, less financial flexibility, and more volatile profit rates, and it will generally be a greater risk than an all-equity corporation. All these factors tend to lower the multipliers used in valuing the firm.

[9] Empirical evidence showing how firms' financial ratios affect their beta systematic risk coefficients are contained in W. H. Beaver, P. Kettler, and M. Scholes, "The Association between Market-Determined and Accounting-Determined Risk Measures," *Accounting Review*, October 1970, vol. 45, pp. 654–682; D. J. Thompson II, "Sources of Systematic Risk in Common Stocks," *Journal of Business*, April 1976, vol. 49, no. 2, pp. 173–188. Essentially, these studies show that more risky firms have higher beta systematic risk coefficients. In turn, the betas determine the firms' cost of capital (that is, k) as shown in the security market line (SML), or capital asset pricing model (CAPM), of Fig. 15-3. The betas and the cost of capital are thus seen to be positive transformations of each other, and both move inversely with the present value (or intrinsic value) of a security. For a summary of how a firm's fundamental factors affect its beta (and thus its discount rate and intrinsic value) see J. C. Francis and S. J. Archer, *Portfolio Analysis*, 2d ed., Prentice-Hall, Englewood Cliffs, N.J., 1979, chap. 4, and app. A, chap. 4. For a popular book about analysis of financial ratios see L. A. Bernstein, *Financial Statement Analysis*, 3d ed., Irwin, Homewood, Ill., 1983.

Income ratios (for example, the rate of return on assets and return on equity) measure the productivity of the money invested in the enterprise and are useful in detecting ineffective uses of capital. If the income ratios are all high, the firm is in the enviable position of having weak or nonexistent competition. On the other hand, low income ratios indicate low productivity of capital and a significant possibility that the firm might default on its debt contracts. Low income ratios will tend to lower the firm's multipliers.

STANDARDS OF COMPARISON FOR FINANCIAL RATIOS After financial ratios are calculated, they are of more value if they can be measured against some standard of comparison. The common standards against which financial ratios are measured are (1) the firm's own historical ratios, (2) competitors' ratios, and (3) published industry average ratios. Competitors' ratios and industry ratios may be used to detect significant deviations from the normal way of doing business. A historical trend in a firm's ratios indicates that some change is occurring within the firm. Once these items of interest are detected, additional analysis will reveal the source of the deviation and whether the deviation is desirable.[10]

The important financial ratios are already calculated for most publicly traded firms. The ratios are published in Moody's *Industrial Manuals*, Standard & Poor's *Corporation Records, Value Line Investment Survey*, and other sources. These sources also suggest some conclusions about the implications of their analysis (they were discussed on pages 147–163).

15-3.5 factors affecting intrinsic value

Numerous studies of varying degrees of sophistication have sought to determine the major factors which determine stock prices. One study used a mathematical statistics process called *multivariate analysis*. This study of 63 firms listed on the NYSE found that, on the average, 31 percent of the variation in a stock's price could be attributed to changes in the level of the whole stock market; 12 percent to changes peculiar to each firm which were assumed to come from within the firm. These percentages varied from industry to industry. The average percentages for six industries are shown in Table 15-4. This study indicates the necessity for the fundamental analyst to look beyond the firm itself in estimating future earnings, dividends, and multipliers.

Figure 15-4 shows how total corporate profits and dividends in the United States varied over recent years. Figure 15-5 shows how the average capitalization rates for dividends and earnings varied during the same time period. The aggregated data conceal many radical fluctuations which affected some firms' multipliers and earnings. Nevertheless, these two figures show that earnings, dividends, and the reciprocals of their multipliers all vary consider-

[10] Altman has shown how to use financial ratios to foretell bankruptcy: Edward I. Altman, "Corporate Bankruptcy Potential: Shareholder Returns and Share Valuation," *Journal of Finance*, December 1969. Also see Altman's "Financial Ratios, Discriminant Analysis, and the Prediction of Corporate Bankruptcy," *Journal of Finance*, September 1968. For a more complete review of Altman's work see E. I. Altman, *Corporate Financial Distress*, Wiley, New York, 1983. For an investigation of stock price behavior see S. Katz, S. Lillien, and B. Nelson, "Stock Market Behavior Around Bankruptcy Model Distress and Recovery Predictions," *Financial Analysts Journal*, January–February 1985, pp. 70–74.

TABLE 15-4 proportion of stock price variation due to various factors, 1927 to 1960

industry	firm	market	industry	industry subgroups
Tobacco	.25	.09	.17	.49
Oil	.15	.37	.20	.28
Metals	.15	.46	.08	.31
Railroad	.19	.47	.08	.26
Utilities	.22	.23	.14	.41
Retail	.27	.23	.08	.42
Overall	.20	.31	.12	.37

Source: B. J. King, "Market and Industry Factors in Stock Price Behavior," *Journal of Business*, January 1966, pp. 139–190.

ably. Fundamental analysts must be able to forecast these and the other factors which introduce this volatility into the determinants of market value if they are to *time* their purchases and sales advantageously.

15-4 TIMING OF STOCK PURCHASES AND SALES

Some investors buy securities whose market prices are at or below the intrinsic value they estimate and then hold these securities to obtain the long-run price appreciation and the dividends normally attained from common stocks. This is called a *buy-and-hold strategy*. It involves no attempt to "buy low and sell high" or otherwise outguess the market. Most life insurance companies, for example, follow a buy-and-hold strategy. They have millions of dollars of cash premiums flowing in every day, and they invest these funds as they come in

FIGURE 15-5 stock and bond yields.

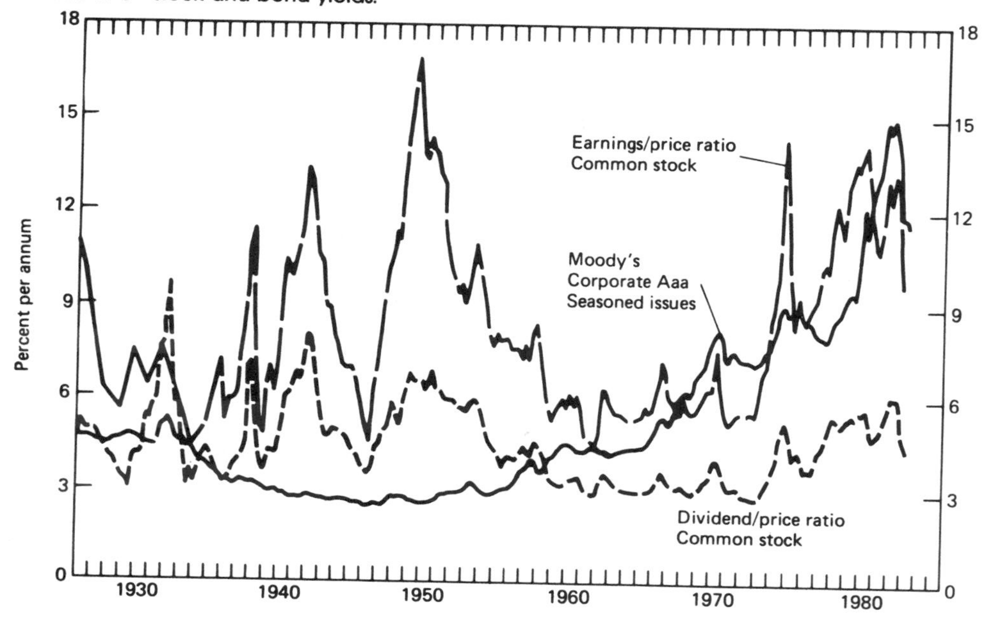

and hardly ever liquidate. In contrast, some investors are *traders*; they try to outguess the rises and falls in the market so they will earn more profits by buying at cyclically low prices and selling at cyclically high prices. Traders hope to beat the buy-and-hold strategy.

Over the past years securities markets in the United States have periodically fallen precipitously, offering traders who can anticipate these turns ample opportunity to profit from timely security trading. Tables 9-3 and 9-4 (on pages 226 and 228, respectively) list the bear markets which have occurred in the United States in the past half century and give summary statistics about them.

The evidence plainly shows that a trader who buys at market low points and sells at market high points can avoid capital losses and earn larger trading profits than a buy-and-hold strategy would earn. However, this is easier said than done. For example, studies of the performance of mutual funds which have the published objective of maximizing their investors' income by using "professional management" to trade actively reveal that they have been unable to earn a significantly higher rate of return than has been earned with a naive buy-and-hold strategy.[11] Mutual fund performance is examined in Chap. 28. Here the difficulties in forecasting the market's turns and the timing of security purchases and sales so as to earn trading profits are examined.

The purpose of this section is to discuss the tools a fundamental analyst who is an active trader can use to try to forecast the rises and falls in security markets. To predict the timing of security price movements, economic forecasts are utilized. Other approaches also are employed to anticipate the timing of rises and falls in security prices. A group of security analysts called *technical analysts* study charts of stock prices in order to predict the market's turns; they tend to ignore fundamental financial and economic factors. Technical analysis is explained in detail in Chap. 18. Of these two approaches to the timing problem, that of the fundamental analyst who studies the underlying economic forces is considerably more difficult because it requires formal training in macroeconomic forecasting. However, to utilize economic forecasts the security analyst need not be capable of actually preparing them.

15-4.1 leading indicators

It is important to be able to predict the course of the national economy because it affects corporate profits, investor optimism, and therefore security prices. Figures 15-2 and 15-4 show the manner in which gross national product (GNP), aggregate corporate profits after taxes, and Standard & Poor's 500 stocks average have varied together over time. These economic time series do not move exactly concurrently across time, however. Several economic variables rise and fall some months ahead of similar changes in the GNP; they are called *leading economic indicators*.

15-4.2 economic forecasts

After viewing Table 15-5 and noting that the stock market *leads* the national economy, an investor may seem well advised not to bother to forecast the national economy but simply to follow those indicators which lead stock

[11] William F. Sharpe, "Mutual Fund Performance," *Journal of Business*, January 1966, supplement, "Security Prices," pp. 119–138.

TABLE 15-5 economic indicators which lead GNP

indicator	recent lead times ahead of GNP, months
Private home-building activity	2–37
New durable goods orders	1–30
Average workweek	0–20
S&P's 500 stock average	4–11

Source: Jesse Levin, "Prophetic Leaders," *Financial Analysts Journal,* July–August 1970, p. 89.

prices. This can be a valuable forecasting tool—especially in predicting bear markets. Home-building activity, durable goods orders, and the number of hours in the average workweek all usually turn down several months before a bear market begins. However, obtaining the most valuable information for making timing decisions in security trading requires a detailed sector forecast of the national economy which extends at least a year into the future.

Since the significant rises and falls (that is, the major bull and bear markets) in security prices have preceded the associated turns in the national economy by as much as 11 months in recent years, a forecast of the economy must extend more than 11 months into the future if it is to be useful in anticipating turns in the stock market. This prediction should thus extend at least 1 year into the future. Furthermore, the forecast should be broken down into a series of quarterly figures to give more insight into the timing of the expected changes.

A good economic forecast which discloses the timing of changes and provides some detail about inflation and other matters is useful in investment decisions. Much more detailed economic forecasts may be purchased from economic consultants. For example, some of the economic forecasting firms prepare 10-year economic projections showing the quarterly development of the U.S. economy broken down into intricate detail. These forecasts can usually predict the dollar amounts of economic activity in various sectors of the economy for a year into the future with only small errors. Such details are quite useful in pinpointing growth industries and other facts necessary in timing decisions for profitable investment. Table 15-6 lists the names and addresses of some of the better-known economic forecasting firms in the world. These firms may be hired for consulting work or some provide their periodic forecasts on a subscription basis.

Ultimately, the ability of an economic model to predict dollar quantities is not so important to the security analyst as the ability to foretell the *timing* and *direction* of the changes in the various rates of economic growth. Indications of shifts in the direction of the economy are most useful in anticipating similar changes in the stock market. This type of information allows portfolio managers to assume a defensive position when bear markets are foreseen and to assume an aggressive stance when bullish conditions are expected.[12]

[12] For an analysis of the ability of different security models to pick the best times to buy or sell see R. D. Arnott and W. A. Copeland, "The Business Cycle and Security Selection," *Financial Analysts Journal,* March–April 1985, pp. 26–33.

BASIS FOR ECONOMIC FORECASTS Economic forecasts which extend very far into the future and/or show very much detail within the national economy are always based upon a fairly detailed set of basic assumptions about the world situation and its impact on the fiscal and monetary policy of the nation. Assumptions about the particular industry in which a company is located and its competitors are also important to a security analyst who is estimating the impact of economic developments on a given industry or firm. Figure 15-6 shows the series of decisions which form the basis for any given forecast of the intrinsic value of a corporation's shares.

Since forecasting models rest squarely on assumptions about international, national, and industry conditions, a fundamental analyst trying to relate the effects of economic developments to security prices should take part in the formulation of these assumptions. This participation will ensure that factors such as large government contracts, labor relations, and technical development—all of which affect security prices—are considered. The economic forecasting services allow their customers to suggest their own assumptions on which to base a forecast (although an added fee may be charged).

VARYING THE ASSUMPTIONS Working with the economic forecasters allows the security analyst to ask the "what if" questions that are so important in the timing of investment decisions. For example, in 1969 when the United States began reducing its involvement in Vietnam, it was desirable to make different assumptions about the rate of U.S. withdrawal from that war. Each different assumption implied a different economic forecast and a different set of intrinsic values in U.S. securities markets. As shown in Fig. 15-6 (page 446), a wide array of intrinsic values are forecast for a given firm's share, depending upon the underlying assumptions about the world and the economy. Interaction between the security analyst and the economist will facilitate preparation of the best possible intrinsic value estimates. Multiple forecasts allow security traders to make immediate investment decisions as news is released because they will have estimates of the price implications of various possible economic developments.

15-4.3 crux of the timing question

In forecasting the times when any given security's price will rise above or fall below the intrinsic value which will prevail under normal market conditions, the fundamental analyst must ultimately estimate both (1) what each quarter's earnings per share will be and (2) what the earnings multipliers will be in each quarter.

FORECASTING EARNINGS PER SHARE Chapters 16 and 17 discuss the measurement of historical growth in a firm's earnings. Methods are suggested to adjust historical growth rates so they can be used to forecast earnings. The following basic relation is suggested for forecasting earnings:

$$e_t = (1 + g)^t e_0$$

where

e_t = earnings per share in period t

g = estimated earnings growth rate

TABLE 15-6 a partial listing of domestic and foreign econometric service bureaus

company	contact	SERVICES OFFERED			
		macro forecasting	data access	consulting	other
Domestic					
1. A. Gary Shilling & Co. 111 Broadway New York, NY 10006 (212) 349-6000	Dr. Glenn C. Picou	Yes	No	Yes	Industry level analysis
2. Center for Economic Research Chapman College Orange, CA 92666	Dr. James L. Doti	Yes	Yes	Yes	
3. Chase Econometrics 150 Monument Road Bala Cynwyd, PA 19004 (215) 667-6000	Dr. Lawrence Chimerine	Yes	Yes	Yes	
4. Data Resources, Inc.* 29 Hartwell Ave. Lexington, MA 02173 (617) 816-0165	Mr. Geo. F. Brown, Jr.	Yes	Yes	Yes	
5. Economic Forecasting Georgia State University Atlanta, GA 30303 (404) 658-3282	Dr. Donald Ratajczak	Yes	No	Yes	Regional Analysis
6. Indiana University Bloomington, IN 47401	Dr. Eugene A. Brady	Yes	No	Yes	
7. Kent Econ. & Dev. Inst. Kent, Ohio 44242 (216) 672-2222	Dr. Vladimir Simunek	Yes	Yes	Yes	Special economic studies
8. Merrill Lynch Economics 165 Broadway New York, NY 10080 (212) 637-6211	Dr. Raymond Cosman	Yes	Yes	Yes	Special economic studies
9. UCLA Business Forecasting Los Angeles, CA 91436 (213) 825-1623	Dr. Larry Kimbell	Yes	Yes	Yes	
10. Wharton Econometric 3624 Science Center Philadelphia, PA 19104 (215) 386-9000	Mr. Petralia	Yes	Yes	Yes	

11. Williams Trend Indicators 6 Devon Dr. Orangeburg, NY 10962 (914) 359-1129	Dr. Roger Williams	Yes	No	Yes	
Foreign					
1. Informetrica Limited P.O. Box 828, Station B Ottawa, Ontario Canada KIP 5P9	Dr. Michael C. McCracken	Yes	Yes	Yes	Software application packages
2. Centre for Economic Forecasting London Business School Sussex Place, Regents Park London, NW1 4SA England 01-262-5050	Dr. Bill Robinson	Yes	Yes	No	On-line access to large econometric model of the UK economy
3. Henley Centre for Forecasting London, England 01-353-9961	Dr. Aleck Kellaway	Yes	Yes	Yes	Forecasting services & publications
4. Phillips & Drew London, England 01-628-4444	Dr. Paul Neild	Yes	No	No	
5. Institute of Economics Taipei, Taiwan Republic of China 115 7822019	Dr. Paul K. C. Liu	No	Yes	Yes	
6. Centre D'Observation Economique de la Chambre de Commerce et d'Industrie de Paris Paris, France 75008 561-99-00	Dr. Monsieru Devaud	Yes	Yes	No	
7. Gama 2 Rue de Rouen Nanterre, France 92001 (1) 725-92-34	Dr. R. Courbis	Yes	No	Yes	Publishes quarterly global forecasts and annually global sectoral forecasts

Source: **A. Migliaro and C. L. Jain, *An Executive's Guide to Econometric Forecasting*, Graceway, Flushing, N.Y., 1983.**

*** Data Resources, Inc., is owned by McGraw-Hill.**

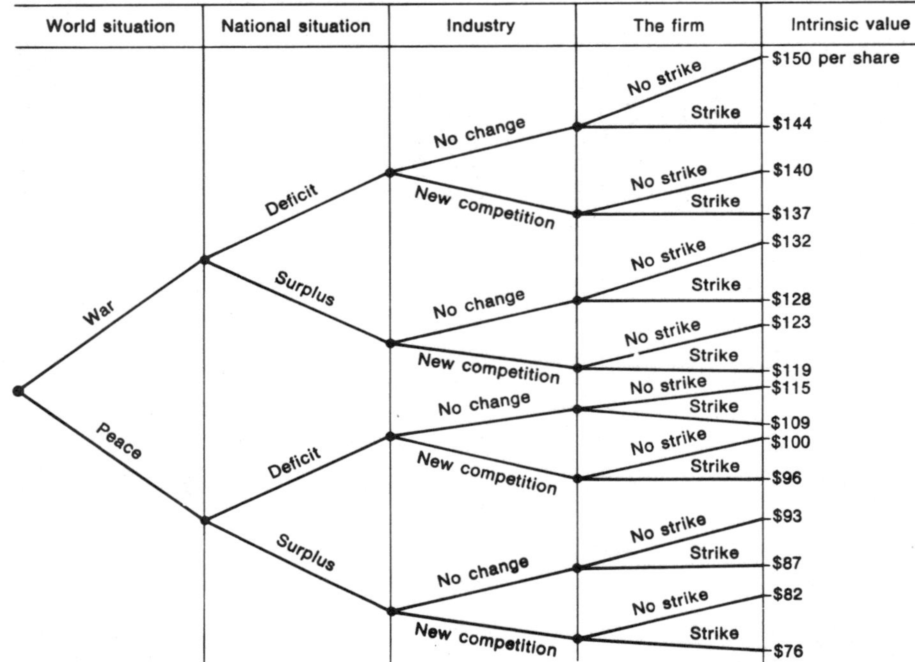

FIGURE 15-6 the basic assumptions underlying economic forecasts have impact on intrinsic value estimates.

This technique can be used to furnish one forecast of earnings per share. A second earnings forecast can be devised by using the economic forecast.[13]

Detailed economic forecasts showing the quarter-by-quarter economic activity in the various industries comprising the national economy can be obtained. These industry sales forecasts can be broken down by company by using historical data on market shares and current information about new competitive developments. These sales forecasts can yield information about expected earnings.[14]

[13] Evidence exists which suggests that earnings per share fluctuate randomly. See J. Lintner and T. Glauber, "Higgledy Piggledy Growth in America," in J. Lorie and R. Brealy (eds.), *Modern Developments in Investment Management*, 2d ed., Dryden, Hinsdale, Ill., 1978. Nevertheless, econometric models which rationalize a large proportion of earnings per share have been published. See J. C. Francis, "Analysis of Equity Returns: A Survey with Extensions," *Journal of Economics and Business*, Spring/Summer 1977, vol. 29, no. 3, pp. 181–192. Also, a different approach to forecasting a corporation's earnings is to use a simultaneous equation econometric model of the firm. See J. C. Francis and D. R. Rowell, "A Simultaneous Equation Model of the Firm for Financial Analysis and Planning," Spring 1978, *Financial Management*, pp. 29–44.

[14] For an exploration of earnings per share forecasts and stock prices see E. H. Hawkins, S. C. Chamberlin, and W. E. Daniel, "Earnings Expectations and Security Prices," *Financial Analysts Journal*, September–October 1984, pp. 24–39. See also D. Givoly and J. Lakonishok, "The Quality of Analysts Forecasts of Earnings," *Financial Analysts Journal*, September–October 1984, pp. 40–48; E. J. Elton, M. J. Gruber, and M. N. Gultiken, "Professional Expectations: Accuracy and Diagnosis of Errors," *Journal of Financial and Quantitative Analysis*, September 1984, vol. 19, no. 4, pp. 351–364.

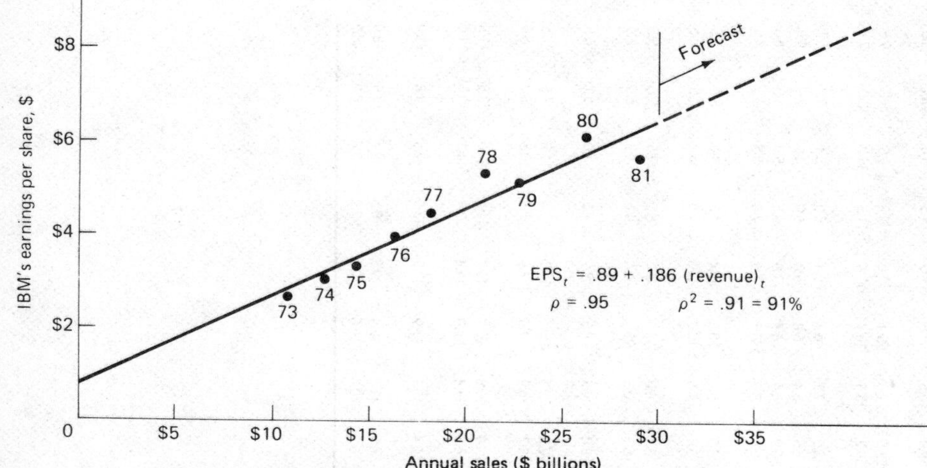

FIGURE 15-7 sales-earnings per share regression for IBM useful in forecasting.

For example, the graph in Fig. 15-7 shows how earnings per share of IBM have varied with the firm's annual sales revenues over the 9 years from 1973 to 1981. Note that an accurate sales forecast would have been able to explain 91 percent (that is, the correlation coefficient squared) of the variation in IBM's annual earnings per share. When stationary sales-earnings relationships exist, they can be used along with an economic forecast and sales projection to provide a second earnings forecast. Furthermore, information gained from interviews with the executives of a firm and its competitors can also be useful in forecasting earnings.

FORECASTING EARNINGS MULTIPLIERS The advance notice given by the leading economic indicators (shown in Table 15-5) reveals that security prices have anticipated the economy from 4 to 11 months in the United States in recent years. This fact implies that an economic forecast for 1 year into the future can be expected to lead changes in the level of security prices from 1 to 8 months. Since the time lag between changes in a 1-year economic forecast and the associated changes in security prices varies from 4 to 11 months, even the best economic forecasts cannot be expected to pinpoint the turn in the securities markets within much less than a 3-month range. However, the economic forecast is still quite useful in indicating the direction of the market and in giving information about the extent of coming changes.

Forecasts of the market levels can be expressed most usefully for security analysis by stating them in terms of the average price-earnings ratio for the market. A study of past price-earnings ratios for some market average and the then-prevailing economic conditions will aid the fundamental analyst in converting the economic forecast into a forecast of the market's average earnings multiplier. Table 15-7 shows how the Dow Jones Industrial Average and Standard & Poor's 500 earnings multipliers have varied in recent years.

After the analyst has forecast an average earnings multiplier, a scatter diagram such as the one shown in Fig. 15-8 can be used to convert this market forecast into earnings multipliers for individual securities. The price-earnings

TABLE 15-7 price-earnings ratios for selected firms*

Industry	1963	1964	1965	1966	1967	1968	1969	1970	1971	1972	1973	1974	1975	1976	1977	1978	1979	1980	1981
Airlines																			
American	11.6	10.9	12.9	10.9	16.3	17.2	16.3	loss	loss	18.0	loss	12.7	loss	6.3	4.5	4.0	5.0	loss	loss
Northwest	9.5	8.8	10.2	15.9	17.0	14.8	13.9	10.3	30.5	51.2	11.2	7.3	8.4	12.4	5.8	10.0	9.0	78.0	65.0
Pan American	7.4	13.0	12.6	13.4	15.2	17.1	loss	loss	loss	loss	loss	loss	loss	loss	4.6	3.0	6.0	4.0	loss
Automobiles																			
Chrysler	7.8	9.3	10.1	11.0	10.2	9.8	24.2	loss	17.7	8.2	6.1	loss	loss	2.3	6.4	loss	loss	loss	loss
Ford	11.4	12.2	8.9	8.5	61.7	9.5	9.4	9.9	10.1	8.3	6.6	10.8	15.9	5.0	3.2	3.5	4.0	loss	loss
General Motors	13.4	14.9	13.8	13.9	13.9	13.5	12.5	33.9	12.2	10.4	7.8	12.9	10.5	6.8	6.0	4.5	6.0	loss	43.0
Photographic equipment																			
Eastman Kodak	27.9	30.4	31.3	loss	31.6	32.4	30.6	28.5	33.1	35.8	31.5	22.5	22.8	25.1	17.0	9.5	9.5	8.0	9.5
Polaroid	58.4	34.0	47.0	46.7	56.5	59.5	64.7	48.9	51.9	90.6	66.0	59.7	15.3	15.7	11.4	11.5	35.0	10.0	27.5
Petroleum																			
Exxon (Standard Oil of N.J.)	14.2	17.2	17.0	14.2	11.7	12.8	12.6	10.5	11.1	11.5	8.6	5.5	7.1	8.4	9.4	8.0	5.4	5.6	5.6
Shell	14.1	16.1	16.2	14.8	14.7	14.3	13.3	12.2	13.2	13.2	11.5	5.6	6.4	6.3	6.8	6.0	6.0	9.0	9.0
Standard Oil of California	14.0	14.2	14.3	12.9	11.4	12.0	11.5	8.7	9.4	10.6	7.2	5.0	6.1	6.7	7.0	6.5	5.0	6.0	6.0
Standard Oil of Indiana	10.9	13.8	14.7	13.2	12.8	13.5	12.4	9.7	12.3	13.9	12.3	6.6	8.3	8.7	7.6	7.0	6.5	10.5	9.5
Steel																			
Bethlehem	15.0	12.7	11.7	9.2	12.1	8.5	8.7	12.2	8.1	9.9	6.4	3.8	5.9	10.5	loss	4.5	3.6	8.4	5.5
U.S. Steel	15.3	14.7	11.0	9.9	13.8	8.9	10.2	12.4	10.7	10.7	5.4	3.6	5.8	10.2	23.2	9.5	loss	4.0	2.6
Rubber																			
Goodyear	16.2	15.7	16.2	14.8	13.5	13.2	13.6	15.0	13.4	11.3	8.8	6.9	8.0	13.5	7.1	5.5	7.5	5.0	5.5
Goodrich	16.8	15.1	13.5	11.7	20.4	13.8	17.2	31.6	14.7	8.4	5.3	5.3	10.3	25.1	6.6	4.6	4.5	6.0	5.0
Communications																			
American Telephone & Telegraph	21.2	22.1	19.3	15.4	14.8	14.2	13.3	11.8	11.9	10.9	10.1	8.8	9.4	8.5	8.9	7.5	7.0	6.1	6.5
Electronics																			
Texas instruments	25.4	21.6	29.4	35.3	58.2	41.7	38.7	36.1	34.2	35.4	29.1	22.3	33.3	26.2	16.7	12.5	11.5	7.5	21.5
International Telephone & Telegraph	18.0	16.6	16.9	21.6	loss	20.8	18.4	14.3	16.4	14.8	10.2	5.7	6.2	7.0	7.9	6.5	10.5	5.0	6.5
Office equipment																			
Burroughs	18.5	16.1	19.7	32.1	39.4	41.6	41.8	34.7	33.0	39.9	36.3	23.8	20.8	20.7	13.7	11.4	10.0	33.5	11.5
IBM	36.6	35.2	35.0	43.1	42.5	40.2	40.2	34.1	34.7	34.4	27.8	16.2	14.4	16.0	14.4	13.1	14.1	10.1	11.0
Mining																			
Homestake	23.8	21.4	24.2	26.5	39.3	66.1	57.4	36.1	45.8	19.1	11.7	16.4	40.1	17.9	17.2	13.0	7.5	9.8	21.0
Averages:																			
Dow Jones Industrial Average	18.5	19.0	18.0	15.5	16.0	17.0	14.5	14.6	16.1	15.1	9.9	6.2	11.3	10.4	9.3	8.5	7.4	7.9	8.0
Standard & Poor's 500	16.6	17.5	17.0	15.1	16.5	16.2	16.1	16.0	16.1	17.2	13.0	9.1	10.4	10.0	9.1	7.9	7.0	8.0	8.2

* Average of each year's high and low values.

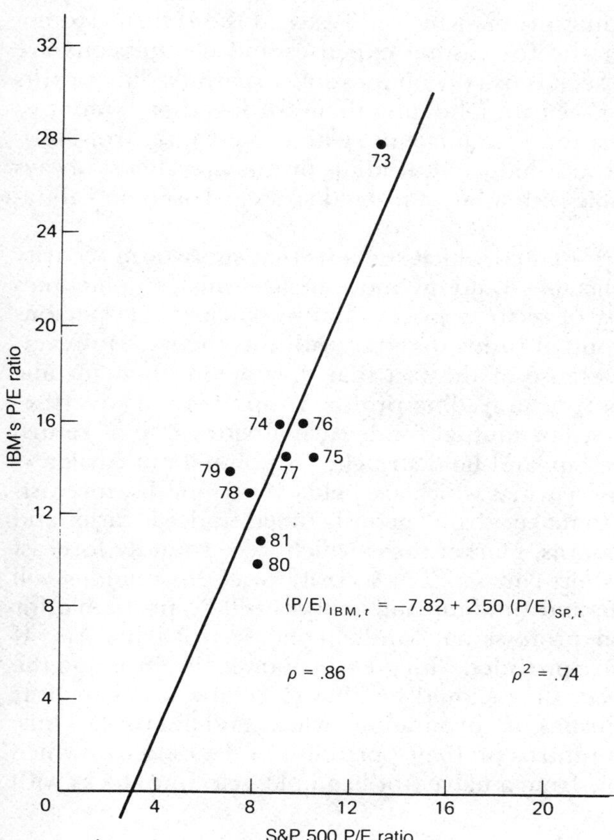

FIGURE 15-8 IBM's price-earnings (P/E) ratio regressed on S&P 500 average price-earnings (P/E) ratio.

ratio may be viewed as an index of investor confidence. Since investors' confidence in all securities tends to rise and fall with the level of the market, useful relationships between the market's average earnings multiplier and individual securities earnings multipliers, such as IBM shows in Fig. 15-8, are not uncommon.[15] Note that 74 percent (that is, the correlation squared) of the variation in IBM's price-earnings ratio from 1973 to 1981 can be explained in terms of the Standard & Poor's 500 stocks average price-earnings ratio. Thus, a forecast of the market's average earnings multiplier has valuable implications for individual common stocks.

15-4.4 conclusions about timing

Because of the uncertainties involved in forecasting quarterly earnings per share, earnings growth rates, the risk of the firm, and the exact date when the market will begin expected changes in direction, it is difficult, if not impossi-

[15] Refined estimates of the relationship between the price-earnings ratios of individual firms and the market averages (as well as a theoretical justification for their existence) may be found in J. C. Francis, "Analysis of Equity Returns: A Survey with Extensions," *Journal of Economics and Business*, Spring/Summer 1977, vol. 29, no. 3, pp. 181–192. This article is reprinted in *Readings in Investment*, edited by J. C. Francis, C. F. Lee, and D. E. Farrar, McGraw-Hill, New York, 1980.

ble, to earn short-term trading profits which will exceed the returns from a buy-and-hold strategy after the forecasting expenses and commissions are deducted. To be more precise, it is usually not possible to earn trading profits over many trades by buying securities, holding them for less than 6 months, and selling them. Such short-term trading can yield a positive return. However, after the commissions are deducted, trading profits are almost always less than the return attainable with a buy-and-hold strategy based on fundamental analysis.

In Chap. 19 evidence is presented which suggests that short-term security price changes are unpredictable random movements—this is sometimes called the *random-walk theory* of security prices. Many securities salespersons and managers of "go-go" mutual funds disagree with this theory. However, their opinions are biased because of the fact that they derive their income from investors who seek short-term trading profits. In spite of the advertisements implying the contrary, few mutual funds earn a better rate of return than investors using a naive buy-and-hold strategy, as pointed out earlier.

For the long run, say, for securities which are held over 6 months, forecasting security prices in order to make advantageously timed trades is easier and more profitable. After 6 months, market turns which were soundly forecast will usually come to pass, short-run random security price fluctuations will tend to average out to zero, and fundamental analysis will be profitable for those who are experienced professional fundamental security analysts. If these professional analysts are provided with good economic forecasts and the other information they need, they should be able to escape losses in bear markets and avoid the securities of corporations which go bankrupt. Thus, they should be able to earn returns on their portfolios in the long run which exceed the returns attainable from a naive (for example, selecting stocks with a dart) buy-and-hold strategy.

15-5 CONCLUSIONS ABOUT FUNDAMENTAL SECURITY ANALYSIS

As might be expected, it is not easy to find underpriced and overpriced securities. Professional fundamental analysts have usually forecasted changes in a corporation's income fairly accurately, and security prices have adjusted to the new intrinsic value before the latest income figures are announced to the public.

When significantly different earnings and dividends which were *not* expected are announced by a corporation, some analysts will reach buy or sell decisions immediately. By merely applying recent multipliers to the new income data and then comparing the intrinsic value estimates with the market price, it is possible to get some indication as to whether the security is priced correctly. This explains why security prices sometimes react noticeably to announcements of changed levels of income and/or dividends.[16]

[16] P. Brown and R. Ball, "An Empirical Evaluation of Accounting Income Numbers," *Journal of Accounting Research*, Autumn 1968, pp. 159–178. P. C. Jain, "The Effect of Voluntary Sell-off Announcements on Shareholder Wealth," *Journal of Finance*, March 1985, vol. 40, no. 1, pp. 209–223; J. D. Rosenfield, "Additional Evidence on the Relation between Divestiture An-

Regardless of how sophisticated the techniques used, a complete, painstaking fundamental analysis, based on relevant facts, is a logical way to estimate the true value of a going concern. Understandably, fundamental analysis is the most widely used method of estimating security prices. Erroneous intrinsic value estimates can be attributed to several facts: (1) The analyst did not have all the relevant information. (2) The analyst simply did not do the necessary work thoroughly. (3) The market was in a temporary disequilibrium (for example, President Kennedy's assassination caused the stock market to drop temporarily, although fundamental values were unchanged). Hindsight is always better than foresight in these matters. Nevertheless, even under ideal conditions, fundamental analysis can suggest only a range of prices rather than a specific value.

QUESTIONS

15-1. "A fundamental analyst's estimate of intrinsic value is different from the present value of all income." Is this statement true, false, or uncertain? Explain.

15-2. Compare and contrast the earnings multiplier with the dividend multiplier. Why do they differ?

15-3. Does an increase in a firm's growth rate of earnings always mean an increase in its intrinsic value? Explain.

15-4. Why is the growth rate in dividends per share not a good measure of the firm's growth rate?

15-5. Can factors which are external to the firm, such as national economic conditions, affect the intrinsic value of a share of stock? Explain.

15-6. "An increase in a firm's liquidity ratios means that the firm is well managed and safe. This will always increase its multipliers." Is this statement true, false, or uncertain? Explain.

15-7. Can fundamental analysis be used for quick, short-range value forecasts, or is it useful only for determining long-run equilibrium values? Explain.

15-8. Will accounting gimmicks (like accelerating depreciation) affect or distort the intrinsic-value estimates made by fundamental analysts?

15-9. An experienced fundamental security analyst claims that the intrinsic value estimating procedures used by members of the profession lead to realistic estimates of true value which are based on "all the facts" and realistic assumptions. Comment on this claim.

15-10. The Blume Company is a small, growing manufacturer of lawn equipment which is planning to go public for the first time. Assume that Mr. Blume, the president of the firm, has hired you as a financial consultant to estimate

---

nouncements and Shareholder Wealth," *Journal of Finance*, December 1984, vol. 39, no. 5, pp. 1437–1448; A. Kane, Y. K. Lee, and A. Marcus, "Earnings and Dividend Announcements: Is There a Corroboration Effect?" *Journal of Finance*, September 1984, vol. 39, no. 4, pp. 1091–1099; G. J. Alexander, P. G. Benson, and J. M. Kampmeyer, "Investigating the Valuation Effects of Announcements of Voluntary Corporate Selloffs," *Journal of Finance*, June 1984, vol. 39, no. 2, pp. 503–518.

the price per share at which stock should be sold. The Westerfield Corporation and the Pettit Corporation are also young lawn equipment manufacturers which have recently gone public and have similar product lines (they all even have the same accountant). Data on these three corporations are:

earnings per share (EPS)	Westerfield	Pettit	Blume's totals
Earnings per share, 19 X 5	$ 5	$ 11	$1,000,000
Average EPS, 19 X 0 – 19 X 5	$ 5	$ 8	$ 780,000
Median market price, 19 X 5	$29	$145	?
Average price, 19 X 0 – 19 X 5	$27	$110	–
Dividends per share, 19 X 5	$ 3	$ 7.20	$ 500,000
Average dividends, 19 X 0 – 19 X 5	$ 2.80	$ 6.50	$ 390,000
Book value per share, 19 X 5	$81.23	$112.10	$ 131,500
Growth in EPS, 19 X 0 – 19 X 5	0	5%	6%
Debt-equity ratio, 19 X 5	9%	42%	45%
Current assets–current liabilities	3.1	1.9	2.0
Employees	180	90	80
Sales	$17,000,000	$9,800,000	$8,800,000

The sales, earnings, and stock prices of all lawn equipment manufacturers have followed rates of change in national income (that is, GNP) in the past few years. Historical data show that the two public firms have beta coefficients (of systematic risk) of about 1. The future for the lawn equipment industry is bright. Because of increased suburban living and rising affluence, it is expected that the market for lawn equipment will continue to expand. The economic outlook promises steady growth, and securities markets are normal. What data above will you ignore in pricing Blume's stock? If Blume issues 1 million shares, what price per share will you recommend?

15-11. The Archer Corporation has a beta volatility coefficient (measuring its systematic risk) of 1, and, as Fig. 15-3 leads us to expect, the market has been applying a $k = 10$ percent capitalization rate in valuing its earnings. Archer's normalized earnings of $2 per share are all paid out in cash dividends. Per-share earnings have been growing at 3 percent per annum for some time, and the current market price of $28.60 reflects this growth experience. However, because of a technological breakthrough, Archer's earnings are expected to grow at the increased rate of 6 percent per year for the foreseeable future. What effect do you think this technological innovation will have on Archer's market price per share when the news becomes public?

SELECTED REFERENCES

Brealey, R. A., *An Introduction to Risk and Return from Common Stocks*, 2d ed., M.I.T., Cambridge, Mass., 1983. A readable, nonmathematical summary of various studies; chaps. 2 through 5 throw light on some issues relevant to fundamental analysis.

Francis, Jack Clark, "Analysis of Equity Returns: A Survey with Extensions," *Journal of Economics and Business*, Spring/Summer 1977, reprinted in J. C. Francis, C. F. Lee, and Donald E. Farrar, (eds.) *Readings in Investments*, McGraw-Hill, New York, 1980. Econometric analysis of earnings per share, price-earnings multipliers, and stock price changes reveals insights.

Graham, B., D. Dodd, and S. Cottle, *Security Analysis*, 4th ed., McGraw-Hill, New York, 1962. This nonmathematical book is used by most fundamental analysts; it should be read by anyone who aspires to be a fundamental analyst.

Malkiel, B. G., "The Valuation of Public Utility Equities," *The Bell Journal of Economics and Management Science*, 1970. A statistical test of the valuation model Eq. (15-3*a*).

Whitbeck, V., and M. Kisor, A New Tool in Investment Decision Making," *Financial Analysts Journal*, May–June 1963. An easy-to-read empirical study of earnings per share and multipliers.

avon products inc.

The Avon Products Corporation is well known for two reasons. First, Avon is the world's largest manufacturer of women's cosmetics and toiletries, which are sold by door-to-door salespeople. Second, Avon's common stock was a favorite of many investors during the early 1970s until it let them down in 1974. Let us analyze the performance of Avon's stock price in terms of fundamental analysis.

The price of Avon's common stock had been bid up to $140, or 60 times earnings, in early 1973 on the basis of its fine earnings record. Over the previous decade Avon's earnings per share had grown at a compound annual rate of 17 percent—an impressive growth record.

Could Avon keep up the pace? Despite the popularity of Avon's stock, the company was showing familiar signs of aging, a gradual decline in profitability and in its ability to reinvest its earnings internally to earn rates of profit as high as in the past. Avon's rate of return on equity slipped from 37 percent in 1965 to 33 percent in 1972. Moreover, its cash dividend payout ratio had crept up from 55 percent in 1965 to 63 percent in 1972 because its earnings were sagging.

In October 1973, *Fortune* magazine published an article that suggested that in the years ahead Avon would suffer a steadily declining earnings growth rate and, as a result, a steadily rising dividend payout ratio. Discounting the projected dividend stream at a suitable risk-adjusted discount rate, the author of the article estimated Avon's intrinsic value per share to be a mere $42.50, although the stock's market price was then over $100 per share.

Avon's stock had slipped from a February 1973 high of $140 to $102 at the time of publication of the article in *Fortune*, partly because of disappointing gains in earnings in the second quarter of 1973. Then, however, the fundamental logic of considering the present value of Avon's future cash dividends began to sink in with investors. After the *Fortune* article was published, Avon's stock price collapsed along with the rest of the market, reaching a low of 10

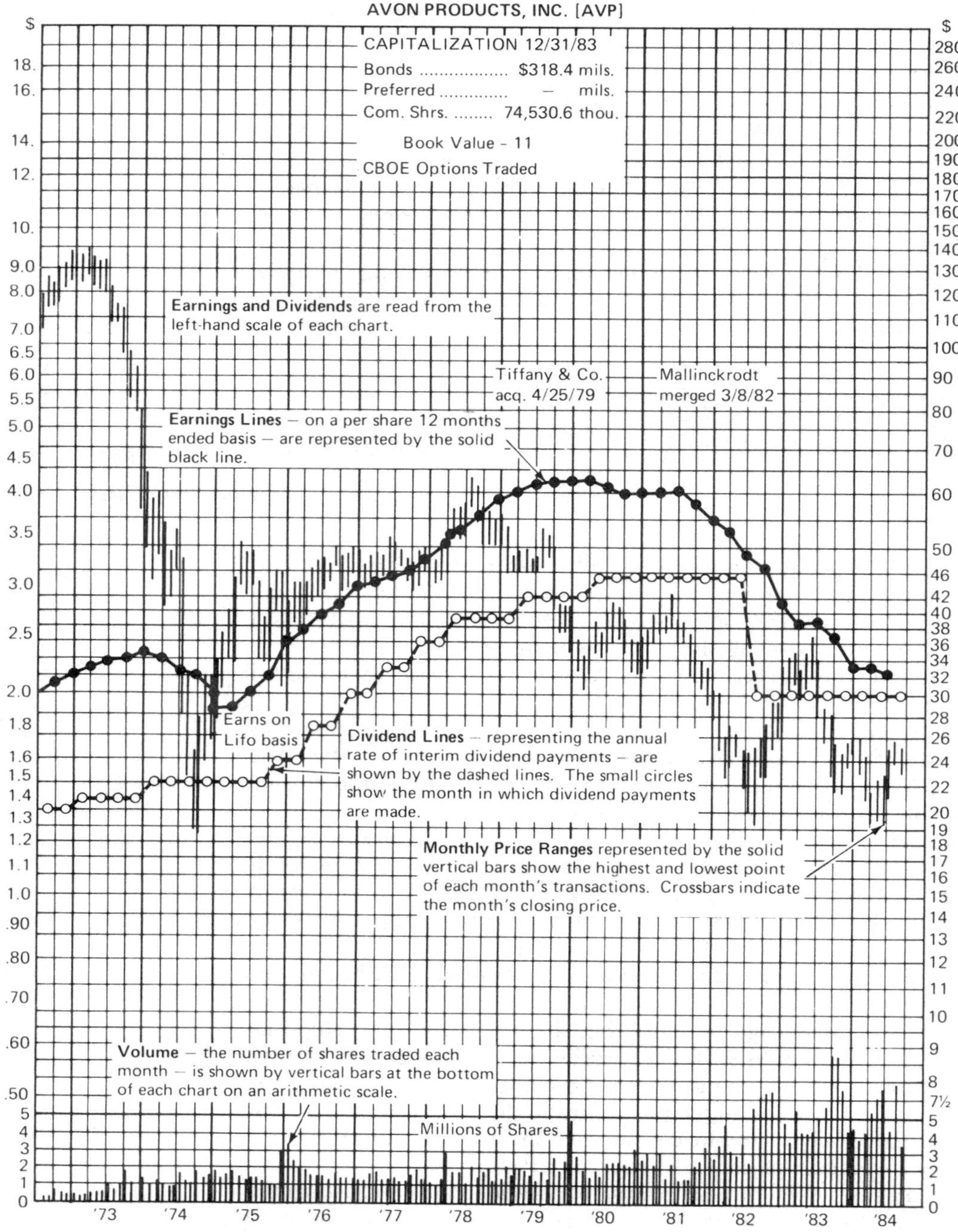
AVON PRODUCTS, INC. [AVP]
CAPITALIZATION 12/31/83
Bonds .... $318.4 mils.
Preferred .... — mils.
Com. Shrs. .... 74,530.6 thou.
Book Value - 11
CBOE Options Traded
Earnings and Dividends are read from the left-hand scale of each chart.
Tiffany & Co. acq. 4/25/79
Mallinckrodt merged 3/8/82
Earnings Lines — on a per share 12 months ended basis — are represented by the solid black line.
Earns on Lifo basis
Dividend Lines — representing the annual rate of interim dividend payments — are shown by the dashed lines. The small circles show the month in which dividend payments are made.
Monthly Price Ranges represented by the solid vertical bars show the highest and lowest point of each month's transactions. Crossbars indicate the month's closing price.
Volume — the number of shares traded each month — is shown by vertical bars at the bottom of each chart on an arithmetic scale.
Millions of Shares
$
18.
16.
14.
12.
10.
9.0
8.0
7.0
6.5
6.0
5.5
5.0
4.5
4.0
3.5
3.0
2.5
2.0
1.8
1.6
1.5
1.4
1.3
1.2
1.1
1.0
.90
.80
.70
.60
.50
5
4
3
2
1
0
$
280
260
240
220
200
190
180
170
160
150
140
130
120
110
100
90
80
70
60
50
46
42
40
38
36
34
32
30
28
26
24
22
20
19
18
17
16
15
14
13
12
11
10
9
8
7½
5
4
3
2
1
0
'73
'74
'75
'76
'77
'78
'79
'80
'81
'82
'83
'84

PER SHARE DATA ($)

Yr. end Dec. 31	1983	1982	1981	1980	[1]1979	1978	1977	1976	1975	1974
Book Value	10.96	11.08	15.51	15.31	14.25	12.69	11.27	10.15	9.04	8.13
Earnings	2.21	2.75	3.66	4.01	4.17	3.92	3.30	2.90	2.40	1.93
Dividends	2.00	2.50	3.00	2.95	2.75	2.55	2.20	1.80	1.51	1.48
Payout Ratio	91%	95%	82%	74%	66%	65%	67%	62%	63%	77%
Prices—High	36⅞	30½	42⅜	40¾	56	63	52⅛	50¼	51¼	65
Low	21¼	19⅜	29⅛	31⅛	37¼	43⅞	43¼	32¾	27⅞	18⅝
P/E Ratio—	17–10	11–7	12–8	10–8	13–9	16–11	16–13	17–11	21–12	34–10

Data as orig. reptd. 1. Reflects merger or acquisition. 2. See Text. E—Estimated.

INCOME DATA (MILLION $)

year ended Dec. 31	revs.	oper. inc.	% oper. inc. of revs.	cap. exp.	depr.	int. exp.	net bef. taxes	Eff. tax rate	net inc.	% net inc. of revs.
1983	3,000	409	13.6%	128	67.3	53.7	[2]310	47.0%	164	5.5%
[1]1982	3,001	472	15.7%	129	56.7	56.4	[3]392	49.8%	197	6.6%
1981	2,614	428	16.4%	114	31.5	16.8	446	50.7%	[2]220	8.4%
1980	2,569	467	18.2%	118	27.4	12.3	472	48.9%	241	9.4%
[1]1979	2,378	466	19.6%	116	23.4	[2]10.9	480	47.8%	251	10.5%
1978	2,015	455	22.6%	75	20.5	5.4	456	50.0%	228	11.3%
1977	1,648	381	23.1%	35	19.6	4.5	381	49.8%	191	11.6%
1976	1,434	333	23.2%	27	18.8	3.3	339	50.4%	168	11.7%
1975	1,295	291	22.5%	26	17.5	5.1	281	50.5%	139	10.7%
1974	1,260	252	20.0%	21	16.8	7.9	239	53.2%	112	8.9%

Data as orig. reptd. 1. Reflects merger or acquisition. 2. Reflects accounting change. 3. Incl. equity in earns. of nonconsol. subs.

BALANCE SHEET DATA (MILLION $)

		--current--									
Dec. 31	cash	assets	liab.	ratio	total assets	ret. on assets	long term debt	com-mon equity	total cap.	% LT debt of cap.	ret. on equity
1983	184	1,030	594	1.7	2,286	7.3%	318	1,204	1,642	19.4%	13.6%
1982	161	1,005	556	1.8	2,233	9.4%	297	1,219	1,623	18.3%	16.6%
1981	258	988	527	1.9	1,568	14.0%	5	933	993	0.5%	23.7%
1980	308	1,051	550	1.9	1,571	16.2%	3	921	971	0.3%	27.1%
1979	307	979	471	2.1	1,406	18.8%	4	857	887	0.5%	30.9%
1978	340	909	430	2.1	1,226	20.1%	3	738	757	0.4%	32.7%
1977	384	784	333	2.4	1,039	19.5%	5	655	674	0.7%	30.8%
1976	382	687	290	2.4	926	19.3%	7	589	611	1.1%	30.2%
1975	290	588	249	2.4	816	17.8%	9	524	546	1.6%	27.9%
1974	181	526	234	2.2	749	15.3%	18	472	497	3.6%	24.3%

Data as orig. reptd. 1. Reflects merger or acquisition. 2. Reflects accounting change. 3. Incl. equity in earns. of nonconsol. subs.

Contributions in 1983 by industry segment were:	sales	profits
Cosmetics, fragrances & toiletries	63%	61%
Fashion jewelry	11%	12%
Health care products	10%	14%
Other	16%	13%

Foreign operations accounted for about 36% of sales and 31% of profits in 1983.

times earnings or $19 per share in the fall of 1974. Soon, however, events took a turn for the better.

Avon's sales and profits grew nicely from 1975 through 1978—a shock for many people who thought that the "women's liberation" movement would discourage the use of cosmetics. This sales growth caused the stock price to reach $63 in 1978; that price represents a price-earnings multiple of 16 times. After 1978, however, Avon's profit margins shrank, the growth rates in sales and profits both declined, and cash dividend payouts kept consuming a larger proportion of the company's earnings.

A particularly slow sales growth and decreased profits in 1981 disenchanted Avon's investors. The stock price slid down to $19 per share in 1982 for a new low price-earnings ratio of seven times. The firm diversified into profitable health care products by acquiring Mallinckrodt in 1982 and Foster Medical Corporation in 1984. But, Avon's stock price nevertheless slid back down to $19 in 1984 after total revenues lagged and profits shrank again in 1983. Furthermore, Avon was paying out over 90 percent of its earnings as cash dividends, and competition kept chiseling down its profit margins—a situation that makes it difficult for a corporation to finance growth opportunities.

What lies ahead for investors who buy Avon's stock? Explain.[17]

[17] For the views of some fundamental analysts that were released while this book was in production see "Avon Products, Market's One-Time Darling, Appears to Show Hint of Former Blush," *Wall Street Journal,* June 21, 1985, p. 47.

CHAPTER 16 earnings analysis

Chapter 8 explained that, in order to buy underpriced common stocks and sell overpriced stocks profitably, it is necessary to estimate the intrinsic economic *value* of the equity share and then compare the stock's price with its value. The present value model of Eq. (8-1) was introduced for this valuation work in Box 8-2 on page 196.

$$\text{Present value} = \sum_{t=1}^{\infty} \frac{\text{Income}_t}{(1 + \text{discount rate})^t} \tag{8-1}$$

Chapter 8 went on to explain that, in order to use this model to value common stocks or other risky assets, one must answer two questions. First, what discount or capitalization rate should be used? The discussion of default risk in Secs. 9-2, 12-1, and 12-4 went into some detail answering this question. The second question is, how does the investor measure the income from common stocks, which, unlike bonds, do not clearly specify the stream of income payments in advance? Discussion of this income question is the subject of this chapter. The economist's concept of income is explained; then it is suggested that the concept of economic income is generally more suitable than reported accounting income for fundamental security analysis.

Economists define the *income of a firm* as the maximum amount which can be consumed by the owners of the firm in any period without decreasing their future consumption opportunities. This is more than a definition; it is an important concept[1] that financial analysts should keep in mind when they analyze income statements. The economist's definition of income is intuitively more appealing than the accountant's definition because it relates directly to

[1] This concept of income is discussed in J. R. Hicks, *Value and Capital*, 2d ed., Oxford, New York, 1965, chap. 14.

the owner's real consumption. After all, what good is income that some accountant says you have if you cannot consume it?[2]

The periodic income statements issued by a firm's accountants are the most highly visible and well-known source of income measurements. This chapter, therefore, examines the accountant's procedure for determining income. Accountants provide the basic figures an analyst typically uses when estimating a firm's economic income and intrinsic value.

16-1 THE ACCOUNTING INCOME STATEMENT

Table 16-1 outlines the essentials of the model underlying accountants' income statements. Despite the model's seeming simplicity, in practice many questions arise concerning the definitions and measurements of the various items determining income. For decisions on these questions, the accounting profession can turn to several sources.

In most cases, acceptable accounting procedures are determined by the general acceptance of the practicing accountants. As the phrase *general acceptance* readily suggests, more than one procedure may exist for reporting the same type of business transaction; that is, accounting principles are inexact. There are, however, limitations. The American Institute of Certified Public Accountants (AICPA), through its Accounting Principles Board, hands down opinions on which practices are acceptable and which are unacceptable. Often these opinions eliminate the less desirable (that is, the extreme or the completely ambiguous) alternatives while still allowing several accounting choices. The result is a narrowing of practices, but not the creation of uniform

[2] In addition to the accountants' definition of a firm's earnings and the economists theory of income, a third income concept is employed by those economists who are macroeconomic model builders. For a capsule view of the differences between the accountants' earnings model and the macroeconomists' earnings concept, see G. Thomas Friedlob, "How Economic Statisticians View Accounting Profits," *Journal of Accounting, Auditing and Finance,* Winter 1983, pp. 100–107.

TABLE 16-1 model of accounting income statement

sales	sales
Less: Cost of goods sold	– COGS
Gross operating margin	GM
Less: Selling and administrative expenses and depreciation	– Op. Exp.
Net operating income (earnings before interest and taxes)	NOI (EBIT)
Less: Interest expense	– Int.
Taxable Income	T. Inc.
Less: Taxes	– Tax
Net income	NI
Less: Dividends on preferred stock	– P. Div.
Net income for common equity	C. Inc.
Less: Dividends for common equity	– C. Div.
Retained earnings	Ret. E

accounting. Thus, the same economic event can often legitimately be reported in several different ways.

The existing body of accounting practice has also been shaped by certain professional organizations, government agencies, and legislative acts. The most important institutions influencing accounting practices are the Securities and Exchange Commission (SEC), the American Institute of Certified Public Accountants, the American Accounting Association, and the Internal Revenue Code.

The AICPA, between 1939 and 1959, published 51 Accounting Research Bulletins on topics of importance in financial reporting at the time. A formal committee, the Accounting Principles Board (APB), was established in 1959 by the AICPA and charged with the responsibility for formulating accounting principles. Between 1959 and 1973, this committee published 31 influential opinions. The importance of these opinions is that, since October 1964, the AICPA has required that any accounting practice that deviates from an APB opinion must either be so indicated in the audit reports of the accountant or disclosed in footnotes to financial statements. The result of this requirement by the AICPA was that the accountant faced substantial potential liability if he or she certified financial statements that departed from acceptable practices as established by the APB published statements, which were recommendations of the board but did not carry the weight of opinions.

In 1972 the APB was dissolved and replaced by the Financial Accounting Standards Board (FASB). The FASB has seven full-time, well-paid members, only four of whom are certified public accountants in public practice. The remaining three members are professionals in fields related to financial reporting. The FASB and its staff work as an accounting "think-tank" at offices in the suburbs of New York City.[3]

The Internal Revenue Service (IRS) also limits the range of permissible accounting. The IRS can say, and has said, "If a given accounting procedure is used by a firm for tax purposes, it also must be used in the published financial statements of that firm." The possibility that the IRS may hand down such rulings causes increased consistency between the accounting statements given to shareholders and the statements given to the IRS in any given year, but they do not cause published financial statements of firms to be identical with their tax return statements. The IRS also may contest the propriety of certain generally acceptable accounting procedures when they tend to evade income taxes. Such questions, however, do not necessarily tend to align a firm's reported income with its economic income. This is especially true with depreciation, as explained in more detail below. In the final analysis, the responsibility to ferret out a firm's economic income lies with the fundamental security analyst.

The Securities and Exchange Commission also has influenced accounting practices. It requires that companies which intend to offer their securities to

[3] The FASB headquarters is located in Stamford, Conn., a small town with a population of only slightly over 100,000. In spite of its small size Stamford has more headquarters of *Fortune* 500 corporations than any other city in the United States, except New York City. But, corporate headquarters continue to leave New York City for southern Connecticut, so Stamford may wind up with the most before much longer.

the public provide adequate disclosure so that the investing community can evaluate the investment merits of the issue. The SEC has regulations which have been published in its *Federal Reporting Release* (FRR).[4] In recent years, the SEC has worked closely with the AICPA and has endorsed the role established for the FASB. Most of the publications of the SEC elaborate on the opinions of the AICPA and apply the principles to specific situations.

Regulatory agencies establish accounting rules for the companies (like banks, savings and loan associations, and public utilities) under their jurisdiction. These accounting rules are established so that the regulatory agency can determine the prices or rates that the company can charge its customers. In some cases, the accounting rules required may conflict with opinions promulgated by the AICPA.

Persons unfamiliar with the complexity of accounting procedures understandably obtain the erroneous impression that the accounting income is a narrowly defined quantity. The neatly published financial statements in annual reports seem to imply that these statements are the last word and are not open to dispute. However, reference to an accounting textbook will reveal a multiplicity of generally accepted accounting procedures which may be used in many situations.

The following quotation opens the chapter entitled "Measuring and Reporting Income" in a widely used intermediate accounting textbook.

> Arriving at an estimate of the periodic income of a business enterprise is perhaps the foremost objective of the accounting process. The word *estimate* is, unfortunately, proper because income is one of the most elusive concepts in the business and economic world. The art of accounting has not progressed (and never will) to the point where periodic business income can be measured with certainty.[5]

Although this quotation may come as a shock to neophyte accountants and fundamental analysts, experienced accountants and analysts have long recognized the vagaries in accountants' procedures for determining income.

The latitude of alternative, generally accepted procedures which the accountant may follow in deriving a firm's income is often not the cause of income reports by accountants which differ significantly from the firm's economic income. The accountant needs some leeway in order to use a procedure which most clearly reports the true economic consequence of a business transaction. When accountants produce income statements which fundamental analysts find necessary to alter significantly in order to obtain income estimates, the cause is usually (1) the accountant's use of an accounting procedure which is inappropriate for the relevant economic transaction and/or (2) pressure brought to bear on the accountant from top management to minimize the firm's income taxes or to window-dress the corporation's financial statements. In order to explain most of the adjustments the financial

[4] Until May 1982 the SEC's regulations were *Regulations S-X* and its *Accounting Series Releases* (which were called *ASRs*). However, since 1982 the *Federal Reporting Release* (*FRR*) codified all previously existing ASRs into one document, named *FRR One*.

[5] W. D. Meigs, C. E. Johnson, and T. F. Keller, *Intermediate Accounting*, 3d ed., McGraw-Hill, New York, 1974, p. 89.

analyst may find it necessary to make in a firm's income statement, a numerical example is explained below.

16-2 CONTRAST OF INCOME STATEMENTS FROM IDENTICAL FIRMS

Table 16-2 shows income and expense statements for two companies which are identical in every way except for their accounting procedures. The statement on the left, for Firm B, tends to minimize taxable income. The income statement for Firm A, on the right, represents the economic income from both firms. The divergent accounting procedures followed in developing the income statements for Firms A and B are legal, commonplace, and generally accepted by practicing accountants. In essence, both income statements are correct on the basis of accounting practices, but only income statement A is correct in the sense that it provides a true picture of the economic results of the firm's transactions.

Firms A and B may be thought of as being two identical manufacturers whose identical sales are expected to remain constant in the future. The firms are assumed to be equally well managed, to have identical labor forces and identical assets, and to be carrying on identical research and development programs in search of cost reductions in their manufacturing process.

Some firms prepare two different income statements, each statement being

TABLE 16-2 two income statements for the same year

		company B, in thousands of dollars		company A, in thousands of dollars	key (see text)
Sales revenue		$9,200		$11,000	
Less: Returns and allowances		−1,000		− 1,000	
Net sales		8,200		10,000	(1)
Beginning inventory	2,000		2,000		
Purchases and freight in	6,000		6,000		
Net purchases	8,000		8,000		
Less: Ending inventory	−2,000		−3,000		(2)
Cost of goods sold		6,000		5,000	
Gross margin		2,200		5,000	
Operating expenses:					
Selling costs	1,500		1,500		
Depreciation	500		300		(3)
Pension	100		20		(4)
Other costs	200		50		(5)
Salaries	200		200		
Bonuses	100		100		
Total operating expenses		−2,600		−2,170	
Net operating expenses		(400)		2,830	
Less: Interest		− 100		− 100	
Taxable income (loss)		(500)		2,730	
Less: Federal taxes (50%) (refund)		(250)		−1,365	
Net income from operations (loss)		(250)		1,365	

completely rational, legal in its own right, and compatible with the other. One income statement which minimizes taxable income may be prepared for the IRS, and a second income statement may be kept confidential and used by management as a basis for decision making. Presumably, this second statement would be the better reflection of the firm's economic income. The two income statements A and B in Table 16-2 may alternatively be regarded, if so desired, as two different statements for the same firm instead of different statements for two identical firms.

The five items where statements A and B differ are keyed at the right margin of Table 16-2. These differences are explained below; they are a representative but far from exhaustive list of points where confusion and deception can enter into income measurements.

16-2.1 sales (1)

Statement A includes in its sales item both cash sales and all current sales made on installment contract. Both firms factor their accounts receivable as soon as they arise and thus realize the cash proceeds of the installment contract sales immediately. But Company B does not recognize these sales until the customer's final cash payment is actually received and the factoring company has no potential bad debt claims against it. Both practices of installment sales recognition are acceptable. However, the procedure shown in statement A is a truer reflection of the actual sales transaction and cashflow and should thus be used to obtain estimates of the firm's economic income. There are, however, some conditions which must be present before a cash-collection method may be used.

Sales can be realized as early as the date the sales order is signed. Or, as with some long-term construction contracts, the sale may not be recognized until as late as the day the delivery is made; this may be years after the contract is signed. Between these extremes are many points in time when the accountant may choose to recognize the sales revenue in the financial statements.

In an attempt to improve current income, some firms have abused the revenue recognition principle. For example, real estate development corporations at one time reported the sale of land at the time of the sale even though the purchaser may have made only a small down payment.[6] In the franchising business, a company that granted a franchise in exchange for a note rather than cash would report a sale in the current period for the total value of the transaction. In both instances, the collectibility of future payments from the purchaser raises questions about the appropriateness of recording the transaction as revenue in the current period.

With the issuance of APB Opinion 21, companies must now record transactions resulting in notes receivable at the fair market value instead of the face value of the note.[7] In instances when the fair market value cannot be determined, the value of the note is taken as the present value of the future

[6] The SEC responded to this practice with *Accounting Series Release 95* ("Accounting for Real Estate Transactions Where Circumstances Indicate That Profits Were Not Earned at the Time the Transactions Were Recorded").

[7] "Interest on Receivables and Payables," APB Opinion 21, AICPA, New York, 1971.

payments required by the issuer of the note. The discount rate is determined by the rate of interest which most appropriately reflects the credit rating of the issuer. Although this requirement reduces the value of the note in order to take into account the timing of cash receipt, it does not directly answer the question of when the sale should be recognized.

16-2.2 inventory (2)

Statement A used the FIFO (*first in, first out*) method of inventory valuation while B used the LIFO (*last in, first out*) method. During periods of inflation the FIFO method tends to result in higher reported profits.

Perhaps the easiest way to understand LIFO and FIFO is by an example. Imagine that 1-ton steel ingots are the inventory items and that one ingot is always carried in inventory. Assume that, early in the accounting year represented in Table 16-2, the cost of ingots rose from $2000 apiece to $3000. The inventory is valued at cost, and the beginning inventory value of the one-ingot inventory is assumed to be $2000 whether LIFO or FIFO is used. This value is shown in Tables 16-2 and 16-3.

If FIFO had been used, the ending inventory (of one ingot purchased for $3000) would be valued at $3000. This means that the cost of goods sold in Table 16-3 would be $5000 if FIFO had been employed instead of LIFO.

Some consideration of these methods reveals that FIFO incorporates inventory capital gains or losses into regular income, LIFO does not. Thus, the FIFO method often causes profit to be more volatile than the LIFO method. FIFO is assumed to be the most realistic (although least advantageous for tax purposes) method of inventory valuation in this case for two main reasons: First, most manufacturers usually sell the oldest items in their inventories first. Second, profits and losses on the inventory are reflected in reported income as they occur.

Not only does the use of LIFO versus FIFO have different effects on income, but switching from one of these inventory valuation techniques to the other can result in some spectacular changes. Chrysler Corporation's 1970 income statement provides good examples of (1) how to detect that a company reports a substantially different set of books to its stockholders from the one it reports to the IRS and (2) what switching from LIFO to FIFO can do to reported earnings.

Comparison of the federal income taxes a company reports paying to see whether they are about 50 percent of its reported pretax income is a good way to detect if the company keeps "two sets of books." Thus, when Chrysler reported a $34 million loss before taxes in early 1970 and, at the same time, showed an $80 million asset on its balance sheet with the title "Refundable

TABLE 16-3 LIFO during inflation (firm B)

	inventory value
Beginning inventory (1 ingot at $2000)	$2000
Plus: purchases (2 ingots at $3000 each)	6000
Cost of goods available for sale	$8000
Less: Ending inventory (1 ingot at $2000)	−2000 (undervalued)
Cost of goods sold	$6000 (*overvalued*)

U.S. Taxes on Income," something strange was suspected. Some scrutiny to determine Chrysler's economic income revealed that the company's losses were probably over $74 million rather than the $34 million which was reported by its accountants and certified by its CPAs. This creative bit of accounting was accomplished by switching from LIFO to FIFO, as explained below.

In 1970, Chrysler switched some of its inventory from LIFO to FIFO with the result that consolidated inventories were revised upward from $110 to $150 million. This $40 million bookkeeping gain was then added to Chrysler's accounting profit, or, more precisely, subtracted from the losses its accountants reported to its shareholders. Thus, Chrysler's actual loss was probably somewhere between the $34 million reported loss and the ($34 million + $40 million =) $74 million loss before the change in inventory valuation methods.

In its second set of books, that is, in the set it keeps for the IRS, Chrysler reported the economic loss of $74 million plus some other things so that it could get a larger income tax refund. These tricks entitled Chrysler to the $80 million of "Refundable U.S. Taxes on Income" which appeared as a balance sheet asset and first called attention to the unusual entry.[8]

16-2.3 depreciation (3)

Assuming that no new technology or unusually heavy use is likely to depreciate the value of the assets used by Firms A and B before they are worn out, the straight-line depreciation used by Firm A is more honest (but less desirable for tax purposes) than the accelerated sum-of-the-digits depreciation procedure employed by Firm B.

Several depreciation techniques may be used in the financial statements that a firm reports to the public.

1. Straight-line method
2. Units of production method
3. Double declining balance method
4. Sum-of-the-digits method

The third and fourth methods are accelerated methods of depreciation. The second method may be used to accelerate depreciation during a period of rapid production. To understand how depreciation affects profit, a numerical example using the first and fourth methods will be used.

Imagine an asset that costs $1,000 with an expected life of $n = 3$ years. By use of the straight-line method, depreciation is $333.33 (= $1000/3 = cost/$n$) for each of the 3 years. By use of the sum-of-the-digits method, the annual depreciation starts large and diminishes each year, because a decreasing fraction is multiplied by the cost of the asset (a stable amount) to determine each year's depreciation. The numerator of this fraction decreases by 1 each year, as shown below. The numerator represents the number of years left in the life of the asset. The denominator of the fraction remains stable; it is the sum of the years in the life of the asset (for example, if the life expectancy of an asset were 3 years, the denominator would be $1 + 2 + 3 = 6$).

[8] Abraham Briloff, *Unaccountable Accounting,* Harper & Row, New York, 1972, pp. 36–39.

year	depreciation as fraction of cost	sum-of-the-digits annual dollar depreciation
1	$n \div \sum_{i=1}^{n=3} i = \frac{3}{6}$	\$500.00
2	$n - 1 \div \sum_{i=1}^{n=3} i = \frac{2}{6}$	\$333.33
3	$n - 2 \div \sum_{i=1}^{n=3} i = \frac{1}{6}$	\$166.66
	1.0	1000.00

Accelerated depreciation increases depreciation costs in the early years of a new asset's life; it thereby decreases profit, income tax, and net accounting profit when the asset is new. Accelerated depreciation postpones taxes on income. Postponing taxes is like obtaining an interest-free loan from the federal government. The total depreciation expense is unchanged; only the timing is altered. As Table 16-2 shows, however, it can affect any particular year's reported accounting income significantly. Depreciation accounting for tax purposes is an altogether different story.

As a result of a ruling that went into effect in 1981, the IRS has purposefully *increased* the disparity between the depreciation techniques it requires for tax reporting and the depreciation techniques allowed for use in publicly reported accounting statements. Today the IRS requires firms to depreciate their assets for tax purposes using the *accelerated cost recovery system (ACRS)*. The ACRS depreciation technique typically differs markedly from the traditional techniques that the firm uses in its publicly reported accounting statements.

For tax accounting, the IRS requires firms to explicitly assign all depreciable assets into one of four different categories (based on the life of the asset) and then to depreciate these assets using the narrowly defined accelerated depreciation technique specified under the ACRS. The ACRS guidelines do not allow the accountant much leeway in tax accounting for depreciation. In almost every case the ACRS guidelines result in more rapid write-offs than is realistic, and also, more rapid write-offs than would be allowed under the traditional accelerated depreciation techniques outlined above. The ACRS was adopted as a fiscal measure that is designed to renew American technology more rapidly by accelerating asset renewal. As a result of the new ACRS requirements, the disparities between the depreciation techniques used in published financial statements and the depreciation techniques used for tax accounting are wider than ever before. The ACRS also makes depreciation accounting a more complex problem for the financial analyst to unravel in an effort to discern the firm's true economic income.

16-2.4 pension costs (4)

Statement B reflects the maximum allowable pension cost and statement A the minimum. The maximum is the normal cost for current employee services, plus 10 percent of any unpaid past employee service costs and/or 10 percent of any change in prior service costs.[9] The minimum is the normal cost plus the equivalent of an interest payment on any unfunded prior employee service costs. The maximum allowable cost is based on the notion that pension payments are due to individual employees. The minimum cost is based on the idea that payments are put into a pension fund from which all present and all future retired employees can draw payment. The former recognizes prior services' expense during the life span of individuals (short time span), whereas the latter spreads it over the life of the pension plan (perhaps to infinity). On the assumption that the firms have a youthful labor force with few workers near the age when they will draw retirement benefits, Firm A's treatment of pension costs is the more forthright approach (although, again, it furnishes the least income tax shelter).

There are several methods of determining pension costs. For pension funds established in advance of the actual payment of the employees' benefits, these costs must be estimated. Usually an actuary analyzes a company's contractual pension liabilities, its labor turnover, the age pattern of the employees, the rate of return that can be earned on the funds invested, and the mortality rates of the pensioners. Based on these data, future costs are estimated. The pension costs deducted in any given year thus depend on both the accounting procedure and the actuary's estimates.

Although companies are required to disclose in a footnote to the financial statements the pension accounting and funding policy, the pension charge for the year, and the unfunded vested liability of the company, two important pieces of information are not provided. First, the company need not disclose the amount of unfunded past service obligations. Such obligations can exceed the net worth of a company. Second, the rate of return that the actuary assumes is not disclosed. If an unrealistically high rate of return is assumed to be earned on funds now invested in the pension plan, pension costs can be reduced on the income statement. Yet the company may then have to make large cash contributions in the future to make up any deficiency.

16-2.5 expensing versus capitalizing (5)

There are many items which the accountant may either (1) write off as current expenses or (2) capitalize and then amortize over a period of years. For example, motion picture production costs, oil well exploration costs, advertising campaign costs, and many other items are simply not clearly either an expense or an asset purchase; they are matters of managerial discretion which the fundamental analyst should scrutinize. Prior to the issuance of FASB statement 2, companies were entitled to either capitalize research and development (R&D) outlays or expense them. The new rule prohibits capitalizing R&D outlays.[10]

9 "Accounting for the Cost of Pension Plan," APB Opinion 8, AICPA, New York, 1966, pp. 85–86. Also, see Appendix C to Chap. 11 for an explanation of a sophisticated new financial strategy that allows a company to recover some funds from its pension fund and count these past pension fund payments as current income while the funds remaining in the pension fund fully defease the company's pension liability.

10 FASB 2, "Accounting for Research and Development Costs," Stamford, Conn., October 1974. An exception to the rule is material, equipment, or facilities that have "alternative future uses." For a list of activities that should be included in R&D and examples of activities that should be excluded, see paragraphs 9 and 10 of FASB 2.

Statements A and B differ because some outlays were expensed by B but capitalized by A. A fundamental analyst would consider that practice in comparing the two income statements. If the outlays appear to be expenses, the analyst will adjust A's income statement accordingly.

16-2.6 effects on accounting income

Table 16-2 summarizes the five differences in accounting procedures which were just discussed and shows the effects on accounting income. Firm B paid no income taxes; instead, it received a $250,000 federal income tax refund to partially offset its losses. In contrast, Firm A paid $1,365,000 in federal income taxes. These tax differences make it difficult to recall that both firms were identical except for the accounting procedures used. Thus, the taxpayers of the United States and Firm B's shareholders were misled by the accounting income reported by the company. However, both firms would have little difficulty getting a certified public accountant to certify that their respective income statements were within current "generally accepted accounting principles."

Some financial executives and accountants take advantage of the discretionary leeway in the accounting procedures which were highlighted in Table 16-2. These persons use the variables at their discretion to manipulate their firms' income to suit their current purposes.

Many investors do not have the time or training to make the proper adjustments in reported income figures. Therefore, the accounting profession should continue to narrow the areas left to the discretion of firms in reporting their own incomes.[11] The numerical example summarized in Table 16-2 dramatically pinpoints major ambiguities in accountants' procedures for estimating income. The point-by-point discussion keyed to this table suggests how fundamental security analysts could derive estimates of a firm's true economic income from accounting statements which are misleading.

In interpreting this example, the reader should bear at least two caveats in mind. First, the true economic income which a firm earns may be less than its reported income (as represented by statement B, for example) instead of larger. The example in Table 16-2 is a teaching device and is not intended to show all possible misrepresentations.

Second, the amount of difference between the reported earnings in statements A and B is not meant to be suggestive of some average amount of misrepresentation. In the final analysis, it is difficult to specify the amount of misrepresentation present in any given set of accounting procedures, since different analysts may interpret a given situation in quite different ways. However, well-trained, astute, but unethical financial managers can manage their accountants' and other affairs to make their firms' reported earnings come out to be any number they wish within a wide range. Thus, analysts should not use firms' reported income figures without due caution.[12]

[11] One study suggests that financial statements can be meticulously examined for the quality of corporate earnings in order to help increase the likelihood of avoiding stocks that will underperform the market. See Frank J. Fabozzi, "Quality of Earnings: A Test of Market Efficiency," *Journal of Portfolio Management*, Fall 1978, pp. 53–56.

[12] There is a body of academic thought called the *efficient markets theory* which argues that the market prices of securities reflect all available public information; this thinking is explained in detail in Chap. 19. According to the efficient markets theory, it does not matter whether a firm accounts for its income using method A or B in the example above, because financial analysts will

After a financial analyst has ferreted out and resolved the various ambiguities that may creep into a firm's income and expense statement, the income analysis work is not finished. The financial analyst should go on to examine the firm's income as it is reported on a per-share basis.

16-3 REPORTING EARNINGS PER SHARE

Investors should be concerned with earnings per share when they are estimating the value of the share. This figure measures the dollar amount of net income earned on a share of common stock during the reporting period.[13] If a company has convertible securities, warrants, stock options, or other contracts which permit the number of shares of common stock outstanding to be increased in future periods, more than one measure of earnings per share may be reported. Moreover, income or losses caused by extraordinary events will result in additional earnings per share measures being reported. The alternative measures of earnings per share are discussed below.

16-3.1 potential dilution of earnings per share[14]

Although the total earnings of a company may increase over time, analysts are aware that an increase in the number of shares of common stock outstanding may *dilute* earnings per share. An increase in the outstanding common stock can occur because management elects to sell more shares or because of the existence of contracts which permit investors to purchase common stock from the company. Examples of such contracts are convertible bonds, convertible preferred stock, and options or warrants to purchase common stock.

If the potential dilution due to the existence of convertible security contracts may result in a decline of less than 3 percent in earnings per share, the potential dilution need not be reported. Only a single presentation of earnings per share need be made. For companies in which the impact on earnings per share is greater than 3 percent, earnings per share will be presented two ways. First, dilution which considers only *common stock equivalents* is used to determine earnings per share.[15] This measure is called *primary earnings per*

---

see through these accounting gimmicks and ferret out the underlying economic truth. As a result, the price of the stock should be the same, whether method A or method B is used. An experienced CPA argues against the efficient markets theory by providing salient contrary examples, see Arthur R. Wyatt, "Efficient Market Theory: Its Impact on Accounting," *Journal of Accountancy*, February 1983, pp. 56–65.

[13] Technically speaking, earnings per share on the common stock is net income after taxes less preferred stock dividend payments divided by the weighted average number of shares of common stock outstanding. To compute the weighted average number of shares outstanding, the weights are determined by the length of time the shares are outstanding. For example, if there were 1.2 million shares outstanding for the first 8 months of the reporting year and 1.5 million shares in the last 4 months, then the weighted average number of shares is 1.3 million, determined as follows: (1.2 million shares × 8/12) + (1.5 million shares × 4/12) = 1.3 million shares.

[14] Based on "Earnings per Share," APB Opinion 15, AICPA, New York, 1969.

[15] *Common stock equivalents* are defined as options or warrants to purchase common stock and certain convertible securities. For a convertible security to be considered a common stock equivalent, the cash yield of the security at the time of issuance has to be less than two-thirds of the price rate existing when the security was issued. Common stock equivalents may be used when the result will be a decline in a loss per share.

share. Second, the maximum potential dilution of earnings per share must be reported. This measure is termed *fully diluted earnings per share.*[16]

16-3.2 extraordinary gains and losses

Analysts attempt to estimate the future "normal" economic income of the companies they investigate. However, certain events may distort this "normal" economic income. For example, suppose a company takes a considerable loss by closing down an unprofitable division or wins a legal case in which a substantial award is received. How should the event be recorded?

Accountants have debated how to treat extraordinary items on the income statement. On the one hand, some accountants took the view that extraordinary items should be reported on the income statement for the current period. The opposing view was that extraordinary items would distort income and hence should simply be charged or credited directly to retained earnings. In 1966, the controversy was virtually ended with the issuance of APB Opinion 9, "Reporting the Results of Operations." The opinion requires that extraordinary items be reported separately in the income statement, net of taxes. The exception to this reporting rule was prior period adjustments, which the opinion[17] defines as

> those material adjustments which (*a*) can be specifically identified with and directly related to the business activities of particular prior periods, and (*b*) are not attributable to economic events occurring subsequent to the date of the financial statements for the prior period, and (*c*) depend primarily on determinations by persons other than management, and (*d*) were not susceptible to reasonable estimation prior to such determination. Such adjustments are rare in modern financial accounting.

Examples of prior period adjustments are substantial settlements on lawsuits and adjustments or settlements of income taxes. Stringent requirements for an item to be classified as "extraordinary" were established in APB Opinion 30 issued in 1973.[18] The opinion requires that the item be both unusual in nature and not expected to recur in the foreseeable future.[19] Two examples of extraordinary items are losses due to a major casualty, such as a flood, and losses due to an expropriation of business assets from foreign operations. Three examples of transactions or events that are not included as extraordi-

[16] A study of the impact on financial statement users of the requirement in APB Opinion 15 calling for reporting of fully diluted earnings per share indicates that investors do react to information on potential dilution (Steven J. Rice, "The Information Content of Fully Diluted Earnings per Share," *The Accounting Review*, April 1978, vol. LIII, no. 2, pp. 429–438).

[17] APB Opinion 9, paragraph 23.

[18] APB Opinion 30, "Reporting the Results of Operations," AICPA, New York, 1973.

[19] The SEC requires a company to file Report Form 8-K within 10 days after the close of any month in which any problem arises. One disclosure that is required in the 8-K is extraordinary items. For a discussion of how the requirements for disclosure of this nature have been circumvented by companies required to file, see A. J. Lurie and V. S. Pastena, "How Promptly Do Corporations Disclose Their Problems?" *Financial Analysts Journal*, September–October 1975, pp. 55–61. The SEC requirements were extended in 1982. Now the 8-K must also be filed promptly to report the following: (1) changes in control of the corporation and how these changes occurred, (2) information about mergers, acquisitions, and dispositions, (3) bankruptcy or receivership judgments affecting the corporation, (4) changes in the corporation's certifying accountant, (5) resignation of any corporate directors, and (6) additional financial information to include pro forma financial information on acquired subsidiaries.

nary items are the write-down of inventory, gains or losses due to foreign exchange fluctuations,[20] and gains or losses from the disposition of a segment of the business.

16-4 INFLATION AND EARNINGS

One major criticism of published financial statements in recent years is that they do not recognize the impact of inflation. For example, one economist has estimated that reported after-tax profits of nonfinancial corporations were overstated by more than 300 percent in 1974 and by almost 60 percent in 1975. When profits were measured in 1965 dollars, real profits in 1975 were approximately $38.8 billion—which is the same as reported profits in 1965. On the other hand, reported profits in 1975 were $58.8 billion.[21]

Because profits are eroded as a result of inflation, the ability of a firm to maintain its operating capacity in the future is reduced. This occurs for two reasons: First, the profits retained in the corporation will have less purchasing power for replacing capital equipment. Second, fewer dollars will be retained, since dividends and taxes are based on reported profits rather than on profits adjusted for inflation. For example, using 1965 as the base year, it is estimated that, in 1975, nonfinancial corporations added $6 billion to retained earnings compared with an addition of $20 billion in 1965. In 1974 dividends exceeded real profits by $12.7 billion. The effective tax rate on 1974 profit dollars was overstated.

Two approaches have been suggested for adjusting for the impact of inflation on financial statements: general price-level accounting (GPLA) and current value accounting (CVA). The former deals with changes in the general price level; the latter adjusts for changes in individual items. The two approaches should be considered not as alternatives but rather as complementary responses to independent questions.[22] In 1969, the Accounting

[20] The accounting rules for reporting the impact of foreign exchange fluctuations on earnings were set forth in FASB Statement 8, "Accounting for the Translation of Foreign Currency Transactions and Foreign Currency Statement," AICPA, Stamford, Conn., 1975. For a summary of the statement see David Norr, "Currency Translation and the Analyst," *Financial Analysts Journal*, July–August 1976, pp. 46–54. In the article immediately following David Norr's, John K. Shank discusses the pitfalls of FASB Statement 8 ("FASB Statement 8 Resolved Foreign Currency Accounting—or Did It?"). Rita M. Rodriquez has examined the impact of FASB 8 on a sample of large U.S. multinational firms ("FASB 8: What Has It Done to Us?" *Financial Analysts Journal*, March–April 1977, pp. 40–47). She found that there was no significant impact on the earnings of the companies in her sample. More recently, FASB Statement 52 has been issued to modify FASB 8. FASB Statement 52 revises the accounting requirements for translation of foreign currency transactions and foreign currency financial statements. FASB 52 adopts the functional currency approach and requires each financial statement to be stated in its functional foreign currency before being translated into dollars. In contrast, FASB 8 specified the dollar as the measuring unit for all entities.

[21] "Focus on Balance Sheet," *Business Week*, June 7, 1976, p. 59. The economist whose estimate is cited is George Terbough, economic consultant for the Machinery & Allied Products Institute. For estimates of the impact of inflation on earnings for the years 1965 to 1973 see George Terbough, "Inflation and Profits," *Financial Analysts Journal*, May–June 1974, pp. 19–23.

[22] Paul Rosenfield, "The Confusion between General Price Level Restatement and Current Value Account," *Journal of Accountancy*, October 1972, pp. 63–68.

Principles Board recommended that supplementary financial statements using GPLA be voluntarily presented by companies.[23] The motion was later dropped because few companies responded to the request. The Financial Accounting Standards Board, in December 1974, issued an exposure draft of a proposal "Financial Reporting in Units of General Purchasing Power," which would require that financial statements be disclosed on a general price-level-adjusted basis.

Sidney Davidson and Roman Weil have estimated income by using general price-level accounting for 30 Dow Jones companies and a selected sample of other large companies for the years 1973 and 1974.[24] Their findings indicate that the effects of general price-level restatement differ significantly among firms. For almost all companies in the sample, adjusted income before monetary gain[25] was less than income as conventionally reported. However, when monetary gains were included, the adjusted income was a high percentage of reported income.

The SEC has supported the use of replacement cost accounting for financial reporting. Replacement cost accounting is one form of current value accounting.[26] Beginning with the 1976 10-K forms,[27] the SEC has required that certain registrants disclose current replacement cost for the cost of goods sold and depreciation.[28] According to the SEC, replacement cost "is the lowest amount that would have to be paid in the normal course of business to obtain a new asset of equivalent operating or productive capacity."

One major criticism of replacement cost accounting is that the SEC did not provide specific guidelines for companies to estimate replacement cost. Consequently, it is argued that it is difficult to compare companies because of the alternative methods for measuring replacement cost. In a survey of chief financial officers of the country's largest corporations conducted by the National Association of Accountants to determine the usefulness of replacement cost data, many of the respondents indicated that they think that the SEC requirement will mislead investors and further aggravate uncertainty among

[23] APB Accounting Series Release 3, "Financial Statements Restated for General Price Level Changes," AICPA, June 1969.

[24] Sidney Davidson and Roman L. Weil, "Inflation Accounting: What Will General Price Level Adjusted Income Statements Show?" *Financial Analysts Journal*, January–February 1975, pp. 27–31, 70–84. This article presents the results for 1973. The following article by the same authors presents the results for 1974: "Impact of Inflation Accounting on 1974 Earnings," *Financial Analysts Journal*, September–October 1975, pp. 42–45.

[25] A monetary gain occurs when the company is, on balance, a net borrower and the price level increases. There is a gain, since the company pays back creditors in cheaper dollars.

[26] Davidson and Weil, in "Inflation Accounting: The SEC Proposal for Replacement Cost Disclosures," *Financial Analysts Journal*, March–April 1976, have described the essential difference between general price-level restatement and replacement cost accounting as follows: "Replacement cost income measurements change in the timing, but not the ultimate amounts, of income. Income over a sufficiently long period is still cash inflows less outflows. General price-level-adjusted accounting changes the amounts, but not the timing, of reported income." (p. 65)

[27] The 10-K report is a detailed financial report which publicly held companies are required to file with the SEC; this report is discussed in Chap. 4. Corporations' 10-K statements are publicly available at the SEC.

[28] The requirement was set forth in Accounting Release 190, March 23, 1976. Companies that have gross property and inventories that are valued at more than $100 million and which represent more than 10 percent of total assets are required to disclose the necessary data.

the common stock analysts.[29] It was also felt that the requirement would be too costly to implement.

A methodology for estimating replacement cost data and income was developed by Angela Falkenstein and Roman Weil.[30] These two researchers applied their methodology to the financial statements of the 30 Dow Jones Industrials for 1975. They found that, for some companies which reported profits by using generally accepted accounting procedures (GAAP), losses occurred when replacement costs were used. Moreover, the payout ratio (that is, the percentage of earnings which is paid out in cash dividends) on a conventional basis was about 50 percent. However, when income was adjusted for replacement costs, the payout ratio was about 125 percent. A payout ratio in excess of 100 percent implies that new sources of funds will be required if the company is to operate at the same level it has operated at in the past; it is impossible for a firm to maintain a payout ratio in excess of 100 percent.

Realizing that a consensus could not be reached within the accounting profession about exactly how to report the effects of inflation on a business, the Financial Accounting Standards Board (FASB) issued its Statement 33 entitled "Financial Reporting and Changing Prices." This statement mandates inflation accounting disclosures in annual reports to shareholders of public corporations having either assets in excess of $1 billion or $125 million of inventories and gross properties. The following items are required to be reported under two fundamentally different measurement approaches.

current year data	historical cost–constant dollar	current cost
1. Income from continuing operations	x	x
2. Purchasing power gain or loss on monetary assets and liabilities	x	x
3. Increases or decreases in the current costs of inventories and properties, net of inflation		x
4. Inventories and properties at year end		x
5. Five-year summary of selected data	x	x
6. Footnotes and narrative explanations	x	x

[29] Management Accounting Survey, "Corporations Doubt Usefulness of Replacement Cost Data," *Management Account*, August 1976.

[30] Angela Falkenstein and Roman Weil, "Replacement Cost Accounting: What Will Income Statements Based on the SEC Disclosure Show?—Part 1," *Financial Analysts Journal*, January–February 1977, pp. 46–56. Part 11 appears in the March–April issue. The estimates obtained did not use the replacement cost increments provided in the 10-K forms, since prior to 1976 not much information was reported. Should the SEC continue to require that companies provide replacement cost estimates, security analysts will need a methodology to construct a time series of earnings based on replacement costs. A study of 1976 earnings by 17 companies in the pharmaceutical industry using the methodology developed by Falkenstein and Weil and the replacement cost data provided in the 10-K forms found that for all firms the income estimate using the reported replacement costs exceeded the income estimate using the Falkenstein and Weil methodology. See also F. J. Fabozzi and Lawrence Shiffrin, "Replacement Cost Accounting: Application to the Pharmaceutical Industry," *Quarterly Review of Economics and Business*, Spring 1979, vol. 19, pp. 163–171.

The historical cost–constant dollar accounting deals with general inflation (which must be measured by the Consumer Price Index, according to the FASB); this technique is also popularly called price-level accounting. The current cost basis of accounting focuses on specific price changes for individual assets rather than on price changes caused by general inflation. Annual reports for years ending after December 24, 1980, are required to provide the new supplementary information about the effects of inflation according to FASB 33. The FASB expects to review Statement 33 and revise (and probably extend) it in the years ahead. That is, FASB 33 is viewed as merely a first step toward better reporting of price-level changes by the accounting profession.

16-5 HOW ACCOUNTING INCOME AFFECTS THE BALANCE SHEET

A *balance sheet* is a summary of account balances carried after the appropriate closing of the books. Income statements deal with *flows*, whereas the balance sheets deal with *stocks*. Of course, stocks are merely accumulations of flows. Thus, the vagaries which undermine the estimates of accounting income are cumulated in certain balance sheet items. Table 16-4 shows a model of the balance sheet.

There is a great deal of debate in the accounting profession concerning the treatment of items in the balance sheet. The impact of inflation has made the balance sheet in its present form of questionable value to users of financial statements. Some of the reforms suggested or actually adopted for particular balance sheet items will be discussed below.

16-5.1 asset reporting

Two reforms have been suggested to improve the valuation of current assets on the balance sheet. For marketable securities it has been advocated that the value reported in the balance sheet should be the current market value. For inventories it has been proposed that all inventories should be valued at replacement cost (that is, what the company must pay in the current market to replenish inventories rather than the misleading inventory valuation methods presently permitted). Some worthwhile changes in the reporting of long-term assets are considered next.

Rather than reporting plant and equipment on the basis of historical cost less depreciation, it has been argued that this account should reflect how much it would take to replace the company's entire productive capacity. Adjustments to historical costs might be based on a variety of indices. For land and natural resources, some accountants have suggested that these assets,

TABLE 16-4 balance sheet model

uses of funds	sources of funds
Current assets	Current liabilities
Long-term assets	Long-term liabilities
Other assets	Net worth
Total assets	Total liabilities and N. W.

since they are unique and cannot be reproduced, should be shown at net realizable value. This value represents current market price minus any future development, selling, or interest costs. There are other accountants who prefer a value based on the future expected cashflows from these assets, discounted at an appropriate interest rate. No professional consensus has emerged to specify exactly how to value the long-term assets.

The balance sheet category headed Other Assets may contain intangible assets such as goodwill or capitalized expenses. However, this balance sheet category was aided by FASB 2, which prohibits capitalizing research and development (R&D) expenses on the balance sheet as Other Assets. Before FASB 2 some firms capitalized large amounts of R&D expense each year and showed them as a balance sheet asset which was depreciated over a number of years, rather than writing off the cost as a current expense. As a result of this now-unsanctioned practice, some firms' historically reported earnings are inflated by the amount of the R&D expenses which were not written off as current expenses. The item of goodwill under the Other Assets category is also reported more realistically today than it was in the past because of certain rulings about reporting business combinations which may arise through mergers and acquisitions.

16-5.2 business combination reporting

A business *combination* can be accounted for by one of two accounting methods: purchase of assets or pooling of interest. Because of abuses that have resulted from permitting accountants leeway in selecting the method of handling business combinations for financial reporting, the APB issued an opinion which sets forth the conditions under which each method must be used.[31] When the purchase-of-assets method is employed, the payment by one company of an excess amount for another company results in an intangible asset referred to as "goodwill." For reporting purposes, the company must amortize goodwill over its useful life or, at most, 40 years.[32] However, some companies abuse the write-off requirement, with the result that goodwill is carried at an inflated value on the balance sheet and reported income is overstated.

16-5.3 reporting liabilities

On the liabilities side of the balance sheet, there are three controversies facing accountants. The first surrounds the advantages that accrue to a company during an inflationary period when it has issued debt. Some accountants argue that since the company must repay the debt in the future in cheaper dollars (that is, dollars which have less purchasing power because of inflation), there is a gain to shareholders. This gain can be reflected in the financial statement by increasing net worth.

A second controversy involves the treatment of deferred taxes. A deferred tax liability must be established when the company reports a lower income to the Internal Revenue Service than to its shareholders. There is a question as to whether this amount should actually appear as a liability. Some argue that such an amount should be part of net worth if the company can continue to report lower earnings to the IRS than it is reporting to shareholders. This can

[31] "Business Combinations," APB Opinion 16, AICPA, New York, 1970.

[32] "Intangible Assets," APB Opinion 17, AICPA, New York, 1970.

result if a company continually increases its capital expenditures and employs accelerated depreciation. In such cases, the deferred taxes will be, in effect, a long-term interest-free loan from the government that may not have to be repaid in the foreseeable future.[33]

The third controversy on the liability side of the balance sheet concerns the treatment of lease arrangements. The primary users of leases prior to 1960 were retail companies who leased their premises. The popularity of leases since 1960 has been such that lease financing now constitutes an important source of financing for different types of capital assets. Rather than borrow funds or raise equity to acquire capital assets, a company can elect to lease an asset from an asset leasing firm.

In the absence of uniformity in accounting for leases and disclosure of leases by lessees, comparisons of certain financial ratios of companies in the same industry may be inappropriate and misleading. For example, if Company *X* and Company *Y* are in the same industry and the former company *leases* its fixed assets whereas the latter firm *owns* its fixed assets, then an examination of the debt-equity ratio of the two companies would be misleading.[34]

Because a lease is a contractual agreement, the provisions of the lease may vary widely. The FASB has classified leases as either operating or capital (financing) leases.[35] The FASB has established criteria for classifying a lease as a capital lease. If at least one of the financing criteria is met, then the lease is classified as a capital lease. The criteria attempt to identify whether a transaction is a purely financing device for the purchase of the asset.

The accounting treatments of the two types of leases differ because it is necessary to portray the substance of each economic transaction. Rental payments on an operating lease are expensed. On the other hand, for a capital lease, the lessee records the lease as if an asset is being financed and an obligation is being created. More specifically, an asset and a liability of an amount equal to the present value of the minimum lease payments during the term of the lease are created on the balance sheet.[36] The FASB has also established disclosure requirements for lease arrangements of lessees.[37]

[33] In any event, the present value or discounted value of the deferred tax liability should in theory be recorded as a liability. The further into the future that this liability can be expected to be repaid, the lower the present value or discounted value of the liability.

[34] For examples see A. Thomas Nelson, "Capitalizing Leases—The Effects on Financial Ratios," *Journal of Accountancy*, July 1963, pp. 49–58.

[35] "Accounting for Leases," Statement of Financial Accounting Standards, no. 13, Stamford, Conn., July 22, 1976, par. 7.

[36] FASB 13. There are several problems related to the determination of the recorded value. These problems involve the treatment of executory costs (for example, insurance, maintenance, and tax expenses), the discount rate for determining the present value, amortization of the leased asset, and the reduction of the liability over time.

[37] In 1973, subsequent to the issuance of four APB opinions on the treatment of leases, the SEC established its own policy on lease disclosure (see "Notice of Adoption of Amendments to Regulation S-X Requiring Improved Disclosure of Leases," *Accounting Series Release* 147, SEC, Washington, D.C., October 1973). FASB 13 includes substantially all the lease disclosure requirements promulgated by the SEC. Following FASB 13, the SEC also proposed that regulated companies, including public utilities, comply with the statement, since it was unclear whether FASB 13 applied to regulated companies.

16-5.4 accounting earnings can exaggerate growth in owners' equity

The conventions the accounting profession uses for handling the balance item called Retained Earnings can mislead investors and unsophisticated financial analysts. For an example of the type of confusion that can arise, consider the equity section of the balance sheet shown in the hypothetical example below. Essentially, this section of the so-called right-hand side of the balance sheet contains the firm's nonliability sources of financing.

Common stock at $1 par (100,000 shares outstanding)	100,000
Paid-in surplus	900,000
Retained earnings	7,000,000
Total equity, or net worth	$8,000,000

There are three components of a corporation's net worth: (1) The par value of the outstanding common stock can only be increased if more shares are sold. Accountants define it to be the specified par value per share multiplied by the number of shares outstanding. (2) The Paid-In Surplus is the excess over and above the par value per share that the common stock investors paid for the stock when they originally bought it; this quantity is also fixed—unless more shares are sold. In the example above, for instance, it appears that the average share of stock was sold for $10 per share and thus contributed $9 per share to the Paid-In Surplus account. (3) Retained Earnings, however, can increase or decrease every year for most corporations. Positive net earnings (that remain after all cash dividends are deducted) are added to Retained Earnings to increase it. Or, if the firm had a bad year, net losses are deducted from Retained Earnings to reduce it.

After the board of directors reaches its decision every quarter about how much of the corporation's quarterly accounting earnings to pay out in cash dividends, the remainder of the company's accounting earnings is designated as Retained Earnings, according to a deeply entrenched accounting convention. Since the average American corporation pays out about 50 percent of its accounting earnings as cash dividends, the remaining 50 percent of the corporation's accounting earnings becomes Retained Earnings and gets added to the Equity section of the corporate balance sheet. Thus, Retained Earnings increases in those years in which the corporation is profitable. Every time that Retained Earnings is increased, the corporation's total Owners' Equity (or Net Worth) account increases correspondingly, and this raises the corporation's Book Value per Share. These are all merely accounting definitions which cannot be argued with and have some financial consequence only if financial analysts cannot discern the truth in the misleading cases. However, the way that Retained Earnings affects future years' earnings is a matter which can have more serious financial consequences.

Retained Earnings initially show up in the corporate financial statements in some asset category to offset the equal increase on the other side of the balance sheet under the Owners' Equity heading. Retained Earnings gets spent on something, call it "bricks and mortar" if there is a need for an example of a possible asset, which should make the corporation larger and more profitable in the years ahead. Two insights about these so-called Retained Earnings are worth noting here. First, Retained Earnings is not really economic income which the investor can spend at will. Since Retained Earnings are not really earnings available for the investors' consumption, it is wrong and misleading to label Retained Earnings as a form of "earnings" and thus imply that it is part of the investors' income.

A second important point is also worth noting about Retained Earnings. Retained Earnings gets reinvested somewhere in the corporation so that some of the future earnings actually grow out of past earnings which were reinvested in Retained Earnings. This is circular. Part of a corporation's future earnings are actually only a return on past earnings that were reinvested under the heading of Retained Earnings. This is a form of double counting which inflates the accounting measure of corporate income.[38] In order to help investors see what is truly being done with the corporation's earnings, Retained Earnings should be renamed with a more descriptive title. Titles such as "Involuntary Reinvestment" or "Usurped Earnings" may sound overly dramatic; but these titles would be more likely to alert investors to the way that their corporation is actually being financed than would continued use of that misleading item called "Retained Earnings." In the final analysis, retained earnings is like a warrant or a stock rights offering that the Board of Directors forces its shareholders to purchase whether or not they want to.

16-6 HOW TO ADJUST A SERIES OF INCOME STATEMENTS

Since income is so important in determining the value of a security and since the concept of accounting profit is so vague, it is usually necessary to adjust or normalize the reported income figure to a more realistic value that is defined consistently from year to year.

The key word in analyzing a series of income statements from one firm is "consistency." Since there are so few clear-cut definitions in income accounting, some definitions must be adopted and used consistently. This is where the economists' concept becomes useful (see Box 16-1).

The financial analyst's job is to detect misleading accounting statements and restate them consistently, using the definition of economic income (rather than some accountant's reported profit which may contain tax gimmicks or window-dressing manipulations). In this manner a company's true earning

[38] For a more detailed explanation of how corporate investors are misled by the title and usage of "Retained Earnings" see the article by A. J. Merrett and Gerald D. Newbould entitled "CEPS: The Illusion of Corporate Growth," *Journal of Portfolio Management*, Fall 1982, pp. 5–10.

BOX 16-1
a person's economic income

DEFINITION OF ECONOMIC INCOME FOR A PERSON A person's economic income is the maximum he or she can consume without diminishing a future period's consumption opportunities.

BOX 16-2
a shareholder's economic income

DEFINITION OF A STOCK SHARE'S ECONOMIC INCOME The economic income from an equity share during a given period equals the maximum amount of real, physical consumption opportunities which can be withdrawn from the share during that period without diminishing the consumption opportunities which can be obtained from it in future periods.

power can be analyzed and the *trend* in income can be detected. Typically, financial statements for several past years are gathered from the company's 10-K reports. Then, by referring to the notes to the financial statements, the various years' statements can be adjusted so the items in all years are consistently defined. After these adjustments, year-by-year comparisons of the share's economic income may be made. Box 16-2 defines the economic income from a share of stock.

The definition of an equity share's economic income furnishes the financial analyst a stable guiding light which suggests how to adjust a share of stock's reported (or accounting) income so that it is realistic, consistent, and suitable for informative comparisons with other years' incomes and other firms' incomes. Some key aspects of this guiding definition are worthy of further discussion.[39]

1. *Inflation adjustments*. The economic income definition's reference to "real, physical consumption opportunities" refers to inflation-adjusted dollars rather than to inflated (or nominal) dollars.
2. *Withdrawals*. An equity share's economic income does not actually have to be withdrawn and consumed, but the consumption *opportunity* must genuinely exist or the income is not real. For example, if a firm must retain some of its earnings to survive, then those retained earnings are not true economic income which the share's owner could consume without diminishing the share's future income.[40]
3. *Depreciation*. The economic income must be the income left after an allowance for wear and tear of the assets is deducted. This depreciation or depletion allowance must be reinvested in the assets to maintain their future productivity undiminished and is thus not consumable income.
4. *Market values*. A share's current economic income includes its current capital gains and losses at current market values, regardless of whether the gains and losses are realized. Thus, for example, if a supermarket firm discovered oil wells (which were totally unrelated to its basic food enterprise) on its customer

[39] Milton Friedman, *A Theory of the Consumption Function*, Princeton University Press, 1957. For a deeper discussion of many of the problems raised here, see R. K. Jaedicke and R. T. Sprouse, *Accounting Flows: Income, Funds and Cash*, Prentice-Hall Foundations of Finance Series, Prentice-Hall, Englewood Cliffs, N.J., 1965. Any intermediate accounting textbook will explain the details of the various procedures accountants use in handling different transactions.

[40] For more discussion of how earnings are double-counted and mistaken for growth because Retained Earnings is erroneously called a source of income rather than a source of mandatory equity financing see "CEPS: The Illusion of Corporate Growth," *The Journal of Portfolio Management*, Fall 1982, pp. 5–10.

parking lots, the appreciation which the firm enjoyed from the mineral deposits would constitute economic income regardless of whether the oil was sold.

The income statement for firm A in Table 16-2 provides an example of how some of the concepts above should be employed in an effort to delineate a firm's economic income.

16-7 MEASURING AND PROJECTING EARNINGS STATISTICALLY

The preceding paragraphs discussed the concept of economic income and how to derive estimates of it from the accountant's income statements. After a firm's past accounting income figures have been normalized to yield a series of consistently defined estimates of the firm's economic income, the growth rate of a firm's economic income may be estimated. Knowledge of a firm's historical earnings growth rate is helpful when forecasting future earnings.[41]

[41] The impact of reported accounting earnings on the market price of the corporation's stock has been actively researched. An easy-to-read article which surveys these studies and offers some suggestions is O. M. Joy and C. P. Jones, "Earnings Reports and Market Efficiencies: An Analysis of the Contrary Evidence," *The Journal of Financial Research*, vol. II, no. 1, Spring 1979, pp. 51–63. See the following studies for details: (1) R. Ball and P. Brown, "An Empirical Evaluation of Accounting Income Numbers," *Journal of Accounting Research*, Autumn 1968, pp. 159–178. (2) S. Basu, "The Information Content of Price-Earnings Ratios," *Financial Management*, Summer 1975, pp. 53–63. (3) S. Basu, "Investment Performance of Common Stocks in Relation to Their Price-Earnings Ratios: A Test of the Efficient Market Hypothesis, *The Journal of Finance*, June 1977, pp. 663–681. (4) W. Beaver, "The Information Content of Annual Earnings Announcements," *Journal of Accounting Research, Empirical Research in Accounting: Selected Studies*, 1968. (5) W. Breen, "Low Price-Earnings Ratios and Industry Relatives," *Financial Analysts Journal*, July–August 1968, pp. 125–127. (6) W. Breen and J. Savage, "Portfolio Distributions and Tests of Security Selection Models," *The Journal of Finance*, December 1968, pp. 805–819. (7) S. Brown, "Earnings Changes, Stock Prices and Market Efficiency," *The Journal of Finance*, March 1978, pp. 17–28. (8) D. Cassidy, "Investor Evaluation of Accounting Information: Some Additional Empirical Evidence," *Journal of Accounting Research*, Autumn 1976, pp. 212–229. (9) G. Foster, "Quarterly Accounting Data: Time-Series Properties and Predictive-Ability Results," *The Accounting Review*, January 1977, pp. 1–21. (10) J. C. Francis, "Analysis of Equity Returns: A Survey with Extensions," *Journal of Economics and Business*, Spring/Summer 1977, pp. 181–192. (11) J. C. Francis and D. R. Rowell, "A Simultaneous Equation Model of the Firm for Financial Analysis and Planning," *Financial Management*, Spring 1978, vol. 7, no. 1, pp. 29–44. (12) N. Gonedes, "Properties of Accounting Numbers: Models and Tests," *Journal of Accounting Research*, Autumn 1973, pp. 212–237. (13) P. Griffin, "The Time-Series Behavior of Quarterly Earnings: Preliminary Evidence," *Journal of Accounting Research*, Spring 1977, pp. 71–83. (14) C. Jones and R. Litzenberger, "Quarterly Earnings Reports and Intermediate Stock Price Trends," *The Journal of Finance*, March 1970, pp. 143–148. (15) O. Joy, R. Litzenberger, and R. McEnally, "The Adjustment of Stock Prices to Announcements of Unanticipated Changes in Quarterly Earnings," *Journal of Accounting Research*, Autumn 1977, pp. 207–225. (16) R. Kaplan and R. Roll, "Investor Evaluation of Accounting Information: Some Empirical Evidence," *The Journal of Business*, April 1972, pp. 225–257. (17) H. Latané and C. Jones, "Measuring and Using Standardized Unexpected Earnings," presented at the American Finance Association Meetings, New York, 1977. (18) H. Latané, O. Joy, and C. Jones, "Quarterly Data, Sort-Rank Routines, and Security Evaluation," *The Journal of Business*, October 1970, pp. 427–438. (19) H. Latané, C. Jones, and R. Rieke, "Quarterly Earnings Reports and Subsequent Holding Period Returns," *Journal of Business Research*, April 1974, pp. 119–132. (20) H. Latané and C. Jones, "Standardized Unexpected Earnings—A Progress Report," *The Journal of Finance*, December 1977, pp. 1457–1465.

It is necessary to estimate a stock's future income because the value of the share is the present value of its *future* economic income.[42] Chapter 17 discusses industry analysis and closes by explaining some tools which are valuable in analyzing a firm's earnings growth rate and in forecasting its future earnings.

For short-term forecasts (for example, 1 year or less in the future), a firm's earnings may usually be estimated from discussions with the firm's management and the firm's competitors, from publicly available information, and from other more-or-less subjective sources. More scientific forecasting techniques useful for longer-run earnings projections are explained in Chap. 17. A firm's long-run earning power is ultimately what determines its intrinsic value.

16-7.1 forecasting earnings per share

Once the growth trend has been satisfactorily estimated, future values of earnings per share may be forecasted. First, the earnings trend line may be extrapolated (as shown by the dotted segment in Fig. 17-7 on page 497). If the points do not "fit" fairly closely on the trend line, it may be difficult to obtain a good forecast. In this case a larger sample (change from annual to quarterly data and/or increase in the sample period) may help. Or Eq. (16-1) may be useful:

$$e_t = (1 + g)^t(e_0) \qquad (16\text{-}1)$$

where e_t denotes earnings per share at period t. These methods should be satisfactory for short forecasts of a few years into the future if no change in the firm's growth rate is anticipated.

16-7.2 forecasting the growth rate for earnings

Forecasting earnings per share may not be as simple as indicated in the preceding paragraph if the firm's rate of growth is expected to change. The rate of growth may change for several reasons. Products have life cycles, as explained in Chap. 17, which can affect their earnings growth rates. Furthermore, old patents expire and/or new patents are obtained, competition becomes more or less aggressive, periods occur that are economically accelerating or depressed, or other factors cause growth rates to change. One of the purposes of fundamental analysis is to anticipate these factors accurately in order to make a good estimate of the growth rate of a firm's income.

16-7.3 can earnings be forecasted?

Methods for forecasting earnings are explained in Chap. 17 and in the paragraphs above. However, an important question which the financial analyst should address is whether earnings can, in fact, be accurately forecasted by using historical earnings. Studies by both American and British researchers

(21) R. Litzenberger, O. Joy, and C. Jones, "Ordinal Predictions and the Selection of Common Stocks," *Journal of Financial and Quantitative Analysis*, September 1971, pp. 1059–1068. (22) J. McWilliams, "Prices, Earnings and P. E. Ratios," *Financial Analysts Journal*, May–June 1966, pp. 137–142. (23) F. Nicholson, "Price Ratios in Relation to Investment Results," *Financial Analysts Journal*, January–February 1968, pp. 105–109.

[42] C. C. Holt, "The Influence of Growth Duration on Share Prices," *Journal of Finance*, September 1962, pp. 465–475. R. A. Haugen and D. W. Wichern, "The Elasticity of Financial Assets," *Journal of Finance*, September 1974, pp. 1229–1240.

suggest that earnings per share follow a random walk.[43] That is, the study of successive changes in historical earnings per share suggests that they fluctuate randomly up and down and that they are not helpful in forecasting future changes.

The hypothesis that earnings per share follow a random walk does not imply that earnings per share cannot be predicted. What it simply means is that a security analyst will not usually improve the ability to forecast future earnings per share by simply projecting historical earnings.[44]

16-8 CONCLUSIONS ABOUT EARNINGS ANALYSIS

The economic income from an equity share is the maximum amount of consumption which the share can yield during some period such that the consumption opportunities from the share are undiminished at the end of the period. This economic quantity may not coincide with accountants' concept of income. Therefore, accounting income figures must be adjusted or normalized to obtain as nearly as possible a consistently defined series of eco-

[43] This was first observed for British firms by Professor Ian M. D. Little ("Higgledy Piggledy Growth," *Institute of Statistics*, Oxford, November 1962, vol. 24, no. 4). The results were supported in a later study with Professor A. C. Rayner entitled *Higgledy Piggledy Growth Again*, Blackwell, Oxford, 1966. The following studies support the British findings. Joseph E. Murphy, Jr., "Relative Growth in Earnings per Share—Past and Future," *Financial Analysts Journal*, November–December 1966, pp. 73–76. John Lintner and Robert Glauber, "Higgledy Piggedly Growth in America?" Paper presented to the Seminar on the Analysis of Security Prices, University of Chicago, May 1967. Richard A. Brealey, *An Introduction to Risk and Return from Common Stocks*, 2d ed., M.I.T., Cambridge, Mass., 1983, chap. 5, "The Behavior of Earnings." W. S. Albrecht, L. L. Lookabill, and J. C. McKeown, "The Time-Series Properties of Annual Earnings," *Journal of Accounting Research*, Autumn 1977, vol. 15, pp. 226–244. R. J. Ball and R. Watts, "Some Time Series Properties of Accounting Income," *Journal of Finance*, June 1972, vol. 27, pp. 663–682. W. H. Beaver, "The Time Series Behavior of Earnings," *Empirical Research in Accounting: Selected Studies, Journal of Accounting Research* (supplement), 1970, vol. 8, pp. 62–99. R. A. Brealey, "Some Implications of the Comovement of American Company Earnings," *Applied Economics*, 1971, vol. 3, pp. 183–196. N. Dopuch and R. L. Watts, "Using Time-Series Models to Assess the Significance of Accounting Changes," *Journal of Accounting Research*, Spring 1972, vol. 10, pp. 180–194. L. L. Lookabill, "Some Additional Evidence on the Time Series Properties of Accounting Signals," *Accounting Review*, October 1976, vol. 51, pp. 724–738. R. L. Watts and R. W. Leftwich, "The Time Series of Annual Accounting Earnings," *Journal of Accounting Research*, Autumn 1977, vol. 15, pp. 253–271. In addition, the following book reviews the literature on the behavior and comovement of earnings: G. Foster, *Financial Statement Analysis*, Prentice-Hall, Englewood Cliffs, N. J., 1978.

[44] The value of earnings reported in interim financial statements for forecasting annual earnings has been debated in the investment literature. See David Green, Jr., and Joel Segall, "The Predictive Power of First-Quarter Earnings Reports," *Journal of Business*, January 1967, vol. 40, pp. 44–45, and Phillip Brown and Victor Niederhoffer, "The Predictive Content of Quarterly Earnings," *Journal of Business*, October 1968, vol. 41, pp. 488–497. The Francis model also has a high degree of explanatory power over the empirically observed quarterly earnings per share of NYSE stocks; see J. C. Francis, "Analysis of Equity Returns: A Survey with Extensions," *Journal of Business and Economics*, Spring-Summer 1977, vol. 29, no. 3, pp. 181–192. The Francis article is reprinted in J. C. Francis, C. F. Lee, and D. E. Farrar (eds.), *Readings in Investments*, McGraw-Hill, New York, 1980, pp. 459–470. For a discussion of the pitfalls of interim financial statements see Lee J. Seidler and William Benjes, "The Credibility Gap in Interim Financial Statements," *Financial Analysts Journal*, September–October 1967, pp. 109–115.

nomic income. The present value of this latter series is then taken to determine the value of that equity share. The procedures utilized by fundamental security analysts in determining the intrinsic value of an equity's economic income were explained in Chap. 15.

QUESTIONS

16-1. Write out the model used by accountants in determining taxable income.

16-2. How would reported assets, expenses, and accounting income be affected by a switch from LIFO to FIFO inventory valuation during an inflationary period? Explain.

16-3. Explain three ways in which a company can manipulate its earnings within the framework of generally accepted accounting principles.

16-4. "During an inflationary period the balance sheet of a firm may be of questionable value." Discuss.

16-5. How does primary diluted earnings per share differ from fully diluted earnings per share? Will all firms report both statistics in financial statements?

16-6. Distinguish between an extraordinary item and a prior period adjustment.

16-7. What two approaches have been suggested for adjusting financial statements for the impact of inflation? Are these two methods alternative methods for handling inflation? Which of the two methods was required by the SEC's new FRR One?

16-8. What is the present method of handling leases on a financial statement?

16-9. What are some accounting factors which could cause a firm's historical average growth rate to decrease in future years? To increase?

16-10. "Retained earnings are like a new issue of common stock that the old shareholders are forced to buy." True, false, or uncertain? Explain.

SELECTED REFERENCES

Briloff, Abraham, *Unaccountable Accounting*, Harper & Row, New York, 1972. A nonmathematical, case-by-case discussion, giving names of large corporations and large CPA firms, dates, and numerous actual examples of accounting entries which do not reflect the economic realities.

Davidson, Sidney, Clyde P. Stickney, and Roman L. Weil, *Inflation Accounting*, McGraw-Hill, New York, 1976. A book which illustrates the impact of inflation on reported earnings and presents the results of the authors' research for specific companies.

Foster, George, *Financial Statement Analysis*, Prentice-Hall, Englewood Cliffs, N. J., 1978. A new and modern approach to financial analysis which is based on economic theory and which uses simple econometrics is explained in this book.

Graham, B., D. Dodd, and S. Cottle, *Security Analysis*, 4th ed., McGraw-Hill, New York, 1962. This book is a standard reference of many practicing fundamental security analysts. It is a nonmathematical, detailed description of security analysis based on financial statements and other basic facts about the firm. Chapter 33 deals with earnings forecasting.

industry analysis

Sometimes people ask "Why should a security analyst do industry analysis?" This is a good question, and there is a good answer: The mediocre stocks in a growth industry usually outperform the best stocks in a stagnant industry. Therefore, it is worthwhile for a security analyst to pinpoint growth industries in which to search for firms that will be good investment prospects. Stated simply, industry analysis can be viewed as one aspect of security analysis.

17-1 THE IMPORTANCE OF INDUSTRY ANALYSIS

The portion of economic theory which deals with the organization of industries[1] suggests that firms which manufacture homogeneous products should maximize their profits by adopting fairly similar policies with respect to the following factors.

1. The labor-capital ratio utilized by each firm.
2. Markups, profit margins, and selling prices.
3. Advertising and promotional programs.
4. Research and development expenditures.
5. Reliance on legislated competitive aids (such as tariffs in the import-export business, or monopoly franchises by public utilities).

[1] The classic theories about industrial organization are E. H. Chamberlin, *The Theory of Monopolistic Competition*, 7th ed., Harvard University Press, Cambridge, Mass., 1956, and also Joan Robinson, *The Economics of Imperfect Competition*, Macmillan, London, 1933. More recently, see Roger Sherman and Robert Tollison, "Technology, Profit and Market Performance," *Quarterly Journal of Economics*, August 1972, vol. 86, pp. 448–462.

Since each different industry usually uses some unique technological process and similar set of operating policies to produce its particular product, economic theory also suggests that the competitive firms in each industry should experience similar levels of risk and similar rates of return. In fact, empirical research by people like Marc Nerlove have shown that the firms in each different industry do typically experience similar average rates of return that are typical of their industry. Furthermore, the industry average rates of return do differ significantly from industry to industry.[2] Fabozzi and Francis have shown empirical evidence that different investments result in different levels of risk which are the result of, among other things, significantly different levels of average risk from industry to industry.[3] Table 17-1 lists the average beta systematic risk coefficients which Rosenberg and Guy reported for 39 different industries, for instance.

17-1.1 intertemporal stability of industry returns

After reviewing the theoretical and empirical reasons why we should expect significant differences in the performance of different industries, the next logical question that arises is "Do certain industries *always* perform either best or worst?" Various researchers have uniformly reported a negative reply to this question.[4]

Researchers have ranked the performance of different industries over one period of years and then ranked the performance of the same industries over a subsequent period of years in order to compare the rankings. The correlation coefficients between one period's rankings and the next period's rankings were near zero in every case reported. These findings imply that an industry that was either best or worst during one period of time cannot be expected to retain that ranking in the future. Or, stated differently, the past is not a good predictor of the future—if one looks very far into the future.

17-1.2 rankings within an industry

Changing our perspective from the industry rankings to the rankings of the individual firms within an industry raises the question "Do the firms within an industry typically experience similar performance rankings within their industry with the passage of time?" After all, if the rankings of firms within an industry were consistent over time, it would reduce the need for company analysis. Industry analysis combined with consistent rankings of the firms in that industry would show which firms to select without further research.

Benjamin King analyzed the price movements of 63 stocks over a period of

[2] Marc Nerlove, "Factors Affecting Differences among Rates of Return on Investments in Individual Common Stocks," *The Review of Economics and Statistics*, August 1968, vol. 50, pp. 312–331.

[3] Frank J. Fabozzi and J. C. Francis, "Industry Effects and the Determinants of Risk," *The Quarterly Review of Economics and Business*, Autumn 1979, vol. 19, no. 3, pp. 61–74.

[4] Henry A. Latané and Donald L. Tuttle, "Framework for Forming Probability Beliefs," *Financial Analysts Journal*, 1968, vol. 24, pp. 51–61. Eugene F. Brigham and James L. Pappas, "Rates of Return on Common Stock," *Journal of Business*, 1969, vol. 42, pp. 302–316. Frank K. Reilly and Eugene Drzycimski, "Alternative Industry Performance and Risk," *Journal of Financial and Quantitative Analysis*, 1974, vol. 9, pp. 423–446. Milford S. Tysseland, "Further Tests of the Validity of the Industry Approach to Investment Analysis," *Journal of Financial and Quantitative Analysis*, 1971, vol. 6, pp. 835–847. Harlan L. Cheney, "The Value of Industry Forecasting as an Aid to Portfolio Management," *Appalachian Financial Review*, 1970, vol. 1, pp. 331–339.

TABLE 17-1 average beta coefficients for 39 industries

industry	industry's average value for beta
Nonferrous metals	.99
Energy raw materials	1.22
Construction	1.27
Agriculture, food	.99
Liquor	.89
Tobacco	.80
Apparel	1.27
Forest products, paper	1.16
Containers	1.01
Media	1.39
Chemicals	1.22
Drugs, medicine	1.14
Soaps, cosmetics	1.09
Domestic oil	1.12
International oil	.85
Tires, rubber goods	1.21
Steel	1.02
Producer goods	1.30
Business machines	1.43
Consumer durables	1.44
Motor vehicles	1.27
Aerospace	1.30
Electronics	1.60
Photographic, optical	1.24
Nondurables, entertainment	1.47
Trucking, freight	1.31
Railroads, shipping	1.19
Air transport	1.80
Telephone	.75
Energy, utilities	.60
Retail, general	1.43
Banks	.81
Miscellaneous finance	1.60
Insurance	1.34
Real property	1.70
Business services	1.28
Travel, outdoor recreation	1.66
Gold	.36
Miscellaneous, conglomerate	1.14

Source: Barr Rosenberg and James Guy, "Prediction of Beta from Investment Fundamentals," *Financial Analysts Journal*, July–August 1976, vol. 32, pp. 62–70.

33 years and found the results summarized in Table 15-4, on page 440. King used a mathematical statistics process called multivariate analysis to decompose the causes of price movements in the stocks he studied. Averaged over all the industries he studied, King found that 20 percent of the stock price movements were the result of factors unique to each firm, 31 percent were due to general market factors, 12 percent were the result of *industry factors*, and 37 percent were the result of factors tied to *industry subgroups*. These findings have several implications.

King's findings once again document the importance of industry analysis in explaining stock price movements. But, the fact that slightly over half, on average, of the variance in the stocks' prices was due to firm and market effects is evidence that industry factors alone cannot explain all the price movements of a common stock. The high proportion of each firm's stock price movements determined by factors which are unique to that firm attest to the need for analysis of the individual firms to supplement the industry analysis.

Other research has reported wide variations between the firms in a given industry. Cheney reported a tendency for the firms in nongrowth industries to behave somewhat similarly. On the other hand, Cheney found that firms in growth industries tended to perform dissimilarly.[5] Gaumnitz, Meyers, and Livingston all found strong positive comovement between the stock prices of firms within some industries. In the majority of industries, however, this comovement was only weakly positively correlated.[6] Thus, after reviewing different research findings, the conclusion seems to be that industry analysis is worthwhile, but that it does not obviate the need for analysis of the individual firms within the industry.

17-2 ANALYSIS OF INDUSTRY DATA

The first step of industry analysis is to obtain information and raw data about the industry or industries to be analyzed. Let us begin by considering a few of the most valuable sources of industry information.

17-2.1 some sources of industry information

The Board of Governors of the Federal Reserve System in Washington publishes a monthly magazine entitled *Federal Reserve Bulletin* which can be a helpful source of information. In particular, the pages of statistical appendixes at the end of each month's issue contain valuable industry data under the headings: Nonfinancial Business Activity; Output, Capacity, and Capacity Utilization; Labor Force, Employment, and Unemployment; Industrial Production Indexes and Gross Value; Housing and Construction; Consumer and Producer Prices; and other topics.

Value Line Investment Survey is an investment advisory service, which was described above in Chap. 6, that contains informative industry analysis of numerous different industries. Subscribers to *Value Line* will obtain several industry surveys each month (for example, see Fig. 6-13 on page 163).

Many industries have trade associations which are supported by at least the major firms in the industry. These trade associations usually publish periodicals about the industry, its current problems, and its operating results. The quality and dependability of these periodicals varies from publisher to pub-

[5] Harlan L. Cheney, "The Value of Industry Forecasting as an Aid to Portfolio Management," *Appalachian Financial Review*, vol. 1, 1970, pp. 331–339.

[6] Jack E. Gaumnitz, "The Influence of Industry Factors in Stock Price Movements," paper presented at the Southern Finance Association Meeting, October 1970. Stephen L. Meyers, "A Re-Examination of Market and Industry Factors in Stock Price Movements," *Journal of Finance*, 1973, pp. 695–705. Miles Livingston, "Industry Movements of Common Stocks," *Journal of Finance*, 1977, vol. 32, pp. 861–874.

lisher. However, good trade association journals can furnish insightful material to potential investors.

Standard & Poor's Corporation (S&P hereafter) prepares industry financial index data for dozens of different industries. Utility industry indices (such as telephone companies and electric companies, for example), transportation industry indices (namely, air, railroad, and truckers), financial industry indices (for example, life insurance companies or banks), and industrial industry indices (such as aerospace, drugs, foods, and steel) are compiled. All these data are published by Standard & Poor's in books called the *Analysts Handbook* and *Industry Surveys*.[7] Since these Standard & Poor's publications can be very helpful to industry analysts, they will be discussed in more detail below. In particular, these S&P publications will be discussed because they furnish some of the same kinds of data that the other publications mentioned above contain and because they furnish a concrete example of how industry data can be used.

17-2.2 industry data from two industries

Standard & Poor's maintains about 30 years of annual financial data for each industry index it prepares. Tables 17-2 and 17-3 each show a page of financial data on two separate industries of the type that is found in both S&P's *Analysts Handbook* and its *Industry Survey*. Figure 17-1 is from both the *Analysts Handbook* and *Industry Survey*.

Figure 17-1 illustrates that stock prices for the chemical industry have done worse than the S&P 400 Industrial Stock Price Index over the past few decades. Common stock prices for the radio and television broadcasting industry, in contrast, did about as well as the S&P 400 average during the late 1950s. However, Fig. 17-2 shows that the radio and TV stocks, on average, surpassed the average industrial stock's price during the 1960s and late 1970s. Tables 17-2 and 17-3 contain financial data about the two industries which helps explain the disparity in the performance of these industries' stock prices.

Comparing the sales data in Tables 17-2 and 17-3 reveals that while the radio and television industry is one of growth, which has enjoyed sales increases every year for three decades, the chemical industry has not fared so well. Chemicals are a basic raw material used in the production of numerous other products. Therefore, the chemical industry experiences sales that fluctuate with the business cycle, because consumers postpone some of their purchases during recessions. This reduced consumer spending is reflected in reduced output of numerous products which use chemicals as a raw material. As a result of this cyclical sales pattern, the chemical industry's sales suffer periodic declines during recessions (see the 1958 and 1975 sales declines in Table 17-3 for examples). Furthermore, even in the good years, chemicals sales did not grow as rapidly, on average, as did the sales of radio and television companies.

[7] Standard & Poor's *Industry Survey* is a two-volume set containing basic analysis, current analysis, financial statistics, and graphs of the stock price indices for dozens of major industries. A subscription may be obtained by writing to Standard & Poor's Corporation, 25 Broadway, New York.

TABLE 17-2 S&P's radio and television industry data (per-share data—adjusted to stock price index level; average of stock price indices, 1941–1943 = 10)

	sales	operating profit	profit margin, %	depreciation	income taxes	EARNINGS per share	EARNINGS % of sales	DIVIDENDS per share	DIVIDENDS % of earnings	PRICE-1941–1943 = 10 high	PRICE-1941–1943 = 10 low	PRICE-EARNINGS RATIO high	PRICE-EARNINGS RATIO low	DIVIDEND YIELDS, % high	DIVIDEND YIELDS, % low	BOOK VALUE per share	BOOK VALUE % of return	working capital	capital expenditures
1951	40.75	4.29	10.53	0.56	2.26	1.56	3.83	1.04	66.67	22.11	17.19	14.17	11.02	6.05	4.70	11.32	13.78	9.94	...
1952	53.95	4.93	9.14	0.79	2.45	1.79	3.32	1.04	58.10	25.68	21.57	14.35	12.05	4.82	4.05	12.51	14.31	8.31	4.53
1953	65.68	7.05	10.73	1.10	3.46	2.46	3.75	1.20	48.78	32.39	25.20	13.17	10.24	4.76	3.70	13.00	18.92	10.06	3.27
1954	76.04	7.66	10.07	1.42	3.20	3.10	4.08	1.23	39.68	56.85	27.77	18.34	8.96	4.43	2.16	16.51	18.78	15.49	3.20
1955	85.21	9.73	11.42	1.76	4.44	3.60	4.22	1.51	41.94	64.10	46.57	17.81	12.94	3.24	2.36	18.56	19.40	17.74	1.56
1956	80.27	11.68	14.55	1.75	5.19	4.57	5.69	2.32	50.77	67.93	46.50	14.86	10.18	4.99	3.42	19.42	23.53	16.53	2.35
1957	86.40	13.72	15.88	1.71	6.57	5.59	6.47	2.54	45.44	72.01	49.64	12.88	8.88	5.12	3.53	22.92	24.39	20.47	2.96
1958	94.62	14.96	15.81	2.03	7.22	6.15	6.50	2.67	43.41	80.62	53.04	13.11	8.62	5.03	3.31	26.89	22.87	18.64	5.05
1959	98.92	15.60	15.77	2.31	6.77	6.28	6.35	3.06	48.73	97.86	72.99	15.58	11.62	4.19	3.13	29.69	21.15	21.00	2.58
1960	103.66	14.67	14.15	2.33	6.96	5.92	5.71	3.39	57.26	93.99	77.26	15.88	13.05	4.39	3.61	32.71	18.10	20.91	6.07
1961	105.98	13.72	12.95	2.23	6.39	5.57	5.26	3.47	62.30	93.17	74.58	16.73	13.39	4.65	3.72	34.11	16.33	24.70	2.21
1962	110.99	17.80	16.04	2.21	8.61	7.29	6.57	3.48	47.74	101.01	76.68	13.86	10.52	4.54	3.45	35.85	20.33	26.70	2.87
1963	125.91	23.41	18.59	2.62	10.94	10.11	8.03	3.66	36.20	177.40	100.34	17.55	9.92	3.65	2.06	38.76	26.08	31.09	9.46
1964	145.37	27.01	18.58	2.91	12.08	12.15	8.36	4.81	39.59	207.06	165.77	17.04	13.64	2.90	2.32	43.44	27.97	29.03	16.02
1965	158.04	27.84	17.62	3.50	11.81	12.53	7.93	5.54	44.21	233.77	163.65	18.66	13.06	3.39	2.37	46.36	27.03	28.15	11.97
1966	181.52	32.93	18.14	4.17	13.78	15.20	8.37	5.39	35.46	303.39	221.40	19.96	14.57	2.43	1.78	53.09	28.63	42.57	10.55
1967	179.27	28.99	16.17	5.16	10.42	11.89	6.63	5.85	49.20	362.90	253.97	30.52	21.36	2.30	1.61	32.85	36.19	45.38	9.92
1968	193.27	34.84	18.03	6.03	14.55	12.84	6.64	6.00	46.73	343.79	241.85	26.77	18.84	2.48	1.75	39.85	32.22	46.04	6.84
1969	279.32	40.03	14.33	7.81	15.93	14.35	5.14	6.09	42.44	317.79	229.17	22.15	15.97	2.66	1.92	58.25	24.64	68.15	11.09
1970	288.37	36.43	12.63	7.98	13.28	12.97	4.50	6.58	50.73	262.89	143.08	20.27	11.03	4.60	2.50	65.18	19.90	74.17	11.68
1971	290.85	36.59	12.58	8.10	13.08	13.07	4.49	6.65	50.88	315.02	194.44	24.10	14.88	3.42	2.11	57.78	22.62	68.64	11.76
1972	311.37	44.80	14.39	6.90	17.96	18.99	6.10	6.52	34.33	410.44	308.57	21.61	16.25	2.11	1.59	75.68	25.09	73.67	12.71
1973	336.68	51.60	15.33	7.13	21.67	21.92	6.51	6.90	31.48	369.01	168.78	16.83	7.70	4.09	1.87	85.49	25.64	79.41	9.86
1974	370.57	56.35	15.21	6.94	24.63	23.89	6.45	7.09	29.68	232.48	150.74	9.73	6.31	4.70	3.05	98.81	24.18	84.47	15.60
1975	403.68	57.14	14.15	8.23	23.64	22.97	5.69	7.42	32.30	294.20	159.48	12.81	6.94	4.65	2.52	118.88	19.32	100.98	11.22
1976	480.90	84.13	17.49	8.48	38.69	37.78	7.86	8.79	23.27	373.25	282.40	9.88	7.47	3.11	2.35	145.37	25.99	118.90	14.90
1977	603.47	105.96	17.56	11.88	47.81	46.74	7.75	10.95	23.43	385.41	317.96	8.25	6.80	3.44	2.84	153.59	30.43	120.60	23.78
1978	715.76	126.86	17.72	14.46	55.76	55.26	7.72	13.55	24.52	502.92	325.41	9.10	5.89	4.16	2.69	183.03	30.19	141.53	34.20
1979	812.80	133.85	16.47	16.58	56.54	62.11	7.64	15.73	25.33	517.22	407.54	8.33	6.56	3.86	3.04	210.63	29.49	145.80	48.91
1980	891.43	131.77	14.78	18.54	55.25	62.48	7.01	17.88	28.62	567.98	403.37	9.09	6.46	4.43	3.15	242.68	25.75	160.52	58.18
1981	945.29	144.00	15.23	25.70	55.02	65.33	6.91	18.29	28.00	640.61	494.02	9.81	7.56	3.70	2.86	270.12	24.19	165.12	58.29

Stock price indices for this group extend back to 1941.
* American Broadcasting (5-14-69) (9-8-48 to 5-22-51)
* CBS Inc. (formerly Columbia Broadcasting) (1-8-41)
* Capital Cities Communications (formerly Capital Cities Broadcasting) (10-12-66)
* Cox Broadcasting (7-19-67)
* Metromedia (9-11-63)
* Taft Broadcasting (10-31-62)
American Broadcasting (9-8-48 to 5-22-51)
Storer Broadcasting (11-28-56 to 10-5-66)

Source: Standard & Poor's *Analysts Handbook*, 1982 annual edition, p. 61.

TABLE 17-3 S&P's chemical industry data (per share data—adjusted to stock price index level; average of stock price indices, 1941–1943 = 10)

	sales	operating profit	profit margin, %	depreciation	income taxes	EARNINGS per share	EARNINGS % of sales	DIVIDENDS per share	DIVIDENDS % of earnings	PRICE 1941–1943 = 10 high	PRICE 1941–1943 = 10 low	PRICE-EARNINGS RATIO high	PRICE-EARNINGS RATIO low	DIVIDEND YIELDS, % high	DIVIDEND YIELDS, % low	BOOK VALUE per share	BOOK VALUE % of return	working capital	capital expenditures
1951	12.47	3.93	31.52	0.61	2.29	1.33	10.67	0.90	67.67	25.84	20.90	19.43	15.71	4.31	3.48	7.95	16.73	3.21	1.63
1952	12.53	3.58	28.57	0.74	1.84	1.26	10.06	0.91	72.22	25.94	22.05	20.59	17.50	4.13	3.51	8.69	14.50	4.01	1.85
1953	13.84	3.92	28.32	0.94	1.88	1.34	9.68	0.95	70.90	26.79	23.35	19.99	17.43	4.07	3.55	9.31	14.39	4.40	1.74
1954	13.79	3.73	27.05	1.06	1.35	1.60	11.60	1.16	72.50	37.44	26.23	23.40	16.39	4.42	3.10	9.91	16.15	4.82	1.36
1955	16.14	4.77	29.55	1.17	1.82	2.13	13.20	1.39	65.26	50.25	35.54	23.59	16.69	3.91	2.77	11.15	19.10	5.13	1.21
1956	16.83	4.44	26.38	1.22	1.62	1.98	11.76	1.38	69.70	52.30	41.55	26.41	20.98	3.32	2.64	12.29	16.11	5.01	1.95
1957	17.38	4.44	25.55	1.28	1.59	1.95	11.22	1.43	73.33	47.21	37.97	24.21	19.47	3.77	3.03	13.11	14.87	5.18	2.36
1958	16.89	4.01	23.74	1.36	1.25	1.69	10.01	1.36	80.47	49.76	38.27	29.44	22.64	3.55	2.73	13.81	12.24	5.14	1.79
1959	19.34	5.16	26.68	1.40	1.90	2.23	11.53	1.47	65.92	61.60	48.57	27.62	21.78	3.03	2.39	14.75	15.12	5.76	1.62
1960	19.97	4.82	24.14	1.50	1.65	2.08	10.42	1.46	70.19	60.80	44.15	29.23	21.23	3.31	2.40	15.79	13.17	5.67	2.29
1961	20.67	4.96	24.00	1.66	1.64	2.08	10.06	1.55	74.52	56.69	47.55	27.25	22.86	3.26	2.73	16.66	12.48	5.68	2.17
1962	23.55	5.92	25.14	1.88	2.01	2.42	10.28	1.67	69.01	54.31	39.16	22.44	16.18	4.26	3.07	17.34	13.96	6.75	2.33
1963	26.69	6.60	24.73	2.10	2.22	2.75	10.30	1.83	66.55	62.36	52.50	22.68	19.09	3.49	2.93	18.61	14.78	7.77	2.71
1964	31.88	7.99	25.06	2.41	2.58	3.34	10.48	1.99	59.58	72.87	62.96	21.82	18.85	3.16	2.73	20.09	16.63	8.99	3.85
1965	34.52	8.59	24.88	2.64	2.55	3.41	9.88	1.89	55.43	76.78	68.78	22.52	20.17	2.75	2.46	21.94	15.54	9.90	4.88
1966	38.18	8.97	23.49	2.88	2.58	3.50	9.17	1.94	55.43	75.38	49.82	21.54	14.23	3.89	2.57	23.51	14.89	9.93	5.41
1967	38.63	8.12	21.02	3.15	1.99	2.84	7.35	1.87	65.85	60.53	50.87	21.31	17.91	3.68	3.09	24.40	11.64	10.21	5.07
1968	43.96	9.37	21.31	3.51	2.56	3.16	7.19	2.00	63.29	61.43	50.20	19.44	15.89	3.98	3.26	26.25	12.04	11.21	4.59
1969	47.18	9.55	20.24	3.70	2.52	3.17	6.72	1.94	61.20	57.95	40.08	18.28	12.64	4.84	3.35	27.17	11.67	11.79	5.40
1970	47.51	8.89	18.71	3.90	1.95	2.70	5.68	1.90	70.37	47.11	36.93	17.45	13.68	5.14	4.03	27.77	9.72	11.75	5.95

1971	49.55	9.36	18.89	3.99	2.07	2.93	5.91	1.90	64.85	58.71	47.56	20.04	16.23	3.99	3.24	29.48	9.94	12.97	5.25
1972	54.18	10.77	19.88	4.15	2.66	3.61	6.66	1.97	54.57	67.13	56.40	18.60	15.62	3.49	2.93	30.64	11.78	14.51	5.00
1973	64.00	13.54	21.16	4.23	3.91	5.10	7.97	2.08	40.78	72.95	55.46	14.30	10.87	3.75	2.85	33.84	15.07	16.39	6.39
1974	85.47	17.01	19.90	4.76	5.10	6.79	7.94	2.21	32.55	68.80	47.20	10.13	6.95	4.68	3.21	38.34	17.71	18.71	10.26
1975	80.33	15.24	18.97	4.92	4.18	5.51	6.86	2.18	39.56	74.63	48.76	13.54	8.85	4.47	2.92	39.26	14.03	17.59	11.95
1976	91.16	17.47	19.17	5.49	4.52	6.59	7.23	2.48	37.63	89.70	67.27	13.61	10.21	3.69	2.76	43.27	15.23	18.93	12.97
1977	101.01	18.33	18.15	6.37	4.31	6.16	6.10	2.78	45.13	72.45	52.70	11.76	8.56	5.28	3.84	46.55	13.23	19.77	12.10
1978	112.76	20.82	18.46	7.21	5.07	7.16	6.35	3.10	43.30	59.62	46.05	8.33	6.43	6.73	5.20	50.65	14.14	22.27	12.13
1979	129.30	22.59	17.47	7.51	5.13	9.17	7.09	3.38	36.86	61.04	51.75	6.66	5.64	6.53	5.54	54.58	16.80	24.8	12.48
1980	140.37	20.64	14.70	7.52	4.03	8.07	5.75	3.56	44.11	64.88	49.70	8.04	6.16	7.16	5.49	60.53	13.33	25.83	15.11
1981	143.65	21.09	14.68	7.72	4.78	7.71	5.37	3.37	43.71	73.84	52.81	9.58	6.85	6.38	4.56	65.84	11.71	29.45	15.26

Stock price indices for this group extend back to 1926.

* Dow Chemical (7-30-47)
* du Pont de Nemours (1-16-35)
* Hercules Inc. (9-17-30)
* Monsanto Co. (1-16-35)
* Stauffer Chemical Co. (7-25-79)
* Union Carbide Co. (12-31-25)

Airco Inc. (Formerly Air Reduction) (1-2-18 to 2-5-75)

Allied Chemical Corp. (1-2-18 to 7-25-79)

American Cyanamid (9-17-30 to 7-25-79)

American Potash & Chemical (2-14-62 to 1-3-68)

Atlas Powder (1-16-35 to 7-23-47)

Chemetron Corp. (Formerly Nat'l Cylinder Gas) (4-16-58 to 2-5-75)

Columbian Carbon (12-31-25 to 2-7-62)

Commercial Solvents (12-31-25 to 6-16-65)

GAF Corp. (Formerly General Aniline & Film) (6-16-65 to 2-5-75)

Hooker Chemical (1-3-68 to 7-30-68)

Olin Corp. (1-2-18 to 2-5-75) (Formerly Olin-Mathieson Chemical)

United Carbon (1-16-35 to 7-23-47)

U.S. Industrial Chemicals (5-11-38 to 8-1-51)

Source: Standard & Poor's *Analysts Handbook,* 1982 annual edition, p. 16.

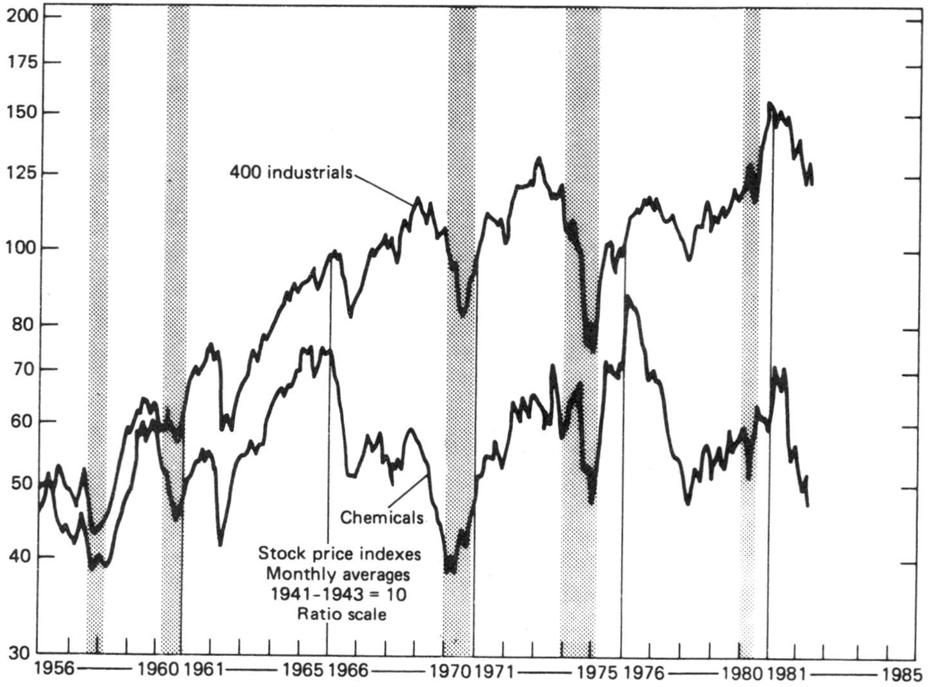

FIGURE 17-1 graph of S&P's chemical industry stocks price index.

FIGURE 17-2 graph of S&P's radio and TV industry stocks price index.

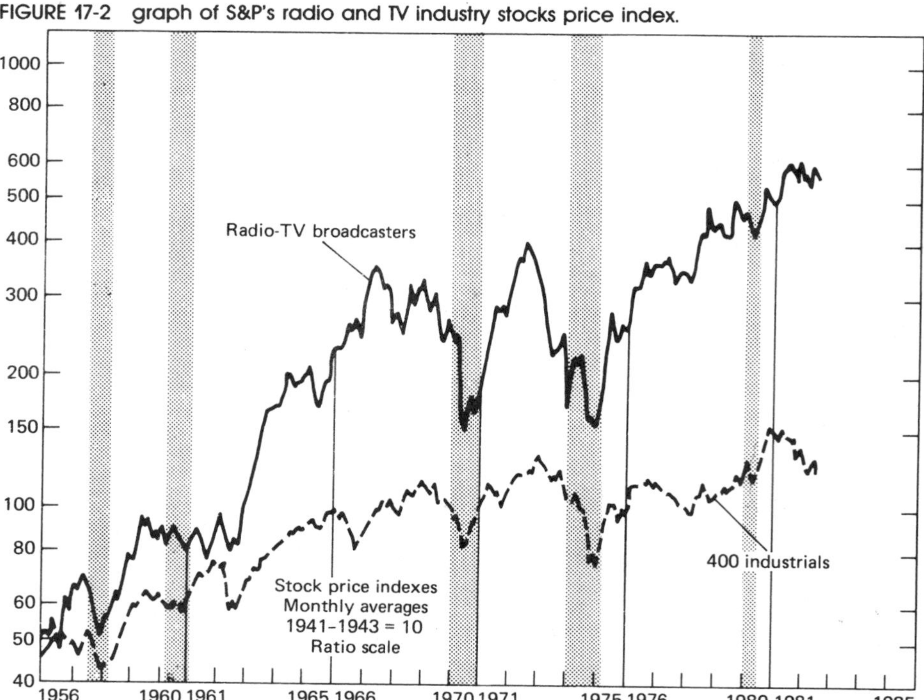

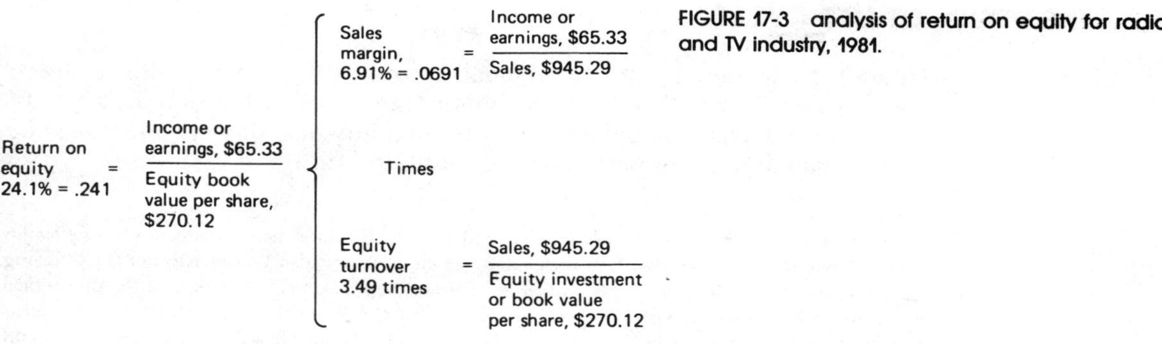

FIGURE 17-3 analysis of return on equity for radio and TV industry, 1981.

The annual financial data in Tables 17-2 and 17-3 indicate that, in addition to slower and more erratic sales growth, the chemical industry suffered from sagging profit margins. The average annual profit margins in the chemical industry were gradually shrinking while the radio and TV profit margins were growing over the past few decades.

The data in Tables 17-2 and 17-3 may be useful for other types of financial analysis of an industry. Figure 17-3 illustrates the algebraic and financial relationships between several well-known financial ratios. S&P's 1981 data for the chemical industry and for the radio and television industry have been inserted into this analytical framework to gain further insights into the profitability of these industries. (This type of analysis is equally useful for the analysis of individual firms.)

The data in Figs. 17-3 and 17-4 analyze how the radio and television industry earned more than twice as much return on the owners' equity, on average, in 1981 as did the chemical industry. The analysis goes on to reveal that this higher rate of profitability was the product of both higher sales profit margins and higher equity turnover for the radio and television industry.

In addition to the financial facts revealed in Figs. 17-1, 17-2, 17-3, and 17-4 and also Tables 17-2 and 17-3, the *Industry Surveys* contain more information of value to investment analysts. Forecasts of the future growth prospects for each industry and financial data about every individual company which is used to compile the industry index data are presented. Such reports provide potential investors with a quick and easy source of investment information about every major domestic industry in the United States.

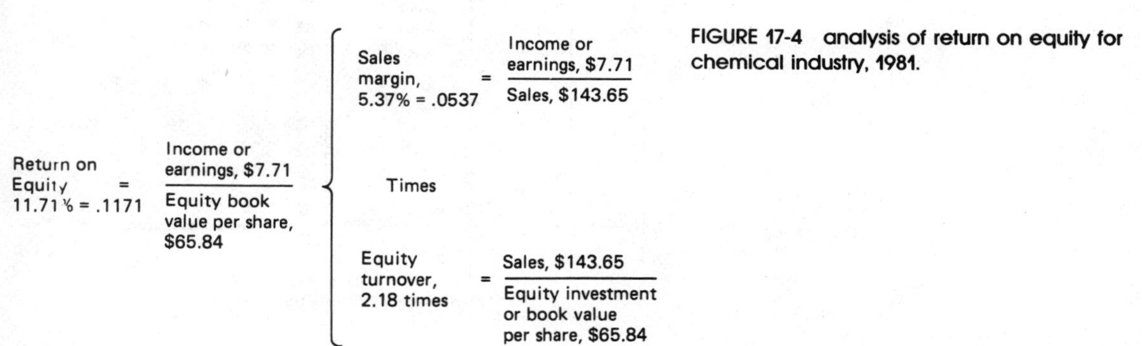

FIGURE 17-4 analysis of return on equity for chemical industry, 1981.

17-3 THE PRODUCT LIFE CYCLE

In addition to figures and facts about an industry, such as those reviewed above in Sec. 17-2, a theoretical economic framework can enrich the analysis. Figure 17-5 depicts the industry (or product) life cycle theory, which may be useful in analyzing the past and forecasting the future of an industry.[8]

[8] The industry life cycle theory is discussed in Sam R. Goodman, *Techniques of Profitability Analysis,* Wiley, New York, 1970; in particular, see chap. 4. See also Walter Kiechel III, "Playing by the Rules of the Corporate Strategy Game," *Fortune,* Sept. 24, 1979, for some of the theoretical apparatus which underlies the life cycle theory. Also see Simon S. Kuznets, *Modern Economic Growth,* Yale University Press, New Haven, 1966. See also Julius Grodinsky, *Investments,* Ronald Press, New York, 1953.

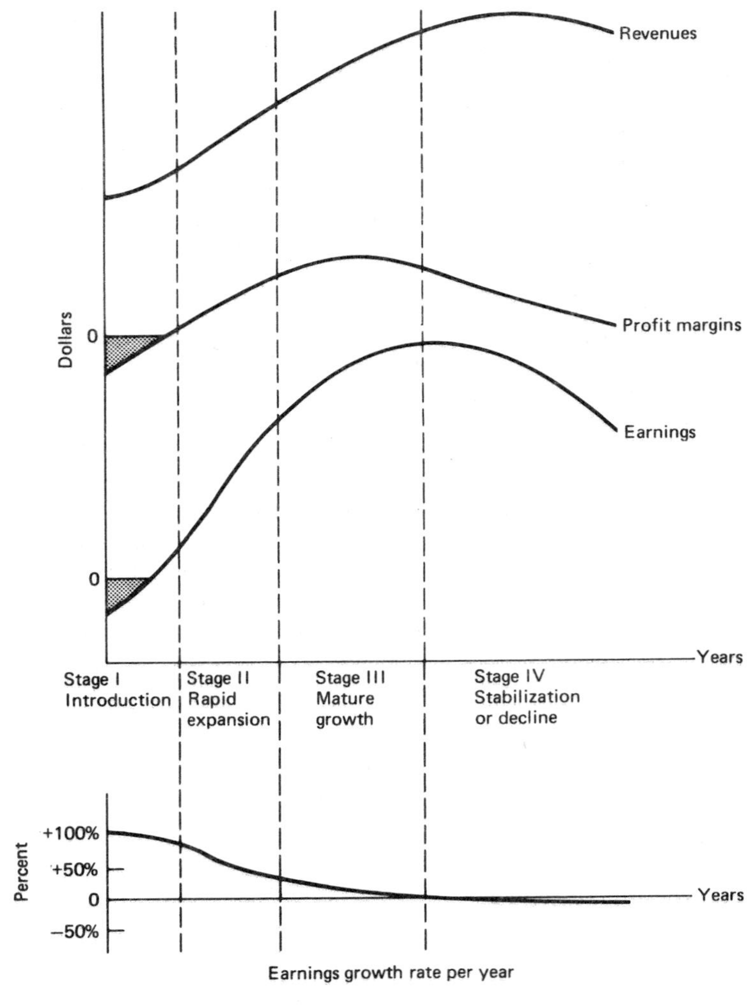

FIGURE 17-5 the life cycle of products and their industry.

The product life cycle curves in Fig. 17-5 pass through four phases of development as the industry grows older.

STAGE ONE: INTRODUCTION In this beginning phase the product or industry starts with sales of zero and operates at a loss as initial sales are obtained. If the product survives and continues to grow, its new industry may be recognized by the best security analysts; such industries are sometimes called an *emerging growth industry* toward the end of stage one.

STAGE TWO: RAPID EXPANSION Sales grow rapidly, and consistent annual profits usually begin to emerge during the second stage of a product's development. In spite of their new-found profitability, however, firms in this second stage must reinvest much of their earnings and also borrow heavily in order to finance the new plant, equipment, inventory, and accounts receivable needed to sustain this period of rapid growth. Solvency is difficult to maintain as a firm expands rapidly.

STAGE THREE: MATURE GROWTH Following years of rapid growth, during which the firms in an industry tend to acquire stable market shares, come years of slower growth which comprise the third stage. Mature growth companies may be large corporations, they may begin to pay consistent cash dividends, and they repay any excessive debt they acquired during their period of rapid expansion. Profit margins stated as a percent of sales typically start to shrink because of price competition during the third stage, but annual dollar profits continue to grow, although at a slower rate.

STAGE FOUR: STABILIZATION OR DECLINE When a product reaches stage four of its life cycle, unit sales at both the level of the individual firms and for the aggregate industry stabilize—unit sales may even decline if the product becomes obsolete. However, dollar sales and dollar profits may continue to grow slowly at a rate about equal to the rate of inflation. Firms in this fourth stage are usually very liquid but have few profitable investment opportunities left within the firms. Such stable firms must typically diversify into new fields of endeavor in order to sustain the growth of the corporation. The automobile is an example of a product in its fourth stage.

The life cycle theory is better for explaining the behavior of industries than it is for explaining the behavior of individual firms because many firms fall into bankruptcy during stages one and two. Even in those cases where it is applicable, the life cycle theory can be difficult to interpret because there are no set time dimensions on a product's life. For instance, cameras that develop pictures internally (such as the Polaroid) and most fad goods reach stage four of their life cycles in a fraction of the number of years it took for the automobile and the printing industries to mature and stabilize. In spite of these difficulties, the theory can still yield valuable insights for some industries.

The life cycle theory can be particularly valuable to the analyst who is endeavoring to estimate *growth rates* in sales, earnings, and/or dividends. After an industry is successfully categorized into one of the four stages, the theory suggests rough values for the industry's growth and goes on to suggest whether these growth rates should be increasing or slowing from their previous values. Considering the importance and difficulty of forecasting growth, a theory that may yield good insights is an important tool for the industry analyst.

17-4 FORECASTING

For short-term forecasts of 1 year or less into the future, forecasts can often be assembled from information gained in discussions with the management of different firms in an industry and from publicly available information (such as an article from a good trade association journal or other magazine). Scientific forecasting techniques which are useful for longer-run projections of various kinds are explored below.

17-4.1 measuring past growth

Before future growth rate is forecast, it is usually necessary to start by considering historical data. A common method of analyzing historical data is to fit a line through successive values of historical data on semilogarithmic graph paper. Consider the earnings data shown in Table 17-4.

The arithmetic graph in Fig. 17-6 seems to indicate that the growth rates of the earnings in Industries A and B are about equal, since the slopes of the trend lines that fit through the points are equal. However, the semilogarithmic graph in Fig. 17-7 shows that earnings of Industry B are growing much faster (100 percent in 5 years) than those of Industry A (which increased only 25 percent in 5 years). This is because the slope of a line on the semilog paper represents the percentage increase (that is, the growth rate per year) instead of merely a fixed dollar increase per period. A constant dollar increase per period implies a declining growth rate. The average growth rate in percentage form is more useful than the average dollar growth per period because growth rates measured in percentages are not distorted by changes in the dollar level. Thus, semilogarithmic time series graphs such as the one in Fig. 17-7 are preferable.

After a straight trend line has been fit through 5 or 10 years of data points plotted on semilog paper (as shown in Fig. 17-7), the growth rate per period may be estimated. The growth rate is determined from the numerical value at

TABLE 17-4 earnings data for hypothetical Industries A and B, in millions

year	earnings for A, $	earnings for B, $	years	status
19X6	4.00	1.00	0	Known
19X7	4.10	1.10	1	Known
19X8	4.25	1.30	2	Known
19X9	4.45	1.50	3	Known
19X0	4.75	1.90	4	Known
19X1	5.00	2.00	5	Known
19X2	?	?	6	Unknown
19X3	?	?	7	Unknown
19X4	?	?	8	Unknown

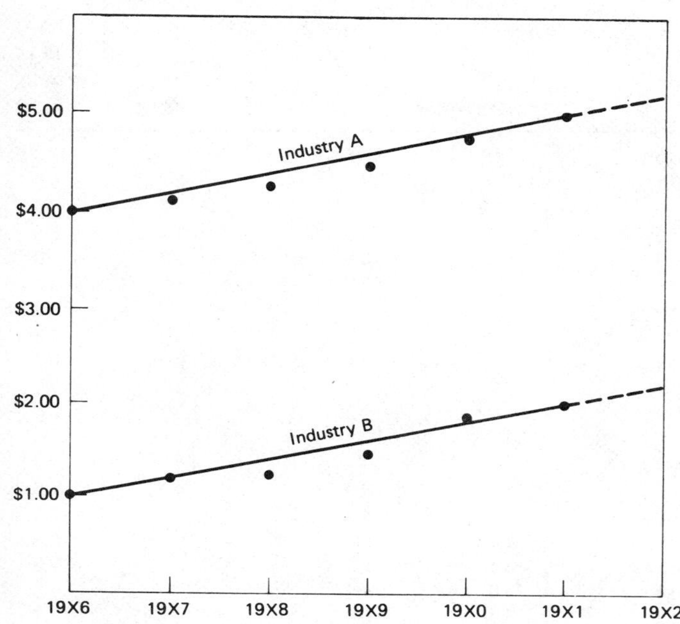

FIGURE 17-6 time-series graph of earnings per share on arithmetic graph paper.

the top and bottom ends of the historical trend line. The relation between a constant growth rate, denoted g, and the ratio of the ending value of the trend line over the beginning value is given in Eq. (17-1*a*).

$$(1 + g)^t = \frac{V_t}{V_0} = \frac{\text{ending value after } t \text{ periods}}{\text{beginning value}} \tag{17-1a}$$

Table 17-5 shows the ratios of ending values, denoted V_t, over beginning values, denoted V_0, of a trend line which has grown at a constant growth rate for 5, 10, 20, or 40 years. To determine an annual growth rate in Industry B's earnings, for example, the end points of its trend line in Fig. 17-6 are first observed to be $V_0 = \$1$ and $V_5 = \$2$ earnings. Substituting these values into Eq. (17-1*a*) yields the values shown in Eq. (17-1*b*).

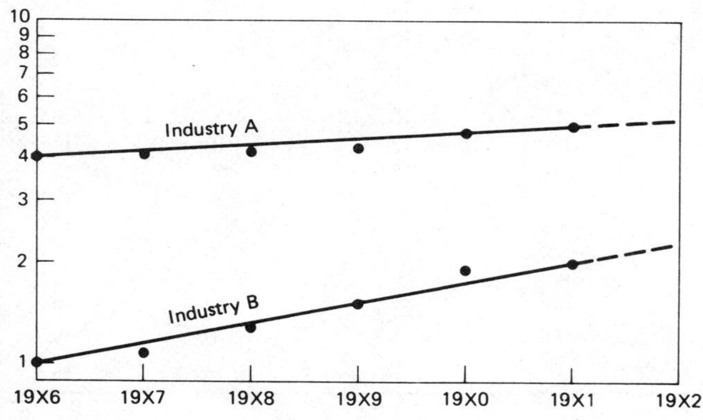

FIGURE 17-7 time-series graph of earnings per share on semilogarithmic graph paper.

TABLE 17-5 the effects of different growth rates over 5, 10, 20, and 40 years of constant growth

5 YEARS		10 YEARS		20 YEARS		40 YEARS*	
$(1+g)^5 = V_5/V_0$	rate of growth, g	$(1+g)^{10} = V_{10}/V_0$	rate of growth, g	$(1+g)^{20} = V_{20}/V_0$	rate of growth, g	$(1+g)^{40} = V_{40}/V_0$	rate of growth, g
.01	−60.2%	.01	−36.9%	.01	−20.6%	.01	−10.9%
.02	−54.3	.02	−32.4	.02	−17.8	.02	−9.3
.03	−50.4	.03	−29.6	.03	−16.1	.05	−7.2
.04	−47.5	.04	−27.5	.05	−13.9	.1	−5.6
.05	−45.1	.05	−25.9	.1	−10.9	.2	−4.0
.07	−41.2	.1	−20.6	.2	−7.7	.3	−3.0
.1	−36.9	.2	−14.9	.3	−5.8	.4	−2.3
.2	−27.5	.3	−11.3	.4	−4.5	.6	−1.3
.3	−21.4	.4	−8.8	.5	−3.4	1.0	0.0
.4	−16.7	.5	−6.7	.7	−1.8	1.5	1.0
.5	−12.9	.6	−5.0	.9	−0.5	2.2	2.0
.6	−9.7	.7	−3.5	1.1	0.5	3.2	3.0
.7	−6.9	.8	−2.2	1.4	1.7	4.6	3.9
.8	−4.4	.9	−1.0	1.8	3.0	6.4	4.8
.9	−2.1	1.1	1.0	2.3	4.3	8.6	5.5
1.0	0	1.3	2.7	2.8	5.3	12.0	6.4
1.1	1.9	1.5	4.1	3.4	6.3	15.	7.0
1.3	5.4	1.8	6.1	4.0	7.2	18.	7.5
1.4	7.0	2.0	7.2	4.7	8.0	22.	8.1
1.6	9.9	2.2	8.2	5.4	8.8	25.	8.4
1.7	11.2	2.4	9.1	5.9	9.3	28.	8.7
1.8	12.5	2.6	10.0	6.4	9.7	31.	9.0
1.9	13.7	2.7	10.4	6.8	10.1	34.	9.2
2.0	14.9	2.8	10.8	7.0	10.2	35.	9.3
2.1	16.0	2.9	11.2	7.1	10.3	36.	9.4
2.2	17.1	3.0	11.6	7.2	10.4	37.	9.5
2.3	18.1	3.1	12.0	7.3	10.5	38.	9.5
2.4	19.1	3.2	12.3	7.4	10.5	39.	9.6
2.5	20.1	3.3	12.7	7.6	10.7	40.	9.7
2.6	21.1	3.4	13.0	7.9	10.9	42.	9.8
2.7	22.0	3.5	13.3	8.3	11.2	44.	9.9
2.8	22.9	3.7	14.0	8.8	11.5	48.	10.2
2.9	23.7	4.0	14.9	9.4	11.9	53.	10.5
3.0	24.6	4.3	15.7	11.	12.7	60.	10.8
3.2	26.2	4.8	17.0	12.	13.2	70.	11.2
3.6	29.2	5.3	18.1	13.	13.7	80.	11.6
4.1	32.6	6.0	19.6	14.	14.1	90.	11.9
4.6	35.7	6.9	21.3	15.	14.5	100.	12.2
5.3	39.6	7.9	23.0	17.	15.2	120.	12.7
6.2	44.0	9.2	24.8	20.	16.2	150.	13.4
7.2	48.4	11.	27.1	22.	16.7	200.	14.2
8.6	53.8	13.	29.2	26.	17.7	250.	14.8
11.0	61.5	16.	32.0	30.	18.5	300.	15.4
13.0	67.0	19.	34.2	35.	19.5	350.	15.8
16.0	74.1	23.	36.8	42.	20.5	400.	16.2
19.0	80.2	29.	40.0	50.	21.6	500.	16.8
24.0	88.8	36.	43.1	60.	22.7	700.	17.8
30.0	97.4	46.	46.6	73.	23.9	1,000.	18.9
38.0	107.0	58.	50.1	90.	25.2	1,300.	19.7
49.0	117.8	75.	54.0	111.	26.6	1,715.	20.5

* The 40-year growth rate is actually for $39\frac{11}{12}$ years.

Source: L. Fisher and T. Lorie, "Some Studies of Variability of Returns on Investments in Common Stock," *Journal of Business*, April 1970, p. 103.

$$(1 + g)^t = 2.0 = \frac{\$2}{\$1} = \frac{V_5}{V_0} \tag{17-1b}$$

Looking up the ratio of $V_t/V_0 = 2.0$ for a 5-year period in Table 17-5 shows that $g = 14.9$ percent. That is, \$1 growing at a constant rate of 14.9 percent for 5 years will become \$2.

To solve for the growth rate for Industry A for 5 years, the ratio $V_5/V_0 = \$5/\$4 = 1.25$ is observed to be between the values 1.1 and 1.3 in Table 17-5. Interpolating between the growth rates associated with 1.1 and 1.3 yields a growth rate, denoted g, of approximately 4.5 percent per year. Thus, Industry A's earnings grew at about 4.5 percent per annum while Industry B's earnings grew at about 15 percent per year over the 5-year period.[9]

17-4.2 forecasting earnings

Once the growth trend has been satisfactorily estimated, future values of earnings (or sales or many other economic quantities) may be forecasted. First, the earnings trend line on semilog paper may be extrapolated as shown by the dotted segment in Fig. 17-7. If the points do not "fit" fairly closely on the trend line, it may be difficult to determine its slope. In this case a larger sample (change from annual to quarterly data and/or increase in the sample period) may help; or Eq. (17-2) may be used.

$$e_t = (1 + g)^t e_o \tag{17-2}$$

where

e_t = earnings per share at period t

These methods should be satisfactory for short forecasts of a few years into the future if no change in the firm's growth rate is anticipated.

17-4.3 forecasting the growth rate

Forecasting earnings or any other economic variable may not be as simple as indicated in the preceding paragraph if the rate of growth is expected to change. The rate of growth may change for several reasons. Products have life cycles. Figure 17-5 shows how earnings growth might behave over the life cycle of a product. Note that the growth rate is depicted as decreasing each year. Since the growth rate is such an important factor in determining the stock prices, not only its size but its duration must be estimated.[10]

If a firm's managers are aggressive and farsighted, they will phase out products which are becoming obsolete and phase in new products which they have developed through a continuing research and development program. In this manner a firm could grow indefinitely. However, managers frequently become tied to their products and the company dies as its original product becomes outdated.

[9] Fitting a trend line as described above is equivalent to taking the logarithm of n different periods' earnings and using regression analysis to estimate the following equation

$$e_t = e_0(1 + g)^t \qquad \text{for } t = 1, 2, \ldots, n \text{ periods}$$

This equation is linear in the logarithms, and t is the independent variable in the regression. Taking the antilog of the regression slope coefficient will yield an unbiased estimate of the $(1 + g)$ quantity. Negative earnings present a numerical problem.

[10] C. C. Holt, "The Influence of Growth Duration on Share Prices," *Journal of Finance*, September 1962, pp. 465–475.

Sometimes patents expire, competition within an industry becomes more aggressive because foreign firms begin to compete, economically depressed periods occur, or other factors cause growth rates to drop. One of the purposes of industry analysis is to anticipate these factors accurately in order to make a good estimate of the growth rate for either the industry as a whole or firms within the industry. In order to best stay abreast of this type of information, professional fundamental security analysts typically specialize in one industry. They attend trade conventions for that industry, get to know each firm's products, meet with various firms' managers, follow news reports about any legislation which may affect the industry, and take other steps to ensure that they constantly have up-to-date estimates of the growth rates for the industry. For shorter-range forecasts the earnings figure suggested by Eq. (17-2) is merely adjusted to reflect things which can cause earnings to vary from their long-run trend in the short run.

17-5 CHAPTER SUMMARY—INDUSTRY ANALYSIS

It is better to invest in a growth industry than in a declining industry. As a result, industry analysis can be an important step in the analysis of individual securities.

Each industry tends to have unique risk and return characteristics which result from the most efficient economic patterns that have been developed for the production of that industry's product. Economic competition between the firms in any given industry usually forces them all to adopt the one most efficient production method, and this is the reason why all firms in a given industry tend to have similar risk and return characteristics.

Significant differences exist between the risk and return of various industries because of differing degrees of foreign competition which each industry may face, different labor-capital ratios which may be most economic for the manufacture of each industry's product, differences in the stage of the life cycle of each industry's product, and other factors. These differences between the industries' average risk and return characteristics are what make industry analysis worthwhile to perform.

Although all the firms in most industries tend to be somewhat similar, they are not homogeneous. Differences in the quality of similar products, the adeptness of the different firms' managements, the aggressiveness of each firm's sales efforts, differences in the sizes of the competing firms, differences in the legal patents held by each firm, and other factors can result in significant variations among firms which are all competing in an industry to manufacture a similar product. As a result of these differences in competing firms, it is necessary to supplement industry analysis with company analysis.

QUESTIONS

17-1. Define the word *industry*. Why is a knowledge of an industry's product important to the industry analyst?

17-2. Assume that after studying all the firms in a particular industry you become aware that they all perform almost identically to that industry's average rate of return. What does this imply about the importance of industry analysis for that industry? What does it imply about analysis of the individual firms in the industry?

17-3. "Although the risk and return statistics of individual firms vary, there are no significant differences between the average risk and return statistics of the different industries." Is this statement true, false, or uncertain? Explain.

17-4. Select two industries from the Standard & Poor's *Analysts Handbook* which are essentially different (such as the chemical industry and the radio and TV industry). Explain what economic data you would use to explain the sales and profits of these two different industries.

17-5. Categorize which stage of their product's life cycle the following industries are in, in your opinion. Explain. (*a*) Radio and television industry, (*b*) mainframe computers, (*c*) personal computers, (*d*) machine tools, (*e*) fast-food restaurants.

17-6. Consider the product life cycle theory. How can the theory be used by the industry analyst? How can this theory be used by the fundamental security analyst in analyzing individual securities?

17-7. How would you forecast the future of a conglomerate corporation?

17-8. Answer the following questions about the product life cycle theory. (*a*) At which stage in an industry's life cycle is it most desirable to invest? (*b*) Discuss the possible limitations of the theory. (*c*) Why do most industries tend to grow at a decreasing rate?

SELECTED REFERENCES

Fabozzi, Frank J., and J. C. Francis, "Industry Effects and the Determinants of Risk," *The Quarterly Review of Economics and Business,* Autumn 1979, vol. 19, no. 3, pp. 61–74. This statistical investigation of systematic risk determinants documents significant industry differences in risk levels.

Goodman, Sam R., *Techniques of Profitability Analysis,* Wiley, New York, 1970. The book discusses various economic theories that relate to industrial organization. In particular, see chap. 4 on product life cycle theory.

King, B. J., "Market and Industry Factors in Stock Price Behavior," *Journal of Business,* January 1966, pp. 139–190. This sophisticated analysis of stock price movements documents the important influence of industry factors in the determination of stock market prices.

part five

SECURITY PRICE MOVEMENTS

There are two schools of thought about security price movements. Chapters 18 and 19 review these two viewpoints.

CHAPTER 18—*technical analysis* shows graphs of stock prices and discusses the patterns in these graphs.

CHAPTER 19—*security price movements* reviews economic and statistical analysis of security price movements.

CHAPTER 18 technical analysis

There are two main approaches to analyzing securities: technical analysis and fundamental analysis. This chapter introduces technical analysis.

A technical analyst is a particular kind of security analyst who prefers not to work through the infinite number of fundamental facts about the issuing corporation, such as the earnings of a company and its competitive products, or about forthcoming legislation which may affect the firm. Instead, technical analysts search for a quick-and-easy summary of these innumerable fundamental facts by studying the way that the market price of a security behaves. Over the past decades technical analysts almost totally focused their attention on *charts* of security market prices and a few related summary statistics about security trading. That is, technical analysts prepared and studied charts of various financial variables in order to make forecasts about security prices. Today, however, technical analysis includes the work of some nonchartists who use quantitative rather than graphical tools.[1] Dozens of different techniques are used by professional technical analysts. In this chapter, a few of the more prominent technical analysis tools are explained. Before the tools of technical analysis are examined, however, concepts which are at the core of all technical analysis are reviewed.

18-1 THE THEORY OF TECHNICAL ANALYSIS

Technical analysis is based on the widely accepted premise that security prices are determined by the supply of and the demand for securities. The tools of technical analysis are therefore designed to measure supply and demand.

[1] One of the modern technicians is R. A. Levy, President, Computer Directions Advisors, Inc., Silver Spring, Md. Levy has stated his position in various articles and in a book: R. L. Levy, "Conceptual Foundations of Technical Analysis," *Financial Analysts Journal*, July–August 1966,

Typically, technical analysts record historical financial data on charts, study these charts in an effort to find meaningful *patterns*, and use these patterns to predict future prices. Some charting techniques are used to predict the movements of a single security, some are used to predict movements of a market index, and some are used to predict both the action of individual securities and the market action.

Edwards and Magee[2] articulated the basic assumptions underlying technical analysis as follows:

1. Market value is determined solely by the interaction of supply and demand.
2. Supply and demand are governed by numerous factors, both rational and irrational.
3. In disregard of minor fluctuations in the market, stock prices tend to move in trends which persist for an appreciable length of time.
4. Changes in trend are caused by shifts in supply and demand.
5. Shifts in supply and demand, no matter why they occur, can be detected sooner or later in charts of market action.
6. Some chart patterns tend to repeat themselves.

In essence, technical analysts believe that past patterns of market action will recur in the future and can therefore be used for predictive purposes.

Chapters 15, 16, and 17 explained how fundamental analysts estimate the intrinsic *value* of a security. Technical analysts, on the other hand, seek to estimate security *prices* rather than values; that is, they try to forecast short-run shifts in supply and demand which will affect the market price of one or more securities. They tend to ignore factors such as the firms' risks and earnings growth in favor of various barometers of supply and demand that they have devised.

One text[3] on technical analysis lyrically asserts that

> It is futile to assign an intrinsic value to a stock certificate. One share of United States Steel, for example, was worth $261 in the early fall of 1929, but you could buy it for only $22 in June 1932. By March 1937, it was selling for $126 and just one year later for $38. . . . This sort of thing, this wide divergence between presumed value and actual value, is not the exception; it is the rule; it is going on all the time. The fact is that the real value of a share of U.S. Steel common is determined at any given time solely, definitely and inexorably by supply and demand, which are accurately reflected in the transactions consummated on the floor of the . . . Exchange.
>
> Of course, the statistics which the fundamentalists study play a part in the supply and demand equation—that is freely admitted. But there are many other factors affecting it. The market price reflects not only the differing fears and guesses and

---

p. 83; *The Relative Strength Concept of Common Stock Forecasting,* Investors Intelligence, Larchmont, N.Y., 1968). *Fortune* magazine reported that Levy's own work indicated that many technical analysis tools of the traditional charting type were worthless: *Fortune,* September 1970, p. 188.

[2] R. D. Edwards and John Magee, Jr., *Technical Analysis of Stock Trends,* 4th ed., Magee, Springfield, Mass, 1958, p. 86.

[3] R. D. Edwards and John Magee, Jr., *Technical Analysis of Stock Trends,* 4th ed., Magee, Springfield, Mass., 1958, p. 3.

> moods, rational and irrational, of hundreds of potential buyers and sellers, as well as their needs and their resources—in total, factors which defy analysis and for which no statistics are obtainable, but which are nevertheless all synthesized, weighted and finally expressed in one precise figure at which a buyer and seller get together and make a deal (through their agents, their respective brokers). This is the only figure that counts.
>
> In brief, the going price as established by the market itself comprehends all the fundamental information which the statistical analyst can hope to learn (plus some which is perhaps secret to him, known only to a few insiders) and much else besides of equal or even greater importance.

The preceding quotation makes some strong assertions, stresses the impact of the investor emotion in an unscientific manner, and is an extremely flattering interpretation of one set of facts; but it does convey the spirit of technical analysis.

In defending their practices, most technical analysts do not accuse fundamental analysts of being illogical or conceptually in error. In fact, many technical analysts would agree with fundamental analysts that security prices do fluctuate around their true intrinsic values. Nevertheless, they assert the superiority of their methods over fundamental analysis by pointing out that technical analysis is easier and faster or that it can be simultaneously applied to more stocks than fundamental analysis. This latter claim is certainly true. Of course, if technical analysis does not accomplish what it is purported to do, its relative simplicity does not justify its use.

Many technical analysts would not say that fundamental analysis is worthless, but rather that it is just too troublesome to bother with. First, they point out that even if a fundamental analyst does find an underpriced security, he must wait and hope that the rest of the market recognizes the security's true value and bids its price up. Second, fundamental analysis is hard, time-consuming work. Technical analysis, on the other hand, requires less schooling and is easier to use. Third, technical analysts cite the inadequacy of the income statements produced by accountants (as discussed in Chap. 16) which form the basis for much fundamental analysis. Finally, technical analysts point out the highly subjective nature of the earnings multipliers used by fundamental analysts. In view of these deficiencies of fundamental analysis, consider some of the tools used by technical analysts to measure supply and demand and to forecast security prices.[4]

18-2 THE DOW THEORY

The Dow theory is one of the oldest and most famous technical tools; it was originated by Charles Dow, who founded the Dow Jones Company and was the editor of *The Wall Street Journal* around 1900. Mr. Dow died in 1902, and the Dow theory was developed further and given its name by members of *The Wall Street Journal* staff. Down through the years, numerous writers have altered, extended, and in some cases abridged the original Dow theory.

[4] Although this chapter focuses on charting of common stock prices, technical analysis of other market indicators and other types of financial instruments is also widely practiced. For a favorable report about the profitability of technical analysis in commodity trading see Shawn Tully, "Princeton's Rich Commodity Scholars," *Fortune*, Feb. 9, 1981, pp. 94–98.

Today, many versions of the theory exist and are used; it is the basis for many other techniques used by technical analysts.

The Dow theory rose to a peak of prominence during the 1930s. At that time, *The Wall Street Journal* published editorials written by its staff members which interpreted market action in terms of the theory. On October 23, 1929, *The Wall Street Journal* published a still-famous editorial, "A Turn in the Tide," which correctly stated that the bull market was then over and a bear market had started. This forecast was based on the Dow theory. The horrendous market crash which followed the forecast drew much favorable attention to the Dow theory.

18-2.1 how the Dow theory works

The Dow theory is used to indicate reversals and trends in the market as a whole or for individual securities. According to Mr. Dow himself, "The market is always considered as having three movements, all going at the same time. The first is the narrow movement from day to day. The second is the short swing, running from two weeks to a month or more; the third is the main movement, covering at least 4 years in duration."[5] Dow theory practitioners refer to these three components as: (1) daily fluctuations, (2) secondary movements, and (3) primary trends. The primary trends are commonly called bear or bull markets. Secondary trends last only a few months. The theory asserts that daily fluctuations are meaningless. However, the chartist must plot the asset's price or the market average day by day in order to outline the primary and secondary trends.

Figure 18-1 is a line chart which a Dow theorist might develop. This figure shows a primary uptrend existing from period t to the peak price which occurred just before day $t + j$. On trading day $t + j$, an "abortive recovery" occurs, signaling a change in the direction of the market's primary movement. An abortive recovery occurs when a secondary movement fails to rise above the preceding top. Before $t + j$, all the tops are ascending; but after the abortive recovery, the tops are descending until just before day $t + k$. At $t + k$, a secondary movement fails to reach a new bottom, signaling the start of a bull market. Most Dow theorists do not believe that the emergence of a new

[5] *The Wall Street Journal,* Dec. 19, 1900.

FIGURE 18-1 a line chart of daily closing prices with Dow theory signals.

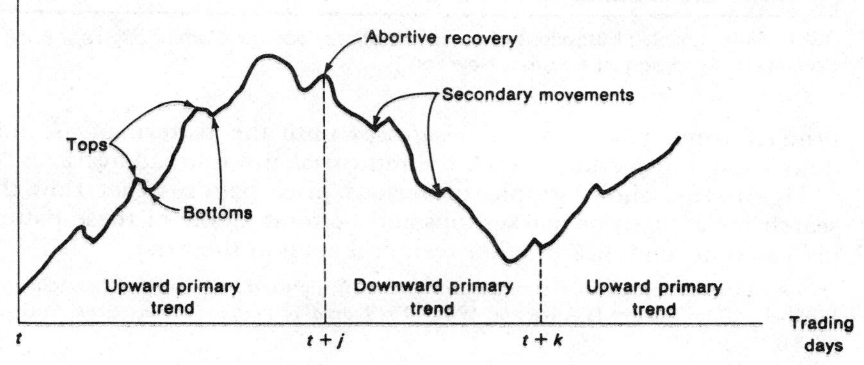

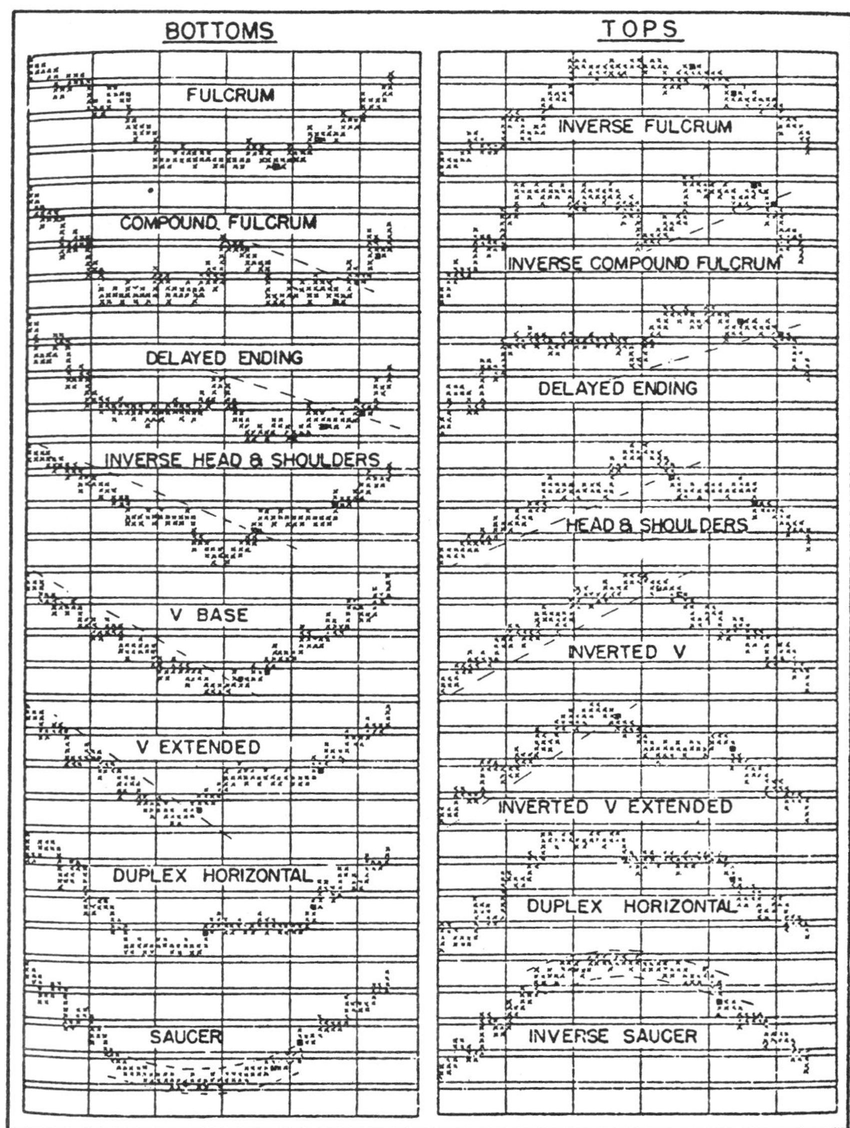

FIGURE 18-2 graphic illustrations of chart formations. (*Source*: *Commodity Year Book*, Commodity Research Bureau, Inc., New York.)

primary trend has been truly *confirmed* until the pattern of ascending or descending tops occurs in both the industrial and railroad averages.[6]

Figure 18-2 shows graphs of various price patterns that Dow theorists search for as signs of market tops and bottoms. Some of these patterns are discussed in reference to other technical analysis theories.

[6] A supportive empirical test of the Dow theory is reported by David A. Glickstein and Rolf E. Wubbels, "Dow Theory Is Alive and Well," *The Journal of Portfolio Management*, April 1983, pp. 28–31.

18-3 BAR CHARTS

Technical analysts use three basic types of charts: (1) line charts, (2) bar charts, and (3) point and figure charts. Figure 18-1 shows a line chart; lines are used to connect successive days' prices. Figure 18-3 shows a bar chart. *Bar charts* have vertical bars representing each day's price movement. Each bar spans the distance from the day's highest price to the day's lowest price; a small cross on the bar marks the closing price.

FIGURE 18-3 bar chart of head and shoulders top formation. (*Source*: W. L. Jiler, *How Charts Can Help You in the Stock Market*, Trendline, New York, p. 114.)

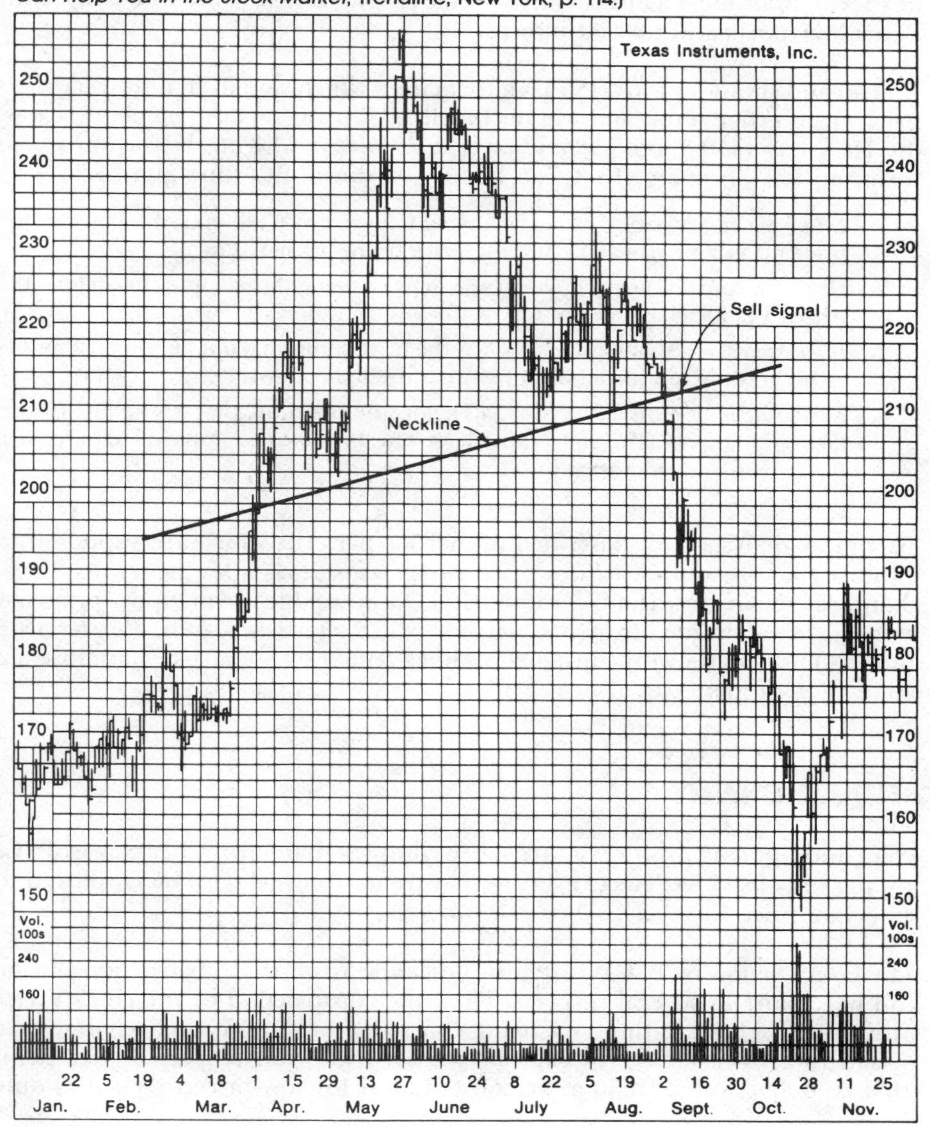

Point and figure charts (PFCs) are made of X's and O's and are more complex than line and bar charts; they will be discussed in the next section. Charts of the price movements of both individual assets and the market indices are kept on all three types of charts.

Line charts, bar charts, and PFCs usually have bar graphs along the bottoms of the charts showing the volume of shares traded at each price change. Figure 18-3 shows such volume data. Trading volume is of lesser importance to the chartists than the security prices themselves, but it is probably the second most important statistic they follow. As an example of how technical analysts try to relate stock price moves and the volume of shares traded, consider a pattern called the head and shoulders formation. Chartists find the head and shoulders pattern in line charts, bar charts, and PFCs for both individual assets and market indices.

18-3.1 head and shoulders top on a bar chart

A head and shoulder top (HST) is a formation which signals that the security's price has reached a top and will decline in the future. As the name indicates, the HST has a left shoulder, and a right shoulder. The market action which forms an HST (see Fig. 18-3) can be broken down into four phases:

1. *Left shoulder* A period of heavy buying followed by a lull in trading pushes the price up to a new peak before the price begins to slide down.
2. *Head* A spurt of heavy buying raises a price to a new high and then allows the price to fall back below the top of the left shoulder.
3. *Right shoulder* A moderate rally lifts the price somewhat but fails to push prices as high as the top of the head before a decline begins.
4. *Confirmation or breakout* Prices fall below the neckline, that is, the line drawn tangent to the left and right shoulders. This breakout is supposed to precede a price drop and is a signal to sell.

18-3.2 other formations

Technical analysts have described numerous patterns which are supposed to indicate the direction of future price movements. Triangles, pennants, flags, channels, rectangles, double tops, triple tops, wedge formations, and diamonds are only some of the patterns for which chartists search. Figures 18-2 and 18-3 are charts with construction lines added by a chartist that illustrate some of these patterns.

18-4 POINT AND FIGURE CHARTS

Point and figure charts (PFCs) are more complex than line or bar charts. PFCs are not only used to detect reversals in a trend; they can also be employed to set actual price forecasts, called *price targets*.

18-4.1 construction of PFCs

The construction of PFCs differs significantly from the construction of line and bar charts in several respects. First, the construction of the chart varies with the price level of the stock being charted. Only "significant" changes are posted to a PFC. Thus, for high-priced securities only three- or five-point (that is, dollar) price changes are posted, and for low-priced securities only one-point changes are posted. As a result, there are one-point PFCs, two-point PFCs, three-point PFCs, and five-point PFCs.

A second unusual feature of PFCs is their lack of a time dimension. On line and bar charts, each vertical column represents a trading day, but on a PFC, determining the days is sometimes impossible because each column represents a *significant reversal* instead of a trading day. As a result, a trading day in

FIGURE 18-4 explanation of point and figure charts from technical analysis book. (*Source*: Chartcraft Chart Book, Larchmont, N.Y.)

INTRODUCTION

THE ESSENTIAL FEATURE OF A POINT-AND-FIGURE CHART

A line or a bar chart is two-dimensional. The vertical spaces measure price. The horizontal spaces measure calendar time, whether daily, weekly, or monthly.

A point-and-figure chart is one dimensional. Both vertical and horizontal spaces measure price. There is no measurement of arbitrary calendar time. Each successive horizontal space on the chart represents a change of direction in the price, from up to down or from down to up.

WHY A POINT-AND-FIGURE CHART?

A point-and figure chart is indigenous to stock market trading. It originated in the stock market and has been used exclusively in the stock market. It is not a new-fangled idea or method. It was used in stock trading long before line or bar charts were introduced from other fields.

A point-and-figure chart is easier to construct and maintain than any other type of chart. This is because entries do not have to be made on a calendar basis. Days or weeks may go by without any entries being made.

A point-and-figure chart is easier to read and interpret than other charts. It is easier to recognize bases of accumulation and tops of distribution. It is easier to see ascending bottoms and tops and descending tops and bottoms.

READING THE CHARTS CONTAINED IN THIS BOOK

Xs are used when the price of a stock is going up and Os are used when the price of a stock is going down. Rows of Xs and Os alternate-they never appear in the same column. Passage of time is indicated by months. "1" stands for January "2" for February, etc. In charts printed out by computer, "A" is used instead of "10" for October, "B" instead of "11" for November and "C" instead of "12" for December. These figures appear in place of an X or an O.

The charts contained in this book are 3-point or, more correctly, 3-box reversal charts. A full 3 boxes of price change are necessary. before one moves from Xs to Os or from Os to Xs. Once a direction has been established, each one point or 1 box change in the same direction is recorded.

Units of charting -

From 20 to 100, 1 point units are used (each box represents \$1)
Above 100, 2 point units are used (each box represents \$2)
Below 20, ½ point units are used (each box represents 50 cents)
Below 5, ¼ point units are used (each box represents 25 cents)

TRENDLINES

Each chart in this book contains at least one trendline; 99% of them contain two trendlines. These trendlines are the Bullish Support Line and the Bearish Resistance Line.

The BULLISH SUPPORT LINE is drawn upwards by intersecting each successive higher square on the chart. It does not connect two price points. It is drawn from a low point on the chart immediately after the first upturn. If there are only two columns of price changes above this trendline then it should be considered as tentative. If there are more than two columns then it is a valid Bullish Support Line. This line will disappear when it is touched by a downward price change.

The BEARISH RESISTANCE LINE is drawn downwards by intersecting each successive lower square on the chart. It does not connect two price points. It is drawn from a high point on the chart immediately after the first downturn. If there are only two columns of price changes below this trendline then it should be considered as tentative. If there are more than two columns then it is a valid Bearish Resistance Line. This line will disappear when it is touched by an upward price change.

The Bullish Support Line is a guide to where a downmove may find support and reverse itself. The Bearish Resistance Line is a guide to where an upmove may find resistance and reverse itself. Long term traders may use these trendlines as guides for how long to hold their positions. If they are long of the stock, they may hold as long as the Bullish Support Line is not penetrated. If they are short of the stock they may hold as long as the Bearish Resistance Line is not penetrated.

The best stock to buy is: (1) a stock that has given a buy signal by penetrating a previous top, (2) has a valid Bullish Support Line, and (3) has no valid Bearish Resistance Line.

The best stock to sell short is: (1) a stock that has given a sell signal by penetrating a previous bottom, (2) has a valid Bearish Resistance Line, and (3) has no valid Bullish Support Line.

On page V, there is an exercise in point-and-figure chart construction. We suggest that you go through this practice exercise at your leisure. This will enable you to continue posting the charts in this book without any difficulty. The figures used for such posting are obtained from the daily highs and lows of the stock market tables carried in your newspaper. A complete explanation of point-and-figure charting and interpretation is contained in our book, "How to Use The Three-Point Reversal Method of Point and Figure Trading" which sells for \$3.95 a copy.

Before taking positions on any of the chart patterns in this book, please consult the Technical Indicator Review pages. We do not believe that the average trader should trade against the trend of the market. We believe in following the line of least resistance.

NOTES: Each chart is marked with a short term indication of Bullish or Bearish. The figure after the word "Bullish" or "Bearish" is the Price Objective (decimal point is omitted, i.e. 1950 is \$19.50). When none appears, none exists or has already been attained.

The eight digit number appearing to the right of the stock name over each chart is the CUSIP number. This is the number assigned by NASDAQ to identify each stock.

The number appearing in the upper right hand corner of certain charts refers to S & P's group index to which that stock is assigned. (See complete listing under Industry Groups in Table of Contents, page 111).

Occasionally throughout the Chartbook you will find two charts for a single stock. This means that the first chart has run off either the top or bottom of the price scale. The second chart shows a new price scale and picks up where the first one left off.

The Chartcraft Weekly Service now supplies the recordable price changes for each of the stocks contained in this book. Thus, by using the service you can bring your charts up-to-date once a week with a minimum of time and effort. The combination rate for the monthly Chart Book and the Weekly Service is \$300 per year.

PRACTICE EXERCISE IN CHART CONSTRUCTION

Date	High	Low	Chart Entries
5/2	22-7/8	21	O 22-21
5/3	21	20	(5) 20
5/4	20-3/4	20-1/8	
5/5	19-7/8	19-1/2	O $19\frac{1}{2}$
5/6	20-1/2	19-1/2	
5/9	20-1/2	20-1/4	
5/10	20-1/4	20-1/8	
5/11	20-1/4	20	
5/12	20-1/4	19-7/8	
5/13	21-1/2	20-1/8	
5/16	21-1/2	21	
5/17	21-1/4	20-3/4	
5/18	22-1/2	21-1/2	X 20-21-22
5/19	22-1/2	22	
5/20	22-3/8	21-1/4	
5/23	22	21-1/4	
5/24	22	21	
5/25	21	20-1/4	
5/26	21-1/2	20-1/2	
5/27	22-1/4	21-1/2	
5/31	22-7/8	22	
6/1	24-7/8	24	(6)23-X 24
6/2	25	24	X 25
6/3	24	23-1/4	
6/6	23-3/8	23	
6/7	24-1/4	23-1/2	
6/8	24-1/4	23-3/4	
6/9	24	23-5/8	
6/10	23-5/8	23-1/8	
6/13	23-1/2	23	
6/14	23-3/4	22-1/2	
6/15	22-7/8	21-1/2	O 24-23-22
6/16	22	21-1/4	
6/17	22-1/4	21-5/8	
6/20	22-1/4	21-3/4	
6/21	22-1/4	22	
6/23	21-1/4	20-1/2	O 21
6/24	20-3/4	20-1/2	
6/27	21	20-3/4	
6/28	20-7/8	20-1/4	
6/29	20-1/2	20	O 20
6/30	21-1/8	19-1/2	O $19\frac{1}{2}$
7/1	21-5/8	20-7/8	
7/5	21-1/4	21	
7/6	21	20-7/8	
7/7	20-7/8	20-1/2	
7/8	20-1/4	19-3/4	
7/11	20	19-3/4	
7/12	19-3/4	19-1/4	
7/13	19-3/4	19-3/8	
7/14	20	19-5/8	
7/15	20	19-5/8	
7/18	21	19-3/4	
7/19	20-1/2	20	
7/20	20	20	
7/21	20-1/8	19-7/8	
7/22	19-7/8	19-7/8	
7/25	19-7/8	19	(7) 19
7/26	19-3/4	19	
7/27	19	18-1/2	O $18\frac{1}{2}$
7/28	19	18-1/2	
7/29	19	18-3/4	
8/1	19-1/4	19	
8/2	-	-	
8/3	19-1/2	19	

Date	High	Low	Chart Entries
8/4	19	19	
8/5	19-1/4	19	
8/8	19-1/4	19	
8/9	19-3/8	18-1/2	
8/10	18-1/2	18-1/2	
8/11	19	18-1/8	
8/12	20	19	X 19-$19\frac{1}{2}$-(8)20
8/15	20	20	
8/16	20	20	
8/17	19-5/8	19-1/4	
8/18	19-1/8	19-1/8	
8/19	19-1/8	19	
8/22	19-1/4	19-1/4	
8/23	19-1/2	19-1/8	
8/24	19-1/2	19-1/8	
8/25	19-1/4	19	
8/26	19	19	
8/29	18-7/8	18-1/2	O $19\frac{1}{2}$-19-$18\frac{1}{2}$
8/30	18-3/4	18-1/4	
8/31	18-1/2	18-1/4	
9/1	20-7/8	19-3/4	X 19-$19\frac{1}{2}$-(9)20
9/2	20-3/8	19-7/8	
9/6	19-3/4	19-1/2	
9/7	19-1/4	18-1/4	O $19\frac{1}{2}$-19-$18\frac{1}{2}$
9/8	18-1/4	18-1/4	
9/9	19	19	
9/12	18-3/4	18-1/4	
9/13	18-3/4	18-1/4	
9/14	18-5/8	18-1/8	
9/15	18-1/2	18	O 18
9/16	18-1/2	18	
9/19	18-1/4	17	O $17\frac{1}{2}$-17
9/20	17-1/2	17-1/2	
9/21	18	17-1/2	
9/22	18	18	
9/23	18	17-3/4	
9/27	17-3/8	16-1/4	O $16\frac{1}{2}$
9/28	16-1/4	15-1/2	O16-$15\frac{1}{2}$
9/29	16	15-5/8	
9/30	17	16-1/4	X 16-$16\frac{1}{2}$-17
10/3	17	16-1/2	
10-4	16-7/8	16-1/4	
10/5	16-1/2	16	
10/6	16-1/2	16-1/4	
10/7	16-1/2	16-1/4	
10/10	16-3/4	16-1/2	
10/11	16-3/4	16-1/2	
10/12	17-1/4	16-1/2	
10/13	16-7/8	16-3/4	
10/14	16-5/8	16-5/8	
10/17	16-1/2	16-1/4	
10/18	16-1/4	16-1/4	
10/19	16-1/8	16	
10/20	16	15-1/2	O $16\frac{1}{2}$-16-(A)$15\frac{1}{2}$
10/21	15-1/2	14	O 15-$14\frac{1}{2}$-14
10/24	14-1/4	13	O $13\frac{1}{2}$-13
10/25	14-1/8	13-1/8	
10/26	14	13-3/8	
10/27	15	14	X $13\frac{1}{2}$-14-$14\frac{1}{2}$-15
10/28	15-1/2	14-3/4	X $15\frac{1}{2}$
10/31	14-7/8	14-1/4	
11/1	15-1/4	15	
11/2	15-3/8	15	
11/3	15	15	
11/4	15	15	

Date	High	Low	Chart Entries
11/7	15-3/8	15-1/8	
11/9	15-3/8	15-1/9	
11/10	15-3/4	15-3/4	
11/11	15-3/4	15-3/8	
11/14	15-5/8	15-3/8	
11/15	15-1/2	15-1/4	
11/16	15-3/4	15-1/2	
11/17	15-3/4	15-3/8	
11/18	15-7/8	15-1/2	
11/21	15-3/4	15-3/8	
11/22	16-1/2	16	(B)16-X $16\frac{1}{2}$
11/23	16-3/8	16-1/4	
11/25	17-1/8	16-1/8	X 17
11/28	17-1/4	16-/34	
11/29	17	16-5/8	
11/30	16-1/2	16-1/2	
12/1	16-1/4	16	
12/2	15-5/8	15-5/8	
12/5	15-5/8	15-1/4	O $16\frac{1}{2}$-16-C$15\frac{1}{2}$
12/6	15-1/4	15	O 15
12/7	15	15	
12/8	15-7/8	15-1/8	
12/9	15-1/2	15-1/2	
12/12	15-1/2	15-1/4	
12/13	15-1/2	15	
12/14	16	15	
12/15	16	15-5/8	
12/16	15-3/4	15-5/8	
12/19	15-3/4	15	
12/20	15-1/8	14-3/4	
12/21	15	14-3/8	O $14\frac{1}{2}$
12/22	15-1/2	14-1/2	
12/23	14-7/8	14-1/4	
12/27	14-7/8	14-3/8	
12/28	14-3/4	14-1/2	
12/29	15	14-1/2	
1/3/72	16	14-3/4	X 15-$15\frac{1}{2}$-(1)16
1/4	17-1/8	16-1/4	X $16\frac{1}{2}$-17
1/5	16-7/8	16-5/8	
1/6	16-7/8	16-1/2	
1/9	17-1/4	16-1/2	
1/10	18-1/2	17-1/8	X $17\frac{1}{2}$-18-$18\frac{1}{2}$
1/11	18-5/8	18-1/4	
1/12	18-1/2	17-7/8	
1/13	18	17-3/4	
1/16	18	17-3/4	
1/17	17-3/4	17-1/2	
1/18	17-1/2	17	O 18-$17\frac{1}{2}$-17
1/19	17-3/4	17-1/2	
1/20	18-1/4	17-1/2	
1/23	18-5/8	17-1/2	X $17\frac{1}{2}$-18-$18\frac{1}{2}$
1/24	19-3/4	18-1/4	X 19-$19\frac{1}{2}$
1/25	18-3/8	18-1/8	
1/26	19	18-1/4	
1/27	20-1/8	19-1/4	X 20
1/30	21-7/8	20-1/4	X 21
1/31	21-7/8	21-1/4	

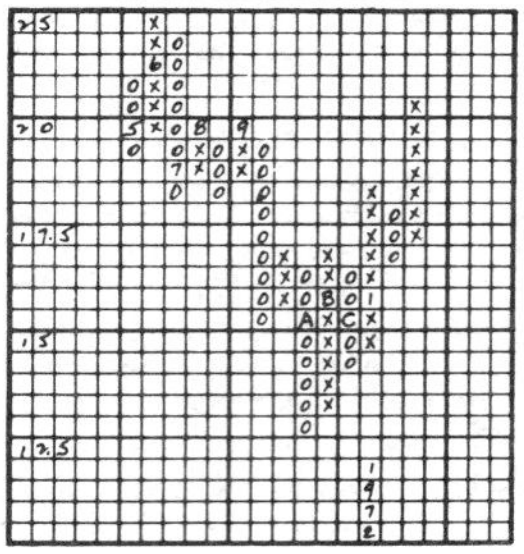

If your last chart entry is an X, look at the daily high. If the stock has gone up, enter the additional X or Xs and forget about the lows. If the stock has not gone up, look at the low for a possible 3-box reversal.

If your last chart entry is an O, look at the daily low. If the stock has gone lower, enter the additional Os and forget about the highs. If the stock has not gone lower, look at the daily high for a possible 3-box reversal.

SAMPLE CHART

FIGURE 18-4 *(continued)*

which the direction of the price made two significant reversals would generate two new columns on a PFC. Consider the instructions shown in Fig. 18-4. These two pages are from a point and figure chartbook, and they are provided along with the accompanying explanation as a PFC teaching vehicle.

18-4.2 interpretation of PFCs

To set the price target (that is, forecasted price) which a stock is expected to attain, PFC chartists begin by finding "congestion areas." A *congestion area* is a horizontal band of X's and O's created by a series of reversals around a given price level. Congestion areas are supposed to result when supply and demand are equal. A breakout is said to have occurred when a column of X's rises above the top of a congestion area. A *penetration* of the top of a congestion area is a signal for a continued price rise. Penetration of the bottom of a congestion area by a column of O's is a bearish signal.

Figure 18-5 shows PFCs where top and bottom penetrations have occurred. It shows that the PFC of the Standard & Poor's 500 composite average gave some sell signals late in the summer of 1969 as the 1969–1970 bear market began. The months of the year are indicated by the numbers from 1 through 12, which are used in place of an X or O when the first significant change occurs in a new month. At the end of 1969, some weak buy signals were given only to be followed by a strong sell signal in December 1969. If investors had followed all these signals, they would have been "whipsawed." That is, securities could have been sold, bought back at higher prices, and then later sold again at even lower prices for a considerable cumulative loss. In December

FIGURE 18-5 point and figure chart of Standard & Poor's composite 500. (*Source*: A. W. Cohen, *Technical Indicator Analysis*, Chartcraft, Inc., Larchmont, N.Y.)

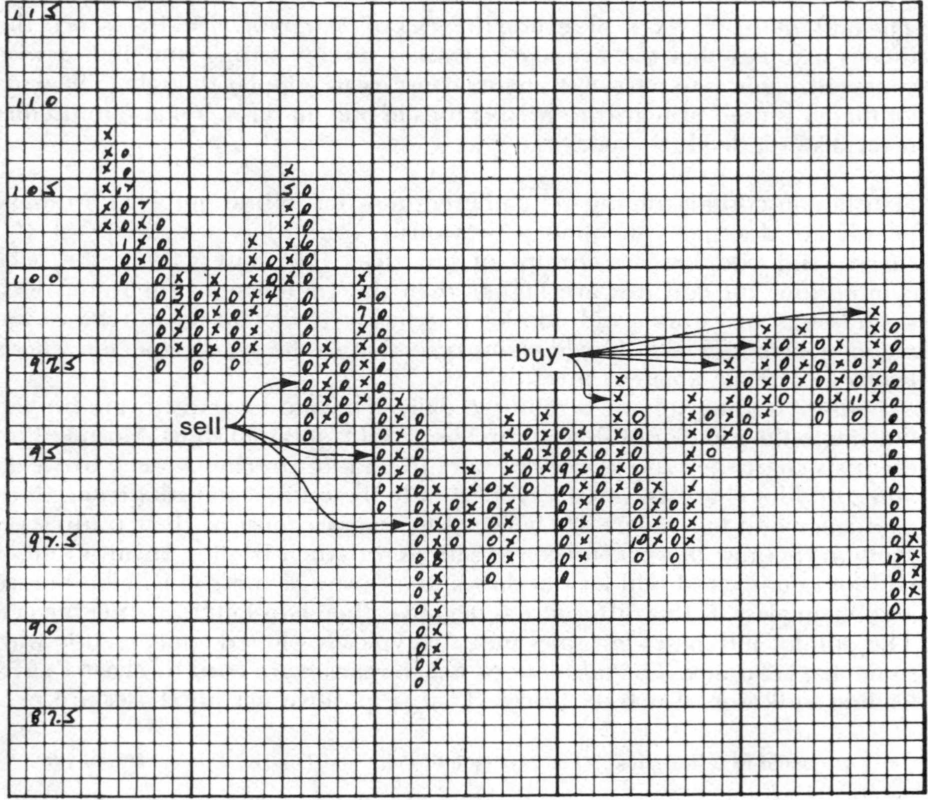

1969 when the PFC issued a strong sell signal, the bear market of 1969–1970 was already under way; so this signal merely pointed to something which was already obvious.

18-4.3 establishing price targets

To establish estimates of the new prices which a security should attain, PFC chartists measure the *horizontal count*—the horizontal width of a congestion area—as they watch for a breakout. *Breakout* refers to a price rise or fall in which the price rises above or falls below the horizontal band which contained the congestion area. When a breakout occurs, the chartist projects the horizontal count upward or downward in the same direction as the breakout to establish the new price target. The reason a particular price target is appropriate is not clear; even the PFC chartists themselves have difficulty explaining the establishment of price targets. John Schulz, a PFC chartist who has written columns for *Forbes* magazine, once wrote that "on the question of where, in actual practice, measurements of lateral action should be taken, we are far from doctrinaire. . . . we advocate the utmost flexibility because this tends to obviate the dangerous rigidity of preconceived notions."[7] Such flexibility also tends to obviate use of the technique.

18-5 CONTRARY OPINION THEORIES

The odd-lot theory is one of several theories of *contrary opinion*. In essence, the theory assumes that the average person is usually wrong and that a wise course of action is to pursue strategies contrary to popular thought. The odd-lot theory is used primarily to predict tops in bull markets, but also to predict reversals in individual securities.

18-5.1 the odd-lot theory

Statistics on odd-lot trading are gathered in order to find out what ordinary people are doing. As mentioned previously, round lots are groups of 100 shares, and odd lots are groups of less than 100 shares. Since the sales commissions on odd lots are higher than the commissions on round lots, professional investors avoid odd-lot purchases. Most odd-lot purchases are made by investors with limited resources—that is, the average person who is probably a small, amateur investor.

Odd-lot trading volume is reported daily. The odd-lot statistics are broken down into the number of shares purchased, sold, and sold short. Most odd-lot theorists chart the ratio of odd-lot sales to odd-lot purchases week by week. Some odd-lot chartists, however, chart only the odd-lot statistics from Mondays since odd-lot traders are believed to transact most of their trading on Mondays because of weekend conversations with their friends. In any event, if odd-lot sales exceed odd-lot purchases, the "average" person is selling more and buying less. If this difference is negative, then odd-lotters are net buyers. The odd-lot purchases-less-sales index is typically plotted concurrently with some market index. The odd-lotters' net purchases are used by chartists as a leading indicator of market prices. That is, positive net purchases are pre-

[7] As quoted in D. Seligman, "The Mystique of Point and Figure," *Fortune,* March 1962.

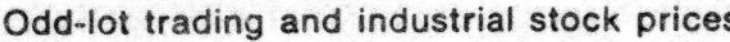

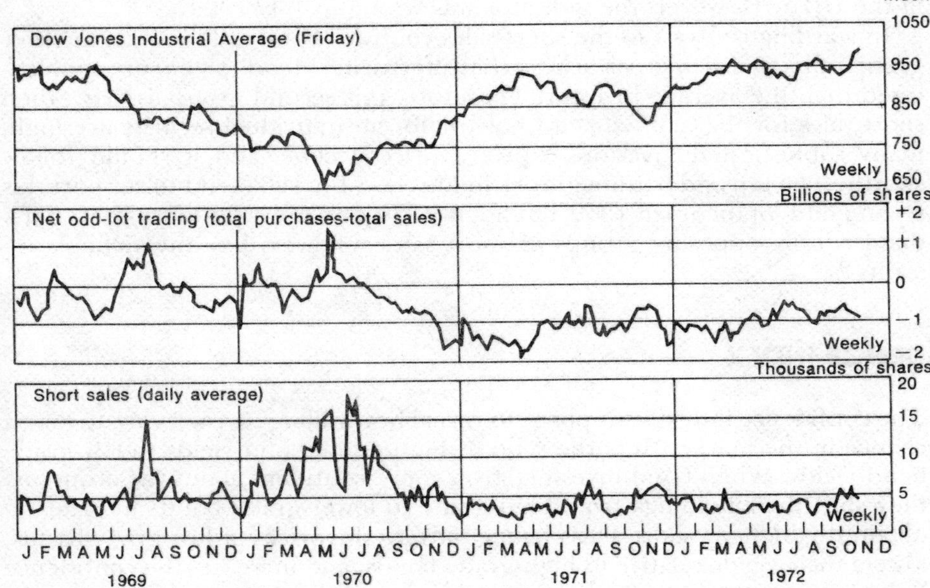

FIGURE 18-6 graphs for odd-lot and short sales technical indicators. (*Source*: Cleveland Trust Company Bulletin, November 1972.)

sumed to forecast falls in market prices, and net sales (or negative net purchases) are presumed to occur at the end of bear markets.

Figure 18-6 shows data for the Dow Jones Industrial Average (DJIA) in the top panel; concurrent odd-lotter net purchases are shown in the center panel for the period during and after the 1969–1970 bear market. Contrary to the odd-lot theory of contrary opinion, the odd-lotters were net buyers during low points in the DJIA. That is, the odd-lotters have "bought low and sold high" in recent years and thus have defied the theory about them.[8]

18-5.2 the short sellers theories

Some chartists follow statistics on short sales. (Short sales are defined on pages 593 to 596.) Some short-sales theorists use aggregate statistics as an indicator of overall market sentiment, and some follow the short sales for individual securities in search of information about that security. However, both groups may interpret a high level of outstanding short sales (that is, uncovered short positions or short interest, as it is variously called) as a sign of increased future demand for securities with which to cover the outstanding short positions. Therefore, rising short sales foretell future demand for the security and thus increments in future prices. This is the *short sales contrary opinion* theory. The empirical data for 1970, graphed in the top and bottom panels of Fig. 18-6,

[8] T. J. Kewley and R. A. Stevenson, "The Odd-Lot Theory for Individual Stocks," *Financial Analysts Journal*, January–February 1969. This study suggests that the theory gives good "buy" signals but not good "sell" signals.

tend to confirm the theory; the peak in short sales preceded the 1970 upturn in the DJIA. However, the indicator was wrong in July 1969.

In startling contrast to the short sales contrary opinion followers, another group of technical analysts believe that short sellers tend to be more sophisticated than the average investor. Therefore, this second group asserts, when short sales for the market as a whole or for an individual security are high, many sophisticated investors expect a price decline, and it should follow shortly. The top and bottom graphs in Fig. 18-6 for 1969 tend to support this second odd-lot theory in 1969, but not in 1970. It is not clear that either of the diametrically opposing groups of short sales followers has any valuable insights.[9]

18-6 THE CONFIDENCE INDEX

The confidence index is supposed to reveal how willing investors are to take a chance in the market. It is the ratio of high-grade bond yields to low-grade bond yields. When bond investors grow more confident about the economy, they shift their holdings from high-grade to lower-grade bonds in order to obtain the higher yields. This change bids up the prices of low-grade bonds, lowers their yields relative to high-grade bonds, and increases the confidence index.

Markets for bonds are frequented mostly by large institutional investors who are believed to be less emotional about their portfolio decisions than many investors in the stock market. In an effort to measure the market expectations of these "smart money" managers and assess their confidence in the economy, some chartists study the confidence index.

18-6.1 calculating the confidence index

Barron's, the weekly financial and business newspaper, publishes figures on the confidence index regularly in its Market Laboratory section. The *Barron's* confidence index is the ratio of the average yield from its list of the 10 highest-grade bonds over the average yield from the Dow Jones 40 bonds. Equation (18-1) defines the *Barron's* confidence index (BCI).

$$BCI_t = \frac{\text{average yield of } \textit{Barron's} \text{ 10 highest-grade bonds at period } t}{\text{average yield of Dow Jones 40 bonds at time period } t} \tag{18-1}$$

The *Barron's* definition of the confidence index is widely used because it is published each week, but it has no intrinsic superiority over, say, the confidence index (CI) defined in Eq. (18-2).

$$CI_t = \frac{\text{average yield of Aaa bonds at time period } t}{\text{average yield of Baa bonds at time period } t} \tag{18-2}$$

Other valid definitions of the confidence index exist, too.

[9] For an empirical report which is favorable to short interest technicians read Thomas J. Kerrigan, "The Short Interest Ratio and Its Component Parts," *Financial Analysts Journal*, November–December 1974, pp. 45–49.

18-6.2 interpretation of the confidence index

The confidence index has an upper limit of unity (that is, CI < 1.0), since the yields on high-quality bonds will never rise above the yields on similar low-quality bonds. In periods of economic boom when investors grow optimistic and their risk-aversion diminishes, the yield spread between high- and low-quality bonds narrows and the confidence index rises. A rising confidence index is interpreted by chartists as an indication that the managers of the "smart money" are optimistic. On the assumption that the wisdom of these investors will be borne out, confidence index technicians predict that the stock market (where fewer sophisticated investors are assumed to trade) will follow the leadership of the smart money. Some confidence index technicians claim that the confidence index leads the stock market by 2 to 11 months. Thus, an upturn in the confidence index is supposed to foretell rising optimism and rising prices in the stock market.

Just as a rise in the confidence index is expected to precede a rising stock market, so a fall in the index is expected to precede a drop in stock prices. A fall in the confidence index represents the fact that low-grade bond yields are rising faster or falling more slowly than high-grade yields. This movement is supposed to reflect increasing risk-aversion by smart money managers who foresee an economic downturn and rising bankruptcies and defaults.

Figure 18-7 shows a point and figure chart of the *Barron's* confidence index plotted on the vertical axis at increments of half percentage points. Each block represents ½ of 1 percent. A change of 1½ percentage points in the opposite direction is considered a significant reversal which warrants starting a new column. The chart shows that the *Barron's* confidence index issued a weak sell signal when it broke out of the bottom of the congestion area in early 1968.

FIGURE 18-7 point and figure chart of *Barron's* confidence index. (*Source*: Chartcraft, Inc., Larchmont, N.Y.)

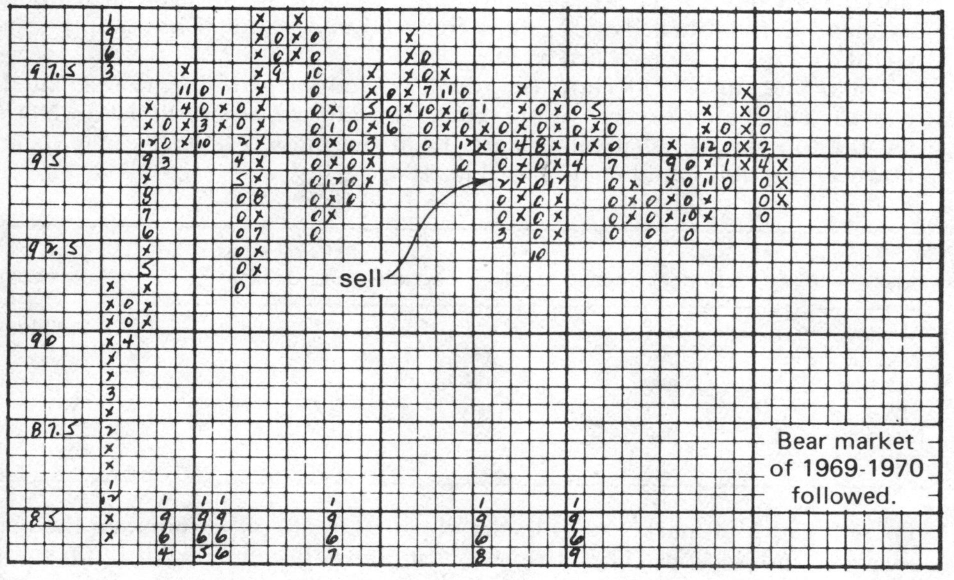

This would have been a good sell signal to heed. A recession and bear stock market occurred soon after in the period 1969–1970.

There is no question that the confidence index is positively correlated with the stock market. However, in view of the numerous other economic series which are also correlated with the stock market, this is of no unique value. The confidence index is usually, but not always, a leading indication. Furthermore, the confidence index has sometimes issued erroneous signals.

Many observers who have examined the confidence index conclude that it does measure what it is supposed to measure and thus that it conveys some worthwhile information. But, in view of its inconsistent lead-lag relationship with the stock market, if the confidence index is to be used it should be used in conjunction with other technical indicators or aids.

18-7 BREADTH OF MARKET

Breadth-of-market indicators are used to measure the underlying strength of market advances or declines. For example, it is possible that the Dow Jones Industrial Average of only 30 blue-chip stocks which are very popular would still be rising for some time after the market for the majority of lesser-known stocks had already turned down. Thus, to gauge the real underlying strength of the market, tools are needed to measure the *breadth* of the market's moves.

18-7.1 breadth-of-market calculations

Numerous methods exist for measuring the breadth of the market. One of the easiest methods is to compare the number of issues that advanced in price and the number that declined on some particular market such as the New York Stock Exchange (NYSE). More specifically, subtract the number of issues whose prices declined from the number of issues whose prices advanced each day to get *net advances or declines*. The data on advances and declines are published daily in most financial and national newspapers—a typical example is reproduced as Fig. 18-8.

The net advances or declines (sometimes called the *plurality*) are calculated from the newspaper excerpt of Fig. 18-8, for example, as shown below. Note that the top row of calculations starts from the most recent Tuesday data, shown in the right-hand column of Fig. 18-8.

day	advances	minus	declines	equals	net advances and declines	breadth
Tuesday	745		634		+111	111 (start)
Wednesday	994		391		+603	714
Thursday	468		914		−446	268
Friday	255		1118		−863	−595
Monday	669		589		+ 80	−515
Tuesday	582		657		− 75	−590

These breadth-of-market statistics are obtained by simply cumulating the net advances and declines. The breadth statistics may become negative during a bear market, as they did in the example above. This is no cause for alarm,

FIGURE 18-8 daily advances and declines.

MARKET DIARY

	Tues	Mon	Fri	Thur	Wed	Tues
Issues traded	1,531	1,532	1,562	1,597	1,582	1,616
Advances	582	669	255	468	994	745
Declines	657	589	1,118	914	391	634
Unchanged	292	274	189	215	197	237
New highs, 1970	3	4	1	9	14	8
New lows, 1970	49	41	42	31	24	38

since the breadth level is entirely arbitrary; it depends on the date when the cumulative breadth series was begun. Only the direction, not the level, of the breadth-of-market statistics is relevant.

18-7.2 interpretation of breadth data

Breadth-of-market data are frequently plotted on line charts. Figure 18-9 shows a line chart of breadth data for the NYSE; the chart calls the breadth data the advance-decline line. Technical analysts compare the breadth of market with one of the market averages or, as done in Fig. 18-9, with two of them. The breadth and market averages usually move in tandem. What technical analysts watch for is breadth to follow a path which diverges from the path of a market average.

Suppose the DJIA, with its 30 blue-chip stocks that are popular with amateur and professional investors alike, is moving upward. If breadth follows a divergent downward path, it indicates that many small stocks are starting to turn down while the blue chips continue to rise. This is an indicator of weakening market demand and signals a possible market downturn.

18-8 RELATIVE STRENGTH ANALYSIS

Dr. R. A. Levy suggests that the prices of some securities rise relatively faster in a bull market or decline more slowly in a bear market than other securities—that is, some securities exhibit *relative strength*. Relative strength technicians believe that by investing in securities which have demonstrated relative strength in the past, an investor will earn higher returns because the relative strength of a security tends to remain undiminished over time.[10]

18-8.1 measuring relative strength

The relative strength concept may be applied to individual securities or to whole industries. Technicians measure relative strength in several ways. Some simply calculate rates of return and classify those securities with historically high average returns as securities with high relative strength. More frequently, technicians observe certain ratios to detect relative strength in a

[10] Dr. Levy is one of the few technical analysts who has published a study of his techniques. The interested reader is directed to the following articles by Levy; all appeared in *Financial Analysts Journal:* (1) "Conceptual Foundations of Technical Analysis," July–August 1966, pp. 83–89. (2) "Random Walks: Reality or Myth," November–December 1967, pp. 69–76. An article by M. C. Jensen commenting on Levy's article follows directly in the same issue: "Random Walks: Reality or Myth—Comment," November–December 1967, pp. 77-85. (3) "Random Walks: Reality or Myth—Reply," January–February 1968, pp. 129–132. See also M. C. Jensen and G. A. Bennington, "Random Walks and Technical Theories: Some Additional Evidence," *Journal of Finance*, May 1970, pp. 469–482.

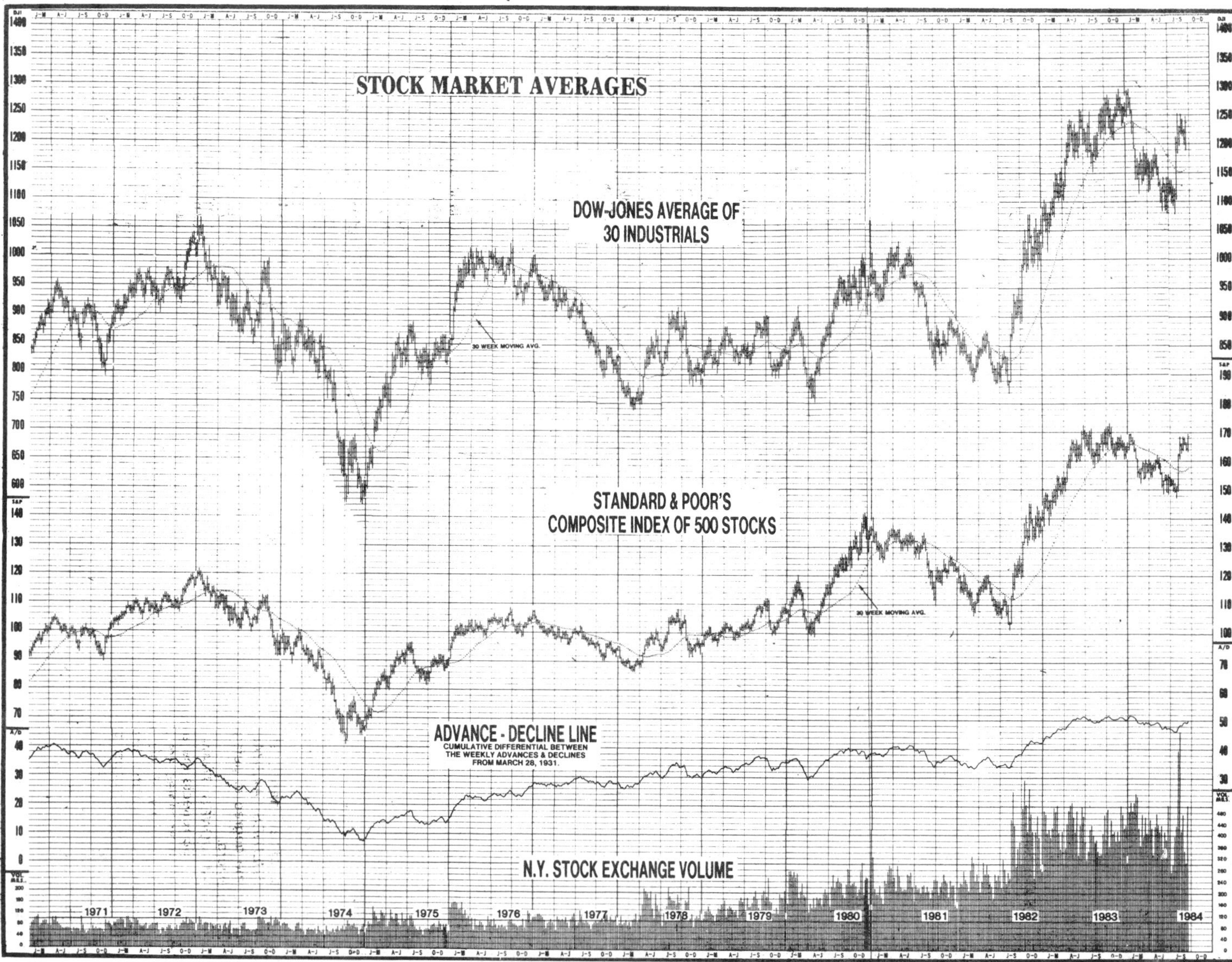

FIGURE 18-9 chart of stock market averages, trading volume, and advance-decline index, 1971–1984. (*Source*: Trendline's *Current Market Perspectives*, September 1984, p. 5.)

TABLE 18-1 relative strength data for Anonymous Corp.

year	P_A*	P_{EIA}†	P_{MIA}‡	P_A/P_{EIA}	P_A/P_{MIA}	P_{EIA}/P_{MIA}
19X3	30	17	210	30/17 = 1.78	30/210 = .144	17/210 = .081
19X4	36	18	250	36/18 = 2	36/250 = .144	18/250 = .072
19X5	72	20	285	72/20 = 3.6	72/285 = .253	20/285 = .070

* P_A = average price of Anonymous Corp. for the year.
† P_{EIA} = Moody's electronics industry average for the year.
‡ P_{MIA} = Moody's industrial average for the year.

security or an industry. For example, consider the data for Anonymous Corp., denoted *A*, a hypothetical growth firm in the electronics industry, denoted EI, shown in Table 18-1.

From 19x3 to 19x4 Anonymous did slightly better than most of the firms in the electronics industry, as evidenced by the fact that its price grew relatively more than the electronics industry average; the ratio P_A/P_{EIA} rose from 1.78 to 2. From 19x3 to 19x4 the electronics industry showed weakness relative to all industrial stocks: the ratio P_{EIA}/P_{MIA} declined from .081 to .072. Thus, Anonymous had to beat the electronics industry average merely to keep up (relatively speaking) with the rest of the market. From 19x3 to 19x4 Anonymous did not demonstrate any particular strength relative to the market average: the ratio P_A/P_{MIA} remained .144. From 19x4 to 19x5 Anonymous showed considerable strength relative to its industry and to the market; during that time the electronics industry advanced at nearly as fast a rate as the market.

18-8.2 interpretation of relative strength data

A relative strength technician would typically plot the ratios of (1) the security relative to its industry and (2) the security relative to the entire market. A chart like the one shown in Fig. 18-10 might result for the Anonymous Corp.

Figure 18-10 shows that although the electronics industry is failing to keep pace with the market, the Anonymous Corp. is developing relative strength

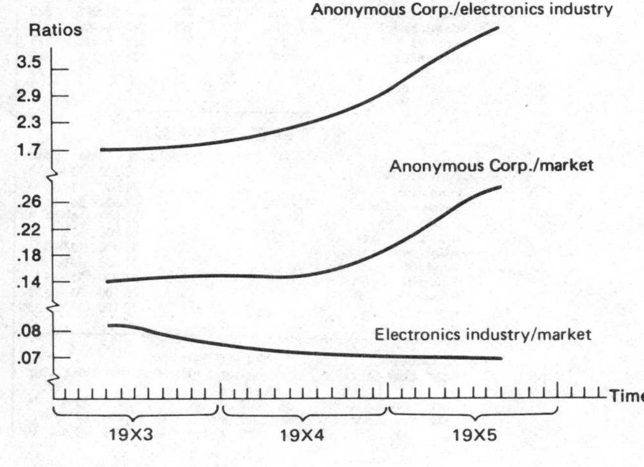

FIGURE 18-10 hypothetical relative-strength data for Anonymous Corp. and the electronics industry. (*Source*: Table 18-1.)

both in its industry and in the market. After preparing charts like this for numerous firms from different industries over a length of time, the technician would select certain industries and firms which demonstrated relative strength to be the most promising investment opportunities.

18-9 CHARTING VOLUME OF TRADING DATA

On the day following each trading day many newspapers across the United States publish statistics giving the total number of shares traded in certain security markets. Some financial newspapers also publish the number of shares traded in selected individual issues. For example, Fig. 18-11 shows an excerpt from a typical financial newspaper giving data for the volume of shares traded for the NYSE.

Many technical analysts believe that it is possible to detect whether the market in general and/or certain security issues are bullish or bearish by studying the volume of trading. Volume is supposed to be a measure of the intensity of investors' emotions. There is a Wall Street adage that "it takes volume to really move a stock" either up or down in price. This saying is often, but not always, true. Frequently, a large amount of trading volume tends to be

FIGURE 18-11 volume data for the NYSE, AMEX, and ASE from a typical newspaper.

Thursday's Volume
Total, 2,469,050 Shares
Amex, 2,320,000 Shares

Amex Composite

Volume since Jan. 1:	1979	1978	1977
Total sales	76,112,950	55,829,780	79,247,080

American Stock Exchange

Since Jan. 1:	1979	1978	1977
Total sales	71,620,000	52,350,000	74,810,000

MARKET DIARY

	Thu.	Wed.	Tue.	Mon.	Fri.	Thu.
Issues traded	802	855	817	857	842	823
Advances	234	218	249	296	362	351
Declines	319	399	311	324	225	229
Unchanged	249	238	257	237	255	243
New highs	7	10	9	7	13	13
New lows	3	6	2	2	2	2

ACTIVE STOCKS

	Volume	Close	Chgs.
ResrtInt A	115,800	33⅛	+ ¾
HouOilM	76,000	16⅜	− ¼
Syntex Corp	69,600	36	− ¼
GtBas Pet	57,800	6½	+ ¾
Instrum Sys	44,800	1¼	.....
AtlasCM	38,400	2⅞	.....
Amdahl	32,300	45⅛	.....
Carnatn	29,900	25¼	−1
BrownFor B	28,100	33¼	+ ¼
LoewsTh wt	28,100	17⅝	+ ⅜

52 Weeks High	Low	Stock	Div.	Yld %	P-E Ratio	Sales 100s	High	low	Close	Net Chg.
			−	A−A−A		−				
13⅝	9⅝	AAR	.38	3.1	8	x9	12¼	12	12⅛	+ ¼
6⅝	3½	AAV	.29e	7.3	6	1	4	4	4	.....
12	6⅝	APS	.36	3.9	7	21	9¼	9⅛	9⅛	− ⅛

associated with big security price changes. Thus it is reasonable for stock price chartists to study volume data in an effort to discern what might be the cause of specific stock price movements. However, the cause-and-effect relationship between the volume of shares traded and the price change in the traded security is vague and hard to unravel.[11]

Volume technicians watch volume most closely on days when prices move, that is, on days when supply and demand move to a new equilibrium. If high volume occurs on days when prices move up, the overall nature of the market is considered to be bullish. If the high volume occurs on days when prices are falling, the market is bearish.

Figure 18-9 shows bar charts of the DJIA and the Standard & Poor's index of 500 composite stocks plotted with the daily volume on the NYSE along the bottom of the chart.

There is one occasion when falling prices and high volume are considered bullish. When technicians feel the end of a bear market is near, they watch for a high volume of selling as the last of the bearish investors liquidate their holdings—this is called a *selling climax*. A selling climax is supposed to eliminate the last of the bears who drive prices down by selling, clearing the way for the market to turn up.

Some technicians also look for a speculative blowoff to mark the end of a bull market. A *speculative blowoff* is a high volume of buying which pushes prices up to a peak; it is supposed to exhaust the enthusiasm of bullish speculators and make way for a bear market to begin. Technicians who believe that a speculative blowoff marks the end of a bull market sometimes say "the market must die with a bang, not a whimper."

18-10 MOVING AVERAGE ANALYSIS

Moving average technicians, or rate-of-change technicians, as they are also called, focus on prices and/or a moving average of the prices. The *moving average* is used to provide a smoothed, stable reference point against which the daily fluctuations can be gauged. *Rate-of-change analysis* is used for individual securities or market indices.

18-10.1 construction of chart

Selecting the span of time over which to calculate the moving average affects the volatility of the moving average. Many technicians who perform rate-of-change analysis use a 200-day moving average of closing prices. The moving average changes each day as the most recent day is added and the two-hundred-and-first day is dropped. To calculate a 200-day moving average (MA_t) of the DJIA on day t, Eq. (18-3) is employed.

[11] Robert L. Crouch, "The Volume of Transactions and Price Changes on the New York Stock Exchange," *Financial Analysts Journal*, July–August 1970, pp. 104–109. Thomas W. Epps, "Security Price Changes and Transaction Volumes: Theory and Evidence," *American Economic Review*, September 1975, pp. 586–597. Paul C. Grier and Peter S. Albin, "Nonrandom Price Changes in Association with Trading in Large Blocks," *The Journal of Business*, July 1973, pp. 425–433. Seha Tinic, "The Economics of Liquidity Services," *Quarterly Journal of Economics*, vol. 86, February 1972, pp. 79–93.

$$MA_t = \left(\frac{1}{200}\right)\sum_{j=1}^{200} DJIS_{t-j} \tag{18-3}$$

Figure 18-9 shows the moving average of the DJIA and Standard & Poor's index of 500 composite stocks as dotted lines; the daily values of the two indices are represented by the bar charts. It is this relationship between the actual values and the moving average from which the technician obtains information.

18-10.2 interpreting rate-of-change charts

When the daily prices penetrate the moving average line, technicians interpret this penetration as a signal. When daily prices move downward through the moving average, they frequently fail to rise again for many months. Thus, a downward penetration of a flattened moving average suggests selling. When actual prices are above the moving average but the difference is narrowing, this is a signal that a bull market may be ending. A summary of buy and sell signals followed by moving average chartists is given below.

Moving average analysts recommend buying a stock when (1) the 200-day moving average flattens out and the stock's price rises through the moving average, (2) the price of a stock falls below a moving average line which is rising, and (3) a stock's price which is above the moving average line falls but turns around and begins to rise again before it ever reaches the moving average line.

Moving average chartists recommend selling a stock when (1) the moving average line flattens out and the stock's price drops downward through the moving average line, (2) a stock's price rises above a moving average line which is declining, and (3) a stock's price falls downward through the moving average line and turns around to rise but then falls again before getting above the moving average line.

Adherence to the moving average trading rules over many months and many different stocks shows that sometimes profitable trades are signaled. However, the rules touch off unprofitable trades, too. This is why most technical analysts use more than one technique of technical analysis and compare the buy and sell signals issued by these different technical tools before they decide to trade securities.

18-11 CONCLUSIONS

Many more tools for technical analysis could be discussed; the discussion in this chapter has been limited to a mere sampling of the techniques.

All technical analysis tools have one thing in common: They attempt to measure the supply and demand for some group of investors. Technical analysis seems to presume that these shifts in supply and demand occur *gradually*, rather than instantaneously. More specifically, when shifting prices are detected, they are presumed to be the result of gradual shifts in supply and demand rather than a series of instantaneous shifts which all coincidently happen to be moving in the same direction. Since these *shifts are expected to continue as the price gradually reacts* to news or other factors, the price change pattern is extrapolated to predict further price changes.

Many economists believe that technical analysis cannot measure supply and demand or predict prices. They suggest that security markets are efficient markets in which news is impacted into security prices instantaneously and without delay.[12] That is, news that causes changes in the supply and/or demand for a security is supposed to cause sudden once-and-for-all changes rather than gradual adjustments in supply and demand. As a result, economists believe that security *price changes* are a series of random numbers which occur in reaction to the random arrival of news. When a security's price moves in the same direction for several days, most economists interpret these movements as a series of independent changes in supply and/or demand—all of which coincidentally happen to move the price in the same direction. They assert that technical analysts are wrong in believing that supply and/or demand adjust gradually, causing trends which may be used for predicting future prices. The evidence provided by economists to support their efficient markets hypothesis will be examined in Chap. 19.

QUESTIONS

18-1. "Fundamental analysts' estimates of intrinsic value are different from the security prices determined by supply and demand." True, false, or uncertain? Explain.

18-2. According to the Dow theory, what is the significance of an abortive recovery which follows a series of ascending tops?

18-3. What factual information is contained in the markings on a bar chart?

18-4. What does each column on a point and figure chart represent? How is the time dimension shown on a point and figure chart?

18-5. What significance is attributed to the volume of odd-lot trading by technical analysts?

18-6. Explain what the confidence index is supposed to measure. What relevance does this measure of confidence have for stock prices?

18-7. How are data on the number of shares which advanced and declined on a given trading day used by technical analysts?

18-8. Compare and contrast relative strength and systematic risk. What implications does high relative strength have for rates of return?

18-9. What are a *speculative blowoff* and a *selling climax*?

18-10. How is the moving average used in rate-of-change analysis?

18-11. Do most experienced technical analysts have one tool they believe in and follow closely? Explain.

[12] Eugene F. Fama, "Efficient Capital Markets: A Review of Theory and Empirical Work," *Journal of Finance*, May 1970, pp. 383–417, and "The Behavior of Stock Market Prices," *Journal of Business*, January 1965, pp. 34–105.

SELECTED REFERENCES

Bookstaber, R., *The Complete Investment Book,* Scott Foresman & Co., Glenview, Ill., 1985. Chapters 14–20 present computer programs for technical systems.

Edwards, R. D., and John Magee, Jr., *Technical Analysis of Stock Trends*, 5th ed., Stock Trends Service, Springfield, Mass., 1966. A book that has been used for years by technical analysts. Many different techniques are explained.

Jiler, William L., *How Charts Can Help You in the Stock Market*, Trendline, New York, 1962. This popular book on charting explains many techniques and gives examples.

Levy, R. A., *The Relative Strength Concept of Common Stock Forecasting*, Investors Intelligence, Larchmont, N.Y., 1968. This book explains some of the new nonchart-oriented quantitative technical tools.

Wu, Hsiu-Kwant, and Alan Z. Zakon, *Elements of Investments: Selected Readings*, Holt, New York, 1965, sec. 5. This book of readings in investments devotes an entire section to technical analysis.

the behavior of stock market prices

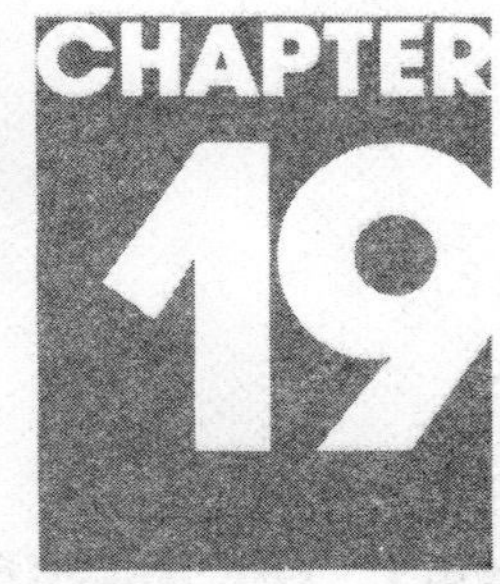

The economic model of capitalism, free markets, and private enterprise that the United States economy is patterned after requires (among other things) efficient capital markets that allocate investable funds where they are needed most so that they will be used most productively. Essentially, this requires that the highest bidder get the resource. Security prices must be allowed to fluctuate freely. If the prices are manipulated or controlled, financial capital will be misallocated to less productive uses.[1]

This chapter reviews empirical evidence about the capital markets in the United States. Evidence is reviewed which suggests that the capital markets are free of price manipulation and are thus able to *allocate capital efficiently*. Some anomalous evidence is reported too. In effect, Chap. 19 treats the assertion that capital markets are efficient price setters as a testable hypothesis to be affirmed or denied with empirical evidence from scientific studies.

The investigation of security price movements which fills this chapter and its appendix is not undertaken solely to determine the *capital allocational efficiency* of security markets in the United States. The degree of efficiency with which a market allocates capital and how efficiently it sets prices also has implications for investment analysts. For example, if markets price their securities inefficiently, fundamental security analysis will be profitable because underpriced securities will await the perceptive analyst. Likewise, overpriced securities can be worthwhile to search for too, as they can be profitably sold short. Market pricing inefficiencies would also make it profitable to

[1] A market may be considered *allocationally efficient* when prices adjust so that the risk-adjusted marginal rates of return are equal for all savers and all investors. As discussed in Chap. 3, a securities market is *operationally efficient* when transactions costs are zero, or, more realistically, when transactions costs are kept down to a level where market-makers earn no economic profits. As suggested in Chap. 8, a market achieves *pricing efficiency* when its prices reflect all available information so that prices equal their underlying economic values. These three concepts of market efficiency are all interdependent. This chapter focuses on pricing efficiency.

perform technical analysis. If security prices respond inefficiently to new information, learning lags which slow security price adjustments will cause trends which can be seen in charts and used to make trading profits. Also, if markets post inefficient prices, the risk-return analysis, which is based on the long-run equilibrium tendencies of a rational market, will not be a worthwhile pursuit. This chapter presents and reviews evidence about the efficiency of security prices with an eye toward reaching conclusions about these considerations.

19-1 THE MARKET MECHANISM

Before examining the facts about market efficiency, let us review the securities market mechanism. Securities markets are large institutions where many independent buyers and sellers meet. It is easy for newcomers to enter the market and for others to leave it. The existing securities regulations control price manipulation and require that security issuers disclose much information about themselves for the investing public. These factors are necessary for efficient markets, but they are not sufficient to guarantee market efficiency. However, additional aspects of the market mechanism are worthy of consideration.

19-1.1 dissemination of information

News is generated in a random fashion. The various competing news services rush this news to the presses in an effort to "make the headlines." The news is not delayed or controlled in any systematic manner; it is widely dispersed and available to the public at virtually no cost. Public libraries contain current books published by the various financial services, and radio and television announcements are available at virtually no cost.

There are no significant learning lags associated with news dissemination. That is, an investor in the middle west or on the west coast can obtain financial news as quickly as a resident of New York City. Of course, different investors may develop different price forecasts based on the same news. Upon receiving financial news, some investors will underreact to it, while other investors will overreact. However, the reaction is immediate and continuous until the news is fully impacted into security prices.

19-1.2 prices fluctuate freely

Security prices are not controlled by any one buyer or seller. There are many independent buyers and sellers. Most security traders are not large enough to affect prices. The few institutions that are large enough to do so are restrained by law from manipulating prices (although they do sometimes reluctantly affect prices by their actions).

There are many independent sources of opinion about security prices. Fundamental analysts and technical analysts develop expectations and valuation techniques which are widely divergent and independent of one another. Thus, at any moment some "experts" will predict price rises for a security which other "experts" may consider overvalued.

19-1.3 fundamental analysis widespread

There are many full-time fundamental analysts; over 12,000 are listed in the directory of the Financial Analysts Federation alone. These analysts follow the financial news and adjust their intrinsic value estimates accordingly. Many of them are in a position to affect prices through the buy or sell recommendations they make to their employers. Of course, all these analysts will never reach a uniform opinion about a security's intrinsic value, but they generally agree as to whether a given piece of news should tend to raise or lower prices.

19-1.4 continuous equilibrium and degrees of disequilibrium

If securities markets are perfectly efficient in allocating capital, the market will be in continuous equilibrium. This *continuous equilibrium* will not be static through time, however. Every time a new piece of news is released, one or more securities' intrinsic values will change, and the securities market prices will adjust toward their new values. It is the speed of this price adjustment process which gauges how efficient a market is. Since a *perfectly efficient market* is in *continuous equilibrium*, the intrinsic values of securities *vibrate randomly*, and *market prices always equal the underlying intrinsic values at every instant* in time.[2] If any disequilibrium (of even a temporary nature) exists, then securities markets are less than perfectly efficient, and some capital will be misallocated as a result. Stated differently, allocational inefficiency results from irrational price movements.

19-2 TESTABLE HYPOTHESES ABOUT MARKET EFFICIENCY

When tests of the efficient markets hypothesis are being carried out, securities markets will be tested for varying degrees of efficiency. First, the *weakly efficient market hypothesis* is examined. The weakly efficient hypothesis says that *historical* price and volume data for securities contain no information which can be used to earn a trading profit above what could be attained with a naive buy-and-hold investment strategy.[3] This hypothesis suggests that technical analysis, which was discussed in Chap. 18, is merely well-recorded market folklore. Empirical evidence supports this hypothesis.

Also examined is the *semistrong efficient market hypothesis*, which says that markets are efficient enough for prices to reflect all *publicly available* information. Consequently, only a few insiders, trading on short-run price changes, can earn a profit larger than what could be earned by using a naive buy-and-hold strategy. It is concluded that securities markets in the United States are semistrong efficient.

Finally, the *strongly efficient market hypothesis* is examined; it claims that *no one* can consistently earn a profit larger than what could be earned with a naive buy-and-hold strategy by trading on short-run security price movements. The

[2] Paul Samuelson, "Proof That Properly Discounted Present Values of Assets Vibrate Randomly," *Bell Journal of Economics and Management Science*, Autumn 1973, pp. 369–374. See also Samuelson's article "Proof That Properly Anticipated Prices Fluctuate Randomly," *Industrial Management Review*, vol. 6, no. 2, pp. 41–49. The articles employ advanced mathematics.

[3] The naive buy-and-hold strategy refers to the investment policy of randomly selecting securities (for example, with a dart), buying them, and holding them over the same time period as the alternative investment strategy is being tested while reinvesting all dividends. Studies indicate that about 10 or 11 percent per annum before taxes could have been earned in the New York Stock Exchange over the last 40 years by following a naive buy-and-hold strategy. L. Fisher and J. Lorie, "Rates of Return on Investments in Common Stock: The Year-by-Year Record, 1926–1965," *Journal of Business*, January 1964. Ibbotson Associates, *Stocks, Bonds, Bills and Inflation: 1985 Yearbook*, Capital Market Research Center, Chicago, Ill.

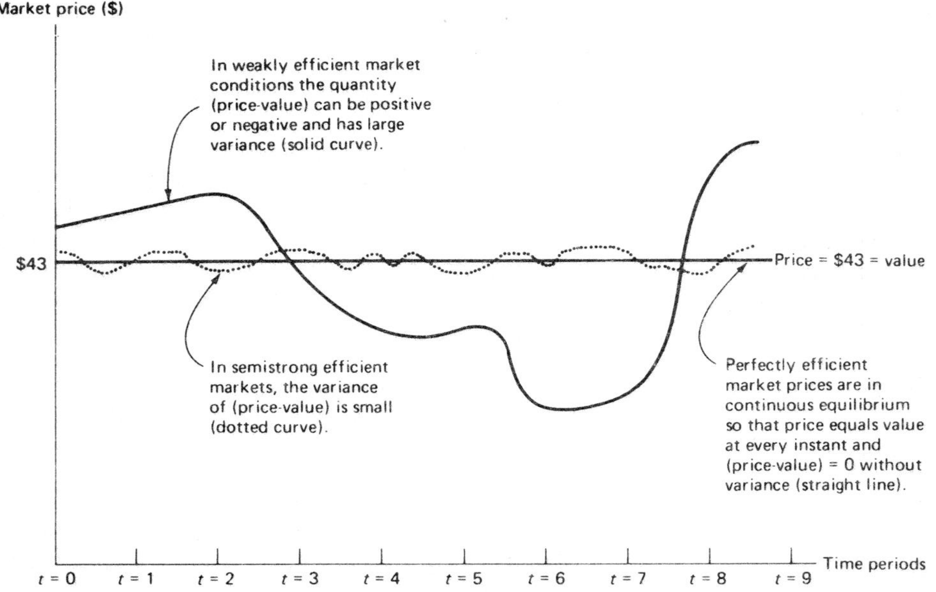

FIGURE 19-1 illustration of different degrees of market price efficiency.

reason given is that security price changes are independent random variables and that *no one* has monopolistic access to valuable inside information. The strongly efficient market hypothesis is found to be not quite acceptable. A few cases of monopolistic profit making have been found which violate this hypothesis.

Differences in the degree of security price efficiency are contrasted graphically in Fig. 19-1. The three hypotheses about pricing efficiency are not mutually exclusive: They differ only in the *degree* of market efficiency they suggest. The review of evidence about pricing efficiency below begins with the weakest hypothesis and ends with evidence about the strongest hypothesis.[4] Some anomalous evidence is reviewed too.

19-3 THE WEAKLY EFFICIENT MARKETS HYPOTHESIS

In this section the hypothesis highlighted in Box 19-1, that markets are weakly efficient, is examined.

Some lucky traders do beat the naive buy-and-hold strategy, and some unlucky ones lose everything they have. However, we will not illogically reason from these specific cases to reach general conclusions. Instead, we will scientifically analyze massive data in an effort to reach accurate general conclusions.

[4] Eugene F. Fama, "Efficient Capital Markets: A Review of Theory and Empirical Work," *Journal of Finance*, May 1970, pp. 383–417, and "The Behavior of Stock Market Prices," *Journal of Business*, January 1965, pp. 34–105.

BOX 19-1
definition of weakly efficient markets

> Weakly efficient markets were defined to be markets in which past prices provide no information about future prices which would allow a short-term trader to earn a return above what could be attained with a naive buy-and-hold strategy. This definition does not mean that short-term traders and speculators will not earn a positive rate of return. It means that, on average, they will not beat a naive buy-and-hold strategy with information obtained from historical data.

19-3.1 filter rules

An x percent filter rule is a mechanical security trading rule which operates as defined in Box 19-2.

By varying the value of x, one can test an infinite number of filter rules. If stock price changes are a series of independent random numbers, filter rules should not yield more return than a naive buy-and-hold strategy. The filter rules should earn a significant profit, however, if some of the patterns chartists talk about (such as the primary trends of the Dow theory) actually exist.

Various studies have been conducted using different stocks and different filters. Filters as small as ½ of 1 percent (that is, $x = .005$), as large as 50 percent ($x = .5$), and many values between these extremes have been tested. The tests were performed with stock price data gathered at various intervals. One test used daily stock prices covering several years. Some of the filter rules earn a return above the naive buy-and-hold strategy if the commissions incurred in buying and selling are ignored. However, after commissions are deducted, no filter outperformed the naive strategy.[5] In fact, some ran up considerable net losses. If patterns do exist which can be used as bases for a profitable trading strategy, filter rules are unable to detect them. This is one piece of evidence in support of the weakly efficient markets hypothesis.

19-3.2 serial correlation

Security price changes do not appear to have significant momentum or inertia which causes changes of a given sign to be followed by changes of that same

[5] S. Alexander, "Price Movements in Speculative Markets: Trends or Random Walks," *Industrial Management Review*, May 1961, pp. 7–26. E. F. Fama and M. E. Blume, "Filter Rules and Stock Market Trading," *Journal of Business*, January 1966, pp. 226–241. Readers who are interested in commodities trading may study the application of filter rules and other tests explained in this chapter to commodity prices. See Richard A. Stevenson and Robert M. Bear, "Commodity Futures: Trends or Random Walks?" *Journal of Finance*, March 1970, pp. 65–81.

BOX 19-2
definition of a filter rule

> If the price of a security rises at least x percent, buy and hold the security until its price drops at least x percent from a subsequent high. Then, when the price decreases x percent, liquidate the long position, and assume a short position until the price rises x percent.

sign; the filter rules should have detected this pattern if it existed. However, security prices may follow some sort of *reversal* pattern in which price changes of one sign tend to be followed by changes of the opposite sign. Filter rules might not detect a pattern of reversals, but serial correlation tests should.

Serial correlation (or *autocorrelation*) measures the correlation coefficient between a series of numbers with lagging numbers in the same time series. Trends or reversal tendencies in security price changes can be detected with serial correlation. We can measure the correlation between security price changes in period t (denoted Δp_t) and price changes in the same security which occur k periods later and are denoted Δp_{t+k}; k is the number of periods of lag. Of course, there is a long-term upward trend in security prices; so if one "period" covers a number of years, a positive serial correlation should be observed. But long-term trends are of no interest; they were already known to exist, as shown in Table 7-2 and Fig. 7-2 on pages 183 and 190, respectively. In question here is the existence of patterns in short-term (for example, daily, weekly, or monthly) price changes which can be used to earn a larger profit after commissions from aggressive trading than what the naive buy-and-hold strategy would yield. If such patterns exist, this would tend to indicate that security prices do not adjust to follow their randomly changing intrinsic values.

In effect, tests for serial correlation in a security's price changes are searching for patterns like the two in Fig. 19-2. The x's in Fig. 19-2 are what would occur if positive changes (denoted $\Delta p > 0$, or Δp^+) were followed by positive changes k periods later and/or if negative changes (denoted $\Delta p < 0$ or Δp^-) were followed by other negative changes k periods later. That is, the x's above the horizontal axis in Fig. 19-2 depict upward-trending prices, and the x's beneath the horizontal axis represent downward-trending prices. If prices kept reversing direction every kth period, the observations represented by the o's in Fig. 19-2 would result.

Various serial correlation studies about security prices have been published. Many different securities, many different lags (that is, different values of k), and many different time periods have been used from which to draw the

FIGURE 19-2 scatter diagram of price changes and lagged price changes in security.

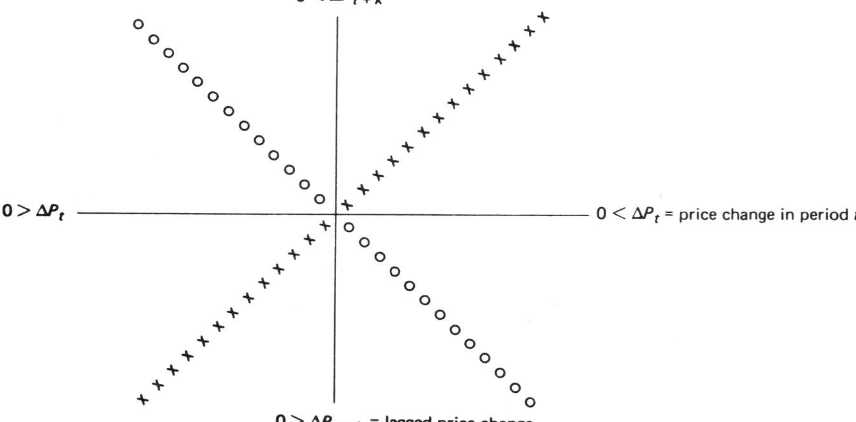

data for the tests. The serial correlation studies failed to detect any significant trends (that is, any significant correlations).[6] Again, a scientific evaluation of stock price movements tends to support the weakly efficient markets hypothesis.

19-3.3 runs tests

It is possible that security prices might fluctuate randomly but occasionally follow upward, sideways, or downward trends which filter rules and serial correlations could not detect as deviations from random wiggles. That is, price changes may be random most of the time but *occasionally* become serially correlated for *varying periods* of time. To examine this possibility, runs tests may be used to determine if there are runs in the price changes. A *run* occurs in a series of numbers whenever the changes in the numbers switch signs. For instance, six price *changes* that comprise four runs are listed below.

$$\Delta p^+, \Delta p^+, 0, \Delta p^-, \Delta p^+, \Delta p^+$$

The four runs illustrated above are positive, zero, negative, and positive. Runs vary in length from one to any large number. For example, in a bear market, a security price that declines for ten consecutive trading days will generate nine negative daily price changes but only one negative run.

Mathematical statisticians are able to determine how many positive, negative, zero, or total runs may be expected to occur in a series of truly random numbers of any size. Therefore, if a time series of security price changes has either a positive, negative, zero, or total number of runs which occur either more frequently or less frequently than would be expected in a series of random numbers, this is evidence that some kind of nonrandomness occurs. The runs tests which have been published suggest that the runs in the price changes of various securities are not significantly different from the runs in a table of random numbers.[7] It seems that short-run traders who search for various types of nonrandom trends from which to earn a profit will not be able to beat a naive buy-and-hold strategy, on average.

19-3.4 anomalous evidence about weakly efficient markets

The preceding evidence suggests that studying charts of historical stock prices will not reveal any patterns that contain profitable insights about prices in the future. However, two patterns of minor proportion have been reported.

Kenneth R. French has reported a small but statistically significant "weekend effect."[8] He found that stock prices tend to rise all week long to a peak price level on Fridays. Then, the stocks tend to trade on Mondays at reduced

[6] Eugene F. Fama, "The Behavior of Stock Market Prices," op. cit. S. Alexander, ibid. M. G. Kendall, "The Analysis of Economic Time Series, part I," *Journal of the Royal Statistical Society*, 1953, vol. 96, pp. 11–25. More recent studies which embrace a more heterogeneous sample of stocks and extend the previous serial correlation studies may be found in Gabriel A. Hawawini, "On the Time Behavior of Financial Parameters: An Investigation of the Intervaling Effect," unpublished doctoral dissertation, New York University, 1977. See also Robert A. Schwartz and David K. Whitcomb, "Evidence on the Presence and Causes of Serial Correlation in Market Model Residuals," *Journal of Financial and Quantitative Analysis*, June 1977, pp. 291–315. These more recent studies find significant positive serial correlations for one-day trends in some stocks.

[7] Eugene F. Fama, op. cit.; S. Alexander, op. cit. See also Table App. 19-A5.

[8] Kenneth R. French, "Stock Returns and the Weekend Effect," *Journal of Financial Economics*, March 1980.

prices, before they begin the next week's ascent. This tendency is so small that if a trader bought stocks on Mondays and sold them on Fridays, the trading profits gained would be too little to pay the brokerage commissions associated with weekly trading. The week-end deviation from perfectly random price movements is an unexplained anomaly in the weakly efficient markets theory.

Another anomalous pattern in stock price movements is called the "year-end effect." Several researchers have discerned a tendency for stock prices, especially the prices of stock in small firms, to fall two or three percentage points late in December and then rise early in January.[9] It has been suggested that the year-end effect might result from last minute selling by those investors who have accumulated losses on stocks and who want to realize some of these losses to reduce their income taxes for the year. However, the cause of this second anomaly remains as much a mystery as the cause of the week-end effect. Some difficulties have been reported in getting accurate measurements too.[10] Whether or not someone will be able to devise a trading rule that profitably exploits the year-end effect on an after-commissions basis remains to be seen.

The two anomalies reported above make it difficult to conclude that stock prices conform completely to the weakly efficient markets hypothesis. However, they are not yet the basis for any profitable trading strategies. Therefore, they appear to be of only limited significance.[11]

19-3.5 weakly efficient markets hypothesis accepted

In testing the weakly efficient markets hypothesis, filter rules, serial correlations, and runs tests have been employed. Other tests could be reviewed, but their findings are similar.[12] These are scientific studies which support the weakly efficient hypothesis. Studies by unbiased scientists using analytical

[9] Ben Branch, "A Tax Loss Trading Rule," *Journal of Business*, April 1977, vol. 50, no. 2, pp. 198–207. Marc R. Reinganum, "The Anomalous Stock Market Behavior of Small Firms in January: Empirical Tests for Tax-Loss Selling Effect," *Journal of Financial Economics*, 1983, vol. 12, no. 1. Richard Roll, "The Turn of the Year Effect and the Return Premium on Small Firms," *Journal of Portfolio Management*, 1982.

[10] Marshall E. Blume and Robert F. Stambaugh, "Biases in Computed Returns: An Application of the Size Effect," *Journal of Financial Economics*, November 1983. Richard Roll, "On Computing Mean Returns and the Small Firm Premium," *Journal of Financial Economics*, November 1983, vol. 12, no. 3. These two studies reach similar conclusions.

[11] Two studies reported a tendency for stock market prices to reverse and move in the opposite direction from one transaction to the next. This pattern does not suggest profitable trading schemes for people who do not own seats on the exchange so that they may trade without paying commissions. Victor Niederhoffer and M. F. M. Osborne, "Market Making and Reversal on the Stock Exchange," *Journal of American Statistical Association*, December 1966, vol. 61. Clive W. T. Granger and Oskar Morgenstern, "Spectral Analysis of New York Stock Market Prices," *KYKLOS*, vol. 16, 1963.

[12] A. B. Larson reports that corn futures prices appear to fluctuate randomly in "Measurement of a Random Process in Futures Prices," Paul Cootner (ed.), *The Random Character of Stock Market Prices*, MIT Press, Cambridge, Mass., 1964, pp. 219–230. Benoit Mandelbrot reports that spot cotton prices fluctuate randomly in "The Variation in Certain Speculative Prices," in Paul Cootner (ed.), *The Random Character of Stock Market Prices*, MIT Press, Cambridge, Mass., 1964, pp. 307–332. Richard Roll documents random Treasury bill rates in *The Behavior of Interest Rates*, Basic Books, New York, 1970. W. Schwert finds that the prices of seats on the NYSE fluctuate randomly in "Stock Exchange Seats as Capital Assets," *Journal of Financial Economics*, January 1977, pp. 51–78. J. P. Stein's research uncovers randomly fluctuating prices for art in

techniques which deny the weakly efficient hypothesis are conspicuously absent. Unscientific assertions that short-run security price changes are not random continue to emanate from persons who earn their living by selling charting services. However, the latter may be dismissed because of their bias and the paucity of scientific evidence they produce. Thus, a reasonable individual would have little trouble accepting the weakly efficient markets hypothesis.

19-4 THE SEMISTRONGLY EFFICIENT MARKETS HYPOTHESIS

The semistrongly efficient markets hypothesis requires more evidence of market efficiency than the previous hypothesis. In essence, the weakly efficient hypothesis asserts only that security prices do not tend to follow patterns repetitively. Semistrongly efficient markets are defined in Box 19-3.

In a free and competitive market, prices adjust so that they equate supply and demand. When supply and demand functions do not change, an equilibrium price will emerge which represents a consensus of opinion. For securities this equilibrium price would be the intrinsic value. That price will prevail until supply and/or demand are changed by *new information*. When a new piece of information reaches the market, supply and/or demand will react, and a new price will be formed. The faster the news is assimilated and the new equilibrium price emerges, the more efficient the markets.

19-4.1 learning lags

In order for markets to be semistrong efficient, there can be no lags as the latest news is disseminated to the public. Prompt news dispersion is important if prices are to reflect all relevant information immediately. Consider what would occur if learning lags existed.

Suppose that financial news released in New York City did not spread beyond the state's boundaries on the day it was released because of some learning lag. If the news favorably affected some corporation's stock, the price would move up slightly as New Yorkers acted upon it. Then, on the second day after the announcement, suppose the news traveled as far west as the

---

"The Monetary Appreciation of Paintings," *Journal of Political Economy*, October 1977, pp. 1021–1036. Several different commodity prices are found to fluctuate with little deviation from randomness by Richard Stevenson and Robert Bear, "Commodity Futures: Trends or Random Walks?" *Journal of Finance*, March 1970. Brad Cornell and David Mayers report that foreign exchange prices fluctuate randomly in "The Efficiency of the Market for Foreign Exchange under Floating Rates," *Review of Economics and Statistics*, February 1978.

BOX 19-3
definition of semistrongly efficient markets

> The semistrongly efficient markets hypothesis requires that all *public* information be fully reflected in security prices. This means that information in *The Wall Street Journal*, *Moody's*, and *Standard & Poor's* publications, for example, is worthless to investors.

Mississippi River. The rest of the eastern investors would bid the price up a bit further the second day. By the third day, suppose the news traveled as far west as the Rocky Mountains. As a result, middle western investors would bid prices up farther as they learned the news. Finally, on the fourth day after the announcement, the news would spread to the rest of the western states. By that time, a price would be bid up for a fourth consecutive day. As a result of this hypothetical learning lag, two events would occur. First, there would be a 4-day trend in a security's price rather than one immediate effect. Second, for over 3 days the security's price would not have fully reflected all available information. The studies discussed in Sec. 19-3 revealed essentially no instances of trends such as the one just hypothesized. This lack of such trends indicates that financial news is widely and quickly disseminated. As a result, securities prices do tend to reflect all publicly available information at any moment.

The market may over- or underreact to news. However, as long as it reacts instantly and continuously in a series of unbiased movements around the true intrinsic value (or equilibrium price), the semistrong hypothesis is supported.

19-4.2 reaction to earnings announcements

It is possible that securities prices fully reflect most news immediately but react imperfectly, irrationally, or slowly to a certain few kinds of news. Although investigating the reaction to every type of news is not possible, we can examine a few particularly interesting cases. One of the most important pieces of information determining a security's price is the earnings of the corporation which issued the security. If securities markets are semistrongly efficient, prices will reflect changes in firms' earning power.

A study by Ball and Brown analyzed the effects of the annual earnings announcements made by 261 corporations over a 20-year period.[13] First, Ball and Brown estimated the simple linear regression Eq. (19-1) to measure each firm's changes in earnings.

$$\Delta \text{eps}_{it} = a_i + b_i(\Delta \text{eps}_{Mt}) + u_{it} \tag{19-1}$$

where

Δeps_{it} = change in the ith firm's earnings per share in the tth time period

Δeps_{Mt} = change in earnings per share averaged over all other firms

a_i and b_i = regression intercept and slope coefficient, respectively, for firm i

u_{it} = unexplained residual for firm i in period t

After Eq. (19-1) was estimated for each firm, Eq. (19-2) was derived from Eq. (19-1) to forecast the next year's earnings per share.

[13] R. Ball and P. Brown, "An Empirical Evaluation of Accounting Income Numbers," *Journal of Accounting Research*, Autumn 1969, pp. 159–178. Ball and Brown acknowledged in their article that their results may be biased because the earnings were scaled by dividing them by market prices, a process which probably introduces spurious correlation. This possibility is evaluated by Nicholas J. Gonedes, "Evidence of the Information Content of Accounting Numbers: Accounting-Based and Market-Based Estimates of Systematic Risk," *Journal of Financial and Quantitative Analysis*, June 1973, pp. 407–443.

$$E(\Delta \text{eps}_{it}) = a_i + b_i (\Delta \text{eps}_{Mt}) \tag{19-2}$$

where

$E(\Delta \text{eps}_{it})$ = forecasted or expected change in eps for the ith firm in the tth time period

Δeps_{Mt} = change in the market average eps which actually occurred in time period t

Based on the 1-year forecasts prepared with Eq. (19-2), each year's earnings for every firm were classified into two possible categories. First, there were those firms that did worse than expected—that is, the disappointing growth in earnings category. Second, there were the firms that did better than expected—that is, the category where growth in earnings was a pleasant surprise. The effects of these earnings changes on the common stock prices of the firms in each category were analyzed separately.

To determine the effects of the announcements on a security's price while holding other factors (namely, the market's movement) constant, Ball and Brown calculated characteristic lines relating the rate of change in the 261 firms' market prices to the rate of change in the level of the market.

$$r_{it} = a_i + b_i r_{Mt} + e_{it} \tag{10-1}$$

where

r_{it} = the ith stock's 1-month rate of return in time period t

r_{Mt} = the market's rate of return in month t

a_i and b_i = regression intercept and slope statistics, respectively, for the ith asset

e_{it} = the unsystematic residual return for stock i in month t which was left unexplained by the characteristic line

The number of percentage points above or below the firm's characteristic line where the actual rates of return occurred (that is, the residual error, denoted e_{it}) measures the portion of the price change which was caused by unsystematic factors other than the market's movements. The percentage points above or below the characteristic line were determined for all securities in the two categories—that is, disappointing earnings or pleasantly surprising earnings—for each of the 12 months before and the 6 months after each firm's 20 annual earnings announcements. Equation (19-3) was employed to calculate the abnormal performance index (API) over the 12 months before and the 6 months after (for a total of 18 months before and after) the earnings announcement for all 261 stocks.

$$\text{API} = \frac{1}{261} \sum_{i=1}^{261} (1 + e_{i,1})(1 + e_{i,2}) \ldots (1 + e_{i,18}) \tag{19-3}$$

Figure 19-3 shows the compounded rates of residual return averaged over all 261 firms in the sample. It shows that, on average, the market correctly anticipated earnings changes *before* they were announced to the public. That is, the firms which had disappointing earnings experienced unfavorable downward pressure on their prices in the months preceding the actual an-

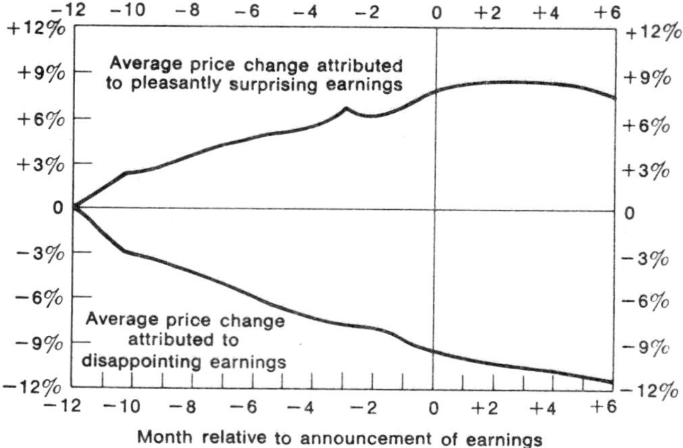

FIGURE 19-3 average percentage price movements preceding and succeeding 20 annual earnings announcements of 261 firms.

nouncement to the market. Firms whose earnings were higher than expected enjoyed upward pressure on the prices of their securities in the months preceding the earnings announcement. On the average, only about 10 percent of the cumulative unsystematic price adjustment occurred *after* the earnings were announced. This was hardly enough of a price change to yield a net trading profit *after commissions.*

The analysis of earnings announcement effects supports the semistrongly efficient markets hypothesis. The securities prices reflected, and even anticipated, the new information about changes in firms' earnings.

Before going on to other subjects, we must pause to realize that the tendency of securities prices to anticipate changes in announced earnings does not result in *trends* in securities prices. First of all, earnings tend to change in a random manner, so that patterned reactions to earnings will not cause price patterns.[14] Second, none of the 261 firms in the sample experienced the smooth price changes indicated by the aggregate data shown in Fig. 19-3. Each individual firm's price moved up or down in a series of erratic random price changes which could not be predicted in advance. Only the cumulative unsystematic errors in the subsamples accumulated smoothly to nonzero sum over time.[15]

19-4.3 announcement effects from changes in the discount rate

The discussion of interest rate risk in Chap. 9 explained why interest rates affect security prices. Essentially, market interest rates determine the appropriate discount rate to use in determining the security's present values. Therefore, changes in the discount rate announced by the Federal Reserve Board may be expected to affect security prices. This is particularly true because

[14] R. A. Brealey, *An Introduction to Risk and Return from Common Stocks*, MIT Press, Cambridge, Mass., 1983, chap. 5. Chapter 5 discusses the randomness of earnings research.

[15] Other studies have reached similar conclusions about the reaction of stock prices to earnings changes. J. Aharony and I. Swary, "Quarterly Dividend and Earnings Announcements and Stockholders Returns: An Empirical Analysis," *Journal of Finance*, March 1980, pp. 1–12. M. Joy, R. Litzenberger, and R. McEnally, "The Adjustment of Stock Prices to Announcements of Unanticipated Changes in Quarterly Earnings," *Journal of Accounting Research*, Autumn 1977. R. Watts, "Systematic Abnormal Returns after Quarterly Earnings Announcements," *Journal of Financial Economics*, June–September 1978, pp. 127–150.

announcements of changes in the discount rate are so widely publicized by financial newspapers.

Research into the effects of discount rate changes has shown that the average security's price changes a tiny but significant amount (never exceeding ½ of 1 percent) on the first trading day following the public announcement by the Federal Reserve of a change in the discount rate.[16] This change is not enough to yield a trading profit. Most of the price change associated with the announcement seems to occur *before* the actual announcement. Thus, the semistrong hypothesis is again supported by the empirical facts.

19-4.4 leading and lagging stocks

Some Wall Street veterans refer to General Motors as a "bellwether stock" because it is supposed to initiate, and sometimes lead, trends in the movements of stock prices. A diversified stock market average, like Standard & Poor's 500 stocks composite average, is thus an average of some leading and some lagging stocks, according to this thinking.

If some securities tended to lead market movements and other stocks tended to be laggers, economic logic suggests that profit-seeking price speculators would reduce these leads and lags to zero. These speculators would buy (sell) the lagging stocks whenever the leading stocks rose (fell) in price in order to profit from the price rise (to avoid losses on the price fall). As long as any stock tended to be a consistent leader or lagger, this simple rule would yield short-run trading profits.

The existence of consistent leading or lagging stocks would disprove the semistrongly efficient markets hypothesis, because consistent leads or lags must presumably be the result of some investors consistently getting valuable news before other investors. That is, leading and lagging security prices would result from the fact that for some securities (the leaders), new news which systematically affected all securities prices was impacted into their prices before the same news was reflected in the prices of other securities. Such intertemporal differences in the reaction of prices to new public information would refute the semistrong efficient markets hypothesis.

To test for leading and lagging stock prices, the modified characteristic regression line shown in Eq. (19-4) was estimated empirically by Dr. Jack Clark Francis.[17]

$$r_{it} = a_i + b_i\,(r_{m,t+k}) + e_t \qquad (19\text{-}4)$$

Equation (19-4) is like the characteristic lines explained in Chap. 10 except that it also allows for leads and lags in the reaction of the ith security to systematic changes in the market, as measured by r_m. The subscript k, which is added to or subtracted from the time period subscript for r_m in Eq. (19-4), measures the lead or lag in months. For example, if Eq. (19-4) yielded a significant goodness of fit for the ith stock when $k = -2$, the ith stock would

[16] R. N. Waud, "Public Interpretation of Discount Rate Changes: Evidence on the 'Announcement Effect,' " *Econometrica*, 1971.

[17] J. C. Francis, "Intertemporal Differences in Systematic Stock Price Movements," *Journal of Financial and Quantitative Analysis*, June 1975. A later study employing daily returns found some significant 1-day leads and lags in NYSE and AMEX stocks—especially AMEX. See G. A. Hawawini and A. Vora, "Evidence of Intertemporal Systematic Risks in the Daily Price Movement of NYSE and AMEX Common Stocks," *Journal of Financial and Quantitative Analysis*, 1979. These leads and lags are so small, however, that they do not obviate the Francis conclusions.

lead the rate of change in the market by 2 months. But if the regression had a significant correlation for $k = 4$, this would mean the stock's rate of price change r_i tended to lag 4 months behind the rate of change in the market index r_m. When $k = 0$, Eq. (19-4) is identical with the characteristic regression line, Eq. (10-1), with no leads or lags.

The leading-concurrent-lagging-characteristic regression line, Eq. (19-4), was estimated for values of $k = 6, 5, 4, 3, 2, 1, 0, -1, -2, -3, -4, -5$, and -6 months for 770 different NYSE stocks: that is (770 stocks × 13 leads and lags for each equals) 10,010 regressions were run on the sample. The model was estimated over two different 3-year sample periods (that is, $t = 1, 2, \ldots, 36$ months) to determine whether leaders or laggers existed over temporary short-run periods. Then the model was estimated over one 10-year (that is, $t = 1, 2, \ldots, 120$ months) sample to test for stocks which might consistently lead or lag in the long run. Thus, in total 30,030 (= 3 samples × 13 lags × 770 stocks) regressions were fitted.

Over the two 3-year sample periods, about 10 percent of the 770 stocks showed some statistically significant tendency to lead or lag the market in each sample period. But the stocks which tended to lead or lag in one 3-year sample usually did not show any tendency to lead or lag in the other 3-year sample. When the same 770 stocks were tested over a 10-year period, only 6 of them (that is, less than 1 percent of the sample) showed any significant tendency to lead or lag the market. Six significant regressions could be expected if 10,010 regressions on 770 stocks were run with *random numbers* simply because of coincidences called sampling errors.

The temporary leads and lags which were found in about 10 percent of the 770 stocks in one of the two 3-year subsamples help explain why chartists can think that some stocks lead or lag the market: They are observing spurious correlation errors which occur because of coincidence. But these temporary coincidences are not consistent enough to suggest that some stocks do in fact lead or lag the market or to violate the semistrong efficient markets hypothesis.

19-4.5 effects of stock splits

Stock splits and stock dividends are essentially paper-shuffling operations which do not change the total value of the firm or the owner's wealth. For example, a 100 percent stock dividend or a 2 for 1 stock split results in twice as many shares outstanding and in each share being worth half as much.[18] If security markets efficiently equate security prices with security values, the *total value* of the firm's outstanding shares will not be affected.

Some firms occasionally have stock splits to broaden the market for their shares. For example, if a firm's shares are selling for $120 each, a 3 for 1 stock split (or 200 percent stock dividend) will reduce the cost of a round lot (100 shares) from $12,000 to $4000. Therefore, splitting the high-priced shares

[18] To accountants and attorneys, stock splits are different from stock dividends, the difference being due to the treatment of the equity section of the balance sheet. With a stock split, the par value per share is decreased to reflect the splitting of the shares; the number of shares outstanding is simultaneously increased so as to leave the total amount in the capital account unchanged. With stock dividends, a portion of retained earnings equal to the value of the stock dividend is transferred from retained earnings to the capital account. Both adjustments are pure bookkeeping entries which leave total equity and total assets unchanged and hence have no real economic significance.

may be advisable if a firm is seeking to broaden its shareholder group to include families that may not have $12,000 but do have $4000 to invest. This is particularly true because shareholders may make good customers. However, the additional small investors gained by such actions cannot be expected to control enough purchasing power to raise the price of the firm's shares significantly.

The study which will be discussed here is based on a sample of 940 stock splits and stock dividends that occurred on the NYSE between 1927 and 1959.[19] In essence, the study asked if stock splits or stock dividends had any influence on investors' one-period rates of return, as defined below.

$$r_t = \frac{\text{capital gains or loss} + \text{cash dividends}}{\text{purchase price}}$$

All the shares were adjusted for the stock splits and stock dividends before the rates of return were calculated . This adjustment ensured that only actual changes in the investor's wealth would be measured rather than the meaningless price changes which are associated with a stock dividend or split. For example, if a 2 for 1 split or 100 percent stock dividend occurred, the share prices would be halved before the stock dividend or split (or doubled afterward) so that no changes in the investor's wealth would be attributed to it in calculating rates of return.

The numerical example below shows how a share of stock, originally selling for $100 per share, can fall to $50 per share owing to a 2 for 1 split or 100 percent stock dividend without changing the owner's 5 percent rate of return. The change in the unit of account (that is, the stock dividend or stock split) occurred between periods 2 and 3. Since the investor owns twice as many shares after the stock split but since each share has half the previous market price, the investor's wealth is unchanged. Moreover, the investor's income in this simple example is $5 of cash dividends per period per $100 of investment before and after the change in the unit of account, that is, a constant 5 percent rate of return.

time period (t)	$t = 1$	$t = 2$	$t = 3$	$t = 4$
Market price per share	$100	$100	$50	$50
Cash dividend per share	$5	$5	$2.50	$2.50
Earnings per share	$10	$10	$5	$5
Number of shares held per $100 original investment	1	1	2	2
Rate of return per period	5%	5%	5%	5%

[19] E. Fama, L. Fisher, M. Jensen, and R. Roll, "The Adjustment of Stock Prices to New Information," *International Economic Review*, February 1969, vol. 10, no. 1, pp. 1–21. The FFJR study was replicated with allowance for shifting beta statistics and similar results were obtained; see Sasson Bar-Yosef and Lawrence D. Brown, "A Reexamination of Stock Splits Using Moving Betas," *Journal of Finance*, September 1977, vol. XXXII, no. 4, pp. 1069–1080. More recently, it has been reported that stock splits increase the day-to-day and week-to-week price fluctuations approximately 30 percent. See James A. Ohlson and Stephen H. Penman, "Volatility Increases Subsequent to Stock Splits: An Empirical Aberration," *Journal of Financial Economics*, June 1985, vol. 14, no. 2, pp. 251–266.

CHARACTERISTIC LINE USED In order to have a standard of comparison against which the rates of return may be evaluated, we must make adjustments for the differences in returns resulting from bull- or bear-market swings in price. The characteristic line, defined in Eq. (10-1), was calculated for each security studied in order to adjust for these changes in the market conditions. Each stock's characteristic line was fit using 60 monthly returns from the 30 months before and 30 months after the change in the unit of account.

RESIDUAL ERRORS The residual errors e_t around the time of the stock split or stock dividend were the focus of the study. Figure 19-4 shows the characteristic line for some hypothetical firm.

If the residual error at the time of stock split or stock dividend was zero, $e_{it} = 0$, the security's actual rate of return was right on the characteristic line, and the change had no positive or negative effects on an investor's normal pattern of returns. If the residual error was positive (that is, if it had a positive e_{it}) at the time of the change, then the actual return (that is, the r_{it}) was above the characteristic line, and the stock split or stock dividend was apparently boosting returns above the normal pattern. A negative residual error (that is, a negative e_{it}) occurs when the actual rate of return is below the characteristic line and some negative influence is affecting that period's rate of return. If the beliefs that most investors and businesspeople hold about stock splits and stock dividends somehow creating something of value are true, the residual errors will tend to be positive after the split or dividend because the value of the firm should increase at that time.

MONTHLY RESIDUAL ERRORS AVERAGED The residual errors about the characteristic line are the results of many influences other than stock splits and stock dividends. Therefore, it is not practical to examine the residuals of *individual* firms following a split or dividend and draw conclusions. To overcome this problem, the residual errors averaged over 940 stocks were calculated for each month before and after the split or dividend. In effect, this approach averages the influences which are not due to the stock dividend or stock split to zero. If the *average* residuals are significantly different from zero in the months after the change, this disparity indicates that the change affected the value of the firm. Equation (19-5) defines the average residuals $\bar{e}_t$ for the tth month before or after the split or dividend month.

FIGURE 19-4 characteristic line.

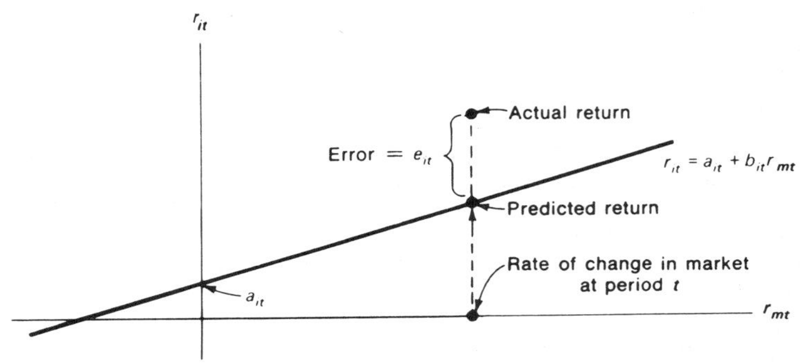

$$\bar{e}_t = \left(\frac{1}{940}\right) \sum_{i=1}^{940} e_{it} \tag{19-5}$$

The average residual, say, 6 months before the split month is denoted $\bar{e}_{-6}$, for example.

CUMULATIVE AVERAGE RESIDUALS (CARs) In order to measure the cumulative month-by-month effect that the stock dividend or split may have, the average monthly residuals from Eq. (19-5) were summed chronologically over 60 months. Equation (19-6) defines these cumulative abnormal (or unsystematic) average monthly residual returns, denoted CARs.

$$\text{CARs} = \sum_{t=-30}^{30} \bar{e}_t = \sum_{t=-30}^{30} \sum_{i=1}^{940} e_{it} \tag{19-6}$$

Note that the cumulative abnormal residuals (CARs) graphed in Fig. 19-5 are increasing in the months *preceding* the stock split or stock dividend. This rise in returns in the few months prior to the change can be attributed to the information content of an *anticipated cash dividend.* In the majority of cases, a stock split or stock dividend is accompanied by an increase in the cash dividend. Thus, the stock split or stock dividend is interpreted by the market as evidence of an upcoming increase in cash dividends. These anticipated increases in the firm's cash dividends usually *contain information.* When a board of directors declares an increased cash dividend, this decision tends to indicate that the majority of the directors are confident that the sustainable earnings power of the firm has risen enough to maintain a higher level of future dividends. It is this implied earnings rise which is the basis for the higher returns preceding the stock split or stock dividend.

INTERPRETING THE RESULTS The preceding explanation for the increasing cumulative abnormal residuals (CARs) prior to a stock dividend or split involves some complicated logic. Let us retrace this reasoning and examine it more closely. The cause-and-effect logic for positive residuals preceding the

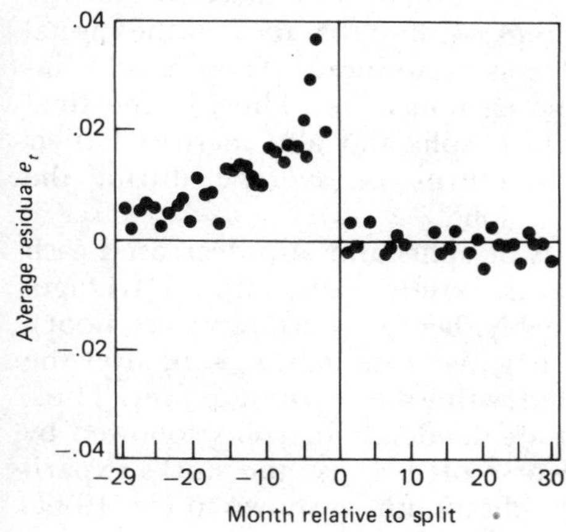

FIGURE 19-5 the average residual errors surrounding the item of a stock split or stock dividend. (*Source*: E. Fama, L. Fisher, M. Jensen, and R. Roll, "The Adjustment of Stock Prices to New Information," *International Economic Review*, February 1969, vol. 10, no. 1, fig. 2*a*.)

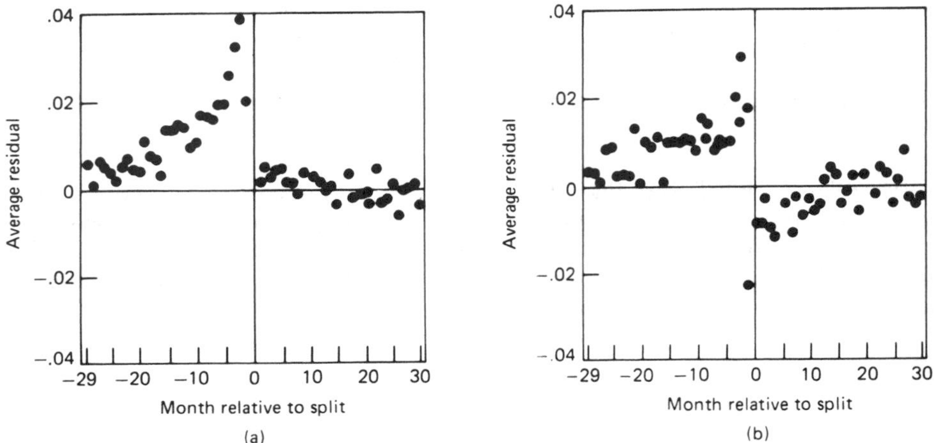

FIGURE 19-6 the average residual errors before and after stock dividends and splits: (*a*) average residuals for dividend "increases"; (*b*) average residuals for dividend decreases. (*Source*: E. Fama, L. Fisher, M. Jensen, and R. Roll, "The Adjustment of Stock Prices to New Information," *International Economic Review*, February 1969, vol. 10, no. 1, pp. 1–21.)

changes goes as follows. A stock dividend or split implies an increase in cash dividends; increased cash dividends imply a permanent rise in earnings; and higher anticipated earnings cause capital gains, pushing returns up and causing positive residual errors. If this line of logic is correct, a firm which declares a stock dividend or split and subsequently fails to raise its cash dividend must be disappointing the market; its price and returns can be expected to rise in anticipation of the stock split or dividend and then fall when cash dividends and earnings fail to rise. Figure 19-6 shows graphs of the cumulative average residuals (CARs) for firms which had stock dividends or splits and then either (1) increased their cash dividend or (2) decreased their cash dividend.

Figure 19-6*a* shows that firms which had stock dividends or splits and subsequently raised cash dividends had small positive residuals, on average, in the months after the stock dividend or split. This is an indication that the market had correctly anticipated the earnings rise and that most of the capital gains occurred before the earnings rise was announced. These stocks' increased cash dividends merely reflect the earnings rise. Thus, in the final analysis, the owners of the securities which split and also increased their earning power enjoyed abnormally high returns, on average, during the months surrounding the stock dividend or split.

Those firms which had stock dividends or splits and also decreased cash dividends experienced high returns (that is, positive residuals, on average) until the cash dividend declined (presumably, because earnings were poor). Then the value of the stock fell, causing negative residuals, $e_{it} < 0$, after the stock dividend or split which was associated with lower earning power. Thus, investors who bought stocks that had stock dividends or splits followed by decreases in their cash dividends were worse off because the stocks experienced capital losses, on average, after the split month, as shown in Fig. 19-6*b*.

CONCLUSIONS The evidence indicates that stock dividends and splits by themselves are worthless but that they may convey valuable information about the firm's earning power. Earning power is the basic source of stock values. Stock dividends and splits alone cause high returns only for several months before cash dividends are paid because the market expects an increase in dividends and, more basically, an increase in earnings. If the expected increase in dividends (and, also, in earnings) does not materialize, the information content of the stock dividend or split is discounted, and returns fall temporarily below normal before resuming their pattern along the characteristic line. In the final analysis, neither the market value of the firm nor the return to the investor is changed by stock splits and dividends. Such changes are essentially paper-shuffling operations which the market expects to convey information about earnings. Any effects from stock dividends and splits can be attributed to their implicit information content and nothing else.

If an investor can correctly anticipate stock dividends and stock splits, the data seem to indicate that it is possible to earn speculative capital gains. However, further studies of the average residuals show that the gains tend to be zero after the announcement date of the stock dividend or split.[20] Therefore, speculation anticipating the announcement of stock dividends or stock splits should precede the public announcement if it is to be profitable. This is probably possible only by spending the capital gains before they are earned to detect announcements which are associated with increasing earnings. The investor would be better off by ignoring stock dividends and splits and instead concentrating on forecasts of the earning power of firms.

The study of stock dividends and splits furnishes additional support for the semistrongly efficient markets hypothesis that markets are efficient. The stock dividends and stock splits themselves had no discernible effects on prices. This evidence is impressive in view of the popular folklore about the importance of stock dividends and stock splits. It seems that the rational investors' evaluations prevailed over those of their less sophisticated counterparts. The unusual price changes which did occur near the time of the splits were attributable to rational investor reactions to changes in cash dividends and earnings.

19-4.6 anomalies in the semistrongly efficient markets hypothesis

Two anomalies in the semistrongly efficient markets hypothesis are noteworthy. First, there is a "price-earnings ratio effect." Second, there is a "size effect." Both of these anomalies have been found to cause statistically significant aberrations in stock prices as a result of publicly available information.

STOCKS WITH LOW PRICE-EARNINGS RATIOS The use by fundamental security analysts of price-earnings ratios (or synonymously, earnings multipliers) was explained in some detail in Chap. 15. The following paragraphs present empirical evidence about a well-known and highly regarded investment scheme which is based on this form of analysis. The decision rule to employ the scheme is simple and easy to apply: Buy stocks which have low price-earnings ratios in order to earn excessively high risk-adjusted rates of return.

[20] W. H. Hausman, R. R. West, and J. A. Largay, "Stock Splits, Price Changes, and Trading Profits: A Synthesis," *Journal of Business,* January 1971, pp. 69–77.

Respected investment advisory firms (for example, Value Line Investment Company of New York City) and money management firms use low price-earnings ratios as investment criteria with acknowledged success.[21] Further, several academic researchers and financial analysts have published studies which advocate selection of stocks with low price-earnings ratios (called simply P/E's hereafter).[22] The most thorough study published recently which advocates the selection of low P/E stocks was done by Dr. S. Basu; it is explained below.[23]

Dr. Basu analyzed market data on over 750 NYSE listed stocks from the 14-year period between September 1956 and August 1971. The first step in his analysis was to array all the stocks under analysis based on the values of their year-end P/E's. Second, Basu formed five equal-sized portfolios from the quintiles of each year's array of the stocks' P/E's. Third, the monthly rates of return of the five P/E quintile portfolios were calculated over the next year. Fourth, Basu computed the characteristic line in risk-premium form for each of the five quintile portfolios.

$$r_{pt} - R_t = A_p + B_p(r_{mt} - R_t) + u_{pt} \tag{19-7}$$

where

$r_{pt} - R_t$ = the risk-premium on the pth P/E quintile portfolio in the tth month, also called excess return

$r_{mt} - R_t$ = the rate of return risk-premium in the tth month from the Lorie-Fisher market index

[21] Fischer Black, "Yes Virginia, There Is Hope: Tests of the Value Line Ranking System," *Financial Analysts Journal,* September–October 1973. T. E. Copeland and D. Mayers, "The Value Line Enigma, 1965–1978: A Case Study of Performance Evaluation Issues," *Journal of Financial Economics,* 1984 forthcoming. J. Shelton, "The Value Line Contest: A Test of Predictability of Stock Price Changes," *Journal of Business,* July 1967, pp. 251–269. W. Hausman, "A Note on the Value Line Contest: A Test of the Predictability of Stock Price Changes," *Journal of Business,* July 1969, pp. 317–320. R. S. Kaplan and R. Weil, "Risk and the Value Line Contest," *Financial Analysts Journal,* July–August 1973, pp. 56–60. L. Brown and M. Rozeff, "The Superiority of Analysts Forecasts as Measures of Expectations: Evidence from Earnings," *Journal of Finance,* March 1978, pp. 1–16. C. Holloway, "A Note on Testing an Aggressive Strategy Using Value Line Ranks," *Journal of Finance,* June 1981, pp. 711–719.

[22] Paul F. Miller and Ernest R. Widmann, "Price Performance Outlook for High and Low P/E Stocks," *1966 Bond and Stock Issue, Commercial and Financial Chronicle,* Sept. 29, 1966, pp. 26–28. Francis Nicholson, "Price Ratios in Relation to Investment Results," *Financial Analysts Journal,* July–August 1960, pp. 43–45. J. Peter Williamson, *Investments: New Analytic Techniques,* Praeger, New York, 1971, pp. 160–168. Volkert S. Whitbeck and Manown Kisor, Jr., "A New Tool in Investment Decision-Making," *Financial Analysts Journal,* May–June 1973, pp. 55–62.

[23] S. Basu, "The Investment Performance of Common Stocks in Relation to Their Price-Earnings Ratios: A Test of the Efficient Markets Hypothesis," *Journal of Finance,* June 1977, vol. XXXII, no. 3, pp. 663–682. Basu used Jensen's characteristic line estimated in terms of risk premiums. M. C. Jensen, "Risk, the Pricing of Capital Assets, and the Evaluation of Investment Portfolios," *Journal of Business,* April 1969, vol. 42, no. 2, pp. 167–247. More recently, assertions that the P/E ratio subsumes the size effect are made by S. Basu, "The Relationship between Earnings Yield, Market Value, and the Return for NYSE Stocks: Further Evidence," *Journal of Financial Economics,* 1983, vol. 12, no. 1.

A_p = alpha regression intercept coefficient = Jensen's portfolio performance measure for the *p*th quintile portfolio

B_p = beta regression slope coefficient for portfolio p = an index of the *p*th portfolio's systematic risk

u_{pt} = residual return for portfolio p in month t which was left unexplained by the regression

Basu replicated the four steps outlined above Eq. (19-7) each year for 14 years. Table 19-1 contains summary statistics. Quintile portfolio 5 contains the 20 percent of the stocks with the highest P/E's. Portfolio 1 contains the stocks with the lowest P/E's and, purportedly, the highest risk-adjusted rates of return. Essentially, each of the quintile portfolios in Table 19-1 may be viewed as a mutual fund which has the policy of acquiring all NYSE stocks in a given P/E quintile (but no others) each year on April 1, holding the portfolio 1 year, and then liquidating and reinvesting in a similar P/E quintile portfolio on April 1 of next year.

The top three lines of Table 19-1 support the venerable folklore about P/E's. The first and second quintile portfolios, with their low median P/E's, earned much higher average rates of return and higher average risk-premiums than the other quintile portfolios with higher median P/E's. The inverse relationship between the P/E and the average return is clearly visible in the top three lines. However, these statistics in the top three lines ignore the effects of risk.

The fourth line of Table 19-1 lists the five quintile portfolios' beta systematic risk coefficients. There is no obvious relationship between the five portfolios' P/E's and their betas. Thus, it appears that the differences in returns documented in the second and third lines of Table 19-1 may be purely the result of P/E's.

The fifth and sixth lines in Table 19-1 present Treynor's and Sharpe's risk-adjusted investment performance measures, respectively. Treynor's measure is defined in Eq. (28-4) and illustrated in Fig. 28-7. Sharpe's portfolio performance measure is defined in Eq. (28-2) and illustrated graphically in Fig. 28-4. Both measures vary inversely with the P/E of the quintile portfolio. This is evidence which supports the notion that, on average, low P/E stocks earn better risk-adjusted rates of return than high P/E stocks. These results from two different investment performance measures, both of which measure return per unit of risk borne, are even more impressive than the simple return data shown in the first three lines of Table 19-1.

The resounding success of simply buying stocks with low P/E's which is documented in Table 19-1 gave Dr. Basu some pause; it appeared to be too easy to beat the market. Furthermore, the superior risk-adjusted rates of return from low P/E stocks implies that the semistrongly efficient market hypothesis explained above was violated. Therefore, Dr. Basu pressed his inquiry further before jumping hastily to the conclusion that the semistrongly efficient markets hypothesis had been violated.

Basu simulated deducting the security analysis and portfolio management expenses which are appropriate for a large portfolio in order to determine the returns net of these costs which could have been earned from quintile

TABLE 19-1 performance measures and related summary statistics (April 1957–March 1971)

	QUINTILE P/E PORTFOLIO*					MARKET PORTFOLIO*	
performance	**5**	**4**	**3**	**2**	**1**	**S**	**F**
Median P/E ratio†	35.8	19.1	15.0	12.8	9.8	15.1	
Average annual rate of return r_p‡	.0934	.0928	.1165	.1355	.1563	.1211	.1174
Average annual excess return r'_p§	.0565	.0558	.0796	.0985	.2260	.0841	.0804
Systematic beta risk B_p	1.1121	1.0387	.9678	.9401	.9866	1.0085	1.0000
Treynor's reward-to-volatility measure¶	.0508	.0537	.0822	.1047	.1237	.0834	.0804
Sharpe's reward-to-variability measure[a]	.0903	.0967	.1475	.1886	.2264	.1526	.1481
Jensen's measure of average excess return, and	−.0330	−.0277	.0017	.0228	.0467	.0030	
t value in parentheses	(−2.62)	(−2.85)	(.18)	(2.73)	(3.98)	(.62)	

* 5 = highest P/E quintile, 1 = lowest P/E quintile, S = total sample, and F = Fisher stock market index.

† Based on 1957–1971 pooled data.

‡ $\bar{r}_p = \left(\sum_{t=1}^{168} r_{pt}\right)/14$, where r_{pt} is the continuously compounded return of portfolio p in month t (April 1957 to March 1971).

§ $\bar{r}_p = \left(\sum_{t=1}^{168} r'_{pt}\right)/14$, where r_{pt} is the continuously compounded excess return (r_{pt} minus r_{ft}) of portfolio p in month t (April 1957 to March 1971).

¶ Mean excess return on portfolio p divided by its systematic risk, Eq. (22-3).

[a] Mean excess return on portfolio p divided by its standard deviation, Eq. (22-1).

Source: S. Basu, "The Investment Performance of Common Stocks Relative to Their Price-Earnings Ratios: A Test of the Efficient Markets Hypothesis," *Journal of Finance*, June 1977, table 1.

portfolio 1. He deducted (1) the high, fixed NYSE commissions which existed during his sample period, (2) a research fee of ¼ of 1 percent each year, and (3) federal income taxes which were appropriate for an investor in the 50 percent tax bracket. After these costs were deducted from the quintile portfolio with the lowest P/E, Dr. Basu found that the portfolio earned from ½ of 1.0 to 2½ percent per annum more than a randomly selected portfolio (that is, selected without regard to the stocks' P/E's) in the same risk-class.

Basu's after-costs results are well worth considering when selecting common stocks, especially for tax-exempt investors and NYSE insiders who do not have to pay stock brokerage commissions. However, the one or two percentage points per year additional rate of return which the average (that is, commission- and tax-paying) investor could hope to attain from the lowest P/E portfolio hardly represents a breathtaking way to beat the market. Rather, the annual incremental return to be gained from selecting low P/E stocks could better be described as a slow, but fairly steady, little gain.

THE SIZE EFFECT—A SECOND ANOMALY Several studies were published in the early 1980s indicating that common stock investments in small-sized firms earned significantly higher rates of return than similar investments in medium- or large-sized corporations.[24] In one early study Banz, for instance, showed that NYSE-listed firms with market values of total common stock outstanding in the smallest 20 percent earned 19.8 percent per year more than the largest 20 percent of the firms in this NYSE sample.[25] There were times when the firms in the largest quintile outperformed the firms in the smallest quintile. However, the rates of return from common stock investments in the smallest quintile outperformed those in the larger quintiles by an amount that was both economically and statistically significant over the longer sample intervals. Since the total market value of all common stock outstanding is a matter of public record for most corporations, the size effect appears to be a second flaw in the semistrongly efficient markets hypothesis.

[24] Rolf W. Banz, "The Relationship between Return and Market Value of Common Stocks," *Journal of Financial Economics,* vol. 9, March 3–18, 1981. P. Brown, A. W. Kleidon, and T. A. March, "New Evidence on the Nature of Size Related Anomalies in Stock Prices," *Journal of Financial Economics,* 1983, vol. 12, pp. 33–56. R. G. Ibbotson and R. A. Sinquefield, *Stocks, Bonds, Bills and Inflation: The Past and the Future,* 1982 edition, Financial Analysts Research Foundation, Charlottesville, Va. Donald Keim, "Size Related Anomalies and Stock Return Seasonality: Further Empirical Evidence," *Journal of Financial Economics,* June 1983, vol. 12, pp. 13–32. M. R. Reinganum, "Misspecification of Capital Asset Pricing: Empirical Anomalies Based on Earning's Yields and Market Values," *Journal of Financial Economics,* 1981*a*, vol. 9, pp. 19–46. M. R. Reinganum, "The Arbitrage Pricing Theory: Some Empirical Results," *Journal of Finance,* 1981*b*, vol. 36, pp. 313–321. M. R. Reinganum, "A Direct Test of Roll's Conjecture on the Firm Size Effect," *Journal of Finance,* 1982, vol. 37, pp. 27–35. M. R. Reinganum, "The Anomalous Stock Market Behavior of Small Firms in January: Empirical Tests for Tax-Loss Selling Effects," *Journal of Financial Economics,* 1983, vol. 12, pp. 89–104. M. R. Reinganum, "Portfolio Strategies Based on Market Capitalization," *Journal of Portfolio Management,* Winter 1983, vol. 9, pp. 29–36. R. Roll, "A Possible Explanation of the Small Firm Effect," *Journal of Finance,* 1981, vol. 36, 879–888.

[25] Rolf W. Banz, "The Relationship between Return and Market Value of Common Stocks," *Journal of Financial Economics,* March 1981, vol. 9, pp. 3–18.

Much research effort has gone into investigating the size effect. Statistical measurement problems have been encountered. Furthermore the economic rationale for the size effect has been difficult to unravel. It appears as if the size effect may be a proxy for one or more other fundamental economic determinants of common stock returns. For example, some researchers have found that small firms are typically riskier than larger firms. If so, economic theory suggests that riskier investments must yield higher returns to induce investors to assume the risk. Risk-adjusted rates of return (like those explained in Chap. 28) were calculated to see if the small firms yielded sufficiently high returns to compensate for their level of riskiness. These tests generally indicated that the small-sized firms outperformed the larger firms on a risk-adjusted return basis. However, some statistical problems in measuring the risk clouded these results.[26] Also, problems in measuring the investors' returns further obscured the results of the early tests of the size effect.[27]

Several different economic variables may ultimately be shown to be the cause of the size effect. The small firms may have low price-earnings ratios[28] or low market prices[29] or freedom from agency costs[30]—any of which may explain what appears at first to be a size effect. Or one of the other reasons cited above may explain the reason for the size effect. Further research may show that it is merely a statistical measurement error or some other logical economic variable which was simply difficult to discern in the early research into the size effect.[31] Nevertheless, the size effect stands as an anomaly in the

[26] R. Roll, "A Possible Explanation of the Small Firm Effect," *Journal of Finance*, 1981, vol. 36, pp. 879–888. Andrew A. Christie and Michael Hertzel, *Capital Asset Pricing Anomalies: Size and Other Correlations*, University of Rochester, 1981. M. R. Reinganum, "Misspecification of Capital Asset Pricing: Empirical Anomalies Based on Earning's Yields and Market Values," *Journal of Financial Economics*, 1981, vol. 9, pp. 19–46.

[27] Marshall Blume, and Robert F. Stambaugh, "Biases in Computed Returns: An Application to the Size Effect," *Journal of Financial Economics*, November 1983, vol. 12, no. 3. R. Roll, "On Computing Mean Returns and the Small Firm Premium," *Journal of Financial Economics*, November 1983, vol. 12, no. 3. H. R. Stoll and R. E. Whaley, "Transaction Costs and the Small Firm Effect," *Journal of Financial Economics*, 1983, vol. 12, pp. 57–79.

[28] S. Basu, "The Investment Performance of Common Stocks in Relation to Their Price-Earnings Ratios: A Test of the Efficient Markets Hypothesis," *Journal of Finance*, June 1977, vol. XXXII, no. 3, pp. 663–682. S. Basu, "The Relationship between Earnings Yield, Market Value and the Return for NYSE Common Stocks: Further Evidence," *Journal of Financial Economics*, 1983, vol. 12, no. 1.

[29] Some financial analysts have attached significance to the absolute dollar level of the price of a common stock. B. Graham, D. L. Dodd, and S. Cottle, *Security Analysis*, 4th ed., McGraw-Hill, New York, 1962, p. 649. L. H. Fritzemeier, "Relative Price Fluctuation of Industrial Stocks in Different Price Groups," *Journal of Business*, April 1936, pp. 113–154. M. E. Blume and F. Husic, "Price, Beta, and Exchange Listing," *Journal of Finance*, May 1973, vol. 28, no. 2, pp. 283–299. Dan Galai and Benjamin Bachrach, "The Risk-Return Relationship and Stock Prices," *Journal of Financial and Quantitative Analysis*, June 1979. More recent research, however, suggests that the low-priced stocks which earn the highest rates of return may be significantly positively correlated with the size and riskiness of the issuing corporation. Thus, the price level of the stock may really only be a proxy for the size and/or the riskiness of the issuing firm.

[30] M. Jensen and W. Meckling, "Theory of the Firm: Managerial Behavior, Agency Costs, and Ownership Structure," *Journal of Financial Economics*, October 1976, pp. 305–360.

[31] It has been suggested that stocks that are not widely held by institutional investors offer superior investment returns. This finding may be the result of underlying size effects, low P/E

semistrongly efficient markets hypothesis until a better explanation for its existence is determined.

CONCLUSIONS ABOUT THE SEMISTRONGLY EFFICIENT MARKETS HYPOTHESIS Moody's manuals, Standard & Poor's reports, and audited financial information filed with the Securities and Exchange Commission are readily available to investors across the United States. This background information about corporations provides the perspective needed to evaluate new information. Financial newspapers and the news services compete to deliver news as quickly as possible. As a result, investors can obtain the latest financial news quickly at minimal cost. They tend, on average, to interpret this news correctly. When news affects the value of a security, it will cause reevaluations and security trading. This trading begins immediately after news is announced and affects prices at once. Prices adjust through a series of erratic but unbiased movements toward their intrinsic value. The studies reviewed above show that security prices not only react immediately and rationally to news; they often anticipate it. As a result, it may be concluded that security prices reflect practically all publicly available information, as suggested by the semistrongly efficient hypothesis.

19-5 THE STRONGLY EFFICIENT MARKETS HYPOTHESIS

The strongly efficient markets hypothesis is defined in Box 19-4.

Before looking at the evidence, common sense suggests that such an extreme hypothesis should be refutable: All that need be done would be to find one insider who has profited from inside information, and the hypothesis would be disproved. It is not hard, moreover, to find evidence that several investors have enough valuable inside information with which to earn trading profits.

19-5.1 monopolistic access to valuable information

Specialists on the organized security exchanges who make the markets in securities have valuable inside information. They keep a book of unfilled limit orders to buy and sell at different prices. This information allows them to see the outlines of the supply and demand curves for the securities in which they make a market. The specialists' book is kept confidential in order to stop

ratios, agency costs, or some other underlying factor. See Avner Arbel, Steven Carvell, and Paul Strebel, "Giraffes, Institutions and Neglected Firms," *Financial Analysts Journal,* May–June 1983, pp. 2–8.

BOX 19-4
definition of the strongly efficient markets hypothesis

> The strongly efficient markets hypothesis is that *all* (not just publicly available) information is fully reflected in security prices. This is sometimes called a *perfectly efficient market* in which prices and values are always equal as they fluctuate randomly together as new information arrives.

possible price manipulation schemes by outsiders. As a result, specialists have monopolistic access to valuable information which they use to make a speculative trading profit.[32] This is one of the reasons why the seats on the NYSE sell for thousands of dollars.[33]

Various studies, actions taken by the SEC, and court cases also suggest that some corporate insiders are able to profit (sometimes illegally) from monopolistic access to information.[34]

19-5.2 trading on inside information

Federal law defines *insiders* as the directors, officers, significant shareholders, and any other persons who have access to valuable inside information about a firm. This section examines the profitability of trading on inside information.

Federal law requires all insiders to notify the Securities and Exchange Commission (SEC) in writing of all trades they have made in their corporation's stock within 1 month. The SEC then publishes these insider trades in its monthly pamphlet *Official Summary of Insider Trading,* which is available to the public through the U.S. Government Printing Office. Professor Jeffrey F. Jaffe analyzed the *Official Summary* of many years to measure insiders' trading profits.[35] The capital asset pricing model (CAPM), or security market line (SML), furnished the engine for Dr. Jaffe's analysis of insiders' trading profits.

[32] V. Niederhoffer and M. F. M. Osborne, "Market Making and Reversal on the Stock Exchange," *Journal of the American Statistical Association,* December 1966, pp. 897–916.

[33] Another reason why seats have value is that members of the NYSE can also earn sales commissions by acting as floor brokers.

[34] The Texas Gulf Sulphur case, discussed in Box 4-3 on page 107, is a well-known example of insiders trading illegally for their own profit. See also the Securities and Exchange Commission's *Institutional Investor Study Report,* Government Printing Office, 1971, vols. 1–8.

[35] J. F. Jaffe, "Special Information and Insider Trading," *Journal of Business,* July 1974, pp. 410–428. Other studies about insider trading include the following: J. H. Lorie and V. Niederhoffer, "Predictive and Statistical Properties of Insider Trading," *Journal of Law and Economics,* April 1968, pp. 35–51. J. B. Baesel and Garry R. Stein, "The Value of Information: Inferences from the Profitability of Insider Trading," *Journal of Financial and Quantitative Analysis,* September 1979, pp. 553–572. Joseph Finnerty, "Insiders and Market Efficiency," *Journal of Finance,* September 1976, pp. 1141–1148. S. H. Penman, "Insider Trading and the Dissemination of Firm's Forecast Information," *Journal of Business,* October 1982.

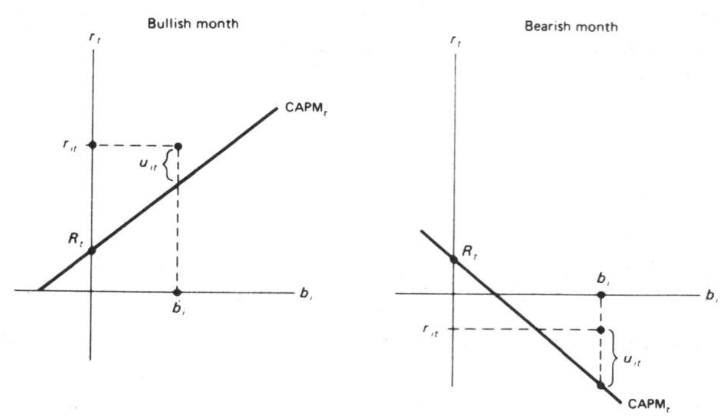

FIGURE 19-7 security market lines estimated with *ex post* monthly returns measured from bull and bear markets.

Using the CAPM for empirical work is complicated by the discontinuity which exists in going from the *ex ante* (that is, future-oriented) theoretical CAPM to the *ex post* (that is, observed in historical sample periods) CAPM. When dealing with the *ex post* data, the CAPM shifts every month. As shown in Fig. 19-7, the high beta stocks have the highest returns in bull markets and the lowest returns in bear markets.

Jaffe estimated the CAPMs for different months by first estimating the characteristic regression lines of all NYSE stocks, Eq. (10-1). Each stock's beta systematic risk coefficient and monthly returns were then taken from these first-pass regressions for the second-pass regression estimates of each month's CAPM. Regression Eq. (19-8) shows the regression model for the *t*th month's CAPM.

$$r_{it} = R_t + c_t(b_i) + u_{it} \qquad \text{for } i = 1, 2, \ldots, n \text{ stocks} \tag{19-8}$$

The intercept R_t and slope c_t coefficients for month *t*'s CAPM were found by regressing stocks' 1-month rate of return in month t, r_{it}, on their beta systematic risk coefficients b_i. The *i*th stock's residual error from the CAPM in month t, denoted u_{it}, measures whether the stock did better or worse than the capital market theory (explained in Chaps. 10 and 26) suggests.

To see whether insiders' trades in their own corporation's stock were based on valuable insider information, Dr. Jaffe measured the residual errors for the *i*th stock in month t, as illustrated in Fig. 19-7. These residual errors are positive (that is, the observed monthly return is above the CAPM) if the stock beats the risk-adjusted market return. In other words, after allowing for current bullish or bearish market conditions and the stock's individual reaction to these conditions (as measured by its beta coefficient), the u_{it} term measures the *i*th stock's positive or negative unsystematic return in month t.

To discern which stocks were being actively traded by insiders, Dr. Jaffe studied each month's *Official Summary of Insider Trading* from the SEC. He selected the stocks in each month which had three more inside sellers than buyers; Jaffe labeled this event a *selling plurality* by insiders. Three more insiders buying than selling in the same month was called a *buying plurality*. Then he recorded the monthly residual errors u_{it} for each of these stocks in which the insiders seemed to exhibit some consensus about buying or selling. After recording such facts for many stocks and for many years, Dr. Jaffe summed up the residual errors for all stocks traded actively by a plurality of insiders in the *t*th month. Equations (19-9) and (19-10) define the average residual error from the CAPM in month t for stocks which the plurality of insiders bought or sold, respectively. The upper limits of summation B and S refer to the number of stocks bought and sold, respectively, by the plurality of insiders in month t.

$$\text{Buyers' average plurality residual} = bu_t = \frac{1}{B}\sum_{i=1}^{B} u_{it} \tag{19-9}$$

$$\text{Sellers' average plurality residual} = su_t = \frac{1}{S}\sum_{i=1}^{S} u_{it} \tag{19-10}$$

Combining the absolute values of the sums in Eqs. (19-9) and (19-10), as shown in Eq. (19-11), yields the average residual for all insiders' trades in month t; it is denoted U_t.

$$U_t = |bu_t| + |su_t| \tag{19-11}$$

The average residual from the CAPM for all insider plurality trading in month t is a measure of extra returns which these insiders earned, on average, from trades which are assumed to be motivated by inside information.

A 1 percent buying commission and a 1 percent selling commission were subtracted from each insider's trade to obtain net profit. Then the average residuals after commissions were cumulated over $C = 1, 2,$ and 8 months after the month in which the plurality of insiders originally made its trades. This yielded the cumulative average residuals denoted U_{tc}, defined in Eq. (19-12) and shown in Table 19-2.

$$U_{tc} = \sum_{m=1}^{C=1,2,8} U_{t+m} \tag{19-12}$$

Table 19-2 shows that 1 month, $C = 1$, after a plurality of insider buying or selling, the insiders' net profit after commissions averaged ($-.0102$ equals a loss of) -1.02 percent of the value of the stock. After the stock was held 2 months (that is, $C = 2$), the insiders broke about even, $U_{tc} = .0009$. But only after 8 months did the plurality of insiders' stocks experience enough price change to pay the commissions and yield (.0307 =) 3.07 percent net profit. Statistically speaking, this rate of insiders' trading profit is significantly above zero. But practically speaking, the average insider certainly is not getting rich quick. Alas, investors aspiring to hitting the jackpot by using inside information must lower their sights and plan on working hard to earn a slightly better rate of return than they could by picking stocks with a dart.

MONOPOLISTIC ACCESS TO INFORMATION LIMITED The fact that specialists and some insiders can earn trading profits from their information refutes the strongly efficient markets hypothesis. However, discovery of these market flaws prompts one to wonder how many people have monopolistic access to valuable information. That is, given that there are imperfections which rule out strongly efficient markets, how deeply do these imperfections permeate the market?

After an examination of corporate insiders and specialists, who undeniably have monopolistic access to valuable information, it would seem that a group of well-endowed professional portfolio managers should be examined next. That is, the latter group would seem to be the next most likely to be able to obtain and profit from valuable investment information before it is fully

TABLE 19-2 cumulative average residual measures of insiders' profit rates, net of commissions

months cumulated	cumulative average residual
$C = 1$	$U_{t1} = -.0102$
$C = 2$	$U_{t2} = .0009$
$C = 8$	$U_{t8} = .0307$

impacted into the market prices. Since mutual funds fall into this category, we shall examine them.

In Chap. 28 various aspects of mutual fund performance are analyzed. Rankings of the annual returns achieved by 39 funds showed (in Table 28-1) that no individual fund was able to earn a better-than-average return consistently over a 10-year period. This tended to indicate that no individual fund (or funds) within the group had any relative advantage in obtaining valuable information. Plotting the performance of a sample of 23 mutual funds relative to the efficient frontier in risk-return space (in Fig. 28-3) showed that none was an efficient investment. In another sample, 34 mutual funds' performances were compared with the Dow Jones Industrial Average (DJIA) using Sharpe's portfolio performance index (which measures the risk-premium over risk). This comparison (which is illustrated in Fig. 28-5) showed that 23 out of the 34 funds ranked below the DJIA. These mutual fund studies all seem to point clearly to the fact that no funds possess any knowledge which is not already fully impacted into security prices.

Another study of 115 mutual funds over the decade from 1955 to 1964 showed similar findings. In particular, this study[36] concluded that

> Although these tests certainly do not imply that the strong form of the [efficient markets] hypothesis holds for all investors and for all time, they provide strong evidence in support of that hypothesis. One must realize that these analysts are extremely well endowed. Moreover they operate in the securities markets every day and have wide-ranging contacts and associations in both the business and financial communities. Thus, the fact that they are apparently unable to forecast returns accurately enough to recover their research and transactions costs is a striking piece of evidence in favor of the strong form of the [efficient markets] hypothesis.

19-6 CONCLUSIONS ABOUT SECURITY PRICES

The weakly efficient and semistrongly efficient markets hypotheses are well supported by the facts. The strongly efficient markets hypothesis is not, however. A few cases—namely, insiders and specialists—were found which violated the strongly efficient hypothesis. The evidence seems to indicate that, for all practical purposes, security markets in the United States are *intrinsic-value random-walk markets.*

Dr. Paul Cootner has summarized this process, and has suggested that security prices can be viewed as a series of constrained random fluctuations around the true intrinsic value.[37] He hypothesizes the existence of two groups of investors. The first group can be referred to as the "naive investors," those who have access only to the public news media for their information. They

[36] M. Jensen, "Risk, the Pricing of Capital Assets, and the Evaluation of Investment Portfolios," *Journal of Business,* April 1969, p. 170. Words in brackets added.

[37] P. H. Cootner, "Stock Prices: Random versus Systematic Changes," *Industrial Management Review,* Spring 1962, pp. 24–45. E. F. Fama elaborated on his interpretations of the intrinsic-value random-walk market model on pp. 36–37 of "The Behavior of Stock Market Prices," *Journal of Business,* January 1965, pp. 34–105; essentially, he agreed with Cootner.

might be chartists, amateur fundamental analysts, dart throwers, or speculators; they base their investment decisions upon their interpretations of the public news and their financial circumstances. Naive investors will recognize few, if any, divergences from intrinsic values.[38] They are more likely to invest on the basis of "hot tips" when they have excess liquidity, and at other more-or-less random times which may or may not be wise.

The second group of investors are the "professional investors"—those who have the resources to discover news and develop clear-cut estimates of intrinsic value. As a result, the professionals will recognize significant deviations from intrinsic value and initiate trading that tends to align the market price with the intrinsic value.

Figure 8-2, on page 199, shows how security prices might fluctuate over time in the market Cootner describes. The dashed lines represent the true intrinsic value of the security as estimated by the professional investors. Trading by the naive investors is not necessarily based on a correct interpretation of the latest news. As a result, naive investors may be buying securities whose market prices are above their intrinsic values, or vice versa. These naive traders are largely responsible for the aimless price fluctuations which can cause prices to diverge from intrinsic values.

When a security price does differ significantly from its true intrinsic value, the professional investors find it profitable to correct this disequilibrium. Small deviations will not be profitable to correct, but when prices are significantly out of line, the professionals will bid up low prices or liquidate overpriced securities. In effect, the professionals erect "reflecting barriers" around the true intrinsic value.[39] These reflecting barriers are represented by the solid lines above and below the intrinsic-value lines in Fig. 8-2. Prices will fluctuate freely within the reflecting barriers, but when they reach these barriers, the action of the professionals will cause prices to move toward their intrinsic value.

The intrinsic-value estimates of the professionals may change as the latest news is learned. The reflecting barriers around the intrinsic value will therefore change accordingly. As a result, it is not usually possible to observe the true intrinsic value or the reflecting barriers from charts of historical security prices. Price charts like the one in Fig. 8-2*b* will occur when a security experiences changes in its intrinsic value. The preceding evidence suggests certain investment policies.

19-6.1 fundamental security analysis

In an intrinsic-value random-walk market, fundamental analysis plays a major role in determining security prices. Expert fundamental analysts who discover new financial information and quickly interpret it correctly will earn higher-than-average returns, but most fundamental analysts will not earn a return above what could be achieved with a naive buy-and-hold strategy.

In an intrinsic-value random-walk market, security prices are unbiased estimates of the true intrinsic value and reflect all current public information. Searching for undervalued securities will therefore be largely unfruitful.

[38] Intrinsic-value estimation is discussed in Chap. 15.

[39] William Feller, *An Introduction to Probability Theory and Its Applications*, vol. I, 3d ed., Wiley, New York, 1968, pp. 436–438. Provides a discussion of a random walk with reflecting barriers.

Only the most expert fundamental analysts who have discovered new information will find it profitable to perform fundamental analysis, and any underpriced securities they discover will be bid up in price into line with their intrinsic value very quickly. Therefore, all but the few most expert fundamental analysts will not profit (above what a naive strategy would yield) from their activity. It will not be worthwhile for amateur investors to learn fundamental analysis in an intrinsic-value random-walk market. The amateur can expect to accumulate more wealth by selecting securities randomly and devoting the time which would have been spent on fundamental analysis to his or her own profession earning more wages or salary. The only fundamental analysts that will repeatedly earn unusual profits while experiencing few losses will be hard-working professional analysts with experience and resources to support their costly search for information.

19-6.2 technical analysis

The various tests to measure the randomness of stock price changes which were described earlier cannot detect absolutely every conceivable pattern which might be formed. Some extremely complex patterns might go undetected. However, technical analysts do not usually search for extremely complex patterns. Their concepts are simple at best. Therefore, the evidence that patterns do not exist tends to indicate that technical analysis will not be worthwhile to perform in an intrinsic-value random-walk market. Chartists can expect to earn an average rate of return, but they could expect to earn the same return by selecting securities with an unaimed dart. They would therefore be wiser to devote their time to more profitable activities and to select securities by some other method. There would be no reason for an institutional portfolio to employ a chartist in an intrinsic-value random-walk market.

19-6.3 risk-return analysis

In an intrinsic-value random-walk market, most securities' rates of return will conform to probability distributions which are stationary over time. In such a market it will be worthwhile for investors to estimate the risk and return statistics for their investment alternatives. The investor can then select the investments with the maximum return in the preferred risk-class. In this manner investors can maximize their utility. Selecting the most efficient portfolio in the preferred risk-class will enable investors to attain their highest level of happiness from their investments. This investment may or may not earn an above-average rate of return; the outcome depends upon the risk-class the investor selects and when the investment is liquidated. Such analysis, however, will maximize the investor's expected utility (as defined in App. 27A).

Of course, risk-return relationships represent theoretical market equilibriums. In the real world of continuous dynamic disequilibrium, the positive relation between risk and average return can be expected to emerge only if investments are held for at least one *complete business cycle*. For example, risky assets purchased at the end of an inflated bull market and sold at the end of a long bear market will have had the *highest* risk and *lowest* rates of return during such a period. However, if risky assets are held over a complete market cycle (for example, from peak to peak), they will earn higher-than-average returns and the positive relationship between risk and return will be evident.

19-6.4 the negativism of the efficient markets theory

The efficient markets theory is a very negative statement. It declares that no patterns exist in price changes, that technical analysis techniques which some persons have spent their lives developing are merely worthless folklore, and that the daily changes in the DJIA which security sales representatives talk about are really random numbers containing no information. But it is not fruitful to try to reach general conclusions from a few specific cases. The efficient markets theory should be viewed as an unbiased scientific statement supported by a body of published evidence. The available data indicate that security markets in the United States are intrinsic-value random-walk markets.

19-6.5 internal versus external market efficiency

Primarily as a result of large investments in "social overhead capital" which exists externally to the stock markets in the United States, the conclusion was reached that these markets are semistrongly efficient.[40] This *external market efficiency* or *pricing efficiency* differs from *internal efficiency*, or synonymously, *operational efficiency*.[41]

In order for a given securities market such as the NYSE or the American Stock Exchange to be *internally efficient*, the securities traded there must be immediately marketable at low commissions to any investor-customer who wishes to trade. Internal market efficiency results from (1) publicly posted bid-and-ask prices which are backed by market-makers who stand ready to buy or sell large quantities at the posted prices, (2) brokerage commissions which are determined competitively rather than fixed at high levels that take large brokers' profits out of every trade, (3) market-makers who do not manipulate the prices of the securities in which they deal, and (4) a requirement that the companies whose securities are traded make public their audited financial statements. Since May Day (that is, May 1, 1975), when the Securities and Exchange Commission ordered the NYSE to stop using its fixed minimum commission schedule, the internal efficiency of the NYSE has improved because its commission rates were driven down by healthy competition between competing market-makers and the different brokers. However, in terms of external efficiency, the NYSE was a semistrongly efficient market before May Day.

If a particular market is terribly inefficient *internally* because its market-makers manipulate the prices of the securities in which they deal, or because its brokers charge unreasonably high commissions, or because it does not provide adequate information about the companies which issue its securities, or because all the preceding problems exist, then that market will probably not be *externally* efficient. In fact, some of the lesser-developed foreign coun-

[40] The essential *social overhead capital* includes free public libraries; large international news services like UPI and AP; low-cost, publicly available investment advice publications like *Value Line*; good, inexpensive, daily financial newspapers; and an ample supply of qualified financial analysts who do the good financial research that should underlie all portfolio management decisions.

[41] R. R. West, "On the Difference between Internal and External Market Efficiency," *Financial Analysts Journal*, November–December 1975, pp. 30–34. The phrases "internal efficiency" and "external efficiency" were defined and discussed in App. 3, pages 82–85.

tries and some of the small, local securities markets in the United States are not externally efficient capital markets because of internal market problems. As long as competing market-makers exist and anticompetitive practices are forbidden by law, however, competition should lead to the development of externally efficient markets.

QUESTIONS

19-1. Explain the weakly efficient, semistrongly efficient, and strongly efficient markets hypotheses.

19-2. "An investor who learned that General Motors' earnings per share had increased by an unusually large amount a few days before the news was announced publicly could probably buy GM stock and profit from a quick capital gain when the announcement was made." True, false, or uncertain? Explain.

19-3. Characterize the nature and behavior of stock prices in a large public securities market. That is, what do stock prices represent and what patterns do they follow? Why do stock prices behave in this manner? What does this imply about the investments management policies that should be followed?

19-4. Why are runs tests, serial correlation, and filter rules used in testing the random-walk hypothesis? What do these tests reveal?

19-5. "Stock prices are random numbers." Is this statement true, false, or uncertain? Explain.

19-6. "The managers of large institutional portfolios (such as mutual funds) should instruct their fundamental security analysts to collect and evaluate the 'hot tips' which are discussed on Wall Street so their portfolios can profit from monopolistic access to this valuable information." True, false, or uncertain? Explain.

19-7. Suppose your long-time next-door neighbor is a business executive who watches the stars through a telescope and studies the physical sciences as a hobby. He has earnestly explained to you on several occasions that he has observed that the spots on the sun's surface are more active during bull markets. He has shown you books about sunspots to prove he can recognize them and records of his observations of sunspot activity and the stock market. If you believe and trust your neighbor, should you begin to study sunspot activity as a way to beat the stock market?

19-8. "If rates of return are distributed as a Paretian distribution with a characteristic exponent less than 2 (that is, theoretically infinite variance), then risk-return analysis is hopeless." To what problem is this statement referring? Is the statement true, false, or uncertain? Explain. *Hint*: See App. 19A.

19-9. "Rates of return conform to mathematical statisticians' random-walk model." True, false, or uncertain? Explain. *Hint*: See App. 19A.

19-10. Compare and contrast the random-walk theory of rates of return with the martingale model. *Hint*: See App. 19A.

SELECTED REFERENCES

Brealey, R. A., *An Introduction to Risk and Return from Common Stocks*, 2d ed., MIT Press, Cambridge, Mass., 1983. This book summarizes much current investments literature. The book is nonmathematical, easy-to-read, and relevant to the so-called random-walk theory.

Fama, Eugene F., "The Behavior of Stock Market Prices," *Journal of Business*, January 1965, pp. 34–105. This paper rationalizes the existence of an intrinsic-value random-walk market and shows various types of evidence in support of the theory. The stationary stable symmetric distribution with Paretian tails is discussed, and an appendix shows some theorems about such distributions. Mathematics and statistics are used.

Tinic, S. M., and R. R. West, *Investing in Securities: An Efficient Markets Approach*, Addison-Wesley, Reading, Mass., 1979. This investments textbook is written from the viewpoint that securities markets are efficient. It rationalizes the determination of securities prices using joint tests of market efficiency in conjunction with various other asset pricing models.

APPENDIX 19A

random-walk and martingale models

A *model* is a simplified version of reality. It is a toylike construct which is "played with" in order to learn the essential nature of the more complex thing being modeled. Consider the random-walk model defined in Box App. 19A-1.

When introducing the random-walk model to a class, mathematical statistics professors sometimes use the aimless lurchings of an intoxicated person as an example. At each step the drunk's direction may be at any of the 180 degrees emanating from his location (assuming he cannot fall backward), and the distance of each step is a random variable with the range from zero to, say, 4 feet. Furthermore, the number of steps per minute is a random variable with a range from zero to dozens. If the probability distributions describing the direction, distance, and frequency of the drunk's steps are realistic, the random-walk model can tell the probability that the drunk reaches any given position at any point in time. This appendix examines the behavior of security prices to see whether the random-walk model of mathematical statistics can be adapted to characterize their movements.

BOX APP. 19A-1
definition of random-walk model

A *random-walk model* is a mathematical model in which a series of numbers are (1) independent and (2) identically distributed.

APP. 19A-1 PROBABILITY DISTRIBUTIONS FOR SECURITIES

Suppose that the market prices of certain common stocks were recorded at the close of each trading day for 4 years. If the relative frequency (that is, the objective historical probabilities) of each security's price were determined, a distribution of past prices could be prepared. Figure App. 19A-1 represents two hypothetical relative-frequency distributions for 4 years of common stock prices. One distribution is for the first 2 years, and the other distribution is for the second 2 years.

Distributions of security *prices* are of little value for two reasons which should be apparent after a glance at Fig. App. 19A-1. First, the distributions are not stable over time. Nearly all securities' prices increase with the passage of time at about 6 percent per year.[42] As a result, each year's relative-frequency distribution shifts a little farther to the right and has a higher mean price. Second, the shape of the distribution changes each year. Each year, as the security's price rises, the distribution's tail on the right side grows a little longer. In statistical language, the positive skewness of a security's price tends to increase with the price.[43]

As a result of these two changes, the distributions of security prices are of little value: one year's distribution cannot be used to predict the probability that a certain price will occur in the next year. In statistical language, the distributions are not stable over time. This is unfortunate because stable distributions are the most useful in forecasting.[44]

distributions of price changes unstable

In a search for stable distributions which could be useful in making probability statements about future security prices, analysts examined the price *changes* (denoted Δp) which occur daily, rather than the prices themselves.

[42] L. Fisher and J. Lorie, "Rates of Return on Investments in Common Stock: The Year-by-Year Record, 1926–1965," *Journal of Business*, January 1964, p. 315, table A2. The average NYSE stock's price rose 6.8 percent per annum from 1926 to 1960. This does not include cash dividends.

[43] See Mathematical App. C for a definition and discussion of skewness. Essentially, positive skewness means that the distribution has an unusually long tail on the right side and is therefore lopsided.

[44] The frequency distributions of historical security prices can be made more useful by adding subscripted time variables to the parameters of the distribution and building an appropriate growth rate into them. However, such complications should be avoided whenever possible by constructing stable probability distributions.

FIGURE APP. 19A-1 hypothetical frequency distribution of a common stock's prices.

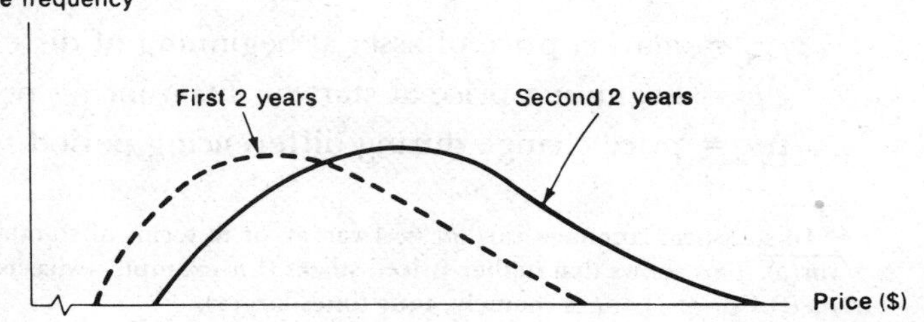

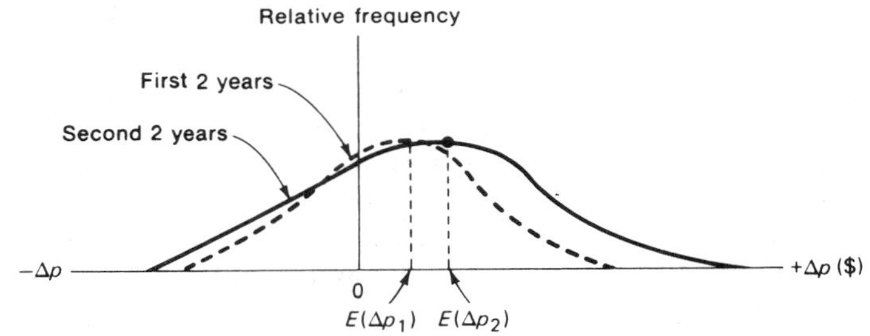

FIGURE APP. 19A-2 frequency distributions of a hypothetical common stock's price changes.

Figure App. 19A-2 shows two relative-frequency distributions of price changes for a hypothetical common stock like the one shown in Fig. App. 19A-1.

The distributions in Fig. App. 19A-2 represent 4 years of daily price changes. One distribution represents the first 2 years of daily changes, and the other distribution represents the second 2 years. The distributions of price changes for most securities have positive means because stock prices tend to drift upward with the passage of time.

Unfortunately, the frequency distributions of price changes are diminished in value because historical price changes tend to be unstable too. Security prices tend to fluctuate up and down in terms of a fixed range of *percentages*; so, as the security's price rises over time, the dollar amounts of the price changes grow, too. To see this intuitively, consider the variance of price changes before and after a stock split. If a $100 stock is split into two $50 shares, the variance of the stock price changes will be smaller after the split (unless the percentage price fluctuations increase, an occurrence that is highly unlikely).[45] As a result of this phenomenon, the mean and the standard deviation of price changes increase with the price of the security in most cases.

stable distributions of rates of return

Although the distributions of price changes are not stationary, studying these distributions reveals that security prices tend to change by *percentages* that conform to a stable distribution. Let us denote the percentage price changes by the rate of change as defined in Eq. (App. 19A-1).

$$r_t = \frac{p_{t+1} - p_t}{p_t} \qquad \text{(App. 19A-1)}$$

$$= \frac{\Delta p_t}{p_t}$$

where

p_{t+1} = market price of asset at beginning of differencing period $t + 1$

p_t = beginning price at start of differencing period t

Δp_t = price change during differencing period $t = p_{t+1} - p_t$

[45] In statistical language $\text{var}(2p) = 4\ \text{var}(p)$, or in terms of standard deviations $\sqrt{\text{var}(2p)} = 2\sqrt{\text{var}(p)}$. This shows that higher-priced stocks (for example, twice as high for $2p$) have a larger variance of price changes (namely, four times larger).

The rates of change of daily, weekly, monthly, quarterly, semiannual, or yearly price changes tend to conform to a stable relative-frequency distribution as shown in Fig. App. 19A-3 if the price changes are drawn from at least one *complete* business cycle.

Dividends d_t are sometimes included when rates of return are calculated, as shown in Eq. (App. 19A-2*a*).

$$r_t = \frac{p_{t+1} - p_t + d_t}{p_t} \qquad \text{(App. 19A-2}a\text{)}$$

$$= \frac{p_{t+1} + d_t}{p_t} - 1 \qquad \text{(App. 19A-2}b\text{)}$$

Most corporations pay the *same* dividends quarter after quarter, only occasionally increasing them slightly or canceling them altogether; so dividends may be treated as a constant in dealing with most corporations. Thus, whether rates of return are calculated with Eq. (App. 19A-2*a*) or rates of change are calculated with Eq. (App. 19A-1), the distribution is shifted to the right by the amount of the dividend yield (that is, d/p) but has the same shape and stability.[46] It is better to use Eq. (App. 19A-2*a*) than Eq. (App. 19A-1) when measuring returns, so that the dividend income is considered in measuring the investor's income (and to compensate for the ex-dividend price drop-off).

Not every security has a relative-frequency distribution of historical rates of return which remains stationary. If the firm nears bankruptcy, changes products, enjoys major technological breakthroughs which confer a competitive advantage, or experiences other major changes, the distribution may shift. However, the distributions of returns for the vast majority of firms are fairly stationary over time if the distribution is observed over at least one complete business cycle. This is usually true even though the firm has executive shakeups, enters new market areas, or alters its product line.

The existence of *stable* distributions of returns allows analysts to do several valuable things. First, probability statements may be made about the percentage price changes that may be expected to occur. Second, a security's historical average return and standard deviation of returns furnish estimates of the security's future risk and return. Thus, a stable random-walk model may be construed for rates of return (or rates of price change), although it is not possible to construct a stable distribution with the raw price data.

[46] A third way to measure rates of return is to take the natural or Naperian logarithm of the value relatives. Symbolically $r_t = \ln (p_{t+1}/p_t) = \ln (p_{t+1}) - \ln (p_t)$.

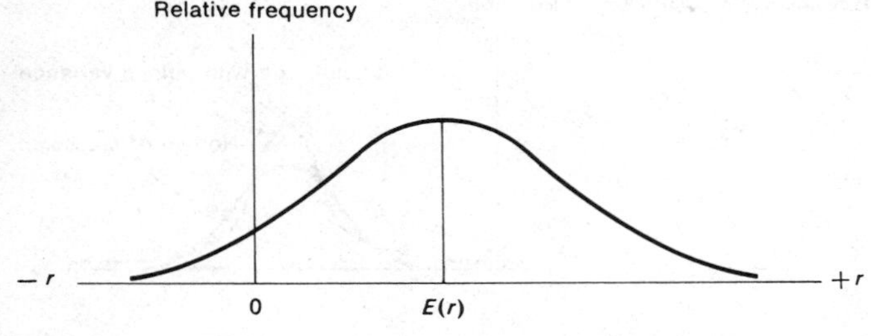

FIGURE APP. 19A-3 frequency distribution of historical rates of return and rates of change for a hypothetical security.

It will be recalled that for a series to be classified as random walk, the two major requirements are that the successive members in the series be (1) independent and (2) identically distributed. *Identically distributed* is a technical statistical phrase which means all the numbers conform to the same probability distribution. Since the probability distributions of historical rates of return tend to be stable for any given security, this fact indicates that the second condition necessary to classify securities as a random walk is fulfilled. The precise form of the probability distribution is considered below.

advantages of using gaussian or normal distributions

Many researchers were hopeful that rates of change and rates of return are *normally distributed* for several reasons. First, normal distributions are completely described by only two statistics, the mean and the variance. Thus, skewness and kurtosis could be ignored.[47] Second, normal distributions have a finite variance; that is, their tails come down to the horizontal axis of the probability distribution. Figure App. 19A-4 compares a normal distribution, which has a finite variance (and standard deviation), with a distribution with infinite variance. It is highly desirable that a probability distribution possess a finite variance because statistics from populations possessing finite variance are dependable statistics which do not erratically vary from sample to sample.[48] Third, the normal distribution is well known and has a well-developed sampling theory.

infinite variance

As computers analyzed larger files of accurate historical data, the normal distributions of rates of price change and rates of return were called into question. The occasional extremely large and extremely small rates of return which had previously been attributed to error or ignored repeatedly appeared in securities distributions. These extreme values lie beyond the tails of a normal distribution; they are sometimes referred to as *outliers*.

Closer examination of the distributions of returns indicated that they may not be normal or Gaussian, as had been thought. The distributions were *leptokurtic* and had large variances. Drs. Benoit Mandelbrot and Eugene Fama published studies suggesting that the rates of return were distribu-

[47] See Mathematical App. C for definitions and discussions of skewness and kurtosis.

[48] Statistically speaking, an erratic statistic is said to be *inefficient*, a technical statistical word which means the statistic varies erratically from sample to sample. An *efficient* statistic varies less than any other statistic. Efficiency is a desirable statistical property. Statistics from populations with finite variances are more efficient than statistics from populations with infinite variances. Another advantage of having a finite variance is that the central limit theorem applies only to distributions with finite variances.

FIGURE APP. 19A-4 normal distribution compared with leptokurtic distribution with infinite variance.

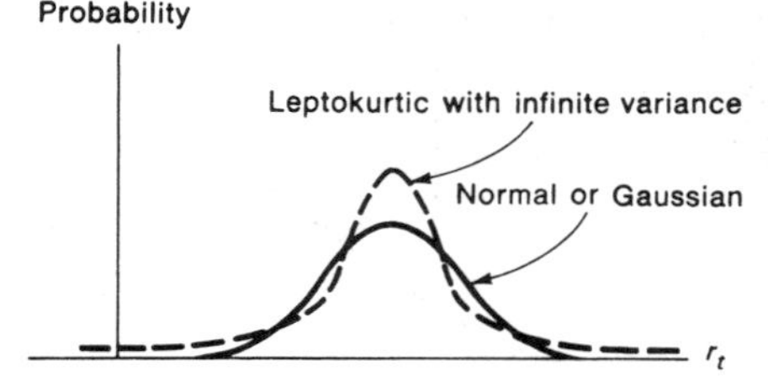

ted according to a stable symmetric distribution with *infinite* variance.[49] Of course, any sample of actual returns which was analyzed had a finite variance, since the actual rates of return were not infinitely large or infinitely small. Occasionally, however, outliers appeared which suggested that the probability distribution of returns implied a theoretically infinite variance. Figure App. 19A-4 outlines such a distribution with a dashed line and compares it with the normal distribution. The tails of the distribution represented by the dashed line are very long. As a result, there is a tiny probability that rates of return reach very large positive or negative values and cause the distribution to have a theoretically infinite variance.

problems with infinite variance populations

The existence of outliers and a theoretically infinite variance presents problems for risk-return analysis. Equation (App. 19A-3) shows the formula for calculating the standard deviation of returns from a sample of n observations.

$$\sigma = \sqrt{\frac{1}{n} \sum_{t=1}^{n} [r_t - E(r)]^2} \qquad \text{(App. 19A-3)}$$

If risk is being estimated with Eq. (App. 19A-3) using historical returns, inefficient and erratic statistics will be obtained. Every time an extreme value of r_t (that is, an outlier) is included in the computation of the risk with Eq. (App. 19A-3), the standard deviation will increase erratically instead of smoothly approaching the true population value. Figure App. 19A-5 represents the problem graphically.

In order to develop efficient and unerratic risk statistics from a population with an infinite variance, some other financial risk surrogate may be used. Equation (App. 19A-4) defines the mean absolute deviation of returns (MAD).

[49] Benoit Mandelbrot, "The Variation of Certain Speculative Prices," *Journal of Business*, October 1963, pp. 394–419. Eugene F. Fama, "The Behavior of Stock Market Prices," *Journal of Business*, January 1965, pp. 39–105.

FIGURE APP. 19A-5 sequential values of the standard deviation and mean absolute deviation from population with infinite variance. (*Source:* Eugene F. Fama, "The Behavior of Stock Prices," *Journal of Business*, January 1965, p. 96.)

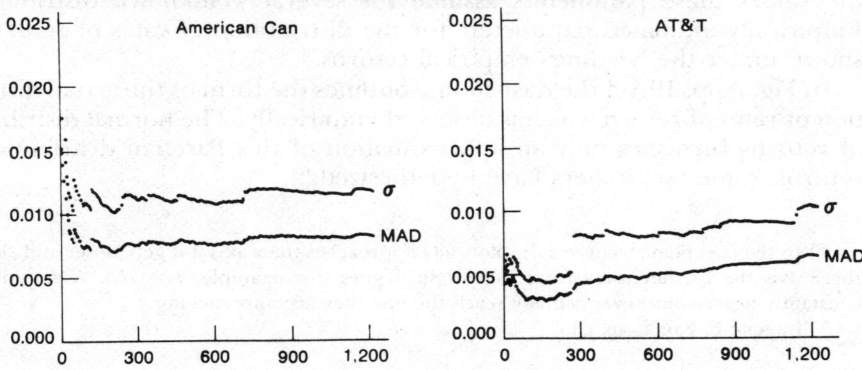

$$\text{MAD} = \frac{1}{n} \sum_{t=1}^{n} |r_t - E(r)| \qquad \text{(App. 19A-4)}$$

where

$|r_t - E(r)|$ = absolute value of the deviation from the mean

Since the deviations around the expected value are not squared in Eq. (App. 19A-4) as they are in Eq. (App. 19A-3), the MAD does not increase dramatically as the standard deviation does when an outlier enters into the computations. Figure App. 19A-5 compares the MAD with the standard deviation in a sequential sampling experiment. The MAD is both smaller and less erratic than the standard deviation.

stable Paretian distribution

Drs. Mandelbrot and Fama suggested that the relative-frequency distributions of returns were a particular form of the stable, nonnormal distribution which is a member of a family of four-parameter distributions. This distribution can assume many forms as the parameters vary. The normal, the Cauchy, the t distribution with one degree of freedom, and other distributions are merely special cases of this four-parameter distribution. The distribution is called a *Paretian distribution* because the tails of the distribution follow the law of Pareto. The four parameters of the Paretian distribution are α, β, γ, and δ.

The parameter α is called the characteristic exponent of the Paretian distribution. The characteristic exponent varies in the range $0 < \alpha < 2$ with the height of the tails of the distribution. When $\alpha = 2$, the tails asymptotically approach the horizontal axis, and the distribution has a finite variance.[50] The normal distribution, for example, is a Paretian distribution with $\alpha = 2$.

The parameter β is an index of skewness. This skewness parameter varies in the range $-1 < \beta < +1$ with $\beta = 0$ for a symmetric distribution such as the normal distribution. The parameter δ is a location parameter for the Paretian distribution. When $\alpha > 1$ and $\beta = 0$, then δ is the mean, mode, or median of the distribution.

The fourth parameter γ defines the scale of a Paretian distribution. When $\alpha = 2$ (as it does for the normal distribution), γ is one-half the variance. When $\alpha < 2$, the distribution has an infinite variance, but γ still assumes a finite value which varies with the width of the distribution. Table App. 19A-1 shows the values these parameters assume for several well-known distributions. Empirically estimated parameters for the distribution of rates of return are shown under the heading "empirical returns."

In Fig. App. 19A-4 the dashed line outlines the form of the actual distribution of rates of return which is observed empirically. The normal distribution of returns furnishes only an approximation of this Paretian distribution of returns, some researchers have hypothesized.[51]

[50] In the (x,y) plane a curve asymptotically approaches the x axis if it gets closer and closer to the x axis the further away from the origin it goes (for example, $y = c/x$). Asymptotes get constantly nearer but never actually reach the line they are approaching.

[51] Eugene F. Fama, op. cit.

TABLE APP. 19A-1 various forms of Paretian distribution

Paretian parameter		normal	empirical returns*	Cauchy
α	Characteristic exponent	2	1.75	1
β	Skewness parameter	0	0	0
γ	Scale parameter	Half of variance	$\left(\frac{f.72 - f.28}{1.654}\right)^{.57}$	Semi-interquartile range
δ	Location parameter	Mean	Mean	Mean

* f.72 denotes the 72 percent fractile.

subordinated normal distribution

Several researchers have suggested that short-term stock prices are, in fact, distributed normally if time is defined correctly.[52] They view stock prices as being generated in transaction time or operational time rather than in terms of calendar time. These researchers argue that the economic variable which is observable and which closely approximates *operational time* is a stock's trading volume. For example, Dr. Westerfield[53] hypothesizes that every time a piece of new information arrives in the market which causes a change in some security's value, it tends to result in security trading. Stock prices, Westerfield maintains, are changed by such trading activity rather than by the mere passage of trading days.

APP. 19-2 INDEPENDENCE OF SECURITY PRICE CHANGES

It will be recalled that the successive values in a random walk must be (1) identically distributed according to some stable distribution and (2) independent of preceding or subsequent observations. It has been explained that short-term rates of return are distributed according to a stable symmetric distribution, which fulfills the first requirement to classify rates of return as conforming to the random-walk model. However, in order for rates of return to fully conform to the random-walk model, they must also be independent. To be *independent*, the rates of price change and rates of return for a security must not possess any detectable cycle or other pattern.

52 It has been shown that stock price returns are normally distributed in terms of transaction time (that is, per transaction) rather than per unit of calendar time (for example, per day). C. W. J. Granger and O. Morgenstern, *Predictability of Stock Market Prices* (Heath, Lexington, Mass, 1970) appear to be first to present this evidence. Also see P. K. Clark, "A Subordinated Stochastic Process Model with Finite Variance for Speculative Prices," *Econometrica*, January 1973, pp. 135–155; R. Westerfield, "The Distribution of Common Stock Price Changes: An Application of Transactions Time and Subordinated Stochastic Models," *Journal of Financial and Quantitative Analysis*, December 1977; and I. G. Morgan. "Stock Prices and Heteroscedasticity," *Journal of Business*, October 1976, pp. 496–508. Recently, even Eugene Fama has suggested using the normal distribution. See his *Foundations of Finance*, Basic Books, New York, 1976, chaps. 2 and 3.

53 R. Westerfield, op. cit.

Next, some of the tests used to determine whether the rates of return from security price changes are a statistically independent series of numbers are examined. If these rates of return are independent, however, two conclusions may be drawn. First, a finding of perfect statistical independence will fulfill the requirements to classify the percentage changes of security prices as a random walk. Second, if the percentage changes in security prices are perfectly independent, then they are random. As a result, technical analysis will not be worth performing. Various statistical procedures are reviewed below in order to determine if rates of return and rates of price change are statistically independent.

serial correlation: a test for independence

Serial correlation is one of the many statistical tools used to measure dependence of successive numbers in a series. It has been widely used to measure possible dependence in security prices' rates of change. The linear regression model shown in Eq. (App. 19A-5) is the model for which the correlation coefficient is determined when measuring serial correlation in rates of return.

$$r_{i,t+k} = a_i + b_i r_{i,t} + e_{i,t} \tag{App. 19A-5}$$

where

$r_{i,t}$ = rate of return from the ith asset during the tth period (that is, day, week, or year) as measured by Eq. (App. 19A-1) or (App. 19A-2)

$r_{i,t+k}$ = rate of return on the same security k periods later; k is called the lag

$e_{i,t}$ = a random error which averages zero

a_i and b_i = least-squares regression intercept and slope coefficient for asset i[54]

The correlation coefficient for model Eq. (App. 19A-5) is the serial correlation coefficient for a k-period lag. A simple graphical explanation should make this clearer.

[54] Correct measurement of the serial correlation which is associated with regression Eq. (App. 19A-5) is possible only if var($r_{i,t}$) is constant over the period under examination, that is, homoscedasticity is essential.

FIGURE APP. 19A-6 cyclical rates of return.

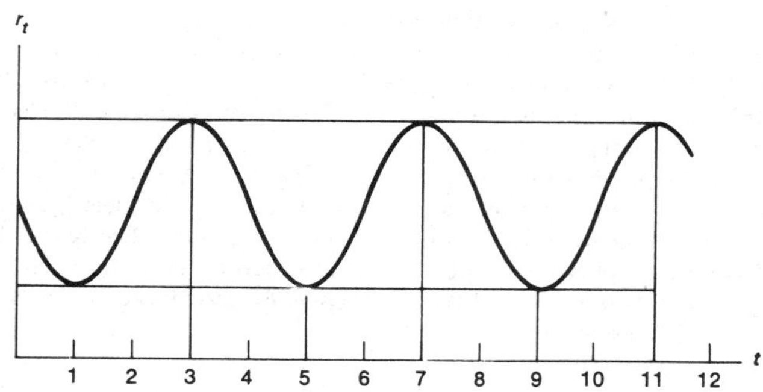

Figure App. 19A-6 is a graph of a time series of rates of return for some hypothetical security. These rates of return conform to a perfectly repetitive four-period cycle. If the lagged regression model Eq. (App. 19A-5) is fitted to the data graphed in Fig. App. 19A-6, the serial correlations (denoted ρ_k) will vary with the lag. For a four-period ($k = 4$) lag, the data graphed in Fig. App. 19A-6 will yield a perfect positive correlation ($\rho_4 = +1$), indicating the existence of a four-period perfectly repetitive cycle. For a two-period lag, a perfectly negative serial correlation ($\rho_2 = -1$) will result, indicating that rates of return two periods apart move inversely. For a one-period lag ($k = 1$), zero serial correlation ($\rho_0 = 0$) will result, indicating that rates of return from adjoining periods move inversely half the time and directly the other half. The data would thus indicate that no pattern of dependence can be detected for $k = 1$; but for two- and four-period lags, complete dependence is implied by their correlations.

When performing serial correlation tests, the analyst tries all possible lags which may exist. For example, Table App. 19A-2 shows the serial correlation coefficients Fama found for each of the 30 securities in the Dow Jones Industrial Average for lags from 1 to 10 days' length (that is, $k = 1, 2, 3, 4, 5, 6, 7, 8, 9, 10$). It will be noted that few of the serial correlation coefficients in Table App. 19A-2 are significantly different from zero.[55] Fama and others have used serial correlation to test different securities and different lags. These studies detected no significant serial correlations which could be used to earn speculative profits. However, some significant serial correlations were found, particularly in the less actively traded stocks.[56]

Table App. 19A-3 presents serial correlation coefficients which are in some respects significantly different from Fama's statistics in Table App. 19A-2. Dr. Gabriel Hawawini used a more heterogeneous sample of securities to analyze than Fama used. Fama's sample was limited to actively traded, NYSE-listed, blue-chip stocks. Hawawini's more representative sample results shown in Table App. 19A-3 reveal many significant 1-day serial correlations in both individual stocks and stock market indices. For lags of 3 days and longer, however, Hawawini reports few significant serial correlations above what are expected to occur simply as a result of normal sampling error. Thus, some statistically significant serial correlation appears to exist, but it is of dubious economic significance. After all, how much after-commissions profit could a speculator earn if armed with the knowledge of some marginally significant 1- and 2-day serial correlations?

If rates of return were calculated by using long-enough differencing intervals (for example, one-period returns from 5-year periods), then a positive serial correlation of returns would emerge owing to the upward trend in the

[55] Correlation coefficients more than 1.96 standard errors from zero are significantly different from zero at the .05 level of significance if the underlying distribution is normal. Such coefficients are noted with an asterisk in Table App. 19A-2.

[56] G. A. Hawawini, "On the Time Behavior of Financial Parameters; An Investigation of the Intervaling Effect," unpublished doctoral dissertation, New York University, 1977. Robert A. Schwartz and David K. Whitcomb, "Evidence on the Presence and Causes of Serial Correlation in the Market Model Residuals," *Journal of Financial and Quantitative Analysis*, June 1977, vol. XII, no. 2, pp. 291–315, and "The Time-Variance Relationship: Evidence of Autocorrelation in Common Stock Returns," *Journal of Finance*, March 1977, vol. 1, no. 1, pp. 41–56.

TABLE APP. 19A-2 daily serial correlation coefficients for lag $k = 1, 2, \ldots, 10$

	LAG									
stock	(1)	(2)	(3)	(4)	(5)	(6)	(7)	(8)	(9)	(10)
Allied Chemical	.017	−.042	.007	−.001	.027	.004	−.017	−.026	−.017	−.007
Alcoa	.118*	.038	−.014	.022	−.022	.009	.017	.007	−.001	−.033
American Can	−.087*	−.024	.034	−.065*	−.017	−.006	.015	.025	−.047	−.040
AT&T	−.039	−.097*	.000	.026	.005	−.005	.002	.027	−.014	.007
American Tobacco	.111*	−.109*	−.060*	−.065*	.007	−.010	.011	.046	.039	.041
Anaconda	.067*	−.061*	−.047	−.002	.000	−.038	.009	.016	−.014	−.056
Bethlehem Steel	.013	−.065*	.009	.021	−.053	−.098*	−.010	.004	−.002	−.021
Chrysler	.012	−.066*	−.016	−.007	−.015	.009	.037	.056*	−.044	.021
Du Pont	.013	−.033	.060*	.027	−.002	−.047	.020	.011	−.034	.001
Eastman Kodak	.025	.014	−.031	.005	−.022	.012	.007	.006	.008	.002
General Electric	.011	−.038	−.021	.031	−.001	.000	−.008	.014	−.002	.010
General Foods	.061*	−.003	.045	.002	−.015	−.052	−.006	−.014	−.024	−.017
General Motors	−.004	−.056*	−.037	−.008	−.038	−.006	.019	.006	−.016	.009
Goodyear	−.123*	.017	−.044	.043	−.002	−.003	.035	.014	−.015	.007
International Harvester	−.017	−.029	−.031	.037	−.052	−.021	−.001	.003	−.046	−.016
International Nickel	.096*	−.033	−.019	.020	.027	.059*	−.038	−.008	−.016	.034
International Paper	.046	−.011	−.058*	.053*	.049	−.003	−.025	−.019	−.003	−.021
Johns Manville	.006	−.038	−.027	−.023	−.029	−.080*	.040	.018	−.037	.029
Owens Illinois	−.021	−.084*	−.047	.068*	.086*	−.040	.011	−.040	.067*	−.043
Procter & Gamble	.099*	−.009	−.008	.009	−.015	.022	.012	−.012	−.022	−.021
Sears	.097*	.026	.028	.025	.005	−.054	−.006	−.010	−.008	−.009
Standard Oil (Calif.)	.025	−.030	−.051*	−.025	−.047	−.034	−.010	.072*	−.049*	−.035
Standard Oil (N.J.)	.008	−.116*	.016	.014	−.047	−.018	−.022	−.026	−.073*	.081*
Swift & Co.	−.004	−.015	−.010	.012	.057*	.012	−.043	.014	.012	.001
Texaco	.094*	−.049	−.024	−.018	−.017	−.009	.031	.032	−.013	.008
Union Carbide	.107*	−.012	.040	.046	−.036	−.034	.003	−.008	−.054	−.037
United Aircraft	.014	−.033	−.022	−.047	−.067*	−.053	.046	.037	.015	−.019
U.S. Steel	.040	−.074*	.014	.011	−.012	−.021	.041	.037	−.021	−.044
Westinghouse	−.027	−.022	−.036	−.003	.000	−.054*	−.020	.013	−.014	.008
Woolworth	.028	−.016	.015	.014	.007	−.039	−.013	.003	−.088*	−.008

* Coefficient is twice its computed standard error.
Source: Eugene F. Fama, "The Behavior of Stock Market Prices," *Journal of Business*, January 1965, p. 72.

market. These long-run trends can be seen with the naked eye in graphs like Fig. 7-2, on page 190. The so-called random-walk theory, however, applies only to *short-run* rates of return from which speculative traders and technical analysts try to profit. The random-walk theory does not deny the existence of a long-run upward trend in security prices; it requires only that short-run price movements be random. The data reveal that short-run price changes and rates of return are not highly serially correlated. In essence, this means there is not a significant cycle or pattern in security price changes that repeats itself or that can be used to predict future security prices. The simple linear model underlying the serial correlation tests indicates that successive security price changes tend to behave somewhat like a series of random numbers. However, other more complicated patterns may exist.

TABLE APP. 19A-3 evidence of serial correlation in securities and market returns January 1970–December 1973

	ORDER OF SERIAL CORRELATION, IN DAYS							
securities	**1**	**2**	**3**	**4**	**5**	**10**	**15**	**20**
Wayne Gossard	−.170*	−.040	−.034	.022	−.011	.025	−.001	.051
Mich. Seamless Tube	−.185*	.046	−.096*	.051	−.044	−.065*	−.024	−.011
Allied Products Corp.	−.368*	−.002	−.014	−.020	.014	.030	−.010	−.012
Maryland Cup Corp.	.201*	.091*	.011	−.014	−.012	−.038	−.007	−.005
Big Three Inds.	.145*	.074*	.047	.047	−.007	.010	−.014	−.019
Thomas & Betts Corp.	.145*	.061	.019	−.017	−.040	.043	.023	−.017
Cleveland Cliffs	.210*	.106*	.003	−.022	−.076*	−.030	.029	−.018
N.Y.S. Gas & Electric	−.137*	.076*	.004	.013	.019	−.010	−.010	−.029
Great West. Finance	.161*	.020	−.010	−.001	−.041	−.056	.029	−.040
Genuine Parts Co.	.126*	.001	−.031	−.060	−.085*	−.032	.004	.013
Union Electric Co.	−.155*	.037	.011	.048	−.001	.022	−.061	−.059
Searle, G. D.	.136*	.077*	−.038	−.031	−.060	−.020	−.060	−.020
Pacific Gas & Elec.	.154*	.080*	.037	.005	−.002	−.007	−.008	−.005
Shell Oil Co.	.123*	.022	−.020	−.033	−.001	−.026	.014	.003
Kresge, S. S. Co.	.143*	.015	−.064*	−.059	−.006	−.071	−.023	−.038
% of significant corr. for 50 securities	66%	20%	6%	6%	10%	8%	4%	4%
Market indices								
Dow-Jones Industrial	.248*	.003	−.034	−.022	−.075*	−.049	.044	.005
Standard & Poor's Corp.	.285*	.043	.027	−.013	−.005	−.053	.047	.022
NYSE Composite	.338*	.048	.006	.007	−.002	−.052	.054	−.005

* Asterisks indicate correlations significantly different from zero.

Source: Gabriel A. Hawawini, "On the Time Behavior of Financial Parameters: An Investigation of the Intervaling Effect," unpublished doctoral dissertation, New York University, 1977.

runs tests

A runs test is a statistical tool used to detect the presence of occasional nonrandom trends in a series of numbers. For testing security prices, a *run* can be defined as a sequence of price changes of the same sign. Table App. 19A-4 shows how runs are determined from a series of daily closing prices. There are 12 price changes between the 13 successive security prices p_t shown in the table. There are three runs of positive changes, one run of zero change, and two runs of negative changes for a total of six runs.

A runs test is performed by comparing the number of runs in the data with the number of runs which would be present in a sample of random numbers. It is possible to determine the number of total runs, the number of positive-change runs, the number of zero-change runs, and the number of negative-change runs which can be expected in a series of random numbers of any length.[57] Then if the runs which were actually found in the data are significantly different (that is, either too few or too many) from the numbers which are expected from truly random numbers, it is inferred that the successive changes are dependent. Table App. 19A-5 shows some of the results of a

[57] Eugene F. Fama, op. cit., pp. 74–80. Fama explains the runs tests and gives the formulas.

TABLE APP. 19A-4 determining runs in a time series of hypothetical security prices

time period (t)	security prices (p_t)	$\Delta p_t = p_{t+1} - p_t$	runs	type run
1	$67	+1	1	positive
2	68	−5		
3	63	−3	2	negative
4	60	−3		
5	57	0	3	zero
6	57	0		
7	57	+3	4	positive
8	60	+1		
9	61	−1	5	negative
10	60	+2		
11	62	+1	6	positive
12	63	+2		
13	65			

study of the 30 stocks in the DJIA. About 1400 daily stock prices from 1957 to 1962 were analyzed for each stock. Since the actual number of runs was not significantly different from the number of runs expected if the series were random, the test implies that stock price changes are random. Runs analyses of other securities by other analysts have also indicated that security price changes are a series of independent numbers.

testing independence with filter rules

A *filter rule* is a mechanical trading rule which can detect trends in data. An x percent filter rule operates as follows:

> If the price of a security rises at least x percent, buy and hold the security until its price drops at least x percent from a subsequent high. Then, when the price decreases x percent or more, liquidate any long position and assume a short position until the price rises at least x percent.

By varying the value of x, an infinite number of filter rules can be tested. If stock price changes are a series of independent random numbers, filter rules should not yield more return than a naive buy-and-hold strategy.

Several analysts have applied filter rules to series of historical daily prices for various securities. The historical data were stored in the memory of a computer. Then, the computer was programmed to simulate trading activity using many different filters. Filters as small as ½ of 1 percent ($x = .005$) and as large as 50 percent ($x = .5$) were used. Each study showed that the filter rules were less profitable than a naive buy-and-hold strategy. If brokers' commissions are ignored, a few of the filter rules were able to earn a rate of return as high as 15 percent per year, a rate of return above what could have been achieved by using a naive buy-and-hold strategy during that period. Nevertheless, the vast majority of the filter rules earned very poor returns (that is, less than could be obtained with a naive buy-and-hold strategy) or even incurred losses. Many buy and sell transactions are generated by some filter rules (namely, $x = .005$). To perform a realistic test of a filter rule, sales

TABLE APP. 19A-5 runs analysis by sign (daily changes)

stock	POSITIVE			NEGATIVE			NO CHANGE		
	actual	expected	actual – expected	actual	expected	actual – expected	actual	expected	actual – expected
Allied Chemical	286	290.1	– 4.1	294	290.7	3.3	103	102.2	0.8
Alcoa	265	264.4	0.6	262	266.5	– 4.5	74	70.1	3.9
American Can	289	290.2	– 1.2	285	284.6	0.4	156	155.2	0.8
AT&T	290	291.2	– 1.2	285	285.3	– 0.3	82	80.5	1.5
American Tobacco	296	300.2	– 4.2	295	294.0	1.0	109	105.8	3.2
Anaconda	271	272.9	– 1.9	276	278.8	– 2.8	88	83.3	4.7
Bethlehem Steel	282	286.4	– 4.4	300	294.6	5.4	127	128.0	–1.0
Chrysler	417	414.9	2.1	421	421.1	– 0.1	89	91.0	–2.0
Du Pont	293	300.3	– 7.3	305	299.2	5.8	74	72.5	1.5
Eastman Kodak	306	308.6	– 2.6	312	308.7	3.3	60	60.7	–0.7
General Electric	404	404.5	– 0.5	401	404.7	– 3.7	113	108.8	4.2
General Foods	346	340.8	5.2	320	331.3	–11.3	133	126.9	6.1
General Motors	340	342.7	– 2.7	339	340.3	– 1.3	153	149.0	4.0
Goodyear	294	291.9	2.1	292	293.0	– 1.0	95	96.1	–1.1
International Harvester	303	300.1	2.9	301	298.8	2.2	116	121.1	–5.1
International Nickel	312	307.0	5.0	296	301.9	– 5.9	96	95.1	0.9
International Paper	322	330.2	– 8.2	338	333.2	4.8	102	98.6	3.4
Johns Manville	293	292.6	0.4	296	293.5	2.5	96	98.9	–2.9
Owens Illinois	297	293.7	3.3	295	291.2	3.8	121	128.1	–7.1
Procter & Gamble	343	346.4	– 3.4	342	340.3	1.7	141	139.3	1.7
Sears	291	289.3	1.7	265	271.3	– 6.3	144	139.4	4.6
Standard Oil (Calif.)	406	417.9	–11.9	427	416.6	10.4	139	137.5	1.5
Standard Oil (N.J.)	272	277.3	– 5.3	281	277.9	3.1	135	132.8	2.2
Swift & Co.	354	354.3	– 0.3	355	356.9	– 1.9	169	166.8	2.2
Texaco	266	265.6	0.4	258	263.6	– 5.6	76	70.8	5.2
Union Carbide	266	268.1	– 2.1	265	265.6	– 0.6	64	61.3	2.7
United Aircraft	281	280.4	0.6	282	282.2	– 0.2	98	98.4	–0.4
U.S. Steel	292	293.5	– 1.5	296	295.2	0.8	63	62.3	0.7
Westinghouse	359	361.3	– 2.3	364	362.1	1.9	106	105.6	0.4
Woolworth	349	348.7	0.3	350	345.9	4.1	148	152.4	–4.4

Source: Eugene F. Fama, "The Behavior of Stock Market Prices," *Journal of Business*, January 1965, p. 79.

commissions must be deducted to determine the *net* profitability of a trading technique. When allowance was made for sales commissions, the filter rules earned even poorer returns. No filter rule earned a rate of return above what a naive buy-and-hold strategy earned, and most filters resulted in losses after deduction of the commissions they generated.

Some studies of filter rules figured the rate of return from long positions and the return from short positions separately. Using a filter rule to select short positions nearly always resulted in losses even before allowance was made for commissions. Sometimes the long positions initiated by a filter rule earned positive returns. In fact, a ½ percent filter ($x = .005$) resulted in an annual return before commissions as high as 20 percent, according to one study. After sales commissions were deducted, however, a higher return could have been achieved by using a naive buy-and-hold strategy. In general, filter rules do not earn net rates of return as high as those that could be gained with a naive buy-and-hold strategy.

simplified numerical example of random walk

Thus far, the notions of a stable probability distribution and statistical independence have been developed in an effort to clarify the nature of a random walk. Before reaching conclusions, let us consider a simplified random-walk numerical example to pull these ideas together.

Imagine a security whose rates of return either increase or decrease by one percentage point each period with equal probability. Denote the expected return of this security as $E(r_0)$. Table App. 19A-6 traces the course of all possible outcomes over several periods.

In this table the probability of any outcome is shown in parentheses following that outcome. Examination of the table will reveal the following characteristics: (1) The expected return is constant at $E(r_0)$ in every period and for every differencing interval. Thus, the expected return is stationary as the future unfolds and actual returns fluctuate around $E(r_0)$. (2) The variance of returns tends to increase with the length of the differencing period. (3) The probability distribution of possible returns is stationary although the actual returns vary randomly. That is, the actual rates of return over time are a

TABLE APP. 19A-6 simplified random walk in returns

period (t)	0	1	2	3	4
Possible outcomes (and their probabilities)				$E(r_0) + 3(1/8)$	. . .
			$E(r_0) + 2(1/4)$		
		$E(r_0) + 1(1/2)$		$E(r_0) + 1(3/8)$	. . .
	$E(r_0)$		$E(r_0)$ (1/2)		
		$E(r_0) - 1(1/2)$		$E(r_0) - 1(3/8)$	. . .
			$E(r_0) - 2(1/4)$		
				$E(r_0) - 3(1/8)$	. . .
$E(r_1)$	$E(r_0)$	$E(r_1) = E(r_0)$	$E(r_2) = E(r_0)$	$E(r_3) = E(r_0)$	. . .
var(r_1)	0	1	2	3	4

series of independent values which can be assigned probabilities but cannot be predicted in advance.

The example shown in Table App. 19A-6 is a random walk in rates of return because the returns are independent and identically distributed. An examination of actual historical rates of return will reveal that characteristics 1 and 2 above also occur in the empirical data and that characteristic 3 is a rough approximation of a stable distribution to which the empirical data conform. Thus, this simple random-walk model is a good first approximation of the way rates of return actually perform.

conclusions regarding independence

Some of the simplest and most common tests used to determine the independence of series of security price changes and rates of return have been presented. It was shown that the data are not *perfectly* statistically independent in every case. A few cases were found (namely, small serial correlations, actual runs not exactly equal to expected runs, a few filter rules which earned a small profit before commissions, and year-end and week-end anomalies) where variations from perfect statistical independence existed. These cases of dependence were found to be very slight; no profit could be earned from a knowledge of these small variations from pure independence. Nevertheless, a mathematical statistician would not say that rates of return are perfectly independent over time. Therefore, rates of return are not perfectly described by a rigorously defined random-walk model.

A practical businessperson need not adhere to the rigorous conventions of the mathematical statistician. Investors' criteria are simpler. As long as rates of return are sufficiently independent that profit cannot be increased by using whatever statistical dependency exists, it may be concluded that rates of return are independent for business purposes. Thus, as a first approximation, we may say rates of return follow a random walk as far as businesspeople need be concerned.

The random-walk conclusion casts serious doubts on the efficiency of technical analysis. It will be recalled that technical analysts' methods are largely based upon statistical dependency and patterns in security price changes. There is little doubt that some of the patterns described by the technical analysts actually exist; such patterns can also be found in series of random numbers or in ink blots. Also, some of the market indicators used by chartists (for example, the confidence index) are actually correlated with security market indices. But technical tools *do not furnish dependable leading indicators:* they are frequently concurrent or lagging indicators, or they may even fail to formulate the proper signal at all. The patterns, moreover, are ambiguous. Different technicians interpret the same chart to mean different things. Furthermore, the charts issue erroneous signals about as frequently as they issue correct signals. The few studies which have been published in support of technical analysis are weak. The evidence presented by the random-walk advocates is more voluminous and more scientific than evidence presented by the technical analysts. A reasonable person who objectively studied the existing literature would most likely conclude that technical analysis tools were (in some cases) crude attempts to measure risk or (in most cases) not worth performing at all.

BOX APP. 19A-2 definition of a martingale

> A martingale process is a mathematical process in which the conditional expectation of the $(n + 1)$st value equals the nth value in some set of data.[58]

APP. 19A-3 MARTINGALE MODELS

The random walk is a mathematical model in which a series is both independent and identically distributed; it is a special, more narrowly defined case of a *martingale process*. A martingale does not require that successive members of the series be either independent or identically distributed. Box App. 19A-2 defines a martingale.

Symbolically, rates of return follow a martingale if Eq. (App. 19A-6) is not violated.

$$E({}_jr_{t+1} | {}_jr_t, \ldots, {}_jr_{t-n}) = {}_jr_t \qquad \text{(App. 19A-6)}$$

where

${}_jr_t$ = return for security j at period t.

Equation (App. 19A-6) is a symbolic representation of the weakly efficient markets hypothesis. It says that knowledge of all historical returns of some security suggests only that the next period's return is expected to equal the last period's return.

A stronger form of the martingale exists if Eq. (App. 19A-7) is not violated.

$$E({}_jr_{t+1} | N_t) = {}_jr_t \qquad \text{(App. 19A-7)}$$

where

N_t = all the public news and information which existed at period t

This is the semistrongly efficient markets hypothesis. Equation (App. 19A-7) implies that all available news is already reflected in prices. Equations (App. 19A-6) and (App. 19A-7) imply that future returns are independent of past data, but they do not imply complete independence of the entire series of returns.[59] Security prices are a *submartingale* process, since they drift upward over time. Equation (App. 19A-8) defines the submartingale process followed by most security prices.

$$E({}_jp_{t+1} | {}_jp_t, {}_jp_{t-1}, \ldots, {}_jp_{t-n}) > {}_jp_t \qquad \text{(App. 19A-8)}$$

where

${}_jp_t$ = price of security j at period t

[58] William Feller, *An Introduction to Probability Theory and Its Implications*, vol. II, Wiley, New York, 1966; see pp. 210–212 for a more rigorous discussion of martingales.

[59] John T. Emery, "The Information Content of Daily Market Indicators," *Journal of Financial and Quantitative Analysis*, March 1973, pp. 183–190.

In contrast to the martingale, the random-walk model is much more narrowly defined. Rates of return are a random walk if Eq. (App. 19A-9) is not violated.

$$f({}_jr_{t+1}|{}_jr_t, {}_jr_{t-1}, \ldots, {}_jr_{t-n}) = f({}_jr_t) \qquad \text{(App. 19A-9)}$$

where

$f({}_jr_t)$ = the probability distribution of returns for security j at period t

Equation (App. 19A-9) implies Eq. (App. 19A-6). Furthermore, Eq. (App. 19A-9) implies that rates of return are independent and identically distributed according to some stationary distribution.

Technically speaking, Eq. (App. 19A-9) is not true because the percentage price changes for securities are not all perfectly independent—only nearly so. Equations (App. 19A-6) and (App. 19A-8) are weaker assertions which are true, however.

The distinction between Eqs. (App. 19A-6) and (App. 19A-9) is not great where stock price changes are concerned. It took mathematicians and economists several years to determine that Eqs. (App. 19A-6) and (App. 19A-8) were true and that (App. 19A-9) was an overstatement. But, when using language precisely, it is best to refer to security prices as a submartingale and to rates of return as a martingale. The random-walk term is an exaggeration.

The efficient market hypothesis may be formalized by using the compact functional notation for probability distributions. Suppose that $f(p_{it}, p_{i,t-1}, p_{i,t-2}, p_{i,t-3}, \ldots |\phi_{t-1})$ is the joint probability distribution of the ith security's prices with all other securities prices in period t. Suppose further that this distribution is conditional upon ϕ_{t-1}, which is the set of *all information* that determines security prices in period t. Also, define $g(p_{it}, p_{i,t-1}, p_{i,t-2}, p_{i,t-3}, \ldots |\phi_{t-1}{}^M)$ to be the joint probability distribution of the ith security's price with all other prices, which is conditional upon $\phi_{t-1}{}^M$, the set of all information that the *market uses* to determine the security prices in period t. Capital markets are perfectly efficient if Eq. (App. 19A-10) is true.[60]

$$f(p_{it}, p_{i,t-1}, p_{i,t-2}, p_{i,t-3}, \ldots |\phi_{t-1}) = g(p_{it}, p_{i,t-1}, p_{i,t-2}, p_{i,t-3}, \ldots |\phi_{t-1}{}^M) \qquad \text{(App. 19A-10)}$$

[60] Stephen F. LeRoy, "Efficient Capital Markets: Comment," *Journal of Finance*, March 1976, vol. XXI, no. 1, pp. 139–141. E. F. Fama, "Reply," ibid, pp. 143–145.

part six

OTHER INVESTMENTS

The five chapters in Part 6 discuss marketable securities and some institutional arrangements surrounding them which are typically used by more experienced and professional investors in the United States. The securities explained in Chaps. 20 through 24 are useful in constructing well-diversified and profitable portfolios.

CHAPTER 20—*preferred stock* a hybrid combination of the debt and equity securities that is analyzed in the risk-return context and contrasted with the pure equity and pure debt securities.

CHAPTER 21—*speculating and hedging* compares and contrasts long and short positions and explains hedges and the options: puts, calls, strips, straps, straddles, warrants, and convertible securities.

CHAPTER 22—*commodities* starts by listing the commodities and the exchanges where futures contracts are traded. Cash, spot, and futures positions are defined and risk-averting hedges are explained.

CHAPTER 23—*financial futures* extends Chap. 22 by explaining the new futures contracts on financial assets. Futures on stock and bond market indices are discussed.

CHAPTER 24—*international investing* begins by analyzing the benefits to be obtained from multinational diversification. Then foreign exchange risks and the way foreign securities are handled in the United States are examined.

preferred stock

The various characteristics which a preferred stock issue may possess were initially described in Sec. 2-7.[1] This chapter reconsiders those aspects of preferred stocks and goes on to analyze preferred stock in a risk-return framework. One-period market rates of return from nonconvertible preferred stocks will be used to estimate the risk and return characteristics for 100 different preferreds. Then these market-determined risk measures for preferreds will be compared with the risk and return statistics from bonds and common stocks in order to see how the different securities' various legal limitations and privileges affect their market behavior.[2]

20-1 TRADITIONAL VIEW OF PREFERRED STOCK

Legally speaking, preferred stock represents a portion of the ownership of a corporation and is thus similar to common stock. Nonconvertible preferred stock is a perpetual security too; it never matures and has to be repaid like a debt security. Preferred stockholders are paid cash dividends as common stockholders are; these cash dividends are not a tax-deductible expense like the interest payments that corporations make to the owners of debt securities. In addition, some issues of preferred stock give their owners the same voting rights that the owners of common stock shares have, although voting rights of preferreds vary greatly from issue to issue. Preferred stock has a claim on the business's assets in the event of bankruptcy which is junior to the bond

[1] Further details about preferred stock issues are discussed by D. E. Fisher and Glen Wilt, Jr., "Nonconvertible Preferred Stock as a Financing Instrument, 1950–1965," *Journal of Finance*, September 1968, vol. XXIII. See, also W. S. Curran, "Preferred Stock in Public Utility Finance—A Reconsideration," *Financial Analysts Journal*, March–April 1972; and B. Graham, D. L. Dodd, and S. Cottle, *Security Analysis*, 4th ed., McGraw-Hill, New York, 1962, chaps. 27, 28, and 47.

[2] This chapter presumes Chap. 10 has been mastered.

owners' claims. In all these respects, then, preferred stock is similar to common stock.

However, preferred stock is also similar to bonds in several respects. Preferred stock pays contractual payments each period which, just like bond interest coupons, are stipulated as some fixed percent of the security's par value. If the issuing corporation falls upon hard times and does not have earnings sufficient to pay the preferred stockholders their contractual dividend payments, then the preferred stockholders can file a suit against the corporation if their shares have the cumulative provision (that is, missed dividends are accumulated as debts owed by the corporation). However, preferred stockholders do not enjoy increased dividends when the corporation is prosperous in the way common stockholders do (except for those rare issues of participating preferred stock). Furthermore, preferred stock does have a claim on assets in the event of bankruptcy which is prior to the claims of common stockholders. Preferred stockholders are repaid the full face value of their securities before the common shareholders can be paid a cent from bankruptcy proceeds. Preferred stock is similar to bonds in these respects.

Finance textbooks have traditionally summarized the similarities which preferred stock has to both common stocks and bonds by concluding that preferred stock is a *hybrid* or compromise security. The risk, income, and voting control of preferred stock lies somewhere between the high-risk, high-income, and maximum voting control of common stock and the lower-risk, lower-income, and lesser control of bonds (as illustrated in Table 2-1). The most discerning textbooks argue that only preferred stock issued by corporations with high quality ratings should be approached in the same fashion as bonds. However, one classic book on security analysis explains that it is "by no means asserting the investment equivalence of bonds and preferred stocks in general" and goes on to add "the sounder and more fruitful approach to the field of speculative senior securities lies in the direction of common stocks."[3] Preferred stocks should certainly not be equated with common stocks, since preferred stocks receive only a limited dividend no matter how well the firm may be doing. Moreover, if the firm suffers reverses and has difficulty paying expected dividends, owners of preferred stock are likely to suffer less severely than the owners of common shares.

After reviewing the traditional wisdom about preferred stocks, it is difficult to consider simultaneously all the various facets of an investment in preferred stock. Traditional discussions may sound lyrical, but, unfortunately, they leave analytical investors asking whether preferred stocks are like bonds, like common stocks, or like some combination of the two or whether they are a unique class of securities with widely varying characteristics. One way to be able to categorize preferred stock issues more effectively is to start by categorizing the issuing corporation on the basis of its quality ratings.

Most texts define *quality* to mean the chance of default in dividend or interest payment or principal repayment.[4] The methods used by the major commercial rating agencies exemplify this traditional approach. Moody's Investors Service, for example, says that the purpose of ratings "is to provide the

[3] See Graham, Dodd, and Cottle, op. cit., p. 309.

[4] D. E. Vaughn, *Survey of Investments*, Holt, New York, 1967, p. 5.

American investor with a simple system of gradation by which the relative investment qualities . . . may be noted."[5] See Fig. 6-5 on page 153 for an example of the type of quality ratings which the Standard & Poor's Corporation (S&P) assigns to preferred stocks. Moody's ratings are analogous to the S&P ratings. Moody's[6] describes its preferred stock rating process as follows:

> Since ratings involve a judgment about the future, on the one hand, and since they are used by investors as a means of protection, on the other, the effort is made, when assigning ratings, to look at "worst" potentialities in the "visible" future rather than solely at the past record and the status of the present. Investors using the ratings should not, therefore, expect to find in them a reflection of statistical factors alone. They are not statistical ratings but an appraisal of long-term risks, such appraisal giving recognition to many nonstatistical factors.

After dichotomizing preferred stocks into high-quality and low-quality groups based on their quality ratings, it will be seen that the high-quality preferred stocks "behave" in the market like bonds and the low-quality preferred stocks "behave" like common stocks. The behavior of the securities is measured statistically by periodically observing their market prices in order to calculate risk and return statistics for preferred stocks. This econometric analysis of market data essentially measures how actual market participants evaluate the meanings and implications of the various rights, priorities, and the other implications which legal documents assign to preferred stock.

If preferred stock prices are unbiased and efficient estimates of preferred stock values (as explained in Chap. 8), then all relevant investment information should be compounded into the market price of the asset. As a result, the *market-determined statistics* are indirectly based on the information used to develop a traditional quality rating of an asset, and the market statistics may also include insider or other additional nonpublic information. Thus, the traditional quality ratings will be associated with the empirical risk statistic for a preferred stock if the market price reflects all relevant information, that is, if the market prices are efficient prices.

If market prices of securities do, in fact, reflect all relevant information in an efficient manner (and some evidence in Chap. 19 suggests that they do), then there are certain advantages to be gained from using market-determined risk statistics like the beta coefficient or the standard deviation. The market-determined risk statistics are capable of comparing the quality or risk of several different types of investments. A market measure of quality would not be restricted to comparing only securities which are relatively similar, since it has no explicit dependence on the type of security under analysis. Instead, such a measure would respond to the effects of changes in all securities. The measure could also have a continuous arithmetic scale. This allows small pieces of information affecting the quality of a security in a less than catastrophic way to be reflected adequately in the quality measure.

At first glance, there appear to be differences between the meaning of quality or risk as measured in the marketplace and as measured in traditional fashion. However, after investigation these differences turn out to be more

[5] Moody's *Industrial Manual*, 1956–1966, Moody's Investors Services, New York.
[6] Ibid.

imagined than real. Traditional measures of quality purport to focus on the "worst possibilities" of ruin for the security. They ignore period-to-period changes and returns, and they estimate, instead, the possibility of dividend or interest default. They are meant to be of interest primarily to investors intending to hold the rated securities for long periods of time.

Quality, as measured with actual market data, considers all the risks encountered when holding a security. As a result, statements that "high-quality preferreds are like bonds" take on additional meanings. In the case of market risk this means that high-quality preferreds suffer essentially the same risks as bonds (namely, interest rate risk). Similarly, statements saying that low-quality preferreds are "like common stocks" mean that low-quality preferreds suffer essentially the same risks as common stocks. Another interpretation of the word *like* in this context is that the preferred stock in question is significantly positively (but not perfectly positively) correlated with whatever stock or bond index may be under discussion.

To facilitate comparing and contrasting various preferred stocks with bonds and common stocks, some market indices are defined in the following section.

20-2 MARKET INDICES FOR OTHER TYPES OF SECURITIES

A representative sample of U.S. Treasury bonds (that is, bonds which are free of default risk) was prepared for comparison with the preferred stocks. The sample was first used to construct a bond market index. This bond market index was based on percentage price changes in the bonds in order to facilitate comparisons with the preferred stocks' simultaneous percentage price changes. The single-period bond returns are defined in Eq. (20-1) and denoted r_{Bt}.

$$r_{Bt} = \frac{m_{B,t+1} - m_{B,t}}{m_{B,t}} \tag{20-1}$$

In Eq. (20-1) the convention $m_{B,t}$ represents the dollar value of the Treasury bond index at the start of time period t.[7]

[7] The month-long holding period returns for any coupon-bearing bond or note are calculated as follows:

$$r_B = \frac{\left(p_{t+1} + \frac{n+1}{m}d\right) - \left(p_t + \frac{n}{m}d\right)}{p_t + \frac{n}{m}d} = \frac{p_{t+1} - p_t + \frac{1}{m}d}{p_t + \frac{n}{m}d}$$

where

d = amount of interest due when it becomes payable
m = number of periods between interest payments
n = number of periods accrued toward the next payment at the end of period t

Then $1/m$ indicates the one period of "straight-line" accrual of the interest payment from period t to period $t + 1$.

The interest accrual is shown explicitly, since the purchase of a bond consists of two parts. The first is payment of the quoted price ex-interest, and the second is payment for any interest that

R_t is a riskless rate surrogate (namely, a U.S. Treasury bill rate) observed during time period t. The risk-premium for an index of bonds is calculated with Eq. (20-2).

$$r_{Bt} - R_t = \text{the risk-premium for bond } B \text{ in the } t\text{th period} \tag{20-2}$$

Market returns from the bond index calculated with Eqs. (20-1) and (20-2) can be compared and contrasted directly with the market returns from a preferred stock index. Equations (20-3) and (20-4) show how the returns and risk-premiums, respectively, are calculated for the preferred stocks.

$$r_{pt} = \frac{p_{t+1} - p_t + d_t}{p_t} \tag{20-3}$$

The right-hand side of Eq. (20-3) represents a one-period price change plus cash dividend rate of return from the ith preferred stock during time period t. The p_t variable denotes the market price of the preferred stock at the beginning of the ith time period, and d_t represents the cash dividend (if any) received during period t.

$$r_{pt} - R_t = \text{risk-premium from preferred stock } p \text{ in the } t\text{th time period} \tag{20-4}$$

A common stock index also was prepared for comparison with the preferred stocks. Equation (20-5) defines the one-period rate-of-return formula used in constructing the returns from the common stock index.

$$r_{mt} = \frac{m_{t+1} - m_t + d_{mt}}{m_t} \tag{20-5}$$

Here the right-hand side of the equation represents the one-period capital gain plus the cash dividend rate of return from the Lorie-Fisher market index[8] made from equal portions of all NYSE stocks. The m_t denotes the dollar value of the market index at the start of period t, and d_{mt} stands for the cash dividend from the market index which was paid during period t.

$$r_{mt} - R_t = \text{the risk-premium earned with the stock market index during time period } t \tag{20-6}$$

In the remainder of this chapter a sample of 100 different preferred stocks issued by 81 different NYSE companies (100 stocks because some of the 81 firms had more than one preferred stock issue) will be analyzed. Before delving into this analysis, however, it is worthwhile to consider some general

---

has accrued toward the next interest payment. Then sale of the bond at the end of a period (after it has been bought at the beginning of the period) entitles the bondholder to claim the new market value of the interest accrual for the period. The same formula may be used for the period return on bills if interest accrual is set to zero. The r_B is a measure of the price change for the period.

The sampled securities and index construction are explained in more detail by John S. Bildersee, "Risk and Return on Preferred Stocks," Ph.D. dissertation, University of Chicago, 1971.

[8] J. Lorie and Lawrence Fisher, "Rates of Return on Investments in Common Stocks," *Journal of Business*, vol. XXXVII, January 1964.

characteristics of common stocks, Treasury bonds, and preferred stocks. A preferred stock index was prepared for this comparison. The one-period rates of return for the 100 preferred stocks were calculated monthly from March 1956 to March 1966 with Eq. (20-3). Then the equally weighted average of the 100 different preferred stocks' rates of return was converted into risk-premium form with Eq. (20-4), and a preferred stock index was thus obtained.

After the representative market indices were constructed for common stocks, preferred stocks, and the U.S. Treasury bonds as explained above, an overall market index was constructed by combining these three specialized security market indices. Various proportions of the three pure security market indices were used to construct a market index for heterogeneous assets. Table 20-1 shows summary statistics describing proportions of the specialized security market indices which were combined in the construction of different overall market indices along with the correlation coefficients between the different portfolios' monthly returns. A mere glance at all the high positive correlations throughout Table 20-1 reveals the high degree of commonality among the various market indices which were constructed.

The particular overall market index made up from the following components was arbitrarily selected to be *the overall market index* (TOMI) used in further analysis.

65%	Common Stock Index
5%	Preferred Stock Index
30%	U.S. Treasury Bond Index
100%	The overall market index (TOMI)

TABLE 20-1 correlations among several market indices, March 1956 to March 1966

OVERALL MARKET INDEX WITH PROPORTIONS AS FOLLOWS:				CORRELATION WITH OTHER INDICES:				
				Cmm. stk. %	100	75	65	60
common stock index, %	preferred stock index, %	U.S. Treasury bond index, %	total, %	Prf. stk. %	0	0	5	5
				Treas. bd. %	0	25	30	35
				Total percent:	100%	100%	100%	100%
100	0	0	100		1.00	.99	.99	.99
75	0	25	100			1.00	.99	.99
65	5	30	100				1.00	.99
60	5	35	100 ←	TOMI				→ 1.00
50	0	50	100		.98	.99	.99	.99
50	5	45	100		.99	.99	.99	.99
50	10	40	100		.99	.99	.99	.99
60	0	40	100		.99	.99	.99	.99
70	0	30	100		.99	.99	.99	.99
80	0	20	100		.99	.99	.99	.99
90	0	10	100		.99	.99	.99	.99

Source: John S. Bildersee, "Risk and Return on Preferred Stocks," Ph.D. dissertation, University of Chicago, 1971.

TABLE 20-2 correlations among various market indices

index	gov't bonds	high-quality preferred stocks	all 100 preferred stocks	low-quality preferred stocks	common stocks	TOMI
Government bonds	1.00	.57	.30	.04	−.15	−.01
60 high-quality preferred stocks		1.00	.41	.16	.22	.23
All 100 preferred stocks			1.00	.37	.57	.62
40 low-quality preferred stocks				1.00	.75	.81
Common stocks					1.00	.99
TOMI						1.00

Source: John S. Bildersee, "Risk and Return on Preferred Stocks," Ph.D. dissertation, University of Chicago, 1971.

Table 20-2 shows the correlations between TOMI and the pure security market indices. The Common Stock Index, the U.S. Treasury Bond Index, and the index made from 100 different preferred stocks were explained above. In addition to these three pure security indices, two new preferred stock indices are shown in Tables 20-2 and 20-3. An index made from the 60 preferred stocks which had the highest quality (that is, the least systematic beta risk) and also another preferred stock index composed of the remaining 40 preferreds which had the lowest quality (that is, the highest beta systematic risk coefficients) were formed.[9] The summary statistics in Tables 20-2 and 20-3 include these new preferred stock indices so that additional comparisons can be made and more can be learned about the risk and return characteristics of preferred stocks.

The correlations in Table 20-2 are much lower than the correlations in Table 20-1. They are evidence of significant differences among returns from

[9] The quality of the 100 preferred stocks was determined by ranking their 100 beta systematic risk coefficients. These betas were calculated by regressing each preferred stock issue's monthly risk-premiums calculated with Eq. (20-4) onto the common stock market index returns calculated with Eq. (20-6). As a result, a characteristic regression line was calculated for each of the 100 preferred stocks in order to categorize its quality. The characteristic line in terms of risk premiums was originated by Jensen. See M. C. Jensen, "Risk, the Pricing of Capital Assets and the Evaluation of Investment Portfolios," *Journal of Business*, April 1969, vol. 42, pp. 167–247.

TABLE 20-3 risk and return statistics for various pure market indices and TOMI

market index	$E(r_i - R)$ = average risk-premium, a return measure	standard deviation, a risk measure, %
Government bonds	.034% per month	.531
60 high-quality preferred stocks	.082% per month	1.262
All 100 preferred stocks	.165% per month	1.316
40 low-quality preferred stocks	.278% per month	2.002
TOMI	.568% per month	2.441
Common stocks	.846% per month	3.722

Source: John S. Bildersee, "Risk and Return on Preferred Stocks," Ph.D. dissertation, University of Chicago, 1971.

the security indices for the 60 high-quality preferreds, the 40 low-quality preferreds, all 100 preferred stocks together, the common stocks, the Treasury bonds, and TOMI. The common stock prices fluctuate with the corporations' earnings prospects (as explained in Chaps. 15, 16, and 17); the bond prices fluctuate inversely with market interest rates (as explained in Chaps. 11, 12, and 13); and the preferred stock prices are influenced by both the issuing corporation's earnings prospects and market interest rates. The index of the 60 highest-quality preferreds is most highly correlated with U.S. Treasury bonds. The 40 lowest-quality preferreds are most highly correlated with the Common Stock Index. The index made up of all 100 preferred stocks is correlated with both the stock and the bond indices. These findings suggest the following conclusions:

1. In general, preferred stocks have elements in common with both common stocks and default-free U.S. Treasury bonds.
2. The high-quality preferred stocks *behave* more like the default-free U.S. Treasury bonds than like common stocks.
3. The low-quality preferreds *behave* more like common stocks than like bonds.

20-3 RISK-RETURN DIFFERENCES IN BASIC SECURITY TYPES

Some comparative risk and average return (that is, average risk-premium) statistics are shown in Table 20-3 in order to delineate additional differences between the security types in terms of market statistics. U.S. Treasury bonds (which are essentially incapable of undergoing bankruptcy) experience the least variability of monthly return. In marked contrast to the Treasury bonds, the common stock index experiences the greatest total risk of any of the indices (or portfolios) shown in Table 20-3.

It is expected that the common stock would experience more risk in the market because the corporate laws attach more bankruptcy risk to common stock ownership than to the ownership of preferred stock or bonds if all the securities are issued by firms of equal quality. Thus, the higher market risk reflected in the common stock indices and the lower market risks experienced by the senior securities (namely, preferred stock and bonds) are merely efficient market reflections of the respective bankruptcy risks legislated into each type of security by U.S. corporate laws. Furthermore, even the more subtle risk differentials between the 60 highest-quality preferreds and the 40 lowest-quality preferreds are reflected in the market risk statistics shown in Table 20-3.

Further perusal of the risk and return statistics for the three pure security indices in Table 20-3 reveals that the securities with the highest risk also yield the highest returns, on average. This direct relation between risk and return is exactly what economic theory suggests should occur. Investors are risk-averse and therefore require higher average (or expected) rates of return to induce them to invest in riskier securities.

Summarizing briefly, the market statistics shown in Tables 20-2 and 20-3 accurately reflect the different driving forces, the different levels of risk, and the different levels of return, respectively, from investing in different types of securities. The average risk and return statistics for the basic types of se-

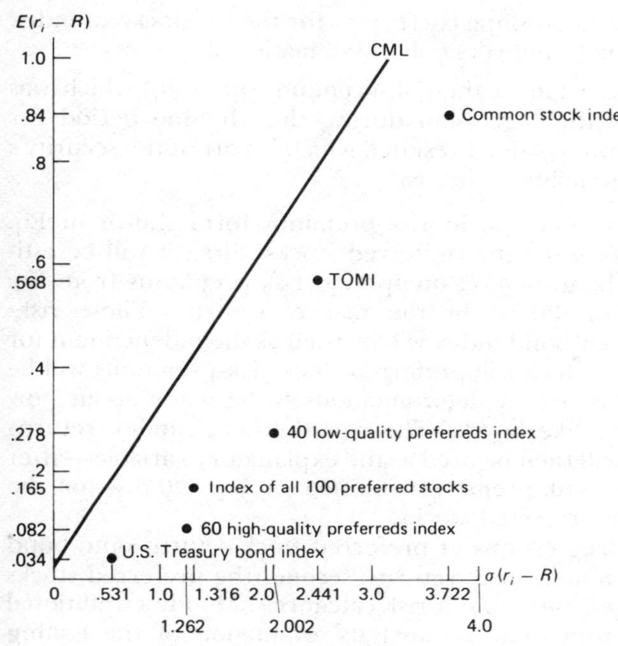

FIGURE 20-1 investment opportunities in risk-return space.

curities discussed above are graphically placed in perspective beneath the efficient frontier of Markowitz diversified portfolios in Fig. 20-1. TOMI also is illustrated in Fig. 20-1 as merely the diversified average of the three pure security indices.

The market data apparently reflect a consensus evaluation of all the characteristics of securities which have traditionally been discussed verbally and in texts. However, market statistics have the additional advantage of being concise, being part of the risk-return theory (see Chap. 10), which lends valuable investment insights, and being easy to categorize rather than being somewhat vague. The characteristic regression line and its associated risk-return statistics furnish the primary tools for the analysis of other aspects of preferred stocks' market behavior.

20-4 THE CHARACTERISTIC LINE FOR PREFERRED STOCKS

The characteristic-line model in risk-premium form is restated below.[10]

$$r_{it} - R_t = \alpha_i + \beta_i(r_{mt} - R_t) + e_{it} \tag{20-7}$$

where

α_i = alpha = the regression intercept for the ith market asset, a measure of unusually good (if positive) or unusually bad (if negative) risk-adjusted returns for the ith asset

[10] The characteristic line in risk-premium form was presented and explained in appendix A to chap. 14 of J. C. Francis: *Investment: Analysis and Management*, 3d ed., McGraw-Hill, New York, 1980. The model was originally developed by M. C. Jensen, "Risk, the Pricing of Capital Assets and the Evaluation of Investment Portfolios," *Journal of Business*, April 1969, vol. 42, pp. 167–247.

β_i = beta = the regression slope coefficient for the ith stock, an index of the ith security's undiversifiable systematic risk

e_{it} = epsilon = the portion of the risk-premium $(r_{it} - R_t)$ which was unexplained by the regression during the tth time period for security i = an unexplained residual which is part of the security's unsystematic variability of return

The characteristic regression line in risk-premium form shown in Eq. (20-7) will be estimated twice for the preferred stocks. First, it will be estimated with the Treasury bond market one-period risk-premiums from Eq. (20-2) substituted into Eq. (20-7) for the market returns. These risk-premiums from the Treasury bond index will be used as the independent (or explanatory) variable upon which the preferred stock risk-premiums will be regressed. Such regressions permit determinations to be made about how much preferred stocks are like bonds. The common stock index returns calculated with Eq. (20-5) will then be used as the explanatory variable—after they are converted to the risk-premiums defined in Eq. (20-6)—for the second regression with the preferred stocks.

Before performing the regressions of preferred stock returns onto bond returns, first, and onto common stock returns, second, the preferred stocks were grouped into homogeneous default-risk categories. Moody's traditional quality ratings (derived from financial analysts' evaluation of the issuing firms' financial ratios) were used to delineate the following three homogeneous default-risk categories:

1. High-grade preferred stocks (11)
2. Medium-grade preferred stocks (20)
3. Speculative-grade preferred stocks (10)

The exact number of preferreds used in each grouping is shown in the parentheses after each group's name. Preferred stocks which experienced quality rating changes during the sampled decade were deleted from this phase of the analysis in order to eliminate any ambiguities about the assignment of the default-risk categories. As a result, only (11 + 20 + 10 =) 41 out of the total of 100 preferred stocks were used to form the three Moody's default-risk groupings.[11]

The three default-risk groupings were used to form three homogeneous default-risk preferred stock indices. Then each of the three preferred stock index returns was regressed, first, onto the bond market index returns and, second, onto the common stock index returns. The statistics from these characteristic-line regressions in risk-premium form are summarized in Table 20-4.

The statistics in Table 20-4 suggest conclusions similar to those indicated

[11] Preferred stock can be meaningfully analyzed in terms of two variables simultaneously: (1) Macaulay's duration to measure interest rate risk, and (2) beta to measure default risk. For an example of theoretical and empirical analysis of preferred stock in terms of these two variables see "Risk and Security Returns," by Patrick Casabona, Jack Francis, and Ashok Vora in the Spring 1983 issue of *Review of Business*, St. John's University, Jamaica, N.Y., pp. 14–20. See also P. A. Casabona, F. J. Fabozzi, and J. C. Francis, "How to Apply Duration to Equity Analysis," *Journal of Portfolio Management*, Winter 1984, pp. 52–59.

TABLE 20-4 regression* of indices representing various Moody's quality preferred stocks on the bond index alone and the common stock index alone

		BOND INDEX			COMMON STOCK INDEX		
Preferred stock index†	Cos.	α	β	R^2	α	β	R^2
High grade	11	−.013	1.692‡	.393	−.139	.051	.017
Medium grade	20	.021	.842‡	.123	−.113	.190‡	.294
Speculative grade	10	.128	.231	.008	−.257	.228‡	.368

* The characteristic regression line in risk-premium form; Eq. (20-7) was the econometric model.

† Based on traditional subjective financial ratio analysis executed by Moody's Inc.

‡ The observation is over two standard errors from zero.

Source: John S. Bildersee, "Risk and Return on Preferred Stocks," Ph.D. dissertation, University of Chicago, 1971.

above by the data in Tables 20-2 and 20-3. The high-grade preferred stock index is more highly correlated and moves systematically more closely with the U.S. Treasury Bond Index than with the Common Stock Index. This suggests that high-quality preferred stocks behave more like bonds than like common stocks. The statistics in Table 20-4 also indicate that the index made up of 10 speculative-grade (that is, the low-quality) preferreds behaved more like the Common Stock Index than like the Treasury Bond Index. Summarizing all the results shown in Table 20-4, it appears that preferred stocks are, in fact, hybrid securities which are like both bonds and common stocks in some respects. The high-quality preferreds are more like bonds; they are primarily responsive to interest rate factors rather than to the issuing corporation's earnings prospects. The low-quality preferreds, in contrast, are more similar to common stocks. These conclusions based on the traditional Moody's quality rating groups correspond to, and thus verify, the conclusions reached above (in Tables 20-2 and 20-3), which were based on market-determined risk measures (namely, beta coefficient groupings).[12]

20-5 CONCLUSIONS ABOUT PREFERRED STOCKS

This chapter analyzed nonconvertible preferred stocks from three different viewpoints. First, the traditional discussion of the legal intricacies of preferred stocks relative to senior (namely, bond) and junior (namely, common stock) securities was reviewed. The discussion was informative but verbose at best. Moreover, it was impossible to reach precise or incisive conclusions about the relative merits of preferred stock investing. The second viewpoint considered was quantitative and more analytical; market-determined risk and return statistics were analyzed.

The analysis of market-determined risk and return statistics yielded some concise conclusions (see Tables 20-2 and 20-3). This second approach to

[12] F. J. Fabozzi, "A Note on the Association between Systematic Risks and Common Stock and Bond Rating Classifications," *Journal of Economics and Business*, April 1982, pp. 159–164. This study reports a significant relation between the quantitative and qualitative risk measures that is supportive of this chapter's conclusions.

preferred stock analysis suggested that, in fact, the preferreds were a hybrid offspring of bonds and stocks. The preferreds were found to possess behavior similar to bonds if they were of high quality (that is, if they had low betas) but to be more similar to common stocks if they were of lower quality (that is, if they had high betas).

The third and final approach used to analyze preferred stocks was based on the traditional quality ratings prepared by Moody's Inc. After grouping the preferred stocks into the high-, medium-, and speculative-quality categories determined by Moody's, the return, correlation, and beta risk statistics were calculated for each of the three categories. Concise conclusions which were highly supportive of the previous qualitative and quantitative analysis of preferred stocks were obtained.

It was found (see Table 20-4) that preferred stocks' market returns covaried significantly with both Treasury bond returns and common stock returns; this became scientific evidence that the preferreds are like both stocks and bonds—as the traditional writers had long suspected. Furthermore, the Moody-rated high-quality bonds behaved more like the bond index while the Moody's speculative-rated preferreds behaved more like the common stock index. Thus, the risk-return analysis based on Moody's ratings corresponded precisely with the risk-return analysis based solely on market-determined statistics. And both types of analytical findings were supportive of the contentions which had been qualitatively asserted by the traditional writers. These similar conclusions reached by the three different approaches to preferred stock analysis reinforce their own credibility. Furthermore, the empirical work helped delineate the risk and return characteristics of preferred stock investing relative to the other basic types of investment securities.

QUESTIONS

20-1. What underlying legal restrictions on all preferred stocks may cause the stocks' market prices to behave like a U.S. Treasury bond? After explaining why all preferred stocks might behave like bonds if the conditions were correct, explain the financial and legal conditions which cause many preferred stocks to behave differently than bonds.

20-2. What U.S. law makes every preferred stock issue behave more like a common stock than a bond if the issuing corporation is weak? After explaining about the U.S. law that can cause any preferred stock to behave more like a common stock than a bond, explain why the preferred issues of some corporations behave more like bonds than common stocks.

20-3. Consider calculating the risk and return statistics listed below in terms of both (*a*) returns and (*b*) risk-premiums (that is, returns less the riskless rate).

	(*a*) returns	(*b*) risk-premiums
Expected return	$E(r_{it})$	$E(r_{it} - R_t)$
Variance (or total risk)	$\text{var}(r_{it})$	$\text{var}(r_{it} - R_t)$
Correlation with market	$\rho(r_{it}, r_{mt})$	$\rho[(r_{it} - R_t), (r_{mt} - R_t)]$

If the preferred stock empirical statistics in Chap. 20 had been prepared in terms of returns instead of risk-premiums, how would the chapter have been changed?

20-4. Why were no convertible preferred stocks included in the sample of 100 preferreds analyzed in Chap. 20? Explain. *Hint*: You may find it helpful to review Secs. 2-7 and 2-8.

20-5. With what index is the preferred stock index made up of 60 high-quality preferreds most highly correlated in Table 20-2? Explain why.

20-6. Why does the index made up of 40 low-quality preferred stocks in Table 20-3 have a higher risk-premium than the preferred stock index made up of the 60 high-quality preferreds?

20-7. Mrs. Pam Chase is an investment officer from the First National Bank of Arcadia (FNBA). The FNBA is in the 40 percent corporate income tax bracket. She is analyzing the two fixed-income securities below to determine which investment will pay FNBA the highest after-tax rate of cashflow: (*a*) A corporate bond selling at par and offering to pay a yield to maturity of 12 percent and (*b*) a preferred stock selling at par and paying a 9 percent cash dividend annually. *Hint*: Consult Chaps. 2 and 5.

20-8. What is the present value of a 10 percent preferred stock selling at its par value of $100 per share if the appropriate risk-adjusted discount rate is 12 percent? *Hint*: Consult Chaps. 2, 9, and 11.

20-9. If a corporation misses paying preferred stock cash dividends for a few years, the preferred stockholders are typically given the right to elect several members to the corporation's board of directors until the preferred cash dividends are paid. In contrast, if a corporation omits paying coupon interest on its bonds, the bondholders are not allowed to elect any directors. How can you explain this difference? *Hint*: Consult Chaps. 2, 4, and 9.

SELECTED REFERENCES

Bildersee, John S., "Some Aspects of the Performance of Nonconvertible Preferred Stocks," *Journal of Finance*, vol. XXVIII, no. 5, pp. 1187–1201, December 1973. A risk-return analysis of the nonconvertible preferred stock investment security. Simple correlation and regression analysis used. This article distills Bildersee's unpublished doctoral dissertation entitled "Risk and Return on Preferred Stocks," University of Chicago, 1971. This research provided the statistics used in Chap. 20.

Fisher, Donald E., and Glenn Wilt, Jr., "Non-convertible Preferred Stock as a Financing Instrument, 1950–1965," *Journal of Finance*, vol. XXIII, September 1968. Various characteristics of nonconvertible preferred stocks are explained from the point of view of the issuing corporation.

Graham, B., D. L. Dodd, and S. Cottle, *Security Analysis*, 4th ed., McGraw-Hill, New York, 1962. Chapters 27, 28, and 47 present an articulate example of the traditional security analysts' views of preferred stock investing. No mathematics used.

CHAPTER 21

speculating and hedging

This chapter introduces various speculative positions and assets. The short position, put and call options, warrants, and convertible securities are explained. Hedging is investigated as one of the uses for these speculative assets. Before exploring these positions, however, it is worthwhile to distinguish between three different economic activities: gambling, speculating, and investing.

A *gamble* involves the purchase of an opportunity to win some game of chance that will typically be completed in a few seconds. The results of a gamble are quickly resolved by the roll of the dice or a turn of a card. *Gambling differs from speculating and investing* in several respects. First of all, a gamble is completed much quicker than a speculation or an investment. Second, rational, risk-averse people undertake gambles as a form of entertainment, not as a way to earn an income. Casino gambling typically involves transactions that have a negative expected value for the gambler. Third, astute financial analysis cannot change the roll of the dice or the turn of a card. Essentially, the expected value of a gamble is invariant with respect to financial research insights.

Speculations last longer than gambles, but they have shorter durations than investments. *Speculation* involves the purchase of a marketable asset in hopes of making a profit from an increase in price that is expected to occur within a few weeks or months. Speculators can expect to avoid some unprofitable speculations and exploit some profitable ones by working to gain research insights. Unfortunately, speculating is perceived to be wasteful and unproductive by some observers. Actually, speculating is a productive economic activity that can benefit both the astute financial analyst and society in general.

Investing occurs when someone buys an asset and holds it in order to earn interest, dividends, or some other kind of income and, typically, in order to benefit from some long-term price appreciation. Financial analysts are employed to research out the investments with the best potential long-run investment rewards. There is no precise dividing line between the time involved in a speculation and an investment. The Internal Revenue Service (IRS) charges lower tax rates on what it calls "long-term capital gains." Long-term capital gains (or profits) are defined by the IRS to be increases in prices of assets that are owned for more than 6 months. Evidently, the members of Congress who wrote the tax laws hope to stimulate investment activity by taxing the gains from long-term investments at a lower tax rate than the similar gains from short-term speculating and/or gambling. In any event, if a dividing line between speculating and investing is needed, the IRS guideline suggests itself as a separating point.

Speculators may assume a number of different financial positions that differ from the typical long-run investment position of buying a market asset, holding it, and hoping for price appreciation and other income. Each of these different speculative positions and assets can be used for different purposes: to obtain entertainment from a quick gamble, to profit from a short-run price change speculation, or to earn the long-run reward associated with successful investment. For example, bearish investors (that is, those who expect price declines) can assume short positions to profit from the price declines that they expect. These short positions can be taken for an hour-long gamble on a quick price drop or for a short-run speculation that the price will come down, or they can be held open for longer in order to profit from a long-run price decline in an investment asset. Another possibility is that short-run price speculators who want the breathtaking thrills that accompany highly leveraged positions may buy or sell puts, calls, strips, straps, spreads, straddles, warrants, or some combination of these options. Some of these positions are profitable if prices rise; some are profitable if prices fall; some are profitable if prices either rise or fall; and some are profitable if prices do not change at all. Further, some of the positions are best-suited for long-term investing, and some are tailor-made for short-term speculation. This chapter explains various positions from which speculators and investors may select. Whether the position turns out to be a speculation or an investment depends in each case on how long and why the position was kept open.

21-1 LONG AND SHORT POSITIONS

Investors may assume either or both of two basic positions in a market asset. A *long position* involves simply buying and holding the asset; this is the only position of which many investors are aware. The short position is more complicated.

21-1.1 the short position

A *short sale* occurs when one person sells a second person something that the first person does not yet own. Does it sound illegal? It is not. Short sales are routine transactions which just require more explanation than the buy-and-hold position.

Short sellers usually sell an asset (such as a stock or a bond) short because they expect its price to fall and they want to profit from that price fall. The short seller, therefore, actually sells an asset he or she does not own to a second party, who takes a long position in the asset; the long buyer expects the price to rise. Thus, a short sale requires a short seller who is bearish and a long buyer who is bullish (that is, one who expects price appreciation) about the same asset at the same time; it is a case of opposites attracting each other in search of profit. The short seller borrows the shares of stock (or whatever asset is involved) to be sold short from a third party in order to make delivery on the short sale. Then the short seller waits for the asset's price to fall so that the asset can be purchased at the anticipated lower price and so that the third party who loaned the asset can be repaid. If the asset's price does fall (rise), the short seller profits (loses) by the difference between the price paid for the asset to give to the third party and the price at which the asset was sold earlier to the long buyer, less any commission costs. Therefore, aside from the commission costs taken out of the transaction by the stockbroker, the short seller's profit equals the long buyer's loss—or vice versa, if the asset's price rises after the short sale. Table 21-1 outlines the parties, suggests some average times, and explains all the transactions in a hypothetical short sale.

A second reason to create a short position is to create another new position that is negatively correlated with an existing long position in order to reduce risk in the aggregate position. That is, a short position may be taken to establish a risk-reducing *hedged* portfolio comprised of an existing long position and the newly created offsetting short position. This risk-reducing strategy is discussed further in Sec. 21-2.

21-1.2 complicated aspects of short positions

Short sales are more complicated than the example in Table 21-1 may seem to indicate for several reasons. First, short sales of NYSE common stocks, for instance, can be made only on an "*up-tick*"—that is, after a trade in which the stock's price was bid up. This is an NYSE rule designed to keep short sellers from accenting a downturn in the price of a stock. A second complication involves dividends. If a common stock which is sold short pays a *cash dividend* while on loan to the short seller, the short seller must pay that dividend from personal funds to the third party who lent the shares. Third, the short seller may be required to put up *guarantee money* equaling as much as 100 percent of the value of the borrowed shares as collateral for the third party who lent the shares. A fourth problem which can arise with short sales is that the short seller can get "*closed out*" of the short position at any time if the third party who lent the shares demands them back. For example, if the price of the security which was sold short goes up so that the third party who lent the shares wants to sell and recognize a capital gain, the third party can call for the shares to be returned immediately. This can force the short seller, for example, to cover the short position by buying the shares at a disadvantageous higher price. This can throw the short seller for a loss unless the shares can be borrowed elsewhere (which they usually can).

21-1.3 profit-loss illustrations for long and short positions

Figure 21-1 illustrates the long and the short positions in a fashion which should help clarify the two concepts further. The vertical axis in these two profit-loss graphs shows the dollars of profit above the origin and the dollars of loss below the origin. The horizontal axis shows the market prices of the assets.

The profit-loss graph for the long position in Fig. 21-1*a* has a slope of positive unity, indicating that the person holding the long position makes a dollar of profit (loss) for each dollar the market price rises (falls). In contrast,

TABLE 21-1 outline of the parties and transactions in a hypothetical short sale of securities

date	Mr. First Bull	Mr. Bear	Broker A	Mr. Second Bull
January 15: An independent purchase is made	First Bull buys 100 shares of XYZ, leaves them in an account with Broker A, and retires to Florida. Broker A holds the shares in the brokerage's name without First Bull's knowing that he is doing so (a common practice).			
February 10: A short sale occurs.		Mr. Bear expects the price of XYZ to drop, so he calls Broker A and requests a short sale. So 100 shares of XYZ are sold short from Bear's account.	Broker A executes a short sale for Mr. Bear and a purchase for Mr. Second Bull, both for XYZ stock.	Mr. Second Bull buys 100 shares of XYZ through Broker A without knowing they are being sold by a short seller.
February 15: Delivery is made on short sale	First Bull's 100 shares of XYZ are loaned to Bear by Broker A (without telling First Bull).	Bear makes delivery by borrowing First Bull's shares through Broker A. Now Bear is in a short position.	Broker A delivers First Bull's 100 shares of XYZ to Mr. Second Bull, collects cash for the shares, and marks Bear's account short 100 shares which are owed to First Bull.	First Bull's 100 shares of XYZ are received by Second Bull without his knowing he has purchased them from a short seller.
March 3: The short position is covered.		Bear covers his short position by buying 100 shares of XYZ at today's market price and has Broker A return them to First Bull.	Broker A buys 100 shares of XYZ for Bear and places them in First Bull's safe deposit box. If these shares cost less (more) than the sale price on Feb. 10, Bear gets the profit (loss).	
March 8: Borrowed shares are replaced.	The 100 shares of XYZ are replaced in First Bull's account without his ever being aware they were gone.			

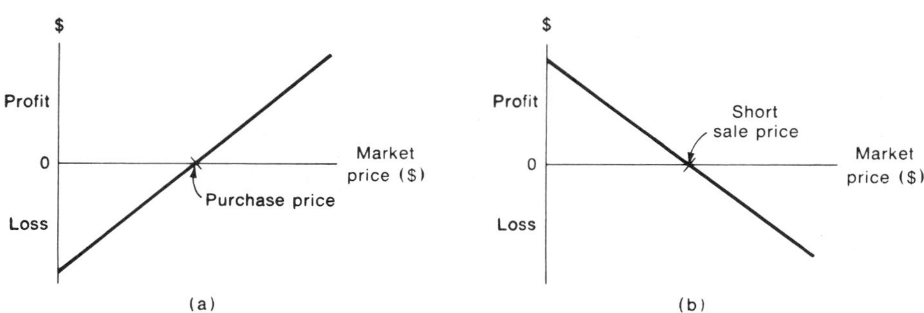

FIGURE 21-1 profit graphs: (*a*) long position; (*b*) short position.

the profit-loss graph for the short position in Fig. 21-1*b* has a slope of negative unity, indicating a dollar of loss (profit) for the short seller for each dollar the market price rises (falls).

Short sales have been conducted on the floor of the New York Stock Exchange (amidst what is predominantly long trading) for decades. The volume of short sales is reported daily in the financial newspapers under the heading "Short Interest." The short interest is the total number of shares that brokers have listed in their accounts as being sold short. The short interest is usually below 5 percent of the total volume of shares traded (and the NYSE specialists do most of it).

There are different reasons why an individual may take a short position. First, and most obvious, is the desire to make a speculative gain from a short-term price fall. Second, a *risk-averse* investor may sell short to "hedge" against possible losses. Hedging is an important investment strategy which should be considered carefully.

21-2 HEDGING AND ARBITRAGE

Hedging may be defined as arranging for two different positions such that the potential losses from one of the positions tends to be, more or less, offset by profits from the other position. Alternatively, hedging can be defined as the establishment of offsetting long and short positions in order to diminish the portfolio's risk that could result from an adverse price movement. There are many different types of hedges. Some hedges are undertaken to reduce potential losses from adverse price movements. Other hedges are set up with the expectation of reaping profits. The easiest hedge of all to explain is discussed first; it is the perfect hedge from which no profits or losses can be earned. Figure 21-2 is a profit-loss graph which illustrates the position of an investor who is perfectly hedged.

Figure 21-2 is a profit-loss graph which combines the long position from Fig. 21-1*a* and the short position from Fig. 21-1*b* at the same purchase and sale price, respectively. The hedger is thus *perfectly hedged* so that the profits and the losses from these two positions sum up to zero at any value the market price may assume. Figure 21-2 might result, for instance, if an investor

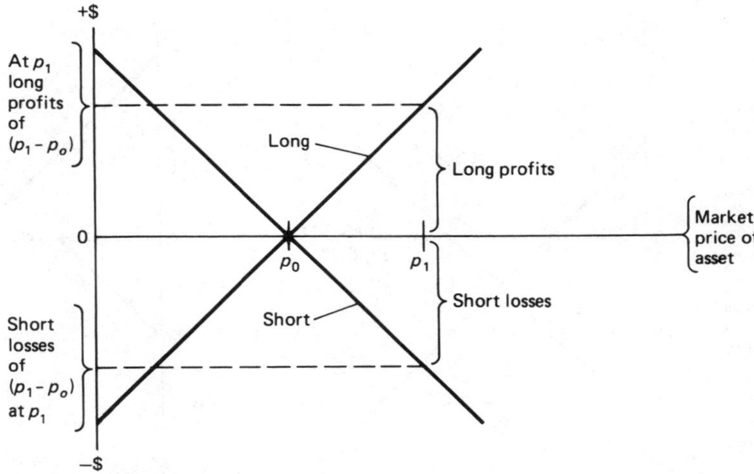

FIGURE 21-2 the perfect hedge.

purchased a long position of 100 shares of the Alpha Corporation's common stock at $64 per share. Simultaneously, the investor sold 100 shares of Alpha's stock short at $64 per share. Figure 21-2 shows that if the market price of the hedged asset rises above the identical purchase price p_0 for the long position and sales price for the short position, to the higher price of, say, p_1 dollars, then the profit on the long position will be exactly offset by the loss on the short position. The hedger, therefore, cannot earn either profits or losses because the hedge is perfect.

The conditions essential for a hedge to be perfect are (1) equal dollar amounts must be held in both the long and the short positions, and (2) the purchase price for the long position must be identical to the sales price for the short sale. Not all hedges are perfect.[1]

21-2.1 imperfect hedges

A hedge may be imperfect for either of two reasons. First, if the dollar commitments to the long and the short positions are not equal, the hedge will be imperfect; or, second, a hedge will be imperfect if the short sales price is not equal to the purchase price for the long position. This second imperfection often results from assuming the long and the short positions at different points in time.

Figure 21-3 illustrates two *imperfect hedges*. Since the size of the dollar commitments to the long and the short positions cannot be illustrated in such figures, let us assume that these dollar commitments are equal. Thus, the two hedges are imperfect because their short sales price, denoted p_s, differs from the purchase price for the long position, designated p_p in Fig. 21-3.

[1] Later it will be explained that the long and short positions do not have to be of equal dollar magnitude to create a perfect hedge. For instance, an investment that involved only half as many dollars in an offsetting short position that had twice the price volatility could result in a perfect hedge too.

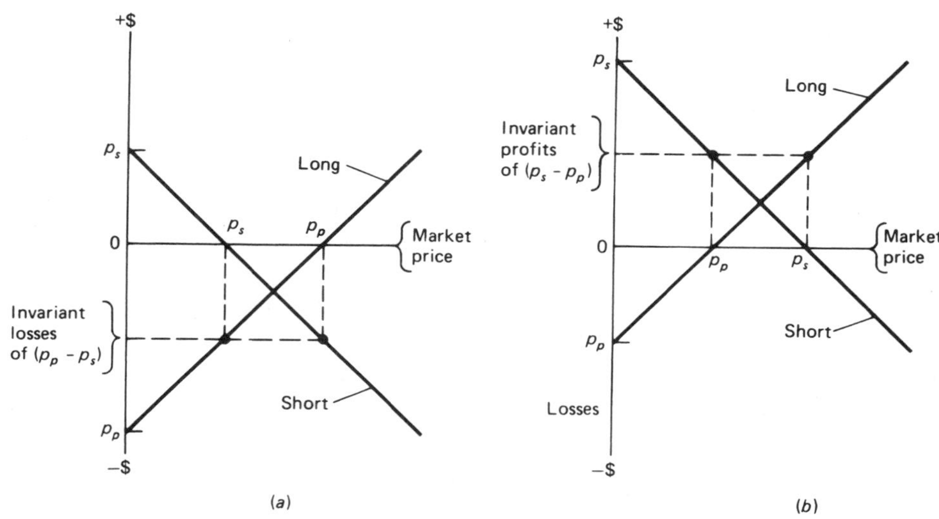

FIGURE 21-3 imperfect hedges: (*a*) unprofitable hedge; (*b*) profitable hedge.

The hedge in Fig. 21-3*a* involves a purchase price for the long position which is above the sales price for the short position, $p_p > p_s$. The resulting hedge will yield an *invariant loss* at whatever value the market price may assume. This loss will equal the excess of the purchase price over the short sale price, $(p_p - p_s)$.

The hedge in Fig. 21-3*b* is imperfect because its short sales price is above the purchase price for its long position. As a result the hedge will yield an *invariant profit* equal to the excess of the short sale price over the purchase price. It is impossible for the imperfect hedge in Fig. 21-3*b* to do anything except yield a profit of $(p_s - p_p)$ regardless of what value the market price of the hedged asset assumes.[2]

21-2.2 various reasons for a short sale

As mentioned above, short sales are used to accomplish different objectives. First, they can be used by bearish speculators in search of profits from a price decline. Second, they can be used by risk-averse hedgers. For example, consider a hypothetical investor named Mr. Ford who owns a controlling interest in a corporation which he wishes to maintain. If Mr. Ford expects the price of his stock to fall because of inside information he has about the firm, he may hold his long position and sell short to establish a hedge that will minimize his anticipated loss.[3] If the price falls after Mr. Ford sets up a hedge, the losses on his long position are matched by gains on his short position. Thus, the

[2] For additional discussion of hedging see Frank J. Fabozzi and Gregory M. Kipnis, *Stock Index Futures*, Dow Jones-Irwin, Homewood, Ill., 1984, chap. 12.

[3] If the security involved in the short selling to maintain control is required to be listed with the SEC (see Chap. 4), then the transaction described is illegal because "insiders" are not allowed to sell short. Thus, Mr. Henry Ford of Ford Motor Company, for instance, would be legally denied the privilege of selling Ford stock short against the box.

investor has maintained control and hedged his loss. Since Mr. Ford always actually owned the shares (presumably they were in his safe-deposit box) that he sold short, he did what is commonly referred to as *selling short against the box*. Selling short against the box is not risky because the short seller is hedged against adverse price moves.

When selling short against the box, short sellers can borrow shares to use for delivery and then purchase shares to repay the loan, or they may simply deliver the shares they hold in their boxes. It is a common procedure to borrow shares. The borrower may give the lender cash to hold equal to the value of the shares borrowed. This protects the lender. The lender of the shares can use this cash at will while still benefitting from income from the shares. The lender of the shares may even be able to charge the borrower a fee for loaning the shares. Many brokers can arrange for such loans of shares in order to complete a short sale—the practice is common, and it may be unnecessary for the short seller to put up the cash collateral in some cases.

An investor may sell short against the box in order to carry a taxable gain from a high-income year into a low-income year and thus decrease income taxes. For example, suppose that Ms. Gaynor is having a high-income year which puts her in a high income tax bracket. If she has a $10,000 price gain on December 15, she might not want to liquidate the shares and take the gain until the next year, when she expects to be in a lower tax bracket. However, if this investor fears the price of the securities she holds may decline before the new year, she can sell short against the box. This "locks her into" her gain because the long and short positions' profits and losses cancel each other and any subsequent price decline does not diminish the $10,000 profit. Then after January 1 Ms. Gaynor can deliver her shares against the short sale to terminate both positions. Thus the $10,000 gain occurs and is taxable in the year when Ms. Gaynor anticipates a lower tax rate.

21-2.3 arbitrageurs are hedged short sellers

A fourth reason someone may be short in a security is to carry on arbitrage. *Arbitrage* involves simultaneously, or almost simultaneously, buying long and selling short the same, or different but related, assets in an effort to profit from unrealistic price differentials. Arbitrage may take place in the same or different markets. For an example of arbitrage between different markets consider GM's common stock. If GM stock is sold in the United States and also in a European market at different prices, arbitrage can be profitable. Profit seeking arbitrageurs facilitate enforcement of the economic *law of one price* by buying the stock in the market where its price is lowest and selling in the market where the stock's price is highest. Arbitrageurs will go on buying at the low price and selling at the high price until the price of GM stock is the same in all free markets around the world. The price of GM stock may never be exactly identical in all markets because of transactions costs such as brokers' commissions, foreign exchange restrictions, long-distance telephone costs, mail costs, and other "frictions" that slow up arbitrage and erode arbitrage profits. However, with the exception of these transactions costs (of a few cents per share), GM stock should cost the same no matter where in the world you buy it.

Some arbitrage is risky and some is riskless. In order to earn riskless trading profits, an arbitrageur simultaneously sells equal amounts of the security short in the market where its price is high and buys the security long in the market where the price is low. Figure 21-3*b* illustrates a profitable hedge of the type that arbitrageurs strive to establish. Arbitrageurs keep buying the security in the market where it is cheapest until they bid its price up to a higher level. Simultaneously, these same arbitrageurs keep selling everything they bought in the low-priced market in the market where the price is higher until they drive down the high price. As the short sale and the long purchase prices are thus driven together by the actions of profit-seeking arbitrageurs, the arbitrage pays off regardless of what other price fluctuations occur.

Short selling is also used by hedgers and arbitrageurs in foreign exchange markets and commodity exchanges, as explained in Chaps. 22, 23, and 24.

It should be noted from the preceding examples that short sales are not always undertaken in order to attain a speculative profit. Short sales may be used like insurance to hedge away risks, or they may be used to maintain control, reallocate income tax burdens to later years, or arbitrage differential prices into equilibrium. Thus, risk-averse investors and risk-taking speculators both use short selling.

In addition to taking long, short, and hedged positions, market participants can buy and sell options. Options are financial instruments[4] which offer high leverage and limited liability to their buyers.

21-3 PUT AND CALL OPTIONS

Options are contracts giving their holder the right, but not the obligation, to buy or sell securities at a predetermined price. More specifically, options are marketable legal contracts which entitle their owner to buy or sell a stated number of shares (usually 100) of a particular security at a fixed price within a predetermined time period. There are two basic types of options. A *put* is an option to sell, that is, an option to "put" shares on someone else. It is a marketable contract giving the owner (or holder or buyer) the option to sell 100 shares of some security at any time he or she selects within a fixed period at a predetermined price. The predetermined price at which an option is to be exercised is variously called the *exercise price* or *contract price* or *striking price*.

A *call* is an option to buy, that is, an option to call in shares for purchase. It is a marketable contract giving its owner (or holder or buyer) the option of buying 100 shares of some security at a predetermined price within some specified time interval. The puts and calls traded on listed option exchanges are usually written for 30, 60, 90, 180, or 270 days.[5] *American options* may be

[4] Although it may seem natural to call options and futures contracts "securities," this usage would offend some lawyers and regulatory bureaucrats who are embroiled in a jurisdictional dispute over which federal agency should exercise control over these different financial markets. The interests of certain parties are best served if the word *securities* is used only to refer to stocks and bonds.

[5] Option contracts can be written to cover any length of time. The fact that no options with terms to maturity in excess of 1 year are written on the organized exchanges does not limit the ability of two parties to draw up an option contract of any duration they please. Only the standardized options originated there are actively traded on the exchanges, however.

exercised by their holder at any time before they mature. On the other hand, since they are marketable securities, instead of being exercised to obtain the gain, unexpired options can be sold in the secondary market in order to realize any gains in their market prices (or premiums). *European options* are identical to American options in every respect except one: the European options can be exercised only on the day when they expire. The term European options can be confusing, however, because many options traded in Europe are American options which can be exercised or bought or sold at any time during their life.

Other kinds of options are a combination of puts and calls. However, these other options are discussed below, after the option markets are described.

21-3.1 puts and calls markets—over the counter

Only a handful of firms make up the over-the-counter option market. The exchanges where the standardized listed options are traded have taken most of the trading volume away from the older over-the-counter options market.

The over-the-counter put and call dealers publish lists suggesting premiums for options in the financial newspapers. This advertising is done to inform customers that they stand ready to do business. Interested option buyers and option writers contact the dealer, who acts as negotiator, helping a buyer and a writer who are interested in a given security to (1) settle on a mutually satisfactory premium, (2) settle on a contract price or exercise price at which the security may be put or called, and (3) determine what length of time they want the option contract to cover. To a certain extent these final arrangements depend upon the "haggling power" of the buyer and the writer of the options in the over-the-counter market for options. However, as a first approximation, the premium on 90-day calls averages around 9 percent of the cost of the 100 shares, while 6-month premiums average roughly 14 percent of the price of the round lot. These relative premiums vary considerably from stock to stock and from time to time depending on the degree of optimism or pessimism attached to any given security at that particular moment. However, in dollar terms, most premiums range from $137.50 to $1000 per 100-share option. Today relatively few options are traded in the over-the-counter options market, compared to the exploding new markets for listed options.

21-3.2 the exchanges where listed options are traded

In 1973 the Chicago Board of Options Exchange (CBOE) began operation. It was America's first options exchange and organized secondary market for options. The CBOE began trading only call options on about two dozen stocks. Soon, trading volume flourished, and the CBOE expanded the number of options traded to over 200 by the early 1980s. To understand how the CBOE originated, it is helpful to know that it was originally established by the oldest and, contemporarily, the largest futures exchange in the United States—the Chicago Board of Trade. As a result, the CBOE clears its transactions through a clearing house that resembles the commodity futures contracts clearing house at the Chicago Board of Trade.

Today the organized market for listed options flourishes on the trading floors of the following four securities exchanges.

1. The Chicago Board of Options Exchange (CBOE)
2. American Stock Exchange (AMEX)

3. Philadelphia Stock Exchange (PHLX)
4. Pacific Stock Exchange (PSE)

Members of each respective exchange come together during the trading hours on the floor of the exchange and buy and sell options by open outcry. The phrase "open outcry" is used emphatically by exchange members to emphasize the fact that designated market-makers (like the specialists) or clandestine deals are not part of the price determination process in the options exchanges. Most of the trades that the members of the various option exchanges transact are done for the clients of securities brokerages—the members of the exchanges are essentially brokers for the brokerage firms.

The four security exchanges that make markets in listed options all clear their option transactions through the Options Clearing Corporation (OCC). The OCC has its headquarters in Chicago, but it is owned by the four security exchanges. The OCC is regulated by the SEC, as are all option markets in the U.S.

The options traded at all four exchanges are issued by the OCC. The OCC does not write options. Instead, the OCC interposes itself between every option writer and every option buyer and acts as an *intermediary* and a clearing house for the options. In so doing, the OCC substitutes its ability to deliver in place of the option writer's ability to deliver.

Having the OCC as intermediary in every option transaction facilitates option trading by supplying the OCC's guarantee of financial integrity for every option contract it handles. This guarantee lowers transactions costs. For instance, transactions costs are lowered by eliminating the need for credit investigation that would be necessary if a reputable organization like the OCC did not stand behind every contract. Owners of options can choose to close out their positions at any time before the option expires by simply selling the option back to the OCC at the current market price for the option. The OCC then simply resells the position to another option buyer at that same current market price. Having the OCC as the centralized intermediary and clearing agent is fundamental to the maintenance of a smoothly functioning secondary market where options can be traded actively at any time before they expire.

The four organized options markets keep track of all of their trades in the memories of computers which are operated by the Options Clearing Corporation (OCC) and brokerage firms which are clearing members of the OCC. All buyers and sellers who may have owned the option at any time prior to its being closed out are successively crossed out of the computer's memory as they buy out the previous owner of the option. In addition to its clearing functions, the OCC also performs a guarantee function.

The OCC stands behind and guarantees every option it issues on the four options exchanges. Thus, if some option seller defaults on a contractual option obligation, the OCC steps in and delivers on the contract at its own expense. As a result of the OCC's guarantee, the options issued at the four organized options exchanges are perfectly marketable securities and the buyer need not check the credit of the party who wrote an option before buying it.

In order for speculators to buy an option, they need only examine the security prices and/or option prices published daily in most newspapers, and

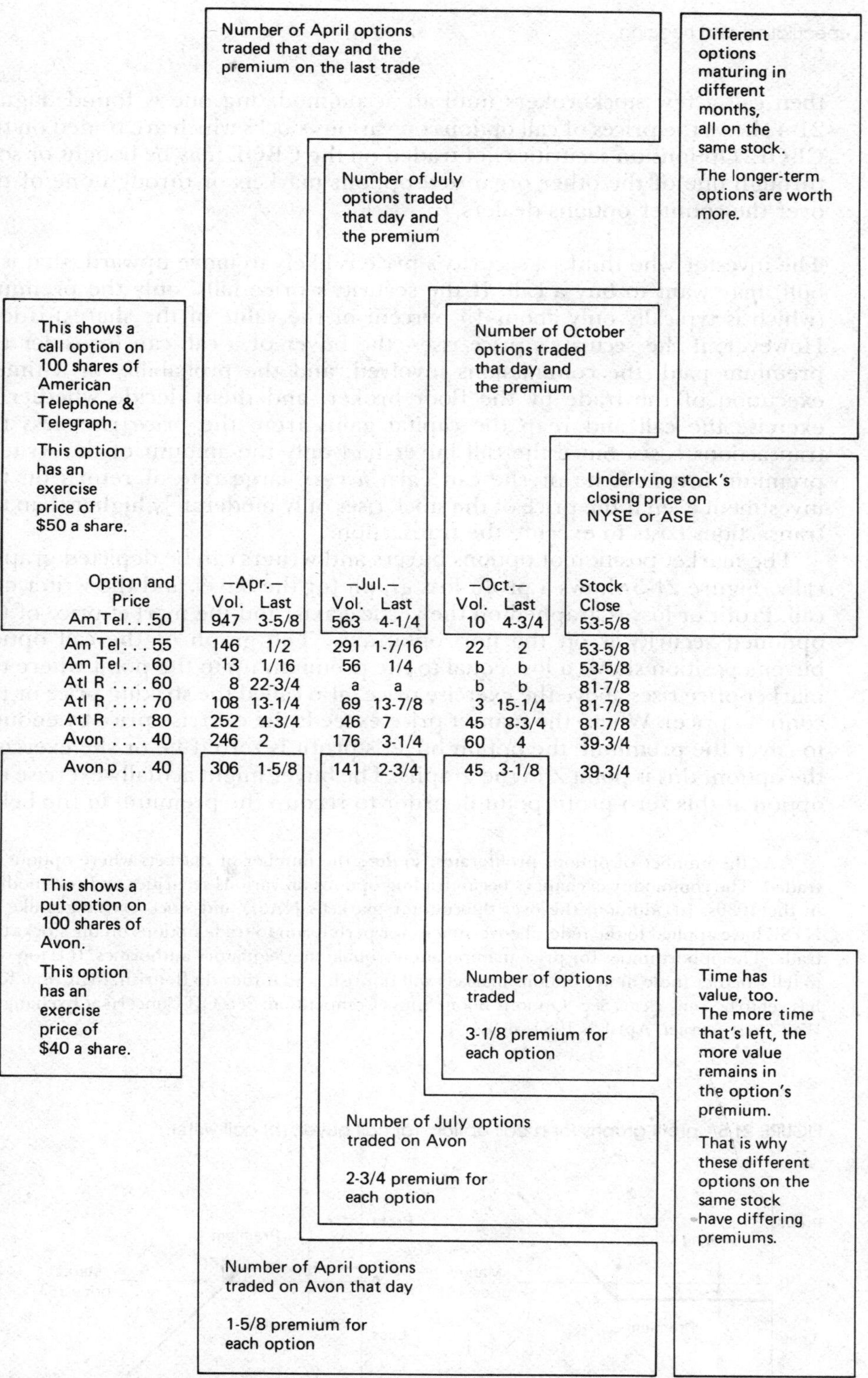
Number of April options traded that day and the premium on the last trade
Different options maturing in different months, all on the same stock.
The longer-term options are worth more.
Number of July options traded that day and the premium
This shows a call option on 100 shares of American Telephone & Telegraph.
This option has an exercise price of $50 a share.
Number of October options traded that day and the premium
Underlying stock's closing price on NYSE or ASE
This shows a put option on 100 shares of Avon.
This option has an exercise price of $40 a share.
Number of options traded
3-1/8 premium for each option
Time has value, too. The more time that's left, the more value remains in the option's premium.
That is why these different options on the same stock have differing premiums.
Number of July options traded on Avon
2-3/4 premium for each option
Number of April options traded on Avon that day
1-5/8 premium for each option

Option and Price	—Apr.— Vol.	Last	—Jul.— Vol.	Last	—Oct.— Vol.	Last	Stock Close
Am Tel . . . 50	947	3-5/8	563	4-1/4	10	4-3/4	53-5/8
Am Tel . . . 55	146	1/2	291	1-7/16	22	2	53-5/8
Am Tel . . . 60	13	1/16	56	1/4	b	b	53-5/8
Atl R 60	8	22-3/4	a	a	b	b	81-7/8
Atl R 70	108	13-1/4	69	13-7/8	3	15-1/4	81-7/8
Atl R 80	252	4-3/4	46	7	45	8-3/4	81-7/8
Avon 40	246	2	176	3-1/4	60	4	39-3/4
Avon p . . . 40	306	1-5/8	141	2-3/4	45	3-1/8	39-3/4

FIGURE 21-4 explanation of hypothetical newspaper quote of option prices.

then call a few stockbrokers until an accommodating one is found. Figure 21-4 shows the prices of call options on various stocks which are traded on the CBOE. Options on securities not traded on the CBOE may be bought or sold through one of the other organized options markets or through one of the over-the-counter options dealers.[6]

21-3.3 profit-loss graph for a call option

The investor who thinks a security's price is likely to move upward (that is, a bull) may want to buy a call. If the security's price falls, only the premium (which is typically only about 15 percent of the value of the shares) is lost. However, if the security's price rises, the buyer of a call can (consider the premium paid, the commissions involved, and the probability of a timely execution of the trade by the floor broker, and then) decide whether to exercise the call and reap the capital gains from the price rise, less the transactions costs. Since the call buyer had only the amount of the writer's premium invested, he or she can earn a very large rate of return on the investment even if the price of the stock rises only moderately higher than the transactions costs to execute the transaction.

The market position of options buyers and writers can be depicted graphically. Figure 21-5 shows a profit-loss graph for the buyer and the writer of a call. Profit or loss is graphed on the vertical axis, and the market price of the optioned security is on the horizontal axis. The graph of the call option buyer's position shows a loss equal to the premium up to the point where the market price rises above the exercise price (also called the striking price or the contract price). Where the market price exceeds the exercise price by enough to cover the premium, the option buyer's profit is zero if he or she exercises the option; this is point *Z* in the graphs. The buyer might actually exercise the option at this zero-profit point in order to recoup the premium in the belief

[6] As the number of options proliferates, so does the number of markets where options are traded. The commodity exchanges began trading options on various securities and commodities in the 1980s. In addition, the over-the-counter market's NASD and stock exchanges like the NYSE have applied to the federal government for permission to trade options on the stocks they trade. The opportunities for price manipulation trouble the regulatory authorities. It is too soon to tell whether these newer options markets will flourish, and if they do flourish, their final form has yet to become clear. See "Options Boom Spurs Competition, Sets Off Concern at Exchanges," *Wall Street Journal*, April 3, 1984, p. 1.

FIGURE 21-5 profit graphs for a call option: (*a*) call buyer; (*b*) call writer.

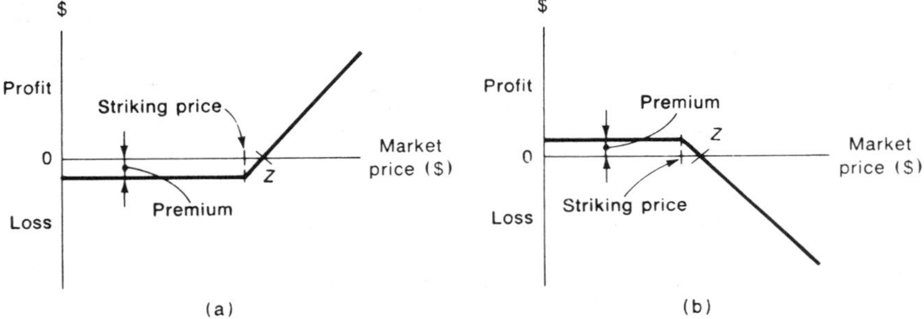

that the market price would not rise any more. If the market price rises above Z, the buyer reaps a profit (after the cost of the premium) by exercising the call.

21-3.4 profit-loss graph for the put option

The profit positions of the writer and the buyer of a put option are shown in Fig. 21-6. The buyer of the put hopes the optioned security's price will fall, just as a short seller would. But unlike the short seller, the buyer has limited losses (that is, only the premium) if the security turns capricious and experiences a price rise. If the security's price falls, the put owner's profit cannot exceed the exercise price times 100 shares less the premium paid. Thus, the writer of the put has limited losses if the price falls. The put writer cannot lose more than 100 times the exercise price less the premium received. If the price of the security rises, the writer gains the premium and no more. Options writers' gains are always limited to their premiums.

Any investor who wants to speculate that the price of some security will fall may choose between buying a put or selling short. The purchase of a put is usually more desirable than taking a short position for two main reasons. First, the investment in a put is limited to the premium, whereas a short seller usually must invest a larger sum. This means that the put option offers more *financial leverage* than the short position. Second, the holder of a put loses no more than the premium if the price of the optioned security rises, but a short seller's losses are unlimited if the security's price rises. A third reason that buying a put may be more desirable than selling short derives from the way cash dividends are handled. Short sellers must make up for any cash dividends the securities they borrowed may pay. That is, the short seller must pay from personal funds an amount of cash equal to any cash dividends which are declared on the borrowed stock to the party who lent the securities which were sold short.

Although the put option is a useful security, it is not always the preferred choice over a short sale. One of the big disadvantages of buying options is that they expire and become worthless. Therefore, if the speculator is not confident that the price of the security about which he or she is bearish will decline before the put expires, then a short position may be more advisable. Paying a series of put premiums while waiting for the price of the optioned security to

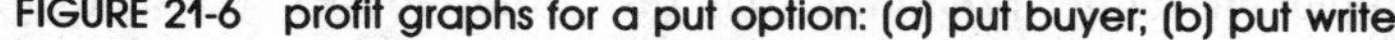
FIGURE 21-6 profit graphs for a put option: (*a*) put buyer; (b) put writer.

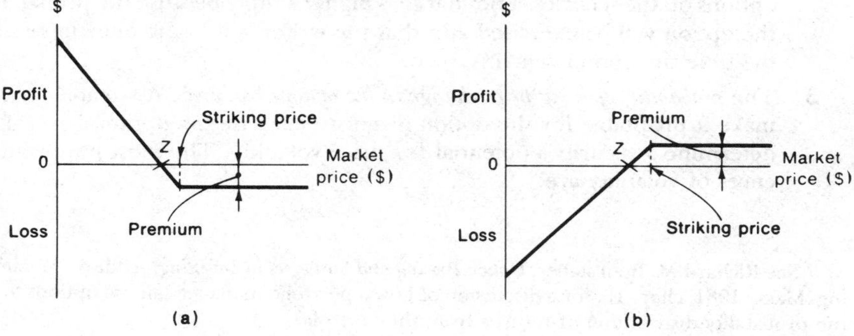

decline is certainly not an optimal strategy. Each case must be judged on its own merits in the final analysis.

Put and call options can be used for four different types of financial activities: (1) gambles on immediate price changes, (2) speculations on short-run price changes, (3) long-run investments involving either long-term options or continuous reinvestment in a series of short-term options,[7] and (4) forming more complex options. The more complex options which can be formed from puts and calls are called *combinations* of options; they will be explained later in this chapter. Before examining these combinations however, let us consider what determines the prices (or premiums) for which put and call options sell.

21-4 THE DETERMINANTS OF PUT AND CALL PREMIUMS

Options need not be exercised to realize the profits from an advantageous price move in the underlying asset. Advantageous price moves in the underlying asset make the option itself worth more. Therefore, the option may be sold in the secondary options market before it matures in order to realize the profits. The price for which an option sells is called the *premium* for the option. In order to understand how to profit from selling unexpired options, let us consider the determinants of option premiums.

The option buyer pays the premium to some option writer to induce the writer to grant the option. The main factors which determine the price the option buyer must pay for an option are discussed below.

1. The *price of the optioned security.* It takes a larger premium to induce the option writer to assume the risks associated with 100 shares of high-priced stock because the possible losses are larger than for 100 shares of low-priced stock. For example, if market prices drop 10 percent, then the decrease in value of 100 shares of a \$20 stock is only (\$20 × 100 − \$18 × 100 =) \$200, whereas the 10 percent decrease in value of 100 shares of a \$150 stock is (\$150 × 100 − \$135 × 100 =) \$1500. The writers of both puts and calls must charge larger premiums to write options on high-priced securities because their potential losses are larger.
2. The *length of time the option remains open.* Writers of 6-month options charge about 40 percent higher premiums than they would to write the same 3-month options on the security. The charge is higher simply because the probability that the option will be exercised and that the writer will lose money increases with the time the option remains open.
3. The *probability of a big price change in the optioned security.* A sizeable change can make it profitable for the option owner to exercise the option. Several factors determine a security's potential for price volatility. The most important influences of volatility are:

[7] See Richard M. Bookstaber, *Option Pricing and Strategies in Investing*, Addison-Wesley, Reading, Mass., 1981, chap. 10, for a discussion of how a portfolio manager can use options to reshape the probability distribution of returns from the portfolio.

a. The historical price volatility of the security (for example, airline stocks have always been more volatile than public utility stocks).
b. The trend of the market (that is, bullish or bearish).
c. Recent news which may affect the security's price.

Essentially, options on riskier securities enjoy higher premiums.

4. The *exercise price*. The exercise price (or striking price) of an option usually approximates the market price of the security on the day the option was written. Sometimes, however, the exercise price of a put or a call is "points away" from the market price (that is, the exercise price is above or below the market price by several dollars). For example, if the exercise price of a call is several dollars above the optioned security's price, the probability that the call will be exercised is decreased. As a result, the call writer will be willing to accept a smaller premium.

Cash dividend payments and market interest rates also have some effect on the premium for which an option sells. These two factors are discussed later in this chapter.

21-4.1 the call option's premium

Figure 21-7 illustrates the interaction between the various factors which determine the market price (or premium) for which a call option may be purchased. The dashed curves represent the prices for calls with different characteristics.

In the space below the (horizontal) stock price axis in Fig. 21-7, some phrases which are popular with security brokerage personnel are illustrated. They refer to the value of the call which is under discussion; they are defined as follows:

1. A call which is "out of the money" is worthless when it matures because the market price of the optioned security is less than the exercise price. That is,

FIGURE 21-7 the determinants of call prices (or premiums).

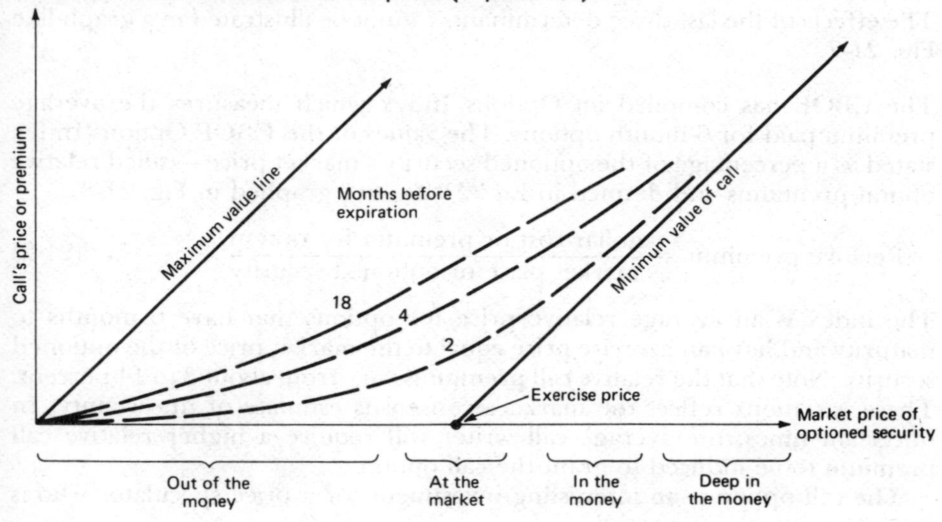

$$\text{Exercise price}_{it} > \text{market price of the optioned security}_{it}$$

for the *i*th optioned security at the *t*th instant in time. A call which is out of the money will probably still have a positive premium before its maturity date, however, because optimists expect that the price of the optioned security may rise before the option matures.

2. "At the market" a call option has a market price for the optioned security which is approximately equal to the call's exercise price; that is,

$$\text{Exercise price}_{it} = \text{market price of the optioned security}_{it}$$

3. A call which is "in the money" has a market price for its optioned securities which has risen above the call's exercise price. A call which is "deep in the money" is highly valued because the market price of its optioned security is far above the call's exercise price; symbolically,

$$\text{Exercise price}_{it} < \text{market price of the optioned security}_{it}$$

21-4.2 a call option's premium over intrinsic value

The vertical distance between the minimum value line and the price curve for an option's premium is called the *premium over the intrinsic value*. Equation (21-1) defines the premium over intrinsic value for a call option.

$$\begin{matrix}\text{Premium over} \\ \text{intrinsic value}\end{matrix} = \begin{matrix}\text{call option's} \\ \text{premium}\end{matrix} + \begin{matrix}\text{exercise} \\ \text{price}\end{matrix} - \begin{matrix}\text{price of} \\ \text{optioned} \\ \text{stock}\end{matrix} \tag{21-1}$$

Observance of Fig. 21-7 shows that the premium over intrinsic value of a call option is greatest when the market price of the optioned asset equals the exercise price of the option. More specifically, the premium over intrinsic value of a call option (1) increases with the time-to-maturity value portion of a call's premium—that is, it increases with the length of time remaining until the call expires, (2) increases with the riskiness of the optioned security, (3) increases very slightly with the level of market interest rates, and (4) decreases with the payment of cash dividends by the optioned stock (because the price of the stock drops off by the amount of the cash dividend payout). The effects of the last three determinants cannot be illustrated in a graph like Fig. 21-7.

21-4.3 relative option premiums

The CBOE has compiled an Options Index which measures the average premium paid for 6-month options. The values of this CBOE Options Index stated as a percentage of the optioned security's market price—called relative option premiums and defined in Eq. (21-2)—are graphed in Fig. 21-8.

$$\text{Relative premium} = \frac{\text{dollar cost or premium for option}}{\text{market price of optioned security}} \tag{21-2}$$

The index is an average relative price for options that have 6 months to maturity and have an exercise price equal to the market price of the optioned security. Note that the relative call premiums vary from about 8 to 14 percent. These variations reflect the market's consensus estimate of uncertainty. In uncertain times, the average call writer will require a higher relative call premium to be induced to grant the call option.

The call option is an interesting investment for a price speculator who is

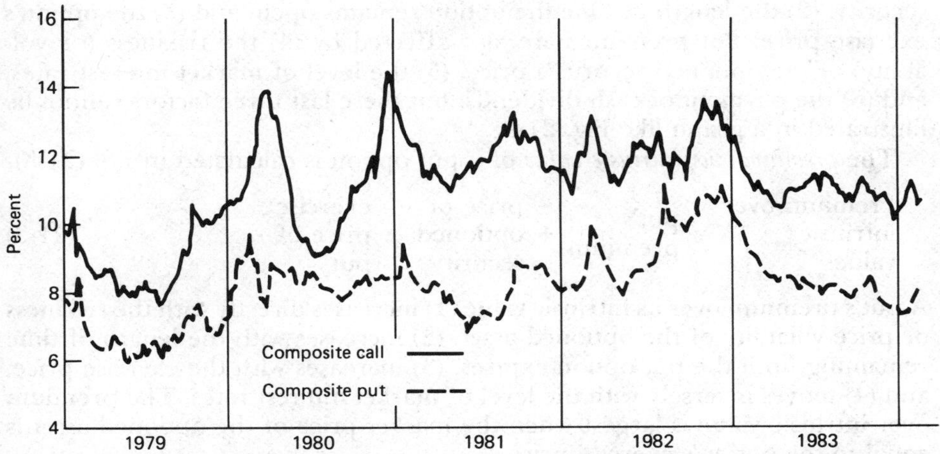

FIGURE 21-8 relative option premiums for CBOE composite call and put indices, 1979–1984.

bullish. A bearish price speculator might wish to sell (or write) a call option but would not want to buy a call. On the other hand, the bear might buy a *put option* in order to profit from a security price decline. A put option offers profit possibilities which are similar in some respects to those derived from the short position, but the put option offers some additional benefits.[8]

21-4.4 the premium for the put option

The market price (or synonymously, the premium) of a put option is determined by the four factors which were discussed a few paragraphs above in reference to the prices of call options. However, these four factors have completely different effects on put prices than they do on call prices. Figure 21-9 illustrates how put prices are determined by (1) the price of the optioned

[8] For a discussion of option indices see Walter L. Eckardt, Jr., and Stephen L. Williams, "The Complete Options Indexes," *Financial Analysts Journal*, July–August 1984, pp. 48–57, and Gary L. Gastineau and Albert Mandansky, "Some Comments on the CBOE Call Options Index," *Financial Analysts Journal*, July–August 1984, pp. 58–67.

FIGURE 21-9 the determinants of put prices (or premiums).

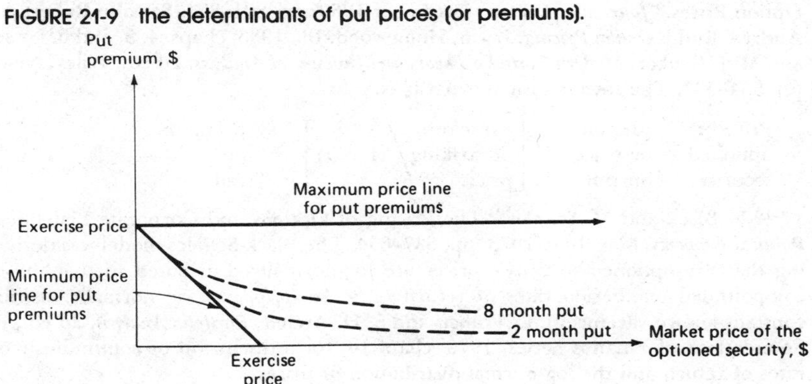

security, (2) the length of time the option remains open, and (3) the option's exercise price. Put premiums are also affected by (4) the riskiness (or volatility) of the optioned security's price, (5) the level of market interest rates, and (6) the payment of cash dividends, but these last three factors cannot be illustrated in a graph like Fig. 21-9.

The *premium over intrinsic value* of a put option is calculated in Eq. (21-3).

$$\text{Premium over intrinsic value} = \text{put's premium} + \text{price of optioned security} - \text{exercise price of put} \qquad (21\text{-}3)$$

A put's premium over its intrinsic value (1) increases directly with the riskiness or price volatility of the optioned asset, (2) increases with the length of time remaining until the put option expires, (3) increases with the exercise price, and (4) moves inversely with the level of market interest rates. The premium over intrinsic value is largest when the market price of the optioned asset is equal to the option's exercise price.

Put premiums fluctuate with call premiums as illustrated in Fig. 21-8. The relative put premiums for 6-month puts range from 6 to 11 percent. These relative put and call premiums tend to fluctuate together because calls may be converted into puts, and thus there is a parity between the two premiums.[9]

The next section explains mathematical formulas with which to calculate option premiums.

21-5 THE BLACK-SCHOLES OPTION MODEL

Doctors Fischer Black and Myron Scholes have derived mathematical formulas for the values of put and call options.[10] These formulas are viewed as a formal theory called the Black-Scholes option valuation model; this theory is widely accepted. The mathematics used in deriving the Black-Scholes option valuation formulas are beyond the scope of this book. However, the final formulas are explained below.

[9] There is a parity between put and call premiums which is maintained by an arbitrage process. This reasoning is explained by Hans R. Stoll, "The Relationship between Put and Call Option Prices," *Journal of Finance*, December 1969, pp. 801–824. See also Robert A. Jarrow and Andrew Rudd, *Option Pricing*, Irwin, Homewood, Ill., 1983, chaps. 4, 5, and 6. Or see E. J. Elton and M. J. Gruber, *Modern Portfolio Theory and Investment Analysis*, 2d ed., Wiley, New York, 1984, pp. 534–537. The formula for this parity is:

$$\text{Price of optioned security} + \text{premium or price on put} - \left[\text{exercise or striking price} \Big/ (1 + r)\right] = \text{premium on call}$$

[10] F. Black and M. Scholes, "The Pricing of Options and Corporate Liabilities," *Journal of Political Economy*, May–June 1973, pp. 637–654. The Black-Scholes model was derived by assuming that the optioned security's prices are log-normally distributed so that the continuously compounded one-period rates of return $r_{it} = \ln (p_{it}/p_{i,t-1})$ are normally distributed with a constant known variance. J. C. Francis and S. H. Archer, *Portfolio Analysis*, 2d ed., Prentice-Hall Foundations of Finance Series, 1979, chap. 14, for a discussion of continuously compounded rates of return and the log-normal distribution of prices.

21-5.1 the Black-Scholes call valuation formula

The Black-Scholes call option pricing formula is shown as Eq. (21-4) in Box 21-1 below. The call prices suggested by the Black-Scholes model are represented by the dashed curves in Fig. 21-7.

21-5.2 numerical example

All that is needed to use the Black-Scholes model are (1) a table of natural logarithms and (2) a table of cumulative normal distribution probabilities. The values for $N(x)$ and $N(y)$ are shown in Table 21-2. Most algebra and statistics books contain tables of logarithms.

To show an illustrative numerical example of how to apply the Black-Scholes model, the following data are used: $p_s = \$60$, $p_e = \$50$, $d = .333$ (which represents 120 days out of a 360-day year), $R = .07$ (which represents 7 percent per annum), and $\text{var}(r_i) = .144$. The quantity x is evaluated below using Eq. (21-5).

$$x_i = \frac{\ln (60/50) + [.07 + .5(.144)](.333)}{\sqrt{.144}\sqrt{.333}}$$

$$= \frac{.182 + .142(.333)}{.379(.577)} = \frac{.2296}{.2191} = 1.048$$

BOX 21-1 the Black-Scholes call formula

$$c_i = p_{si}N(x_i) - p_{ei}\,[e^{(-Rd_i)}]N(y_i) \tag{21-4}$$

where x and y are defined below.

$$x_i = \frac{\ln (p_{si}/p_{ei}) + [R + .5 \text{ var } (r_i)]d_i}{[\text{var}(r_i)]^{1/2}d_i^{1/2}} \tag{21-5}$$

$$y_i = x_i - [\text{var}(r_i)]^{1/2}d_i^{1/2} \tag{21-6}$$

where

c = the call's price or premium

p_s = market price of the optioned stock

p_e = exercise or striking price

ln = natural (base e) logarithm

e = the exponential number = 2.7183 = antiln

$\text{var}(r_i)$ = variance of the rates of price change for the ith optioned stock, a risk measure

R = riskless rate of interest

d_i = duration or time until expiration of the ith call, stated as a fraction of 1 year (for example, 1 month means $d = 1/12$)

$N(x)$ = cumulative normal-density function of the argument x; $N(x)$ gives the probability that a value of less than x will occur in a normal probability distribution which has a mean of zero and a standard deviation equal to unity: $N(-\infty) = 0$, $N(0) = .5$, and $N(+\infty) = 1.0$, for instance

The quantity y_i is evaluated using Eq. (21-5).

$$y_i = x_i - (\sqrt{.144}\ \sqrt{.333}) = 1.048 - .2191 = .829$$

Substituting the values from above in Eq. (21-4) yields the figures below:

$$c_i = \$60[N(1.048)] - \$50\{\text{antiln}[-.070(.333)]\}[N(.829)]$$

Looking up the values of the antilog for natural logs and the cumulative normal distribution in tables and completing the calculations yields the results below:

$$c_i = \$60(.851) - \$50(.9769)(.800) = \$51.060 - 39.076 = \$11.98$$

The calculations indicate that the *i*th call option's intrinsic value is \$11.98. As a result of slight differences in the way various people interpolate between the values in Table 21-2, slightly different answers are possible. Another place where different estimates can arise when using the Black-Scholes model is in the risk statistic, var(r_i). Because the risk statistic must be estimated different analysts are likely to develop differing estimates of it.[11]

21-5.3 the hedge ratio

The *hedge ratio* of an option may be defined as the dollar change in the option's premium (or price) that is associated with a one-dollar change in the price of the optioned asset. Graphically speaking, the hedge ratio is the slope of the dashed call price curve in Fig. 21-7.

From the standpoint of the risk-averse investor, the optimal hedge ratio is the ratio of shares of optioned stock per 100-share option that must be held to fully hedge against movements in the stock's price. Mathematically, this optimal hedge ratio is given by the value of the quantity $N(x)$ in the Black-Scholes call Eq. (21-4), as shown below.

$$N(x) = \Delta c/\Delta p = \text{slope of call price curve} = \text{hedge ratio} \qquad (21\text{-}7)$$

If an investor uses the hedge ratio so that $(-1)N(x)$ times as much stock is held in a position opposite to the option position, then any movement in the value of the stock position will be exactly offset by an opposite and equal movement in the value of the option position. For instance, if a call option for 100 shares of ABC stock is owned in a long position and the hedge ratio based on the current price of ABC is $N(.808) = -.790$, then 79 shares of ABC should be sold short in order to establish a perfect hedge.[12]

Unfortunately, the hedges formed using the hedge ratio are perfect only as long as the price of the optioned stock does not change. As soon as the stock's price changes, then the value of $N(x)$ changes, and the hedge has to be recomputed. After the new hedge ratio is computed, the securities position has to be correspondingly rebalanced.[13]

[11] Computer programs are available to calculate the prices of puts and calls using the Black-Scholes model. One such program is the TK!Solver program produced by Software Arts Inc. Software Arts is a computer software manufacturer that is probably best known for its spreadsheet program named Visi-Calc. The TK!Solver program is a sophisticated equation processor that is totally different from the Visi-Calc program. TK!Solver will solve virtually any equation for the value of any variable in the equation if the values of all other variables are known. Hand calculators are also available to solve the Black-Scholes formula.

[12] The hedge ratio is discussed in Richard M. Bookstaber, *Option Pricing and Strategies in Investing*, Addison-Wesley, Reading, Mass., 1981, chap. 8.

TABLE 21-2 values of $N(x)$ for given values of x for a cumulative normal distribution with zero mean and unit variance

x	$N(x)$	x	$N(x)$	x	$N(x)$	x	$N(x)$	x	$N(x)$	x	$N(x)$
		−2.00	.0228	−1.00	.1587	.00	.5000	1.00	.8413	2.00	.9773
−2.95	.0016	−1.95	.0256	−.95	.1711	.05	.5199	1.05	.8531	2.05	.9798
−2.90	.0019	−1.90	.0287	−.90	.1841	.10	.5398	1.10	.8643	2.10	.9821
−2.85	.0022	−1.85	.0322	−.85	.1977	.15	.5596	1.15	.8749	2.15	.9842
−2.80	.0026	−1.80	.0359	−.80	.2119	.20	.5793	1.20	.8849	2.20	.9861
−2.75	.0030	−1.75	.0401	−.75	.2266	.25	.5987	1.25	.8944	2.25	.9878
−2.70	.0035	−1.70	.0446	−.70	.2420	.30	.6179	1.30	.9032	2.30	.9893
−2.65	.0040	−1.65	.0495	−.65	.2578	.35	.6368	1.35	.9115	2.35	.9906
−2.60	.0047	−1.60	.0548	−.60	.2743	.40	.6554	1.40	.9192	2.40	.9918
−2.55	.0054	−1.55	.0606	−.55	.2912	.45	.6736	1.45	.9265	2.45	.9929
−2.50	.0062	−1.50	.0668	−.50	.3085	.50	.6915	1.50	.9332	2.50	.9938
−2.45	.0071	−1.45	.0735	−.45	.3264	.55	.7088	1.55	.9394	2.55	.9946
−2.40	.0082	−1.40	.0808	−.40	.3446	.60	.7257	1.60	.9452	2.60	.9953
−2.35	.0094	−1.35	.0885	−.35	.3632	.65	.7422	1.65	.9505	2.65	.9960
−2.30	.0107	−1.30	.0968	−.30	.3821	.70	.7580	1.70	.9554	2.70	.9965
−2.25	.0122	−1.25	.1057	−.25	.4013	.75	.7734	1.75	.9599	2.75	.9970
−2.20	.0139	−1.20	.1151	−.20	.4207	.80	.7881	1.80	.9641	2.80	.9974
−2.15	.0158	−1.15	.1251	−.15	.4404	.85	.8023	1.85	.9678	2.85	.9978
−2.10	.0179	−1.10	.1357	−.10	.4602	.90	.8159	1.90	.9713	2.90	.9981
−2.05	.0202	−1.05	.1469	−.05	.4801	.95	.8289	1.95	.9744	2.95	.9984

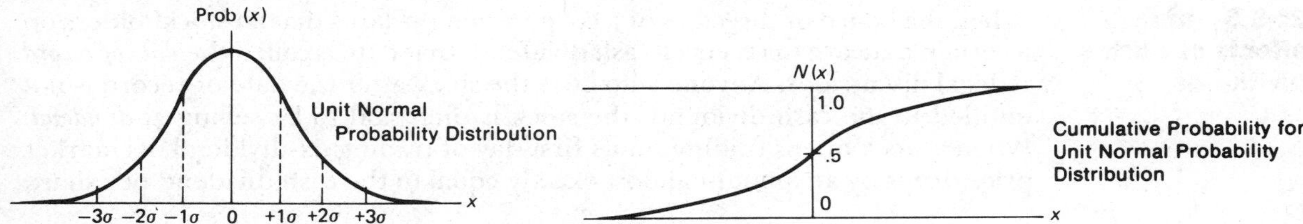

21-5.4 estimating risk for the optioned stocks

Since the Black-Scholes model's derivation presumes a normal distribution of continuously compounded rates of one-period return, the variance of continuously compounded rates of return should be used as a risk measure.[14]

[13] Mr. Gary L. Gastineau, Vice President, Webster Management, a subsidiary of Kidder, Peabody and Co., 20 Exchange Place, New York, has developed a competing option valuation model. Gastineau's model is explained in an article he authored, "An Index of Listed Option Premiums," *Financial Analysts Journal*, May–June 1977, pp. 3–8, see especially the appendix. Or see G. L. Gastineau, *The Stock Options Manual*, 2d ed., McGraw-Hill, New York, 1979, chap. 7, pp. 254–264. Other option valuation models that have been derived include the following: J. Cox and S. Ross. "The Valuation of Option for Alternative Stochastic Processes," *Journal of Financial Economics*, March 1976, vol. 3, pp. 145–166. Also see J. Cox, S. Ross, and M. Rubinstein, "Option Pricing: A Simplified Approach," *Journal of Financial Economics*, October 1979, vol. 7, pp. 229–264. See also R. Roll, "An Analytic Method for Valuing American Call Options on Dividend Paying Stocks," *Journal of Financial Economics*, November 1977, vol. 85, pp. 251–258. See also M. Rubinstein, "Displaced Diffusion Option Pricing," *Journal of Finance*, March 1983, vol. 38, pp. 213–218. These and other approaches to valuing puts and calls are analyzed by R. Geske and K. Shastri, "Valuation by Approximation: A Comparison of Alternative Option Valuation Techniques," *Journal of Financial and Quantitative Analysis*, March 1985, vol. 20, no. 1, pp. 45–72.

[14] Although systematic (or beta or covariance) risk is relevant in analyzing individual assets with the Security Market Line (SML) or Capital Asset Pricing Model (CAPM), only *total* risk is relevant in the Black-Scholes model.

Equation (21-8) shows the definition for the one-period continuously compounded rate of return.

$$r_t = \ln_e \frac{p_{st}}{p_{s,t-1}} \tag{21-8}$$

The noncompounded one-period rate of return of Eq. (2-2) furnishes an acceptable approximation to Eq. (21-8), especially for small rates of return—that is, for short periods. Regardless of how the rates of return are calculated, the variance of returns is defined in Eqs. (C-3*a*) and (C-3*b*) of Mathematical App. C.

Table 21-3 presents some annualized variances for optioned New York Stock Exchange common stocks which are traded on the Chicago Board of Options Exchange to be used as a guideline. However, these risk statistics may change with the passage of time, and thus they need to be rechecked every time they are used.[15] One common way to obtain current risk statistics is to (1) estimate the variance using recent empirical returns and then (2) subjectively adjust the empirically estimated variance to reflect expected changes in the optioned security's risk which are not reflected in the historical statistics.[16]

After the value of a call option has been estimated, this value may need to be adjusted to reflect the effects of cash dividends. The next section shows how to adjust for a cash dividend.[17]

21-5.5 the effects of cash dividends

When the board of directors of a corporation declares that all stockholders on a certain date are to receive a cash dividend, that date is called the *date of record* in legal discussions. Anyone who buys the stock after the date of record is not entitled to the cash dividend; the stock is then said to be selling *ex-dividend*. When a stock opens trading on its first day of trading ex-dividend, its market price drops by an amount almost exactly equal to the cash dividend per share

[15] J. C. Francis, "Statistical Analysis of Risk Surrogates for NYSE Stocks," *Journal of Financial and Quantitative Analysis*, December 1979. H. Latane and R. J. Rendelman, Jr., "Standard Deviation of Stock Price Ratios Implied in Option Prices," *Journal of Finance*, May 1976, pp. 369–381. M. Brenner and D. Galai, "On Measuring the Risk of Common Stocks Implied by Option Prices: A Note," *Journal of Financial and Quantitative Analysis*, December 1984, vol. 19, no. 4, pp. 403–404.

[16] For a discussion about estimating risk statistics, see Michael Parkinson, "The Extreme Value Method for Estimating the Variance of the Rate of Return," *Journal of Business*, January 1980, vol. 53, no. 1, pp. 61–67, and (in the same issue) Mark B. Garman and Michael J. Klass, "On the Estimation of Security Price Volatilities from Historical Data," pp. 67–78.

[17] Computer programs for the Black-Scholes model and various option pricing statistics are available for microcomputers from Dr. Richard Bookstaber, Morgan Stanley Co., New York. These programs may be purchased at a fraction of the price of some commercially available programs. The programs were discussed above on page 173 of this book.

TABLE 21-3 some historical annualized variance statistics

optioned stock	annual variances
McDonald's	.50
Northwest Airlines	.35
Delta Airlines	.25
International Harvester	.15
Sears, Roebuck & Co.	.10

which was paid to shareholders on the date of record. This ex-dividend price *drop-off* decreases the value of any call options against the stock and should therefore be considered in determining when to exercise an American call. Since European calls can be exercised only on their maturity dates, the decision to exercise these options before they trade ex-dividend is not relevant.

Figure 21-7 illustrates the minimum call boundary and the Black-Scholes value curve for some hypothetical American call option. The minimum-value line (or stock price parity line) establishes the minimum value of the call if it is exercised at any time. Upon its exercise, the call is said by option traders to be "dead." The curve gives the option's value if it is still "alive" (that is, if it has not been exercised prior to maturity). An American call is always worth at least as much alive as dead if it has any time remaining before it expires. The vertical distance between the minimum value (or dead or parity) line and the live value curve measures the value of the time remaining until the option expires. The graph is useful in illustrating some key considerations involved in deciding whether to exercise a call before the stock goes ex-dividend.

If a call on an optioned security with a market price of $p_s{}^d$ is exercised, this call's value of $p_c{}^d$ is given by reference to the minimum value boundary Op_eZ in Fig. 21-10. If the optioned stock goes ex-dividend, its price will drop off from $p_s{}^d$ to $p_s{}^e$. However, the option's premium will not fall as much as the price of the optioned stock if the option is alive. At an ex-dividend market price for the optioned stock of $p_s{}^e$, the value of the live call is $p_c{}^e$. The Black-Scholes formula can be used to find the value of live calls. If the option's drop-off of $(p_c{}^d - p_c{}^e)$ dollars when exercised ex-dividend is less than the amount of the cash dividend, then the call should be kept alive to maximize the investor's wealth. The call should be exercised before it goes ex-dividend if inequality (21-9) is true.[18]

$$\text{Cash dividend per share}_{it} < (p_c{}^d - p_c{}^e)_{it} \tag{21-9}$$

[18] Rational call premium adjustments to reflect the payment of cash dividends and other factors are analyzed by Robert C. Merton, "The Theory of Rational Option Pricing," *Bell Journal of Economics and Management Science*, Spring 1973, pp. 141–183. Also see R. E. Whaley, "Valuation of American Call Options on Dividend Paying Stocks: Empirical Tests," *Journal of Financial Economics*, March 1982. Also see C. A. Ball and W. N. Torous, "On Jumps in Common Stock Prices and Their Impact on Call Pricing," *Journal of Finance*, March 1985, vol. 40, no. 1, pp. 155–174.

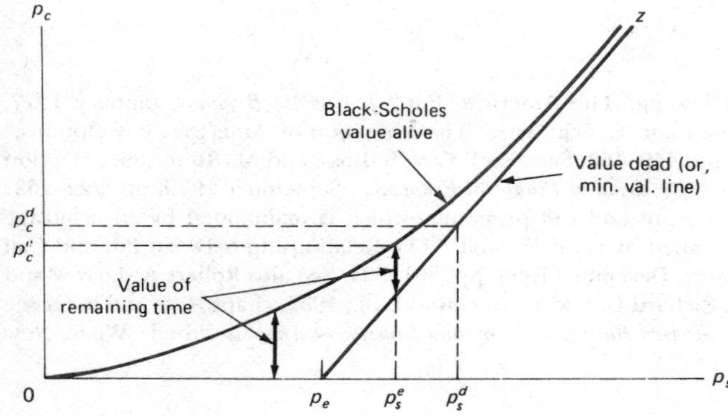

FIGURE 21-10 security values before and after ex-dividend trading.

21-5.6 valuing the put option

Black and Scholes derived a formula for pricing European puts—that is, puts which may only be exercised on their expiration date. However, no one has been able to analytically derive a formula for valuing American puts (that may be exercised on any day of their life) which is as accurate as the numerical approximation techniques available to value American puts.[19] Therefore, some people use the put-call parity formula in Eq. (21-10a) to derive the value of a put option after the value of a call option on the same security has been determined.[20]

$$\begin{matrix}\text{Premium}\\ \text{or price}\\ \text{on put}\end{matrix} = \begin{matrix}\text{premium}\\ \text{or price}\\ \text{of call}\end{matrix} + \left[\left(\begin{matrix}\text{exercise}\\ \text{or striking}\\ \text{price}\end{matrix}\right) \Big/ (1 + r)^d\right] - \begin{matrix}\text{price of}\\ \text{optioned}\\ \text{security}\end{matrix} \qquad (21\text{-}10a)$$

where

r = a short-term market interest rate (such as the 90-day Treasury bill rate) which is used to find the present value of the exercise price

d = the time until the option expires

The same values from the numerical example of how to apply the Black-Scholes call valuation model are employed to determine the value of a put option on the same stock. The following data are used: $p_s = \$60$, $p_e = \$50$, $d = .333$ (which represents 120 days out of a 360-day year), $R = .07$ (which represents 7 percent per annum), and $\text{var}(r_i) = .144$. The Black-Scholes model placed a value on this 4-month call of \$11.98. The value of the put is calculated below by substituting these values into Eq. (21-10a).

$$\begin{aligned}&(\$11.98) + [(\$50)\ /\ (1.0 + .07)^{.333}] - (\$60) = \qquad (21\text{-}10b)\\ &(\$11.98) + [(\$50)\ /\ (1.0227)] - (\$60) =\\ &(\$11.98) + (\$48.89) - (\$60) =\\ &\$60.87 - \$60 = 87 \text{ cents}\end{aligned}$$

If the optioned stock recently paid a cash dividend, the market price of the stock probably experienced an *ex-dividend drop-off* that exactly equaled the amount of the cash dividend. In this case, the amount of the recent cash dividend should be added back into the current market price of the stock, and this total amount should be used in place of the stock's price in valuing the put option. For instance, if the stock just paid a 25-cent cash dividend, then the \$60 stock price should be increased to \$60.25 in Eq. (21-10b) for valuing the put.

[19] M. Parkinson, "Option Pricing: The American Put," *Journal of Business*, January 1977, pp. 21–36. See also M. Brennan and E. Schwartz, "The Valuation of American Put Options," *Journal of Finance*, May 1977, pp. 449–462. See also J. Cox, S. Ross, and M. Rubinstein, "Option Pricing: A Simplified Approach," *Journal of Financial Economics*, September 1979, pp. 229–263.

[20] There is a parity between put and call premiums which is maintained by an arbitrage process. This reasoning is explained by Hans R. Stoll, "The Relationship between Put and Call Option Prices," *Journal of Finance*, December 1969, pp. 801–824. See also Robert A. Jarrow and Andrew Rudd, *Option Pricing*, Richard D. Irwin, Homewood, Ill., 1983, chaps. 4, 5, and 6. Or see E. J. Elton and M. J. Gruber, *Modern Portfolio Theory and Investment Analysis*, 2d ed., Wiley, New York, 1984, pp. 534–537.

21-6 COMBINATIONS

Straddles, strips, spreads, and straps are the names of option positions which are constructed from various combinations of puts and calls. These combinations are analyzed below.

21-6.1 straddles

The buyer of a straddle is actually simultaneously purchasing both a put and a call on the same optioned asset. The buyer thus pays a premium for a straddle that equals the sum of the premiums for both a put and a call purchased separately. Straddle buyers are willing to pay the large premium for a put plus a call because they are reasonably confident that the price of the optioned security will deviate, either up or down, from the exercise price. The straddle buyer gains if the price of the optioned asset makes either an upward, a downward, or a both an upward and a downward price move. The writer of a straddle has the opposite view. Straddle writers are sufficiently confident that the security's price will not vary before the option matures that they are willing to write a contract that guarantees it will not move, if they are paid the straddle premium as an inducement.

The profit positions of the buyer and the writer of a straddle are depicted in Fig. 21-11. Since a straddle is a put and a call at the same exercise price, the profit positions for the straddle in Fig. 21-11 are merely Figs. 21-5 and 21-6 added for the case when the exercise prices of the put and the call are identical.

Figure 21-11 shows that the straddle writer loses if the optioned security's price either rises or falls. For taking this large risk, the straddle writer receives a premium which is equal to a put premium plus a call premium. In fact, there may be two writers to a straddle, both a put writer and a call writer. This could occur if the puts and calls dealer is not able to find one person to write the entire straddle.[21] Or, the person desiring to buy a straddle might buy a put

[21] The dealer probably owns a seat on one or more of the options exchanges and earns income either (1) from being a broker for other parties who are willing to write options, or (2) by selecting some of the options to be written by him- or herself in order to earn the premium income for writing.

FIGURE 21-11 profit graphs for a straddle option: (*a*) straddle buyer; (*b*) straddle writer.

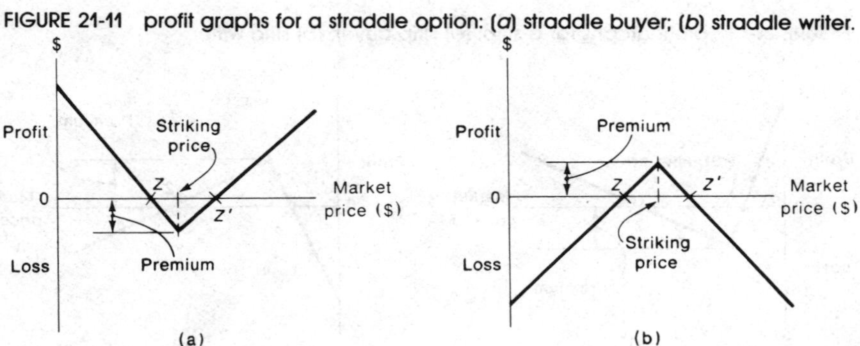

and a call separately on the same security in order to create a straddle position.

21-6.2 strip

The buyer of a strip is speculating that the price of some security will change from the exercise price, but strip buyers believe that the security's price is more likely to fall than it is to rise. Figure 21-12 represents the profit positions for the buyer and the writer of a strip.

Since a strip equals two puts and one call on the same asset, the buyer evidently believes a decrease in the price of the optioned security is more probable than an increase. The premium for writing a strip usually equals the premium for writing two puts plus one call. In order for the buyer to recoup this large premium, the market price of the optioned security must either drop to Z or rise to Z' in Fig. 21-12. The drop from the exercise price to Z is only half as far as the rise from the exercise price to Z' because the line through Z has twice as steep a slope as the line through Z'. Figure 21-12, representing the strip, is quite similar to Fig. 21-11 for the straddle. The only differences are in the size of the premium and the slope of the line through point Z'.

21-6.3 spread

Figure 21-13 represents the profit position of the buyer and the writer of a spread and is similar to Fig. 21-11 for the straddle. The difference between these two figures is that the exercise price of the spread is "points away" from the market. The exercise price for the put portion of the spread is point A in Fig. 21-13. The market price of the optioned security when the option was written is represented by point B. Point C is the exercise price for the call portion of the spread. The premium on the spread is less than the premium on the straddle because the market price of the security which is optioned with a spread must rise or fall more than if it were optioned with a straddle in order for the option buyer to profit. Graphically, this means the distance from Z to Z' in Fig. 21-11 is less than the distance from Q to Q' in Fig. 21-13. Symbolically, $(Z' - Z) < (Q' - Q)$.

21-6.4 strap

Straps consist of two calls and one put on the same security at the same exercise price. Thus, a strap is like a strip which is skewed in the opposite direction. The buyer of a strap evidently foresees bullish and bearish pos-

FIGURE 21-12 profit graphs for a strip: (*a*) strip buyer; (*b*) strip writer.

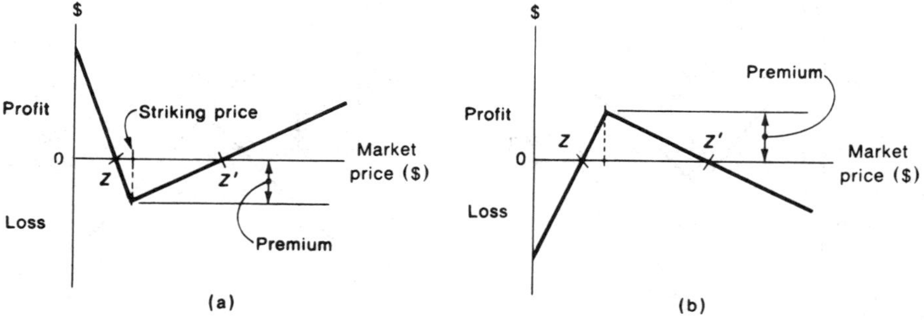

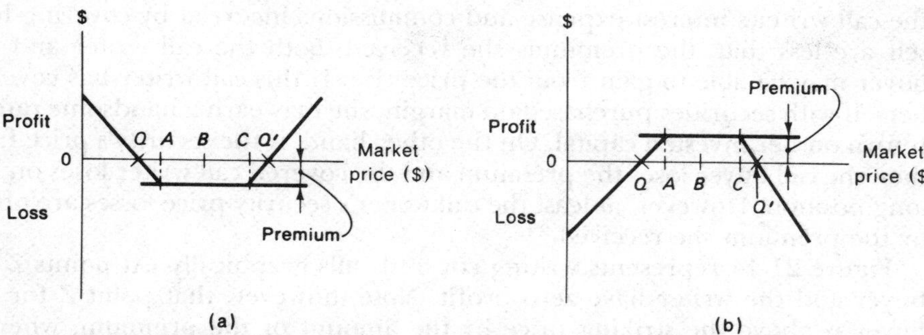

FIGURE 21-13 profit graphs for a spread: (*a*) spread buyer; (*b*) spread writer.

sibilities for the optioned security, with a price rise being more likely. Graphs of the profit positions for the buyers and sellers of a strap are left as an exercise for the interested reader to construct.[22]

OTHER OPTIONS In addition to the strips, straps, spreads, and straddles that can be formed from puts and calls, numerous other option packages can be developed. For example, the *down-and-out option* is basically a call option with two complications added. The first complication is that the option expires any time the market price of the optioned security falls below some specified price level. The second complication is that the call's writer will return a portion of the purchase price paid for the call option if the call is exercised prior to its maturity. There is also the *up-and-out option*, which is a put option with two added provisions: (1) The option expires and becomes worthless if the market price of the optioned security rises above some prespecified level. (2) If the option is exercised prior to its maturity, the writer must refund some prespecified portion of the premium received for writing the up-and-out option. These less popular options will not be analyzed here.[23] However, there is a more popular option strategy involving the basic positions which is worthwhile to consider; it is called "writing covered calls."

21-6.5 writing covered and uncovered (or naked) options

Sometimes options writers buy the security on which they are writing the option. When they do so, they are said to have *covered* themselves. For example, consider a woman who wrote a call. This call writer might buy 100 shares of the security on which she is writing the call if she expects (as does the call's buyer) that the price of the optioned security might rise. Then, if the security's price does rise and the call is exercised, the writer will simply deliver the shares she has already purchased and not suffer any loss. Assuming that

[22] The combination position called a strap is discussed and graphically illustrated in William W. Welch, *Strategies for Put and Call Option Trading*, Winthrop, Cambridge, Mass., 1982, p. 163.

[23] The down-and-out option is analyzed by R. C. Merton, "The Theory of Rational Option Pricing," *Bell Journal of Economics and Management Science*, Spring 1973, vol. 4, no. 1, sec. 6. The down-and-out option, compound options, options on more than one security, options on futures, and other options are discussed in chap. 7 of *Options Markets* by J. C. Cox and M. Rubinstein, Prentice-Hall, Englewood Cliffs, N.J., 1985. The appendix to chap. 23 of this book also discusses options on futures. Warrants and convertibles are the topic of the appendix to this chapter.

the call writer's interest expense and commissions incurred by covering herself are less than the premiums she received, both the call writer and the buyer may be able to gain from the price rise. If this call writer has covered herself with securities purchased on margin, she may earn a handsome rate of return on her invested capital. On the other hand, if the security's price falls, then the call buyer loses the premium and the covered call writer loses on her long position. However, at least the call writer's security price losses are offset by the premium she received.[24]

Figure 21-14 represents writing covered calls graphically. At points *Z* the buyer and the writer have zero profit. Note, however, that point *Z* for the buyer is above the striking price by the amount of the premium, whereas point *Z* is below the striking price for the writer.

An option writer who writes a call against some security without owning that security is said to be *writing naked* or *writing against cash* or *writing uncovered*. Figure 21-5*b* shows the profit position for a call writer who was writing naked. That is, this particular call writer had not covered himself by buying the securities for which he wrote the option. In this case, the call buyer's profits are the call writer's losses. A comparison of the call writer's exposure to loss in Figs. 21-5*b* and 21-14*b* shows that writing calls *naked* is risky in a bull (rising) market and that writing calls *covered* is risky in a bear (falling) market.

The writers of options may write any option naked or choose to cover themselves. The final decision depends on the particular option being written and the option writer's beliefs about the direction of the market. In any event, the naked option writer's profits are limited to the premium, while the naked writer's potential losses are unlimited.[25]

[24] C. R. Grube, D. B. Panton, and T. J. Michael, "Risks and Rewards in Covered Call Positions," *Journal of Portfolio Management*, vol. 5, 1979.

[25] For a discussion of how the manager of an options portfolio can reshape the probability distribution of returns attainable from the various options see Richard M. Bookstaber and Roger G. Clarke, *Option Strategies for Institutional Investment Management*, Addison-Wesley, Reading, Mass., 1983.

Research suggests that the prices of options in at least some international options exchanges are determined by the same factors suggested by the option theory. However, markets outside the United States may be less efficient. See P. J. Holpern and S. M. Turnbull, "Empirical Tests for

FIGURE 21-14 profit graphs for a call: (*a*) call buyer; (*b*) covered writer.

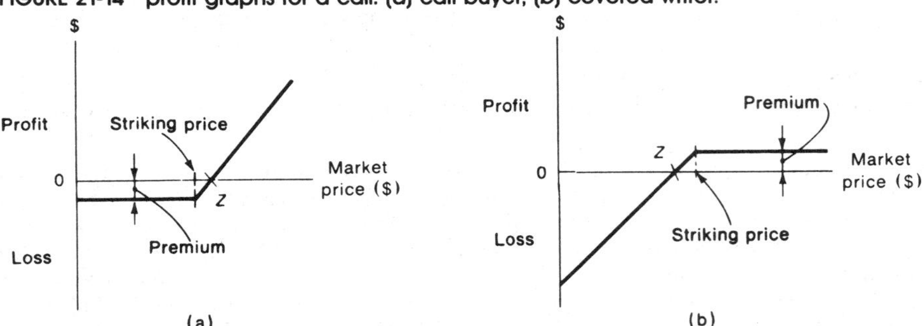

The federal margin requirements mandate that option sellers who write options naked put up the appropriate initial margin; in recent years this has been at least 50 percent of the total market value of the optioned shares. Thus the leverage attainable by writing naked is not infinite, but it is more leverage than can be obtained in nonmargined long or short transactions. Option writers who have an offsetting position in the security on which the option is being written (that is, covered writers) on deposit at their brokers' offices are not required to put up any additional margin.

In the final analysis, it is not correct to assume that covered option writers always gain from their activity. Covered call writers will gain from their call writing only if the price of their optioned stock remains almost unchanged so that it is never exercised. If the price of the stock advances significantly, the covered call writer would have been better off not to have written the options because the appreciating securities are called away at a lower price. If the price of the optioned stock declines, the covered call writer suffers the loss in market value just as if the call had never been written; however, the loss from the price drop is at least partially offset by the premium income.

21-6.6 federal income taxes and options

The cost of an option is a nondeductible capital expenditure, and the option represents a capital asset in the hands of the holder. Gain or loss occurring upon the sale of an option in a closing sale transaction constitutes capital gain or loss, long-term or short-term, depending upon how long the option has been held. If an option is allowed to expire, it is treated as having been sold on the expiration date. Upon the exercise of an option, its cost is added to the exercise price to determine the basic cost of the underlying stock acquired.

The premium received for writing an option is not included in the writer's taxable income at the time of receipt (when the option is written); it is deferred until such time as the writer's obligation terminates. The writer's obligation may terminate (1) by the passage of enough time for the option to expire, (2) by delivery of the underlying stock pursuant to the terms of the option, or (3) the writer may sell the written call to another call writer for a premium which may be more, the same, or less.

If a writer's obligation terminates by reason of the passage of enough time for the option to expire, or if the call writing obligation is sold to another call writer, the premium constitutes a short-term capital gain which the writer realized on the day the call expired or was sold. If the option is exercised, the premium received by the writer is treated as an increase in the proceeds realized upon the sale of the underlying stock in the exercised transaction. The gain or loss on such a sale constitutes capital gain or loss, long-term or short-term, depending upon how long the stock has been held.[26]

Boundary Conditions for Toronto Stock Exchange Options," *Journal of Finance*, June 1985, vol. 40, no. 2, pp. 481–500.

[26] For a detailed discussion of how options are taxed see Gary L. Gastineau, *The Stock Options Manual*, 2d ed., McGraw-Hill, New York, 1979, chap. 5. See also Max G. Ansbacher, *The New Options Market*, 2d ed., Walker, New York, 1979, chap. 10. Also see J. Cox and M. Rubinstein, *Options Markets*, Prentice-Hall, Englewood Cliffs, N.J., 1985. The appendix to chap. 5 also explains taxes.

21-7 SUMMARY AND CONCLUSIONS

Research by one of the Nobel Prize winners in economics has shown that resources within a nation can be allocated better if there are more different contingent claims on assets than are provided by only the long position.[27] That is, the existence of short positions, hedges, and options actually increases the nation's average per capita wealth, regardless of whether every person owns securities. Stated differently, the existence of short positions and options increases the chances that an investor will find a set of financial claims which are consistent with his or her preferences, thus inducing the investor to make a comfortable increase in investment. This additional investment can create more jobs and more goods for consumption and also shape security prices so that they more clearly reflect investors' wishes and forecasts. This scientific finding refutes the naive notion that speculation is some worthless form of gambling.

The people who buy and sell put and call options have obligations and rights that are summarized in Table 21-4.

The spectrum of possible positions which participants in securities markets may assume is wide. For example, individuals who want to speculate that the market price of an asset will rise or fall may set themselves up to profit from such moves, if they materialize, by assuming a long or short position, respectively. If a speculator desires more financial leverage and/or wants only a limited liability—which are not obtainable with the long and short positions—then call or put options are appropriate. On the other hand, a speculator who thinks that the price of some security will not change and wants to profit from this expectation can do so. By writing strips, straps, and straddles, the person can profit if the security's price remains stationary. Positions exist from which thoughtful individuals may profit from practically every other situation too. The existence of such profitable opportunities encourages good securities research, helps keep securities prices aligned with their true intrinsic values, and makes securities markets more efficient allocators of capital.

Both risk-taking speculators and risk-averse hedgers use options. Risk-averse investors who must maintain a long (short) position during a period of time when they expect the price of the asset to decline (rise) may buy put (call) options or take the opposite position to protect themselves from adverse price

[27] Kenneth Arrow, "The Role of Securities in the Optimal Allocation of Risk-Bearing," *Review of Economic Studies*, April 1964, pp. 91–96.

TABLE 21-4 the buyers and sellers of options have different rights and obligations

	call option	put option
Buyer or owner	Right to buy on or before the expiration date at the exercise price	Right to sell on or before the expiration date at the exercise price
Writer or seller	Obligation to sell at the exercise price on or before the expiration date	Obligation to buy at the exercise price on or before the expiration date

movements. Thus, options perform an important risk-reducing function, somewhat analogous to the function performed by insurance.

Other kinds of options exist. Appendix 21A delves into Warrants and Convertible Securities—both of which are essentially options added to other securities. In addition, following Chaps. 22 and 23, which introduce futures contracts, 23A explains options on futures contracts.

QUESTIONS

21-1. "Risk-averters do not sell short. Short selling is done by speculators." Is this statement true, false, or uncertain? Explain.

21-2. Who are the parties to put and call options and what function is performed by each party?

21-3. What are the main factors determining put and call premiums?

21-4. Graph the profit positions showing the positions of the buyer and the writer of a strap.

25-5. Compare and contrast writing a call naked and selling a common stock short.

21-6. Is it possible to create a short position from options? Explain.

21-7. Compare and contrast call options and warrants.

21-8. Does the Chicago Board of Options Exchange ever trade options of any type with the same expiration date but different exercise prices? Why?

21-9. Should the price of a strip option bear any relation to the prices of put and call options? Explain.

21-10. Is there any kind of basic relation between the prices of puts and calls on the same security which may be expected to exist permanently? Explain.

21-11. Use the Black-Scholes call option pricing formula to find the value of call options on the following optioned stocks:

	ABC stock	XYZ stock
Time to maturity	4 months	88 days
Standard deviation	30	40
Exercise price	$40	$60
Price of optioned stock	$40	$68
Interest rate	.12	.06

SELECTED REFERENCES

Black, F., and M. Scholes, "The Pricing of Options and Corporate Liabilities," *Journal of Political Economy*, June 1973, pp. 637–654. A seminal mathematical paper which develops a static equilibrium pricing model for options.

Bookstaber, R. M., *The Complete Investment Book*, Scott, Foresman and Company,

Glenview, Ill., 1985. Chapter 3 discusses cash-futures arbitrage. Chapter 5 discusses interest rate arbitrage. Chapter 23 discusses the Black-Scholes option pricing formula. Chapter 24 discusses Black's commodity options pricing model. Chapter 25 discusses volatility estimation using historical data. Chapter 26 discusses the implied volatility statistics derived from option prices. Each chapter contains a computer program to perform the calculations, as explained on page 173 of this book.

Cox, J. C., and M. Rubinstein, *Options Markets*, Prentice-Hall, Englewood Cliffs, N.J., 1985. This comprehensive book covers both the institutional material and option theory in detail.

Gastineau, Gary L., *The Stock Options Manual*, 2d ed., McGraw-Hill, New York, 1979. The first six chapters contain easy-to-read descriptions of options and option markets. Chapter 7 through 10 discuss quantitative call pricing models, options on bonds and commodities, and other topics.

APPENDIX 21A

warrants, convertibles, and the newer options

The options industry has enjoyed explosive growth since the organized option exchanges opened in the 1970s. Moreover, this growth is continuing into the 1980s as entirely new types of options are created and as more of the traditional options on securities are listed and traded. Options on commodities, options on financial indices, and options on futures contracts are all exciting new products. Understanding these new products well enough to sell them has been straining the capacity of the securities industry since the 1980 decade started. In contrast, warrants and convertible bonds are well-known option-type securities. Let us consider them first.

APP. 21A-1 WARRANTS

Stock purchase warrants, or more simply, warrants, are options to buy shares of stock. They are like *calls* to the extent that they are options to buy a fixed number of shares at a predetermined price during some specified time period. However, warrants are different from calls in certain respects. Warrants are written by the corporation to whose stock they apply rather than by an independent option writer. They are given as attachments to the corporation's issue of bonds or preferred stock. Warrants are "sweeteners" given with an issue of senior securities in order to increase the proceeds of the issue and thereby lower the interest cost. These options may expire at a certain date, or they may be perpetual. They are usually detached from the securities with which they were issued and traded as separate securities.

The price stated on the warrant which the owner must pay to purchase the stated number of shares is called the *exercise price*. The minimum value of a warrant, denoted MVW, may be calculated with Eq. (App. 21A-1).

$$MVW = (p_s - p_e)N \qquad \text{(App. 21A-1)}$$

where

p_s = market price per share of the optioned stock
p_e = conversion or exercise price
N = number of shares of common stock obtained with one warrant

For example, a warrant which entitles its owner to buy two shares (that is, $N = 2$) of stock at an exercise price of \$50 per share (p_e = \$50) while the market price is \$60 per share (p_s = \$60) has a minimum value of [(\$60 − \$50) (2) =] \$20 per warrant. Figure (App. 21A-1) depicts Eq. (App. 21A-1) graphically as the minimum-value line. The slope of the MVW line is N.

Figure App. 21A-1, depicting the determination of warrant prices, is also appropriate to explain the price of calls since call options and warrants are identical except for some minor details. Figure App. 21A-1 shows that when the market price of the optioned security is above the exercise price, the warrant has some positive minimum value. The actual market price of the warrant actually follows the dashed curves in Fig. App. 21A-1 (like call prices). This shows that warrants typically have a market value above the MVW. The excess of a warrant's price over its minimum value (p_w − MVW) is determined by expectations about future stock prices in the same way that call option premiums are determined.[28]

The terms governing a warrant are specified in detail in a legal contract (like a bond indenture) called the *warrant agreement*. The warrant agreement stipulates such important details as when the warrant may be exercised. Most

[28] J. P. Shelton, "The Relation of the Pricing of a Warrant to the Price of Its Associated Common Stocks," *Financial Analysts Journal*. This two-part article is in the May–June 1967 issue and also the July–August 1967 issue. Also see D. Leabo and R. L. Rogalski, "Warrant Price Movements and the Efficient Market Model," *Journal of Finance*, March 1975; A. H. Y. Chen, "A Model of Warrant Pricing in a Dynamic Market," *Journal of Finance*, December 1970; A. J. Boness, "Elements of a Theory of Stock-Option Value," *Journal of Political Economy*, April 1964.

FIGURE APP. 21A-1 the determinants of a warrant's price.

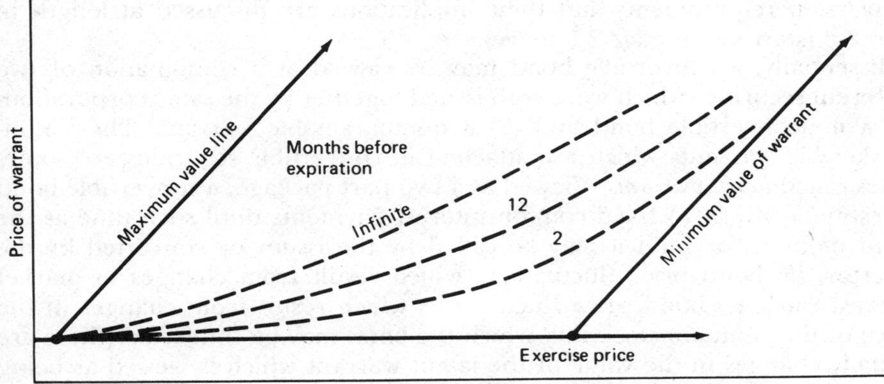

warrants are like long-term American call options; that is, they may be exercised anytime within their life of 5 or 10 years. A few warrants have perpetual lives, and a few other warrants are like European calls and may be exercised only at specific points in time.

Most warrants are protected against stock splits and stock dividends. Thus, if the security to which the warrant applies undergoes a 2 for 1 split, for instance, the warrant likewise is adjusted so that it entitles its owner to two of the new split shares (which are worth half of what the old shares would have been worth if they had not been split). However, most warrants are not protected against the eroding effect of cash dividends on the price of the optioned security. Thus, when a common stock starts to trade ex-dividend, its market price drops off by an amount approximately equal to the cash dividend which was just paid. This ex-dividend price drop-off moves the price of the optioned stock further below the exercise price of the warrant and thus tends to decrease the value of the warrant.

Some warrants are *nondetachable*, which means that they cannot be detached from their associated securities. However, many warrants are detachable, and they may be separated from the securities to which they were attached as sweeteners and traded separately as independent financial instruments. The warrant agreement outlines all such rights and provisions for its particular issue of warrants.

APP. 21A-2 CONVERTIBLE BONDS

Convertible bonds are corporate debt securities, usually debentures. However, convertible bonds are unlike most other bonds because, at the option of the bondholder, they may be *converted* into equity shares in the same corporation that issued the convertible bonds, if certain conditions are met. However, from their investors' point of view, most convertible bond issues are encumbered by an unfortunate call provision. That is, most convertible bond issues have provisions in their indenture contracts which allow their issuers to call them in before maturity. When an issuer calls in an outstanding issue, this action is taken for the issuer's benefit, and whatever the issuer gains from the conversion essentially comes out of the investors' pockets. These call and conversion requirements and their implications are discussed at length in Sec. 2-8 (starting on page 37 above).

Essentially, a convertible bond may be viewed as a combination of two different securities which were both issued together by the same corporation: (1) a nonconvertible bond and (2) a nonmarketable warrant. These nonmarketable warrants which are attached to convertible securities are sometimes called *latent warrants*. Viewed as a two-part package, a convertible bond investment offers (*a*) fixed coupon interest payments until such time as the bond defaults, or until it may be called by the issuer or converted by the investor, (*b*) bond price fluctuations which result from changes in market interest rates, (*c*) bond price fluctuations which result from changes in the price of the common stock into which the bond may be converted (these are actually changes in the value of the latent warrant which is viewed as being "attached" to the bond), (*d*) downside risk protection provided by a "floor" or

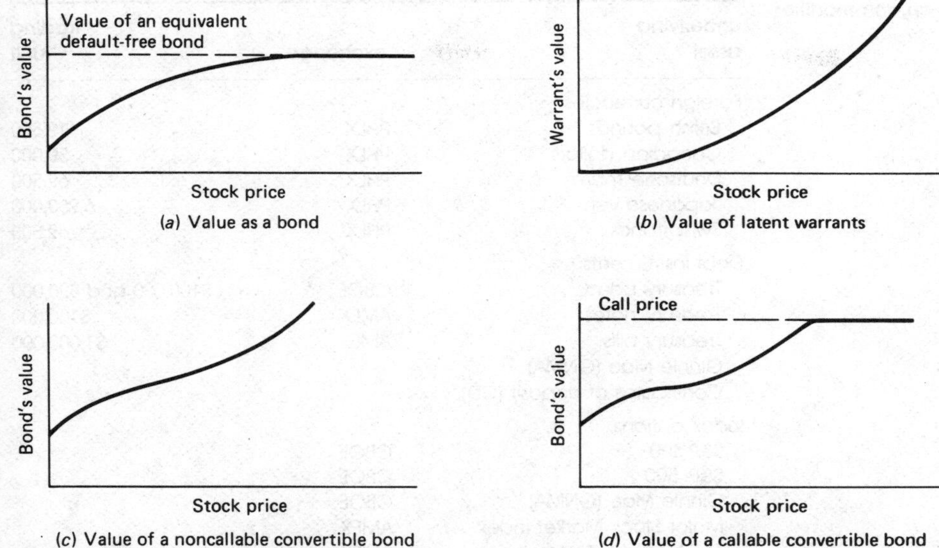

(a) Value as a bond

(b) Value of latent warrants

(c) Value of a noncallable convertible bond

(d) Value of a callable convertible bond

FIGURE APP. 21A-2 the elements of value in a convertible bond.

"safety net" under the investment's price which equals the present value of the nonconvertible bond's coupon payments, and (*e*) cashflows from the bond coupons which would normally exceed the cash dividend cashflows from a common stock investment of equal size. Calculating a value for such a package is a complicated task. To make matters even worse, as mentioned above, most convertible bond issues are callable at the issuer's discretion. Figure App. 21A-2 illustrates the general principles which are applicable in valuing convertible bonds.[29]

Figure App. 21A-2*a* illustrates how the value of a noncallable, nonconvertible corporate bond increases directly with the value of the issuing corporation's common stock price. This relationship derives from the fact that as the corporation prospers and its common stock's value rises, the probability decreases that bonds issued by the same corporation might fall into default. However, an upper limit or "ceiling" on the bond's price is established by the fact that the bond can never be worth more than a default-free bond with similar coupon and maturity provisions.

Figure App. 21A-2*b* shows that the value of the *latent warrant* which is implicit in every convertible security package rises in value directly with the value of the common stock into which it might be converted. Adding together the values indicated in Fig. App. 21A-2*a* and *b* results in the series of values illustrated in Fig. App. 21A-2*c*. Figure App. 21A-2*c* indicates how the value of a noncallable convertible bond varies directly with the price of the underlying

[29] Valuing convertible bonds is discussed by M. J. Brennan and E. S. Schwartz, "Convertible Bonds: Valuation and Optimal Strategies for Call and Conversion," *Journal of Finance*, December 1977, vol. XXXII, no. 5, pp. 1699–1716.

TABLE APP. 21A-1 options on commodities and economic indices

underlying asset	exchange	trading unit
Foreign currencies:		
British pounds	PHLX	12,500
Canadian dollars	PHLX	50,000
Deutsche marks	PHLX	62,500
Japanese yen	PHLX	6,250,000
Swiss francs	PHLX	62,500
Debt instruments:		
Treasury bonds	CBOE	\$100,000 and \$20,000
Treasury notes	AMEX	\$100,000
Treasury bills	AMEX	\$1,000,000
Ginnie Mae (GNMA)		
Certificates of deposit (CD)		
Index options:		
S&P 100	CBOE	
S&P 500	CBOE	
Ginnie Mae (GNMA)	CBOE	
Major Stock Market Index	AMEX	
AMEX Market Value	AMEX	
Consumer Price Index	CSC	
Subindex options:		
Computer technology	AMEX	
Oil and gas	AMEX	
International oils	CBOE	
Aerospace	NYSE	
Banking	NYSE	
Pharmaceutical	NYSE	
Precious metal	NYSE	
Technology	NYSE	
Telecommunications	NYSE	
Aerospace	AMEX	
Defense	AMEX	
Drugs	AMEX	
Electronics	AMEX	
Financial services	AMEX	
Health care	AMEX	
Leisure businesses	AMEX	
100 Hi-tech stocks	PSE	
Options on Futures Contracts: See App. 23A		

common stock. However, life is usually more complicated than even Fig. App. 21A-2*c* reveals.

As mentioned before, most convertible bonds are callable by the issuer at some call price which is prespecified in the indenture contract governing the bond issue. This call price imposes some sort of "ceiling effect" which limits the callable, convertible bond's price rise. To see how the "ceiling effect" works, consider a hypothetical corporation which starts to enjoy prosperity. Suppose this prosperity pushes up the prices of the corporation's common stock and convertible bonds. Eventually the corporation will probably call the convertible bonds, in order to force their owners to convert them into common stock. After all, the corporation does not want an overhanging issue of convertible bonds which limits its ability to issue new securities. Therefore, when the market price of the convertible bonds rises to about 125 percent of the call price, the issuing corporation usually calls the issue. Figure App. 21A-2*d* summarizes all of this; it is merely Fig. App. 21A-2*c* redrawn with a constraint or ceiling equal to the price the market thinks will cause the bonds to be called inserted as a "lid" on the price of the callable convertible bond.

APP. 21A-3 OPTIONS ON COMMODITIES AND ECONOMIC INDEXES

Table App. 21A-1 lists options on assets which were never optioned until the 1980s. Options on oil stocks, debt instruments, and economic indices are exciting new opportunities to speculate on the values of important variables which differ from the stock price options which dominated the option market for decades. Furthermore, options contracts on futures contracts are another new development. Options on futures are discussed at length in App. 23A.

commodity futures contracts

As the name suggests, commodity futures contracts are legal contracts. The terms of a futures contract stipulate the type of commodity covered by the contract, the future date for which delivery of the goods is scheduled, the sales price per unit for the commodity, the number of units (that is, the quantity) of the commodity that was sold, the quality specifications of the commodity that must be delivered under the contract, and related details. These stipulated details cannot be changed once a contract is executed because the futures contracts traded on any particular commodity in any given market are all standardized contracts that vary only with respect to the price and quantity of the particular sale covered by that specific contract.

The *uniformity* of the futures contract makes it more marketable to new buyers. For example, rapid trading is expedited if a homogeneous commodity is uniformly specified in all the futures contracts traded in a given market. Nevertheless, the second, third, and later buyers of any futures contract can, and usually do, pay a different price per unit for the contracted commodity than was agreed upon in the original contract. A futures contract is traded at successively different prices by transferring the contract through a third party called the *clearing house.* The clearing house inserts itself between every buyer and every seller. That is, the clearing house pays the original commodity seller the current price for the agreed-upon quantity and then turns around and sells a new, but identical, futures contract to the new buyer at the same current price. As a result of the clearing house positioning itself as the *intermediary* in every trade, a commodity contract may be resold at a price per unit that differs from the originally contracted unit price. The ultimate future delivery price and deliverer are reassigned by the clearing house each time the contract is resold. Thus, commodity futures contracts are *marketable financial instruments* that are actively traded on commodity futures exchanges.

Commodity futures contracts are usually called simply *futures.* Futures should be viewed as another type of financial instrument that portfolio managers may wish to consider.[1] Commodity futures contracts are useful to both risk-taking speculators and risk-averse hedgers in ways that are explained in the chapter that follows. The opportunities to earn a diverse mix of returns from a portfolio made up of stocks, bonds, options, and futures are too rich to ignore.

22-1 COMMODITIES TRADING

Commodities include farm products such as cotton, soybeans, hogs, and their derivatives, like soybean meal, soybean oil, and pork bellies (which refers to unsliced bacon). Other homogeneous raw materials, such as silver and copper, are also actively traded commodities.

Commodity prices are determined by the supply of and the demand for the underlying commodity. Commodity supplies are subject to all such capricious acts of nature as fire, flood, disease, insects, and drought, plus various unpredictable governmental acts like import-export quotas, subsidies, and foreign exchange revaluations. In contrast to erratic supply, the demand for most commodities is fairly steady. Farm products are traded in what economists call nearly perfect markets where there are many small sellers (namely, farmers) and many buyers—none of whom is large enough to affect prices.

The physical commodities are traded in what are synonymously called the cash, physicals, or actuals markets. Grain elevators and stockyards where farmers deliver and sell their products for cash are examples of *cash markets*. Large cash markets exist in the cities of Kansas City and Minneapolis in the United States, but no commodity futures contracts are traded at those cash markets. The commodity futures contracts are traded at markets for financial instruments called *futures exchanges*. Some cash markets are supplemented by associated futures contract markets, but most cash markets are not associated directly with a futures exchange.

Since the supply of harvested new crops arrives erratically to meet a demand function that is typically not so seasonal, some commodities must be stored for future delivery. Perhaps that is why contracts to deliver stocks of stored commodities came to be called commodity futures contracts. No one knows for sure where the word "futures" gained its first usage in the commodities business. Technically speaking, commodity futures contracts that do not fall due for delivery in the next few days are called *futures contracts*. Futures contracts that are near expiration and ready for the commodity to be delivered instantaneously are usually called *spot contracts* instead of futures contracts in the United States.[2] In spite of the fact that they are different, however, some people (in particular, the British) equate the spot market and the cash market in their market vernacular. Maybe the British refer to the

[1] C. V. Harlow and R. J. Tewles, "Commodities and Securities Compared," *Financial Analysts Journal*, September–October 1972, pp. 64–70. Futures contracts and securities are different financial instruments. Securities include stocks and bonds; the SEC oversees the securities markets in the United States. Futures contracts are not called securities. In the United States, futures markets are governed by the CFTC, as explained in chap. 4 at pages 112–113.

[2] Futures contracts are not traded in spot market transactions. Bills of lading and warehouse receipts are used in the spot market transactions.

TABLE 22-1 commodities

UNITED STATES COMMODITY EXCHANGES

commodity & exchange	trading hours (local time)	contract unit	MINIMUM PRICE CHANGE per unit	MINIMUM PRICE CHANGE per contract	value of 1¢/1$ move	MAXIMUM DAILY price change	MAXIMUM DAILY price range	contract value of maximum move
Cattle, feeder (CME)	9:05–12:45	44,000 lb	$.000025 lb	$11	$440	1½¢	3¢	$660
Cattle (CME)	9:05–12:45	40,000 lb	2½¢ 100¢ lb	$10	$400	1½¢	3¢	600
Cattle (MACE)	9:05– 1:00	20,000 lb	.00025 lb	$5	$200	1½¢	3¢	$300
Certificates of deposit (CBT)	7:30– 2:00	$1,000,000	1 B.Pt.* .01	$25	100 B.Pt. = $2500*	80 B.Pt.*	160 B.Pt.*	$2000
Certificates of deposit (IMM)	7:30– 2:00	$1,000,000	1 B.Pt.* .01	$25	100 B.Pt. = $2500*	80 B.Pt.*		$2000
Citrus (FCOJ) (NYCE)	10:15– 2:45	15,000 lb	5/100¢ lb	$7.50	$150	5¢	10¢	$750
Cocoa (NYCSC)	9:30– 3:00	10 tt	$1 tt	$10	$10	88¢	$176	$880
Coffee C (NYCSC)	9:45– 2:28	37,500 lb	1/100¢ lb	$3.75	$375	4¢	8¢	$1500
Copper (COMEX)	9:50– 2:00	25,000 lb	05/100¢ lb	$12.50	$250	5¢	10¢	$1250
Corn (CBT)	9:30– 1:15	5,000 bu	1/4¢ bu	$12.50	$50	10¢	20¢	$500
Corn (MACE)	9:30– 1:15	1,000 bu	1/8¢ bu	$1.25	$10	10¢	20¢	$100
Cotton (NYCE)	10:30– 3:00	50,000 lb	1/100¢ lb	$5	$500	2¢	4¢	$1000
Cotton (NOCE)	9:15– 2:00	50,000 lb	$.0001 lb	$5	$500	2¢	4¢	$1000
Currencies, foreign (IMM)								
British pound	7:30– 1:24	25,000	.0005	$12.50		.05	.1000	$1250
Canadian dollar	– 1:26	100,000	.0001	$10		.0075	.0150	$750
Deutschemark	– 1:20	125,000	.0001	$12.50		.01	.0200	$1250
Dutch guilder	– 1:30	125,000	.0001	$12.50		.01	.0200	$1250
French franc	– 1:28	250,000	.0005	$12.50		.005	.010	$1250
Japanese yen	– 1:22	12,500,000	.00001	$12.50		.0001	.0002	$1250
Mexican peso	– 1:18	1,000,000	.00001	$10		.0015	.003	$1500
Swiss franc	– 1:16	125,000	.0001	$12.50		.015	.03	$1875
Eurodollar CDs	7:30– 2:00	$1,000,000	1 B.Pt.* .01	$25	100 B.Pt. = $2500*	100 B.Pt.*	200 B.Pt.*	$2500
Crude oil, sour (NYMEX)		1,000 bbl	$.01 bbl	$10	$10	$1	$2	$1000
Crude oil, sweet (NYMEX)		1,000 bbl	$.01 bbl	$10	$10	$1	$2	$1000
Crude oil, sweet (CBT)		1,000 bbl	$.01 bbl	$10	$10	$1	$2	$1000
Gasoline, leaded NY (NYMEX)	9:30– 3:30	42,000 gal	$.001	$4.20	$420	2¢	4¢	$840
Gasoline, leaded (CBT)		42,000 gal	$.00025 gal	$10.50	$420	3¢	6¢	$1260
Gasoline, unleaded Gulf (CBT)	8:30– 2:30	42,000 gal	$.00025 gal	$10.50	$420	3¢	6¢	$1260
Gasoline, leaded (CME)		42,000 gal	$.00025 gal	$10.50	$420	2¢	4¢	$840
Gasoline, unleaded (CME)		42,000 gal	$.00025 gal	$10.50	$420	2¢	4¢	$840
Gold (CBT)	8:00– 1:30	100 oz t‡	10¢ oz	$10	$100	$40	$80	$4000
Gold (COMEX)	9:00– 2:30	100 oz t	10¢ oz	$10	$100	$25	$50	$2500

Gold (IMM)	8:00– 1:30	100 oz t	10¢ oz	$10	$100	$50	$100	$5000
Gold (MACE)	8:00– 1:40	33.2 oz t	2.5¢ oz	83¢	$33.20	$25	$50	$830
GNMA CDR (CBT)	8:00– 2:00	$100,000	1/32 pt	$31.25	1 pt = $1,000	64/32nds	128/32nds	$2000
Heating oil, no. 2 NY (NYMEX)	10:00– 2:45	42,000 US gal	$.0001 gal	$4.20	$420	2¢	4¢	$840
Heating oil, no. 2 (CBT)		42,000 US gal	$.00025 gal	$10.50	$420	3¢	6¢	$1260
Hogs, live (CME)	9:10– 1:00	30,000 lb	2½/100¢ lb	$7.50	$300	1½¢	3¢	$450
Hogs, live (MACE)	9:10– 1:15	15,000 lb	.025¢ lb	$3.75	$150	1½¢	3¢	$225
Lumber (CME)	9:00– 1:05	130,000 board ft	10¢ MBF	$13.00	$130	$5	$10	$850
NYSE composite index (NYFE)	10:00– 4:15	$500 X	.05	$25.00		none	none	
		futures price						
Oats (CBT)	9:30– 1:15	5,000 bu	1/4¢ bu	$12.50	$50	6¢	12¢	$300
Oats (MACE)	9:30– 1:30	5,000 bu	1/8¢ bu	$6.25	$50	6¢	12¢	$300
Palladium (NYMEX)	9:00– 2:20	100 oz t	5¢ oz t	$5.00	$100	$6	$12	$600
Platinum (NYMEX)	9:10– 2:30	50 oz t	10¢ oz t	$5.00	$50	$20	$40	$1000
Plywood, western (CBT)	9:00– 1:05	76,032 ft²	10¢ MSF	$7.60	$76	$7	$14	$532
Pork bellies (CME)	9:10– 1:00	38,000 lb	$.00025 lb	$9.50	$380	2¢	4¢	$760
Potatoes, white round (NYME)	9:45– 2:00	50,000 lb	1¢ cwt	$5.00	$5	50¢	$1	$250
Propane (LPG) (NYCE)	9:45– 2:35	42,000 gal	$.001	$4.20	$420	1¢	2¢	$420
Rice, milled (NOCE)	9:45– 1:45	1,200 cwt	$.005 cwt	$6.00		50¢	$1	$600
Rice, rough (NOCE)	9:45– 1:45	2,000 cwt	$.005 cwt	$10.00		30¢	60¢	$600
Silver, NY (COMEX)	9:05– 2:25	5,000 oz t	10/100¢ oz	$5.00	$50	50¢	$1	$2500
Silver, Chicago (CBT)	8:05– 1:25	5,000 oz t	10/100¢ oz	$5.00	$50	50¢	$1	$2500
Silver, Chicago (CBT)	8:05– 1:25	1,000 oz t	10/100¢ oz	$1.00	$10	50¢	$1	$500
Silver, Chicago (MACE)	8:05– 1:40	1,000 oz t	.005¢ oz	$.50	$5	50¢	$1	$500
Silver, NY (MACE)	8:30– 1:40	1,000 oz t	$.001 oz	$1.00	$10	50¢	$1	$500
Soybeans (CBT)	9:30– 1:15	5,000 bu	1/4¢ bu	$12.50	$50	30¢	60¢	$1500
Soybeans (MACE)	9:30– 1:30	1,000 bu	1/8¢ bu	$1.25	$10	30¢	60¢	$300
Soybeans (NOCE)	9:30– 1:15	5,000 bu	$.0025 bu	$12.50	$50	30¢	60¢	$1500
Soybean meal (CBT)	9:30– 1:15	100 tons (200,000 lb)	10¢ ton	$10.00	$100	$10	$20	$1000
Soybean oil (CBT)	9:30– 1:15	60,000 lb	1/100¢ lb	$6.00	$600	1¢	2¢	$600
S & P 500 stocks index (CME)	9:00– 3:15	$500 X	.05	$25.00		none		$2500
		futures price						
Sugar, no. 11 (NYCSC)	10:00– 1:43	112,000 lb	1/100¢ lb	$11.20	$1120	1¢	2¢	$1120
Sugar, no. 12 (NYCSC)	10:00– 1:43	112,000 lb	1/100¢ lb	$11.20	$1120	1¢	2¢	$1120
Sugar, refined (MACE)	9:00– 1:00	40,000 lb	1/100¢ lb	$4.00	$400	1/2¢	1¢	$200
Treasury bills (90-day) (IMM)	8:00– 2:00	$1,000,000	1 B.Pt. .01*	$25.00	100 B.Pt. = $2500*	60 B.Pt.*	120 B.Pt.*	$1500
Treasury bonds (CBT)	8:00– 2:00	$100,000	1/32 pt.	$31.25	32/32nds = $1000	64/32nds	128/32nds	$2000
Treasury bonds (NYFE)	9:00– 3:00	$100,000	1/32 pt.	$31.25	32/32nds = $1000	96/32nds		$3000
Treasury notes (10-year) (CBT)	8:00– 2:00	$100,000	1/32 pt.	$31.25	32/32nds = $1000	64/32nds		$2000
Treasury notes (2-year) (CBT)		$400,000	1/128 pt.	$31.25		96/128 pt.		$3000
Value Line composite index (KCBT)	9:00– 3:15	$500 X	.05	$25.00		none		
		futures price						
Wheat (CBT-KC-MPLS)	9:30– 1:15	5,000 bu	1/4¢ bu	$12.50	$50		50¢	$1500
Wheat (MACE)	9:30– 1:30	1,000 bu	1/8¢ bu	$1.25	$10	20¢	40¢	$200

TABLE 22-1 commodities *(continued)*

LONDON COMMODITY EXCHANGES *(continued)*

commodity & exchange	trading hours (local time)	contract unit	MINIMUM PRICE CHANGE per unit	MINIMUM PRICE CHANGE per contract	value of 1¢/1$/£1 move	MAXIMUM DAILY price change	MAXIMUM DAILY price range	contract value of maximum move
Barley, domestic feed (WCE)	9:30–1:15	100 tons (bd lot)		$10	$100			
		20 tons (job lot)	10¢ ton	$2 CDN§	$20	$5	$10	
Flaxseed (WCE)	9:30–1:15	100 tons (bd lot)		$10	$100			
		20 tons (job lot)	10¢ ton	$2 CDN	$20	$10	$20	
Oats, domestic feed (WCE)	9:30–1:15	100 tons (bd lot)		$10	$100			
		20 tons (job lot)	10¢ ton	$2 CDN	$20	$5	$10	
Rye (WCE)	9:30–1:15	100 tons (bd lot)		$10	$100			
		20 tons (job lot)	10¢ ton	$2 CDN	$20	$5	$10	
Rapeseed, Vancouver (WCE)	9:30–1:15	100 tons (bd lot)		$10	$100			
		20 tons (job lot)	10¢ ton	$2 CDN	$20	$5	$10	
Wheat, domestic feed (WCE)	9:30–1:15	100 tons (bd lot)		$20	$100			
		20 tons (job lot)	10¢ ton	$100	$20	$5	$10	
Treasury bills (90 days) (TSE)	9:00–3:15	$1,000,000 board lot	1 B.Pt. .005*	$50 CDN	100 B.Pt. = $2500*	Pt. .150	.300	
Gold (WCE)	8:25–1:30	20 oz	10¢ oz	$2	$20	$30	$60	
Silver (WCE)	8:40–1:25	200 oz	1¢ oz	$2	$2	.50¢	$1	
Treasury bonds (TSE)	9:00–3:15	$100,000 at 9%	$31.25	$31.25	32/32nd = $1000	64/32nds	128/32nds	

HONG KONG COMMODITY EXCHANGES

commodity & exchange	trading hours (local time)	contract unit	MINIMUM PRICE CHANGE per unit	MINIMUM PRICE CHANGE per contract	value of 1¢/1$/£1 move	MAXIMUM DAILY price change	MAXIMUM DAILY price range	contract value of maximum move
Cotton	9:30–11:30		1/100¢ US	$5				
(Hong Kong Commodity Exchange)	15:30–16:30	50,000 lb	lb					
Soybeans	4 sessions: 9:50 a.m., 10:50 a.m.,							
(Hong Kong Commodity Exchange)	12:50 p.m., 2:50 p.m.	500 bags of 60 kg	20¢ HK	HK $600				
Sugar	10:30–12:00	50 long tons						
(Hong Kong Commodity Exchange)	14:25–16:00	(112,000 lbs)	1/100¢ US	$11.20	$1120			
Gold (Hong Kong Commodity Exchange)	9:00–12:00	100 oz t‡	10¢ US					
	14:30–17:30		10¢ US	$10		10¢/oz t		
Palm oil (Kuala Lumpur Commodity Exchange)	11:00–12:30	25 tt	$1	$25		1st day	$5	
	3:30– 6:00		Malaysia	Malaysia		2nd day	$75	
						3rd day	$100	
						4th day	none	
						5th day	$50	

Aluminum (LME)	Kerb 13:15–13:25, 11:55–12:00, 12:55–13:00 Kerb 16:40–17:00, 15:45–15:50, 16:25–16:30	25 ††	£0.50	£12.50	£.25	none	none
Cocoa (London Cocoa Terminal Marketing Association)	10:00–13:00 14:30–16:45	10 †† (1000 kg)	£.1 tons	£.10	£.40	£.40	none
Coffee Robusta (London Coffee Terminal Marketing Association)	10:30–12:30 14:30–17:00	5 ††	£.1 tons	£.5	£.5	none	none
Coffee no. 2 Arabica (London Coffee Terminal Marketing Association)	10:15–16:45	17,250 k (250 bags of 69 k)	$.05 50 k	$17.25	$3.45	none	none
Copper, high-grade (LME)	12:00–12:05, 12:30–12:35, 15:35–15:40, 15:10–16:15, 13:15–13:25, 16:40–17:00 (Kerb)	25 ††	£0.50	£12.50	£.25	none	none
Standard copper cathodes (LME)	12:00–12:05, 16:15–16:20, 15:35–15:40, 16:15–16:20, 13:15–13:25, 16:40–17:00 (Kerb)	25 ††	£0.50	£12.50	£.25	none	none
Gold (London Bullion Market)	8:30–19:30 Fixes held at 10:30 a.m. *15:00 p.m.	minimum order outside of fixes is 100 oz *Minimum order for covering versus Amsterdam Market is 10 oz		No minimum on fix		none	none
Silver (London Bullion Market)	8:30–19:15 Fixes held at 12:15	Minimum order is 5000 oz outside fix	N.A.	N.A. No minimum on fix	N.A.	none	none
Crossbred, greasy wool no. 2 (London Wool Term Marketing Association)	10:30–12:00, 15:00–16:30, Kerb Until 17:30	1,500 k	1 pence/k				
Greasy wool (Sydney)	11:00–12:30 15:00–16:30	1,500 k	10¢/k	$1.50 (Aust.)			
Lead (LME)	12:00–12:15, 12:45–12:50, 15:30–15:35, 16:00–16:05, 13:15–13:25, 16:40–17:00 (Kerb)	25 ††	£0.25	£6.25	£.25	none	none
Nickel (LME)	12:20–12:25, 13:00–13:05, 15:45–15:50, 16:30–16:35, 13:15–13:25, 16:40–17:00 (Kerb)	6 ††	£.1 tons	£.60	£.60	none	none
Rubber (London Rubber Term Market Association)	8:45– 9:30, Kerb 9:45–12:45, 14:30–16:45, Unofficial after hours trading	15 †	0.10 pence/k	£1.50		3 pence	none
Silver (LME)	11:50–11:55, 13:05–13:10, 15:50–15:55, 16:35–16:40, 13:15–13:25, 16:40–17:00 (Kerb)	10,000 oz †‡	0.5 oz †‡	£50.00	N.A.	none	none
Soybean meal (London Gafta Soymeal Futures Market)	10:30–12:30, 14:30–17:00, Kerb After Official Call Until 19:15	100 †† (1000 k each)	10 pence	£.10	£.100		£5

TABLE 22-1 commodities *(continued)*

LONDON COMMODITY EXCHANGES *(continued)*

commodity & exchange	trading hours (local time)	contract unit	MINIMUM PRICE CHANGE per unit	MINIMUM PRICE CHANGE per contract	value of 1¢/1$/£1 move	MAXIMUM DAILY price change	MAXIMUM DAILY price range	contract value of maximum move
Sugar raws no. 4 (London Term. Sugar Market Association)	10:30–12:30, 14:30–17:00, 17:00–19:10 (Kerb)	50 tt	£0.05 tons	£2.50	£50	*	£.40	
Tin (LME)	Kerb 13:15, 13:25, 12:05–12:10, 12:40–12:45, Kerb 16:40, 17:00, 15:40–15:45, 16:20–16:25	5 tt	£.1 tons	£.5	£.5	none	none	
Zinc (LME)	12:15–12:20, 12:50–12:55, 15:30–15:35, 16:05–16:10, 13:15–13:25, 16:40–17:00 (Kerb)	25 tt	£0.025	£6.25	£25	none	none	
Gas oil in bulk (Intl. Pet. Ex. of London)	9:30–12:30 2:45– 5:20	100 tt	25¢ US tons	$50	$100		none	

CME = Chicago Mercantile Exchange
MACE = Mid-America Commodity Exchange
CBT = Chicago Board of Trade
IMM = International Monetary Market of the CME
NYCE = New York Cotton Exchange
NYCSC = New York Coffee, Sugar and Cocoa Exchange
COMEX = Commodity Exchange, N.Y. City
NOCE = New Orleans Cotton Exchange
NYMEX = New York Mercantile Exchange
KCBT = Kansas City Board of Trade
WCE = Winnepeg Commodity Exchange
TSE = Toronto Stock Exchange
LME = London Metal Exchange
* B.Pt.—basis point.
† t—metric tons.
‡ oz t—troy ounces.
§ CDN—Canadian dollars.

physicals or cash market as the "spot market" because spot contracts are due to be delivered instantaneously and, thus, to be turned into the physical or cash commodity. In the United States both spot and futures contracts are traded on commodity exchanges. The physical or cash commodity, however, is never traded on a commodity exchange in the U.S.

Table 22-1 lists the major commodity exchanges in the United States and the commodity futures contracts that are traded at each. The Chicago Board of Trade, now more than a century old, is the largest commodity exchange in the United States. Interestingly, there are no significant cash markets for commodities in Chicago although two of the largest commodity futures exchanges in the world, the Chicago Board of Trade and the Chicago Mercantile Exchange, operate in that city. Since it is very expensive to accept delivery on a futures contract in Chicago, the commodity exchanges in Chicago primarily support trading by hedgers and speculators instead of farmers.

Figure 22-1 shows a floor plan of a trading room found in a typical commodity exchange. There are usually several trading rooms at an exchange, and only the exchange members may enter them. Trading actually occurs in the *trading ring*, or *trading pit*, shown in Fig. 22-1. Exchange members who want to buy or sell futures in some commodity go to the appropriate trading room, step into the trading pit, and indicate by *open outcry* or by making appropriate hand signals that are visible to all who are present their intention to transact business. This is how commodity buyers and sellers get together to consummate a legitimate trade on domestic futures exchanges in the United States. When the buyer and the seller settle on the contract terms, news of the latest price is posted to the board on the trading room wall and also sent out by wire to the boardrooms of brokerage houses around the world.

Floor brokers are independent members of the commodity exchange who transact most of the trading on the exchange floor. For a commission, they buy and sell futures for their customers. Orders to buy and sell come into the exchange by telephone and/or telegraph to the floor brokers from their customers. The floor brokers step into the appropriate pit, execute the trades, and then notify their customers. The *independents*, as these floor brokers are

FIGURE 22-1 trading floor of a commodity exchange.

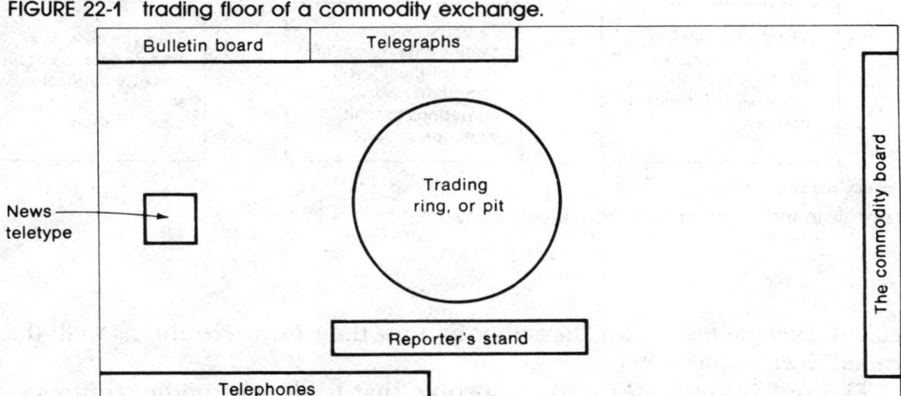

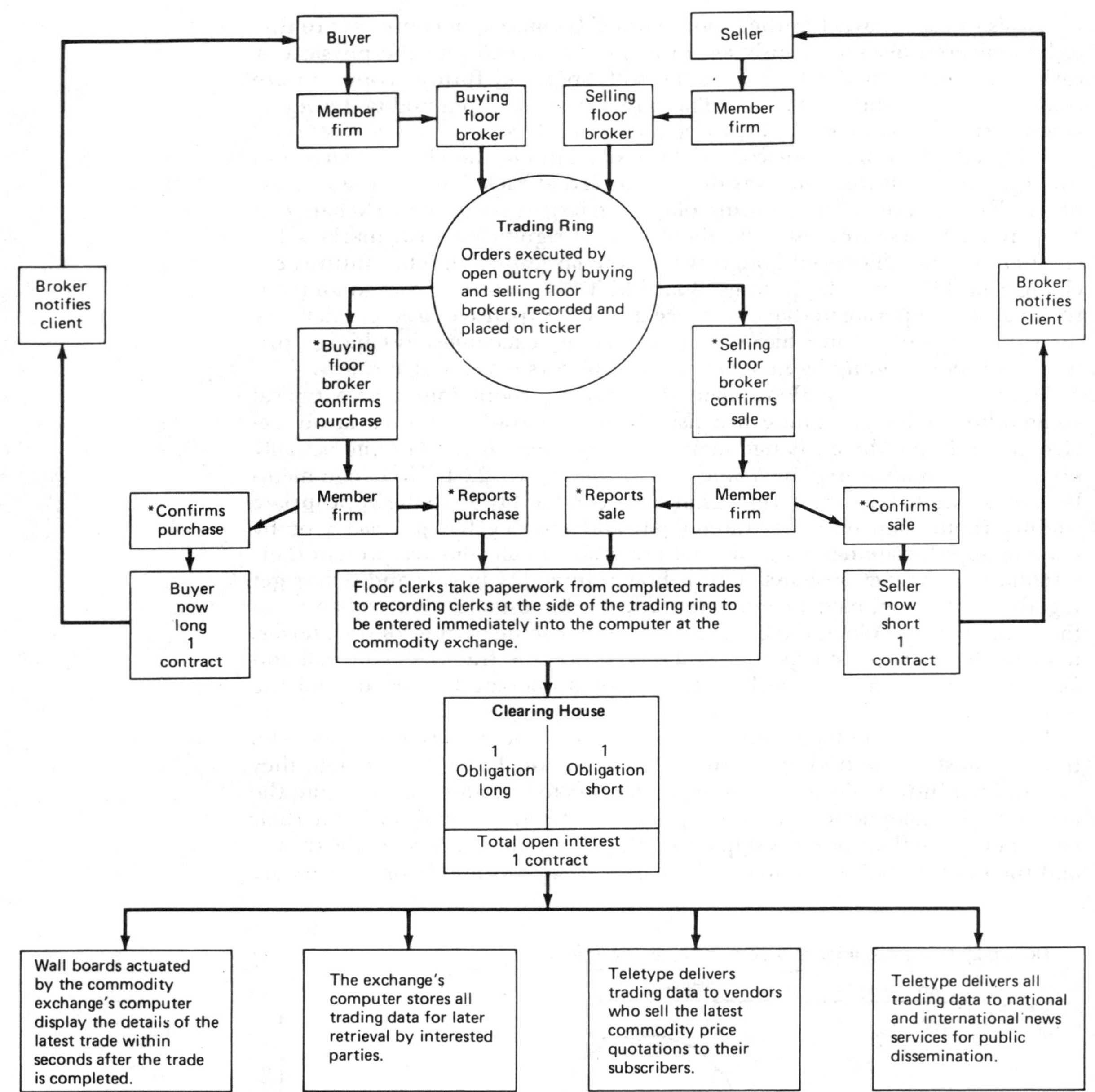

FIGURE 22-2 flowchart of events in the origination of one futures contract.

called, execute orders for the public and for their own accounts as well; this is called *dual trading*.

Figure 22-2 indicates who the people that trade commodity futures contracts interact with, where some of the more important of these contacts occur, and how the news of the trades is channeled around the world. Figure 22-2 is an event flowchart that traces out the flow of events and information that accompany every commodity futures trade.

22-1.1 futures contracts

The phrase "commodity exchange" can be misleading, because the commodities themselves are not traded at commodity exchanges. It is the commodity futures contracts that are actively traded at the exchanges. Today, the futures contracts themselves are not even traded. *Trading cards* are what are actually traded. Modern futures contracts are, in fact, a set of legal contract provisions, rules, regulations, and exchange bylaws that govern every transaction that flows through a futures exchange. Years ago, however, preprinted contractual forms were traded on the floors of the commodity exchanges.

In years past, a different commodity futures contract form existed for each commodity which specified the standard trading unit for the commodity in pounds, bushels, or whatever unit was appropriate; what grade of commodity was to be delivered; where the commodity was to be delivered; and what

FIGURE 22-3 futures contract for Brazilian coffee from yesteryear.

CONTRACT "B" (new)
(BRAZIL COFFEE CONTRACT)
(Variable Differentials)
New York______________19_____

____________________________ *(has)/(have) this day (sold)/(bought)*

*and agreed to (deliver to)/(receive from)*________________________

32,500 lbs. (in about 250 bags) of Brazilian COFFEE shipped through the ports of Santos, Paranagua, Angra dos Reis or Rio de Janeiro, grading from No. 2 to No. 6 inclusive, provide the average grade shall not be above No. 3, nor below No. 5. Nothing in this contract, however, shall be construed as prohibiting a delivery averaging above No. 3 at the premium for No. 3 grade. No premium shall be allowed for Softish Coffee grading above No. 4.

At the price of _______ cents per pound for Santos No. 4, Strictly Soft, Fair to Good Roast, Solid Bean with additions or deductions for grades, ports of shipment and description (quality) according to the differentials established or to be established by the Committee on Coffee of the New York Coffee and Sugar Exchange for the delivery month specified below in accordance with Section 88(8) (a) of the By-Laws of said Exchange. The delivery must consist of Coffee from one port only.

The Coffee to be Fair to Good Roast, Solid Bean, and the description (quality) to be Strictly Soft, Soft, or Softish. No delivery permitted of Hard Coffee.

Deliverable from licensed warehouse in the Port of New York between the first and last days of ________________________inclusive, the delivery within such time to be at the seller's option upon either five, six or seven days' notice to the buyer as prescribed by the Trade Rules.

Either party may call for margin as the variations of the market for like deliveries may warrant, which margin shall be kept good.

This contract is made in view of, and is in all respects subject to, the By-Laws, Rules and Regulations of the New York Coffee and Sugar Exchange, Inc.

____

(Across the face is the following): *(Brokers)*

*For and in consideration of One Dollar to*______________
*in hand paid, receipt whereof is hereby acknowledged,*______________
accept this contract with all its obligations and conditions.

penalties would be imposed if the delivery were made at another place or in another grade. When a futures contract was signed, the buyer and the seller merely filled in blanks on the contract specifying their names, the date, the quantity, the price, and the month in which delivery was to be made. Figure 22-3 shows a blank futures contract from the "old days," before computer memories were used to store the details of all the "open interest" futures contracts.

22-1.2 the commodity board

For any given commodity there are several delivery months which may be specified in the futures contract. The price of the futures in any given commodity varies with the month in which the commodity is to be delivered. Thus, March No. 2 grade soft red winter wheat deliverable at Chicago has a different price per bushel from the price of the same type of wheat delivered at the same place in May. As a result, commodity futures prices are listed on a *commodity board* like the one shown in Table 22-2.

The top line of the commodity board gives the highest and lowest prices at which that particular commodity has ever been traded since the contract's inception. All prices are in cents per bushel for this particular commodity. The second line of the board lists the delivery months. It will be noted that Chicago wheat futures, like most futures, are not available for delivery every month. The *delivery months* for futures are determined by the commodity exchange with the approval of the Commodity Futures Trading Commission (CFTC). The third line of the board gives the closing price of the commodity on the last day the exchange was open for business. The bottom four lines of the board give the current day's opening price, the highest price attained so far that day, the lowest price for the day, and the current price for the commodity in each of its delivery months. The board is kept current by clerks employed by the exchange. The current prices are also wired to the boardrooms of brokerage houses around the country.

22-1.3 price fluctuations in the United States

Commodity futures prices have both minimum and maximum price limit fluctuations imposed on them by the commodity exchanges. The fifth column of Table 22-1 lists the *minimum price fluctuations* on the major commodities. New bids must be higher than the old (or existing) bids, and new asked (or offering) prices must be less than the old (or existing) asked prices by at least the amount of the minimum fluctuation limit; otherwise the exchange will not accept the new bid or asked price. The minimum price limit fluctuations are

TABLE 22-2 commodity board for Chicago wheat

High and low	490–311	499–350	491–366	479–344	484–360
Delivery months	December	March	May	July	September
Previous close	370	377⅛	379	355	363⅜
Opening today	371½	377	378⅞	353	362
Today's high	371	379	379	353	362
Today's low	368⅝	377¼	377	350½	361
Ticker	369	379	378	350	361⅛

designed to prevent bids involving price changes that are not significantly different from zero.

Column seven of Table 22-1 lists the *maximum price fluctuations* permitted on most commodities. The purpose of these maximum limits is to prohibit large and potentially destabilizing price changes. Thus, if a commodity's price rises the *day's limit,* trading in that commodity for the remainder of the day cannot exceed that day's maximum price. Trading may thus be stopped. The next day, trading resumes at the previous day's high price but still cannot rise higher than the daily maximum or trading will be halted again. Luckily, the maximum price fluctuation limits seldom halt trading in any commodity. Some economists suggest that price restrictions distort natural supply and demand relationships and thus misallocate resources when they do come into play. However, there is a perennial debate among market economists about whether the price change limits do more good than bad.

22-1.4 the clearing house

In addition to the buyer and the seller, there is a third party to every futures contract, the *clearing house,* which guarantees that every futures contract will be fulfilled even if one of the parties defaults. Every commodity exchange has a clearing house.

The clearing house acts as buyer if the buyer defaults or as seller if the seller defaults. The clearing house thus provides a performance guarantee for every futures contract. It saves part of the fees it collects for insuring futures contracts in a guarantee fund. When one of the parties to a futures contract defaults, the clearing house pays whatever costs are necessary to carry out the contract from this fund. This provision frees futures traders from checking one another's credit every time they transact a trade and thus helps make the futures contract a freely negotiable financial instrument.

The clearing house also facilitates trading of futures contracts before they are due for delivery. If the original buyer of a future sells the contract to reverse the trade, and if the second buyer in the series sells the contract to reverse that trade, and then if a third buyer in the series sells the contract to reverse that trade, the clearing house keeps track of this series of buyers. Then, when the time comes to deliver on the contract, the clearing house arranges for the original seller of the contract to make delivery to the last buyer of the contract. In practice, the clearing house actually rewrites every futures contract as two separate contracts and substitutes its name into both. That is, the clearing house becomes the seller from which all buyers obtain delivery and the buyer to whom all sellers make delivery. Thus, when several subsequent buyers are involved in a given futures contract, these various buyers and sellers do not even need to know each other's names to ensure that the contract gets delivered.[3] The clearing house keeps track of these details and deals directly with each buyer and seller separately, as shown in Fig. 22-4.

[3] Technically, the traders on the floor of a commodity exchange make it a point to know the names of the other sides of all their trades in order to expeditiously clear up any mistakes, called *out trades.* By knowing the other party that was part of the out trade, the trader can negotiate a settlement of the mistake directly. Such direct negotiation avoids costly and inconvenient arbitration of the out trade.

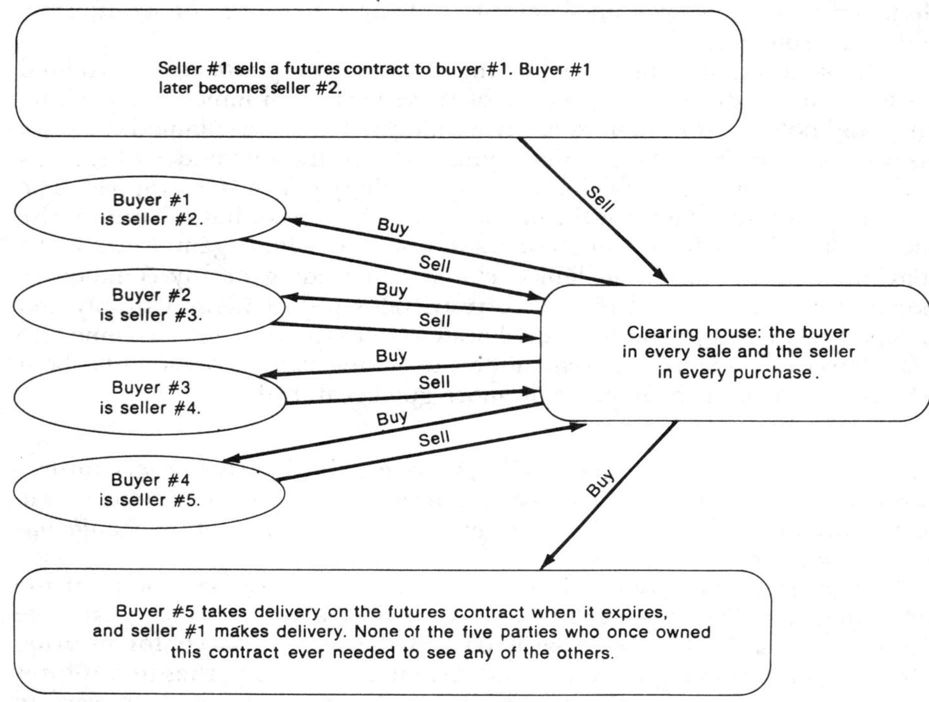

FIGURE 22-4 flowchart of a series of trades of one futures contract which is reversed.

22-1.5 the mechanics of trading commodity futures

Futures traders need not be involved in a business utilizing the commodities they trade; they need not ever see the commodities. Commodity traders usually start by opening a trading account with a futures commission merchant (FCM hereafter) at a brokerage house which deals in commodities. The brokerage firm will either purchase or lease a *membership* at a commodity exchange, or the FCM will make arrangements with a floor trader who is a member of a commodity exchange to carry out the trades.

The major full-service brokerage firms like Merrill Lynch, Pierce, Fenner and Smith, Inc.; E. F. Hutton; and others have commodities departments or subsidiaries (such as Merrill Lynch Futures Inc.) to assist the general public in trading futures. Some firms like Conti-Commodity and Phibro specialize in being FCMs and dealers for the larger buyers of commodities. In addition, there are discount brokers in the commodity futures business. Like the discount brokers in the common stock markets, the discount FCMs do not provide free research, nice offices for clients to visit, and other expensive amenities. As a result, the FCMs charge their clients commissions that are about one-fourth as much as one of the full-service FCMs would charge for the same transaction. Lind-Waldock, Macro-Source, Murias Commodities Inc., and Jack Carl Associates are all discount FCM firms. The discount FCMs are not as large as the full-service FCM firms, do not have offices in as many cities, and do very little advertising. However, almost all of them have offices in Chicago and can be contacted by telephone from anywhere in the world.

Futures contracts are denominated in a single quantity of a commodity. For example, on the Chicago Board of Trade 100 tons is one unit or one contract of soybean meal, a wheat contract consists of 5000 bushels, and a unit of lard is 40,000 pounds. Table 22-1 shows the standard contract units for every major commodity in the third column. To sell a futures contract, the trader notifies the broker. The broker obtains all the needed details about whether the customer wants to sell futures (that is, to take a short position) or buy futures (to assume a long position); what the current prices, margin requirements, relevant unit, and total costs are; and in what trading months the future may be bought and sold.

The broker prepares the order and transmits it to the commodity exchange. For example, if the customer wanted to go short 200 tons of soybean meal until November, the broker could notify the floor trader at the soybean trading room of the Chicago Board of Trade to "sell two November soy meals." This message would be transmitted by telephone or direct wire to the floor trader. This floor trader would probably execute the order and send word back to the broker that the transaction had been consummated—all within a few minutes. At that time the customer would be required to put up the initial margin requirement of approximately 5 to 10 percent. Then, anytime before November, when the soybean meal contract expired and came due to be delivered, the broker's short-selling customer could either buy back the contract in the futures market or buy physical soybean meal in the cash market and deliver it to fulfill the futures contract. If the short seller defaulted on the contract, the clearing house would carry out the contracted delivery of 200 tons of soybean meal as scheduled and initiate a lawsuit against the defaulted short seller. Actually, very few commodity market traders ever make delivery on their futures contracts; most settle by "rolling over" their position into a later delivery month or reversing the trade so that they are left without a position.

22-2 ACTIVELY TRADED COMMODITIES

Commodities that are actively traded in the futures markets include both the traditional (for example, agricultural products) and the newer financial instruments.

22-2.1 the traditional and the new commodities

AGRICULTURAL COMMODITIES Some of the actively traded farm commodities include meats (like unsliced bacon and broiler chickens), grains (like wheat, corn, and soybeans), and other commodities (like coffee, sugar, rice, and cotton).

Various other traditional commodities which have been traded for a long time exist too; these include metals (like gold and silver), wood (like plywood and stud lumber), and rubber.

The farm goods and other traditional commodities mentioned above were the earliest commodities traded. Investors started trading them centuries ago in crude markets. The most recent items traded at commodities exchanges are financial futures contracts.

FINANCIAL FUTURES The financial commodities traded in futures markets are contracts on foreign currencies (like the British pound, the Canadian dollar, the Swiss franc, and the Japanese yen), contracts on bonds (like U.S. Treasury bonds, U.S. Treasury bills, and commercial paper), and contracts on financial indices (like a stock market index).[4]

It is natural to have financial futures markets because money is a commodity. Like wheat or corn or any other commodity, money has one price for current delivery and a different price for future delivery. The difference between the current price and the future price of money is essentially the market interest rate, or basis, for the commodity called money.

22-2.2 characteristics of actively traded commodities

When we say a given commodity is "traded successfully," we are speaking from the point of view of the commodity exchange. *Successfully traded* commodity futures contracts are those that enjoy sufficient trading volume (or, what is a closely related measure, the open interest) to make active markets for the contract and generate sufficient trading fees to pay the commodity exchange's cost of keeping the market operating. In general, the following list of statements apply to actively traded commodities.

- The commodity should be gradable into *homogeneous quality categories*. This means that one lot of any commodity (such as a boxcar load of sugar) should be interchangeable with any other lot of that commodity.
- *Raw materials* (such as wheat) are traded successfully more frequently than finished goods (such as flour). Money is also a raw material; it is used to produce a finished product called profits.
- The commodity's cash market price should be determinable by a *clear price discovery process*; there should be no arbitrariness about the price. For example, the price should be determined by supply and demand facts rather than by the whim of an individual or by a nonmarket process.
- *Storability* is important; perishable commodities (for example, lettuce or fresh flowers) cannot be stored or shipped easily. Since commodity hedgers endeavor to buy at a low price and sell at a high price, they want commodities they can hold in storage cheaply until prices rise.
- The commodity must exist in *volume*. Rare objects (for example, art objects) cannot generate the trading volume needed to sustain an active market.
- Large amounts of *risk capital* must be committed to carrying the risky inventories needed to make liquid markets. That is, hedgers must be willing to invest millions of dollars in inventories that will fluctuate in value. Then, when the parties investing in inventories of physicals enter the futures market to hedge, they, in turn, create more needs for risk capital to finance the speculators' positions that bear the risk the hedgers are hedging.
- The futures contract should be *conveniently written* for both buyer and seller. Contracts cannot be written in such dense legal language that only lawyers can read them.
- The commodity should be *cheaply transportable*. The marketability of a commodity is maximized if it can be shipped inexpensively to buyers.

[4] Financial futures are the topic of Chap. 23 of this book.

- The commodity should be *readily describable*. There can be no ambiguity about what is going to be delivered.
- The *price* of the commodity must be *volatile*. The more that the price of a commodity fluctuates, the more risk-averters will want to hedge their inventories and, in turn, the more speculative trading will occur to create these hedges.
- A liquid cash market where the physical commodity is traded should be active before trading in commodity futures contracts is begun. The *prior existence of a viable cash market* means that the price discovery process for the commodity already exists and is discernible.
- The public, and the risk-averse manufacturers who will want to hedge their inventories, need to be *educated* about the commodity and its futures contract. No one will invest in something they do not understand.

Most of these statements apply to most actively traded commodities. However, not every one of the statements above applies to every successfully traded commodity. For example, although most U.S. farm commodities are not easily gradable into homogeneous quality categories, the U.S. government nevertheless grades and inspects these commodities. The above list merely suggests what is usually required to trade a contract successfully.[5]

Usually, any given commodity is traded successfully at only one U.S. commodity exchange. For example, the Chicago Mercantile Exchange (nicknamed the "Chicago Merc") is primarily a meat market, although it also successfully trades other commodities. There are exceptions to this tendency, however; wheat and several other commodities are traded successfully on various U.S. commodity exchanges. No foreign commodity exchanges are as large as the ones in the United States, but several are nevertheless efficient commodity exchanges.

22-3 PRICES AND RETURNS

Commodity prices are determined by the supply of and the demand for the commodity. However, the relationships between the cash price, spot price, and futures price for any given commodity at any given instant are determined by different factors.

22-3.1 normal and inverted markets

For any storable commodity on a given day, the futures price is normally higher than the spot price.[6] The excess of the futures price over spot price is called the *premium*, or the *positive basis*. In *normal markets*, the premium is just

[5] Lester Telser and Harlow Higginbotham, "Organized Futures Markets: Costs and Benefits," *Journal of Political Economy*, October 1977, pp. 969–1000. Henry Bakken, *Futures Trading in Livestock—Origins and Concepts*, Mimir, Madison, Wis., 1970.

[6] Some commodities (such as fresh eggs, fresh potatoes, and live cattle) are not storable. For these nonstorable commodities it is not uncommon for spot prices to exceed futures prices. Also, just before harvest time when current supplies of a storable commodity are short but the forthcoming new crop is expected to be large, inverted markets are not unusual for storable commodities. Holbrook Working, "Theory of the Inverse Carrying Charge in Futures Markets," *Journal of Farm Economics*, February 1948, vol. XXX, and also, "The Theory of Price of Storage," *American Economic Review*, December 1949, vol. XXXIX.

sufficient to cover storage, inspection, interest expense, insurance, and the other carrying charges incurred while holding a commodity for future delivery. This premium is necessary to compensate speculators like grain elevator operators for buying commodities when their cash prices are low (for example, at harvest time) so that they will store them until their prices are bid higher, at which time they will sell the commodity to fill the excess demand. Such storage by grain elevator operators and other similar commodity dealers provides a supply of commodities all year long, although the entire crop in the commodity may be harvested in one month of the year. It is so common for futures prices to exceed spot prices by the amount of carrying charges in commodity markets that this situation is called a *normal carrying charge market.*

More generally, the difference between futures and spot prices on the same commodity at a given moment is called the *basis.* If futures exceed spot prices, this situation is called a positive basis, a premium, or *contango.*[7] However, a negative basis, or *discount* situation, can also occur.

$$\text{Basis} = (\text{futures price}) \text{ less } (\text{spot price}) \tag{22-1a}$$

A *normal market* is defined as one in which the basis, as measured in Eq. (22-1*a*), is a positive amount that equals the carrying cost.[8]

The premium of futures prices over spot prices may be slightly less than the cost of carrying the commodity in inventory if a "convenience yield" exists.[9]

> The "convenience" yield can be defined as the sum of extra advantages (other than appreciation in the market value) which a manufacturer may derive from carrying stocks above his immediate requirements rather than holding the equivalent value in cash and buying stocks at a later date.[10]

The higher selling price which a manufacturer could obtain by being a dependable supplier of substantial quantities of some raw material is one example of how a convenience yield is obtained from carrying a commodity in inventory. Some users of the commodity would be willing to pay the dependable supplier's higher selling price simply to establish a good relationship with the supplier and thus free themselves of worry about suffering from a costly and troublesome out-of-stock condition.

Occasionally the market in some storable commodity becomes "inverted." In an *inverted market* the futures price is less than the spot price. This excess of

[7] J. M. Keynes was first observed to use the word *contango* in an article he wrote for the *Manchester Guardian Commercial* in 1923. The word is more popular in England than in the United States today. However, the word *contango* seems to be used more frequently by silver futures traders than others for some unknown reason—perhaps because silver is such an international commodity.

[8] If the basis is restated as shown in Eq. (22-1*b*), then the basis is negative and has an absolute value equal to the carrying costs in normal markets.

$$\text{Basis} = (\text{spot price}) \text{ less } (\text{futures price}) \tag{22-1b}$$

[9] The convenience yield concept was first introduced by Nicholas Kaldor, "Speculation and Economic Stability," *Review of Economic Studies,* 1939, vol. 7, pp. 1–27.

[10] Gerda Blau, "Some Aspects of the Theory of Futures Trading," *Review of Economic Studies,* 1944–1945, vol. XII, no. 1, pp. 9–14.

spot over futures prices is called a *discount*. Futures can sell at a discount to spot, for example, when the current supply of a commodity is very low, keeping cash and spot prices high, but the currently growing crop is expected to yield a large harvest, so that future supplies will be plentiful and futures prices low.

22-3.2 one risk-averter plus one speculator can equal one futures contract

Between most risk-averting hedged sellers and most risk-averting hedged buyers is a risk-taking speculator. This speculator dislikes risk too. However, like an insurance company, the professional speculator takes many risks in both buying and selling. If the majority of the speculator's decisions are based on correct forecasts, he or she earns a trading profit over many transactions.

Professional speculators may or may not be members of a commodity exchange. Speculators prepare commodity forecasts and then, on the basis of their forecasts, either sell short to or buy futures contracts from hedging sellers or other speculators. For instance, one hedging seller and one speculator might consummate a trade that created one hedged inventory position for the hedger who sold the contract and one long futures position for the speculator who bought the contract. Later, the speculator might liquidate the long futures position by selling the contract to, say, a futures buyer who was hedging a short position in the physical commodity. As a result of this second transaction one speculator with a futures contract to sell and one hedging futures buyer can create another hedged position.

The final result is that the hedging buyer and the hedging seller have passed the risks they sought to avoid on to the professional speculator (who is probably well hedged and earns a profit for providing insurance). However, if the number of hedging buyers does not exactly equal the number of hedging sellers (and it rarely will), the speculator is left holding some long or short positions which are unhedged. In such situations, speculators hope that the price forecasts on which they based their decisions are correct. The fact that commodity exchanges have been growing for over a century suggests that, typically, many parties to these arrangements profit from them.

Not all trades need take place between a hedger and a speculator. Sometimes speculators can trade with each other (through the clearing house) merely because of differing price expectations.

22-3.3 the argument about normal backwardation

Financial economists are not all in agreement about exactly how large the basis should be in normal market conditions with storable commodities. Let us consider the determination of the size of the basis in more detail.

Two famous English economists, Keynes and Hicks, have argued independently that futures prices (fp) for storable commodities should normally be slightly less than the expected spot prices, $E(sp)$, by the amount of an insurance premium they called "normal backwardation."[11] The Keynes-Hicks viewpoint can be represented symbolically as Eq. (22-2).

$$fp = E(sp) + \text{a tiny positive "insurance premium"} \qquad (22\text{-}2)$$

[11] J. M. Keynes, *A Treatise on Money*, vol. II, and also *The Applied Theory of Money*, Macmillan, London, 1924. J. R. Hicks, *Value and Capital*, 2d ed., Clarendon, Oxford, 1946, chaps. IX and X, especially pp. 136–139.

Since the *expected spot price* is expected to occur at the *future* delivery date, it can never really be observed and measured. Thus, the Keynes-Hicks hypothesis does not yield to direct empirical testing.

Keynes and Hicks hypothesize that speculators provide a valuable insurance function for hedgers, and thus, hedgers must pay a risk-premium called *normal backwardation* in order to induce speculators to assume the risks associated with providing this insurance. More specifically, Keynes and Hicks argue that hedgers will usually be long the physical commodity and thus hedge themselves with offsetting short positions in the futures markets. This hedging activity, according to Keynes and Hicks, will force speculators, in the *aggregate*, to hold a net long position in futures contracts. Keynes and Hicks reasoned that in order to entice speculators to perennially take the net long positions that they envisioned, the futures markets would have to allow speculators to buy futures at prices which were slightly below their expected spot price. The difference between the futures price and the expected spot price is the insurance premium paid by the hedgers to the speculators. Stated differently, the normal backwardation theory implies that there is a positive net cost for hedgers to use the futures markets.

Mr. C. O. Hardy has suggested that the Keynes-Hicks theory is wrong. In contrast to Hicks and Keynes, Hardy argues that futures prices should normally be at a slight premium over the expected spot prices.[12] Mr. Hardy hypothesizes[13] that special types of "speculative insurance" have been developed to meet the need for

> protection against various types of loss where no proper distribution of risk can be obtained. In this type of contract, a large group of private insurers enters into a contract by which they agree to recompense the insured for his loss, dividing the cost between themselves. If the individual insurer writes many policies, and none are large, he secures a combination of risks which protect him against excessive loss. But there is a large speculative element involved in fixing the premium rates.

Mr. Hardy's speculators are like gamblers who are willing to pay for the opportunity to gamble. Furthermore, it appears as if Mr. Hardy's speculators view futures markets as being somewhat like gambling casinos that exist for their enjoyment. As a result, Hardy hypothesizes that speculators will bid futures prices up above what they actually expect the spot prices to be in the future. Mr. Hardy's hypothesis is summed up by Eq. (22-3).

$$fp = E(sp) + \text{a tiny negative "gamblers fee"} \tag{22-3}$$

Some of the opponents of Mr. Hardy argue that his view is inappropriate for futures prices because diversification is not very useful at reducing the insurer's risk exposure against *systematic* fluctuations in futures prices. Thus, the situation envisioned by Mr. Hardy is not economically self-perpetuating.

[12] C. O. Hardy and L. S. Lyon, "The Theory of Hedging," *Journal of Political Economy*, April 1923, vol. 31, no. 2, pp. 276–287.

[13] C. O. Hardy, *Risk and Risk Bearing*, Chicago, 1923, pp. 67–69.

Professors Telser[14] and Cootner[15] formulated empirical tests which were intended to discern whether futures prices were biased estimates of their expected spot prices. However, the results of these tests are not decisive. Thus, the debate about whether futures prices normally lie a little above or a little below their expected spot prices is still unresolved. Fortunately, the amount of this discrepancy is a modest amount for any given commodity contract.

22-3.4 the relationship between spot and futures prices

The market prices for storable commodities conform to Eq. (22-4) when the markets are normal.

$$fp_t \leq sp_0 + tC \tag{22-4}$$

where

fp_t = the market price of a futures contract that provides delivery t time periods in the future

sp_0 = the current (that is, at time $t = 0$) market price of a spot contract

C = the total carrying cost for the commodity for one month. This varies from commodity to commodity, but it is the sum of items like the following: (1) storage costs, (2) insurance, (3) insect spray, (4) interest expense (either direct or imputed) for financing the inventory, plus (5) whatever else is appropriate, minus (6) the commodity's convenience yield (if any exists)

t = the number of months the commodity is stored for future delivery

Note the inequality sign in Eq. (22-4). The inequality implies that futures prices cannot normally rise above the combination of spot prices plus the carrying costs. This inequality results from the fact that current inventories can be carried into future months for consumption at a later date merely by paying the carrying cost. On the other hand, the reverse is not possible. Future harvests cannot be consumed before they are harvested. Therefore, futures prices for storable commodities increase by the amount of the monthly carrying costs each month under normal market conditions.

The logic of inequality (22-4) can be extended to explain the difference between the prices of two futures contracts on the same storable commodity which have different expiration (or delivery, or unwinding) dates. Under normal market conditions inequality (22-5) can be used to establish limits on the spot-futures price relationship.

[14] Lester G. Telser, "Future Trading and the Storage of Cotton and Wheat," *Journal of Political Economy,* June 1958, vol. LXV, pp. 233–255. Telser was not testing Hardy's hypothesis; his study was instead directed at disproving the normal backwardation theory of Keynes and Hicks.

[15] Paul H. Cootner, "Returns to Speculators: Telser versus Keynes," *Journal of Political Economy,* no. 4a, August 1960, vol. LXVIII. See also Cootner's "Rejoinder" to Telser's "Reply," in the same issue. A recent piece of evidence supporting the Hicks-Keynes position was reported by Eric C. Chang, "Returns to Speculators and the Theory of Normal Backwardation," *Journal of Finance,* March 1985, vol. 40, no. 1, pp. 193–208.

$$fp_{t_2} \leq fp_{t_1} + C(t_2 - t_1) \tag{22-5}$$

The time period subscript t_2 is assumed to occur further in the future than time subscript t_1 so that $t_2 > t_1$. Thus, the quantity $(t_2 - t_1)$ measures the time difference between the expiration dates of the two futures contracts.

If inequality (22-5) was ever violated (namely, if it were reversed), profit-seekers would quickly and profitably restore its integrity by simultaneously performing the following transactions at the instant the violation is observed (some time before t_1). (1) Take a long position in the futures contract for delivery at time period t_1. (2) Take a short position in the contract for delivery at time t_2. (3) Take delivery at time t_1 at price fp_1 and store the commodity for C cents per month per bushel (or barrel, or pound, or whatever is appropriate). (4) At time t_2 deliver the stored commodity at a price of fp_2 to reap a certain profit. (5) Keep doing this transaction for as many times as you can because you will earn a riskless profit until such time as inequality (22-5) is restored. Actually, this five-step arbitrage process is such an easy "money pump" that Eq. (22-5) is not frequently violated.

22-3.5 one-period futures returns and margins

The one-period rate of return from purchasing a futures contract in period t and selling it in period $t + 1$ is defined in Eq. (22-6). Essentially, the rate of return is the rate of price fluctuation. The price of the futures contract in period t is denoted p_t.

$$r_t = \frac{p_{t+1} - p_t}{p_t} \tag{22-6}$$

$$= \frac{\text{net income or loss from price change}}{\text{invested cash capital (that is, 100\% margin)}}$$

Equation (22-6) ignores the broker's commission; commissions should be deducted from the numerator to reduce the holding period return.[16]

Speculators buy and sell futures contracts with the hope of profiting from price changes. They usually never hold a futures contract long enough for the delivery date to arrive. Instead, they trade contracts actively and only make small down payments, called the initial (or original) *margin*, to bind their purchase or sales agreements.[17] Margin requirements are set and enforced by

[16]Dusak defines the return as in Eq. (22-6); Katherine Dusak, "Futures Trading and Investor Returns: An Investigation of Commodity Market Risk Premiums," *Journal of Political Economy*, December 1973, pp. 1387–1406. Fischer Black, in contrast, argues that it is not possible to define the rate of return for a highly leveraged futures contract in "The Pricing of Commodity Contracts," *Journal of Financial Economics*, January 1976. Returns on margined futures contracts are defined by Zvi Bodie and Victor Rosansky, "Risk and Return in Commodity Futures," *Financial Analysts Journal*, May–June 1980, pp. 38–39. Professor Lester Telser argues that margins affect the rates of return but does not explicitly show how he thinks they should be measured. L. Telser, "Margins and Futures Contracts," *Journal of Futures Markets*, 1981, vol. 11, no. 2.

[17] Commodity brokerages define a client's margin to be equal to the equity value in the client's account. The equity equals the sum of the following amounts: (1) cash, (2) cashlike securities (namely, U.S. Treasury bills which are left on deposit at the broker's office), and (3) the net total of the unrealized gains on open positions less the unrealized losses (that is, net "paper profits," which may be positive or negative).

the commodity exchanges to accomplish several objectives. First, margin requirements are supposed to help maintain the integrity of futures contracts and futures traders by limiting their risk exposure. Second, margins are supposed to control the pyramiding of debt which could contribute to a market crash.

All major commodity exchanges in the United States require purchasers or short sellers of futures contracts to put up margin money to guarantee that they perform as contracted. *Initial margin* requirements of 5 and 10 percent are common.[18] The initial margin is like a down payment that is supposed to be sufficient to guarantee payment by the speculator unless the margined commodity's price falls by more than the maintenance margin on a long position (or rises by more than the maintenance margin on a short position). If adverse price fluctuations decrease the value of the trader's initial margin too much, then the trader receives a margin call to put up additional margin money which is called the maintenance (or variation) margin.

Maintenance margin or *variation margin* requirements are additional amounts of guarantee money that margin traders may be required to pay to their brokerage to ensure their performance of the futures contract if the price of the commodity fluctuates adversely. For example, if a speculator buys a futures contract long on 5 percent initial margin and then the commodity's price falls 5 percent, the speculator's original margin is completely wiped out. In this case the broker will ask the speculator to put up some maintenance margin money. If the speculator does not quickly put up the maintenance margin money, the broker will liquidate the futures contract being held as collateral on the 95 percent loan granted the speculator to buy the contract. In order to avoid the losses and ill feelings that can result from a *margin call,* the clearing house requires the broker to do what is called "mark to the market." Then, the broker will, in turn, force the speculator to "mark to the market." A futures trader or futures brokerage firm is said to *mark to the market* when they pay the additional margin money, called the maintenance margin, to keep from having a futures position liquidated to pay off margin debt.[19]

Varying the use of margins changes futures traders' financial leverage and risk. Equation (22-6) is rewritten as Eq. (22-7) to show mr_t, the one-period rate of return to a margined buyer of a long position when the initial margin is the fraction, $0 < m < 1.0$, of the purchase price.

$$mr_t = \frac{p_{t+1} - p_t}{p_t m_t} \tag{22-7}$$

The variability of return, or risk, in margin trading increases, as shown by Eq. (22-8), as the margin decreases. The r_t term was defined in Eq. (22-6).[20]

[18] Note that commodity futures margins are much lower than the common stock margin requirements set by the Federal Reserve Board. Common stock margin requirements were 55 percent while futures margins were 5 to 10 percent for initial margins in 1985, for instance.

[19] Maintenance margins are approximately 75 percent of the initial margins at most commodity brokerage firms; however, this relationship varies from broker to broker. In any event, any time the customer's equity falls below the required maintenance margin, the customer receives a margin call. Margins are discussed more fully in Thomas A. Hieronymus, *Economics of Futures Trading,* Commodity Research Bureau Inc., New York, chap. 3, p. 63—a detailed numerical example of how maintenance margins are calculated.

[20] See Mathematical App. B, Theorem B-2, for proof of Eq. (22-8).

$$\text{var}(mr_t) = \left(\frac{1}{m_t}\right)^2 \text{var}(r_t) \tag{22-8}$$

Equation (22-8) shows that trading on ($m = .1 =$) 10 percent margin increases the margined trader's variance of return $[(1/m)^2 = (1/.1)^2] = 100$ times larger than the nonmargin trader's. Clearly, margin trading can be breathtaking.

22-3.6 using T-bills to meet margin requirements

Clients of most commodity brokerages are allowed to give the brokerage either cash or an interest-bearing U.S. Treasury bill or some combination of both to meet their margin requirement. This is good for the client and bad for the brokerage. It is bad for the brokerage because the broker loses cash deposits on which no interest was being paid and in its place receives the client's T-bill which pays interest to the client rather than to the brokerage. This is good for the client because the brokerage's loss is the client's gain.

Suppose that a commodity investor buys a T-bill and asks the broker to hold it in order to meet the margin requirement. If the commodity client buys T-bills that are worth p_1 and p_2 dollars at the beginning and end of the investment period, respectively, the client has an average of $[(p_1 + p_2) / 2]$ dollars invested during that period. Equation (22-9) shows how much income the T-bill will receive during the period if the interest rate on T-bills is the riskless interest rate, denoted R.

$$\text{Interest income} = R\,[(p_1 + p_2) / 2] \tag{22-9}$$

Equation (22-9) can be combined with Eq. (22-6), as shown in Eq. (22-10). Equation (22-10) defines the total rate of return from both the interest income on the T-bill and the commodity investment for the owner of the margined commodity account; it is denoted *br*.

$$br = \frac{1}{p_t}(p_{t+1} - p_t) + R\,\frac{(p_1 + p_2)}{2} \tag{22-10}$$

A commodity investor can earn a one-period rate of return from a commodity account in three different ways; they are defined in Eqs. (22-6), (22-7), and (22-10). Equation (22-6) is for a cash (that is, it is like a 100 percent margin) account, and Eqs. (22-7) and (22-10) are appropriate for margin accounts.[21]

22-4 COMMODITY HEDGING

People who wish to limit their losses from an adverse move in commodity prices may do so by hedging. That is, hedgers "cover" themselves in anticipation of an adverse price movement so that they are not later forced to make a disadvantageous purchase or sale. Hedging is not an activity which is designated to maximize profits. Hedging results in less than maximum profits; this is the cost of averting a possible loss. *Hedging* may be defined as arranging (or synchronizing) a requirement to coincide with its fulfillment. There are basi-

[21] The mathematical relationship between the three different holding period rates of return for commodity positions is shown below.

$$1.0 + br_t = (1.0 + R_t)\,(1.0 + r_t)$$

See footnote 16 for more details about the rate of return measure.

cally three types of hedges: the so-called "perfect" hedge, a buying hedge, and a selling hedge.

22-4.1 the so-called perfect commodity hedge

Someone who owns identical long and short positions has a position that is sometimes called a *perfectly hedged position* or *perfectly hedged portfolio*.[22] The owner of a perfectly hedged position has contracted to buy and to sell the same goods at the same price at the same time. Thus, future price fluctuations cannot affect holders of a perfect hedge. The owner of a perfectly hedged position is contractually bound to a zero profit and zero loss situation.

For an example of what might be called a perfectly hedged position, consider a hypothetical silverware manufacturer. Suppose that as of July 198X this silversmith owns a futures contract that obligates her to take delivery on 10,000 ounces (one contract) of silver in July 198X. Stated differently, the silverware manufacturer is long silver futures to guarantee that needed raw materials will be supplied. Further suppose that our hypothetical silversmith is also obligated by another futures contract to sell 10,000 ounces of silver in July 198X; she is now short physical silver. This manufacturer is perfectly hedged against changes in the level of silver prices and also is assured of needed supply. In effect, a perfectly hedged position is like having no position or holding cash until such time as the hedge is lifted. Before July 198X, the silverware manufacturer can lift the hedge by taking delivery of the silver needed to produce the firm's product and buying back the July 198X futures contract. If the price level of silver has changed, the profits on one position will be exactly offset by the losses on the other position, and so the silverware manufacturer can neither suffer losses nor enjoy gains from the price change in silver bullion.[23]

Figure 22-5 illustrates the profit from a long and a short position which offset each other to form a perfect hedge.

[22] No commodity futures hedge is a truly perfect hedge. Unavoidable risks called "basis risks" introduce small elements of risk into every commodities hedge. These "basis risks" are explained later in this section, after the concept of the so-called perfect hedge is introduced. Perfect and imperfect hedges are analyzed graphically in Sec. 21-2, starting at page 596.

Discussions of a perfectly hedged options position may be interpreted to refer to an option hedge ratio of unity, as explained in Sec. 21-5 beginning at page 612.

[23] If the silver manufacturer negotiated a sales contract that tied the delivery prices of the finished silverware advantageously above the market price of the raw silver bullion, then the manufacturer has also "locked in" profits and "locked out" price fluctuation risks.

FIGURE 22-5 profit graphs of *(a)* long position, *(b)* short position, and *(c)* perfect hedge.

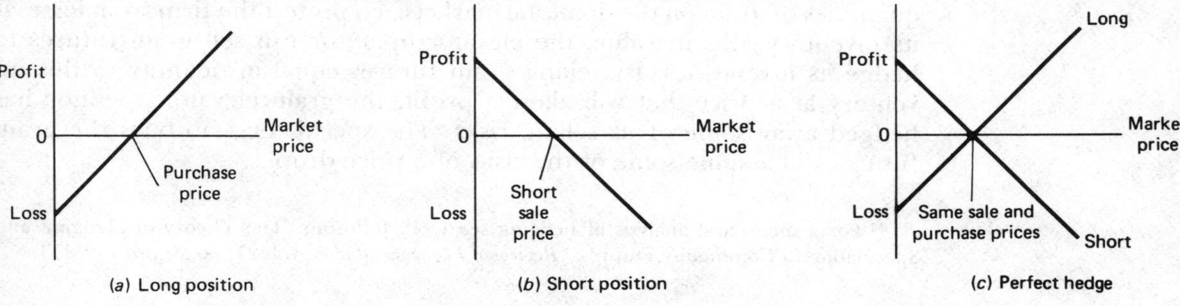

22-4.2 buying hedges

A *buying hedge* is a purchase of futures to protect against price rises. Many people call a buying hedge a *long hedge,* because the hedger is long the futures contract. Breakfast cereal manufacturers who buy grain commodities, shoe manufacturers who buy hides, and other commodity users frequently use buying hedges to protect themselves from price fluctuations in the commodities that are their raw material. For example, consider the plight of a manufacturer of breakfast cereals who has contracted to deliver fixed quantities of breakfast cereals to supermarkets at a fixed price every month for a year. Essentially, this cereal manufacturer has contracted to be short physical cereal. If the price of the grain used to manufacture the cereal rises above the price for which the cereal manufacturer has contracted to sell it, the cereal manufacturer would be legally obligated to perform under a contract that entailed losses and perhaps even resulted in bankruptcy. To be free of this risk, the cereal manufacturer need only buy grain futures providing for delivery of the quantity of grain needed to fill the orders at a cost which allows a margin for profit. The cereal manufacturer has thus hedged away the buying risks and can earn the profit needed to survive by concentrating on *manufacturing* cereal efficiently. The speculator who sells the grain futures contract to the cereal manufacturer will bear all the risks of an increase in the price of the grain.

Hedging reduces both potential losses and, unfortunately, potential profits. To see how a hedger's profits are reduced, consider what happens if the price of the hedged commodity falls. If the price of a commodity drops, a hedged buyer (like the cereal manufacturer in the paragraph above) cannot gain from the price decline. The speculator who sold the futures contract captures the profit from a price drop or absorbs the loss from a price rise, respectively, whichever the case may be. Thus, commodity markets allow specialization of the risk-taking function. The manufacturers who use commodities may hedge away their commodity risks and concentrate on manufacturing efficiently, and the commodity speculators can concentrate on forecasting commodity prices and specialize in assuming the risks of commodity price fluctuation; thus, they perform an insurance function.[24]

22-4.3 selling hedge

A *selling hedge* (or *short hedge,* as it is also called) involves selling futures to avoid losses from possible price declines on an item carried in inventory. Commodity handlers who buy commodities in the cash markets frequently use selling hedges to protect themselves from losses in inventory values. For example, the operator of a grain elevator may own the tons of grain which are stored in the company facility. Now suppose that during the spring the elevator operator hears rumors that a foreign country is dumping large quantities of grain on the domestic markets. To protect the firm from losses if its inventory falls in value, the elevator operator can sell grain futures to hedge its inventories. By selling grain futures equal in quantity to this inventory at a price that will allow a profit, the grain elevator operator has hedged away some of its selling risks. The speculator who buys the grain futures will assume some of the risks of a price drop.

[24] For a theoretical analysis of hedging see L. L. Johnson, "The Theory of Hedging and Speculation in Commodity Futures," *Review of Economic Studies,* vol. 27, no. 3, pp. 139–151.

If the price of the grain in the example above rises in the future, the hedged sellers may not profit from the rising value of their inventories. A selling hedge removes some of the profit from a price rise as well as the possibility of loss from a price fall. There are many risk-averse commodity processors who prefer to earn their income from manufacturing operations rather than commodity speculation and therefore use selling hedges regularly.[25]

Consider how farmers might sell a growing crop before it is harvested to protect themselves from uncertainty. They commonly use the transaction called a selling hedge as a safeguard against losses if the market value of their crop falls. Unfortunately, hedging can also limit the hedged farmer's potential profits if the market value of the crop goes up.

Suppose, for example, a wheat producer named Mr. Brown can profitably produce at least 20,000 bushels of wheat if, at the time of planting, he is assured of a price of $4.50 per bushel. Farmer Brown expects to harvest his crop in late June, and notices that the present futures price of July wheat is $4.50 per bushel. To assure himself of this price, he decides to sell futures (that is, take a short position in the futures market) for 20,000 bushels of wheat. Assume that in June, when Mr. Brown harvests and markets his crop, the cash price of wheat has fallen to $4.25 per bushel. Since futures and cash prices converge near the contract expiration date, the futures price will also be near $4.25 per bushel. At the same time that farmer Brown sells his crop in the cash market for $4.25 per bushel, he executes a buy order in the futures market for the same price, thus canceling (or reversing) his earlier July contract committing him to delivery in July. He realizes a net gain of 25 cents

[25] All the incentive to hedge is not subsumed under the aegis of risk-aversion. Many hedges are profitable—in addition to reducing the risk from an adverse price fluctuation. However, since risk-aversion is the central purpose of most hedging activity, the profits to be gained from hedges are not discussed here for the sake of expedition.

TABLE 22-3 advantageous selling hedge

in cash market		in futures market		farmer's action
October 1, 19X1		October 1, 19X1		Lays down hedge
Expected harvest:	20,000 bu	Sells:	20,000 bu July futures	
Expected price: (at harvest)	$4.50/bu	Price:	$4.50/bu	
July 1, 19X2		July 1, 19X2		Lifts hedge
Sells:	20,000 bu	Buys:	20,000 bu July futures	
Price:	$4.25/bu	Price:	$4.25/bu	
Loss:	$ .25/bu	Gain:	$ .25/bu	

Hedged position: No net gain or loss from expected price of $4.50 per bushel because cash losses equal future gains.

per bushel on his futures transactions while the cash market value of wheat was 25 cents per bushel less than the price upon which he based his planting plans. Excluding the brokerage commissions, the three transactions (the cash sales and the two futures contracts) have the net result that farmer Brown receives the $4.50 per bushel he anticipated. This is all summarized in Table 22-3. Note that if farmer Brown had not hedged his harvest against a price change, he would have lost 25 cents per bushel. Unfortunately, not all hedges are profitable; some only neutralize risk, at best.

22-4.4 disadvantageous selling hedge

While a well-constructed hedge should always lessen the hedger's risk exposure, few if any hedges are able to totally eliminate all risks. For example, farmer Brown's hedge, shown in Table 22-3, might not have worked out quite so advantageously. If the cash price increases during the production season, as in the similar example shown in Table 22-4, then farmer Brown would be worse off than if he had not hedged. The important point is that the farmer has, within fairly narrow limits, protected himself from *downside* price risk by hedging some fraction of his anticipated crop at the time it was planted.

If farmer Brown had not hedged in the rising market example shown in Table 22-4, he would have made 25 cents per bushel additional profit. On 20,000 bushels, the possible $5000 profit was lost because of the disadvantageous hedge.

22-4.5 reversing or unwinding a position

In both the advantageous and the disadvantageous examples of a selling hedge above, our wheat farmer, Mr. Brown, lifted the hedge with a *reversing trade*. That is, farmer Brown purchased another July wheat futures which was as *similar as could be obtained* to the one which was originally sold. Figure 22-4 illustrates a series of futures trades which might represent the wheat contract's life. In spite of the fact that the selling hedge may reduce farmer Brown's risk-exposure to price declines, there are other risks which are still inherent in every hedge. These risks, called *basis risks*, are listed and defined

TABLE 22-4 disadvantageous selling hedge

in cash market		in futures market		farmer's action
October 1, 19X1		October 1, 19X1		Lays down hedge
Expected harvest:	20,000 bu	Sells:	20,000 bu July futures	
Expected price: (at harvest)	$4.50/bu	Price:	$4.50/bu	
July 1, 19X2		July 1, 19X2		Lifts hedge
Sells:	20,000 bu	Buys:	20,000 bu July futures	
Price:	$4.75/bu	Price:	$4.75/bu	
Gain:	$ .25/bu	Loss:	$ .25/bu	

Hedged position: No net gain or loss from expected price of $4.50 per bushel because cash losses equal future gains.

below. As a result of any of these four different basis risks, a commodity's basis may become larger (or smaller) rather than remain constant. If the basis changes, the hedger can suffer losses (or reap gains) of a few cents per bushel. These losses (or gains) can be substantial over a position of several units (that is, tens of thousands of bushels of grain, for example).

1. *Quantity risk.* The unit of measurement used in a futures contract may not correspond to the amount of commodity that has to be hedged. Since the futures contracts are all uniform and cannot be tailor-made, the hedged quantities may not always correspond exactly. As a result, any unhedged quantity is exposed to risk.
2. *Quality risk.* An undesirable grade of the commodity may be all that is available for sale in the future market. If so, the party who sold the futures contract will deliver the undesirable grade and be forced to pay a penalty fee to the buyer. Nevertheless, the satisfactory grade of the desired commodity may be unavailable at any price. This possibility could cause the buyer who received the unsatisfactory grade of the commodity considerable expense.
3. *Location risk.* The only futures contracts which are available to be purchased may provide for delivery at an undesirable location. Thus, the buyer could incur unexpected shipping costs that contribute to basis risk.
4. *Expiration date risk.* A futures contract that offers delivery in the month the goods are needed may not exist. For instance, reconsider the example of farmer Brown's July wheat contract from a few paragraphs above. In this case, if a July wheat contract was nonexistent, the wheat farmer would be forced to buy a wheat contract for delivery in the nearest possible month to July. Such a contract might sell at a significantly different price than the desired contract. This price difference is a source of basis risk.

As a result of the four types of basis risks listed above, the perfect hedge is in fact a rarity. The truth is that hedging will reduce the large risks associated with a price-level change but will not always eliminate the four basis risks described above. In fact, the basis risks can be so substantial that some speculators earn their livings by doing what is called *trading on the basis risks.* Of course, the unskilled speculators can also go bankrupt at trading on the basis.

22-5 INFORMATION FOR COMMODITY SPECULATORS AND INVESTORS

Having current information that is accurate can mean the difference between gains or losses to active investors and speculators.[26] Therefore, let us consider some sources of commodity information.

22-5.1 sources of information

Spot and futures prices are largely determined by supply and demand expectations. Since demand is fairly steady, it is usually not too difficult to forecast. Forecasting commodity supplies is more difficult and requires accurate, up-

[26] Michael Gorham, "Public and Private Sector Information in Agricultural Commodity Markets," *Economic Review,* San Francisco Federal Reserve Bank, Spring 1978. Copies of this study of the determinants of grain prices are available free upon request from the bank's research department.

to-date information. In particular, profitable speculation in commodities requires information about inventories held in storage, current harvests, exports and imports, and any changes in the government's policies which will affect supply. The main sources of commodity information are listed below.

GOVERNMENT REPORTS The U.S. Department of Agriculture (USDA) issues periodic crop reports and news bulletins for farm commodities. These reports are released to the public and are quite accurate. The USDA also gathers and publishes information from U.S. embassies abroad about the commodity situation in foreign lands. These foreign agriculture bulletins are typically more accurate than official commodity reports issued by the foreign governments themselves.[27]

The agricultural information disseminated publicly by some foreign governments is sometimes untrue and self-serving. For instance, consider a hypothetical South American country whose main export is coffee. If this hypothetical country experiences a bumper coffee crop one year, that country's government might be tempted to tell public lies and announce to foreign newspapers (in the United States, to make this example more specific) that the coffee crop was expected to be small. The hypothetical country's lies might drive up the price of coffee and help that country's balance of trade and its balance of payments. United States government agricultural reports are more believable and unbiased.

SITUATION REPORTS Various magazines discuss the major price-making influences in specific commodities. For example, two of the many situation reports are *The Poultry and Egg Situation* and *The Wheat Situation*. Situation reports are available for every major commodity; they discuss any issue which might affect prices. Since there are so many factors to consider in commodity speculating, most speculators specialize in contracts for only a few commodities. Such speculators would subscribe to the situation reports about the commodities in which they specialize.

COMMODITY RESEARCH ORGANIZATIONS Some research companies publish newsletters, price analyses, supply and demand statistics, and analyses of current news, and some even publish buy and sell recommendations about commodities. The Commodity Research Bureau in New York City is the largest of these services. However, there are many other commodity advisory services.

BROKERAGE HOUSES Most brokerage houses which handle commodity trading have commodity research departments which issue free newsletters to customers.

[27] G. Gunnelson, W. D. Dobson, and S. Pamperin, "Analysis of the Accuracy of USDA Forecasts," *American Journal of Agricultural Economics,* November 1972. For a review of the price determining factors for all the major commodities, see Perry J. Kaufman, *Handbook of Futures Markets,* a Wiley-Interscience Publication, John Wiley and Sons, New York, 1984. A commodity information company that sells subscriptions for up-to-the-minute price graphs is Commodity Perspective, Suite 1200, 30 South Wacker Drive, Chicago, Ill. 60606.

NEWSPAPERS *The Journal of Commerce* has what many people consider to be the best newspaper coverage of commodity market developments; it has an entire section devoted to commodities. *The New York Times* and *The Wall Street Journal* publish valuable commodity news, too.

22-5.2 important news items

In reading these various sources of information, the commodity speculator should watch for news about factors which can influence commodity prices. The major news items which affect these prices are cited in the following paragraphs.

CHANGES IN THE U.S. GOVERNMENT'S AGRICULTURAL PROGRAM Changes in government subsidies, acreage allotments, marketing quotas, export programs, and commodity "loan" programs have a major impact on commodity prices.

INTERNATIONAL NEWS International tensions have a strong effect on prices of imported and exported commodities. Currency restrictions, war rumors, or loss of imports can touch off a wave of stockpiling which will send prices skyrocketing.

GENERAL BUSINESS CONDITIONS Commodity prices tend to rise and fall with the general price level. Moreover, the level of business activity affects both the inflation rate and the demand for some commodities.

AGRICULTURAL PRODUCTION NEWS Unusual weather in areas where a commodity is produced can cause changes in the price of the commodity. Planting crop reports should be followed closely for news of changes in the number of acres under cultivation, news of insect damage, or news of disease in the crop. Harvest reports should be compared with previous expectations to see if the supply and demand expectations upon which current prices are based were correct.

Successful speculation is based on fast and accurate information processing. After all, prices are determined by buyers' and sellers' *expectations*. Only by studying the information which shapes these expectations can speculation be profitable in the long run.

22-5.3 open interest

One of the more widely watched commodity futures statistics is called the *open interest*. Many daily newspapers publish both the commodity futures prices, as shown in Fig. 22-6, and the open interest statistics for every commodity contract, as shown in Fig. 22-7.

When a new futures contract of any kind is originated and the first contract is sold, the open interest advances from zero to one. During the early months of a contract's trading life (of 1 year for most grain commodities, for example) many contracts are opened, and the open interest soars to become thousands of contracts within a few months. Later, as the contract's delivery date nears, more positions are closed out with reversing trades. Thus, the open interest declines back to zero on the delivery date. Only about a few percent of all the futures contracts which are opened are ever actually delivered; all the rest disappear as reversing trades wipe them out. The typical pattern of a futures

Futures Prices

Open Interest Reflects Previous Trading Day.

–GRAINS AND OILSEEDS–

CORN (CBT) 5,000 bu.; cents per bu.

	Open	High	Low	Settle	Change	Lifetime High	Lifetime Low	Open Interest
Sept	....	....	....	....	....	....	....	80
Dec	284¼	284¾	282½	283¼	– 1	330	275¼	95,222
Mar85	287¾	288½	286½	287½	– ¾	325½	283¾	25,387
May	290½	292½	290	291¼	– ½	330	289¾	8,176
July	292	293½	291	292¼	....	331	291	7,701
Sept	284	284	282½	283¾	+ ¼	321½	282½	433
Dec	274	275½	273½	275½	+ 1½	295	273½	1,002
Mar86	282½	282½	282½	282½	+ ½	288	282	2

Est vol 25,500; vol Mon 23,912; open int 138,003, +685.

CORN (MCE) 1,000 bu.; cents per bu.

	Open	High	Low	Settle	Change	Lifetime High	Lifetime Low	Open Interest
Dec	284¼	285	282½	283¼	– 1	330	275¼	6,172
Mar85	287¾	288¾	286½	287½	– ¾	325¼	284	671
May	291¾	292¼	290	291¼	– ½	328	290	170
July	292¼	293¼	291	292¼	....	330	291	171
Sept	....	....	....	283¾	+ ¼	315½	285	24
Dec	275¾	275¾	274	275½	+ 1¼	290	274	103

Est vol 650; vol Mon 885; open int 7,311, +141.

OATS (CBT) 5,000 bu.; cents per bu.

	Open	High	Low	Settle	Change	Lifetime High	Lifetime Low	Open Interest
Dec	175¾	177¼	175¾	176¼	– ½	193¼	168½	3,064
Mar85	174½	175½	174½	174¾	– ¾	196½	173	1,152
May	172½	172½	172½	172½	– ½	191	171	320
July	170½	171¼	170½	171¼	+ ¼	178½	169½	143

Est vol 400; vol Mon. 352; open int 4,679, +43.

SOYBEANS (CBT) 5,000 bu.; cents per bu.

	Open	High	Low	Settle	Change	Lifetime High	Lifetime Low	Open Interest
Nov	593	599	590	597½	+ 5¾	772¼	568½	34,983
Jan85	604	609	600	608¼	+ 6½	779	580½	10,484
Mar	615	621	613	619¾	+ 4¼	790½	593½	4,890
May	626	631½	624	631	+ 5¾	797	601	1,806
July	630	635	626½	634½	+ 4¾	799	607	2,657
Aug	628	633	627	633	+ 3	756	610½	292
Sept	621	625	620	625	+ 3	667	605	147
Nov	620	623½	618	623	+ 2	660	602	930

Est vol 35,400; vol Mon 19,763; open int 56,189, +810.

SOYBEANS (MCE) 1,000 bu.; cents per bu.

	Open	High	Low	Settle	Change	Lifetime High	Lifetime Low	Open Interest
Nov	592½	599	590	597½	+ 5¾	772¼	568	11,038
Jan85	603½	609½	600	608¼	+ 6½	779	580	1,038
Mar	615	620½	614	619¾	+ 4¼	788	596	555
May	626	630	625	631	+ 5¾	796½	602	202
July	630	635	628	634½	+ 4¾	798	609	271
Aug	632	632	631	633	+ 3	672⅛	612	50
Sept	....	....	....	625	+ 3	647	624	12
Nov	621⅜	624	620	623	+ 2	660	602	68

Est vol 1,650; vol Mon 2,901; open int 13,234, –497.

SOYBEAN MEAL (CBT) 100 tons; $ per ton.

	Open	High	Low	Settle	Change	Lifetime High	Lifetime Low	Open Interest
Oct	146.00	147.00	145.20	146.90	+ .30	240.00	141.00	12,153
Dec	152.00	153.20	151.50	153.00	+ .40	227.00	148.00	19,808
Jan85	154.60	156.20	154.50	155.80	+ .40	208.00	151.30	8,244
Mar	159.50	161.00	159.00	160.20	+ .50	209.00	155.50	3,609
May	163.70	165.00	163.30	164.00	– .50	205.00	160.00	1,501
July	168.00	168.00	166.50	167.50	– .30	196.50	163.20	948
Aug	167.00	167.00	166.00	166.80	– .70	176.00	163.50	252
Sept	167.00	167.00	166.00	166.00	– .50	175.00	163.00	37
Oct	....	....	....	165.60	– .40	177.00	163.50	36

Est vol 11,000; vol Mon 10,079; open int 46,588, –1,100.

SOYBEAN OIL (CBT) 60,000 lbs.; cents per lb.

	Open	High	Low	Settle	Change	Lifetime High	Lifetime Low	Open Interest
Sept	....	....	....	....	....	....	....	23
Oct	25.00	25.28	25.00	25.28	+ .21	33.05	23.50	14,390
Dec	24.15	24.52	24.13	24.47	+ .24	30.90	22.74	16,861
Jan85	24.05	24.40	24.00	24.37	+ .27	30.50	22.85	5,468
Mar	23.95	24.13	23.85	24.15	+ .23	30.40	22.95	3,516
May	23.80	24.10	23.75	24.00	+ .25	30.10	22.80	1,567
July	23.55	23.80	23.45	23.75	+ .12	30.02	22.70	734
Aug	....	....	....	23.40	– .20	27.00	22.50	250
Sept	....	....	....	23.08	+ .14	24.75	22.50	67
Oct	....	....	....	22.75	....	26.00	22.00	50

Est vol 10,500; vol Mon 11,285; open int 42,926, –513.

WHEAT (CBT) 5,000 bu.; cents per bu.

	Open	High	Low	Settle	Change	Lifetime High	Lifetime Low	Open Interest
Sept	....	....	....	....	....	....	....	1
Dec	352	352½	350½	350¾	– 1¾	418	337½	26,963
Mar85	357½	359	357	357½	– ¾	404	344	9,750
May	355	356½	355	355	– ¾	405	350	3,569
July	340	340¾	339½	339¾	– 1	390	335	1,500
Sept	....	....	....	343½	– 1	376½	340½	83
Dec	355½	355½	355½	355½	– ½	356	355½	1

Est vol 6,300; vol Mon 5,947; open int 41,867, –286.

WHEAT (KC) 5,000 bu.; cents per bu.

	Open	High	Low	Settle	Change	Lifetime High	Lifetime Low	Open Interest
Dec	373¾	374½	373¼	373½	– ¼	397	355	18,523
Mar85	370½	371¾	370	371	+ ¼	407½	362	9,473
May	360¼	361½	359¼	359¾	....	384½	356½	1,135
July	349½	349½	348	348	– ¼	373½	346¼	526
Sept	....	....	....	354	....	358	356¾	2

Est vol 2,879; vol Mon 305; open int 29,659, +213.

WHEAT (MPLS) 5,000 bu.; cents per bu.

	Open	High	Low	Settle	Change	Lifetime High	Lifetime Low	Open Interest
Dec	376¾	378½	376½	378¼	+ 1½	414	366½	4,361
Mar85	384¼	387	384	386¾	+ 2¾	413½	380¾	2,364
May	....	....	....	391½	+ 2½	412	386	390
July	....	....	....	386	+ 1	407	381	43

Est vol 1,436; vol Mon 1,628; open int 7,158, –93.

WHEAT (MCE) 1,000 bu.; cents per bu.

	Open	High	Low	Settle	Change	Lifetime High	Lifetime Low	Open Interest
Dec	352½	352½	350¼	350¾	– 1¾	408¾	340	5,476

	Open	High	Low	Settle	Change	Lifetime High	Lifetime Low	Open Interest
Dec	65.00	65.29	64.90	65.17	+ .21	78.40	64.43	12,109
Mar85	66.55	66.95	66.55	66.84	+ .25	79.35	66.36	5,591
May	67.65	68.00	67.65	67.90	+ .20	79.20	67.60	580
July	69.10	69.15	69.00	69.05	+ .15	79.85	68.70	728
Oct	69.50	69.50	69.50	69.55	+ .40	77.50	69.20	55
Dec	69.90	69.90	69.67	69.85	+ .10	73.00	69.67	620
Mar86	....	....	....	70.36	+ .06	70.60	70.60	6

Est vol 1,500; vol Mon 1,798; open int 20,792, –122.

ORANGE JUICE (CTN)–15,000 lbs.; cents per lb.

	Open	High	Low	Settle	Change	Lifetime High	Lifetime Low	Open Interest
Sept	....	....	....	....	....	....	....	603
Nov	181.60	181.70	180.15	181.00	– 1.35	185.65	107.50	3,125
Jan85	182.20	182.80	181.10	182.60	– .55	185.60	109.00	3,269
Mar	182.25	182.95	181.30	182.90	+ .15	185.50	118.50	1,777
May	182.10	182.80	181.60	182.80	– 1.00	185.00	151.00	974
July	182.00	182.00	182.00	183.15	+ .15	184.80	155.00	665
Sept	180.50	180.50	180.00	180.50	– .90	181.50	165.00	142
Nov	179.00	179.00	179.00	179.90	....	181.00	164.50	46

Est vol 1,500; vol Mon 2,478; open int 10,601, +167.

SUGAR–WORLD (CSCE)–112,000 lbs.; cents per lb.

	Open	High	Low	Settle	Change	Lifetime High	Lifetime Low	Open Interest
Oct	3.90	4.05	3.87	4.04	+ .03	15.30	3.80	14,330
Jan85	4.60	4.80	4.59	4.75	+ .09	13.10	4.41	1,024
Mar	5.15	5.30	5.13	5.30	+ .08	13.60	4.94	47,702
May	5.52	5.70	5.49	5.70	+ .15	10.50	5.25	9,734
July	5.82	6.05	5.81	6.05	+ .17	9.95	5.57	3,380
Sept	6.15	6.40	6.15	6.40	+ .21	9.75	5.86	274
Oct	6.30	6.55	6.30	6.54	+ .19	9.05	6.03	5,869
Jan86	6.75	6.75	6.69	6.85	+ .15	7.45	6.45	82

Est vol 13,570; vol Mon 8,483; open int 82,395, –2,253.

SUGAR–DOMESTIC (CSCE)–112,000 lbs.; cents per lb.

	Open	High	Low	Settle	Change	Lifetime High	Lifetime Low	Open Interest
Nov	21.45	21.45	21.45	21.45	– .01	22.19	21.43	1,142
Jan85	21.55	21.62	21.55	21.61	+ .07	22.20	21.54	2,104
Mar	21.80	21.80	21.76	21.79	+ .02	22.30	21.70	3,400
May	21.97	21.99	21.95	21.97	....	22.40	21.75	1,740
July	22.10	22.15	22.10	22.13	+ .03	22.43	21.85	2,064
Sept	22.10	22.10	22.10	22.10	....	22.23	21.90	1,071
Nov	21.94	21.97	21.94	21.95	– .05	22.15	21.90	1,784
Jan	22.00	22.00	22.00	22.00	+ .02	22.00	21.95	10

Est vol 413; vol Mon 610; open int 13,315, +160.

–METALS & PETROLEUM–

COPPER (CMX)–25,000 lbs.; cents per lb.

	Open	High	Low	Settle	Change	Lifetime High	Lifetime Low	Open Interest
Sept	56.20	56.20	56.00	56.05	– .40	90.80	54.95	89
Oct	56.00	56.00	56.00	56.05	– .45	61.45	56.00	50
Dec	57.50	57.70	56.90	57.35	– .40	92.70	55.90	47,933
Jan85	....	....	....	57.95	– .40	92.00	57.05	270
Mar	59.25	59.50	58.90	59.15	– .40	93.20	57.75	18,306
May	60.45	60.45	60.30	60.30	– .40	92.50	59.45	6,064
July	61.45	61.45	61.45	61.45	– .40	88.25	60.25	3,470
Sept	62.65	62.75	62.50	62.60	– .40	82.10	61.15	3,564
Dec	64.70	64.70	64.15	64.35	– .45	84.25	63.20	1,950
Jan86	....	....	....	64.90	– .45	84.20	69.50	73
Mar	66.30	66.30	66.25	66.05	– .45	80.00	64.70	695
May	....	....	....	67.15	– .45	74.00	66.20	397
July	68.50	68.60	68.50	68.25	– .45	72.55	68.50	231

Est vol 6,500; vol Mon 7,983; open int 83,092, +714.

GOLD (CMX)–100 troy oz.; $ per troy oz.

	Open	High	Low	Settle	Change	Lifetime High	Lifetime Low	Open Interest
Sept	345.50	345.50	345.50	345.70	+ .20	354.80	334.50	9
Oct	345.00	346.80	344.50	345.90	+ .10	597.00	335.50	8,272
Dec	351.20	353.30	351.20	352.40	+ .10	608.00	341.60	47,437
Feb85	357.50	359.50	357.20	358.90	+ .10	522.00	348.00	26,921
Apr	363.50	366.00	363.50	365.30	+ .20	514.50	355.00	26,644
June	371.90	371.90	371.90	372.20	+ .20	510.00	362.70	16,463
Aug	379.00	379.00	379.00	379.10	+ .20	485.00	370.00	7,750
Oct	....	....	....	386.30	+ .20	493.00	377.00	3,321
Dec	393.40	393.40	393.00	393.80	+ .20	489.50	383.90	5,476
Feb86	401.00	401.00	401.00	401.60	+ .20	485.50	392.00	3,710
Apr	....	....	....	409.40	+ .20	496.80	401.80	2,123
June	....	....	....	417.90	+ .20	433.50	407.00	504

Est vol 23,000; vol Mon 36,834; open int 148,630, +467.

PLATINUM (NYM)–50 troy oz.; $ per troy oz.

	Open	High	Low	Settle	Change	Lifetime High	Lifetime Low	Open Interest
Sept	....	....	....	324.50	+ 2.80	356.00	320.50	0
Oct	322.00	326.00	321.50	325.20	+ 2.60	463.00	316.50	4,980
Dec	....	....	....	330.70	+ 2.60	337.50	332.00	2
Jan85	330.70	335.00	330.50	334.40	+ 2.70	447.00	325.00	7,273

	Open	High	Low	Settle	Change	Lifetime High	Lifetime Low	Open Interest
Nov	126.20	129.20	125.30	127.30	+ 1.50	229.00	120.20	4,314
Jan85	137.00	139.00	135.50	137.70	+ 1.70	221.30	130.30	1,913
Mar	147.50	149.30	146.30	147.90	+ 1.20	220.40	139.30	965
May	156.30	157.70	155.30	156.10	+ .40	225.00	147.40	258
July	165.00	166.20	164.50	166.00	+ .50	230.50	153.00	284
Sept	170.60	171.70	170.50	171.10	+ .80	197.50	157.50	200
Nov	173.60	174.60	173.60	174.00	....	186.10	167.30	66
Jan86	....	....	....	181.50	....	182.00	176.50	13

Est vol 3,154; vol Mon 2,023; open int 8,020, –147.

–FINANCIAL–

BRITISH POUND (IMM)–25,000 pounds; $ per pound

	Open	High	Low	Settle	Change	Lifetime High	Lifetime Low	Open Interest
Dec	1.2345	1.2405	1.2330	1.2375	– .0085	1.5100	1.2145	16,483
Mar85	1.2400	1.2445	1.2360	1.2405	– .0090	1.5170	1.2155	598
June	....	....	....	1.2440	– .0095	1.3050	1.2240	26
Sept	....	....	....	1.2490	– .0095	1.2735	1.2450	7

Est vol 4,951; vol Mon 7,005; open int 17,114, +898.

CANADIAN DOLLAR (IMM)–100,000 dlrs.; $ per Can $

	Open	High	Low	Settle	Change	Lifetime High	Lifetime Low	Open Interest
Dec	.7584	.7584	.7574	.7580	–.0003	.8048	.7451	5,264
Mar85	.7577	.7577	.7550	.7573	–.0005	.8050	.7443	1,364
June	.7574	.7574	.7574	.7573	–.0005	.7835	.7483	185

Est vol 569; vol Mon 1,093; open int 6,813, –27.

JAPANESE YEN (IMM) 12.5 million yen; $ per yen (.00)

	Open	High	Low	Settle	Change	Lifetime High	Lifetime Low	Open Interest
Dec	.4111	.4118	.4108	.4114	–.0019	.4663	.4074	17,362
Mar85	.4175	.4175	.4165	.4167	–.0019	.4695	.4133	598
June	.4225	.4230	.4218	.4230	–.0019	.4570	.4205	107
Dec		....	....	.4355	–.0019	.4483	.4370	3

Est vol 5,546; vol Mon 10,268; open int 18,070, –81.

SWISS FRANC (IMM)–125,000 francs-$ per franc

	Open	High	Low	Settle	Change	Lifetime High	Lifetime Low	Open Interest
Dec	.4008	.4033	.4008	.4031	–.0021	.5000	.3938	18,290
Mar85	.4078	.4098	.4073	.4096	–.0021	.5035	.3995	496
June	.4160	.4160	.4145	.4160	–.0021	.4900	.4102	58
Sept	.4200	.4215	.4195	.4215	–.0020	.4830	.4175	11
Dec	.4275	.4280	.4260	.4280	new	.4280	.4260	0

Est vol 12,693; vol Mon 16,967; open int 18,855, –1,372.

W. GERMAN MARK (IMM)–125,000 marks; $ per mark

	Open	High	Low	Settle	Change	Lifetime High	Lifetime Low	Open Interest
Dec	.3305	.3313	.3289	.3303	–.0042	.4080	.3204	34,422
Mar85	.3355	.3355	.3333	.3348	–.0043	.4110	.3244	1,241
June	.3400	.3405	.3395	.3401	–.0044	.3710	.3338	86
Sept		....	....	.3460	–.0045	.3460	.3424	1

Est vol 20,795; vol Mon 30,633; open int 35,750, –1,191.

EURODOLLAR (LIFFE)–$1 million; pts of 100%

	Open	High	Low	Settle	Change	Lifetime High	Lifetime Low	Open Interest
Dec	88.61	88.76	88.59	88.74	+ .07	89.36	85.92	5,767
Mar85	88.33	88.48	88.32	88.46	+ .03	88.85	85.49	3,014
June	88.06	88.25	88.03	88.19	+ .02	88.58	85.66	1,512
Sept		....	....	87.97	+ .02	88.39	85.50	424

Est vol 3,803; vol Mon 3,631; open int 10,717, +151.

STERLING DEPOSIT (LIFFE)–£250,000; pts of 100%

	Open	High	Low	Settle	Change	Lifetime High	Lifetime Low	Open Interest
Dec	89.65	89.71	89.59	89.71	– .01	90.91	88.13	3,147
Mar85	89.61	89.67	89.60	89.70	– .02	90.86	87.85	1,456
June	89.49	89.59	89.47	89.55	– .05	90.60	87.94	457

Est vol 986; vol Mon 1,017; open int 5,108, –87.

LONG GILT (LIFFE)–£50,000; pts of 100%

	Open	High	Low	Settle	Change	Lifetime High	Lifetime Low	Open Interest
Sept	106-16	107-05	106-14	107-05	+ 0-15	109-12	97-27	617
Dec	105-28	106-18	105-22	106-17	+ 0-16	108-31	97-06	1,990
Mar85		....	....	105-28	+ 0-15	108-19	96-21	41
June	105-06	105-06	105-06	105-25	+ 0-15	105-26	96-17	101
Sept		....	....	108-28	+ 0-15	101-01	99-00	0

Est vol 2,929; vol Mon 1,802; open int 2,749, +39.

EURODOLLAR (IMM)–$1 million; pts of 100%

	Open	High	Low	Settle	Chg	Yield Settle	Yield Chg	Open Interest
Dec	88.39	88.48	88.36	88.37	– .03	11.63	+ .03	40,406
Mar85	88.11	88.21	88.07	88.09	– .04	11.91	+ .04	22,035
June	87.92	87.92	87.76	87.77	– .07	12.23	+ .07	11,157
Sept	87.62	87.65	87.51	87.51	– .07	12.49	+ .07	3,174
Dec	87.38	87.41	87.27	87.27	– .06	12.73	+ .06	1,994
Mar86	87.19	87.20	87.06	87.07	– .05	12.93	+ .05	209
June	86.95	87.00	86.88	86.90	– .04	13.10	+ .04	11

Est vol 17,965; vol Mon 19,000; open int 78,985, +202.

GNMA 8% (CBT)–$100,000 prncpl; pts. 32nds. of 100%

	Open	High	Low	Settle	Chg	Yield Settle	Yield Chg	Open Interest
Sept	....	....	....	....	....	....	....	159
Dec	67-08	67-14	66-29	66-31	– 7	13.846	+ .052	7,725
Mar85	66-15	66-20	66-05	66-06	– 7	14.034	+ .053	2,260
June	65-25	65-25	65-14	65-14	– 8	14.218	+ .062	679
Sept	....	....	....	64-27	– 9	14.365	+ .070	196
Dec	64-25	64-25	64-10	64-10	– 9	14.499	+ .071	310
Mar86	64-09	64-09	63-27	63-27	– 9	14.619	+ .072	344
June	63-27	63-27	63-15	63-15	– 9	14.715	+ .072	522

Est vol 2,500; vol Mon 2,169; open int 12,195, +45.

TREASURY BONDS (CBT)–$100,000; pts. 32nds of 100%

	Open	High	Low	Settle	Chg	Yield Settle	Yield Chg	Open Interest
Sept	....	....	....	....	....	....	....	18,092
Dec	67-13	67-21	66-30	66-30	– 12	12.547	+ .071	134,655
Mar85	66-25	67-02	66-11	66-12	– 12	12.655	+ .072	22,388
June	66-11	66-18	65-28	65-28	– 12	12.753	+ .073	6,734
Sept	65-27	65-28	65-15	65-15	– 12	12.833	+ .074	6,001
Dec	65-15	65-25	65-03	65-03	– 13	12.908	+ .081	7,721
Mar86	65-11	65-14	64-25	64-25	– 13	12.971	+ .082	6,482

CBT–Chicago Board of Trade; CME–Chicago Mercantile Exchange; CMX–Commodity Exchange, New York; CRCE–Chicago Rice & Cotton Exchange; CSCE–Coffee, Sugar & Cocoa Exchange, New York; CTN–New York Cotton Exchange; IMM–International Monetary Market at CME, Chicago; KC–Kansas City Board of Trade; LIFFE–London International Financial Futures Exchange; MCE–MidAmerica Commodity Exchange; MPLS–Minneapolis Grain Exchange; NYFE–New York Futures Exchange, unit of New York Stock Exchange. NYM–New York Mercantile Exchange; WPG–Winnipeg Commodity Exchange.

FIGURE 22-6 futures price quotations from hypothetical newspaper.

Open Interest

Wednesday, August 30
(Changes from Tuesday)

WHEAT (CBT): Sept. 5,278, Dec. 23,196, March'79, 8,842, May 7,297, July 2,166, Sept. 10. Total: 46,789, down 459. **CORN**: Sept. 10,415, Dec. 59,230, March'79, 25,692, May 10,426, July 3,507, Sept. 172. Total: 109,442, down 2,710. **OATS**: Sept. 1,060, Dec. 5,254, March'79, 1,033, May 923, July 6. Total: 8,276, up 150. **SOYBEANS**: Aug. 1, Sept. 6,271, Nov. 35,983, Jan.'79, 18,574, March 17,172, May 12,922, July 6,070, Aug. 834. Total: 97,827, up 493. **SOYBEAN MEAL**: Sept. 4,441, Oct. 12,111, Dec. 18,882, Jan.'79, 9,439, March 6,719, May 3,464, July 1,067, Aug. 112. Total: 56,235, down 567. **SOYBEAN OIL**: Sept. 6,654, Oct. 9,089, Dec. 18,084, Jan.'79, 4,891, March 4,610, May 3,733, July 2,266, Aug. 433. Total: 49,760, down 418. **BROILERS**: Sept. 446, Oct. 627, Nov. 689, Dec. 260, Jan.'79, 252. Total: 2,274, down 34. **PLYWOOD**: Sept. 1,[illegible], Nov. 2,159, Jan.'79, 1,288, March 490, May 628, July 45, Sept. 15. Total: 6,527, down 166. **GNMA**: Sept. 2,[illegible], Dec. 8,643, March'79, 7,234, June 5,924, Sept. 3,225, Dec. 3,518, March'80, 2,753, June 3,341, Sept. 2,329, Dec. 2,[illegible], March'81, 1,556. Total: 43,362, down 558. **TREASURY BONDS**: Sept. 2,382, Dec. 3,176, March'79, 1,395, June 1,[illegible], Sept. 1,308, Dec. 870, March'80, 450, June 444, Sept. 521, Dec. 359, March'81, 328. Total: 12,312, down 209.

CATTLE: Aug. 13, Oct. 24,434, Dec. 2,903, Jan.'79, 1,[illegible], Feb. 14,676, April 10,611, June 8,524, Aug. 2,503, Oct. 1,[illegible], Dec. 348. Total: 85,080, up 1,264. **FEEDER CATTLE**: Aug. 8, Sept. 1,620, Oct. 4,565, Nov. 3,703, Jan.'79, 1,817, March 2,517, April 2,108, May 2,223, Aug. 48. Total: 28,609, down 498. **EGGS**: Sept. 671, Oct. 94, Nov. 112, Dec. 390, Jan.'79, 14, Feb. 9. Total: 1,290, down 91. **HOGS**: Aug. 7, Oct. 5,442, Dec. 5,486, Feb.'79, 2,361, April 1,863, June 633, July 299, Aug. 139, Oct. 86, Dec. 5. Total: 16,321, down 97. **FROZEN PORK BELLIES**: Aug. 16, Feb.'79, 5,805, March 1,281, May 259, July 125, Aug. 104. Total: 7,590, up 88. **LUMBER**: Sept. 2,579, Nov. 2,692, Jan.'79, 1,685, March 749, May 309, July 18. Total: 8,032, down 48. **TREASURY BILLS**: Sept. 2,901, Dec. 5,257, March'79, 4,817, June 5,174, Sept. 4,714, Dec. 5,298, March'80, 3,550, June 2,590. Total: 34,301, up 781.

MAINE POTATOES: Nov. 2,241, March'79, 2,305, April 558, May 6,417. Total: 11,521, down 43. **COCOA**: Sept. 299, Dec. 2,516, March'79, 1,368, May 640, July 264, Sept. 125, Dec. 196. Total: 5,408, up 208. **WORLD SUGAR NO. 11**: Sept. 1,139, Oct. 10,840, Jan.'79, 117, March 14,205, May 4,323, July 1,562, Sept. 831, Oct. 1,188. Total: 34,205, up 100. **COFFEE**: Sept. 294, Dec. 1,687, March'79, 1,085, May 469, July 253, Sept. 57, Dec. 55. Total: 3,900, down 2. **COTTON**: Oct. 3,588, Dec. 20,915, March'79, 6,822, May 1,345, July 460, Oct. 110, Dec. 628. Total: 33,868, up 475. **ORANGE JUICE**: Sept. 2,097, Nov. 3,972, Jan.'79, 4,098, March 1,959, May 1,145, July 296, Sept. 185, Jan.'80, 13. Total: 31,765, down 178. **COPPER**: Sept. 1,007, Oct. 13, Dec. 26,274, Jan.'79, 898, March 9,115, May 3,690, July 3,808, Sept. 1,980, Dec. 2,499, Jan.'80, 666, March 717, May 241. Total: 50,864, down 2,387. **GOLD (CMX)**: Sept. 31, Oct. 3,002, Dec. 24,207, Feb.'79, 7,452, April 8,798, June 6,822, Aug. 4,996, Oct. 2,493, Dec. 4,865, Feb.'80, 1,267, April 1,221, June 272. Total: 65,426, up 412. **GOLD (IMM)**: Sept. 4,690, Dec. 17,064, March'79, 14,221, June 19,138, Sept. 13,763, Dec. 5,589, March'80, 2,514, June 6. Total: 76,985, up 273. **GOLD (WPG)**: Oct. 118, Jan.'89, 118, April 34, July 7, Oct. 10. Total: 287, up 14. **SILVER (CMX)**: Sept. 1,390, Oct. 7, Dec. 22,463, Jan.'79, 13,432, March 28,942, May 28,907, July 27,926, Sept. 32,665, Dec. 31,339, Jan.'80, 12,571, March 10,837, May 2,517. Total: 212,996, down 1,828. **SILVER (CBT)**: Aug. 18, Sept. 28, Oct. 8,069, Nov. 1, Dec. 12,729, Feb.'79, 24,790, April 46,464, June 37,850, Aug. 35,954, Oct. 23,570, Dec. 13,030, Feb.'80, 8,719, April 5,841, June 5,369, Aug. 3,064, Oct. 509, Dec. 321, Feb. 6. Total: 226,332, down 293.

FIGURE 22-7 statistics on open interest from a hypothetical newspaper.

contract's lifetime open interest is shown in Fig. 22-8*a* for several grain contracts.

Figure 22-8*b* illustrates the average volume of contracts traded per month for the same three grain contracts shown in Fig. 22-8*a*. Note that there is a high positive correlation between the monthly average open interest and the monthly average volume of contracts traded for any specific commodity

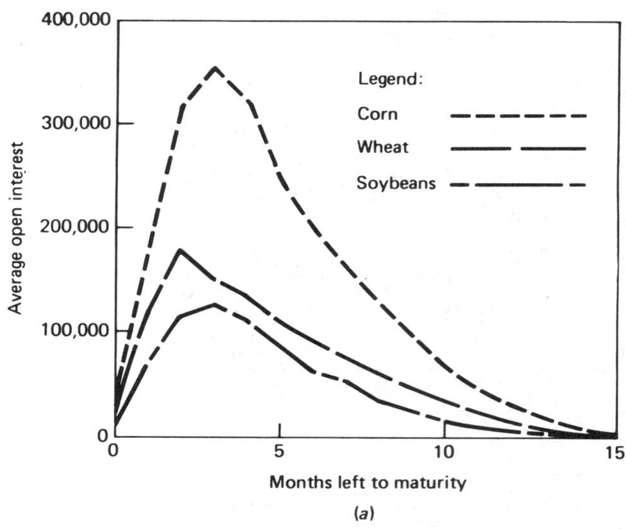

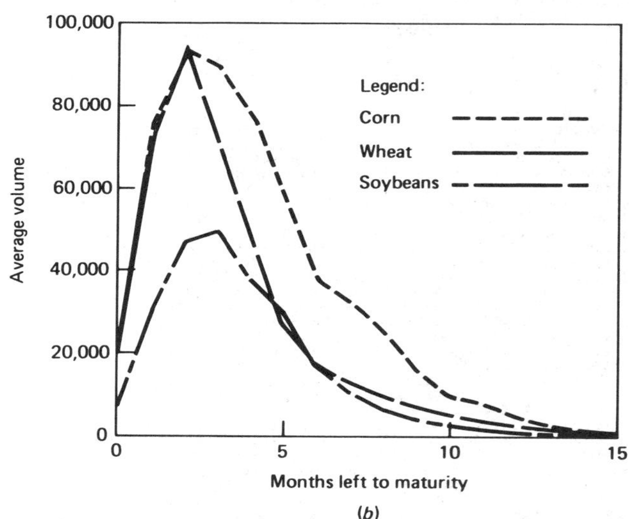

FIGURE 22-8 (*a*) average open interest and time to maturity for grains (*Source*: Mr. Nikolaos T. Milonas, "Liquidity, Price Variability, and Storage Asymmetry: Prices in Futures Markets," Ph.D. dissertation, Baruch College, City University of New York, 1984); (*b*) average volume and time to maturity for grains (*Source*: Mr. Nikolaos T. Milonas, "Liquidity, Price Variability, and Storage Asymmetry: Prices In Futures Markets," Ph.D. dissertation, Baruch College, City University of New York, 1984).

futures contract. Similar patterns also exist for other commodity futures contracts.

During the life of a futures contract the futures price rises and falls in unison with the underlying commodity's cash (or physicals) price. Throughout these positively correlated price fluctuations, however, the futures price remains above the cash price by the amount of the carrying charges in normal markets. However, as the delivery date nears, the futures price converges with the cash price. This occurs because as the futures contract expires, it becomes a substitute for holding the physical commodity. Even after the contract expires and the commodity is delivered, however, the futures prices and the cash prices are still affected by carrying costs because many futures traders "roll their hedges forward" again and again rather than take delivery on them. Restated in market vernacular, the "basis strengthens" (that is, the basis shrinks) in a normal market as the delivery date draws nearer, but the cash and the futures prices still covary closely. Finally, on the last permissible delivery date (when the contract will cease to exist), the futures price converges with the cash price because the basis reflects almost nothing except an allowance for the tiny remaining carrying costs. Essentially, the spot and the futures prices interact so closely that they are determined simultaneously. Figure 22-9 illustrates how futures prices and spot prices move together through time for a storable commodity.

22-5.4 the simultaneous determination of spot and futures prices

To see the manner in which spot and futures prices are determined simultaneously, consider a hypothetical example of some commodity which is easily stored, such as coffee, sugar, cocoa, or cotton. Imagine that this year's new crop of, say, coffee is very small. The scarcity could occur for several reasons. Nearly all coffee comes from Latin America. If international trade relations with Latin America become poor because of political tensions; if foreign exchange restrictions were raised by Latin America; if Latin American revolutionaries burned the coffee crop; or if the coffee crop was wiped out by insects, drought, disease, or flood, existing inventories would have to last until the next new crop became available. Current coffee inventories would become more valuable as soon as news arrived that the new crop would not be forthcoming.

The rise in spot prices would decrease current coffee consumption and cause coffee processors to process their supplies more carefully to minimize

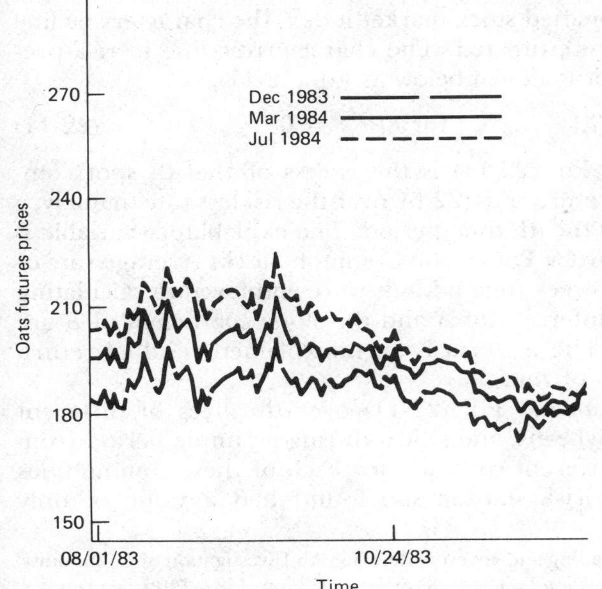

FIGURE 22-9 market prices of oats contracts with different delivery dates.

waste. Speculators would bid up coffee futures prices in order to profit from expected price rises. Coffee futures, as a result, would stay at a premium above the rising spot prices, and higher premiums would provide for higher coffee storage expenses. As a result, coffee inventories would receive unusually good care. Some coffee inventories might be moved to better leakproof, fireproof, humidity-controlled storage facilities and would be treated with insect repellent. Thus, the current supply would be conserved. Spot and futures prices could rise until consumption was cut back to a level which existing inventories could be expected to meet. Then supply and demand would be equated in both the spot and futures markets, and coffee prices would stabilize at a new higher level.

The speculators who were first to obtain, interpret, and act upon the news indicating that future commodity supplies would be decreased would earn a speculative profit. By buying both spot and futures contracts before the news spread and prices were bid up, they would obtain inventories of the spot commodity and futures contracts which could later be sold at a profit (after news of the shortage spread and prices were bid up).

22-6 DIVERSIFICATION AND COMMODITY RETURNS

Unsystematic risk was defined (in Chap. 10) to be variability of return caused by factors which are unique to an asset; it is *diversifiable* risk. Since the prices of many commodities are primarily influenced by acts of God (such as droughts, floods, and insect hordes), the weather during the growing season, and political considerations (such as wars, import quotas for foreign goods, and acreage allotments for domestically grown commodities), there is good reason to suspect that commodity prices are independent of security prices, which are mainly determined by business earnings and other financial factors. In order to evaluate the degree of interdependence between commodity returns and the returns from a diversified stock market index, the characteristic line and its related statistics were estimated. The characteristic line in risk-premium form was employed; it is shown below as Eq. (22-11).

$$r_{it} - R_t = A + B(r_{mt} - R_t) + u_{it} \qquad \text{for } E(u_{it}) = 0 \tag{22-11}$$

The dependent variable in Eq. (22-11) is the excess of the ith spot commodity's one-period rate of return, Eq. (22-6), over the riskless rate (namely, a 15-day Treasury bill rate) in the tth time period. The explanatory variable is the risk-premium for Standard & Poor's 500 Common Stocks Average rate of return in time period t. Two-week time periods were employed in calculating all returns. The regression intercept of A and the slope coefficient of B are simple regression statistics. The u_{it} term is an unexplained residual return which has an expected value of zero.

Dr. Katherine Dusak estimated Eq. (22-11) over the lives of different futures contracts on corn, soybeans, and wheat during a sample period from 1952 to 1967.[28] Over the different contracts for each of these commodities the highest beta systematic risk statistic she found had a value of only

[28] Katherine Dusak, "Futures Trading and Investor Returns: An Investigation of Commodity Market Risk Premiums," *Journal of Political Economy*, December 1973, pp. 1387–1406. See Dusak's

$b = .119$. Practically none of the beta coefficients she estimated by regressing the spot commodity returns onto the stock market average returns was significantly different from zero. Moreover, the largest coefficient of determination she found had a value of only $R^2 = .011$; it was for the same soybean contract which had the highest beta. This soybean statistic of $R^2 = .011$ suggests that at least ($1.0 - .011 = .989 =$) 98.9 percent of the total risk of most agricultural commodities is unsystematic risk. This type of risk can be easily diversified away to zero in a portfolio of diversified common stocks and commodities. Thus, common stock investors who are seeking the risk-reducing benefits of diversification would be well-advised to consider putting some of their investment funds into commodities.

Over the different commodity investments which she examined, Dr. Dusak found that the commodity spot contracts earned average rates of return which were only about as large as the riskless rate of return, *R*. This is the rate of return which the capital asset pricing model (CAPM) suggests is appropriate for market assets with beta values of approximately zero (a reassuring piece of evidence for those who may wonder if the risk-return analysis is appropriate for commodity analysis). This finding, however, also has implications for commodity speculators who may hope to "get rich quick" in the commodity markets. It suggests that only those few commodity speculators who do their homework carefully and then exercise their trades expeditiously can expect to earn rates of return above what they could earn by putting their money in a riskless savings account. That is, commodity speculation does not appear to be a likely place for reckless playboys who hope to "strike it rich" and "get something for nothing" merely by gambling in commodities. Only the experts with years of experience who work hard can expect to enjoy large returns from commodity speculation.

22-7 IS COMMODITY SPECULATION HARMFUL?

"Speculation" is a word which has undesirable connotations to some people who do not understand speculation and who may erroneously identify it with market corners or similar activities. Market corners are socially and economically undesirable. These and other price manipulation schemes use the brute force of centrally controlled wealth to destabilize prices so that a few unethical people can profit therefrom; such results are clearly not beneficial. In fact, laws have been passed making the obviously harmful commodity price manipulation schemes and fraud illegal in the United States. On the other hand, the legal forms of speculation discussed here are socially and economically desirable. Consider the costs and benefits to the community which result from speculation.[29]

---

table 3 for the beta estimates. The characteristic line in risk-premium form used by Dusak is very similar to the traditional characteristic line in one-period rates of return that is explained above in chap. 10. The characteristic line in risk-premiums is explained by M. C. Jensen, "Risk, the Pricing of Capital Assets, and the Evaluation of Investment Portfolios," *Journal of Business*, April 1969.

[29] A study of financial futures which found no price destabilization was reported by Kenneth C. Froewiss, "GNMA Futures: Stabilizing or Destabilizing," *Economic Review*, Spring 1978, Federal Reserve Bank of San Francisco, pp. 20–29.

22-7.1 speculation may destabilize prices

Only one issue has been seriously suggested by economists considering the undesirable effects of futures and options speculation, that is, price destabilization. There is an unresolved academic debate on this point.[30] Some economists have argued that profitable speculation in commodities or other investments must stabilize the price of the asset. In essence, this group argues that, to earn a profit, the speculator must "buy low and sell high" and that this activity will be stabilizing. Purchases made at low prices, such as point *L* in Fig. 22-10, will tend to drive prices up, and sales at high prices, like point *H*, will tend to lower prices. The overall effect of such speculation will be to (1) maximize speculators' profits and (2) stabilize prices. It is reasoned that speculators who do not "buy low (*L*) and sell high (*H*)" will remain a near-bankrupt, nonpowerful force and that their destabilizing effects will be small.

The second group of economists disagrees. They assert that it is possible for speculation to be both profitable and destabilizing at the same time. These economists assert that purchases can be made after prices have started to rise (at points like purchase point *P* in Fig. 22-10), which accents the price rise. They also point out that sales can be made after prices have started to fall (at points like sale point *S* in Fig. 22-10), causing prices to fall faster and perhaps farther. Yet, as long as the purchase price is below the sales price, symbolically, $P < S$, a speculative profit will result. In this case, speculation will be both profitable and destabilizing.

Unnecessarily unstable prices are undesirable because they increase business executives' uncertainty, frustrate planning, discourage long-range investment programs, and cause capital to be allocated to projects which yield only short-run profits with very little risk. Furthermore, as speculators destabilize

[30] M. Friedman, "In Defense of Destabilizing Speculation," in R. W. Pfouts, *Essays in Economics and Econometrics*, pp. 133–141; W. J. Baumol, "Speculation, Profitability and Stability," *Review of Economics and Statistics*, August 1957; L. G. Telser, "A Theory of Speculation Relating Profitability and Stability," ibid., August 1959, pp. 295–301; W. J. Baumol, "Reply," ibid.; J. L. Stein, "Destabilizing Speculation Can Be Profitable," ibid., August 1961. More recently, studies have been published providing new evidence that speculation is a beneficial social activity. See William L. Silber, "Marketmaker Behavior in an Auction Market: An Analysis of Scalpers in Futures Markets," *Journal of Finance*, September 1984, vol. 39, no. 4, pp. 937–953. See also Robert Forsythe, Thomas R. Palfrey, and Charles R. Plott, "Futures Markets and Informational Efficiency: A Laboratory Experiment," *Journal of Finance*, September 1984, vol. 39, no. 4, pp. 955–981.

FIGURE 22-10 graph of price fluctuations across time.

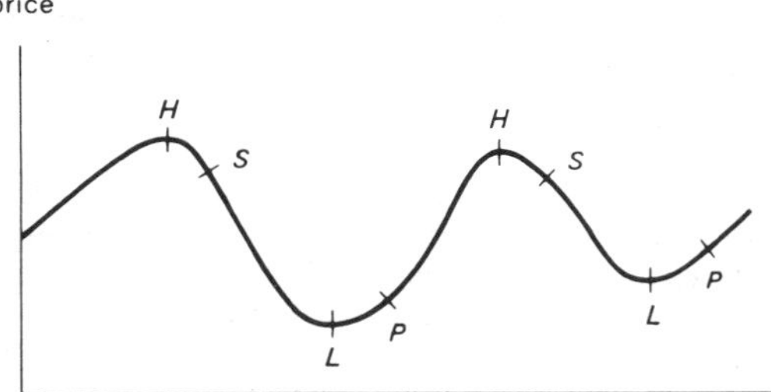

the prices of futures contracts this might destabilize the prices in the cash markets for the commodity.

Unfortunately, no empirical tests have been published to substantiate either the claim that speculation is destabilizing or the claim that it is a stabilizing influence. The conclusion that can be drawn is that speculation can destabilize prices if the speculator is not adept at maximizing profit (that is, buying at or near the lowest price and selling at or near the highest price). However, such inept speculators will probably not become very powerful in the price formation process.

22-7.2 socially desirable effects of speculation

Several desirable economic benefits result from speculation. For example, society enjoys the following benefits from speculation:

1. Consumption is expeditiously allocated over time.
2. Some risks may be hedged away.
3. Publicly available forecasts are contained in futures prices.
4. Prices adjust more efficiently.
5. Resources are allocated more efficiently.
6. Active markets provide liquidity for traders.
7. Arbitrage helps ensure uniform prices.

These points are advantageous in the following ways:

ALLOCATION OF CONSUMPTION OVER TIME Commodities and most investments are items which may be used either now or later. The price at which an item is expected to sell later, relative to the current price, will largely determine when the item is used. For example, if the premium on some commodity exceeds its carrying costs, it will be profitable to stockpile the commodity for use later.

Speculators prepare the forecasts and conduct the activity which help determine spot and futures prices. Thus, speculators help allocate consumption over time. It is fairly well recognized that futures speculators are necessary to keep farm prices from dropping to near zero at harvest time (that is, during the new-crop month), to store goods for the future, and to sell goods at reasonable prices long after the harvest and during years when the harvest is poor.

RISKS HEDGED AWAY In the preceding pages, buying hedges and selling hedges were discussed. It was explained how futures contracts are utilized by risk-averters to hedge away risk. Speculators can relieve business executives of their buying and selling risks and leave them free to concentrate on efficient production. Thus, speculation allows separation and specialization of the risk-bearing function, and thus expedites efficient production.

PUBLIC FORECASTS Speculators' fortunes depend on their ability to forecast. As a result, professional speculators devote considerable time, expense, and efforts to forecasting the supply of and demand for commodities and other investments. Such speculators actively search out news. Any new information contains a profit potential if it will affect the price of an asset in which they are prepared to speculate. After the new information becomes public and prices adjust accordingly, the information is worthless to the speculators' efforts to earn a profit. Therefore, in order to maximize their profits, speculators act upon such new information *immediately*.

Speculators' forecasts and news discoveries enable them to make timely profit-oriented purchases and sales. As a result, the prices of speculative assets reflect the latest information—frequently even before it reaches the news media. These prices are widely published. Therefore, the general populace may avail itself of a free, up-to-the minute, expert forecast of the future price of any commodity simply by observing the published prices of futures contracts.

EFFICIENT PRICE ADJUSTMENT Efficient prices may be defined as prices which react immediately and continuously to all relevant information so that prices at every instant fully reflect the latest relevant facts. Efficient prices are characterized by continuous, unpredictable moves. Although seasonal or other trends may be evident in efficient prices, the day-to-day price changes should be random as they adjust to the random arrival of news.

Although unnecessary price movement of the type caused by price manipulation is undesirable, the price movement characterizing efficient markets is valuable. Only if prices reflect all the latest information about supply and demand may resources be allocated in such a manner as to maximize society's welfare. Efficient prices may overreact or underreact to any given piece of information. Nevertheless, it is essential that prices react continuously as they pursue an ever-changing equilibrium price. Efficient prices may be imperfect estimates of equilibrium prices (or, if you prefer, the intrinsic economic value of the commodity), but they are *unbiased* estimates which fluctuate around the equilibrium price. Since stable equilibriums with constant prices are impossible in this world of uncertainty, efficiently fluctuating prices are the best that can be hoped for.

Efficient prices are partially the result of profit-maximizing speculators. These persons will uncover the relevant facts about supply and demand and act upon them without delay in an effort to maximize their profits.[31] This action causes continuous, unbiased price adjustments.

EFFICIENT RESOURCE ALLOCATION The supplies of resources which are available in the world at any time are limited. If these resources are not allocated in an

[31] Aggressive forecasting and news prospecting do not necessarily earn a profit for the speculator. These activities are necessary merely to avoid bankruptcy. Only the experts will profit from their forecasts. Empirical research suggesting that commodity prices are random has been published. R. A. Stevenson and R. M. Bear, "Commodity Futures: Trends or Random Walks," *Journal of Finance,* March 1970. T. F. Cargill and G. C. Rausser, "Time and Frequency Domain Representations of Futures Prices as a Stochastic Process," *Journal of the American Statistical Association,* March 1972. S. Smidt, "A Test of the Independence of Price Changes in Soybean Futures," *Food Research Institute Studies,* 1965, vol. 5, no. 2. A. B. Larson, "Measurement of a Random Process in Futures Prices," *Food Research Institute Studies,* 1960, vol. 1, no. 3. D. J. S. Rutledge, "A Note on the Variability of Futures Price," *Review of Economics and Statistics,* 1976, vol. LVIII, no. 1, pp. 118–120. P. A. Samuelson, "Is Real-World Price a Tale Told by the Idiot of Chance?" *Review of Economics and Statistics,* 1976, vol. LVIII, no. 1, pp. 120–123. Thomas Cargill and Gordon C. Rausser, "Temporal Price Behavior in Commodity Futures Markets," *Journal of Finance,* September 1975.

optimum manner, the welfare of society cannot attain its full potential. In order for these limited resources to be allocated to the proper place at the proper time, they must be mobile and must react swiftly to changing demands.

In a market economy such as that in the United States, resources tend to go to the highest bidder. Thus, efficient resource allocation requires (1) efficient prices and (2) resources which may be readily shifted between places and time periods. The activities of speculators facilitate these needs by (1) making prices adjust in an efficient manner and (2) making inventories available when and where demand is high.

LIQUIDITY FOR TRADERS The existence of a commodity market provides a place where commodity producers, speculators, and users all can meet and enjoy free entry and exit (perhaps through their brokers) to the market. If the trading activity on the commodity exchange is flourishing, liquidity (of both long and short positions) is increased.[32] This liquidity reduces cash budgeting problems and frees business executives to transact their primary business.

ARBITRAGE TO ENSURE UNIFORM PRICES As explained before, if the prices of a given commodity sold in different markets differ by more than the transportation costs between the two markets, arbitrage will bring the prices together. A speculator can buy the commodity in the market where its price is low and simultaneously sell it where the price is high. This transaction will yield a riskless profit and may be continued until the two prices differ by no more than the transportation costs between the two markets. A uniform price between markets will ensure that a commodity is not in excess supply and that it is not being wasted in one place because its price is low while the same commodity is in short supply in another place.[33]

22-7.3 speculation is beneficial

The preceding review of the undesirable and desirable effects of commodity speculation points fairly clearly to the conclusion that speculation is beneficial to the public welfare. The probability does exist that prices will occasionally be destabilized by some speculator who ineptly tries to maximize profits. However, this seems to be a small cost to pay in comparison with the benefits society derives from speculation. In view of the net benefits that futures markets provide the nation, it is difficult to understand why Congress outlawed futures trading in onions in 1958 and nearly outlawed potato futures a few years after that.

[32] William L. Silber, "Marketmaker Behavior in an Auction Market: An Analysis of Scalpers in Futures Markets," *Journal of Finance*, September 1984, vol. 39, no. 4, pp. 937–953.

[33] Pure arbitrage can be defined as taking identical long and short positions at the same time and in the same quantities so that the resulting position involves no risk. Quasi-arbitrage involves selling items from an existing portfolio in order to obtain the funds to buy similar but different goods in an equivalent portfolio at a lower price. For an example of quasi-arbitrage in the financial futures markets see Richard J. Rendelman, Jr., and Christopher E. Cabrini, "The Efficiency of the Treasury Bill Futures Market," *Journal of Finance*, September 1979, vol. 34, no. 4, pp. 895–914. Quasi-arbitrage is just as useful as pure arbitrage at stopping equivalent goods from selling at different prices. See Sec. 21-2 on page 596 for more information about arbitrage.

QUESTIONS

22-1. Compare and contrast selling a futures contract without owning an inventory in the commodity and selling a common stock short.

22-2. What functions are performed by the clearing house in a commodity futures contract?

22-3. Define an inverted market and suggest how it might occur.

22-4. "Futures prices are determined after spot prices are known. Adding carrying costs to spot prices yields futures prices." Is this statement true, false, or uncertain? Explain.

22-5. Explain what a selling hedge is, and give an example.

22-6. "Speculation is an evil pastime for wealthy playboys. It destabilizes prices and misallocates resources, and it should be declared illegal." True, false, or uncertain? Explain.

22-7. The following data are reported on the commodity prices of wheat futures:

July	\$3.49 per bushel
September	\$3.57
December	\$3.69¼
March	\$3.81½
May	\$3.88
July	\$3.75⅞
September	\$3.84

From these data, estimate (*a*) the cost of storing a bushel of wheat per month and (*b*) the month in which wheat is harvested. Explain how you obtain these estimates.

22-8. Explain why there are no futures markets for coal, raisins, and salt. Does the absence of such markets mean that no speculation in these commodities occurs?

22-9. If wheat futures were selling at \$3 per bushel and some event occurred which changed wheat's new equilibrium price to \$3.50 per bushel, what would this do to trading in the relevant wheat future?

22-10. Assume that you are hired by the Chicago Board of Trade (CBT) to manage its New Products Committee. You are directed to do research to discern new commodities in which the CBT might advantageously initiate trading in futures contracts. List and explain six criteria you would adopt for screening commodities in order to select high-volume possibilities for the CBT to consider trading.

22-11. Define and discuss the determinants of the basis in commodity trading.

22-12. What factors prevent any hedge from being a perfect hedge? Explain.

22-13. Define the one-period rate of return for a commodity investor who purchased a futures contract on margin and gave the commodity broker a U.S. Treasury bill to hold as the margin.

SELECTED REFERENCES

Kaufman, Perry J., *Handbook of Futures Markets*, Wiley-Interscience, John Wiley and Sons, New York, 1984. A thick volume that discusses a comprehensive range of commodity topics nonmathematically.

Labys, W. C., and C. W. J. Granger, *Speculation, Hedging and Commodity Price Forecasts,* Heath, Lexington Books, Lexington, Mass., 1970. An econometric study of commodity price fluctuations.

Peck, Anne E., *Selected Writings on Futures Markets,* Chicago Board of Trade, vols. 1 and 2, 1977. These two volumes contain scholarly articles which were compiled by Anne Peck of the Food Research Institute at Stanford University. The first volume contains only papers written by Dr. Holbrook Working. The second volume contains papers by selected writers. Mathematics is used in most of the papers. The Chicago Board of Trade has also prepared other volumes.

Tewles, R. J., H. L. Stone, and C. V. Harlow, *The Commodity Futures Game,* McGraw-Hill, New York, 1977. A nonmathematical textbook that explains various facets of commodity futures trading.

APPENDIX 22A

fundamental determinants of storable agricultural commodity prices

This appendix supplements the material in Chap. 22 with an explanation of the principal factors which determine the market prices of storable agricultural commodities and their futures contracts.[34]

APP. 22A-1 ANALYSIS OF SPOT PRICES

The market prices of spot commodities are determined by the demand for and the supply of the physical commodity.[35] For agricultural commodities the supply comes from essentially two aggregate sources:

1. Harvests (H) of new crops
2. Inventories (I) carried forward in storage

The demand for commodities comes from two types of aggregated needs:

1. Consumption (C) demand

[34] This appendix draws heavily on Paul Samuelson, "Intemporal Price Equilibrium: A Prologue to the Theory of Speculation," *Weltwirtschaftliches Archiv*, 1957, vol. 79, pp. 181–219, reprinted in *Collected Scientific Papers of Paul A. Samuelson*, vol. II, edited by J. E. Stiglitz, chap. 73, pp. 946–984, MIT Press, 1966.

[35] This section draws on J. L. Stein, "The Simultaneous Determination of Spot and Future Prices," *American Economic Review*, December 1961, pp. 1012–1025.

2. Demand for a storable quantity (Q) for inventory

The market for a given spot commodity is in static equilibrium when the prices have no tendency to change because the aggregate supply of physicals (that is, $H + I$) equals the aggregate demand for physicals (that is, $C + Q$), as shown in Eqs. (App. 22A-1*a*) and (App. 22A-1*b*).

$$\text{Supply} = \text{demand} \tag{App. 22A-1a}$$

$$H + I = C + Q \tag{App. 22A-1b}$$

At any given instant in time the aggregate supply of a commodity is a constant; this is illustrated in Fig. App. 22A-1 by the vertical supply function denoted S_0. The aggregate demand function, in contrast to the inelastic supply function, is negatively sloped to indicate that consumption increases at lower prices. At harvest time the quantity of a given physical commodity which is available increases by H units (such as bushels or barrels or whatever unit is used to measure quantity). This is represented in Fig. App. 22A-1 by the rightward shift of the before-harvest supply function, denoted S_0, to the after-harvest supply function S_1. The demand function is presumed to remain fixed through time because the commodity is consumed at a rate which is an unchanging function of the commodity's price.

dynamic analysis of equal annual harvests

In order to present clear-cut examples of how the price of a given commodity fluctuates as the quantity available for sale varies, some simplifying assumptions are necessary. Assume that

1. The aggregate demand function shown in Fig. App. 22A-1 never shifts.
2. An aggregate quantity of H units of the commodity is harvested each year.
3. The entire harvest is gathered on July 15 of each year.
4. A carrying cost of 4 cents per bushel per month is incurred regardless of how many bushels of the given commodity are stored.

FIGURE APP. 22A-1 static equilibrium analysis of a commodity harvest.

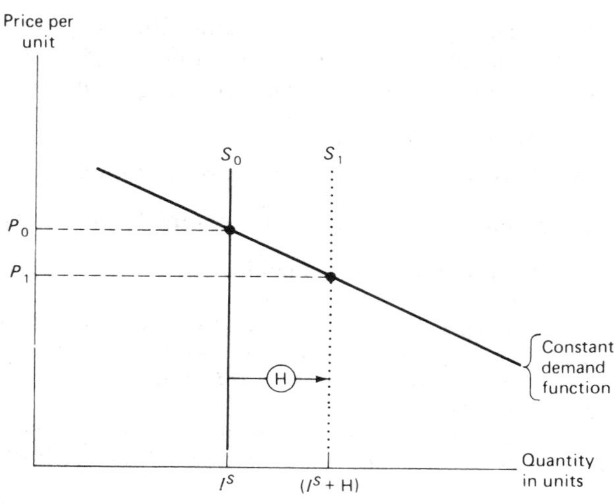

5. Speculators will buy the commodity and carry it in their inventory to earn a speculative profit if, and only if, they expect the commodity's price to increase by at least the carrying charge (of 4 cents per bushel per month).
6. The price of the commodity will not rise more than an amount equal to the carrying charge per period for the commodity because, if it did, speculators, in order to maximize their profits, would buy all the commodity and hold it for later sale at a higher price until none was left for sale. As a result of this hoarding, the price would be quickly bid up until storing more inventory was no longer profitable. Sales would then resume at a new, higher price level, and this price would then increase slowly at a normal rate per month equal to the carrying charge.
7. Finally, risk and uncertainty are assumed away. This allows clear-cut graphs to be drawn; the graphs need not have the wild and erratic price fluctuations caused by uncertain transactions which are later reversed in a world confused by uncertainty.

Figure App. 22-2*a* and *b* illustrates how the aggregate quantity of the commodity carried in inventory and the market price of the spot commodity will vary together under the preceding seven simplifying assumptions. Figure App. 22A-2*a* shows that the *aggregate inventory* increases by *H* bushels on the harvest day of July 15 each year and then is consumed at a steady rate. Figure App. 22A-2*b* shows that the commodity's *price* drops each year on July 15 when the new crop increases the aggregate supply. Then, after July 15, the market price rises steadily by 4 cents per bushel per month until the next harvest. Figure App. 22A-2*a* and *b* depicts the simplest possible case. Next consider what happens if the size of the harvest changes every year; this is a more complex case.

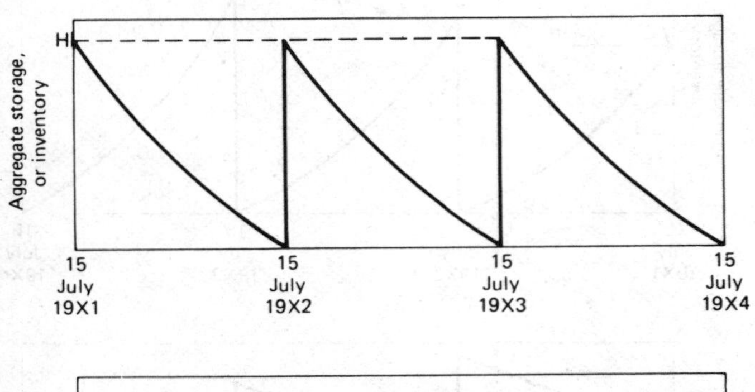

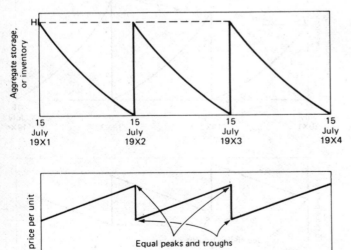

FIGURE APP. 22A-2 the interaction of price and aggregate inventory for a commodity with equal annual harvests: (*a*) aggregate inventory; (*b*) price per unit.

dynamic analysis of increasing harvests

Let the second simplifying assumption be changed as indicated in Eq. (App. 22A-2).

$$H_t = H_{t-1} + h \qquad \text{(App. 22A-2)}$$

Equation (App. 22A-2) suggests that the size of each year's harvest increases by h bushels. This modified assumption means that the vertical supply functions in Fig. App. 22A-1 shift farther to the right at each harvest. This more realistic situation is analyzed in Fig. App. 22A-3*a* and *b*.

Figure App. 22A-3*a* illustrates how the aggregate inventory increases, on July 15 of each year, to a new peak which is h bushels higher than the previous inventory peak. The commodity's price reacts to this situation by falling to a new lower level each year on July 15 and then rising steadily by 4 cents per bushel per month until the next harvest. However, each year's price peak is lower than the previous year's peak because each year's aggregate supply available for sale is larger.

dynamic analysis of decreasing annual harvests

To analyze what may happen if each year's harvest decreases, Eq. (App. 22A-2) is rewritten as Eq. (App. 22A-3).

$$H_t = H_{t-1} - h \qquad \text{(App. 22A-3)}$$

Equation (App. 22A-3) suggests that each harvest's vertical supply function in Fig. App. 22A-1 shifts further to the left as the successive harvests dwindle in the face of unchanging demand. Figure App. 22A-4a and *b* illustrates one possible outcome from successively smaller harvests which occur while demand is invariant.

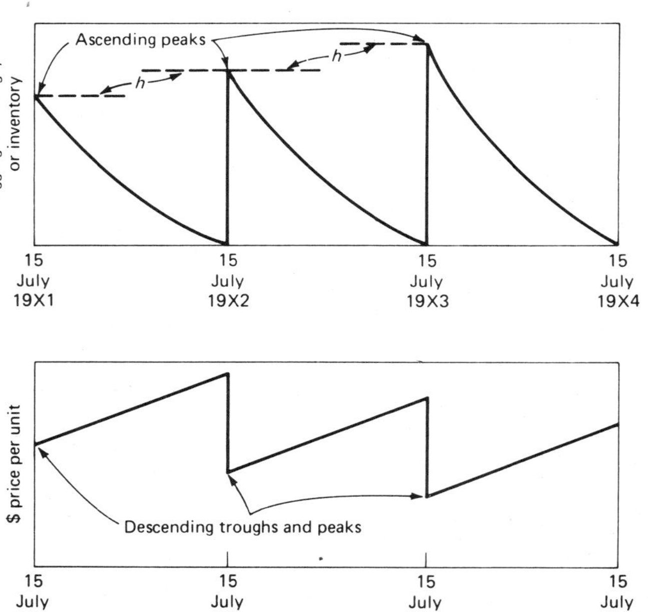

FIGURE APP. 22A-3 the interaction of price and aggregate inventory for a commodity with increasing annual harvests: (*a*) aggregate inventory; (*b*) price per unit.

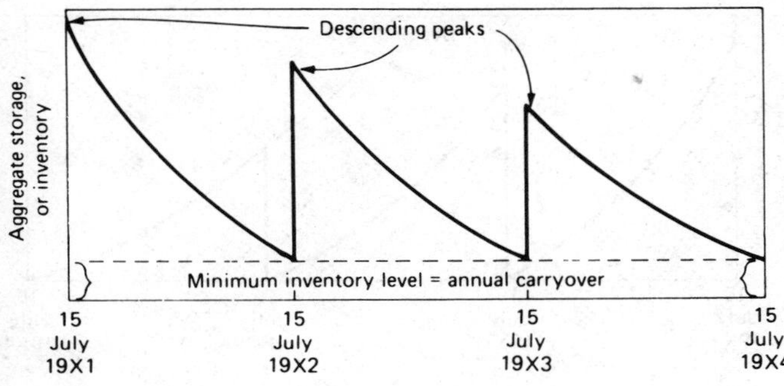

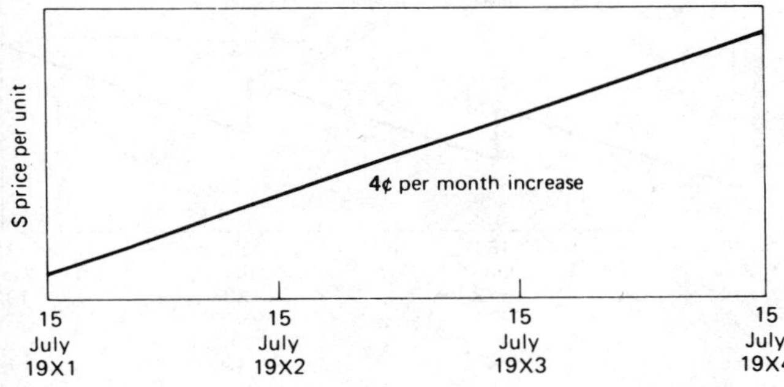

FIGURE APP. 22A-4 the interaction of price and aggregate inventory for a commodity with decreasing harvests and inventory carryover: (*a*) aggregate inventory; (*b*) price per unit.

minimum inventory maintained

Figure App. 22A-4*a* shows that the amount of commodity carried forward increases to a series of successively lower peaks at each year's harvest. However, it is also assumed that, because of one or both of the two following reasons, the aggregate inventory levels never fall all the way to zero.

1. Speculators never let their inventories fall all the way to zero in case some act of God (for example, locusts or a drought) destroys the growing crop and causes the commodity's price to skyrocket and yield large profits as their inventory appreciates.
2. Some commodity processors always maintain a minimum inventory level in order to keep their production lines running without delays in case some shortages develop. That is, the commodity processors obtain some "convenience yield" from carrying minimum levels of inventory and thus are willing to incur some losses if necessary in order to maintain a minimum inventory level.[36]

As a result of the continual existence of some inventory carry-over into each new year's ever-tightening supply situation, the price of the commodity increases steadily by 4 cents per bushel per month year after year. The price does not fall at harvest time because the price speculators, who expect continued price gains, and/or the commodity processors, who obtain a conve-

[36] The concept of a convenience yield was developed by Nicholas Kaldor, "Speculation and Economic Stability," *Review of Economic Studies,* 1939, vol. VII, p. 6.

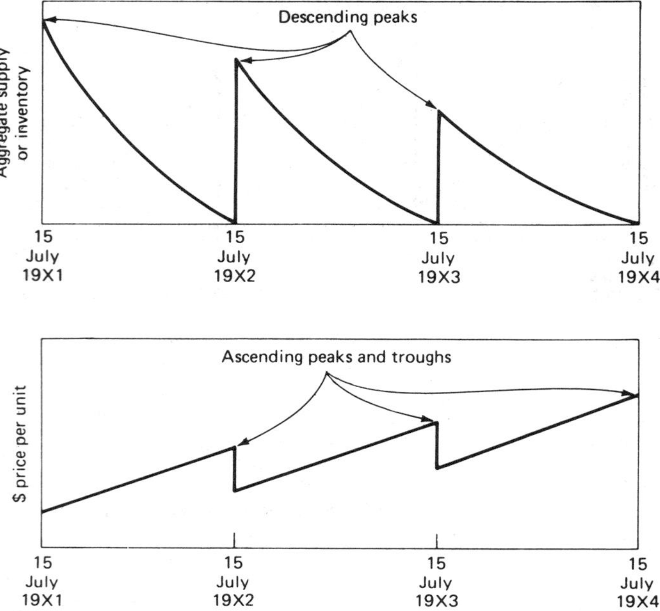

FIGURE APP. 22A-5 the interaction of price and aggregate inventory for a commodity with decreasing harvests and zero inventory carryover: (*a*) aggregate inventory; (*b*) price per unit.

nience yield from maintaining their inventories, buy the entire harvest at current prices and store it for the future at a cost of 4 cents per bushel (or whatever the unit may be) per month.

if inventory can fall to zero

If it is assumed (1) that there are no price speculators to buy and hold inventories in the hope of earning profits and (2) that no one obtains a convenience yield from maintaining some minimum level of inventory, then the inventory level can fall to zero. In this case, Fig. App. 22A-5*a* and *b* (rather than Fig. App. 22A-4*a* and *b*) illustrates the results of decreasing harvests. Figure App. 22A-5*a* shows a series of descending aggregate inventory peaks as each year's smaller harvest is gathered. Moreover, after each year's harvest, all the commodity carried in storage is consumed before the next harvest. As a result, the price rises steadily by the amount of the carrying charge each month, as shown in Fig. App. 22A-5*b*. Then on July 15 of each year, the price drops back in a series of ascending trough prices as the supply situation shrinks each year and demand continues undiminished.

APP. 22A-2 MORE REALISTIC HARVESTS AND STORAGE COSTS

In order to gain realism, consider the effects of relaxing the third and fourth simplifying assumptions while the harvests are constant, as shown in Fig. App. 22A-2*a*. First, the third assumption is relaxed; later, the fourth will be relaxed too. Instead of assuming that all the harvest occurs on July 15, suppose that it begins on July 15 and continues until August 15. This modifies the example depicted in Figure App. 22A-2*a* and *b* to become the more realistic situation illustrated in Figure App. 22A-6*a* and *b*.

month-long harvests

Figure App. 22A-6*a* shows that the amount of inventory starts increasing on July 15, when the harvest begins each year. This increase continues every day for 1 month until the harvest ends on August 15 and the aggregate inventory reaches its annual peak. Then the inventory is steadily consumed until it reaches a low point just before the next year's harvest. As a result, the inventory graphed in Fig. App. 22A-6*a* reaches *curved peaks* (rather than the pointed peaks caused by the 1-day harvests which were illustrated in the preceding figures).

The month-long harvest smooths the inventory fluctuations somewhat, and this in turn dampens the price reactions. Figure App. 22A-6*b* shows how the commodity's *price fluctuations are smoothed by the longer harvest periods*. Figure App. 22A-6*b* is more realistic than its counterpart Figure App. 22A-2*b*, which was developed under the third simplifying assumption that all the harvest occurred on one day. Next, the fourth assumption will be realigned to reflect more realistic circumstances.

nonconstant storage costs

The fourth simplifying assumption, that storage costs are constant, could be represented graphically by a perfectly horizontal line, such as the one shown in Fig. App. 22A-7*a*. In fact, the S-shaped curve shown in Fig. App. 22A-7*b* is more realistic than the simple assumption of a horizontal line.

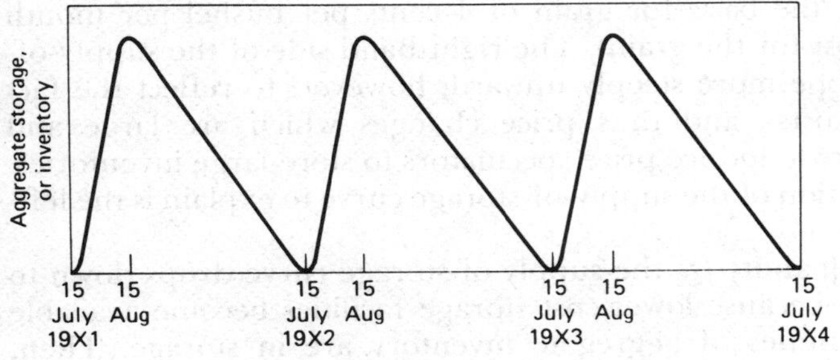

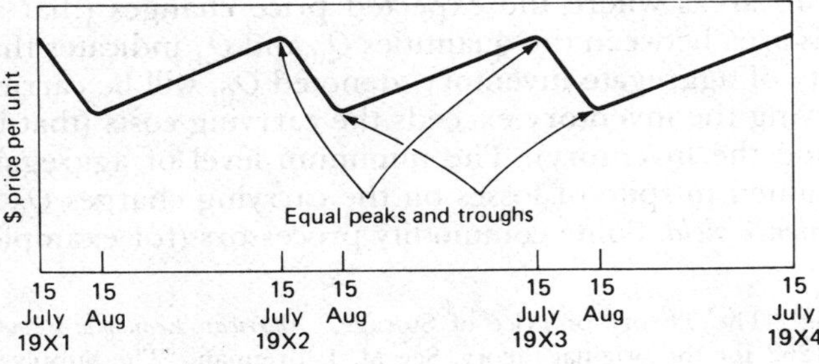

FIGURE APP. 22A-6 the interaction of price and aggregate inventory for a commodity with equal annual month-long harvests: (*a*) aggregate inventory; (*b*) price per unit.

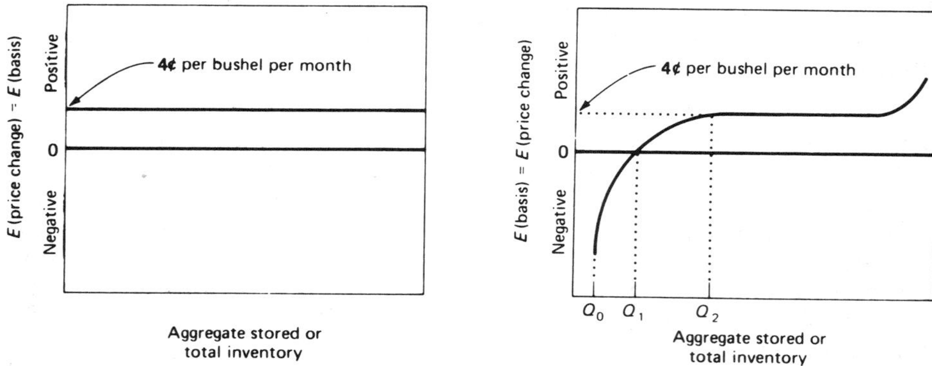

FIGURE APP. 22A-7 two different supply-of-storage functions: (*a*) constant storage cost per unit; (*b*) increasing storage cost per unit.

Figure App. 22A-7*b* illustrates what is referred to as the *supply-of-storage curve*.[37] It relates the aggregate amount of any given physical commodity which is carried in inventory (that is, stored) to the basis (that is, the price change) expected for that commodity. The supply-of-storage curve slopes upward to reflect the fact that speculators (such as grain elevator operators) will store more of a commodity when they think its price will increase more rapidly. The curve is horizontal over its midrange because some of the storage space available for wheat can be rented to store corn, for example, without bidding up the rent for storage space. This represents the normal market condition in which the expected basis equals the typical carrying cost for storage (for example, the basis for grain of 4 cents per bushel per month equals the carrying cost for the grain). The right-hand side of the supply-of-storage curve does slope more steeply upward, however, to reflect the fact that large carrying costs—and thus price changes which are large and positive—are necessary to induce price speculators to store large inventories. The most difficult portion of the supply-of-storage curve to explain is the left-hand side.

To the left of the quantity Q_2 the supply-of-storage curve drops down to the point denoted Q_1 because lower-cost storage facilities become available when only small quantities of aggregate inventory are in storage. Then, strange as it may seem, the supply-of-storage curve drops off steeply at quantities below Q_1, into areas where the expected price changes (that is, basis) are negative. This area between the quantities Q_0 and Q_1 indicates that some minimum quantity of aggregate inventory, denoted Q_0, will be carried even if the cost of carrying the inventory exceeds the carrying costs (that is, money is lost in carrying the inventory). The minimum level of aggregate inventory that is maintained in spite of losses on the carrying charges Q_0 is explained by the *convenience yield*. Some commodity processors (for example,

[37] See Holbrook Working, "The Theory of Price of Storage," *American Economic Review*, December 1949, pp. 1254–1262 for the original theory. See M. J. Brennan, "The Supply of Storage," *American Economic Review*, March 1958, for empirical evidence.

food manufacturers who make flour from wheat) maintain some minimum level of inventory at any cost because they find it convenient and economical to keep their production process running smoothly rather than be forced to shut down their plants because of, say, delayed raw material deliveries. This valuable convenience obtained from maintaining minimum levels of inventory is called the convenience yield; it is the reason minimum inventories are maintained even on a loss basis.

As a result of the nonconstant storage costs indicated by the supply-of-storage curve, it is necessary to modify Fig. App. 22A-6*a* and *b* as shown in Fig. App. 22A-8*a* and *b;* Fig. App. 22A-8*a* is similar to Fig. App. 22A-6*a*. However, Fig. App. 22A-8*b* differs from Fig. App. 22A-6*b* because the constant storage cost assumption was dropped. Allowing for the supply-of-storage schedule of Fig. App. 22A-7*b* causes the commodity prices in Fig. App. 22A-8*b* to fall less at low inventory levels and rise less at high inventory levels (namely at harvest time) and thus demonstrate smoother curves than the analogous price graph in Fig. App. 22A-6*b*.

Figure App. 22A-8*a* and *b* represents the most realistic examples of aggregate inventory and price interactions for commodities in the spot market which have been developed in this appendix. However, they were drawn with the seventh simplifying assumption, that uncertainty was absent, so that all speculators would visualize the same forecasts of supply, demand, and prices. This seventh assumption can make the price graphs appear deceptively simplistic.

If the *actual market prices* of spot contracts for a given commodity were graphed, the graphs would exhibit random price fluctuation rather than the

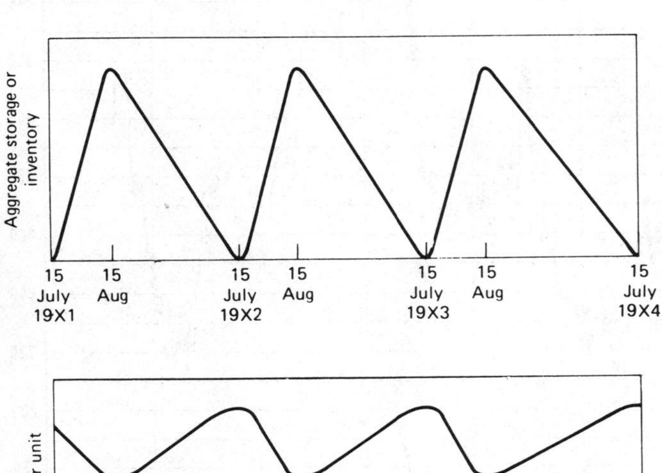

FIGURE APP. 22A-8 the interaction of price and aggregate inventory for a commodity with equal annual month-long harvests and increasing storage costs: (*a*) aggregate inventory; (*b*) price per unit.

clear-cut pattern shown in Fig. App. 22A-8*b*.[38] Compare the spot corn prices shown in Fig. App. 22A-9 with those shown in Fig. App. 22A-8*b*. The random and sometimes wild price changes visible in graphs of actual commodity prices result from new information about supply and demand conditions which affects the commodity prices in an unpredictable fashion. For exaple, if news of a drought destroying a growing grain crop or news of a foreign exchange complication which affected coffee prices became public, the prices of the affected commodity would be disrupted and react instantly to the important

[38] T. F. Cargill and G. C. Rausser, "Time and Frequency Domain Representations of Futures Prices as a Stochastic Process," *Journal of the American Statistical Association*, March 1972, pp. 23–30. T. C. Cargill, "Temporal Behavior in Commodity Futures Markets," *The Journal of Finance*, September 1975, vol. 30, no. 4, pp. 1043–1053.

FIGURE APP. 22A-9 market price fluctuation of corn.

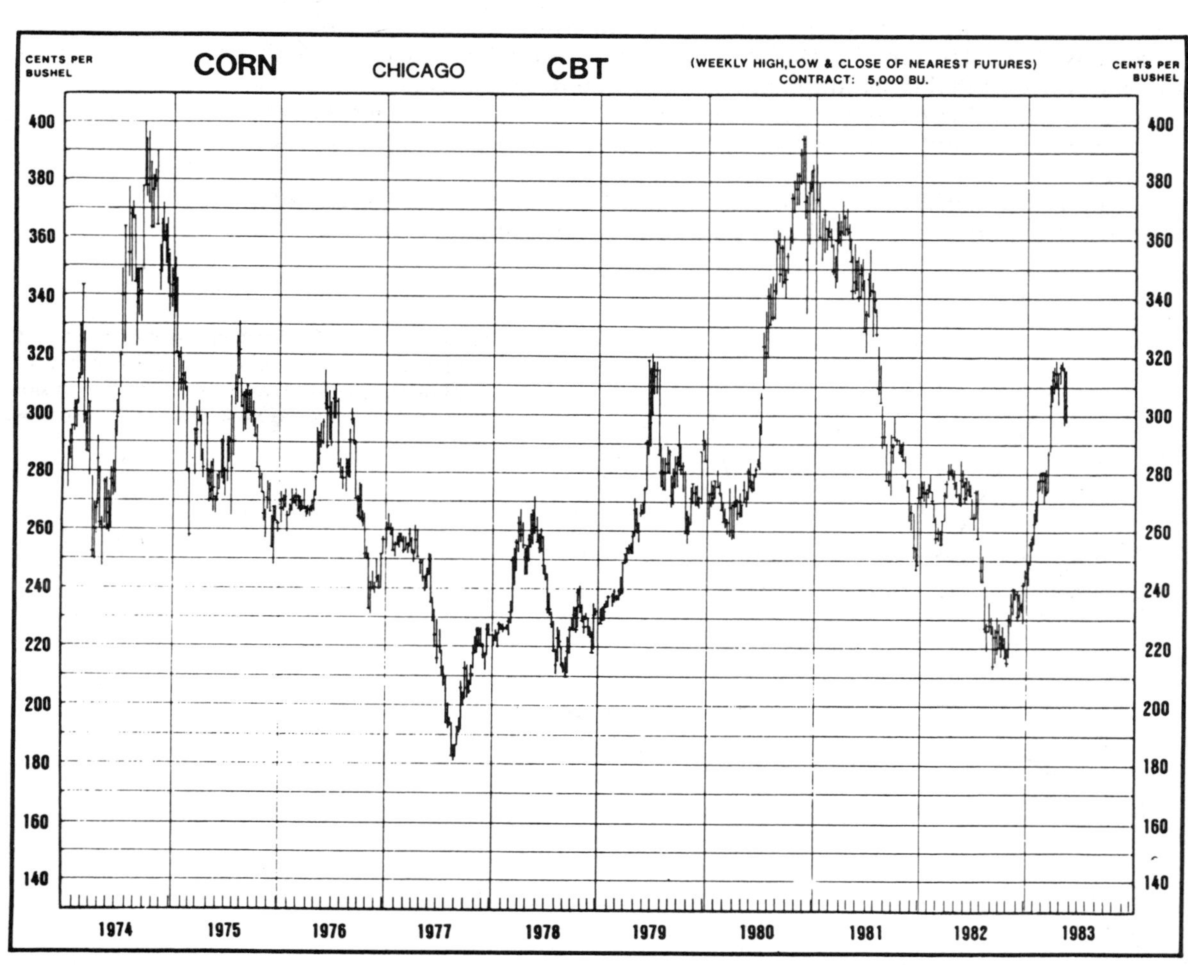

news. It is the continual arrival of good and bad news which causes commodity speculators to adjust supply and demand estimates and thus causes commodity prices to resemble the random-walk staggerings of an intoxicated person rather than follow simple seasonal patterns. The prices of both the spot and futures contracts fluctuate randomly together in this manner, as shown in Fig. 22-9 on page 663.

financial futures contracts*

Financial futures contracts are a new category of commodity futures contract; they were first traded in the United States in 1972.[1] Financial futures contracts, usually called *financial futures,* have rapidly grown in popularity since the inception. Figure 23-1 illustrates the growth of financial futures trading at the Chicago Board of Trade (CBT). The graph indicates that the aggregate number of T-bond futures, T-note futures, GNMA futures, and options on bond futures grew from .5 million contracts in 1977 to 23.7 million contracts in 1983. The cash market value of those 23.7 million contracts was over $2 trillion. Other commodity exchanges also enjoyed soaring rates of growth in new financial futures contracts they introduced during this time period.

23-1 FINANCIAL FUTURES DEFINED

Financial futures are standardized futures contracts whose market prices are established through open outcry and hand signals in a regulated commodity exchange. Like all futures contracts, financial futures represent a legally enforceable commitment to buy or sell a prespecified quantity and quality of a specific financial instrument during a predetermined future delivery month. Unlike the traditional commodity futures contracts, however, delivery is not made in a voluminous physical commodity. Instead, either financial securities or a cash settlement are delivered to fulfill a financial futures contract. The physically small financial security or check to be delivered, and also the

[1] Foreign exchange futures started trading at the International Monetary Market (IMM) of the Chicago Mercantile Exchange in 1972—the United States' first financial futures contract. Previous to this almost all foreign exchange in the United States was traded informally through an interbank forward market.

* Chapter 23 presumes a knowledge of the material in Chaps. 2, 21, and 22. Chapter 23 has an appendix entitled "Options on Futures" that presumes a mastery of Chap. 23.

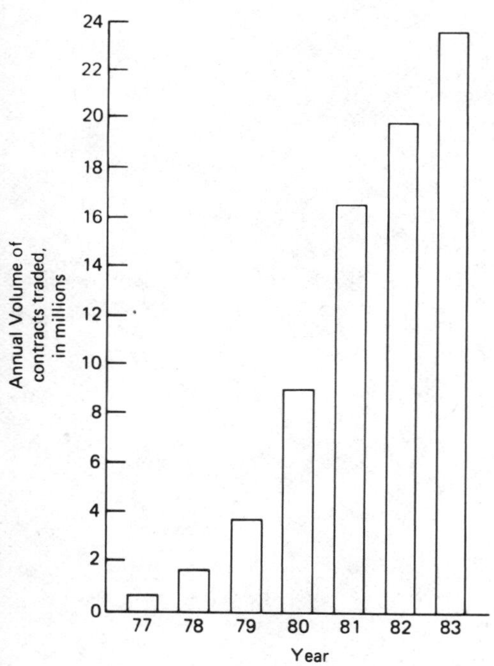

FIGURE 23-1 annual volume of T-bond, T-note, and GNMA futures and options on futures traded at CBOT. (*Source*: The Financial Futures Professional, Chicago Board of Trade, January 23, 1984, vol. 8, no. 1, p. 1.)

economic variables that determine the market price of the financial future, are two principal factors that differentiate these new contracts from the traditional futures contracts.

Financial futures contracts are traded on the following financial securities, precious metals, and economic indices. The number(s) after each financial futures item refer to one or more of the exchanges, listed below on p. 684, where the contract is traded.

U.S. Treasury bonds (1, 5, 10)

U.S. Treasury notes (6½–10-year) (1)

U.S. Treasury notes (2-year) (1)

U.S. Treasury bills (up to 1-year) (2)

Eurodollar time deposits (3-month) (2)

GNMA collateralized deposit receipts (CDR) (1)

Domestic U.S. certificates of deposit (3-month) (2)

Deutsche mark (2, 8)

Canadian dollar (2)

French franc (2)

Swiss franc (2, 8)

Dutch guilder (2)

British pound (2, 8)

Mexican peso (2)

Japanese yen (2, 8)
U.S. dollar (11)
Standard & Poor's 500 Stock Composite Index (3)
Value Line Stock Index (4)
NYSE Composite Stock Index (6)
NYSE Financial Stocks Index (6)
Canadian bonds (8-year) (7)
Canadian bonds (3–5-year) (7)
Canadian T-bills (13-week) (7)
Toronto equity futures contract (7)
Long-term bonds (8)
20-Year UK gilt interest rate (8)
3-Month Eurodollar interest rate (8)
3-Month sterling interest rate (8)
Share price index of Australia (11)
90-Day bank accepted bills of exchange (11)
Silver (1, 5, 12)
Gold (1, 2, 5, 12)
Consumer Price Index (13)

The list of financial futures contracts now being traded is growing rapidly. The financial futures on additional securities and economic indices that are awaiting approval of the federal government's Commodity Futures Trading Commission (CFTC) is almost as long as the list above.

The financial futures contracts listed above are traded at the commodity exchanges listed below. Slightly different versions of the same financial futures contract are traded on more than one exchange in some cases.

1. Chicago Board of Trade
2. International Monetary Market (IMM) of the Chicago Mercantile Exchange
3. Index and Option Market (IOM) of the Chicago Mercantile Exchange
4. Kansas City Board of Trade
5. Mid-America Commodity Exchange
6. New York Futures Exchange (NYFE)
7. Toronto Stock Exchange
8. Winnipeg Commodity Exchange
9. London International Financial Futures Exchange (LIFE)
10. International Futures Exchange (INTEX) of Bermuda
11. Sydney Futures Exchange Ltd. (of Australia)
12. Commodity Exchange (COMEX) in NYC
13. New York Coffee, Sugar, and Cocoa Exchange (NYCSC)

In order to sharpen our focus of exactly what comprises a financial future and how it works, the futures contract based on the Standard and Poor's 500 Stocks Composite Index is discussed below in some detail.

23-2 THE FINANCIAL FUTURES CONTRACT ON S&P 500 INDEX

The Chicago Mercantile Exchange (CME) has a subsidiary named the Index and Option Market (IOM). The IOM obtained permission from the federal government's Commodity Futures Trading Commission (CFTC) in 1982 to begin trading futures contracts on the Standard and Poor's 500 Stocks Composite Index (S&P 500).[2] Let us investigate this ingenious new financial future because it is interesting both in its own right and as a way to learn about financial futures in general.

23-2.1 long or short the contract?

Some investors feel more adept at forecasting the trend of the stock market's average price than they do at selecting individual issues. These investors may take one of two basic positions with the S&P 500 futures contract.

1. Bullish traders should buy the S&P 500 futures contract—that is, they should take a *long position.* If their optimistic expectations are borne out, they will profit in proportion to the increase in the index's value.
2. Bearish investors should sell the S&P 500 futures contract. By selling the contract *short,* pessimistic investors can gain earnings in proportion to the decrease in the S&P 500 index.

Daily changes in the S&P 500 index are highly correlated with the changes in other stock market indices, as shown in Table 23-1. Furthermore, Table 7-1 on page 182 shows that the monthly price changes tend to be more highly correlated than the day-to-day changes shown in Table 23-1.

Almost all futures contract buyers close out their long positions by selling their contract before it matures—this is called making a *reversing transaction*—rather than holding the contract until it expires and then taking delivery. Essentially, these buyers take their profits or losses at a time they think is advantageous for them, rather than waiting for their contract to expire. However, a small fraction of futures contract buyers hold their contracts until they expire and take delivery on the contracted commodity. The natural question is, "What do buyers of a S&P 500 futures contract *receive* if they hold the contract until its delivery (or expiration) date?"

[2] The CFTC and the legislation that governs the commodity exchanges and the commodity futures industry is discussed briefly in Sec. 4-3 of Chap. 4. Section 4-3 also provides references where more legal details can be obtained.

TABLE 23-1 correlation coefficients between daily changes in stock market index, 1971–1982

	S&P 500	Value Line	NYSE*	DJIA†
S&P 500	1.0			
Value Line	.88	1.0		
NYSE	.98	.93	1.0	
DJIA†	.73	.51	.64	1.0

* New York Stock Exchange.

† Dow Jones Industrial Average.

23-2.2 what is delivered on the S&P 500 futures contract?

Like the other stock market index futures, the S&P 500 index future is a cash settlement contract—only cash may be used to "make delivery" on the expiring contract. Each S&P 500 index futures contract is quoted at $500 times the value of the S&P 500 index. For instance, if the S&P 500 index reaches 121, then every S&P 500 index futures contract is quoted at (121 times $500 equals) $60,500 at that instant in time. Thus, if an investor had previously bought the S&P 500 index future long when the S&P 500 index had a value of 118, the investor profited $1500, as shown below, if the S&P 500 index reached 121 and the contract was sold.

value of S&P 500 index	×	$500	=	contract's market value	description
121		$500		$60,500	Selling price
118		$500		– $59,000	Buying price
				1,500	Profit

If, instead of taking a long position, our hypothetical trader had first sold S&P 500 futures short when the S&P 500 had a value of 118, the story would have ended differently. A short sale would have resulted in a $1500 loss from the ensuing rise in the index—as shown below.

value of S&P 500 index	×	$500	=	contract's market value	description
121		$500		– $60,500	Bought to cover short
118		$500		$59,000	Sold short
				$ 1,500	Loss

The example of the long and short positions above makes it clear that no attempt is made to deliver the S&P 500 index. Instead, the profit or loss on a financial futures contract held until maturity is resolved by cash settlement.

23-2.3 delivery months and margins

The Index and Option Market (IOM) of the Chicago Mercantile Exchange applied to the Commodity Futures Trading Commission (CFTC) and received permission to trade S&P 500 futures contracts for delivery in March, June, September, and December of each year. These are the only 4 months in which delivery on a S&P 500 futures contract can be obtained. The Kansas City Board of Trade makes a market in futures on the Value Line Stock Market Index. And, the New York Futures Exchange makes a market in futures contracts on the New York Stock Exchange Composite Index. All three of the stock market index futures have the same four delivery months to facilitate hedging and spreading transactions between them.

When investors buy a futures contract, they may either pay cash or use credit to guarantee the purchase. If a security of any kind is purchased on credit, the customer must post a performance bond which is called the *margin*. Margins on commodity futures contracts are much less than most margins required in the security markets. (For instance, margins are about one-half the value of the transaction for common stocks.) Margins on futures contracts range from 2 to 10 percent of the contract's market value. This margin money must be posted "up front" by both long buyers and short sellers to ensure that they will make good any losses on their positions.

If a trader buys one December 19X9 S&P 500 futures contract on July 18, 19X9, when the value of the index is 150 and a 5 percent *initial margin* is required, the trader must pay $3750 (equals .05 times 150 times $500) to the broker, for example. If the market value of the contract does not change, the required margin remains constant. When the contract is liquidated the initial margin is returned if the contract's price remains unchanged. However, additional margin may be either demanded from or paid to the trader if the market price of the contract fluctuates adversely or beneficially, respectively.

23-2.4 settlement prices and marking to the market

Variation margin is the additional margin required as a result of fluctuations in the market value of a futures contract; this is sometimes also called the *maintenance margin.* If the futures trader has a long (short) position and the contract's market value increases, then the position is earning (losing) money and margin payments (demands called *margin calls*) are made to (upon) the trader. When a brokerage house demands that one of its customers immediately pay cash to bring the margin level back up to an acceptable level, this is referred to as a *variation margin call.* If the customer doesn't meet this demand quickly, the brokerage house may liquidate the account rather than take a chance of suffering uncompensated losses if the value of the margined accounts suffers declines that more than wipe out the initial margin.

Variation margin requirements are based on the *closing (or settlement) price* of every commodity futures account every day. Thus, every day computers or margin clerks at all brokerage houses in the United States calculate every client's required margin and then issue variation margin calls in those cases where losses have reduced the customer's margin (or equity) in the account to unacceptable levels. A numerical example should clarify this daily procedure.

Suppose that Mr. Samuel Speculator is bullish about the outlook for common stock prices in general. As a result, let us further assume that Sam bought one December 19X1 futures contract on the S&P 500 index on July 18, 19X1, when the value of the index was 150. Mr. Speculator's initial margin requirement would be (.05 times $500 times 150 equals) $3750. Sam holds this long position open for 4 trading days and then liquidates it on July 21, 19X1, for a net profit of $5000 before brokerage commissions and income taxes. Mr. Speculator receives this $5000 net gain over the 4-day period in the form of the following outflows and inflows:

date	Sam's cashflow	explanation
7/18	− $3,750	Initial margin
7/19	− $1,900	Variation margin call
7/20	+ $1,900	Variation margin payment
7/21	+ $8,750	Liquidating value
	$5,000	Net gain over 4 days

The cashflows above are explained in Table 23-2.

TABLE 23-2 Mr. Sam Speculator's margined position in the S&P 500 contract for 4 days

item no.	titles	DAILY DATES POSITION OPEN 7/18	7/19	7/20	7/21
1	S&P 500 index's settlement price	150	146	150	160
2	Value of one contract (= item 1 × $500)	$75,000	$73,000	$75,000	$80,000
3	$ value of change in contract's value (= daily change in item 2)	NA	− $2,000	+ $2,000	+ $5,000
4	Daily owner's margin (= item 3 + previous day's values in items 4 and 6)	$3,750	$3,750 −2,000 0 $1,750	$1,750 +2,000 +1,900 $5,650	$5,650 +5,000 −1,900 $8,750
5	5% margin requirement (= .05 × item 2)*	$3,750	$3,650	$3,750	$4,000
6	Variation margin call or excess margin (= item 5 − item 4)†	0	+ $1,900	− $1,900	− $4,750

* The numerical example shown in Table 23-2 is oversimplified to make it easier to explain. In actuality, the margin requirements are more complicated than the constant 5 percent used in the table. Initial margins are usually at least double the maintenance margin requirements. Furthermore, the margin requirements on a hedged position are usually only half as much as the margins required on an unhedged long or short position.

† Payments to client are shown as negative amounts in item 6.

Commodity futures traders are required to *mark to the market* each trading day. This means that at the close of trading each day cashflows to and from the brokerage must be paid or received, respectively, to maintain the variation margin requirements. The $1900 variation margin call that Sam Speculator had to pay on July 19, 19X1, is an example of how Sam's position was "marked to the market." And the $1900 and $4750 excess margins that Sam withdrew from his account on July 20 and 21, 19X1, respectively, are examples of how marking to the market can generate cashflows for a trader if his or her position is profitable.

23-2.5 a short hedge to eliminate undiversifiable risk

Financial futures on stock market indices like the S&P 500 are excellent vehicles for constructing hedges that can eliminate some of the undiversifiable stock market risks that result from bull and bear market swings.[3] An example should clarify the value of a hedge to eliminate undiversifiable stock market risks.

HEDGING A PORTFOLIO Assume that a financial manager is responsible for a $40 million portfolio that is diversified across 30 different blue-chip stocks from 10 different industry groups. The portfolio's manager is concerned about the prospect of an upcoming bear market that could drive down the market value of the portfolio significantly. To avoid such losses the manager is considering a hedge to protect the $40 million investment's value.

[3] Chapter 10 defines undiversifiable risk, diversifiable risk, and the beta coefficient.

Since the $40 million portfolio is made up of 30 blue-chip stocks from 10 different industry groups, it occurs to the portfolio's manager that the portfolio is behaving similarly to the Dow Jones Industrial Average (DJIA). The DJIA is an average of 30 blue-chip stocks which, as shown in Table 23-1, is highly correlated with the other stock market indices.[4] Thus, the portfolio's manager concludes (correctly) that the S&P 500 futures contract should experience fluctuations in market value that are similar to the $40 million portfolio's fluctuations. Stated differently, the S&P 500 financial futures contract is an excellent financial instrument with which to hedge away some of the undiversifiable market risk from systematic market swings that affect almost all stocks' prices simultaneously.

The portfolio manager is satisfied with the 30 stocks in the portfolio. Liquidating the portfolio and buying it back after the bear market decline passes would be costly in terms of brokerage commissions alone. Therefore, the manager decides to sell short $40 million worth of S&P 500 index financial futures. Being short the S&P 500 index futures in an amount equal to the value of the long position in the stock market should substantially hedge the portfolio's value against bear market declines. If the market does decline as expected, the short position in the S&P 500 financial futures should earn about a dollar for each dollar of portfolio value that is lost in a systematic market decline. As a result, the combined value of the portfolio's long position and the short position in financial futures should remain unchanged at about $40 million until the futures contract expires, regardless of whether the stock market advances or declines. This futures transaction to minimize potential losses from an expected decline in the value of the portfolio will entail much smaller commission costs than selling the shares of stock and repurchasing them at a later date.

SAVINGS IN COMMISSION COSTS The savings to a portfolio in commission costs alone are, in most cases, sufficient to justify using futures contracts to hedge a common stock position—rather than using the common stock directly to form an offsetting position. Consider the round-turn (that is, both the buy and the sell) commissions for the $40 million portfolio (which is modest in size by Wall Street standards).

Assuming that $40 million of common stock can be sold and repurchased at a total round-turn commission cost of 1 percent suggests that this transaction would involve $400,000 in commission costs. In contrast, the round-turn commission cost for a futures contract on the Standard & Poor's 500 index is only about $25 per contract. Since 500 of these futures contracts would be needed to hedge the $40 million portfolio, the total commission cost of using the futures contracts would be (500 contracts times $25 commission apiece equals) $12,500. The estimated commission savings is ($400,000 less $12,500 equals) $387,500 from using the futures contracts to hedge the $40 million portfolio of common stocks. The disadvantage of hedging with futures contracts is that after some months the contracts reach their delivery date. So, after the contracts expire a new hedge with new hedge costs must be established if the need for the hedge remains.

[4] Chapter 7 analyzes the DJIA in some detail and compares it to other market indices.

The portfolio hedging transaction hypothesized above in which the trader hedges a long position by selling futures short is called a *short hedge.* The risks inherent in this strategy are the basis risks that result (1) because the basis between the S&P 500 index and the portfolio will not remain constant as their values fluctuate similarly but not in perfect harmony, and (2) if the futures contracts expire before the expected systematic market decline is past. The example provided was simple; more sophisticated hedging procedures exist.[5]

23-2.6 spreading between different stock index futures

The S&P 500 index financial futures contract is not the only financial future based on a stock market index. Table 23-3 lists details about three similar but different stock market index futures contracts. The primary difference between the three contracts is the indices on which they are based.

The correlation coefficients in Table 23-1 above indicate that the prices of the three different stock market futures should move together, since the indices on which they are based are highly correlated. Since none of the correlations are equal to 1, however, none of the stock market futures should move together in perfect unison—small differences remain. These differences are basis risk differences similar to the differences in grain prices that may exist, for instance, because different qualities of the same grain are delivered under similar grain contracts.

Other types of basis risk exist too. Even though three similar financial futures contracts on different stock market indices have the same delivery months, the fact that their delivery days differ slightly will introduce additional small elements of basis risk between the contracts. These small basis risks provide the incentive for a form of arbitrage that is referred to as *intermarket spreading.*[6]

An intermarket spread could be set up by (1) taking a long position with the S&P 500 index contract and (2) *simultaneously* selling short an equal quantity of financial futures on the NYSE Composite Index that have the same delivery months, for instance. Any changes in the market values of these long and short positions will almost, but not quite, offset each other. However, the basis risk associated with the small spread between the two different contracts is what provides the profit opportunity that motivates the spread. The spreader's goal is to gain more on one "leg" of the spread than is lost on the other "leg."

Some people say that spreading is less risky than taking an unhedged long or short position alone.[7] However, the appearance of the safe hedge can be

[5] See Frank J. Fabozzi and Gregory M. Kipnis, *Stock Index Futures,* Dow Jones-Irwin, Homewood, Ill., 1984. See also Nancy H. Rothstein (ed.), *Handbook of Financial Futures,* McGraw-Hill, New York, 1983, chaps. 9–12. See Allan M. Loosigian, *Interest Rate Futures,* Dow Jones-Irwin, Homewood, Ill., 1980; Allan M. Loosigian, *Foreign Exchange Futures,* Dow Jones-Irwin, Homewood, Ill., 1981.

[6] Arbitragers create different kinds of spreads—intermonth spreads, butterfly spreads, intercommodity spreads, and intermarket spreads. For a discussion see James M. Little, "Strategies for Speculation," in Nancy H. Rothstein (ed.), *Handbook of Financial Futures,* McGraw-Hill, New York, 1983, see chap. 9, especially pp. 145–153.

[7] Mark Castelino and Ashok Vora, "Spread Volatility in Commodity Futures: The Length Effect," *Journal of Futures Market,* Spring 1984, vol. 4, no. 1, pp. 39–46.

TABLE 23-3 stock index futures contract specifications

contract	exchange	price quotation	minimum fluctuation (tick)/ value	maximum fluctuation (limit)/ value	margin initial/ maintenance	trading hours	contract delivery months	settlement (delivery) date(s)	delivery invoicing method	last trading day
New York Stock Exchange Composite Index (NYSE Composite Index)	New York Futures Exchange (NYFE)	$500 times the NYSE Composite Index	.05 (5 BP)* $25	None (5 BP)*	Speculative: $3,500/$1500 Hedge: $1500/$750	10:00–4:15 EST	Mar., June, Sept., Dec.	Last business day in settlement month	Cash settlement based on the value of the NYSE Composite Index at close of trading at NYSE on the last trading day	Business day prior to last business day in settlement month
Standard & Poor's 500 Stock Index (S&P 500 Index)	Index and Options Market (a division of the Chicago Mercantile Exchange)	$500 times the Standard & Poor's 500 Index	.05 (5 BP)* $25	None	Speculative: $6000/$2500 Hedge: $2500/$750	9:00–3:15 CST	Mar., June, Sept., Dec.	Last day of trading	Cash settlement based on closing quotation of Standard & Poor's Price Index on last day of trading	3d Thurs. of contract month
Value Line	Kansas City Board of Trade (KCBT)	500 times futures price in units of Value Line Composite average	.01 (1 BP)* $5	None	Speculative: $6500/$5100 Hedge: $3500/$3500	9:00–3:15 CST	Mar., June, Sept., Dec.	First business day of month immediately following contract month	Cash settlement via wire transfer through clearing house	Last business day of contract month

* BP stands for basis points, or hundredths of the $500.

misleading. Since the two hedged contracts are likely to move in fairly close tandem (as indicated in Table 23-1), the commodity exchanges and brokerages have smaller margin requirements on hedged positions than on unhedged positions. Therein lies the danger. The lower margin percentage requirements allow the spreader to take a larger position than would have been permitted without the hedge if the same amount of initial margin money were invested. Because of the larger hedged position the spreader may enter, the risk exposure with the spread may be greater than the risk exposure with the seemingly safer unhedged position of lesser size.

23-2.7 price quotations in newspapers

The prices of all actively traded futures contracts are published in the next day's news by large national newspapers like *The New York Times* and *The Wall Street Journal;* the S&P 500 futures is one of those published. Figure 23-2 is a newspaper excerpt showing the S&P 500 index futures contract price quotations for 1 trading day.

The market price of the S&P 500 contract is 500 times the value of the S&P 500 index. Thus, when the S&P 500 index is 170.5, for instance, the price of one contract is a much larger number, as shown below.

170.5	Hypothetical Standard & Poor's 500 index value
× 500	The multiplier of 500 times
$85,250.00	Resulting value of S&P 500 futures contract

In order to conserve newspaper space, the excerpt in Fig. 23-2 shows that only the value of the index is published, not the larger value of the contract's prices. The notes in Fig. 23-2 explain the meanings of the values of the numbers in each column. Each row of the figure represents a S&P 500 futures contract with a different expiration month. At the bottom of the price quotations in Fig. 23-2 are statistics about the volume of contracts traded and the next day's values for the S&P 500 index.

FIGURE 23-2 S&P 500 stock index futures contract price quotations from a newspaper excerpt.

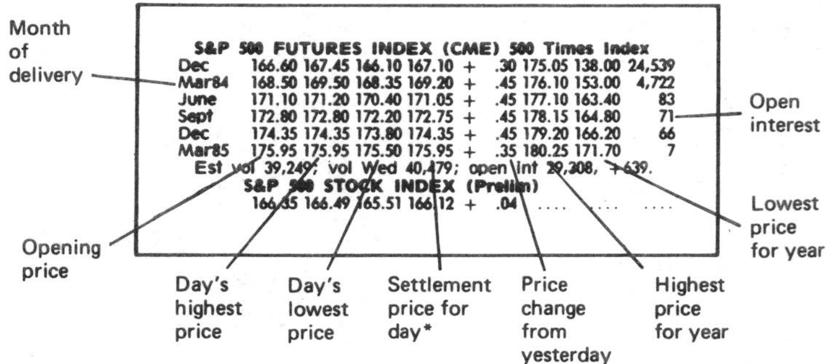

S&P 500 FUTURES INDEX (CME) 500 Times Index

Dec	166.60	167.45	166.10	167.10	+	.30	175.05	138.00	24,539
Mar84	168.50	169.50	168.35	169.20	+	.45	176.10	153.00	4,722
June	171.10	171.20	170.40	171.05	+	.45	177.10	163.40	83
Sept	172.80	172.80	172.20	172.75	+	.45	178.15	164.80	71
Dec	174.35	174.35	173.80	174.35	+	.45	179.20	166.20	66
Mar85	175.95	175.95	175.50	175.95	+	.35	180.25	171.70	7

Est vol 39,249; vol Wed 40,479; open int 29,308, +639.

S&P 500 STOCK INDEX (Prelim)

	166.35	166.49	165.51	166.12	+	.04	....	....	....

*The settlement price is sometimes the same as the closing price. However, if there were several trades made at the closing bell's ring, then the most representative of these closing prices is selected as the settlement price on which mark-to-the-market computations are calculated for that day.

In addition to the stock market index contracts, bond market index contracts exist.[8]

23-3 FINANCIAL FUTURES ON TREASURY SECURITIES

One of the largest securities markets in the world is the market for the debt securities issued by the U.S. Treasury—Treasury bills, Treasury notes, and Treasury bonds. One of the most active categories of financial futures are the contracts on these Treasury securities. Table 23-4 lists financial futures on Treasury securities of various types.

Financial futures on stock market indices differ from the futures contracts on Treasury securities in two major respects. First, the contracts on Treasury securities are called *interest rate futures*, because their prices are determined by market interest rates. In contrast, interest rates are only one of many factors that affect the prices of common stocks. The second major difference between stock index futures and interest rate futures is that Treasury securities, unlike the stock market indices, may actually be delivered when the contract expires. Interest rate futures are not cash settlement contacts, as are the stock index futures. In addition to these two major differences, there are a number of other significant differences. Let us consider futures contracts on Treasury securities in more detail.

Treasury bills are the single most important money market security traded. With over $300 billion in T-bills outstanding, the futures contracts on this underlying security are traded actively in liquid markets. Over $3 billion worth of T-bills are traded on an average day as their prices fluctuate throughout each trading day. Figure 23-3 shows 1 day's T-bill quotations from a daily national newspaper.

23-3.1 reading T-bill price quotations

The first column of Fig. 23-3 shows the maturity date of each T-bill issue. The term to maturity for each T-bill is calculated by counting from November 17, 19X3, the date of the quotations, to the maturity date. No price data are

[8] For additional discussion of the determinants of the value of financial futures consult the following articles: G. M. Constantinides, "Capital Market Equilibrium with Personal Tax," *Econometrica*, 1983; B. Cornell and M. R. Reinganum, "Forward and Futures Prices: Evidence from the Foreign Exchange Markets," *Journal of Finance*, 1981, vol. 36, pp. 1035–1045; B. Cornell and Kenneth R. French, "The Pricing of Stock Index Futures," *Journal of Futures Markets*, 1983, vol. 3, no. 1, pp. 1–14; B. Cornell and K. R. French, "Taxes and the Pricing of Stock Index Futures," *Journal of Finance*, June 1983, pp. 675–694; J. C. Cox, J. E. Ingersoll, and S. A. Ross, "The Relation between Forward and Futures Prices," *Journal of Financial Economics*, 1981, vol. 9, pp. 321–346; E. Elton, M. Gruber, and J. Rentzler, "Intra-day Tests of the Efficiency of the Treasury Bill Futures Markets," *Review of Economics and Statistics*, vol. 66, no. 1, pp. 129–137; Frank J. Fabozzi and Gregory M. Kipnis, *Stock Index Futures*, Dow Jones-Irwin, Homewood, Ill., 1984; K. R. French, "The Pricing of Futures and Forward Contracts," Ph.D. dissertation, University of Rochester, 1982a; K. R. French, "A Comparison of Futures and Forward Prices," working paper, UCLA, 1982b; R. A. Jarrow and G. S. Oldfield, "Forward Contracts and Futures Contracts," *Journal of Financial Economics*, 1981, vol. 9, pp. 373–382; R. J. Rendleman and C. E. Carabini, "The Efficiency of the Treasury Bill Futures Market," *Journal of Finance*, 1979, vol. 34, pp. 895–914; S. F. Richard and M. Sundaresan, "A Continuous Time Equilibrium Model of Forward Prices and Futures Prices in a Multigood Economy," *Journal of Financial Economics*, 1981, vol. 9, pp. 347–372.

TABLE 23-4 interest rate futures contracts on Treasury securities

contract	exchange	contract size	price quotation method	minimum fluctuation (tick)/ value	maximum fluctuation (limit)/ value	margin initial/ maintenance	trading hours	contract delivery months	settlement (delivery) date(s)	deliverable grade	delivery invoicing method	last trading day
U.S. Treasury bonds (20-year)	Chicago Board of Trade (CBT)	$100,000 principal	% of par quoted in 32ds of a pt	1/32d of a pt $31.25	64/32 (2 pts) $2,000	Speculative: $4500/$3000 Hedge: $3000/$3000	8:00–2:00 CST	Mar. June Sept. Dec.	Any business day during month	U.S. Treasury bonds with not less than 15 years to call or maturity	(Conversion factor × futures price × $1000) + accrued interest	7 business days prior to last business day of month
U.S. Treasury bonds (20-year)	MidAmerica Commodity Exchange (MIDAM)	$50,000 principal $15.62	% of par quoted in 32ds of a pt	1/32d of a pt $15.62	64/32 (2 pts) $1,000	$1500/$1000	8:00–2:10 CST	Mar. June Sept. Dec.	Any business day during month	U.S. Treasury bonds with not less than 15 years to call or maturity	(Conversion factor × futures price × $1000) + accrued interest	7 business days prior to last business day of month
U.S. Treasury bills (90-day)	International Monetary Market (IMM)	$1,000,000 face value	Annualized discount yield: 100 − discount yield − price	1/100 of 1% (1 BP) $25.00	6/100 of 1% (60 BP) $1,500	$2500/$2000	8:00–2:00 CST	Mar. June Sept. Dec.	3-day period beginning 1st Thurs. after 3d weekly bill auction in the delivery month	13-week U.S. Treasury bills with $1,000,000 face value	Wire transfer vs. deposit in one of 4 Chicago banks or a registered New York bank	2d day following 3d weekly T-bill auction in contract month
U.S. Treasury bills (90-day)	MidAmerica Commodity Exchange (MIDAM)	$500,000 face value	% of par quoted in 32ds of a pt	1/100 of 1% (1 BP) $12.50	64/32 (2 pts) $1,000	$1250/$1000	8:00–2:15 CST	Mar. June Sept. Dec.	Weds. following 3d Mon. of contract month	Cash settlement. No delivery	Based on settlement price of IMM T-bill contract	2d day following 3d weekly T-bill auction in contract month
U.S. Treasury notes (10-year)	Chicago Board of Trade (CBT)	$100,000 principal	Annualized discount yield: 100 − discount yield − price	1/32d of a pt $31.25	60/100 of a pt (60 BP) $750	Speculative: $3000/$2000 Hedge: $2000/$2000	8:00–2:00 CST	Mar. June Sept. Dec.	Any business day during month	U.S. Treasury notes with maturity of 6½–10 years	(Conversion factor × futures price × $1000) + accrued interest	7 business days prior to last business day of month

U.S. Treas. Bills

Mat. date	Bid Discount	Asked Discount	Yield
-19X3-			
11-25	7.90	7.80	7.94
12- 1	8.38	8.30	8.46
12- 8	8.28	8.20	8.37
12-15	7.90	7.80	7.97
12-22	8.24	8.12	8.31
12-29	8.38	8.30	8.51
-19X4-			
1- 5	8.45	8.35	8.58
1-12	8.48	8.40	8.65
1-19	8.62	8.54	8.81
1-26	8.69	8.61	8.89
2- 2	8.78	8.70	9.00
2- 9	8.80	8.72	9.04
2-16	8.84	8.82	9.16
2-23	8.88	8.80	9.16
3- 1	8.86	8.76	9.13

Mat. date	Bid Discount	Asked Discount	Yield
-19X4-			
3- 8	8.86	8.76	9.15
3-15	8.85	8.75	9.15
3-22	8.90	8.82	9.24
3-29	8.90	8.82	9.26
4- 5	8.94	8.86	9.32
4-84	8.98	8.90	9.38
4-19	8.99	8.91	9.41
4-26	8.99	8.91	9.43
5- 3	8.97	8.89	9.42
5-84	9.04	8.96	9.51
5-17	9.01	8.99	9.57
6-14	9.01	8.95	9.54
7-12	9.01	8.97	9.58
8- 9	9.09	9.01	9.66
9- 6	9.13	9.07	9.77
10- 4	9.12	9.04	9.79
11- 1	9.12	9.06	9.86

FIGURE 23-3 Treasury bill quotations for November 17, 19X3. (*Source:* November 18, 19X3 newspaper excerpt.).

shown in Fig. 23-3; the prices must be computed from the bid yields and asked yields shown in the second and third columns, respectively. The *T-bill yields* shown in columns two and three are calculated with Eq. (23-1*a*).

$$\text{T-bill yield} = \frac{[(\text{face value} - \text{price}) \times 360]/\text{days to maturity}}{\text{face value}} \tag{23-1a}$$

The T-bill yield is synonymously called the *discount yield* and the *bank discount rate.* This is an annualized yield.

For example, a \$1,000,000, 91-day T-bill with a price of \$984,833.33 would have a T-bill yield of 6 percent, as shown below.

$$\frac{[(\$1{,}000{,}000 - \$984{,}333.33) \times 360]/91}{\$1{,}000{,}000} = .06 = 6.0\% \tag{23-1b}$$

Newspaper readers who want to know either the bid price or the asked price can algebraically solve Eq. (23-1*a*) for the price, as shown in Eq. (23-2*a*), substitute in the appropriate values from the newspaper, and calculate the price.

$$\text{Price} = \left[1 - \left(\frac{\begin{matrix}\text{days to} \\ \text{maturity}\end{matrix} \times \begin{matrix}\text{T-bill} \\ \text{yield}\end{matrix}}{360}\right)\right]\text{face value} \tag{23-2a}$$

The fourth column of Fig. 23-3 gives the *bond-equivalent yield,* which is based on asked prices, as defined in Eq. (23-3).

$$\begin{matrix}\text{Bond} \\ \text{equivalent} \\ \text{yield}\end{matrix} = \frac{[(\text{face value} - \text{asked price}) \times 365]/\text{days to maturity}}{\text{price}} \tag{23-3}$$

There are two significant differences between Eqs. (23-1*a*) and (23-3).[9]

[9] Equation (23-3) is true for maturities of less than 182 days. For instruments with maturities in excess of 182 days see Marcia Stigum, *Money Market Calculations: Yields, Break-Evens, and Arbitrage*, Dow Jones-Irwin, Homewood, Ill., 1981, pp. 33–35. See also Bruce D. Fielitz, "Calculating the Bond Equivalent Yield for T-Bills," *Journal of Portfolio Management*, Spring 1983, pp. 58–60.

The T-bill yield definition uses a 360-day year, whereas the bond equivalent yield uses a 365-day year. The second difference is the denominators. Equation (23-3) realistically bases the yield on the *actual* price. In contrast, Eq. (23-1*a*) is based on the face value—a less realistic yield measure results.

Equation (23-4) defines the yield to maturity, denoted r, for a T-bill (or any zero coupon bond).[10] This measure needs to be annualized to facilitate yield comparisons.

$$\text{Price} = \frac{\text{face value}}{(1.0 + r)^t} \tag{23-4}$$

Algebraically solving Eq. (23-4) for the yield to maturity results in Eq. (23-5), which is computationally more handy.

$$r = \sqrt[t]{\frac{\text{face value}}{\text{price}}} - 1.0 \tag{23-5}$$

Equations (23-1*a*), (23-3), and (23-5) are all similar rate-of-return measures. But all three differ slightly, and these differences should not be overlooked.

23-3.2 the IMM's T-bill futures contract

The International Monetary Market (IMM) of the Chicago Mercantile Exchange (CME) started trading the first futures contract with T-bills as the underlying commodity in 1976. Although competing T-bill contracts have been introduced by other exchanges since 1976, the IMM contract remains the most actively traded. Therefore, we will discuss the IMM contract in detail—the concepts also apply to other T-bill futures, although the similar contracts traded on other exchanges have slightly different delivery dates and differ in other details.

The IMM's T-bill futures contract has a $1 million face value. This means that whoever is short the contract must deliver T-bills with $1 million face value when the contract expires. The long buyer, in contrast, buys the contract at a fluctuating market price that varies inversely with market interest rates.[11]

Consider how the price of a T-bill futures contract is derived. It is traditional in securities markets for bid prices (that is, the highest bid made by a potential purchaser) to be lower than the offering price (namely, the lowest price at which any potential seller will sell). Because of the inverse relationship

[10] The yield to maturity for coupon bonds was discussed at length in Sec. 11-3 of Chap. 11. Equation (23-4) measures the same compound rate of return when no coupons exist.

[11] The minimum yield change for T-bill futures contracts is 1 basis point, as indicated in column five of Table 23-4 above. The following formula is used to determine the dollar value of the smallest price change associated with a yield change of 1 basis point.

[(1/100) of 1.0%] × [face value] × [fraction of year to maturity] = [$ value of 1 basis point]

Example 1: a full (360-day) year's contract for $1,000,000

$$.0001 \times \$1{,}000{,}000 \times \frac{360}{360} = \$100$$

Example 2: a 90-day T-bill contract on IMM

$$.0001 \times \$1{,}000{,}000 \times \frac{90}{360} = \$25$$

The formula above shows that the relationship between basis point changes in yields and dollar changes in the price of a contract depends on both the face value and the term to maturity for the contract.

between interest rates and bond prices, it is also traditional and logical for bid yields (not bid prices) to be higher than offer yields. Thus, if a T-bill is sold at a greater yield, its price declines.

When the T-bill futures contract was being written a unique value called the *IMM index* was defined to make the IMM T-bill futures prices conform with all the traditional pricing relationships. The IMM index is defined in Eq. (23-6*a*).

$$\text{IMM index} = 100.0 - (\text{T-bill futures yield}) \qquad (23\text{-}6a)$$

$$94.0 = 100.00 - 6.0 \qquad (23\text{-}6b)$$

Note that the T-bill yield defined in Eq. (23-1*a*) is used in the IMM index rather than one of the other rate-of-return measures. It is also worthwhile to observe that the IMM index is not an actual price of a 90-day bill since the T-bill yield [Eq. (23-1*a*)], from which the IMM index is calculated, is an *annualized* interest rate. This annualization facilitates comparison of the yields and IMM index values of T-bills with different maturities (for example, a 3-month T-bill and a 6-month T-bill), but it does not yield actual market prices for the contracts.

To continue the example of the 6 percent 91-day T-bill from Eq. (23-1*b*), Eq. (23-6*b*) above indicates an IMM index value of 94.0 for the T-bill. The IMM index produces results that conform to the traditional quotation procedures listed below.

1. Bond prices and yields move inversely.
2. Bid prices are always lower than asked prices.
3. Bid yields are always higher than asked yields (as shown in Fig. 23-3, for example).

The final step is to convert the IMM index to an actual T-bill price. Equation (23-2*a*) is used to calculate the price because it considers: (1) the number of days to maturity, (2) the T-bill yield, and (3) the face value of the T-bill in question. All three values are essential price determinants. The price of $1 million face value T-bill with 91 days to maturity and a 6 percent T-bill yield is $984,833.33, as shown below in Eq. (23-2*b*).

$$\text{Price} = \left[1.0 - \left(\frac{\text{days to maturity} \times \text{T-bill yield}}{360}\right)\right]\left(\text{face value}\right) \qquad (23\text{-}2a)$$

$$\$984{,}833.33 = \left[1.0 - \left(\frac{91 \times .06}{360}\right)\right](\$1{,}000{,}000) \qquad (23\text{-}2b)$$

To see how gains or losses are calculated, suppose a speculator expects market interest rates to drop from the T-bill yield of 6 percent shown in Eq. (23-1*b*) and (23-2*b*), to 4 percent. Further assume that this speculator therefore purchases a T-bill future in order to profit from the expected decline in interest rates. If this speculator's expectations are suddenly fulfilled as interest rates drop in the same day the T-bill future is purchased, the speculator enjoys a gain of $25 per basis point, as shown in column five of Table 23-4 for the IMM T-bill contract. Thus, the 200 basis point drop in the yield (times $25 per basis point) equals a $5,000 total gain.

FIGURE 23-4 Treasury bill futures contract's price quotations for November 17, 19X3. (*Source:* November 18, 19X3 newspaper excerpt.)

TREASURY BILLS (IMM)—$1 mil.; pts. of 100%

	Open	High	Low	Settle	Chg	Discount Settle	Discount Chg	Open Interest
Dec	91.00	91.03	90.97	91.02	− .05	8.98	+ .05	26,004
Mar×4	90.59	90.61	90.55	90.60	− .06	9.40	+ .06	18,742
June	90.29	90.29	90.25	90.28	− .06	9.28	+ .06	4,637
Sept	90.03	90.03	89.99	90.03	− .06	9.97	+ .06	1,565
Dec	89.81	89.81	89.78	89.81	− .06	10.19	+ .06	470
Mar×5	89.61	89.62	89.58	89.61	− .06	10.39	+ .06	178
June	89.41	89.41	89.37	89.41	− .07	10.59	+ .07	124
Sept	....	....	....	89.32	+ .02	10.68	− .02	12

Est vol 12,489; vol Wed 14,475; open int 51,732, −749.

23-3.3 price quotations for the IMM T-bill contract

Figure 23-4 shows an excerpt from a newspaper reporting the preceding day's prices for the IMM T-bill contract. The first column lists the delivery months of the contracts traded. Note that the contracts' expiration dates extend up to 2 years into the future. As indicated above in the far right-hand column of row three in Table 23-4, trading in the expiring T-bill contracts terminates 2 business days after the third weekly 3-month T-bill auction of the delivery month. These auctions are held almost every Monday at the Federal Reserve Bank of New York City, but the contracts expire in only the third week of every third month. So, there are no T-bill futures contracts expiring near the dates of more than 90 percent of the weekly T-bill auctions.

The values of the IMM index calculated with Eq. (23-6) are shown in columns two, three, four, and five of Fig. 23-4 for the day's opening value, the day's highest value, the day's lowest value, and the day's settlement price, respectively.[12] The "Chg" heading over column six refers to the change in the settlement price from the preceding day's settlement price.

Columns seven and eight of Fig. 23-4 fall under the word "Discount." Column seven shows the T-bill discount yield calculated with Eq. (23-1*a*) based on the day's settlement price for the IMM index. Column eight gives the change in this T-bill discount yield from the preceding trading day. Column nine, headed "Open Interest," shows the total number of open contracts for each different T-bill contract. Below the price quotations in Fig. 23-4 are figures for the day's estimated volume of contracts traded, the preceding day's volume, the total open interest over all IMM T-bill contracts (that is, the total of column nine), and the change in the total open interest since the preceding trading day.

[12] The settlement price is selected by the clearinghouse of the commodity exchange after every trading day. This settlement price is used in determining net gains or losses, margin requirements, and the next day's price limits. The term *settlement price* is also often used as an approximate equivalent to the term *closing price*. The close in futures trading refers to a brief period of time at the end of the trading day during which transactions frequently take place quickly and at a range of prices. The settlement price is the closing price if there is only one closing price. When there is a *range* of closing prices, the settlement price is as near the midpoint of the closing range as possible, consistent with the contract's price change increments. Thus, the settlement price can be used to provide a single reference point for analysis of marking to the market.

23-3.4 delivery procedures for the T-bill future

When any IMM T-bill future expires and it is time for the contract's seller to make delivery, the procedure illustrated in Fig. 23-5 is followed. The contract buyer and the contract seller each have a responsibility to perform certain steps in the delivery procedure.

Commodity brokerages or full-service security brokerages like E. F. Hutton, Merrill Lynch, Bache, or Paine Webber are members of the IMM's clearinghouse. Every buyer and every seller is represented by one of these so-called "clearing members."

THE SELLER'S DELIVERY COMMITMENT The clearing member representing the seller of a T-bill future is responsible for delivering a seller's delivery commitment to the IMM clearinghouse by noon of the last trading day. This delivery commitment must specify the name of a Chicago bank (1) that is a member of the Federal Reserve System, (2) at which the seller has a bank account, and (3) which must be registered with the IMM. No later than 12:45 PM on the delivery day the seller must transfer from his or her prespecified bank account the T-bills to fulfill the delivery obligation. The seller is responsible for seeing that these T-bills reach the bank selected by the buyer by 12:45 PM and bear whatever costs are incurred to complete the delivery. This process is illustrated in Fig. 23-5.

THE BUYER'S DELIVERY COMMITMENT The buyer's broker must deliver a buyer's delivery commitment to the IMM clearinghouse by noon of the last trading

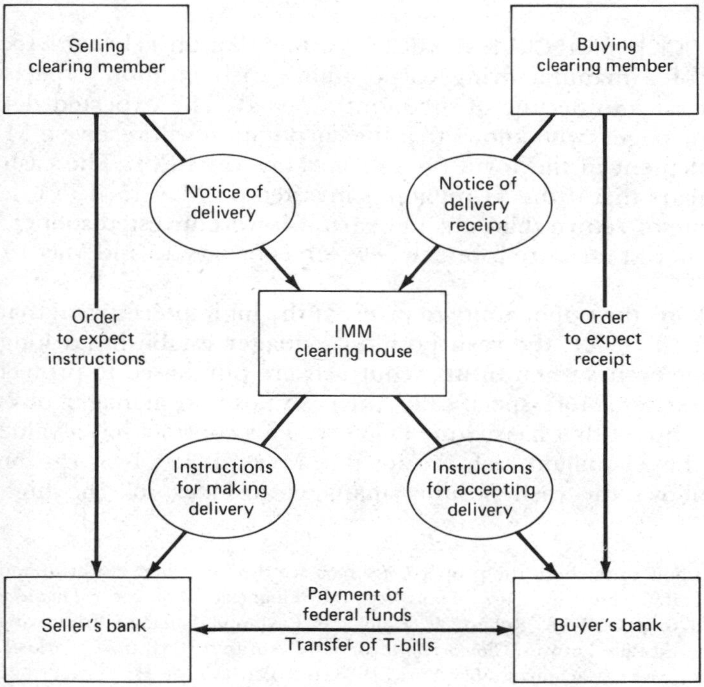

FIGURE 23-5 IMM's delivery procedure diagram.

day of the T-bill contract. This document must specify a bank account to which the T-bills can be transferred. The buyer's clearing member must present to the seller's designated agent a wire transfer of federal funds to pay in full for the purchase by 11 AM on the delivery day.

THE ROLE OF THE CLEARINGHOUSE The IMM clearinghouse matches the buyer's and seller's delivery commitments and also communicates to the buyer's bank and the seller's bank the instructions needed to complete the delivery transaction. The clearinghouse also monitors these delivery procedures to ensure the timely transfer and payment between the buyer and seller. Should either party default in any way, the clearinghouse will complete the transaction on schedule at its own expense. Later, the clearinghouse will collect damages from the defaulted party. As a result of the clearinghouse's role, no IMM contract has ever failed to be delivered on schedule.

As shown in Table 23-4, the IMM is not the only financial futures exchange that makes a market in Treasury securities. Each different exchange's futures contract on a Treasury security is unique in some respect, and each exchange's clearinghouse follows a different delivery procedure. However, all these competing futures markets function smoothly and are growing.

23-3.5 speculating on interest rate changes

Futures contracts on Treasury securities provide a useful vehicle for speculating on forecasted changes in market interest rates. Hedging strategies, spreads of various types, and arbitrage opportunities can be profitably exploited if the speculator can correctly forecast market interest rates. A few possibilities are discussed below.

A LONG HEDGE TO LOCK IN HIGH CURRENT RATES Assume that on February 15, 19X1, a manager of a manufacturing corporation's cash position expects short-term interest rates to decline in the months ahead. The expected decline troubles this manager, who knows that the corporation will receive a $1 million lawsuit settlement in the form of cash on May 15, 19X1. The cash position manager fears that if the $1 million is invested on May 15, 19X1, it will earn a lower rate of return than it could earn if it were invested sooner, because declining interest rates are foreseen between February 15 and May 15 of 19X1.

In order to "lock in" the opportunity to invest at the high interest rate that exists on February 15, 19X1, the cash position manager establishes a long hedge. A long hedge occurs when futures contracts are purchased to protect against future price rises. More specifically, the cash position manager buys one 90-day T-bill contract that has a June delivery. This contract has a value that is as close to the $1 million cash receipt due May 15, 19X1, as can be obtained.[13] This allows the cash position manager to "lock in" the high

[13] For directions on how to establish the proper *hedge ratio* see the following: P. Bacon and R. Williams, "Interest Rate Futures: New Tools for the Financial Manager," *Financial Management,* Spring 1976, pp. 32–38; Robert W. Kolb and Raymond Chiang, "Improving Performance Using Interest Rate Futures," *Financial Management,* Autumn 1981, p. 77; Sarkis J. Khoury, *Investment Management,* Macmillan, New York, 1983, pp. 454–455.

TABLE 23-5 results of a long hedge in 90-day T-bill futures

cash market	futures market	summary for day	
February 15, 19X1: no transaction occurs, but 90-day T-bills are yielding 7.60%	February 15, 19X1: cash position manager buys 90-day T-bill future maturing in June for 91.90	Long hedge laid down to "lock in" high yield of 8.1 percent	February 15, 19X1
May 15, 19X1: $1 million cash received and used to purchase one 90-day T-bill yielding 6.80%	May 15, 19X1: cash manager sells June 90-day T-bill future contract for 92.80	Hedge lifted when cash invested at an effective yield of 7.7%	May 15, 19X1
80 basis points less interest income earned because cash not invested sooner, an opportunity loss	90 basis point profit earned on one T-bill contract (= 92.80 − 91.90)	Effective yield is 7.7% (= 6.8% + .90%) because of hedge.	Overall summary

current yield 4 months before the $1 million cash is actually received and available to be invested. Table 23-5 summarizes the results of such a profitable long hedge.

The long hedge in Table 23-5 was reversed (or unwound) when the cash available for investment arrived as scheduled on May 15, 19X1. If the cash position manager invested the cash without simultaneously selling the T-bill future, the portfolio would have been "doubled up"; that is, the portfolio would have had simultaneous long positions in T-bill futures and in T-bills. Doubling up is sloppy hedge administration—it should be avoided because it exposes the portfolio to double the risk and provides no hedge as protection.

No cash was lost in this example. But Table 23-5 shows that an opportunity loss of 80 (= 7.60% − 6.80%) basis points occurred in the cash market for T-bills by (unavoidably) delaying the investment. This opportunity loss was more than offset by a gain of 90 (= 92.80 − 91.90) basis points on the T-bill future, however. Thus, an effective yield of 7.7% is earned even though the T-bill rate had fallen down to 6.8% (as had been forecasted).

THE DIFFERENCE BETWEEN PRACTICE AND THEORY Unfortunately, interest rate forecasts are not always correct. First of all, if short-term interest rates had increased, instead of decreased as the cash manager had predicted, an out-of-pocket loss would have been suffered in the futures market. A second, but smaller, risk occurs because the market value of the June 90-day T-bill future contract on May 15, 19X1, was not exactly equal to the $1 million amount being hedged. Since fractions of future contracts cannot be obtained, perfect hedges for the exact amount needed are rare.

Figure 23-6 illustrates the objectives that long (or buying) hedgers idealistically seek when they employ interest rate futures contracts. But a long hedge based on a faulty interest rate forecast could work out differently.

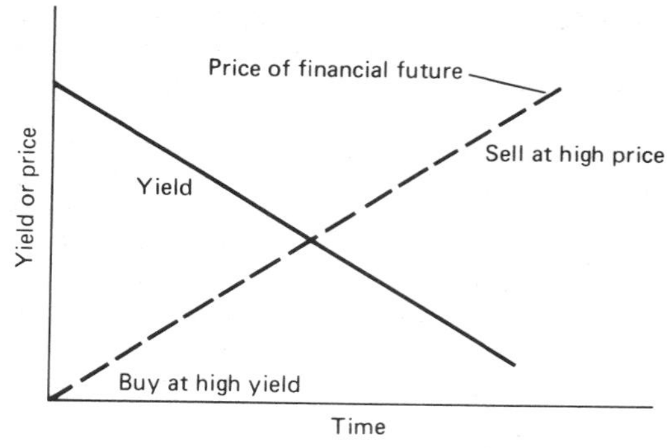

FIGURE 23-6 the objectives of a long hedge with interest rate futures when declining interest rates are expected.

23-3.6 market efficiency and quasi-arbitrage

As explained briefly in Chap. 8 and in more detail in Chap. 19, an *efficient price* fluctuates around its underlying *value* less than does an *inefficient price*. Tests of market efficiency are of interest because market inefficiencies can be profitably exploited. Let's consider a case in point.

One of the basic axioms of economics is that the same good cannot sell at two different prices. If such a price inequality emerged, riskless arbitrage profits would occur until the same good sold at the same price around the world (after allowance is made for differences in the transportation cost). For example, suppose that $1 million T-bills from the same issue (which were perfect substitutes) were selling for $1 million in New York City and only $999,999 in Boston—a tiny $1 difference. This situation could not endure because profit-seeking arbitragers would keep buying millions of dollars of T-bills in Boston and then instantly resell them in New York. The arbitragers would make a $1 profit per T-bill without taking any risk because they would be perfectly hedged with a short position in New York that was offset by a long position in Boston. Using wire transfers, the arbitragers could quickly make many dollars of riskless profits—except for one thing that would surely occur to stop the arbitrage profits: the price of the Boston T-bills would be bid upward by the constant purchases in Boston, and/or the price of the identical T-bills in New York City would be driven down by continual price-depressing sales pressure. When the New York and the Boston prices were equal, the arbitrage would cease, and the T-bill market would enjoy efficient prices as the *law of one price* prevailed.

The pure arbitrage model above should extend to include quasi-arbitrage too. That is, quasi-arbitrage should ensure that a real T-bill and an equivalent position involving a synthetic duplicate T-bill should both sell at the same price too.

Pure arbitrage refers to shorting one asset to fund a position in an economically equivalent asset at a lower price. *Quasi-arbitrage* refers to selling securities from an existing portfolio to fund an economically equivalent synthetically created position at a lower price. Quasi-arbitrage is explained in more detail in the following paragraph.

QUASI-ARBITRAGE WITH T-BILL FUTURES William Pool and Donald Puglisi have argued that it is possible to create a *synthetic* T-bill position that mimics a genuine T-bill position.[14] For example, Poole and Puglisi reason that a long position with a genuine 6-month T-bill is no different from a synthetic 6-month T-bill long position created by combining a genuine 3-month T-bill with a 3-month T-bill futures contract. More specifically, assume that an investor purchases a 6-month T-bill and a 3-month T-bill that both originate on the same date. In addition, the investor purchases a futures contract. This futures contract entitles its owner to take delivery of a 3-month T-bill that originates on the exact date that the other 3-month T-bill expires. Thus, the investor has created a synthetic 6-month T-bill by linking a genuine 3-month T-bill with a 3-month T-bill futures contract that delivers a second genuine T-bill to follow immediately after the first genuine 3-month T-bill.

More formally, let's adopt the following three conventions (which are somewhat similar to the conventions used to define the expectations theory about the term structure of interest rates in Chap. 13).

${}_0R_3$ = the market interest rate on a genuine 3-month T-bill purchased in the cash market that originates at time $t = 0$ and matures at time $t = 3$.

${}_0R_6$ = the market interest rate on a genuine 6-month T-bill purchased in the cash market that originates at time $t = 0$ and matures at time $t = 6$. Note that both this 6-month T-bill and the 3-month T-bill originate at the same time.

${}_3r_6$ = the rate of return earned on a 3-month T-bill futures contract that delivers a 3-month T-bill originating at time $t = 3$ and maturing at time $t = 6$. Note that this latter 3-month T-bill originates on the same date that the other 3-month T-bill expires, and it matures on the same date as the 6-month T-bill.

The relationship between these three rates of interest defined above can be stated as shown in Eq. (23-7).

$$(1.0 + {}_0R_6) = (1.0 + {}_0R_3)(1.0 + {}_3r_6) \tag{23-7}$$

$$\begin{pmatrix}\text{1.0 + interest rate} \\ \text{on genuine 6-month T-bill}\end{pmatrix} = \begin{pmatrix}\text{1.0 + interest rate on} \\ \text{synthetic 6-month T-bill}\end{pmatrix}$$

The right-hand side of Eq. (23-7) represents the rate of return from the synthetic 6-month T-bill. If the T-bill futures market is efficient, the return from the genuine 6-month T-bill, on the left-hand side of Eq. (23-7), should exactly equal the return on the synthetic 6-month T-bill because they are perfect substitutes (assuming we ignore whatever differences in taxes and transactions costs may exist). If the equality of Eq. (23-7) were an inequality, quasi-arbitrage would occur until such time as the equality were restored.

Quasi-arbitrage could be done with zero initial investment. First, the genuine 6-month T-bill could be sold short. Then, the proceeds from this short sale could be used to purchase a long position in a synthetic 6-month T-bill in a long position. Equation (23-8) indicates that the profit from this quasi-arbitrage should be zero if T-bill futures markets are efficient.

[14] William Poole, "Using T-Bill Futures to Gauge Interest Rate Expectations," *Economic Review*, Federal Reserve Bank of San Francisco, Spring 1978. Also see Donald J. Puglisi, "Is the Futures Market for Treasury Bills Efficient?" *Journal of Portfolio Management*, Winter 1978, vol. 4.

$$[(1.0 + {}_0R_3)(1.0 + {}_3r_6)] - (1.0 + {}_0R_6) = 0 \tag{23-8}$$

$$\text{Long position's return} - \text{short position's return} = \text{return from quasi-arbitrage}$$

EMPIRICAL TESTS OF T-BILL FUTURES MARKET EFFICIENCY Different researchers have constructed various forms of empirical tests to determine if quasi-arbitrage of the type outlined above can actually generate profits. Although the results were mixed, it seems that the T-bill futures market is sufficiently efficient to deny quasi-arbitragers the opportunity to get rich quick.

Some inefficiencies were discovered, however. Anthony Vignola and Charles Dale concluded that the T-bill futures market is slightly inefficient and that this inefficiency has not diminished as the market has grown and matured.[15] Poole analyzed only short-term T-bill futures and concluded that the market is efficient.[16] However, Poole's test included an inappropriate assumption about using T-bills to meet margin requirements. Richard Lang and Robert Rasche reviewed Poole's results; their own results did not suggest that all T-bill futures contracts are efficiently priced. They found that only the contracts closest to delivery, which were the contracts Poole found to be efficient, are efficient.[17] Lang and Rasche went on to conclude that

> On the basis of this evidence, we cannot conclude that the differences between the futures and forward rates have been narrowing consistently over time as the futures market for Treasury bills has become more developed.

Richard Rendelman and Christopher Carabini tested observed IMM index values to see if they fall within their expected price range. Their conclusion was that:

> To the extent that quasi-arbitrage opportunities have existed in the market, there appears to have been a tendency for the market to become less efficient over time. The pricing of the near term contract has become less efficient while the pricing of the third contract has become more efficient. However, it is doubtful that these inefficiencies have been large enough to induce portfolio managers to alter their investment policies.[18]

Additional empirical evidence about the efficiency of T-bill futures prices is forthcoming.[19]

[15] Anthony J. Vignola and Charles J. Dale, "Is the Futures Market for Treasury Bills Efficient?" *Journal of Portfolio Management,* Winter 1979, vol. 5.

[16] William Poole, "Using T-Bill Futures to Gauge Interest Rate Expectations," published by Federal Reserve Bank of San Francisco, *Economic Review,* Spring 1978.

[17] Richard W. Lang and Robert H. Rasche, "A Comparison of Yields on Futures Contracts and Implied Forward Rates," *Review,* Federal Reserve Bank of St. Louis, December 1978. Reprinted in *Interest Rate Futures: Concepts and Issues,* Gerald D. Gray and Robert W. Kolb (coeditors), Robert F. Dame, Inc. Richmond, Va., 1982, chap. 8. Several of the other articles about quasi-arbitrage referenced here are also reprinted in the book.

[18] Richard J. Rendleman, Jr., and Christopher E. Carabini, "The Efficiency of the Treasury Bill Futures Market," *Journal of Finance,* September 1979, vol. 34.

[19] Ben Branch, "Testing the Unbiased Expectations Theory of Interest Rates," *The Financial Review,* Fall 1978, vol. 13, pp. 51–66; Brian G. Chow and David J. Brophy, "The U.S. Treasury

The conclusion that quasi-arbitrage profits are not substantial does not necessarily imply that the T-bill futures market is efficient. Quasi-arbitrage profits are the easiest to detect and most blatant form of market inefficiency. Additional research into other, more subtle market strategies is needed before conclusions about the efficiency of T-bill futures prices can be attained.

In addition to stock market index futures and Treasury bill futures, there are other actively traded financial futures contracts.

23-4 T-BOND AND T-NOTE FUTURES CONTRACTS

Table 23-4 above lists the specifications for futures contracts on two different Treasury bond futures and one Treasury note future. Treasury bonds and notes are similar coupon interest-paying debt securities that differ primarily with respect to the length of time until they mature. T-bonds have longer lives than the T-notes (as explained in Chap. 2).

23-4.1 contract specifications

Figure 11-1 on page 288 is an excerpt from a daily newspaper that shows the market prices of the security underlying the T-bond futures contract. The prices of both the underlying T-bonds and T-notes and the futures contracts on them are all quoted in thirty-seconds of one percentage point. For example, 94.16 means 94$^{16}/_{32}$ percent of face or par value. Thus, a $100,000 T-bond or T-bond future quoted at 94.16 would have a market price of 94.5 percent of $100,000, or $94,500.

Both the T-bond and T-note contracts come in $100,000 denominations. And both require that 8 percent coupon securities be tendered for delivery. However, T-bonds or T-notes with coupon rates that differ from 8 percent can be delivered if suitable price adjustments are made—the price adjustments are defined in the futures contract.

The T-note and T-bond contracts have longer maturities than the money market securities on which futures contracts are traded (such as T-bills, CDs, commercial paper, and banker's acceptances). Therefore, the futures contracts on T-notes and T-bonds may be used for different purposes than T-bill futures. Consider an example of how T-bond futures have been used to short hedge a long position in corporate bonds.

23-4.2 an investment banker short hedges an underwriting

Consider the dilemma of a large investment banking firm, Salomon Brothers in this example, when they underwrite a large bond issue for a large corporation. Salomon Brothers agreed to buy and distribute a primary issue of IBM bonds maturing in 1999 with a 9 percent coupon rate that had a $1 billion face value. On October 4, 1979, Salomon paid IBM $990 million for this bond issue. The prospect of unstable market interest rates at that time worried the managers of this underwriting firm. These veteran debt underwriters were

---

Bill Futures Market and Hypotheses Regarding the Term Structure of Interest Rates," *The Financial Review,* Fall 1978, vol. 13, pp. 36–50; Dennis R. Capozza and Bradford Cornell, "Treasury Bill Pricing in the Spot and Futures Markets," *Review of Economics and Statistics,* November 1979, vol. 61, no. 4.

worried that after they paid the IBM Corporation $990 million for the long-term bond issue, but before they could sell the bonds to the public for $1 billion, market interest rates might rise and decrease the market value of the bonds while they were trying to distribute them. In order to foreclose such possible losses, let us suppose that Salomon Brothers laid down the short hedge summarized in Table 23-6.

An investment banker took legal possession of a long position in bonds with, if market interest rates stayed constant, a market value of $1 billion on October 4, 1979. To hedge the possibility that a sudden rise in market interest rates would wipe out all or part of Salomon's $10 million spread, the investment banker sold short $1 billion worth of T-bond futures. T-bond futures were used instead of T-note futures or T-bill futures because the deliverable T-bonds are required to have maturities in excess of 15 years. Thus, the T-bond futures price would be more highly correlated with any changes in the long-term corporate bond's price than would the price of a futures contract on a debt instrument with a shorter maturity. Although a futures contract on a long-term corporate bond index would provide an even better hedge for the IBM bond position, this was not possible since no futures contracts on any long-term corporate bond index existed in 1979.

TABLE 23-6 an underwriter's short hedge of a corporate bond issue

cash market	futures market	event
11 AM on Oct. 4, 1979, Salomon Bros. gives IBM a cashier's check to purchase a primary bond issue with $1 billion market value.	11 AM Oct. 4, 1979, Salomon Bros. sells 10,000 T-bond futures contracts short on the CBT with $1 billion total value.	The short hedge is laid down.
Oct. 10, 1979, at 2 PM Salomon sells $680 million of IBM bonds for $679 million, so its overnight inventory has a $320 million face value. A rise in market interest rates caused an opportunity loss of $1 million on the IBM bonds sold.	Oct. 10, 1979, at 2 PM Salomon buys back $680 million of futures (or 680 contracts) for $678 million, so it retains a $320 million short position in futures at face value. A $2 million gain on futures resulted from rising interest rates.	The short hedge is balanced so long cash and short futures positions are equal. A gain of $2 million earned on the futures more than offset $1 million lost on the inventory of bonds.
Oct. 11, 1979, Salomon sells its remaining $320 million inventory of IBM bonds for $319.5 million because interest rates stayed high. An opportunity loss of $500,000 results.	Oct. 11, 1979, Salomon buys 320 T-bond contracts with $320 million face value for $319.4 million, because interest rates stay high. A gain of $600,000 results.	The last part of the short hedge is lifted and an additional net gain of ($600,000 − $500,000 =) $100,000 is recognized.
$1,000,000 plus $500,000 equals a total opportunity loss of $1,500,000 on the inventory of IBM bonds as market interest rates rise.	$2,000,000 plus $600,000 equals $2,600,000 total profit from being short futures as market interest rates rise and remain high.	$2,600,000 gain less $1,500,000 opportunity loss equals $1,100,000 net benefit from the short hedge.

By October 10, 1979, Salomon Brothers had been able to distribute over half the issue of bonds.[20] IBM bonds with a par value of $320 million had to be carried in Salomon Brothers' overnight inventory at risk. In order to avoid being short $680 million worth of unhedged T-bond futures, Salomon Brothers covered (or bought back or unwound or reversed) $680 million of their $1 billion short position in T-bond futures. This transaction rebalanced the overnight hedged position in IBM bonds. As indicated in Table 23-6, the investment banker sold the last of the IBM bond issue on October 11, 1979. At that time the remaining $320 million short position in T-bond futures was reversed with a purchase of $320 million of futures contracts.

In constructing this hypothetical example, it was assumed that Salomon Brothers' advance fears of rising market interest rates were vindicated. As a result, the investment banker suffered an opportunity loss of $1 million between October 4 and October 10, 1979. This opportunity loss occurred when IBM bonds with a par value of $680 million could be sold for only $679 million. However, the T-bond futures simultaneously also dropped in price. So, when Salomon Brothers covered $680 million of its short T-bond position, these contracts were repurchased for $678—or $2 million less than the amount received when the short position was established. This $2 million gain in the futures market more than offset the investment banking firm's $1 million opportunity loss on the IBM bond inventory.

Table 23-6 further indicates that market interest rates rose and stayed high. The investment banker's $320 million inventory of IBM bonds had to be sold for $319.5 million, resulting in an opportunity loss of $500,000 on October 11, 1979. As with the preceding days, however, the $320 million short position in T-bond futures profited as market interest rates rose. So, Salomon made a $600,000 gain on the T-bond futures by buying back the still outstanding $320 million of futures contracts for $319.4 million. This $600,000 gain more than offset the $500,000 opportunity loss incurred on October 11, 1979.

Overall, the investment banker's short hedge in Table 23-6 was well executed and profitable. The hedge protected the value of the long position in IBM bonds and, since it was not a perfect hedge, was able to earn a $2.6 million total gain on the T-bond futures. This profit more than compensated for the $1.5 million opportunity loss incurred when the issue of IBM bonds with a face value of $1 billion could be sold for only $998.5 million when they were distributed over the 1-week distribution period.

[20] This underwriting example is taken from a true story. See, for example, *Business Week*, Oct. 29, 1979, p. 50. There actually was a $1 billion IBM bond issue on Oct. 4, 1979, underwritten by Salomon Brothers. However, the facts have been simplified here to expedite the teaching points. One of the largest simplifications is that Salomon handled the large IBM underwriting without the aid of an underwriting syndicate. In fact, a syndicate of 227 investment banking firms participated in the IBM bond issue.

This IBM bond issue was noteworthy on Wall Street because IBM, which had been a long-time client of the highly prestigious Morgan Stanley investment banking firm, gave the deal to Salomon Brothers. Losing this lucrative deal is one of the factors that led Morgan Stanley to become slightly less of an elitist organization. For details see "Morgan Stanley Banks on a Hybrid Strategy As Its World Changes," *Wall Street Journal*, June 27, 1985, pp. 1 and 32.

23-4.3 generalizations about short hedges

Figure 23-7 below illustrates what Salomon Brothers and every other short hedger idealistically *hopes* to accomplish when establishing a short hedge. Compare the idealistic Fig. 23-7 with the IBM Salomon case in Table 23-6 for further insight into the short hedge.

In Salomon's case, the loss they incurred from their cash position in IBM bonds was more than compensated for by the gain from their short position in T-bond futures. However, consider what would have happened if market interest rates had fallen instead of rising as Salomon (correctly) feared. If interest rates had fallen instead of rising, Salomon's profits and losses on their futures and cash positions, respectively, would have been reversed. More specifically, there would have been a gain from appreciating IBM bonds in the inventory and a loss on the short futures position, leaving Salomon's net position largely unchanged. This effect is the essence of hedging with interest rate futures: interest rate risk is reduced or eliminated.

23-5 CHAPTER SUMMARY AND CONCLUSIONS

The volume of financial futures contracts traded every day is exploding. Furthermore, there are new financial futures contract applications waiting to be approved by the federal government's Commodity Futures Trading Commission (CFTC). The financial futures business is one of the most rapidly growing parts of the U.S. financial community.

Section 23-1 of this chapter listed dozens of financial futures contracts already being actively traded at over a dozen different commodity exchanges. There are simply too many different financial futures contracts in existence to be discussed in this chapter. Only the more popular contracts were explained to provide familiarity with these new financial instruments.

Stock market averages and indices, indicators that track the average price of the securities in a given market, were explained in Chap. 7. And Chap. 22 introduced futures contracts and explained how commodity exchanges work. Section 23-2 of this chapter (1) brought this preceding material together and introduced futures contracts on stock market indices; (2) explained the use of the Standard & Poor's 500 Stocks Composite Average, not as a deliverable commodity, but as an indicator for a cash settlement futures contract; (3) reviewed initial margins, variation or maintenance margins, and the re-

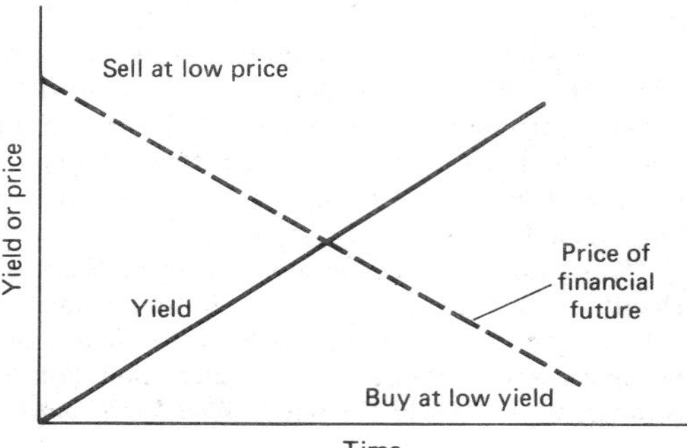

FIGURE 23-7 the objectives of a short hedge with financial futures when rising interest rates are forecasted.

quirement that exists in all commodity exchanges to mark to the market at the close of each day's trading; (4) examined various strategies available to those who foresee either bull or bear markets and want to speculate accordingly; and (5) discussed strategies for risk-averse hedgers.

Interest rate futures are financial futures too. But unlike the stock market index futures, whose prices are determined by numerous factors, the prices of the interest rate futures are determined by one primary factor—market interest rates. Market interest rates determine bond prices, as explained in Chaps. 11 and 13. Interest rate futures, however, have bonds or other interest rate-sensitive assets as the deliverable commodity. This chapter examined different speculative and hedging strategies and the delivery process for interest rate futures used at the Chicago Mercantile Exchange's International Monetary Market (IMM). It also introduced quasi-arbitrage, which was used to analyze the efficiency of the T-bill futures markets.

Treasury notes and Treasury bonds are different from Treasury bills in two major respects. First, T-bills are short-term money market securities, while T-notes are intermediate-term assets and T-bonds are long-term assets. A second important difference is that T-bills are issued on a discount basis and pay no coupons. In contrast, T-notes and T-bonds both pay periodic coupons (as previously explained in Chap. 2). Futures contracts on T-notes and T-bonds are popular instruments that can be used by both speculators and hedgers. Therefore, this chapter briefly reviewed both the T-note and T-bond contracts, and their use was demonstrated by an investment banking example. Financial futures contracts are still a fairly new product on the American scene; new products are rapidly emerging, and much remains to be learned.[21]

[21] The research articles listed below and other articles published in the same periodicals may be informative.

Fisher Black, "The Pricing of Commodity Contracts," *Journal of Financial Economics,* January–March 1976; vol. 3, no. 1.

Marcelle Arak and Christopher J. McCurdy, "Interest Rate Futures," *Quarterly Review,* Federal Reserve Bank of New York, Winter 1979–1980.

Peter W. Bacon and Richard E. Williams, "Interest Rate Futures: New Tool for the Financial Manager," *Financial Management,* Spring 1976; vol. 5, no. 1.

Robert W. McLeod and George M. McCabe, "Hedging for Better Spread Management," *The Bankers Magazine,* July–August 1980, vol. 163, no. 4.

Richard W. McEnally and Michael L. Rice, "Hedging Possibilities in the Flotation of Debt Securities," *Financial Management,* Winter 1979, vol. 8, no. 4.

Louis H. Ederington, "The Hedging Performance of the New Futures Markets," *Journal of Finance,* March 1979, vol. 34.

Charles T. Franckle, "The Hedging Performance of the New Futures Markets: Comment," *Journal of Finance,* December 1980, vol. 35, no. 5.

Robert W. Kolb and Raymond Chiang, "Improving Hedging Performance Using Interest Rate Futures," *Financial Management,* August 1981, pp. 72–79.

Edward J. Kane, "Market Incompleteness and Divergences between Forward and Futures Interest Rates," *Journal of Finance,* May 1980, vol. 35, no. 2.

Edward Miller, "Tax-Induced Bias in Markets for Futures Contracts," *The Financial Review,* vol. 15, pp. 35–38.

In conclusion, it is informative to review the difference between option contracts and futures contracts. Table 21-4 on page 622 summarizes the rights and obligations of the buyers and sellers of both put and call options. The primary difference between options and futures is the difference between the rights and obligations of the buyers of these two different financial instruments. The buyer of a futures contract is legally obligated to perform. In contrast, the option buyer has the right *but not* the obligation to perform. The sellers of both options and futures are obligated to perform; it is only the option buyers who are not obligated to do anything after they pay the premium to buy their option. The appendix to Chapter 23 explains option contracts on futures contracts.

QUESTIONS

1. Define the "basis" for an interest rate future contract. What determines the basis on interest rate futures?
2. Why might speculators prefer futures markets over the cash market in the underlying asset?
3. Forward contracts were the predecessor of futures contracts. Why didn't speculators and hedgers use forward contracts as much as they use futures contracts?
4. "The existence of two almost identical T-bill futures contracts traded at competing commodity exchanges is economically undesirable because it fragments the market." Is the preceding sentence true, false, or uncertain? Explain.
5. Define "spreading." (*Hint:* You might check one of the books referenced in this chapter for more spreading information.) Why do some commodity

---

J. E. Hilliard, "Hedging Interest Rate Risk with Futures Portfolios under Term Structure Effects," *Journal of Finance*, December 1984, vol. 39, no. 5, pp. 1547–1570.

James G. O'Brien, "Tax Topics: Interest Rates Futures—Commercial Banks," *The Banking Law Journal*, March 1981, vol. 98, no. 2.

James Kurt Dew, "Bank Regulations for Futures Accounting," *Issues in Bank Regulation*, Spring 1981.

Robert C. Lower and Scott W. Ryan, "Futures Trading by National Banks," *The Banking Law Journal*, March 1981, vol. 98, no. 3.

Phillip Cagan, "Financial Futures Markets: Is More Regulation Needed?" *Journal of Futures Markets*, Summer 1981, no. 2.

Louis H. Ederington, "Living with Inflation: A Proposal for New Futures and Options Markets," *Financial Analysts Journal*, January–February 1980.

"Ready or Not, Here Come Financial Futures," *Institutional Investor*, March 1983, pp. 51–66.

Victor Niederhoffer and Richard Zeckhauser, "Market Index Futures Contracts," *Financial Analysts Journal*, January–February 1980.

J. C. Francis and Mark Castelino, "Basis Speculation in Commodity Futures: The Maturity Effect," *Journal of Futures Markets*, 1982, vol. 2, no. 2, pp. 195–206.

Many of the papers above and others as well have been published in Gerald D. Gay and Robert W. Kolb (eds.), *Interest Rate Futures*, Robert F. Dame, Inc., Richmond, Va., 1982.

speculators use spreading strategies rather than simply take a long or short position?

6. Do you expect trading in stock market index futures contracts to have any impact on stock market prices? Explain.
7. If an investor buys a Treasury bond in a long position and then realizes that the T-bond price is going to decline because of a previously unforeseen turn in interest rates, what can the investor do to avoid losses? Describe more than one way to avoid the imminent loss.
8. Compare and contrast a long position in futures contracts with owning a call option position of the same size on the same asset. (*Hint:* Refer to Chap. 21 about call options.)
9. Suppose that long-term Treasury bonds are currently yielding higher interest rates than Treasury notes—that is, the yield curve is sloping upward. Assume that your research makes you confident that the yield curve will flatten out, causing the yield spread between T-notes and T-bonds to narrow. How can you profit from this flattening of the yield curve if your expectations are borne out?
10. Is quasi-arbitrage riskier than pure arbitrage? Explain.

SELECTED REFERENCES

Commodity futures exchanges. Each exchange will gladly provide free printed material describing its products and procedures.

Frank J. Fabozzi and Gregory M. Kipnis (eds.), *Stock Index Futures*, Dow Jones-Irwin, Homewood, Ill., 1984. An easy-to-read collection of articles about different aspects of stock index futures written by experts in their respective segments of the subject.

Robert W. Kolb, *Understanding Futures Markets*, (Scott, Foresman, and Company, Glenview, Ill., 1985. This college-level textbook starts by describing the institutions of futures markets, explains the present value calculations that permeate financial futures work, and analyzes various aspects of market efficiency, speculation, and hedging in financial futures contracts. Algebra and statistics are used, but the book is easy to read.

Allan M. Loosigian, *Foreign Exchange Futures*, Dow Jones-Irwin, Homewood, Ill., 1981. A nonmathematical description of the foreign exchange aspect of the financial futures markets. This book comprehensively reviews international economic agreements, defines the foreign exchange vocabulary, discusses the futures markets, and reviews numerous hedging and speculation applications.

______, *Interest Rate Futures*, Dow Jones-Irwin, Homewood, Ill., 1980. An easy-to-read, nonmathematical description of the commodity exchanges and the major interest rate futures contracts, with details about brokerage services, speculation, hedging, arbitraging, and the determinants of market interest rates.

Nancy H. Rothstein (ed.), *The Handbook of Financial Futures*, McGraw-Hill, New York, 1984. This collection of essays written by businesspeople uses virtually no mathematics, is easy to read, and is replete with examples. The book contains a comprehensive discussion of institutional arrangements and examples of applications.

Andrew D. Seidel and Philip M. Ginsberg, *Commodities Trading*, Prentice-Hall,

Englewood Cliffs, N.J., 1983. A comprehensive advanced undergraduate- or MBA-level textbook about options and commodity futures. The book uses mathematics. The main focus of the book is on financial futures.

APPENDIX 23A

options on futures

Chapter 21 defined put and call options. Chapter 22 introduced commodity futures contracts. And Chap. 23 went on to explain financial futures contracts. This appendix considers all these elements at once as it discusses a financial instrument that is a combination of options and futures contracts—it is called an option on a futures contract, or a commodity option.

Options on futures were traded actively in London and Canada before World War II. And some options on futures were traded on the Chicago Board of Trade until 1934. But options on futures were outlawed by some 1936 amendments to the Grain Futures Trading Act. Then, in 1982 commodity exchanges in the United States began trading options on a few futures contracts under the supervision of a Commodity Futures Trading Commission (CFTC) pilot program. Table App. 23A-1 lists the options on futures that started trading in the fall of 1982.

APP. 23A-1 CHARACTERISTICS OF OPTIONS ON FUTURES

All options on futures are two steps removed from the underlying asset. First, there is the futures contract on the underlying asset. Second, there is the put or call option on the futures contract. At first, this seems complicated. But options on futures are actually like ordinary futures contracts that have only limited liability and different margin procedures.

TABLE APP. 23A-1 options on futures contracts

option	U.S. Treasury bond futures	gold futures	Standard & Poor's 500 stock index futures
Exchange	Chicago Board of Trade	Commodity Exchange, Inc. (COMEX)	International Monetary Market (IMM), a division of Chicago Mercantile Exchange
Trading unit	$100,000 face value U.S. Treasury bond futures contract	100 troy ounces	One S&P 500 stock index futures contract

TABLE APP. 23A-1 *(continued)*

option	U.S. Treasury bond futures	gold futures	Standard & Poor's 500 stock index futures
Price quotation method	Points & 64ths of a pt Each full point = $1,000 1/64 = $15.63 (e.g., 2-16 = 2 pts and 16/64 = $2,500)	Dollars per ounce (e.g., a quote of 2.45 means $2.45 per ounce, or $2,450 per option)	Quoted in index points, i.e., each .01 point (1 BP). Each BP is worth $5 (e.g., a quote of 2.45 represents $1,225)
Strike price interval	Integral multiples of 2 points ($2,000) per T-bond futures contract (e.g., 68, 70, 72, etc.)	If the strike price is between $300 & $500, intervals are $10; if between $500 & $800, interval is $30; if over $800, strike prices trade in intervals of $40.	Integer divisible by 5 without remainder (e.g., 110, 115, 120)
Minimum fluctuation (tick value)	Multiples of 1/64 of 1% of a $100,000 T-bond futures contract ($15.63)	10¢ per ounce ($10)	.05 index points (i.e., 5 BP) ($25)
Maximum fluctuation (limit value)	Same as limit for T-bond futures, currently 2 points (128/64 = $2,000)	No limit	No limit
Trading hours	8–2 CST	9:25–2:30 EST	9:00–3:15 CST
Trading months	Same as CBT T-bond futures: Mar., June, Sept., Dec.	Apr., Aug., Dec. (4-month cycle)	Mar., June, Sept., Dec. (4-month cycle)
Exercise	Buyer may give notice by 8 PM any business day prior to expiration; clearing corporation will establish future position for buyer (long if a call, short if a put) & opposite position for seller prior to opening on next business day	Until 3 PM on any business day on which the option is trading	Until last day of trading (i.e., 3d Thurs. of contract month for underlying futures contract)
Last day of trading	12 PM on 1st Friday preceding by at least 5 business days, the first notice day for the T-bond futures contract	2d Friday of month prior to expiration of underlying contract month; 2:30 PM	Last trading day of underlying contract (i.e., 3d Thurs. of contract month)
Expiration	10 AM on first Saturday following last day of trading	2d Friday of month prior to expiration of underlying futures contract	Last day of trading of underlying contract (i.e., 3d Thurs. of contract month)

buying or selling an option on a future

The *buyer* of one option on a future may exercise the option to assume a position in one future. But the position assumed depends on whether the option buyer purchases a put or a call. If a *call option is purchased,* the buyer has the right to exercise the call option by purchasing a long (but not a short) position in the specified future at the exercise (or striking) price stipulated in the option contract. In contrast, if a *put option is purchased,* the buyer has the option to exercise that put by establishing a short (not a long) position in the specific future at the exercise price stipulated in the put option contract. Put and call options must be exercised before some maturity date agreed upon when the option seller sells the option to the option buyer or else the option expires and becomes worthless. The buyers of put and call options on futures have the right, but are under no obligation of any kind, to exercise the options they have purchased. Options need not be exercised to be profitable, however. Options are marketable financial instruments. Therefore, owners of profitable put and call options often choose to realize their profits by selling the option for a higher price than they paid for it instead of exercising its privileges and entering a futures market position.

Consider the irrevocable obligation of the seller, or writer, of the option on the future. Unlike the option buyer, the option writer has a legal *obligation* to perform—the writer has no other option. What the option writer is obligated to perform, however, depends on whether he or she sold a put or a call option.

If the seller or *writer of one call option* on a futures contract is notified that the buyer is exercising the option, the call seller must instantly assume a short position in the particular futures contract that was optioned. More specifically, the call seller must deliver the optioned futures contract at the stipulated exercise price. If the writer of the option does not have a long position in the underlying instrument when the option is exercised the writer must assume a short position in the optioned futures contract by paying the initial margin.

Now let's consider the position of someone who writes a put option on a future. If the *writer of one put option on a futures contract* is notified that the buyer is exercising the option, the put seller is obliged to instantly assume a long position. That is, the put writer must let the option buyer put (that is, deliver) the optioned commodity futures contract to him or her at the exercise price (which is typically above the current market price or the put would not be profitable to exercise).

Graphs to illustrate the gains or losses of the various positions involved may be helpful. These graphs illustrate the expiration date profits attainable by exercising an option to enter a position in the futures market. The profits that may be attained from simply selling the option for more than its purchase price are considered later in this appendix, when the determinants of option prices are analyzed.

illustrations of the various positions' gains and losses

Figure App. 23A-1 illustrates the profit position of the option buyer on a financial future. Movements in financial option prices are determined by changes in the prices of the underlying asset. In Fig. App. 23A-1, the buyer of an option contract gains as the price of the option rises. For a call option on an interest rate future, such gains occur when interest rates fall, or for a put option, when interest rates rise. As the option price falls, however, the buyer's maximum loss is limited to the premium paid. In Fig. App. 23A-2 the position of an option writer on a financial futures contract is illustrated. This option writer loses as the price of the option rises, but if the option price falls the maximum gain is limited to the initial premium received.

Figure App. 23A-3 shows that the buyer of a futures contract on an underlying financial asset gains as the price of the contract rises. In the lower left quadrant of Fig. App. 23A-3, losses occur as the price of the contract falls. In Fig. App. 23A-4, the short seller of a financial futures contract gains as prices fall and loses as prices rise.

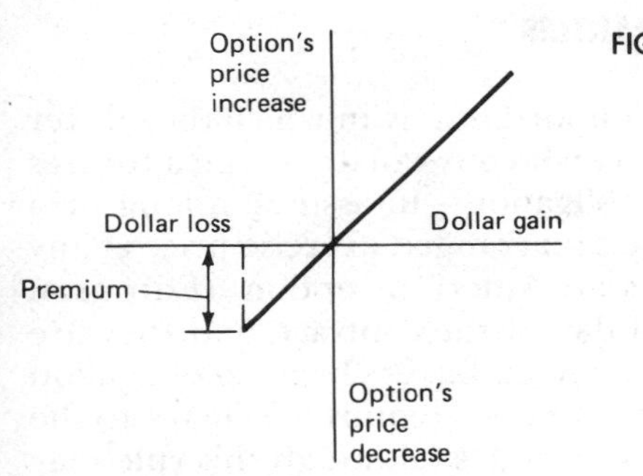

FIGURE APP. 23A-1 option buyer's position.

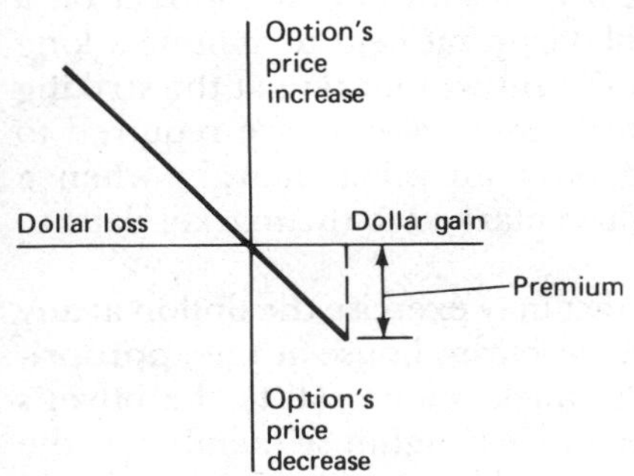

FIGURE APP. 23A-2 option writer's position.

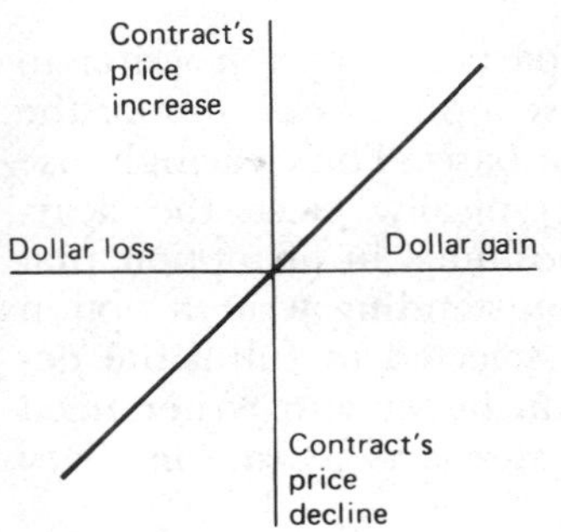

FIGURE APP. 23A-3 position of a future's buyer.

FIGURE APP. 23A-4 position of a future's seller.

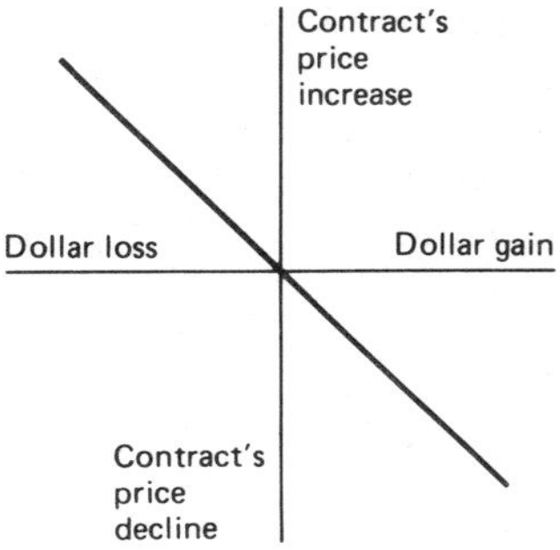

Contract's price increase

Dollar loss

Dollar gain

Contract's price decline

APP. 23A-2 RIGHTS VERSUS OBLIGATIONS FOR THE OPTION PARTIES

Options are *unilateral* contracts—this is an important way in which they differ from the bilateral futures contract. Any party who buys an option on a futures contract acquires the right—but not the obligation—to assume a long or a short position in one futures contract at the prearranged exercise price at any time during the life of the option, if it is an American option. (European options can be exercised only on the final day of the contract, and they are usually written on forward contracts.) Since option buyers have no obligation to perform after their premium is paid, they are not required to mark to the market as are the sellers of futures options contracts (although this rule may be changed in the future).

In contrast to option buyers, anyone who writes an option contract on a future undertakes a firm (legally enforceable) commitment to assume a long (for a call) or a short (for a put) position in the futures market at the striking price if the buyer exercises the option. Since option writers are required to perform, these writers are required to deposit an initial margin when a position is opened. Furthermore, this margin is marked to the market daily to reflect changes in the value of the option.

The buyer of an option on a futures contract may exercise the option at any time before it expires merely by notifying the clearinghouse at the appropriate commodity exchange. All this takes is a quick phone call to the buyer's broker, who then notifies the clearinghouse (or clearinghouse member, if the broker is not a member of the clearinghouse). Then the clearinghouse will proceed to establish a futures position for the buyer. At the same time, the seller of the option is obliged to instantly assume the opposite futures position at the prearranged exercise price.

In the large exchanges, a computer assigns a particular option writer to respond to an option buyer who decides to exercise a put or call option; the assignment is given randomly on a first-in-first-out basis. The clearinghouse computer, which keeps an inventory of writers, typically selects the clearinghouse member with the largest number of positions in an option that expires in the relevant month. Then the oldest outstanding written option within that clearinghouse member's inventory is selected to fulfill the demands of the exercising option buyer. The option buyer and writer need never know each other's identity. The clearinghouse acts as intermediary between the buyer and the writer.

How the writer of the option on the futures contract responds depends on the particular underlying financial instrument. If the instrument is a U.S. Treasury bond, the relevant bond can be delivered to fulfill the contract if the contract is obtained and held for delivery. But if the futures contract underlying the option is on some stock market index, then a cash settlement is the only possible mode of delivery if the contract is obtained and held for delivery. Delivery on stock market futures contracts is explained in Sec. 23-2 of this chapter.

The option writer's response to notification that the option is being exercised depends on whether the writer was writing "naked" or "covered," as explained in Sec. 21-6 at page 620. If the option writer owns the underlying financial instrument, then that position can be delivered to fulfill the buyer's demand for it—if such a demand ever emerges. If the option writer was writing naked, then if delivery of the contract is ultimately demanded, the writer is placed in a short position.

App. 23A-2.1 OPTIONS ON FUTURES SPECIFICATIONS FOR T-BONDS

As indicated in Tables App. 23A-1 and 23-4, the expiration months for options on T-bond futures are identical to the T-bond futures delivery months—March, June, September, and December of each year, for 2 years into the future.

The market prices of both T-bonds and T-bond futures are quoted in terms of percentage points followed by thirty-seconds of a percentage point. For example, a T-bond quoted at 99-16 is worth $99^{16}/_{32}$ or 99.5 percent of the bond's face value. Thus, a $100,000 T-bond quoted at 99-16 is worth $99,500. Each full percentage point is worth $1,000 of market value, and each thirty-second of a point is worth $31.25.

Unlike T-bond futures, options on T-bond futures are quoted in sixty-fourths of a percentage point. Thus, for instance, a premium of 2-32 represents a premium of $2,500. Each sixty-fourth is worth $15.63. The next section explains how the premiums on options on T-bond futures are determined.

determinants of premiums for a call on T-bond futures

For the sake of clarity, consider an option on a T-bond futures contract that has an exercise (or striking) price of exactly 60 percentage points of face value. Figure App. 23A-5 illustrates the determination of this option's price or premium. When the underlying T-bond futures contracts are trading at 62-00, the call option on these contracts has a *minimum value* of 2 points, denoted 2-00. However, option prices (or premiums) rise farthest above their minimum value line when the price of the optioned asset lies near the exercise (or striking) price, as shown in Fig. App. 23A-5. Thus, the premium (or price) on this call option is 3-00 points (that is, $3,000) because the premium is 1 point above its minimum value when the T-bond future's price is 62-00.

The vertical distance between the minimum value line and the curve representing the market price of the call option is called the *time value* of the option. The time value of a call option is calculated as follows:

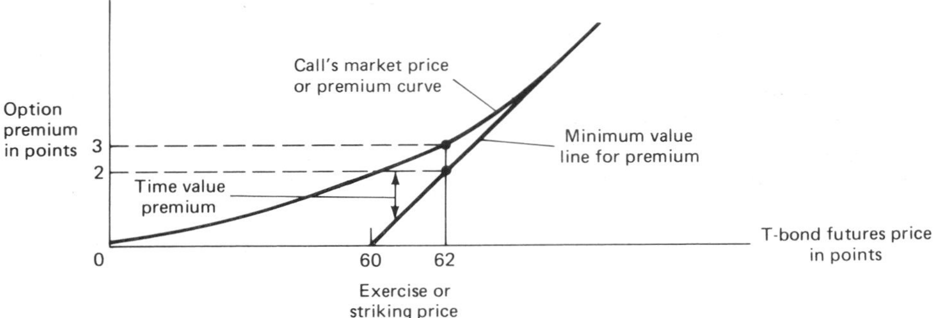

FIGURE APP. 23A-5 price breakdown for call option on T-bond future.

$$\begin{pmatrix}\text{Time}\\\text{value}\\\text{of call}\end{pmatrix} = \begin{pmatrix}\text{call}\\\text{option's}\\\text{premium}\end{pmatrix} + \begin{pmatrix}\text{exercise}\\\text{price}\end{pmatrix} - \begin{pmatrix}\text{market}\\\text{price of}\\\text{underlying}\\\text{asset}\end{pmatrix}$$

$$(1) = (3) + (60) - (62)$$

The time value for a call option on a financial futures contract increases directly with the riskiness (namely, the price volatility) of the underlying futures contract and the time remaining until the call option expires, if all other factors are held equal. Essentially, the same factors that explained the premiums of options on common stocks in Chap. 21 on pages 606 and 607 determine the values of options on futures contracts.

determinants of premiums for a put on T-bond futures

Figure App. 23A-6 illustrates the primary determinants that influence premiums for a put option on a T-bond future when the exercise (or striking) price is 60-00. If the underlying T-bond future is trading at 58-00 (that is, \$58,000 for a \$100,000 T-bond), the put option's premium is 3-00 points (namely, \$3,000). This 3-00 point market price is comprised of a minimum value of 2-00 plus a time value premium of 1 point, as calculated below.

$$\begin{pmatrix}\text{Time}\\\text{value}\\\text{of put}\end{pmatrix} = \begin{pmatrix}\text{put's}\\\text{premium}\\\text{or price}\end{pmatrix} + \begin{pmatrix}\text{put's}\\\text{market}\\\text{price}\end{pmatrix} - \begin{pmatrix}\text{put's}\\\text{exercise}\\\text{price}\end{pmatrix}$$

$$(1) = (3) + (58) - (60)$$

The time value premium over the minimum value line is illustrated by a vertical arrow in Fig. App. 23A-6. The factors that determine the size of the time value premiums on puts also determine the time value premiums on calls.

APP. 23A-3 THE ADVANTAGES AND DISADVANTAGES OF OPTIONS ON FUTURES

After considering options on futures for a while, the question arises: "Are there any advantages to buying options on futures instead of simply buying the same futures contract directly?" The answer is: "Yes, there is an advan-

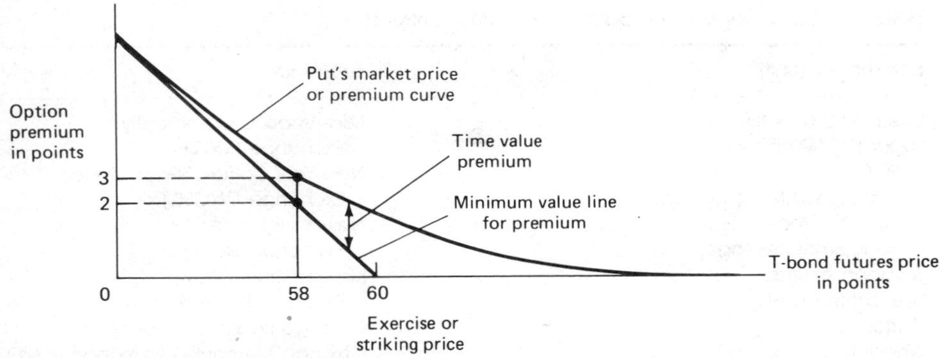

FIGURE APP. 23A-6 price breakdown for put option on T-bond future.

tage." Speculators who buy options on futures enjoy a so-called safety net that inherently keeps the buyer of an option on a futures contract from losing more than the premium paid for the put or call option.

Speculators who buy futures contracts directly must put down an initial margin and then mark to the market based on each day's settlement price—this requirement is explained in this chapter. As a result, the owner of a futures contract can lose much more than the cost of an option's premium. Figure App. 23A-1 illustrates the fact that option buyers' losses are limited to the premium they paid to purchase the option. Of course, option buyers do not enjoy this safety net or limited liability for free. Options do not become profitable until the price of the underlying asset moves far enough in the appropriate direction to cover the cost of the option's premium. As a result of this built-in difference, speculators who forecasted the market's move correctly will always make a larger gain from a futures contract than they would have if they had used an option on the same futures contract.

When considering the desirability of using options on futures, it would also be appropriate to inquire: "Is there any reason to buy an option on a futures contract instead of simply buying an option on the underlying asset directly?" The answer is: "Yes. The advantage from using options on futures is that less cash may be required." This advantage becomes evident only when a comparison is made after the two different options have been exercised. When a direct option is exercised on the underlying asset, the underlying asset must be purchased with cash—this is a large outlay. In contrast, a speculator who exercises an option on a futures contract need only pay enough cash to cover the cost of the required initial margin—the entire value of the contract need not be expended simply to exercise the option. However, this exercising advantage may be valueless to some speculators. After all, the options need not be exercised to be profitable. Options that have appreciated over their initial premium can simply be sold to another speculator in the secondary market in order to realize the gain. Buying the option on a future rather than buying the direct option is advantageous primarily to buyers who may not want to exercise the option to recognize a gain.

Options on different futures contracts are similar. Table App. 23A-1 lists the options on futures that were initially traded in 1982. Options on the

TABLE APP. 23A-2 options on additional futures contracts

commodity (unit)	exchange
Gold (33.2 ounces)	Mid-America Commodity Exchange (MACE)
Sugar (112,000 pounds)	New York Coffee, Sugar, Cocoa Exchange (NYCSC)
NYSE Composite Stock Index ($500 times average)	New York Futures Exchange (NYFE)
Value-Line Stock Average ($500 times average)	Kansas City Board of Trade (KCBT)
Soybean futures	Chicago Board of Trade (CBT)
Live cattle futures	Chicago Mercantile Exchange (CME)
Cotton futures	New York Cotton Exchange
Wheat futures	Minneapolis Grain Exchange
Wheat futures	Mid-America Commodity Exchange

futures contracts in Table App. 23A-2 have received CFTC approval to begin trading.[22]

APP. 23A-4 SELECTED REFERENCES

Michael T. Belongia and Thomas H. Gregory, "Are Options on Treasury Bond Futures Priced Efficiently?" *Review,* St. Louis Federal Reserve Bank, January 1984, vol. 66, no. 1, pp. 5–13.

Fischer Black, "The Pricing of Commodity Contracts," *Journal of Financial Economics,* January 1976, vol. 3, no. 1 and 2, pp. 167–179.

Eugene Moriarity, Susan Phillips, and Paula Tosini, "A Comparison of Options and Futures in the Management of Portfolio Risk," *Financial Analysts Journal,* January–February 1981, pp. 61–67.

Avner Wolf, "Fundamentals of Commodity Options on Futures," *Journal of Futures Market,* 1982, vol. 2, no. 4, pp. 391–408.

[22] "An Underwhelming Debut for Agricultural Options," *Business Week,* Nov. 26, 1984, p. 159.

international investing

The corporate form of business ownership with multiple owners, limited liability for investors, and separate debt and equity securities exists in some form in most industrial countries of the world. International investing is a routine transaction at many banks and stock brokerage firms. So let's begin our exploration of the opportunities available to international investors by considering the financial economics of international investing.

24-1 MULTINATIONAL DIVERSIFICATION

The possibility of investing in different countries of the world introduces another dimension to diversification. Portfolio theory is a useful tool with which to analyze these possibilities.

24-1.1 Grubel's classic analysis

The initial application of portfolio theory in an international context was by Herbert Grubel.[1] Grubel's model assumes that there are two countries that are economically isolated. In each of these countries, there are three types of wealth: real assets, money, and marketable bonds. The model explores what happens when the initial economic barriers are removed, assuming that only marketable bonds and consumer goods (such as food) are traded. In this model a portfolio of marketable bonds from both countries would have an expected return that is determined by the expected returns in each country and the proportion of assets invested in each country, as specified in Eq. (24-1*a*).

[1] Herbert Grubel, "Internationally Diversified Portfolios: Welfare Gains and Capital Flows," *American Economic Review*, December 1968, pp. 1299–1314.

$$E(r_p) = (x)E(r_1) + (1-x)E(r_2) \qquad (24\text{-}1a)$$

where

$E(r_p)$ = expected return on an international portfolio of marketable bonds from countries 1 and 2

$E(r_1)$ = expected return on bonds in country 1

$E(r_2)$ = expected return on bonds in country 2

x = proportion of assets invested in country 1, where $1.0 > x > 0$

$(1-x)$ = proportion of assets invested in country 2

The conventions employed in Eq. (24-1*a*) are all presumed to be adjusted to reflect foreign exchange risk, or else it is assumed that the foreign exchange rates are pegged. (Foreign exchange risk will be treated separately, later in this chapter.)

The variance of this two-country bond portfolio, $\text{var}(r_p)$, would be determined by the variances of returns in each country, denoted $\text{var}(r_1)$ and $\text{var}(r_2)$, respectively, the proportion of assets in each country, x and $(1 - x)$, respectively, and the correlation of returns between both countries' bonds, denoted $\rho_{1,2}$, as shown in Eq. (24-2*a*)

$$\text{var}(r_p) = x^2 \text{ var}(r_1) + (1 - x)^2 \text{ var}(r_2) + + 2(x)(1 - x)(\sigma_1)(\sigma_2)(\rho_{1,2}) \qquad (24\text{-}2a)$$

BOX 24-1
the impact of intercountry return correlations on the variance from an international portfolio

$E(r_1) = E(r_2) = 10\%$ = expected returns in the two countries

$\sigma_1^2 = \sigma_2^2 = 16\%$ = variance of expected returns

$(x) = (1 - x) = .50$ = proportion of assets invested in each country, $x > 0$

$$E(r_p) = (x)\, E(r_1) + (1 - x)\, E(r_2) \qquad (24\text{-}1a)$$

$$E(r_p) = (.5)(.1) + (1.0 - .5)(.1) = .1 = 10.0\% \qquad (24\text{-}1b)$$

$$\text{var}(r_p) = x^2 \text{ var}(r_1) + (1 - x)^2 \text{ var}(r_2) + + 2(x)(1 - x)(\sigma_1)(\sigma_2)(\rho_{1,2}) \qquad (24\text{-}2a)$$

$$\text{var}(r_p) = (.5)^2(.16)^2 + (1.0 - .5)^2(.16)^2 + + 2(.5)(1.0 - .5)\sqrt{(.16)}\sqrt{(.16)}(\rho_{1,2}) \qquad (24\text{-}2b)$$

$$\text{var}(r) = .08 + .08(\rho_{1,2}) \qquad (24\text{-}2c)$$

numerical illustration of the portfolio's variance reduction

correlation, ρ	+1.0	+.50	0.0	−.50	−1.0
$\text{var}(r_p)$	.16	.12	.08	.04	0

where

$\text{var}(r_1)$ = variance of returns in country 1 = σ_1^2

$\text{var}(r_2)$ = variance of returns in country 2 as seen from country 1 and adjusted for any changes in the foreign exchange rate = σ_2^2

$\rho_{1,2}$ = correlation coefficient between the two countries' bond returns

Box 24-1 illustrates the risk reduction benefits available to the international investor as the correlation between the two countries' bond portfolios varies. The correlation between international investment returns is seen to be the key to risk reduction through international diversification. Table 24-1 presents empirical estimates of the correlations between common stock portfolios in the United States and various foreign countries; these estimates can be used to quantify and refine the claim of potential risk reduction.

Table 24-1 shows that estimates of the correlation between the U.S. stock market and foreign stock markets have ranged from as high as .8598 with the Canadian market and as low as −.26 with the Japanese market. The correlations from Table 24-1 in the risk analysis model shown in Box 24-1, for example, show that equal investments in Canada and the United States would produce a portfolio variance of only 14.88 percent versus 16 percent for a total investment in the United States. Or, for equal investments in the United States and Japan, the portfolio variance would be only 5.92 percent. These

TABLE 24-1 summary of intercountry correlations

country	(1)*	(2)	(3)	(4)	(5)
USA	1.0000				
Canada	.7025		.8598	.4895	
United Kingdom	.2414	.578	.5836	.6420	.26
West Germany	.3008	.335	.4062	.4337	.43
France	.1938	.542	.4139	.1820	.34
Italy	.1465				.09
Belgium	.1080	.621			.83
Netherlands	.2107	.583			.53
Japan	.1149		.1796	.5279	−.26
Australia	.0584		.4311	.6626	
South Africa	−.1620				.08
Switzerland		.685			
Spain			.0098	.3230	
Venezuela					−.17
Austria					.26
Denmark					.19
Mexico					.02
New Zealand					.08

* *Author*	*Sampled period*	*Publication*
(1) H. Grubel	1959–66 annual	1968 AER
(2) B. Jacquillat and B. Solnik	1974–76 monthly	1978 JPM
(3) A. M. Rugman	1951–75 annual	1977 JEB
(4) A. M. Rugman	1970–75 monthly	1977 JEB
(5) H. Levy and M. Sarnat	1951–67 annual	1970 AER

statistics suggest that international diversification could aid U.S. investors and foreign investors as well.[2]

24-1.2 the international investor's efficient frontier

It is possible to analyze the effect of multinational diversification on the Markowitz efficient frontier using Grubel's model. As might be expected, as the number of countries in which investments are made increases, more desirable efficient frontiers become attainable. That is, as the number of countries in the investment universe increases, the rate of return for any given level of risk increases, or conversely, the level of risk attainable at any given rate of return decreases.

Point F in Fig. 24-1 indicates the risk level and rate of return for the U.S. stock market alone. Efficient frontier E shows the risk and return combinations available from investing in only developing countries; this option is dominated by all the other investment alternatives illustrated in Fig. 24-1. Even though point F in the figure represents a portfolio that is fully diversified within the United States, this portfolio is not efficient in an international context. Efficient frontier D indicates the efficient frontier if investments are limited to the countries in the European Economic Community (EEC)—that

[2] Monthly rates of return from foreign investments in common stocks which are adjusted to reflect changes in the foreign exchange rate can be calculated with Eq. (24-3) below.

$$\text{Effective monthly rate of return} = \left(\frac{\dfrac{\text{an. cash dividend}}{12 \text{ mos.}} + p_t}{p_{t-1}} \right)^{12} - 1.0 \qquad (24\text{-}3)$$

where

p_t = market price of the foreign security (or foreign stock market index) that existed at the end of the period

p_{t-1} = market price at the beginning of that period

FIGURE 24-1 various efficient frontiers derived from different investment opportunities. (*Source*: H. Levy and M. Sarnat, "International Diversification of Investment Portfolios," *American Economic Review*, September 1970, pp. 668–675.

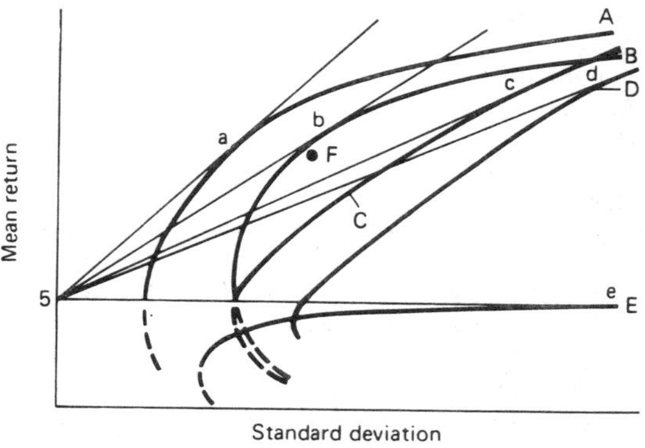

is, the Common Market countries. If the investment universe is expanded beyond the EEC to include all western European countries, efficient frontier C becomes attainable. When all high-income countries are considered, the possibilities expand to efficient frontier B. Finally, when all countries, including the developing countries, are allowed into the solution, efficient frontier A is reached. Efficient frontier A dominates all other investment opportunities in Fig. 24-1. This analysis suggests that the portfolio with the highest rate of return in whatever risk class is selected should be composed of investments from many countries, if possible. As a practical matter, however, barriers to capital flows (such as government-imposed foreign exchange restrictions) may not make the theoretically optimal portfolio feasible.

24-1.3 correlations for the multinational investor

The key factor that accounts for the change in the risk-return opportunities available in an open international capital market is the low correlation between the different countries' securities markets. For international diversification the relevant market index changes; that is, a domestic market index is replaced by a *world market index*. As a result, the correlation of each security with the broader world is lower.[3] Table 24-2 shows empirical statistics about what percent of each domestic portfolio is explained by a worldwide investment index. The statistics in Table 24-2 are the coefficient of determination

[3] Correlation and regression are introduced in Mathematical App. D. The characteristic line is introduced in Chap. 10.

TABLE 24-2 percentage of the variance of different countries' stock market indices explained by a worldwide index*

country	*R*-squared for a market value weighted index, %	*R*-squared for an equally weighted index, %
Australia	11.1	20.2
Austria	4.5	20.1
Belgium	26.2	50.1
Canada	66.7	38.2
Denmark	.8	11.6
France	9.6	40.2
Germany	22.3	49.0
Italy	6.2	25.6
Japan	7.9	15.5
Netherlands	45.4	52.7
Norway	2.0	22.2
Spain	.4	8.9
Sweden	13.1	28.5
Switzerland	29.5	54.5
United Kingdom	16.9	22.6
United States	88.0	30.0
Simple Average	21.9	30.6

* Monthly returns from January 1959 to October 1973 were used.

Source: Donald R. Lessard, "World, Country and Industry Relationships in Equity Returns: Implications for Risk Reduction through International Diversification," *Financial Analysts Journal*, January–February 1976, pp. 2–8.

(that is, the correlation squared, or the R-squared, as it is also called) for the international characteristic line shown in Eq. (24-4).

$$r_{ct} = a_c + b_c r_{wt} + e_{ct} \tag{24-4}$$

In Eq. (24-4) the symbol r_{ct} is the dependent variable in this simple linear regression model—it is the one-period rate of return from country c in time period t. The independent variable is r_{wt}, the one-period rate of return in time period t from a portfolio that is diversified worldwide and is therefore not highly correlated with the portfolio from any one individual country. The regression intercept for country c is denoted a_c, and its regression slope (or beta) coefficient is b_c. This regression slope coefficient is a *country-world beta*. The unexplained residual return for country c in time period t is denoted e_{ct}.

The coefficient of determination for regression Eq. (24-4) is inversely related to the desirability of investing in each country. Stated differently, the countries with the lowest R-squared statistics are the most desirable for the purposes of obtaining beneficial international diversification.

24-1.4 fundamental reasons for low intercountry correlations

The intercountry correlations between security markets are not low merely because random good or bad luck strikes different countries at different times. There are sound economic reasons why the different countries and their economic prospects are not tied closely together.

Different countries have different political systems (for example, capitalism versus socialism), different currencies (such as French francs and Japanese yen), different foreign exchange regulations (for example, fixed versus floating exchange rates), different trade restrictions (such as import and export limitations and tariffs), different political alliances (such as the communist block countries), and various other different kinds of barriers to international trade. Furthermore, different countries may be at different phases in their business cycle (for example, the United States may be starting a recovery just as some other countries are in the trough of a recession), undergoing foreign exchange rate changes (because of different intercountry inflation rates, interest rates, monetary policies, and/or fiscal policies), or in differing military postures (such as peace versus cold war versus hot war) at the same time. As a result of all these important differences, the different countries' security markets are not expected to be highly synchronized or highly positively correlated with each other.[4]

Figure 24-2 illustrates how the inflation rates and security market indices of the major industrial countries of the world move together through time. The various panels of the figure highlight the differences in different countries' economic conditions.

24-2 DIVERSIFICATION IN DIFFERENT COUNTRIES

Multinational diversification is beneficial if there are barriers to investment such as restrictions on currency flows, lack of English translations of foreign

[4] R. A. Cohn and J. J. Pringle, "Imperfections in International Financial Markets: Implications for Risk Premia and the Cost of Capital to Firms," *Journal of Finance*, March 1973, pp. 59–66.

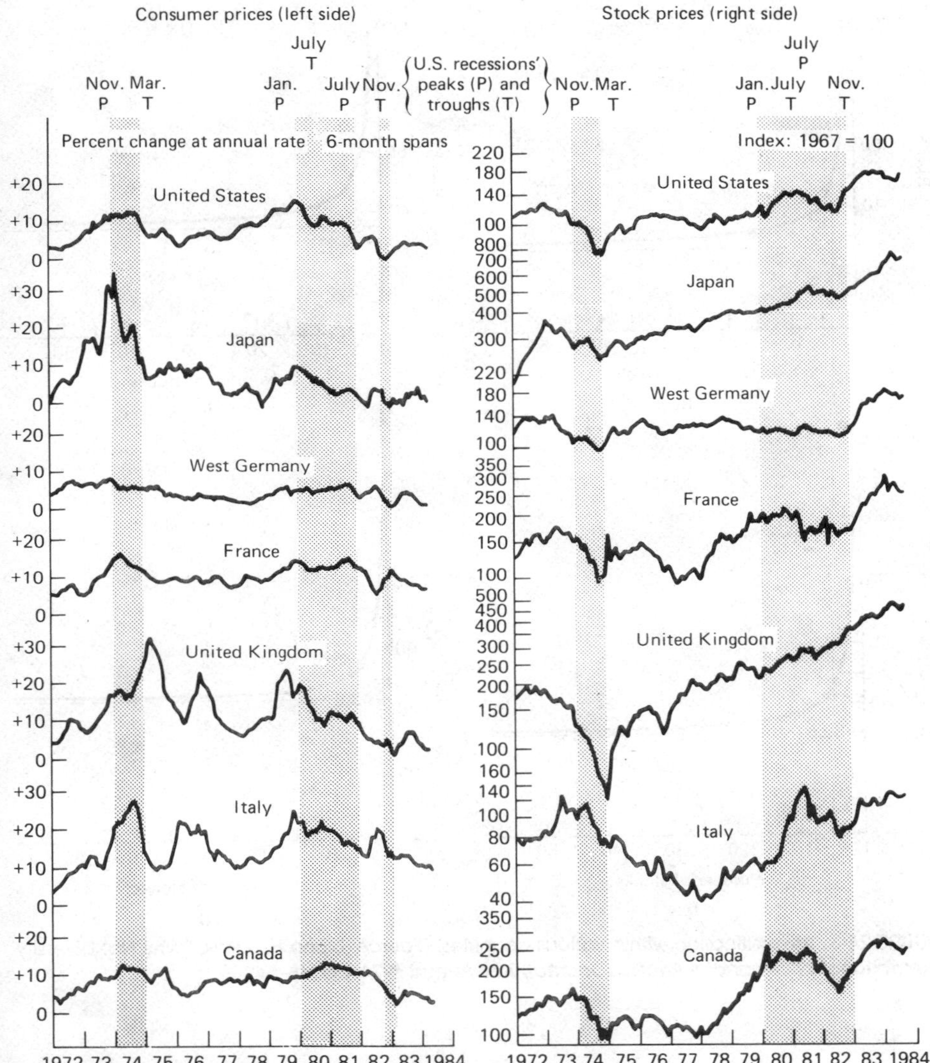

FIGURE 24-2 international comparisons of inflation rates and stock prices.

financial statements, lack of information about local accounting conventions, lack of information about social and cultural differences, or markets that are thin with respect to volume of trading or number of traders.[5] If such barriers do exist, the international market structure will be segmented and diversification will be beneficial. If such barriers to international diversification do not exist, the markets will be *homogeneous*. Multinational diversification would not

[5] Gunter Dufey and Ian Giddy, *The International Money Market*, Prentice-Hall, Englewood Cliffs, N.J., 1978.

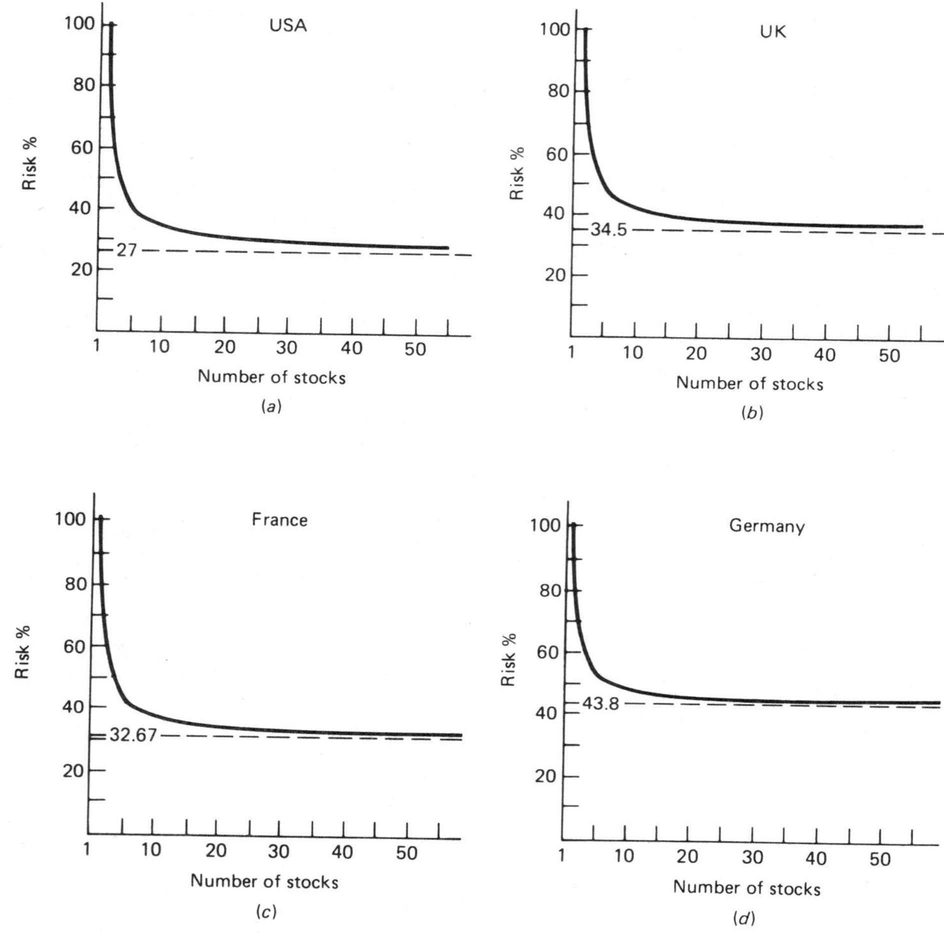

FIGURE 24-3 diversification within various countries. (*Source*: Bruno H. Solnik, "Why Not Diversify Internationally?" *Financial Analysts Journal*, July-August 1974, pp. 48–54).

TABLE 24-3 randomly diversified portfolio's variance as percent of variance of the average individual stock

USA	27.0%
UK	34.5%
France	32.7%
W. Germany	43.8%
Italy	38.0%
Belgium	19.0%
Netherlands	24.1%
Switzerland	44.0%
International	11.7%

Source: Bruno H. Solnik, "Why Not Diversify Internationally?" *Financial Analysts Journal*, July–August 1974, pp. 48–54.

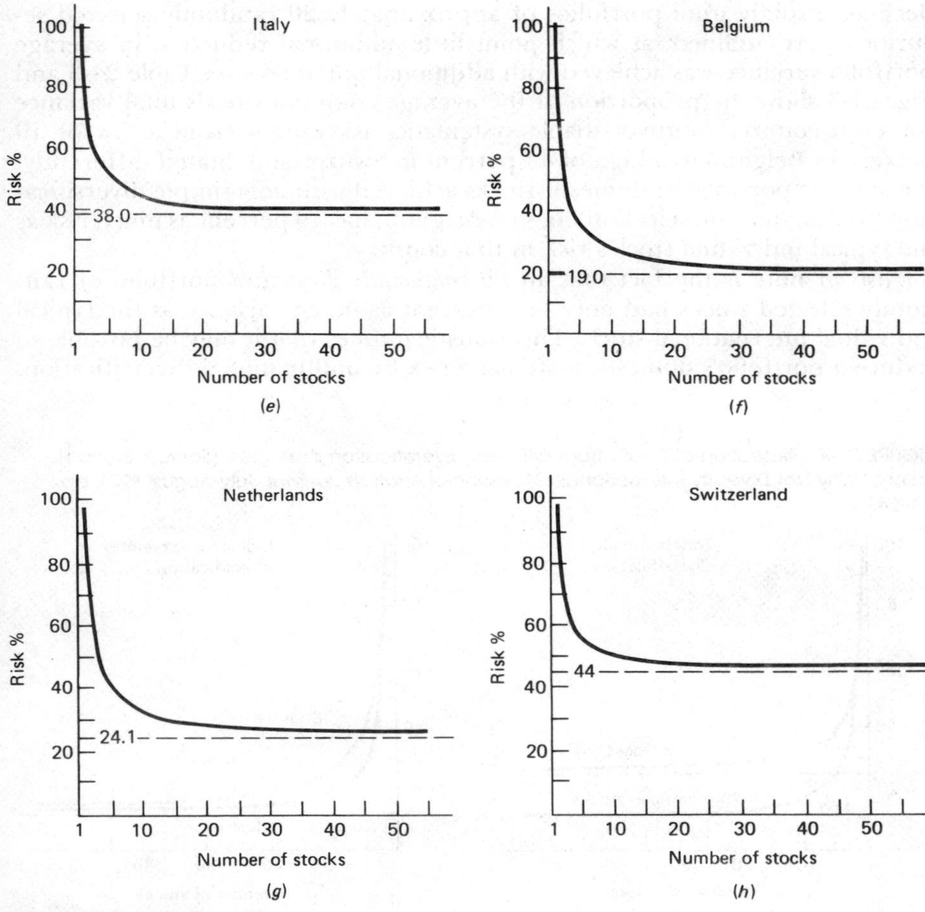

FIGURE 24-3 *(continued)*

be expected to offer any beneficial risk-reducing opportunities if the international markets were homogeneous.

Because individuals have limited funds, the amount of diversification that is possible is limited. Even large investment companies may experience limits to effective diversification. Consequently, it is valuable to know how best to diversify across countries for an international portfolio. Using weekly returns for eight different countries from 1966 to 1971, Bruno Solnik calculated the proportion of variance that could be eliminated from portfolios by increasing the number of assets included in the portfolio. For each country, portfolios of various sizes were constructed from randomly selected stocks from that country and the variances of these portfolios were calculated. These variances were averaged for each portfolio size.[6] In each country, average portfolio variance

[6] Solnik was, essentially, applying the methodology originally developed by John L. Evans and Stephen H. Archer in "Diversification and the Reduction of Dispersion: Empirical Analysis," *Journal of Finance*, December 1968. The Evans-Archer results are presented in Sec. 25-2 on page 747.

declined rapidly until portfolios of approximately 20 randomly selected securities were attained, at which point little additional reduction in average portfolio variance was achieved with additional portfolio size. Table 24-3 and Fig. 24-3 show the proportion of the average common stock's total variance for each country; undiversifiable systematic risk ranges from a low of 19 percent in Belgium to a high of 44 percent in Switzerland. Stated differently, the average portfolio of domestic stocks achieved with only simple diversification (that is, random selection) in, say, Belgium, has 19 percent as much risk as the typical individual stock's risk in that country.

Also of note is the fact that an *internationally diversified* portfolio of randomly selected stocks had only 11.7 percent as much variance as the typical individual international stock. This statistic implies that it may be possible to reduce a portfolio's domestic systematic risk by multinational diversification.

FIGURE 24-4 **Illustration of results from different diversification strategies.** (*Source*: Bruno H. Solnik, "Why Not Diversify Internationally?" *Financial Analysts Journal*, July-August 1974, pp. 48–54.)

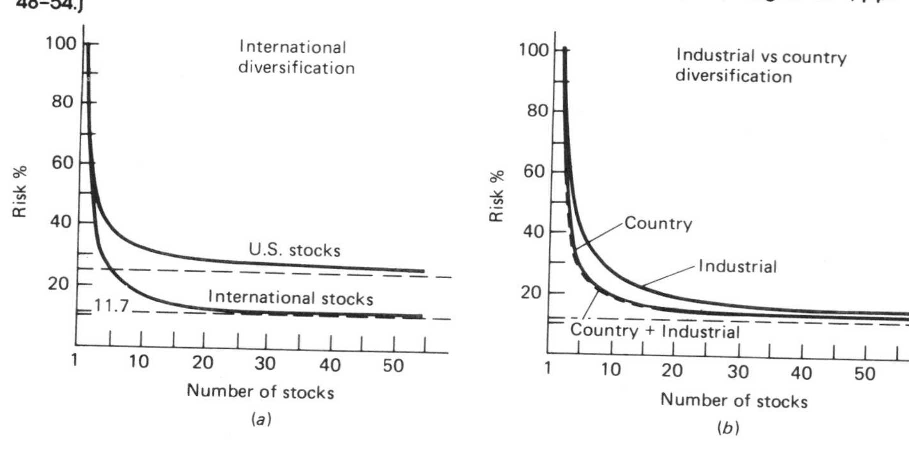

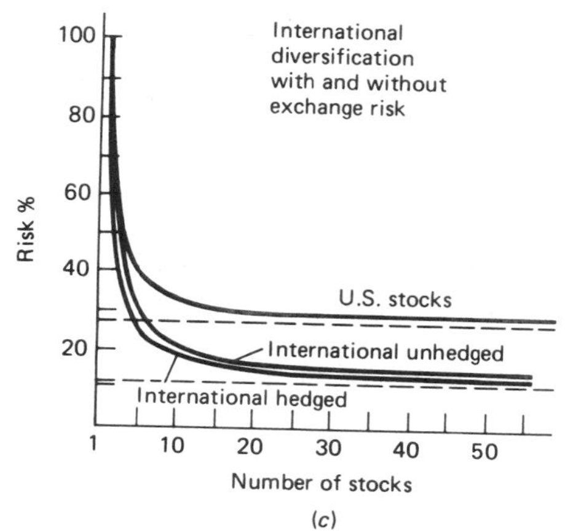

Panels *a* through *c* of Fig. 24-4 illustrate some risk reduction possibilities. Unfortunately, the benefits from Solnik's study cannot be taken too literally because his study did not make adjustments to hold the rates of return *equivalent* from country to country as diversification was employed to reduce the risk. That is, the international investor may have had to suffer undesirably low rates of return to obtain the variance reduction that the Solnik study suggests.

To determine how best to diversify, three strategies of selecting different numbers of randomly selected common stocks were examined. Stocks were selected (1) across countries, (2) across industries, and (3) across both countries and industries. Panels *a*, *b*, and *c* of Fig. 24-4 illustrate that both selection across countries and selection across countries and industries are superior strategies to selecting only across industries. These experiments with random diversification suggest that the optimal portfolio should contain approximately 20 common stocks diversified across countries.[7]

An important consideration of investors in foreign securities is foreign exchange risk. However, panel *c* of Fig. 24-4 indicates that a substantial portion of the risk reducing value of multinational diversification occurs whether or not international portfolios are hedged against foreign exchange losses. Although the hedged portfolio has lower risk than the unhedged portfolio, unfortunately its total return is also greatly reduced. Thus, the value of international diversification exists with or without a concurrent currency hedge.[8]

Let's consider the foreign exchange risk more closely.

24-3 THE EFFECTS OF FOREIGN EXCHANGE RATES THAT VARY

If we view the rate of return on the multinational common stock portfolio in terms of capital gains and cash dividend yield, the investor's one-period rate of return, r_t, is the difference between the portfolio value at the beginning of the period, p_{t-1}, and the portfolio's value at the end of the period, p_t, plus any cash distributions during the period, d_t, all divided by the portfolio's beginning value. This well-known relationship is restated as Eq. (24-5*a*).

$$r_t = (p_t - p_{t-1} + d_t)/p_{t-1} \tag{24-5a}$$

The rate of return in local currency (LC) for multinational investment, denoted $R(\mathrm{N,LC})$, is equal to the terminal value of the investment, denoted $V1'$, less the initial value of the investment, $V0'$, plus any distributions during the period, $D1'$, all divided by the initial investment, $V0'$. All these terms are denominated in local currency in Eq. (24-6).

[7] One simple way to diversify internationally without bumping into problems with foreign languages and foreign accounting conventions is to simply buy shares in one large corporation that is active multinationally. Ford Motor Company has over 30 percent of its sales outside the United States, for instance. And Sony is a Japanese corporation that has 35 percent of its sales in the United States.

[8] The capital asset pricing model (CAPM), or security market line (SML), for the international investor has been worked out in a seminal article by Rene Stulz, "On the Effects of Barriers to International Investment," *Journal of Finance*, September 1981, vol. 36, no. 4, pp. 923–934.

$$R(\text{N,LC}) = (V1' - V0' + D1')/V0' \tag{24-6}$$

Note that Eqs. (24-5*a*) and (24-6) are similar, except that Eq. (24-6) restates any foreign returns into local currency amounts.[9]

If the exchange rate between dollars and local currency, at time period $t = 0$, denoted $S0$, is constant over the period, there will be no foreign exchange effect, as the amounts $V0$, $V1$, and $D1$ will all be converted to dollars at an exchange rate that remains invariant throughout the period. In this case Eqs. (24-5*a*) and (24-6) produce identical results.

In the case when the exchange rate remains unchanged we can substitute the identities $[(S1)\,(V1)] = (V1')$, $[(S0)\,(V0)] = (V0')$, and $[(S1)\,(D1)] = (D1')$ into Eq. (24-6) to obtain Eq. (24-7*a*). Equations (24-6) and (24-7*a*) are mathematically equivalent. Equation (24-7*a*) assumes the local currency is dollars.

$$R(\text{N},\$) = \frac{(S1)\,(V1) - (S0)\,(V0) + (S1)\,(D1)}{(S0)\,(V0)} \tag{24-7a}$$

However, if the current exchange rate $S0$ changes to $S1$ at the end of one period, then $V1$ and $D1$ will be converted at the $S1$ exchange rate and $V0$ will be converted into dollars at the $S0$ exchange rate. Thus, the rate of return on multinational investment, in dollar terms, changes because the foreign exchange rate changes, as shown below. Rearranging Eq. (24-7*a*) above yields Eqs. (24-7*b*) and (24-7*c*).

$$R(\text{N},\$) = \frac{[(S0 - S0 + S1)\,(V1)] - [(S0)\,(V0)] + [(S0 - S0 + S1)\,(D1)]}{[(S0)\,(V0)]} \tag{24-7b}$$

Rearranging Eq. (24-7*b*) above yields the following equivalent equations.

$$R(\text{N},\$) = \frac{[(S0)\,(V1 - V0 + D1)]}{[(S0)\,(V0)]} + \frac{[(S1 - S0)\,(V1 + D1)]}{[(S0)\,(V0)]} \tag{24-7c}$$

$$R(\text{N},\$) = R(\text{N,LC}) + [1 + R(\text{N,LC})]\left(\frac{S1 - S0}{S0}\right) \tag{24-7d}$$

$$= (\text{pure nominal rate of return}) + (\text{foreign exchange factor}) \tag{24-7e}$$

The dollar return on foreign investment is determined by two elements that are visible in Eqs. (24-7*d*) and (24-7*e*)—they are (1) the return on assets in local currency, $R(\text{N,LC})$, plus (2) a foreign exchange factor. Thus, we have seen algebraic proof that the investor's rate of return is explicitly affected by the foreign exchange factor. For example, assume that a portfolio is composed of \$100 of investment in a foreign market at an exchange rate of 20 units of local currency for \$1, denoted 20 LC = \$1. The total investment thus

[9] The discussion assumes that all local currency cashflows remain unchanged—an oversimplification in many cases. For a detailed and comprehensive discussion of all possible cases see David K. Eiteman and Arthur I. Stonehill, *Multinational Business Finance*, 3d ed., Addison-Wesley, Reading, Mass., 1982, chap. 14. See also Gunter Dufey and S. L. Srinivasuler, "The Case for Corporate Management of Foreign Exchange Risk," *Financial Management*, Fall 1983.

costs 2000 units of local currency. One year later, the value of the investment is 2200 LC and, in addition, a 200-LC dividend is paid. If the exchange rate is still 20 LC:\$1, the return on investment is 20 percent, as shown below using Eq. (24-7*a*).

$$\frac{(20{:}1)\ (2200\ \text{LC}) - (20{:}1)\ (2000\ \text{LC}) + (20{:}1)\ (200\ \text{LC})}{(20{:}1)\ (2000\ \text{LC})} = .2 = 20\%$$

The amounts in Eq. (24-7*a*) above may be equivalently restated using the 20 to 1 exchange ratio; the results are restated below in terms of Eq. (24-5*a*).

$$\frac{\$110 - \$100 + \$10}{\$100} = .2 = 20\% \qquad (24\text{-}5b)$$

Consider an *x* percent change in the foreign exchange rate; this quantity is defined below.

$$\frac{S1 - S0}{S0} = \text{an } x \text{ percent change in the exchange ratio}$$

If the exchange rate rises (falls) by 5 percent, the new return on investment in dollars will be 26.3 percent (14.3 percent), as shown below.

First, let's consider the 5 percent increase from (20:1) to (21:1) in terms of Eq. (24-7*a*), as shown below.

$$\frac{(21{:}1)\ (2{,}200\ \text{LC}) - (20{:}1)\ (2{,}200\ \text{LC}) + (21{:}1)\ (200\ \text{LC})}{(20{:}1)\ (2{,}000\ \text{LC})} = .143$$

The formula above is equivalently restated below in terms of Eq. (24-5*a*) by adjusting with the two different exchange rates.

$$\frac{\$104.7619 - \$100 + \$9.523}{\$100} = \frac{\$14.28}{\$100} = .143 = 14.3\% \qquad (24\text{-}5c)$$

Next, let's evaluate the 5 percent decrease in the exchange rate from (20:1) to (19:1) in terms of Eq. (24-7*a*), as shown below.

$$\frac{(19{:}1)\ (2{,}200\ \text{LC}) - (20{:}1)\ (2{,}000\ \text{LC}) + (19{:}1)\ (200\ \text{LC})}{(20{:}1)\ (2{,}000\ \text{LC})} = .263$$

The values above are equivalently restated in terms of Eq. (24-5*a*) by using the two different exchange rates.

$$\frac{\$115.789 - \$100 + \$10.526}{\$100} = \frac{\$26.315}{\$100} = .263 = 26.3\% \qquad (24\text{-}5d)$$

The two preceding numerical examples of appreciation and depreciation in the exchange rate were informative. The two examples showed that a foreign investment with a 20 percent rate of return in the foreign country could pay either a 14.3 or a 26.3 percent rate of return to the multinational investor if the foreign currency's exchange rate varied by 5 percent in either direction. Foreign exchange risk is thus seen to be an additional risk consideration of significant importance to multinational investors.

As the volatility of the exchange rate increases, swings in return due to the foreign exchange factor may also increase—this can be seen explicitly in the

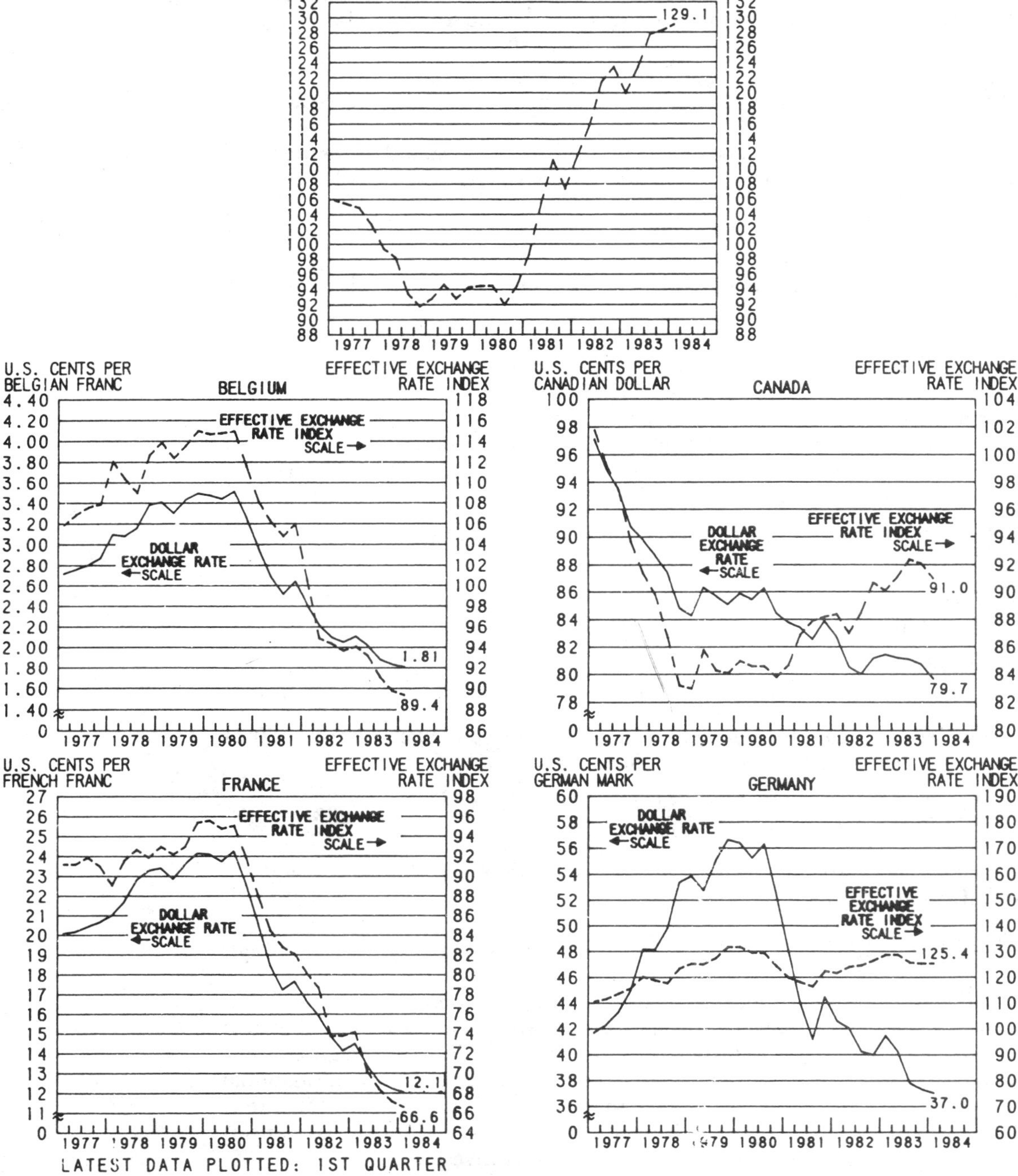

FIGURE 24-5 movements in exchange rates. (*Source*: International Economic Conditions, Federal Reserve Bank of St. Louis, August 1984, pp. 2 and 3.)

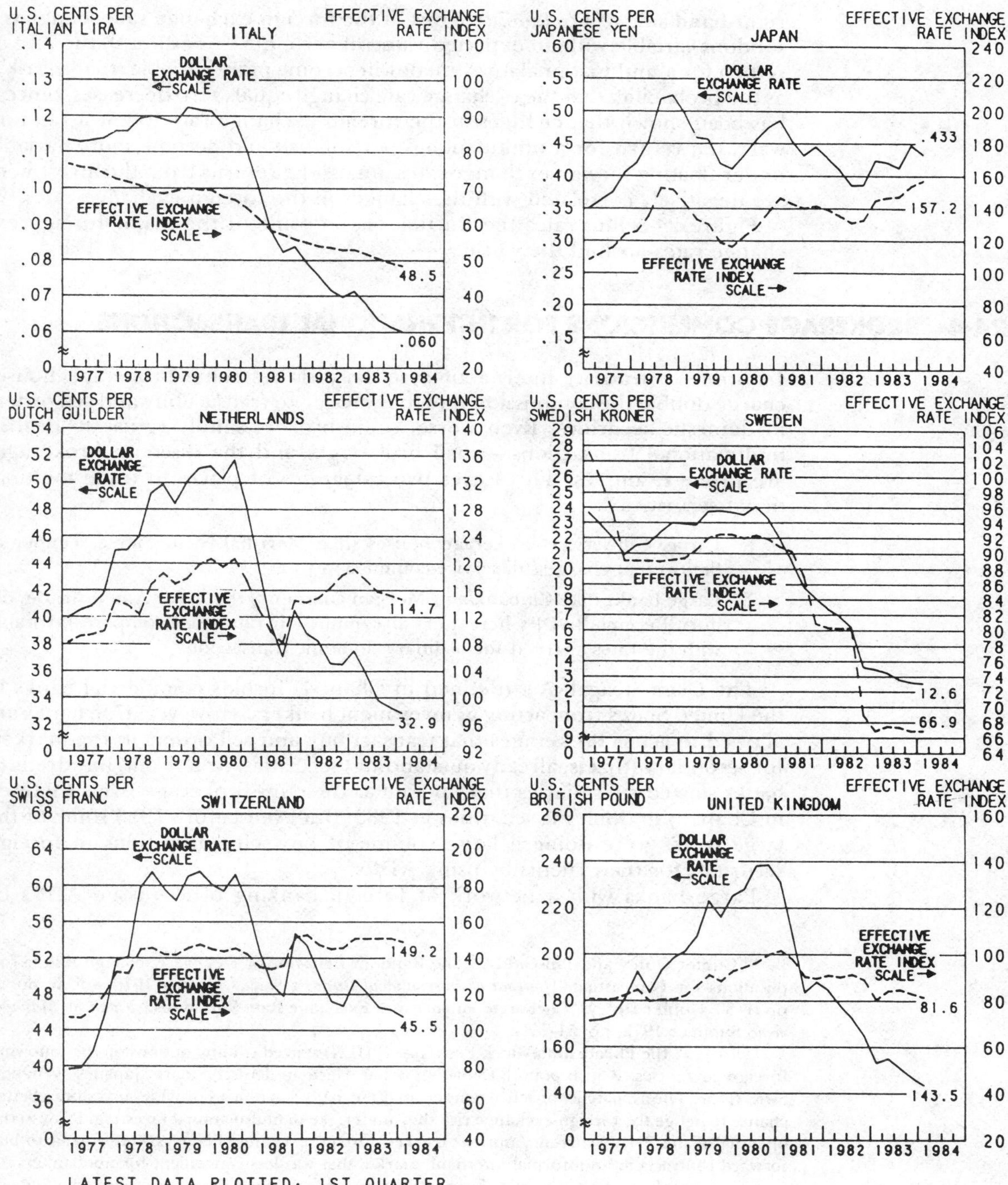

FIGURE 24-5 *(continued)*

right-hand side of Eq. (24-7d). Thus, if the foreign exchange rate change is a random variable with an expected value of zero, $E(S1 - S0) = 0$, the rate of return for a multinational investment will become more variable (that is, risky) as the probability that the exchange rate change equals zero decreases. Since it has been shown that changes in the foreign exchange rate follow a random walk, the return for a multinational portfolio should become more variable under floating foreign exchange rates, unless the returns from the investment are negatively correlated with the changes in the foreign exchange rates.[10]

Figure 24-5 illustrates the fluctuations in some of the major foreign exchange rates around the world.[11]

24-4 BROKERAGE COMMISSIONS FOR INTERNATIONAL TRANSACTIONS

In order to transact international security trades some brokerage houses charge double the commission rate they charge to transact buy and sell orders in domestic securities. Even worse, some brokers simply refuse to deal in multinational transactions—small brokerages and the discount brokerages are prime examples. This leaves two categories of places to trade multinational securities.

1. Large, full-service brokerage houses (like Merrill Lynch, Pierce, Fenner & Smith) that charge full service commission rates
2. Large banks (like Citibank and Morgan Guaranty) that issue American Depository Receipts (ADRs hereafter) at commission rates that compare favorably with the rates charged for ordinary domestic transactions

The Glass-Steagall Act (defined in Chap. 4) forbids commercial banks in the United States from acting as investment bankers. However, U.S. banks are allowed to act as brokerages that transact buy and sell orders in the markets for secondary (that is, already outstanding) securities. As a result, hundreds of banks started subsidiaries that operate as discount brokerage firms (defined in Chap. 3) in domestic securities in 1983. But even before 1983 some of the large banks were doing a large volume of buy-sell transactions in foreign securities for their clients by using ADRs.

Large banks with a network of foreign banking offices issue ADRs by

[10] Gunter Dufey and Ian Giddy, "The Random Behavior of Flexible Exchange Rates: Implications for Forecasting," *Journal of International Business Studies*, Spring 1975, vol. 6, no. 1, pp. 1–32. Gunter Dufey, "Corporate Finance and Exchange Rate Variations," *Financial Management*, Summer 1972, pp. 51–57.

[11] In 1983 the Philadelphia Stock Exchange (PHLX) started trading options on the following foreign currencies: British pound, Canadian dollar, German deutsche mark, Japanese yen, and Swiss franc. The availability of active markets in these major currencies provides investors a better chance to hedge the foreign exchange risk they undertake in multinational investing. Prior to the opening of the PHLX currency options market, foreign exchange hedgers were forced to buy forward contracts in an informal interbank market that was less convenient for nonbankers.

For more information, the following pamphlet may be obtained free by writing to the Federal Reserve Bank of Philadelphia, Research Dept., 10 Independence Mall, Philadelphia, Pa. 19106; ask for Brian Gendreau, "New Markets in Foreign Currency Options," *Business Review*, July–August 1984, pp. 3–12.

purchasing securities in a foreign corporation (Sony Corporation, for instance) for their domestic U.S. clients (say, Susan Doe, in New York City). The bank keeps these securities in the vault of its foreign branch (in Tokyo, in this case) registered in the bank's own name. The client (namely, Ms. Doe) is issued an ADR stating that the bank is holding (Sony, in this example) securities for the client. The bank collects cash dividends or coupon interest for the client and either reinvests the money or converts it into U.S. dollars and pays it out to the client—whichever alternative is requested—for a modest fee of a penny or two out of each security's cash payment. The bank also stores the foreign securities in a safe place where they may be sold quickly.

Although most of the corporations represented by banks' ADRs are large and reputable, these issuers enjoy a kind of diplomatic immunity from most of the rules and regulations of the Securities and Exchange Commission (SEC). But this immunity hasn't hurt the marketability of these foreign securities. Every day hundreds of thousands of foreign shares represented by ADRs are traded in the organized security exchanges and over the counter in the United States. In fact, sometimes more shares of a popular stock (like Sony) are traded using ADRs in the United States than are traded in the issuer's homeland.

In conclusion, ADR holders receive all the benefits that someone who owns the underlying security would receive without paying any additional brokerage commission, without losing any marketability, and without being bothered with collecting cash dividends in a foreign currency.

24-5 CHAPTER SUMMARY AND CONCLUSIONS

International investors face all the same risks that domestic investors face, plus four additional risks—international marketability risk, international political risk, foreign exchange risk, and the risk of being forced to work with inferior investment information.

Virtually no foreign markets are as efficient as the large, deep, and resilient securities markets in the United States. Billions of dollars change hands smoothly in the U.S. security markets daily without most of the sellers being forced to give up large price markdowns or pay large commissions to sell their investments. Dealing with these marketability risks in a foreign market can be an unpleasant new experience. Furthermore, there is the added marketability risk in some foreign countries—security price manipulation that is illegal in the United States may be permitted or go unnoticed in some foreign markets.

International political risk and foreign exchange risk are usually interrelated. Many of the foreign exchange rates in the world are fixed by the governments of the countries that issue the currencies, rather than being freely floating exchange rates determined by supply and demand. And since the administration of every country is some form of political organization, the foreign exchange rate authorities are typically high-level bureaucrats who are subject to political pressures from their country's top administrators. The United States is rare and lucky to have a foreign exchange authority (namely, the central bank called the Federal Reserve System) that is fairly immune from political pressures.

The risk of being forced to compete against foreign investors who have inside information, who have faster access to the public information about their country, and who may even be able to manipulate security prices in their country places the outside investor at a distinct disadvantage, in terms of information. Some large institutional investors (such as international banks like Citibank, Bank of America, and others) have foreign offices that manage investments in the host country and are partly staffed by the local citizens of the foreign country. Such foreign nationals not only are low-cost employees, but they may also be able to gather valuable information for their employer. Or, a foreign investor can simply purchase a highly diversified portfolio of securities in the foreign country without doing intensive investments research—buying shares in an index fund is an example of this passive kind of investment management. Such a passive international investor is essentially investing in the overall economic prospects of the foreign country.

Investors may be willing to assume the international political risk, the foreign exchange risk, and the information risks in order to obtain the impressive risk reduction available in the international security markets. That is, the risk-reducing benefits from international investing may more than offset the disadvantages from possible traumas arising from political considerations, the risk that the investment be harmed by a currency devaluation, and/or the disadvantage that the foreign investor may suffer relative to the domestic investors in the foreign country when it comes to getting valuable information in a timely fashion.

The correlations between the securities markets in different countries are usually lower than the correlations available to the purely domestic investor. As a result, multinational investing opportunities offer a more dominant efficient frontier of investment opportunities from which to choose.

QUESTIONS

1. How might a multinational investor based in the United States use foreign exchange futures to hedge against the risk that the foreign exchange rate changes? (*Hint*: Some of the material about financial futures in Chap. 23 may be helpful.)
2. Are there any risks that are peculiar to international investing? Stated differently, what factors in addition to the usual investment risks should be of particular concern to the multinational investor?
3. What are the advantages that induce investors to invest internationally when they have to face additional new risks peculiar to multinational investing?
4. Does every international investment opportunity provide the investor with new investment opportunities that dominate the old opportunities in a risk-return analysis?
5. What factors explain why the intercountry correlations between securities markets are low? (*Hint*: You may benefit from consulting an international economics textbook or an international finance textbook.)
6. What do the following mutual funds have in common? Explain each fund's investment objective.

(*a*) International Investors Incorporated
New York City
(*b*) Research Capital Fund
San Mateo, California
(*c*) Templeton Growth Fund
Toronto, Ontario, Canada
(*Hint*: Consult the latest edition of a book entitled *Investment Companies*, published each year by Warren, Gorham and Lamont.

7. If an investor is interested in multinational diversification but does not have the time or expertise to select individual foreign securities in which to invest, is there another way this investor can invest internationally?
8. Since the intercountry correlation between securities markets plays such an important role in international diversification, consider the trend in these statistics. Do you think that, in general, these correlations should increase, stay the same, or decrease with the passage of time? Explain why.

SELECTED REFERENCES

Gunter Dufey and Ian Giddy, *The International Money Market*, Prentice-Hall, Englewood Cliffs, N.J., 1978. This book analyzes international business finance from a monetary economics viewpoint with liberal usage of empirical data. No mathematics.

Edwin J. Elton and Martin J. Gruber (eds.), *Studies in International Capital Markets*, North-Holland, Amsterdam, 1975. A collection of studies that analyze international finance in terms of modern portfolio theory and efficient markets. Mathematics and statistics are used.

Charles N. Henning, William Pigott, and Robert Haney Scott, *International Financial Management*, McGraw-Hill, New York, 1978. Three monetary economists present their analysis of international business finance. The discussion is supplemented with some empirical data. No mathematics.

Maurice Levi, *International Finance*, McGraw-Hill, New York, 1983. A discussion of international finance that uses algebra and empirical data. Modern portfolio theory and the efficient markets theories are employed.

part seven

PORTFOLIO THEORY

CHAPTER 25—*diversification and portfolio analysis* explains why and how wealth-seeking, risk-averse investors should diversify. Portfolios, rather than individual securities, are shown to be the objects of choice for rational investors.

CHAPTER 26—*capital market theory* explicates models for the determination of the prices of risky marketable securities.

CHAPTER 27—*different investment goals* rationalizes the coexistence of both daring and timid investors and shows their common, rational grounds by using utility analysis to analyze investment decisions.

CHAPTER 28—*portfolio performance evaluation* introduces the tools used to evaluate the performance of the managers of investment portfolios; mutual fund data are analyzed.

CHAPTER 29—*multiperiod wealth maximization* explains how to use the one-period Markowitz portfolio analysis in the long-run context involving multiple planning horizons.

In Part 7 the focus shifts from individual assets to portfolios of assets. The concepts essential to portfolio management are introduced and analyzed.

diversification and portfolio analysis*

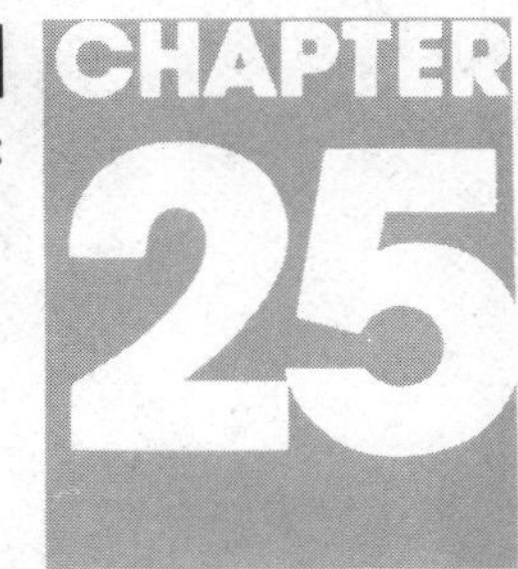

Dictionaries explain that *efficient* things produce the desired result with a minimum of waste. This chapter shows how to apply the concept of efficiency to investment management. The desired result investors seek is returns, or income. And the waste they seek to avoid is lost returns—that is, they seek to minimize their investment's *variability of return*. Diversification is essential to the creation of an efficient investment because diversification reduces variability of the investment returns.

The portfolio manager seeking efficient investments works with two statistics—the expected return, and risk statistics. The expected return and risk statistics for individual stocks and bonds serve as input data that are analyzed in order to develop a diversified portfolio having the maximum rate of return that can be expected at whatever level of risk is deemed appropriate. All information available to the security analyst is supposed to be summarized in the risk-return statistics for the stocks and bonds that are under consideration. These statistics furnish the input information for the portfolio analysis. This chapter explains how the portfolio manager selects which assets to buy and how much of each one to buy based only on each asset's risk and expected return statistics.

25-1 DOMINANCE AND EFFICIENT PORTFOLIOS

When a portfolio manager is confronted with the expected return and risk statistics of hundreds of different bonds, stocks, options, mortgages, and whatever other assets that are investment candidates, he or she may select the assets worthy of investment by using the dominance principle.

25-1.1 dominance principle

The *dominance principle* states that (1) among all investments with any given expected rate of return, the one with the least risk is the most desirable or

*Chapter 25 presumes a knowledge of Chaps. 9 and 10.

TABLE 25-1 the risk and expected return of five assets

security	expected return, $E(r)$, %	risk σ, %
American Telephone Works (ATW)	7	3
General Auto Corporation (GAC)	7	4
Fuzzyworm Tractor Co. (FTC)	15	15
Fairyear Tire and Rubber Co. (FTR)	3	3
Hotstone Tire Corporation (HTC)	8	12

(2) among all the assets in a given risk-class, the one with the highest expected rate of return is the most desirable.

Application of the dominance principal to the assets in Table 25-1 reveals that Fairyear Tire and Rubber (FTR) is dominated by American Telephone Works (ATW) because they both have the same risk (σ = 3 percent) but ATW has a higher expected return than FTR. Figure 25-1 shows this graphically. That is, FTR can be eliminated from consideration because it is a *dominated investment.* ATW dominates General Auto Corporation (GAC); their expected returns are the same, but ATW has less risk. So GAC is dominated and can be ignored too.

Use of the dominance principle shows FTR and GAC to be inferior investments. The nondominated assets are Fuzzyworm Tractor Co. (FTC), Hotstone Tire Corporation (HTC), and ATW. Part of the work of investment decision making seems to be done, since the investment choices have been narrowed from five to three. However, this example is simplified because it has ignored diversification and assets called portfolios.

FIGURE 25-1 five assets in risk-return space.

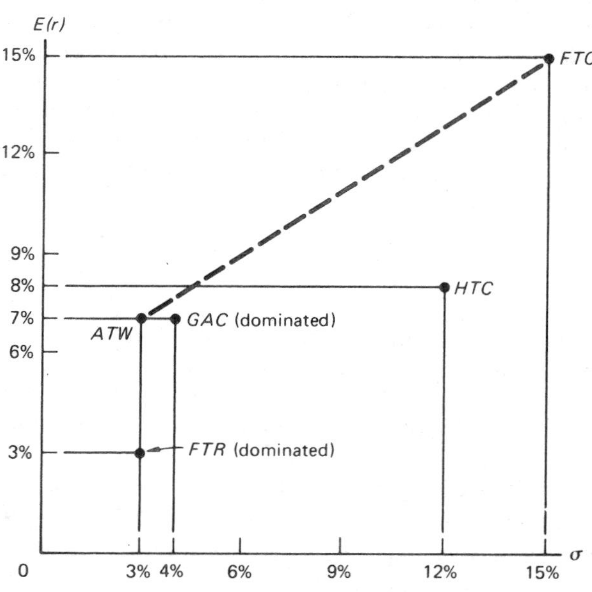

25-1.2 efficient portfolios

Although HTC is a nondominated asset, a close examination of Fig. 25-1 shows that its relative risk and return opportunities are somehow not as appealing as those of ATW and FTC. The reason is that *portfolios* have not been considered.

Suppose a portfolio were constructed of ATW and FTC. The portfolio's expected return is simply the weighted average of the expected rates of return of the assets in the portfolio. Equation (25-1) defines the expected return for a portfolio, denoted $E(r_p)$ for an n-asset portfolio.

$$E(r_p) = \sum_{i=1}^{n} x_i E(r_i) \tag{25-1}$$

where x_i is the fraction of the total value of the portfolio invested in the ith asset (the x_i's are called *weights* or *participation levels*) and $E(r_i)$ denotes the expected rate of return from the ith asset. It is assumed that the weights sum to 1 (that is, $\sum_{i=1}^{n} x_i = 1$), since it is pointless to account for more or less than 100 percent (which is equal to 1.0) of the funds in the portfolio.

To be more specific, suppose that seven-eights of the portfolio's funds are put into ATW and the other one-eighth into FTC. In this case $n = 2$; the weight in ATW is $x_{ATW} = 7/8$; and the weight in FTC is $x_{FTC} = 1/8$. The computations for this two-asset portfolio's expected return are as follows:

$$\begin{aligned} E(r_p) &= x_{ATW}E(r_{ATW}) + x_{FTC}E(r_{FTC}) \\ &= \frac{7}{8}(7\%) + \frac{1}{8}(15\%) \\ &= .875(.07) + .125(.15) \\ &= .08 = 8\% \end{aligned}$$

The two-asset portfolio with seven-eighths in ATW and the other one-eighth in FTC has the same expected rate of return as HTC. The dashed line from ATW to FTC in Fig. 25-1 represents the risk and return of all possible portfolios that can be formed from various proportions of ATW and FTC.[1] HTC is a dominated asset if portfolios are considered as possible assets, that is, the dashed line from ATW to FTC dominates HTC in Fig. 25-1.

It appears that the concept of dominant assets should be extended to include portfolios. Hereafter, dominant assets will be called *efficient portfolios* whether they contain one or many assets. An efficient portfolio, then, is any asset or combination of assets that has: (1) the maximum expected return in its risk-class, or conversely, (2) the minimum risk at its level of expected return.

The objective of portfolio management is to develop efficient portfolios. As the dashed line in Fig. 25-1 shows, there are a number of efficient portfolios. The group of all efficient portfolios will be called the efficient set of port-

[1] The linear opportunity locus representing portfolios composed of ATW and FTC ignores beneficial diversification effects, which will be explained later in this chapter.

folios, or, simply, the *efficient set*. The efficient set of portfolios composes the efficient frontier in risk-return space (if borrowing and lending are ignored). The *efficient frontier* is the locus of points in risk-return space having the maximum return at each risk-class.

The efficient frontier dominates all other assets. Consider how different kinds of diversification can be used to reduce a portfolio's risk and improve the efficient frontier from which a rational, risk-averse, wealth-seeking investor will select his or her investments.

25-2 SIMPLE DIVERSIFICATION

Simple diversification can be defined as "not putting all the eggs in one basket," or "spreading the risks." These vague definitions are analyzed in the paragraphs below.

25-2.1 effects of simple diversification

Simple diversification implies that a portfolio made up of 200 different securities is 10 times more diversified than a portfolio made up of 20 different securities. (It will be shown later in this chapter that this is not true.) Simple diversification can usually be expected to reduce the risk of a portfolio somewhat. As the number of securities added to a simply diversified portfolio increases to 10 or 15, the portfolio's risk will usually decrease toward the systematic level of risk in the market. After the portfolio's assets have been spread across more than about 15 randomly selected securities, further decreases in portfolio risk usually cannot be attained, on average, simply by investing in additional securities.

Several studies have shown that the total risk of most securities, as measured by their variance in rates of return over time, can be divided into two parts.[2] The exact proportions of systematic and unsystematic risk vary from security to security and industry to industry, but for a large number of common stocks listed on the New York Stock Exchange (NYSE), systematic

[2] Given the ith security's characteristic line,

$$r_{it} = a_i + b_i r_{mt} + e_{it}$$

the variance of the security's returns can be partitioned as follows:

$$\begin{aligned} \text{var}(r_{it}) &= \text{var}(a + br_{mt} + e_{it}) \\ &= b_i^2 \text{ var}(r_{mt}) + \text{var}(e_{it}) \\ &= \text{systematic risk} + \text{unsystematic risk} \\ &= \text{total risk} \end{aligned}$$

Here $\text{var}(e_{it})$ is the residual variance and $\text{var}(r_{it})$ is the total variance. Independent studies show that systematic risk is typically between one-fourth and one-third of a security's total risk. J. Evans and S. H. Archer, "Diversification and the Reduction of Dispersion: An Empirical Analysis," *Journal of Finance*, December 1968, pp. 761–767. K. H. Johnson and D. S. Shannon have extended the Evans-Archer study in "A Note on Diversification and the Reduction of Dispersion," *Journal of Financial Economics*, December 1974, pp. 365–372. See also W. H. Wagner and S. Lau, "The Effect of Diversification on Risk," *Financial Analysts Journal*, November–December 1971, pp. 48–53. More recent research has shown that it may take a few more securities to achieve a satisfactory level of diversification than the pioneering empirical studies indicated. See E. Elton and M. Gruber, "Risk Reduction and Portfolio Size: An Analytical Solution," *Journal of Business*, October 1977, pp. 415–437; T. Tole, "You Can't Diversify without Diversifying," *Journal of Portfolio Management*, Winter 1982, pp. 5–11.

risk has been shown to compose about one-quarter of the securities' total risk on average.

systematic variability of return	25%
Plus: unsystematic variability of return	75%
Equals: total variability of return	100% of total risk

Simple diversification will usually decrease the unsystematic portion of total risk toward zero until approximately 15 securities are added to the portfolio, because unsystematic risk is (by definition) uncorrelated with the market. That is, the unsystematic variabilities in different firms' rates of return are independent with an average value of zero, and therefore they average out to zero when added together into a portfolio. Adding more than about 15 securities to a portfolio cannot be expected to reduce its unsystematic risk (or to increase it, in most cases).

Figure 25-2 shows the manner in which simple diversification works. Drs. Evans and Archer prepared the figure using empirical data on 470 common stocks from the NYSE. The figure shows that the average standard deviation of returns for all 470 stocks was .21. The level of systematic risk in the market was estimated at .12 (that is, $\sigma_m = 12$ percent).

For preparation of Fig. 25-2, 60 different portfolios of each size were constructed randomly, that is, 60 one-security portfolios, 60 two-security portfolios, 60 three-security portfolios, and so on up to the forty-security portfolios. Every portfolio was constructed from randomly selected stocks. These portfolios were constructed so that each *randomly selected* security was allocated an *equal weight* in all the random portfolios. Then the average standard deviation of returns was calculated for the 60 portfolios of each size. Figure 25-2 shows these average standard deviations at each size of portfolio. From it we can see that, on the average, randomly combining 10 to 15 stocks will reduce the portfolio's risk to the systematic level of variation found in the market average, but spreading the portfolio's assets over twice or three times as many stocks cannot be expected to further reduce risk.

FIGURE 25-2 naive diversification reduces risk to the systematic level in randomly selected portfolios. (*Source*: J. H. Evans and S. H. Archer, "Diversification and the Reduction of Dispersion: An Empirical Analysis," *Journal of Finance*, December 1968, pp. 761–767.)

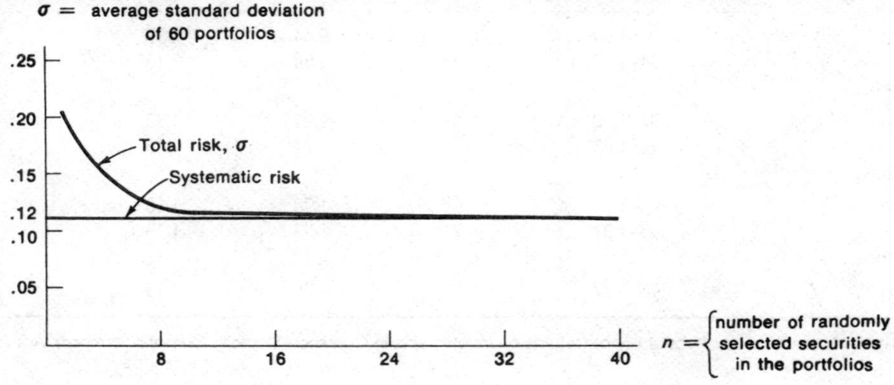

25-2.2 diversifying across industries

Some investment counselors advocate selecting securities from different and unrelated industries to achieve better diversification. It is certainly better to follow this advice than to select all the securities in a portfolio from one industry. But it turns out that diversifying across industries is not much better than simply selecting securities randomly. Either procedure is simple diversification—as explained below.

Studies of the rates of return of securities in many industries have shown that nearly all industries are highly correlated with one another. The easiest way to see the meager benefits of diversifying across various industries is to examine the movement of Standard & Poor's indices for industrial, railroad, and utility stocks. Figure 10-1 on page 253 shows how these three different indices move up and down together month after month. This *systematic variability* of return cannot be diversified away merely by selecting securities from different industries.

One study sought to test the effectiveness of diversifying across different industries and also of increasing the number of different assets in the portfolio. Portfolios containing 8, 16, 32, and 128 common stocks, all listed on the NYSE, were formed by two separate techniques. Technique 1 involved simple random selection of assets (for example, with a dart). Technique 2 drew each asset in the portfolio from a different industry. Numerous portfolios were constructed in this study, and statistics were tabulated about the portfolio's rates of return.[3]

Table 25-2 presents the findings of the study. The rates of return were calculated from portfolios constructed in each of 20 consecutive years.

[3] The study actually investigated wealth relatives, or link relatives, as they are sometimes called, rather than the rates of return.

$$\text{Wealth relative} = p_t/p_{t-1} = 1 + r_t = \text{link relative}$$

However, the variance of the wealth relatives is the same as the variance of the percentage price change over the same period since $\text{var}(1 + r) = \text{var}(r)$. See Mathematical App. B for proof.

TABLE 25-2 statistics obtained by use of different diversification techniques

stocks in portfolio	technique used to diversify	20th and 80th percentiles (the middle 60%)	min. return	max. return	mean return	average std. dev. of returns
8	Random	.94–1.29	.53	2.64	1.13	.22
	Across industries	.94–1.30	.53	2.58	1.13	.22
16	Random	.94–1.28	.63	2.21	1.13	.21
	Across industries	.94–1.28	.65	2.21	1.13	.21
32	Random	.95–1.27	.69	1.98	1.13	.20
	Across industries	.95–1.27	.71	1.93	1.13	.20
128	Random	.96–1.27	.71	1.76	1.13	.19

Source: L. Fisher and J. Lorie, "Some Studies of Variability of Returns on Investments in Common Stocks," *Journal of Business*, April 1970, p. 112, table 5.

The two main conclusions that may be drawn from Table 25-2 are that (1) diversification across industries is not better than random diversification and (2) increasing the number of different assets held in the portfolio above eight does not substantially reduce the portfolio's risk.

25-2.3 superfluous diversification

Simple diversification will ordinarily reduce risk to the systematic level in the market (as indicated by Fig. 25-2). However, portfolio managers should not become overzealous and spread their assets over too many assets. If 10 or 15 different assets are selected for the portfolio, the maximum benefits from simple diversification most likely have been attained. Further spreading of the portfolio's assets is *superfluous diversification* and should be avoided. Superfluous diversification will usually result in the following poor portfolio management practices:

1. *Purchasing lackluster performers.* The search for numerous different assets to buy will ultimately lead to the purchase of investments that will not yield an adequate rate of return for the risk they bear.
2. *Using out-of-date securities information.* If the portfolio contains dozens of different securities, the portfolio's management cannot hope to stay informed on the status of them all simultaneously.
3. *Incurring higher search costs.* The larger the number of assets to be selected for the portfolio, the more expensive the search for potential investments.
4. *Incurring high transaction costs.* Frequent purchases of small quantities of shares will result in larger broker's commissions than will less frequent purchases of larger quantities.[4]

Although more money is spent to manage a superfluously diversified portfolio, there will most likely be no concurrent improvement in the portfolio's performance. Thus, superfluous diversification may lower the net return to the portfolio owners after the portfolio management expenses are deducted.

25-2.4 portfolio returns unaffected by diversification

Wagner and Lau, two investment analysts who were employed at a large west coast bank, analyzed the effect of simply diversifying across randomly selected securities in terms of both return and risk. Table 25-3 summarizes their statistics from portfolios created with simple diversification that range in size from 1 to 20 common stocks.

The far right-hand column of Table 25-3 reveals that the portfolios made up of a few randomly selected stocks earned the same rate of return as the simply diversified portfolios that contained a larger number of stocks. The small differences in the average monthly returns shown in Table 25-3 are only normal *sampling errors* and not significantly different rates of return. These similar returns are exactly what was expected because the portfolios' returns are simply the arithmetic averages of the returns of their securities, and diversification does not affect the arithmetic average rate of return calculated with Eq. (25-1). The portfolios' correlation statistics are affected by diversification, however.

[4] As the third market, fourth market, block positioners, and discount brokers compete, negotiated brokerage commissions continue to be chiseled down on larger trades.

TABLE 25-3 return and risk statistics from simply diversified portfolios, June 1960 to May 1970

number of random stocks	standard deviation of monthly returns	portfolios' correlation with market	portfolios' average monthly returns
1	.70	.54	.0110
2	.50	.63	.0084
3	.48	.75	.0102
4	.46	.77	.0096
5	.46	.79	.0101
10	.42	.85	.0096
15	.40	.88	.0107
20	.39	.90	.0109

Source: W. H. Wagner and S. C. Lau, "The Effects of Diversification on Risk," *Financial Analysts Journal*, November–December 1971, pp. 49–51.

25-2.5 correlation between diversification effects and the market

The second column of statistics in Table 25-3 shows that the standard deviations of the simply diversified portfolios declined as the number of randomly selected stocks was increased. These results further confirm those of the Evans-Archer study (shown in Fig. 25-2) and the Fisher-Lorie study (shown in Table 25-2). The Wagner-Lau risk statistics offer an additional insight, however.

The correlation coefficients in the third column of Table 25-3 increase as the number of different equally weighted securities held in the randomly diversified portfolios increases. These correlations result when the unsystematic returns are averaged out to zero in the portfolios made up of the larger numbers of different stocks. The unsystematic returns are uncorrelated with the returns from the market portfolio (or any market index, for that matter). So the more widely diversified portfolios made up of a larger number of stocks contain only systematic (or undiversifiable) returns that are highly correlated with the market.

Care must be taken in interpreting the correlation statistics shown in column three of Table 25-3. These correlations should not be misinterpreted to mean that systematic risk increases in the more widely diversified portfolios. Quite to the contrary, the systematic risk is invariant. Both the portfolios' total risks and the unsystematic (or diversifiable) risks are reduced by simple diversification. The portfolios' correlation with the market increases with the level of simple diversification because both the market and the large portfolios contain the same undiversifiable systematic variations after the unsystematic variations are diversified down toward zero.

25-2.6 simple diversification across quality rating categories

Wagner and Lau extended their study of diversification to include simple diversification across different stocks that all have the same Standard & Poor's quality ratings. Quality ratings are based on what is essentially the risk of bankruptcy. Standard & Poor's own explanations of its common stock quality ratings are shown in Fig. 6-5 on page 153. Table 25-4 shows the relationships between the quality ratings, standard deviations, beta systematic risk coefficients, and average monthly returns from six simply diversified portfolios;

TABLE 25-4 **risk and return statistics for simply diversified portfolios with homogeneous quality ratings**

portfolios' homogeneous quality rating	portfolios' beta risk coefficient	portfolios' standard deviation	portfolios' average monthly return
A+	.74	.039	.67
A	.80	.042	.69
A−	.89	.045	.78
B+	.87	.045	1.04
B	1.23	.063	1.05
B− to C+	1.23	.063	1.03

Source: W. H. Wagner and S. Lau, "The Effect of Diversification on Risk," *Financial Analysts Journal,* November–December 1971, p. 52.

each portfolio contains 20 equally weighted common stocks *identical in quality rating*.

Economic theory suggests that risk-averse investors should require higher average rates of return in order to induce them to assume higher levels of risk. The empirical statistics shown in Table 25-4 support the theory. A direct relationship between the return and the various risk statistics is clearly discernible in Table 25-4. This positive risk-return relationship is particularly interesting because bankruptcy risk (as measured by the quality ratings) contains unsystematic elements (such as management errors and acts of God) that Evans and Archer showed were easy to diversify away to zero. Stated differently, portfolio theory (as exemplified by the Evans-Archer findings) suggests that *unsystematic risks should not affect portfolio returns*, since this type of risk may be diversified away to zero. Unsystematic risk should therefore affect only the prices of individual assets, but not the prices and returns of diversified portfolios. Wagner and Lau analyzed this interesting result to obtain additional investment management insights.

25-2.7 increasing simple diversification within quality categories

Wagner and Lau used the same methodology as Archer and Evans (see Fig. 25-2) to generate the risk statistics for portfolios that were *simply diversified within quality ratings*. Their results are illustrated in Fig. 25-3. Comparison of Fig. 25-2 with Fig. 25-3 reveals that simple diversification yields significant risk reductions within homogeneous quality rating categories, just as it did across the more heterogeneous sample used by Evans and Archer.

Further insights can be discerned by considering Fig. 25-3; it shows that the standard deviations of the homogeneous-quality-rating portfolios decreased to different levels of undiversifiable (or systematic) risk. In particular, the highest-quality simply diversified portfolios were able to achieve lower levels of undiversifiable risk than the simply diversified portfolios of lower-quality stocks. This result stems from the fact that bankruptcy risk (as measured by the quality ratings) also contains elements of systematic risk. More specifically, the higher-quality portfolios in Fig. 25-3 contained assets with less systematic risk and were thus less likely to experience portfolio variability of return (that is, risk) from individual assets that go bankrupt from systematic factors. This

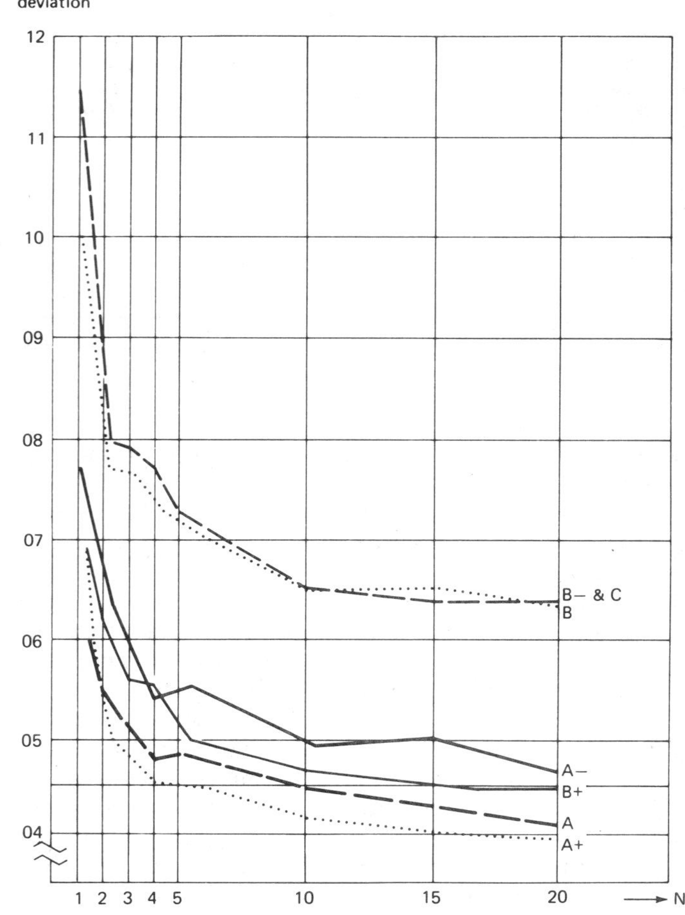

FIGURE 25-3 naive diversification increases within different categories of stocks with identical quality ratings. (*Source*: W. H. Wagner and S. Lau, "The Effects of Diversification on Risk," *Financial Analysts Journal*, November–December 1971, exhibit 1.)

finding suggests that portfolio managers may be able to reduce portfolio risk to levels lower than those attainable with simple diversification by not diversifying across assets for which security analysts foresee the possibility of bankruptcy. But, as Fig. 25-3 shows, these risk reductions are modest.

The next section explains a more sophisticated method of diversification that considers *both* the risk and the return of the portfolio simultaneously.

25-3 MARKOWITZ DIVERSIFICATION

Named after its originator, Harry M. Markowitz, *Markowitz diversification* may be defined as the process of combining assets that are less than perfectly positively correlated[5] in order to reduce portfolio risk without sacrificing any

[5] Mathematical App. D, in Part 9, defines correlation and discusses it briefly.

TABLE 25-5 numerical example of Markowitz diversification with inverse correlation

Time period	$t = 1$	$t = 2$	$t = 3$	$t = 4$	var(r)*
Return from X Return from Y	$r_{r1} = 5\%$ $r_{y1} = 25\%$	$r_{r2} = 10\%$ $r_{y2} = 20\%$	$r_{r3} = 15\%$ $r_{y3} = 15\%$	$r_{r4} = 5\%$ $r_{y4} = 25\%$	$\sigma_r^2 = .0015$ $\sigma_y^2 = .0021$
Return for portfolio of half X and Y	$\frac{25 + 5}{2} = 15\%$	$\frac{10 + 20}{2} = 15\%$	$\frac{15 + 15}{2} = 15\%$	$\frac{5 + 25}{2} = 15\%$	$\sigma_p^2 = 0$

* $\text{var}(r_x) = \Sigma\ 1/4(r_s - .008)^2 = .00612/4 = .00153$
$\text{var}(r_y) = \Sigma\ 1/4(r_y - .2125)^2 = .0085/4 = .00212$
$\text{var}(r_p) = \Sigma\ 1/4(r_p - .15)^2 = 0$

portfolio returns.[6] It can sometimes reduce risk below the systematic level. Markowitz diversification is more analytical than simple diversification and considers assets' correlations (or covariances). The lower the correlation between assets, the more it will be able to lower risk.[7]

25-3.1 numerical example

The simplest way to see the benefits of combining securities with low correlations is by numerical example. Consider what happens when two assets, denoted X and Y, which have perfectly negatively correlated rates of return, are combined into a portfolio. Table 25-5 shows the results.

The portfolio of half asset X and half Y has *zero variability of returns*. This complete reduction of risk is due to the perfect negative correlation of the rates of return of X and Y; their returns move inversely so that the gains on one asset offset the losses on the other.

25-3.2 general two-asset analysis of Markowitz diversification

Numerical examples represent only specific cases. It is a well-known (but often made) error in logic to draw general conclusions from specific cases. Therefore, a more general mathematical analysis of Markowitz diversification is needed. Consider the risk and return of a simple two-asset portfolio as the correlation coefficient between the two assets varies. Table 25-6 gives the risk and return of two hypothetical common stocks issued by the Apex and Bean Corporations.

[6] H. Markowitz, "Portfolio Selection," *Journal of Finance*, March 1952, p. 89.

[7] There is a trade-off between risk and return in the market. But at any given level of expected return, Markowitz diversification can reduce risk lower than can simple diversification. This reduction in risk need not be accompanied by a reduction in the portfolio's expected rate of return.

TABLE 25-6 statistics for Apex and Bean

stock	expected return $E(r)$, %	risk, %
Apex	5	20
Bean	15	40

FORMULA FOR PORTFOLIO RETURN For the Apex and Bean stocks, Eq. (25-2*a*) is a special case of Eq. (25-1) that defines the two-asset portfolio's expected return.

$$E(r_p) = x_A E(r_A) + x_B E(r_B) \qquad (25\text{-}2a)$$

$$= x_A(5\%) + x_B\,(15\%)$$

$$= .05x_A + .15x_B \qquad (25\text{-}2b)$$

The portfolio's return formula is a linear function, since the weight variables in Eq. (25-2*a*) or Eq. (25-2*b*) have exponents of unity. The portfolio risk formula is more complex.

RISK FORMULA Total risk, as measured by the standard deviation of returns from a portfolio made up of n assets, is defined for the general n-asset case by Eq. (25-3*a*).

$$\sigma_p = \sum_{i=1}^{n} \sum_{j=1}^{n} x_i x_j \sigma_{ij} \qquad (25\text{-}3a)$$

$$= \sqrt{\sigma_i^2 x_i^2 + \sigma_j^2 x_j^2 + 2x_i x_j \sigma_{ij}} \qquad \text{if } n = 2 \qquad (25\text{-}3b)$$

where

σ_p = standard deviation of the portfolio's rates of return

$\sigma_i^2 = \sigma_{ii}$ = variance of returns of the ith asset, that is, the standard deviation squared

$\sigma_{ij} = \text{cov}(r_i, r_j)$ = covariance of returns for assets i and j[8]

The covariance is related to the correlation coefficient, as shown in Eq. (25-4).[9]

$$\sigma_{ij} = (\sigma_i)\,(\sigma_j)\,(\rho_{ij}) \qquad (25\text{-}4)$$

where ρ_{ij} is the correlation coefficient between variables i and j.

The covariance measures how two variables covary. If two assets move together, their covariance is positive. For example, most common stocks have a positive covariance with each other. If two variables are independent, their covariance is zero. If two variables move inversely, their covariance is negative.

Equation (25-3) defines a portfolio's risk. For the two-asset portfolio of Apex and Bean, Eq. (25-5) gives the standard deviation of returns.[10]

$$\sigma_p = \sqrt{x_A^2 \sigma_A^2 + x_B^2 \sigma_B^2 + 2x_A x_B \sigma_{AB}} \qquad (25\text{-}5)$$

Substituting Eq. (25-4) into (25-5) yields (25-6*a*), which shows exactly how the correlation between the returns from Apex and Bean affects the portfolio's risk.

[8] Mathematical App. B, in Part 9, explains the covariance, σ_{ij}.

[9] Mathematical App. D explains correlation and the correlation coefficient in more detail.

[10] The portfolio risk formula shown in Eqs. (25-5) and (25-6) and elsewhere is derived and explained in Mathematical App. E.

$$\sigma_p = \sqrt{x_A^2\sigma_A^2 + x_B^2\sigma_B^2 + 2x_Ax_B\rho_{AB}\sigma_A\sigma_B} \tag{25-6a}$$
$$= \sqrt{x_A^2\,(20\%)^2 + x_B^2\,(40\%)^2 + 2x_Ax_B\rho_{AB}\,(20\%)\,(40\%)} \tag{25-6b}$$
$$= \sqrt{.04x_A^2 + .16x_B^2 + .16x_Ax_B\rho_{AB}}$$

Figure 25-4*a*, *b*, *c*, and *d* is a set of graphs in risk-return space of the two assets Apex and Bean and the portfolios that can be formed from them at three different values for their correlation coefficient, $\rho_{AB} = -1, 0,$ and $+1$. These four figures were prepared by plotting the risk and return of the various portfolios composed of Apex and Bean stocks for which the participation levels summed to unity (that is, $x_A + x_B = 1$) and for three different correlation coefficients, $\rho_{AB} = -1.0$, 0, and $+1.0$.

In order to understand Fig. 25-4, it is informative to verify a few points in the figures by substituting some appropriate numbers into Eq. (25-2*b*) and (25-6*b*) and calculating the portfolio's expected return and risk. For example,

FIGURE 25-4(*a*) two perfectly positively correlated assets generate linear portfolio investment opportunities; (*b*) two zero correlated assets generate a curve of portfolio possibilities; (*c*) two perfectly negatively correlated assets can create a riskless portfolio; (*d*) the assets' correlation affects the portfolio's risk.

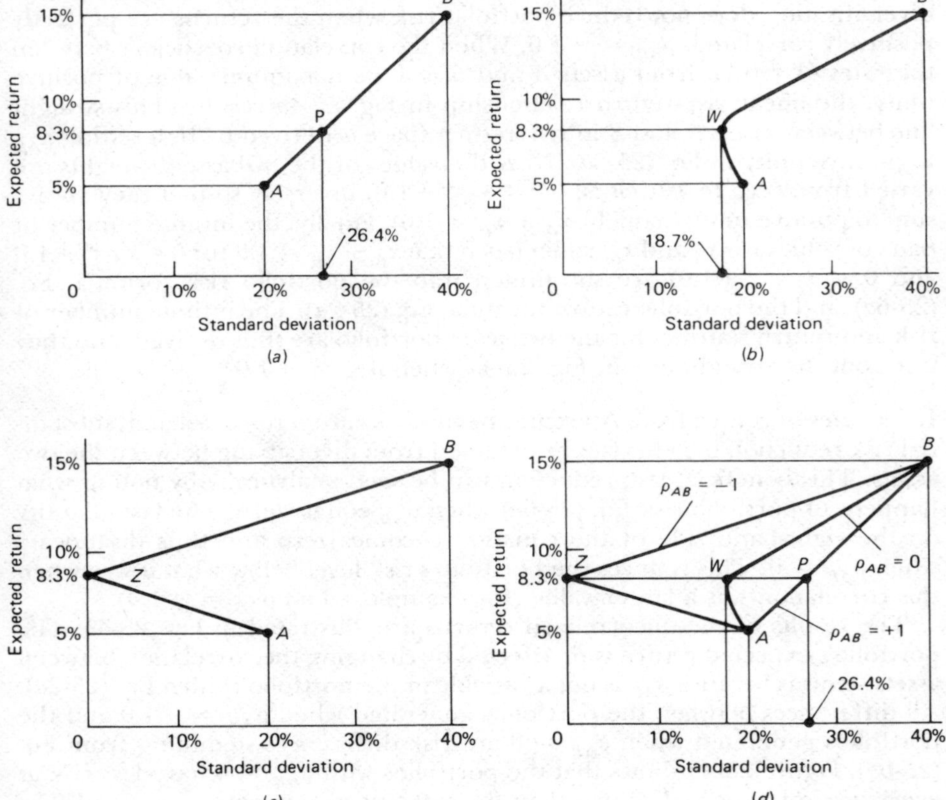

for the portfolio which has $x_A = 2/3$ and $x_B = 1/3$, the expected return is fixed at 8.3 percent regardless of what value the correlation coefficient assumes.

$$E(r_p) = \sum_{i=1}^{2} x_i E(r_i)$$
$$= x_A E(r_A) + x_B E(r_B)$$
$$= x_A\,(.05) + x_B\,(.15)$$
$$= \frac{2}{3}(.05) + \frac{1}{3}(.15) = .083 = 8.3\%$$

The risk for this portfolio with $x_A = 2/3$ and $x_B = 1/3$ varies with the correlation coefficient, ρ_{AB}.

$$\sigma_p = \sqrt{x_A^2\,\sigma_A^2 + x_B^2\,\sigma_B^2 + 2x_A x_B \rho_{AB}\sigma_A\sigma_B} \qquad (25\text{-}6a)$$
$$= \sqrt{(2/3)^2\,(20\%)^2 + (1/3)^2\,(40\%)^2 + 2(\rho_{AB})\,(2/3)\,(1/3)\,(20\%)\,(40\%)}$$
$$= .0175 + .0175 + .035\,(\rho_{AB}) \qquad (25\text{-}6c)$$
$$= .035 + .035(\rho_{AB})$$

25-3.3 perfectly positively correlated returns, Fig. 25-4*a*

Portfolio analysis of the two-asset portfolio illustrated in Fig. 25-4*a* shows that diversification does not reduce portfolio risk when the returns are perfectly positively correlated, $\rho_{AB} = +1.0$. When the correlation coefficient between the rates of return from assets *A* and *B* is at its maximum value of positive unity, the linear risk-return relationship in Fig. 25-4*a* results. This straight line between assets *A* and *B* in risk-return space is derived by first setting ρ_{AB} to positive unity in Eq. (25-6*a*). Next the values of the two assets' weights are varied from zero to 1 (that is, $0.0 < x < +1.0$) inversely so that they always sum to positive unity (namely, $x_A + x_B = 1.0$). Finally, the infinite number of pairs of values for x_A and x_B values (such that $x_A + x_B = 1.0$ for $0 < x_A < +1.0$ and $0 < x_B < +1.0$) are substituted into the portfolio risk formula, Eq. (25-6*a*), and the portfolio return formula, Eq. (25-2*a*). The infinite number of risk and return statistics for the two-asset portfolio are thus derived, and they trace out the straight line in Fig. 25-4*a* when $\rho_{AB} = +1.0$.

25-3.4 uncorrelated assets, Fig. 25-4*b*

If the rates of return from Apex and Bean stocks are zero-correlated, substantial risk reduction benefits can be obtained from diversifying between the two assets. This beneficial risk reduction can be seen analytically by noting what happens to portfolio risk Eq. (25-6*a*) when ρ_{AB} equals zero. The last quantity on the right-hand side of the equation becomes zero and thus disappears when $\rho_{AB} = 0$. This reduces the portfolio's risk level below what it was when this correlation was a larger value (for example, when $\rho_{AB} = +1.0$).

The results of the uncorrelated returns are illustrated in Fig. 25-4*b*. The portfolio's expected return is unaffected by changing the correlation between assets—this is because ρ_{AB} is not a variable in the portfolio return Eq. (25-2*a*). All differences between the portfolios generated when $\rho_{AB} = +1.0$ and the portfolios generated when $\rho_{AB} = 0$ are risk differences stemming from Eq. (25-6*a*). Figure 25-4*b* shows that the portfolios with $\rho_{AB} = 0$ have less risk at every level of expected return than the same portfolios with $\rho_{AB} = +1.0$ in Fig. 25-4*a*.

The substantial risk reductions available by diversifying across uncorrelated assets are readily available to all investors. Empirical research has shown that common stock price indices, bond price indices, and commodity price indices all tend to be uncorrelated.[11] Thus, any investor who diversifies across these different market assets can expect to benefit from the diversification between uncorrelated assets as indicated in Fig. 25-4*b*.

25-3.5 perfectly negatively correlated returns, Fig. 25-4c

The lowest possible value for any correlation coefficient is negative unity. When the correlation coefficient in portfolio risk Eq. (25-6*b*) reaches negative unity, the last term on the right-hand side of the equation assumes its maximum negative value for any given pair of values for x_A and x_B. In fact, the portfolio's risk can be reduced to zero risk when $\rho_{AB} = -1.0$ for one set of portfolio weights. For example, for the portfolio made of Bean and Apex stocks, Fig. 25-4*c* shows that when $x_A = 2/3$ and $x_B = 1/3$ and $\rho_{AB} = -1.0$, the portfolio's risk vanishes to zero. For all other weights the portfolio's risk is above zero, but portfolio risk is always at its lowest possible level over all possible sets of portfolio weights when $\rho_{AB} = -1.0$.

If it seems dubious that two perfectly negatively correlated *risky assets* like Apex and Bean can be combined in just the correct proportions to form a *riskless portfolio* like the one at $x_A = 2/3$ and $x_B = 1/3$ in Fig. 25-4*c*, reconsider the example in Table 25-5.

25-3.6 analysis using Markowitz diversification

Figure 25-4*d* summarizes the three illustrated examples from Fig. 25-4*a*, 25-4*b*, and 25-4*c*. To summarize, Fig. 25-4*a* shows that at point *P*, $x_A = 2/3$ and $x_B = 1/3$ and, for a correlation of $\rho_{AB} = +1$, the portfolio's total risk is $\sigma_p = \sqrt{.07} = 26.4$ percent. Figure 25-4*b* shows that if $\rho_{AB} = 0$, then $\sigma_p = \sqrt{.035} = 18.7$ percent at point *W*. And Fig. 25-4*c* illustrates the case when $\rho_{AB} = -1$; then $\sigma_p = \sqrt{0} = 0$ at point Z. Figure 25-4*d* was constructed by plotting all the points (like *P*, *W*, and *Z*, respectively) from Fig. 25-4*a*, 25-4*b*, and 25-4*c* together in risk-return space.

Markowitz diversification can lower risk below the systematic level if the security analyst can find securities whose rates of return have low enough correlations. Unfortunately, there are only a precious few securities that have low correlations. Therefore, using Markowitz diversification requires a data bank of financial statistics for many securities, and a computer.

Applying Markowitz diversification to a collection of potential investment assets with a computer is called *Markowitz portfolio analysis*. It is a scientific way to manage a portfolio, and its results are quite interesting. Since Markowitz portfolio analysis considers both the risk and return of dozens, or hundreds, or thousands of different securities simultaneously (the number is limited only by the size of the computer and the number of securities for which one has risk and return statistics), it is a more powerful method of analyzing a portfolio than using one's head or selecting investments with a committee. A person's mind (even the mind of a genius) or an investment committee cannot simultaneously evaluate hundreds of different investment opportunities and

[11] R. G. Ibbotson and R. A. Sinquefield, *Stocks, Bonds, Bills, and Inflation: The Past (1926–1976) and the Future (1977–2000)*, Financial Analysts Research Foundation, Charlottesville, Va., 1977, exhibit 7; K. Dusak, "Future Trading and Investor Returns: An Investigation of Commodity Risk Premiums," *Journal of Political Economy*, December 1963, vol. 81, no. 6, pp. 1387–1406.

balance the risks and returns of them all with one another to find efficient portfolios that dominate all other investment opportunities. Markowitz portfolio analysis is essentially a mathematics problem requiring that many different equations be solved simultaneously. This can be done on a large scale only by using a computer program that does what is called quadratic programming. *Quadratic programming* minimizes the portfolio's risk (a quadratic equation) at each level of average return for the portfolio.[12]

The type of portfolio manager who is not sufficiently analytical to use quadratic programming is sometimes lightly referred to as a "financial interior decorator."

FINANCIAL INTERIOR DECORATING Many investment counselors are financial interior decorators, meaning that they *design* portfolios of securities to match the investors' personalities. Thus, an elderly widow completely dependent on the income from a modest fixed investment (such helpless women are referred to as "Aunt Janes" in the brokerage industry) would be advised to invest in low-risk, low-return assets like bonds and utility stocks on the assumption that they would minimize risk. The financial interior decorator would give little or no consideration to the correlation coefficients among assets. On the other hand, a young professional man or woman with a promising future would be advised to invest in high-risk, high-return securities. A financial interior decorator would make this suggestion on the oversimplified assumption that the high-risk stocks must combine to make a portfolio with the highest long-run rate of return, an assumption that is not necessarily true.

In spite of the superficial intuitive appeal of the financial interior decorating approach to portfolio management, the preceding analysis reveals its weakness. A Markowitz diversified portfolio of risky assets will earn a higher average return in the long run than a simply diversified portfolio because it will not experience the large losses that periodically hurt the long-run performance of a simply diversified portfolio. Or, on the other hand, two high-risk, high-return securities might yield the minimum risk portfolio if they are negatively correlated.

25-4 CONVEXITY OF THE EFFICIENT FRONTIER

If the risk and return of all individual assets on all security exchanges were plotted in risk-return space, they would be dominated by portfolios. Figure 25-5 represents the set of investment opportunities available in the securities

[12] Computer programs to perform portfolio analysis and other forms of investment analysis are publicly available. See William B. Riley, Jr., and Austin H. Montgomery, Jr., *Guide to Computer Assisted Investment Analysis*, McGraw-Hill, New York, 1982. Chapter 8 contains a simplified Markowitz portfolio analysis computer program that can be run on a personal computer. This and other programs can be purchased from McGraw-Hill on a floppy disk called "Investpak" for about $40. For information write to: Investpak, McGraw-Hill Book Co., 27 Floor, 1221 Avenue of the Americas, New York, NY 10020. Also see chap. 10 of *The Complete Investment Book* by Richard Bookstaber, Scott, Foresman, and Company, Glenview, Ill., 1985. The chapter lists a quadratic program written in Basic language on pp. 119–126. Dr. Bookstaber's computer programs may be purchased on floppy disks to run on personal computers for a modest fee, as explained above on page 173.

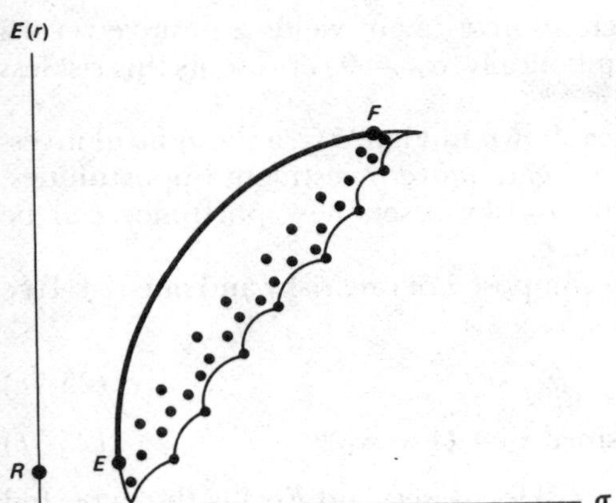

FIGURE 25-5 the set of investment opportunities.

markets. The escalloped, quarter-moon-shaped opportunity set in this figure contains individual assets (stocks and bonds) represented by dots in the lower right-hand side of the opportunity set. The efficient frontier is represented by the heavy dark curve from E to F. Only portfolios will lie along the efficient frontier. Portfolios will always dominate individual assets because of the risk-reducing benefits of diversification that portfolios enjoy. Only the highest-return portfolio F in Fig. 25-5 is likely to be a one-asset efficient portfolio.

The opportunity set is constructed of curves that are all convex toward the $E(r)$ axis. This is because all assets have correlation coefficients between positive unity and negative unity. As shown in Fig. 25-4, this fact results in a locus of portfolios that traces a curve convex to the $E(r)$ axis in $[\sigma, E(r)]$ space. Only perfectly positively correlated (that is, $\rho = +1$) assets will generate linear combinations of risk and return; under no circumstances will a portfolio possibility locus ever curve away from the $E(r)$ axis in $[\sigma, E(r)]$ space.

Not all portfolios will lie on the efficient frontier; some will dominate others. For example, Markowitz diversification will generate portfolios that are more efficient than simply diversified portfolios. If Markowitz diversification is applied to all marketable assets, the resulting portfolios are the efficient set of portfolios that forms the efficient frontier in Fig. 25-5. Appendix 25A shows how to perform the portfolio analysis required to find the efficient frontier when more than two assets are involved.

25-5 DERIVATION OF THE CAPITAL MARKET LINE

Earlier in this chapter the concept of the efficient frontier was examined. It was explained that the efficient frontier that can be constructed without borrowing or lending is rarely a straight line. Rather, it is a curve that is convex toward the $E(r)$ axis in risk-return space. However, if borrowing and lending opportunities are included in the analysis, a linear set of investment opportunities called the *capital market line* (CML) emerges.

25-5.1 one riskless asset assumed

If investors were surveying *all* investment opportunities, they would find that opportunities to borrow and lend exist. Figure 25-5 depicts a *riskless asset* at a point R on the expected-return axis. Point R might represent U.S. Treasury bonds that are held to maturity. Such an investment yields a positive return and has zero variability of return. Symbolically, $\sigma_R = 0$ represents this riskless condition.

After considering the opportunities shown in Fig. 25-5, a thoughtful investor would realize that it is possible to create more investment opportunities. By combining the riskless asset with a risky asset, new portfolios can be created that are not shown in this figure.

The expected return of a portfolio composed of one risky and one risk-free asset is shown in Eq. (25-7*a*).

$$E(r_p) = x_R R + x_i E(r_i) \qquad (25\text{-}7a)$$

$$= x_R R + (1 - x_R)E(r_i) \qquad \text{since } x_i = (1 - x_R) \qquad (25\text{-}7b)$$

R denotes the expected return of the riskless asset, and $E(r_i)$ is the expected return of some risky asset. The risk of a portfolio of R and a risky asset is shown in Eq. (25-8*a*).

$$\sigma_p = \sqrt{x_R^2\sigma_R^2 + x_i^2\sigma_i^2 + 2x_R x_i \sigma_{iR}} \qquad (25\text{-}8a)$$

$$= 0 + x_i\sigma_i + 0 \qquad \text{since } \sigma_R = \sigma_{iR} = 0 \qquad (25\text{-}8b)$$

The opportunity locus in risk-return space representing the portfolios that can be formed from a risky asset and R is a straight line since Eqs. (25-7*a*) and (25-8*b*) are both linear. Figure 25-6 shows four of the infinite number of opportunity loci representing portfolios containing R and a risky asset. These opportunity loci all start at R and pass through the opportunity set of risky assets.

In Fig. 25-6 the portfolios between R and the efficient frontier (point T, for example) represent portfolios containing both R and the risky asset m; that is, part of the portfolio is invested in the riskless asset. But those portfolios lying on the section of the opportunity loci above point m on the line $RTmAL_1$ (point

FIGURE 25-6 several portfolio possibility lines for portfolios containing risk-free asset *R*.

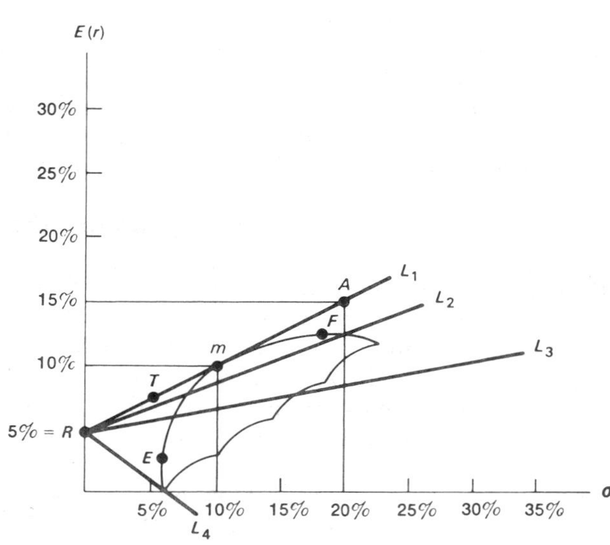

A, for example) contain negative amounts of R, $x_R < 0$. A negative amount of R may be interpreted as borrowing at interest rate R to buy more of a risky asset like m—buying on margin. Thus, an aggressive investor might create a leveraged portfolio like A in Fig. 25-6 to increase his or her expected return. Of course, financial leverage also increases the financial risk, as shown in the figure.

25-5.2 numerical example of a leveraged portfolio

Suppose one share of investment m costs \$1,000 and offers a 50-50 chance of returning either \$1,000 or \$1,200. The expected return for the holding period is 10 percent, as shown below.

$$
\begin{aligned}
E(r_m) &= \sum_{i=1}^{2} p_i r_i \\
&= .5\left(\frac{1{,}000 - 1{,}000}{1{,}000}\right) + .5\left(\frac{1{,}200 - 1{,}000}{1{,}000}\right) \\
&= .5(0) + .5(20\%) \\
&= 0 + 10\% = 10\%
\end{aligned}
$$

The standard deviation of returns is 10 percent for m (still assuming the zero and 20 percent outcomes are equally likely).

$$
\begin{aligned}
\sigma_m &= \sqrt{\Sigma p_i[r_i - E(r)]^2} \\
&= \sqrt{.5(0 - .1)^2 + .5(.2 - .1)^2} \\
&= \sqrt{.5(.01) + .5(.01)} \\
&= \sqrt{.01} \\
&= .1 = 10\%
\end{aligned}
$$

Now if an investor borrows \$1,000 at $R = 5$ percent and buys a second share of m, $x_m = 2$ and $x_R = -1$. In this case the investor has a 50-50 chance of receiving \$950 or \$1,350 on the \$1,000 of original equity, as shown below.

	TWO ALTERNATIVE OUTCOMES	
	bad	good
Original equity	\$1,000	\$1,000
Principal amount borrowed at 5%	1,000	\$1,000
Total amount invested in m	\$2,000	\$2,000
Return on two shares of m	\$2,000	\$2,400
Repayment of loan principal	(1,000)	(1,000)
Payment of interest at 5%	(50)	(50)
Net return on original equity	\$ 950	\$1,350
Probability of outcome	.5	.5

Thus, the expected return on m leveraged is 15 percent. The calculations follow.

$$
\begin{aligned}
E(r) &= \sum p_i r_i \\
&= .5\left(\frac{950 - 1{,}000}{1{,}000}\right) + .5\left(\frac{1{,}350 - 1{,}000}{1{,}000}\right) \\
&= .5(-5\%) + .5(35\%) \\
&= -2.5\% + 17.5\% \\
&= 15\%
\end{aligned}
$$

The standard deviation of returns on the leveraged portfolio is 20 percent, as follows.

$$
\begin{aligned}
\sigma &= \sqrt{\Sigma p_i[r_i - E(r_i)]^2} \\
&= \sqrt{.5(-5\% - 15\%)^2 + .5(35\% - 15\%)^2} \\
&= \sqrt{.5(-20\%)^2 + .5(20\%)^2} \\
&= \sqrt{.5(.04) + .5(.04)} \\
&= \sqrt{.02 + .02} \\
&= \sqrt{.04} \\
&= .2 = 20\%
\end{aligned}
$$

These results are shown graphically in Fig. 25-6 as portfolios m and A on line L_1. Equations (25-7*a*) and (25-8*b*) may be checked by substituting in the values from this example.

25-5.3 the CML emerges

Rational investors who use Markowitz diversification will recognize the various opportunities shown in Fig. 25-6. These investors will also recognize that the opportunity locus designated L_1 dominates *all* other opportunities. The portfolios that can be created from R and risky assets other than m (along lines L_2, L_3, and L_4, for example) and even most of the efficient set of portfolios (along curve EF) are dominated by the opportunities represented by the line L_1 in Fig. 25-6. Therefore, investors will all want the portfolio denoted m in Fig. 25-6 because this is the risky asset needed to generate the dominant opportunity locus L_1. Hereafter, L_1 will be called the capital market line (CML). The CML is a separate and distinct relation from the security market line (SML), or capital asset pricing model (CAPM), which was developed in Chap. 10. The CAPM or SML is a linear relationship between expected return and *systematic risk* for portfolios and individual assets. The CML, on the other hand, is a linear relationship between expected return and *total* risk on which *only portfolios* will lie.[13]

25-5.4 the market portfolio

Imagine a capital market, such as the ones shown in Figs. 25-6 and 25-7, that is at equilibrium. By the definition of an economic equilibrium in a market, supply and demand are equal for all goods. So every security in the market

[13] The rationale for the CML and CAPM (or SML) and the assumptions underlying them both are explained in detail in Chap. 26.

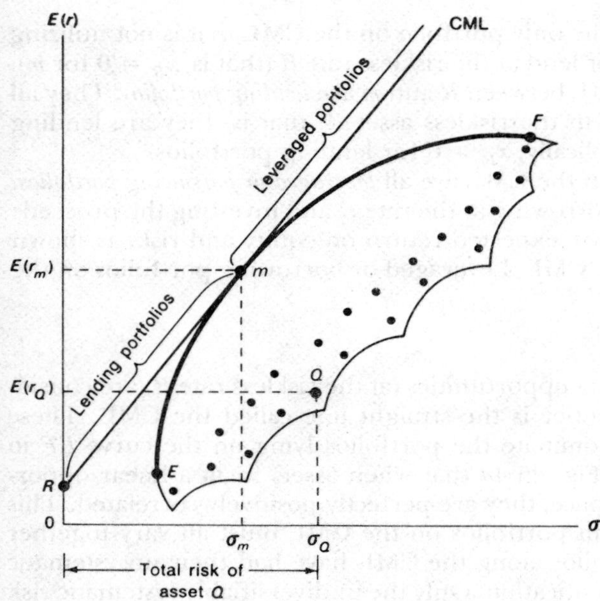

FIGURE 25-7 the capital market line (CML) tangent to the efficient frontier.

must be held by some owner. Since all investors unanimously want m, it follows that, in equilibrium, m must be a huge portfolio containing all securities in the proportions x_i^* where

$$x_i^* = \frac{\text{total value of the } i\text{th firm's securities}}{\text{total value of all securities in the market}}$$

Let m be designated as the *market portfolio*, the unanimously desirable portfolio containing all securities in exactly the proportions in which they are supplied.[14] The return on the market portfolio is the weighted average return on all securities in the market. In equilibrium R must be the interest rate that equates the supply of and demand for loanable funds.

In reality there is no market portfolio. However, it is a useful theoretical construct, since the return on m is the return the Dow Jones average, the Standard & Poor's average, the NYSE index, and others are estimating. The return on m would be the optimum market index.

[14] For the original discussion of the market portfolio see E. Fama, "Risk, Return and Equilibrium: Some Clarifying Comments," *Journal of Finance,* March 1968, pp. 32–33. For empirical estimates of the market portfolio see Roger G. Ibbotson and Carol L. Fall, "The United States Market Wealth Portfolio," *Journal of Portfolio Management,* Fall 1979. See also Roger G. Ibbotson and Lawrence B. Siegel, "The World Market Wealth Portfolio," *Journal of Portfolio Management,* Winter 1983, pp. 5–17.

The geometric shape of the opportunity set in risk-return [that is, (σ, $E(r)$)] space has been analyzed by R. C. Merton, "An Analytic Derivation of the Efficient Portfolio Frontier," *Journal of Financial and Quantitative Analysis,* September 1972, pp. 1151–1172.

25-5.5 lending and leveraged portfolios on the CML

In Fig. 25-7, portfolio m is the only portfolio on the CML that is not utilizing the opportunity to borrow or lend at the riskless rate R (that is, $x_R = 0$ for m). The portfolios along the CML between R and m are *lending portfolios*. They all have some money invested in the riskless asset R; that is, they are lending money at the rate R. Symbolically, $x_R > 0$ for lending portfolios.

The portfolios above m on the CML are all *leveraged or borrowing portfolios*. They were constructed by borrowing at the rate R and investing the proceeds in m, increasing the portfolios' expected return on equity and risk, as shown by the upper portions of the CML. Leveraged or borrowing portfolios on the CML have $x_R < 0$.

25-5.6 systematic risk

When borrowing and lending opportunities (at the riskless rate R) are considered, the true efficient frontier is the straight line called the CML. These investment opportunities dominate the portfolios lying on the curve EF in Fig. 25-7. It was shown in Fig. 25-4a that when assets form a linear opportunity locus in risk-return space, they are perfectly positively correlated. This means that the returns from portfolios on the CML must all vary together systematically. These portfolios along the CML have had their unsystematic risk reduced to zero by diversification. Only the undiversifiable systematic risk remains. Their returns are perfectly positively correlated because of systematic variability in returns.

Individual assets represented by dots like point Q in Fig. 25-7 are not efficient because their total risk includes both systematic and unsystematic risk. These individual assets have not had their total risk reduced by diversification. The total risk of asset Q is equal to the distance from 0 to σ_Q along the horizontal axis of Fig. 25-7. The total risk can be partitioned into two pieces—systematic and unsystematic risk.[15] As explained in Chap. 10, the systematic part of an asset's total risk is due to the systematic parts of market risk, purchasing power risk, interest rate risk, managerial risk, industry risk, default risk, and whatever other systematic factors may exist.[16]

25-5.7 CML is simplified but realistic

The preceding analysis is a simplified version of reality. The CML was mathematically derived from the efficient frontier by unrealistically assuming that money could be freely borrowed or lent at the risk-free rate R. Of course, private citizens cannot borrow money at the same low rate as the federal government, that is, at interest rate R. Such assumptions, however, keep the model simple and manageable. In spite of the simplifications used to derive the market model shown in Fig. 25-7, it is still realistic. Most portfolios' rates

[15] Partitioning the total risk of asset Q statistically proceeds as shown below:

$$\begin{aligned}\text{var}(r_Q) &= \text{var}(a_Q + b_Q r_m + e) \qquad \text{since } r_Q = a + b_Q r_m + e \\ &= b_Q{}^2\,\text{var}(r_m) + \text{var}(e_Q) \\ &= \text{systematic} + \text{unsystematic risk} \\ &= \text{total risk of asset } Q\end{aligned}$$

[16] B. F. King, op. cit., pp. 139–190. King partitions the risk of 316 stocks listed on the NYSE from 89 different industrial categories. Factor analysis is used. The factors that make up an asset's systematic risk are discussed further in Chap. 30, entitled "Arbitrage Pricing Theory."

of return are highly positively correlated and lie along a curve like the efficient frontier *EF* in Fig. 25-7.

Table 25-7 lists the risk and return statistics of 34 mutual funds. These portfolios' average returns were regressed on their risk. The results are shown in Fig. 25-8.

The correlation coefficient for the regression line shown in Fig. 25-8 is high and positive. The empirical data indicate that the trade-off of risk for return available in the market does resemble the theoretical CML model shown in Fig. 25-7.

TABLE 25-7 **performance of 34 mutual funds, 1954–1963**

	average annual return, %	std. dev. of annual return, %
Affiliated Fund	14.6	15.3
American Business Shares	10.0	9.2
Axe-Houghton, Fund A	10.5	13.5
Axe-Houghton, Fund B	12.0	16.3
Axe-Houghton, Stock Fund	11.9	15.6
Boston Fund	12.4	12.1
Board Street Investing	14.8	16.8
Bullock Fund	15.7	19.3
Commonwealth Investment Company	10.9	13.7
Delaware Fund	14.4	21.4
Dividend Shares	14.4	15.9
Eaton and Howard, Balanced Fund	11.0	11.9
Eaton and Howard, Stock Fund	15.2	19.2
Equity Fund	14.6	18.7
Fidelity Fund	16.4	23.5
Financial Industrial Fund	14.5	23.0
Fundamental Investors	16.0	21.7
Group Securities, Common Stock Fund	15.1	19.1
Group Securities, Fully Administered Fund	11.4	14.1
Incorporated Investors	14.0	25.5
Investment Company of America	17.4	21.8
Investors Mutual	11.3	12.5
Loomis-Sales Mutual Fund	10.0	10.4
Massachusetts Investors Trust	16.2	20.8
Massachusetts Investors—Growth Stock	18.6	22.7
National Investors Corporation	18.3	19.9
National Securities—Income Series	12.4	17.8
New England Fund	10.4	10.2
Putnam Fund of Boston	13.1	16.0
Scudder, Stevens & Clark Balanced Fund	10.7	13.3
Selected American Shares	14.4	19.4
United Funds—Income Fund	16.1	20.9
Wellington Fund	11.3	12.0
Wisconsin Fund	13.8	16.9

Source: William F. Sharpe, "Mutual Fund Performance," *Journal of Business*, January 1966 suppl., p. 125.

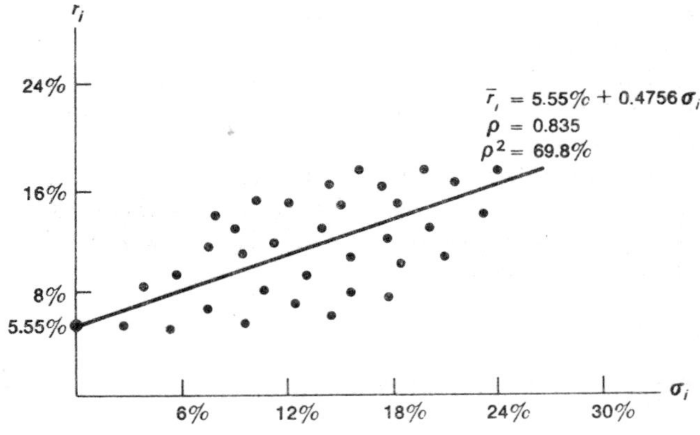

FIGURE 25-8 empirical test of the capital market line (CML). (*Source*: William F. Sharpe, "Risk Aversion in the Stock Market: Some Empirical Evidence," *Journal of Finance*, September 1965, pp. 416–422.)

25-6 CONCLUSION: RATIONAL INVESTORS DIVERSIFY

In the preceding pages of this chapter, it was shown how the dominance principle could be used to delineate desirable assets. Then various diversification practices were reviewed. It was seen that simple diversification of even the most naive variety (for example, selecting securities with a dart) was beneficial in reducing risk. Markowitz diversification was seen to be the most effective way of attaining risk reduction.

After derivation of the efficient frontier was explained in terms of Markowitz diversification, borrowing and lending opportunities were introduced. It was seen that the dominant assets were always portfolios (as opposed to individual assets) and usually involved lending or leverage. Thus, we reach the conclusion that *diversification is essential* to the investment program of a rational, risk-averse, wealth-seeking investor. Furthermore, Markowitz diversification helps the investor attain a higher level of expected utility (or happiness) than any other risk reduction technique. Thus, rational investors will be concerned with the *correlation* between assets, in addition to the assets' expected returns and standard deviations.

After investors somehow (that is, by using either simple or Markowitz diversification) delineate the most dominant investment opportunities to be found (that is, their own most efficient frontier), they still must select one in which to invest their funds. Essentially, once the efficient frontier is delineated, portfolio selection is a personal choice.

QUESTIONS

1. Write a few sentences explaining the mathematical calculations used to find the portfolio's expected return.
2. What is assumed about the weights or participation levels of the assets in a portfolio? Why?
3. Define an efficient portfolio.

4. Define simple diversification. Will simple diversification reduce total risk? Unsystematic risk? Systematic risk?
5. Define superfluous diversification. What problems frequently result from superfluous diversification?
6. Define Markowitz diversification. Draw a graph of a two-asset portfolio's risk and return possibilities and explain how Markowitz diversification can reduce risk.
7. What does it mean to say that two variables are perfectly positively correlated? Uncorrelated or independent? Inversely correlated? Graph realistic examples of each and explain. (*Hint*: Mathematical App. D may be helpful reading.)
8. Define financial interior decorating and explain the shortcoming of this popular approach to portfolio management.
9. Why are all the curves in the opportunity set drawn convex rather than concave to the expected return axis?
10. "A portfolio of many different assets from many different industries will be a well-diversified portfolio." Is this statement true, false, or uncertain? Explain.
11. "Apart from negatively correlated stocks, all the gains from diversification come from 'averaging over' the independent components of the returns and risks of individual stocks. Among positively correlated stocks, there would be no gains from diversification, if independent variations [unsystematic risk] were absent." Quotation from John Lintner, "Security Prices, Risk, and Maximal Gains from Diversification," *Journal of Finance*, December 1965, p. 589 (bracketed words added). Explain this statement.

Note: The following questions are more technical and presume a knowledge of the appendixes to this chapter.

12. What assumptions describe an investor who prefers to use Markowitz portfolio analysis?
13. What is the objective of portfolio analysis?
14. What statistical inputs are required for a portfolio analysis of four assets?
15. Expand the following formula for a portfolio's variance of returns for four assets into a form showing all four assets' variances and covariances.

$$\text{var}(r_p) = \sum_{i=1}^{n} \sum_{j=1}^{n} x_i x_j \sigma_{ij} \qquad \text{for } n = 4$$

16. Below are the possible rates of returns for two assets:

r_1, %	r_2, %	prob. (r_1 and r_2)
15	15	⅓
30	12	⅓
45	9	⅓
$E(r_1) = 30\%$	$E(r_2) = 12\%$	1.0

Assume that a security analyst has forecasted these returns, based on three different possible ratės of economic growth. Also assume that the analyst has also calculated the expected return for each asset. Calculate the two variances and $\text{cov}(r_1,r_2)$. If assets 1 and 2 are combined 50-50 into a portfolio, what is the variance of this portfolio? Show your formulas and calculations.

SELECTED REFERENCES

Gordon Alexander and J. C. Francis, *Portfolio Analysis*, 3d ed., Prentice-Hall, Englewood Cliffs, N.J., 1986. The CML and other more sophisticated models are developed. Graphical utility analysis, statistics, and advanced mathematics are used.

H. Markowitz, *Portfolio Selection*, Wiley, New York, 1959. Chapters 1 through 5 present the foundations for portfolio analysis. Chapters 7 and 8 present different techniques for performing portfolio analysis. Algebra is used.

F. Modigliani and G. A. Pogue, "An Introduction to Risk and Return: Concepts and Evidence," part 1, *Financial Analysts Journal*, March–April 1974, vol. 30, no. 2, part 2, ibid., May–June 1974. An easy-to-read tutorial article explaining Markowitz diversification and its various implications. Important research is reviewed.

APPENDIX 25A

mathematical portfolio analysis

Markowitz portfolio analysis performed graphically cannot handle more than a few securities. The graphical analysis does serve well as an introduction to portfolio analysis and may result in a better understanding of the analysis and of the solution obtained.[17] However, a more efficient solution technique for portfolio analysis which uses differential calculus and linear algebra is explained in this appendix.

APP. 25A-1 A CALCULUS RISK MINIMIZATION SOLUTION: GENERAL FORM

Calculus can be used to find the minimum risk portfolio for any given expected return E^*. Mathematically, the problem involves finding the minimum portfolio variance. That is,

$$\text{Minimize: } \text{var}(r_p) = \sum_{i=1}^{n}\sum_{j=1}^{n} x_i x_j \sigma_{ij} \qquad \text{(App. 25A-1)}$$

[17] Informative examples of Markowitz portfolio analysis performed graphically may be found in: Harry Markowitz, *Portfolio Selection*, Wiley, New York, 1959, chap. 7; J. C. Francis and S. H. Archer, *Portfolio Analysis*, 2d ed., Prentice-Hall, Englewood Cliffs, N.J., 1979, chap. 5; J. C. Francis, *Investments: Analysis and Management*, 3d ed., McGraw-Hill, New York, 1980, apps. A and B to chap. 18, and app. B contains a short Fortran computer program to plot the isovariance ellipses.

subject to two Lagrangian constraints. The first constraint requires that the desired expected return E^* be achieved. This is equivalent to requiring the following equation:

$$\sum_{i=1}^{n} x_i E(r_i) - E^* = 0 \qquad \text{(App. 25A-2)}$$

The second constraint requires that the weights sum to unity. This constraint is equivalent to requiring the following equation:

$$\sum_{i=1}^{n} x_i - 1 = 0 \qquad \text{(App. 25A-3)}$$

Combining these three quantities yields the Lagrangian objective function of the risk minimization problem with a desired return constraint:

$$z = \sum_{i=1}^{n} \sum_{j=1}^{n} x_i x_j \sigma_{ij} + \lambda_1 \left(\sum_{i=1}^{n} x_i E(r_i) - E^* \right) + \lambda_2 \left(\sum_{i=1}^{n} x_i - 1 \right) \qquad \text{(App. 25A-4)}$$

The minimum risk portfolio is found by setting $dz/dx_i = 0$ for $i = 1, \ldots n$ and $dz/d\lambda_i = 0$ for $i = 1, 2$ and then solving the system of equations for the x_i's. The number of assets analyzed, n, can be any positive integer. Martin solved this problem and has shown the relationship between the solution and the graphical critical line solution in a well-written article.[18]

25A-2 CALCULUS MINIMIZATION OF RISK: A THREE-SECURITY PORTFOLIO

For a three-security portfolio, the objective function to be minimized is shown below.

$$\begin{aligned} z = {} & x_1^2\sigma_{11} + x_2^2\sigma_{22} + x_3^2\sigma_{33} + 2x_1x_2\sigma_{12} + 2x_1x_3\sigma_{13} + 2x_2x_3\sigma_{23} \\ & + \lambda_1(x_1E_1 + x_2E_2 + x_3E_3 - E^*) + \lambda_2(x_1 + x_2 + x_3 - 1) \end{aligned} \qquad \text{(App. 25A-5)}$$

Setting the partial derivatives of z with respect to all variables equal to zero yields equation system (App. 25A-6).

$$\frac{dz}{dx_1} = 2x_1\sigma_{11} + 2x_2\sigma_{12} + 2x_3\sigma_{13} + \lambda_1E_1 + \lambda_2 = 0$$

$$\frac{dz}{dx_2} = 2x_2\sigma_{22} + 2x_1\sigma_{12} + 2x_3\sigma_{23} + \lambda_1E_2 + \lambda_2 = 0$$

$$\frac{dz}{dx_3} = 2x_3\sigma_{33} + 2x_1\sigma_{13} + 2x_2\sigma_{23} + \lambda_1E_3 + \lambda_2 = 0 \qquad \text{(App. 25A-6)}$$

[18] A. D. Martin, Jr., "Mathematical Programming of Portfolio Selections," *Management Science*, January 1955, pp. 152–166. Reprinted in E. B. Frederickson, *Frontiers of Investment Analysis*, International Textbook, Scranton, Pa., 1965, pp. 367–381.

$$\frac{dz}{d\lambda_2} = x_1 + x_2 + x_3 - 1 = 0$$

$$\frac{dz}{d\lambda_1} = x_1E_1 + x_2E_2 + x_3E_3 - E^* = 0$$

This system is linear, since the weights (x_i's) are the variables and they are all of degree one; thus the system may be solved as a system of linear equations. The matrix representation of this system of linear equations is shown below as matrix Eq. (App. 25A-7), a Jacobian matrix.

$$\underbrace{\begin{bmatrix} 2\sigma_{11} & 2\sigma_{12} & 2\sigma_{13} & E_1 & 1 \\ 2\sigma_{21} & 2\sigma_{22} & 2\sigma_{23} & E_2 & 1 \\ 2\sigma_{31} & 2\sigma_{32} & 2\sigma_{33} & E_3 & 1 \\ 1 & 1 & 1 & 0 & 0 \\ E_1 & E_2 & E_3 & 0 & 0 \end{bmatrix}}_{C} \cdot \underbrace{\begin{bmatrix} x_1 \\ x_2 \\ x_3 \\ \lambda_1 \\ \lambda_2 \end{bmatrix}}_{x} = \underbrace{\begin{bmatrix} 0 \\ 0 \\ 0 \\ 1 \\ E^* \end{bmatrix}}_{k} \qquad \text{(App. 25A-7)}$$

This system may be solved several different ways. With matrix notation, the inverse of the coefficient matrix, denoted C^{-1}, may be used to find the solution (weight) vector x as shown below. I denotes the identity matrix.

$$\begin{aligned} Cx &= k \\ C^{-1}Cx &= C^{-1}k \\ Ix &= C^{-1}k \\ x &= C^{-1}k \end{aligned} \qquad \text{(App. 25A-8)}$$

The solution will give the n ($n = 3$, in this case) weights in terms of E^*.

$$\begin{aligned} x_1 &= a_1 + d_1E^* \\ x_2 &= a_2 + d_2E^* \\ x_3 &= a_3 + d_3E^* \end{aligned} \qquad \text{(App. 25A-9)}$$

where the a_i and d_i are constants. For any desired E^* the equations give the weights of the minimum-risk portfolio. These are the weights of a portfolio in the efficient frontier. By varying E^* the weights may be generated for the entire efficient frontier. Then the risk, var(r_p), of the efficient portfolios may be calculated, and the efficient frontier may be graphed.

As a numerical example, the data from the three-security portfolio problem indicated in Table 25A-1 are solved to obtain the following coefficients matrix.

TABLE APP. 25A-1 statistical inputs for portfolio analysis of three common stocks

Asset	$E(r_i)$	$\text{var}(r_i) = \sigma_{ii}$	$\text{cov}(r_i,r_j) = \sigma_{ij}$
Homestake Mining	$E(r_1) = 5\% = .05$	$\sigma_{11} = .1$	$\sigma_{12} = -.1$
Kaiser Aluminum	$E(r_2) = 7\% = .07$	$\sigma_{22} = .4$	$\sigma_{13} = 0$
Texas Instruments	$E(r_3) = 30\% = .3$	$\sigma_{33} = .7$	$\sigma_{23} = .3$

$$\begin{bmatrix} 2\sigma_{11} & 2\sigma_{12} & 2\sigma_{13} & E_1 & 1 \\ 2\sigma_{21} & 2\sigma_{22} & 2\sigma_{23} & E_2 & 1 \\ 2\sigma_{31} & 2\sigma_{32} & 2\sigma_{33} & E_3 & 1 \\ 1 & 1 & 1 & 0 & 0 \\ E_1 & E_2 & E_3 & 0 & 0 \end{bmatrix} = \begin{bmatrix} 2(.1) & 2(-.1) & 2(0) & .05 & 1 \\ 2(-.1) & 2(.4) & 2(.3) & .07 & 1 \\ 2(0) & 2(.3) & 2(.7) & .3 & 1 \\ 1 & 1 & 1 & 0 & 0 \\ .05 & .07 & .3 & 0 & 0 \end{bmatrix} = C$$

Multiplying the inverse of this coefficients matrix by the constants vector (k) yields the weights vector ($C^{-1}k = x$) as shown below in matrix Eq. (App. 25A-10).

$$\overset{C^{-1}}{\begin{bmatrix} .677 & -.736 & .059 & .789 & -1.433 \\ -.736 & .800 & -.064 & .447 & -2.790 \\ .059 & -.064 & .005 & -.236 & 4.223 \\ -1.433 & -2.790 & 4.223 & .522 & -15.869 \\ .789 & .447 & -.236 & -.095 & .552 \end{bmatrix}} \overset{k}{\begin{bmatrix} 0 \\ 0 \\ 0 \\ 1 \\ E^* \end{bmatrix}} = \overset{x}{\begin{bmatrix} x_1 \\ x_2 \\ x_3 \\ \lambda_1 \\ \lambda_2 \end{bmatrix}} \qquad \text{(App. 25A-10)}$$

Evaluating the weights vector yields the system of Eq. (App. 25A-11), below.

$$\left.\begin{aligned} x_1 &= .789 - 1.433E^* \\ x_2 &= .447 - 2.790E^* \\ x_3 &= -.236 + 4.223E^* \end{aligned}\right\} x_1 + x_2 + x_3 = 1 \text{ for any given } E^* \qquad \text{(App. 25A-11)}$$

$$\lambda_1 = .522 - 15.869E^*$$

$$\lambda_2 = -.095 + .522E^*$$

The weights in the first three equations in (App. 25A-11) sum to unity, are a linear function of E*, and represent the weights of the three securities in the efficient portfolio at the point where $E(r_p) = E^*$. Varying E^* generates the weights of all the efficient portfolios.

APPENDIX 25B

stochastic dominance

Stochastic dominance selection rules utilize every bit of information in the probability distributions rather than simply focusing on the probability distribution's first two moments (that is, the expected return and the variance). As a result, stochastic dominance selection rules can sometimes yield portfolios that maximize expected utility, are not Markowitz efficient portfolios, and (sometimes) dominate Markowitz efficient portfolios.

Figure App. 25B-1 shows the locations of three assets, denoted A, B, and C, in relation to the efficient frontier. Figure App. 25B-2 shows three uniform probability distributions of returns for these three assets. Figure App. 25B-3 shows cumulative probability distributions for the three assets. In terms of the logic of stochastic dominance, inefficient portfolio A is more desirable than

FIGURE APP. 25B-1 points in risk-return space.

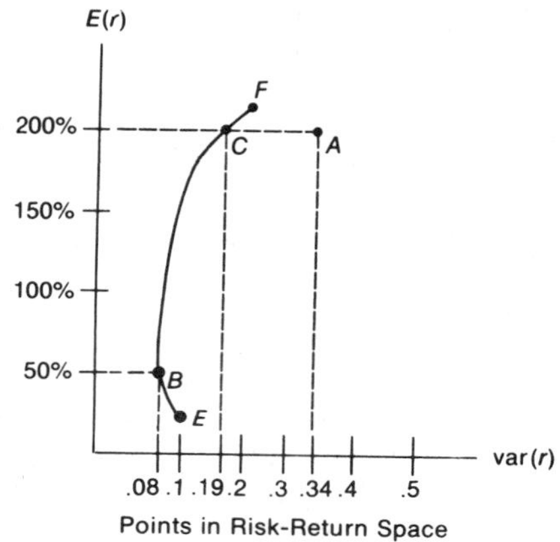

efficient portfolio B, for example. This example demonstrates that portfolio analysis methods that consider only the first two moments may waste some information that could be used to maximize investors' expected utility.

Probability distribution A is said to stochastically dominate probability distribution B if the cumulative probability of achieving any rate of return up to some specified level for distribution A is less than, or equal to, that same cumulative probability for asset B and, at least at one point, the less than inequality holds. This means that the chances of earning a low rate of return from asset A are lower than the chances of earning a low return from asset B.

Figure App. 25B-3 graphically depicts how portfolio A stochastically dominates portfolio B even though A is an inefficient portfolio. For any given rate of return, the cumulative probability that asset B earns up to that return is larger than the cumulative probability that A earns up to that same return. This is obvious since portfolio A's lowest return (of 100 percent) equals portfolio B's highest possible return.[19]

[19] More rigorous mathematical statements are usually used to define stochastic dominance. Some writers distinguish between first-degree, second-degree, and third-degree stochastic dominance. In the interest of brevity these distinctions are not developed here. For a more detailed discussion, see J. P. Quirk and R. Saposnik, "Admissibility and Measurable Utility Functions," *Review of Economic Studies*, 1962, vol. 29, pp. 140–146.

FIGURE APP. 25B-2 uniform probability distribution for three assets.

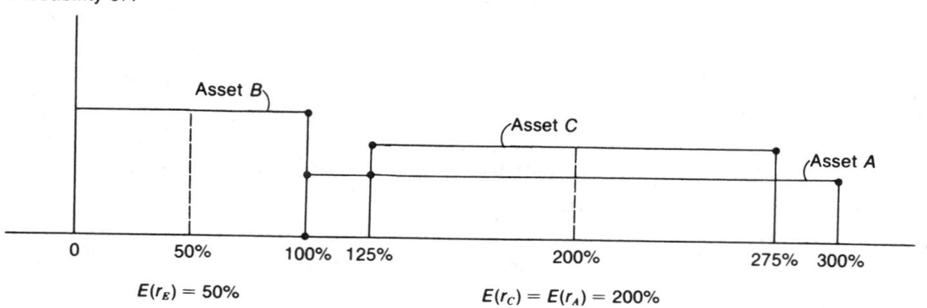

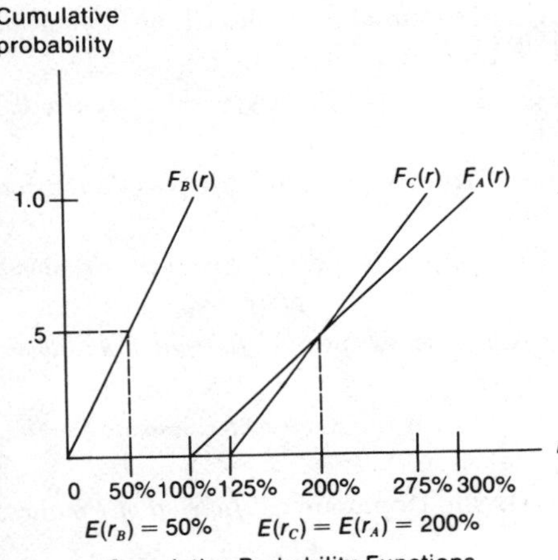

FIGURE APP. 25B-3 cumulative probability function: for the three risky assets the graphs are uniform probability distributions from b to c. It is well known that the expected value of such distribution is $E(r) = (b + c)/2$; the variance is $\sigma^2 = (c-b)^2/12$; and the cumulative probability of a return less than or equal to r_c is $F(r_0) = (r_0 - b)/c - b)$.

The advantages of selecting investments with the stochastic dominance criteria instead of risk-return criteria are:

1. Stochastic dominance orderings do not presume a certain form of probability distribution.
2. Fewer restrictions on the investor's utility function are implied by use of the stochastic dominance criteria.
3. Undesirable portfolios, such as those on the lower section of the efficient frontier, can be eliminated from further consideration.[20]
4. The stochastic dominance selection criteria do not waste information about the probability distribution; every point is considered.

Although stochastic dominance selection rules are logically superior to simpler selection criteria, their practical value is dubious, since they require knowledge of *every point* on the probability distribution rather than, for example, merely the first two moments. It requires rather heroic confidence to try to estimate every point on a probability distribution in this world of uncertainty and changing expectations. The cost of estimating the entire probability distribution not only exceeds the cost of estimating the first two moments, but this cost probably is not justified in terms of the additional benefits it could realistically be expected to yield. This is an empirical question that has not yet been resolved.

APP. 25B-1 SELECTED REFERENCES

M. M. Ali, "Stochastic Dominance and Portfolio Analysis," *Journal of Financial Economics*, 1975, vol. 2, pp. 205–229.

V. S. Bawa, "Optimal Rules for Ordering Uncertain Prospects," *Journal of Financial Economics*, 1975, vol. 2, pp. 95–121.

[20] W. J. Baumol, "An Expected Gain-Confidence Limit Criterion for Portfolio Section," *Management Science*, October 1963, pp. 171–182.

———, "Safety-First, Stochastic Dominance and Optimal Portfolio Choice," *Journal of Financial and Quantitative Analysis*, 1978, vol. 13, pp. 255–271.

P. A. Diamond and J. E. Stiglitz, "Increases in Risk and in Risk Aversion," *Journal of Economic Theory*, 1974, vol. 8, pp. 337–360.

J. Hadar and W. R. Russell, "Diversification of Interdependent Prospects," *Journal of Economic Theory*, 1974, vol. 7, pp. 231–240.

——— and ———, "Rules for Ordering Uncertain Prospects," *American Economic Review*, 1969, vol. 59, pp. 25–34.

——— and ———, "Stochastic Dominance and Diversification," *Journal of Economic Theory*, 1971, vol. 3, pp. 288–305.

———, ———, and K. Seo, "Gain from Diversification," *Review of Economic Studies*, 1977, vol. 44, pp. 363–368.

W. H. Jean, "The Geometric Mean and Stochastic Dominance," *Journal of Finance*, March 1980.

O. M. Joy and R. B. Porter, "Stochastic Dominance and Mutual Fund Performance," *Journal of Financial and Quantitative Analysis*, 1974, vol. 9, pp. 25–31.

R. C. Kearns and R. C. Burgess, "An Effective Algorithm for Estimating Stochastic Dominance Efficient Sets," *Journal of Financial and Quantitative Analysis*, September 1979.

H. Levy and G. Hanoch, "Relative Effectiveness of Efficiency Criteria for Portfolio Selection," *Journal of Financial and Quantitative Analysis*, 1970, vol. 5, pp. 63–76.

———, and Y. Kroll, "Efficiency Analysis with Borrowing and Lending: Criteria and Their Effectiveness," *Review of Economics and Statistics*, February 1979.

H. M. Markowitz, "An Algorithm for Finding Undominated Portfolios," in H. Levy and M. Sarnat (eds.), *Financial Decision Making Under Uncertainty*, Academic Press, New York, 1977, pp. 3–10.

R. B. Porter, "An Empirical Comparison of Stochastic Dominance and Mean-Variance Choice Criteria," *Journal of Financial and Quantitative Analysis*, 1973, vol. 8, pp. 587–608.

———, "Semi-Variance and Stochastic Dominance: A Comparison," *American Economic Review*, 1974, vol. 64, pp. 200–204.

——— and R. P. Bey, "An Evaluation of the Empirical Significance of Optimal Seeking Algorithms in Portfolio Selection," *Journal of Finance*, December 1974.

——— and R. C. Pfaffenberger, "Efficient Algorithms for Conducting Stochastic Dominance Tests on Large Numbers of Portfolios: Reply," *Journal of Financial and Quantitative Analysis*, 1975, vol. 10, pp. 181–185.

R. C. Scott and P. A. Horvath, "On the Direction of Preference for Moments of Higher Order than the Variance," *Journal of Finance*, September 1980.

G. A. Whitmore, "Third Degree Stochastic Dominance," *American Economic Review*, 1970, vol. 60, pp. 457–459.

capital market theory

This chapter discusses five aspects of the capital market theory, some of which have been touched on previously.

1. The assumptions which underlie the theory
2. The definition of the market portfolio
3. The capital market line (CML)
4. The capital asset pricing model (CAPM)—or the security market line (SML), as it is also called
5. What happens to the theory when the underlying assumptions used to simplify the theory are dropped

Capital market theory is an economic equilibrium theory about asset valuation. The theory considers all marketable investments—that is, thousands of stocks, bonds, options, commodities, warrants, and other things—simultaneously and explains how their prices should behave. Parts of this theory have already been introduced in this book. The notions of a security's total risk, systematic risk, and unsystematic risk were explained and the concept of the CAPM, or SML, was presented in Chap. 10. Then in Chap. 25, when the discussion turned to portfolios instead of individual assets, the CML emerged as a portfolio pricing model. The present chapter pulls all these ideas together and shows how they interact to form one unified economic theory.

26-1 INVESTMENT OPPORTUNITIES IN RISK-RETURN SPACE

Chapter 25 explained how to determine the efficient frontier for a group of assets. Suppose that all investment assets in the world were analyzed—stocks, bonds, paintings, entrepreneurships, foreign exchange, commodities, and many other marketable assets would be considered. By use of a large computer and advanced mathematics, it is possible to perform portfolio analysis

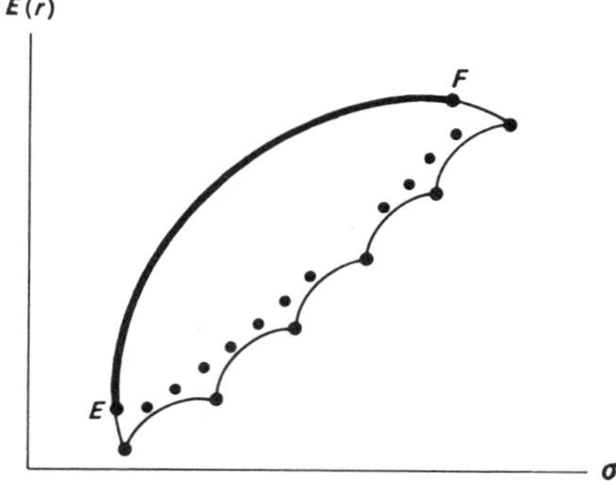

FIGURE 26-1 the opportunity set without borrowing and lending opportunities.

upon these thousands of assets and thus to determine the efficient frontier. Figure 26-1 shows the investment opportunities that might be shown to exist by undertaking such a massive analysis.

26-1.1 the efficient frontier

All the thousands of investment opportunities in the world are assumed to be represented by the escalloped quarter-moon-shaped design in Fig. 26-1. The individual assets lie along the *bottom* of this set of investment opportunities and are represented by the dots.

Individual assets (like stocks, bonds, and other securities) contain both systematic risk and unsystematic risk and are not efficient. Only *portfolios* using Markowitz diversification have had the unsystematic risk reduced to zero and can attain the curved efficient frontier. The efficient frontier is represented by the heavy dark curve from E to F in Fig. 26-1. The portfolios lying on the efficient frontier contain only systematic risk caused by variations in the economic, political, and sociological environment, which simultaneously affects nearly every asset in some way. As a result, the efficient assets along the curve EF in Fig. 26-1 are highly positively (but not perfectly) correlated.

26-1.2 borrowing and lending at a riskless rate

The investment opportunities shown in Fig. 26-1 may be extended by considering the possibilities of borrowing and lending. To keep the model simple and easy to conceptualize, suppose that all investors can borrow or lend at one riskless rate of return, denoted R. By definition, the riskless asset has no variability of return, $\text{var}(R) = 0$.

Figure 26-2 represents the investment, borrowing, and lending opportunities which would exist in equilibrium if all investors were Markowitz portfolio analysts, could borrow or lend at rate R, and had homogeneous expectations. The term *homogeneous expectations* means that all investors visualize the same expected return, risk, and correlation statistics for any specific asset in the world. Different assets can and will be perceived differently. But, any particular asset will be perceived homogeneously. Assuming homogeneous expectations allows us to represent the investment opportunities visualized by every investor with just one graph; we are spared the work of drawing separate graphs to represent differences of opinion over the risk and return statistics of specific assets. The capital market line shown in Fig. 26-2 is specified mathematically in Eq. (26-1).

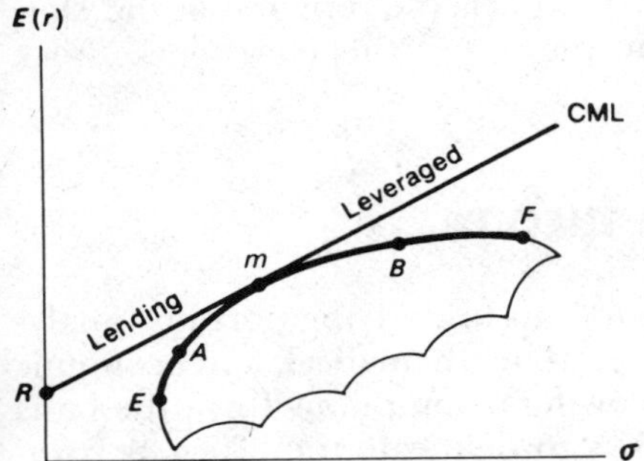

FIGURE 26-2 borrowing, lending, and investment opportunities in a market of Markowitz diversifiers.

$$E(r_i) = R + \left[\frac{\{E(r_m) - R\}}{\sigma_m}\right]\sigma_i \tag{26-1}$$

where

$E(r_i)$ = expected rate of return from the ith portfolio (and its total risk is measured by the standard deviation σ_i)

R = riskless rate of interest

$E(r_m)$ = expected rate of return from the market portfolio, denoted M

σ_m = market portfolio's standard deviation of returns

The market portfolio is defined in more detail in the following paragraph.

26-1.3 the market portfolio

Portfolio m in Fig. 26-2 is a huge portfolio containing all assets in the world in the proportions $x_i{}^*$ where

$$x_i{}^* = \frac{\text{total value of the } i\text{th security}}{\text{total value of all securities in the market}}$$

Let m be designated as a *market portfolio.* It contains all securities in exactly the proportions they are supplied in equilibrium because it is the one unique portfolio that all investors would buy. The return on the market portfolio is the weighted average return on all securities in the market.[1]

Of course, there is no real-life analog to the market portfolio, but it is a

[1] The market portfolio was originally Eugene Fama's concept. See E. Fama, "Risk, Return and Equilibrium: Some Clarifying Comments," *Journal of Finance,* March 1968, pp. 32–33. However, William Sharpe had previously published the conclusions discussed in this chapter before anyone else, without the market portfolio notion. See W. Sharpe, "Capital Asset Prices: A Theory of Market Equilibrium under Conditions of Risk," *Journal of Finance,* September 1964, pp. 425–552. For empirical estimates of the market portfolio see R. G. Ibbotson and Lawrence B. Siegel, "The World Market Wealth Portfolio," *Journal of Portfolio Management,* Winter 1983, pp. 5–17. For an explanation of the critical role of the market portfolio in empirical tests of the capital market theory see Richard Roll, "A Critique of the Asset Pricing Theory's Tests," *Journal of Financial Economics,* March 1977, pp. 129–176. Roll's critique is made in a general-equilibrium context. Thus, Roll's critique does not obviate the usefulness of empirical characteristic line statistics based on some narrowly defined market index—this is partial-equilibrium analysis rather than general-equilibrium analysis.

useful theoretical construct, since the return on m is the return that the Dow Jones average, the Standard & Poor's average, and the New York Stock Exchange index are estimating.

26-2 ASSUMPTIONS UNDERLYING CAPITAL MARKET THEORY

Capital market theory is based on the assumptions underlying portfolio analysis. The theory consists essentially of the logical, mathematical, and economic implications of portfolio analysis. The following assumptions form the basis for performing Markowitz portfolio analysis to delineate the efficient frontier:

1. The rate of return from an investment adequately summarizes the outcome from the investment, and investors see the various possible rates of return in a probabilistic fashion (that is, they visualize a probability distribution of rates of return, either consciously or subconsciously).
2. Investors' risk estimates are proportional to the variability of return (namely, the standard deviation or variance) they perceive for a security or portfolio.
3. Investors are willing to base their decisions on only two parameters of the probability distribution of returns: the expected return, and the variance (or its square root, the standard deviation) of returns. Symbolically, $U = f\{E(r), \sigma\}$ where U denotes the investors' utility.
4. For any risk-class, investors prefer a higher rate of return to a lower one. Symbolically, $\delta U/\delta E(r) > 0$. Conversely, among all securities with the same rate of return, investors prefer less rather than more risk. Symbolically, $\delta U/\delta\sigma < 0$.

Investors who conform to the preceding assumptions will prefer efficient portfolios. Such investors will be referred to as *Markowitz diversifiers.* With this background information, it is possible to begin to discuss capital market theory. The assumptions necessary to generate the capital market theory are listed below.

1. All investors are Markowitz efficient diversifiers who delineate and seek to attain the efficient frontier. Thus, the four assumptions in the preceding list are also part of the assumptions on which the capital market theory is constructed.
2. Any amount of money can be borrowed or lent at the risk-free rate of interest R. The return on short-term U.S. Treasury bills may be used as a proxy for R. Essentially, this assumption allows investors to have idealized margin accounts. No other borrowing is permitted.
3. *Idealized uncertainty* prevails; that is, all investors visualize identical probability distributions for the future rates of return on any specific asset. They have *homogeneous expectations.* This assumption does not imply that different assets are not perceived to have different risk and/or rate-of-return statistics, however.
4. All investors have the same "one-period" time horizon.
5. All investments are infinitely divisible; fractional shares may be purchased in any portfolio or any individual asset.
6. No taxes and no transaction costs for buying and selling securities exist. Thus, trading is "frictionless."

7. No inflation and no change in the level of interest rates exist (or all changes are fully anticipated).
8. The capital markets are in equilibrium.

Readers unaccustomed to economic analysis are probably confused and discouraged by a theory based upon a list of unrealistic assumptions, but they should not be. The assumptions provide a concrete foundation upon which a theory can be derived by applying the forces of logic, intuition, and mathematics. Without these assumptions, the analysis would degenerate into a polemical discussion of which historical facts, folklore, and institutions are significant, which are insignificant, what their relationships are, and what conclusions might be reached by a "reasonable person." Such discussions are usually not productive.

Traditionally, economists have based their analyses on as few and as simple assumptions as possible. Then a theory is derived with conclusions and implications that are incontestable, given the assumptions. Later, the assumptions are relaxed to determine what can be expected in more realistic circumstances. In the final analysis, the test of a theory is not how realistic its assumptions are; rather, it is the predictive power of a model that should be judged. Later in this chapter, the assumptions underlying the capital market theory are aligned with reality in order to see whether the implications of the model are changed. Before this alignment is made, however, the parts of the capital market theory will be examined in a unified presentation.

26-3 THE CAPITAL ASSET PRICING MODEL (CAPM)

Thus far in this chapter, the analysis has determined that in an equilibrium situation characterized by the given assumptions, the expected return of a *portfolio* is a linear function of the portfolio's standard deviation of returns. This linear relation has been called the CML. Thus far, however, the discussion has ignored the determination of the equilibrium rate of return on *individual assets* (such as individual stocks and bonds). Reconsider the rationale lying behind the CAPM, or SML, to understand how the prices of the individual assets are determined.

26-3.1 covariance with the market

The variance of a two-security portfolio is given in Eq. (26-2*a*).

$$\text{var}(r_p) = x_1^2\text{var}(r_1) + x_2^2\text{var}(r_2) + 2x_1x_2\text{cov}(r_1, r_2) \qquad (26\text{-}2a)$$

For an n-security portfolio, the variance is given by Eq. (26-2*b*).

$$\text{var}(r_p) = \sum_{i=1}^{n} x_i^2\text{var}(r_i) + \sum_{i=1}^{n}\sum_{j=1}^{n} x_i x_j \sigma_{ij} \qquad \text{for } i \neq j \qquad (26\text{-}2b)$$

Note that within the expression for the risk of a portfolio of any size are covariance terms between all possible pairs of securities in the portfolio. The essence of Markowitz diversification is to find securities with low positive covariances or negative covariances. As a result, demand will be high for individual securities or portfolios that have low positive covariance or negative covariance of returns with the market portfolio. Securities that have high covariance with the market portfolio, that is, high systematic risk, will experience low demand. As a result, the prices of securities with high systematic risk will fall, and prices of securities with low systematic risk will be bid up. Since equilibrium rates of return move inversely with the price of the security, securities having a high covariance with the market will have *relatively* low prices (that is, low relative to their income but not necessarily low in absolute dollars) and high expected returns. Conversely, securities with low or negative covariances will have relatively high prices and therefore experience low expected rates of return in equilibrium. This relationship is depicted in Fig. 26-3. Equation (26-3*a*) is a mathematical statement of the CAPM, or SML, in terms of the covariance.[2]

$$E(r_i) = R + \left[\frac{E(r_m) - R}{\sigma_m^2}\right] \operatorname{cov}(r_i, r_m) \tag{26-3a}$$

where

$[E(r_m) - R]/\sigma_m^2$ = slope of CAPM = the market price of systematic risk

R = riskless rate of return

$\operatorname{cov}(r_i, r_m)$ = ith asset's covariance of returns with market

$E(r_i)$ = equilibrium expected return for ith asset

[2] For the first rigorous mathematical derivation of the CAPM, or SML, see W. F. Sharpe, "Capital Asset Prices: A Theory of Market Equilibrium under Conditions of Risk," *Journal of Finance*, September 1964, vol. XIX, no. 3, footnote 22. For a review of several different mathematical derivations of the CAPM, or SML, as it is also called, see J. C. Francis and S. H. Archer, *Portfolio Analysis*, 2d ed., Prentice-Hall, Englewood Cliffs, N.J., 1979, appendix to chap. 8. Jack L. Treynor also developed the CAPM, or SML, model in an unpublished paper he prepared at about the same time that W. F. Sharpe prepared his "Capital Asset Prices . . ." paper. Treynor was working alone and mailed copies of his paper to various interested people; for example, W. F. Sharpe acknowledges Treynor's paper in the sixth footnote of "Capital Asset Prices . . ." Unfortunately, Treynor never did publish his paper. Later developments of the CAPM can be found in John Lintner, "The Valuation of Risk Assets and the Selection of Risky Investments in Stock Portfolios and Capital Budgets," *The Review of Economics and Statistics*, February 1965, pp. 13–27. For a different formulation of the same model see Jan Mossin, "Equilibrium in a Capital Asset Market," *Econometrica*, October 1966, pp. 768–783.

FIGURE 26-3 the CAPM in terms of the covariance.

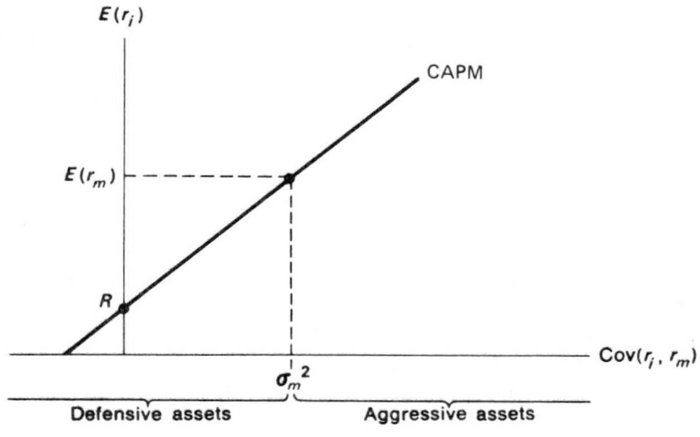

The expected return $E(r_i)$ is the appropriate discount rate to use in valuing the *i*th security's income; it is the cost of capital for that security's amount of systematic risk.

Expressed in words, Fig. 26-3 and Eq. (26-3*a*) say that in equilibrium an individual security's or a portfolio's expected return is a linear function of its covariance of return with the market. That is, the expected return from any market asset is an increasing function of its systematic risk. Since systematic risk is the portion of a security's total risk that hinders rather than helps diversification, the relationship is intuitively appealing. The more risk a security has that cannot be eliminated by diversification, the more return investors will require to induce them to hold that risky security in their portfolios.

26-3.2 components of expected return

The expected rate of return, which the CAPM suggests is appropriate for any asset, is made up of two separate components:

1. The CAPM's intercept R represents the *price of time*. This component of the *i*th asset's expected rate of return compensates the investor for delaying consumption in order to invest.
2. The CAPM's *market price of risk*. This component is measured by the slope of the CAPM, $[E(r_m) - R]/\sigma^2_{im}$.

The market price of risk is multiplied by the *i*th asset's systematic covariance risk, as shown in Eq. (26-3*a*). The product of this multiplication determines the appropriate *risk-premium* that should be added to the riskless rate to find the appropriate expected rate of return for the *i*th asset. This risk-premium is what induces investors to invest in risky instead of riskless assets.

The locus of equilibrium expected returns shown in Fig. 26-3 is the CAPM, or SML; it is a separate and distinct relation from the CML shown in Fig. 26-2.

In equilibrium, an *individual* security's expected return and risk statistics will lie on the CAPM, or SML, and *off* the CML. Likewise, in equilibrium, efficient *portfolios* $[E(r), \sigma]$ pairs will lie *on* the CML, and portfolio $[E(r), \text{cov}(r_i, r_m)]$ pairs will lie on the CAPM. Thus, even under idealistic assumptions and at static equilibrium, the CML will not include all points if portfolios and individual securities are plotted together on one graph. Individual securities and inefficient portfolios will not lie on the CML.

The returns of individual securities and portfolios are not determined by *total* risk. The unsystematic risk of a security is not particularly undesirable since it washes out to zero in a portfolio. Unsystematic risk is the stuff that makes simple diversification useful.

26-3.3 defensive and aggressive securities

In Fig. 26-3, the portion of the horizontal axis representing low or negative covariances is marked as including *defensive securities*. These securities are defensive in the sense that they offer the opportunity to reduce portfolio risks by including them in a portfolio that is correlated with m (as nearly all portfolios will be). Defensive assets have less than average covariance with the market. Symbolically, $\text{cov}(r_i, r_m) < \text{cov}(r_m, r_m) = \sigma_m{}^2$ for defensive assets.

The *aggressive securities* are those that offer opportunities for speculation; their dividend and price reactions to changes in market conditions are more dramatic and volatile than the reactions of defensive securities. Aggressive assets have more than average covariances with the market; that is, $\text{cov}(r_i, r_m) > \text{cov}(r_m, r_m) = \sigma_m^2$ for aggressive assets.

26-3.4 the CAPM restated

In the discussion of systematic risk in Chap. 10 the regression coefficient b_i from Eqs. (10-1) and (10-10) was suggested as an *index* of systematic risk. The covariance of returns with m was suggested as a *measure* of systematic risk earlier in this chapter. Two methods of defining the CAPM are possible. In Fig. 26-4*a*, the CAPM, or SML, is defined in terms of the beta regression coefficient b_i. In terms of b_i, defensive and aggressive securities can be delineated more simply. It is intuitively appealing to think of securities with $b_i < 1$ as being defensive and aggressive securities as having $b_i > 1$.

The CAPM in terms of the $\text{cov}(r_i, r_m)$ is shown in Fig. 26-4*b*. The two presentations of the CAPM in Fig. 26-4 are equivalent. The only difference between the two graphs of the CAPM is that the horizontal scale of the CAPM in terms of the beta coefficient is $1/\sigma_m^2$ times the length of the horizontal scale of the other graph. This is due to the definition of the slope coefficient shown in Eq. (26-4).

$$b_{(i|m)} = \frac{\text{cov}(r_i, r_m)}{\sigma_m^2} \tag{26-4}$$

$$= \text{cov}(r_i, r_m)\left(\frac{1}{\sigma_m^2}\right)$$

where $1/\sigma_m^2$ is constant for all assets. Equation (26-3*a*) may be equivalently restated in terms of the beta coefficient as shown in Eq. (26-5).

$$E(r_i) = R + \left[\frac{E(r_m) - R}{\sigma_m^2}\right]\text{cov}(r_i, r_m) \tag{26-3a}$$

$$= R + [E(R_m) - R]\left[\frac{\text{cov}(r_i, r_m)}{\sigma_m^2}\right]$$

$$= R + [E(r_m) - R]b_i \tag{26-5}$$

FIGURE 26-4 the CAPM restated in terms of (*a*) the beta coefficient; (*b*) the covariance.

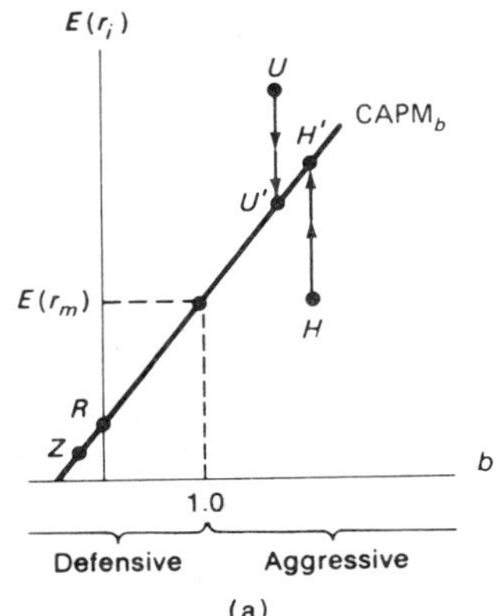

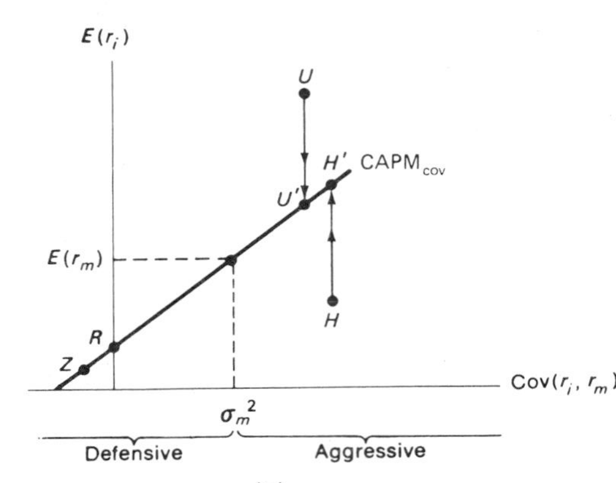

Equation (26-5) is the CAPM graphed as in Fig. 26-4*a*. But, Fig. 24-4*a* is equivalent to the graph in Fig. 26-4*b*, which represents Eq. (26-3*a*). Note that when $b_{(i|m)} = 1$, then $\text{cov}(r_i, r_m) = \sigma_m{}^2$. This relation reveals why the divisions between defensive and aggressive securities in the two graphs in Fig. 26-4 are comparable.

26-3.5 overpriced and underpriced indications

The CAPM, or SML, has asset pricing implications for both portfolios and individual securities. Points between the CAPM, or SML, and the $E(r)$ axis like point U in Fig. 26-4 represent securities whose prices are lower than they would be in equilibrium. Since points like U represent securities with unusually high returns for the amount of systematic risk they bear, these securities enjoy strong demand that will bid their prices up until their equilibrium rate of return is driven back onto the CAPM or SML at point U'.

Likewise, assets lying between the CAPM, or SML, and the systematic risk axis represent securities whose prices are too high. The asset at point H in Fig. 26-4 does not offer sufficient return to induce rational investors to accept the amount of systematic risk it bears. As a result, the asset's price will fall owing to lack of demand. The prices of such assets will continue to fall until the denominator of the rate-of-return formula is low enough to allow the expected return to reach the CAPM at a point like H'.

$$E(r) = \frac{E(\text{capital gains or losses + dividends})}{\text{purchase price}} \tag{26-6a}$$

$$= \frac{[E(p_t) - p_{t-1}] + E(d_t)}{p_{t-1}} \tag{26-6b}$$

Then the capital loss will cease, and an equilibrium purchase price will emerge until a change in the firm's systematic risk, a change in R, or some other change causes another disequilibrium. These asset pricing implications of the *security market line* model are why it is often called the *capital asset pricing model.*

26-3.6 negative correlation with portfolio *m*

Consider point Z in Fig. 26-4; it represents a defensive security with an equilibrium rate of return *below* the return on riskless asset R. Upon observing rates of return that were consistently below R, the traditional financial analyst would typically attribute the low return to a high price for the security, which was bid up in expectation of growth. But capital market theory provides a second rationalization of points like Z: Their price is maintained at high levels by the Markowitz diversification benefits they offer (an example is Homestake Mining stock, which is listed on the NYSE). Asset Z is negatively correlated with the market portfolio.

26-3.7 ex ante theory and ex post data

This analysis implies that equilibrium *expected* returns are determined by *expected* risk—this is called the *ex ante theory*. Historical, or *ex post,* returns are not used by investors as a basis for their decisions about the future, although their expectations can be affected by ex post behavior. Their investment plans for the future are based on their expectations about the future. Thus it should be noted that a "jump" is made in going from the capital market theory, which is stated in terms of expectations, to actual historical data. If the probability distribution of historical returns has remained fairly stable over time, then historical average returns and variances can be used to estimate expected returns and expected variances. However, historical data play *no role* in the theory itself.

To test capital market theory, expectations must be observed—an impossible task if conducted on a meaningful scale. Of course, expectations may be formed from historical observations, but unless investors' past expectations were always correct, historical data will not be satisfactory to validate or deny the theory.

26-4 RELAXING THE ASSUMPTIONS

The assumptions underlying capital market theory will now be aligned more closely with conditions existing in the "real world." First, assumption 2 on page 778, that one riskless interest rate exists at which everyone may borrow or lend, will be relaxed.

26-4.1 multiple interest rates

In a more realistic model, the borrowing rate B is higher than the lending rate L. In Fig. 26-5, this is represented by two unchanging rates (that is, $\sigma_L = \sigma_B = 0$) at points L and B. The lines emerging from points L and B represent the dominant lending and borrowing opportunities, respectively. The dashed portions of these two lines do not represent actual opportunities and are included merely to indicate the construction of the figure. Two tangency portfolios, denoted m_L and m_B, are shown for lenders and borrowers, respectively. They replace the market portfolio. The kinked line formed by the solid sections of the two lines and a section of the opportunity locus is the relevant efficient frontier when the borrowing and lending rates differ. As a result, the CML has a curved section between m_L and m_B in Fig. 26-5. The curved section is part of the efficient frontier.[3]

[3] K. L. Hastie, "The Determination of Optimal Investment Policy," *Management Science*, August 1967, pp. B757–B774. Hastie was the first analyst to study relaxing the assumptions. See also M. J. Brennan, "Capital Market Equilibrium and Divergent Borrowing and Lending Rates," *Journal of Financial and Quantitative Analysis*, December 1971, vol. 6, no. 5, pp. 1197–1206. Brennan shows that, under certain assumptions, a weighted average of the borrowing and lending rates would emerge as a single rate.

FIGURE 26-5 the capital market line (CML) when borrowing and lending rates differ.

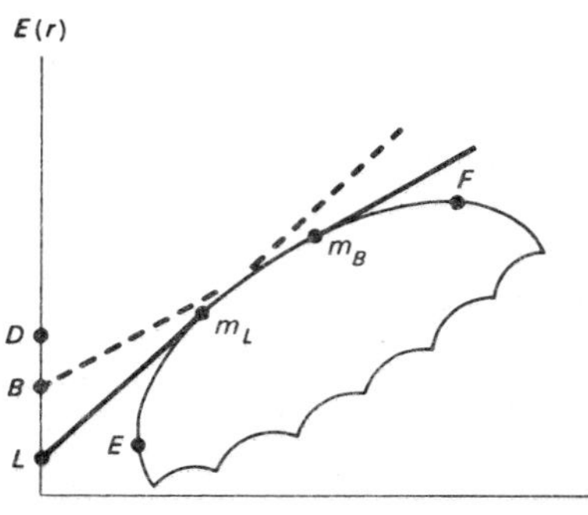

Of course, not all investors can borrow at rate B; those with poor credit ratings must pay a higher borrowing rate than those with good credit ratings. The proverbial *deadbeat* might be able to borrow money only by paying rate D in Fig. 26-5. Obviously, the greater the difference between the lending and the various borrowing rates, the greater the curve of the CML. Furthermore, the CML will change for each individual as that person's credit rating changes, and the CML for the market in general will change with credit conditions, that is, as the borrowing and lending rates change. The reader may graph these complications as an exercise.

In Fig. 26-5 points m_L and m_B are two separate tangency portfolios for lending and borrowing, respectively, if one lending rate and one borrowing rate are recognized. The existence of two tangency portfolios creates problems. Equation (26-3) is a mathematical representation of the CAPM in terms of the covariance.

$$E(r_i) = R + \left[\frac{E(r_m) - R}{\sigma_m^2}\right]\text{cov}(r_i, r_m) \qquad (26\text{-}3a)$$

where $[E(r_m) - R]/\sigma_{im}^2$ is the slope that measures the market price of risk.

If separate borrowing B and lending L rates are assumed to exist, two CAPM's emerge:

$$E(r_i) = B + \left[\frac{E(r_{mB}) - B}{\sigma_{mB}}\right]\text{cov}(r_i, r_{mB}) \quad \text{for } E(r_i) > E(r_{mB}) \qquad (26\text{-}3b)$$

$$E(r_i) = L + \left[\frac{E(r_{mL}) - L}{\sigma_{mL}^{\ 2}}\right]\text{cov}(r_i, r_{mL}) \quad \text{for } E(r_i) < E(r_{mL}) \qquad (26\text{-}3c)$$

These two CAPMs will have not only different vertical axis intercepts, but also different slopes, since $[E(r_m) - R]/\sigma_m^{\ 2}$ will be different. Also, since their covariances are measured with respect to two different tangency portfolios (namely, m_L and m_B), even their covariances differ. As a result, two CAPMs emerge. Figure 26-6 shows the relationship between CAPM_L and CAPM_B. Since further relaxation of assumption 2 would clutter Figs. 26-5 and 26-6 without yielding any additional insights, this task is left to the reader.

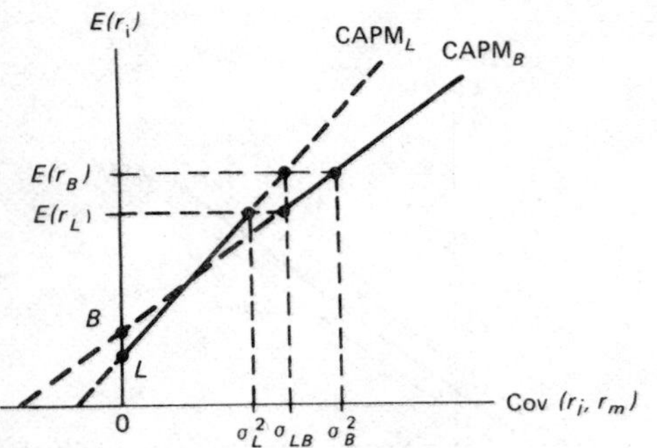

FIGURE 26-6 two CAPM's when borrowing and lending rates differ.

FIGURE 26-7 transaction costs obscure the capital market line (CML).

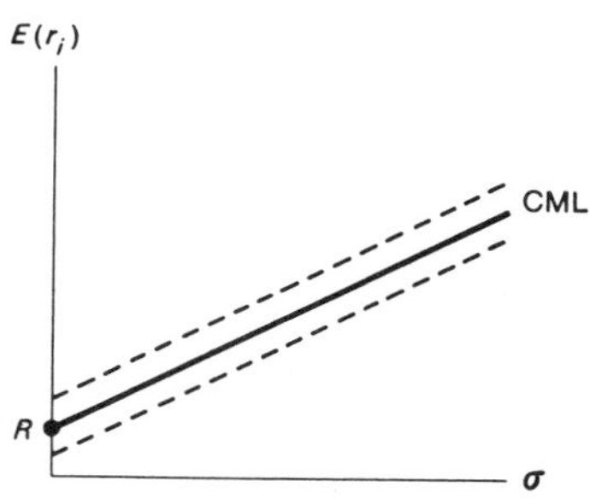

26-4.2 transaction costs

If assumption 6 (which assumes away transaction costs) is dropped, the CML and CAPM have "bands" on their sides, as shown in Figs. 26-7 and 26-8. Within these bands, it would not be profitable for investors to buy and sell securities and generate the price revisions necessary to attain equilibrium; transaction costs would consume the profit that induces such trading. As a result, the markets would never reach the theoretical equilibrium described earlier, even if the other assumptions were retained.

The effects of simple diversification, which were explained in Sec. 25-2, show that investors need not diversify over many securities to obtain portfolios near the CML. Instead they may buy larger quantities of fewer different market assets and thereby obtain the lower brokerage fees associated with large block transactions. Therefore, the effect of transaction costs need not be particularly detrimental to the attainment of equilibrium; that is, the "bands" around the CML and CAPM may not be wide.

26-4.3 general uncertainty of heterogeneous expectations

To jettison assumptions 3 and 4 about homogeneous expectations over a common planning horizon would require drawing an efficient frontier, CML, and CAPM composed of "fuzzy" curves and lines. The more investors' expectations differed, the fuzzier and more blurred all lines and curves would become. In effect, they would become bands. As a result of general uncertainty, the analysis becomes determinate only within limits. Only major disequilibriums will be corrected. Statements cannot be made with certainty, and predictions must contain a margin for error.

FIGURE 26-8 transaction costs obscure the capital asset pricing model (CAPM).

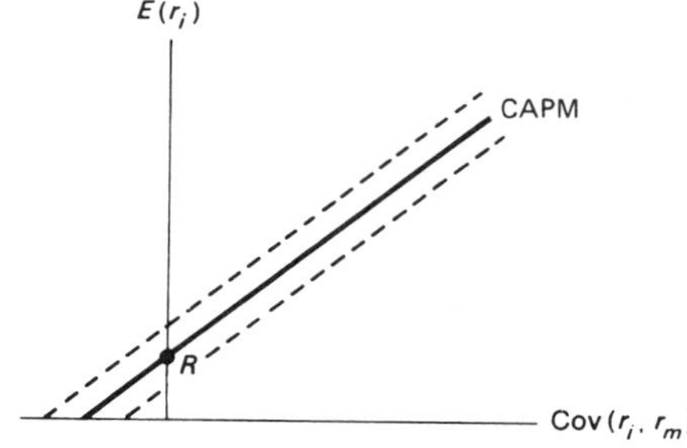

26-4.4 different tax brackets

Recognition of the existence of different tax rates on ordinary income and capital gains would also blur the picture. The after-tax rate of return atr_t is defined as follows:

$$atr_t = \frac{\text{capital gains} \times (1 - T_G) + \text{dividends} \times (1 - T_O)}{\text{price at beginning of holding period}} \tag{26-7}$$

where T_G is the capital gains tax rate and T_O is the tax rate applicable to ordinary income. In terms of after-tax returns, every investor would see a slightly different CML and CAPM depending on his or her particular tax situation. Thus, a static equilibrium could never emerge under existing tax laws even if all the other assumptions were rigorously maintained.

26-4.5 indivisibilities

If all assets were not infinitely divisible, that is, if assumption 5 were discontinued, the CAPM would degenerate into a dotted line. Each dot would represent an opportunity attainable with an *integral* number of shares. Little profit is to be gained from further examination of this trivial problem.

26-4.6 varying rates of inflation

The interest rates observed in reality are nominal interest rates, or equivalently yields to maturity (*ytm*), on marketable bonds rather than real interest rates (*rr*). The market *ytm* of a bond is determined by several factors, as indicated below.

$$ytm_t = rr + E\left(\frac{\Delta P}{P}\right) + \theta + f(n) \tag{26-8}$$

where

ytm_t = nominal yield to maturity in period t for a bond that is published in the news media

rr = real rate of return or real rate of interest per period

$E(\Delta P/P)$ = expected percentage change in the general price level per period, that is, the expected rate of inflation or deflation

θ = risk-premium

$f(n)$ = function of the number n of years until the bond's maturity.

This discussion will omit the impact of risk-premiums, transaction costs, and the term structure of interest rates in determining the market yields to maturity, ytm_t. One of the primary factors that makes market yields to maturity and other market interest rates fluctuate is changes in the rate of inflation. The rate of inflation fluctuates with the level of investment, monetary policy, fiscal policy, and other factors. Thus, it follows that ytm_t fluctuates, too.

Relaxing assumption 7 means that even if ytm_t is the market interest rate on default-free U.S. Treasury bills, for instance, it must nevertheless *vary* in both the money and the real sense. Thus, there is no true riskless asset, $\text{var}(R) > 0$;

FIGURE 26-9 lack of riskless rate obscures the capital market line (CML).

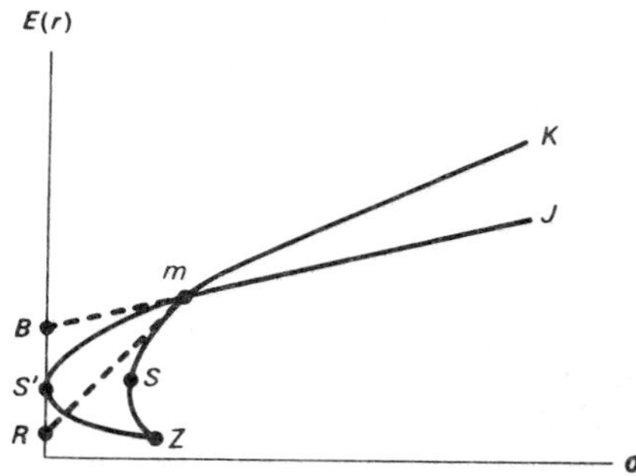

even default-free U.S. government securities will experience some variability of real return.[4]

Graphically, this means point R in Fig. 26-9 ceases to exist as a lending possibility and is replaced by a risky nominal interest rate at a point like Z. The efficient frontier is now the curve from S to K or from S' to K, assuming all money is borrowed at rate Z. Portfolio S or S' is the minimum-risk portfolio—it may or may not contain default-free securities, and it may not actually have zero risk, as S' does. A point like S will be the minimum-variance portfolio if returns on Z and m are uncorrelated but not perfectly negatively correlated.[5] If borrowing at rate B, rather than at rate R, is considered, the efficient frontier becomes SmJ or $S'mJ$, depending on whether S or S' is the minimum-variance portfolio. If it is assumed that funds may be lent (but not borrowed) at rate R, then the efficient frontier becomes the nonlinear set of opportunities through points RmK (unless point S' exists).

26-4.7 zero-beta portfolio

Point Z in Fig. 26-9 will be called the *zero-beta portfolio* hereafter. Portfolio Z has a beta of zero, in spite of its positive variance, because its variability of return is all unsystematic risk that is uncorrelated with the returns from the market portfolio. The existence of portfolio Z causes the CML to bend. The CAPM is still linear when Z is employed, as shown in Fig. 26-10.

The CAPM derived with portfolio Z is a slightly different asset pricing model. The CAPM remains linear when the portfolio Z is employed (instead of the riskless rate R) because the expected return and beta risk of all

[4] K. L. Hastie, op. cit., pp. B–771 and B–772. More recently, Black has extended Hastie's work by developing a portfolio, called the zero-beta portfolio (ZBP), which is free of systematic risk. Black derived the ZBP mathematically and derived some theorems about it (see Fischer Black, "Capital Market Equilibrium with Restricted Borrowing," *Journal of Business*, 1972, vol. 45, pp. 444–445). Empirical estimates of the returns on the ZBP were also prepared by F. Black, M. C. Jensen, and M. Scholes [see "The Capital Asset Pricing Model: Some Empirical Tests," in M. C. Jensen (ed.), *Studies in the Theory of Capital Markets*, Praeger, New York, 1972]. Essentially, the ZBP is an all-equity portfolio with positive variance but zero correlation with the market portfolio. Borrowing and lending at some riskless interest is an unneeded assumption if it is instead assumed that funds may be borrowed (for example, by short selling) and lent (that is, invested) in the ZBP.

[5] See Fig. 25-4 and the accompanying discussion of how the correlation coefficient determines the degree of convexity.

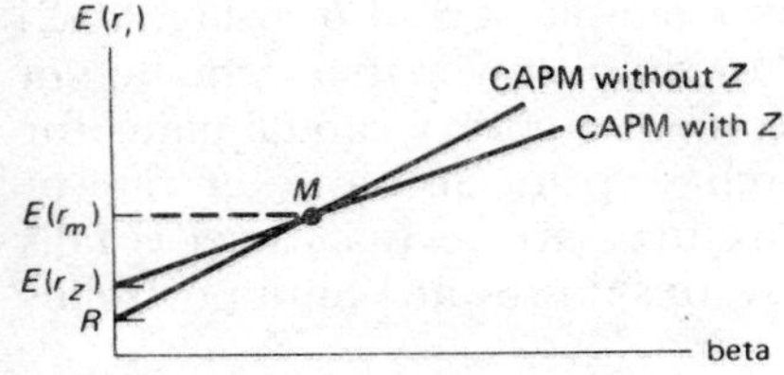

FIGURE 26-10 the CAPM shifts with portfolio *Z*.

portfolios are *linear* weighted averages of the expected returns and betas from assets *m* and *Z*. The portfolio expected rate of return formula is shown in Eqs. (26-9*a*) and (26-9*b*).

$$E(r_p) = x_1E(r_1) + x_2E(r_2) + \cdots + x_nE(r_n) \tag{26-9a}$$

where $\sum_{i=1}^{n} x_i = 1.0$. But for a two-asset portfolio comprised of assets *Z* and *m*, Eq. (26-9*a*) can be equivalently rewritten as Eq. (26-9*b*).

$$E(r_p) = x_mE(r_m) + x_Zb_Z \tag{26-9b}$$

where $x_Z = (1.0 - x_m)$.

The beta of a portfolio is also a linear weighted average of the beta of the assets in the portfolio.

$$b_p = x_1b_1 + x_2b_2 + \cdots + x_nb_n \tag{26-10a}$$

where $\sum_{i=1}^{n} x_i = 1.0$. But for a two-asset portfolio made up of assets denoted *Z* and *m* the portfolio's beta can be equivalently rewritten as Eq. (26-10*b*).

$$b_p = x_mb_m + x_Zb_Z \tag{26-10b}$$

where $x_Z = (1.0 - x_m)$. Thus, if it is assumed that funds may be raised by selling portfolio *Z* short (that is, let x_Z be negative), then the new linear CAPM with a flatter slope, illustrated in Fig. 26-10, emerges.

26-4.8 some investors are simple diversifiers

Thus far, all the assumptions underlying capital market theory except the first have been relaxed. Finally, let us relax this first assumption—that all investors are Markowitz diversifiers. Simply diversified investors would most likely adjust asset prices until returns were proportional to the *total* risk (as measured by the variance or standard deviation) of an asset. They will not delineate the efficient frontier and therefore will not recognize that portfolio *m* in Fig. 26-2 is the single most desirable portfolio. Only the Markowitz diversifiers will recognize that *m* is the most desirable asset; they will bid up the price of portfolio *m*. Consequently, the purchase price of asset *m* will rise, and its expected return will be lower after these temporary capital gains cease if systematic risk is unchanged (because the expected return moves inversely to the purchase price).

$$E(r) = \frac{E(\text{capital gains + dividends})}{\text{purchase price}} \tag{26-11}$$

The prices of portfolios other than *m* (for example, *A* and *B* in Fig. 26-2) will tend to remain constant as they are held by simple diversifiers who do not realize the unique desirability of *m*. After some temporary capital gains for portfolio *m*, a new, higher equilibrium purchase price and a lower rate of return emerge. Thus, prices and expected returns are revised, asset *m* falls downward in [σ, $E(r)$] space, and the CML swings downward until portfolios *A*, *m*, and *B* are all tangent to the CML.

As a result of these price revisions, which occur in a market where some investors are simple diversifiers, a condition represented by Fig. 26-11 emerges. Several portfolios lie along the CML in Fig. 26-11, all those along the line segment *AmB*. Equilibrium is attained when all assets are included in combinations lying along *AmB*, and they are included in such proportions as they are supplied to the market.

Consider the implications of the equilibrium shown in Fig. 26-11. It was shown that when two or more assets plot in a straight line in [σ, $E(r)$] space, they must be perfectly positively correlated. Thus, assets like *A*, *m*, and *B* and all other combinations along *AmB* must be perfectly positively correlated. The risky combinations of assets along *AmB* vary owing to some common cause, such as variation in the overall economic, psychological, and market situations. The returns on combinations *A*, *m*, and *B* will vary together *systematically*. All other variability of return (namely, unsystematic risk) due to causes unrelated to movements in market conditions has been reduced by diversification. Only undiversifiable risk remains in the assets on the efficient frontier.

In a capital market partially inhabited by simple diversifiers, an equilibrium such as the one shown in Fig. 26-11 is expected to emerge.[6] In this model the efficient frontier is flattened out along the CML, since simple diversifiers cannot delineate the efficient frontier. This suggests that the regression line

[6] If all investors were simple diversifiers who focused only on total risk, all assets (that is, both portfolios and individual assets) would lie on the CML in equilibrium. The CAPM, or SML, would cease to exist because simple diversifiers would not recognize the importance of undiversifiable systematic risk.

Empirical data supporting an equilibrium such as the one shown in Fig. 26-11 could also arise from heterogeneous expectations. That is, if each investor delineated a different efficient frontier, each would seek to attain a different market portfolio. As a result, many portfolios could lie along a ray like *AmB* in Fig. 26-11.

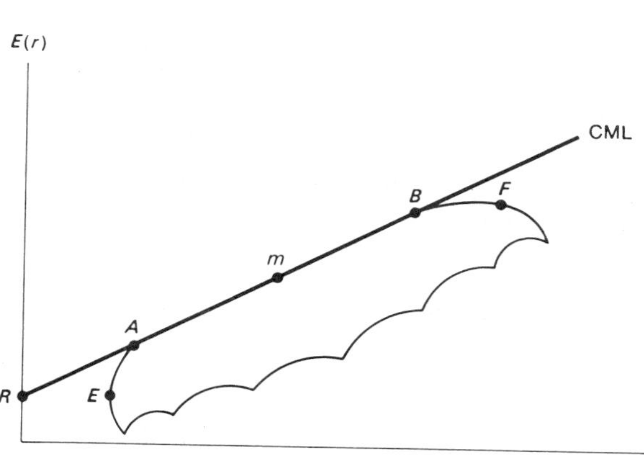

FIGURE 26-11 market equilibrium with simple diversification.

shown in Eq. (26-12) should fit the empirical data for portfolios and yield high correlations.

$$r_i = R + c\sigma_i \qquad \text{for } i = 1, 2, \ldots, n \text{ portfolios} \tag{26-12}$$

In Eq. (26-12), r_i and σ_i are the historical average return and risk statistics for portfolio i, and c is the regression slope coefficient, a positive constant. In fact, it was explained in Chap. 25 (see Fig. 25-8 on page 766) that such a simple linear regression, using a sample of 34 mutual funds, yielded a + .83 correlation coefficient.[7] The inclusion of individual assets in this regression would decrease the correlation because individual assets are not efficient enough to lie on the CML.

26-4.9 infinite borrowing and lending opportunities

Suppose that assumption 2, that infinite amounts of money could either be borrowed or lent at the riskless rate of interest, were true. This outcome is unlikely because there are legal margin requirements, capital adequacy requirements for brokerage houses, short sales restrictions, and other impediments to restrict investors' ability to either borrow or lend without limit. However, if these restrictions were somehow not binding, the opportunity set in $[\sigma, E(r)]$ space would extend infinitely far.[8] As illustrated in Fig. 26-12, even with divergent borrowing and lending rates of interest, infinite extensions of the upper and lower boundaries of the investment opportunity set are indicated by the arrowheads—an interesting but unlikely consideration.

26-5 CHAPTER SUMMARY

Capital market theory is an economic equilibrium theory that explains how the market prices of stocks, bonds, mutual fund shares, and other assets are determined. Assuming that investors are risk-averse, the theory is derived from the distinction between diversifiable and undiversifiable risk. Since

[7] William F. Sharpe, "Risk Aversion in the Stock Market: Some Empirical Evidence," *Journal of Finance*, September 1965, pp. 416–422; W. F. Sharpe, "Mutual Fund Performance," *Journal of Business*, January 1966, pp. 123–125.

[8] R. C. Merton, "An Analytic Derivation of the Efficient Portfolio Frontier," *Journal of Financial and Quantitative Analysis*, September 1972, pp. 1151–1172.

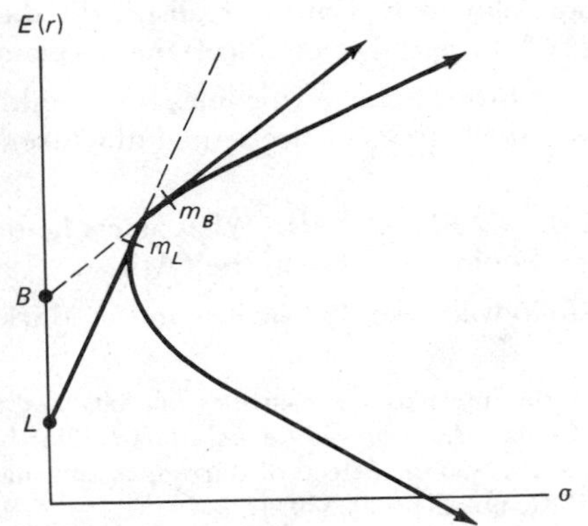

FIGURE 26-12 unrestricted short sales and leverage leave risk and return unbounded on the right-hand side in $[\sigma, E(r)]$ space.

unsystematic risk may be easily eliminated through diversification, it has no effect on the rates of return that risk-averse investors should expect in equilibrium. The capital asset pricing model shows that expected returns are a linear function of only one kind of risk—the undiversifiable risk.

The capital market theory was derived with the aid of some simplifying assumptions. However, all the assumptions underlying the theory were relaxed one at a time. In each case the implications of the model were slightly obscured. If all were relaxed simultaneously, the result would be even less determinate. However, the fact that the analysis is not exactly determinate under realistic assumptions does not mean it has no value. The analysis still rationalizes much observed behavior, explains such hitherto unexplained practices as diversification, and offers realistic suggestions about the directions that prices and returns should follow when they deviate significantly from equilibrium. The theory is a powerful engine for analysis.[9]

QUESTIONS

1. Compare and contrast the two terms *dominant asset* and *efficient asset*. Use graphs to show what you mean.
2. Which of the two graphs below is incorrect? Why?

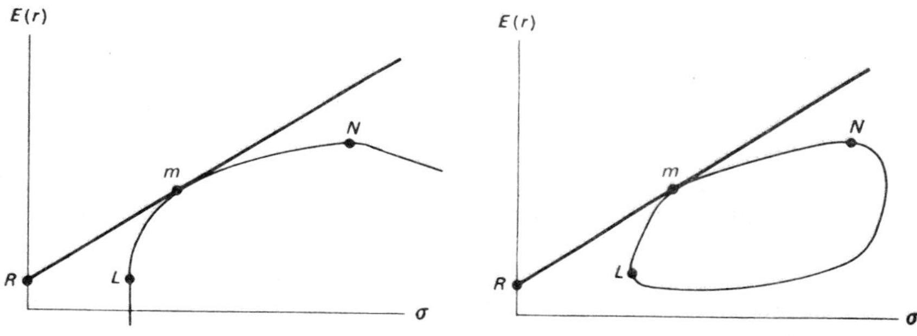

3. Draw a graph in risk-return space showing the various parts of the total risk for one inefficient asset. Hint: See Fig. 25-7 on page 763 for a start.
4. Define the market portfolio.
5. "Since the assumptions underlying portfolio analysis are unrealistic, the theory is not a valid description of reality." True, false, or uncertain? Explain.
6. Compare and contrast your conception of the characteristic lines for a highly leveraged tool manufacturer's common stock and a cigarette manufacturer's common stock.
7. Compare and contrast the CML and the CAPM, or SML. What assets lie on both lines in equilibrium? What assets should never lie on the CML?
8. John Lintner said that the "best portfolio will never be the one in the Mark-

[9] Capital market theory has been extended into the international securities markets. See a book of readings edited by E. J. Elton and M. J. Gruber, *International Capital Markets*, North-Holland, Amsterdam, 1975. In particular, see Rene Stulz, "On the Effects of Barriers to International Investment," *Journal of Finance*, September 1981, no. 4, pp. 923–934.

owitz efficient set with the lowest attainable risk."[10] Explain Lintner's remark.

9. Compare and contrast the behavior of aggressive securities and defensive securities in a bear market.
10. Explain how you would find the beta coefficient for some firm using historical data. What data would you need? What would you do with the data? What can you use this beta for? Graph two different models in which the beta coefficient is an important factor and explain them.
11. Given the assumptions underlying capital market theory, rationalize the following *separability theorem*: The investment decision of which asset to buy is a separate and independent decision from the financing decision of whether to borrow or lend.
12. What does it mean to assume that all investors have "homogeneous expectations" or that "idealized uncertainty" exists? Why is this assumption necessary to capital market theory?
13. Basic Scientific Research, Inc. (BSRI) is composed of a group of scientists working to develop new products that can be patented, manufactured, and sold to obtain large monopolistic profits. Investors in BSRI stock are told that the corporation has a small chance of inventing a highly lucrative product like Xerox or Polaroid. They are also told that, quite frankly, it is much more likely that BSRI will simply consume its original capital with no payoff at all. The best possible outcome is the long shot that BSRI's research will be fruitful and thus will turn their investment into a multimillion-dollar capital gain. Use risk-return analysis to evaluate this investment opportunity.

SELECTED REFERENCES

The reader who wishes to follow the original development of capital market theory is directed to the following articles, especially the second one by Sharpe. All use calculus and probability theory. This list is not exhaustive.

Gordon Alexander and J. C. Francis, *Portfolio Analysis*, 3d ed., Prentice-Hall, Englewood Cliffs, N.J., 1986. This monograph derives the capital market theory mathematically using consistent notation.

Harry Markowitz, *Portfolio Selection*, Cowles Foundation Monograph 16, Wiley, New York, 1959. Footnote 1 on page 100 appears to be the first seed of the capital market theory.

William F. Sharpe, "Capital Asset Prices: A Theory of Market Equilibrium under Conditions of Risk," *Journal of Finance*, September 1964, pp. 425–552. Reprinted in J. C. Francis, C. F. Lee and D. Farrar, *Readings in Investments*, McGraw-Hill, New York, 1980, pp. 109–126.

———, "A Simplified Model for Portfolio Analysis," *Management Science*, January 1963, pp. 277–293. See especially part 4 on the diagonal model, later called the characteristic line.

James Tobin, "Liquidity Preference as Behavior Towards Risk," *Review of Economic Studies*, vol. 26, no. 1, February 1958, pp. 65–86. This article derived a seminal market equilibrium model from Markowitz's portfolio analysis theory. Sharpe's work is based on the Markowitz and Tobin models.

[10] In "Security Prices, Risk, and Maximal Gains from Diversification," *Journal of Finance*, December 1965, p. 589.

CHAPTER 27 different investment goals

This chapter deals with the economic analysis of risky decision making. The economist's concept of "utility" is used to explain why different investors select different investments in an effort to maximize their happiness. In particular, the investor's expected utility from investment returns is defined and analyzed in this chapter.[1]

Utility means about the same thing as happiness; thus, utility is a measure of psychic gain. Punishment, for example, is designed to decrease the recipient's level of utility; it yields disutility. The recipient would pay money in order to avoid the punishment. On the other hand, eating sweet fruit increases utility for most people. They would pay money for the psychic gain to be derived from eating, say, a grape. Every activity provides some level of utility. If eating an apple is more enjoyable than eating a grape and eating a grape is preferable to receiving punishment, this situation can be represented symbolically as follows:

$$U(\text{apple}) > U(\text{grape}) > U(\text{punishment})$$

where U(apple) denotes the utility from an apple, etc.

Investors' basic reason for investment activity is to maximize their personal happiness, or utility. They hope to increase their happiness by investing so they will have more money to buy the things they want. This is summarized in Eq. (27-1).

$$\max U = g(w) \tag{27-1}$$

where

[1] The utility analysis in Chap. 27 is a more well-defined and rigorous concept than the dominance concept, which was initially used in Chap. 25 to explain why some investments are more desirable than others. And for readers who wish to see a more formal statement of the utility theory, the appendix to Chap. 27 presents some basic mathematics about utility analysis of choices involving risk.

U = investor's utility
w = personal wealth
g = some positive function

so the investor's utility rises as that wealth increases ($dU/dw = g' > 0$, mathematically speaking).[2]

Essentially, Eq. (27-1) says that an investor's happiness is a function of how much wealth the investor has. This does not mean that all wealthy people are necessarily happy. Instead, it means that persons can be happier (that is, achieve a higher level of utility) if they have more wealth with which to buy the things that bring them happiness.

27-1 MAXIMIZING UTILITY

Maximizing an investor's utility-of-wealth function, like $U(w) = g(w)$ in Eq. (27-1), is related to the investor's one-period rate of return because the rate of return measures the percentage change in wealth, $r = h(w)$, as shown explicitly in Eq. (27-2*a*).

Maximize: One-period rate of return from invested wealth, r:

$$\text{Maximize: } r = h(w) = \frac{w_T - w_0}{w_0} \tag{27-2a}$$

where w_0 is the beginning level of wealth and w_T is the terminal wealth, or wealth at the end of period; and the symbol h denotes the one-period rate of return from wealth function of Eq. (27-2*a*). Equation (27-3) is the inverse function of Eq. (27-2*a*)—it states terminal wealth as a function, denoted $f(r)$, of the rate of return.

$$w_T = f(r) = w_0(1.0 + r) \tag{27-3}$$

In Eqs. (27-2*a*) and (27-3), maximizing $r = h(w)$ is equivalent to maximizing $w = f(r)$. Stated differently, if $w_T > w_0$, this implies $r > 0$, and vice versa. For example, if an investor invests \$75 of beginning wealth and one period later liquidates the investment for \$100 of terminal wealth, the rate of return from the invested wealth is 33 percent.

$$r = \frac{\$100 - \$75}{\$75} = 33\% \tag{27-2b}$$

Conversely, if $w_T < w_0$, then, $r < 0$ because the invested wealth diminishes. In summary, there is a one-to-one correspondence between the investor's terminal wealth and the investor's one-period rate of return.

[2] The functional notation may be unfamiliar. Functions f, g, and h are some unspecified functions performed on the variables in parentheses. The symbols f, g, and h represent three different functions. Three examples of the form a function in the variable w might assume are

$U = aw$ a linear function denoted $U = f(w)$

$U = a + bw^2$ a second-degree equation denoted $U = g(w)$

$U = a + b\,[\log(cw)]$ a logarithmic function denoted $u = h(w)$

where a, b, and c are some constants in the explicit formulas.

It is better to discuss the rates of return from investments than it is to discuss the dollar amount of their gain or loss, because the rates of return from different assets are in directly *comparable units*. But dollar amounts are *not comparable* between assets with different price levels. For example, consider a different investment that also has a 33.3 percent rate of return but costs twice as much to purchase as the investment of Eq. (27-2*b*). This higher-priced asset's rate of return is shown in Eq. (27-2*c*).

$$r = \frac{\$200 - \$150}{\$150} = 33\% \tag{27-2c}$$

These two different investments had vastly different dollar gains, \$25 and \$50, from the mathematically equivalent Eq. (27-2*b*) and (27-2*c*), respectively. But the investment of Eq. (27-2*c*) may simply represent twice as many shares of the same stock represented by Eq. (27-2*b*). The different-sized dollar gains hinder recognition of the fact that the two similar investments have the same rate of return and are equally desirable. This example shows that it is better to discuss different assets' rates of return because they are directly comparable, whereas the dollar amounts are hard to compare.

The mathematical relationships between the investor's utility function (or happiness function), denoted U; the investor's utility (or happiness) from the terminal value of the invested wealth, denoted $U(w_T) = g(w_T)$; and the investor's terminal wealth stated as a function of the one-period rate of return, denoted $w_T = f(r)$, are all summarized in Eq. (27-4*a*), below.

$$\max U(w_T) = g[w_T] \tag{27-1}$$

$$= g[f(r)] \tag{27-4a}$$

$$= \text{some function of rate of return, } r \tag{27-4b}$$

Equation (27-4*a*) follows from substituting the quantity $w_T = f(r)$ from Eq. (27-3) for w_T in Eq. (27-1). Essentially, Eq. (27-4*a*) shows that maximizing the investor's happiness is simply a function of the investor's rate of return.

In an uncertain world, investors cannot know in advance which investment will yield the highest return. Even if investors have a hot tip or inside information about an investment, they are still uncertain that the tip is true or precisely how to act upon it. In an *uncertain* world, investors can maximize only their *expected* utility. Expected utility is determined by the function denoted c of expected return and risk. Symbolically, this is summarized in Eq. (27-5).

$$\max E(U) = c[E(r), \text{risk}] \tag{27-5}$$

$$= c[E(r), \sigma]$$

where

$E(U)$ = expected utility

$E(r)$ = expected return

risk = defined as variability of returns and measured by the standard deviation of returns (denoted σ)

c = some mathematical function

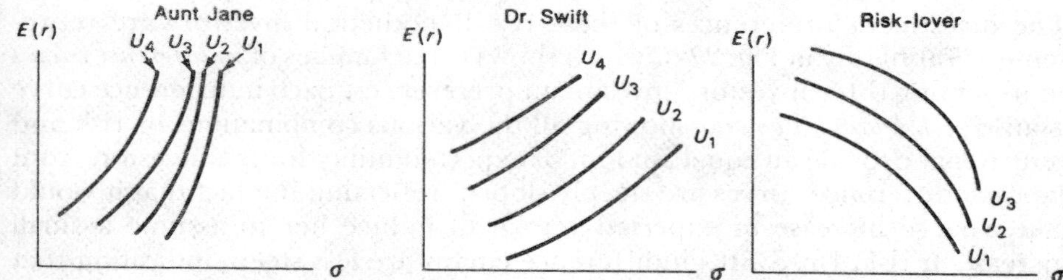

FIGURE 27-1 different investment preferences in risk-return space.

An increase in expected return will increase the investor's expected utility if risk does not also increase. Mathematically speaking, this means that the following partial derivative is positive, $\delta E(U)/\delta E(r) > 0$. A decrease in risk, denoted σ, will increase expected utility if expected return does not decrease simultaneously. That is, $\delta E(U)/\delta\sigma < 0$. The two preceding statements (that are both restated as partial derivatives) together mean that the investor will prefer efficient investments over inefficient ones. Such utility-maximizing behavior is analyzed graphically by using utility (or happiness) isoquants to measure investor utility in risk and expected return space (Fig. 27-1).

27-2 INDIVIDUAL'S INVESTMENT GOALS

Investment goals are determined in large part by the age and socioeconomic status of the individual investor. For example, consider the fictitious Aunt Jane, a little, old, frail widow who is all alone in the world. Aunt Jane lives modestly on social security and the income from a small portfolio. She is terrified, and rightfully so, of the prospect of a decrease in the value of her portfolio. She does not know how to manage the portfolio for herself and has no idea how many more years she will live. In order to conserve her meager wealth, she consumes only the income from her portfolio and none of the principal.

In marked contrast to Aunt Jane is Dr. Swift, an aggressive young man who can expect a successful professional career as a physician, dentist, lawyer, or scientist.[3] Dr. Swift's income began at a comfortable level shortly after he completed a terminal college degree, and it can be expected to rise in years to come if he works hard. The financial future for this person is fairly secure.

Dr. Swift has different investment objectives from those of Aunt Jane. He is willing to take risks in order to gain a larger return. If his risky investments are wiped out, his family will not suffer—he may merely have to work a few more years before retirement or do without some luxuries. However, Dr. Swift is not a reckless person. He dislikes risk and is willing to assume it only because he wants the high returns that might be attained. Thus, Aunt Jane and Dr. Swift are both risk-averters, and Aunt Jane is the more risk-averse of the two.

[3] Both Aunt Jane and Dr. Swift represent stereotypes in the investment world; there are also plenty of helpless widower Uncle Sams and upwardly mobile women.

27-2.1 indifference maps in risk-return space

The investment preferences of these two hypothetical investors are represented graphically in Fig. 27-1, which shows three families of *indifference curves* representing three investors' investment preferences. Each indifference curve is an *expected utility isoquant* showing all the various combinations of risk and return that provide an equal amount of expected utility for the investor. Aunt Jane's indifference curves are steeply sloped, reflecting the fact that it would take a large increase in expected return to induce her to assume a small increase in risk. Dr. Swift's indifference curves are less steep, indicating that he is more willing to assume risk to attain an increase in his expected return than Aunt Jane.

The indifference map of a risk-lover is also shown in Fig. 27-1. The risk-lover's indifference curves are negatively sloped, indicating a willingness to give up expected return in order to gain risk. This author has never actually observed this type of behavior; it is graphed only as an intellectual exercise.

In order to see how the three investment preferences shown in Fig. 27-1 will result in different investments, they must be graphed with some investment opportunities in risk-return space. Figure 27-2 shows a hypothetical set of investment opportunities in $[\sigma, E(r)]$ space. These opportunities might represent all the stocks, bonds, real estate, and art objects in the world at a given point in time, plus the opportunity to borrow or lend at R.

Aunt Jane's utility isoquants are $AJU_4 > AJU_3 > AJU_2 > AJU_1$ and appear in the lower left portion of Fig. 27-2. Aunt Jane will maximize her expected utility by selecting the low-risk, low-return portfolio at point J on the capital market line (CML). Portfolio J is the weighted average of investments R and M.

Dr. Swift maximizes his expected utility higher on the CML by purchasing portfolio S, which will provide him with the level of expected utility represented by his indifference curve DSU_2. This is the highest level of utility he can hope to achieve, given the investment opportunities shown in Fig. 27-2.

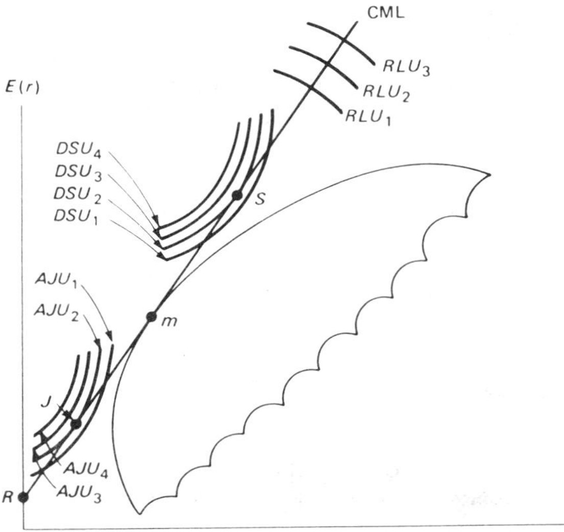

FIGURE 27-2 selection of an investment in $[\sigma, E(r)]$ space.

In contrast with rational investors, risk-loving investors will maximize their expected utility by borrowing all that they can to leverage themselves as high on the CML as possible.

Thus far, the discussion has focused on investors' preferences at a point in time. People's preferences change with the passage of time; so we shall see how this tendency can affect their investment decisions.

27-2.2 the typical family's changing investment preferences

For most young couples, the first three investments are life insurance, an emergency fund, and a home—in about that order.

LIFE INSURANCE Most newly married people are advised that they should make provisions to care for their spouse, any children, and any large expenses (such as hospital and funeral expenses) in the event that they die or are killed. This is advice that most couples follow. However, the newly married person must be wary not to buy (or be sold) more life insurance than necessary to meet family needs.

After the amount of coverage is determined, the question arises as to whether term insurance or whole-life insurance with cash values is best. After looking at the facts, many young people find that decreasing term insurance that has no cash value other than the death payment is a good buy. However, life insurance sales agents prefer to sell whole-life or endowment policies because the sales commissions are larger than for term insurance. And the whole-life insurance policies are also more profitable for the life insurance companies because the policies allow an insurance company to invest the cash values in a whole-life or endowment policy until the policy is cashed in, while paying the policyholder a smaller rate of interest for the funds. Thus, most life insurance buyers are better off purchasing term insurance and investing the money they saved by not buying an equal amount of whole-life or endowment life insurance.

A *term insurance policy* is essentially a bet with the insurance company that the insured will not die—nothing more, no frills or savings plans. The insured pays the insurer a premium to issue a contract that legally binds the insurer to pay if the insured dies within some specified time period. If the insured does not die within the time span of the policy, the policyholder and the beneficiaries receive nothing from the insurer. When the term insurance policy expires, a new policy must be purchased. As the insured grows older, the probability of dying increases; therefore, the cost of a given amount of term insurance increases with the age of the insured. When the insured reaches old age, term insurance will be very expensive, and it should be discontinued. Table 27-1 shows some typical costs of term insurance at various ages. This is the type of insurance policy that is best for many people; it is the cheapest, simplest type. By purchasing term insurance instead of more expensive policies, the insured will save hundreds of dollars each year. If these savings are saved at compound interest, they will grow to thousands of dollars by the time the insured reaches old age. At that time, the insured can cancel the term insurance because the accumulated savings on insurance premiums will exceed the face value of the term life insurance policy.

If the insured does not have the self-discipline to save the difference in cost between term insurance and the whole-life or endowment policies, he or she should consider those policies that include contractual savings plans.

TABLE 27-1 costs per $1,000 of term life insurance per year at various ages

age	annual cost per $1,000, $*
20	3.66
25	3.71
30	3.78
35	3.89
40	4.44
45	6.04
50	9.06
55	14.41
60	21.56
65	32.06

* These figures are the averages of several rates quoted by large insurance companies.

Whole-life and *endowment insurance policies* are a combination of decreasing term insurance and rising cash values. These policies are more expensive than term insurance. Table 27-2 shows the costs of various types of cash value life insurance purchased at different ages. The cash values associated with these policies arise because the insurance company invests the extra revenue from whole-life and endowment policies in the insured's name, and it grows at a low rate of interest. Figure 27-3 graphically depicts how the $123.50 annual premium on a straight-life policy paying a $10,000 death benefit, purchased at age 25, will be divided between actual insurance costs and savings.

The interest paid by the insurer on the cash values is low and may not equal inflation in some years.[4] But the insured who lacks self-discipline to buy term

[4] For example, during several recent time periods the rate of inflation has been over 10 percent. During some of these same time periods the interest that some older life insurance policies were paying on cash values was about 3 or 4 percent. Savings accounts at some banks and savings and loan associations were paying about 6 percent. Thus, these types of savings lose purchasing power. Furthermore, if the policyholder has any investment skills, higher rates of return are available.

TABLE 27-2 annual premium cost per $1,000 of various types of life insurance with cash values*

age	5-year term renewable and convertible, $	straight or ordinary life, $	life paid up at 65, $	20-pay life, $	20-year endowment, $
25	4.33	12.35	13.86	21.07	41.69
30	4.41	14.65	16.83	23.73	42.01
35	5.04	17.61	20.93	26.93	42.63
40	6.61	21.55	26.68	30.80	43.76
45	9.08	26.58	35.49	35.49	45.67
50	13.40	32.81	49.66	41.19	48.65
55	21.05	40.37	78.10	48.25	53.14

* Averages of several quoted rates.

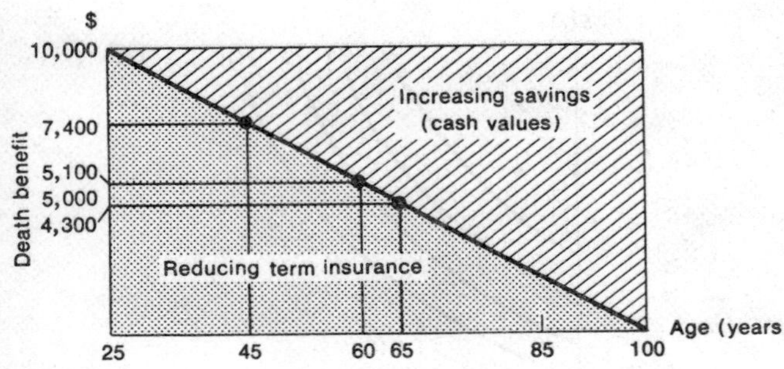

FIGURE 27-3 whole- or straight-life insurance policy is a combination of term insurance and a savings plan; the figures are the average of several quoted rates.

insurance and invest the money so saved should buy the more expensive policies that have automatic savings provisions. In this manner the insured will have a paid-up insurance policy with cash values.

AN EMERGENCY FUND AND A HOME The new family also needs an emergency fund to cover unforeseen problems not covered by insurance. This fund should be held in a form that is liquid and available if needed. After a new family has life insurance, an emergency fund, and some furniture, it usually invests in a home. Home ownership can be a good investment. There are positive economic benefits for home owners. The mortgage interest and property tax on the home are (unlike rent) tax-deductible, so the costs of home ownership are partially offset by income tax reductions. The home owner builds equity in the home; this equity can be recovered if the house is sold at a price advantageous to the seller. In addition, a home is an inflation hedge because the values of houses tend to rise during inflation while the real value (in terms of purchasing power) of the fixed mortgage debt decreases.

Most of the disadvantages of home ownership are difficult to assess in money terms. Home ownership decreases many people's willingness to move to a new job even if it offers better pay and opportunities. Home and yard care often consumes time that could be used more productively elsewhere—such as taking a self-improvement course in night school, for instance. Home owners make "home improvements" that are sometimes poor investments when viewed from a purely financial point of view. Home ownership involves the risk that the neighborhood may depreciate in value. All in all, it is difficult to base home-ownership decisions purely on investment criteria unless the house is to be used solely as a rental property. Home owners who live in their homes obtain "psychic income" that can obscure the dollar economics of the home purchase.

One of the purposes of the low-risk, low-return investments of life insurance, an emergency fund, and a home is to assure the young family of some fixed minimum-level financial support and security. After these basic investments are made, and if no health or education expenses are straining the family budget, the family's willingness and ability to undertake risky investments increase. Figure 27-4 shows the risk and return preferences for a hypothetical family as it matures.

The investment in life insurance and an emergency fund are represented by point *R*. After the young family has accumulated sufficient wealth, typ-

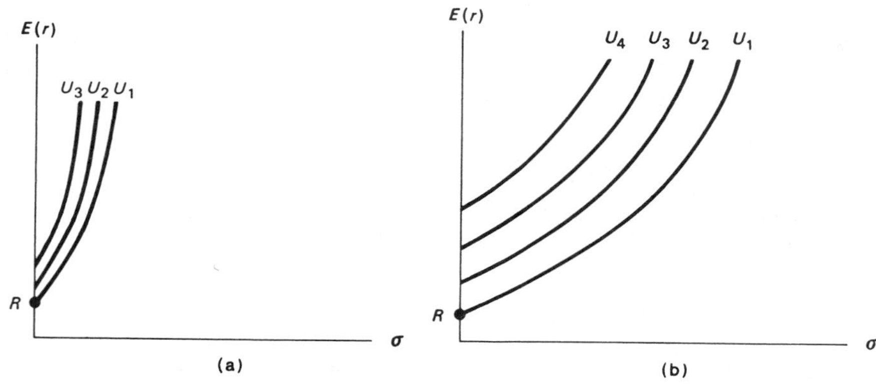

FIGURE 27-4 investment preferences: (*a*) a young family; (*b*) a mature family.

ically it purchases a home. In the next few years, families mature and their preferences for risk and return shift. The indifference map in Fig. 27-4*b* represents the typical risk-averse, wealth-maximizing behavior of most mature families whose homes are paid for and whose children are educated. At retirement, the families' risk-return preferences will shift again. Most families in retirement will have investment preferences similar to those of Aunt Jane; they become very risk-averse after their income ceases. They move back to an attitude like the one shown in Fig. 27-4*a*.

27-3 INSTITUTIONAL INVESTORS

Many of the marketable securities in the United States are managed by *institutional investors* such as insurance companies, pension funds, and trusts, although they are actually owned by individuals. Table 27-3*a* shows the total dollar value of all NYSE-listed securities owned by institutional investors. Table 27-3*b* shows the characteristics of the individuals who are NYSE investors. Some of the institutional investors in particular own more bonds, mortgages, and other financial instruments than they do stock.

Owing to the fact that the institutional investors manage such a large quantity of financial assets, many portfolio management job opportunities exist within these institutions. Consider the type of investments some institutional investors select and the reasons.

27-3.1 mutual funds

The Securities and Exchange Commission (SEC) requires that all mutual funds (that is, open-end investment companies) state their investment policies and objectives as explicitly as possible in a report filed with the SEC and also in the prospectuses they give to prospective investors. The funds are expected to follow these stated objectives so investors will know what kind of investment management services they are buying. The main categories of mutual funds can be delineated by these statements of objectives:

TABLE 27-3*a* estimated holdings of NYSE-listed stock by selected institutional investors (billions)

	YEAR ENDED					
type of institution	1955	1960	1965	1970	1975	1980
U.S. Institutions:						
Insurance companies:						
Life	$2.2	$3.2	$6.3	$11.7	$21.6	$38.1
Non-life	4.2	6.0	10.1	12.2	11.6	26.9
Investment companies:						
Open-end	6.3	12.4	29.1	39.0	35.0	38.1
Closed-end	4.6	4.2	5.6	4.1	5.5	5.1
Noninsured pension funds:						
Corporate & other private	3.4	14.3	35.9	60.7	82.5	166.0
State & local government	0.1	0.3	1.4	9.6	24.4	53.0
Nonprofit institutions:						
Foundations	6.9	8.0	16.4	17.0	20.8	32.4
Educational endowments	2.3	2.9	5.9	6.6	7.7	12.1
Common trust funds	0.9	1.4	3.2	4.1	5.2	9.5
Mutual savings banks	0.2	0.2	0.5	1.4	2.4	1.5
Subtotal	$31.1	$52.9	$114.4	$166.4	$216.7	$382.7
Foreign institutions	N/A	N/A	N/A	N/A	25.1	57.5
Total	$31.1	$52.9	$114.4	$166.4	$241.8	$440.2
Market value of all NYSE-listed stock	$207.7	$307.0	$537.5	$636.4	$685.1	$1,242.8
Estimated % held by Institutional Investors	15.0%	17.2%	21.3%	28.1%	35.3%	35.4%

N/A Not Available

Source: 1983 Fact Book, NYSE, pp. 51–52.

1. Common stock funds:
   (a) *Income and growth funds.* The income and growth funds take a middle-of-the-road approach in selecting between high returns and low risk. They keep the vast majority of their invested capital in blue-chip common stocks. Capital gains and dividend income are sought, but these funds do not invest in high-risk situations in an effort to maximize their rates of return.
   (b) *Growth funds.* Growth funds, which are also called "go-go" or performance funds, seek to maximize their returns. The prospectuses of these funds usually refer to the fact that risks will be assumed in pursuit of high capital gains. Dividend income is desired by the performance funds, but it is second to price appreciation.

TABLE 27-3*b* selected characteristics of individual shareowners (thousands)

	1959	1962	1965	1970	1975	1980	1981
Age							
Under 21	197	450	1,280	2,221	1,818	2,308	2,321
Adults (21 and over)	12,087	16,256	18,490	28,271	23,388	27,892	29,939
21–34	2,444	2,390	2,626	4,500	2,838	6,407	7,653
35–44	2,064	3,528	4,216	5,801	3,976	5,925	5,624
45–54	2,800	4,519	4,752	7,556	5,675	5,456	5,439
55–64	2,666	3,202	3,549	6,084	5,099	5,144	6,144
65 and over	2,113	2,617	3,347	4,330	5,088	4,589	5,079
Education							
3 Years high school or less	2,804	3,007	3,106	3,566	1,621	1,746	1,861
4 Years high school	3,130	4,828	5,344	8,697	6,580	5,737	6,045
1–3 Years college	2,587	3,284	4,012	5,867	5,301	9,353	10,093
4 Years college or more	3,566	5,137	6,028	9,999	9,886	10,613	11,880
Occupation							
Professional & technical	1,934	2,682	3,136	6,320	4,273	6,096	6,708
Clerical & sales	1,801	2,959	2,903	4,415	3,399	3,928	4,102
Managers & proprietors	1,982	2,276	2,330	3,981	3,726	5,322	5,841
Craftsmen & foremen	580	927	924	1,377	1,154	1,548	1,665
Operative & laborers	411	439	647	849	748	1,321	1,133
Service workers	326	423	414	622	452	236	284
Farmers & farm laborers	73	65	64	170	234	147	115
Housewives, retired persons, & nonemployed adults	4,000	5,462	8,072	10,320	9,402	8,108	9,140
Household Income							
Under $5,000	3,518	2,991	2,977	2,389	780	—	—
$ 5,000–$ 9,999	5,826	7,348	7,100	5,779	2,636	1,742	2,164
$10,000–$14,999	1,741	3,170	4,862	8,346	4,552	3,180	2,537
$15,000–$24,999	689	1,967	2,477	7,670	8,778	6,930	6,829
$25,000 & over	314	780	1,073	4,114	6,642	15,605	17,547
Portfolio							
Under $10,000	N/A	N/A	N/A	8,810	11,647	17,912	17,038
$10,000–$14,999	N/A	N/A	N/A	9,001	3,072	2,290	1,945
$15,000–$24,999	N/A	N/A	N/A	8,272	2,760	1,847	2,115
$25,000 & over	N/A	N/A	N/A	4,437	5,909	4,489	5,871

Note: Except for age, selected characteristics are those of adult shareowners only. "Not classified" responses excluded from some tabulations.

Source: 1983 Fact Book, NYSE, pp. 51–52.

(*c*) *Index funds.* Index funds have appeared in recent years as the mutual fund industry began to admit publicly that it was unable to achieve rates of return that were as good as most stock market indices could report. Although index funds do not have to limit their investments to common stocks, they have tended to do so as they typically sought to emulate Standard & Poor's 500 Stocks Composite Index. All the other types of mutual funds utilize an *active management,* which works to find the best investments available in the market. In contrast, index funds have a *passive management,* which does little more than try to keep the fund's investments aligned with the securities that make up the market index the fund is seeking to emulate.[5]

(d) *Specialized common stock funds.* These funds specialize in certain types of common stocks. For example, such a fund might specialize in stock in gold companies (for those who think that a gold investment has special advantages), shares in "sinless product" manufacturers (for religious investors who do not want their money invested in cigarette or liquor stocks, for example), or pollution-control companies' stock (for the ecology-oriented investor).

2. Special-purpose funds:
   (a) *Balanced or income funds.* A balanced fund typically holds most of its invested assets in bonds and preferred stocks. The other part of the fund's investment is usually diversified over 100 different common stocks. Balanced funds stress risk minimization and conservation of principal. These funds are conservatively managed and do not seek high-return investments that are risky.
   (b) *Money market funds.* These mutual funds began as a result of double-digit inflation and the related double-digit interest rates that started late in the 1960s. Money market funds typically invest entirely in money market assets (that is, loans with less than 1 year to maturity). Thus, they own large-denomination certificates of deposit issued by large commercial banks, Treasury bills, and commercial paper, which all pay rates of interest in excess of the current inflation rate.
   (c) *Municipal bond funds.* These portfolios invest only in the bonds issued by municipal governments to finance local schools, sewers, bridges, and so on. The interest income paid to municipal bond investors is completely income-tax exempt. This is the federal government's way of helping cities and other municipalities in the United States to sell their bonds; the investors get a tax exemption on their interest income. Medical doctors, senior business executives, wealthy people, and others in high income tax brackets are the typical investors in these funds.

Figure 27-5 shows indifference maps characterizing the risk-return preferences of the three main types of mutual funds. The actual operating performances of mutual funds are analyzed in Chap. 28.

27-3.2 commercial banks

The banks' activities are highly regulated because the federal government allows them to create money by making loans against fractional deposits. If banking activities are not stable, the nation's money supply and the national economy cannot be stable either. With the exception of their trust departments, which manage other people's investments, banks are practically forbid-

[5] For an analysis of passive portfolio analysis rendered scientifically, see Andrew Rudd, "Optimal Selection of Passive Portfolios," *Financial Management,* Spring 1980, vol. 9, no. 1, pp. 57–66. For a discussion of active versus passive portfolio management see the following: Keith P. Ambachtsheer and James L. Farrell, "Can Active Management Add Value?" *Financial Analysts Journal,* November–December 1979. Walter Good, R. Ferguson, and Jack Treynor, "An Investor's Guide to the Index Fund Controversy," *Financial Analysts Journal,* November–December 1976.

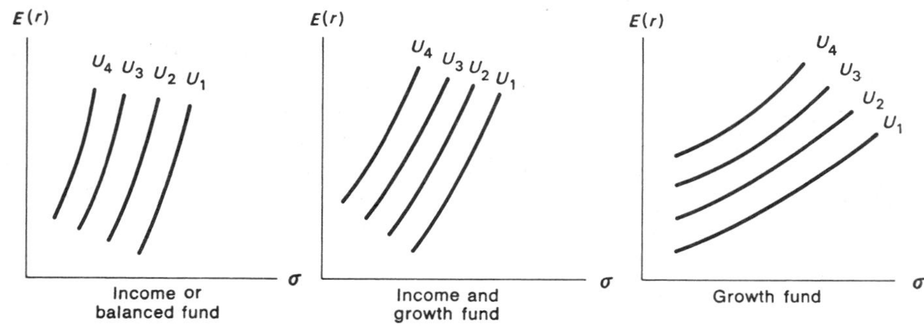

FIGURE 27-5 different mutual fund objectives represented in [σ, E(r)] space.

den from investing in common stocks. In fact, banks are forced into investing heavily in federal, state, and local bonds because of actions taken by the Federal Reserve Board and rules handed down by the comptroller of the currency and enforced by bank examiners.

Table 27-4 shows the balance sheet of a typical commercial bank in common-sized percentages. Each balance sheet item in the table is stated as a percent of owner's equity. That is, the bank's equity is defined as unity (or 100.0% = 1.0), and everything else is some multiple of equity. Liabilities are negative and assets are positive, so that the sum of all the weights is unity—thus, the balance sheet balances. For example, the average bank's total demand deposits are 470 percent of (or 4.7 times) the bank's equity, and the sign is negative because demand deposits are a liability to the bank. It is the convention to state all assets and liabilities as a percentage (or weight) of equity for the purposes of Markowitz portfolio analysis in order to calculate the risk and rate of return on equity.[6]

[6] For an example of balance sheet analysis see J. C. Francis, "Portfolio Analysis of Asset and Liability Management in Small-, Medium-, and Large-Sized Banks," *Journal of Monetary Economics*,

TABLE 27-4 common-sized balance sheet for the average large-sized banks, 1971

assets	weights as percent of equity	liabilities	weights as percent of equity	
Cash and uncoll. funds	180% = 1.8	Demand deposits	−470% = −4.7	total
Gov't bonds	290% = 2.9	Savings deposits	−230% = −2.3	liabili-
Home and other mortgages	150% = 1.5	Cert. of deposit	−250% = −2.5	ties: −9.5
Business loans	333% = 3.3	Equity	−100% = −1.0	
Installment loans	100% = 1.0	Total liabilities and equity	−1,050% = −10.5 times equity	
Total assets	1,050% = 10.5 times equity			

Source: J. C. Francis, "Portfolio Analysis of Asset and Liability Management in Small-, Medium-, and Large-Sized Banks," *Journal of Monetary Economics*, August 1978, vol. 4, no. 3, table 1, p. 461.

CONSTRAINTS ON BANK MANAGERS Banks must remain liquid and continuously able to instantly repay any funds that demand depositors (that is, checking account depositors) wish to withdraw from their accounts. Bank examiners from the Federal Reserve, the comptroller of the currency, the FDIC, and various state bank agencies regularly inspect banks to ensure that they are holding the legally required reserves in vault cash and non-interest-earning deposits at other banks (primarily the Federal Reserve Bank). The government regulates bank liquidity in this fashion to prevent another money panic and run on the banks like the catastrophic event that occurred in the early 1930's when the United States had its Great Depression. As a result of this legal liquidity requirement, banks must hold more of their assets in non-interest-earning required reserves than they wish. Of course, this hurts the banks' profitability. This is an important fact; Table 27-4 shows that these required reserves (namely, cash and uncollected funds) are a substantial part of the banks' total assets. In addition to required reserves, there are other assets that are not totally within the control of a bank's management.

The main asset on the balance sheet, commercial loans, is only partially controlled by the bank. The quantity of commercial loans demanded by businesses depends on the rate of business expansion and market interest rates. The interest rates on commercial loans are largely determined by economic conditions. Mortgage loans are long-term loans, the demand for which varies with credit conditions and home-building activity. Management of those portions of a bank's investments represented by commercial loans and mortgages largely involves evaluating customers' credit-worthiness and collateral at the time the loans are made. Risk can be assessed only subjectively for most of a bank's assets that are direct loans. Furthermore, some mortgages are insured with the Federal Housing Administration or Veterans Administration. This all makes risk-return analysis difficult. Asset and liability management within a bank are further complicated by credit conditions, which vary over the business cycle.

It is common for banks' liquidity to alternate with economic conditions. During an economically slow period, banks may be saturated with liquidity for which they cannot find borrowers. During an economic boom, banks may be rationing loans, raising loan rates, and liquidating reserves to meet loan demand. In effect, the opportunities open for adept investment management are limited mainly to anticipating shifts in interest rates in the bond markets and so operating as to minimize federal income taxes. Banks are so highly *constrained by regulations* that only their trust departments need be concerned with seeking an efficient frontier that is not highly constrained.

PORTFOLIO ANALYSIS OF BANK BALANCE SHEETS In spite of the legal constraints and other external forces touched upon above, it is still possible to delineate an efficient banking frontier and select an efficient portfolio of bank assets and liabilities. This efficient banking frontier will be dominated by other

---

August 1978, vol. 4, no. 3, pp. 459–480. Reprinted in J. C. Francis, Cheng-Few Lee, and Donald E. Farrar (eds.), *Readings in Investments*, McGraw-Hill, New York, 1980. See also J. C. Francis and S. H. Archer, *Portfolio Analysis*, 2d ed., Prentice-Hall, Englewood Cliffs, N.J., 1979, chap. 13.

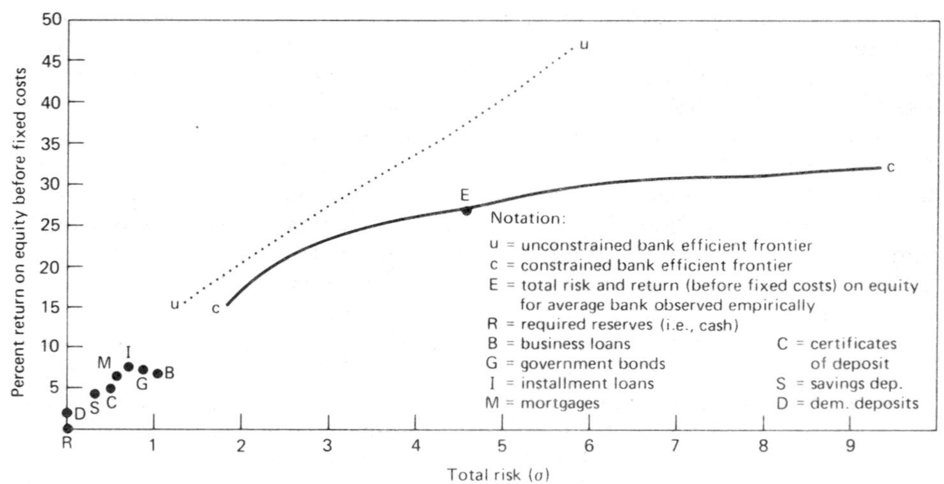

FIGURE 27-6 unconstrained and constrained efficient banking frontiers for average large bank. (*Source*: J. C. Francis, "Portfolio Analysis of Asset and Liability Management in Small-, Medium-, and Large-Sized Banks," *Journal of Monetary Economics*, August 1978, vol. 4, no. 3, figs. 1 and 2.)

efficient frontiers, selected from more assets and not constrained by banking regulations. But the constrained risk-return analysis is still a worthwhile bank management exercise.

Figure 27-6 illustrates the risk and return statistics for the average large U.S. bank's five major asset categories, three major liability categories, and its owner's equity. The dotted curve marked *UU* in the figure represents the unconstrained efficient banking frontier that Markowitz portfolio analysis can delineate from the five assets and the three liabilities. These efficient bank balance sheets contain no required reserves, for example, and are thus not realistically feasible. The curve *CC* illustrates the more realistic constrained efficient banking frontier. The bank balance sheets along the *CC* efficient frontier offer the minimum risk at each level of return on equity that can be attained while holding the required legal reserves, and also while relying on only a realistic amount of demand deposits as a source of funds (that is, the bank is constrained not to do all its borrowing through interest-free checking deposits). The average large bank's actual balance sheet is at point *E* in risk-return space, just below the *CC* efficient frontier in Fig. 27-6.

It is impossible to construct an indifference map in risk-return space that represents the investment preferences of a group of people. And in this case in particular, it is thus not possible to rationalize the preferences of bank owners in this fashion. Therefore, Fig. 27-6 contains no utility isoquants. Point *E*, however, does represent the bank shareholders' revealed preference within the various legal and competitive constraints which impinge upon banks. This is a portfolio worthy of further examination.

The average large bank's portfolio of assets and liabilities (that is, point *E*) lies far above the eight dots that lie in the lower left corner of Fig. 27-6. These eight dots represent the characteristics of the five assets and the three liabilities that make up bank balance sheets. At first it may seem strange that point E lies so far above the risk and return statistics of the component assets and liabilities that make up the balance sheet. This difference between risk and return is easily explained in terms of *financial leverage*. The average large bank's debt-to-equity ratio is 9.5 to 1.0, whereas most U.S. manufacturing corporations have debt-to-equity ratios of less than unity. It appears that most bank investors are willing for their banks to undertake considerable financial leverage to generate rates of return on equity sufficient to reward them for investing in the banks' equity shares.

Table 27-4 shows the exact ingredients in the average large bank's portfolio, represented by point E in Fig. 27-6. Comparison of this actual portfolio (that is, point E) with the nearest efficient banking portfolio (represented by the point on the curve CC that is nearest to point E) reveals a high degree of similarity. Both the actual bank and the most similar bank on the constrained efficient frontier borrowed funds from all three liability sources. And both the actual bank and the most similar efficient bank invested their funds in a diversified fashion: they placed similar proportions in each of the five asset categories. This analysis shows that even the complicated behavior of a large commercial bank can be analyzed and explained using portfolio theory. As mentioned above, however, it is not possible to construct an indifference map for the banks' shareholder group to show why point E in Fig. 27-6 was selected. Furthermore, the banks' activities are so highly regulated that all the holdings shown in Table 27-4 were not freely selected.

The investment activities that bank trust departments undertake in managing other people's investment funds are less constrained and therefore easier to analyze than the banks' investments of their own funds.

27-3.3 trusts

A *trust* is a fiduciary agreement in which a trustee or trustees administer assets placed in trust by a creator (donor, or grantor). In general, trusts are established to place responsibility for the administration of a person's estate or assets into the hands of someone other than the creator or the beneficiary of the trust. They are managed by trust companies, the trust departments of commercial banks, or insurance companies. Trust contracts are called *fiduciary agreements*.

Personal trusts may be set up by a deceased person's will (a testamentary trust), or a living person may put assets in trust (a living trust) for some designated beneficiary. *Living trusts* may be classed as either revocable or irrevocable. Irrevocable trusts have tax advantages not available through revocable trusts.

About one-third of all employee pension funds are set up as common trusts in which the retired employees are the beneficiaries. Some banks' trust departments also have *common trusts* in which many small accounts are commingled and managed as one. *Endowment trusts* are also set up; these trusts may designate schools, research facilities, libraries, art groups, and others as beneficiaries. Under most of these arrangements, the trustee has the power of attorney to buy and sell the assets of the trust in any manner he or she chooses as long as (1) the transactions are conducted in accordance with any provisions stated in the trust agreement and (2) the trustee (man or woman) acts as what the courts interpret to mean a "prudent man."[7]

Under some personal trusts the trustee acts only as an advisor and caretaker of the trust; in these situations some other person, usually the beneficiary, holds the ultimate decision power over the way the trust is managed. The trustee receives a fee for his or her services that ranges from ¼ of 1 percent to 2 percent per year on the value of the assets in trust, depending mainly upon the size of the trust.

The total assets held in trust are much larger than most people realize. For example, the total value of common stock held in all trusts in the United States exceeds the total value of the common stocks owned by all mutual funds by a sizable margin. Trusts are large institutional investors.

In some cases, an entire business or other asset will be turned over to a trustee to administer. However, most assets held in trusts are marketable securities. About 60 pecent of all assets in trusts are stocks, and about 25 percent are bonds. Trust funds are managed in accordance with the provisions set out in the trust agreement. Most trusts specify maintenance of principal as the main objective. The trustee can violate the trust agreement only under penalty of law; that is, the trustee's own personal risk-return preferences should not affect the manner in which the trust is managed. The risk-return preferences used in trust management are specified by the creator of each trust and usually reflect that creator's risk-return preferences and the purpose for which that trust was created. Thus, no single preference map in risk-return space is suitable for all the trust portfolios at one bank.

In addition to the individual trust accounts for substantial individuals, bank trust departments may operate a commingled or *common trust fund*. A common trust fund operates in a manner similar to that of a mutual fund. Numerous investors place their funds in a commingled portfolio that the bank's trust department manages for a fee. Every investor in a common trust fund is treated the same and earns the same rate of return. Large bank trust departments operate these commingled accounts for small investors who do not have enough funds to start private trust accounts of their own but still need investment management services. Most bank trust departments require a minimum of $100,000 to open a private trust account. The common trusts are also used by some corporations that want professional money management for their pension funds. Some bank trust departments even have several different common trust funds. One might be managed as a growth portfolio, one might be managed as a bond portfolio, and one might be managed as a real estate portfolio. The individual investors in a common trust have no voice in the management of their portfolio—they are typically told in advance of investing what investment goal is used to govern the portfolio. Thus, selecting a common trust fund is like selecting a mutual fund to manage your money.

[7] The "prudent man" legal guidelines that govern trust portfolio managers are discussed in C. W. Buck, "Managing Our Trusts as Prudent Men Would Do," *Commercial and Financial Chronicle*, Mar. 3, 1960. Reprinted in H. Wu and A. Zakon (eds.), *Elements of Investments*, Holt, New York, 1965, reading 4.3. Also, see Chap. 4 of this book (page 114) for a brief outline of the "prudent man" legal guideline.

27-3.4 life insurance companies

Most life insurance policies are more than mere insurance policies—they are combinations of insurance and savings plans. As the insured grow older, their risk of death mounts and their insurance rates rise. But by this time the savings portions of most life insurance policies (other than term insurance) have attained cash values that can offset the purchase of increasingly expensive insurance. The investment activities performed by life insurance companies arise from a need to invest the savings portion of the whole-life or endowment life insurance policies that represent cash values to the insured.

Life insurance companies pay a small fixed rate of dividends or interest on the cash value of the savings. Then they invest these funds at a higher rate of return. Table 27-5 shows the balance sheet of a typical life insurance company.

The balance sheet in common-sized percentages in Table 27-5 shows that life insurance companies invest heavily in interest-income-bearing assets, that is, bonds and mortgages. The companies enjoy a very favorable treatment under the income tax laws; among other things, these laws make life insurance companies indifferent between interest and capital gains income. Thus, these companies can earn satisfactory after-tax returns on their investments by specializing in corporate bonds and mortgages rather than by seeking the more risky capital gains.

Life insurance companies buy about half of all corporate bonds in the United States. They are such large purchasers of corporate bonds that they sometimes capture part of the broker's commissions from the bond market by buying *entire* bond issues directly from the issuer. *Direct placements,* as these purchases of an entire bond issue are called, allow the issuer to avoid the delays, uncertainties, red tape, and underwriting costs of a public bond issue. Instead, the issuer sells the entire issue directly to a life insurance company at an interest rate slightly above the appropriate market rate. Thus, the issuer of the bonds passes along some of the savings of the direct placement to the purchasing life insurance company by paying the slightly higher interest rate.

Some large life insurance companies have also developed very efficient mortgage investment operations. These companies employ full-time forces of

TABLE 27-5 typical balance sheet for a life insurance company

assets	%	liabilities	%
Cash and short-term U.S. government bonds	3	Policy reserves	80
Long-term federal, state, and local government bonds	10	Dividends and other obligations	12
Corporate bonds	36	Net worth	
Mortgages	25	Contingency reserves	1
Policy loans	8	Equity and surplus	7
Preferred and common stock	9	Total liabilities and net worth	100
Real estate	4		
Company premises	5		
Total assets	100		

Source: Adopted from *1984 Life Insurance Fact Books,* American Council of Life Insurance, Washington, D.C.

agents who go into the field and originate mortgages, with the life insurance company lending home buyers the money they need. Small- and medium-sized life insurance companies whose volume of mortgage credit in any given area is not large enough to justify the expense of originating their own mortgages simply buy them from *mortgage bankers* who originate the mortgages and then resell them to life insurance companies and other mortgage investors.

It is interesting to note insurance companies' lack of interest in common stocks. Although even the tightest state restrictions allow life insurance companies to hold up to 5 percent of their total assets in common stocks, a few companies do not even own any common stock. Their reluctance to hold common stocks is particularly unusual in view of their lack of need for liquidity. They usually have premium inflows that exceed their outflow for loans, death payments, and operating expenses and thus are in the enviable position of being able to wait for favorable market conditions to buy and sell common stocks. In fact, there is a controversy in the life insurance industry as to whether more or less common stock should be purchased. This discussion revolves around technicalities involving legal reserves and the treatment of capital gains.

Another reason life insurance companies do not invest more aggressively in common stock is the "legal list" restrictions imposed on them. According to state laws which govern the majority of life insurance companies in New York, the company can buy only common stocks which (1) have paid dividends continuously for over 10 years and (2) have paid dividends from current earnings rather than borrowed funds. Common stocks which meet these and other restrictions are included on the *legal list* of stocks in which life insurance companies are permitted to invest. Such arbitrary restrictions have caused life insurance companies to invest their funds in other sources. Some have been putting funds into sale-and-lease-back arrangements which involve some risk and a higher return. In any event, the rigid investment restrictions imposed on life insurance companies make it impossible to accurately represent their investment preferences in terms of risk and return statistics.

Life insurance companies also administer about one-third of all pension fund assets. Most of these portfolios are heavily invested in common stock, but these assets are separate from the assets which provide backing for life insurance policies' cash values. These pension fund portfolios can be viewed as being a separate group of assets aside from the insurance companies' own assets, which are invested in different ways. The life insurance companies manage these pension funds for a fee somewhat in the way a mutual fund is managed. A company may operate one or more commingled funds, each of which contains funds from several different clients' pension funds. Or it may manage a separate and independent portfolio for each of its large clients; in that case each client can dictate the investment goal to the insurance company's investment managers.

27-4 CONCLUSIONS ABOUT INVESTMENT PREFERENCES

Institutional investors' investment choices are often severely constrained by federal and state laws. Thus, it is often impossible to represent the investment objectives of these institutions by preference maps in risk-return space. Mutual funds, whose investment practices are only moderately constrained, are one of the few institutional investors whose investment objectives may be represented by an indifference map.[8]

An individual investor's preferences can be represented with an indifference map in risk-return space. The point at which an investor's highest indifference curve is just tangent to the efficient frontier is the portfolio that will maximize the investor's expected utility. When investment preferences change, this may be represented by drawing a new set of indifference curves in risk-return space.

QUESTIONS

1. Draw an indifference map in risk-return space for an investor who is absolutely fearless but loves high returns. Have you ever known anyone who actually had such investment preferences? Explain.
2. "Term insurance is the best buy for the person who has the self-discipline for regular savings." Is this statement true, false, or uncertain? Explain.
3. "Life insurance companies' holdings of common stocks are predominantly in low-risk stocks." Is this statement true, false, or uncertain? Is the investment area, as implied by your answer, the desirable one? Explain.
4. Define a trust and explain the roles of the parties to a trust. Do trusts tend to be managed conservatively, or do they tend to seek high risks and high returns?
5. Explain what difficulties you would have in constructing the indifference map for an institutional investor like a bank or life insurance company.
6. Do you think that the legislators and government policymakers who developed the investment regulations for publicly owned institutional investors understood Markowitz diversification? Explain your view.

SELECTED REFERENCES

Marshall E. Blume and Jack P. Friedman (eds.), *Encyclopedia of Investments*, Warren, Gorham and Lamont, Boston, 1982. This nonmathematical volume explains numerous financial securities, real assets, and other investment vehicles appropriate for various investors.

Lawrence J. Gitman and Michael D. Joehnk, *Fundamentals of Investing*, Harper & Row, New York, 1981. Chapters 14 through 18 of this elementary investments textbook discuss different investment programs that are suitable to achieve different investment objectives.

John L. Maginn and Donald L. Tuttle (eds.), *Managing Investment Portfolios*, Warren Gorham and Lamont, Boston, 1983. This easy-to-read volume explains how to set an investment goal, what assets are appropriate for different investment objectives, and how to monitor an investment to see that it progresses according to plan.

[8] Unfortunately, mutual funds' published statements of investment objectives do not always align with the investment preferences implied by their actual investments. This latter problem is one of the points taken up in Chap. 28, where the ability of mutual funds to maximize their shareholders' expected utility is evaluated.

Herbert Phillips and John C. Ritchie, *Investment Analysis and Portfolio Selection,* 2d ed., South-Western Publishing Company, Cincinnati, 1983. Chapters 25 through 29 of this investments textbook discuss the merits of different types of investments in light of differing investor goals.

APPENDIX 27A

utility analysis

Utility analysis and decision making in uncertainty are complex. To discuss all the important issues in the field would take several volumes.[9] Therefore, Chap. 27 has merely touched on the main points necessary to understand (1) what utility is; (2) how utility is related to consumption, wealth, and the rate of return; and (3) how a utility map in risk-return space may be used to maximize investor utility. This appendix extends that analysis and shows proof of several of the important assertions made in the chapter about single-period utility maximization. Multiperiod utility analysis is discussed in Chap. 29.

APP. 27A-1 GRAPHICAL UTILITY ANALYSIS

The principal elements of utility analysis underlying investments management are explained graphically in the following few pages. To begin with, a utility-of-wealth function is a formula or a graph of a formula that shows how much utility (how many utils, or how much happiness) a person derives from different levels of wealth. A utility-of-wealth function might be mathematically written as $U = g(w)$, or simply $U(w)$, for example. Figure App. 27A-1 shows a graph of a utility-of-wealth function. The notion of marginal utility is a little more complex; it involves segments of the utility-of-wealth function. In words, *marginal utility* of wealth may be defined as the additional utility a person enjoys from a change in his or her wealth. Mathematically, marginal utility is the first derivative of the utility function—that is, $dU/dw = U'(w)$. To determine whether marginal utility is rising or falling, the slope of the utility function or the sign of the second derivative of the utility function must be observed. Decreasing marginal utility is present when the utility function rises

[9] Here is some of the important literature: S. Archer and C. D'Ambrosio, *The Theory of Business Finance: A Book of Readings,* Macmillan, New York, 1967, readings 2–4, 39, and 40; Harry Markowitz, *Portfolio Selection,* Cowles Foundation Monograph 16, Wiley, New York, 1959, chaps. 10–13; and J. L. Bicksler and P. A. Samuelson, *Investment Portfolio Decision-Making,* Lexington Books, Lexington, Mass., 1974, readings 1–8 and 14–18.

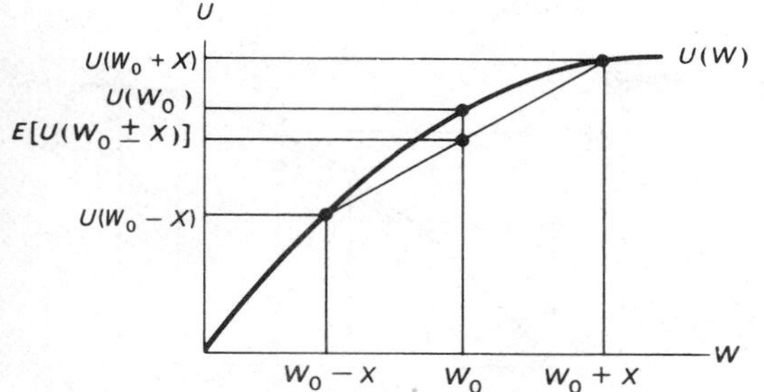

FIGURE APP. 27A-1 diminishing marginal utility of wealth.

at a less steep rate or when the second derivative of the utility function is negative, $d^2U/dw^2 < 0$, or equivalently $U''(w) < 0$.

Utility analysis is useful for analyzing the logic, or lack of it, in decisions involving risk. The analysis of such decisions is based on the expected-utility principle (see Box App. 27A-1).

Maximizing *expected* utility is different from simply maximizing utility if the possible outcomes are risky. To understand the difference, consider the definition of expected utility. (Mathematical App. B, in Part 9, explains the mathematical expectation.) The expected utility from a decision to undertake some risky course of action is the weighted average of the utils from the possible outcomes calculated, using the probability of each outcome as the weights. For example, if you decide to enter into a coin-tossing gamble, you have made a decision to undertake a risky course of action. There are two possible outcomes—heads or tails. The probability of heads is denoted P (heads) and the probability of tails is written as P(tails). The utility from the gamble that results if heads turns up is represented by U(heads) and the utility of getting tails is U(tails). Thus, the expected utility of the gamble is written symbolically as

$$E[U(\text{coin toss})] = P(\text{head}) \times U(\text{head}) + P(\text{tail}) \times U(\text{tail})$$

To understand this more clearly, consider some more specific examples.

App. 27A-1.1 diminishing marginal utility and risk-aversion

Risk-averse behavior will result if the investor has diminishing marginal utility of wealth or returns. Diminishing marginal utility-of-wealth and utility-of-returns functions are graphed in Figs. App. 27A-1 and App. 27A-2, respectively. They are both concave to the horizontal axis.[10]

Diminishing marginal utility of wealth or of returns leads to risk-avoiding

[10] By definition, a function U is concave if and only if $U(x) \geq \alpha U(x - y) + (1 - \alpha)\, U(x + y)$ for $1 \leq \alpha \leq 0$. A concave (to the horizontal axis) utility function results in risk-aversion.

BOX APP. 27A-1 expected-utility principle

Decision makers make decisions that maximize their *expected* utility.

FIGURE APP. 27A-2 diminishing marginal utility of returns.

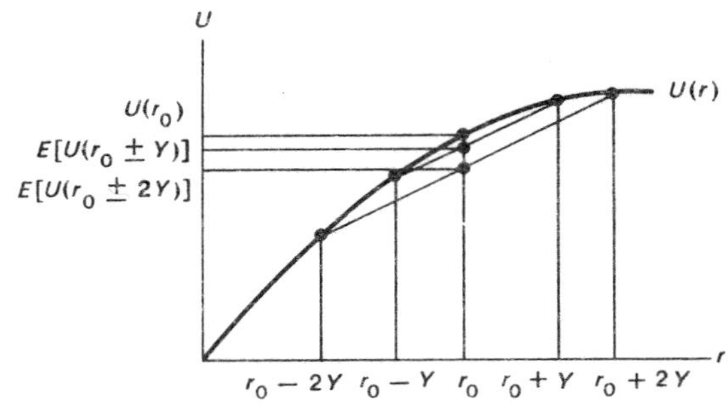

behavior since, from any point on the utility-of-wealth or utility-of-returns curve, a risky investment has a lower expected utility than a safe investment with the same expected outcome. That is, if an investment ofers a 50-50 chance of increasing or decreasing a given level of starting wealth by X dollars, the loss of utility from the bad outcome is larger than the gain in utility from the favorable outcome. Symbolically, $.5U(W_0 - X) + .5U(W_0 + X) \le U(W_0)$. Thus, the person with diminishing utility of wealth would prefer to keep W_0 rather than make a risky investment or bet to attain $W_0 + X$ or $W_0 - X$ with equal probability. Figure App. 27A-1 represents this situation graphically. Since the utility of the certain starting wealth $U(W_0)$ is larger than the expected utility of an equal amount of uncertain wealth $E[U(W_0)]$, the risk-averter prefers not to assume the risk, $U(W_0) > E[U(W_0)]$. The risk-averter prefers simply to hold W_0 cash rather than assume risks in an effort to increase this wealth. If the chance for gains from the risky investment were large enough, however, the risk-averse investor would find it sufficient compensation to assume the risk. Thus, risk-averters may gladly accept risky investments if they feel the odds are in their favor. People everywhere commonly exhibit diminishing marginal utility of wealth (for example, people require higher wages per hour to work overtime).

App. 27A-1.2 equality of wealth and return utility functions

Utility preference orderings are *invariant* under a positive linear transformation of the utility function. Graphically speaking, this means that any utility curve (such as the ones in Figs. App. 27A-1 and App. 27A-2) can be raised or lowered (that is, can have a constant added or subtracted), can be scaled down without having its shape changed (that is, can be divided by a positive constant), or can be expanded without changing its curvature (that is, can be multiplied by a positive constant) without changing the way the utility curve would rank the desirability of a set of investment opportunities. These transformations would change the number of utils assigned to any given outcome, but the preference rankings would be invariant under a positive linear transformation. Since the one-period rate of return is just a positive linear transformation of the investor's wealth, this implies that a given investor's utility-of-returns function is simply a linear transformation of his or her utility-of-wealth function, and the two will yield the same preference orderings for any given group of investment opportunities. Thus, the investor's utility curves shown in Figs. App. 27A-1 and App. 27A-2 are merely linear transformations of each other and result in *identical preferences* for single-period changes in wealth or equivalent one-period rates of return. The positive linear transformation between one-period changes in wealth and the rate of return is

$$r_t = \frac{w_T - w_0}{w_0}$$

where

w_0 = beginning-of-period wealth (a positive constant)
w_T = end-of-period wealth (a random variable)
r_t = one-period rate of return (also a random variable)

App. 27A-1.3 graphical analysis

Suppose, for example, that an investor can earn a rate of return of r_0 with certainty or can invest in a risky investment that will return $r_0 + y$ or $r_0 - y$ with equal probability. Symbolically, $P(r_0 - y) = P(r_0 + y) = ½$. Both the riskless and the risky investment have an expected return of r_0.

$$\begin{aligned} E(r) &= P_1(r_0 + y) + P_2(r_0 - y) \\ &= \frac{1}{2}(r_0 + y) + \frac{1}{2}(r_0 - y) \\ &= r_0 \end{aligned}$$

Since the expected returns are the same, a risk-averse investor will prefer the sure return because the risk-averter's diminishing marginal utility will cause the disutility from a return of $r_0 - y$ to exceed the gain in utility from a return of $r_0 + y$.

Furthermore, suppose that this risk-averter had a third investment opportunity in an even riskier investment expected to yield either $r_0 - 2y$ or $r_0 + 2y$ with equal probability. This latter investment is riskier (that is, has more variability of return) than the other risky investment, but it offers the same expected return. The calculations below show that the two risky investments have equal expected returns.

$$E(r) = \overbrace{P_1(r_0 - y) + P_2(r_0 + y)}^{\text{Small risk}} = r_0$$

$$\begin{aligned} E(r) &= \overbrace{P_1(r_0 + 2y) + P_2(r_0 + 2y)}^{\text{Larger risk}} \\ &= \frac{1}{2}(r_0 - 2y) + \frac{1}{2}(r_0 + 2y) = r_0 \end{aligned}$$

A risk-averse investor will rank the desirability of the riskiest investment last, since its expected return is the same as the other two investments but it entails more risk. Therefore, the riskiest investment will have the least expected utility. Symbolically, $U(r_0) > E[U(r_0 \pm y)] > E[U(r_0 \pm 2y)]$. This is shown graphically in Fig. 27A-2.

App. 27A-1.4 expected utility, expected return, and risk formulas

In an uncertain world, expected utility is determined by expected return *and* risk.[11] Symbolically, this is summarized in Eq. (App. 27A-1*a*)

$$E(U) = f[E(r), \text{risk}] \quad \text{(App. 27A-1}a\text{)}$$

$$= f[E(r), \sigma] \quad \text{(App. 27A-1}b\text{)}$$

where

$E(U)$ = expected utility
$E(r)$ = expected return
risk = variability of returns, measured by the standard deviation of returns (denoted σ)
f = some unspecified mathematical function

An increase in expected return will increase the investor's expected utility if risk does not also increase. Or a decrease in risk will increase expected utility if expected return does not decrease simultaneously.[12] Expected returns and expected utility are defined in Eqs. (App. 27A-2) and (App. 27A-3), respectively.

$$E(r) = \sum_{i}^{N} p_i r_i \quad \text{(App. 27A-2)}$$

where

p_i = probability of ith outcome
r_i = ith possible rate of return
N = number of possible outcomes

BOX APP. 27A-2 the expected-utility formula

Expected utility is calculated as follows:

$$E(U) = \sum_{i}^{N} p_i U_i \quad \text{(App. 27A-3)}$$

where U_i = utility of ith outcome.

The expected value is like a weighted average of the possible outcomes where the probabilities are the weights.[13]

[11] The standard deviation of returns is, of course, only a risk surrogate rather than a risk synonym, as this discussion implies. See Chap. 9 for a more complete discussion of risk. Throughout this book, σ is used as a symbol standing for *total* risk. Sometimes it is convenient to use the variance σ^2 rather than the standard deviation. Both are used interchangeably to denote total risk.

[12] Technically, expected utility is a function of $E(r)$ and σ only if the utility function is quadratic or if the distribution of terminal wealth is a two-parameter distribution (such as a normal distribution).

[13] Mathematical App. B discusses the mathematical expectation.

Measurement of total risk was examined in detail in Chap. 9. Equation (App. 27A-4) shows the formula used to calculate the standard deviation of returns for the *i*th security from expected rates of return.[14]

$$\sigma = \sqrt{\sum_{t=1}^{T} P_t[r_{it} - E(r_i)]^2} \qquad \text{(App. 27A-4}b\text{)}$$

Before the utility analysis of risky investment alternatives can be performed, the investment analyst must be supplied with probability distributions of outcomes and a utility function in order to find the expected utility for each object of choice. For example, in selecting among alternative investments, a probability distribution of returns representing the possible investment outcomes and their probabilities is required. And a utility function assigning utils to each possible rate of return that the investment might earn is also needed. Only after the utility function and the probability distributions are known can utility analysis proceed.

App. 27A-1.5 numerical example

Consider three objects of choice, say, investments *A*, *B*, and *C*, with probability distribution of returns as defined in Table App. 27A-1.

Figures App. 27A-3 to App. 27A-5 represent the utility functions for a risk-averting, a risk-indifferent, and a risk-seeking investor, respectively. Since investments *A*, *B*, and *C* all offer the same expected return of 3 percent, it is clear that the three investors will rank these three investments differently *purely* because of their differences in risks.

The risk-averter's expected utility from *A*, *B*, and *C* is calculated thus:

$$E[U(A)] = \sum_{i=1}^{2} P_i U(r_i)$$

$$= \frac{1}{2}[U(-.03)] + \frac{1}{2}[U(.09)]$$

[14] When calculating the standard deviation of returns from historical rates of return, the probabilities become relative frequencies, so substitute $P = 1/T$ and rewrite Eq. (App. 27A-4*a*) as (App. 27-4*b*):

$$\sigma = \sqrt{\sum_{t=1}^{T} \left(\frac{1}{T}\right)[r_t - E(r)]^2} \qquad \text{(App. 27A-4}b\text{)}$$

TABLE APP. 27A-1 probability distributions of returns for three investments

	INVESTMENT OUTCOMES AND THEIR PROBABILITIES							CHARACTERISTICS	
investments	outcomes	−3%	0	3%	6%	9%	$\Sigma p = 1$	$E(r)$	σ
A	↑	.5		+		.5	1	$E(r_A) = 3\%$	$\sigma_A = 6\%$
B	Probabilities		.5	+	.5		1	$E(r_B) = 3\%$	$\sigma_B = 3\%$
C	↓			1			1	$E(r_C) = 3\%$	$\sigma_C = 0$

FIGURE APP. 27A-3 risk-averter's quadratic utility-of-returns function.

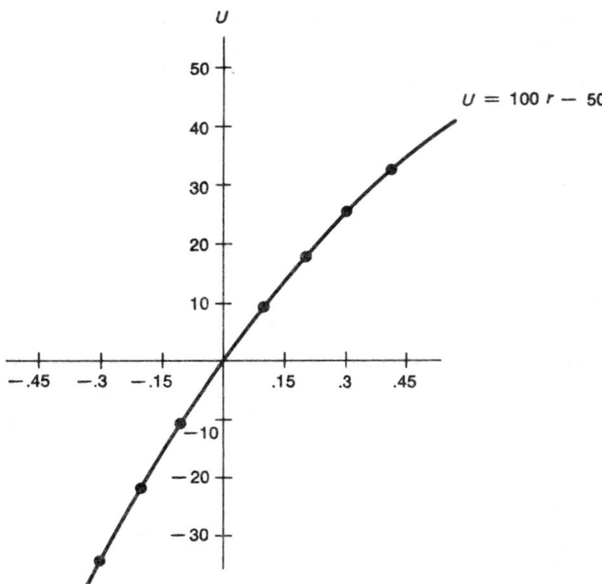

FIGURE APP. 27A-4 risk-indifferent investor's linear utility-of-returns function.

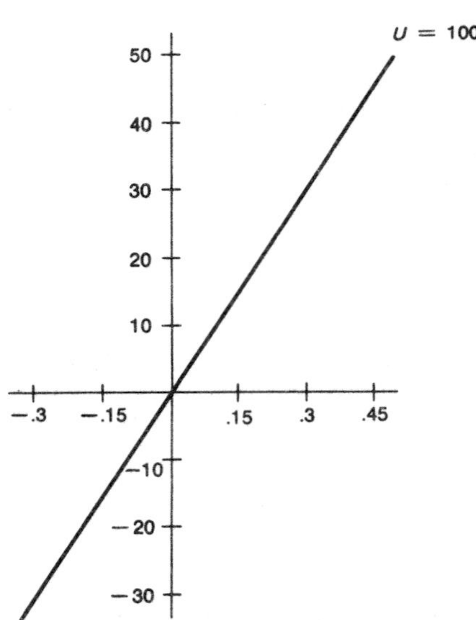

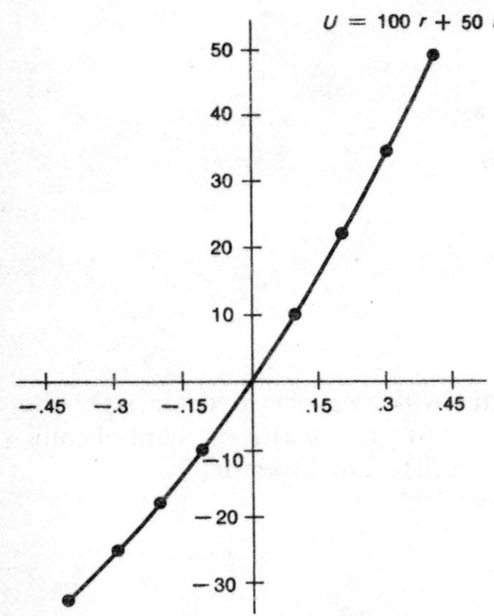

FIGURE APP. 27A-5 risk-lover's quadratic utility-of-returns function.

$$= \frac{1}{2}(-3.045) + \frac{1}{2}(8.595)$$

$$= 2.785 \text{ utils}$$

$$E[U(B)] = \frac{1}{2}[U(0)] + \frac{1}{2}[U(.06)]$$

$$= 0 + \frac{1}{2}(5.82)$$

$$= 2.91 \text{ utils}$$

$$E[U(C)] = 1[U(.03)]$$

$$= 1(2.955)$$

$$= 2.955 \text{ utils}$$

The risk-averter derives the most satisfaction from investment C, which has the least variability of return.

The risk-indifferent investor's expected utils from the three investments are calculated below:

$$E[U(A)] = \frac{1}{2}[U(-.03)] + \frac{1}{2}[U(.09)]$$

$$= \frac{1}{2}(-3) + \frac{1}{2}(9)$$

$$= 3 \text{ utils}$$

$$E[U(B)] = \frac{1}{2}[U(0)] + \frac{1}{2}[U(.06)]$$
$$= 0 + \frac{1}{2}(6)$$
$$= 3 \text{ utils}$$
$$E[U(C)] = 1[U(.03)]$$
$$= 1(3)$$
$$= 3 \text{ utils}$$

Since investments A, B, and C differ only with respect to their risk, the risk-indifferent investor assigns the same utility to all three. Symbolically, $E[U(A)] = E[U(B)] = E[U(C)]$ for the risk-indifferent investor.

The risk-lover's utility calculations follow.

$$E[U(A)] = \frac{1}{2}[U(-0.3)] + \frac{1}{2}[U(.09)]$$
$$= \frac{1}{2}(-2.055) + \frac{1}{2}(9.405)$$
$$= 3.225 \text{ utils}$$
$$E[U(B)] = \frac{1}{2}[U(0)] + \frac{1}{2}[U(.06)]$$
$$= 0 + \frac{1}{2}(6.18)$$
$$= 3.09 \text{ utils}$$
$$E[U(C)] = 1[U(0.3)]$$
$$= 1(3.045)$$
$$= 3.045 \text{ utils}$$

The risk-lover prefers the large variability of return exhibited by investment A. The three investors' expected utilities are summarized in Table App. 27A-2.

Investments A, B, and C all have identical expected returns of 3 percent, $E(r) = 3$ percent; only their variability of returns differs. The lower expected

TABLE APP. 27A-2 different investment preferences for risky investments

investor	asset *A*—most risky $E(r_A) = 3\%, \sigma_A = 6\%$	asset *B* $E(r_B) = 3\%, \sigma_B = 3\%$	asset *C*—least risky $E(r_C) = 3\%, \sigma_C = 0$
Risk-averter	$E[U(A)] = 2.785$	$E[U(B)] = 2.91$	$E[U(C)] = 2.955$
Risk-indifferent	$E[U(A)] = 3$	$E[U(B)] = 3$	$E[U(C)] = 3$
Risk-lover	$E[U(A)] = 3.225$	$E[U(B)] = 3.09$	$E[U(C)] = 3.045$

utilities assigned to *A* and *B* by the risk-averse investor are due to their larger variability of returns, which seems distasteful. And the larger expected utility the risk-lover associates with investments *A* and *B* reflects this investor's preference for risk. Thus, the two parameters—mean and variance of returns—are *both* reflected in expected utility. In all cases, expected utility measures the effects of both $E(r)$ and σ. Symbolically, $E(U) = f[\sigma, E(r)]$.

The preceding numerical example showed how a rational, risk-averse, wealth-seeking investor will select investments that minimize risk at any given level of expected return and thus maximize expected utility in a world of uncertainty.

App. 27A-1.6 selecting investments in terms of risk and return

Given the investor's utility function, we have seen how an individual will be able to select investment assets (either consciously or subconsciously) in terms of the investments' expected return and risk. Figure App. 27A-6 shows graphically how an investor will select between investments by examining only their expected returns and risk. The exhibit is a graph in risk-return space of the seven hypothetical securities listed below:

name of security	expected return, $E(r)$, %	Risk, σ, %
American Telephone Works (ATW)	7	3
General Auto Corporation (GAC)	7	4
Fuzzyworm Tractor Company (FTC)	15	15
Fairyear Tire & Rubber (FTR)	3	3
Hotstone Tire Corporation (HTC)	7	12
Rears and Sawbuck Co. (RS)	9	13
Treasury IOUs (IOU)	2	0

FIGURE APP. 27A-6 opportunities and preferences in risk-return space.

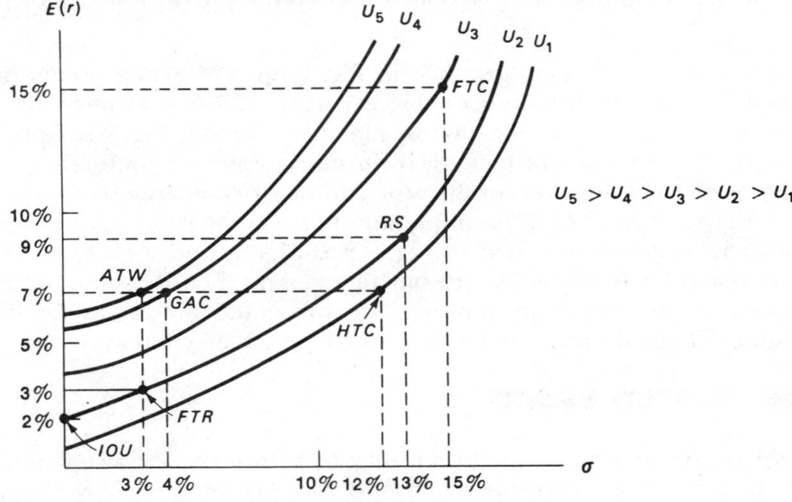

Figure App. 27A-6 also shows a utility map in risk-return space representing the preference of some risk-averse investor (like the one whose utility from rates of return curve was shown in Fig. App. 27A-3). In this indifference map the investor's utility is equal all along each curve. These curves are called *utility isoquants* or *indifference curves*. The graph is called an *indifference map in risk-return space*. Since investments RS, IOU, and FTR are all on the same indifference curve (that is, U_2), the investor obtains equal expected utility from them although their expected returns and risk differ considerably.

An infinite number of indifference curves could be drawn for the risk-averter depicted in Fig. App. 27A-6, but they would all be similar in shape and would all possess the following characteristics:

1. Higher indifference curves represent more investor satisfaction. Symbolically, $U_5 > U_4 > U_3 > U_2 > U_1$, because the investor likes higher expected return and dislikes higher risk.
2. All indifference curves slope upward. This is because the investor requires higher expected returns as an inducement to assume larger risks. Consider, for example, the investor's indifference between FTR, IOU, and RS. This indifference results from the fact that RS's expected return is just enough above the expected return of FTR to compensate the risk-averse investor for assuming the additional risk incurred in going from FTR to RS. Riskless investment IOU has just enough reduction in risk below the risk of FTR to compensate the investor for accepting IOU's lower rate of return and still be as happy as with FTR or RS. Investment IOU is called the *certainty equivalent* of investments FTR and RS because it involves no risk.
3. The indifference curves grow steeper at higher levels of risk. This reflects the investor's diminishing willingness to assume risk as returns become higher.

Given the investment opportunities and the investor preferences shown in Fig. App. 27A-6, we see that the investor prefers ATW over any of the other investments since ATW lies on a higher indifference curve than any other investment. In fact, Fig. App. 27A-6 shows that

$$U(\text{ATW}) > U(\text{GAC}) > U(\text{FTC}) > U(\text{IOU}) = U(\text{RS}) = U(\text{FTR}) > U(\text{HTC})$$

App. 27A-1.7 unusual risk attitudes

The indifference map graphed in Fig. App. 27A-6 represents rational normal, risk-averse preferences. Figure App. 27A-6 is implied by a utility-of-returns function like the one in Fig. App. 27A-3. Figures App. 27A-4 and App. 27A-5 represent *radically* different investment preferences, the preferences of a risk-indifferent investor and of a risk-loving investor, respectively.

Figure App. 27A-7 is simply another way of representing the utility-of-returns function graphed in Fig. App. 27A-4, and Fig. App. 27A-5 results from a utility function like the one in Fig. App. 27A-8. These two pathological cases of investment preferences are presented merely as intellectual curiosities. They do not represent rational, risk-averse behavior.

APP. 27A-2 MATHEMATICAL UTILITY ANALYSIS

For quadratic utility functions it may be shown that expected utility is determined by expected return $E(r)$ and risk (as measured by the variance of returns σ^2 or standard deviation σ). This finding can be generalized to other

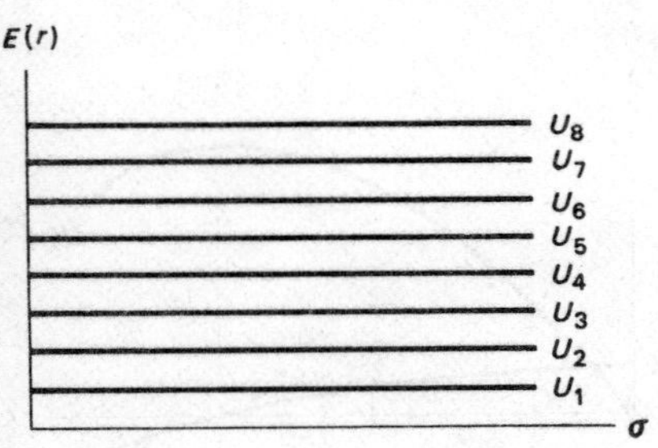

FIGURE APP. 27A-7 risk-indifferent wealth maximizer's preferences in risk-return space.

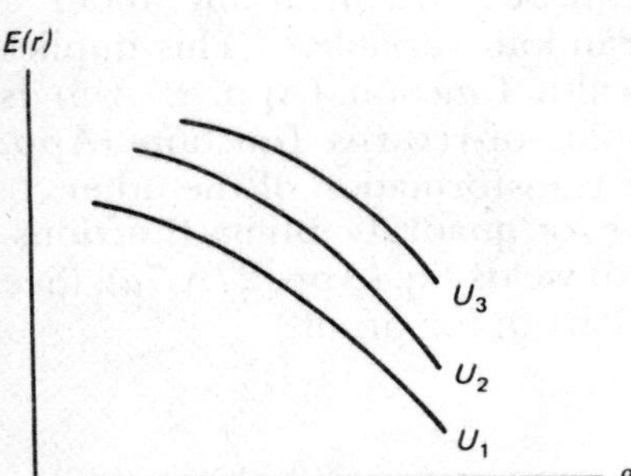

FIGURE APP. 27A-8 risk-lover's preferences in risk-return space.

utility functions if the probability distribution of returns is a two-parameter distribution.

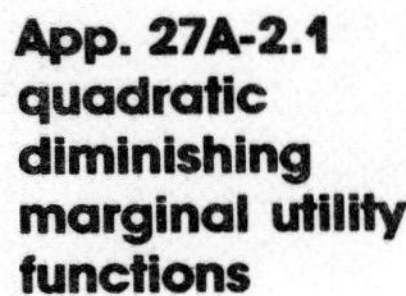

App. 27A-2.1 quadratic diminishing marginal utility functions

Consider the quadratic utility of wealth and return functions (App. 27A-5) and (App. 27A-6).

$$U = w - aw^2 \qquad w < \left(\frac{1}{2a}\right) \qquad \text{for } a > 0 \qquad \text{(App. 27A-5)}$$

$$U = r - br^2 \qquad r < \left(\frac{1}{2b}\right) \qquad \text{for } b > 0 \qquad \text{(App. 27A-6)}$$

Equations (App. 27A-5) and (App. 27A-6) are graphed in Figs. App. 27A-9 and App. 27A-10, respectively. Figures App. 27A-9 and App. 27A-10 also show the marginal-utility curves; they are denoted MU. The marginal utility diminishes as larger returns are obtained.

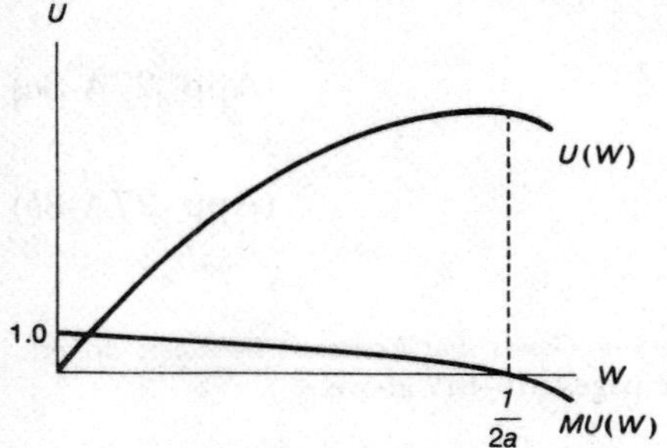

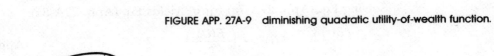

FIGURE APP. 27A-9 diminishing quadratic utility-of-wealth function.

FIGURE APP. 27A-10 diminishing quadratic utility-of-returns function.

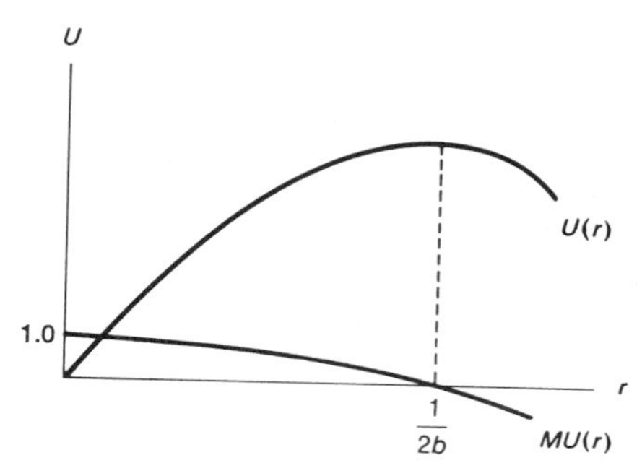

The preference orderings of a utility function are invariant under a positive linear transformation of the basic random variable.[15] This implies that the diminishing quadratic utility-of-wealth function (App. 27A-5) is equivalent to the diminishing quadratic utility-of-returns function (App. 27A-6), since one variable is a positive linear transformation of the other.

Expected utility is a function of $E(r)$ and σ for quadratic utility functions. Taking the expected value of Eq. (App. 27A-6) yields Eq. (App. 27A-7*a*). (See Mathematical Expectation Theorem B-2, in Part 9, for proof.)

$$\begin{aligned} E(U) &= E(r - br^2) \\ &= E(r) - bE(r^2) \\ &= E(r) - b\sigma^2 - bE(r)^2 \quad \text{since } E(r^2) = \sigma^2 + E(r)^2 \qquad \text{(App. 27A-7a)} \\ &= f[E(r), \sigma^2] \qquad \text{(App. 27A-7b)} \end{aligned}$$

Equation (App. 27A-7*b*) shows that expected utility is a function of expected return and risk as measured by the variance of returns. Expected utility varies directly with $E(r)$ and inversely with risk, since

$$\frac{dE(U)}{dE(r)} = 1 - 2bE(r) > 0$$

and

$$\frac{dE(U)}{d\sigma} = -2b < 0$$

for the values to which b and r are constrained. Thus, investors with diminishing quadratic utility of wealth from returns desire both higher $E(r)$ and less risk.

Solving Eq. (App. 27A-7*a*) for σ^2 yields Eq. (App. 27A-8*a*).

$$\sigma^2 = \left(\frac{E(r)}{b}\right) - E(r)^2 - \left(\frac{E(U)}{b}\right) \qquad \text{(App. 27A-8a)}$$

$$= \left(\frac{E(r)}{b}\right) - E(r)^2 - \text{constant} \qquad \text{(App. 27A-8b)}$$

[15] J. von Neumann and O. Morgenstern, *Theory of Games and Economic Behavior*, 3d ed., Princeton, Princeton, N.J., 1953, pp. 22–24. Or, see pages 816–817 above.

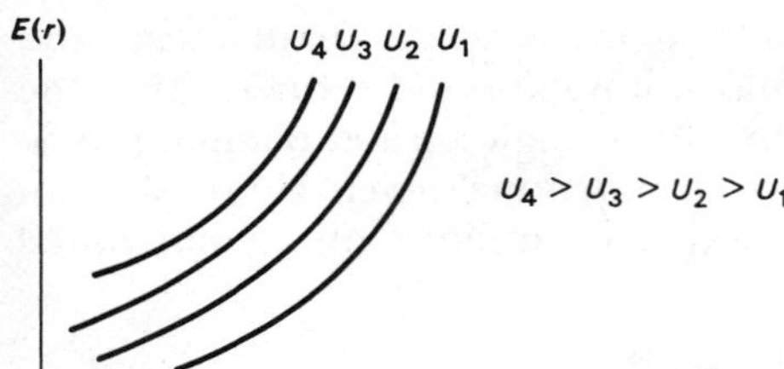

FIGURE APP. 27A-11 indifference map for risk-averter.

Varying the constant term in Eq. (App. 27A-8*a*) generates the quadratic indifference map in $[E(r), \sigma]$ space shown in Fig. App. 27A-11. Figure App. 27A-11 shows that investors whose utility is well approximated by Eqs. (App. 27A-6) and (App. 27A-7*a*) will maximize their expected utility by selecting investments with the maximum return in some risk-class, that is, by selecting efficient portfolios.

App. 27A-2.2 quadratic utility not required for $[E(r), \sigma]$ analysis

It can be shown that if the probability distribution of rates of return or wealth is a two-parameter distribution and the investor has a diminishing single-period utility function, the investor can maximize expected utility by selecting investments with the minimum risk at each rate of return (or, conversely, the maximum return at each risk-class).[16]

$$E[U(r)] = U(r)f(r|m_1, m_2)\,dr \qquad \text{(App. 27A-9}a\text{)}$$

$$= F(r|m_1, m_2) \qquad \text{(App. 27A-9}b\text{)}$$

where $f(r|m_1, m_2)$ is a two-parameter probability distribution of returns that is completely specified by m_1 and m_2. For example, if Ms. Investor has a logarithmic utility function (that is, diminishing marginal utility) and if the probability distribution is a two-parameter distribution (such as a normal distribution), she will maximize her expected utility by maximizing returns at any given risk-class, since $dE(U)/dE(r) = dF/dm_1 > 0$ and $dE(U)/\sigma^2 = dF/dm_2 < 0$. Thus, selection of investments in terms of $E(r)$ and σ does not require a quadratic utility function.

APP. 27A-3 CONCLUSIONS

This book deals with investors who have diminishing but positive marginal utility of wealth and/or returns. Such investors, this chapter has shown, prefer more wealth to less wealth but prefer less risk to more risk. In an uncertain world, these investors will maximize the expected utility from their investment activities by selecting assets that have (1) the maximum expected return in their risk-class, or conversely, (2) the minimum risk at any particular level of expected return.

[16] J. Tobin, "Liquidity Preference as Behavior Towards Risk," *Review of Economic Studies,* February 1958, pp. 65–86, and M. K. Richter, "Cardinal Utility, Portfolio Selection of Taxation," *Review of Economic Studies,* June 1960, pp. 152–160.

The objective of rational investment management, then, is to delineate and select those investments that have the maximum expected return within the risk-class the investor prefers over the investor's single-period planning horizon. The investor need not always select an individual asset. He or she can construct a portfolio that yields higher expected utility than an individual asset.

APP. 27A-4 QUESTIONS

1. If people's utility is determined largely by what they consume, how do investors derive utility from the rates of return on their investments? After all, a rate of return cannot be eaten.
2. Draw a graph of the utility-of-wealth function for a risk-lover. What are the characteristics of a risk-lover's marginal utility of wealth?
3. If their risk is the same, is investment *A* or *B* better? Show how you choose between them.

	A	*B*
Cost at time $t = 0$	$W_0 = \$500$	$W_0 = \$40$
Proceeds at time $t > 0$	$W_T = \$800$	$W_T = \$95$

4. How does risk affect utility? Use formulas and/or graphs to explain.
5. Rank the desirability of the following investments. Show your work graphically.

investment	$E(r)$, %	σ, %
A	10	5
B	10	10
C	5	5
D	12	10

6. Write down your social security number. Assume that you can purchase a risky investment that will pay one of two equally likely rates of return. This investment will pay the rate of return indicated by the last digit in your social security number with a .5 probability and the rate of return indicated by the next-to-last digit with a .5 probability. Calculate the expected return of this investment. For example, for the social security number 307-38-3152, the expected return is $.5(5\%) + .5(2\%) = 3.5\% = E(r)$. If you were the risk-averse investor shown in Fig. App. 27A-3, would you rather have a certain (that is, one riskless) investment paying the expected return calculated from the last two digits of your social security number, or the risky investment based on the equal probability of the last two digits? Explain. Explain what the risk-indifferent investor in Fig.

App. 27A-4 and the risk-lover in Fig. App. 27A-5 would do if confronted with this same choice between a certain expected return and a risky investment with the same expected return.

APP. 27A-5 SELECTED REFERENCES

M. Friedman and L. J. Savage, "The Utility Analysis of Choices Involving Risk," *The Journal of Political Economy,* August 1948, pp. 279–304. A classic paper rationalizing choice in uncertainty with the expected-utility hypothesis. Only algebra is used.

H. Markowitz, *Portfolio Selection,* Wiley, New York; 1959. Chapters 10 through 13 discuss the utility theory underlying the selection of efficient assets. Most of the mathematics is first-year college algebra.

portfolio performance evaluation

Billions of dollars are kept invested in marketable securities in the United States. Most of these funds are managed by professional investment managers (or money managers) who earn their living by providing portfolio management services for fees. The largest and most popular types of publicly available portfolio management services are provided by the *institutional investors* below.[1]

1. The trust departments of large, big-city commercial banks
2. Investment advisory services (which are usually subsidiaries of mutual fund management companies, security brokerage firms, or investment newsletter services)
3. The investment management departments of life insurance companies
4. Investment companies (primarily, the open-end companies called mutual funds)

The publicly available portfolio management services receive the funds they manage from the following major sources of investable wealth.

1. Pension funds[2]

[1] *Institutional Investor*, "America's Largest Money Managers," August 1984. Pages 115–174 list the 300 largest money management organizations in the U.S. The smallest of these managed over $1 billion in 1983. The article gives the names, addresses, amount of funds managed for the last 2 years, size, ranking, and categorical breakdown of where the managed money is invested.

[2] *Institutional Investor*, "1984 Pensions Directory." January 1984. Pages 99–215 list the names and addresses of the 500 largest pensions in the U.S., tells how much money was in each fund, and lists the professional money managers that are paid to manage part of the funds. The most popular pension fund managers are also listed separately.

2. Substantial individuals (for example, wealthy widows and orphans)
3. College endowments
4. Charitable foundations

These investors own and ultimately control the funds, but they frequently turn temporary control of the investment decisions over to some external portfolio management service. Before delegating the investment management function to a hired consultant, however, they ask themselves two questions. First, "Should we try to manage the funds ourselves?" Most of them have decided to seek investment management services externally in the hope of obtaining expert advice that would more than pay for itself in better returns for their portfolios. This leads to the second question, "Which portfolio management service should we select?"

This chapter addresses itself to the question of how to select the "best" portfolio management service. The tools taught in this chapter are also useful to the portfolio managers themselves, if they wish to be able to evaluate and improve their own money management skills. The remainder of the chapter explains both good and bad ways to evaluate the portfolio performance of the hundreds of bank trust departments, investment advisors, investment management departments of life insurance companies, mutual funds, and other money managers. Tools that can be used to rank the historical performance of all these different portfolios will be explained. Some naive methods and some logical methods of portfolio performance will be considered and compared.

All the logical methods are derived from various parts of the risk-return analysis presented in Chaps. 9 and 10. Regardless of whether the old, naive methods or the newer, more logical methods of portfolio performance are used, however, one common problem exists: *data availability*. Historical-rate-of-return data are required in order to evaluate the investment performance of any portfolio. Unfortunately, not all portfolio management services make adequate data about their past performance publicly available.

The performance of dozens of mutual funds is evaluated in this chapter. Mutual funds are examined rather than other portfolios because, by law, mutual funds must publicly disclose their operating results. Also, provisions of the Investment Company Act of 1940 limit mutual funds' use of leverage (that is, issuing debt), buying on margin, taking more than 9 percent of the proceeds from the sales of new shares for sales commissions, selling the funds' shares on margin, and short selling. These requirements ensure a certain amount of similarity among mutual funds. Because of these similarities, plus their tax-exempt income status,[3] the requirements that they disclose their holdings and income, and their popularity with investors, mutual funds make a valuable subject for study. Before evaluating the investment performance of mutual fund managers, let's first investigate the organizations and objectives of mutual funds.

[3] Mutual funds are exempt from paying income taxes on the income they earn for their shareholders only if they immediately pay almost all of it out to the shareholders.

28-1 INVESTMENT COMPANIES DEFINED

Investors with modest amounts to invest may be well advised not to buy securities, because they have insufficient funds to buy a diversified portfolio. Since investors should buy stock in lots of 100 shares or more to incur lower stockbroker round-lot commissions, and since the average New York Stock Exchange (NYSE) stock costs about $30 per share, it takes, on average, $3,000 per issue (100 shares times an average price of $30 per share), to buy one round lot of stock. Multiplication of $3,000 per stock issue by 10 different stock issues needed to obtain diversification gives $30,000 (10 issues times $3,000 per issue) as the minimum needed to begin investing in individual securities in a diversified manner. Diversification is, of course, valuable as a means of reducing investment risk.[4]

Since millions of aspiring investors lack (1) sufficient capital to buy a diversified portfolio, (2) the expertise to manage a portfolio, and/or (3) the time to manage a portfolio, enterprising portfolio managers have created public portfolios of diversified securities in which investors can buy a small or large number of shares. These public portfolios, called investment companies, typically assume one of two basic forms: (1) the open-end investment company, usually called a mutual fund, and (2) the closed-end investment fund.

28-1.1 mutual funds

More than 17 million individuals, companies, and other organizations own shares in over 600 different *open-end investment companies* in the United States.[5] The size of these individual accounts ranges from a child's single share, valued at only a few dollars, to a multimillion-dollar pension fund's numerous shares in several different mutual funds. Likewise, the total asset holdings of individual mutual funds range from only a few million dollars to hundreds of millions of dollars.

Mutual funds are conduits from savings to investment. The funds commingle the savings of many people into one large, diversified investment portfolio. Many mutual funds own over 100 different issues of stocks and/or bonds. But no single investor owns any particular asset. Instead, an investor who has purchased a certain percentage of the mutual fund's total shares outstanding owns that percentage of every asset and every liability the fund obtains. Investors can cash in their shares in the fund whenever they wish, at the net asset value per share on that day. The *net asset value per share* equals the value of the fund's total net assets after liabilities divided by the total number of shares outstanding on that day. Thus, the net asset value per share fluctuates every time any asset experiences a change in its market price.

According to Subchapter M of the Internal Revenue Code, all income earned by a mutual fund is tax-exempt if the fund (1) distributes at least 90 percent of its cash dividend and interest income as it is received, (2) diversifies by placing no more than 5 percent of its total assets in any one security issue,

[4] Selection of the number 10 as the minimum number of stock issues needed to obtain diversification is discussed analytically in Chap. 25. The discussion is based on the work by John H. Evans and S. H. Archer, "Diversification and the Reduction of Dispersion: An Empirical Analysis," *Journal of Finance*, December 1968, pp. 761–767. (See page 747 above.)

[5] Investment Company Institute, *Mutual Fund Fact Book*, 1983.

and (3) is registered with the Securities and Exchange Commission under the provisions of the Investment Company Act of 1940. Since practically every mutual fund meets these provisions, there is no double taxation (that is, taxation paid by both the fund and the shareholder on the fund's earnings).

By law, open-end investment companies are required to publish and adhere to a statement of the fund's investment objective. These statements are typically one or two paragraphs long and can be grouped into the following main categories:

1. *Growth funds.* These funds tend to invest only in common stock and plan to assume some risks to obtain stocks that are expected to yield higher returns. Figure 28-1 shows a page from a book entitled *Investment Companies* that describes one of the larger and older growth funds.
2. *Income funds.* Investment in stocks and bonds that pay high cash dividends and coupon interest is the objective of income funds. Risky stocks offering higher potential capital gains tend to be avoided in favor of "blue-chip" stocks (that is, those of large, old, stable companies).
3. *Balanced funds.* These funds divide their holdings between fixed-income securities and low-risk common stocks in order to avoid the risk of loss. These conservative funds usually have the lowest rates of return.
4. *Liquid asset funds.* These mutual funds are also called *money market funds* because they invest in money market instruments such as Treasury bills. One of the main assets of some liquid asset funds is bank deposits (called certificates of deposit, or CDs) of over \$100,000, which are left with the bank for a specified number of days. The 90-day or 180-day CDs sometimes pay one of the highest rates of interest available on practically riskless bank deposits. The liquid asset funds started in the 1960s when interest rates rose above 10 percent. Their objective is to earn high rates of interest from liquid, low-risk, short-term bonds, bank deposits, and other money market instruments. Figure 28-2 shows a page from *Donoghue's Money Fund Report* that lists many of the liquid asset mutual funds in the United States.
5. *Municipal bond funds.* These funds buy only municipal bonds to obtain their tax-exempt income. Only substantial individuals (a stockbroker's euphemism for rich people) who are in high income tax brackets usually buy shares in municipal bond mutual funds. Within the major category of municipal bond funds are two subcategories of funds: (a) short-term municipal bond funds, and (b) long-term municipal bond funds. The short-term municipal bond funds are essentially money market funds that invest only in tax-exempt, short-term debt instruments.
6. *Corporate bond funds.* These mutual funds invest in the bonds of business corporations in order to earn interest rates that are higher than U.S. States Treasury bonds pay, but, at the same time, without taking as much bankruptcy risk as do the common stock investors.

INVESTORS' RETURN FROM MUTUAL FUND INVESTING Investors obtain three types of income from owning mutual fund shares: (1) cash dividend or interest disbursements, denoted d, (2) capital gains disbursements, denoted c, and (3) changes in the fund's net asset value (nav) per share from capital gains and cash dividends not distributed to the owners, denoted $(\text{nav}_{t+1} - \text{nav}_t)$ for the

T. ROWE PRICE GROWTH STOCK FUND, INC.

The major objectives of the fund are to seek long-term appreciation of capital and increased future income through investment in well-established growth companies. Ordinarily, the assets of the fund will be invested primarily in common stocks, but policy is sufficiently flexible to permit the fund to establish and maintain reserves which will enable it to take advantage of buying opportunities.

At the 1983 year-end, the fund had 95.3% of its assets in common stocks, of which a sizable proportion was concentrated in five industry groups: information processing (9.1% of assets), electronic components (8.1%), general merchandise (6.3%), electronic systems (6.1%), and media & communications (4.9%). The five largest individual common stock investments were IBM (9.1% of assets), Motorola and General Electric (each 3.5%), Hewlett-Packard (3.2%), and Times-Mirror (2.9%). The rate of portfolio turnover during the year was 62.7% of average assets. Unrealized appreciation was 19.4% of year-end assets.

Statistical History

	AT YEAR-ENDS								ANNUAL DATA				
					% of Assets in								
Year	Total Net Assets ($)	Number of Share-holders	Net Asset Value Per Share ($)	Yield (%)	Cash & Equiv-alent	Bonds & Pre-ferreds	Com-mon Stocks	Income Div-idends ($)	Capital Gains Distribu-tion ($)	Expense Ratio (%)	Offering Price ($) High	Offering Price ($) Low
1983	1,013,083,410	100,202	15.21	3.3	5	—	95	0.50	—	0.50	16.26	13.39
1982	1,007,506,534	99,898	14.07	3.8	6	—	94	0.534	0.089	0.50	14.72	9.97
1981	919,426,628	98,614	12.72	3.9	6	—	94	0.497	0.044	0.49	15.27	11.81
1980	1,133,745,871	105,748	15.08	2.8	11	—	89	0.419	—	0.49	15.58	10.39
1979	942,946,894	116,794	12.02	2.8	5	—	95	0.331	—	0.51	12.33	10.43
1978	974,832,394	138,034	11.12	2.5	4	—	96	0.277	—	0.52	12.64	9.24
1977	986,066,265	159,140	10.25	2.2	2	—	98	0.226	—	0.51	11.23	9.46
1976	1,174,928,903	179,108	11.26	2.1	3	—	97	0.231	—	0.51	11.68	10.26
1975	1,112,897,758	196,103	10.19	1.3	6	1*	93	0.129	—	0.53	11.21	7.73
1974	797,177,531	197,742	7.65	2.7	12	—	88	0.215	0.23	0.55	12.05	6.87
1973	1,121,029,445	198,438	11.91	1.1	9	1	90	0.14	0.54	0.51	16.81	11.19

* Includes a substantial proportion of convertible issues.
Note: Figures adjusted for 2-for-1 split, effective 5/1/73.

An assumed investment of $10,000 in this fund, with capital gains accepted in shares and income dividends reinvested, is illustrated below. The explanation on Page 163 must be read in conjunction with this illustration.

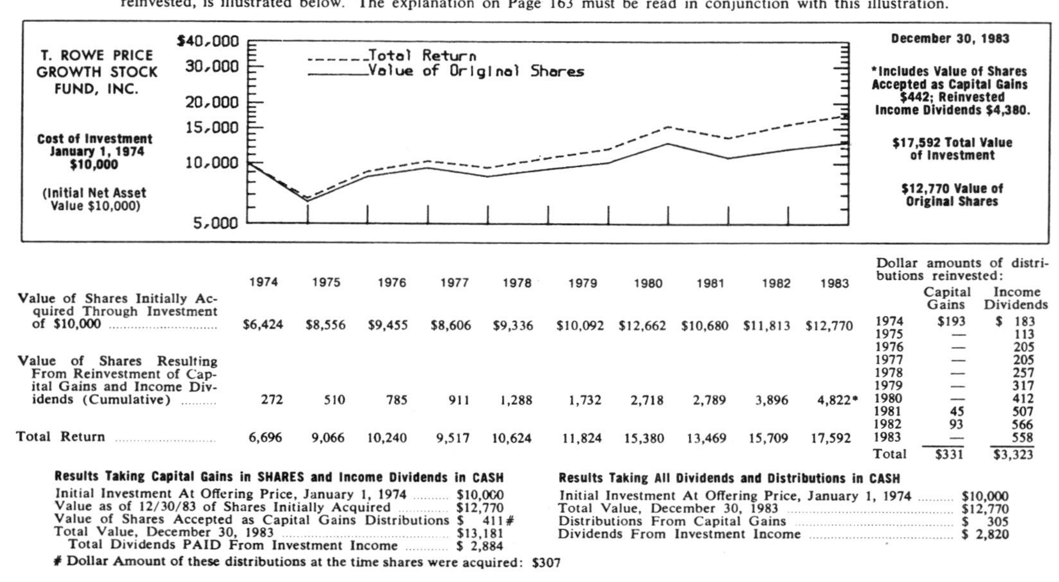

	1974	1975	1976	1977	1978	1979	1980	1981	1982	1983
Value of Shares Initially Acquired Through Investment of $10,000	$6,424	$8,556	$9,455	$8,606	$9,336	$10,092	$12,662	$10,680	$11,813	$12,770
Value of Shares Resulting From Reinvestment of Capital Gains and Income Dividends (Cumulative)	272	510	785	911	1,288	1,732	2,718	2,789	3,896	4,822*
Total Return	6,696	9,066	10,240	9,517	10,624	11,824	15,380	13,469	15,709	17,592

Dollar amounts of distributions reinvested:

	Capital Gains	Income Dividends
1974	$193	$ 183
1975	—	113
1976	—	205
1977	—	205
1978	—	257
1979	—	317
1980	—	412
1981	45	507
1982	93	566
1983	—	558
Total	$331	$3,323

Results Taking Capital Gains in SHARES and Income Dividends in CASH

Initial Investment At Offering Price, January 1, 1974	$10,000
Value as of 12/30/83 of Shares Initially Acquired	$12,770
Value of Shares Accepted as Capital Gains Distributions	$ 411#
Total Value, December 30, 1983	$13,181
Total Dividends PAID From Investment Income	$ 2,884

\# Dollar Amount of these distributions at the time shares were acquired: $307

Results Taking All Dividends and Distributions in CASH

Initial Investment At Offering Price, January 1, 1974	$10,000
Total Value, December 30, 1983	$12,770
Distributions From Capital Gains	$ 305
Dividends From Investment Income	$ 2,820

FIGURE 28-1 mutual fund information from one sample page of book entitled *Investment Companies*. (*Source*: *Investment Companies*, 1984 Edition, Wiesenberger Financial Services, a division of Warren, Gorham and Lamont Inc., New York, p. 424.)

SLYC Money Fund Performance

Week Ending August 1, 1984

ASSETS ($mil)	SLYC Family Taxable Money Funds	30-Day Avg. 8/1	12-Mo. YTD 6/84	Avg Mat days	Portfolio Holdings (%): U.S. Treas.	U.S. Other	Repos	CDs	Banker's Accept	Comm'l Paper	Euro$, CDs, TDs	Yankee$, CDs, BAs	Non-Prime
1.3	Babson M.M.F. Federal Port.	9.7	9.0	17	7	63	30m	–	–	–	–	–	–
61.9	Babson M.M.F. Prime Port.	10.5	9.4	27	–	–	2m	10	44	44	–	–	–
233.9	Boston Company Cash Mgt	10.9	9.5	55	–	–	5m	–	12	52	19	12	–
22.7	Boston Company Gov't M.F.	9.9	9.0	20	48	–	52m	–	–	–	–	–	–
103.6	Bull & Bear Dollar Reserves	10.5	9.2	28	–	–	–	–	2	85	9	4	–
471.7	Columbia Daily Income	10.2	9.2	31	8	12	2	–	15	63	–	–	–
7,857.3	Dreyfus Liquid Assets	10.6	9.5	56	9	–	–	8	4	4	75	–	–
880.7	Dreyfus M.M. Instruments Gov't	9.9	9.3	68	63	–	37m	–	–	–	–	–	–
4,195.6	Fidelity Cash Reserves	10.6	9.5	36	2	–	–	4	2	25	19	47	1
2,717.4	Fidelity Daily Income	10.5	9.7	31	6	–	–	30	20	42	–	–	2
384.0	Fidelity U.S. Gov't Res.	10.2	9.3	29	8	33	59m	–	–	–	–	–	–
254.7	Financial Daily Income	10.9	9.8	36	–	–	–	–	2	67	–	–	31
63.3	Founders Money Market	10.2	9.3	20	–	–	–	–	–	100	–	–	–
4,286.9	Kemper Money Market+	11.0	9.9	23	–	–	–	4	–	45	20	18	13
19.2	Lexington Gov't Secs. M.M.F.	10.3	9.1	31	11	21	68m	–	–	–	–	–	–
231.1	Lexington Money Market	10.7	9.6	51	–	–	12m	6	–	58a	–	24	–
6.8	Money Fund of U.S. Treas. Secs.+	9.0	8.4	1	–	–	100m	–	–	–	–	–	–
34.4	SAFECO M.M.M.F.	10.9	9.8	35	–	3	–	–	–	44	–	–	53
1,001.7	Scudder Cash Investment Trust	10.5	9.3	35	27	–	4	18	23	28	–	–	–
127.4	Scudder Gov't Money Fund	9.7	8.9	36	87	–	13m	–	–	–	–	–	–
923.6	SteinRoe Cash Reserves	10.7	9.5	31	–	–	–	22	36	42	–	–	–
34.2	SteinRoe Gov't Reserves	9.7	8.8	28	49	–	51m	–	–	–	–	–	–
3,007.6	T. Rowe Price Prime Reserve	10.8	9.7	30	–	–	–	9	3	55	18	1	14
171.2	T. Rowe Price U.S. Treas. M.F.	9.9	9.0	28	52	–	48m	–	–	–	–	–	–
27.1	USAA Federal Secs. M.M.F.	9.3	8.6	76	100	–	–	–	–	–	–	–	–
280.6	USAA Money Market Fund	11.0	9.5	33	–	4	–	17	3	76	–	–	–
545.8	Value Line Cash Fund	10.8	9.6	25	–	–	–	–	–	12	–	–	88
34.0	Vanguard M.M.T. Insured Port.	10.3	9.1	21	3	–	10m	–	13	74	–	–	–
436.3	Vanguard M.M.T. Federal	10.2	9.4	33	4	81	15	–	–	–	–	–	–
1,367.8	Vanguard M.M.T. Prime	10.9	9.7	38	–	–	3m	29	21	47	–	–	–

Net Assets ($ mil)	SLYC Family Tax-Free Money Funds	Investment Results (%): 30 Day 8/1	12-Mo YTD as of 6/84	Avg Mat (days)	Portfolio Holdings (%): Demand Notes MIG 1 & MIG 2	Project Notes	Gen'l Obligation Notes & Bonds: MIG 1	MIG 2	Revenue Notes & Bonds: MIG 1	MIG 2	Comm'l Paper A-P1 MIG	Other
52.4	Boston Co. MA Tax-Free M.F.	5.1	–	55	17	20	–	–	42	–	21	–
10.5	Boston Co. Tax-Free Money Fund	5.5	–	27	40	29	–	–	–	–	31	–
1,729.2	Dreyfus Tax-Exempt M.M.F., Inc.	5.5	5.2	81	25	13	20	4	19	3	12	4
64.3	Fidelity Mass. Tax-Free/M.M.P.	5.0	–	37	–	46	–	5	–	–	27	22
2,437.8	Fidelity Tax-Exempt M.M. Trust	5.6	5.3	42	28	28	9	7	–	–	20	8
3.3	Financial Tax-Free Money Fund	5.3	5.0	28	61	2	5	–	2	2	26	2
60.9	Lexington Tax Free M.F., Inc.	6.0	5.5	108	52	–	1	10	25	11	–	1
214.7	Scudder Tax-Free Money Fund	5.4	4.9	55	47	30	10	–	–	–	13	–
147.0	SteinRoe Tax-Exempt M.F.	5.4	5.1	49	30	1	4	–	8	–	57	–
795.3	T. Rowe Price Tax-Exempt M.F.	5.9	5.4	112	41	–	8	1	10	2	12	26
16.8	USAA Tax Exempt M.M.F.	5.9	–	84	32	3	9	7	–	–	2	47
5.4	Value Line Tax-Exempt Fund	6.4	–	18	84	–	–	–	–	–	4	12
393.0	Vanguard Muni. Bond Fund M.M.	5.9	5.4	85	45	2	–	–	46	–	7	–

FIGURE 28-2 statistics about money market mutual funds. (*Source*: *Donoghue's Moneyletter*, August 1984, vol. 5, no. 16)

tth period. The one-period rate of return for a mutual fund share is defined in Eq. (28-1).

$$r_t = \frac{c_t + d_t + (\text{nav}_{t+1} - \text{nav}_t)}{\text{nav}_t} \tag{28-1}$$

Mutual fund investors do not receive the entire rate of return defined in Eq. (28-1) because of two deductions. First, the fund's management fee of from .5 to 1.5 percent per year of the net asset value is deducted to pay the portfolio's management expenses. Second, some mutual funds, called *load funds*, deduct from 1 to 8.5 percent (usually the latter) of the mutual fund owner's original investment to pay a commission to the mutual fund salesperson. *No-load funds* are mutual funds that sell their shares by mail without sales representatives and charge their investors no sales commission. Some mutual funds may charge no up-front load, but a liquidation fee of from 1 to 8 percent may be charged.

All mutual funds are called open-end because they can keep selling more shares and thus keep growing larger as long as investors will buy more shares. Fund managers want their funds to grow larger so they can charge their management-fee percentage on a larger amount of total assets and thus pay themselves higher salaries. The investment performance of actual mutual funds is analyzed and ranked later in this chapter.

28-1.2 closed-end funds

Closed-end investment companies are like mutual funds to the extent that both are publicly owned investment portfolios. But closed-end funds differ in several important respects. First, as their name implies, closed-end funds cannot sell more shares after their initial offering—thus, the size is limited. Second, the shares of closed-end funds are not redeemable at their net asset value, as are the shares in a mutual fund. Instead, the shares of the closed-end funds trade on stock exchanges at market prices that may be above or below their net asset values.[6] These two distinctions between closed-end and open-end funds are essentially the best way to define the closed-end funds. Closed-end funds have diversification and investment objectives that differ over a much wider range than the open-end funds, making them very difficult to describe.

Over the years, the two distinguishing features of closed-end funds have fallen into enough disfavor to limit growth and importance of the funds. Thus, there are fewer closed-end funds than open-end funds, and their numbers have not grown significantly in recent years.

Since closed-end funds are essentially marketable shares of common stock, their one-period rates of return are calculated by using Eq. (2-2), on page 32 of Chap. 2, just like common stock returns.

The rest of this chapter analyzes mutual fund returns data. These data are analyzed in order (1) to show how investment performance analysis can be

[6] For a discussion of the prices of closed-end shares, see Ken J. Boudreaux, "The Pricing of Mutual Fund Shares," *Financial Analysts Journal*, January–February 1974, pp. 26–32. Also see Burton G. Malkiel, "The Valuation of Closed-End Investment Company Shares," *Journal of Finance*, June 1977, vol. 32, no. 3, pp. 847–860. See also Rex Thompson, "The Information Content of Discounts and Premiums on Closed-End Shares," *Journal of Financial Economics*, June–September 1978, pp. 151–186.

accomplished, and (2) to see if mutual fund managers can earn returns for their investors that exceed the returns available from other investment alternatives.

28-2 RANKING FUNDS' AVERAGE RETURNS

When an investor considers the purchase of shares in mutual funds, the first question to be asked is: "Can the mutual funds earn a higher return for me than I can earn for myself?" Table 28-1 shows data for 39 mutual funds' performances for the decade from 1951 to 1960 inclusive.[7]

Column 1 of Table 28-1 shows the average rate of return for each mutual fund. These returns are what would have been earned if a tax-exempt investor had purchased shares in each fund on January 1,1951, held them 10 years while reinvesting the dividends, and sold the shares at the end of December 1960. It will be noted that only 18 of the mutual funds (that is, less than half of them) were able to earn a rate of return above the 14.7 percent that the investor could have expected to earn by randomly picking stocks listed on the New York Stock Exchange or using some other naive buy-and-hold strategy.[8] Of the 39 funds, the best performance exceeded the average by only four percentage points. The data indicate that, on the average, the mutual funds did not earn returns for investors that a naive investor could not attain alone at less cost.

Columns 2 through 11 of Table 28-1 show the rankings of the 39 funds' yearly rates of return. The most striking feature of the rankings is their lack of consistency. None of the 39 funds was able to consistently outperform the naive buy-and-hold strategy over the decade.

28-3 EFFICIENCY AND RELIABILITY OF THE FUNDS' PERFORMANCES

One might question whether the mutual funds are really as poor at managing investments as the data in Table 28-1 indicate. After all, they might be maximizing their returns in a very low risk-class where high returns were not

[7] For a ranking of mutual fund performances from 1970 to 1979 see J. C. Francis, *Management of Investments*, McGraw-Hill, New York, 1983, table 27-1, p. 588.

[8] A naive buy-and-hold strategy means randomly selecting securities (for example, with an unaimed dart), buying them, and holding them regardless of what information becomes available about them or the market. The naive buy-and-hold strategy is used as a standard of comparison because it represents an investment that someone with no skill should be able to earn with average luck—no unusual good luck or unusual bad luck is involved. The actual returns from a naive buy-and-hold strategy have been estimated by different researchers. See J. Lorie and L. Fisher, "Rate of Return on Investments in Common Stocks: The Year-by-Year Record, 1926–1965," *Journal of Business*, July 1968, pp. 291–316. Also see R. G. Ibbotson and R. A. Sinquefield, *Stocks, Bonds, Bills, and Inflation: The Past and the Future*, Financial Analysts Research Foundation, Charlottesville, Va., 1982; see pages 182–185 above. Estimates of more diversified portfolios were also prepared. See R. G. Ibbotson and Carol L. Fall, "The U.S. Wealth Portfolio: Components of Capital Market Values and Returns," *Journal of Portfolio Management*, Fall 1979. Also see R. G. Ibbotson and Laurence B. Siegel, "The World Wealth Portfolio," *Journal of Portfolio Management*, Winter 1983. More recently, see *Stocks, Bonds, Bills, and Inflation: 1985 Yearbook*, Ibbotson Associates, Chicago, Ill., 1985.

TABLE 28-1 year-by-year ranking of individual fund returns

fund	return on net (1)	YEAR 1951 (2)	1952 (3)	1953 (4)	1954 (5)	1955 (6)	1956 (7)	1957 (8)	1958 (9)	1959 (10)	1960 (11)
Keystone Lower Price	18.7	29	1	38	5	3	8	35	1	1	36
T Rowe Price Growth	18.7	1	33	2	8	14	15	2	25	7	4
Dreyfuss	18.4	37	37	14	3	7	11	3	2	3	7
Television Electronic	18.4	21	4	9	2	33	20	16	2	4	20
National Investors Corp.	18.0	3	35	4	19	27	4	5	5	8	1
De Vegh Mutual Fund	17.7	32	4	1	8	14	4	8	15	23	36
Growth Industries	17.0	7	34	14	17	9	9	20	5	6	11
Massachusetts Investors Growth	16.9	5	36	31	11	9	1	23	4	9	4
Franklin Custodian	16.5	26	2	4	13	33	20	16	5	9	4
Investment Co. of America	16.0	21	15	14	11	17	15	23	15	15	15
Chemical Fund, Inc.	15.6	1	39	14	27	3	33	1	27	4	23
Founders Mutual	15.6	21	13	25	8	2	20	16	11	13	28
Investment Trust of Boston	15.[illegible]	6	3	25	3	14	26	31	20	29	20
American Mutual	15.5	14	13	4	22	14	13	16	25	25	4
Keystone Growth	15.3	29	15	25	1	1	1	39	11	18	38
Keystone High	15.2	10	7	3	27	23	36	5	27	25	11
Aberdeen Fund	15.1	32	23	9	25	9	7	10	27	7	30

Massachusetts Investors Trust	14.8	8	9	14	16	9	15	20	18	32	28
Texas Fund, Inc.	14.6	3	15	9	32	23	26	5	27	37	7
Eaton & Howard Stock	14.4	14	9	4	17	20	15	13	37	29	17
Guardian Mutual	14.4	21	26	25	34	31	29	13	20	15	2
Scudder, Stevens, Clark	14.3	14	23	14	19	27	15	29	9	15	30
Investors Stock Fund	14.2	8	28	21	22	27	20	23	5	29	23
Fidelity Fund, Inc.	14.1	21	6	31	6	23	29	33	11	25	23
Fundamental Inv.	13.8	14	15	31	15	9	11	31	18	25	30
Century Shares	13.5	14	28	35	25	3	20	23	31	34	2
Bullock Fund Ltd.	13.5	29	9	21	19	14	9	20	34	34	20
Financial Industries	13.0	26	15	31	13	19	29	34	20	9	35
Group Common Stock	13.0	38	8	25	27	27	33	8	20	34	17
Incorporated Investors	12.9	14	13	37	6	3	13	37	11	18	39
Equity Fund	12.9	14	27	21	32	31	33	13	31	18	23
Selected American Shares	12.8	21	15	21	31	23	20	23	15	32	30
Dividend Shares	12.7	32	7	14	34	20	32	4	37	37	11
General Capital Corp.	12.4	10	28	9	38	35	39	23	34	13	23
Wisconsin Fund	12.3	32	26	4	37	35	38	10	34	18	7
International Resources	12.3	10	37	39	22	35	1	37	39	1	11
Delaware Fund	12.1	36	23	25	27	39	26	29	9	23	30
Hamilton Fund	11.9	38	28	9	34	35	36	10	31	18	17
Colonial Energy	10.9	10	15	35	39	20	4	36	20	39	10

Source: E. F. Fama, "The Behavior of Stock Prices," *Journal of Business*, January 1965, table 18, p. 93.

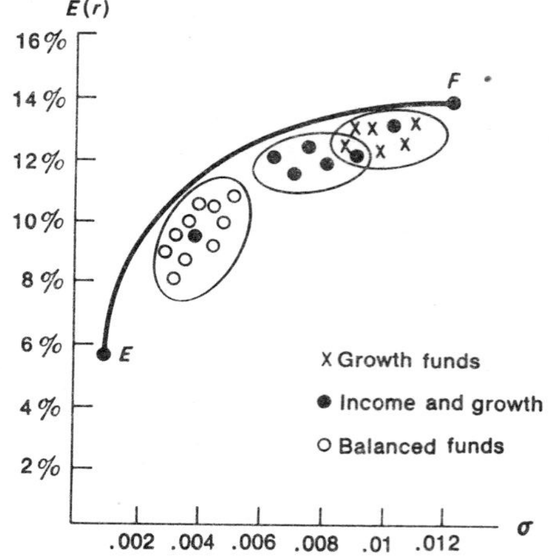

FIGURE 28-3 performance of 23 mutual funds from 1946 to 1956 in risk-return space. (*Source*: Donald E. Farrar. *The Investment Decision Under Uncertainty*, Prentice-Hall, Englewood Cliffs, N.J., 1962, p. 73.)

available. This would mean the funds were efficient investments along the bottom portion of the efficient frontier. Figure 28-3 shows the actual performance of 23 mutual funds in risk-return space relative to the efficient frontier (that is, the curve *EF*) that existed at that time.

Figure 28-3 was prepared from monthly data on the 23 mutual funds from 1946 to 1956. It shows that none of the funds was an efficient asset and only a few had average returns that were within one percentage point of the efficient frontier. It is interesting to note, however, that the funds tended to cluster into groups. The funds that sought growth and were willing to assume risk to attain it formed a cluster that tends to lie above that of the less aggressive funds, and the income-growth funds clearly lie above the risk-avoiding balanced funds. Mutual fund managers evidently are able to distinguish between the risk and return characteristics of their investments and stay in some preferred risk-class fairly consistently. Unfortunately, they do not all seem to be able to follow their published objectives very well.

According to the Investment Company Act of 1940, mutual funds must publish a written statement of their investment objectives and make it available to their shareholders. An objective can be changed only if the majority of the shareholders consent in advance to the new objective. These investment objectives fall into the following four categories.

1. Growth
2. Growth and income
3. Income and growth
4. Income, growth, and stability (called a balanced fund)

These objectives are listed in descending order with respect to the aggressiveness with which the fund's management implies it will seek high average rate of return and assume the corresponding risks.

The stated objectives that mutual funds issue to their shareholders are not dependable; that is, there is sometimes no relation between the stated investment objectives and the actual performance of some mutual funds. Although the funds shown in Fig. 28-3 tended to remain in fairly consistent risk-return groupings over time, the risk-return grouping did not align with the funds' stated objectives in some cases. As a matter of fact, *quantitative risk measures* give a clearer picture of the funds' investment objectives than what the fund managements say in their published statements.

28-3.1 portfolio's risk-classes

All portfolios' average rates of return vary widely over time as the market alternates between bullish and bearish periods. Therefore, average rates of return are not satisfactory measures with which to classify mutual funds' risk and return. Certain quantitative risk measures, however, are fairly stationary over time. And, since risk and return are positively related, they also furnish an indication of whether the portfolio can be expected to earn a high, medium, or low rate of return in the long run—that is, over at least one complete business cycle.

Two quantitative risk surrogates are appropriate for measuring the historical risk of portfolios. First, the *standard deviation* of historical rates of return may be used to measure total risk. Second, portfolios' *beta* coefficients from their characteristic lines (which were fit with historical data) may be used to measure systematic or undiversifiable risk. Either of these risk surrogates is satisfactory for categorizing portfolio risk. Examples of both will be explained later in this chapter.

Mutual funds' beta coefficients may be classified as explained in Table 28-2. Table 28-3 shows the relationship between the two risk surrogates and the average rates of return for 103 mutual funds. The data for these statistics were gathered from January 1960 to June 1968. Table 28-3 shows the two risk

TABLE 28-2 portfolio systematic risk measures defined

range of beta	level of funds' risk	description of price volatility
.5– .7	Low	Share prices vary about half the rate of the market index.
.7– .9	Medium	Share prices rise about 80% of the rate of the market index.
.9–1.3	High	Share prices vary directly with the rate of change in the market index.

TABLE 28-3 risk-return relationships for mutual funds

risk-class	range of betas	number of mutual funds	average beta	average variance, σ^2	average rate of return
Low	.5– .7	28	.619	.000877	.091 = 9.1%
Medium	.7– .9	53	.786	.001543	.106 = 10.6%
High	.9–1.1	22	.992	.002304	.135 = 13.5%

Source: Irwin Friend, Marshall E. Blume, and Jean Crockett, *Mutual Funds and Other Institutional Investors: A New Perspective*, McGraw-Hill, New York, 1970, p. 150.

TABLE 28-4 comparison of mutual funds performances with their stated objectives, January 1960 to June 1968*

beta coefficient	NUMBER OF FUNDS IN CATEGORY				AVERAGE RATE OF RETURN, %			
	growth	growth & income	income & growth	income, growth, & stability	growth	growth & income	income & growth	income, growth, & stability
.5 to .7	3	5	4	16	6.9	10.1	9.7	9.1
.7 to .9	15	24	7	7	11.2	10.0	10.0	12.2
.9 to 1.1	20	1	0	1	13.8	9.5		13.5

* Investment objectives as classified by Arthur Wiesenberger Services in 1967.

Source: Irwin Friend, Marshall E. Blume, and Jean Crockett, *Mutual Funds and Other Institutional Investors: A New Perspective*, McGraw-Hill, New York, 1970, p. 150.

surrogates are highly positively related with each other and with the portfolios' average rates of return.

Table 28-4 compares the portfolios' published investment objectives with their quantitative risk and average return statistics. It shows that the portfolios' beta coefficients were much better indicators of the portfolios' actual performance than were their published statements.

28-4 SHARPE'S PORTFOLIO PERFORMANCE MEASURE

In assessing the performance of a portfolio, it is necessary to consider both risk *and* return. In the ranking of portfolios' average returns, the skill with which management minimized risk is not considered; rank is therefore an oversimplified performance measure. However, it is often desirable to be able to *rank* portfolios' performance. Determining the relative efficiency of portfolios, as done in Fig. 28-3, is a more comprehensive analysis of portfolios' performance. The real need is for an index of portfolio performance that is determined by *both* the return and the risk of a portfolio. Equation (28-2*a*) defines a single-parameter portfolio performance index that calculates its index number from both the risk and return statistics. The numerator of Eq. (28-2*a*), $r_i - R$, is called the risk-premium for portfolio i. The *risk-premium* is that return over and above the riskless rate that is paid to induce investors to assume risk. (See Box 28-1 on page 845.)

Sharpe's index of performance generates one (ordinal) number that is determined by both the risk and the return of the portfolio (or other investment) being assessed. Figure 28-4 graphically depicts Sharpe's index. S_i measures the slope of the solid line starting at the riskless rate R in Fig. 28-4 and running out to asset i. Thus, $S_C > S_B > S_A$ indicates that asset C is a better performer than asset B, and B is better than A. The fact that the portfolios have different average returns or risks does not hinder a direct comparison with Sharpe's performance index.[9]

Sharpe gathered data on the risk and return of 34 mutual funds for the decade from 1954 to 1963 inclusive and ranked their performances. Table 28-5 lists the average return, standard deviation, and Sharpe's performance measure for the 34 mutual funds. Sharpe also calculated these same statistics for the Dow Jones Industrial Average (DJIA) to use as a standard of comparison in evaluating the performance of the funds. The DIJA is a sample of 30 stocks of large, old, blue-chip firms that are popular with investors. Figure 28-5 shows a frequency distribution of the S_i's for the 34 mutual funds listed in Table 28-5, with the DJIA included for comparison purposes.

[9] I. Friend and M. Blume, "Measurement of Portfolio Performance under Uncertainty," *American Economic Review*, September 1970, pp. 561–575. This study questions portfolio performance measures. In particular, the authors point out the unrealistic assumption on which both the Sharpe and Treynor portfolio performance measures are based. Both performance rankings can be very sensitive to the value assumed for the riskless rate of interest. Both models are based on the unrealistic assumption that investors can borrow and lend at rate R.

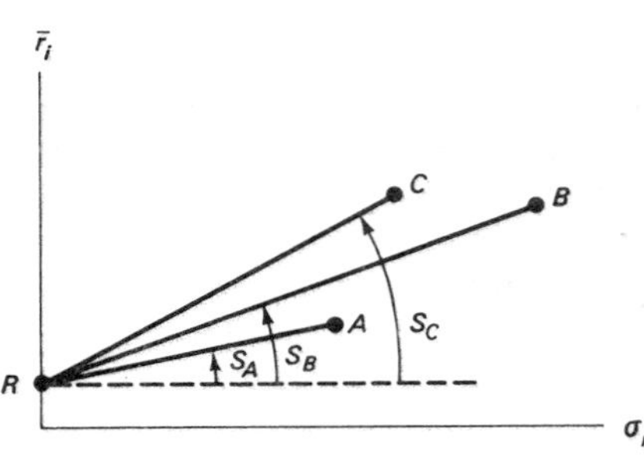

FIGURE 28-4 Sharpe's index of portfolio performance measures the ratio of risk-premium to total risk.

TABLE 28-5 performances of 34 mutual funds, 1954–1963

mutual fund	average ann. return, %	std. dev. of ann. return, %	risk-premium* to std. dev. ratio = S_i
Affiliated Fund	14.6	15.3	.75896
American Business Shares	10.0	9.2	.75876
Axe-Houghton, Fund A	10.5	13.5	.55551
Axe-Houghton, Fund B	12.0	16.3	.55183
Axe-Houghton, Stock Fund	11.9	15.6	.56991
Boston Fund	12.4	12.1	.77842
Broad Street Investing	14.8	16.8	.70329
Bullock Fund	15.7	19.3	.65845
Commonwealth Investment Company	10.9	13.7	.57841
Delaware Fund	14.4	21.4	.53253
Dividend Shares	14.4	15.9	.71807
Eaton and Howard, Balanced Funds	11.0	11.9	.67399
Eaton and Howard, Stock Fund	15.2	19.2	.63486
Equity Fund	14.6	18.7	.61902
Fidelity Fund	16.4	23.5	.57020
Financial Industrial Fund	14.5	23.0	.49971
Fundamental Investors	16.0	21.7	.59894
Group Securities, Common Stock Fund	15.1	19.1	.63316
Group Securities, Fully Administered Fund	11.4	14.1	.59490
Incorporated Investors	14.0	25.5	.43116
Investment Company of America	17.4	21.8	.66169
Investors Mutual	11.3	12.5	.66451
Loomis-Sales Mutual Fund	10.0	10.4	.67358
Massachusetts Investors Trust	16.2	20.8	.63398
Massachusetts Investors—Growth Stock	18.6	22.7	.68687
National Investors Corporation	18.3	19.9	.76798
National Securities—Income Series	12.4	17.8	.52950
New England Fund	10.4	10.2	.72703
Putnam Fund of Boston	13.1	16.0	.63222
Scudder, Stevens & Clark Balanced Fund	10.7	13.3	.57893
Selected American Shares	14.4	19.4	.58788
United Funds—Income Funds	16.1	20.9	.62698
Wellington Fund	11.3	12.0	.69057
Wisconsin Fund	13.8	16.9	.64091

* S_i = (average return − 3%)/variability. The ratios shown were computed from original data and thus differ slightly from the ratios obtained from the rounded data shown in the table.

Source: William F. Sharpe, "Mutual Fund Performances," *Journal of Business,* suppl., January 1966, p. 125.

BOX 28-1
Sharpe's portfolio performance index

Dr. William F. Sharpe has devised an index of portfolio performance, denoted S_i, which is defined in Eq. (28-2a) for the ith portfolio.

$$S_i = \frac{\text{risk-premium}}{\text{total risk}} = \frac{\bar{r}_i - R}{\sigma_i} \tag{28-2a}$$

where

$\bar{r}_i$ = average return on ith portfolio
σ_i = standard deviation of returns for portfolio i
R = riskless rate of interest

Of the 34 funds shown in Fig. 28-5, eleven had risk-premium-to-risk ratios above the .667 of the DJIA.[10] The average of the 34 mutual funds' ratio is .633, which is below .667 for the DJIA. This means that the DJIA was a more efficient portfolio than the average mutual fund in the sample. When one considers that (1) the sales commission of 8 percent paid on the purchase of mutual fund shares exceeds the commissions incurred in purchasing se-

[10] The average return of the DJIA over the period was 16.3 percent, and its standard deviation was 19.94 percent, giving $S_{DJIA} = (16.3 - 3)/19.94 = 13.3/19.94 = .667$. Another study of data for 38 mutual funds from 1958 to 1967 showed similar but not identical results. This study showed that only 18 out of the 38 mutual funds outperformed the Standard & Poor's (S&P) 500 stocks average, but the average risk-premium-to-risk ratio for the 38 funds was slightly above the S&P 500's ratio. K.V. Smith and D. A. Tito, "Risk Return Measures of Ex Post Portfolio Performance," *Journal of Financial and Quantitative Analysis,* December 1969, pp. 464–465.

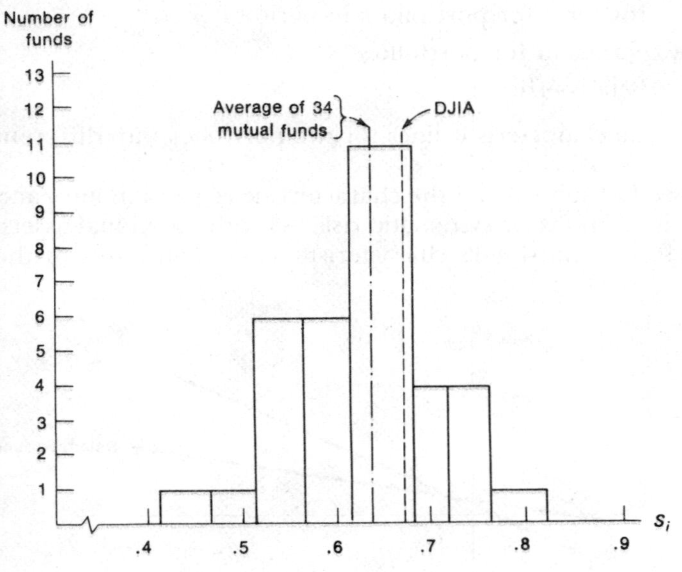

FIGURE 28-5 frequency distribution of Sharpe's risk-premium-to-risk ratio for a sample of 34 mutual funds, 1954–1963.

curities directly (that is, creating your own portfolio) and (2) the efficiency of the average mutual fund investment is below that of the DJIA, it follows that most investors would be better off by creating their own portfolios of randomly selected blue-chip stocks than buying mutual funds.

In calculating the data in Table 28-5, which are shown in Fig. 28-5, the management expenses of the mutual funds were deducted to determine net returns to the funds' investors. If the management expenses of the 34 funds are ignored, 19 of them had better performance index scores than the DJIA. The sample data indicate that before management expenses, the average mutual fund performs about as well as a market average such as the DJIA, but the returns to the funds' shareholders (after the funds' operating expenses are deducted but ignoring the sales commission paid by fund investors) were less than those of the DJIA. It seems that mutual fund managers' salaries and other professional management expenses lowered the net returns to shareholders because these costs were larger than the increase in returns they generated.

28-5 TREYNOR'S PORTFOLIO PERFORMANCE MEASURE

Mr. Jack Treynor conceived an index of portfolio performance that is based on systematic risk, as measured by portfolios' beta coefficients, rather than on total risk, like Sharpe's measure. To use Treynor's measure, the characteristic regression lines of portfolios must first be calculated by estimating Eq. (28-3):

$$r_{pt} = a_p + b_p r_{mt} + e_{pt} \qquad t = 1, 2, \ldots, T \tag{28-3}$$

where

r_{pt} = rate of return on pth portfolio in tth time period

r_{mt} = return on market index in period t

e_{pt} = random-error term for portfolio p in period t

a_p = intercept coefficient for portfolio p

b_p = portfolio's beta coefficient

Figure 28-6 shows typical characteristic lines for two portfolios with different management policies toward risk.

Chapter 10 discussed in some detail the characteristic regression lines and the beta coefficient as an index of systematic risk. As with individual assets, the beta coefficient from a portfolio's characteristic lines is an index of the

FIGURE 28-6 characteristic lines for portfolios.

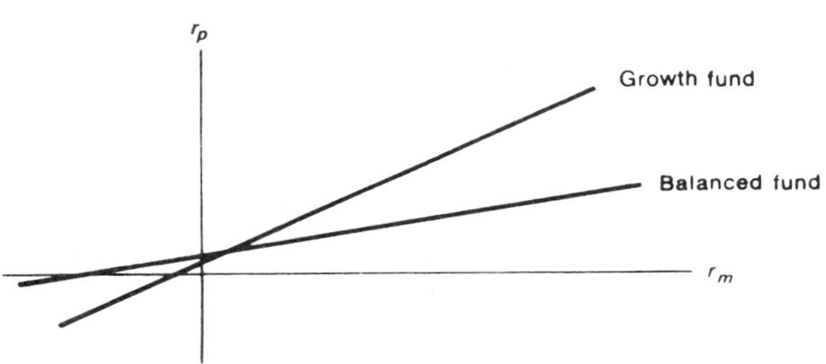

BOX 28-2
Treynor's portfolio performance index

Treynor's single-parameter investment performance index number for ranking purposes is defined in Eq. (28-4*a*).

$$T_p = \frac{\text{risk-premium}}{\text{systematic risk index}} = \frac{r_p - R}{b_p} \qquad (28\text{-}4a)$$

where

r_p = average rate of return on portfolio p
b_p = beta coefficient for portfolio p
R = riskless rate

portfolio's systematic or undiversifiable risk. Using only naive diversification, the unsystematic variability of returns of the individual assets in a portfolio typically average out to zero, and the portfolio is left with only systematic risk. Therefore, Treynor suggests measuring a portfolio's return relative to its *systematic* risk rather than relative to its *total* risk, as does the Sharpe measure.

28-5.1 the Treynor index

Equation (28-4) defines Treynor's index of portfolio performance, denoted T_p for the pth portfolio.[11] Graphically, T_p is a measure of the slope of the line from R to the pth portfolio, as shown in Fig. 28-7. As this figure demonstrates, portfolio P is more desirable than portfolio Q because P earned more risk-premium per unit of systematic risk; that is $T_P > T_Q$.

28-6 COMPARISON OF SHARPE AND TREYNOR MEASURES

Treynor's portfolio performance index T_p is similar to Sharpe's index S_i, which was defined in Eq. (28-2*a*), since they both use the risk-premium as a numerator. But Treynor's index measures systematic risk as its denominator and Sharpe's index uses total risk. In effect, Sharpe's measure ranks assets'

[11] J. Treynor, "How to Rate Management of Investment Funds," *Harvard Business Review*, January–February 1965, pp. 63–75.

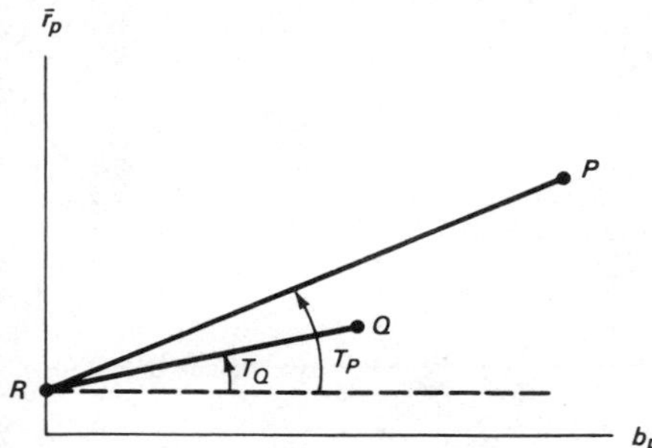

FIGURE 28-7 Treynor's portfolio performance measure in $(b_p, \bar{r}_p)$ space.

degrees of dominance in $[\sigma, E(r)]$ space and Treynor's measure ranks assets' dominance in $[b, E(r)]$ space. Both risk measures implicitly assume that money may be freely borrowed or lent at R. This is the rationalization for the linear investment opportunities that emerge out of R. This somewhat *unrealistic assumption* is also the logical flaw in both the Sharpe and the Treynor indices.

28-6.1 rank correlation

The Sharpe and Treynor portfolio performance indices yield very similar rankings of the portfolios' performances in most cases. Figure 28-8 shows a plot of points representing rankings of 34 mutual funds with the Sharpe and Treynor indices. These two sets of rankings were calculated with the same data used to prepare Table 28-5. Each point represents the ranking of one of the 34 portfolios in terms of both indices. The rank correlation coefficient for the two rankings was .97. Thus, although the Treynor and Sharpe measures differ conceptually, in practice they both tend to rank portfolios' performances similarly.

28-6.2 more recent results

Using 120 monthly rates of return from the 1960 to 1969 decade, John G. McDonald analyzed the performance of 123 mutual funds. The Sharpe and Treynor performance measures were used in the slightly reformulated manner shown in Eqs. (28-2*b*) and (23-4*b*), which follow.

$$S_p = \frac{E(r_{pt} - R_t)}{\sigma_p} \tag{28-2b}$$

$$T_p = \frac{E(r_{pt} - R_t)}{b_p} \tag{28-4b}$$

McDonald used monthly observations of the 30-day commercial paper rate as a surrogate for the riskless rate; this is why the R's in Eqs. (28-2*b*) and (28-4*b*) have subscripts of t for $t = 1, 2, \ldots, 120$ months. These monthly observations of R_t were subtracted from each portfolio's monthly rate of return to

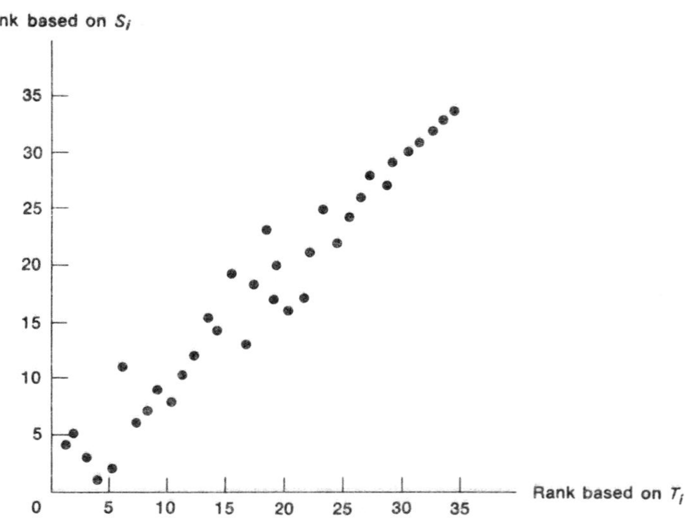

FIGURE 28-8 comparison of portfolio performance rankings in (rank of T_1, rank of S_1) space. (*Source*: William F. Sharpe, "Mutual Fund Performance," *Journal of* Business, suppl., January 1966, p. 129.)

TABLE 28-6 portfolio performance statistics, 1960–1969, for 123 mutual funds

fund's stated objective (sample size)	average beta	average σ_i	average $E(r_{it} - R_f)$	average S_i	average T_i
Maximum capital gain (18)	1.22	5.90	.693	.117	.568
Growth (33)	1.01	4.57	.565	.124	.560
Growth-income (36)	.90	3.93	.476	.121	.529
Income-growth (12)	.86	3.80	.398	.105	.463
Balanced (12)	.68	3.05	.214	.070	.314
Income (12)	.55	2.67	.252	.094	.458
Total sample (123)	.92	4.17	.477	.133	.510
Market average				.133	.510

Source: John G. McDonald, "Objectives and Performance of Mutual Funds," *Journal of Financial and Quantitative Analysis,* June 1974, pp. 311–333.

obtain monthly risk-premiums, denoted $r_{pt} - R_t$. Then the average risk-premium, denoted $E(r_{it} - R_t)$, over the 120 months was divided by the appropriate risk measure to compare the portfolios' performances. Table 28-6 shows a summary of the statistics.

McDonald found that, on average, the funds with more aggressive objectives took more risk and earned higher returns, as was found earlier (see Table 28-3) in the Friend-Blume-Crockett study. The McDonald study also found that a few funds departed from their stated objective; similar results were reported (see Table 28-4) in the Friend-Blume-Crockett study and elsewhere.

Concerning the investment performance of the 123 funds, McDonald's study reported that slightly over half the 123 mutual funds (that is, 67 out of 123) had values for Treynor's performance index that exceeded the stock market average. Using Sharpe's performance measure, about 31.7 percent (that is, 39 out of 123) of the funds outperformed the stock market average. Thus, using a slightly different specification of the Sharpe and Treynor portfolio performance measures, and a more recent sample, did not yield any significantly different conclusions. On average, mutual funds perform about as well as a naive buy-and-hold strategy.[12]

28-7 CONCLUSIONS

The preceding discussion explained certain risk-return portfolio performance tools. These tools were applied to mutual funds to provide examples of

[12] A study that used 10 years of more recent data than McDonald and that included mutual funds, banks, investment advisors, and life insurance companies has been published. J. C. Bogle and J. M. Twardowski, "Institutional Investment Performance Compared," *Financial Analysts Journal*, January–February 1980, pp. 33–41. This study suggests that the mutual funds perform better than the other three categories of investment managers compared in the study. Unfortunately, the Bogle-Twardowski study does not employ risk-adjusted rates of return that are comparable with the results presented in this chapter.

their use. Certain conclusions can be drawn regarding mutual funds and the tools used to evaluate portfolio performance.

28-7.1 conclusions about mutual fund investing

The preceding portfolio performance analysis of mutual funds suggests that many investors who own or are considering buying mutual fund shares could expect higher rates of return and less risk if they invested their own funds by selecting securities blindly and then simply holding them. This statement does not mean that all mutual fund shares represent poor investment decisions. Mutual funds can perform some valuable services for some investors.

Consider an average, amateur investor who has \$6,000 or less to invest. Suppose that Mr. Average will purchase only round lots (to avoid paying the higher odd-lot trading cost) and that the securities he buys have an average cost of \$30 per share; he would probably be well advised to invest in a good mutual fund. Such an investor would be able to buy only two securities, as the following computations show.

$$\$30 \times 100 \text{ shares} = \$3{,}000 \text{ per round lot}$$

$$\$6{,}000 \text{ total investment} = \$3{,}000 \text{ per round lot} \times 2 \text{ round lots}$$

Since two is too few securities to minimize the portfolio's unsystematic portion of total risk, this investor would probably look for a mutual fund. Furthermore, the small private investor cannot usually find time and/or does not have the skills needed to perform the economic and financial analysis that should precede any investment decision.

Although mutual funds do not typically earn high rates of return, they are usually able to reduce their risk to the systematic level of the market fluctuations. So, the fortunes of a mutual fund investor are not tied to the fortunes of only one or two individual securities. Therefore, unless investors have the resources at their disposal to perform Markowitz diversification (namely, access to a computer, data for many securities, and the ability to program the computer), they might be better off investing in a mutual fund.

The majority of mutual funds earn long-run average rates of return that exceed the returns paid by insured savings accounts. Thus, investors receive some added return for assuming risk (unless they are forced to liquidate their holdings in a period of depressed prices).

Finally, mutual funds can help an investor stay in some preferred risk-class (although that risk-class is not necessarily the one the fund says it will pursue in its statement of investment objectives). By examining mutual funds' quantitative risk coefficients, an investor can find a fund that will fairly consistently maintain a given level of risk. Table 28-3 explains the risk implications of various portfolio risk measures. As mentioned before, mutual funds do tend to stay in a given risk-class and select assets that earn a mediocre return for that level of risk.[13] This is a valuable service that amateur or part-time investors might not be able to provide for themselves.

[13] R. S. Carlson, "Aggregate Performance of Mutual Funds, 1948–1967," *Journal of Financial and Quantitative Analysis,* March 1970, pp. 1–32. T. Kim, "An Assessment of the Performance of Mutual Fund Management: 1969–1975," *Journal of Financial and Quantitative Analysis,* September 1978, vol. 8 no. 3, pp. 385–407.

28-7.2 conclusions about portfolio performance measures

Ranking portfolios' yearly rates of return reveals whether any of them are consistently able to outperform their competitors. However, such rankings may make an efficient low-risk portfolio appear to be doing poorly. To evaluate a portfolio adequately, the level of risk it assumes must be considered *with* its rate of return. Unfortunately, some portfolio managers' statements about the degree of risk (and concurrent expected returns) they will seek are sometimes erroneous. In contrast, portfolios' empirically measured risk coefficients furnish stationary indices of the level of risk a portfolio is undertaking. If the standard deviation is used, portfolios' standard deviations and average rates of return may be plotted in $[\sigma, E(r)]$ space and compared with the efficient frontier. Sharpe's index of portfolio performance measures the risk-premium per unit of risk borne by individual portfolios. This index considers both risk and return and yields one index number for each portfolio; these numbers may be used to rank the performances of a group of portfolios that are in different risk-classes.

Some analysts prefer Treynor's portfolio performance measure because systematic risk is more relevant than total risk in certain applications and because Treynor's measure can be used to compare both individual assets and portfolios. On the other hand, Treynor's performance measure has the disadvantage that it is sensitive to the market index used, and it is not clear which market index is "best." The Treynor index uses portfolios' beta systematic risk coefficients and average returns to compare portfolios' performance in $[b, E(r)]$ space. The Treynor and Sharpe portfolio performance measures rank mutual funds similarly in spite of their differences, however.[14]

28-7.3 conclusions about portfolio management practices

There are several common traps a portfolio manager may fall into that can shackle the portfolio's performance. An aimless search for undervalued securities is not likely to yield returns that exceed those attainable by using a naive buy-and-hold strategy. So the portfolio manager should try to limit the portfolio's holdings to a small number of securities so that each one may be watched carefully. Superfluous diversification across hundreds of securities is not good diversification, and it reduces the portfolio's flexibility and diminishes the portfolio's expected return. Portfolio management could benefit considerably from an accurate, detailed economic forecast. Such an economic forecast will reveal the growth industries in the economy and furnish various indicators that are necessary to allocate capital in an optimal manner. Finally, a good economic forecast will provide advance warning of economic downturns and thus of the bear markets that precede them. This advance notice will allow the portfolio manager to shift the portfolio's assets to financial instruments that are advantageous to hold in a bear market.[15] In order to be

[14] Irwin Friend and Marshall Blume, "Measurement of Portfolio Performance under Uncertainty," *American Economic Review*, September 1970, pp. 561–575. The Friend-Blume study compares the Sharpe, Treynor, and Jensen portfolio performance measures numerically and algebraically. For more information about the Jensen portfolio performance measure see M. C. Jensen, "The Performance of Mutual Funds in the Period 1945 through 1964," *Journal of Finance*, May 1968, pp. 389–416. See also M. C. Jensen, "Risk, the Pricing of Capital Assets, and the Evaluation of Investment Portfolios," *Journal of Business*, vol. 42, 1969.

[15] J. L. Treynor and K. K. Mazuy, "Can Mutual Funds Outguess the Market?" *Business Review*, January–February 1965, pp. 63–76. F. J. Fabozzi and J. C. Francis, "Mutual Fund Systematic Risk for Bull and Bear Markets: An Empirical Examination," *Journal of Finance*, December 1979, vol. 34, no. 5, pp. 1243–1250.

efficient, a portfolio's funds must be shifted among various unrelated securities (such as stocks, bonds, options, and commodities) in order to take full advantage of Markowitz diversification and to maximize the expected return. Judging from the performance statistics reviewed above, all mutual fund managers have room for improvement.

QUESTIONS

1. "Closed-end investment companies redeem their shares at the current net asset value." Is this statement true, false, or uncertain? Explain.
2. How is the income of an open-end investment company taxed?
3. "Rankings of portfolios' average returns show that, although the average mutual fund does not outperform the market, a few truly superior funds consistently beat the market." Is this statement true, false, or uncertain? Explain.
4. Why is ranking mutual funds by their rates of return a poor way to evaluate their performance?
5. How well does the mutual fund industry perform relative to some naive buy-and-hold strategy?
6. Consider the following investment advice: "Put your money in the trust department of a good commercial bank. Banks will manage your investments better than the mutual funds, and they won't charge you a load fee." Is this statement true, false, or uncertain? Explain.
7. Consider the following summary statistics about five investment portfolios.

portfolio	average return, %	standard deviation	beta
Alpha (*A*)	7	3	.4
Beta (*B*)	10	8	1.0
Gamma (Γ)	13	6	1.1
Delta (Δ)	15	13	1.2
Epsilon (*E*)	18	15	1.4

Assume that the riskless rate of interest is 3.0 percent.

(*a*) Which of the portfolios performed the best according to Sharpe's measure? The worst?

(*b*) Which performed the best according to Treynor's performance measure? The worst?

(*c*) Assume that the riskless rate of interest is 6 percent. Under this new assumption, which portfolio ranks the best according to Sharpe's measure? According to Treynor's measure? Show your calculations and draw graphs to document the work with all variables labeled.

SELECTED REFERENCES

E. F. Fama, "Components of Investment Performance," *Journal of Finance,* June 1972, pp. 551–568. This paper uses mathematical statistics to analyze and extend the Sharpe and Treynor portfolio performance evaluation tools.

William F. Sharpe, "Mutual Fund Performance," *Journal of Business,* Supplement on Security Prices, January 1966, pp. 119–138. This risk-return analysis of mutual fund performance uses correlation, regression, and statistical inference.

multiperiod wealth maximization*

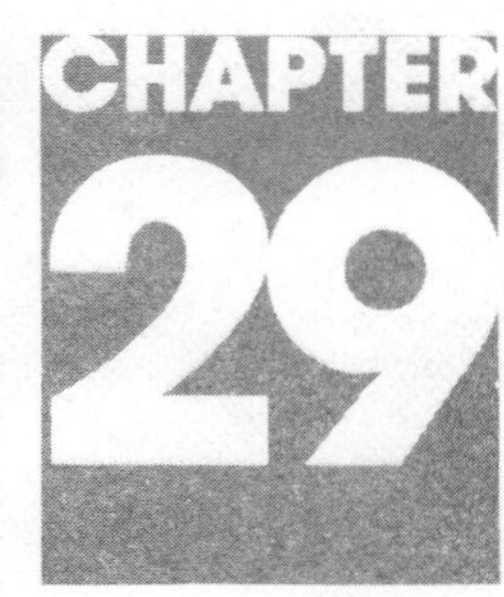

The portfolio management process presented in Chaps. 25, 26, and 27 is a "one-period" form of analysis. At the beginning of each period the following portfolio management process must be repeated.

Step one: *Security analysts* prepare estimates of the one-period risk and return statistics for every asset that is an investment candidate.

Step two: The *portfolio analyst* uses Markowitz portfolio analysis (explained in Chap. 25) to delineate the one-period efficient frontier from all the individual assets' risk and return statistics.

Step three: *Portfolio selection* is made by choosing one of the portfolios on the efficient frontier and making a one-period investment in it.

The length of the one period that a Markowitz efficient portfolio is designed to span is arbitrary. One or 2 years is a likely length of time for the period to encompass, however, because it is difficult to estimate the risk and return statistics over very short or very long time periods. After the portfolio management staff defines the length of their planning horizon period, the risk and return statistics for every individual asset that is being analyzed must be estimated for this *single period*.

Since security analysts have increasing difficulty as they try to estimate expected risk and return statistics further in the future, the length of one period cannot be extended indefinitely. It is difficult to imagine predicting, for example, a security's expected risk and return statistics as far as 5 years ahead. And 10-year forecasts are even more unimaginable. So, what does the portfolio manager do in the *long run*?

When the one-period planning horizon on which a portfolio is constructed comes to its end, the old portfolio must almost always be *revised* for several reasons. First, more current information has probably caused the security analysts to revise their input statistics on which the single-period portfolio

* Chapter 29 presumes a knowledge of Chaps. 25, 26, 27, and 28 and Mathematical App. F.

analysis is based. Second, even if no new information causes the efficient frontier to be revised, price changes and the receipt of cash dividends and coupon interest have passively modified the weights of the assets held in the portfolio. So, long-term investing requires that the one-period portfolio analysis be performed every year or so to calculate the weights in the new efficient portfolios, and then a new portfolio must be selected from the revised efficient frontier. The question to which Chap. 29 addresses itself is: "What kind of investment management policy is appropriate for long-run investing over *multiple periods?*" For example, suppose you should inherit millions of dollars at age 20 and you expect to bequeath it to charity when you are 70 years old. Or suppose you are involved in the management of a multimillion-dollar portfolio for a life insurance company and it is not expected that any of this portfolio need be liquidated within the next two decades. In such real-life situations that involve decades—that is, they clearly involve *multiple periods*—the question naturally arises as to whether the *one-period* Markowitz portfolio analysis procedure is relevant. And if the Markowitz model is relevant for multiple-period investment management, how is portfolio analysis over one period applied to multiple periods?

29-1 UTILITY OF TERMINAL WEALTH

The proper multiperiod or long-run investment policy is assumed to be the one that will maximize the investor's utility (that is, happiness) from his or her consumption in each period, as shown in Eq. (29-1).

$$\max U(C_1, C_2, \ldots, C_T) \tag{29-1}$$

The symbol C_t denotes consumption in the tth period, and the Tth period is the terminal period or last period. For the average person, C_1 and C_2 would probably involve more wining and dining and less geriatric medical care than C_T, for example. Since a person's acquisition of wine, companionship, and geriatric medical care can be expedited with money, economists typically assume that maximizing a person's wealth in each period is equivalent to maximizing the utility from consumption.

If a person owns a portfolio of securities and other market assets, he or she can obtain money for consumption purposes in each period by liquidating part of these assets to finance current consumption.[1] Therefore, let us make the simplifying assumption that investing in order to maximize the terminal value w_T of a portfolio at the end of T periods (for example, at the end of someone's lifetime or at the end of an insurance company's long-run planning horizon), as shown in Eq. (29-2*a*), is equivalent to maximizing utility of consumption Eq. (29-1).[2] Equation (29-2*a*) represents this long-run investment objective.

[1] By pledging the portfolio as collateral, the investment owner can borrow about as much as the portfolio's current value. However, borrowing against an asset involves penalty costs, which complicate the analysis. Since the owner can simply liquidate part of the portfolio to finance consumption, this simpler alternative is employed.

[2] The relationship between consumption and investment decisions over multiple periods is analyzed by E. F. Fama, "Multiperiod Consumption-Investment Decisions," *American Economic Review*, March 1970, pp. 163–174.

$$\max U(w_T) \tag{29-2a}$$

The investor's *beginning wealth* at time period $t = 0$ may be denoted w_0. This allows Eq. (29-2*a*) to be rewritten equivalently as Eq. (29-2*b*), since $w_T = w_0(1 + r)^T$, where r denotes the *average compounded rate of return* over T periods.

$$\max U[w_0(1 + r)^T] = \max [U(w_T)] \tag{29-2b}$$

In the world of uncertainty, an investor cannot expect to foresee the future clearly. Therefore, *expected* (rather than known with certainty) utility must be maximized to acknowledge the existence of risk. This is represented by rewriting Eq. (29-2*b*) with an expectation operator (discussed in Mathematical App. B and the appendix to Chap. 27), as shown in Eq. (29-3*a*).

$$\max E[U(w_T)] = \max E\{U[w_0(1 + r)^T]\} \tag{29-3a}$$

29-1.1 geometric mean return

The compounded rate of return r equals the geometric mean of the T one-period rates of return r_t for $t = 1, 2, \ldots, T$, as shown in Eqs. (29-4*a*) and (29-4*b*). (See Mathematical App. F at the end of this book for a more detailed explanation of the *geometric mean return*.)

$$(1 + r)^T = \frac{w_T}{w_0} \tag{29-4a}$$

$$= (1 + r_1)(1 + r_2) \ldots (1 + r_T) \tag{29-4b}$$

Equation (29-4*a*) shows that maximizing the geometric mean return is *equivalent* to maximizing the ratio of terminal wealth over beginning wealth. Essentially, maximizing the geometric mean also maximizes terminal wealth.

Since the geometric mean return as defined in Eq. (29-4*a*) is a factor in the utility-of-wealth function, Eq. (29-3*a*), it can be seen that increases either in terminal wealth or in the geometric mean return help increase the investor's expected utility. And in the special case in which initial wealth w_0 is a fixed constant that is separable and independent from the geometric mean return, maximizing the geometric mean is equivalent to maximizing the investor's expected utility of terminal wealth. In fact, w_0 is separable and independent of r if the investor's utility is logarithmic.[3]

29-1.2 logarithmic utility of terminal wealth

For the sake of concreteness, assume utility equals the logarithm of wealth, or equivalently, the logarithm of returns. The investor's beginning wealth w_0 is separable from the rate of return r as shown in Eq. (29-5*c*).

[3] Separability occurs in log utility functions

$$U(w) = \ln(w)$$

as shown in Eq. (29-5*c*). For an analysis of these cases, see E. J. Elton and M. J. Gruber, "On the Optimality of Some Multi-Period Portfolio Selection Models," *Journal of Business*, April 1974, pp. 231–243.

Other cases are analyzed by Samuelson and Merton: Paul A. Samuelson, "Lifetime Portfolio Selection by Dynamic Stochastic Programming," *Review of Economics and Statistics*, August 1969, pp. 239–246; and Robert C. Merton, "Lifetime Portfolio Selection under Uncertainty: The Continuous Time Case," ibid., pp. 247–257. The papers by Merton and Samuelson are companion pieces.

FIGURE 29-1 **the natural or Naperian logarithm utility function of terminal wealth.**

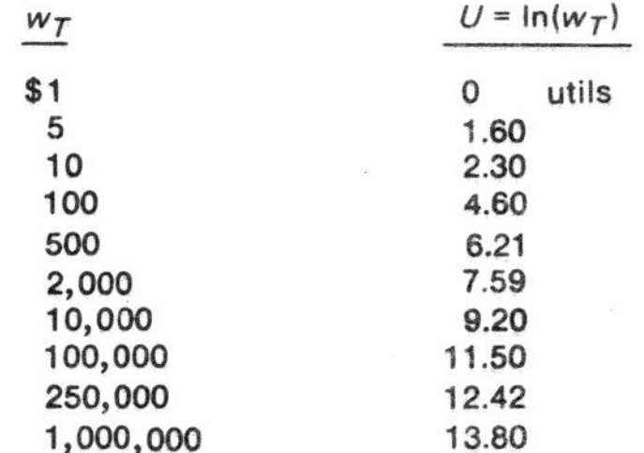

w_T	$U = \ln(w_T)$
$1	0 utils
5	1.60
10	2.30
100	4.60
500	6.21
2,000	7.59
10,000	9.20
100,000	11.50
250,000	12.42
1,000,000	13.80

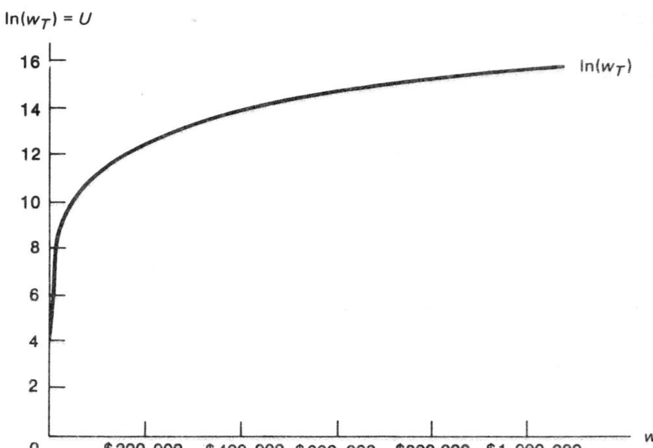

$$U(w_T) = \ln(w_T) \tag{29-5a}$$

$$= \ln[w_0(1 + r^T)] \tag{29-5b}$$

$$= \ln(w_0) + T[\ln(1 + r)] \tag{29-5c}$$

Since the rate of return is *separable* from wealth, this shows that at least the Markowitz procedure of confining the analysis to the rate of return and ignoring the dollar value of the investor's wealth is logical and satisfactory for logarithmic utility functions.

As the analysis focuses explicitly on the log utility function, the plausibility of this popular form is reviewed before proceeding further. Figure 29-1 shows a graph of Eq. (29-5*a*). This utility function is realistic because, first, it exhibits positive marginal utility of wealth. That is, more terminal wealth always increases utility; this means that investors never get tired of more wealth. Second, utility function Eq. (29-5*a*) is realistic because it has diminishing marginal utility of wealth. In other words, each additional wealth increment increases its recipient's happiness less than each preceding increment of the same size. The log utility function possesses other properties that are desirable for analysis, too.[4]

[4] J. W. Pratt, "Risk Aversion in the Small and in the Large," *Econometrica*, April 1964, pp. 122–136.

29-1.3 positive linear transformations

The log utility function yields an invariant preference ordering over a set of objects (for example, investments) if the function undergoes any positive linear transformation. That is, if a and b are positive constants, Eq. (29-6a) is true.

$$\text{Preference ordering } [\ln (w_T)] = \text{preference ordering } [a + b \ln (w_T)] \tag{29-6a}$$

For a more pragmatic and relevant example of transformations that leave the preference ordering invariant, consider the positive constant initial wealth, w_0. If w_0 is subtracted from w_T and the difference is divided by w_0, this is a positive linear transformation of the basic random variable w_T. As shown in Eq. (29-7), it transforms the random variable terminal wealth into a rate of change in wealth or one-period rate of return.

$$r = \frac{w_T - w_0}{w_0} \tag{29-7}$$

Equation (29-7) means that ranking investments based on the log of their expected terminal values or their expected returns will yield identical preference rankings. This is summarized succinctly in Eq. (29-6b).

$$\text{Preference ordering } [U(\ln \{w_T\})] = \text{preference ordering } [U(\ln \{r\})] \tag{29-6b}$$

Other positive linear transformations can be used to vary the shape of the log utility function. The logarithmic utility function can even be transformed to create approximations of nonlogarithmic utility functions.[5] Therefore, the conclusions obtained here with the log utility function are also roughly true for some other classes of utility functions—most particularly, the quadratic utility function. That is, in spite of the fact that a mathematical economist can prove that a quadratic and a logarithmic utility function yield different investment preferences, for example, these differences might be so slight or might be present in such extreme cases that a business investment executive would never notice or encounter them. Furthermore, many business investment decisions are made by committees, and it is not possible to specify one utility function for a group of people. Thus, selecting efficient portfolios must be done without reference to a utility function for group decision making.

Regardless of the numerous business situations for which utility analysis is inappropriate, it is still useful for analyzing the logic of various economic decisions. So, to gain more insights into the proper long-term investment strategy, log utility function Eq. (29-5a) is rewritten in terms of the one-period rates of return below.

[5] Harry Markowitz, *Portfolio Selection*, Wiley, New York, 1959, pp. 120–125. Markowitz shows how the quadratic function can approximate the log function. In particular, he shows that the following equation is a very close approximation over the range of relevant returns.

$$\ln (1 + r) = r - .5r^2$$

29-1.4 one-period returns and utility of terminal wealth

Substituting the logarithmic Eq. (29-5*b*) into the investor's long-term expected utility objective function Eq. (29-3*a*) produces Eq. (29-3*b*).

$$\max E[U(w_T)] = \max E\{U[w_0(1 + r)^T]\} \tag{29-3a}$$

$$= \max E\{\ln [w_0(1 + r)^T]\} \tag{29-3b}$$

Substituting Eq. (29-4*b*) into objective function (29-3*b*) yields Eq. (29-3*c*), which shows explicitly how utility of terminal wealth relates to the T different single-period rates of return $r_1, r_2, \ldots, r_T$.

$$\max E[U(w_T)] = \max E\{\ln [w_0(1 + r)^T]\} \tag{29-3b}$$

$$= \max E\{\ln [w_0(1 + r_1)(1 + r_2) \ldots (1 + r_T)]\} \tag{29-3c}$$

29-1.5 the utility from being bankrupt

One of the insights that can be obtained by restating the investor's long-term objective as Eq. (29-3*c*) is the effect of taking risks period after period. Suppose that in the tth period the investor selects a risky asset that has a one-period rate of return of $r_t = -100$ percent. The link relative for period t becomes zero since -100 percent $= -1.0$ and thus $1 + r_t = 1 - 1 = 0$. This might happen, for example, if an investor becomes too greedy and impatiently speculates in a nondiversified venture that is not prudent in hopes of "getting rick quick."

If any one link relative becomes equal to zero, the investor loses all the wealth that had been accumulated up to period t. When this situation occurs it is commonly called *bankruptcy*. The bankrupt party's utility of returns [namely, Eq. (29-3*c*)] becomes as low as it can possibly be—it becomes the utility of zero, mathematically speaking. This shows that some risk-aversion (that is, the fear of bankruptcy) is essential to maximize expected utility of terminal wealth over multiperiod reinvesting. Merely buying high-risk assets or "taking long shots" at the racetrack will not automatically yield riches or happiness. Quite to the contrary, the assumption of high risks period after period means that $r_t = -100$ percent ($= -1.0$) may occur in one period and cause the terminal wealth to become zero. Such outcomes were what caused some Wall Street speculators to jump from their office windows to their deaths during the Great Crash of the early 1930s.

29-2 SINGLE-PERIOD PORTFOLIO MANAGEMENT

Thus far, three long-run investment strategies have been shown to be equivalent: (1) maximizing the logarithmic utility function, (2) maximizing the geometric mean rate of return, and (3) maximizing terminal wealth.[6] The analysis of these multiperiod objectives ultimately focused on the individual *one-period* rates of return r_t, which are the focal point of Markowitz single-period portfolio analysis. It has been shown at various places in this book (for example, see the CAPM, or SML, and the CML, or the efficient frontier) that the portfolio manager must undertake some risks of investing in order to

[6] Footnote 5 showed that a fourth utility function, a specific quadratic function, is also essentially equal.

obtain significant positive returns. However, it was also shown earlier in this chapter [namely, in the bankruptcy discussion that followed Eq. (29-3*c*)] that it is foolhardy to undertake large risks and expect to maximize multiperiod terminal wealth. To go a step further and reach a conclusion about exactly how the portfolio manager should select a portfolio, it is necessary to assume that the one-period rates-of-return distribution may be described by the two-parameter normal distribution. In fact, there is good evidence that returns are normally distributed.[7]

The *normal probability distribution* is completely defined by its two parameters: the expected value (or mean) and the variance (or standard deviation). Information about higher-order statistical moments is irrelevant when analyzing the normal distribution. The rational investment policy is therefore to select a portfolio with the maximum expected return at whatever level of risk is deemed appropriate—that is, to select an efficient portfolio.[8] The optimum multiperiod strategy is to select any efficient portfolio between the low-return-and-low-risk segment and the high-risk-and-high-return segment that seems likely to maximize terminal wealth in light of the current facts. Coincidently, this is *identical* with the optimal single-period investment strategy.

It is not possible to specify in advance how much risk is wise to undertake when seeking to maximize terminal wealth.[9] However, a study by Sharpe and Cooper throws some light on the question.[10] Over a 36-year sample, they found that large portfolios of New York Stock Exchange (NYSE) stocks with beta systematic risk coefficients slightly above unity had the highest geometric mean rate of return. Table 29-1 shows the average betas for portfolios made

[7] Randolph Westerfield, "The Distribution of Common Stock Price Changes: An Application of Transaction Time and Subordinated Stochastic Models," *Journal of the American Statistical Association*, December 1977; R. C. Blattberg and N. J. Gonedes, "A Comparison of the Stable and Student Distributions as Statistical Models for Stock Prices," *Journal of Business*, April 1974, pp. 244–280; E. Fama, *Foundations of Finance*, Basic Books, New York, 1976. Fama suggests the normal distribution in chaps. 1 through 4.

[8] Mathematical proof that expected utility of terminal wealth is a function of the expected return, $E(r)$, and variance, σ^2, if rates of return are normally distributed, is outlined below. Mathematical statisticians will be able to fill in the missing steps of the proof.

$$E[U(w_T)] = \int U(r|w_0)f[r|E(r), \sigma^2]\, dr$$
$$= E[U(r)|w_0, E(r), \sigma^2]$$

where

r = rate-of-return random variable

U = a logarithmic utility function

$f[r|E(r), \sigma^2]$ = a normal probability distribution of rates of return

The vertical bars indicate that the variables after them are given. The full proof is omitted because it is lengthy and involves integral calculus. See eqs. (3.5), (3.6), (3.7), et al., in James Tobin, "Liquidity Preference as Behavior Towards Risk," *The Review of Economic Studies*, February 1958.

[9] Richard Roll, "Evidence on the Growth Optimum Model," *Journal of Finance*, June 1973, pp. 551–566. Harry Markowitz, "Investment for the Long Run: New Evidence for an Old Rule," *Journal of Finance*, December 1976, vol. 31, no. 5, pp. 1273–1286.

[10] W. F. Sharpe and G. M. Cooper, "Risk-Return Classes of N.Y.S.E. Common Stocks, 1931–1967," *Financial Analysts Journal*, March–April 1972, p. 46.

TABLE 29-1 beta systematic risk coefficients and geometric mean returns for 10 NYSE stock portfolios, 1931–1967

risk-class	portfolio's beta	geometric mean return, %
1	1.42	14.52
2	1.18	14.21
3	1.14	14.79
4	1.24	15.84*
5	1.06	13.80
6	.98	15.06
7	1.00	14.69
8	.76	12.14
9	.65	12.40
10	.58	9.89

* Highest geometric mean return.

from NYSE stocks, constructed from homogeneous *risk deciles*. The table also shows the geometric mean returns for each of the portfolios from the 10 different risk-classes.

The statistics in Table 29-1 tend to indicate that portfolios composed of stocks with beta coefficients between about 1.0 and 1.25 were the most lucrative. A search for either low-risk stocks with betas below about .6 or high-risk stocks with betas above about 1.3 appears to be a counterproductive strategy. However, the stocks for this Sharpe-Cooper study were selected only on the basis of their beta coefficients. Selecting stocks with the aid of an expert security analyst and/or an economic forecaster could change the results in Table 29-1. In the final analysis, the experience of the decision maker and the "luck of the draw" can also be significant factors in investment selection.

The only aspect of multiperiod portfolio management left to be discussed is the question, "How and when should the single-period efficient portfolios be *revised* to take advantage of new information that becomes available during the multiperiod horizon?"

29-3 PORTFOLIO REVISION

As bull- and bear-market periods pass in succession, new stocks are offered, and old securities go bankrupt, the efficient frontier shifts, making portfolio revision necessary. Furthermore, the portfolio will receive cash dividends and interest income that need to be reinvested. Also, new information will arrive continually, causing securities risk and return statistics to change. For these reasons, a multiperiod portfolio strategy will involve *portfolio revision* even though the investor's utility function may never change.

Investors do not usually desire a portfolio that changes its risk-class, even if it shifts along the efficient frontier. For example, a poor, elderly widow would probably not be happy to have her life savings in a "go-go" mutual fund even if it were efficient, like portfolio C in Fig. 29-2. Instead, the widow would probably prefer a less risky balanced fund, like portfolio E' in Fig. 29-2, even

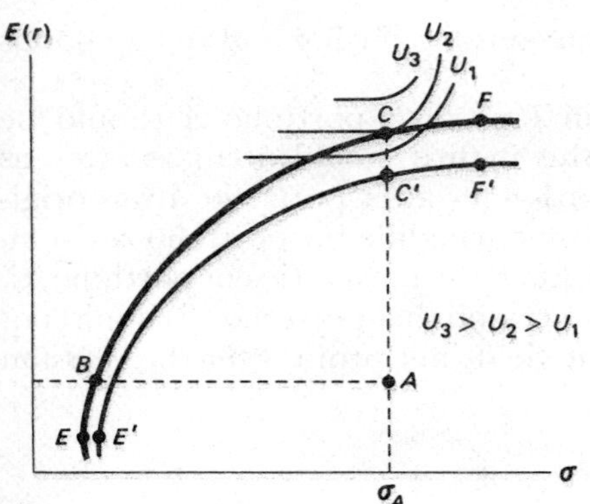

FIGURE 29-2 portfolio revision possibilities.

though it is not on the efficient frontier.[11] Thus, the practical objective of portfolio management in most business and personal situations typically becomes one of simple return maximization in a particular risk-class when the investor's utility map (or indifference curves) is unknown.

For another example, suppose a mutual fund has become suboptimal at point A in Fig. 29-2. This portfolio's manager should not seek just any portfolio that has less risk and/or more expected return, such as the portfolios in the triangle bounded by points A, B, and C. Instead, only portfolios in or near the mutual fund's traditional risk-class (that is, σ_A, which its owners lresumably prefer) that have higher expected returns should be sought. Such portfolios lie along the dotted line $AC'C$ in Fig. 29-2—this dotted line is evidently the *risk-class* that the investor prefers.

29-3.1 revision costs make true efficient frontier unattainable

Portfolio revision is a costly process. When a portfolio is revised, some previously purchased securities may have to be liquidated at a loss. The expense of updating the risk and return statistics for many securities and the computer operation necessary to determine the new efficient frontier are not trivial. And the commissions on any securities bought or sold must be paid, too.

As a result of these costs, it is not possible for a revised portfolio to attain the true efficient frontier along the curve $EBCF$ in Fig. 29-2. Instead, the *constrained* efficient frontier along the curve $E'C'F'$ represents the optimum attainable investments. The vertical difference between the unattainable efficient frontier curve $EBCF$ and the *optimum attainable efficient frontier* curve $E'C'F'$ equals the revision costs as a percentage of the portfolio's total assets.[12] In Fig. 29-2, the optimum attainable efficient frontier is closer to the true efficient frontier for low-risk, low-return portfolios than for efficient portfolios with higher returns because the low-risk, low-return portfolios presumably

[11] The indifference curve representation of the investment preferences of Dr. Swift and Aunt Jane in Fig. 27-1 shows why the widow would prefer portfolio E' instead of C.

[12] A. H. Chen, F. C. Jen, and S. Zionts, "The Optimal Portfolio Revisions Policy," *Journal of Business,* January 1971, pp. 51–61.

contain many bonds, and the sales commissions for buying and selling bonds are lower than for stock.

In situations like the one depicted in Fig. 29-2, portfolio A should be revised to attain point C'. Revisions of this nature should occur as often as they are possible—a month, a quarter, or longer after portfolio A was originally purchased.[13] There is no optimum time schedule for portfolio revision. Owing to revision costs, it is impossible to attain the most efficient portfolio, C, in the desired risk-class, σ_A. But there is no reason that portfolio C' should not be obtained directly and immediately if it yields net profit after the revision costs.

29-4 CONCLUSIONS

When all things are considered, there are unusual circumstances that could arise in selecting an investment portfolio that would make a Markowitz efficient portfolio inadvisable.[14] However, as a pragmatic matter, myopically selecting a one-period Markowitz efficient portfolio in each successive period can maximize expected utility of terminal wealth over a planning horizon that extends many periods into the future, or over a single period.

This discussion about long-run portfolio strategies encompassing multiple periods tends to draw attention away from the portfolio managers who are managing small and/or short-term portfolios. These managers must consider liquidating their portfolios and consuming the wealth, using the money for an emergency, using the proceeds to finance some expenditure for which they were accumulating wealth over one period, ad infinitum. These portfolio managers are not in the position to look more than one period into the future. But they, too, should seek efficient portfolios to maximize their expected utility.[15] Thus, whether portfolio managers are looking one period or multiple periods into the future, they should seek the efficient frontier.

QUESTIONS

1. Why maximize *expected* utility rather than simply the utility of wealth?
2. Find a utility function with positive but diminishing marginal utility that is incompatible with the logarithmic function and graph it. Compare and contrast this function (for example, a quadratic function over its upward-sloping range) with the logarithmic function. Can you make positive linear transformations on the log function so that it closely approximates the other function?

[13] K. H. Johnson and D. S. Shannon, "A Note on Diversification and the Reduction of Dispersion," *Journal of Financial Economics,* December 1974, vol. 1, no. 4, pp. 365–372. For evidence about a workable portfolio revision algorithm, see John Schreiner, "Portfolio Revision—A Turnover-Constrained Approach," *Financial Management,* December 1979; reprinted in J. C. Francis, C. F. Lee, and D. Farrar (eds.), *Readings in Investments,* McGraw-Hill, New York, 1980.

[14] Nils H. Hakansson, "Capital Growth and the Mean-Variance Approach to Portfolio Selection," *Journal of Financial and Quantitative Analysis,* January 1971, pp. 517–555.

[15] E. F. Fama, "Multiperiod Consumption-Investment Decisions," *American Economic Review,* March 1970, pp. 163–174.

3. Assume a portfolio manager has taken *large risks* to attain large returns and has been so successful at this strategy that she has quadrupled her wealth every year for the past 10 years. Now this portfolio manager offers to manage your life savings along with her own funds for free. What do you think of this free chance to get rich quick and retire early?
4. Suppose investor A had as his investment strategy the maximization of a one-period logarithm of returns utility function. In contrast, his twin brother B maximized the log of multiperiod terminal wealth. If A and B were choosing among the same assets from which to form their portfolios, how should their portfolios differ?
5. Compare and contrast the marginal utility of an investor with a log utility function with the quadratic utility function of another investor.
6. If investor P had to pay brokerage fees to trade securities when she revised her portfolio but her twin sister F could trade without paying brokerage fees, how should their portfolios differ after a few periods?

SELECTED REFERENCES

Eugene F. Fama, "Multiperiod Consumption-Investment Decisions," *American Economic Review,* March 1970, pp. 163–174. This article uses integral calculus to show that selecting one-period Markowitz efficient portfolios will yield an optimal multiperiod investment strategy if the investor has current consumption as an alternative to reinvestment each period and if the capital markets are perfect. A knowledge of utility and portfolio theory is presumed.

H. A. Latane', D. L. Tuttle, and C. R. Jones, *Security Analysis and Portfolio Management,* 2d ed., The Ronald Press Co., New York, 1975. This investments textbook suggests how to make investment decisions so as to maximize the geometric mean rate of return or terminal wealth.

Harry Markowitz, "Investment for the Long Run: New Evidence for an Old Rule," *Journal of Finance,* December 1976, vol. 31, no. 5, pp. 1273–1286. Mathematical statistics is used to show that maximizing the geometric mean is compatible with Markowitz's portfolio analysis.

John Schreiner, "Portfolio Revision—A Turnover-Constrained Approach," *Financial Management,* Spring 1980. This article uses algebra and statistics to explain a mathematical portfolio revision algorithm. Numerical results are also discussed.

part eight

ARBITRAGE PRICING THEORY

CHAPTER 30—*arbitrage pricing theory (APT)* presents a powerful new investments theory that first emerged in 1976 and went relatively unnoticed for several years. It is a comprehensive theory in that it embraces different risk factors but yet includes the capital asset pricing model (CAPM) as a special case. APT is also a simple theory that can be derived with only the most modest assumptions about the underlying utility function and the probability distribution of assets' returns. The theory and initial empirical evidence are presented in Chapter 30. Chapter 30 presumes that the material in Chap. 9, 10, and 21 has been mastered.

arbitrage pricing theory (APT)

The modern portfolio theory (MPT) of Harry Markowitz, William Sharpe, Jack Treynor, and others is the most widely accepted investments theory—it was explained previously, in Chaps. 25 through 28.[1] However, Doctor Stephen Ross's arbitrage pricing theory (APT) is a new investments theory that competes with the MPT for the attention of financial researchers.[2] Section 30-1 introduces the APT in a simple two-asset context that is intuitive.

30-1 AN INTRODUCTION TO ARBITRAGE PRICING THEORY (APT)

An *arbitrage opportunity* is a perfectly hedged portfolio that can be acquired at a cost of zero, but that will have a positive value with certainty at the end of the

[1] Portfolio theory was explained above in Chaps. 25 through 28 inclusive. The modern portfolio theory originated in the following articles. H. M. Markowitz, "Portfolio Selection," *Journal of Finance,* March 1952, pp. 71–91; H. M. Markowitz, *Portfolio Selection: Efficient Diversification of Investments,* Wiley, New York, 1959. The single-index model, or the market model, as it is also called, was first published on page 100 of Markowitz's 1959 monograph. Later, additional research on the model was published by Markowitz's student W. F. Sharpe, "A Simplified Model for Portfolio Analysis," *Management Science,* January 1963, pp. 277–293. Today's factor models are simply these earlier index models with their names changed. Then, the CAPM was developed independently by Jack Treynor and W. F. Sharpe: W. F. Sharpe, "Capital Asset Prices: A Theory of Market Equilibrium under Conditions of Risk," *Journal of Finance,* September 1964, pp. 425–442; W. F. Sharpe: "Mutual Fund Performance," *Journal of Business,* January 1966, pp. 119–138; J. L. Treynor, "Toward a Theory of the Market Value of Risky Assets," unpublished manuscript, 1961; and, J. L. Treynor, "How to Rate Management of Investment Funds," *Harvard Business Review,* January–February 1965, pp. 63–75. Many later researchers contributed to the development of the MPT.

[2] S. A. Ross, "The Arbitrage Pricing Theory of Capital Asset Pricing," *Journal of Economic Theory,* December 1976, pp. 344–360; S. A. Ross, "The Current Status of the Capital Asset Pricing Model," *Journal of Finance,* June 1978, pp. 885–901; and Richard Roll and Stephen A. Ross, "An Empirical Investigation of the Arbitrage Pricing Theory," *Journal of Finance,* December 1980, vol. 35, no. 5, pp. 1073–1103.

investment period. An arbitrage opportunity is expressed more formally in Eqs. (30-1), (30-2*a*), and (30-3) below. These three equations are all *dollar-denominated*.

$$\sum_{i=1}^{N} w_i = 0 \tag{30-1}$$

$$E(w_p^T) = \sum_{i=1}^{N} E(w_i^T) > 0 \tag{30-2a}$$

$$0 = \sum_{i=1}^{N}\sum_{j=1}^{N} \sigma_{ij} \tag{30-3}$$

where

w_i = dollars of initial wealth invested in the *i*th asset

$E(w_i{}^T)$ = mathematical expectation of terminal wealth (or value) of asset *i*,

σ_{ij} = covariance between assets *i* and *j*

In this case, the expected dollar profits from the arbitrage portfolio are positive, as indicated in Eq. (30-2*a*).

No money was invested to create this profitable arbitrage portfolio because some securities were sold short to obtain cash inflow (that is, $w_i > 0$) while other securities cost money (that is, $w_j < 0$) when they were purchased to hold in a long position. Essentially, investors are assumed to receive the proceeds (that is, positive cash inflows) from their short sales to invest in their long positions (that cost negative cash outflows) so that Eq. (30-1) is not violated. Eqs. (30-1), (30-2*a*), and (30-3) define the type of arbitrage opportunity that leads to the arbitrage pricing theory (APT).[3]

In the next section the discussion changes from dollar quantities to *rates of return* in order to achieve a higher level of generality.

30-1.1 the returns that underlie the APT

APT is based on the law of one price. The *law of one price* says that the same good cannot sell at different prices. If the same good sells at different prices, arbitrageurs will buy the good where it is cheap (and bid up that low price) and simultaneously sell the good wherever its price is higher (and drive down the high price). Arbitrageurs will continue this activity until the different prices for the good are all equal. Equivalently, the law of one price says that securities with identical risks must have the same expected rate of return. Most specifically, one of the fundamental theorems of APT says that assets with the same stochastic behavior must have the same expected returns. Consider, for instance, the one-period rates of return from two assets with the *equally risky* cashflows indicated in Eqs. (30-4*a*) and (30-4*b*).

[3] S. Ross, "The Arbitrage Pricing Theory of Capital Asset Pricing," *Journal of Economic Theory*, December 1976, pp. 344–360. This mathematical essay derives the APT model. Richard Roll and S. Ross, "An Empirical Investigation of the Arbitrage Pricing Theory," *Journal of Finance*, December 1980, vol. 35, pp. 1073–1103. This second article reviews the APT model and presents initial empirical tests of the APT.

$$r_1 = E(r_1) + e = (w_1^T/w_1) - 1.0 \tag{30-4a}$$

$$r_2 = E(r_2) + e = (w_2^T/w_2) - 1.0 \tag{30-4b}$$

The random variable e in equation series (30-4) is assumed to have a mathematical expectation of zero, $E(e) = 0$, and be identical for the two assets.

In order to prevent arbitrage, the expected returns from equally risky assets one and two must be equal, $E(r_1) = E(r_2)$. However, suppose that these expected rates of return are not equal and $E(r_1) > E(r_2)$. In this case a shrewd investor can create a profitable arbitrage portfolio by taking the proceeds of w_2 dollars from a short sale of asset two and investing this amount in a long position of equal size in asset one. Mathematically, $|-w_1| = w_2$. This arbitrage portfolio requires no initial investment since $-w_1 + w_2 = 0$, as specified in Eq. (30-1). The portfolio is hedged to zero risk, as indicated by Eq. (30-3). The portfolio is also perfectly hedged to zero risk because any gains (or losses) on the long position will be exactly offset by the simultaneous losses (or gains) from the short position of equal size. But, nevertheless, the arbitrage portfolio has positive expected profits with certainty, as specified by Eq. (30-2*a*), since $[E(r_1) - E(r_2)] > 0$. Thus, this arbitrage portfolio conforms to Eqs. (30-1), (30-2*a*), and (30-3). (A similar profitable arbitrage position was illustrated above in Figure 21-3*b* on page 598.)

30-1.2 undiversifiable risk from a common factor

Suppose that the one-period rates of return for all assets are generated by a single *factor* denoted F in accordance with the linear model of Eq. (30-4*c*).

$$r_{it} = a_i + b_i F_t \qquad i = 1, 2, \ldots \tag{30-4c}$$

Let F_t be a random variable with an expected value of zero, $E(F_t) = 0$. For instance, F_t might be the percentage change in the GNP or the Dow Jones Industrial Average. The b_i coefficient in Eq. (30-4*c*) is a measure of undiversifiable risk—it indicates how sensitive the ith asset is to the common source of variations. According to the law of one price, two risky assets with equal values of b_i must have the same expected rate of return; Eq. (30-5) states this condition formally.

$$E(r_i) = a_i \qquad \text{for } i = 1, 2, \ldots \qquad \text{since } E(F_t) = 0 \tag{30-5}$$

The two assets' expected rates of return should be equal, $E(r_1) = E(r_2)$, because these assets are equally responsive, $b_1 = b_2$, to the common risk factor F. But suppose that $b_1 \neq b_2$. When the riskiness of the two assets differs, the arbitrageur can earn riskless profits by investing a fraction x of the arbitrage portfolio's total wealth in asset one and $(1.0 - x)$ in asset two, where $0 < x < +1.0$. Equation (30-6*a*) defines this portfolio's weighted average rate of return.

$$r_{pt} = x r_{1t} + (1 - x) r_{2t} \tag{30-6a}$$

$$= x(a_1 + b_1 F_t) + (1 - x)(a_2 + b_2 F_t) \tag{30-6b}$$

$$= x(a_1 - a_2) + a_2 + [x(b_1 - b_2) + b_2] F_t \tag{30-6c}$$

If the value of the investment proportion x is selected so that $x^* =$

$[b_2/(b_2 - b_1)]$, then this quantity can be substituted into Eq. (30-6*c*) for x to obtain, after some rearranging, Eq. (30-7).

$$r_p = \frac{a_2 + b_2(a_1 - a_2)}{b_2 - b_1} \tag{30-7}$$

In Eq. (30-7) the portfolio's return is riskless since the random systematic factor F drops out of the equation. In perfect capital markets, a certain investment must yield a risk-free rate of return, denoted R. This allows us to say that $r_p = R$, and it also allows us to rewrite Eq. (30-7) as Eq. (30-8).

$$R = \frac{a_2 + b_2(a_1 - a_2)}{(b_2 - b_1)} \tag{30-8}$$

Multiplying both sides of Eq. (30-8) by the quantity $(b_2 - b_1)$ and rearranging leads to Eq. (30-9*a*).

$$\frac{(a_1 - R)}{b_1} = \frac{(a_2 - R)}{b_2} \tag{30-9a}$$

From Eq. (30-5) we know that $E(r_i) = a_i$. Substituting for a_i allows Eq. (30-9*a*) to be restated as Eq. (30-9*b*).

$$\frac{(a_i - R)}{b_i} = \frac{E(r_i) - R}{b_i} = \lambda \frac{\text{(risk-premium)}}{\text{(risk-measure)}} \tag{30-9b}$$

Equations (30-9*a*) and (30-9*b*) define a constant called lambda, denoted λ, that represents the *factor risk-premium.*

30-1.3 the arbitrage pricing line

Equation (30-9*b*) can be equivalently rewritten as Eqs. (30-10*a*) and (30-10*b*) to obtain the *arbitrage pricing line.* Substituting from Eqs. (30-5) and (30-9*b*) allows Eq. (30-10*a*) to be stated below.

$$E(r_i) = R + b_i \frac{E(r_i) - R}{b_i} \tag{30-10a}$$

$$E(r_i) = R + b_i \lambda \tag{30-10b}$$

Equation (30-10*b*) was derived by substituting from the definition in Eq. (30-9*b*). Figure 30-1 illustrates the arbitrage pricing line of Eq. (30-10*a*).

The factor risk-premium, λ, can be interpreted as the *excess rate of return,* $[E(r_i) - R]$, for a risky asset with $b_i = 1.0$. Equation series (30-10) is the essence of the APT. Equations (30-10*a*) and (30-10*b*) say that, in the absence of profitable arbitrage opportunities, the expected rate of return from any risky asset equals the risk-free rate of return plus a risk-premium that is proportional to the asset's sensitivity, b_i, to the common risk factor, F. This sensitivity is measured by the *factor loading*, b_i, for the ith asset.

The arbitrage pricing line shown in Fig. 30-1 is a risk-return relationship. Risk is measured along the horizontal axis of Fig. 30-1. The APT considers all assets that are in the same risk-class, such as assets O and U in Fig. 30-1, to be perfect substitutes that should yield the same rate of return. Assets' expected

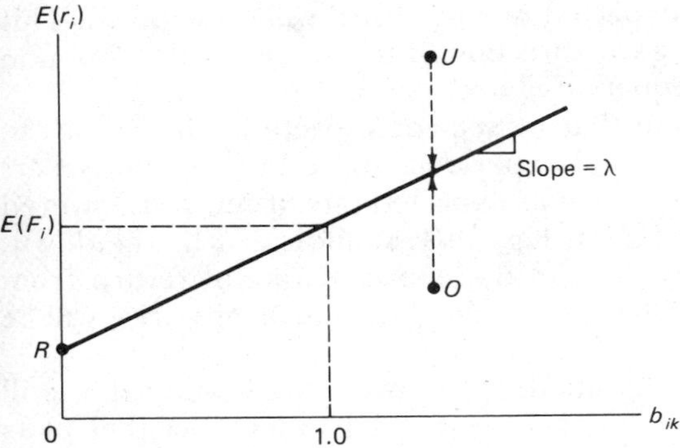

FIGURE 30-1 the APT model for one factor.

rates of return are measured along the vertical axis of Fig. 30-1. The arbitrage pricing line intersects the vertical axis at point R, the riskless rate of interest.

30-1.4 over- and underpriced assets

Consider two assets in the same risk-class, like the two assets at points U and O in Fig. 30-1. Assets U and O both violate the law of one price because they are both in the same risk-class but do not have the same expected rate of return on the arbitrage pricing line. In the economic equilibrium all assets should lie on the arbitrage pricing line. The forces of supply and demand will drive all assets to lie on the arbitrage pricing line as arbitrageurs work to profit from assets that violate the law of one price. The arbitrage process that will tend to move all assets onto the arbitrage pricing line is outlined below.

As investors investigate before they invest, some of them will discover that asset O in Fig. 30-1 offers potential investors a lower rate of return than asset U, even though they both involve *equal* amounts of risk. Therefore, risk-averse investors will sell asset O because it is a less desirable investment. The resulting excess of supply over demand for asset O will drive down its market price. As the price of asset O is driven down, the one-period expected rate of return for asset O will rise; this price-adjustment process is indicated by the arrows in a common stock's expected rate of return equation below.

$$\uparrow E(r) = \frac{[E(p_{t-1}) - p_t] + d_t}{\downarrow p_t} = \frac{[\text{price change}] + [\text{cash dividend, if any}]}{\downarrow \text{purchase price}}$$

Risk-averse investors will continue to sell asset O until its price is driven down and its expected rate of return rises up onto the arbitrage pricing line in Fig. 30-1. The upward-pointing arrow in Fig. 30-1 traces the path that asset O's expected rate of return should follow until it reaches its equilibrium point on the arbitrage pricing line.

Smart investors will not only sell asset O if they own any of it, they will also sell asset O short and use the cash proceeds they obtained from the short sale to buy a long position in asset U. Investors will buy asset U in order to enjoy its expected rate of return, which lies above the arbitrage pricing line in Fig. 30-1 and also above the expected return from asset O. As these profit-seekers buy asset U in order to obtain its high return, they will bid up its price. And, as the price of asset U is bid higher, its expected rate of return will come down. This process can be traced by reversing the direction of the arrows in the common stock's expected rate of return equation above.

The basic economic assumption that most people prefer more wealth to less wealth will assure that asset U will experience more buyers than sellers until its purchase price is bid so high that its expected rate of return is lowered down onto the arbitrage pricing line in Fig. 30-1, as indicated by the downward-pointing arrow in the figure. When the expected rate of return from asset U is driven down onto the arbitrage pricing line, the asset's price will be in equilibrium.

The price adjustment process outlined in the preceding paragraphs will work for all assets in all risk-classes. This means that every asset that plots *above* the arbitrage pricing line in Fig. 30-1 is underpriced, and its price will adjust upward in the same way that the price of asset U rose. Likewise, every asset that plots *below* the arbitrage pricing line is overpriced, and its price will fall by the same market mechanism that lowered the price of asset O in Fig. 30-1.

30-1.5 the arbitrage portfolio

In an effort to maximize the profits they can derive from their research finding, the smartest investors will sell asset O short and *simultaneously* buy a long position of equal dollar value in asset U. These smartest investors will have zero cash invested in their *arbitrage portfolio* made up of a short position in asset O combined with an equal long position in asset U. They will not need to invest a cent of their own funds because they can take the cash proceeds from the short sale of asset O and use these short sale proceeds to buy a long position of equal value in asset U. Furthermore, these smartest investors will not be exposed to any risk because their arbitrage portfolio is perfectly hedged with long and short positions of equal value that offset each other's gains and losses. And finally, the *arbitrage portfolio* will earn a riskless profit of $[E(r_U) - E(r_O)]$. The arbitrage portfolio earns this profit by raising funds from the short sale on which the arbitrageur must pay a rate of return of $E(r_O)$ and, simultaneously, investing these funds in the long position at a higher rate of return of $E(r_U)$. This profit is riskless because the *arbitrage portfolio* is perfectly hedged.

In summary, the *arbitrage portfolio* will (1) have zero money invested, (2) be a riskless investment undertaking, and, (3) earn a predetermined positive profit. Most investors in the world will not even know what the word "arbitrage" means. But, if only a few aggressive investors run arbitrage portfolios for themselves, their actions will be sufficient to generate the APT equilibrium condition illustrated in Fig. 30-1.

30-1.6 implications and extensions of the APT

Note that the capital asset pricing model (CAPM), which happens to be equal to Eq. (30-10*b*), is a special case of the APT.[4] Furthermore, in the case when only one factor exists, that single factor must be the *market portfolio* from the capital market theory of Chap. 26.

[4] William F. Sharpe, "Capital Asset Prices: A Theory of Market Equilibrium under Conditions of Risk," *Journal of Finance*, September 1964, pp. 425–442. The CAPM is derived in this paper. Robert Jarrow and Andrew Rudd, "A Comparison of the APT and CAPM," *Journal of Banking and Finance*, June 1983, vol. 7, no. 2, pp. 295–303.

Another significant aspect of the APT is that it can be extended to include several different common factors. For example, factors like F_1, F_2, and F_3 (or even more factors) could be included as different sources of variation that affect market assets. Much empirical work remains to be done to determine the number of relevant factors that determine asset returns and the identity of these factors. But, before considering the empirical evidence, the APT is developed further in the section below.

30-2 A MORE GENERAL DERIVATION OF THE APT MODEL

Equation (30-11) below may be thought of as an extended characteristic line with k different economic indices as explanatory variables.[5] It is a single asset, time-series return-generating model.

$$r_{it} = a_i + b_{i1}F_{1t} + b_{i2}F_{2t} + \cdots + b_{ik}F_{kt} + e_{it} \tag{30-11}$$

where

r_{it} = one-period rate of return from ith asset in time period t

a_i = expected rate of return for an asset if all risk factors have a value of zero, that is, $a_i = E(r_i)$

F_{jt} = jth risk factor (or communality) that impacts on assets' returns, where $j = 1, 2, \ldots, k$ different risk factors exist. This risk factor has a mathematical expectation of zero, $E(F_{jt}) = 0$

b_{ij} = sensitivity indicator (or factor loading) that measures how respon-sive returns from asset i are to index j for $j = 1, 2, \ldots, k$ indices[6]

e_{it} = random-error term for asset i in period t that measures unex-plained residual return, which has expected value of zero and variance of σ_{ei}

Two statistical conditions must be true of the return-generating function in Eq. (30-11).

1. The unexplained residuals between all assets must be independent, $E(e_ie_j) = 0$ where $i \neq j$.
2. All factors must be independent (or orthogonal) with respect to all assets, $E[e_i \{F_j - E(F_j)\}] = 0$ for all i and j.

Let us derive the APT from a return-generating process like Eq. (30-11).

[5] The characteristic regression line from Chap. 10, Eq. (10-1), is reproduced below as an orientation for those who may already be familiar with it.

$$r_{it} = a_i + b_i r_{mt} + e_{it} \tag{10-1}$$

Although Eqs. (10-1) and (30-11) are different return-generating functions, they have enough in common to make a comparison insightful.

[6] The b_{ij} term is called a factor loading if it is estimated using factor-analytic procedures, or it is called a regression coefficient if it is estimated using regression analysis.

30-1.2 a two-factor return-generating process

A linear additive return-generating process like Eq. (30-11) underlies all APT. It is nevertheless possible to discuss the APT without ever referring to this return-generating model. But we will derive a simple APT model with two indices in order to see how the theory is derived. Equation (30-12) is a simple return-generating process with two unidentified risk factors.

$$r_{it} = a_i + b_{i1}F_{1t} + b_{i2}F_{2t} + e_{it} \tag{30-12}$$

If you want concrete examples, you may imagine that the first risk factor in Eq. (30-12) is the rate of change in Standard & Poor's stock market index and the second risk factor as being an index of cash dividend payout rates. The APT gives us *no clue* as to what indices could be relevant—this is unlike the capital market theory, which is based on a unique index called the *market portfolio.*

30-2.2 three widely diversified portfolios

Consider three risk-averse investors who form portfolios that each contain n assets, where (1) the number of assets (n) must exceed the number of indices ($K = 2$, in this example), and (2) n is some large number. The return on such a portfolio is defined in Eq. (30-13a) as r_p. The x_i term is the weight or participation level for the ith asset in the portfolio.

$$\begin{aligned} r_{pt} &= \sum_{i=1}^{n} x_i r_{it} \\ &= \sum_{i}^{n} x_i a_i + \sum_{i=1}^{n} x_i b_{i1} F_{it} + \sum_{i=1}^{n} x_i b_{i2} F_{2t} + \sum_{i=1}^{n} x_i e_i \end{aligned} \tag{30-13a}$$

Equation (30-14) is the *balance sheet identity*, which cannot be violated if the investor's portfolio is to have any rational financial interpretation. This equation requires that the weights add up to unity (or 100 percent).

$$\sum_{i=1}^{n} x_i = 1.0 \tag{30-14}$$

In a widely diversified portfolio the unsystematic residual risk is *diversifiable* and hence will average out to zero, as indicated in Eq. (30-15).

$$\sum_{i=1}^{n} x_i e_i = 0 \tag{30-15}$$

TABLE 30-1 risk and return statistics for three portfolios

portfolio	expected return	b_{p1}	b_{p2}
B	$E(r_B) = 16.0\%$	1.0	.7
C	$E(r_C) = 14.0\%$	.6	1.0
D	$E(r_D) = 11.0\%$	.5	.4

As a result of Eq. (30-15), Eq. (30-13*a*) will contain only systematic risk and can thus be rewritten as Eq. (30-13*b*).

$$r_{pt} = \sum_{i=1}^{n} x_i a_i + \sum_{i=1}^{n} x_i b_{i1} F_{1t} + \sum_{i=1}^{n} x_i b_{i2} F_{2t} \quad (30\text{-}13b)$$

The systematic risk in portfolio p thus equals $\sum_i x_i b_{i1} = b_{p1}$ and $\sum_i x_i b_{i2} = b_{p2}$ from risk factors one and two, respectively.

Table 30-1 shows the risk and return statistics for the three hypothetical widely diversified portfolios.

30-2.3 the APT model

Equation (30-16) shows the general form of the APT model which can be derived from the two-factor return-generating function of Eq. (30-12). The two sensitivity values, b_{i1} and b_{i2}, are the explanatory variables in Eq. (30-16*a*).

$$E(r_i) = \lambda_0 + \lambda_1 b_{i1} + \lambda_2 b_{i2} \quad (30\text{-}16a)$$

$$E(r_i) = 5.629 + 7.777 b_{i1} + 3.703 b_{i2} \quad (30\text{-}16b)$$

Equation (30-16*b*) shows the specific APT model that can be derived from the numerical values in Table 30-1. The mathematical derivation of the values of λ_0, λ_1, and λ_2 in Eq. (30-16*a*) is explained below.

Any three points, like $E(r_i)$, b_{i1}, and b_{i2}, for example, define a plane in geometry. Equation (30-16*b*) is the formula for a specific three-dimensional plane that is an asset pricing model for the three portfolios in Table 30-1.[7] Figure 30-2 illustrates the APT plane of Eq. (30-16*a*). Substituting the numer-

[7] For other derivations of APT models see Phillip H. Dybvig, "An Explicit Bound on Individual Assets' Deviations from APT Pricing in a Finite Economy," *Journal of Financial Economics*, December 1983, pp. 483–496; Mark Grinblatt and Sheridan Titman, "Factor Pricing in a Finite Economy," *Journal of Financial Economics,* December 1983, vol. 12, no. 4, pp. 497–507.

FIGURE 30-2 APT plane for two-factor model.

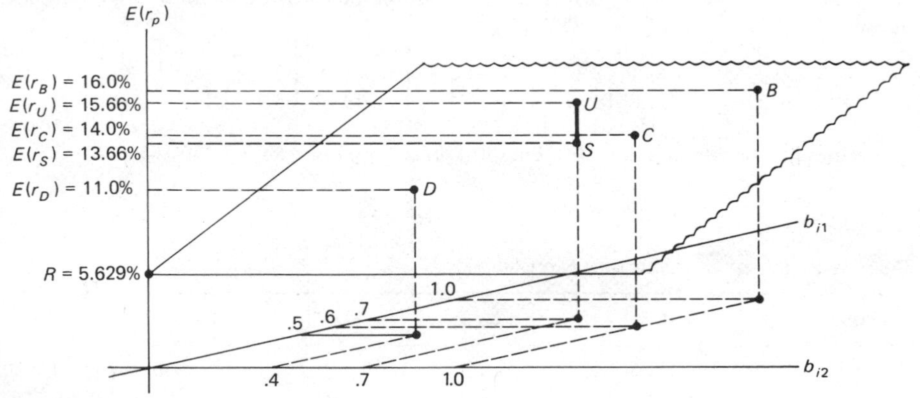

ical value for any of the three portfolios in Table 30-1 into Eq. (30-16b) proves numerically that the three points all fit this APT plane.[8]

30-3 THE ARBITRAGE PORTFOLIO

In equilibrium, the risks and return of every asset should conform to the APT model of Eq. (30-16a) and Fig. 30-2. Consider a specific case where one asset is mispriced to see why the APT has asset pricing implications. Suppose that a wealth-seeking, risk-averse investor analyzes portfolio U in Table 30-2 and discovers that it is underpriced. In order to make this security analysis discovery the investor had to create portfolio S (on paper, without any real transactions). Portfolio S is made up of three equal part investments of one-third each in portfolios B, C, and D from Table 30-1. The two sensitivities and the expected return of portfolio S are calculated below and reported in Table 30-2.

$$E(r_S) = \frac{1}{3}E(r_B) + \frac{1}{3}E(r_C) + \frac{1}{3}E(r_D) \tag{30-19}$$

[8] This footnote shows the mathematical derivation of Eq. (30-16b) and the plane in Fig. 30-2. The APT model of Eq. (30-16a) can be rewritten for the three assets (namely, the portfolios) in Table 30-1, as shown below.

$$E(r_i) = \lambda_0 + \lambda_1 b_{i1} + \lambda_2 b_{i2} \qquad (30\text{-}16a)$$

$$16.0 = \lambda_0(1.0) + \lambda_1\,(1.0) + \lambda_2\,(.7) \qquad (30\text{-}16c)$$

$$14.0 = \lambda_0\,(1.0) + \lambda_1\,(.6) + \lambda_2\,(1.0) \qquad (30\text{-}16d)$$

$$11.0 = \lambda_0\,(1.0) + \lambda_1\,(.5) + \lambda_2\,(.4) \qquad (30\text{-}16e)$$

Equations (30-16c), (30-16d), and (30-16e) are three equations in three unknowns (namely, the λ_0, λ_1, and λ_2), which are equivalently rewritten in matrix Eqs. (30-17a) and (30-17b) below.

$$\begin{bmatrix} 16.0 \\ 14.0 \\ 11.0 \end{bmatrix} = \begin{bmatrix} 1.0 & 1.0 & .7 \\ 1.0 & .6 & 1.0 \\ 1.0 & .5 & .4 \end{bmatrix} \begin{bmatrix} \lambda_0 \\ \lambda_1 \\ \lambda^2 \end{bmatrix} \qquad (30\text{-}17a)$$

$$R = C \quad \lambda \qquad (30\text{-}17b)$$

The matrix (or, more technically, the vector) of unknowns, λ, is evaluated by, first, finding the inverse of the coefficients matrix, C. This inverse is denoted C^{-1}. Second, premultiplying the inverse of matrix C times the return vector, R, yields the values of the vector of unknowns, λ, as shown below in Eqs. (30-18a) and (30-18b).

$$\begin{bmatrix} -.9629 & -.1851 & 2.1481 \\ 2.2222 & -1.1111 & -1.1111 \\ -.3703 & 1.8518 & -1.4814 \end{bmatrix} \begin{bmatrix} 16.0 \\ 14.0 \\ 11.0 \end{bmatrix} = \begin{bmatrix} 5.629 \\ 7.7777 \\ 3.7037 \end{bmatrix} = \begin{bmatrix} \lambda_0 \\ \lambda_1 \\ \lambda_2 \end{bmatrix} \qquad (30\text{-}18a)$$

$$C^{-1} \quad R = \lambda = \lambda \qquad (30\text{-}18b)$$

The values for the lambdas in matrix Eq. (30-18a) are used in APT Eq. (30-16b).

TABLE 30-2 risk-return statistics for two portfolios

portfolio	$E(r_p)$, %	b_{i1}	b_{i2}	identity
S	13.66	.7	.7	(⅓)B + (⅓)C + (⅓)D
U	15.66	.7	.7	Underpriced

$$13.66\% = \frac{1}{3}(16.0\%) + \frac{1}{3}(14.0\%) + \frac{1}{3}(11.0\%)$$

$$b_{S1} = \frac{1}{3}(b_{B1}) + \frac{1}{3}(b_{C1}) + \frac{1}{3}(b_{D1}) \tag{30-20}$$

$$.7 = \frac{1}{3}(1.0) + \frac{1}{3}(.6) + \frac{1}{3}(.5)$$

$$b_{S2} = \frac{1}{3}(b_{B2}) + \frac{1}{3}(b_{C2}) + \frac{1}{3}(b_{D2}) \tag{30-21}$$

$$.7 = \frac{1}{3}(.7) + \frac{1}{3}(1.0) + \frac{1}{3}(.4)$$

Portfolios S and U in Table 30-2 have identical risk statistics, but they have different expected rates of return. According to the *law of one price,* the same good should never sell at two different prices. Since portfolios S and U have identical risks, they are perfect investment substitutes. So, according to the law of one price, investors should buy portfolio U in order to get more return at the same risk as portfolio S. No rational investor would want to buy portfolio S and get less return for the same risk that portfolio U bears.

Some shrewd investor will use the law of one price to earn riskless arbitrage profits. By setting up a hedge with portfolios S and U the shrewd investor can create a profit without investing any money or without taking any risks. Table 30-3 illustrates how a shrewd investor can initially (1) sell \$100 (or any other amount) of portfolio S short and (2) take the \$100 from the short sale and buy a long position in portfolio U. Note that the shrewd investor has a position in the arbitrage portfolio without investing a single penny. This no-money-invested (shown in the second column of Table 30-3) characteristic of the arbitrage portfolio can be formalized as Eq. (30-22).[9]

$$0 = \sum_{p=1}^{p=2} x_p \tag{30-22}$$

[9] Note that Eq. (30-22) is different from Eq. (30-14). They differ because Eq. (30-14) is summing across the n assets that make up portfolio p while, in contrast, Eq. (30-22) is summing across only portfolios S and U in Table 30-3. Conceptually, however, the two equations are identical.

TABLE 30-3 the arbitrage portfolio

portfolio	initial cashflow	ending cashflow	b_{i1}	b_{i2}
S = Short	+ \$100	− \$113.66	−.7	−.7
U = Underpriced (long)	− \$100	\$115.66	.7	.7
A = Arbitrage (hedged)	0	+ \$2.00	0	0

Table 30-3 shows how the shrewd investor has set up a riskless *arbitrage portfolio,* denoted A, which is both long and short assets with identical risks. These identical long and short positions create a riskless hedge that cannot profit or lose from any price changes, because the equal-sized gains and losses from the long and short positions exactly offset each other. The two types of zero-systematic-risk-of-any-kind characteristic of the arbitrage portfolio are formalized in Eqs. (30-23) and (30-24), respectively.[10]

$$0 = \sum_{p=1}^{p=2} x_p b_{p1} \tag{30-23}$$

$$0 = \sum_{p=1}^{p=2} x_p b_{p2} \tag{30-24}$$

At the end of the investment period the closing cash flows sum up in favor of the arbitrageur. This shrewd investor can sell portfolio U and collect the \$100 investment plus the 15.66 percent return for a total of \$115.66 cash inflow. And, at the same time, the shrewd investor can spend \$113.66 to cover the \$100 short position in portfolio S and pay the 13.66 percent interest (or cash dividend) that the person who bought \$100 worth of S expected to receive for making this risky investment. After these cashflows, the shrewd investor earns \$2 profit without investing any money or without taking any risk. Shrewd arbitrageurs will bid up the price of the underpriced portfolio U and therefore drive down its expected return, as indicated in Eq. (30-25).

$$\downarrow E(r_U) = \frac{E(15.66 \text{ income per period})}{\uparrow \text{ purchase price (bid upward)}} \tag{30-25}$$

The arbitrage will continue until portfolio U is priced so that it lies on the APT plane at point S in Fig. 30-2. In fact, if you think about it, similar arbitrage will cause the price of every asset to be revised until its expected return and risk statistics align with the APT model of Eq. (30-16*b*).

30-4 RECONCILING THE CAPM AND APT

Various aspects of the APT can be given economic interpretations that are insightful. For instance, the intercept term, λ_0, in Eq. (30-16*a*) must equal the return on a riskless asset when an asset with zero sensitivities to all the indices is considered. The derivation of the APT is in no way dependent upon the existence of a riskless asset. However, if we define the return on a zero beta or riskless asset to be R, then if such an asset exists, $\lambda_0 = R$. Using this equality allows the APT model of Eq. (30-16*a*) to be equivalently rewritten in *risk-premium form,* as shown in Eqs. (30-26*a*) and (30-26*b*).

$$E(r_i) - \lambda_0 = \lambda_1 b_{i1} + \lambda_2 b_{i2} \tag{30-26a}$$

[10] Note that although they may appear similar at a glance, Eqs. (30-23) and (30-24) are different from Eqs. (30-20) and (30-21) because Eqs. (30-20) and (30-21) are summing across B, C, and D while (30-23) and (30-24) are summing across the objects in the arbitrage portfolio—portfolios S and U.

$$E(r_i) - R = \lambda_1 b_{i1} + \lambda_2 b_{i2} \qquad \text{since } \lambda_0 = R \tag{30-26b}$$

The lambda coefficient associated with the risk sensitivity to the *j*th index, denoted λ_j, measures the increase in expected return the market requires to induce investors to assume a one-unit increase in b_{ij} risk. The λ_j coefficient thus measures the *market price of risk* for whatever risk is measured by b_{ij}.

30-4.1 the CAPM

When $b_{i1} = 1.0$ and $b_{i2} = 0$ then APT Eq. (30-26*b*) reduces to Eqs. (30-27*a*) and (30-27*b*).

$$E(r_i) - R = \lambda_1 b_{i1} \tag{30-27a}$$

$$E(r_i) = R + \lambda_1 b_{i1} \tag{30-27b}$$

Equation (30-27*b*) is simply the capital asset pricing model (CAPM) with λ_1 defined in Eq. (30-28) and b_i as the beta coefficient from the characteristic line of Chap. 10. That is, Eq. (30-27*b*) is the CAPM.

$$\lambda_1 = E(r_m) - R \qquad \text{in Eq. (30-27b)} \tag{30-28}$$

This interpretation of the APT shows that the CAPM is merely a special case of the APT. The derivation of the CAPM in Eq. (30-27*b*) from the APT model of Eq. (30-26*a*) shows that the CAPM and the APT theories do not contradict each other.[11]

30-4.2 the *k*-dimensional APT hyperplane

The *k*-factor return-generating process of Eq. (30-11) was abbreviated to Eq. (30-12) for the sake of expedition. If this simplification were not employed, the *k*-factor APT model shown in Eq. (30-29) would have been derived instead of the two-factor APT model of Eq. (30-16*a*).

$$E(r_i) = \lambda_0 + \lambda_1 b_{i1} + \lambda_2 b_{i2} + \cdots + \lambda_k b_{ik} \tag{30-29}$$

Equation (30-29) is the APT in a *k*-dimensional hyperplane that has all the implications suggested for the two-factor APT model above. In particular, Eqs. (30-22), (30-23), (30-24), and (30-25), which define the arbitrage portfolio, are also true in the *k*-dimensional hyperplane.

30-5 COMPARING APT WITH MPT

The modern portfolio theory (MPT) of Markowitz and Ross's more recent APT are competing for the attention of the finance profession. Let us compare and contrast these two theories so we can understand why proponents of the new APT suggest its superiority over the older and more widely accepted MPT.

30-5.1 APT is more general than MPT

The capital asset pricing model (CAPM), which was discussed in Chaps. 10 and 26, is probably the single most important aspect of the MPT. It has been shown that MPT's important CAPM is merely a special case of the APT. Thus, APT may be viewed as a logical extension, generalization, and natural out-

[11] Robert Jarrow and Andrew Rudd, "A Comparison of the APT and CAPM," *Journal of Banking and Finance*, June 1983, vol. 7, no. 2, pp. 295–303.

growth of the MPT. Other comparisons of the two theories are reviewed in this section as a way to obtain a better perspective on the APT.

30-5.2 APT employs fewer assumptions

All economic theories are based on one or more simplifying assumptions. Economic theories based on fewer and more realistic assumptions are more popular than more highly contrived theories because they are easier to learn, apply, and explain. APT and MPT both employ simplifying assumptions. One of the arguments favoring APT over MPT is that the APT's greater generality is accomplished in spite of the fact that APT is based on fewer simplifying assumptions.

30-5.3 the underlying assumptions

Like MPT, APT assumes that investors prefer more wealth over less wealth. Both theories also assume that investors dislike risk. Stated in terms of the utility theory (explained in the appendix to Chap. 27), both theories assume that all investors have positive but diminishing marginal utility of wealth (or returns) and make investment decisions that will maximize their expected utility. These are realistic assumptions.

Other MPT simplifying assumptions (explained in Chap. 26) that are shared by APT are (1) that capital markets are perfect and (2) that investors have homogeneous expectations. *Perfect markets* is an assumption which is widely used by economists, and it is easy to accept. By assuming that the capital asset markets are perfect, economists assume away the possibility that prices are manipulated or distorted away from the equilibrium values established by supply and demand.

Homogeneous expectations is a more heroic assumption. *Homogeneous expectations* implies that all investors share the same risk and return perceptions for any given asset. The MPT and APT theories both assume that investors have different assessments for different assets. But, investors are assumed to all have the same risk and return perceptions for any particular asset to obviate the need to complicate the model with differences of opinion over how investors view a particular investment opportunity.

Supporters of APT argue its superiority over MPT because of the following assumptions that MPT requires but are not needed in the APT. Unlike MPT, APT is (1) not restricted to a one-period planning horizon; (2) not restricted to rates of price change that conform to a normal empirical probability distribution of returns; (3) not dependent on any strong assumptions about investors' utility functions in order to generate a two-parameter model; (4) not based on a market portfolio that is a uniquely desirable investment; and (5) not based on any requirement for riskless borrowing and lending.

Although the APT requires fewer assumptions than the more specific and restrictive MPT model, the APT does depend on one unique and fairly unrealistic assumption. The APT no-money-invested assumption, Eq. (30-22), presumes that the arbitraging short sellers are able to obtain 100 percent of the proceeds from their short sales to finance the purchase of their equal and offsetting long positions. Realistically, only a few professional investors (such as NYSE specialists) are able to achieve anything approaching this utopian situation. However, it only takes a few well-funded investors who are arbitrageurs to maintain the "law of one price" on which the APT is based.

30-6 EMPIRICAL TESTS OF APT

Empirically testing the APT involves a two-step process. This process employs two different phases of statistical estimates. It is informative to recall how the CAPM is estimated in order to see how the APT tests are structured—the two differing models employ somewhat analogous empirical estimation procedures.

CAPM EMPIRICAL TEST PROCEDURE Empirically testing the CAPM begins with a "first-pass" time-series regression for each different asset, to estimate the characteristic line and the beta coefficient for each asset sampled. Essentially, a list (or vector) of one-period rates of return from the *i*th asset,

$$[r_{it}, r_{i,t+1}, r_{i,t+2}, r_{i,t+3}, \ldots, r_{i,t+T}]$$

are regressed onto a list of concurrent market returns.

$$[r_{mt}, r_{m,t+1}, r_{m,t+2}, r_{m,t+3}, \ldots, r_{m,t+T}]$$

The market returns are the independent variable that is used to explain the behavior of the *i*th asset's returns in a simple regression of the form shown below.

$$r_{it} = a_i + b_i r_{m,t} + e_{i,t} \tag{10-1}$$

where $e_{i,t}$ is a normally distributed random variable with a mean value of zero and a constant variance. After the time-series regression above is estimated for many different assets, one "second-pass" cross-sectional regression is used to measure the risk-return relationship between the average rates of return and the beta risk coefficients for the sampled assets. This second-pass simple regression is of the form below.

$$\begin{pmatrix}\text{Average rate of}\\ \text{return for asset } i\end{pmatrix} = A + B\begin{pmatrix}\text{beta for}\\ \text{asset } i\end{pmatrix} + u_i \tag{30-30}$$

The cross-sectional regression above is an empirical estimate of the CAPM.

APT EMPIRICAL TEST PROCEDURE USING FACTOR ANALYSIS To test or estimate the APT model a statistical methodology called factor analysis is frequently used. *Factor analysis* simultaneously performs two functions in its "first-pass" computation. The factor analysis algorithm analyzes time-series data of $T + 1$ periods' rates of return over a cross section of N different assets and statistically *extracts* those risk factors that systematically affect the returns from the sampled assets. Essentially, factor analysis simultaneously analyzes all the returns from N assets over $T + 1$ time periods—that is, all the data in the matrix below—in the "first-pass" computation.

$$\begin{bmatrix} r_{1,t}, & r_{1,t+1}, & r_{1,t+2}, & \cdots, & r_{1,t+T} \\ r_{2,t}, & r_{2,t+1}, & r_{2,t+2}, & \cdots, & r_{2,t+T} \\ & & \cdot & & \\ & & \cdot & & \\ & & \cdot & & \\ r_{N,t}, & r_{N,t+1}, & r_{N,t+2}, & \cdots, & r_{N,t+T} \end{bmatrix}$$

Factor analysis produces or extracts its own explanatory variables, called *factors,* from the matrix of returns above. The purpose of factor analysis is to reduce the N by $T + 1$ matrix of returns to a smaller k by $T + 1$ matrix that explains all or most of the variation in the matrix of returns. The k factors extracted by factor analysis have *factor scores* like the $F_{i,t}$ value for the ith factor in time period t, shown in the factor matrix below.

$$\begin{bmatrix} F_{1,t}, & F_{1,t+1}, & F_{1,t+2}, & \cdots, & F_{1,t+T} \\ F_{2,t}, & F_{2,t+1}, & F_{2,t+2}, & \cdots, & F_{2,t+T} \\ & & \cdot & & \\ & & \cdot & & \\ & & \cdot & & \\ F_{k,t}, & F_{k,t+1}, & F_{k,t+2}, & \cdots, & F_{k,t+T} \end{bmatrix}$$

The factor scores in the matrix above are used as the independent variables in the second part of the "first-pass" factor analysis computations.

In the second stage of the "first-pass" computation to estimate the APT model empirically, regression analysis is used to estimate the b_{ij} coefficients for the ith asset's sensitivity to the jth factor. These $b_{i,t}$ coefficients are called *factor loadings.* Time-series regressions of the form below yield estimates of the factor loadings.

$$r_{it} = a_i + b_{i1}F_{1t} + \cdots + b_{ik}F_{kt} + e_{it} \tag{30-31}$$

To be more specific about what is obtained, factor analysis yields factor scores in the first portion of the *first-pass* computation that are employed in the second-pass regression to get estimates of the factor loadings, denoted b_{ij} in Eqs. (30-10*b*) and (30-16*a*) in this chapter, for instance. Thus, in the "first pass" the factor analysis computes factor loadings for each asset (i = 1, 2, . . . N) and every risk factor (j = 1, 2, . . . k). These factor loadings are somewhat like the betas obtained from the "first-pass" characteristic line estimates when testing the CAPM.

A "second-pass" regression yields estimates of the APT *factor risk-premiums,* denoted λ_j. The cross-sectional model below is used to regress the assets' average returns, $\bar{r}_i$, on their factor loadings, b_{ij}, and obtain estimates of the λ regression statistics.

$$\bar{r}_i = \lambda_0 + \lambda_1 b_{i1} + \lambda_2 b_{i2} + \cdots + \lambda_k b_{ik} + u_i \tag{30-32}$$

This second-pass regression also produces separate statistics (called t statistics) for each value of lambda, λ, that indicate whether or not the estimated risk-premiums are statistically significant. If these risk-premiums are significantly different from zero, then the jth factor is said to be "priced" or valued by the market in the determination of market prices. The second-pass regression's goodness-of-fit statistics (such as the correlation coefficient) also indicate how well the factors explain the securities' average returns. Let us consider specific empirical studies.

30-7 AN INITIAL STUDY BY ROLL AND ROSS IN 1980[12]

Factor analysis is a technique of statistical analysis with which most financial analysts were unfamiliar in 1976, when Stephen A. Ross's seminal article introducing APT was published.[13] As a result, few empirical tests of the new APT were published soon after the theory's 1976 introduction.[14] Here we will review some of the major findings of an initial inquiry prepared by Stephen Ross and Richard Roll (RR hereafter).

RR employed factor-analytic techniques to analyze 1,260 NYSE stocks divided into 42 groups containing thirty stocks each. Daily stock price returns from 1962 through 1972—that is, 2,619 trading days of returns for each stock—were analyzed. After the factor loadings were estimated in the first step of their tests, RR used multiple regression to perform the second step of their study. RR ran a separate cross-sectional multiple regression for each of the 42 groups of stocks. The factor loadings, b_{ij}, from the first step of the analysis were the independent variables in the multiple regressions of the second step. The cross-sectional regression coefficient, λ_j, for the jth factor loading is an empirical estimate of that factor's risk-premium. One or more of these regression coefficients should be statistically significantly different from

[12] R. Roll and S. Ross, "An Empirical Investigation of the Arbitrage Pricing Theory," *Journal of Finance,* December 1980, vol. 35, pp. 1073–1103.

[13] S. Ross, "The Arbitrage Pricing Theory of Capital Asset Pricing," *Journal of Economic Theory,* December 1976, pp. 344–360.

[14] Some of the earliest empirical studies were A. Gehr, "Some Tests of the Arbitrage Pricing Theory," *Journal of the Midwest Finance Association,* 1978. An interesting factor analysis study not directly related to APT was published by Benjamin F. King, "Market and Industry Factors in Stock Price Behavior," *Journal of Business,* January 1966, supp., vol. 39, pp. 139–190. More recently published APT studies include the following: Nai-fu Chen, "Some Empirical Tests of the Theory of Arbitrage Pricing," *Journal of Finance,* December 1983, vol. 38, no. 5, pp. 1393–1414; Stephen A. Ross, "Return, Risk, and Arbitrage," in Irwin Friend and James Bicksler (eds.), *Risk and Return in Finance,* vol. 1, Ballinger, Cambridge, Mass., 1977; S. Brown and M. Weinstein, "A New Approach to Testing Asset Pricing Models: The Bilinear Paradigm," *Journal of Finance,* 1983, vol. 38, pp. 711–743; J. D. Jobson, "A Multivariate Linear Regression Test for the Arbitrage Pricing Theory," *Journal of Finance,* September 1982, vol. 37, no. 4, pp. 1037–1041; Phillip H. Dybvig, "An Explicit Bound on Deviations from APT Pricing in a Finite Economy," *Journal of Financial Economics,* December 1983, pp. 483–495; Marc R. Reinganum, "The Arbitrage Pricing Theory: Some Empirical Results," *Journal of Finance,* May 1981, vol. 36, no. 2.

zero if APT is to be substantiated. Tables 30-4 and 30-5 summarize some of RR's findings.

Table 30-4 presents the estimates of the APT model of Eq. (30-26*b*), assuming the riskless rate was 6 percent ($R = 6.0\%$) in order to calculate the securities' risk-premiums. At least one of the five risk factors (λ_j for $j = 1, 2, \ldots, 5$) tested was statistically significant at the 95 percent level of significance for 37 out of the 42 (that is, 88.1 percent of the groups). Table 30-4 also shows that two or more factors were significant for 24 out of the 42 groups—that is, 57.1 percent. And, at least three factors were significant for one-third of the 42 groups. About one-sixth of the 42 groups had four or more factors that were significant. Two (or 4.8 percent) of the 42 groups had five significant factors. Two out of 42 groups may not seem like very many—until the fourth column of Table 30-4 is considered. Column four gives the percentage of the

TABLE 30-4 results from 42 cross-sectional regressions for Eq. (30-26*b*), $[E(r_i) - 6\%] = \lambda_1 b_{i1} + \lambda_2 b_{i2} + \cdots$

number of significant factors at 95% level	number of groups (out of 42) with at least as many significant factors as indicated in column one	percentage of 42 groups that were significant	expected percent due to chance if all $\lambda_j = 0$
One factor	37	88.1%	22.6%
Two factors	24	57.1%	2.6%
Three factors	14	33.3%	0.115%
Four factors	7	16.7%	0.003%
Five factors	2	4.8%	0.00003%

Source: R. Roll and S. Ross, "An Empirical Investigation of the Arbitrage Pricing Theory," *Journal of Finance*, December 1980, p. 1092, table III.

TABLE 30-5 results from 42 cross-sectional regressions for Eq. (30-29), $E(r_i) = \lambda_0 + \lambda_1 b_{i1} + \lambda_2 b_{i2} + \cdots$

number of significant factors at 95% level	number of groups (out of 42) with at least as many significant factors as indicated in column one	percentage of 42 groups that were significant	expected percent due to chance if all $\lambda_j = 0$
One factor	29	69.0%	22.6%
Two factors	20	47.6%	2.6%
Three factors	3	7.1%	0.115%
Four factors	2	4.8%	0.003%
Five factors	0	0	0.00003%

Source: R. Roll and S. Ross, "An Empirical Investigation of the Arbitrage Pricing Theory," *Journal of Finance*, December 1980, p. 1094, Table IV.

42 groups that are expected to have the indicated number of significant groups if, in fact, none of the groups were actually significant (that is, due solely to random sampling error). In all five cases, the percent that were actually significant far exceeded the percent that would result from only sampling error. Even though these test results suggest that the APT-based factor analysis can explain a significant amount of common stock returns, RR reformulated their test slightly in order to obtain additional evidence.

Table 30-5 shows the results of RR's test of APT Eq. (30-29). The only difference between RR's test results in Table 30-4 and the results in Table 30-5 is in the riskless rates of interest used in the two tests. The results in Table 30-4 used a 6 percent ($R = 6.0\%$) riskless rate of interest to calculate the excess returns, $[E(r_i) - 6.0\%]$, which served as the independent variable. In contrast, RR used a multiple regression algorithm that estimated its own intercept coefficient, λ_0, to serve as an estimate of the rate of return from an asset that has no systematic risk. The same NYSE common stock data were used for both tests.

The results in Table 30-5 show that 29 out of the 42 groups (that is, 69 percent) had at least one statistically significant factor at the 95 percent level of statistical significance. For 20 of the 42 (or 47.6 percent) groups, at least two factors were significant. For 7 percent (or 3 out of 42) of the groups at least three of the risk factors were significant. And four factors were significant for 2 (or 4.8 percent) of the groups. Although these results do not furnish evidence that is quite as strong as the results in Table 30-4, the results in both tables are much more than would occur merely as the result of normal sampling error.

The results in Table 30-4 suggest that three or possibly even four risk factors exist that systematically influence common stock returns. RR say that the statistically significant risk factors are "priced"—that is, their impact is reflected in the security prices to some statistically significant extent. The results in Table 30-5 support the existence of two statistically significant risk factors. That is, only two risk factors are "priced" according to the results in Table 30-5.

The coefficients of determination (that is, the squared multiple correlation coefficients) associated with RR's cross-sectional regression results in Tables 30-4 and 30-5 were in the range of 50 to 60 percent. This means that the factor loadings explained over half the variance in the common stock's returns. This is a high percentage for individual securities. In comparison, King found that the single-factor characteristic line model explained slightly less than 30 percent of the average common stock's returns.[15]

In an earlier study using longer time periods and different sample data, Gehr found two and possibly three significant risk factors.[16] The high coefficients of determination reported by RR and the similar results of Gehr lend empirical support to the valildity of the APT.

15 B. F. King, "Market and Industry Factors in Stock Price Behavior," *Journal of Business*, January 1966, pp. 139–190.

16 A. Gehr, Jr., "Some Tests of the Arbitrage Pricing Theory," *Journal of the Midwest Finance Association*, 1978, pp. 99–106.

30-8 PROBLEMS WITH APT EMPIRICAL TESTS

Although the initial empirical tests of the APT by Gehr and by Roll and Ross (RR) are supportive, their findings are also clouded by several problems. These problems are essentially problems with factor analysis, not problems with the APT model.

First, one problem inherent in any empirical application of factor analysis is that the statistical procedure is not capable of testing rigorously specified hypotheses. Regression analysis, in contrast, is a statistical tool that can be used to rigorously test specific models and indicate whether or not the data support the model being tested. But factor analysis is such a *flexible procedure*, it is capable of accidentally furnishing support for models that are illogical and/or erroneous because sampling errors may influence the results.[17]

A second problem with the APT tests is that the ability of the factor-analysis process to delineate risk factors to explain securities' returns is highly *dependent upon the sample* of securities being analyzed. Thus, for example, each of the 42 groups of 30 stocks used by RR could conceivably contain different risk factors. Stated differently, if two significant risk factors were found in each of RR's 42 groups, for instance, this hypothetical finding might actually represent as many as 84 different factors, or as few as 2 factors, or any number between 2 and 84. The way to reduce this problem is to increase the sample size so that it becomes equal in size to the population size. This is a costly process, at least, and is simply impossible in some circumstances. Furthermore, it can be so difficult to identify the delineated factors that distinguishing among them can be another whole problem in itself.

Third, "*errors in the variables*" is a statistical problem that results because the factor loadings are statistical estimates that may contain sampling error. As a result, the second-pass cross-sectional regression used in APT tests is likely to have downward-biased goodness-of-fit statistics and regression coefficients.

Fourth, the *signs* on the factor loadings have no logical meaning. The signs of the b_{ij} sensitivity coefficients may be either positive or negative for essentially the same factor from one sample to the next. This, in turn, causes the signs of the λ_j coefficients in the second-pass regression to have no rational economic meaning—since the λ_j's are based on the b_{ij}'s. Furthermore, there is

[17] Jay Shanken, "The Arbitrage Pricing Theory: Is It Testable?" *Journal of Finance*, December 1982, vol. 37, no. 5, pp. 1129–1140. See also M. Reinganum, "The Arbitrage Pricing Theory: Some Empirical Results," *Journal of Finance*, May 1981, vol. 36, pp. 313–321. Both of these studies are critical of the ability of APT to be tested and measured empirically. A comment that disagrees with the nontestability hypothesis is Phillip H. Dybvig and Stephen A. Ross, "Yes, the APT Is Testable," *Journal of Finance*, September 1985, vol. 40, no. 4, pp. 1173–1188. Other critical discussions are furnished by: Phoebus J. Dhrymes, Irwin Friend, and N. Bulent Gultekin, "A Critical Reexamination of the Empirical Evidence on the Arbitrage Pricing Theory," *Journal of Finance*, June 1984, vol. 39, no. 2, pp. 323–346; Phoebus Dhrymes, "Arbitrage Pricing Theory," *Journal of Portfolio Management*, Summer 1984, pp. 35–44. See also Richard Roll and Stephen A. Ross, "A Critical Reexamination of the Empirical Evidence on the Arbitrage Pricing Theory: A Reply," *Journal of Finance*, June 1984, pp. 347–350. D. C. Cho, E. J. Elton, and M. J. Gruber, "On the Robustness of the Roll and Ross Arbitrage Pricing Theory," *Journal of Financial and Quantitative Analysis*, March 1984, vol. 19, no. 1, pp. 1–10.

also a scaling problem. If the b_{ij} is halved, then as a result the associated λ_j is doubled.

Identification is a fifth problem present in most factor-analytic studies. Identifying the factors that are statistically delineated by the factor analysis procedure is one of the most interesting, and also one of the most difficult, aspects encountered with empirical tests of APT.[18]

A sixth problem involves the availability of large and heterogeneous *data* banks and computers that can handle such massive empirical data. The findings of Kryzanowski and To suggest that the number of significant factors delineated by the initial studies was too small because the data sampled were inadequate.

> First, the larger the sample size in terms of time periods, the simpler is the factor structure in terms of the number of relevant factors, and the relatively more "important" is the first factor. Second, the larger the number of securities in the sample studies, the greater is the number of relevant factors. These two biases might help to explain the smaller number of factors found by authors who used a larger sample size and a smaller number of securities.[19]

Our economic intuition can suggest unanticipated risk factors that we think should be delineated by the factor-analysis tests of the APT. Unfortunately, the initial empirical studies of the APT have done very little to identify the factors that significantly influence security prices.[20] In fact, the APT tests

[18] Some preliminary empirical work on factor identification includes the following: George S. Oldfield, Jr., and Richard J. Rogalski, "Treasury Bill Factors and Stock Returns," *Journal of Finance,* May 1981, vol. 36, no. 2, pp. 337–353; H. Russell Fogler, Kose John, and James Tipton, "Three Factors, Interest Rate Differentials and Stock Groups," *Journal of Finance,* May 1981, vol. 36, no. 2, pp. 323–335; William F. Sharpe, "Factors in New York Stock Exchange Security Returns," *Journal of Portfolio Management,* Summer 1982, pp. 5–19; R. Roll and S. Ross, "The Arbitrage Pricing Theory Approach to Strategic Portfolio Planning," *Financial Analysts Journal,* May–June 1984, pp. 14–26. In the preceding *FAJ* article Roll and Ross suggest that their empirical research has identified four factors: (1) unanticipated changes in inflation; (2) unanticipated changes in industrial production; (3) unanticipated changes in risk-premiums (as measured by the yield spread between low-grade and high-grade bonds); and (4) unanticipated changes in the slope of the yield curve.

[19] Lawrence Kryzanowski and Minh Chau To, "General Factor Models and the Structure of Security Returns," *Journal of Financial and Quantitative Analysis,* March 1983, vol. 18, no. 1, pp. 48–49.

[20] Various studies have independently suggested different risk factors that may have a significant impact on security prices. The price-earnings ratio has been suggested by S. Basu, "Investment Performance of Common Stocks in Relation to Their Price-Earnings Ratios: A Test of the Efficient Market Hypothesis," *Journal of Finance,* June 1973, pp. 643–682. Industry factors was suggested by B. F. King, "Market and Industry Factors in Stock Price Behavior," *Journal of Business,* January 1966, pp. 139–190. Farrell suggested more broadly based stock groups: J. L. Farrell, Jr., "Analyzing Covariation of Returns to Determine Homogeneous Stock Groupings," *Journal of Business,* April 1974, pp. 186–207. Some studies of the market reaction to dividend announcements include G. Charest, "Dividend Information, Stock Returns and Market Efficiency—II," *Journal of Financial Economics,* June–September 1978, vol. 6, pp. 297–330; R. R. Pettit, "Dividend Announcements, Security Performance and Capital Market Efficiency," *Journal of Finance,* December 1972, vol. 27, pp. 993–1007; R. H. Litzenberger and Krishna Ramaswamy, "The Effect of Personal Taxes and Dividends on Capital Asset Prices: Theory and Empirical Evidence," *Journal of Financial Economics,* June 1979, pp. 117–162; and others. *(cont'd)*

reported above have not given us a clue as to what risk factors might influence security prices. This is an area where further work is needed.[21]

Many empirical investigations of the new APT will doubtless emerge during the decade of the 1980s to clarify our understanding. Currently, APT tells us that linear combinations of unspecified risk factors determine securities' expected returns. The initial research by Roll and Ross and by Gehr suggested that two, three, or four factors were all that were significant. However, the study by Kryzanowski and To suggested that a larger number of factors may be significant.[22] From the investment managers' viewpoint, identifying the significant factors is the most important aspect of APT research. This latter task will keep many financial researchers busy for the next few years.[23]

The following papers examine the relationship between returns and firm size: R. W. Banz, "The Relationship between Return and Market Value of Common Stocks," *Journal of Financial Economics*, March 1981, vol. 9, pp. 3–18; M. R. Reinganum, "Misspecification of Capital Asset Pricing: Empirical Anomalies Based on Earnings, Yields and Market Values," *Journal of Financial Economics*, March 1981, vol. 9, pp. 19–46.

Some studies of stock prices and the money supply are: R. D. Auerbach, "Money and Stock Prices," *Monthly Review Federal Reserve Bank of Kansas City*, September–October 1976, pp. 3–11, R. V. L. Cooper, "Efficient Capital Markets and the Quantity Theory of Money," *Journal of Finance*, June 1974, vol. 29, pp. 887–908; M. J. Hamburger and L. A. Kochin, "Money and Stock Prices: The Channels of Influence," *Journal of Finance*, May 1972, vol. 27, pp. 231–249; K. E. Homa and D. M. Jaffee, "The Supply of Money and Common Stock Prices," *Journal of Finance*, December 1971, vol. 26, pp. 1045–1066; M. W. Keran, "Expectations, Money and the Stock Market," *Review of the Federal Reserve Bank of Saint Louis*, June 1971, pp. 16–31; M. Palmer, "Money, Portfolio Adjustments and Stock Prices," *Financial Analysts Journal*, July–August 1970, vol. 26, pp. 19–22; J. E. Pesando, "The Supply of Money and Common Stock Prices: Further Observations on the Econometric Evidence," *Journal of Finance*, June 1974, vol. 29, pp. 909–922; R. J. Rogalski and J. D. Vinso, "Stock Prices, Money Supply and the Direction of Causality," *Journal of Finance*, September 1977, vol. 32, pp. 1017–1030; Tom Urich and Paul Wachtel, "Market Response to the Weekly Money Supply Announcements in the 1970s," *Journal of Finance*, December 1981, vol. 36; and others.

In addition, many other risk factors exist that might be significant.

[21] Part of the problem involved in identifying the factors delineated by the factor analysis is related to the esoteric mathematical algorithm employed. Factor analysis simultaneously analyzes N assets' returns over T time periods and "extracts" the "commonalities" we call risk factors. The extraction process is not simple. There are many methods of mathematically extracting orthogonal (that is, essentially, uncorrelated) factors. But they all end up with a maximum of one factor for each variable; each factor represents the "loadings" of the different variables' commonalities on that factor. Interpreting these factors, even the statistically significant ones, is difficult because they are contrived linear combinations of the returns from selected assets. Although factor analysis tells the researcher which assets' returns contributed to each factor, this list of assets' names does not clearly identify the resulting extracted factor. Furthermore, after the first factor is extracted the remaining data are mathematically manipulated (that is, rotated to create either new orthogonal or new oblique residual factors), so these derived factors can be indirect and abstruse.

[22] Lawrence Kryzanowski and Minh Chau To, "General Factor Models and the Structure of Security Returns," *Journal of Financial and Quantitative Analysis*, March 1983, vol. 18, no. 1, pp. 48–49.

[23] Many preliminary APT research studies exist that are not published or are not in a quotable form at the date of this writing.

30-9 AN ALTERNATIVE APPROACH TO ESTIMATING THE APT

There is an old debate among financial analysts and economists about whether the power of economic theory and mathematics should be used to derive a rigorous theoretical model before the model is tested empirically—as in the case of the CAPM, for instance. Those who take the other side in this debate argue that the empirical data should be analyzed to see what relationship can be found on which to base a theory—like factor analysis does in delineating the APT, for example. One relevant consideration is that without a prespecified theoretical model, the statistical tests that can be employed to validate or reject a theory are weaker and harder to interpret. For instance, in the case of the very general APT model, we have no idea about what risk factors to test, or what values the risk-premiums on these risk factors should be expected to have. All we can say in advance of empirically estimating the APT model is that we expect some unknown number of unspecified risk-premiums to emerge and be statistically significant. It is difficult to reject such a vague model.

30-9.1 economic theory suggests risk factors

Economics discussions in the earlier chapters of this book defined the following types of investment risk factors that factor analysis might be expected to delineate empirically if it were employed to estimate an APT model.

Default risk factor
Interest rate risk factor
Market risk factor
Purchasing power risk factor
Management risk factor
Callability risk factor
Convertibility risk factor
Marketability risk factor
Political risk factor
Industry factors

Chapters 9, 10, 17, and the appendix to Chap. 9 discuss these investment influences, review the underlying economic theory about each factor, and present empirical evidence to help identify the different risk factors. All these risks are well known and widely recognized.[24]

Economic intuition suggests that some of the risk factors listed above might be delineated by the factor-analysis tests of the APT. And various studies of the influences that affect security prices have suggested some more specific

[24] Harry Sauvain, *Investment Management*, Prentice-Hall, Englewood Cliffs, N.J., 1973. Sauvain's investments textbook devotes several chapters to discussing the risk factors covered in Chap. 9 of this book. Other books also discuss these different types of investment risk factors.

factors that we might expect empirical estimates of the APT model to find.[25] Unfortunately, the initial empirical studies of the APT have done very little to identify the factors that significantly influence security prices. In fact, the APT tests reported above have not given us a clue as to what risk factors have a significant influence over security prices. This is an area where further work is needed.[26]

30-9.2 an alternative to factor analysis

Most of the initial APT empirical researchers have used factor analysis to endogeneously estimate the indices (or risk factors) and the sensitivity coefficients (or factor loadings) for the indices. Some people even argue that factor analysis (or a similar statistical procedure called principal components analysis) is the only satisfactory way to test the APT model empirically. However, some financial analysts and economists prefer to estimate an APT model using a different empirical testing procedure—a two-step procedure somewhat like the procedure used to empirically estimate the CAPM.[27]

Risk factors that may affect security prices can be developed from exogenous economic theory rather than by endogenous factor-analytic techniques. Developing the risk factors exogenously from economic theory is the first step in the two-step procedure that differs from the factor-analysis approach usually employed to estimate APT models. Then cross-sectional regression analysis can be used in the second step of the empirical work to verify or reject the hypothesized economic variables.

Two basic types of economic theories can be employed to develop indices (or risk factors) in the first step of the two-step alternative to using factor analysis to delineate risk factors. First, macroeconomic theory can be used to develop risk factors like interest rate risk, purchasing power risk, market risk, and other risks of the type defined in Chaps. 9 and 17. Second, the economic theory of the firm can be used to delineate factors such as Macaulay's duration for a firm's securities; a firm's cash dividend yield; the beta coefficient from the characteristic line for a firm's securities; a numeric surrogate for securities' quality ratings, published by Standard & Poor's; and other similar indices. After some economically logical explanatory variables are hypothesized in the first step of the alternative APT estimation procedure, these variables can be tested empirically in the second step by using a cross-sectional regression to estimate an APT model like Eq. (30-16*a*) or (30-29) from this chapter.

The two-step estimation procedure proposed as an alternative to using

[25] Some preliminary empirical work on factor identification includes the following: George S. Oldfield, Jr., and Richard J. Rogalski, "Treasury Bill Factors and Stock Returns," *Journal of Finance,* May 1981, vol. 36, no. 2, pp. 337–353; H. Russell Fogler, Kose John, and James Tipton, "Three Factors, Interest Rate Differentials and Stock Groups," *Journal of Finance,* May 1981, vol. 36, no. 2, pp. 323–335; William F. Sharpe, "Factors in New York Stock Exchange Security Returns," *Journal of Portfolio Management,* Summer 1982, pp. 5–19.

[26] See footnote 20.

[27] Edwin J. Elton and Martin J. Gruber, for instance, argue in favor of using indices with theoretical economics foundations in empirical APT investigations, rather than using indices manufactured by the factor-analysis algorithm. See Elton and Gruber's *Modern Portfolio Theory and Investment Analysis,* 2d ed., Wiley, New York, 1984, pp. 357–366.

factor analysis to estimate an APT model has already been employed by various researchers.[28] Some of these empirical studies were published before the development of the APT, and thus, APT is not mentioned in the reports of those empirical estimates. However, these published tests and extensions of these efforts provide an alternative way to estimate APT models, like Eq. (30-29), without using factor analysis.

30-10 CHAPTER SUMMARY

The APT is a new theoretical model that suggests how to price market assets. Prior to the development of the APT, the capital asset pricing model (CAPM) was the newest financial theory to explain the prices of market assets. So, it is natural to compare and contrast these two important theories.

The APT requires fewer underlying assumptions and admits more different variables into the analysis than the CAPM. Therefore, the APT is a more general and more flexible theory than the CAPM. In fact, it can be shown that the CAPM is a special case of the APT. Thus, the two theories do not contradict each other. In fact, the theories are somewhat similar because both theories delineate *systematic influences* that generate *undiversifiable covariances* between market assets as their basis for risk-premiums.

Since the APT model has been in existence a relatively short time, it has not been tested extensively with empirical data. The results of the initial empirical tests that have been published are favorable—these tests tend to suggest that the APT has more explanatory power than the CAPM. Roll and Ross have stated that

> The well-known Capital Asset Pricing Model asserts that only a single number—an asset's "beta" against the market index—is required to measure risk. Arbitrage Pricing Theory asserts that an asset's riskiness, hence its long-term rate of return, is directly related to its sensitivities to unanticipated changes in four economic vari-

[28] See E. Fama and J. MacBeth, "Risk, Return and Equilibrium: Empirical Tests," *Journal of Political Economy,* May–June 1973, vol. 81, no. 3, pp. 607–636; J. C. Francis, "Skewness and Investors: Decisions," *Journal of Financial and Quantitative Analysis,* March 1975; J. C. Francis, "Analysis of Equity Returns: A Survey with Extensions," *Journal of Economics and Business,* Spring–Summer 1977, vol. 29, no. 3, pp. 181–192; F. J. Fabozzi and J. C. Francis, "Industry Effects and the Determinants of Beta," *Quarterly Review of Economics and Business,* Autumn 1979, vol. 19, no. 3, pp. 61–74; F. J. Fabozzi and J. C. Francis, "Mutual Fund Risk Statistics for Bull and Bear Markets: An Empirical Examination," *Journal of Finance,* December 1979, vol. 34, no. 5, pp. 1243–1250; C. F. Lee, F. J. Fabozzi, and J. C. Francis, "Generalized Functional Form for Mutual Fund Returns," *Journal of Financial and Quantitative Analysis,* December 1980, vol. 15, no. 5, 14 journal pages; C. F. Lee and J. C. Francis, "Investment Horizon, Risk Proxies, Skewness, and Mutual Fund Performance: A Theoretical Analysis and Empirical Investigation," in Haim Levy (ed.), *Readings in Finance,* vol. 4, J.A.I. Press, Greenwich, Conn., 1983, pp. 1–19. See also P. Casabona, A. Vora, and J. C. Francis, "Risk and Security Prices," *Review of Business,* Spring 1983, pp. 14–26; R. H. Litzenberger and K. Ramaswamy, "The Effects of Personal Taxes and Dividends on Capital Asset Prices: Theory and Empirical Evidence," *Journal of Financial Economics,* 1979, vol. 7, pp. 163–196; W. F. Sharpe, "Factors in NYSE Security Returns, 1931–1979," *Journal of Portfolio Management,* Summer 1982, vol. 8, no. 2, pp. 5–19.

ables—(1) inflation, (2) industrial production, (3) risk premiums, and (4) the slope of the term structure of interest rates. Assets, even if they have the same CAPM beta, will have different patterns of sensitivities to these systematic factors.[29]

While some people may expect to discover more risk factors with different identities in later empirical research, the point about multiple patterns of sensitivities that Roll and Ross assert nevertheless makes sense.[30]

QUESTIONS

1. The riskless rate of interest plays a key role in APT. True, false, or uncertain? Explain.
2. Compare and contrast the role of the market portfolio in modern portfolio theory (MPT) with its role in APT.
3. What does APT tell us about the risk factors that should determine the returns from assets?
4. Why is it claimed that APT is a more general theory than MPT?
5. Why is the word "arbitrage" in the name of APT?
6. Does this textbook give you any clues or suggestions as to what risk factors you might expect to be relevant in APT? Explain. (*Hint:* Consult other chapters.)
7. Compare and contrast the beta coefficient from the characteristic regression line with the sensitivity coefficient (or factor loading) in APT.
8. The capital asset pricing model (CAPM) and the arbitrage pricing theory (APT) models are very similar. True, false, or uncertain? Explain.
9. Empirical estimates of the riskless rate of interest obtained from estimates of the APT are far from realistic. True, false, or uncertain? Explain.
10. What problems cloud the results of empirical tests of the APT?

SELECTED REFERENCES

Andrew L. Comrey, *A First Course in Factor Analysis*, Academic Press, New York, 1973. A mathematical statistics book that uses matrix algebra supplemented with easy-to-read examples to explain the various approaches to factor analysis.

Phoebus Dhrymes, "Arbitrage Pricing Theory," *Journal of Portfolio Management*, Summer 1984, pp. 35–44. An empirical study and critique of the APT that uses no rigorous mathematics.

Richard Roll and S. Ross, "An Empirical Investigation of the Arbitrage Pricing Theory," *Journal of Finance*, December 1980, vol. 35, pp. 1073–1103. This article

[29] Richard Roll and Stephen A. Ross, "The Arbitrage Pricing Theory Approach to Strategic Portfolio Planning," *Financial Analysts Journal*, May–June 1984, p. 14.

[30] William F. Sharpe, "Factor Models, CAPMs, and the APT," *Journal of Portfolio Management*, Fall 1984, vol. 11, no. 1, pp. 21–25. Sharpe compares and contrasts the CAPM and the APT and reaches some significant conclusions.

reviews the APT model and presents initial empirical tests of the APT. Matrix algebra is used.

S. Ross, "The Arbitrage Pricing Theory of Capital Asset Pricing," *Journal of Economic Theory,* December 1976, pp. 344–360. This mathematical essay derives the APT model.

Jay Shanken, "The Arbitrage Pricing Theory: Is It Testable?" *Journal of Finance,* December 1982, vol. 37, no. 5, pp. 1129–1140. This article critiques the empirical application of the new APT. Some matrix algebra is used.

part nine

MATHEMATICAL APPENDIXES

MATHEMATICAL APPENDIX A—*the present value concept* explains how the time value of money affects security values.

MATHEMATICAL APPENDIX B—*the expected-value operator* defines the mathematical expectation and derives some relevant theorems.

MATHEMATICAL APPENDIX C—*statistical moments* defines the first four statistical moments of a probability distribution of returns.

MATHEMATICAL APPENDIX D—*elements of correlation and regression analysis* defines the simple correlation coefficient, simple regression, and related terms.

MATHEMATICAL APPENDIX E—*mathematical derivation of formulas for portfolio risk and expected return* shows how the risk and return of the individual assets combine to determine the portfolio's risk and return statistics.

MATHEMATICAL APPENDIX F—*geometric mean return* is explained as the way to measure multiperiod rates of return.

These mathematical appendixes define various terms, concepts, and operations that may become unclear if not used recently.

APPENDIX A

the present value concept

A dollar to be received in 1 year is not worth as much as a dollar to be received today—even if there is no doubt the dollar will be paid in 1 year. This is because a dollar received now can be invested in, say, a 5 percent savings account and $1.05 can be withdrawn in 1 year.

the time value of money

The time value of money can be represented symbolically. Let v_t represent the terminal value of money at the end of time period t, p_0 represent the present value, and r represent the interest rate per period which may be earned on money that is saved for T periods starting at time $t = 0$, that is, the present time.

$$p_0(1 + r)^1 = v_1 \tag{A-1}$$

$$\$1{,}000(1 + .05)^1 = \$1{,}050$$

Equation (A-1) is only a "one-period" formula. If money is invested and left for T periods, then Eq. (A-2) shows the results.

$$p_0(1 + r^T) = v_T \tag{A-2}$$

$$\$1{,}000(1 + .1)^2 = \$1{,}210 \text{ if } T = 2$$

The numerical example above shows that $1,000 saved at $r = 10$ percent for $T = 2$ periods will grow in value to $1,210.

present value

Equations (A-1) and (A-2) can be used to find the *present discounted value* of money to be received at time period t. Dividing both sides of (A-2) by the quantity $(1 + r)^T$ yields (A-3).

$$p_0 = \frac{v_T}{(1 + r)^T} \tag{A-3}$$

$$\$1{,}000 = \frac{\$1{,}210}{(1 + .1)^2} = \frac{1{,}210}{1.21}$$

The calculations above show that the present value of $1,210 to be received $T = 2$ periods in the future is $1,000, if the interest rate or discount rate is $r =$ 10 percent. The quantity $1/(1 + r)^T$ is called the *discount factor* and will sometimes be written $1/(1 + r)^T = D_r^T$. For example, $500 to be received $T =$ 2 periods in the future has a present value of $347.22 when $r = 20$ percent, as shown below:

$$p_0 = \frac{v_T}{(1 + r)^T} = v^T D_r^T \tag{A-3}$$

$$\$347.22 = \frac{\$500}{1.2^2} = \$500 D_2^2$$

Equation (A-3) is a point-input-point-output present value model. This is a very simple transaction. Equation (A-4) is a more general present value model which allows for simultaneous inflows and outflows at multiple points in time. Let c_t denote the cashflow at time period t.

$$p_0 = \sum_{t=1}^{T} \frac{c_t}{(1 + r)^t} \tag{A-4}$$

$$= c_1 D_r^1 + c_2 D_r^2 + \cdots + c_T D_r^T$$

symbols

The discussion of the time value of money which makes up this appendix utilizes the following symbols:

i = stated or coupon interest rate; this is not necessarily the total yield earned from holding the asset. i is an interest rate per period which is printed on a new bond and may bear little relation to the market rate of interest.

p_0 = present value in dollars, or the cost of the asset.

v_T = terminal or ending value in dollars.

T = the number of time periods which the investment lasts.

c_t = net cashflow in period t = cash inflow in period t less cash outflow in period $t = I_t - O_t$.

t = the time period counter index.

$D_r^T = 1/(1 + r)^T$ = the discount factor for T periods in the future at discount rate r.

k = the *appropriate* discount rate. Determining the appropriate discount rate is discussed in Chap. 9. Suffice it to say, the higher the risk, the higher k should be. The symbol k is the cost of capital; it is the discount rate which is appropriate to find the present value of an investment. This k is determined by the asset's risk and the opportunity cost of the investment. The value of k can be determined before the cashflows are estimated.

r = the yield to maturity = the internal rate of return = the market rate = the nominal yield. The value of r will typically vary with credit conditions and other factors. The symbol r is the discount rate which equates the present value of all net cashflows to the cost of the investment. Therefore, r can be determined only after all cashflows and the cost are known.

F = face or par value of a security.

iF = the dollar interest payable per period = the coupon interest rate i multiplied by the face value F.

present value table

It is quite tedious to evaluate all the discount factors, $D_r^T = 1/(1 + r)^T$, when performing present value calculations. To save the analyst this trouble, present value tables have been calculated and printed. Table A-1 is a present value table. This table shows the values of D_r^T for many values of T and r. The D_r^T

TABLE A-1 present value table*

Period	1%	2%	3%	4%	5%	6%	7%	8%	9%	10%	12%	14%	15%	16%	18%	20%	24%	28%	32%	36%
1	.9901	.9804	.9709	.9615	.9524	.9434	.9346	.9259	.9174	.9091	.8929	.8772	.8696	.8621	.8475	.8333	.8065	.7813	.7576	.7353
2	.9803	.9612	.9426	.9246	.9070	.8900	.8734	.8573	.8417	.8264	.7972	.7695	.7561	.7432	.7182	.6944	.6504	.6104	.5739	.5407
3	.9706	.9423	.9151	.8890	.8638	.8396	.8163	.7938	.7722	.7513	.7118	.6750	.6575	.6407	.6086	.5787	.5245	.4768	.4348	.3975
4	.9610	.9238	.8885	.8548	.8227	.7921	.7629	.7350	.7084	.6830	.6355	.5921	.5718	.5523	.5158	.4823	.4230	.3725	.3294	.2923
5	.9515	.9057	.8626	.8219	.7835	.7473	.7130	.6806	.6499	.6209	.5674	.5194	.4972	.4761	.4371	.4019	.3411	.2910	.2495	.2149
6	.9420	.8880	.8375	.7903	.7462	.7050	.6663	.6302	.5963	.5645	.5066	.4556	.4323	.4104	.3704	.3349	.2751	.2274	.1890	.1580
7	.9327	.8706	.8131	.7599	.7107	.6651	.6227	.5835	.5470	.5132	.4523	.3996	.3759	.3538	.3139	.2791	.2218	.1776	.1432	.1162
8	.9235	.8535	.7894	.7307	.6768	.6274	.5820	.5403	.5019	.4665	.4039	.3506	.3269	.3050	.2660	.2326	.1789	.1388	.1085	.0854
9	.9143	.8368	.7664	.7026	.6446	.5919	.5439	.5002	.4604	.4241	.3606	.3075	.2843	.2630	.2255	.1938	.1443	.1084	.0822	.0628
10	.9053	.8203	.7441	.6756	.6139	.5584	.5083	.4632	.4224	.3855	.3220	.2697	.2472	.2267	.1911	.1615	.1164	.0847	.0623	.0462
11	.8963	.8043	.7224	.6496	.5847	.5268	.4751	.4289	.3875	.3505	.2875	.2366	.2149	.1954	.1619	.1346	.0938	.0662	.0472	.0340
12	.8874	.7885	.7014	.6246	.5568	.4970	.4440	.3971	.3555	.3186	.2567	.2076	.1869	.1685	.1372	.1122	.0757	.0517	.0357	.0250
13	.8787	.7730	.6810	.6006	.5303	.4688	.4150	.3677	.3262	.2897	.2292	.1821	.1625	.1452	.1163	.0935	.0610	.0404	.0271	.0184
14	.8700	.7579	.6611	.5775	.5051	.4423	.3878	.3405	.2992	.2633	.2046	.1597	.1413	.1252	.0985	.0779	.0492	.0316	.0205	.0135
15	.8613	.7430	.6419	.5553	.4810	.4173	.3624	.3152	.2745	.2394	.1827	.1401	.1229	.1079	.0835	.0649	.0397	.0247	.0155	.0099
16	.8528	.7284	.6232	.5339	.4581	.3936	.3387	.2919	.2519	.2176	.1631	.1229	.1069	.0930	.0708	.0541	.0320	.0193	.0118	.0073
17	.8444	.7142	.6050	.5134	.4363	.3714	.3166	.2703	.2311	.1978	.1456	.1078	.0929	.0802	.0600	.0451	.0258	.0150	.0089	.0054
18	.8360	.7002	.5874	.4936	.4155	.3503	.2959	.2502	.2120	.1799	.1300	.0946	.0808	.0691	.0508	.0376	.0208	.0118	.0068	.0039
19	.8277	.6864	.5703	.4746	.3957	.3305	.2765	.2317	.1945	.1635	.1161	.0829	.0703	.0596	.0431	.0313	.0168	.0092	.0051	.0029
20	.8195	.6730	.5537	.4564	.3769	.3118	.2584	.2145	.1784	.1486	.1037	.0728	.0611	.0514	.0365	.0261	.0135	.0072	.0039	.0021
25	.7798	.6095	.4776	.3751	.2953	.2330	.1842	.1460	.1160	.0923	.0588	.0378	.0304	.0245	.0160	.0105	.0046	.0021	.0010	.0005
30	.7419	.5521	.4120	.3083	.2314	.1741	.1314	.0994	.0754	.0573	.0334	.0196	.0151	.0116	.0070	.0042	.0016	.0006	.0002	.0001
40	.6717	.4529	.3066	.2083	.1420	.0972	.0668	.0460	.0318	.0221	.0107	.0053	.0037	.0026	.0013	.0007	.0002	.0001	†	†
50	.6080	.3715	.2281	.1407	.0872	.0543	.0339	.0213	.0134	.0085	.0035	.0014	.0009	.0006	.0003	.0001	†	†	†	†
60	.5504	.3048	.1697	.0951	.0535	.0303	.0173	.0099	.0057	.0033	.0011	.0004	.0002	.0001	†	†	†	†	†	†

* Present value of $1 received at the end of T years $= D_r^T = \frac{1}{(1+r)^T}$

† The factor is zero to four decimal places.

values are not perfectly accurate because of rounding at the fifth decimal place.

perpetuities

British consols are perpetual bonds; that is, the bearer of the consol will receive periodic interest to perpetuity, but the principal will never be repaid.

To value a consol, assume that the appropriate discount rate is k. The coupon rate i on bonds almost always differs from the discount rate. The coupon rate is the interest rate paid on the face value of the bond. The face value and coupon rate are printed on the bond itself and never change once the bond is issued. Let F and i denote the face value and coupon rate, respectively. Then iF is the cashflow, which is a fixed constant. The present value of a consol may be determined with Eq. (A-4). The bar over c denotes that it has a fixed constant value.

$$p_0 = \sum_t^T \frac{c_t}{(1+k)^t} \tag{A-4}$$

$$p_0 = \sum_{t=1}^{T=\infty} \bar{c}D_k^t \qquad \text{for a consol, since } T = \infty \text{ and } c_t = \bar{c} = iF$$

$$p_0 = \frac{\bar{c}}{k} \tag{A-5}$$

$$= \frac{iF}{k}$$

It is difficult (to say the least) to evaluate the sum D_k^t an infinitely large number of times, as required above. However, this problem is easily overcome by using Eq. (A-5), which shows how to find the present value p_0 of a *perpetual stream* ($T = \infty$) of *constant cashflows*. When $T = \infty$ and the cashflows are constant, Eqs. (A-4) and (A-5) are equivalent,[1] but Eq. (A-5) saves much computation.

[1] Equation (A-5) is derived from (A-4) as follows:

$$p_0 = \sum_t^T \bar{c}D_k^t \tag{A-4}$$

$$= \bar{c}\sum_t^T D_k^t \qquad \text{since } \sum ax = a\sum x$$

$$p_0 = \bar{c}D_k^1 + \bar{c}D_k^2 + \bar{c}D_k^3 + \cdots + \bar{c}D_k^T \tag{A-4a}$$

$$p_0(1+k) = \bar{c} + \bar{c}D_k^1 + \bar{c}D_k^2 + \cdots + \bar{c}D_k^{T-1} \tag{A-4b}$$

$$p_0(1+k) - p_0 = \bar{c} - \bar{c}D_k^T \qquad \text{by subtracting (A-4}a\text{) from (A-4}b\text{)}$$

$$p_0 + kp_0 - p_0 = \bar{c} - \bar{c}D_k^T$$

$$kp_0 = \bar{c} \qquad \text{since } D_k^T \to 0 \text{ as } T \to \infty\text{, the } \bar{c}D_k^T \text{ term becomes zero}$$

$$p_0 = \bar{c}/k \tag{A-5}$$

Thus, (A-5) is derived from (A-4) for the case when $T = \infty$.

present value of *n* equal cashflows

Sometimes an equal amount is to be received for T consecutive periods, for example, an annuity. Equation (A-4) can be used to find the present value of T equal cashflows ($c = c_t$ for all t).

$$p_0 = \sum_t^T \frac{c_t}{(1 + k)^t} \tag{A-4}$$

$$= c_1(D_i^1) + c_2(D_i^2) + \cdots + c_n(D_k^T)$$

$$= \bar{c}(D_i^1 + D_i^2 + D_i^3 + \cdots + D_i^T) \qquad \text{if } c_t = \bar{c} = \text{constant}$$

$$= \bar{c} \sum_{t=1}^{T} D_k^t \tag{A-6}$$

When $c_t = \bar{c}$ for n periods, Eq. (A-6) is a convenient simplification of (A-4). The sum of the D_k^t quantities in (A-6) is merely the sum of part of a column of Table A-1. This sum of T consecutive values of D_k^t is then multiplied by the constant $\bar{c}$ to find the present value of the T equal cashflows. Table A-2 shows the sums of T consecutive D_k^t quantities, $\sum_{t=1}^{T} D_k^t$, for several values of T and k. This table is useful in finding the present value of T equal cashflows. It shows the present value of $1 received each period for T periods when the discount rate is k.

compounding several times per period

Sometimes it is appropriate to compound the interest factor several times per period. Let b denote the number of times per period the interest is compounded. Equation (A-7) may be used for such present value problems.

$$p_0 = \sum_t^T \frac{c_t}{(1 + r/b)^{bt}} \tag{A-7}$$

Equation (A-7) takes $1/b$ times the interest rate r (that is, r/b) and compounds it b times as frequently (that is, bt) as is done when interest is compounded once a year. Since $(1 + r/b)^b > (1 + r)$, compounding more frequently yields different values. More frequent compounding decreases the present value. For example, at $r = 4$ percent the present value of $1 received in 5 years and compounded annually is $0.82193, as calculated with (A-3) below. But at $r = 4$ percent, the present value of $1 received in 5 years and compounded semiannually (that is, $b = 2$) is $0.82035. The difference is due to compounding semiannually.

$$p_0 = \frac{v_5}{(1 + r)^5} \tag{A-3}$$

$$= \$1(.82193)$$

$$= 82.193¢$$

TABLE A-2 the present value of some annuities*

number of payments	1%	2%	3%	4%	5%	6%	7%	8%	9%	10%	12%	14%	15%	16%	18%	20%	24%	28%	32%
1	0.9901	0.9804	0.9709	0.9615	0.9524	0.9434	0.9346	0.9259	0.9174	0.9091	0.8929	0.8772	0.8696	0.8621	0.8475	0.8333	0.8065	0.7813	0.7576
2	1.9704	1.9416	1.9135	1.8861	1.8594	1.8334	1.8080	1.7833	1.7591	1.7355	1.6901	1.6467	1.6257	1.6052	1.5656	1.5278	1.4568	1.3916	1.3315
3	2.9410	2.8839	2.8286	2.7751	2.7232	2.6730	2.6243	2.5771	2.5313	2.4869	2.4018	2.3216	2.2832	2.2459	2.1743	2.1065	1.9813	1.8684	1.7663
4	3.9020	3.8077	3.7171	3.6299	3.5460	3.4651	3.3872	3.3121	3.2397	3.1699	3.0373	2.9137	2.8550	2.7982	2.6901	2.5887	2.4043	2.2410	2.0957
5	4.8534	4.7135	4.5797	4.4518	4.3295	4.2124	4.1002	3.9927	3.8897	3.7908	3.6048	3.4331	3.3522	3.2743	3.1272	2.9906	2.7454	2.5320	2.3452
6	5.7955	5.6014	5.4172	5.2421	5.0757	4.9173	4.7665	4.6229	4.4859	4.3553	4.1114	3.8887	3.7845	3.6847	3.4976	3.3255	3.0205	2.7594	2.5342
7	6.7282	6.4720	6.2303	6.0021	5.7864	5.5824	5.3893	5.2064	5.0330	4.8684	4.5638	4.2883	4.1604	4.0386	3.8115	3.6046	3.2423	2.9370	2.6775
8	7.6517	7.3255	7.0197	6.7327	6.4632	6.2098	5.9713	5.7466	5.5348	5.3349	4.9676	4.6389	4.4873	4.3436	4.0776	3.8372	3.4212	3.0758	2.7860
9	8.5660	8.1622	7.7861	7.4353	7.1078	6.8017	6.5152	6.2469	5.9952	5.7590	5.3282	4.9464	4.7716	4.6065	4.3030	4.0310	3.5655	3.1842	2.8681
10	9.4713	8.9826	8.5302	8.1109	7.7217	7.3601	7.0236	6.7101	6.4177	6.1446	5.6502	5.2161	5.0188	4.8332	4.4941	4.1925	3.6819	3.2689	2.9304
11	10.3676	9.7868	9.2526	8.7605	8.3064	7.8869	7.4987	7.1390	6.8052	6.4951	5.9377	5.4527	5.2337	5.0286	4.6560	4.3271	3.7757	3.3351	2.9776
12	11.2551	10.5753	9.9540	9.3851	8.8633	8.3838	7.9427	7.5361	7.1607	6.8137	6.1944	5.6603	5.4206	5.1971	4.7932	4.4392	3.8514	3.3868	3.0133
13	12.1337	11.3484	10.6350	9.9856	9.3936	8.8527	8.3577	7.9038	7.4869	7.1034	6.4235	5.8424	5.5831	5.3423	4.9095	4.5327	3.9124	3.4272	3.0404
14	13.0037	12.1062	11.2961	10.5631	9.8986	9.2950	8.7455	8.2442	7.7862	7.3667	6.6282	6.0021	5.7245	5.4675	5.0081	4.6106	3.9616	3.4587	3.0609
15	13.8651	12.8493	11.9379	11.1184	10.3797	9.7122	9.1079	8.5595	8.0607	7.6061	6.8109	6.1422	5.8474	5.5755	5.0916	4.6755	4.0013	3.4834	3.0764
16	14.7179	13.5777	12.5611	11.6523	10.8378	10.1059	9.4466	8.8514	8.3126	7.8237	6.9740	6.2651	5.9542	5.6685	5.1624	4.7296	4.0333	3.5026	3.0882
17	15.5623	14.2919	13.1661	12.1657	11.2741	10.4773	9.7632	9.1216	8.5436	8.0216	7.1196	6.3729	6.0472	5.7487	5.2223	4.7746	4.0591	3.5177	3.0971
18	16.3983	14.9920	13.7535	12.6593	11.6896	10.8276	10.0591	9.3719	8.7556	8.2014	7.2497	6.4674	6.1280	5.8178	5.2732	4.8122	4.0799	3.5294	3.1039
19	17.2260	15.6785	14.3238	13.1339	12.0853	11.1581	10.3356	9.6036	8.9501	8.3649	7.3658	6.5504	6.1982	5.8775	5.3162	4.8435	4.0967	3.5386	3.1090
20	18.0456	16.3514	14.8775	13.5903	12.4622	11.4699	10.5940	9.8181	9.1285	8.5136	7.4694	6.6231	6.2593	5.9288	5.3527	4.8696	4.1103	3.5458	3.1129
25	22.0232	19.5235	17.4131	15.6221	14.0939	12.7834	11.6536	10.6748	9.8226	9.0770	7.8431	6.8729	6.4641	6.0971	5.4669	4.9476	4.1474	3.5640	3.1220
30	25.8077	22.3965	19.6004	17.2920	15.3725	13.7648	12.4090	11.2578	10.2737	9.4269	8.0552	7.0027	6.5660	6.1772	5.5168	4.9789	4.1601	3.5693	3.1242
40	32.8347	27.3555	23.1148	19.7928	17.1591	15.0463	13.3317	11.9246	10.7574	9.7791	8.2438	7.1050	6.6418	6.2335	5.5482	4.9966	4.1659	3.5712	3.1250
50	39.1961	31.4236	25.7298	21.4822	18.2559	15.7619	13.8007	12.2335	10.9617	9.9148	8.3045	7.1327	6.6605	6.2463	5.5541	4.9995	4.1666	3.5714	3.1250
60	44.9550	34.7609	27.6756	22.6235	18.9293	16.1614	14.0392	12.3766	11.0480	9.9672	8.3240	7.1401	6.6651	6.2492	5.5553	4.9999	4.1667	3.5714	3.1250

* Present value of \$1 per year for T consecutive years $= \sum_{t=1}^{T} D_k^t = \sum_{t=1}^{T} \frac{1}{(1+k)^t}$

$$p_0\left(\frac{v_5}{(1 + r/b)^{5b}}\right) \qquad \text{(A-7)}$$

$$= \$1(.82035)$$

$$= 82.035¢$$

Equation (A-7) is a popular approximation that does not yield consistent or exact values because of approximations that are demonstrated in the following inequalities.

$$\left(1 + \frac{r}{4}\right)^4 \neq (1 + r) \neq \left(1 + \frac{r}{2}\right)^2$$

For instance, consider the three following numerical examples when $r = 4.0$ percent.

quarterly, $b = 4$	annual, $b = 1$	semiannual, $b = 2$
$\frac{.04}{4} = .01$	$\frac{.04}{1} = .04$	$\frac{.04}{2} = .02$
$(1.01)^4 = 1.040604$	$(1.04)^1 = 1.04$	$(1.02)^2 = 1.0404$

None of the three values obtained in the numerical examples above are equal. Stated differently, we have employed approximations that have produced inconsistent values. To be exact the correct discount rate to be compounded b times per year should be the quantity below.

$$[(1 + r)^{1/b}] = r' \qquad \text{where } r' < r$$

The two following numerical examples demonstrate the consistent way to calculate the quarterly and semiannual values.

$$\left[\left(1 + \frac{.04}{4}\right)^{1/4}\right]^4 = (1.0098534)^4 = 1.04 \qquad \text{for quarters}$$

$$\left[\left(1 + \frac{.04}{2}\right)^{1/2}\right]^2 = (1.0198039)^2 = 1.04 \qquad \text{for semiannual}$$

The widespread availability of computers and calculators should have made the approximations that were developed in the days of hand computation obsolete. However, many still use Eq. (A-7).[2]

[2] For additional discussion see Philip A. Horvath, "A Pedagogic Note on Intra-Period Compounding and Discounting," *The Financial Review*, February 1985, vol. 20, no. 1, pp. 116–118.

APPENDIX B

the expected-value operator (*E*)

An expectation is like an "average" value. For example, for one toss of a fair coin for $1, we can say the expected value of the outcome is the probability of heads times the $1 loss plus the probability of tails times the $1 gain. Symbolically,

$$\begin{aligned}\text{Expected value} &= P(\text{heads})(-\$1) + P(\text{tails})(+\$1)\\ &= .5(-1) + .5(+1) = 0\end{aligned}$$

The above symbols are a very definite statement of what is meant by the phrase "we expect that fair gambles will break even." Writing the expression for expected value in even more general form, we say:

$$\begin{aligned}E(x) &= \sum_{i=1}^{n} P_i x_i \qquad \text{(B-1)}\\ &= P_1x_1 + P_2x_2 + \cdots + P_nx_n\end{aligned}$$

In words, the expected value of the variable x (for example, x might be the $1 outcome of the gamble or any other number resulting from an experiment involving chance which has n possible outcomes) equals the sum of all n products of $(P_i)(x_i)$, where P_i is the probability of the ith outcome [$P(\text{heads}) = P_i = ½$ in the coin example] and x_i is the ith outcome [$x_i = \$1$ or $-\$1$ in the example].

Mathematicians say that the lettter E as used in Eq. (B-1) is an *operator*, meaning that the lettter E specifies the operation of multiplying all outcomes times their probabilities and summing those products to get the expected value.

Finding the expected value is roughly analogous to finding the weighted average by using probabilities for weights. Do not be confused, however; although the arithmetic is the same, an average is conceptually different from an expectation. An expectation is determined by its probabilities, and it represents a hypothesis about an unknown outcome; but an average is a summarizing measure. There is no conceptual connection between an average and an expectation; there is only the mechanical similarity of the calculations.

The operator E can be used to derive several important formulas. Therefore, let us consider several elementary properties of expected-value operations.

1. The expected value of a constant number is that constant. Symbolically, if c is any constant number (for example, $c = 2, -99$, or 1,064),

   $$E(c) = c$$

Proof of this is given below.

$$E(c) = \sum_{i=1}^{n} P_i c = P_1 c + \cdots + P_n c$$

$$= c \sum_{i=1}^{n} P_i = c(1) = c$$

2. The expected value of a constant times a random variable equals the constant times the expected value of the random variable. Thus, if x is a random variable (for example, the -1 or $+1$ outcome of the gamble) and c is a constant (namely, the number of dollars bet on each toss),

$$E(cx) = cE(x)$$

The proof follows.

$$E(cx) = \sum_{i=1}^{n} P_i(cx_i) = P_1(cx_1) + \cdots + P_n(cx_n)$$

$$= P_1 cx_1 + \cdots + P_n cx_n$$

$$= c(P_1x_1 + P_2x_2 + \cdots + P_nx_n) = c\sum_{i=1}^{n} P_i x_i = cE(x)$$

3. The expected value of the sum of n independent random variables is simply the sum of their expected values. For example, if n = two random variables called, say, x and y,

$$E(x + y) = E(x) + E(y)$$

The proof follows.

$$E(x + y) = \sum_{i=1}^{n} P_i(x_i + y_i) = P_1(x_1 + y_1) + P_2(x_2 + y_2) + \cdots + P_n(x_n + y_n)$$

$$= P_1x_1 + P_1y_1 + P_2x_2 + P_2y_2 + \cdots + P_nx_n + P_ny_n$$

$$= [P_1x_1 + P_2x_2 + \cdots + P_nx_n] + [P_1y_1 + P_2y_2 + \cdots + P_ny_n]$$

$$= \sum_{i=1}^{n} P_i x_i + \sum_{i=1}^{n} P_i y_i = E(x) + E(y)$$

where P_i is the *joint probability* of x_i and y_i occurring jointly.

4. The expected value of a constant times a random variable plus a constant equals the constant times the expected value of the random variable plus the constant. Symbolically, if b and c are constants and x is a random variable,

$$E(bx + c) = bE(x) + c$$

The proof is a combination of the three preceding proofs. These four properties of the expected-value operator may be used to derive the following useful theorems.

THEOREM B-1 The variance of a random variable equals the expected value of the squared random variable less the expected value of the random variable squared.[1]

Stated in equation form,

$$\text{var}(x) = E(x^2) - [E(x)]^2$$

Proof

$$\begin{aligned} \text{var}(x) &= E[x - E(x)]^2 \qquad \text{by definition of var}(x) \\ &= E\{x^2 - 2xE(x) + [E(x)]^2\} \\ &= E(x^2) - 2E(x)^2 + [E(x)]^2 \\ &= E(x^2) - [E(x)]^2 \end{aligned}$$

Q.E.D.

THEOREM B-2 The expected value of a squared random variable equals the variance of that random variable plus its expected value squared.

Stated in equation form,

$$E(x^2) = \text{var}(x) + [E(x)]^2$$

Proof

$$\begin{aligned} \text{var}(x) &= E(x^2) - [E(x)]^2 \qquad \text{by Theorem B-1} \\ [E(x)]^2 + \text{var}(x) &= E(x^2) \end{aligned}$$

Q.E.D.

THEOREM B-3 The variance of a linear transformation of the random variable is not affected by adding or subtracting a constant, but multiplying the random variable by a constant increases the variance of the product by the square of the constant.

Stated in equation form,

$$\text{var}(ax + b) = a^2 \text{ var}(x) \qquad \text{for any constants } a \text{ and } b$$

Proof

$$\begin{aligned} \text{var}(ax + b) &= E[ax + b - E(ax + b)]^2 \qquad \text{by definition} \\ &= E[ax + b - aE(x) - b]^2 \\ &= Ea^2[x - E(x)]^2 \\ &= a^2E[x - E(x)]^2 = a^2 \text{ var}(x) \end{aligned}$$

Q.E.D.

[1] Note that Theorem B-1 implies a computationally efficient way to compute the variance in a real-valued problem. That is, finding the average of the deviations,

$$\frac{1}{n}\sum_{i=1}^{n}(x_i - \bar{x})^2 = \text{var}(x)$$

requires more computation than subtracting the mean squared from the mean of the squares:

$$\frac{1}{n}\sum_{i=1}^{n}x_i^2 - \bar{x}^2 = \text{var}(x)$$

The other theorems also imply similar computational shortcuts which are useful in performing hand calculations or in writing efficient computer programs.

Theorem B-3 implies that the standard deviation of $ax + b$ equals $a\sigma_x$, the square root of a^2 var(x).

THEOREM B-4 If two random variables are independent, the expected value of the product of the two random variables equals the product of their expectations.

Stated in equation form,

$$E(xy) = E(x)E(y) \qquad \text{if } x \text{ and } y \text{ are independent}$$

Proof

$$E(xy) = \sum_i \sum_j [P(x_i \text{ and } y_i)(x_i)(y_i)]$$

but

$$P(x \text{ and } y) = P_x P_y \qquad \text{if } x \text{ and } y \text{ are independent}$$

Therefore

$$E(xy) = \sum_i \sum_j (P_{xi} P_{yj} x_i y_j)$$

$$= \sum_i (P_{xi} x_i) \sum_j (P_{yj} y_j)$$

$$= E(x)E(y) \qquad \text{Q.E.D.}$$

THEOREM B-5 The covariance of two random variables equals the expected value of their product less the product of their expectations.

Stated in equation form,

$$\text{cov}(x,y) = E(xy) - E(x)E(y)$$

Proof

$$\text{cov}(x,y) = E\{[x - E(x)][y - E(y)]\} \qquad \text{by definition}$$

$$= E\{[(xy - xE(y) - yE(x) + E(x)E(y)]\}$$

$$= [E(xy) - E(x)E(y) - E(y)E(x) + E(x)E(y)]$$

$$= E(xy) - E(x)E(y) \qquad \text{Q.E.D.}$$

THEOREM B-6 The covariance of a random variable with any constant is zero.

Stated in equation form,

$$\text{cov}(x,c) = 0 \qquad \text{where } c \text{ is a constant}$$

Proof

$$\text{cov}(x,c) = E(xc) - E(x)E(c) \qquad \text{by Theorem B-5}$$

$$= cE(x) - cE(x) = 0 \qquad \text{Q.E.D.}$$

THEOREM B-7 The covariance of linear transformations of two random variables (x and y) is not affected by adding or subtracting constants to one or both of the variables, but the covariance is increased by a multiple equal to any constants which were multiplied by the random variables.

Stated in equation form,

$$\text{cov}(ax + b, cy + d) = ac \,\text{cov}(x,y) \qquad \text{where } a, b, c, \text{ and } d \text{ are constants}$$

Proof

$$\begin{aligned}
\text{cov}(ax + b, cy + d) &= E\{[ax + b - E(ax + b)][cy + d - E(cy + d)]\} \\
&\qquad \text{by the definition of the covariance} \\
&= E\{[ax + b - aE(x) - b][cy + d - cE(y) - d]\} \\
&= E\{a[x - E(x)]c[y - E(y)]\} \\
&= acE\{[x - E(x)][y - E(y)]\} \\
&= ac \,\text{cov}(x,y) \qquad \text{Q.E.D.}
\end{aligned}$$

THEOREM B-8 The covariance of a sum of random variables with another variable x equals the sum of their covariances with variable x.

Stated in equation form,

$$\text{cov}(x, y + z) = \text{cov}(x,y) + \text{cov}(x,z)$$

Proof

$$\begin{aligned}
\text{cov}(x, y + z) &= E[x(y + z)] - E(x)E(y + z) \qquad \text{by Theorem B-5} \\
&= E(xy + xz) - [E(x)E(y) + E(x)E(z)] \\
&= E(xy) + E(xz) - [E(x)E(y) + E(x)E(z)] \\
&= E(xy) - E(x)E(y) + E(xz) - E(x)E(z) \qquad \text{using B-5 again:} \\
&= \text{cov}(x,y) + \text{cov}(x,z) \qquad \text{Q.E.D.}
\end{aligned}$$

THEOREM B-9 If the random variables x and y both undergo a linear transformation (for example, $ax + b$ and $cy + d$, where a, b, c, and d are constants), their correlation coefficient ρ_{xy} is invariant.

Symbolically,

$$\rho(x,y) = \rho(ax + b, cy + d)$$

Proof

$$\begin{aligned}
\rho(ax + b, cy + d) &= \frac{\text{cov}(ax + b, cy + d)}{(\sigma_{ax+b})(\sigma_{cy+d})} \qquad \text{definition of } \rho_{xy} \\
&= \frac{ac \,\text{cov}(xy)}{a(\sigma_x)c(\sigma_y)} \qquad \text{by Theorems B-3 and B-7} \\
&= \frac{\text{cov}(x,y)}{\sigma_x \sigma_y} \\
&= \rho(x,y) \qquad \text{Q.E.D.}
\end{aligned}$$

THEOREM B-10 The variance of a sum of random variables equals the sum of their variances plus the sum of all their covariances.

Stated in equation form,

$$\text{var}(\Sigma x_i) = \Sigma \sigma_i^2 + \sum_i \sum_j \sigma_{ij} \qquad \text{for } i \neq j$$

Proof

$$\begin{aligned}
\text{var}(\Sigma x_i) &= E\Big(\sum_i x_i - \sum_i u_i\Big)^2 \qquad \text{where } u_i = E(x) \\
&= E\Big[\sum_i (x_i - u_i)^2\Big] \\
&= E\Big[\sum_i \sum_j (x_i - u_i)(x_j - u_j)\Big] \\
&= \sum_i \sum_j E[(x_i - u_i)(x_j - u_j)] \\
&= \sum_i \sum_j \sigma_{ij} \\
&= \sum_i \sigma_i^2 + \sum_i \sum_j \sigma_{ij} \qquad \text{for } i \neq j
\end{aligned}$$

Q.E.D.

THEOREM B-11 The third statistical moment is a simple linear additive sum of the first three moments about the origin, denoted $E(x^n)$ for $n = 1, 2,$ and 3.

Symbolically,

$$M_3 = E[(x - E(x)]^3 = E(x^3) - 3E(x^2)E(x) + 2[E(x)]^3$$

Proof

$$\begin{aligned}
M_3 &= E[x - E(x)]^3 \\
&= E\{[x^3 - 2x^2E(x) + x[E(x)]^2 - x^2E(x) + 2x[E(x)]^2 - [E(x)]^3\}
\end{aligned}$$

since

$$\begin{aligned}
(a - b)^3 &= (a^3 - 2a^2b + ab^2 - a^2b + 2ab^2 - b^3) \\
&= E[x^3 - 3x^2E(x) + 3x[E(x)]^2 - [E(x)]^3] \\
&= E(x^3) - 3E(x^2)E(x) + 3E(x)[E(x)]^2 - [E(x)]^3 \\
&= E(x^3) - 3E(x^2)E(x) + 2[E(x)]^3
\end{aligned}$$

Q.E.D.

This theorem generalizes to the nth statistical moment.

APPENDIX C

statistical moments

Some probability distributions (such as the uniform and normal) may be completely described by their "statistical moments." The moments of a probability distribution are statistical measures.[1]

the expected return and mean

For a probability distribution of returns, the first moment about the *origin* is defined as shown in Eqs. (C-1) and (C-1*a*).

$$E(r) = \sum_{i=1}^{n} P_i r_i \qquad \text{for future returns} \tag{C-1}$$

$$\bar{r} = \frac{1}{T} \sum_{i=1}^{T} r_T \qquad \text{for historical returns} \tag{C-1a}$$

where

$E(r)$ = expected return
n = number of different returns possible
$\bar{r}$ = mean return
r_i = ith possible rate of return
P_i = $1/n$ = relative frequency of ith return = $1/T$
T = terminal time period

It is always assumed that $\sum_i^n P_i = 1$. The first moment about the origin of a distribution is the same as its expected value or mean. The first moment about the origin is a measure of location or central tendency for the distribution.

probability distributions and relative-frequency distributions

Equation (C-1) is similar to Eq. (C-1*a*). The only difference in them is that (C-1) is stated in terms of probabilities and therefore applies to future returns (denoted r_i), whereas Eq. (C-1*a*) is stated in terms of T historical rates of return (denoted r_t) and relative frequencies (denoted $1/n$). Thus, (C-1*a*) defines the mean of a historical relative-frequency distribution.

Equations (C-1) and (C-1*a*) both define first moments about the origin, but (C-1) defines a first moment about the origin of an (expected) probability

[1] For a more rigorous discussion of moments, *see* J. E. Freund, *Mathematical Statistics*, Prentice-Hall, Englewood Cliffs, N.J., 1962, Chap. 4. For a more elementary discussion of moments and various approximations for moments, *see* S. B. Richmond, *Statistical Analysis*, 2d ed., Ronald, New York, 1964, Chap. 4. For those probability distributions (for example, Cauchy) having no moments, this discussion is, of course, irrelevant.

distribution, while (C-1*a*) defines the first moment about the origin of a (historical) relative-frequency distribution.

first moment about the mean always zero

Moments about the mean are different from *moments about the origin*. The *first moment* about the mean is defined by Eqs. (C-2) and (C-2*a*).

$$M_1 = \sum_{i=1}^{n} P_i[r_i - E(r)] = 0 \qquad \text{for future returns} \tag{C-2}$$

$$M_1 = \frac{1}{T}\sum_{t}^{T} [r_t - \bar{r}] = 0 \qquad \text{for historical returns} \tag{C-2a}$$

The first moment about the mean is always zero. However, higher-order moments about the mean, called *statistical moments*, are useful in security and portfolio analysis.

variance or second moment

The *second moment* about the mean of a distribution of returns is defined by Eqs. (C-3) and (C-3*a*).

$$\sigma^2 = \sum_{i}^{n} P[r_i - E(r)]^2 \qquad \text{for future returns} \tag{C-3}$$

$$\sigma^2 = \frac{1}{T}\sum_{t}^{T} [r_t - \bar{r}]^2 \qquad \text{for historical returns} \tag{C-3a}$$

Second statistical moment is a synonym for *variance*. The second statistical moment measures the distribution's dispersion or wideness. The square root of the variance is the *standard deviation*.

the third moment and skewness

The *third moment* of a distribution of returns is defined in Eqs. (C-4) and (C-4*a*).

$$M_3 = \Sigma P_i[r_i - E(r)]^3 \qquad \text{for future returns} \tag{C-4}$$

$$M_3 = \frac{1}{T}\sum_{t}^{T} [r_t - \bar{r}]^3 \qquad \text{for historical returns} \tag{C-4a}$$

The third statistical moment measures the lopsidedness of the distribution; it is normalized by dividing it by the standard deviation cubed. This puts the third moments of different distributions in terms of a relative measure of lopsidedness which is called *skewness*. Equation (C-5) defines the skewness of a distribution of returns.

$$\begin{aligned} \text{sk}(r) &= \frac{M_3}{\sigma^3} \\ &= \frac{\Sigma P[r_i - E(r)]^3}{\{\sqrt{\Sigma P[r_i - E(r)]^2}\}^3} \end{aligned} \tag{C-5}$$

Figure 9-2 on page 209 shows three probability distributions with the three possible types of skewness—positive, zero, and negative. A distribution which is skewed left (*a*) will have a long left tail, a negative third moment, and

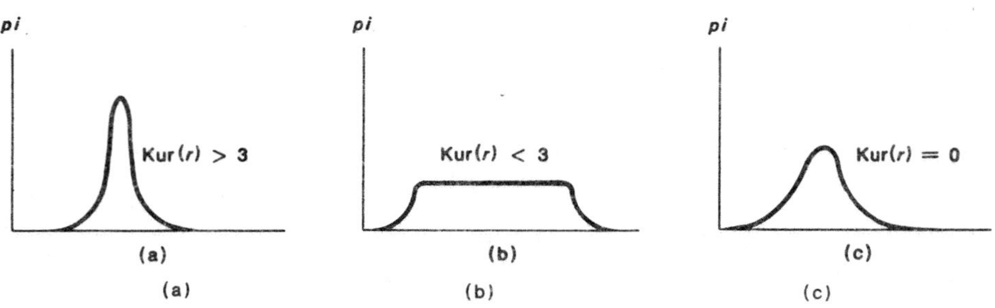

FIGURE C-1 peakedness or kurtosis of distributions. (*a*) leptokurtic; (*b*) platykurtic; (*c*) normal or mesokurtic.

negative skewness. A symmetrical distribution (*b*) will have a third moment and skewness of zero.[2] Distributions which are skewed right (*c*) will have positive third moments, positive skewness, and longer right tails.

fourth moment and kurtosis

The *fourth moment* M_4 measures the peakedness of a probability distribution. For a probability distribution of returns, the fourth moment is defined by Eqs. (C-6) and (C-6*a*).

$$M_4 = \Sigma P_i[r_i - E(r)]^4 \qquad \text{for future returns} \tag{C-6}$$

$$M_4 = \frac{1}{T}\sum_{t}^{T}[\bar{r}_t - \bar{r}]^4 \qquad \text{for historical returns} \tag{C-6a}$$

Figure C-1 shows three probability distributions of returns, leptokurtic (*a*), platykurtic (*b*), and normal or mesokurtic (*c*). Although all three of these distributions may have first, second, and third moments which are identical, they would all have different fourth moments.

The fourth moment of a probability distribution is usually normalized by being divided by the standard deviation raised to the fourth power, allowing direct comparisons of the peakedness of different distributions. This normalized fourth moment is called *a measure of kurtosis*. Kurtosis is defined by Eq. (C-7).

$$\text{kur}(r) = \frac{M_4}{\sigma^4} \tag{C-7}$$

$$= \frac{\Sigma p[r - E(r)]^4}{\{\sqrt{\Sigma p[r - E(r)]^2}\}^4}$$

[2] Skewness may be zero for nonsymmetrical distributions in a few pathological situations. P. G. Hoel, *Introduction to Mathematical Statistics*, 3d ed., Wiley, New York, 1962, pp. 76–77. Skewness can also be difficult to measure econometrically, as shown by J. C. Francis, "Skewness and Investors' Decisions," *Journal of Financial and Quantitative Analysis*, March 1975, pp. 163–172.

APPENDIX D

elements of correlation and regression analysis

Correlation and regression are classical statistical tools used to analyze the interrelation between variables. In this appendix we shall examine simple linear models of correlation and regression.

D-1 REGRESSION

We shall denote the *independent* or *control variable* as x and the *dependent variable* as y. As an example, x and y might be observations of returns on the market and the concurrent returns on some security, respectively. Of course, then we would be discussing the characteristic line—a particular regression line. Or x might represent the average number of cigarettes smoked per month and y might represent the number of chest colds and other respiratory illnesses the smoker suffered per month. Eq. (D-1) shows the basic regression model we shall examine here.

$$y = \alpha + Bx + e \tag{D-1}$$

where

α = intercept coefficient, alpha

B = slope coefficient, beta

e = random error term, epsilon; this is the residual portion of the y value which is left unexplained by the regression $= [y_i - (\alpha + Bx_i)]$

Figure D-1 shows a scattter diagram and the form of Eq. (D-1) which seems to "fit the data best."

FIGURE D-1 graphs of simple linear regression. (*a*) scatter diagram of (x, y) observations; (*b*) least-squares line through scatter of observations

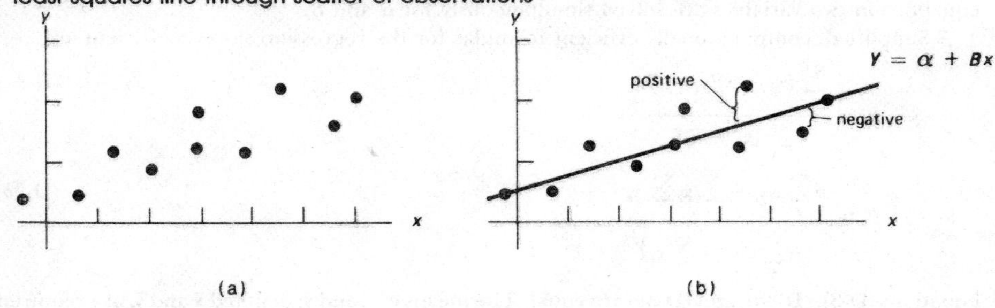

the sample data

Regression analysis begins with n observations of (x_i, y_i) pairs: (x_1, y_1), (x_2, y_2), . . . , (x_n, y_n). These n observations may be graphed as a scatter diagram like the one in Figure D-1. For the characteristic line, the n observations represent observations from n different time periods all for the same asset. For the analysis of the effects of smoking on health, the n observations represent n persons' experiences (or n periods of experience by one person).

fitting the regression line

The objective of regression analysis is to find the line through the points in (x, y) space which "fits the observations." The objective is to minimize the sum of the squared errors around the regression line, or, more specifically, to minimize SSQ in Eq. (D-2).

$$\begin{aligned} \min \text{SSQ} &= \sum_{i=1}^{n} [y_i - (\alpha + Bx_i)]^2 \qquad \text{(D-2)} \\ &= \sum_{i=1}^{n} e_i^2 \\ &= \sum_{i=1}^{n} (y_i - \hat{y}_i)^2 \\ &= \text{the sum of the errors squared} \end{aligned}$$

Here, $\hat{y}_i = \alpha + Bx_i$ = a predicted value of y given that x equals the ith value of x. That is, $\hat{y}_t$ denotes some point lying on the regression line, y_i is an actual observed value of the variable y, and $(y_i - \hat{y}_i) = e_i$ = the ith error. Differential calculus is used to find the formulas for the regression coefficients α and B which "fit a line" through the n observations in such a manner that SSQ is minimized.[1] This line is called a least-squares regression line, or an ordinary least-squares (OLS) line.

the regression coefficients

The formula for the least-squares regression slope coefficient B is defined in Eq. (D-3).[2]

$$B = \frac{\text{cov}(x,y)}{\text{var}(x)} \qquad \text{(D-3)}$$

[1] The partial derivatives $\partial(\text{SSQ})/\partial\alpha$ and $\partial(\text{SSQ})/\partial B$ are set to zero, and the two resulting linear equations in two variables are solved simultaneously for α and B.

[2] Simplified, computationally efficient formulas for the regression slope coefficient are

$$B = \frac{\sum_i (x_i - \bar{x})(y_i - \bar{y})}{\sum (x_i - \bar{x})^2} \qquad \text{(D-3}a\text{)}$$

$$B = \frac{n\sum_i x_i y_i - \sum_i x_i \sum_i y_i}{n\sum_i x_i^2 - \left(\sum_i x_i\right)^2} \qquad \text{(D-3}b\text{)}$$

Equations (D-3), (D-3*a*), and (D-3*b*) are equal. The means of x and y, denoted $\bar{x}$ and $\bar{y}$, are required to calculate (D-3) and (D-3*a*) but not (D-3*b*). Therefore, (D-3*b*) is computationally the simplest formula to use.

The formula for the least-squares regression intercept coefficient α is defined in Eq. (D-4).

$$\alpha = \bar{y} - B\bar{x} \tag{D-4}$$

B from (D-3) is required before α may be determined. After α and B are determined, the line $y = \alpha + Bx$ may be graphed in (x,y) space. This is the least-squares line or line of best fit.

properties of least-squares regression lines

All least-squares regression lines meet the following three conditions if they are calculated correctly.

1. They pass through the centroid $(\bar{x},\bar{y})$.
2. The sum of the squared errors is minimized: SSQ = minimum.
3. The sum of the errors is zero: $\Sigma_{i=1}^{n} e_i = 0$.

If all three of these conditions are not met, some error has been made in calculating the least-squares line intercept and slope coefficients.

D-2 CORRELATION

A correlation coefficient can vary as follows: $-1 \le \rho \le +1$. If $\rho_{xy} = +1$, then x and y are perfectly positively correlated; they move in the same direction in unison. If $\rho_{xy} = 0$, the two variables x and y are uncorrelated; they show no tendency to follow each other. If $\rho_{xy} = -1$, x and y vary inversely; they are perfectly negatively correlated. The definition of ρ_{xy} is given in Eq. (D-5).[3]

$$\rho_{xy} = \frac{\text{cov}\ (x,y)}{\sigma_x \sigma_y} = \rho_{yx} \tag{D-5}$$

pure correlation analysis

The correlation coefficient for x and y may be determined whether or not any regression of y and x is performed. Correlation analysis makes no assumptions as to which variable is the independent variable and which is dependent. The correlation coefficient is a *standardized* measure of the way two variables covary.

a closeness-of-fit measure

If the regression of y onto x (or x onto y) is performed, the correlation coefficient has a second interpretation; the correlation coefficient is a measure of the *closeness of fit* of the observed points to the regression line. Figure D-2 shows some scatter diagrams to which least-squares regression lines have been fitted.

When the (x_i, y_i) points do not follow any linear model of the form shown in Eq. (D-1), the correlation coefficient is zero. If all the (x_i, y_i) points lie exactly on some regression line, the correlation coefficient equals either positive or

[3] A computationally efficient formula for the correlation coefficient is

$$\rho_{yx} = \rho_{xy} = \frac{n\Sigma xy - \Sigma x \Sigma y}{\{[(n\Sigma x^2) - (\Sigma x)^2][(n\Sigma y^2) - (\Sigma y)^2]\}^{.5}} \tag{D-5a}$$

Equation (D-5a) is equivalent to (D-5). Neither formula adjusts for degrees of freedom.

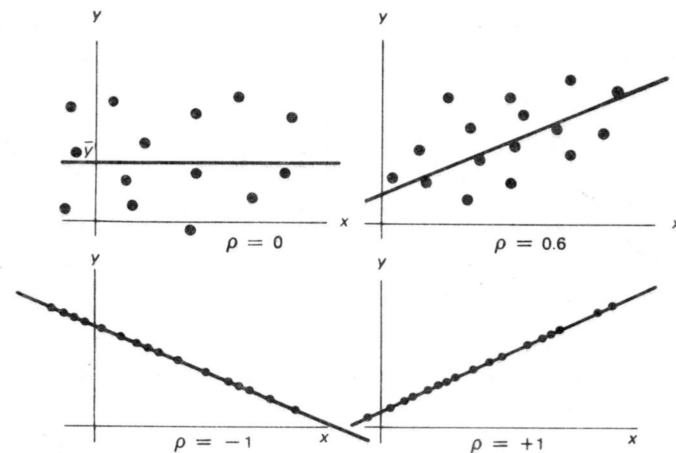

FIGURE D-2 the correlation coefficients for various scatter diagrams.

negative unity, depending on the slope of the line. If the points tend to follow the line but do not lie exactly on the line, the correlation is nonzero and its sign depends on the slope of the regression line.

The correlation coefficient does not vary whether x is regressed onto y or vice versa, although the regression coefficients α and B vary (unless $p = +1$ or -1). Denote the regression slope coefficient for regressing y onto x as $B_y|_x$ and the slope coefficient for regressing x onto y as $B_x|_y$. Equation (D-6) shows the relation of the beta or slope coefficients and the correlation coefficient.

$$\rho_{xy} = \sqrt{(B_x|_y)(B_y|_x)} = \rho_{yx} \qquad \text{(D-6)}$$

coefficient of determination

The correlation coefficient squared is called the *coefficient of determination* and denoted ρ^2. The coefficient of determination gives the percentage of variation in the dependent variable which can be explained by concurrent variance in the independent variable.

serial correlation

The serial correlation coefficient measures the tendency of time series data to run in trends or cycles. If x_t are observations of some variable x at different points in time, then x_t for $t = 1, 2, \ldots, T$ is a *time series* over T periods. The serial correlation or autocorrelation coefficient for a time series of a variable x is defined in Eq. (D-7).

$$\rho_k = \frac{\text{cov}(x_t, x_{t+k})}{(\sigma x_t)(\sigma x_{t+k})} \qquad \text{(D-7)}$$

ρ_k is a serial correlation coefficient of order k, where k is the number of periods of lag which is being examined.

D-3 TOTAL AND UNEXPLAINED VARIANCE

The total variance of the dependent variable in regression model (D-1) is defined in Eq. (D-8).

$$\sigma_y^2 = \frac{1}{n} \sum_{i=1}^{n} (y_i - \bar{y})^2 \tag{D-8}$$

residual variance

Equation (D-9) defines the residual variance.

$$\sigma^2_{(y|x)} = \frac{1}{n} \sum_{i=1}^{n} (y_i - \hat{y}_i)^2 \tag{D-9}$$

$$= \frac{1}{n} \sum_{i=1}^{n} [y_i - (\alpha + bx_i)]^2 \qquad \text{since } \hat{y}_t = \alpha + bx_i$$

$$= \frac{1}{n} \sum_{i=1}^{n} e_i^2$$

The difference between Eqs. (D-8) and (D-9) is that they measure deviations from different points. Equation (D-8) measures deviations of y around the mean of y, whereas (D-9) measures deviations of y around the regression line. If the regression line explains any relation between x and y (that is, if $\rho_{xy} \neq 0$), then the residual variance must be less than the total variance because the regression line is a better estimator of y than the mean, $\bar{y}$. The square root of the residual variance is called the *standard error* of the regression estimate.

The percentage of variance in y unexplained by regression y onto x is defined in Eq. (D-10).

$$\frac{\sigma^2_{(y|x)}}{\sigma_y^2} = \text{percent of var}(y) \text{ unexplained by regression} \tag{D-10}$$

The coefficient of determination is simply unity (100 percent) less the percentage of variance unexplained.

$$\rho^2 = 1 - \frac{\sigma^2_{(y|x)}}{\sigma_y^2} = \text{coefficient of determination} \tag{D-11}$$

D-4 REGRESSION ASSUMPTIONS

Thus far in this appendix we have been discussing least-squares regression lines. Least-squares regression lines are "better" if the following four conditions pertaining to the random error term e exist:

1. e is a random variable with a mean of zero; that is, the error term is unbiased.
2. e has some variance which is constant throughout the length of the regression line. This is called *homoscedasticity*.
3. e_i and e_{i+k} do not covary for any values of k so that $\text{cov}(e_i, e_{i+k}) = 0$; that is, the errors are uncorrelated.
4. e_i and x_i do not covary so that $\text{cov}(e_i, x_i) = 0$; that is, the errors are independent.

If the preceding four conditions are met, the regression line not only minimizes the squared errors, but the following two desirable properties are also obtained (the Gauss-Markov theorem):

1. $E(y \mid x) = \alpha + Bx$; that is, the regression line is an unbiased, linear estimator of y.
2. y_i and y_{i+k} are not serially correlated. Serial correlation can cause the regression coefficients α and B to vary erratically from sample to sample.

If the error term is unbiased and uncorrelated and has homoscedasticity and, in addition, e is a *normally distributed* random variable, the following two additional desirable properties apply to the regression line.

1. e_i and e_{i+k} are independent. This is a stronger condition than being uncorrelated.
2. Probability statements can be made about the various regression statistics. For example, it is possible to draw confidence limits around the regression line.

SELECTED REFERENCES

Brennan, M., *Preface to Econometrics*, 3d ed., South-Western Publishing Co., Cincinnati, 1973. An elementary mathematics and statistics text which gives intuitive nonmathematical explanations of complex topics.

Folger, H. R., and S. Ganapathy, *Financial Econometrics*, Prentice-Hall, Englewood Cliffs, N.J., 1982. This is an econometrics book that employs numerical examples from financial applications.

Pindyck, R. S., and D. L. Rubinfeld, *Econometric Models and Economic Forecasts*, 2d ed., McGraw-Hill, New York, 1981. An easy-to-read intermediate-level econometrics textbook which uses elementary calculus and matrix algebra. The use of real empirical data and numerical examples make this book interesting.

APPENDIX E

mathematical derivation of formulas for portfolio risk and expected return

This appendix explains the risk and return formulas for portfolios and relates them to the risk and return formulas for individual assets.

E-1 RISK AND RETURN FORMULAS FOR INDIVIDUAL ASSETS

The expected return from the ith asset is defined as follows:

$$E(r_i) = \sum_{t=1}^{n} P_t r_t \tag{E-1}$$

where

P_t = probability of tth rate of return

r_t = tth rate of return

n = number of different rates of return possible

It is assumed that the probabilities sum to 1; that is, $\sum_{t=1}^{n} P_t = 1$. The expected-value operator is discussed in Mathematical Appendix B.

In a discussion of investments, it is assumed that the rate of return is the single most meaningful outcome associated with an investment's performance. Thus, discussion of the risk of a security focuses on dispersion of the security's rate of return around its expected return. Following Markowitz, risk is defined as "variability of return."[1] In any event, the standard deviation of rates of return or variance of rates of return is a possible measure of the phenomenon defined above as the risk. Symbolically, for the ith asset,

$$\text{var}(r_i) = \sigma_i^2 = \sigma_{ii} = \sum_{t=1}^{n} P_{it}[r_{it} - E(r_i)]^2 = E[r - E(r)]^2 \tag{E-2}$$

Equation (E-2) defines the variance of returns for asset i. The value of σ_{ii} is in terms of a "rate of return squared." The standard deviation of returns is more intuitively appealing, since it is the square root of the variance. It is defined in Eq. (E-3).

$$\sigma \quad \text{or} \quad \sigma_i = \sqrt{\sum_{t=1}^{n} P_{it}[r_{it} - E(r_i)]^2} \tag{E-3}$$

[1] Harry Markowitz, *Portfolio Selection*, Cowles Foundation Monograph 16, Wiley, New York, 1959, p. 14.

$$= \sqrt{E[r - E(r)^2}$$

$$= \sqrt{\sigma_{ii}}$$

The covariance of returns between assets i and j is denoted by σ_{ij} or $\text{cov}(r_i, r_j)$.

$$\sigma_{ij} = E\{[r_i - E(r_i)][r_j - E(r_j)]\} \tag{E-4}$$

$$= \sum_{t=1}^{T} P_t\{[r_{it} - E(r_i)][r_{jt} - E(r_j)]\}$$

where r_{it} is the tth rate of return for the ith asset. It can be shown that the covariance may also be defined as shown in Eq. (E-4a).

$$\sigma_{ij} = (\rho_{ij})(\sigma_i)(\sigma_j) \tag{E-4a}$$

where ρ_{ij} denotes the correlation coefficient between the returns of assets i and j. Mathematical Appendix B defines the covariance.

Equations (E-1) to (E-4) define the expected return, risk, and covariance of an individual asset. The expected return and risk of a portfolio are broken down in terms of these four components in the following subsection.

E-2 RISK AND RETURN FORMULAS FOR PORTFOLIOS

Assuming that all funds allocated for portfolio use are to be invested, the following constraint is placed on all portfolios.

$$\sum_{i=1}^{n} x_i = 1 \tag{E-5}$$

where x_i denotes the weight, participation level, or fraction of the portfolio's total equity invested in the ith asset. In words, the n fractions of the portfolio's equity invested in n different assets sum up to 1 (or 100 percent). Cash can be one of the assets in the portfolio. Equation (E-5) is a constraint which cannot be violated in portfolio analysis; if it is, the analysis has no rational economic interpretation.

Let r_p denote some actual return from a portfolio, and let $E(r_p)$ denote the expected return for the portfolio. The expected return for the portfolio can be restated in terms of the assets' expected returns as follows:

$$E(r_p) = \sum_{i=i}^{n} x_i E(r_i) \tag{E-6}$$

$$= \sum_{i=1}^{n} x_i \left(\sum_{t=1}^{T} p_{it} r_{it} \right)$$

$$= x_1 E(r_1) + x_2 E(r_2) + \cdots + x_n E(r_n)$$

In words, the expected return of a portfolio is the weighted average of the expected returns from the n securities in the portfolio.

Following the *dispersion of outcome* or *variability of return* definitions of risk, the risk of a portfolio is defined as the variability of its return, that is, the variability of r_p. By denoting the variance of r_p by var(r_p), it is possible to derive an analytical expression for var(r_p) in terms of the r_i's of all securities in the portfolio. This is the form of the expression suitable for portfolio analysis.

Substituting r_p for r_i in Eq. (E-7) yields Eq. (E-8), which defines the variance of the portfolio's rates of return, denoted var(r_p).

$$\sigma_i^2 = \sigma_{ii} = E[r_i - E(r)]^2 \tag{E-7}$$

$$= \sum P_i[r_i - E(r)]^2 \tag{E-7a}$$

$$\sigma_p^2 = \text{var}(r_p) = E[r_p - E(r_p)]^2 \tag{E-8}$$

$$= \sum_i P_i[r_p - E(r_p)]^2 \tag{E-8a}$$

A simple two-security portfolio will be used to illustrate the derivation of the formula for the risk of a portfolio. However, the results are general and follow for an *n*-security portfolio, where *n* is any positive integer. Substituting the quantity $(x_1r_1 + x_2r_2)$ for the equivalent r_p into Eq. (E-8) yields (E-9).

$$\text{var}(r_p) = E[r_p - E(r_p)]^2 \tag{E-8}$$

$$\text{var}(r_p) = E[(x_1r_1 + x_2r_2) - E(x_1r_1 + x_2r_2)]^2 \tag{E-9}$$

Removal of the parentheses and use of property 2 in Mathematical Appendix B for the expectation operator results in an equivalent form:

$$\text{var}(r_p) = E[x_1r_1 + x_2r_2 - x_1E(r_1) - x_2E(r_2)]^2$$

Collecting terms with like subscripts and factoring out the x_i's gives

$$\text{var}(r_p) = E\{x_1[r_1 - E(r_1)] + x_2[r_2 - E(2r_2)]\}^2$$

Since $(ab + cd)^2 = (a^2b^2 + c^2d^2 + 2abcd)$, the above squared quantity can likewise be expanded by letting $ab = x_1[r_1 - E(r_1)]$ and $cd = x_2[r_2 - E(r_2)]$, which gives

$$\text{var}(r_p) = E\{x_1^2[r_1 - E(r_1)]^2 + x_2^2[r_2 - E(r_2)]^2 + 2x_1x_2[r_1 - E(r_1)][r_2 - E(r_2)]\}$$

Bringing the *E* operator inside the braces (by property 2) yields

$$\text{var}(r_p) = x_1^2E[r_1 - E(r_1)]^2 + x_2^2E[r_2 - E(r_2)]^2 + 2x_1x_2E\{[r_1 - E(r_1)][r_2 - E(r_2)]\}$$

Recalling Eqs. (E-2) and (E-4), which define σ_{ii} and σ_{ij}, we recognize that the above expression is equivalent to

$$\text{var}(r_p) = x_1^2\sigma_{11} + x_2^2\sigma_{22} + 2x_1x_2\sigma_{12} \tag{E-10}$$

$$= x_1^2 \text{ var}(r_1) + x_2^2 \text{ var}(r_2) + 2x_1x_2 \text{ cov}(r_1r_2)$$

Equation (E-10) shows that the variance of a weighted sum is not always simply the sum of the weighted variances. The *covariance* term may increase or decrease the variance of the sum depending on its sign.

The derivation of Eq. (E-10) is repeated in a more coherent manner thus:

$$\begin{aligned}
\sigma_p^2 &= \text{var}(r_p) = E[r_p - E(r_p)]^2 \\
&= E[x_1r_1 + x_2r_2 - E(x_1r_1 + x_2r_2)]^2 \qquad \text{by substitution for } r_p \\
&= E[x_1r_1 + x_2r_2 - x_1E(r_1) - x_2E(r_2)]^2 \\
&= E\{x_1[r_1 - E(r_1)] + x_2[r_2 - E(r_2)]\}^2 \qquad \text{by collecting like terms} \\
&= E\{x_1^2[r_1 - E(r_1)]^2 + x_2^2[r_2 - E(r_2)]^2 + 2x_1x_2[r_1 - E(r_1)][r_2 - E(r_2)]\} \\
&= x_1^2E[r_1 - E(r_1)]^2 + x_2^2E[r_2 - E(r_2)]^2 + 2x_1x_2E[r_1 - E(r_1)][r_2 - E(r_2)] \\
&= x_1^2 \text{ var}(r_1) + x_2^2 \text{ var}(r_2) + 2x_1x_2 \text{ cov}(r_1r_2) \qquad \text{(E-10)}
\end{aligned}$$

An understanding of Eq. (E-10) is essential to a true understanding of diversification and portfolio analysis. Next, Eq. (E-10) is expanded (without proof) to measure the risk of more realistic portfolios, that is, portfolios with more than two securities. However, even in its more elaborate versions, this equation is still simply the sum of the weighted variances and covariances.

Equation (E-10) is sometimes written more compactly using summation signs as shown below:

$$\text{var}(r_p) = \sum_i^n x_i^2\sigma_{ii} + \sum_j^n\sum_i^n x_ix_j\sigma_{ij} \qquad \text{for } i \neq j \qquad \text{(E-10}a\text{)}$$

where $n = 2$ or any other positive integer.

To clarify this notation, consider the following table of terms. The subscript i is the row number, and j is the column number.

		col. 1	col. 2	
$\text{var}(r_p)$	=	$+x_1x_1\sigma_{11}+$	$+x_1x_2\sigma_{12}+$	row 1
		$+x_2x_1\sigma_{21}+$	$+x_2x_2x_{22}$	row 2

$$\begin{aligned}
&= x_1x_1\sigma_{11} + x_1x_2\sigma_{12} + x_2x_1\sigma_{21} + x_2x_2\sigma_{22} \\
&= x_1^2\sigma_{11} + 2x_1x_2\sigma_{12} + x_2^2\sigma_{22} \qquad \text{since } x_1x_2\sigma_{12} = x_2x_1\sigma_{21} \\
&= \sum_{i=1}^2 x_i^2\sigma_{ii} + \sum_{j=1}^2\sum_{i=1}^2 x_ix_j\sigma_{ii} \qquad \text{for } i \neq j \qquad \text{(E-10}a\text{)} \\
&= \sum_j^2\sum_i^2 x_ix_j\sigma_{ij} \qquad \text{since cov}(r_i,r_i) = \text{var}(r_i) \qquad \text{(E-10}b\text{)} \\
&= \sum_{i=1}^2 x_i^2\sigma_{ii} + \sum_{i=1}^2\sum_{j=1}^2 x_ix_j\rho_{ij}\sigma_i\sigma_j \text{ since } \sigma_{ij} = \rho_{ij}\sigma_i\sigma_j \qquad \text{for } i \neq j \qquad \text{(E-10}c\text{)}
\end{aligned}$$

The three factors which determine the risk of a portfolio are the weights of the securities, the standard deviation (or variance) of each security, and the correlation coefficient (or covariance) between the securities.

Expressions of $\text{var}(r_p)$ for a large number of securities take the following form:

$$
\begin{array}{lllllll|l}
 & \text{col. 1} & \text{col. 2} & \text{col. 3} & & \text{col. } n-1 & \text{col. } n & \\
\text{var}(r_p) = & x_1x_1\sigma_{11} & + x_1x_2\sigma_{12} & + x_1x_3\sigma_{13} & + \cdots & x_1x_{n-1}\sigma_{1,n-1} & + x_1x_n\sigma_{1n} & \text{row 1} \\
 & + x_2x_1\sigma_{21} & + x_2x_2\sigma_{22} & + x_2x_3\sigma_{23} & + \cdots & x_2x_{n-1}\sigma_{2,n-1} & + x_2x_n\sigma_{2n} & \text{row 2} \\
 & + x_3x_1\sigma_{31} & + x_3x_2\sigma_{32} & + x_3x_3\sigma_{33} & + \cdots & x_3x_{n-1}\sigma_{3,n-1} & + x_3x_n\sigma_{3n} & \text{row 3} \\
 & \vdots & \vdots & \vdots & & \vdots & & \\
 & + x_nx_1\sigma_{n1} & + x_nx_2\sigma_{n2} & + x_nx_3\sigma_{n3} & + & x_nx_{n-1}\sigma_{n,n-1} & + x_nx_n\sigma_{nn} & \text{row } n
\end{array}
$$

These data comprise a matrix, which can be represented more compactly using Eq. (E-10*a*) or (E-10*b*) above. A matrix can be regarded as an array of numbers or a table of numbers. The matrix above represents the weighted sum of all n variances plus all $n^2 - n$ covariances. Thus, in a portfolio of 100 securities (that is, $n = 100$), there will be 100 variances and $100^2 - 100 = 9{,}900$ covariances. The security analyst must supply all these plus 100 expected returns for the securities.

Notice that the elements of the matrix containing terms with identical subscripts form a diagonal pattern from the upper left-hand corner to the lower right-hand corner. There are the n weighted variance terms of the form $x_ix_i\sigma_{ii}$. All the other boxes contain the $n^2 - n$ weighted covariance terms (that is, terms of the form $x_ix_j\sigma_{ij}$, where $i \neq j$). The variance-covariance matrix is symmetric since $x_ix_j\sigma_{ij} = x_jx_i\sigma_{ji}$; each covariance is repeated twice in the matrix. The covariances above the diagonal are the mirror images of the covariances below the diagonal. Thus, the security analyst must actually estimate only $\frac{1}{2}(n^2 - n)$ unique covariances.

APPENDIX F

geometric mean return

When dealing with the average of several *successive rates of return*, the distinction between various multiperiod average rates of return and the *geometric mean* return should be recognized.

F-1 THE MISLEADING ARITHMETIC MULTIPERIOD AVERAGE RETURN

Consider asset A, purchased at \$40. Suppose asset A's price rises to \$60 at the end of the first period, then falls back to \$40, and the asset is sold at that price at the end of the second period. The *arithmetic average rate* of return is the average of 50 percent and -33.3 percent, which is 8.35 percent.

$$\frac{50\% + (-33.3\%)}{2} = 8.35\% = \text{arithmetic average return on } A$$

Next consider asset B, which also has an original price of \$40. But asset B's price falls to \$20 at the end of one period. Then it rises back to \$40 at the end of period 2. The arithmetic average rate of return for asset B is the average of -50 percent and 100 percent, which is 25 percent.

$$\frac{-50\% + 100\%}{2} = 25\% = \text{arithmetic average return for } B$$

The behavior of assets A and B prices over the two periods is summarized graphically in Fig. F-1.

An asset purchased for \$40 and sold for \$40 two periods later did not return 8.35 percent or 25 percent; it clearly earned *zero* return. The arithmetic average of successive one-period returns is obviously not equal to the *true* average rate of return over *multiple periods*.

FIGURE F-1 prices of two assets over two periods.

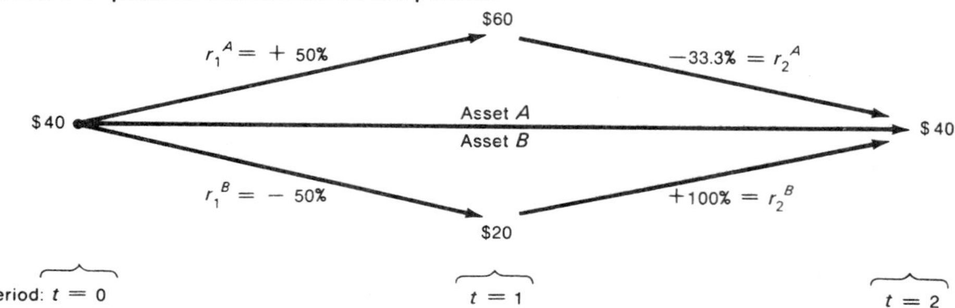

F-2 THE DOLLAR-WEIGHTED RATE OF RETURN

In classes about capital budgeting (or capital expenditures or corporation finance, as it is variously called), the rate of return from a multiperiod investment is defined to be the discount rate which equates the present value of all cashflows c_t to the cost of the investment c_0, as shown below.

$$c_0 = \sum_{t=1}^{T} \frac{c_t}{(1 + r)^t} \tag{F-1a}$$

This rate of return is also sometimes called the *dollar-weighted rate of return*, or the *internal rate of return*. It is represented by the symbol r in Eq. (F-1a).

For only a one-period investment, $n = 1$, the internal rate of return is equivalent to the one-period rate of return, Eq. (2-2), as shown below.

$$c_0 = \frac{c_1}{1 + r} \tag{F-1b}$$

$$c_0 r = c_1 - c_0$$

$$r = \frac{c_1 - c_0}{c_0} \qquad \text{equivalent to Eqs. (2-2) and (2-1)}$$

The quantity $c_1 - c_0$ equals capital gains or losses plus cash dividends or interest for stock or bonds, respectively, as in Eqs. (2-2) and (2-1) in Chap. 2.

For multiperiod investments involving only one cash inflow—namely, the cost of the asset, or c_0—and one cash outflow, c_t, the internal rate of return yields the same solution as the (average compounded or) geometric mean rate of return. For example, for asset A the cashflows were $c_0 = \$40$ and $c_2 = \$40$, which yields $r = 0$, as shown in Eq. (F-1c).

$$\$40 = \frac{\$40}{(1 + r)^2} \qquad \text{only if } r = 0 \tag{F-1c}$$

The internal rate of return is different from the (average compounded or) geometric mean rate of return for multiperiod investments which involve *multiple* cash inflows or outflows, however.

The internal rate of return is also called the dollar-weighted rate of return because it is influenced by how many dollars remain invested in a multiperiod investment. Thus, the dollar-weighted rate of return is not useful for comparing the rates of return for, say, two mutual funds which experience different cashflow patterns over time. The *time-weighted rate of return* is the true (average compounded or geometric mean) rate of return, which is useful for such comparisons because it is not affected by the size of an investment's cash inflows and/or outflows.

F-3 FORMULAS FOR GEOMETRIC MEAN RETURN

The true rate of return over n periods is called average compounded rate of return or geometric mean return (gr) and is defined in Eq. (F-2a). The $1 + r$ terms are called *link relatives* or *value relatives*.

$$gr = \sqrt[T]{(1 + r_1)(1 + r_2) \cdots (1 + r_T)} - 1 \tag{F-2a}$$

$$= \left[\prod_{t=1}^{T} (1 + r_t)\right]^{1/T} - 1 \tag{F-2b}$$

For a common stock, the link relative is the ending price plus dividends divided by the beginning price. Symbolically,

$$1 + r_t = \frac{p_{t+1} + d_t}{p_t} = \text{price plus dividend value relative} \tag{F-3}$$

It is cumbersome to evaluate a Tth root, not to mention the fact that there may be T different roots to consider. The logarithmic transformations may be used to expedite computation of the geometric mean return. Equation (F-4a) shows a computationally efficient formula for calculating the geometric mean of T different one-period returns by using logarithms.[1]

$$gr = \left\{\text{antilog}\left[\frac{1}{T}\sum_{t=1}^{T} \log(1 + r_t)\right]\right\} - 1 \tag{F-4a}$$

Returning to the two-period numerical example, we can calculate the geometric mean with Eq. (F-4a). The natural logs of the value relatives for asset B are shown on the bottom line of Table F-1. The geometric mean return for asset B is zero, as shown below,

$$e^{(1/2)(.693-.693)} - 1 = 0 \tag{F-4b}$$

since $e^0 - 1 = 0$. Obviously, the true rate of return for asset B is the geometric mean return of zero and not the arithmetic average return of 25 percent. The same thing is true for asset A; its geometric mean of zero is calculated below.

$$e^{(1/2)(.405-.405)} - 1 = 0 \tag{F-4c}$$

[1] Either common base-10 logarithms or Naperian, base-e, logarithms may be used; they yield the same geometric return. But natural logs are preferred because the natural log of the value relative is a measure of rate of return. For example, if r = 10 percent = .1, then $1 + r = 1.1$ and ln 1.1 = .095 = 9.5 percent continuously compounded rate of return.

TABLE F-1 multiperiod mean return computations

	time periods	$t = 0$	$t = 1$	$t = 2$
A	Market value of asset A	p_0 = \$40	p_1 = \$60	p_2 = \$40
	One-period return		r_1 = 50%	r_2 = −33.3%
	Natural logarithm of $(1 + r)$		ln(1 + .5) = .405	ln(1 − .333) = −.405
B	Market value of asset B	p_0 = \$40	p_1 = \$20	p_2 = \$40
	One-period return		r_1 = −50%	r_2 = 100%
	Natural logarithm of $(1 + r)$		ln(1 − .5) = −.693	ln(1 + 1) = .693

F-4 COMPARISON OF ARITHMETIC AND GEOMETRIC MEAN RETURNS

The arithmetic average of successive one-period rates of return is defined in Eq. (F-5).

$$\bar{r} = \frac{1}{T}\sum_{t}^{T} r_t \tag{F-5}$$

The arithmetic average return $\bar{r}$ is an approximation of the true multiperiod rate of return. As the variance of the r_t's grows smaller, this approximation becomes better. Equation (F-6) shows the nature of this approximation.

$$\bar{r} \approx [gr^2 + \text{var}(r)]^{1/2} \tag{F-6}$$

F-5 THE IMPACT OF CASH INFLOWS AND OUTFLOWS ON RATE-OF-RETURN MEASURES

If the owner of investment funds is a different person from the manager of the invested funds, the manager of the investment portfolio typically experiences cash inflows when additional money is invested and cash outflows when some of the invested funds are withdrawn by their owner. The managers of most institutional investment portfolios (such as the managers of mutual funds, trust departments of banks, and other large investment programs) can have their investment rate-of-return measurements significantly affected by cash inflows and outflows if they are not analyzed properly. In order to correctly measure the rate of return for an investment portfolio that experiences cashflows in and out of the portfolio, the geometric mean rate of return must be employed. This so-called time-weighted rate of return can yield correct multiperiod rate-of-return measurements if applied properly. In contrast, the internal (or dollar-weighted) rate of return will produce incorrect rate-of-return measurements if any cash inflows or outflows occur during the time period during which the rate of return of the investment portfolio is being measured. A numerical example should clarify the nature of the possible errors that can be caused by analyzing cash inflows and outflows improperly when measuring an investment portfolio's rate of return over multiple time periods.

Consider the rates of return from a hypothetical mutual fund over two consecutive 1-year investment periods. Suppose that the shares in this mutual fund, let us call it asset B, earn a one-period rate of return of -50 percent in the first year and 100 percent in the second year. This hypothetical mutual fund is simply case B indicated in the lower branch of Fig. F-1 above. If the mutual fund has a constant amount of total funds invested over the 2-year period, then the portfolio's geometric mean rate of return is zero—as shown in the lower section of Table F-1.

Let us now consider the more realistic (and more problematical) case that occurs when cash inflows and outflows cause the amount of total funds invested to change. Suppose that our hypothetical mutual fund, or asset B, starts out with a total of $200 million invested in it at the beginning of the first

FIGURE F-2 cash value of a mutual fund's portfolio over two years.

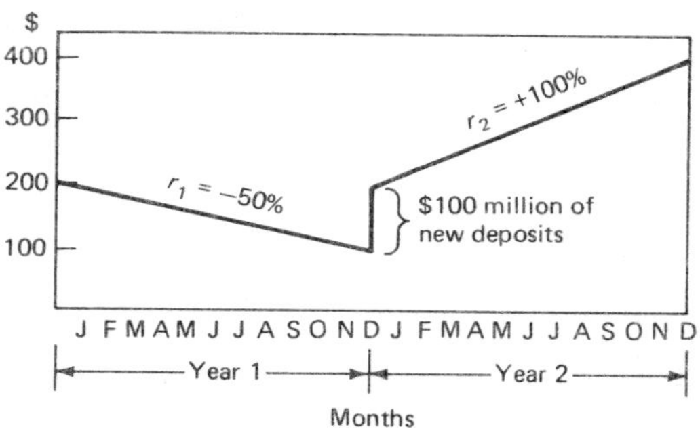

time period. But, at the end of period one the $200 million of total assets declines in market value to only $100 million because the portfolio suffers a −50 percent one-period rate of return in the first of the 2 years being evaluated here. Then, at the end of the first year, or, synonymously, at the start of the second year, $100 million of net purchases of shares by investors in the mutual fund cause an unanticipated cash inflow that raises the total funds invested at the start of the second year to a total of $200 million. And finally, during the second year the mutual fund earns an annual rate of return of 100 percent, pushing its total market value up from $200 million to $400 million at the end of the second period. This pattern of market values and cash flows is illustrated in Fig. F-2. Essentially, there are three cashflows: (1) the original positive amount of $200 million, (2) the $100 million inflow before period two, and, (3) $400 million available to be withdrawn at the end of period two, which can be treated as a negative cashflow. The question to be answered here is, "Given this fact situation, what is this mutual fund's multi-period rate of return over 2 years?"

If the inappropriate dollar-weighted (or internal) rate-of-return measure were employed, an erroneous rate-of-return measure of about 20 percent (or 18.6 percent, to be more exact) would be obtained. That is, the dollar-weighted rate of return would indicate that the beginning $200 million was invested at about 20 percent per year for 2 years, and the additional net investor purchases of $200 million that occurred between the first and the second years were also invested at about 20 percent for the second year. But this answer is obviously in error. If an investment of any amount loses half its value (namely, −50 percent) in one year and then doubles in value (that is, +100 percent) in the second year, such an asset wound up earning an annual average rate of return that is closer to zero than it is to 20 percent. In any event, it is difficult to argue plausibly that such an investment earned about 20 percent per year for 2 consecutive years.

Our hypothetical mutual fund actually earned a rate of return of zero compounded over the 2-year period. To see this intuitively, consider the fortunes of one of the *original dollar bills* invested at the start of the 2-year period. One of these original dollars fell in value to 50 cents at the end of the first year. Then, during the second year this fallen investment's 50-cent value grew to be worth a dollar—the same value it started with 2 years earlier. Thus, we see that the invested dollar earned zero over the 2-year period. This correct answer could have been obtained analytically with the geometric mean rate-of-return formulas. In fact, the calculations for asset B shown in the lower section of Table F-1 are also appropriate for our hypothetical mutual fund. Now you see that the geometric mean rate of return is not affected by cashflows that determine how much money the investment manager has to manage. The geometric mean rate of return is a *time-weighted rate of return* that weights equal time periods equally, regardless how much money is invested in each time period. This is the correct rate-of-return measure to use to evaluate the rate of return for investment managers who have cashflows into and out of the portfolio.

F-6 MAXIMIZING GEOMETRIC MEAN RETURN AS A GOAL

Dr. H. A. Lantane has suggested that maximizing the geometric return is a good investment goal.[2] This suggestion is well taken, since maximizing gr involves maximizing the r_t's each period while minimizing var(r)—that is, risk. To see this more clearly, solve Eq. (F-6) for the geometric mean return.[3]

$$gr = [\bar{r}^2 - \text{var}(r)]^{1/2} \tag{F-7}$$

Equation (F-7) shows that minimizing risk [var(r)] and maximizing the arithmetic average return ($\bar{r}$) will tend to maximize the geometric mean return. Such a policy is equivalent to maximizing terminal wealth because the ratio of terminal wealth, denoted w_r, to beginning wealth, denoted w_0, is simply $(1 + gr)^T = w_T / w_0$. This shows that maximizing the geometric mean return is equivalent to maximizing the ratio of terminal to beginning wealth.

Some financial economists have suggested that maximizing the terminal wealth or geometric mean return of a portfolio is an investment objective which may be preferable to maximizing the portfolio's expected return in a selected risk-class each period. Although this suggestion may be true for some investors, it is not true for all of them. The portfolio which maximizes the geometric mean return or terminal wealth is just one portfolio on or near the efficient frontier.[4] It is shown in Chap. 27 that as an investor's planning horizon and risk-aversion varies, the point on the efficient frontier preferred by that investor varies considerably. Chapter 29 discusses multiperiod portfolio management.

[2] H. A. Lantane, "Criteria for Choice among Risky Ventures," *The Journal of Political Economy*, April 1959, pp. 144–155.

[3] William E. Young and Robert H. Trent, "Geometric Mean Approximations of Individual Security and Portfolio Performance," *Journal of Financial and Quantitative Analysis*, June 1969, pp. 179–199.

[4] Nils H. Hakansson, "Capital Growth and the Mean-Variance Approach to Portfolio Selection," *Journal of Financial and Quantitative Analysis*, January 1971, pp. 517–557; and Jan Mossin, "Optional Multi-Period Portfolio Policies," *Journal of Business*, April 1968, pp. 215–229; E. F. Fama, "Multi-Period Consumption-Investment Decisions," *American Economic Review*, March 1970, pp. 163–174; Harry M. Markowitz, "Investment for the Long-Run: New Evidence for an Old Rule," *Journal of Finance*, December 1976, vol. 31, pp. 1273–1286.

part ten

THE CHARTERED FINANCIAL ANALYST(CFA) DESIGNATION

The Institute of Chartered Financial Analysts (ICFA) is an autonomous professional organization composed of members called *chartered financial analysts,* who have been awarded the registered professional designation CFA. The objectives of the Institute are

- To foster high standards of education and professional development in financial analysis
- To conduct and foster programs of research study, discussion, and publishing, which improve the practice of financial analysis
- To administer a study and examination program in financial analysis for CFA candidates that guides analysts in mastering a professional body of knowledge and in developing analytical skills, and that tests analysts for a reasonable level of competency
- To award the professional designation "Chartered Financial Analyst" (CFA) to persons who meet stipulated standards of competency and standards of conduct for the professional practice of financial analysis, and to permit persons who continue to meet stipulated standards to retain the CFA designation.
- To sponsor and enforce a Code of Ethics and Standards of Professional Conduct

The Institute and its members hold the conviction that the interests of investors and the public will best be served if financial analysts achieve reasonable professional standards of performance. The Institute fosters the achievement of these standards through several programs described below.

BRIEF HISTORY

The Institute of Chartered Financial Analysts was formed in 1959 by and received initial support from The Financial Analysts Federation. The Institute was incorporated under the laws of the Commonwealth of Virginia on January 31, 1962. CFA candidate examinations were first offered in June 1963 to 268 candidates. Over the first twelve years of the Candidate Study Program (1963-74), 3,794 charters were awarded by the Institute, and 18,387 candidates took CFA examinations. The University of Virginia cooperates closely with the Institute in providing educational and logistical support.

CFA CANDIDATE STUDY PROGRAM

Eligible financial analysts are encouraged to become members of the Institute. To become a member, an applicant must (1) meet eligibility requirements, (2) comply fully with the CFA Code of Ethics and Standards of Professional Conduct, (3) study books, journal articles, and other readings prescribed by the Institute, and (4) successfully pass three examinations (each one takes approximately six hours to complete) that are administered by the Institute. The requirements and content of the CFA Candidate Study program are described below.

The specific content of the CFA study materials and examinations are subject to modifications in order to keep pace with changing emphases and techniques in financial analysis.

Candidates who have been approved for a particular study program and who have paid the applicable enrollment fee will receive a Study Guide containing a detailed reading list prepared specifically for CFA candidates. There is no additional charge for this material, and a limited number of copies are available for purchase by noncandidates.

While the Institute itself does not offer classroom-type courses of instruction, it does assist in the organization of local study groups in conjunction with the CFA educational coordinators of local analyst societies and universities. Of special assistance to candidates are the study guides, textbooks, and books of readings published periodically by the Institute.

The CFA is awarded to those candidates who have successfully completed the examinations and other requirements established by The Institute of Chartered Financial Analysts. The candidate must pass three examinations: Examination I—Investment Principles; Examination II—Applied Financial Analysis; and Examination III—Investment Management.

CFA OCCUPATION AND EXPERIENCE REQUIREMENTS

A candidate for the CFA designation must be currently and primarily engaged in one of the following occupational categories:

- A person who is engaged in financial analysis as related to securities investment for a bank, insurance company, investment company, securities firm, financial publishing house, or other similar organization
- A person occupying the position of professor (including assistant and associate professors) or dean of a college or university who is currently teaching or conducting research in the field of securities investment
- A person engaged as an economist in the field of financial analysis as related to securities investment
- A person who is engaged in portfolio management
- A person who is engaged in financial analysis as related to securities investment for a public agency
- A person who is engaged in financial analysis as related to securities investment for a corporate pension, profit sharing, or similar fund
- A person who previously would have qualified for candidacy as a financial analyst or portfolio manager, but who is currently engaged in the professional supervision of financial analysts or portfolio managers as related to securities investment

CFA CANDIDATE APPLICATION PROCEDURES AND FEES

registration and enrollment application

More information and application forms may be obtained from

The Institute of Chartered Financial Analysts
University of Virginia
Post Office Box 3668
Charlottesville, Virginia 22903

initial registration

To be considered for CFA candidacy, the applicant must first complete a detailed registration form. This form together with required supporting documents must be forwarded to the Institute *no later than July 15* preceding the year in which the applicant expects to take the initial examination. A fee of $50 must accompany the registration form. Late registrations (between July 16 and October 1) will be accepted only if accompanied by a $50 late registration fee—total fee, $100. No registrations for the following year's examination are accepted after October 1. The registration fee, which covers the cost of the registration process, is not refundable. Once the applicant has been accepted for candidacy, it will *not be necessary* to file another registration form.

name index

subject index

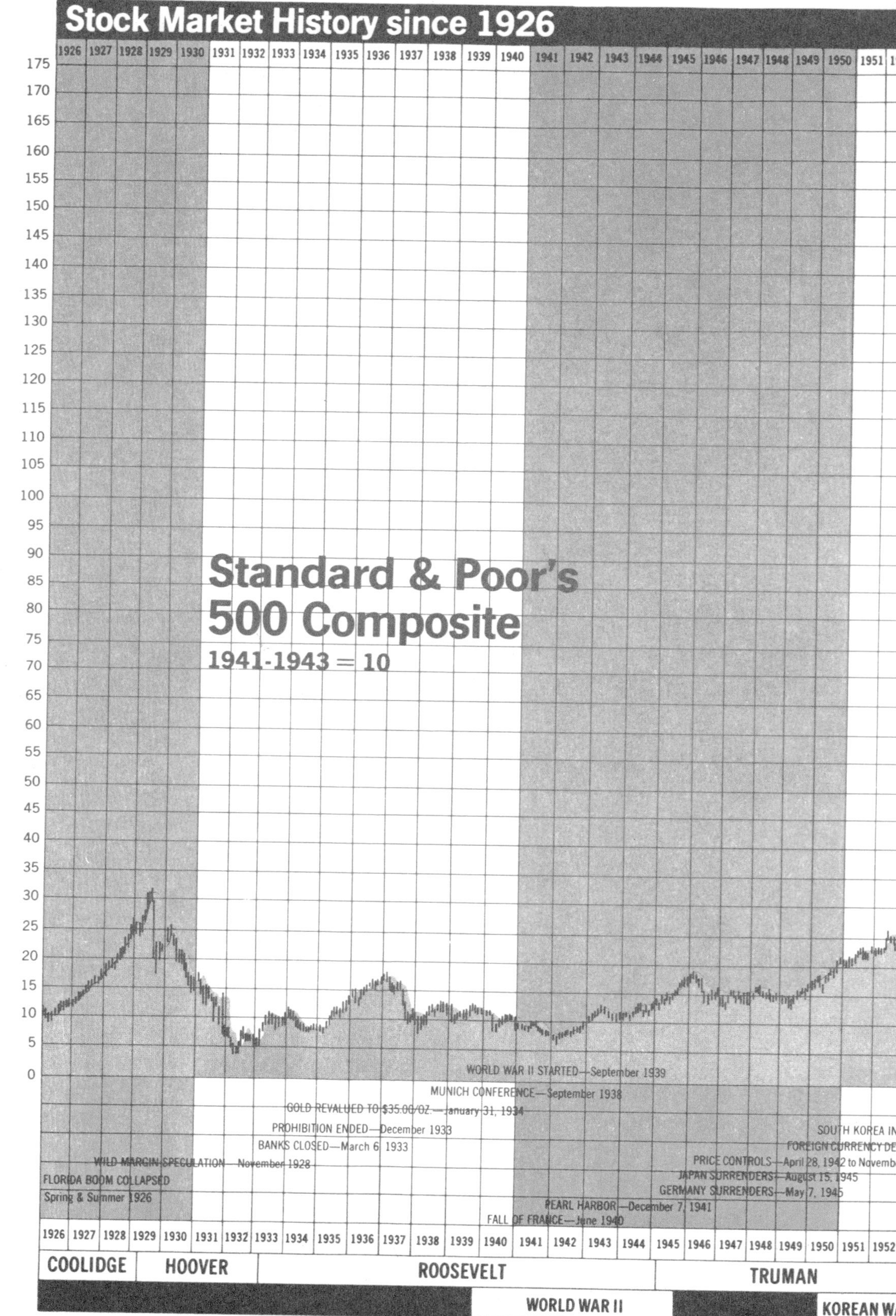

Stock Market History since 1926
1926 1927 1928 1929 1930 1931 1932 1933 1934 1935 1936 1937 1938 1939 1940 1941 1942 1943 1944 1945 1946 1947 1948 1949 1950 1951
175 170 165 160 155 150 145 140 135 130 125 120 115 110 105 100 95 90 85 80 75 70 65 60 55 50 45 40 35 30 25 20 15 10 5 0
Standard & Poor's
500 Composite
1941-1943 = 10
WORLD WAR II STARTED—September 1939
MUNICH CONFERENCE—September 1938
GOLD REVALUED TO $35.00/OZ.—January 31, 1934
PROHIBITION ENDED—December 1933
BANKS CLOSED—March 6 1933
WILD MARGIN SPECULATION—November 1928
FLORIDA BOOM COLLAPSED
Spring & Summer 1926
SOUTH KOREA IN
FOREIGN CURRENCY DEV
PRICE CONTROLS—April 28, 1942 to Novembe
JAPAN SURRENDERS—August 15, 1945
GERMANY SURRENDERS—May 7, 1945
PEARL HARBOR—December 7, 1941
FALL OF FRANCE—June 1940
1926 1927 1928 1929 1930 1931 1932 1933 1934 1935 1936 1937 1938 1939 1940 1941 1942 1943 1944 1945 1946 1947 1948 1949 1950 1951 1952
COOLIDGE
HOOVER
ROOSEVELT
TRUMAN
WORLD WAR II
KOREAN WA

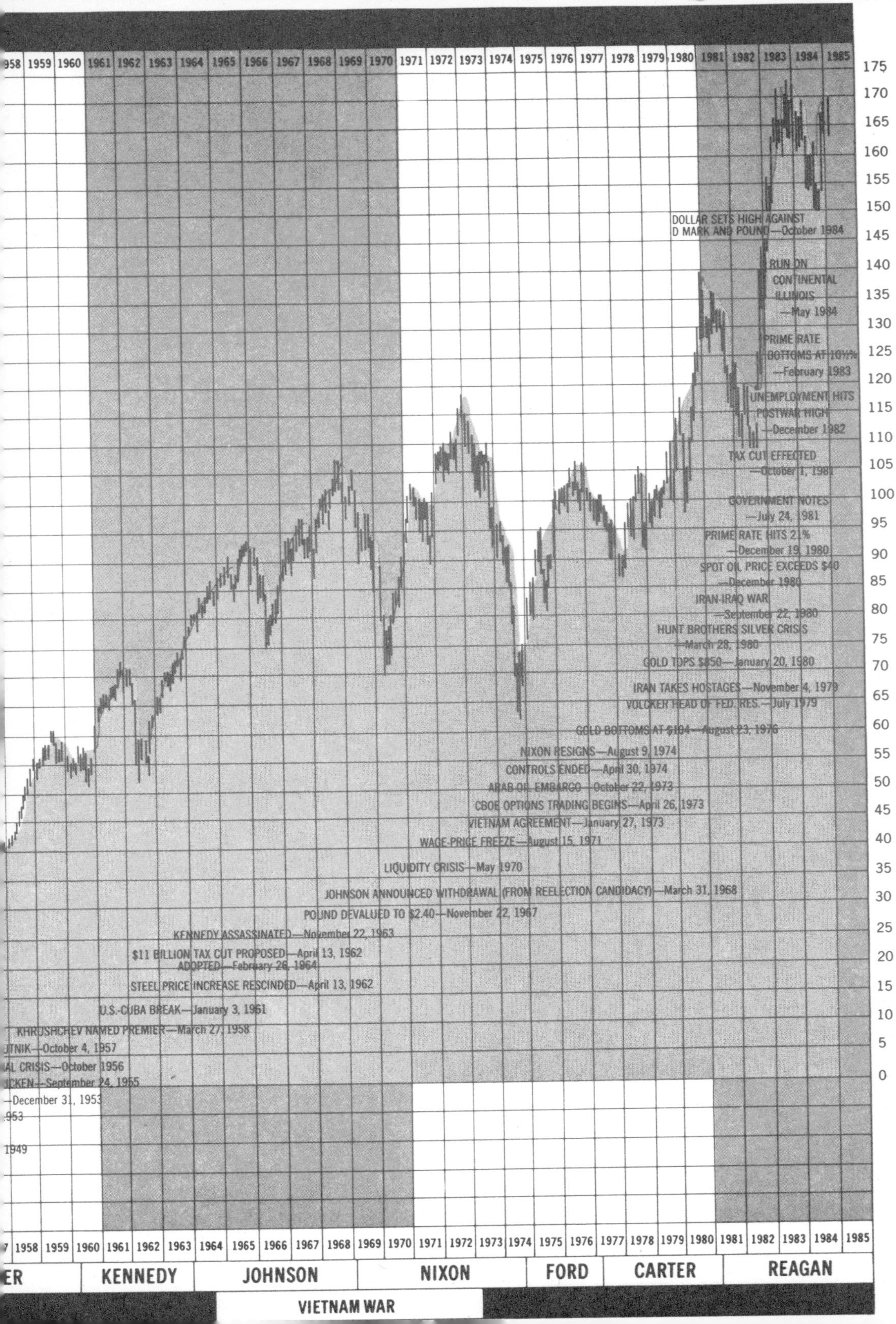

958 | 1959 | 1960 | 1961 | 1962 | 1963 | 1964 | 1965 | 1966 | 1967 | 1968 | 1969 | 1970 | 1971 | 1972 | 1973 | 1974 | 1975 | 1976 | 1977 | 1978 | 1979 | 1980 | 1981 | 1982 | 1983 | 1984 | 1985

175
170
165
160
155
150
145
140
135
130
125
120
115
110
105
100
95
90
85
80
75
70
65
60
55
50
45
40
35
30
25
20
15
10
5
0

DOLLAR SETS HIGH AGAINST D MARK AND POUND—October 1984

RUN ON CONTINENTAL ILLINOIS —May 1984

PRIME RATE BOTTOMS AT 10½% —February 1983

UNEMPLOYMENT HITS POSTWAR HIGH —December 1982

TAX CUT EFFECTED —October 1, 1981

GOVERNMENT NOTES —July 24, 1981

PRIME RATE HITS 21% —December 19, 1980

SPOT OIL PRICE EXCEEDS $40 —December 1980

IRAN-IRAQ WAR —September 22, 1980

HUNT BROTHERS SILVER CRISIS —March 28, 1980

GOLD TOPS $850—January 20, 1980

IRAN TAKES HOSTAGES—November 4, 1979

VOLCKER HEAD OF FED. RES.—July 1979

GOLD BOTTOMS AT $104—August 23, 1976

NIXON RESIGNS—August 9, 1974

CONTROLS ENDED—April 30, 1974

ARAB OIL EMBARGO—October 22, 1973

CBOE OPTIONS TRADING BEGINS—April 26, 1973

VIETNAM AGREEMENT—January 27, 1973

WAGE-PRICE FREEZE—August 15, 1971

LIQUIDITY CRISIS—May 1970

JOHNSON ANNOUNCED WITHDRAWAL (FROM REELECTION CANDIDACY)—March 31, 1968

POUND DEVALUED TO $2.40—November 22, 1967

KENNEDY ASSASSINATED—November 22, 1963

$11 BILLION TAX CUT PROPOSED—April 13, 1962
ADOPTED—February 26, 1964

STEEL PRICE INCREASE RESCINDED—April 13, 1962

U.S.-CUBA BREAK—January 3, 1961

KHRUSHCHEV NAMED PREMIER—March 27, 1958

UTNIK—October 4, 1957

AL CRISIS—October 1956

ICKEN—September 24, 1955

—December 31, 1953

953

1949

7 | 1958 | 1959 | 1960 | 1961 | 1962 | 1963 | 1964 | 1965 | 1966 | 1967 | 1968 | 1969 | 1970 | 1971 | 1972 | 1973 | 1974 | 1975 | 1976 | 1977 | 1978 | 1979 | 1980 | 1981 | 1982 | 1983 | 1984 | 1985

ER | KENNEDY | JOHNSON | NIXON | FORD | CARTER | REAGAN

VIETNAM WAR